Tucker Support Web Site (http://tucker.swcollege.com)

The Tucker Web site provides open access to an interactive study center (with chapter review, quizzing, and more), updates to the text, the opportunity to communicate with the author, direct links to the Internet addresses and activities mentioned in the text, and other teaching and learning resources.

South-Western Economics Resource Center

A unique, rich and robust online resource for economics instructors and students, http://economics.swcollege.com provides customer service and product information, teaching and learning tips and tools, information about careers in economics, and access to all of South-Western's text-supporting Web sites and other cutting-edge educational resources such as our highly regarded EconNews, EconDebate, EconData, and EconLinks Online features.

ECONOMICS

FOR TODAY

THIRD EDITION

IRVIN TUCKER

University of North Carolina at Charlotte

THOMSON

SOUTH-WESTERN

Australia · Canada · Mexico · Singapore · Spain · United Kingdom · United States

THOMSON

SOUTH-WESTERN

Economics for Today, 3rd Edition
Irvin B. Tucker

Editor-in-Chief:
Jack Calhoun

Vice President, Team Director:
Michael P. Roche

Publisher/Acquisitions Editor:
Michael B. Mercier

Developmental Editor:
Andrew McGuire

Senior Marketing Manager:
Lisa Lysne

Production Editor:
Kara ZumBahlen

Manufacturing Coordinator:
Sandee Milewski

Media Technology Editor
Vicky True

Media Developmental Editor:
Peggy Buskey

Media Production Editor:
Pam Wallace

Compositor:
Lachina Publishing Services

Printer:
R. R. Donnelley
Willard, OH

Design Project Manager:
Rik Moore

Internal Designer:
Rik Moore

Cover Designer:
Rik Moore

Cover Photographer/Illustrator:
© PhotoDisc, Inc.

Photography Manager:
Deanna Ettinger

Photo Researcher:
Susan Van Etten

Text and CD:
ISBN 0-324-11475-3

Text only:
ISBN 0-324-17950-2

CD only:
ISBN 0-324-17956-1

Library of Congress Cataloging-in-Publication Data

Tucker, Irvin B.
 Economics for today / Irvin B. Tucker.— 3rd ed.
  p. cm.
 Includes bibliographical references and index.
 ISBN 0-324-11475-3
 1. Economics. 2. United States Economic conditions—1981–2001. I. Title.
 HB171.5 .T748 2002
 330—dc21   2001057819

To Rhett G. Cooper, Jr. and Annie Ruth Cooper

For their commitment to the education
of our family

Brief Contents

Contents

PART 4   MICROECONOMIC POLICY ISSUES   267

CHAPTER 12   Income Distribution, Poverty, and Discrimination   268

CHAPTER 13   Antitrust and Regulation   293

CHAPTER 14   Environmental Economics   321

About the Author

IRVIN B. TUCKER has over twenty years of experience teaching introductory economics at the University of North Carolina at Charlotte and at the University of South Carolina. He earned his B.S. in economics at N.C. State University and his M.A. and Ph.D. in economics from the University of South Carolina.

Dr. Tucker is former Director of the Center for Economic Education at the University of North Carolina at Charlotte and long-time member of the National Council on Economic Education. He is recognized for his ability to relate basic principles to economic issues and public policy. His work has received national recognition by being awarded the Meritorious Leavy Award for Excellence in Private Enterprise Education, the Federation of Independent Business Award for Postsecondary Educator of the Year in Entrepreneurship and Economic Education, and the Freedom Foundation's George Washington Medal for Excellence in Economic Education. In addition, he has published numerous professional journal articles on a wide range of topics including studies of industrial organization, entrepreneurship, and sports economics. Dr. Tucker is also the author of the highly successful third edition of *Survey of Economics*, a text for one-semester economics courses, published by South-Western College Publishing.

PREFACE

Text with a Mission

As with the first edition, the purpose of *Economics for Today, Third Edition,* is to teach, in an engaging style, the basic operations of the U.S. economy to students who will take a two-term economics course. Rather than taking an encyclopedic approach to economic concepts, *Economics for Today* focuses on the most important tool in economics—supply and demand analysis—and applies it to clearly explain real-world economic issues.

In a nutshell, every effort has been made to make *Economics for Today* the most "student-friendly" text on the market. This text was written because so many others expose students to a confusing array of economic analyses that force students to simply memorize in order to pass the course. Instead, *Economics for Today* presents a straightforward and unbiased approach that effectively teaches the application of basic economic principles. After reading this text, the student should be able to say "that economics stuff in the news now makes sense."

How It Fits Together

The text presents the core principles of microeconomics, macroeconomics, and international economics. The first 14 chapters introduce the logic of economic analysis and develop the core of microeconomic analysis. Here students learn the role of demand and supply in determining prices in competitive versus monopolistic markets. This part of the book explores such issues as minimum wage laws, rent control, and pollution. The next 13 chapters develop the macroeconomics part of the text. Using the modern, yet simple, aggregate demand and aggregate supply model, the text explains measurement and changes in the price level, national output, and employment in the economy. The study of macroeconomics also includes how the supply of money and the demand for money influence the economy. Finally, the text concludes with three chapters devoted entirely to international issues. For example, student will learn how the supply of and demand for currencies determine exchange rates and what the complications of a strong or a weak dollar are.

Economics for Today is easily adapted to an instructor's preference for the sequencing of microeconomics and macroeconomics topics. The text can be used in a macroeconomic-microeconomic sequence by teaching the first four chapters and then Part 4 through Part 7. Next, microeconomics is covered in Chapter 5 through Chapter 14. Finally, the course can be completed with Part 8 consisting of three chapters devoted to international economics. Another approach is to select chapters and teach economics in one semester. Also, a customized text might meet your needs. If so, contact your Thomson Learning sales representative for information.

Introductory Chapters

– New discussions of careers in economics in Chapter 1.
– New definition of the "new economy" and its relation to economic growth in Chapter 2.
– New enlarged demand and supply graphs in Chapter 3 clearly explain movements along versus shifts of these curves.

Micro Chapters

– New discussion of the California energy crisis in the chapter on antitrust and regulation.

Macro Chapters

– New four-sector circular flow model in an appendix to the chapter on GDP.
– New self-correcting aggregate demand and supply model in an appendix to the chapter on aggregate demand and supply.
– New history of money box insert in the chapter on money and the Federal Reserve System.

International Chapters

– New box insert on the birth of the euro in the chapter on international trade and finance.

ACKNOWLEDGEMENTS

A deep debt of gratitude is owed to the reviewers for their expert assistance. Each comment and suggestion was carefully evaluated and served to improve the final product. To each of the following reviewers of the first, second, and third editions, I give my sincerest thanks.

Jack E. Adams
University of Arkansas – Little Rock

John W. Alderson, III
East Arkansas Community College

James Q. Aylsworth
Lakeland Community College

Klaus G. Becker
Texas Tech University

Randall W. Bennett
Gonzaga University

John P. Blair
Wright State University

Tantatape Brahmasrene
Purdue University North Central

Juan Castro
East Texas Baptist University

John P. Dahlquist
College of Alameda

William Dougherty
Carroll County Community College

James W. Eden
Portland Community College

Ronald Elkins
Central Washington University

Tommy Eshelman
University of Nebraska – Kearney

John L. Ewing-Smith
Burlington County College

Chris Fawson
Utah State University

Arthur A. Fleisher, III
Metropolitan State College of Denver

Arthur Friedberg
Mohawk Valley Community College

Scott Gabeheart
Mesa Community College

Cindy Gibson
Keuka College

J.P. Gilbert
Mira Costa College

Sanford D. Gordon
University of South Florida

Gary Green
Manatee Community College

Gail A. Hawks
Miami Dade Community College

R. Jack Inch
Oakland Community College

Barbara H. John
University of Dayton

Randall G. Kesselring
Arkansas State University

Harry T. Kolendrianos
Danville Community College

Margaret Landman
Bridgewater State College

Stephen E. Lile
Western Kentucky University

Thomas Maloy
Muskegon Community College

Robert A. Margo
Vanderbilt University

Melanie Marks
Longwood College

Michael Marlow
Cal Polytechnic State U – SLO

James C. McBrearty
University of Arizona

Diana L. McCoy
Truckee Meadows Community College

Donald P. McDowell
Florida Community College

Margaret Moore
Franklin University

Marie Mora
New Mexico State University

Kevin J. Murphy
Oakland University

Lee Nordgren
Indiana University

Peter K. Olson
Indiana University

Patrick B. O'Neill
University of North Dakota

Jan Palmer
Ohio University

Michael L. Palmer
Maple Woods Community College

Kathy Parkison
Indiana University – Kokomo

Donald W. Pearson
Eastern Michigan University

Martin Perline
Wichita State University

Maurice Pfannestiel
Wichita State University

L. Wayne Plumly, Jr.
Valdosta State University

Ray Polchow
Muskingum Area Technical College

Renee Prim
Central Piedmont Community College

Steve Robinson
University of North Carolina – Wilmington

Craig Rogers
Canisius College

Kurt A. Schwabe
Ohio University

Alden W. Smith
Anne Arundel Community College

Rebecca Summary
Southeast Missouri State University

Larry Towle
Eastern Nazarene College

Richard Trieff
Des Moines Area Community College

Roy van Til
University of Maine – Farmington

Lee Van Scyok
University of Wisconsin – Oshkosh

Darlene Voeltz
Rochester Community and Technical College

Harold Warren
Eastern Tennessee State University

Robert G. Welch
Midwestern State University

Herbert D. Werner
University of Missouri

Micheal D. White
St. Cloud State University

Gwen Williams
Alvernia College

Virginia York
Gulf Coast Community College

Paul Young
Dodge City Community College

SPECIAL THANKS

I especially wish to offer my deepest appreciation to Peter Schwarz, my colleague at UNC Charlotte, who provided inspiration and ideas throughout the development of my *Survey of Economics* and this principles text. In particular, many of the ideas in the You're the Economist sections are the result of brainstorming sessions with Professor Schwarz. In addition, Professor Schwarz is author of the environmental economics chapter and the box inset on the California energy crisis. Special thanks also go to Douglas Copeland of Johnson County Community College, who, besides writing and revising the Instructor's Manual, provided invaluable suggestions as well as Internet margin notes and exercises. A sincere thanks also goes to Ken Long of New River Community College for his outstanding work in creating the PowerPoint Presentation Package. Thanks also to William Weber of Eastern Illinois University for his fine work on developing the homework sets.

My appreciation goes to Mike Worls, Acquisitions Editor for South-Western Publishing. My thanks also to Andrew McGuire, Development Editor, and Kara ZumBahlen, Production Editor, who put all the pieces of the puzzle together and brought their creative talent to this text. Pat Lewis was superb in her copyediting of the manuscript. I am also grateful to Vicky True, Media Technology Editor, for developing the text's Web Site and Lisa Lysne for her skillful marketing. Finally, I give my sincere thanks for a job well done to the entire team at South-Western Publishing.

THE SUPPORT PACKAGE

To learn more about the supplements for *Economics for Today* and to download samples, visit the Tucker Web site, http://tucker.swcollege.com. For additional information, contact your South-Western/Thomson Learning sales representative.

FOR THE INSTRUCTOR

Instructor's Manual

This manual, prepared by Douglas Copeland of Johnson County Community College, provides valuable course assistance to instructors. It includes chapter outlines, instructional objectives, critical thinking/group discussion questions, hints for effective teaching, answers to the Analyze the Issue questions, and summary quizzes with answers. It also gives solutions to Homework Sets.

Test Banks

Prepared by the text author, each Test Bank (micro and macro versions) includes over 4,000 multiple-choice, true-false, and short essay questions. The questions are arranged by order presented in the chapter and grouped with concept headings that make it easy to select questions. Most questions have been thoroughly tested in the classroom by the author and classified by topic and degree of difficulty.

ExamView Testing Software

ExamView®—Computerized Testing Software contains all of the questions in the printed test banks. ExamView® is an easy-to-use test creation software compatible with both Microsoft Windows and Macintosh. Instructors can add or edit questions, instructions, and answers, and select questions by previewing them on the screen; selecting them randomly, or selecting them by number. Instructors can also create and administer quizzes online, whether over the Internet, a local area network (LAN), or a wide area network (WAN).

Transparency Acetates

A set of approximately 150 full-color transparency acetates has been created from the key graphs and diagrams in the text. All exhibits in the text are also available as PowerPoint slides that can be downloaded from the Tucker Web site as transparency masters.

PowerPoint Slides

Developed by Ken Long of New River Community College, this state-of-the-art slide presentation provides instructors with visual support in the classroom for each chapter. The package includes vivid highlights of important concepts and graphs.

CNN Video

Professors can bring the real world into the classroom by using the CNN Principles of Economics Video Updates. This VHS video provides current stories of economic interest, and is accompanied by a Multimedia Integration Guide that includes instructional support for each clip. The video is produced by Turner Learning, Inc., using the resources of CNN, the world's first 24-hour, all-news network.

Instructor's Resource CD-ROM

Get quick access to all instructor ancillaries from your desktop. This easy-to-use CD lets you review, edit, and copy exactly what you need in the format you want.

FOR THE STUDENT

Study Guide

The Study Guide is recommended for each student using the text. It is perhaps the best way to prepare for quizzes. Too often, study guides are not written by the author and the material does not really fit the text. Not so here. This Study Guide was prepared by the text author to prepare students before they take tests in class. The Study Guide contains student-friendly features such as the chapter in a nutshell, key concepts review, learning objectives, fill-in-the-blank questions, step-by-step interpretation of the graph boxes, multiple-choice questions, true-false questions, and crossword puzzles.

Homework Sets

These sets of exercises, prepared by William Weber of Eastern Illinois University, review economic concepts presented in the text. They can be given as homework assignments or used by students to practice for exams. Answers are found in the Instructor's Manual.

Tucker Xtra! Web Site & CD-ROM

Students buying a new textbook packaged with the Tucker Xtra! CD-ROM receive complimentary access (via the CD) to the robust set of additional learning tools found at the Tucker Xtra! Web site. Some of the powerful study support features found at this site include THE GRAPHING WORKSHOP, a unique learning system made up of tutorials, interactive tools, and exercises that teach students how to interpret, reproduce, and explain graphs; Frequently Asked Questions and CNN video segments; and extensive self-testing opportunities. Students who do not buy a new text/CD package can purchase access to the site online.

The Wall Street Journal

The Wall Street Journal is synonymous with the latest word on business, economics, and public policy. Tucker *Economics for Today, 3e* makes it easy for students to apply economic concepts to this authoritative publication, and for you to bring the most up-to-date, real-world events into your classroom. For a nominal additional cost, Tucker *Economics for Today, 3e* can be packaged with a card entitling students to a subscription to both the print and interactive versions of *The Wall Street Journal*. Instructors who have at least seven students activate their subscriptions will automatically receive their own free subscription. Contact your South-Western/Thomson Learning sales representative for package pricing and ordering information.

InfoTrac College Edition

With InfoTrac College Edition, your students can receive anytime, anywhere, online access to a database of full-text articles from hundreds of scholarly and popular periodicals such as *Newsweek, Fortune, American Economist,* and the *Quarterly Journal of Economics*. Students can use its fast and easy search tools to find what they're looking for among the tens of thousands of articles—updated daily and dating back as far as four years—all in this single Web site. It's a great way to expose students to online research techniques, while being secure in the knowledge that the content they find is academically based and reliable. An InfoTrac College Edition subscription card is packaged free with new copies of this text. For more information on InfoTrac College Edition, visit http://www.swcollege.com/infotrac/infotrac.html.

FOR STUDENTS AND INSTRUCTORS

Tucker Support Web Site (http://tucker.swcollege.com)

The Tucker Web site provides open access to an interactive study center (with chapter review, quizzing, and more), updates to the text, the opportunity to communicate with the author, direct links to the Internet addresses and activities mentioned in the text, and other teaching and learning resources.

South-Western Economics Resource Center

A unique, rich and robust online resource for economics instructors and students, http://economics.swcollege.com provides customer service and product information, teaching and learning tips and tools, information about careers in economics, access to all of South-Western's text-supporting Web sites, and other cutting-edge educational resources such as our highly regarded EconNews, EconDebate, EconData, and EconLinks Online features.

WebTutor on WebCT and on Blackboard

WebTutor™ *on WebCT* or *WebTutor*™ *on Blackboard* complements *Economics for Today, 3e* by providing interactive reinforcement that helps students grasp complex concepts. WebTutor's online teaching and learning environment brings together content management, assessment, communication, and collaboration capabilities for enhancing in-class instruction or delivering distance learning. For more information and a demo of what *WebTutor*™ can do for your classes, visit http://webtutor.swcollege.com.

Dear Students,

As a principles of economics instructor for over 20 years, I know from firsthand experience that many students are apprehensive about taking economics. In fact, I still recall vividly that as a freshman about to take my first economics course, I had only the vaguest idea what this subject was about. To my delight, my freshman principles of economics course opened my eyes to a new way of thinking. And my years of teaching this powerful reasoning process inspired me to try to write a text that conveyed my excitement about economics to students. I thought that a text that truly did this would have to do two things very well:

1) It would deliver the material in a way that was not boring for students, and
2) It would provide a pedagogical framework that assisted the student in understanding and remembering the concepts presented.

With these two objectives in mind, here's a picture of how I put this book together to help you get the most out of your first economics course:

My writing style is intended to be engaging, clear, and straightforward. As I was writing the text, I viewed myself explaining the concepts to a student in my office. The result is a conversational tone to the text. To avoid boredom, the text uses a fast-paced, action-packed approach that explains all essential concepts without becoming an encyclopedia. Recognizing that today's student lives in a world of visual experiences and sound bites, I combine a very active reading experience with lots of visual reinforcement and integrated hands-on application, analysis, practice, and review. The pedagogical system I have built for you in this book is structured to maximize your comprehension and retention of the material, and if you use the book's features effectively, they should prepare you very well for tests.

In short, my instructional package is designed to provide you with everything you need for success in this course. I have worked hard to make my book the most student-friendly principles of economics text on the market. Please read through the next few pages—they will take you on a tour of how to use the special pedagogical features and ancillary materials that have been created to help you maximize your learning experience with this textbook. If I can help in your endeavor, contact me through the "Talk to the Author" feature on the book's Web site at http://tucker.swcollege.com.

Best Wishes,

THE *ECONOMICS FOR TODAY*
LEARNING SYSTEM

This text combines an extremely active reading experience with superior visual reinforcement of concepts. By using its unique learning system effectively, you should experience better comprehension and retention of the material. The system is built around three main components:

1 READ

This is a textbook that you can actually finish without sacrificing retention. It uses a "less is more," nonencyclopedic approach. You'll find the reading fast-paced. The writing style is engaging, clear, and straightforward. The conversational tone will keep you tuned in.

– You'll find the number of concepts per chapter manageable. The concepts are presented in digestible "bites" followed by **Conclusion Statements** that summarize main ideas. These statements should serve as a stopping point to make sure you grasp the key concept you just read about.

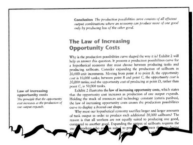

2 REINFORCE

Critical analysis is emphasized throughout each chapter as a way to reinforce concepts by having you apply theory to real-world economic analysis problems.

– **Checkpoints** in each chapter allow you to confirm your understanding of material and exercise your analytical skills by applying your knowledge to a real-world question.

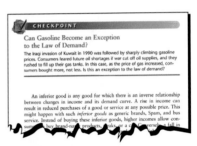

– **"You're the Economist"** articles (2 per chapter) have you connect economic theory to real-world applications. Accompanying **"Analyze the Issue"** features ask specific questions that test your knowledge of the material and sharpen your analytical skills.

An emphasis on visual learning is used to reinforce ideas. Graphical analysis is typically one of the most difficult areas for most students, yet it is extremely important in understanding the concepts.

– **Unique Causation Chains** accompany graphs, helping you to visualize complex economic cause-and-effect relationships in terms of simple box diagrams.

– **End-of-Chapter Visual Summaries** include pertinent mini-graphs and **Causation Chains** from the chapter to provide you with a visual reminder of key chapter concepts.

3 REVIEW

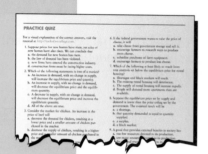

You'll find self-testing features for each chapter to help you review key ideas and assess your mastery of the material.

– Multiple choice **Practice Quizzes** function as a built-in study guide at the end of each chapter. Answers are at the end of the text, and unique visual explanations of the answers can be found at the Web site.

Additional Resources for Students

The following additional print and online resources available with this text are designed to help you in your economics class:

STUDY GUIDE

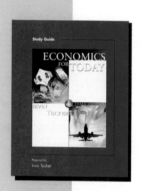

The Study Guide is recommended for each student using the text. It is perhaps the best way to prepare for quizzes. Too often, study guides are not written by the author and the material does not really fit the text. Not so here. This Study Guide was prepared by the text author to prepare you before you take tests in class. The Study Guide contains student-friendly features such as the chapter in a nutshell, key concepts review, learning objectives fill-in-the-blank questions, step-by-step interpretation of the graph boxes, multiple choice questions, true-false questions, and crossword puzzles.

HOMEWORK SETS

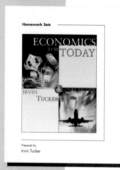

These sets of exercises, prepared by William Weber of Eastern Illinois University, review economic concepts presented in the text. They might be used as homework assignments or as a way for you to practice for exams.

THE WALL STREET JOURNAL EDITION

If you bought a new copy of the special Wall Street Journal Edition of the Tucker textbook, a subscription to both *The Wall Street Journal* Print and Interactive versions was included with your purchase. Be sure to take advantage of all *The Wall Street Journal* has to offer by activating your subscription to this authoritative publication, which is synonymous with the latest word on business, economics, and public policy. It provides an excellent resource for you to observe economics concepts in action, in the real world, every day—and helps you prepare long term for your successful economics/business career.

INFOTRAC COLLEGE EDITION

If you bought a new copy of the InfoTrac College Edition of this text, don't forget to take advantage of your subscription. With InfoTrac College Edition, you can receive anytime, anywhere, online access to a database of full-text articles from hundreds of scholarly and popular periodicals. You can use its fast and easy search tools to find what you're looking for among the tens of thousands of articles—updated daily and dating back as far as four years—all in this single Web site. It's a great way to locate resources for papers and projects without having to travel to the library.

To get started, visit http://www.infotrac-college.com.

TUCKER XTRA! WEB SITE & CD-ROM

If you bought a new textbook packaged with the Tucker Xtra! CD-ROM, this CD provides you with complimentary access to a robust set of additional online learning tools found at the Tucker Xtra! Web site. If you don't have the CD, you can view a demo an purchase access to the site online at http://tucker.swcollege.com. Here is a tour through some of the study support features you will find there:

– The Graphing Workshop

For most students, graphing is one of the most difficult aspects of the Principles course. **THE GRAPHING WORKSHOP** is your one-stop learning resource for help in mastering the language of graphs. You'll explore important economic concepts through a unique learning system made up of tutorials, interactive tools, and exercises that teach you how to interpret, reproduce, and explain graphs:

SEE IT! Animated graphing tutorials provide step-by-step graphical presentations and audio explanations.

TRY IT! Interactive graphing exercises let you practice manipulating and interpreting graphs with GraphIt—a robust, hands-on Java graphing tool. You can check your work online.

APPLY IT! Interactive graphing assignments challenge you to apply what you have learned by creating your own graph from scratch to analyze a specific scenario. You can print out and/or email answers to your instructor for grading.

– Video Lecture and Applications

Via streaming video, difficult concepts from each chapter are explained in two different ways—by an economics instructor and with real-world examples from recent news stories. These video clips can be extremely helpful review and clarification tools if you had trouble understanding an in-class lecture, or if you are more of a visual learner who sometimes has difficulty grasping concepts as they are presented in the text.

– Additional Self-Testing Opportunities

In addition to the open-access chapter-by-chapter quizzes found at the Tucker Product Support Web site, the Tucker Xtra! Web site offers you endless practice for midterms and finals by taking randomly generated online quizzes that span multiple chapters.

– Interactive Games

The **Causation Chains** features that accompany most graphs in the text are brought to life in an interactive format where you must place them into the correct sequence to test your knowledge of the cause-and-effect analysis behind economic events.

Tucker Support Web Site (http://tucker.swcollege.com)

The Tucker Web Site provides you with open access to an online study guide, updates to the text, the opportunity to communicate with the author, direct links to all the Internet addresses and activities mentioned in the text, downloadable learning support tools, and much more.

South-Western College Publishing's Economics Resource Center

A unique, rich and robust online resource for economics students, http://economics.swcollege.com provides customer service and product information, learning tips and tools, information about careers in economics, access to all of South-Western's text supporting Web sites, and other cutting edge educational resources such as our highly regarded EconNews, EconDebate, EconData, and EconLinks Online features.

ECONOMICS
FOR
TODAY

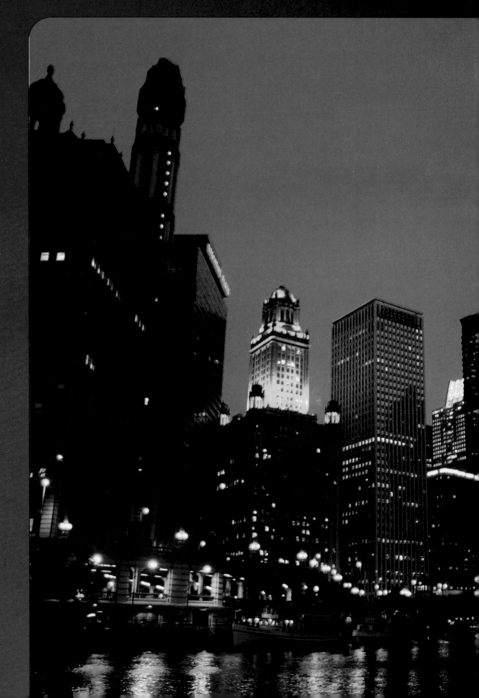

PART 1

Introduction to Economics

The first four chapters introduce you to a foundation of economic knowledge vital to understanding the other chapters in the text. In these introductory chapters, you will begin to learn a valuable reasoning approach to solving economics puzzles that economists call "the economic way of thinking." Part 1 develops the cornerstone of this type of logical analysis by presenting basic economic models that explain such important topics as economic growth and the forces of supply and demand.

CHAPTER 1

Introducing the Economic Way of Thinking

Welcome to an exciting and useful subject economists call "the economic way of thinking." As you learn this reasoning technique, it will become infectious. You will discover that the world is full of economics problems requiring more powerful tools than just common sense. As you master the methods explained in this book, you will appreciate economics as a valuable reasoning approach to solving economics puzzles. Stated differently, the economic way of thinking is important because it provides a logical framework for organizing your thoughts and understanding an economic issue or event. Just to give a sneak preview, in later chapters you will study the perils of government price-fixing for gasoline and health care. You will also find out why colleges and universities charge different

tuitions to students for the same education. You will investigate whether or not you should worry if the federal government fails to balance its budget. You will learn that the island of Yap uses large stones with holes in the center as money. In the final chapter, you will study why some countries grow rich while others remain poor and less developed. And the list of fascinating and relevant topics continues throughout each

chapter. As you read these pages, your efforts will be rewarded by an understanding of just how economic theories and policies affect our daily lives—past, present, and future.

Chapter 1 acquaints you with the foundation of the economic way of thinking. The first building blocks joined are the concepts of scarcity and choice. The next building blocks are the steps in the model-building process that economists use to study the choices people make. Then we look at some pitfalls of economic reasoning and explain why economists might disagree with one another. The chapter concludes with a discussion of why you may wish to be an economics major.

In this chapter, you will learn to solve these economics puzzles:

■ Can you prove there is no person worth a trillion dollars?

■ Why would you purchase more Coca-Cola when the price increases?

■ How can we explain the relationship between the Super Bowl winner and changes in the stock market?

■ What famous people majored in economics?

The Problem of Scarcity

Our world is a finite place where people, both individually and collectively, face the problem of **scarcity**. Scarcity is the condition in which human wants are forever greater than the available supply of time, goods, and resources. Because of scarcity, it is impossible to satisfy every desire. Pause for a moment to list some of your unsatisfied wants. Perhaps you would like a big home, gourmet meals, designer clothes, clean air, better health care, shelter for the homeless, more leisure time, and so on. Unfortunately, nature does not offer the Garden of Eden, where every desire is fulfilled. Instead, there are always limits on the economy's ability to satisfy unlimited wants. Alas, scarcity is pervasive, so "You can't have it all."

You may think your scarcity problem would disappear if you were rich, but wealth does not solve the problem. No matter how affluent an individual is, the wish list continues to grow. We are familiar with the "rich and famous" who never seem to have enough. Although they live well, they still desire finer homes, faster planes, and larger yachts. In short, the condition of scarcity means all individuals, whether rich or poor, are dissatisfied with their material well-being and would like more. What is true for individuals also applies to society. States are debating whether to use lotteries to raise funds to improve the quality of their schools. Even Uncle Sam can't escape the problem of scarcity because the federal government never has enough money to spend for the poor, education, highways, police, national defense, Social Security, and all the other programs it wishes to fund.

Scarcity is a fact of life throughout the world. In much of South America, Africa, and Asia, the problem of scarcity is often life threatening. On the other hand, North America, Western Europe, and some parts of Asia have achieved substantial economic growth and development. Although life is much less grueling in the more advanced countries, the problem of scarcity still exists because individuals and countries never have as much of all the goods and services as they would like to have.

Scarcity

The condition in which human wants are forever greater than the available supply of time, goods, and resources.

Scarce Resources and Production

Resources

The basic categories of inputs used to produce goods and services. Resources are also called factors of production. *Economists divide resources into three categories: land, labor, and capital.*

Because of the economic problem of scarcity, no society has enough **resources** to produce all the goods and services necessary to satisfy all human wants. Resources are the basic categories of inputs used to produce goods and services. Resources are also called *factors of production*. Economists divide resources into three categories: *land, labor,* and *capital* (see Exhibit 1).

Land

Land

A shorthand expression for any natural resource provided by nature.

Land is a shorthand expression for any natural resource provided by nature. *Land* includes those resources that are gifts of nature available for use in the production process. Farming, building factories, and constructing oil refineries would be impossible without land. Land includes anything natural above or below the ground, such as forests, gold, diamonds, oil, wildlife, and fish. Other examples are rivers, lakes, seas, air, the sun, and the moon. Two broad categories of natural resources are *renewable resources* and *nonrenewable resources*. Renewable resources are basic inputs that nature can automatically replace. Examples include lakes, crops, and clean air. Nonrenewable resources are basic inputs that nature cannot automatically replace. There is only so much coal, oil, and natural gas in the world. If these fossil fuels disappear, we must use substitutes.

Labor

Labor

The mental and physical capacity of workers to produce goods and services.

Labor is the mental and physical capacity of workers to produce goods and services. The services of farmers, assembly-line workers, lawyers, professional football players, and economists are all *labor*. The labor resource is measured both by the number of people available for work and by the skills or quality of workers. One reason nations differ in their ability to produce is that human characteristics, such as the education, experience, health, and motivation of workers, differ among nations.

Entrepreneurship

The creative ability of individuals to seek profits by combining resources to produce innovative products.

Entrepreneurship is a special type of labor. Entrepreneurship is the creative ability of individuals to seek profits by combining resources to produce innovative products. An *entrepreneur* is a motivated person who seeks profits by undertaking such risky activities as starting new businesses, creating new products, or inventing new ways of accomplishing tasks. Entrepreneurship is a scarce human resource because relatively few people are willing or able to innovate and make decisions involving greater-than-normal chances for failure.

Entrepreneurs are the agents of change who bring material progress to society. The birth of the Levi Strauss Company is a classic entrepreneurial success story. In 1850, at the age of 24, Levi Strauss sailed from New York to join the California Gold Rush. His intent was not to dig for gold, but to sell cloth. When he arrived in San Francisco, he had sold most of his cloth to other people on the ship. The only cloth he had left was a roll of canvas for tents and covered wagons. On the dock, he met a miner who wanted a pair of pants that would last while digging for gold. Presto! Strauss knew a good thing when he saw it, so he hired workers, built factories, and became

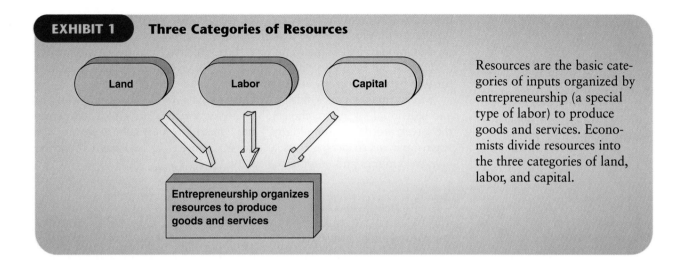

EXHIBIT 1   **Three Categories of Resources**

Land   Labor   Capital

Entrepreneurship organizes resources to produce goods and services

Resources are the basic categories of inputs organized by entrepreneurship (a special type of labor) to produce goods and services. Economists divide resources into the three categories of land, labor, and capital.

the largest pants maker in the world. As a reward for taking business risks, organizing production, and introducing a product, the Levi Strauss Company earned profits, and Strauss became rich and famous.

Capital

Capital is the physical plants, machinery, and equipment used to produce other goods. Capital goods are human-made goods that do not directly satisfy human wants. Before the Industrial Revolution, *capital* meant a tool, such as a hoe, an axe, or a bow and arrow. In those days, these items served as capital to build a house or provide food for the dinner table. Today, capital also consists of factories, office buildings, warehouses, robots, trucks, and distribution facilities. College buildings, the printing presses used to produce this textbook, and pencils are also examples of capital.

The term *capital* as it is used in the study of economics can be confusing. Economists know that capital in everyday conversations means money or the money value of paper assets, such as stocks, bonds, or a deed to a house. This is actually *financial* capital. In the study of economics, capital does not refer to money assets. Instead, capital in economics means a factor of production, such as a factory or machinery. Stated simply, you must pay special attention to this point: "Money is not capital and is therefore not a resource."

Conclusion *Financial capital by itself is not productive; instead, it is only a paper claim on economic capital.*

Capital
The physical plants, machinery, and equipment used to produce other goods. Capital goods are human-made goods that do not directly satisfy human wants.

Economics: The Study of Scarcity and Choice

The perpetual problem of scarcity forcing people to make choices is the basis for the definition of **economics**. Economics is the study of how society chooses to allocate its scarce resources to the production of goods and services in

Economics
The study of how society chooses to allocate its scarce resources to the production of goods and services in order to satisfy unlimited wants.

Browse today's edition of USA Today (http://www.usatoday.com/), The Washington Post (http://www.washingtonpost.com/), *the* International Herald Tribune (http://www.iht.com/). *Can you find a headline story involving economics?*

order to satisfy unlimited wants. You may be surprised by this definition. People often think economics means studying supply and demand, the stock market, money, and banking. In fact, there are many ways one could define *economics*, but economists accept the definition given here because it includes the link between *scarcity* and *choices*.

Society makes two kinds of choices: economywide, or macro choices, and individual, or micro, choices. The prefixes *macro* and *micro* come from the Greek words meaning "large" and "small," respectively. Reflecting the macro and micro perspectives, economics consists of two main branches: *macroeconomics* and *microeconomics*.

Macroeconomics

Macroeconomics

The branch of economics that studies decision making for the economy as a whole.

The old saying "Looking at the forest rather than the trees" describes **macroeconomics.** Macroeconomics is the branch of economics that studies decision making for the economy as a whole. Macroeconomics applies an overview perspective to an economy by examining economywide variables, such as inflation, unemployment, growth of the economy, the money supply, and the national incomes of developing countries. Macroeconomic decision making considers such "big picture" policies as the effect that federal tax cuts will have on unemployment and the effect that changing the money supply will have on prices.

Microeconomics

Microeconomics

The branch of economics that studies decision making by a single individual, household, firm, industry, or level of government.

Examining individual trees, leaves, and pieces of bark, rather than surveying the forest, illustrates **microeconomics.** Microeconomics is the branch of economics that studies decision making by a single individual, household, firm, industry, or level of government. Microeconomics applies a microscope to specific parts of an economy, as one would examine cells in the body. The focus is on small economic units, such as economic decisions of particular groups of consumers and businesses. An example would be to use microeconomic analysis to study economic units involved in the market for ostrich eggs. Will suppliers decide to supply more, less, or the same quantity of ostrich eggs to the market in response to price changes? Will individual consumers of these eggs decide to buy more, less, or the same quantity at a new price?

We have described macroeconomics and microeconomics as two separate branches, but they are related. Because the overall economy is the sum, or aggregation, of its parts, micro changes affect the macro economy, and macro changes produce micro changes.

The Methodology of Economics

Visit this popular economics site (http://www.dismal.com/) *for a survey of economic issues in the study of economics.*

Economists use the same *scientific method* used by other disciplines, such as criminology, biology, chemistry, and physics. The scientific method is a step-by-step procedure for solving problems by developing a theory, gathering data, and testing whether the data are consistent with the theory. Exhibit 2 summarizes the model-building process.

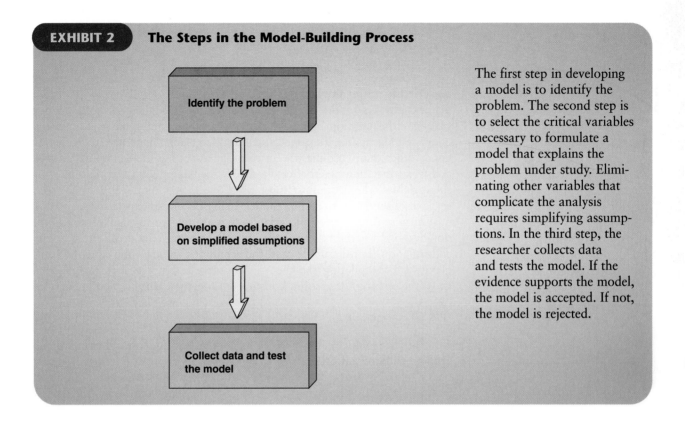

EXHIBIT 2 **The Steps in the Model-Building Process**

Identify the problem

Develop a model based on simplified assumptions

Collect data and test the model

The first step in developing a model is to identify the problem. The second step is to select the critical variables necessary to formulate a model that explains the problem under study. Eliminating other variables that complicate the analysis requires simplifying assumptions. In the third step, the researcher collects data and tests the model. If the evidence supports the model, the model is accepted. If not, the model is rejected.

Problem Identification

The first step in applying the scientific method is to define the problem. Suppose an economist wishes to investigate the microeconomic problem of why U.S. motorists cut back on gasoline consumption in a given year from, for example, 100 billion gallons per month in September to 80 billion gallons per month in December.

Model Development

The second step in our hypothetical example toward finding an explanation is for the economist to build a **model.** A model is a simplified description of reality used to understand and predict the relationship between variables. The terms *model* and *theory* are interchangeable. A model emphasizes only those variables that are most important to explaining an event. As Albert Einstein said, "Theories should be as simple as possible, but not more so." The purpose of a model is to construct an abstraction from real-world complexities and make events understandable. Consider a model airplane that is placed in a wind tunnel to test the aerodynamics of a new design. For this purpose, the model must only represent the shapes of the wings and fuselage, but it does not need to include tiny seats, electrical wiring, or other interior design details. A highway map is another example. To find the best route to drive between two distant cities, you do not want extraneous information on

Model
A simplified description of reality used to understand and predict the relationship between variables.

the location of all roads, streets, potholes, telephones, trees, stoplights, schools, hospitals, and firehouses. This would be too much detail, and the complexity would make it difficult to choose the best route.

A model requires simplified assumptions in order to be useful. Someone must decide, for example, whether a map will include only symbols for the major highways or the details of hiking trails through mountains. In our gasoline consumption example, several variables might be related to the quantity of gasoline consumed, including consumer incomes, the price of goods other than gasoline, the price of gasoline, the fuel economy of cars, and weather conditions. Because a theory focuses only on the main or critical variables, the economist must be a Sherlock Holmes and use a keen sense of observation to form a model. Using his or her expertise, the economist must select the relevant variables that are related to gasoline consumption and reject variables that have only slight or no relationship to gasoline consumption. In this simple case, the economist removes the cloud of complexity by formulating the theory that increases in the price of gasoline *cause* the quantity of gasoline consumed to decrease during the time period.

Testing a Theory

An economic model can be stated as a verbal argument, numerical table, graph, or mathematical equation. You will soon discover that a major part of this book is devoted to building and using economic models. The purpose of an economic model is to *forecast* or *predict* the results of various changes in variables. An economic theory can be expressed in the form "If A, then B, other things held constant." An economic model is useful only if it yields accurate predictions. When the evidence is consistent with a theory that A causes outcome B, there is confidence in the theory's validity. When the evidence is inconsistent with the theory that A causes outcome B, the researcher rejects this theory.

In the third step, the economist gathers data to test the theory that if the price of gasoline rises, then gasoline purchases fall—all other relevant factors held constant. Suppose the investigation reveals that the price of gasoline rose sharply between September and December of the given year. The data are therefore consistent with the theory that the quantity of gasoline consumed per month falls when its price rises, assuming no other relevant factors change. Thus, the theory is valid if, for example, consumer incomes or population size does not change at the same time gasoline prices rise.

To find materials and data resources used by economists on the Internet, visit http://www.helsinki.fi/WebEc/WebEc.html.

Hazards of the Economic Way of Thinking

Models help us understand and predict the impact of changes in economic variables. A model is an important tool in the economist's toolkit, but it must be handled with care. The economic way of thinking seeks to avoid reasoning mistakes. Two of the most common pitfalls to clear thinking are (1) failing to understand the *ceteris paribus assumption* and (2) confusing *association* and *causation*.

CHECKPOINT

Can You Prove There Is No Trillion-Dollar Person?

Suppose a theory says no U.S. citizen is worth $1 trillion. You decide to test this theory and send researchers to all corners of the nation to check financial records to see whether someone qualifies by owning assets valued at $1 trillion or more. After years of checking, the researchers return and report that not a single person is worth at least $1 trillion. Do you conclude that the evidence proves the theory?

The Ceteris Paribus Assumption

As you work through a model, try to think of a host of relevant variables assumed to be "standing still," or "held constant." **Ceteris paribus** is a Latin phrase that means that while certain variables change, "all other things remain unchanged." As in the gasoline example discussed earlier, a key simplifying assumption of the model is that changes in consumer incomes and certain other variables do not occur and complicate the analysis. The ceteris paribus assumption holds everything else constant and therefore allows us to concentrate on the relationship between two key variables: changes in the price of gasoline and the quantity of gasoline purchased per month.

Now suppose an economist wishes to explain a model for the price and quantity purchased of Coca-Cola. The theory is "If the price increases, then the quantity of Coca-Cola purchased decreases, ceteris paribus." Now assume you observe that the price of Coca-Cola increased one summer and some people actually bought more and not less. Based on this real-world observation, you declare the theory is incorrect. Think again! The economist responds that this is a reasoning pitfall because the model is valid based on the assumption of ceteris paribus and your observation gives us no reason to reject the model. The reason the model appeared flawed is that another factor, a sharp rise in the temperature, *caused* people to buy more Coca-Cola in spite of its higher price. If the temperature and all other factors are held constant as the price of Coca-Cola rises, then people will indeed buy less Coca-Cola, as the model predicts.

> **Ceteris paribus**
> *A Latin phrase that means that while certain variables change, "all other things remain unchanged."*

> **Conclusion** *A theory cannot be tested legitimately unless its* ceteris paribus *assumption is satisfied.*

Association versus Causation

Another of the most common errors in reasoning is confusing *association* (or correlation) and *causation* between variables. Stated differently, you err when you read more into a relationship between variables than is actually there. A model is valid only when a cause-and-effect relationship is stable over time, rather than being an association that occurs by chance and eventually disappears. Suppose a witch doctor performs a voodoo dance during three different months and stock market prices skyrocket during each of these months. The voodoo dance is *associated* with the increase in stock

CHECKPOINT

Should Nebraska State Join a Big-Time Athletic Conference?

Nebraska State (a mythical univeristy) stood by while Penn State, Florida State, the University of Miami, and the University of South Carolina joined big-time athletic conferences. Nebraska State officials are pondering whether to remain independent or to pursue membership in a conference noted for high-quality football and basketball programs. An editorial in the newspaper advocates joining and cites a study showing that universities belonging to major athletic conferences have higher graduation rates than nonmembers. Because educating its students is the number-one goal of Nebraska State, will this evidence influence Nebraska State officials to join a big-time conference?

prices, but this does not mean the dance *caused* the event. Even though there is a statistical relationship between two variables in a number of observations, eventually the voodoo dance will be performed, and stock prices will fall or remain unchanged. The reason is that there is no true economic relationship between voodoo dances and stock prices.

Further investigation may reveal that stock prices actually responded to changes in interest rates during the months that voodoo dances were performed. Changes in interest rates affect borrowing and, in turn, profits and stock prices. On the other hand, there is no real economic relationship between voodoo dances and stock prices, and, therefore, the voodoo model is not valid.

The Council of Economic Advisors (http://www.whitehouse.gov/WH/EOP/CEA/html/CEA.html) *and the Bank of America* (http://www.bankamerica.com/) *are just two examples of organizations that hire economists to predict how the economy will behave and also provide the latest data on economic performance.*

Conclusion *The fact that one event follows another does not necessarily mean that the first event caused the second event.*

Throughout this book, you will study economic models or theories that include variables linked by stable cause-and-effect relationships. For example, the theory that a change in the price of a good *causes* a change in the quantity purchased is a valid microeconomic model. The theory that a change in the money supply *causes* a change in interest rates is an example of a valid macroeconomic model. The following You're the Economist gives some amusing examples of the "association means causation" reasoning pitfall.

Why Do Economists Disagree?

Why might one economist say a clean environment should be our most important priority and another economist say economic growth should be our most important goal? If economists share the economic way of thinking and carefully avoid reasoning pitfalls, then why do they disagree? Why are economists known for giving advice by saying, "On the one hand, if you do this, then *A* results, and, on the other hand, doing this causes result *B*?" In

Mops and Brooms, the Boston Snow Index, the Super Bowl, and Other Economic Indicators

Applicable Concept: association versus causation

Although the Commerce Department, the Wharton School, the Federal Reserve Board, and other organizations publish economic forecasts and data on key economic indicators, they are not without armchair competition. For example, the chief executive of Standex International Corporation, Daniel E. Hogan, reports that his company can predict economic downturns and recoveries from sales reports of its National Metal Industries subsidiary in Springfield, Massachusetts. National makes metal parts for about 300 U.S. manufacturers of mops and brooms. A drop in National's sales always precedes a proportional fall in consumer spending. The company's sales always pick up slightly before consumer spending does.[1]

The Boston Snow Index (BSI) is the brainchild of one of the vice presidents of a New York securities firm. It predicts a rising economy for the next year if there is snow on the ground in Boston on Christmas Day. The BSI has predicted correctly about 73 percent of the time over the past 30 years. However, its creator, David L. Upshaw, does not take it too seriously and views it as a spoof of other forecasters' methods.

Greeting card sales are another tried and true indicator, according to a vice president of American Greetings. Before a recession sets in, sales of higher-priced greeting cards rise. It seems that people substitute the cards for gifts, and since there is no gift, the card must be fancier.

A Super Bowl win by an NFC team predicts that the stock market the following December will be higher than the year before. A win by an old AFL team predicts a dip in the stock market.

Several other less well-known indicators have also been proposed. For example, one economist says that the surliness of waiters is a countercyclical indicator. If they are nice, expect that bad times are coming, but if they are rude, expect an upturn. Waiters, on the other hand, counter that a fall in the average tip usually precedes a downturn in the economy.

Finally, Anthony Chan, chief economist for Bank One Investment Advisers, studied marriage trends over a 34-year period. He discovered that when the number of marriages increases, the economy rises significantly, and a slowdown in marriages is followed by a decline in the economy. Chan explains that there is usually about a one-year lag between a change in the marriage rate and the economy.[2]

ANALYZE THE ISSUE

Which of the above indicators are examples of causation? Explain.

---

[1]"Economic Indicators, Turtles, Butterflies, Monks, and Waiters," *Wall Street Journal*, Aug. 27, 1979, pp. 1, 16.
[2]Sandra Block, "Worried? Look at Wedding Bell Indicator," *The Charlotte Observer*, Apr. 15, 1995, p. 8A.

---

fact, President Harry Truman once jokingly exclaimed, "Find me an economist with one hand." George Bernard Shaw offered another famous line in the same vein: "If you took all the economists in the world and laid them end to end, they would never reach a conclusion." These famous quotes imply that economists should agree, but ignore the fact that physicists, doctors, business executives, lawyers, and all professionals often disagree.

It may appear that economists disagree more than other professionals partly because it is more interesting to report disagreements than agreements. Actually, economists agree on a wide range of issues. Many economists, for example, agree on free trade among nations, the elimination of farm subsidies and rent ceilings, government deficit spending to recover from recession, and many other issues. When disagreements do exist, the reason can often be explained by the difference between *positive economics* and *normative economics.*

Positive Economics

Positive economics
An analysis limited to statements that are verifiable.

Positive economics deals with facts and therefore addresses "what is" or "verifiable" questions. Positive economics is an analysis limited to statements that are verifiable. Positive statements can be proven either true or false. Often a positive statement is expressed "If *A,* then *B.*" For example, if the national unemployment rate rises to 7 percent, then teenage unemployment exceeds 80 percent. This is a positive "if-then" prediction, which may or may not be correct. Accuracy is not the criterion for being a positive statement. The key consideration is whether the statement is *testable* and not whether it is true or false. Suppose the data show that when the nation's overall unemployment rate is close to 7 percent, the unemployment rate for teenagers never reaches 80 percent. For example, the overall unemployment rate was 6.9 percent in 1993, and the rate for teenagers was 19 percent—far short of 80 percent. Based on the facts, we would conclude that this positive statement is false.

Now we can explain one reason why economists' forecasts can diverge. The statement "If event *A* occurs, then event *B* follows" can be thought of as a *conditional* positive statement. For example, two economists may agree that if the federal government cuts spending by 10 percent this year, prices will fall about 2 percent next year. However, their predictions about the fall in prices may differ because one economist assumes Congress will not cut spending, while the other economist assumes Congress will cut spending by 10 percent.

> **Conclusion** *Economists' forecasts can differ because, using the same methodology, economists can agree that event* A *causes event* B, *but disagree over the assumption that event* A *will occur.*

Normative Economics

Normative economics
An analysis based on value judgments.

Instead of using objective statements, an argument can be phrased subjectively. **Normative economics** attempts to determine "what should be." Normative economics is an analysis based on value judgments. Normative statements express an individual or collective opinion on a subject and cannot be proven by facts to be true or false. Certain words or phrases, such as *good, bad, need, should,* and *ought to,* tell us clearly that we have entered the realm of normative economics.

The point here is that people wearing different-colored glasses see the same facts differently. Each of us has individual subjective preferences that we apply to a particular subject. An animal rights activist says that no one

Does Raising the Minimum Wage Help the Working Poor?

Applicable Concepts: positive and normative analyses

In 1938, Congress enacted the federal Fair Labor Standards Act, commonly known as the "minimum-wage law." Today, a minimum-wage worker who works full-time still earns a deplorably low annual income. One approach to help the working poor earn a living wage might be to raise the minimum wage.

The dilemma for Congress is that a higher minimum wage for the employed is enacted at the expense of jobs for unskilled workers. Opponents forecast that the increased labor cost from a large minimum-wage hike would jeopardize hundreds of thousands of unskilled jobs. For example, employers may opt to purchase more capital and less expensive labor. The fear of such sizable job losses forces Congress to perform a difficult balancing act to assure that a minimum-wage increase is large enough to help the working poor, but not so large as to threaten their jobs.

Some politicians claim that raising the minimum wage is a way to help the working poor without cost to taxpayers. Others believe the cost is hidden in inflation and lost employment opportunities for marginal workers, such as teenagers, the elderly, and minorities.

Another problem with raising the minimum wage to aid the working poor is that the minimum wage is a blunt weapon for redistributing wealth. Studies show that only a small percentage of minimum-wage earners are full-time workers whose family income falls below the poverty line. This means that most increases in the minimum wage go to workers who are not poor. For example, many minimum-wage workers are students living at home or workers whose spouse earns a much higher income. To help only the working poor, some economists argue that the government should target only those who need assistance, rather than using the "shotgun" approach of raising the minimum wage.

Supporters of raising the minimum wage are not convinced by these arguments. They say it is outrageous that a worker can work full-time and still live in poverty.

Moreover, people on this side of the debate believe that opponents exaggerate the dangers to the economy from a higher minimum wage. Economist Lester Thurow of the Massachusetts Institute of Technology, for example, argues that a higher minimum wage will force employers to upgrade the skills and productivity of their workers. Increasing the minimum wage may therefore be a win-win proposition, rather than a win-lose proposition. Professor Thurow is supported by the research of David Card and Alan B. Krueger. These economists studied data including the 1992 increase in New Jersey's minimum wage, the 1988 rise in California's minimum wage, and the 1990–1991 increases in the federal minimum wage. In each case, their evidence shows that modest increases in the minimum wage have resulted in little or no loss in jobs.[1] Note that we will return to this issue in Chapter 4 as an application of supply and demand analysis.

ANALYZE THE ISSUE

1. Identify two positive and two normative statements given concerning raising the minimum wage. List other minimum-wage arguments not discussed in the You're the Economist, and classify them as either positive or normative economics.

2. Give a positive and a normative argument why a business leader would oppose raising the minimum wage. Give a positive and a normative argument why a labor leader would favor raising the minimum wage.

3. Explain your position on this issue. Identify positive and normative reasons for your decision. Are there alternative ways to aid the working poor?

---

[1] David Card and Alan B. Krueger, *Myth and Measurement: The New Economics of the Minimum Wage* (Princeton, N.J.: Princeton University Press, 1995).

For more on the minimum wage, go to: http://www.dol.gov/dol/esa/public/minwage/main.htm.

should purchase a fur coat. Or one senator argues, "We *ought to* see that every teenager who wants a job has one." Another senator counters by saying, "Maintaining the purchasing power of the dollar is *more important* than teenage unemployment."

Conclusion *When opinions or points of view are not based on facts, they are scientifically untestable.*

When considering a debate, make sure to separate the arguments into their positive and normative components. This distinction allows you to determine if you are choosing a course of action based on factual evidence or on opinion. The material presented in this textbook, like most of economics, takes pains to stay within the boundaries of positive economic analysis. In our everyday lives, however, politicians, business executives, relatives, and friends use mostly normative statements to discuss economic issues. Economists also may associate themselves with a political position and use normative arguments for or against some economic policy. When using value judgments, an economist's normative arguments may have no greater validity than those of others. Biases or preconceptions can cloud an economist's thinking about deficit spending or whether to increase taxes on gasoline. Like beginning economics students, economists are human.

Careers in Economics

The author of this text entered college more years ago than I would like to admit. In those days, economics was not taught in high school, so I knew nothing of the subject. Like many students taking this course, I was uncertain about which major to pursue, but selected electrical engineering because I was an amateur radio operator and enjoyed building radio receivers and transmitters. My engineering curriculum required a course in economics. I signed up thinking that "Econ is boring." Instead, it was an eye-opening experience that inspired me to change my major to economics and pursue an economics teaching career.

The study of economics has attracted a number of well-known people. Both John F. Kennedy and the Rolling Stones' Mick Jagger attended the London School of Economics. Other famous people who majored in economics include Supreme Court Justice Sandra Day O'Connor, actor Arnold Schwarzenegger, and three former presidents—George H. Bush, Ronald Reagan, and Gerald Ford.

An economics major can lead to many career paths. Most economics majors work for business firms. Because economists are trained in analyzing financial matters, they find good jobs in management, sales, or as an analyst interpreting economic conditions relevant to a firm's markets. With an undergraduate degree, private-sector job opportunities exist in banking, securities brokering, management consulting, computer and data processing firms, the utility industry, statistical and market research and analysis, finance, the health care industry, and many others. The remainder of economics majors work for government agencies or in colleges and universities.

For additional information concerning career opportunities in economics, visit the Web site for the publisher of this textbook: http://www.swcollege.com/bef/career_resources_main.html.

EXHIBIT 3 Average Yearly Salary Offers for Selected Majors

Undergraduate Major	Average Offer, January 2001
Computer engineering	$53,443
Computer science	51,581
Electrical engineering	50,850
Management information systems	44,879
Mathematics	44,694
Economics	40,297
Foreign language	37,929
Liberal arts and sciences	37,313
Business administration	36,314
Nursing	34,517
Marketing	33,929
Journalism	33,514
Political science	32,265
Visual & performing arts	29,163
Sociology	28,874
Psychology	28,429
Secondary education	28,261
Animal science	28,323
Environmental science	26,173
Criminal justice	24,944
Social work	24,642

Source: National Association of Colleges and Employers, *Salary Survey*, 40 (Winter 2001): 4–5.

Government economists work for federal, state, and local governments. For example, a government economist might compile and report national statistics for economic growth or work on projects such as how to improve indexes to measure trends in consumer prices. Economists in academe not only enjoy the challenge of teaching economics, but have great freedom in selecting research projects.

Studying economics is also an essential preparation for other careers. Those preparing for law school, for example, find economics an excellent major because of its emphasis on a logical approach to problem solving. Economics is also great preparation for an MBA. In fact, students majoring in any field will benefit throughout their lives from learning how to apply the economic way of thinking to analyze real-world economic issues.

Finally, economics majors shine in salary offers upon graduation. Exhibit 3 shows average yearly salary offers for bachelor degree candidates for January 2001.

KEY CONCEPTS

Scarcity
Resources
Land
Labor

Entrepreneurship
Capital
Economics

Macroeconomics
Microeconomics
Model

Ceteris paribus
Positive economics
Normative economics

SUMMARY

- **Scarcity** is the fundamental economic problem that human wants exceed the availability of time, goods, and resources. Individuals and society therefore can never have everything they desire.

- **Resources** are factors of production classified as land, labor, and capital. Entrepreneurship is a special type of labor. An entrepreneur combines resources to produce innovative products.

- **Economics** is the study of how individuals and society choose to allocate scarce resources in order to satisfy unlimited wants. Faced with unlimited wants and scarce resources, we must make choices among alternatives.

- **Macroeconomics** applies an economywide perspective that focuses on such issues as inflation, unemployment, and the growth rate of the economy.

- **Microeconomics** examines individual decision-making units within an economy. Microeconomics studies such topics as a consumer's response to changes in the price of coffee and the reasons for changes in the market price of personal computers.

- **Models** are simplified descriptions of reality used to understand and predict economic events. An economic model can be stated verbally or in a table, graph, or equation. If the evidence is not consistent with the model, the model is rejected.

- **Ceteris paribus** holds "all other factors unchanged" that might affect a particular relationship. If this assumption is violated, a model cannot be tested. Another reasoning pitfall is to think that *association* means *causation*.

- Use of **positive versus normative economic analysis** is a major reason for disagreements among economists. **Positive economics** uses testable statements. Often a positive argument is expressed as an "*if-then*" statement. **Normative economics** is based on value judgments or opinions and uses words such as *good, bad, ought to,* and *ought not to.*

SUMMARY OF CONCLUSION STATEMENTS

- Financial capital by itself is not productive; instead, it is only a paper claim on economic capital.

- A theory cannot be tested legitimately unless its ceteris paribus assumption is satisfied.

- The fact that one event follows another does not necessarily mean that the first event caused the second event.

- Economists' forecasts can differ because, using the same methodology, economists can agree that event *A* causes event *B*, but disagree over the assumption that event *A* will occur.

- When opinions or points of view are not based on facts, they are scientifically untestable.

STUDY QUESTIONS AND PROBLEMS

1. Explain why both nations with high living standards and nations with low living standards face the problem of scarcity. If you won $1 million in a lottery, would you escape the scarcity problem?

2. Why isn't money considered capital in economics?

3. Computer software programs are an example of
   a. capital.
   b. labor.
   c. a natural resource.
   d. none of the above.

4. Explain the difference between macroeconomics and microeconomics. Give examples of the areas of concern to each branch of economics.

5. Which of the following are microeconomic issues? Which are macroeconomic issues?
   a. How will an increase in the price of Coca-Cola affect the quantity of Pepsi-Cola sold?
   b. What will cause the nation's inflation rate to fall?
   c. How does a quota on textile imports affect the textile industry?
   d. Does a large federal budget deficit reduce the rate of unemployment in the economy?

6. A model is defined as a
   a. value judgment of the relationship between variables.
   b. presentation of all relevant aspects of real-world events.
   c. simplified description of reality used to understand the way variables are related.
   d. data set adjusted for irrational actions of people.

7. Explain the importance of an economic model being an abstraction from the real world.

8. Explain the importance of the ceteris paribus assumption for an economic model.

9. Having won the Cold War, Congress cuts spending for the military, and then unemployment rises in the U.S. defense industry. Is there causation in this situation, or are we observing an association between events?

10. Which of the following is an example of a proposition from positive economics?
    a. If Al Gore had been elected president, taxpayers would have been treated more fairly than under George W. Bush.
    b. The average rate of inflation is higher during George W. Bush's presidency than during Bill Clinton's presidency.
    c. In economic terms, George W. Bush is a better president than Bill Clinton.
    d. Bill Clinton's policies were more just toward poor people than George W. Bush's.

11. "The government should collect higher taxes from the rich and use the additional revenues to provide greater benefits to the poor." This statement is an illustration of a
    a. testable statement.
    b. basic principle of economics.
    c. statement of positive economics.
    d. statement of normative economics.

12. Analyze the positive versus normative arguments in the following case. What statements of positive economics are used to support requiring airbags? What normative reasoning is used?

Should the Government Require Airbags?

Airbag advocates say airbags will save lives and the government should require them in all cars. Airbags add an estimated $600 to the cost of a car, compared to about $100 for a set of regular seat belts. Opponents argue that, because airbags are electronic devices, they are subject to failures and have produced injuries and deaths. For example, airbags have killed both adults and children whose heads were within the inflation zone at the time of deployment. Opponents therefore believe the government should leave the decision of whether to spend an extra $600 or so for an airbag to the consumer. The role of the government should be limited to providing information on the risks of having versus not having an airbag.

ONLINE EXERCISES

Exercise 1

Does the Internet raise or lower the cost of making friends? As you consider this question, visit a virtual meeting place: the American Intercultural Student Exchange (http://www.sibling.org). Or you may wish to participate in a live chat with other people on the Internet—if so, visit Yahoo! (http://chat.yahoo.com). Explain how scarcity relates to the Internet.

Exercise 2

Visit World Factbook (http://www.odci.gov/cia/publications/factbook/index.html) and follow these steps:

1. Select the United States.
2. Note the land area and population in the United States.
3. Compute the land area per person by dividing the land area of the United States by its population size.
4. Select Japan. Repeat steps 2 and 3 for Japan.

5. How does the scarcity of land influence land-use choices? Would you find as many golf courses in Japan as in the United States? Explain.

Exercise 3

Visit Job Openings for Economists (http://www.eco.utexas.edu/joe) and select the most recent issue. Browse the Academic, International, or Nonacademic job openings for economists. Study the job descriptions and earnings for economists.

Exercise 4

Visit the White House home page—http://www.whitehouse.gov/. Look under Current News. Choose a topic you think pertains to economics. Does the subject matter pertain to macroeconomics or microeconomics? Is the analysis primarily normative or positive?

CHECKPOINT ANSWERS

Can You Prove There Is No Trillion-Dollar Person?

How can researchers ever be certain they have seen all the rich people in the United States? There is always the possibility that somewhere there is a person who qualifies. If the researchers had found one, you could have rejected the theory. Because they did not, you can only fail to reject the theory. If you said that the evidence can support, but never prove, the theory, YOU ARE CORRECT.

Should Nebraska State Join a Big-Time Athletic Conference?

Suppose universities that belong to big-time athletic conference do indeed have higher graduation rates than nonmembers. This is not the only possible explanation for the statistical correlation (or association) between the graduation rate and membership in a big-time athletic conference. A more plausible explanation is that improving academic variables, such as tuition, quality of faculty, and student/faculty ratios, and not athletic conference membership increases the graduation rate. If you said correlation does not mean causation, and therefore Nebraska State officials will not necessarily accept the graduation rate evidence, YOU ARE CORRECT.

PRACTICE QUIZ

For a visual explanation of the correct answers, visit the tutorial at http://tucker.swcollege.com.

1. Scarcity exists
   a. when people consume beyond their needs.
   b. only in rich nations.
   c. in all countries of the world.
   d. only in poor nations.

2. Which of the following would eliminate scarcity as an economic problem?
   a. Moderation of people's competitive instincts.
   b. Discovery of sufficiently large new energy reserves.
   c. Resumption of steady productivity growth.
   d. None of the above because scarcity cannot be eliminated.

3. Which of the following is *not* a resource?
   a. Land
   b. Labor
   c. Money
   d. Capital

4. Economics is the study of
   a. how to make money.
   b. how to operate a business.
   c. people making choices because of the problem of scarcity.
   d. the government decision-making process.

5. Microeconomics approaches the study of economics from the viewpoint of
   a. individual or specific markets.
   b. the operation of the Federal Reserve.
   c. economywide effects.
   d. the national economy.

6. A review of the performance of the U.S. economy during the 1990s is primarily the concern of
   a. macroeconomics.
   b. microeconomics.
   c. both macroeconomics and microeconomics.
   d. neither macroeconomics nor microeconomics.

7. An economic theory claims that a rise in gasoline prices will cause gasoline purchases to fall, ceteris paribus. The phrase "ceteris paribus" means that
   a. other relevant factors like consumer incomes must be held constant.
   b. gasoline prices must first be adjusted for inflation.
   c. the theory is widely accepted but cannot be accurately tested.
   d. consumers' need for gasoline remains the same regardless of price.

8. An economist notices that sunspot activity is high just prior to recessions and concludes that sunspots cause recessions. The economist has
   a. confused association and causation.
   b. misunderstood the ceteris paribus assumption.
   c. used normative economics to answer a positive question.
   d. built an untestable model.

9. Which of the following is a statement of positive economics?
   a. The income tax system collects a lower percentage of the incomes of the poor.
   b. A reduction in tax rates of the rich makes the tax system more fair.
   c. Tax rates ought to be raised to finance health care.
   d. All of the above are primarily statements of positive economics.

10. Which of the following is a statement of positive economics?
   a. An unemployment rate greater than 8 percent is good because prices will fall.
   b. An unemployment rate of 7 percent is a serious problem.
   c. If the overall unemployment rate is 7 percent, black unemployment rates will average 15 percent.
   d. Unemployment is a more severe problem than inflation.

11. Which of the following is a statement of normative economics?
   a. The minimum wage is good because it raises wages for the working poor.
   b. The minimum wage is supported by unions.
   c. The minimum wage reduces jobs for less-skilled workers.
   d. The minimum wage encourages firms to substitute capital for labor.

12. Select the normative statement that completes the following sentence: If the minimum wage is raised rapidly, then
   a. inflation will increase.
   b. workers will gain their rightful share of total income.
   c. profits will fall.
   d. unemployment will rise.

Applying Graphs to Economics

Economists are famous for their use of graphs. The reason is "a picture is worth a thousand words." Graphs are used throughout this text to present economics models. By drawing a line, you can use a two-dimensional illustration to analyze the effects of a change in one variable on another. You could describe the same information using other model forms, such as verbal statements, tables, or equations, but the graph is the simplest way to present and understand the relationship between economic variables.

Don't be worried that graphs will "throw you for a loop." Relax! This appendix explains all the basic graphical language you will need. The following illustrates the simplest use of graphs for economic analysis.

A Direct Relationship

Basic economic analysis typically concerns the relationship between two variables, both having positive values. Hence, we can confine our graphs to the upper right (northeast) quadrant of the coordinate number system. In Exhibit A-1, notice that the scales on the horizontal axis (*x*-axis) and the vertical axis (*y*-axis) do not necessarily measure the same numerical values.

The horizontal axis in Exhibit A-1 measures annual income, and the vertical axis shows the amount spent per year for a personal computer (PC). In the absence of any established traditions, we could decide to measure income on the vertical axis and expenditure on the horizontal axis. The intersection of the horizontal and the vertical axes is the *origin* and the point where both income and expenditure are zero. In Exhibit A-1, each point is a coordinate that matches the dollar value of income and the corresponding expenditure

EXHIBIT A-1　A Direct Relationship between Variables

Expenditure for a Personal Computer at Different Annual Incomes

Point	Personal computer expenditure (thousands of dollars per year)	Annual income (thousands of dollars)
A	$1	$10
B	2	20
C	3	30
D	4	40

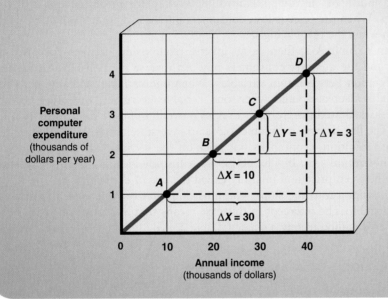

The line with a positive slope shows that the expenditure per year for a personal computer has a direct relationship to annual income, ceteris paribus. As annual income increases along the horizontal axis, the amount spent on a PC also increases, as measured by the vertical axis. Along the line, each 10-unit increase in annual income results in a 1-unit increase in expenditure for a PC. Because the slope is constant along a straight line, we can measure the same slope between any two points. Between points *B* and *C* or between points *A* and *D*, the slope is $(\Delta Y/(\Delta X = +3/+30 = +1/+10 = 1/10$.

for a PC. For example, point *A* on the graph shows that people with an annual income of $10,000 spent $1,000 per year for a PC. Other incomes are associated with different expenditure levels. For example, at $30,000 per year (point *C*), $3,000 will be spent annually for a PC.

　　The straight line in Exhibit A-1 allows us to determine the direction of change in PC expenditure as annual income changes. This relationship is *positive* because PC expenditure, measured along the vertical axis, and annual income, measured along the horizontal axis, move in the same direction. PC expenditure increases as annual income increases. As income declines, so does the amount spent on a PC. Thus, the straight line representing the relationship between income and PC expenditure is a **direct relationship**. A direct relationship is a positive association between two variables. When one variable increases, the other variable increases, and when one variable decreases, the other variable decreases. In short, both variables change in the *same* direction.

Direct relationship

A positive association between two variables. When one variable increases, the other variable increases, and when one variable decreases, the other variable decreases.

Finally, an important point to remember: A two-variable graph, like any model, isolates the relationship between two variables and holds all other variables constant under the ceteris paribus assumption. In Exhibit A-1, for example, such factors as the prices of PCs and education are held constant by assumption. In Chapter 3, you will learn that allowing variables not shown in the graph to change can shift the position of the curve.

An Inverse Relationship

Now consider the relationship between the price of compact discs (CDs) and the quantity consumers will buy per year, shown in Exhibit A-2. These data indicate a *negative* relationship between the price and quantity variables. When the price is low, consumers purchase a greater quantity of CDs than when the price is high.

In Exhibit A-2, there is an **inverse relationship** between the price per CD and the quantity consumers buy. An inverse relationship is a negative association between two variables. When one variable increases, the other variable decreases, and when one variable decreases, the other variable increases. Stated simply, the variables move in *opposite* directions.

The line drawn in Exhibit A-2 is an inverse relationship. By long-established tradition, economists put price on the vertical axis and quantity on the horizontal axis. In Chapter 3, we will study in more detail the relationship between price and quantity called the *law of demand*.

In addition to the slope, you must interpret the *intercept* at point *A* in the exhibit. The intercept in this case means that at a price of $25 no consumer is willing to buy a single CD.

The Slope of a Straight Line

Plotting numbers gives a clear visual expression of the relationship between two variables, but it is also important to know how much one variable changes as another variable changes. To find out, we calculate the **slope**. The slope is the ratio of the change in the variable on the vertical axis (the rise or fall) to the change in the variable on the horizontal axis (the run). Algebraically, if *Y* is on the vertical axis and *X* is on the horizontal axis, the slope is expressed as follows (the delta symbol, Δ, means "change in"):

$$\text{Slope} = \frac{\text{rise}}{\text{run}} = \frac{\text{change in vertical axis}}{\text{change in horizontal axis}} = \frac{\Delta Y}{\Delta X}$$

Consider the slope between points *B* and *C* in Exhibit A-1. The change in expenditure for a PC, *Y*, is equal to +1 (from $2,000 up to $3,000 per year), and the change in annual income, *X*, is equal to +10 (from $20,000 up to $30,000 per year). The slope is therefore +1/+10. The sign is positive because computer expenditure is directly, or positively, related to annual income. The steeper the line, the greater the slope because the ratio of ΔY to ΔX rises. Conversely, the flatter the line, the smaller the slope. Exhibit A-1 also illustrates that the slope of a straight line is constant. That is, the slope between any two points along the line, such as between points *A* and *D*, is equal to +3/+30 = 1/10.

Inverse relationship

A negative association between two variables. When one variable increases, the other variable decreases, and when one variable decreases, the other variable increases.

Slope

The ratio of change in the variable on the vertical axis (the rise or fall) to a change in the variable on the horizontal axis (the run).

EXHIBIT A-2   An Inverse Relationship between Variables

The Quantity of Compact Discs Consumers Purchase at Different Prices

Point	Price per compact disc	Quantity of compact discs purchased (millions per year)
A	$25	0
B	20	25
C	15	50
D	10	75
E	5	100

The line with a negative slope shows an inverse relationship between the price per compact disc and the quantity of CDs consumers purchase, ceteris paribus. As the price of a CD rises, the quantity of CDs purchased falls. A lower price for CDs is associated with more CDs purchased by consumers. Along the line, with each $5 decrease in the price of CDs, consumers increase the quantity purchased by 25 units. The slope = $(\Delta Y/\Delta X = -5/+25 = -1/5$.

What does the slope of 1/10 mean? It tells you that a $1,000 increase (decrease) in PC expenditure each year occurs for each $10,000 increase (decrease) in annual income. The line plotted in Exhibit A-1 has a *positive slope*, and we describe the line as "upward sloping."

On the other hand, the line in Exhibit A-2 has a *negative slope*. The change in Y between points C and D is equal to −5 (from $15 down to $10), and the change in X is equal to 25 (from 50 million up to 75 million CDs purchased per year). The slope is therefore −5/+25 = −1/5, and this line is described as "downward sloping."

What does this slope of −1/5 mean? It means that raising (lowering) the price per CD by $1 decreases (increases) the quantity of CDs purchased by 5 million per year.

EXHIBIT A-3   **An Independent Relationship between Variables**

The flat line with a zero slope shows that the expenditure per year for toothpaste is unrelated to annual income. As annual income increases along the horizontal axis, the amount spent each year for toothpaste remains unchanged at 20 units. If annual income increases 10 units, the corresponding change in expenditure is zero. The slope = $\Delta Y / \Delta X$ = $0/+10$ = 0.

Expenditure for Toothpaste at Different Annual Incomes

Point	Toothpaste expenditure (dollars per year)	Annual income (thousands of dollars)
A	$20	$10
B	20	20
C	20	30
D	20	40

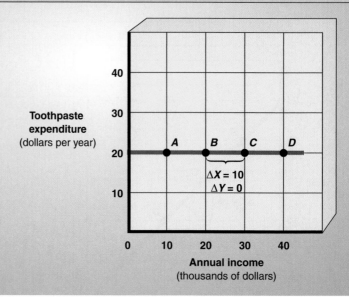

Suppose we calculate the slope between any two points on a flat line—say, points *B* and *C* in Exhibit A-3. In this case, there is no change in *Y* (expenditure for toothpaste) as *X* (annual income) increases. Consumers spend $20 per year on toothpaste regardless of annual income. It follows that $\Delta Y = 0$ for any ΔX, so the slope is equal to 0. The two variables along a flat line (horizontal or vertical) have an **independent relationship**. An independent relationship is a zero association between two variables. When one variable changes, the other variable remains unchanged.

Independent relationship

A zero relationship between two variables. When one variable changes, the other variable remains unchanged.

The Slope of a Curve

The slope of a curve changes from one point to another. Suppose the relationship between the expenditure for a PC per year and annual income is not a straight line, but an upward-sloping curve, as drawn in Exhibit A-4. This means the slope of the curve is *positive* as we move along the curve. To calculate the slope of a given point on the curve requires two steps. For example, at point *A*, the first step is to draw a tangent line that just touches

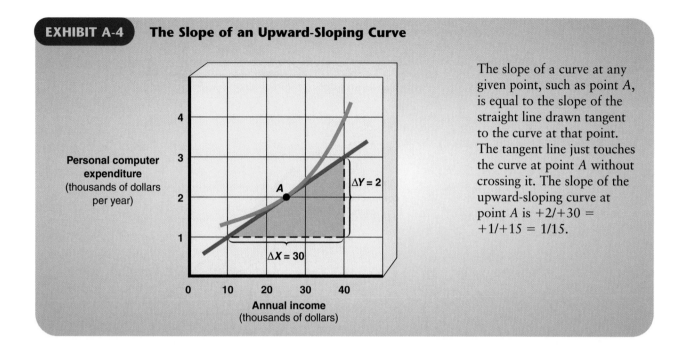

EXHIBIT A-4   **The Slope of an Upward-Sloping Curve**

The slope of a curve at any given point, such as point *A*, is equal to the slope of the straight line drawn tangent to the curve at that point. The tangent line just touches the curve at point *A* without crossing it. The slope of the upward-sloping curve at point *A* is $+2/+30 = +1/+15 = 1/15$.

the curve at this point without crossing it. The second step is to determine the slope of the tangent line. In Exhibit A-4, the slope of the tangent line, and therefore the slope of the curve at point *A*, is $+2/+30 = +1/+15 = 1/15$. What does this slope of $+1/+15$ mean? It means that at point *A* there will be a $1,000 increase (decrease) in PC expenditure each year for each $15,000 increase (decrease) in annual income.

Now consider that the relationship between the price per CD and the quantity demanded by consumers per year is the downward-sloping curve shown in Exhibit A-5. In this case, the slope of the curve is *negative* as we move along the curve. To calculate the slope at point *A*, draw a line tangent to the curve at point *A*. Thus, the slope of the curve at point *A* is $-10/+50 = -1/+5 = -1/5$.

A Three-Variable Relationship in One Graph

The two-variable relationships drawn so far conform to a two-dimensional flat piece of paper. For example, the vertical axis measures the price per CD variable, and the horizontal axis measures the quantity of CDs purchased variable. All other factors, such as consumer income, that may affect the relationship between the price and quantity variables are held constant by the ceteris paribus assumption. But reality is frequently not so accommodating. Often a model must take into account the impact of changes in a third variable (consumer income) drawn on a two-dimensional piece of graph paper.

The Slope of a Downward-Sloping Curve

In this exhibit, the negative slope changes as one moves from point to point along the curve. The slope at any given point, such as point *A*, can be determined by the slope of the straight line tangent to that point. The slope of the downward-sloping curve at point *A* is $-10/+50 = -1/+5 = -1/5$.

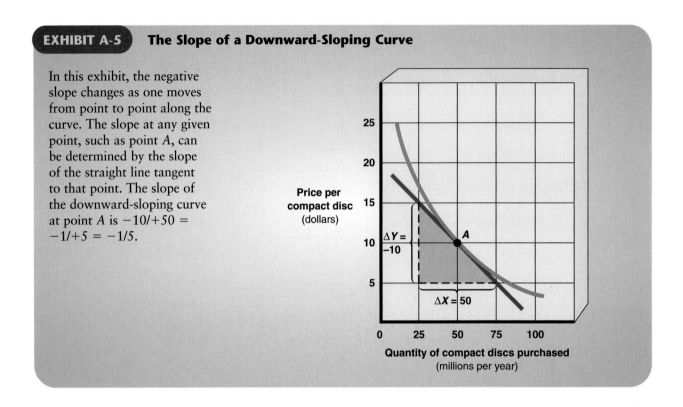

Price per compact disc (dollars)

Quantity of compact discs purchased (millions per year)

Economists' favorite method of depicting a three-variable relationship is shown in Exhibit A-6. As explained earlier, the cause-and-effect relationship between price and quantity of CDs determines the downward-sloping curve. A change in the price per CD causes a movement downward along either of the two separate curves. As the price falls, consumers increase the quantity of CDs demanded. The location of each curve on the graph, however, depends on the annual income of consumers. As the annual income variable increases from $30,000 to $60,000 and consumers can afford to pay more, the price–quantity demanded curve shifts rightward. Conversely, as the annual income variable decreases and consumers have less to spend, the price–quantity demanded curve shifts leftward.

This is an extremely important concept that you must understand: Throughout this book, you must distinguish between *movements along* and *shifts in* a curve. Here's how to tell the difference. A change in one of the variables shown on either of the coordinate axes of the graph causes *movement along* a curve. On the other hand, a change in a variable not shown on one of the coordinate axes of the graph causes a *shift in* a curve's position on the graph.

Conclusion *A shift in a curve occurs only when the* ceteris paribus *assumption is relaxed and a third variable not shown on either axis of the graph is allowed to change.*

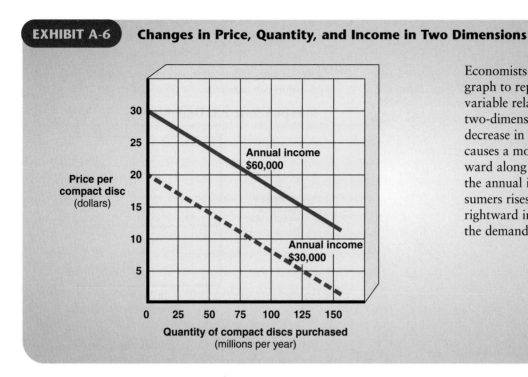

EXHIBIT A-6 **Changes in Price, Quantity, and Income in Two Dimensions**

Economists use a multicurve graph to represent a three-variable relationship in a two-dimensional graph. A decrease in the price per CD causes a movement downward along each curve. As the annual income of consumers rises, there is a shift rightward in the position of the demand curve.

A Helpful Study Hint Using Graphs

To some students, studying economics is a little frightening because many chapters are full of graphs. An often-repeated mistake is to prepare for tests by trying to memorize the lines of graphs. When their graded tests are returned, the students using this strategy will probably exclaim, "What happened?" The answer is that if you learn the economic concepts first, then you will understand the graphs as illustrations of these underlying concepts. Stated simply, superficial cramming for economics quizzes does not work. For students who are anxious about using graphs, in addition to the brief review of graphical analysis in this appendix, the Graphing Workshop on the Tucker Xtra! web site and the Study Guide contain step-by-step features on how to interpret graphs.

KEY CONCEPTS

Direct relationship   Slope
Inverse relationship   Independent relationship

SUMMARY

- **Graphs** provide a means to clearly show economic relationships in two-dimensional space. Economic analysis is often concerned with two variables confined to the upper right (northeast) quadrant of the coordinate number system.

- A **direct relationship** occurs when two variables change in the *same* direction.

Direct relationship

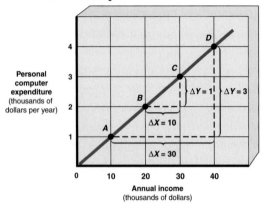

- An **inverse relationship**, occurs when two variables change in *opposite* directions.

Inverse relationship

- An **independent relationship**, occurs when two variables are unrelated.

Independent relationship

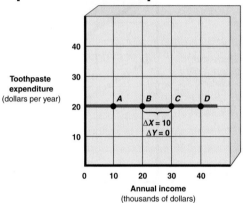

- **Slope** is the ratio of the vertical change (the rise or fall) to the horizontal change (the run). The slope of an *upward-sloping* line is *positive*, and the slope of a *downward-sloping* line is *negative*.

Positive slope of an upward-sloping curve

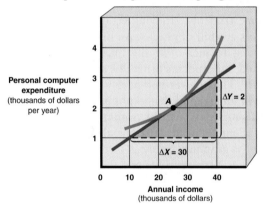

Negative slope of a downward-sloping curve

- A three-variable relationship is depicted by a graph showing a shift in a curve when the ceteris paribus assumption is relaxed and a third variable (such as annual income) not on either axis of the graph is allowed to change.

SUMMARY OF CONCLUSION STATEMENT

- A shift in a curve occurs only when the *ceteris paribus* assumption is relaxed and a third variable not on either axis of the graph is allowed to change.

STUDY QUESTIONS AND PROBLEMS

1. Draw a graph without specific data for the expected relationship between the following variables:
   a. The probability of living and age
   b. Annual income and years of education
   c. Inches of snow and sales of bathing suits
   d. The number of football games won and the athletic budget
   In each case, state whether the expected relationship is *direct* or *inverse*. Explain an additional factor that would be included in the *ceteris paribus* assumption because it might change and influence your theory.

2. Assume a research firm collects survey sales data that reveal the relationship between the possible selling prices of hamburgers and the quantity of hamburgers consumers would purchase per year at alternative prices. The report states that if the price of a hamburger is $4, 20,000 will be bought. However, at a price of $3, 40,000 hamburgers will be bought. At $2, 60,000 hamburgers will be bought, and at $1, 80,000 hamburgers will be purchased.

   Based on these data, describe the relevant relationship between the price of a hamburger and the quantity consumers are willing to purchase, using a verbal statement, a numerical table, and a graph. Which model do you prefer and why?

PRACTICE QUIZ

For a visual explanation of the correct answers, visit the tutorial at http://tucker.swcollege.com.

Exhibit A-7 Straight Line

1. Straight line *CD* in Exhibit A-7 shows that
   a. increasing the value of *X* will increase the value of *Y*.
   b. decreasing the value of *X* will decrease the value of *Y*.
   c. there is a direct relationship between *X* and *Y*.
   d. all of the above.

2. In Exhibit A-7, the slope of straight line *CD* is
   a. 3.
   b. 1.
   c. −1.
   d. 1/2.

3. In Exhibit A-7, the slope of straight line *CD* is
   a. positive.
   b. zero.
   c. negative.
   d. variable.

4. Straight line *AB* in Exhibit A-8 shows that
   a. increasing the value of *X* reduces the value of *Y*.
   b. decreasing the value of *X* increases the value of *Y*.
   c. there is an inverse relationship between *X* and *Y*.
   d. all of the above are true.

5. As shown in Exhibit A-8, the slope of straight line *AB*
   a. decreases with increases in *X*.
   b. increases with increases in *X*.
   c. increases with decreases in *X*.
   d. remains constant with changes in *X*.

Exhibit A-8 Straight Line

6. In Exhibit A-8, the slope of straight line *AB* is
   a. 3.
   b. 1.
   c. −1.
   d. −5.

7. A shift in a curve represents a change in
   a. the variable on the horizontal axis.
   b. the variable on the vertical axis.
   c. a third variable that is not on either axis.
   d. any variable that is relevant to the relationship being graphed.

8. A change in a third variable *not* on either axis of a graph is illustrated by a
   a. horizontal or vertical line.
   b. movement along a curve.
   c. shift of a curve.
   d. point of intersection.

9. What is used to illustrate an independent relationship between two variables?
   a. An upward-sloping curve.
   b. A downward-sloping curve.
   c. A hill-shaped curve.
   d. A horizontal or vertical line.

10. When an inverse relationship is graphed, the resulting line or curve is
    a. horizontal.
    b. vertical.
    c. upward sloping.
    d. downward sloping.

11. Which of the following pairs is the *most* likely to exhibit an inverse relationship?
    a. The amount of time you study and your grade point average.
    b. People's annual income and their expenditure on personal computers.
    c. Baseball players' salaries and their batting averages.
    d. The price of a concert and the number of tickets people purchase.

12. Which of the following pairs is the *most* likely to exhibit a direct relationship?
    a. The price of gasoline and the amount of gasoline that people purchase.
    b. Cholesterol levels and the likelihood of developing heart disease.
    c. Outdoor temperature and heating oil sales.
    d. Annual income and weekly pawn shop visits.

CHAPTER 2

Production Possibilities, Opportunity Cost, and Economic Growth

This chapter continues building on the foundation laid in the preceding chapter. Having learned that *scarcity* forces *choices*, here you will study the choices people make in more detail. This chapter begins by examining the three basic choices: *What, How,* and *For Whom* to produce. The process of answering these basic questions introduces two other key building blocks in the economic way of thinking—*opportunity cost* and *marginal analysis*. Once you understand these important concepts stated in words, it will be easier to interpret our first formal economic model, the *production possibilities curve*. This model illustrates how economists use graphs as a powerful tool to supplement words and develop an understanding of basic economic principles. You will discover that the production possibilities

model teaches many of the most important concepts in economics, including scarcity, the law of increasing opportunity costs, efficiency, investment, and economic growth. For example, the chapter concludes by using the production possibilities curve to explain why underdeveloped countries do not achieve economic growth and thereby improve their standard of living.

In this chapter, you will learn to solve these economics puzzles:

■ Why do so few rock stars and movie stars go to college?

■ Why would you spend an extra hour reading this text, rather than going to a movie or sleeping?

■ Why are investment and economic growth so important?

The Three Fundamental Economic Questions

Whether rich or poor, every nation must answer these same three fundamental economic questions: (1) *What* products will be produced? (2) *How* will they be produced? (3) *For Whom* will they be produced? Later, the chapter on economies in transition introduces various types of economic systems and describes how each deals with these three economic choices.

What to Produce?

Should society devote its limited resources to producing more military goods and fewer consumer goods and services? Should society produce more CDs and fewer computer software programs? Should more small cars and fewer large cars be produced, or should more buses be produced instead of cars? The problem of scarcity restricts our ability to produce everything we want during a given period, so the choice to produce "more" of a good requires producing "less" of another good.

How to Produce?

After deciding which products to make, the second question for society to decide is how to mix technology and scarce resources in order to produce these goods. For instance, a towel can be sewn primarily by hand (labor), partially by hand and partially by machine (labor and capital), or primarily by machine (capital). In short, the How question asks whether a production technique will be more or less capital-intensive.

Education plays an important role in answering the How question. Education improves the ability of workers to perform their work. Variation in the quality and quantity of education among nations is one reason economies differ in their capacities to apply resources and technology to answer the How question. For example, the United States is striving to catch up with Japan in the use of robotics. Answering the question "How to improve our robotics?" requires engineers and employees with the proper training in the installation and operation of robots.

For Whom to Produce?

Once the What and How questions are resolved, the third question is For Whom. Among all those desiring the produced goods, who actually receives them? Who is fed well? Who drives a Mercedes? Who receives organ transplants? Should economics professors earn a salary of $1 million a year and others pay higher taxes to support economists? The For Whom question means that society must have a method to decide who will be "rich and famous" and who will be "poor and unknown."

Opportunity Cost

Because of scarcity, the three basic questions cannot be answered without sacrifice or cost. But what does the term *cost* really mean? The common response would be to say that the purchase price is the cost. A movie ticket *costs* $8, or a shirt *costs* $50. Applying the economic way of thinking, however, *cost* is defined differently. A well-known phrase in economics says, "There is no such thing as a free lunch." This expression captures the links among the concepts of scarcity, choice, and cost. Because of scarcity, people must make choices, and each choice incurs a cost (sacrifice). Once one option is chosen, another option is given up. The money you spend on a movie ticket cannot also buy a videotape. A business may purchase a new textile machine to manufacture towels, but this same money cannot be used to buy a new recreation facility for employees.

The videotape and the recreation facility examples illustrate that the true cost of these decisions is the **opportunity cost** of a choice, not the purchase price. Opportunity cost is the best alternative sacrificed for a chosen alternative. Stated differently, it is the cost of not choosing the next best alternative. This principle states that some highly valued opportunity must be forgone in all economic decisions. The actual good or use of time given up for the chosen good or use of time measures the opportunity cost. We may omit the word *opportunity* before the word *cost*, but the concept remains the same.

Opportunity cost

The best alternative sacrificed for a chosen alternative.

Examples are endless, but let's consider a few. Suppose your economics professor decides to become a rock star in the Rolling in Dough band. Now all his or her working hours are devoted to creating hit music, and the opportunity cost is the educational services no longer provided. Now a personal example: the opportunity cost of dating a famous model or movie star (name your favorite) might be the loss of your current girlfriend or boyfriend. Opportunity cost also applies to national economic decisions. Suppose the federal government decides to spend tax revenues on a space station. The opportunity cost depends on the next best program *not* funded. Assume roads and bridges are the highest-valued projects not built as a result of the decision to construct the space station. Then the opportunity cost of the decision to devote resources to the space station is the forgone roads and bridges and not the money actually spent to build the space station.

What is the opportunity cost of attending college? To learn more about the costs and benefits of attending college, visit the U.S. Department of Education at http://www.ed.gov/.

To personalize the relationship between time and opportunity cost, ask yourself what you would be doing if you were not reading this book. Your answer might be watching television or sleeping. If sleeping is your choice, the opportunity cost of studying this text is the sleep you sacrifice. Rock stars and movie stars, on the other hand, must forfeit a large amount of income to attend college. Now you know why you see so few of these stars in class.

Decisions often involve sacrifice of *both* goods and time. Suppose you decide to see a movie located 15 minutes from campus. If you had not spent the money on the movie ticket, you could have paid for a long-distance phone call to a friend. And the time traveling to and from the movie and sitting through it could have been devoted to studying for your economics exam. The opportunity cost of the movie consists of giving up (1) a phone call and (2) a higher score on the economics exam.

Marginal Analysis

At the heart of many important decision-making techniques used throughout this text is **marginal analysis.** Marginal analysis examines the effects of additions to or subtractions from a current situation. This is a very valuable tool in the economic-way-of-thinking toolkit because it considers the "marginal" effects of change. The rational decisionmaker decides on an option only if the marginal benefit exceeds the marginal cost. For example, you must decide how to use your scarce time. Should you devote an extra hour to reading this book, going to a movie, watching television, talking on the phone, or sleeping? Which of your many options do you choose? The answer depends on marginal analysis. If you decide the benefit of a higher grade in economics exceeds the opportunity cost of, say, sleep, then you allocate the extra hour to studying economics. Excellent choice!

Businesses use marginal analysis. Hotels, for example, rent space to student groups for dances and other events. Assume you are the hotel manager and a student group offers to pay $400 to use the ballroom for a party. To decide whether to accept the offer requires marginal analysis. The marginal benefit of renting otherwise vacant space is $400, and the marginal cost is $300 for extra electricity and janitorial service. Since the marginal benefit exceeds the marginal cost, the manager sensibly accepts the offer.

Similarly, farmers use marginal analysis. For example, a farmer must decide whether to add fertilizer when planting corn. Using marginal analysis, the farmer estimates that the corn revenue yield will be about $75 per acre without fertilizer and about $100 per acre using fertilizer. If the cost of fertilizer is $20 per acre, marginal analysis tells the farmer to fertilize. The addition of fertilizer will increase profit by $5 per acre because fertilizing adds $25 to the value of each acre at a cost of $20 per acre.

Marginal analysis is an important concept when government considers changes in various programs. For example, as demonstrated in the next section, it is useful to know that an increase in the production of military goods will result in an opportunity cost of fewer consumer goods produced.

Marginal analysis
An examination of the effects of additions to or subtractions from a current situation.

The Production Possibilities Curve

The economic problem of scarcity means that society's capacity to produce combinations of goods is constrained by its limited resources. This condition can be represented in a model called the **production possibilities curve.** The production possibilities curve shows the maximum combinations of two outputs that an economy can produce in a given period of time with its available resources and technology. Three basic assumptions underlie the production possibilities curve model:

1. *Fixed Resources.* The quantities and qualities of all resource inputs remain unchanged during the time period. But the "rules of the game" do allow an economy to shift any resource from the production of one output to the production of another output. For example, an economy

Production possibilities curve
A curve that shows the maximum combinations of two outputs an economy can produce in a given period of time with its available resources and technology.

might shift workers from producing consumer goods to producing capital goods. Although the number of workers remains unchanged, this transfer of labor will produce fewer consumer goods and more capital goods.

2. *Fully Employed Resources.* The economy operates with all its factors of production fully employed and producing the greatest output possible without waste or mismanagement.

3. *Technology Unchanged.* Holding existing **technology** fixed creates limits, or constraints, on the amounts and types of goods any economy can produce. Technology is the body of knowledge applied to how goods are produced.

Exhibit 1 shows a hypothetical economy that has the capacity to manufacture any combination of military goods ("guns") and consumer goods ("butter") per year along its production possibilities curve (*PPC*), including points *A*, *B*, *C*, and *D*. For example, if this economy uses all its resources to make military goods, it can produce a *maximum* of 160 billion units of military goods and zero units of consumer goods (combination *A*). Another possibility is for the economy to use all its resources to produce a *maximum* of 100 billion units of consumer goods and zero units of military goods (point *D*). Between the extremes of points *A* and *D* lie other production possibilities for combinations of military and consumer goods. If combination *B* is chosen, the economy will produce 140 billion units of military goods and 40 billion units of consumer goods. Another possibility (point *C*) is to produce 80 billion units of military goods and 80 billion units of consumer goods.

What happens if the economy does not use all its resources to their capacity? For example, some workers may not find work, or plants and equipment may be idle for any number of reasons. The result is that our hypothetical economy fails to reach any of the combinations along *PPC*. In Exhibit 1, point *U* illustrates an *inefficient* output level for any economy operating without all its resources fully employed. At point *U*, our model economy is producing 80 billion units of military goods and 40 billion units of consumer goods per year. Such an economy is underproducing because it could satisfy more of society's wants if it were producing at some point along *PPC*.

Even if an economy fully employs all its resources, it is impossible to produce certain output quantities. Any point outside the production possibilities curve is *unattainable* because it is beyond the economy's present production capabilities. Point *Z*, for example, represents an unattainable output of 140 billion units of military goods and 80 billion units of consumer goods. Society would prefer this combination to any combination along, or inside, *PPC*, but the economy cannot reach this point with its existing resources and technology.

Conclusion *Scarcity limits an economy to points on or below its production possibilities curve.*

Technology
The body of knowledge applied to how goods are produced.

Visit a few pacifist organizations, such as the Center for Economic Conversion at http://www.conversion.org/ *and the American Peace Network at* http://www.apn.org/. *What arguments do these organizations make for decreasing the size of the military? Do these arguments take into account the concept of opportunity cost?*

EXHIBIT 1	**The Production Possibilities Curve for Military Goods and Consumer Goods**

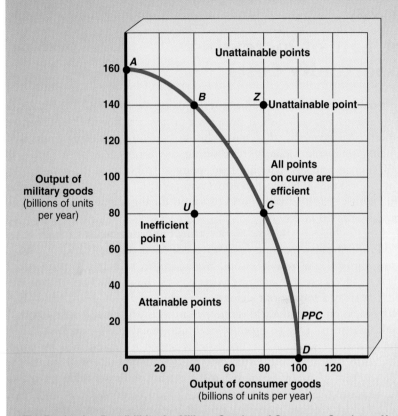

All points along the production possibilities curve (*PPC*) are maximum possible combinations of military goods and consumer goods. One possibility, point *A*, would be to produce 160 billion units of military goods and zero units of consumer goods each year. At the other extreme, point *D*, the economy uses all its resources to produce 100 billion units of consumer goods and zero units of military goods each year. Points *B* and *C* are obtained by using some resources to produce each of the two outputs. If the economy fails to utilize its resources fully, the result is the inefficient point *U*. Point *Z* lies beyond the economy's present production capabilities and is unattainable.

The Production Possibilities for Military Goods and Consumer Goods per Year

Output (billions of units per year)	Production possibilities			
	A	*B*	*C*	*D*
Military goods	160	140	80	0
Consumer goods	0	40	80	100

Because all the points along the curve are *maximum* output levels with the given resources and technology, they are all called *efficient* points. A movement between any two efficient points on the curve means that *more* of one product is produced only by producing *less* of the other product. In Exhibit 1, moving from point *A* to point *B* produces 40 billion additional units of consumer goods per year, but only at a cost of sacrificing 20 billion units of military goods. Thus, a movement between any two efficient points graphically illustrates that "There is no such thing as a free lunch."

Conclusion *The production possibilities curve consists of all efficient output combinations where an economy can produce more of one good only by producing less of the other good.*

The Law of Increasing Opportunity Costs

Why is the production possibilities curve shaped the way it is? Exhibit 2 will help us answer this question. It presents a production possibilities curve for a hypothetical economy that must choose between producing tanks and producing sailboats. Consider expanding the production of sailboats in 20,000-unit increments. Moving from point *A* to point *B*, the *opportunity cost* is 10,000 tanks; between point *B* and point *C*, the *opportunity cost* is 20,000 tanks; and the *opportunity cost* of producing at point *D*, rather than point *C*, is 50,000 tanks.

Exhibit 2 illustrates the **law of increasing opportunity costs,** which states that the opportunity cost increases as production of one output expands. Holding the stock of resources and technology constant (ceteris paribus), the law of increasing opportunity costs causes the production possibilities curve to display a *bowed-out* shape.

Why must our hypothetical economy sacrifice larger and larger amounts of tank output in order to produce each additional 20,000 sailboats? The reason is that all workers are not equally suited to producing one good, compared to another good. Expanding the output of sailboats requires the use of workers who are less suited to producing sailboats than producing tanks. Suppose our hypothetical economy produces no sailboats (point *A*) but decides to produce them. At first, the least-skilled tank workers are transferred to making sailboats, and 10,000 tanks are sacrificed. As the economy moves from point *B* to point *C*, more highly skilled tank makers become sailboat makers, and the opportunity cost rises to 20,000 tanks. Finally, the economy can decide to move from point *C* to point *D*, and the opportunity cost increases even more to 50,000 tanks. Now the remaining tank workers, who are superb tank makers, but poor sailboat makers, must adapt to the techniques of sailboat production.

Finally, it should be noted that the production possibilities curve model could assume that resources can be substituted and the opportunity cost remains constant. In this case, the production possibilities curve would be a straight line, which is the model employed in the chapter on international trade and finance.

Law of increasing opportunity costs
The principle that the opportunity cost increases as the production of one output expands.

Sources of Economic Growth

Economic growth
The ability of an economy to produce greater levels of output, represented by an outward shift of its production possibilities curve.

The economy's production capacity is not permanently fixed. If either the resource base increases or technology advances, the economy experiences **economic growth,** and the production possibilities curve shifts outward. Economic growth is the ability of an economy to produce greater levels of out-

EXHIBIT 2   The Law of Increasing Opportunity Costs

A hypothetical economy produces equal increments of 20,000 sailboats per year as we move from point *A* through point *D* on the production possibilities curve (*PPC*). If the economy moves from point *A* to point *B*, the opportunity cost of 20,000 sailboats is a reduction in tank output of 10,000 per year. This opportunity cost rises to 20,000 tanks if point *C*, instead of point *B*, is selected. Finally, production at point *D*, rather than point *C*, results in an opportunity cost of 50,000 tanks per year. The opportunity cost rises because workers are not equally suited to making tanks and sailboats.

Production Possibilities for Tanks and Sailboats per Year

Output (thousands per year)	Production possibilities			
	A	**B**	**C**	**D**
Tanks	80	70	50	0
Sailboats	0	20	40	60

put, represented by an outward shift of its production possibilities curve. Exhibit 3 illustrates the importance of an outward shift. (Note the causation chain, which is often used in this text to focus on a model's cause-and-effect relationship.) At point *A* on production possibilities curve *PPC*₁, a hypothetical full-employment economy produces 40,000 computers and 200 million pizzas per year. If the curve shifts outward to new curve *PPC*₂, the economy can expand its full-employment output options. One option is to produce at point *B* and increase computer output to 70,000 per year. Another possibility is to increase pizza output to 400 million per year. Yet another choice is to produce more of both at some point between points *B* and *C*.

The Agricultural Research Service (ARS) Department of Agriculture (http://www.ars.usda.gov/) *is the main agricultural research agency of the federal government. What types of research does the ARS conduct, and how might this research push out the production possibilities curve for the subjects of this research?*

EXHIBIT 3   An Outward Shift of the Production Possibilities Curve for Computers and Pizzas

The economy begins with the capacity to produce combinations along production possibilities curve PPC_1. Growth in the resource base or technological advances can shift the production possibilities curve outward from PPC_1 to PPC_2. Points along PPC_2 represent new production possibilities that were previously impossible. This outward shift permits the economy to produce greater quantities of output. Instead of producing combination *A*, the economy can produce, for example, more computers at point *B* or more pizzas at point *C*. If the economy produces at a point between *B* and *C*, more of both pizzas and computers can be produced, compared to point *A*.

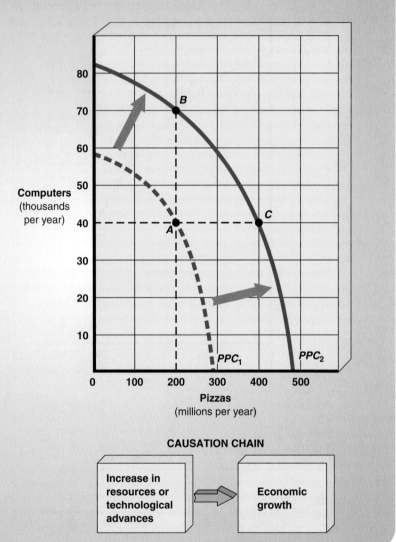

CAUSATION CHAIN

Increase in resources or technological advances ⟹ Economic growth

Changes in Resources

One way to accelerate economic growth is to gain additional resources. Any increase in resources—for example, more natural resources, a "baby boom," or more factories—will shift the production possibilities curve outward. In Exhibit 3, assume curve PPC_1 represents Japan's production possibilities for clothing and food in a given year. Suddenly, Japan discovers within its borders new sources of labor and other resources. As a result of the new resources, Japan will have an expanded capacity to produce any combination along an expanded curve, such as curve PPC_2.

Reductions in resources will cause the production possibilities curve to shift inward. Assume curve PPC_2 describes Japan's economy before World War II and the destruction of its factors of production during the war caused Japan's curve to shift leftward to curve PPC_1. Over the years, Japan trained its workforce, built new factories and equipment, and used new technology to shift its curve outward and surpass its original production capacity at curve PPC_2.

Technological Change and the New Economy

Another way to achieve economic growth is through research and development of new technologies. The knowledge of how to transform a stone into a wheel vastly improved the prehistoric standard of living. Technological change also makes it possible to shift the production possibilities curve outward by producing more from the same resources base. One source of technological change is *invention*. Light bulbs, transistors, computer chips, satellites, and the Internet are all examples of technological advances resulting from the use of science and engineering knowledge.

Technological change also results from the innovations of entrepreneurship introduced in the previous chapter. Innovation involves creating and developing new products or productive processes. Seeking profits, entrepreneurs create new, better, or less expensive products. This requires organizing an improved mix of resources, which expands the production possibilities curve.

One entrepreneur, Henry Ford, changed auto industry technology by pioneering the use of the assembly line for making cars. Another entrepreneur, Chester Carlson, a law student, became so frustrated copying documents that he worked on his own to develop photocopying. After years of disappointment, a small firm named Xerox Corporation accepted Carlson's invention and transformed a good idea into a revolutionary product. These, and a myriad of other business success stories, illustrate that entrepreneurs are important because they transform their new ideas into production and practical use.

Today the phrase the "new economy" is often heard. The **new economy** is economic growth resulting from technological advances that make businesses and workers more productive. Success stories in the new economy are endless. The dizzying array of technological changes marches on cutting costs, boosting productivity and profits. Oil companies, for example, use new computer technology to generate three-dimensional maps and they hit oil with half the number of "dry holes" than previously drilled. McDonald's now uses computer systems that transfer orders at the counter instantly to the cooks. The system also forecasts supply needs, so restaurants throw away less food. New technology is even saving tropical fish. Computer-controlled monitors that track water temperatures, acidity, and chlorine levels are resulting in fewer fish deaths per store. Such widespread technological gains mean real progress in the way we work and live.

New economy

Economic growth resulting from technological advances that make businesses and workers more productive.

Federal Express Wasn't an Overnight Success

Applicable Concept: entrepreneurship

Frederick W. Smith is a classic entrepreneurial success story. Young Fred went to Yale University, had a good new idea, secured venture capital, worked like crazy, made a fortune, and the Smithsonian Institution rendered its ultimate accolade. It snapped up an early Federal Express jet for its collection, displaying it for a time in the Air and Space Museum in Washington, D.C., not far from the Wright brothers' first airplane.

Smith's saga began with a college economics term paper that spelled out a nationwide overnight parcel delivery system that would be guaranteed to "absolutely, positively" beat the pants off the U.S. Postal Service. People, he said, would pay much more if their packages would arrive at their destination the next morning. To accomplish his plan, planes would converge nightly on Memphis, Tennessee with packages accepted at any location throughout the nation. Smith chose this city for its central U.S. location and because its airport has little bad weather to cause landing delays. In the morning hours, all items would be unloaded, sorted, and rerouted to other airports, where vans would battle rush-hour traffic to make deliveries before the noon deadline.

Smith's college term paper got a "C" grade. Perhaps the professor thought the idea was too risky, but lots of others certainly did. In 1969, after college and a tour as a Marine pilot in Vietnam, the 24-year old Smith began pitching his parcel delivery plan and most financiers were skeptical. Nevertheless, with $4 million of his family's money, he persuaded a few venture capitalists to put up $80 million. At this time, this was the largest venture capital package ever assembled. In 1973, delivery service began with 14 jets connecting 25 cities, but on the first night only 16 packages showed up.

It was years before Smith looked like a genius. The company posted a $27 million loss the first year, turned the corner in 1976, and then took off, helped by a 1981 decision to add letters to its basic package delivery service. Today, Smith's basic strategy hasn't changed, but the scale of the operation has exploded. FedEx is the world's largest express transportation company with 3.2 million packages

sorted and routed on an average night. The company flies over 600 planes around the world, painted a distinctive purple, orange, and white. Worldwide there are more than 44,000 computerized delivery vans and a 150,000 person workforce.[1]

The U.S. Postal Service may have been miffed with Smith in the past, but today FedEx is a new "cash cow" to help the Postal Service cut its annual losses. Beginning in 2001, the post office's blue mailboxes were joined by FedEx's familiar orange, white, and purple drop boxes. Also, the post office will ship express and priority mail on FedEx airplanes. This historic alliance means FedEx will pay the Postal Service as much as $230 million over seven years and FedEx will gain revenue because customers will have more conveniently located FedEx drop boxes.

ANALYZE THE ISSUE

Draw a production possibilities curve for an economy producing only pizzas and computers. Explain how Fred Smith and other entrepreneurs affect the curve.

---

[1] Eugene Carlson, "Federal Express Wasn't an Overnight Success," *Wall Street Journal*, June 6, 1989, p. B2.

CHECKPOINT

What Does a Peace Dividend Really Mean?

With the disappearance of the former Soviet Union and the end of the Cold War, the United States is the world's only superpower and is no longer engaged in an intense competition to build up its military. As a result, beginning in the 1990s Congress and the White House had the opportunity to reduce the military's share of the budget and spend more funds for nondefense goods. This situation is referred to as the "peace dividend." Does a peace dividend represent a possible shift of the production possibilities curve or a movement along it?

It can be argued that there is nothing really "new" in the new economy concept. Throughout history, technological advances have fostered economic growth by increasing our nation's productive power. Today, the Internet and computers are "new," but railroads, electricity, and automobiles, for example, were also "new" technologies in their time.

For more information about Federal Express see their Web site at http://www.fedex.com/.

Present Investment and the Future Production Possibilities Curve

When the decision for an economy involves choosing between capital and consumer goods, the output combination for the present period can determine future production capacity.

Exhibit 4 compares two countries producing different combinations of capital and consumer goods. Part (a) shows the production possibilities curve for the low-investment economy of Alpha. This economy was producing combination *A* in 2000, which is an output of C_a of consumer goods and an output of K_a of capital goods per year. Let's assume K_a is just enough capital output to replace the capital being worn out each year (depreciation). As a result, Alpha fails to accumulate the net gain of factories and equipment required to expand its production possibilities curve outward in future years.[1] Why wouldn't Alpha simply move up along its production curve by shifting more resources to capital goods production? The problem is that sacrificing consumer goods for capital formation causes the standard of living to fall.

Comparing Alpha to Beta illustrates the importance of being able to do more than just replace worn-out capital. Beta operated in 2000 at point *A* in part (b), which is an output of C_b of consumer goods and K_b of capital goods. Assuming K_b is more than enough to replenish worn-out capital, Beta is a high-investment economy, adding to its capital stock and creating

---

[1]Recall from the Appendix to Chapter 1 that a third variable can affect the variables measured on the vertical and the horizontal axes. In this case, the third variable is the quantity of capital worn out per year.

EXHIBIT 4   **Alpha's and Beta's Present and Future Production Possibilities Curves**

In part (a), each year Alpha produces only enough capital (K_a) to replace existing capital being worn out. Without greater capital and assuming other resources remain fixed, Alpha is unable to shift its production possibilities curve outward. In part (b), each year Beta produces K_b capital, which is more than the amount required to replenish its depreciated capital. In the year 2010, this expanded capital provides Beta with the extra production capacity to shift its production possibilities curve to the right. If Beta chooses point *B* on its curve, it has the production capacity to increase the amount of consumer goods from C_b to C_c without producing fewer capital goods.

Investment

The accumulation of capital, such as factories, machines, and inventories, that is used to produce goods and services.

extra production capacity. This process of accumulating capital (*capital formation*) is **investment**. Investment is the accumulation of capital, such as factories, machines, and inventories, that is used to produce goods and services. Newly manufactured factories, machines, and inventories in the present provide an economy with the capacity to expand its production options in the future. For example, the outward shift of its curve allows Beta to produce C_c consumer goods at point *B* in the year 2010. This means Beta will be able to improve its standard of living by producing $C_c - C_b$ extra consumer goods, while Alpha's standard of living remains unchanged because the production of consumer goods remains unchanged.

> **Conclusion** *A nation can accelerate economic growth by increasing its production of capital goods in excess of the capital being worn out in the production process.*

INTERNATIONAL ECONOMICS

When Japan Tumbles, Where Is It on the Curve?

Applicable Concept: production possibilities curve

In spite of its recent economic woes, Japan is known for quality products produced by dedicated workers who seek ways to avoid wasting resources—and management listens to them. Although the practice of lifetime employment is changing, workers in large industrial companies still enjoy considerable job security, which diminishes worker resistance to technological change. Japanese industry uses twice as many robots as industry in the United States and Western Europe combined.

One key to Japanese production is a bit of management genius called "just in time delivery." The goal is to produce products at precisely the right time with a minimum inventory on hand. This inventory-on-demand system allows the industrial giants to focus on assembling the final product, while smaller firms make and stock parts. For example, Mazda's workers have a small bin of headlights beside the assembly line so that parts can be quickly picked up and installed. A production manager constantly checks the supply of headlights and other parts to make sure there is no surplus of materials. As soon as more headlights are needed to fill the assembly-line bin, Mazda orders its headlights from an outside small

subcontractor located in Tokyo. The headlights arrive in a matter of hours. Thus, Mazda's only concern is installing the headlights quickly, and it does not have to invest in large inventories of headlights and other auto parts.

Many subcontractors supplying parts to the industrial giants have businesses located in their homes. Mom, Pop, and children operate a small factory in their apartment on the kitchen table and living room floor. Small children are cared for by a female member of the family who works when the children take naps. Women and children usually deliver orders, allowing men to continue producing parts at home.

Scarcity of housing is an acute problem in Japan. In fact, the average poor American has a third more living space than the average Japanese. In Tokyo, for example, few public parks are built because of the opportunity cost in terms of factories or apartment buildings. The typical Japanese family of four in Tokyo lives in an apartment with a tiny kitchen, two small rooms, and no yard. The living room by day serves as the bedroom by night. Each morning family members simply roll up their mattress beds into a closet. In addition to limited space, many houses lack

central heating, so the Japanese must warm themselves with small electric heaters. Moreover, most areas of Japan do not have sewers, so people must use septic tanks. These deficiencies explain why couples save so much in Japan; it is the only way they can hope to afford better housing. (The last chapter of this book explains in more detail how saving allows a country to invest and thereby create economic growth and development by shifting its production possibilities curve outward.)

ANALYZE THE ISSUE

Construct a production possibilities curve that represents Japan's goal of producing both cars and housing. Assume the Japanese economy is in a downturn, and indicate with an *X* the point on your graph where the Japanese are operating. (Hint: Compare an inefficient point to an efficient point.) Give examples to explain the location you have chosen for point X. Also, based on the above article, explain how the Japanese move their production possibilities curve outward.

KEY CONCEPTS

What, How, and For
   Whom questions
Opportunity cost

Marginal analysis
Production possibilities
   curve

Technology
Law of increasing
   opportunity costs

Economic growth
New economy
Investment

SUMMARY

- **Three fundamental economic questions** facing any economy are *What, How,* and *For Whom* to produce goods. The What question asks exactly which goods are to be produced and in what quantities. The How question requires society to decide the resource mix used to produce goods. The For Whom problem concerns the division of output among society's citizens.

- **Opportunity cost** is the best alternative forgone for a chosen option. This means no decision can be made without cost.

- **Marginal analysis** examines the impact of changes from a current situation and is a technique used extensively in economics. The basic approach is to compare the additional benefits of a change with the additional costs of the change.

- A **production possibilities curve** illustrates an economy's capacity to produce goods, subject to the constraint of scarcity. The production possibilities curve is a graph of the maximum possible combinations of two outputs that can be produced in a given period of time, subject to three conditions: (1) All resources are fully employed. (2) The resource base is not allowed to vary during the time period. (3) **Technology,** which is the body of knowledge applied to the production of goods, remains constant. **Inefficient** production occurs at any point inside the production possibilities curve. All points along the curve are **efficient** points because each point represents a maximum output possibility.

Production possibilities curve

- The **law of increasing opportunity costs** states that the opportunity cost increases as the production of an output expands. The explanation for this law is that the suitability of resources declines sharply as greater amounts are transferred from producing one output to producing another output.

- **Economic growth** is represented by the production possibilities curve shifting outward as the result of an increase in resources or an advance in technology. The **new economy** is economic growth resulting from technological advances that make businesses and workers more productive.

Economic growth

- **Investment** means that an economy is producing and accumulating capital. Investment consists of factories, machines, and inventories (capital) produced in the present that are used to shift the production possibilities curve outward in the future.

SUMMARY OF CONCLUSION STATEMENTS

■ Scarcity limits an economy to points on or below its production possibilities curve.

■ The production possibilities curve consists of all efficient output combinations where an economy can produce more of one good only by producing less of the other good.

■ A nation can accelerate economic growth by increasing its production of capital goods in excess of the capital being worn out in the production process.

STUDY QUESTIONS AND PROBLEMS

1. Explain why scarcity forces individuals and society to incur opportunity costs. Give specific examples.

2. Suppose a retailer promotes the store by advertising a drawing for a "free car." Is this car *free* because the winner pays *zero* for it?

3. Explain verbally the statement "There is no such thing as a free lunch" in relation to scarce resources.

4. Which of the following decisions has the greatest opportunity cost? Why?

   a. A decision to use an undeveloped lot in Tokyo's financial district for an apartment building.

   b. A decision to use a square mile in the desert for a gas station.

5. Attending college is expensive, is time-consuming, and requires effort. So why do people decide to attend college?

6. The following is a set of hypothetical production possibilities for a nation.

Combination	Automobiles (thousands)	Beef (thousands of tons)
A	0	10
B	2	9
C	4	7
D	6	4
E	8	0

   a. Plot these production possibilities data. What is the opportunity cost of the first 2,000 automobiles produced? Between which points is the opportunity cost per thousand automobiles highest? Between which points is the opportunity cost per thousand tons of beef highest?

   b. Label a point *F* inside the curve. Why is this an inefficient point? Label a point *G* outside the curve. Why is this point unattainable? Why are points *A* through *E* all efficient points?

   c. Does this production possibilities curve reflect the law of increasing opportunity costs? Explain.

   d. What assumptions could be changed to shift the production possibilities curve?

7. The following table shows the production possibilities for pies and flowerboxes. Fill in the opportunity cost (pies forgone) of producing the first through the fifth flowerbox.

Combination	Pies	Flowerboxes	Opportunity cost
A	30	0	_____
B	26	1	_____
C	21	2	_____
D	15	3	_____
E	8	4	_____
F	0	5	_____

8. Why does a production possibilities curve have a bowed-out shape?

9. Interpret the phrases "There is no such thing as a free lunch" and "A free lunch is possible" in terms of the production possibilities curve.

10. Suppose, unfortunately, your mathematics and economics professors have decided to give tests two days from now and you can spend only a total of 12 hours studying for both exams. After some thought, you conclude that dividing your study time equally between each subject will give you an expected grade of C in each course. For each additional 3 hours study

time for one of the subjects, your grade will increase one letter for that subject, and your grade will fall one letter for the other subject.

a. Construct a table for the production possibilities and corresponding number of hours of study in this case.

b. Plot these production possibilities data in a graph.

c. Does this production possibilities curve reflect the law of increasing opportunity costs? Explain.

11. Draw a production possibilities curve for a hypothetical economy producing capital goods and consumer goods. Suppose a major technological breakthrough occurs in the capital goods industry and the new technology is widely adopted only in this industry. Draw the new production possibilities curve. Now assume that a technological advance occurs in consumer good production, but not in capital good production. Draw the new production possibilities curve.

12. The present choice between investing in capital goods and producing consumer goods affects the ability of an economy to produce in the future. Explain.

 ONLINE EXERCISES

Exercise 1

Visit the Bureau of Labor Statistics at http://www.bls .gov/ceshome.htm and click on Employment Situation Summary. What is happening to unemployment? How would this be reflected on the nation's production possibilities graph?

Exercise 2

Visit http://www.ndsn.org/MARAPR97/PRISONS.html. What is the opportunity cost of funding more prisons according to the author of this article? What long-term impact could the building of more prisons have on the nation's production possibilities curve?

Exercise 3

Visit Resources for Economists on the Internet (http://rfe .org/). Do not visit Neat Stuff and Jokes about Economists and Economics.

Exercise 4

How might the officials of the People's Republic of China answer the three fundamental economic questions? For one perspective, visit the China Council for the Promotion of International Trade (CCPIT): http://www.ccpit.org/.

 CHECKPOINT ANSWER

What Does a Peace Dividend Really Mean?

A "peace dividend" suggests resources are allocated away from military production and used for greater nonmilitary production. If you said that this phrase represents a movement along the production possibilities curve, YOU ARE CORRECT.

PRACTICE QUIZ

For a visual explanation of the correct answers, visit the tutorial at http://tucker.swcollege.com.

1. Which of the following decisions must be made by all economies?
   a. How much to produce? When to produce? How much does it cost?
   b. What is the price? Who will produce it? Who will consume it?
   c. What to produce? How to produce it? For whom to produce?
   d. None of the above.

2. A student who has one evening to prepare for two exams on the following day has the following two alternatives:

Possibility	Score in economics	Score in accounting
A	95	80
B	80	90

   The opportunity cost of receiving a 90, rather than a 80, on the accounting exam is represented by how many points on the economics exam?
   a. 15 points.
   b. 80 points.
   c. 90 points.
   d. 10 points.

3. Opportunity cost is the
   a. purchase price of a good or service.
   b. value of leisure time plus out-of-pocket costs.
   c. best option given up as a result of choosing an alternative.
   d. undesirable sacrifice required to purchase a good.

4. On a production possibilities curve, the opportunity cost of good X in terms of good Y is represented by
   a. the distance to the curve from the vertical axis.
   b. the distance to the curve from the horizontal axis.
   c. the movement along the curve.
   d. all of the above.

5. If a farmer adds 1 pound of fertilizer per acre, the value of the resulting crops rises from $80 to $100 per acre. According to marginal analysis, the farmer should add fertilizer if it costs less than
   a. $12.50 per pound.
   b. $20 per pound.
   c. $80 per pound.
   d. $100 per pound.

6. On a production possibilities curve, a change from economic inefficiency to economic efficiency is obtained by
   a. movement along the curve.
   b. movement from a point outside the curve to a point on the curve.
   c. movement from a point inside the curve to a point on the curve.
   d. a change in the slope of the curve.

7. Any point inside the production possibilities curve is a(an)
   a. efficient point.
   b. unfeasible point.
   c. inefficient point.
   d. maximum output combination.

8. Using a production possibilities curve, unemployment is represented by a point located
   a. near the middle of the curve.
   b. at the top corner of the curve.
   c. at the bottom corner of the curve.
   d. outside the curve.
   e. inside the curve.

9. Along a production possibilities curve, an increase in the production of one good can be accomplished only by
   a. decreasing the production of another good.
   b. increasing the production of another good.
   c. holding constant the production of another good.
   d. producing at a point on the corner of the curve.

10. Education and training that improve the skill of the labor force are represented on the production possibilities curve by a(an)
    a. movement along the curve.
    b. inward shift of the curve.
    c. outward shift of the curve.
    d. movement toward the curve from an exterior point.

11. A nation can accelerate its economic growth by
    a. reducing the number of immigrants allowed into the country.
    b. adding to its stock of capital.
    c. printing more money.
    d. imposing tariffs and quotas on imported goods.

CHAPTER 3

Market Demand and Supply

A cornerstone of the U.S. economy is the use of markets to answer the basic economic questions discussed in the previous chapter. Consider baseball cards, CDs, physical fitness, gasoline, soft drinks, tennis shoes, and cocaine. In a *market economy*, each is bought and sold by individuals coming together as buyers and sellers in markets. Of course, cocaine is sold in an illegal market, but nonetheless it is a market that determines the price and the quantity exchanged. This chapter is extremely important because it introduces basic supply and demand analysis. This technique will prove to be valuable because it is applicable to a multitude of real-world choices of buyers and sellers facing the problem of scarcity. For example, one of the You're the Economist features asks you to consider the highly controversial issue of international trade in human organs.

Demand represents the choice-making behavior of consumers, while supply represents the choices of producers. The chapter begins by looking closely at demand and then supply. Finally, it combines these forces to see how prices and quantities are determined in the marketplace. Market supply and demand analysis is the basic tool of microeconomic analysis.

In this chapter, you will learn to solve these economics puzzles:

■ What is the difference between a "change in quantity demanded" and a "change in demand"?

■ Can Congress repeal the law of supply to control oil prices?

■ Does the price system eliminate scarcity?

The Law of Demand

Economics might be referred to as "graphs and laughs" because economists are so fond of using graphs to illustrate demand, supply, and many other economic concepts. Unfortunately, some students taking economics courses say they miss the laughs.

Exhibit 1 reveals an important "law" in economics called the **law of demand.** The law of demand states there is an inverse relationship between the price of a good and the quantity buyers are willing to purchase in a defined time period, ceteris paribus. The law of demand makes good sense. At a "sale," consumers buy more when the price of merchandise is cut.

In Exhibit 1, the *demand curve* is formed by the line connecting the possible price and quantity purchased responses of an individual consumer. The demand curve therefore allows you to find the quantity demanded by a buyer at any possible selling price by moving along the curve. For example, Bob, a sophomore at Marketplace College, loves listening to music on his stereo while studying. Bob's demand curve shows that at a price of $15 per

Law of demand
The principle that there is an inverse relationship between the price of a good and the quantity buyers are willing to purchase in a defined time period, ceteris paribus.

| EXHIBIT 1 | An Individual Buyer's Demand Curve for CDs |

Bob's demand curve shows how many CDs he is willing to purchase at different possible prices. As the price of CDs declines, the quantity demanded increases, and Bob purchases more CDs. The inverse relationship between price and quantity demanded conforms to the law of demand.

An Individual Buyer's Demand Schedule for CDs

Point	Price per CD	Quantity demanded (per year)
A	$20	4
B	15	6
C	10	10
D	5	16

Visit Haggle Online, an Internet auction site at http://www.haggle.com. *What types of products are being auctioned? Look at the history of the bidding process for a few products. From this information, what can you conclude about the demand for each product?*

Demand
A curve or schedule showing the various quantities of a product consumers are willing to purchase at possible prices during a specified period of time, ceteris paribus.

compact disc (CD) his quantity demanded is 6 CDs purchased annually (point *B*). At the lower price of $10, Bob's quantity demanded increases to 10 CDs per year (point *C*). Following this procedure, other price and quantity possibilities for Bob are read along the demand curve.

Note that until we know the actual price, we do not know how many CDs Bob will actually purchase annually. The demand curve is simply a summary of Bob's buying intentions. Once we know the market price, a quick look at the demand curve tells us how many CDs Bob will buy.

Conclusion *Demand is a curve or schedule showing the various quantities of a product consumers are willing to purchase at possible prices during a specified period of time, ceteris paribus.*

Market Demand

To make the transition from an *individual* demand curve to a *market* demand curve, we total, or sum, the individual demand schedules. Suppose the owner of Rap City, a small chain of retail music stores serving a few states, tries to decide what to charge for CDs and hires a consumer research firm. For simplicity, we assume Fred and Mary are the only two buyers in Rap City's market, and they are sent a questionnaire that asks how many CDs each would be willing to purchase at several possible prices. Exhibit 2 reports their price–quantity demanded responses in tabular and graphical form.

The market demand curve, D_{total}, in Exhibit 2 is derived by summing *horizontally* the two individual demand curves, D_1 and D_2, for each possible price. At a price of $20, for example, we sum Fred's 2 CDs demanded per year and Mary's 1 CD demanded per year to find that the total quantity demanded at $20 is 3 CDs per year. Repeating the same process for other prices generates the market demand curve, D_{total}. For example, at a price of $5, the total quantity demanded is 12 CDs.

The Distinction between Changes in Quantity Demanded and Changes in Demand

Price is not the only variable that determines how much of a good or service consumers will buy. Recall from Chapter 1 that the price and quantity variables in our model are subject to the ceteris paribus assumption. If we relax this assumption and allow other variables held constant to change, a variety of factors can influence the position of the demand curve. Because these factors are not the price of the good itself, these variables are called *nonprice determinants* or simply *demand shifters*. The major nonprice determinants include: (1) the number of buyers, (2) tastes and preferences, (3) income, (4) expectations of future changes in prices, income, and availability of goods, and (5) prices of related goods.

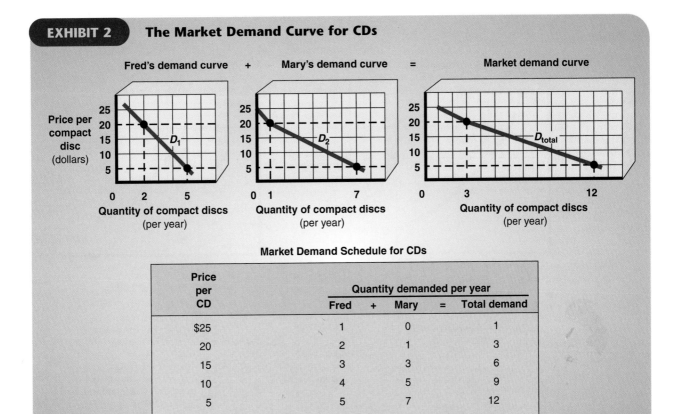

EXHIBIT 2   **The Market Demand Curve for CDs**

Market Demand Schedule for CDs

Price per CD	Quantity demanded per year			
	Fred	+	Mary	=	Total demand
$25	1		0		1
20	2		1		3
15	3		3		6
10	4		5		9
5	5		7		12

Individual demand curves differ for consumers Fred and Mary. Assuming they are the only buyers in the market, the market demand curve, D_{total}, is derived by summing horizontally the individual demand curves, D_1 and D_2.

Before discussing these nonprice determinants of demand, we must pause to explain an important and possibly confusing distinction in terminology. We have been referring to a **change in quantity demanded**, which results solely from a change in the price. A change in quantity demanded is a movement between points along a stationary demand curve, ceteris paribus. In Exhibit 3(a), at the price of $15, the quantity demanded is 20 million CDs per year. This is shown as point *A* on the demand curve, *D*. At a lower price of, say, $10, the quantity demanded increases to 30 million CDs per year, shown as point *B*. Verbally, we describe the impact of the price decrease as an increase in the quantity demanded of 10 million CDs per year. We show this relationship on the demand curve as a movement down along the curve from point *A* to point *B*.

Change in quantity demanded

A movement between points along a stationary demand curve, ceteris paribus.

Conclusion *Under the law of demand, any decrease in price along the vertical axis will cause an increase in quantity demanded, measured along the horizontal axis.*

EXHIBIT 3   **Movement along a Demand Curve versus a Shift in Demand**

Part (a) shows the demand curve, *D*, for CDs per year. If the price is $15 at point *A*, the quantity demanded by consumers is 20 million CDs. If the price decreases to $10 at point *B*, the quantity demanded increases from 20 million to 30 million CDs.

Part (b) illustrates an increase in demand. A change in some nonprice determinant can cause an increase in demand from D_1 to D_2. At a price of $15 on D_1 (point *A*), 20 million CDs is the quantity demanded per year. At this same price on D_2 (point *B*), the quantity demanded increases to 30 million.

Change in demand

An increase or decrease in the quantity demanded at each possible price. An increase in demand is a rightward shift in the entire demand curve. A decrease in demand is a leftward shift in the entire demand curve.

A **change in demand** is an increase (rightward shift) or a decrease (leftward shift) in the quantity demanded at each possible price. If ceteris paribus no longer applies and if one of the five nonprice factors changes, the location of the demand curve shifts.

Conclusion *Changes in nonprice determinants can produce only a shift in the demand curve and not a movement along the demand curve, which is caused by a change in price.*

Comparing parts (a) and (b) of Exhibit 3 is helpful in distinguishing between a change in quantity demanded and a change in demand. In part (b), suppose the market demand curve for CDs is initially at D_1 and there is a shift to the right (an increase in demand) from D_1 to D_2. This means that at *all* possible prices consumers wish to purchase a larger quantity than before the shift occurred. At $15 per CD, for example, 30 million CDs (point *B*) will be consumed each year, rather than 20 million CDs (point *A*).

Now suppose a change in some nonprice factor causes demand curve D_1 to shift leftward (a decrease in demand). The interpretation in this case is that at *all* possible prices consumers will buy a smaller quantity than before the shift occurred.

Exhibit 4 summarizes the terminology for the effects of changes in price and nonprice determinants on the demand curve.

EXHIBIT 4 **Terminology for Changes in Price and Nonprice Determinants of Demand**

Change	Effect	Terminology
Price increases	Upward movement along the demand curve	Decrease in the quantity demanded
Price decreases	Downward movement along the demand curve	Increase in the quantity demanded
Nonprice determinant	Leftward or rightward shift in the demand curve	Decrease or increase in demand

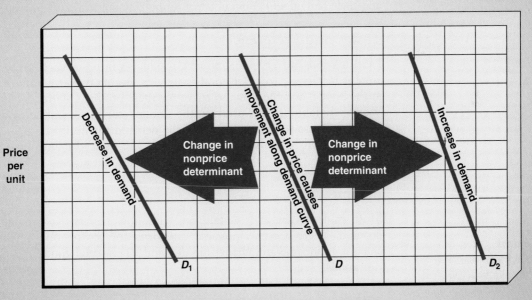

Quantity of good or service per unit of time

Caution! It is important to distinguish between a change in quantity demanded, which is a movement along a demand curve caused by a change in price (*D*), and a change in demand, which is a shift in the demand curve. An increase or decrease in demand (shift to D_1 or D_2) is not caused by a change in price. Instead, a shift is caused by a change in one of the nonprice determinants.

Nonprice Determinants of Demand

Why does Sunkist (http://www.sunkist.com/), a major producer of oranges, provide free orange recipes? To increase the demand for oranges, of course.

Distinguishing between a change in quantity demanded and a change in demand requires some patience and practice. The following discussion of specific changes in nonprice factors will clarify how each nonprice variable affects demand.

Number of Buyers

Look back at Exhibit 2, and imagine the impact of adding more individual demand curves to the individual demand curves of Fred and Mary. At all possible prices, there is extra quantity demanded by the new customers, and the market demand curve for CDs shifts rightward (an increase in demand). Population growth therefore tends to increase the number of buyers, which shifts the market demand curve for a good or service rightward. Conversely, a population decline shifts most market demand curves leftward (a decrease in demand).

Advertising is designed to increase demand. The Clio Awards (http://www.clioawards.com/html/main.cgi) highlight the best advertising campaigns in print, radio, and television.

The number of buyers can be specified to include both foreign and domestic buyers. Suppose the market demand curve D_1 in Exhibit 3(b) is for CDs purchased in the United States by customers at home and abroad. Also assume Japan restricts the import of CDs into Japan. What would be the effect of Japan removing this trade restriction? The answer is that the demand curve shifts rightward from D_1 to D_2 when Japanese consumers add their individual demand curves to the U.S. market demand for CDs.

Tastes and Preferences

Fads, fashions, advertising, and new products can influence consumer preferences to buy a particular good or service. Beanie Babies became the rage in the 1990s, and the demand curve for these products shifted to the right. When people tire of this product, the demand curve will shift leftward. The physical fitness trend has increased the demand for health clubs and exercise equipment. On the other hand, have you noticed many stores selling hula hoops?

Income

Normal good

Any good for which there is a direct relationship between changes in income and its demand curve.

Inferior good

Any good for which there is an inverse relationship between changes in income and its demand curve.

Most students are all too familiar with how changes in income affect demand. There are two possible categories for the relationship between changes in income and changes in demand: (1) **normal goods** and (2) **inferior goods.**

A normal good is any good for which there is a direct relationship between changes in income and its demand curve. For many goods and services, an increase in income causes buyers to purchase more at any possible price. As buyers receive higher incomes, the demand curve shifts rightward for such *normal goods* as cars, steaks, vintage wine, cleaning services, and CDs. A decline in income has the opposite effect, and the demand curve shifts leftward.

CHECKPOINT

Can Gasoline Become an Exception to the Law of Demand?

The Iraqi invasion of Kuwait in 1990 was followed by sharply climbing gasoline prices. Consumers feared future oil shortages if war cut off oil supplies, and they rushed to fill up their gas tanks. In this case, as the price of gas increased, consumers bought more, not less. Is this an exception to the law of demand?

An inferior good is any good for which there is an inverse relationship between changes in income and its demand curve. A rise in income can result in reduced purchases of a good or service at any possible price. This might happen with such *inferior goods* as generic brands, Spam, and bus service. Instead of buying these inferior goods, higher incomes allow consumers to buy brand-name products, steaks, or a car. Conversely, a fall in income causes the demand curve for inferior goods to shift rightward.

Expectations of Buyers

What is the effect on demand in the present when consumers anticipate future changes in prices, incomes, or availability? What happened in 1990 when Iraq invaded Kuwait? Expectations that there would be a shortage of gasoline induced consumers to say "fill-er-up" at every opportunity, and demand increased. Suppose students learn the price of the textbooks for several courses they plan to take next semester will double soon. Their likely response is to buy now, which causes an increase in the demand curve for these textbooks. Another example is a change in the weather, which can indirectly cause expectations to shift demand for some products. Suppose a hailstorm destroys a substantial portion of the peach crop. Consumers reason that the reduction in available supply will soon drive up prices, and they dash to stock up before it is too late. This change in expectations causes the demand curve for peaches to increase.

Prices of Related Goods

Possibly the most confusing nonprice factor is the influence of other prices on the demand for a particular good or service. The term *nonprice* seems to forbid any shift in demand resulting from a change in the price of *any* product. This confusion exists when one fails to distinguish between changes in quantity demanded and changes in demand. Remember that ceteris paribus holds all prices of other goods constant. Therefore, movement along a demand curve occurs solely in response to changes in the price of a product, that is, its "own" price. When we draw the demand curve for Coca-Cola, for example, we assume the prices of Pepsi-Cola and other colas remain unchanged. What happens if we relax the ceteris paribus assumption and

Substitute good

A good that competes with another good for consumer purchases. As a result, there is a direct relationship between a price change for one good and the demand for its "competitor" good.

Complementary good

A good that is jointly consumed with another good. As a result, there is an inverse relationship between a price change for one good and the demand for the "go together" good.

the price of Pepsi rises? Many Pepsi buyers switch to Coca-Cola, and the demand curve for Coca-Cola shifts rightward (an increase in demand). Coca-Cola and Pepsi-Cola are one type of related goods called **substitute goods**. A substitute good competes with another good for consumer purchases. As a result, there is a direct relationship between a price change for one good and the demand for its "competitor" good. Other examples of substitutes include margarine and butter, domestic cars and foreign cars, and audiocassettes and CDs.

CDs and CD players illustrate a second type of related goods called **complementary goods**. A complementary good is jointly consumed with another good. As a result, there is an inverse relationship between a price change for one good and the demand for its "go together" good. Although buying a CD and buying a CD player can be separate decisions, these two purchases are related. The more CD players consumers buy, the greater the demand for CDs. What happens if the price of CD players falls sharply, say, from $250 to $50? The market demand curve for CDs shifts rightward (an increase in demand) because new owners of players add their individual demand curves to those of persons already owning players and buying CDs. Conversely, a sharp rise in college tuition decreases the demand for textbooks.

Exhibit 5 summarizes the relationship between changes in the nonprice determinants of demand and the demand curve, accompanied by examples for each type of nonprice factor change.

The Law of Supply

Law of supply

The principle that there is a direct relationship between the price of a good and the quantity sellers are willing to offer for sale in a defined time period, ceteris paribus.

In everyday conversations, the term *supply* refers to a specific quantity. A "limited supply" of golf clubs at a sporting goods store means there are only so many for sale and that's all. This interpretation of supply is *not* the economist's definition. To economists, supply is the relationship between ranges of possible prices and quantities supplied, which is stated as the **law of supply**. The law of supply states there is a direct relationship between the price of a good and the quantity sellers are willing to offer for sale in a defined time period, ceteris paribus. Interpreting the individual *supply curve* for Rap City shown in Exhibit 6 is basically the same as interpreting Bob's demand curve shown in Exhibit 1. Each point on the curve represents a quantity supplied (measured along the horizontal axis) at a particular price (measured along the vertical axis). For example, at a price of $10 per disc (point C), the quantity supplied by the seller, Rap City, is 35,000 CDs per year. At the higher price of $15, the quantity supplied increases to 45,000 CDs per year (point *B*).

Supply

A curve or schedule showing the various quantities of a product sellers are willing to produce and offer for sale at possible prices during a specified period of time, ceteris paribus.

Conclusion *Supply is a curve or schedule showing the various quantities of a product sellers are willing to produce and offer for sale at possible prices during a specified period of time,* ceteris paribus.

Why are sellers willing to sell more at a higher price? Suppose Farmer Brown is trying to decide whether to devote more of his land, labor, and barn space to the production of soybeans. Recall from Chapter 2 the production

EXHIBIT 5 Summary of the Impact of Changes in Nonprice Determinants of Demand on the Demand Curve

Nonprice determinant of demand	Relationship with the demand curve	Examples
1. Number of buyers	Direct	■ The Japanese remove import restrictions on American CDs, and Japanese consumers increase the demand for American CDs. ■ A decline in the birthrate reduces the demand for baby clothes.
2. Tastes and preferences	Direct	■ For no apparent reason, consumers want Beanie Babies, and demand increases, but after a while, the fad dies, and demand declines.
3. Income		
a. Normal goods	Direct	■ Consumers' incomes increase, and the demand for steaks increases. ■ A decline in income decreases the demand for air travel.
b. Inferior goods	Inverse	■ Consumers' incomes increase, and the demand for hamburger decreases. ■ A decline in income increases the demand for bus service.
4. Expectations of buyers	Direct	■ Consumers expect that gasoline will be in short supply next month and that prices will rise sharply. Consequently, consumers fill the tanks in their cars this month, and there is an increase in demand for gasoline. Months later consumers expect the price of gasoline to fall soon, and the demand for gasoline decreases.
5. Prices of related goods		
a. Substitute goods	Direct	■ A reduction in the price of tea decreases the demand for coffee. ■ An increase in the price of air fares causes higher demand for bus transportation.
b. Complementary goods	Inverse	■ A decline in the price of CD players increases the demand for CDs. ■ A higher price for peanut butter decreases the demand for jelly.

possibilities curve and the concept of increasing opportunity cost developed in Exhibit 2. If Farmer Brown devotes few of his resources to producing soybeans, the opportunity cost of, say, producing milk is small. But increasing soybean production means a higher opportunity cost, measured by the quantity of milk not produced. The logical question is, What would induce Farmer Brown to produce more soybeans for sale and overcome the higher opportunity cost of producing less milk? You guessed it! There must be the *incentive* of a higher price for soybeans.

Conclusion *Only at a higher price will it be profitable for sellers to incur the higher opportunity cost associated with producing and supplying a larger quantity.*

EXHIBIT 6   **An Individual Seller's Supply Curve for CDs**

The supply curve for an individual seller, such as Rap City, shows the quantity of CDs offered for sale at different possible prices. As the price of CDs rises, a retail store has an incentive to increase the quantity of CDs supplied per year. The direct relationship between price and quantity supplied conforms to the law of supply.

An Individual Seller's Supply Schedule for CDs

Point	Price per CD	Quantity supplied (thousands per year)
A	$20	50
B	15	45
C	10	35
D	5	20

Market Supply

To construct a *market* supply curve, we follow the same procedure used to derive a market demand curve. That is, we *horizontally* sum all the quantities supplied at various prices that might prevail in the market.

Let's assume Super Sound Company and High Vibes Company are the only two firms selling CDs in a given market. As you can see in Exhibit 7, the market supply curve, S_{total}, slopes upward to the right. At a price of $25, Super Sound will supply 25,000 CDs per year, and High Vibes will supply 35,000 CDs per year. Thus, summing the two individual supply curves, S_1 and S_2, *horizontally*, the total of 60,000 CDs is plotted at this price on the market supply curve, S_{total}. Similar calculations at other prices along the price axis generate a market supply curve, telling us the total amount of CDs these businesses offer for sale at different selling prices.

EXHIBIT 7　　**The Market Supply Curve for CDs**

The Market Supply Schedule for CDs

Price per CD	Quantity supplied per year		
	Super Sound +	High Vibes =	Total supply
$25	25	35	60
20	20	30	50
15	15	25	40
10	10	20	30
5	5	15	20

Super Sound and High Vibes are two individual businesses selling CDs. If these are the only two firms in the CD market, the market supply curve, S_{total}, can be derived by summing horizontally the individual supply curves, S_1, and S_2.

The Distinction between Changes in Quantity Supplied and Changes in Supply

As in demand theory, the price of a product is not the only factor that influences how much sellers offer for sale. Once we relax the ceteris paribus assumption, there are six principal *nonprice determinants* (or simply *supply shifters*) that can shift the supply curve's position: (1) the number of sellers, (2) technology, (3) resource prices, (4) taxes and subsidies, (5) expectations, and (6) prices of other goods. We will discuss these nonprice determinants in more detail momentarily, but first we must distinguish between a **change in quantity supplied** and a **change in supply**.

Change in quantity supplied

A movement between points along a stationary supply curve, ceteris paribus.

Change in supply

An increase or decrease in the quantity supplied at each possible price. An increase in supply is a rightward shift in the entire supply curve. A decrease in supply is a leftward shift in the entire supply curve.

CHECKPOINT

Can the Law of Supply Be Repealed?

The rising oil prices of the early 1990s in reponse to the Iraqi invasion of Kuwait were nothing new. The United States experienced two oil shocks during the 1970s in the aftermath of Middle East tensions. Congress said no to high oil prices by passing a law prohibiting prices above a legal limit. Supporters of such price controls said this was a way to ensure adequate supply without allowing oil producers to earn excess profits. Did price controls increase, decrease, or have no effect on U.S. oil production during the 1970s?

A change in quantity supplied is a movement between points along a stationary supply curve, ceteris paribus. In Exhibit 8(a), at the price of $10, the quantity supplied is 30 million CDs per year (point *A*). At the higher price of $15, sellers offer a larger "quantity supplied" of 40 million CDs per year (point *B*). Economists describe the effect of the rise in price as an increase in the quantity supplied of 10 million CDs per year.

> **Conclusion** *Under the law of supply, any increase in price along the vertical axis will cause an increase in the quantity supplied, measured along the horizontal axis.*

A change in supply is an increase (rightward shift) or a decrease (leftward shift) in the quantity supplied at each possible price. If ceteris paribus no longer applies and if one of the six nonprice factors changes, the impact is to alter the supply curve's location.

> **Conclusion** *Changes in nonprice determinants can produce only a shift in the supply curve and not a movement along the supply curve.*

In Exhibit 8(b), the rightward shift (an increase in supply) from S_1 to S_2 means that at all possible prices sellers offer a greater quantity for sale. At $15 per CD, for instance, sellers provide 40 million for sale annually (point *B*), rather than 30 million (point *A*).

Another case is that some nonprice factor changes and causes a leftward shift (a decrease in supply) from supply curve S_1. As a result, a smaller quantity will be offered for sale at any price.

Exhibit 9 summarizes the terminology for the effects of changes in price and nonprice determinants on the supply curve.

Nonprice Determinants of Supply

Now we turn to how each of the six basic nonprice factors affects supply.

EXHIBIT 8   **Movement along a Supply Curve versus a Shift in Supply**

(a) Increase in quantity supplied

(b) Increase in supply

CAUSATION CHAIN

Increase in price ⇨ Increase in quantity supplied

CAUSATION CHAIN

Change in nonprice determinant ⇨ Increase in supply

Part (a) presents the market supply curve, *S*, for CDs per year. If the price is $10 at point *A*, the quantity supplied by firms will be 30 million CDs. If the price increases to $15 at point *B*, the quantity supplied will increase from 30 million to 40 million CDs.

Part (b) illustrates an increase in supply. A change in some nonprice determinant can cause an increase in supply from S_1 to S_2. At a price of $15 on S_1 (point A), the quantity supplied per year is 30 million CDs. At this price on S_2 (point B), the quantity supplied increases to 40 million.

Number of Sellers

What happens when a severe drought destroys wheat or a frost ruins the orange crop? The damaging effect of the weather may force orange growers out of business, and supply decreases. When the government eases restrictions on hunting alligators, the number of alligator hunters increases, and the supply curve for alligator meat and skins increases. Internationally, the United States may decide to lower trade barriers on textile imports, and this action increases supply by allowing new foreign firms to add their individual supply curves to the U.S. market supply curve for textiles. Conversely, higher U.S. trade barriers on textile imports shift the U.S. market supply curve for textiles leftward.

EXHIBIT 9   **Terminology for Changes in Price and Nonprice Determinants of Supply**

Change	Effect	Terminology
Price increases	Upward movement along the supply curve	Increase in the quantity supplied
Price decreases	Downward movement along the supply curve	Decrease in the quantity supplied
Nonprice determinant	Leftward or rightward shift in the supply curve	Decrease or increase in supply

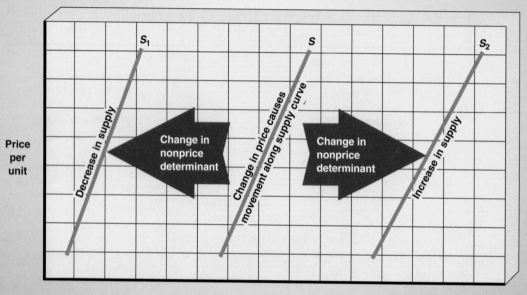

Quantity of good or service per unit of time

Caution! As with demand curves, you must distinguish between a change in quantity supplied, which is a movement along a supply curve in response to a change in price (*S*), and a shift in the supply curve. An increase or decrease in supply (shift to S_1 or S_2) occurs because some nonprice determinant causes the shift.

Technology

Never have we experienced such an explosion of new production techniques. Throughout the world, new and more efficient technology is making it possible to manufacture more products at any possible selling price. For example, new, more powerful personal computers (PCs) reduce production costs and increase the supply of all sorts of goods and services. In the CD industry, robots allow you to select a CD, listen to it, and then just put your money or charge card in the slot if you wish to buy it. Installing these robots makes it possible to offer more discs for sale per year at a lower cost per disc, and the entire supply curve shifts to the right.

Resource Prices

Natural resources, labor, capital, and entrepreneurship are all required to produce products, and the prices of these resources affect supply. Suppose many firms are competing for computer programmers to design their software, and the salaries of these highly skilled workers increase. This increase in the price of labor adds to the cost of production. As a result, the supply of computer software decreases because sellers must charge more than before for any quantity supplied. Any reduction in production cost caused by a decline in the price of resources will have an opposite effect and increase supply.

Taxes and Subsidies

Certain taxes, such as sales taxes, have the same effect on supply as an increase in the price of a resource. The impact of an increase in the sales tax is similar to a rise in the salaries of computer programmers. The higher sales tax imposes an additional production cost on, for example, CDs, and the supply curve shifts leftward. Conversely, a payment from the government for each CD produced (an unlikely subsidy) would have the same effect as lower prices for resources or a technological advance. That is, the supply curve for CDs shifts rightward.

Expectations of Producers

Expectations affect both current demand and current supply. For example, the 1990 Iraqi invasion of Kuwait caused oil producers to believe that oil prices would rise dramatically. Their initial response was to hold back a portion of the oil in their storage tanks so they could make greater profits later when oil prices rose. One approach used by the major oil companies was to limit the amount of gasoline delivered to independent distributors. This response by the oil industry shifted the supply curve to the left. Now suppose farmers anticipate the price of wheat will soon fall sharply. The reaction is to sell their inventories stored in silos today before the price declines tomorrow. Such a response shifts the supply curve for wheat to the right.

Prices of Other Goods the Firm Could Produce

Businesses are always considering shifting resources from producing one good to producing another good. A rise in the price of one product relative to the prices of other products signals to suppliers that switching production to the product with the higher relative price yields higher profit. If the price of tomatoes rises while the price of corn remains the same, many farmers will divert more of their land to tomatoes and less to corn. The result is an increase in the supply of tomatoes and a decrease in the supply of corn. This happens because the opportunity cost of growing corn, measured in forgone tomato profits, increases.

PC Prices Fall Below $400

Applicable Concept: nonprice determinants of demand and supply

Radio was in existence for 38 years before 50 million people tuned in. Television took 13 years to reach that benchmark. Sixteen years after the first PC kit came out, 50 million people were using one. Once opened to the public, the Internet crossed that line in four years.[1]

An Associated Press article reported in 1998:

Personal computers, which tumbled below the $1,000-price barrier just 18 months ago, now are breaking through the $400-price-mark—putting them within reach of the average U.S. family.

The plunge in PC prices reflects declining whole-sale prices for computer parts, such as microprocessors, memory chips and hard drives.

"We've seen a massive transformation in the PC business," said Andrew Peck, an analyst with Cowen & Co., based in Boston.

But PC makers also are responding to a profound shift in U.S. buying habits: Today's consumers care more about bargains than the latest technology for running fancy software, like PC games with 3-D imagery.

Micro Center, a Columbus, Ohio–based chain of 13 computer stores, early this month began selling a $399 computer under the Power Spec label. On Thursday, Precision Tec LLC, a maker based in Costa Mesa, California, introduced its Gazelle machine for

the same price, for sale over the Internet through Egghead.com and other Web-site companies . . .

Many of the new buyers are expected to be from families making less than $30,000 a year, expanding the pool of traditional buyers, who usually come from families making $50,000 or more.

The lower-income buyers "just don't need as much computing power," Matt Sargent, a market research analyst, said. "They are only willing to pay a certain amount of money for it. But for many new computer users and second-time buyers, those lower prices don't necessarily sacrifice computer performance."

Today's computers costing below $1,000 are equal or greater in power than PCs costing $1,500 and more

Exhibit 10 summarizes the relationship between changes in the nonprice determinants of supply and the supply curve, accompanied by examples for each type of nonprice factor change.

A Market Supply and Demand Analysis

Market

Any arrangement in which buyers and sellers interact to determine the price and quantity of goods and services exchanged.

A drumroll please! Buyer and seller actors are on center stage to perform a balancing act in a **market.** A market is any arrangement in which buyers and sellers interact to determine the price and quantity of goods and ser-

just a few years ago—working well for word processing, spread-sheet applications and Internet access, the most popular computer uses.[2]

In 1999, a *Wall Street Journal* article reported that PC makers and distributors are also smashing their industry's time-honored sales channels. PC makers such as Compaq Computer Corporation and Hewlett-Packard Company are using the Internet to sell direct to consumers. In doing so, they are following the successful strategy of Dell Computer Corporation, which for years has bypassed storefront retailers and the PC distributors who traditionally keep them stocked, going instead straight to the consumer with catalogs, an 800 number, and Web sites.[3]

In 2001, a *New York Times* article described a computer price war:

We reached a situation where the market was saturated in 2000. People who needed computers had them. Vendors are living on sales of replacements, at least in the United States. But that doesn't give you the kind of growth these companies were used to. In the past, most price cuts came from falling prices for processors and other components. In addition, manufacturers have been narrowing profit margins for the last couple years. But when demand dried up last fall, the more aggressive manufacturers decided to try to gain market share by cutting prices to the bone. This is an all-out battle for market share.[4]

[1]*The Emerging Digital Economy* (U.S. Department of Commerce, 1998), Chap. 1, p. 1 (http://www/ecommerce.gov/chapter1.htm).
[2]David E. Kalish, "PC Prices Fall Below $400, Luring Bargain-Hunters," Associated Press/*Charlotte Observer*, Aug. 25, 1998, p. 3D.
[3]George Anders, "Online Web Seller Asks: How Low Can PC Prices Go?" *Wall Street Journal*, Jan. 19, 1999, p. B1.
[4]Barnaby J. Feder, "Five Questions for Martin Reynolds: A Computer Price War Leaves Buyers Smiling," *New York Times*, May 13, 2001.

vices exchanged. Let's consider the retail market for tennis shoes. Exhibit 11 displays hypothetical market demand and supply data for this product. Notice in column 1 of the exhibit that price serves as a common variable for both supply and demand relationships. Columns 2 and 3 list the quantity demanded and the quantity supplied for pairs of tennis shoes per year.

The important question for market supply and demand analysis is: Which selling price and quantity will prevail in the market? Let's start by asking what will happen if retail stores supply 75,000 pairs of tennis shoes and charge $105 a pair. At this relatively high price for tennis shoes, consumers are willing and able to purchase only 25,000 pairs. As a result, 50,000 pairs of tennis shoes remain as unsold inventory on the shelves of

EXHIBIT 10 Summary of the Impact of Changes in Nonprice Determinants of Supply on the Supply Curve

Nonprice determinant of supply	Relationship with the supply curve	Examples
1. Number of sellers	Direct	■ The United States lowers trade restrictions on foreign textiles, and the supply of textiles in the United States increases. ■ A severe drought destroys the orange crop, and the supply of oranges decreases.
2. Technology	Direct	■ New methods of producing automobiles reduce production costs, and the supply of automobiles increases. ■ Technology is destroyed in war, and production costs increase; the result is a decrease in the supply of good X.
3. Resource prices	Inverse	■ A decline in the price of computer chips increases the supply of computers. ■ An increase in the cost of farm equipment decreases the supply of soybeans.
4. Taxes and subsidies	Inverse and direct	■ An increase in the per-pack tax on cigarettes reduces the supply of cigarettes. ■ A government payment to dairy farmers based on the number of gallons produced increases the supply of milk.
5. Expectations	Inverse	■ Oil companies anticipate a substantial rise in future oil prices, and this expectation causes these companies to decrease their current supply of oil. ■ Farmers expect the future price of wheat to decline, so they increase the present supply of wheat.
6. Prices of other goods and services	Inverse	■ A rise in the price of brand-name drugs causes drug companies to decrease the supply of generic drugs. ■ A decline in the price of tomatoes causes farmers to increase the supply of cucumbers.

Surplus

A market condition existing at any price where the quantity supplied is greater than the quantity demanded.

sellers (column 4), and the market condition is a **surplus** (column 5). A surplus is a market condition existing at any price where the quantity supplied is greater than the quantity demanded.

How will retailers react to a surplus? Competition forces sellers to bid down their selling price to attract more sales (column 6). If they cut the selling price to $90, there will still be a surplus of 40,000 pairs of tennis shoes, and pressure on sellers to cut their selling price will continue. If the price falls to $75, there will still be an unwanted surplus of 20,000 pairs of tennis shoes remaining as inventory, and pressure to charge a lower price will persist.

Now let's assume sellers slash the price of tennis shoes to $15 per pair. This price is very attractive to consumers, and the quantity demanded is 100,000 pairs of tennis shoes each year. However, sellers are willing and able to provide only 5,000 pairs at this price. The good news is that some consumers buy these 5,000 pairs of tennis shoes at $15. The bad news is that

EXHIBIT 11 Demand, Supply, and Equilibrium for Tennis Shoes (Pairs per Year)

(1) Price per pair	(2) Quantity demanded	(3) Quantity supplied	(4) Difference (3) − (2)	(5) Market condition	(6) Pressure on price
$105	25,000	75,000	+50,000	Surplus	Downward
90	30,000	70,000	+40,000	Surplus	Downward
75	40,000	60,000	+20,000	Surplus	Downward
60	50,000	50,000	0	Equilibrium	Stationary
45	60,000	35,000	−25,000	Shortage	Upward
30	80,000	20,000	−60,000	Shortage	Upward
15	100,000	5,000	−95,000	Shortage	Upward

potential buyers are willing to purchase 95,000 more pairs at that price, but cannot because the shoes are not on the shelves for sale. This out-of-stock condition signals the existence of a **shortage**. A shortage is a market condition existing at any price where the quantity supplied is less than the quantity demanded.

In the case of a shortage, unsatisfied consumers compete to obtain the product by bidding to pay a higher price. Because sellers are seeking the higher profits that higher prices make possible, they gladly respond by setting a higher price of, say, $30 and increasing the quantity supplied to 20,000 pairs annually. At the price of $30, the shortage persists because the quantity demanded still exceeds the quantity supplied. Thus, a price of $30 will also be temporary because the unfulfilled quantity demanded provides an incentive for sellers to raise their selling price further and offer more tennis shoes for sale. Suppose the price of tennis shoes rises to $45 a pair. At this price, the shortage falls to 25,000 pairs, and the market still gives sellers the message to move upward along their market supply curve and sell for a higher price.

Shortage
A market condition existing at any price where the quantity supplied is less than the quantity demanded.

CHECKPOINT

Can the Price System Eliminate Scarcity?

You visit Cuba and observe that at "official" prices there is a constant shortage of consumer goods in government stores. People explain that in Cuba scarcity is caused by low prices combined with low production quotas set by the government. Many Cuban citizens say that the condition of scarcity would be eliminated if the government would allow markets to respond to supply and demand. Can the price system eliminate scarcity?

INTERNATIONAL ECONOMICS

The Market Approach to Organ Shortages

Applicable Concept: price system

The Chinese government has been charged with selling organs from political and criminal prisoners it puts to death. Witnesses report that when prisoners are shot to death, surgeons wait in nearby vans to remove the organs. In the Chinese culture, there are few voluntary organ donations because people believe it desecrates the body.

Economist James R. Rinehart wrote the following in a journal article on this subject:

If you were in charge of a kidney transplant program with more potential recipients than donors, how would you allocate the organs under your control? Life and death decisions cannot be avoided. Some individuals are not going to get kidneys regardless of how the organs are distributed because there simply are not enough to go around. Persons who run

such programs are influenced in a variety of ways. It would be difficult not to favor friends, relatives, influential people, and those who are championed by the press. Dr. John la Puma, at the Center for Clinical Medical Ethics, University of Chicago, suggested recently that we use a lottery system for selecting transplant patients. He feels that the present rationing system is unfair.

The selection process frequently takes the form of having the patient wait at home until a suitable donor is found. What this means is that, at any given point in time, many potential recipients are just waiting for an organ to be made available. In essence, the organs are rationed to those who are able to survive the wait.

In many situations, patients are simply screened out

because they are not considered to be suitable candidates for a transplant. For instance, patients with heart disease and overt psychosis often are excluded. Others with end-stage liver disorders are denied new organs on the grounds that the habits that produced the disease may remain to jeopardize recovery. . . .

Under the present arrangements, owners receive no monetary compensation; therefore, suppliers are willing to supply fewer organs than potential recipients want. Compensating a supplier monetarily would encourage more people to offer their organs for sale. It also would be an excellent incentive for us to take better care of our organs. After all, who would want an enlarged liver or a weak heart. . . ?[1]

Equilibrium Price and Quantity

Equilibrium

A market condition that occurs at any price and quantity where quantity demanded and the quantity supplied are equal.

Assuming sellers are free to sell their product at any price, trial and error will make all possible price-quantity combinations unstable except at **equilibrium**. Equilibrium occurs at any price and quantity where the quantity demanded and the quantity supplied are equal. Economists also refer to *equilibrium* as *market clearing*.

In Exhibit 11, $60 is the *equilibrium* price, and 50,000 pairs of tennis shoes is the *equilibrium* quantity per year. Equilibrium means that the forces of supply and demand are in balance and there is no reason for price or quantity to change, ceteris paribus. In short, all prices and quantities except a unique equilibrium price and quantity are temporary. Once the price of tennis shoes is $60, this price will not change unless a nonprice factor changes demand or supply.

The following excerpt from a newspaper article illustrates the controversy:

Mickey Mantle's temporary deliverance from death, thanks to a liver transplant, illustrated how the organ-donations system is heavily weighted against poor potential recipients who cannot pass what University of Pennsylvania medical ethicist Arthur Caplan calls the "wallet biopsy."... Thus, affluent patients like Mickey Mantle may get evaluated and listed simultaneously in different regions to increase their odds of finding a donor. The New Yorker found his organ donor in Texas' Region 4. Such a system is not only highly unfair, but it leads to other kinds of abuses.[2]

Based on altruism, the current organ donor distribution system continues to result in shortages. In 2001, Health and Human Services Secretary Tommy Thompson stated there were 22,000 transplants in the United States the previous year while 76,000 patients waited on the list for organs. Moreover, he said that the need for organs is increasing twice as fast as the supply. Thompson proposed a national donor card and a new effort by businesses and unions to promote organ donations.[3] Also in 2001, the United Network for Organ Sharing approved a resolution condemning buying and selling organs in other countries.

ANALYZE THE ISSUE

1. Draw supply and demand curves for the U.S. organ market and compare the U.S. market to the market in a country where selling organs is legal.

2. What are some arguments against using the price system to allocate organs?

3. Should foreigners have the right to buy U.S. organs and U.S. citizens have the right to buy foreign organs?

---

[1]James R. Rinehart, "The Market Approach to Organ Shortages," *Journal of Health Care Marketing* 8, no. 1 (March 1988): 72–75. Reprinted by permission from the American Marketing Association.
[2]Carl Senna, "The Wallet Biopsy," *Providence Journal*, June 13, 1995, p. B-7.
[3]Steve Chapman, "Make Organs Pay Off for Donors' Kin," *Chicago Tribune*, April 29, 2001, p. 1–19.

English economist Alfred Marshall compared supply and demand to a pair of scissor blades. He wrote, "We might as reasonably dispute whether it is the upper or the under blade of a pair of scissors that cuts a piece of paper, as whether value is governed by utility [demand] or cost of production [supply]."[1] Joining market supply and market demand in Exhibit 12 allows us to clearly see the "two blades," that is, the demand curve, *D*, and the supply curve, *S*. We can measure the amount of any surplus or shortage by the horizontal distance between the demand and supply curves. At any price *above* equilibrium—say, $90—there is an *excess quantity supplied* (surplus) of 40,000 pairs of tennis shoes. For any price *below* equilibrium—$30, for example—the horizontal distance between the curves tells us there

 For statistics pertaining to organ shortages see http://www.mayo.edu/ news/Mayo_ROCHESTER/ transplant/donorstats.html. *See also United Network for Organ Sharing at* http://www.unos.org/.

---

[1]Alfred Marshall, *Principles of Economics*, 8th ed. (New York: Macmillan, 1982), p. 348.

EXHIBIT 12   The Supply and Demand for Tennis Shoes

The supply and demand curves represent a market for tennis shoes. The intersection of the demand curve, *D*, and the supply curve, *S*, at point *E* indicates the equilibrium price of $60 and the equilibrium quantity of 50,000 pairs bought and sold per year. At any price above $60, a surplus prevails, and pressure exists to push the price downward. At $90, for example, the excess quantity supplied of 40,000 pairs remains unsold. At any price below $60, a shortage provides pressure to push the price upward. At $30, for example, the excess quantity demanded of 60,000 pairs encourages consumers to bid up the price.

CAUSATION CHAINS

Quantity supplied exceeds quantity demanded	⇨	Surplus	⇨	Price decreases to equilibrium price
Quantity demanded exceeds quantity supplied	⇨	Shortage	⇨	Price increases to equilibrium price

is an *excess quantity demanded* (shortage) of 60,000 pairs. When the price per pair is $60, the market supply curve and the market demand curve intersect at point *E*, and the quantity demanded equals the quantity supplied at 50,000 pairs per year.

Conclusion *Graphically, the intersection of the supply curve and the demand curve is the market equilibrium price-quantity point. When all other nonprice factors are held constant, this is the only stable coordinate on the graph.*

Our analysis leads to an important conclusion. The predictable or stable outcome in the tennis shoes example is that the price will eventually come to rest at $60 per pair. All other factors held constant, the price may be above or below $60, but the forces of surplus or shortage guarantee that any price other than the equilibrium price is temporary. This is in theory how the **price system** operates. The price system is a mechanism that uses the forces of supply and demand to create an equilibrium through rising and falling prices. Stated simply, price plays a rationing role. The price system is important because it is a mechanism for distributing scarce goods and services. At the equilibrium price of $60, only those consumers willing to pay $60 per pair get tennis shoes, and there are no shoes for buyers unwilling to pay that price.

Price system

A mechanism that uses the forces of supply and demand to create an equilibrium through rising and falling prices.

KEY CONCEPTS

Law of demand	Normal good	Supply	Surplus
Demand	Inferior good	Change in quantity	Shortage
Change in quantity	Substitute good	supplied	Equilibrium
demanded	Complementary good	Change in supply	Price system
Change in demand	Law of supply	Market	

SUMMARY

- The **law of demand** states there is an inverse relationship between the price and the quantity demanded, ceteris paribus. A market demand curve is the horizontal summation of individual demand curves.

- A **change in quantity demanded** is a movement along a stationary demand curve caused by a change in price. When any of the nonprice determinants of demand changes, the demand curve responds by shifting. An *increase in demand* (rightward shift) or a *decrease in demand* (leftward shift) is caused by a change in one of the nonprice determinants.

- **Nonprice determinants of demand** are as follows
  a. The number of buyers
  b. Tastes and preferences
  c. Income (normal and inferior goods)
  d. Expectations of future price and income changes
  e. Prices of related goods (substitutes and complements)

- The **law of supply** states there is a direct relationship between the price and the quantity supplied, ceteris paribus. The market supply curve is the horizontal summation of individual supply curves.

- A **change in quantity supplied** is a movement along a stationary supply curve caused by a change in price. When any of the nonprice determinants of supply changes, the supply curve responds by shifting. An *increase in supply* (rightward shift) or a *decrease in supply* (leftward shift) is caused by a change in one of the nonprice determinants.

Change in quantity demanded

Change in quantity supplied

(a) Increase in quantity supplied

(b) Increase in supply

■ **Nonprice determinants of supply** are as follows

   a. The number of sellers
   b. Technology
   c. Resource prices
   d. Taxes and subsidies
   e. Expectations of future price changes
   f. Prices of other goods and services

■ A **surplus** or **shortage** exists at any price where the quantity demanded and the quantity supplied are not equal. When the price of a good is greater than the equilibrium price, there is an excess quantity supplied, or a *surplus*. When the price is less than the equilibrium price, there is an excess quantity demanded, or a *shortage*.

■ **Equilibrium** is the unique price and quantity established at the intersection of the supply and demand curves. Only at equilibrium does quantity demanded equal quantity supplied.

Equilibrium

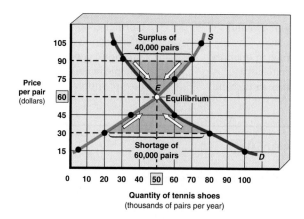

■ The **price system** is the supply and demand mechanism that establishes equilibrium through the ability of prices to rise and fall.

SUMMARY OF CONCLUSION STATEMENTS

■ Demand is a curve or schedule showing the various quantities of a product consumers are willing to purchase at possible prices during a specified period of time, *ceteris paribus*.

■ Under the law of demand, any decrease in price along the vertical axis will cause an increase in quantity demanded, measured along the horizontal axis.

■ Changes in nonprice determinants can produce only a shift in the demand curve and not a movement along the demand curve, which is caused by a change in price.

■ Supply is a curve or schedule showing the various quantities of a product sellers are willing to produce and offer for sale at possible prices during a specified period of time, *ceteris paribus*.

■ Only at a higher price will it be profitable for sellers to incur the higher opportunity cost associated with producing and supplying a larger quantity.

■ Under the law of supply, any increase in price along the vertical axis will cause an increase in quantity supplied, measured along the horizontal axis.

■ Changes in nonprice determinants can only produce a shift in the supply curve and not a movement along the supply curve.

■ Graphically, the intersection of the supply curve and the demand curve is the market equilibrium price-quantity point. When all other nonprice factors are held constant, this is the only stable coordinate on the graph.

STUDY QUESTIONS AND PROBLEMS

1. Some people will pay a higher price for brand-name goods. For example, some people buy Rolls Royces and Rolex watches to impress others. Does knowingly paying higher prices for certain items just to be a "snob" violate the law of demand?

2. Draw graphs to illustrate the difference between a decrease in the quantity demanded and a decrease in demand for Mickey Mantle baseball cards. Give a possible reason for change in each graph.

3. Suppose oil prices rise sharply for years as a result of a war in the Persian Gulf. What happens and why to the demand for

   a. cars?

   b. home insulation?

   c. coal?

   d. tires?

4. Draw graphs to illustrate the difference between a decrease in quantity supplied and a decrease in supply for condominiums. Give a possible reason for change in each graph.

5. Use supply and demand analysis to explain why the quantity of word processing software exchanged increases from one year to the next.

6. Predict what will be the direction of change for either supply or demand in the following situations:

   a. Several new companies enter the home computer industry.

   b. Consumers suddenly decide large cars are unfashionable.

   c. The U.S. Surgeon General issues a report that tomatoes prevent colds.

   d. Frost threatens to damage the coffee crop, and consumers expect the price to rise sharply in the future.

   e. The price of tea falls. What is the effect on the coffee market?

   f. The price of sugar rises. What is the effect on the coffee market?

   g. Tobacco lobbyists convince Congress to remove the tax paid by sellers on each carton of cigarettes sold.

   h. A new type of robot is invented that will pick peaches.

   i. A computer game company anticipates that the future price of its games will fall much lower than the current price.

7. Explain and illustrate graphically the effect of the following situations:

   a. Population growth surges rapidly.

   b. The prices of resources used in the production of good X increase.

   c. The government is paying a $1.00-per-unit subsidy for each unit of a good produced.

   d. The incomes of consumers of normal good X increase.

   e. The incomes of consumers of inferior good Y decrease.

   f. Farmers are deciding what crop to plant and learn that the price of corn has fallen relative to the price of cotton.

8. Explain why the market price is not the same as the equilibrium price.

9. If a new breakthrough in manufacturing technology reduces the cost of producing CD players by half, what will happen to the

   a. supply of CD players?

   b. demand for CD players?

   c. equilibrium price and quantity of CD players?

   d. demand for CDs?

10. The U.S. Postal Service is facing increased competition from firms providing overnight delivery of packages and letters. Additional competition has emerged because messages can be sent over computers and fax machines. What will be the effect of this competition on the market demand for mail delivered by the post office?

11. There is a shortage of college basketball and football tickets for some games, and a surplus occurs for other games. Why do shortages and surpluses exist for different games?

12. Explain the statement "People respond to incentives and disincentives" in relation to the demand curve and supply curve for good X.

Equilibrium your Reubil

ONLINE EXERCISES

Exercise 1

Visit the U.S. Department of Labor's Bureau of Labor Statistics at http://stats.bls.gov/newsrels.htm.

1. Click on Real Earnings under Major Economic Indicators. What has been happening recently to earnings of workers?
2. What impact is this likely to have on the demand for Spam? Reflect this change graphically.

Exercise 2

Visit the U.S. Department of Labor's Bureau of Labor Statistics at http://stats.bls.gov/newsrels.htm.

1. Click on Productivity and Costs. What has been happening recently to productivity and costs of production?

2. Would the productivity change impact the demand of the supply curve for a product? Illustrate graphically the effect of the change in productivity and costs on a demand or supply curve.

Exercise 3

If water is inexpensive and readily available, why does the demand for bottled water, which can cost more than $2 for a 12-ounce bottle, remain strong? Why are consumers willing to pay such a steep price for bottled water? For references, visit the Evian water Web site at http://www.evian.com/home.htm.

Exercise 4

Go to http://price.bus.okstate.edu/archive/Econ3113_963/Shows/Chapter2/chap_02.htm to view a slide show on supply, demand, and market equilibrium.

CHECKPOINT ANSWERS

Can Gasoline Become an Exception to the Law of Demand?

As the price of oil began to rise, the expectation of still higher prices caused buyers to buy more now, and, therefore, demand increased. As shown in Exhibit 13 (right), suppose the price per gallon of gasoline was initially at P_1 and the quantity demanded was Q_1 on demand curve D_1 (point A). Then the Iraqi invasion caused the demand curve to shift rightward to D_2. Along the new demand curve, D_2, consumers increased their quantity demanded to Q_2 at the higher price of P_2 per gallon of gasoline (point B).

The expectation of rising gasoline prices in the future caused "an increase in demand," rather than "an increase in quantity demanded" in response to a higher price. If you said there are no exceptions to the law of demand, YOU ARE CORRECT.

Can the Law of Supply Be Repealed?

There is not a single quantity of oil—say, 3 million barrels—for sale in the world on a given day. The supply curve for oil is not vertical. As the law of supply states, higher oil prices will cause greater quantities of oil to be offered for sale. At lower prices, oil producers have less incentive to drill deeper for oil that is more expensive to discover.

The government cannot repeal the law of supply. Price controls discourage producers from oil exploration and production, which causes a reduction in the quantity supplied. If you said U.S. oil production decreased in the 1970s when the government put a lid on oil prices, YOU ARE CORRECT.

Exhibit 13

Can the Price System Eliminate Scarcity?

Recall from Chapter 1 that scarcity is the condition in which human wants are forever greater than the resources available to satisfy those wants. Using markets free from government interference will not solve the scarcity problem. Scarcity exists at any price for a good or service. This means scarcity occurs at any disequilibrium price where a shortage or surplus exists, and scarcity remains at any equilibrium price where no shortage or surplus exists.

Although the price system can eliminate shortages (or surpluses), if you said it cannot eliminate scarcity, YOU ARE CORRECT.

PRACTICE QUIZ

For a visual explanation of the correct answers, visit the tutorial at http://tucker.swcollege.com.

1. If the demand curve for good *X* is downward sloping, an increase in the price will result in
   a. an increase in the demand for good *X*.
   b. a decrease in the demand for good *X*.
   c. no change in the quantity demanded for good *X*.
   d. a larger quantity demanded for good *X*.
   e. a smaller quantity demanded for good *X*.

2. The law of demand states that the quantity demanded of a good changes, other things being equal, when
   a. the price of the good changes.
   b. consumer income changes.
   c. the prices of other goods change.
   d. a change occurs in the quantities of other goods purchased.

3. Which of the following is the result of a decrease in the price of tea, other things being equal?
   a. A leftward shift in the demand curve for tea.
   b. A downward movement along the demand curve for tea.
   c. A rightward shift in the demand curve for tea.
   d. An upward movement along the demand curve for tea.

4. Which of the following will cause a movement along the demand curve for good *X*?
   a. A change in the price of a close substitute.
   b. A change in the price of good *X*.
   c. A change in consumer tastes and preferences for good *X*.
   d. A change in consumer income.

5. Assuming beef and pork are substitutes, a decrease in the price of pork will cause the demand curve for beef to
   a. shift to the left as consumers switch from beef to pork.
   b. shift to the right as consumers switch from beef to pork.
   c. remain unchanged, since beef and pork are sold in separate markets.
   d. none of the above.

6. Assuming coffee and tea are substitutes, a decrease in the price of coffee, other things being equal, results in a(an)
   a. downward movement along the demand curve for tea.
   b. leftward shift in the demand curve for tea.
   c. upward movement along the demand curve for tea.
   d. rightward shift in the demand curve for tea.

7. Assuming steak and potatoes are complements, a decrease in the price of steak will
   a. decrease the demand for steak.
   b. increase the demand for steak.
   c. increase the demand for potatoes.
   d. decrease the demand for potatoes.

8. Assuming steak is a normal good, a decrease in consumer income, other things being equal, will
   a. cause a downward movement along the demand curve for steak.
   b. shift the demand curve for steak to the left.
   c. cause an upward movement along the demand curve for steak.
   d. shift the demand curve for steak to the right.

9. An increase in consumer income, other things being equal, will
   a. shift the supply curve for a normal good to the right.
   b. cause an upward movement along the demand curve for an inferior good.
   c. shift the demand curve for an inferior good to the left.
   d. cause a downward movement along the supply curve for a normal good.

10. Yesterday seller *A* supplied 400 units of good *X* at $10 per unit. Today seller *A* supplies the same quantity of units at $5 per unit. Based on this evidence, seller *A* has experienced a(an)
    a. decrease in supply.
    b. increase in supply.
    c. increase in the quantity supplied.
    d. decrease in the quantity supplied.
    e. increase in demand.

11. An improvement in technology causes a(an)
    a. leftward shift of the supply curve.
    b. upward movement along the supply curve.
    c. firm to supply a larger quantity at any given price.
    d. downward movement along the supply curve.

12. Suppose autoworkers receive a substantial wage increase. Other things being equal, the price of autos will rise because of a(an)
    a. increase in the demand for autos.
    b. rightward shift of the supply curve for autos.
    c. leftward shift of the supply curve for autos.
    d. reduction in the demand for autos.

13. Assuming soybeans and tobacco can be grown on the same land, an increase in the price of tobacco, other things being equal, causes a(an)
    a. upward movement along the supply curve for soybeans.
    b. downward movement along the supply curve for soybeans.
    c. rightward shift in the supply curve for soybeans.
    d. leftward shift in the supply curve for soybeans.

14. If Q_d = quantity demanded and Q_s = quantity supplied at a given price, a shortage in the market results when
    a. Q_s is greater than Q_d.
    b. Q_s equals Q_d.
    c. Q_d is less than or equal to Q_s.
    d. Q_d is greater than Q_s.

15. Assume that the equilibrium price for a good is $10. If the market price is $5, a
    a. shortage will cause the price to remain at $5.
    b. surplus will cause the price to remain at $5.
    c. shortage will cause the price to rise toward $10.
    d. surplus will cause the price to rise toward $10.

16. In the market shown in Exhibit 14, the equilibrium price and quantity of good X are
    a. $0.50, 200.
    b. $1.50, 300.
    c. $2.00, 100.
    d. $1.00, 200.

Exhibit 14 Supply and demand curves

17. In Exhibit 14, at a price of $2.00, the market for good X will experience a
    a. shortage of 150 units.
    b. surplus of 100 units.
    c. shortage of 100 units.
    d. surplus of 200 units.

18. In Exhibit 14, if the price of good X moves from $1.00 to $2.00, the new market condition will put
    a. upward pressure on price.
    b. no pressure on price to change.
    c. downward pressure on price.
    d. no pressure on quantity to change.

CHAPTER 4

Markets in Action

O nce you understand how buyers and sellers respond to changes in equilibrium prices, you are progressing well in your quest to understand the economic way of thinking. This chapter begins by showing that changes in supply and demand influence the equilibrium price and quantity of goods and services exchanged around you every day. For example, you will study the impact of changes in supply and demand curves on the markets for Caribbean cruises, new homes, and AIDS vaccinations. Then you will see why the laws of supply and demand cannot be repealed. Using market supply and demand analysis, you will learn that government policies to control markets have predictable consequences. For example, you will understand what happens when the government limits the maximum rent landlords can charge and who

benefits and who loses from the federal minimum-wage law.

In this chapter, you will also study situations in which the market mechanism fails. Have you visited Los Angeles and lamented the smog that blankets the beautiful surroundings? Or have you ever wanted to swim or fish in a stream, but could not because of industrial waste? These are obvious cases in which market-system magic failed and the government must consider cures to reach socially desirable results.

In this chapter, you will learn to solve these economics puzzles:

■ How can a spotted owl affect the price of homes?

■ Why might government warehouses overflow with cheese and milk?

■ What do ticket scalping and rent controls have in common?

Changes in Market Equilibrium

Using market supply and demand analysis is like putting on glasses if you are nearsighted. Suddenly, the fuzzy world around you comes into clear focus. In the following examples, you will open your eyes and see that economic theory has something important to say about so many things in the real world.

Changes in Demand

The Caribbean cruise market shown in Exhibit 1(a) assumes market supply, S, is constant and market demand increases from D_1 to D_2. Why has the demand curve shifted rightward in the figure? We will assume the popularity of cruises to these vacation islands has suddenly risen sharply due to extensive advertising (changes in tastes and preferences). Given supply curve S and demand curve D_1, the initial equilibrium price is $600 per cruise, and the initial equilibrium quantity is 8,000 cruises per year, shown as point E_1. After the impact of advertising, the new equilibrium point, E_2, becomes 12,000 cruises per year at a price of $900 each. Thus, the increase in demand causes both the equilibrium price and the equilibrium quantity to increase.

It is important to understand the force that caused the equilibrium to shift from E_1 to E_2. When demand initially increased from D_1 to D_2, there was a temporary shortage of 8,000 cruises at $600 per cruise. Firms in the cruise business responded to the excess demand by hiring more workers, offering more cruises to the Caribbean, and raising the price. The cruise lines therefore move upward along the supply curve (increasing quantity supplied, but not changing supply). During some period of trial and error, Caribbean cruise sellers increase their price and quantity supplied until a shortage no longer exists at point E_2. Therefore, the increase in demand causes both the equilibrium price and the equilibrium quantity to increase.

What will happen to the demand for gas-guzzler automobiles (for example, SUVs) if the price of gasoline triples? Because gasoline and automobiles are complements, a rise in the price of gasoline decreases the demand for such automobiles from D_1 to D_2 in Exhibit 1(b). At the initial equilibrium price of $30,000 per gas guzzler ($E_1$), the quantity supplied now exceeds the quantity demanded by 20,000 automobiles per month. This unwanted inventory forces automakers to reduce the price and quantity supplied. As a result of this movement downward on the supply curve, market equilibrium changes from E_1 to E_2. The equilibrium price falls from $30,000 to $20,000, and the equilibrium quantity falls from 30,000 to 20,000 gas guzzlers per month.

Changes in Supply

Now reverse the analysis by assuming demand remains constant and allowing some nonprice determinant to shift the supply curve. In Exhibit 2(a), begin at point E_1 in the video rental industry with an equilibrium price of $3 per rental and 40 million video rentals per month. Then word spreads to entrepreneurs that the video business is a hot prospect for earning profits. New firms enter the video rental market, and the market supply curve shifts

EXHIBIT 1   **The Effects of Shifts in Demand on Market Equilibrium**

In part (a), demand for Caribbean cruises increases because of extensive advertising, and the demand curve shifts rightward from D_1 to D_2. This shift in demand causes a temporary shortage of 8,000 cruises per year at the initial equilibrium of E_1. This disequilibrium condition encourages firms in the cruise business to move upward along the supply curve to a new equilibrium at E_2.

Part (b) illustrates a decrease in the demand for gas-guzzler automobiles caused by a sharp rise in the price of gasoline (a complement). This leftward shift in demand from D_1 to D_2 results in a temporary surplus of 20,000 gas guzzlers per month at the initial equilibrium of E_1. This disequilibrium condition forces sellers of these cars to move downward along the supply curve to a new equilibrium at E_2.

from S_1 to S_2. This creates a temporary surplus of 40 million video rentals at point E_1. Video rental firms respond to stacks of unrented videos on their shelves by reducing the rental price and the number available for rent. As the price falls, buyers move down along their demand curve and rent more videos per month. When the rental price falls to $2, the market is in equilibrium again at point E_2, instead of E_1, and consumers rent 60 million videos per month.

Exhibit 2(b) illustrates the market for lumber. Suppose this market is at equilibrium E_1, the going price is $400 per thousand board feet, and 8 billion board feet are bought and sold per year. Now suppose a new Endangered Species Act is passed, and the federal government sets aside huge forest resources to protect the spotted owl and other wildlife. This means the

EXHIBIT 2   **The Effects of Shifts in Supply on Market Equilibrium**

(a) Increase in supply

Surplus of 40 million rental videos

Price per video rental (dollars)

Quantity of video rentals (millions per month)

(b) Decrease in supply

Shortage of 4 billion board feet

Price per 1,000 board feet (dollars)

Quantity of lumber (billions of board feet per year)

CAUSATION CHAIN

| Increase in supply | ⇨ | Decrease in equilibrium price | ⇨ | Increase in quantity demanded |

CAUSATION CHAIN

| Decrease in supply | ⇨ | Increase in equilibrium price | ⇨ | Decrease in quantity demanded |

In part (a), begin at equilibrium E_1 in the video rental industry, and assume an increase in the number of video rental firms shifts the supply curve rightward from S_1 to S_2. This shift in supply causes a temporary surplus of 40 million video rentals per month. This disequilibrium condition causes a movement downward along the demand curve to a new equilibrium at E_2. At E_2, the equilibrium rental price declines, and the equilibrium quantity rises.

In part (b), steps to protect the environment cause the supply curve for lumber to shift leftward from S_1 to S_2. This shift in supply results in a temporary shortage of 4 billion board feet per year. Customer bidding for the available lumber raises the price. As a result, the market moves upward along the demand curve to a new equilibrium at E_2, and the quantity demanded falls.

market supply curve shifts leftward from S_1 to S_2 and a temporary shortage of 4 billion board feet of lumber exists at point E_1. Suppliers respond by hiking their price from $400 to $600 per thousand board feet, and a new equilibrium is established at E_2, where the quantity is 6 billion board feet. This higher cost of lumber, in turn, raises the price of a new 1,800-square-foot home by $4,000, compared to the price of an identical home the previous year. One proposed solution to higher lumber prices is to reduce sales of logs to foreign countries. Why might this be a good idea?

Exhibit 3 gives a concise summary of the impact of changes in demand and supply on market equilibrium.

EXHIBIT 3 Effect of Shifts in Demand and Supply on Market Equilibrium		
Change	**Effect on equilibrium price**	**Effect on equilibrium quantity**
Demand increases	Increases	Increases
Demand decreases	Decreases	Decreases
Supply increases	Decreases	Increases
Supply decreases	Increases	Decreases

Can the Laws of Supply and Demand Be Repealed?

The government intervenes in some markets with the objective of preventing prices from rising to the equilibrium price. In other markets, the government's goal is to intervene and maintain a price higher than the equilibrium price. Market supply and demand analysis is a valuable tool for understanding what happens when the government fixes prices. There are two types of price controls: *price ceilings* and *price floors*.

Price Ceilings

What happens if the government prevents the price system from setting a market price "too high" by mandating a **price ceiling**? A price ceiling is a legally established maximum price a seller can charge. Rent controls are an example of the imposition of a price ceiling in the market for rental units. New York City, Washington, D.C., Los Angeles, San Francisco, and Boston are among the many U.S. cities that have adopted rent controls. Since World War I, rent controls have been widely used in Europe. The rationale for rent controls is to provide an "essential service" that would otherwise be unaffordable by many people at the equilibrium rental price. Let's see why most economists believe that rent controls are counterproductive.

Exhibit 4 is a supply and demand diagram for the quantity of rental units demanded and supplied per month in a hypothetical city. We begin the analysis by assuming no rent controls exist and equilibrium is at point *E*, with a monthly rent of $600 per month and 6 million units occupied. Next, assume the city council imposes a rent control (ceiling price) that by law forbids any landlord to rent a unit for more than $400 per month. What does market supply and demand theory predict will happen? At the low rent ceiling of $400, the quantity demanded of rental units will be 8 million, but the quantity supplied will be only 4 million. Consequently, the price ceiling creates a persistent market shortage of 4 million rental units because suppliers cannot raise the rental price without being subjected to legal penalties.

Price ceiling
A legally established maximum price a seller can charge.

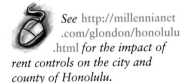

See http://millennianet .com/glondon/honolulu .html *for the impact of rent controls on the city and county of Honolulu.*

EXHIBIT 4   **Rent Control Results in a Shortage of Rental Units**

If no rent controls exist, the equilibrium rent for a hypothetical apartment is $600 per month at point *E*. However, if the government imposes a rent ceiling of $400 per month, a shortage of 4 million rental units occurs. Because rent cannot rise by law, one outcome is that consumers must search for available units instead of paying a higher rent. Other outcomes include a black market, bribes, discrimination, and other illegal methods of dealing with a shortage of 4 million rental units per month.

CAUSATION CHAIN

Rent ceiling ⇨ Quantity demanded exceeds quantity supplied ⇨ Shortage

Note that a rent ceiling at or above $600 per month would have no effect. If the ceiling is set at the equilibrium rent of $600, the quantity of rental units demanded and the quantity of rental units supplied are equal regardless of the rent control. If the rent ceiling is set above the equilibrium rent, the quantity of rental units supplied exceeds the quantity of rental units demanded, and this surplus will cause the market to adjust to the equilibrium rent of $600.

What is the impact of rent controls on consumers? First, as a substitute for paying higher prices, consumers must spend more time on waiting lists and searching for housing. This means consumers incur an *opportunity cost* added to the $400 rent set by government. Second, an illegal market, or *black market*, can arise because of the excess quantity demanded. Because the price of rental units is artificially low, the profit motive encourages tenants to risk breaking the law by subletting their unit to the highest bidder over $400 per month.

From the seller's perspective, rent control encourages two undesirable effects. First, a mandated low rent means landlords may cut maintenance expenses, and housing deterioration will reduce the stock of rental units in the long run. Second, landlords may use discriminatory practices to replace the price system. Once owners realize there is an excess quantity demanded

CHECKPOINT

Why the Higher Price for Lower Cholesterol?

A few years ago a number-one best-selling book proclaimed the virtues of oat bran in reducing cholesterol. More and more consumers added oat bran cereal and muffins to their diets. At the same time, producers switched over to oat bran production from other agricultural crops. Within a two-month period, the price of a pound of oat bran shot up from $0.99 to $2.59. During this two-month period, which increased more—demand, supply, or neither?

for rentals at the controlled price, they may resort to preferences based on pet ownership, family size, or race to determine how to allocate scarce rental space.

The government placed ceilings on most nonfarm prices during World War II and, to a lesser extent, during the Korean War. In 1971, President Nixon "froze" virtually all wages, prices, and rents for 90 days in an attempt to control inflation. As a result of an oil embargo in late 1973, the government imposed a price ceiling of 55 cents per gallon of gasoline. To deal with the shortage, nonprice rationing schemes were introduced in 1974. Some states used a first-come, first-served system, while other states allowed consumers with even-numbered license plates to buy gas on even-numbered days and those with odd-numbered license plates to buy on odd-numbered days. Gas stations were required to close on Friday night and not open until Monday morning. Regardless of the scheme, long waiting lines for gasoline formed, just as the supply and demand model predicts. Finally, in the past legally imposed price ceilings have been placed on such items as natural gas shipped in interstate commerce and on interest rates for loans. Maximum interest rate laws are called *usury laws,* and state governments have adopted these ceilings in the past to regulate home mortgages and other types of loans. Internationally, as discussed later in the chapter on economies in transition, price ceilings on food and rent were common in the former Soviet Union. Soviet sociologists estimated that members of a typical urban household spent a combined total of 40 hours per week standing in lines to obtain various goods and services.

Price Floors

The other side of the price-control coin is a **price floor** set by the government because it fears that the price system might establish a price viewed as "too low." A price floor is a legally established minimum price a seller can be paid. We now turn to two examples of price floors. The first is the minimum wage, and the second is agricultural price supports.

Case 1: The Minimum-Wage Law. In the first chapter, the second You're the Economist applied *normative* and *positive* reasoning to the issue of the minimum wage. Now you are prepared to apply market supply and demand analysis (positive reasoning) to this debate. Begin by noting that the demand for unskilled labor is the downward-sloping curve shown in Exhibit 5. The

Price floor
A legally established minimum price a seller can be paid.

EXHIBIT 5   **A Minimum Wage Results in a Surplus of Labor**

When the federal or state government sets a wage-rate floor above the equilibrium wage, a surplus of unskilled labor develops. The supply curve is the number of workers offering their labor services per year at possible wage rates. The demand curve is the number of workers employers are willing and able to hire at various wage rates. Equilibrium wage, W_e, will result if the price system is allowed to operate without government interference. At the minimum wage of W_m, there is a surplus of unemployed workers, $Q_s - Q_d$.

CAUSATION CHAIN

Minimum wage ⟹ Unemployment

---

wage rate on the vertical axis is the price of unskilled labor, and the amount of unskilled labor employers are willing to hire varies inversely with the wage rate. At a higher wage rate, businesses will hire fewer workers. At a lower wage rate, they will employ a larger quantity of workers.

On the supply side, the wage rate determines the number of unskilled workers willing and able to work per year. At higher wages, workers will give up leisure or schooling to work, and at lower wages, fewer workers will be available for hire. The upward-sloping curve in Exhibit 5 is the supply of labor.

Assuming the freedom to bargain, the price system will establish an equilibrium wage rate of W_e and an equilibrium quantity of labor employed of Q_e. But suppose the government enacts a minimum wage, W_m, which is a price floor above the equilibrium wage, W_e. The intent of the legislation is to "wave a carrot" in front of people who will not work at W_e and to make lower-paid workers better off with a higher wage rate. But consider the undesirable consequences. One result of an artificially high minimum wage is that the number of workers willing to offer their labor increases upward along the supply curve to Q_s, but there are fewer jobs because the number of workers firms are willing to hire decreases to Q_d on the demand curve.

The predicted outcome is a labor surplus of unskilled workers, $Q_s - Q_d$, who are unemployed. Moreover, employers are encouraged to substitute machines and skilled labor for the unskilled labor previously employed at equilibrium wage W_e. The minimum wage is therefore considered counter-productive because employers lay off the lowest-skilled workers, who are ironically the type of workers minimum-wage legislation intends to help.

Supporters of the minimum wage are quick to point out that those employed (Q_d) are better off. Even though the minimum wage causes a reduction in employment, some economists argue that a more equal or fairer income distribution is worth the loss of some jobs. Moreover, the shape of the labor demand curve may be much more vertical than shown in Exhibit 5. If this is the case, the unemployment effect of a rise in the minimum wage would be small. In addition, they claim opponents ignore the possibility that unskilled workers lack bargaining power versus employers.

Finally, a minimum wage set at or below the equilibrium wage rate is ineffective. If the minimum wage is set at the equilibrium wage rate of W_e, the quantity of labor demanded and the quantity of labor supplied are equal regardless of the minimum wage. If the minimum wage is set below the equilibrium wage, the forces of supply of and demand for labor establish the equilibrium wage regardless of the minimum wage rate.

For another rather common economic view of the impact of the minimum wage see http://www.ncpa.org/ba/ba270.html.

Case 2: Agricultural Price Supports. A farm price support is a well-known price floor, which results in government purchases of surplus food and in higher food prices. Agricultural price support programs began in the 1930s as a means of raising the income of farmers, who were suffering from low market prices during the Great Depression. Under these programs, the government guarantees a minimum price above the equilibrium price and agrees to purchase any quantity the farmer is unable to sell at the legal price.

A few of the crops that have received price supports are corn, peanuts, soybeans, wheat, cotton, rice, tobacco, and dairy products. As predicted by market supply and demand analysis, a price support above the equilibrium price causes surpluses. Government warehouses therefore often overflow with such perishable products as butter, cheese, and dry milk purchased with taxpayers' money. The following You're the Economist on the dairy industry examines one of the best-known examples of U.S. government interference with agricultural market prices.

For more information of agricultural price supports see http://www.infoplease.com/ce6/sci/A0802771.html.

Market Failure

In this chapter and the previous chapter, you gained an understanding of how markets operate. Through the price system, society coordinates economic activity, but markets are not always "Prince Charmings." It is now time to step back with a critical eye and consider markets that become "ugly frogs" by allocating resources inefficiently. **Market failure** occurs when market equilibrium results in too few or too many resources being used in the production of a good or service. In this section, you will study four important cases of market failure: lack of competition, externalities, public goods, and income inequality.

Market failure

A situation in which market equilibrium results in too few or too many resources being used in the production of a good or service.

Rigging the Market for Milk

Applicable Concept: price supports

Each year the question in the milk industry is: What does the federal government plan to do about its dairy price support program, which has helped boost farmers' income since 1949? Under the price support program, the federal government agrees to buy storable milk products, such as cheese, butter, and dry milk. If the farmers cannot sell all their products to consumers at a price exceeding the support price level, the federal government will purchase any unsold grade A milk production. Although state-run dairy commissions set their own minimum prices for milk, state price supports closely follow federal levels and are kept within 3 percent of levels in bordering states to reduce interstate milk price competition.

Members of Congress who advocate changes in the price support programs worry that milk surpluses are costing taxpayers too much. Each year the federal government pays billions of dollars to dairy farmers for milk products held in storage at a huge cost. Moreover, the problem is getting worse because the federal government encourages dairy farmers to use ultramodern farming techniques to increase the production per cow. Another concern is that the biggest government price support checks go to the largest farmers, while the number of dairy farmers continues to decline.

Congress is constantly seeking a solution to the milk price-support-program problem. The following are some of the ideas that have been considered:

1. Freeze the current price support level. This prospect dismays farmers, who are subject to increasing expenses for feed, electricity, and other resources.

2. Eliminate the price support gradually in yearly increments over the next five years. This would subject the milk market to the price fluctuations of the free market, and farmers would suffer some bad years from low milk prices.

3. Have the Department of Agriculture charge dairy farmers a tax of 50 cents for every 100 pounds of milk they produce. The farmers oppose this approach because it would discourage production and run small farmers out of business.

4. Have the federal government implement a "whole herd buyout" program. The problem is that using taxpayers' money to get farmers out of the dairy business pushes up milk product prices and rewards drop out dairy farmers who own a lot of cows. Besides, what does the government do with the cows after it purchases them?

Finally, opponents of the dairy price support program argue that the market for milk is inherently a competitive industry and that consumers and taxpayers would be better served without government price supports for milk.

ANALYZE THE ISSUE

1. Draw a supply and demand graph to illustrate the problem described in the case study, and prescribe your own solution.

2. Which proposal do you think best serves the interests of small dairy farmers? Why?

3. Which proposal do you think best serves the interests of consumers? Why?

4. Which proposal do you think best serves the interest of a member of Congress? Why?

CHECKPOINT

Is There Price-Fixing at the Ticket Window?

At sold-out concerts, sports contests, and other events, some of those with tickets try to resell their tickets for more than they paid—a practice known as scalping. For scalping to occur, must the original ticket price be set by a price floor, at the equilibrium price, or by a price ceiling?

Lack of Competition

There must be competition among both producers and consumers for markets to function properly. But what happens if the producers fail to compete? In *Wealth of Nations,* Adam Smith stated: "People of the same trade seldom meet together, even for merriment and diversion, but the conversation ends in a conspiracy against the public, or in some diversion to raise prices."[1] This famous quotation clearly underscores the fact that in the real world businesses seek ways to replace consumer sovereignty with "big business sovereignty." What happens when a few firms rig the market and they become the market's boss? By restricting supply through artificial limits on the output of a good, firms could enjoy higher prices and profits. As a result, firms may waste resources and retard technology and innovation.

Exhibit 6 illustrates how IBM, Apple, Gateway, and other suppliers of personal computers (PCs) could benefit from rigging the market. Without collusive action, the competitive price for PCs is $1,500, the quantity of 200,000 per month is sold, and efficient equilibrium prevails at point E_1. It is in the best interest of sellers, however, to take steps that would make PCs artificially scarce and raise the price. Graphically, the sellers wish to shift the competitive supply curve, S_1, leftward to the restricted supply curve, S_2. This could happen for a number of reasons, including: an agreement among sellers to restrict supply (collusion) and government action. For example, the sellers could lobby the government to pass a law allowing an association of PC suppliers to set production quotas. The proponents might argue this action raises prices and, in turn, profits. Higher profits enable the industry to invest in new capital and become more competitive in world markets.

Opponents of artificially restricted supply argue that although the producers benefit, the lack of competition means the economy loses. The result of restricting supply is that the efficient equilibrium point, E_1, changes to the inefficient equilibrium point, E_2. At point E_2, the higher price of $2,000 is charged, and the lower equilibrium quantity means that firms devote too few resources to producing PCs and charge an artificially high price. Note that under antitrust laws in the United States, the Justice Department is responsible for prosecuting firms that collude to restrict supply to force higher prices.

[1]Adam Smith, *An Inquiry into the Nature and Causes of the Wealth of Nations* (1776; reprint, New York: Random House, The Modern Library, 1937), p. 128.

EXHIBIT 6   **Rigging the PC Market**

At efficient equilibrium point E_1, sellers compete. As a result, the price per PC charged is $1,500, and the quantity of PCs exchanged is 200,000. Suppose suppliers use collusion, government intervention, or other means to restrict the supply of this product. The decrease in supply from S_1 to S_2 establishes inefficient equilibrium E_2. At E_2, firms charge the higher price of $2,000, and the equilibrium quantity of PCs falls to 150,000. Thus, the outcome of restricted supply is that the market fails because firms use too few resources to produce PCs at an artificially higher price.

Externalities

Externality

A cost or benefit imposed on people other than the consumers and producers of a good or service.

Even when markets are competitive, some markets may still fail because they suffer from the presence of side effects economists call **externalities.** An externality is a cost or benefit imposed on people other than the consumers and producers of a good or service. Externalities are also called *spillover effects* or *neighborhood effects*. People other than consumers and producers who are affected by these side effects of market exchanges are called *third parties*. Externalities may be either negative or positive; that is, they may be detrimental or beneficial. Suppose you are trying to study and your roommate is listening to Steel Porcupines at full blast on the stereo. The action of your roommate is imposing an unwanted *external cost* or *negative externality* on you and other third parties who are trying to study or sleep. Externalities can also result in an *external benefit* or *positive externality* to nonparticipating parties. When a community proudly displays its neat lawns, gorgeous flowers, and freshly painted homes, visitors are third parties who did none of the work, but enjoy the benefit of the pleasant scenery.

For some new ideas in pollution regulation see the World Bank's Internet site at http://www.worldbank.org/ nipr/newappr.htm.

A Graphical Analysis of Pollution. Exhibit 7 provides a graphical analysis of two markets that fail to include externalities in their market prices unless the government takes corrective action. Exhibit 7(a) shows a market for steel in which steel firms burn high-sulfur coal and pollute the environment. Demand curve *D* and supply curve S_1 establish the inefficient equilibrium E_1 in the steel market. Not included in S_1 are the *external costs* to the public

EXHIBIT 7   **Externalities in the Steel and AIDS Vaccination Markets**

In part (a), resources are overallocated at inefficient equilibrium E_1 because steel firms do not include the cost per ton of pollution in the cost per ton of steel. Supply curve S_2 includes the external costs of pollution. If firms are required to purchase equipment to remove the pollution or to pay a tax on pollution, the economy achieves the efficient equilibrium of E_2.

Part (b) demonstrates that external benefits cause an underallocation of resources. The efficient output at equilibrium point E_2 is obtained if people are required to purchase AIDS shots or if the government pays a subsidy equal to the external benefit per shot.

because the steel firms are not paying for the damage from smoke emissions. If steel firms discharge smoke and ash into the atmosphere, foul air reduces property values, raises health care costs, and, in general, erodes the quality of life. Because supply curve S_1 does not include these external costs, they are also not included in the price of steel, P_1. In short, the absence of the cost of pollution in the price of steel means the firms produce more steel and pollution than is socially desirable.

S_2 is the supply curve that would exist if the external costs of respiratory illnesses, dirty homes, and other undesirable side effects are included. Once S_2 includes the charges for environmental damage, the equilibrium price rises to P_2, and the equilibrium quantity becomes Q_2. At the efficient equilibrium point, E_2, the steel market achieves allocative efficiency. At E_2, steel firms are paying the full cost and using fewer resources to produce the lower quantity of steel at Q_2.

Conclusion *When the supply curve fails to include external costs, the equilibrium price is artificially low and the equilibrium quantity artificially high.*

Regulation and pollution taxes are two ways society can correct the market failure of pollution:

1. *Regulation.* Legislation can set standards that force firms to clean up their emissions as a condition of remaining in business. This means a firm must buy, install, and maintain pollution-control equipment. When the extra cost of the pollution equipment is added to the production cost per ton of steel, the initial supply curve, S_1, shifts leftward to supply curve S_2. This means regulation has forced the market equilibrium to change from E_1 to E_2. At point E_2, the firm uses fewer resources to produce Q_2 compared to Q_1 output of steel per year, and, therefore, the firm operates efficiently.

2. *Pollution Taxes.* Another approach would be for the government to levy a tax per ton of steel equal to the external cost imposed on society when the firm emits pollution into the air. This action inhibits production by imposing an additional production cost per ton of steel from the pollution taxes and shifts the supply curve leftward from S_1 to S_2. Again, the objective is to change the equilibrium from E_1 to E_2 and eliminate the overuse of resources devoted to steel production and its pollution. The tax revenue could be used to compensate those damaged by the pollution.

A Graphical Analysis of AIDS Vaccinations. As explained above, the supply curve can understate the *external costs* of a product. Now you will see that the demand curve can understate the *external benefits* of a product. Suppose a vaccination is discovered that prevents AIDS. Exhibit 7(b) illustrates the market for immunization against AIDS. Demand curve D_1 reflects the price consumers would pay for shots to receive the benefit of a reduced probability of infection by AIDS. Supply curve S shows the quantities of shots suppliers offer for sale at different prices. At equilibrium point E_1, the market fails to achieve an efficient allocation of resources. The reason is that when buyers are vaccinated, other people who do not purchase AIDS shots (called *free riders*) also benefit because this disease is less likely to spread. Once demand curve D_2 includes external benefits to nonconsumers of AIDS vaccinations (increase in the number of buyers), the efficient equilibrium of E_2 is established. At Q_2, sellers devote greater resources to AIDS vaccinations, and the underallocation of resources is eliminated.

How can society prevent the market failure of AIDS vaccinations? Two approaches follow:

1. *Regulation.* The government can boost consumption and shift the demand curve rightward by requiring all citizens to purchase AIDS shots each year. This approach to capturing external benefits in market demand explains why all school-age children must take polio and other shots before entering school.

2. *Special Subsidies.* Another possible solution would be for the government to pay consumers for each AIDS vaccination. This would mean the government pays each citizen a dollar payment equal to the amount of external benefits per shot purchased. Since the subsidy amount is payable at any price along the demand curve, the demand curve shifts rightward until the efficient equilibrium price and quantity are reached.

Conclusion *When externalities are present, market failure gives incorrect price and quantity signals, and as a result, resources are misallocated. External costs cause the market to overallocate resources, and external benefits cause the market to underallocate resources.*

Public Goods

Private goods are produced through the price system. On the other hand, national defense is an example of a **public good** provided by the government because of its special characteristics. A public good is a good or service that, once produced, has two properties: (1) users collectively consume benefits, and (2) there is no way to bar people who do not pay (free riders) from consuming the good or service.

To see why the marketplace fails, imagine that Patriot Missiles, Inc., offers to sell missile defense systems to people who want private protection against attacks from incoming missiles. First, once the system is operational, everyone in the defense area benefits from increased safety. Second, the *nonexclusive* nature of a public good means that it is impossible or very costly for any owner of a Patriot missile defense system to prevent nonowners, the free riders, from reaping the benefits of its protection.

Given the two properties of a public good, why would any private individual purchase a Patriot missile defense system? Why not take a free ride and wait until someone else buys a missile system? Thus, each person wants a Patriot system, but does not want to bear the cost of the system when everyone shares in the benefits. As a result, the market fails to provide Patriot missile defense systems, and everyone hopes no missile attacks occur before someone finally decides to purchase one. Government can solve this public goods problem by producing Patriot missiles and taxing the public to pay. Unlike a private citizen, the government can use force to collect payments and prevent the free-rider problem. Other examples of public goods include the judicial system, the national emergency warning system, air traffic control, prisons, and traffic lights.

Conclusion *If public goods are available only in the marketplace, people wait for someone else to pay, and the result is an underproduction or zero production of public goods.*

Public good

A good or service with two properties: (1) users collectively consume benefits, and (2) there is no way to bar people who do not pay (free riders) from consuming the good or service.

Can Vouchers Fix Our Schools?

Applicable Concept: public goods versus private goods

In their book, *Free to Choose*, published in 1980, economists Milton Friedman and his wife Rose Friedman proposed a voucher plan for schools.[1] The objective of their proposal was to retain government financing, but provide parents greater freedom to choose the schools their children attend. The Friedmans pointed out that under the current system parents face a strong incentive not to remove their children from the public schools. This is because if parents decide to withdraw their children from a public school and send them to a private school, they must pay private tuition in addition to the taxes that finance enrollment of children in the public schools.

To remove the financial penalty that limits the freedom of parents to choose schools, the government could give parents a voucher, which is a piece of paper redeemable for a sum of money payable to any approved school. For example, if the government spends $6,000 per year to educate a student, then the voucher could be for this amount. The voucher plan embodies exactly the same principle as the GI bill that provides educational benefits to military veterans. The veteran receives a voucher good only for educational expenses and is completely free to choose the school where it is used, provided it satisfies certain standards.

The Friedmans argue that parents could, and should, be permitted to use the vouchers not only at private schools but also at other public schools—and not only at schools in their own district, city, or state, but at any school that is willing to accept their child. That would give every parent a greater opportunity to choose and at the same time require public schools to charge tuition. The tuition would be competitive because public schools must compete for students both with one another and with private schools. It is important to note that this plan relieves no one of the burden of taxation to pay for schooling. It simply gives parents a wider choice as to which competing schools their children attend given the amount of funding per student that the community has obligated itself to provide. The plan also does not affect the present standards imposed on private schools to assure that students attending them satisfy the compulsory attendance laws.

In 1990, Milwaukee began an experiment with school vouchers. The program gave selected children from low-income families taxpayer-funded vouchers to allow them to attend private schools. There has been a continuing heated debate among parents, politicians, and educators over the results. In 1998, Wisconsin's highest court ruled in a 4–2 decision that Milwaukee can use public money for vouchers for students who attend religious schools without violating the constitutional separation of church and state.[2]

In 2001, President George W. Bush unveiled an education plan that included a proposal to provide annual vouchers averaging $1,500 to students from low-income families who attend failing schools. These vouchers could be used to attend a private school, public school, or to receive tutoring. However, the president's voucher proposal failed to gain enough support in Congress, and it was withdrawn from the education plan.

ANALYZE THE ISSUE

1. In recent years, school choice has been a hotly debated issue. Explain whether or not education is a public good. If education is not a public good, why should the government provide it?

2. The Friedmans present a very one-sided view of the benefits of a voucher system. Other economists disagree about the potential effectiveness of vouchers. Do you support a voucher system for education? Explain your reasoning.

---

[1]Milton Friedman and Rose Friedman, *Free to Choose: A Personal Statement* (New York: Harcourt Brace Jovanovich, 1980), pp. 160–161.

[2]Mary Beth Marklein, "Voucher Use in Religious Schools Ruled Constitutional in Wisconsin," *USA Today*, June 11, 1998, p. 1A.

CHECKPOINT

Should There Be a War on Drugs?

The U.S. government fights the use of drugs, such as marijuana and cocaine, in a variety of ways, including spraying crops with poisonous chemicals; imposing jail sentences for dealers and users; and confiscating drug-transporting cars, boats, and planes. What market failure motivates the government to interfere with the market for drugs: lack of competition, externalities, public goods, or income inequality?

Income Inequality

In the cases of insufficient competition, externalities, and public goods, the marketplace allocates too few or too many resources to producing output. Although a very controversial issue, the market may also result in a very unequal distribution of income. Under the impersonal price system, Tom Cruise earns a huge income for acting in movies, while homeless people roam the streets penniless. Thus, the controversy is over how equal the distribution of income should be and how much government intervention is required to achieve this goal. Some people wish to remove most inequality of income. Others argue for the government to provide a "safety net" minimum income level for all citizens. Still others see high income as an incentive and a "fair" reward for productive resources.

To create a more equal distribution of income, the government uses various programs to transfer money from people with high incomes to those with low incomes. Unemployment compensation and food stamps are examples of such programs. The federal minimum wage is another type of government attempt to raise the earnings of low-income workers.

KEY CONCEPTS

Price ceiling   Market failure   Public good
Price floor   Externality

SUMMARY

- **Price ceilings** and **price floors** are maximum and minimum prices enacted by law, rather than allowing the forces of supply and demand to determine prices. A *price ceiling* is a maximum price mandated by government, and a *price floor*, or *support price* for agricultural products, is a minimum legal price. If a price ceiling is set below the equilibrium price, a shortage will persist. If a price floor is set above the equilibrium price, a surplus will persist.

Price Ceiling

Price Floor

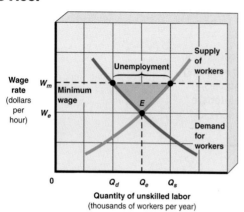

Quantity of unskilled labor
(thousands of workers per year)

Externalities

(a) External costs of pollution

Quantity of steel
(tons per year)

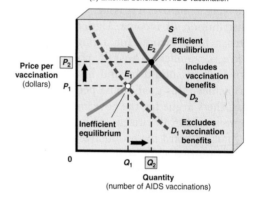

(b) External benefits of AIDS vaccination

Quantity
(number of AIDS vaccinations)

- **Market failure** occurs when the market mechanism does not achieve efficient allocation of resources. Sources of market failure include lack of competition, externalities, public goods, and income inequality. Although controversial, government intervention is a possible way to correct market failure.

- An **externality** is a cost or benefit of a good imposed on people who are not buyers or sellers of that good. Pollution is an example of an *external cost,* which means too many resources are used to produce the product responsible for the pollution. Two basic approaches to solve this market failure are regulation and pollution taxes. Vaccinations provide *external benefits,* which means sellers devote too few resources to produce this product. Two basic solutions to this type of market failure are laws to require consumption of shots and special subsidies.

- **Public goods** are goods that are consumed by all people in a society regardless of whether they pay or not. National defense, air traffic control, and other public goods can benefit many individuals simultaneously and are provided by the government.

SUMMARY OF CONCLUSION STATEMENTS

- When the supply curve fails to include external costs, the equilibrium price is artificially low and the equilibrium quantity artificially high.

- When externalities are present, market failure gives incorrect price and quantity signals, and as a result, resources are misallocated. External costs cause the market to overallocate resources, and external benefits cause the market to underallocate resources.

- If public goods are available only in the marketplace, people wait for someone else to pay, and the result is an underproduction or zero production of public goods.

STUDY QUESTIONS AND PROBLEMS

1. Market researchers have studied the market for milk, and their estimates for the supply of and the demand for milk per month are as follows:

Price per gallon	Quantity demanded (millions of gallons)	Quantity supplied (millions of gallons)
$2.50	100	500
2.00	200	400
1.50	300	300
1.00	400	200
0.50	500	100

a. Using the above data, graph the demand for and the supply of milk. Identify the equilibrium point as E, and use dotted lines to connect E to the equilibrium price on the price axis and the equilibrium quantity on the quantity axis.

b. Suppose the government enacts a milk support price of $2 per gallon. Indicate this action on your graph, and explain the effect on the milk market. Why would the government establish such a support price?

c. Now assume the government decides to set a price ceiling of $1 per gallon. Show and explain how this legal price affects your graph of the milk market. What objective could the government be trying to achieve by establishing such a price ceiling?

2. Use a graph to show the impact on the price of Japanese cars sold in the United States if the United States enacts import quotas on Japanese cars. Now draw another graph to show how the change in the price of Japanese cars affects the price of American-made cars in the United States. Explain the market outcome in each graph and the link between the two graphs.

3. Using market supply and demand analysis, explain why labor union leaders are strong advocates of raising the minimum wage above the equilibrium wage.

4. What are the advantages and disadvantages of the price system?

5. Suppose a market is in equilibrium and both demand and supply curves increase. What happens to the equilibrium price if demand increases more than supply?

6. Consider this statement: "The government is inherently inefficient." Do you agree or disagree? Explain.

7. Suppose coal-burning firms are emitting excessive pollution into the air. Suggest two ways the government can deal with this market failure.

8. Explain the impact of external costs and external benefits on resource allocation.

9. Why are public goods not produced in sufficient quantities by private markets?

10. Which of the following are public goods?

   a. Airbags
   b. Pencils
   c. Cycle helmets
   d. Smoking
   e. Contact lenses

ONLINE EXERCISES

Exercise 1

View the Economic Report of the President (http://w3 .access.gpo.gov/eop/). Click on Economic Report of the President. Scroll to page 343 to view Table B-60 (in Appendix B), and follow these steps:

1. Look at the Entertainment and Food and Beverage series for the last 10 years.

2. Plot both series on a graph.

3. Explain each of the series in terms of how demand and supply affected the price trend for each of the series over the last 10 years.

Exercise 2

Visit the Bureau of Labor Statistics' Most Requested Series (http://stats.bls.gov/top20.html). Under Prices and Living Conditions, select Average Price Data. Choose Milk, All Types, Per Gallon. Follow these steps:

1. Select All Years, and observe changes in the average price per gallon of milk for January of each year.

2. Choose the Back button, and choose Eggs. Select Large and Per Dozen. Select All years, and observe changes in the average price for January of each year.

3. Using demand and supply analysis, explain the observed differences in the price changes for milk and eggs.

Exercise 3

One solution often suggested for lessening the parking problems at colleges and universities is to promote alternative forms of transportation. For example, some people propose the increased use of bicycles to alleviate automobile parking problems during peak hours. Review "Bicycle Parking at the Workplace" at http://www.bts.gov/NTL/DOCS/mapc.html, a study conducted by the Metropolitan Area Planning Council. What suggestions does this study offer? Does the study advance a viable argument? Why or why not?

Exercise 4

Many areas of the country experience water shortages, especially in the hot, dry summer months. Municipalities in these areas have requested or required conservation plans. For a general overview of these plans, review "How to Conserve Water and Use It Effectively" at http://www.epa.gov/OW/you/chap3.html, an Environmental Protection Agency report. What economic strategies might a municipality employ to prevent water shortages and promote the conservation of water?

 CHECKPOINT ANSWERS

Why the Higher Price for Lower Cholesterol?

As shown in Exhibit 8, an increase in demand leads to higher prices, while an increase in supply leads to lower prices. Because the overall direction of price in the oat bran market was up, the demand increase must have been larger than the supply increase.

If you said demand increased by more than supply because consumers reacted more quickly than producers, YOU ARE CORRECT.

Exhibit 8

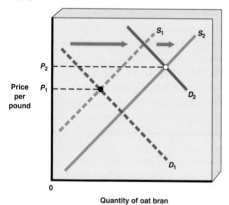

Quantity of oat bran

Is There Price Fixing at the Ticket Window?

Scalpers are evidence of a shortage whereby buyers are unable to find tickets at the official price. As shown in Exhibit 9, scalpers (often illegally) profit from the shortage by selling tickets above the official price. Shortages result when prices are restricted below equilibrium, just as is the

case when there is a price ceiling. If you said scalping occurs when there is a price ceiling because scalpers charge more than the official maximum price, YOU ARE CORRECT.

Exhibit 9

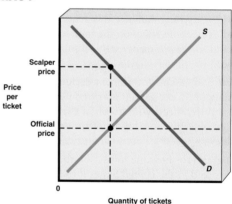

Quantity of tickets

Should There Be a War on Drugs?

Drug use often affects not only the person using the drugs, but other members of society as well. Higher crime rates are largely attributable to increased drug usage. Even the spread of AIDS often begins with users injecting drugs with nonsterile needles. When one person's actions affect others not involved in the decision to buy or sell, the market fails to operate efficiently. If you said the market failure motivating government intervention in the drug market is externalities because drug users impose costs on nonusers, YOU ARE CORRECT.

PRACTICE QUIZ

For a visual explanation of the correct answers, visit the tutorial at http://tucker.swcollege.com.

1. Suppose prices for new homes have risen, yet sales of new homes have also risen. We can conclude that
   a. the demand for new homes has risen.
   b. the law of demand has been violated.
   c. new firms have entered the construction industry.
   d. construction firms must be facing higher costs.

2. Which of the following statements is *true* of a market?
   a. An increase in demand, with no change in supply, will increase the equilibrium price and quantity.
   b. An increase in supply, with no change in demand, will decrease the equilibrium price and the equilibrium quantity.
   c. A decrease in supply, with no change in demand, will decrease the equilibrium price and increase the equilibrium quantity.
   d. All of the above are true.

3. Consider the market for chicken. An increase in the price of beef will
   a. decrease the demand for chicken, resulting in a lower price and a smaller amount of chicken purchased in the market.
   b. decrease the supply of chicken, resulting in a higher price and a smaller amount of chicken purchased in the market.
   c. increase the demand for chicken, resulting in a higher price and a greater amount of chicken purchased in the market.
   d. increase the supply of chicken, resulting in a lower price and a greater amount of chicken purchased in the market.

4. An increase in consumers' incomes increases the demand for oranges. As a result of the adjustment to a new equilibrium, there is a(an)
   a. leftward shift of the supply curve.
   b. downward movement along the supply curve.
   c. rightward shift of the supply curve.
   d. upward movement along the supply curve.

5. An increase in the wage paid to grape pickers will cause the
   a. demand curve for grapes to shift to the right, resulting in higher prices for grapes.
   b. demand curve for grapes to shift to the left, resulting in lower prices for grapes.
   c. supply curve for grapes to shift to the left, resulting in lower prices for grapes.
   d. supply curve for grapes to shift to the left, resulting in higher prices for grapes.

6. If the federal government wants to raise the price of cheese, it will
   a. take cheese from government storage and sell it.
   b. encourage farmers to research ways to produce more cheese.
   c. subsidize purchases of farm equipment.
   d. encourage farmers to produce less cheese.

7. Which of the following is *least* likely to result from rent controls set below the equilibrium price for rental housing?
   a. Shortages and black markets will result.
   b. The existing rental housing will deteriorate.
   c. The supply of rental housing will increase rapidly.
   d. People will demand more apartments than are available.

8. Suppose the equilibrium price set by supply and demand is lower than the price ceiling set by the government. The eventual result will be
   a. a shortage.
   b. that quantity demanded is equal to quantity supplied.
   c. a surplus.
   d. a black market.

9. A good that provides external benefits to society has
   a. too few resources devoted to its production.
   b. too many resources devoted to its production.
   c. the optimal resources devoted to its production.
   d. not provided profits to producers of the good.

10. Pollution from cars is an example of
    a. a harmful opportunity cost.
    b. a negative externality.
    c. a production dislocation.
    d. none of the above.

11. Which of the following is the *best* example of a public good?
    a. Pencils
    b. Education
    c. Defense
    d. Trucks

12. A public good may be defined as any good or service that
    a. allows users to collectively consume benefits.
    b. must be distributed to all citizens in equal shares.
    c. is never produced by government.
    d. is described by answers (a) and (c) above.

Applying Supply and Demand Analysis to Health Care

One out of every seven dollars spent in the United States is spent for health care services. This is a greater percentage than in any other industrialized country.[1] The topic of health care arouses deep emotions and generates intense media coverage. How can we understand many of the important health care issues? One approach is to listen to the normative statements made by politicians and other concerned citizens. Another approach is to use supply and demand theory to analyze the issue. Here again the objective is to bring textbook theory to life and use it to provide you with a deeper understanding of health service markets.

The Impact of Health Insurance

There is a downward-sloping demand curve for health care services just as there is for other goods and services. Following the same law of demand that applies to cars, clothing, entertainment, and other goods and services, movements along the demand curve for health care occur because consumers respond to changes in the price of health care. As shown in Exhibit A-1, we assume that health care, including doctor visits, medicine, hospital bills, and other medical services, can be measured in units of health care. Without health insurance, consumers buy Q_1 units of health care services per year at a price of P_1 per unit. Assuming supply curve S represents the quantity supplied, the market is in equilibrium at point A. At this point, the

---

[1]*Statistical Abstract of the United States,* 2000, http://www.census.gov/prod/www/statistical-abstract-us.html, Table 1358.

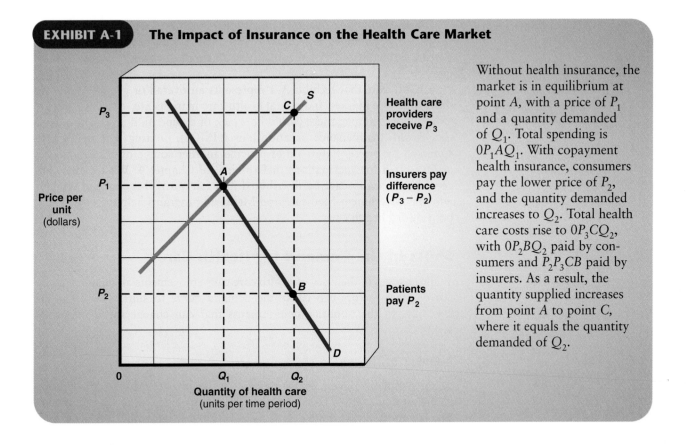

EXHIBIT A-1   **The Impact of Insurance on the Health Care Market**

Without health insurance, the market is in equilibrium at point *A*, with a price of P_1 and a quantity demanded of Q_1. Total spending is $0P_1AQ_1$. With copayment health insurance, consumers pay the lower price of P_2, and the quantity demanded increases to Q_2. Total health care costs rise to $0P_3CQ_2$, with $0P_2BQ_2$ paid by consumers and P_2P_3CB paid by insurers. As a result, the quantity supplied increases from point *A* to point *C*, where it equals the quantity demanded of Q_2.

total cost of health care can be computed by the price of health care (P_1) times the quantity demanded (Q_1) or represented geometrically by the rectangle $0P_1AQ_1$.

Analysis of the demand curve for health care is complicated by the way health care is financed. About 80 percent of all health care is paid for by *third parties*, including private insurance companies and government programs, such as Medicare and Medicaid. The price of health care services therefore depends on the *copayment rate*, which is the percentage of the cost of services consumers pay out-of-pocket. To understand the impact, it is more realistic to assume consumers are insured and extend the analysis represented in Exhibit A-1. Because patients pay only 20 percent of the bill, the quantity of health care demanded in the figure increases to Q_2 at a lower price of P_2. At point *B* on the demand curve, insured consumers pay an amount equal to rectangle $0P_2BQ_2$, and insurers pay an amount represented by rectangle P_2P_3CB. Health care providers respond by increasing the quantity supplied from point *A* to point *C* on the supply curve *S*, where the quantity supplied equals the quantity demanded of Q_2. The reason that there is no shortage in the health care market is that the combined payments from the insured consumers and insurers equal the total payment required for the movement upward along the supply curve. Stated in terms of rectangles, the total health care payment of $0P_3CQ_2$ equals $0P_2BQ_2$ paid by consumers plus P_2P_3CB paid by insurers.

For more information on Medicare, visit the federal government's official Internet site concerning Medicare (http://www.medicare.gov/).

Conclusion *Compared to a health care market without insurance, the quantity demanded, the quantity supplied, and the total cost of health care are increased by copayment health care insurance.*

Finally, note that Exhibit A-1 represents an overall or general model of the health care market. Individual health care markets are subject to *market failure*. For example, there would be a lack of competition if hospitals, doctors, health maintenance organizations (HMOs), or drug companies conspired to fix prices. Externalities provide another source of market failure, as illustrated for vaccinations in Exhibit 7 of Chapter 4. We are also concerned that health care be distributed in a fair way. This concern explains why the government Medicare and Medicaid programs help the elderly and poor afford health care.

Shifts in the Demand for Health Care

While changes in the price of health care cause movements along the demand curve, other factors can cause the demand curve to shift. The following are some of the nonprice determinants that can change the demand for health care.

Number of Buyers

As the population increases, the demand for health care increases. In addition to the total number of people, the distribution of older people in the population is important. As more people move into the 65-and-older age group, the demand for health care services becomes greater because older people have more frequent and prolonged spells of illness. An increase in substance abuse, involving alcohol, tobacco, or drugs, also increases the demand for health care. For example, if the percentage of babies born into drug-prone families increases, the demand for health care will shift rightward.

Tastes and Preferences

Changes in consumer attitudes toward health care can also change demand. For example, television, movies, magazines, and advertising may be responsible for changes in people's preferences for cosmetic surgery. Moreover, medical science has improved so much that we believe there must be a cure for most ailments. As a result, consumers are willing to buy larger quantities of medical services at each possible price.

Doctors also influence consumer preferences by prescribing treatment. It is often argued that some doctors guard against malpractice suits or boost their incomes by ordering more tests or office visits than are really needed. Some estimates suggest that fraud and abuse account for about 10 percent of total health care spending. These studies reveal that as many as one-third of some procedures are inappropriate.[2]

---

[2]*Economic Report of the President, 1994*, Chart 4-5, p. 144.

Income

Health care is a normal good. Rising inflation-adjusted incomes of consumers in the United States cause the demand curve for health care services to shift to the right. On the other hand, if real median family income remains unchanged, there is no influence on the demand curve.

Prices of Substitutes

The prices of medical goods and services that are substitutes can change and, in turn, influence the demand for other medical services. For example, treatment of a back problem by a chiropractor is an alternative for many of the treatments provided by orthopedic doctors. If the price of orthopedic therapy rises, then some people will switch to treatment by a chiropractor. As a result, the demand curve for chiropractic therapy shifts rightward.

Shifts in the Supply of Health Care

Changes in the following nonprice factors change the supply of health care.

Number of Sellers

Sellers of health care include hospitals, nursing homes, physicians in private practice, HMOs, drug companies, chiropractors, psychologists, and a host of other suppliers. To ensure the quality and safety of health care, virtually every facet of the industry is regulated and licensed by the government or controlled by the American Medical Association (AMA). The AMA limits the number of persons practicing medicine primarily through medical school accreditation and licensing requirements. The federal Food and Drug Administration (FDA) required testing that delays the introduction of new drugs. Tighter restrictions on the number of sellers shift the health care supply curve leftward, and reduced restrictions shift the supply curve rightward.

Resource Prices

An increase in the costs of resources underlying the supply of health care shifts the supply curve leftward. By far the single most important factor behind increasing health care spending has been technological change. New diagnostic, surgical, and therapeutic equipment is used extensively in the health care industry, and the result is higher costs. Wages, salaries, and other costs, such as the costs of malpractice suits, also influence the supply curve. If hospitals, for example, are paying higher prices for inputs used to produce health care, the supply curve shifts to the left because the same quantities may be supplied only at higher prices.

Health Care Reform Proposals

In October 1993, the Clinton administration submitted a 1,336-page proposal for health care reform to Congress. After a much-publicized and heated debate, Congress rejected this complex and controversial proposal. The cornerstone of President Clinton's plan was universal health care. First, all employers would be required to provide their employees with health insurance. Second, those persons who were unemployed or not in the labor force would obtain health care through regional health alliances established in each state. In addition, the plan considered taxing destructive personal behavior that increases health care costs, such as cigarette smoking and alcohol abuse.

The critics of the Clinton plan argued that the quantity of health care cannot be extended to meet the demands of everyone without enormous additional costs. The result would be price controls and the rationing of health care (recall Exhibit 4 of Chapter 4). In short, critics viewed the Clinton proposal as creating a system of new bureaucracies and employer mandates that would produce an unwarranted increase in the government's role in the health care industry.

In 1996, Congress passed a bill cosponsored by former Republican Senator Nancy Kassebaum from Kansas and Democratic Senator Edward Kennedy from Massachusetts that bars insurance companies from denying coverage because of preexisting medical conditions of the employee or members of the employee's family. This bill allows workers changing jobs to retain their coverage. The Kassebaum-Kennedy bill does not set rates the insurance companies can charge for being forced to accept higher risks.

As this text is written in 2001, various versions of a "patients' bill of rights" are being debated. For example, legislation sponsored by Senators John Edwards, Edward Kennedy, and John McCain would give patients much more leeway in suing HMOs and insurance companies. Critics argue this proposal would enrich lawyers and increase the cost of health care.

PART 2

Microeconomic Fundamentals

The three chapters in Part 2 build on the basic concepts learned in Part 1 and establish a foundation for further study of microeconomics. Chapter 5 takes a closer look at movements along the demand and supply curves introduced in Chapter 3. Chapter 6 returns to the law of demand and explores in more detail exactly why consumers make their choices among goods and services. And Chapter 7 extends the concept of supply by developing a theory that explains how various costs of production change as output varies.

CHAPTER 5

Price Elasticity of Demand and Supply

Suppose you are the manager of the Steel Porcupines rock group. You are considering raising your ticket price, and you wonder how the fans will react. You have studied economics and know the law of demand. When the price of a ticket rises, the quantity demanded goes down, ceteris paribus. So you really need to know how many tickets fans will purchase if the band boosts the ticket price. If the ticket price for a Steel Porcupines concert is $25, 20,000 tickets will be sold. At $30 per ticket, only 10,000 tickets will be sold. Thus, a $5 increase per ticket cuts the number of tickets sold in half.

Which ticket price should you choose? Is it better to charge a higher ticket price and sell fewer tickets or to charge a lower ticket price and sell more tickets? The answer depends on changes in

total revenue or sales as we move upward along points on Steel Porcupines' demand curve. At $30 per ticket, sales will be $300,000. If you charge $25, the group will take in $500,000 for a concert. Okay, you say, what happens at $20 per ticket?

This chapter teaches you to calculate the percentage change in the quantity demanded when the price changes by a given percentage. Then you will see how

this relates to total revenue. This knowledge of the sensitivity of demand is vital for pricing and targeting markets for goods and services. Next, you will see how changes in consumer income and the prices of related goods affect percentage changes in the quantity demanded. The chapter concludes by relating the concept of price elasticity to supply and the impact of taxation.

In this chapter, you will learn to solve these economics puzzles:

■ Can total revenue from a Steel Porcupines concert remain unchanged regardless of changes in the ticket price?

■ How sensitive is the quantity of cigarettes demanded to changes in the price of cigarettes?

■ What would happen to sales of Mercedes, BMWs, and Jaguars in the United States if Congress prevents sales of luxury Japanese cars in this country?

Price Elasticity of Demand

In Chapter 3, when you studied the demand curve, the focus was on the law of demand. This law states there is an inverse relationship between the price and the quantity demanded of a good or service. In this chapter, the emphasis is on measuring the *relative size* of changes in the price and the quantity demanded. Now we ask, By *what percentage* does the quantity demanded rise when the price falls by, say, 10 percent?

The Price Elasticity of Demand Midpoints Formula

Economists use a **price elasticity of demand** formula to measure the degree of consumer responsiveness, or sensitivity, to a change in price. Price elasticity of demand is the ratio of the percentage change in the quantity demanded of a product to a percentage change in its price. Suppose a university's enrollment drops by 20 percent because tuition rises by 10 percent. Therefore, the price elasticity of demand is 2 (−20 percent/+10 percent). The number 2 means that the quantity demanded (enrollment) changes 2 percent for each 1 percent change in price (tuition). Note there should be a minus sign in front of the 2 because, under the law of demand, price and quantity move in *opposite* directions. However, economists drop the minus sign because we know from the law of demand that quantity demanded and price are inversely related.

The number 2 is an *elasticity coefficient,* which economists use to measure the degree of elasticity. The elasticity formula is

$$E_d = \frac{\text{percentage change in quantity demanded}}{\text{percentage change in price}}$$

where E_d is the elasticity of demand coefficient. Here you must take care. *There is a problem using this formula.* Let's return to our rock group example from the Chapter Preview. Suppose Steel Porcupines raises its ticket price from \$25 to \$30 and the number of seats sold falls from 20,000 to 10,000. We can compute the elasticity coefficient as

$$E_d = \frac{\%\Delta Q}{\%\Delta P} = \frac{\dfrac{10{,}000 - 20{,}000}{20{,}000}}{\dfrac{30 - 25}{25}} = \frac{50\%}{20\%} = 2.5$$

Price elasticity of demand
The ratio of the percentage change in the quantity demanded of a product to a percentage change in its price.

Now consider the elasticity coefficient computed between these same points on Steel Porcupines' demand curve when the price is lowered. Starting at $30 per ticket and lowering the ticket price to $25 cause the number of seats sold to rise from 10,000 to 20,000. In this case, the rock group computes a much different elasticity coefficient, as follows:

$$E_d = \frac{\%\Delta Q}{\%\Delta P} = \frac{\dfrac{20{,}000 - 10{,}000}{10{,}000}}{\dfrac{25 - 30}{30}} = \frac{100\%}{17\%} = 5.9$$

There is a reason for the different elasticity coefficients between the same two points on a demand curve (2.5 if price is raised, 5.9 if price is cut). The natural approach is to select the initial point as the base and then compute a percentage change. But price elasticity of demand involves changes between two possible initial base points (P_1, Q_1 or P_2, Q_2). Economists solve this problem of different base points by using the *midpoints* as the base points of changes in prices and quantities demanded. The *midpoints formula* for price elasticity of demand is

$$E_d = \frac{\text{change in quantity}}{\text{sum of quantitites}/2} \div \frac{\text{change in price}}{\text{sum of prices}/2}$$

which can be expressed as

$$E_d = \frac{\%\Delta Q}{\%\Delta P} = \frac{\dfrac{Q_2 - Q_1}{(Q_1 + Q_2)/2}}{\dfrac{P_2 - P_1}{(P_1 + P_2)/2}}$$

where Q_1 represents the first quantity demanded, Q_2 represents the second quantity demanded, and P_1 and P_2 are the first and second prices. Expressed this way, we divide the change in quantity demanded by the *average* quantity demanded. Then this value is divided by the change in the price divided by the *average* price.[1]

It does not matter if Q_1 or P_1 is the first or second number in each term because we are finding averages. Also note that you can drop the 2 as a divisor of both the $(Q_1 + Q_2)$ and $(P_1 + P_2)$ terms since the 2s in the numerator and the denominator cancel out. Now we can use the midpoints formula to calculate the price elasticity of demand of 3.7 regardless of whether Steel Porcupines raises the ticket price from $25 to $30 or lowers it from $30 to $25.

---

[1]The midpoints formula is also commonly called the *arc elasticity formula.*

$$E_d = \frac{\dfrac{Q_2 - Q_1}{Q_1 + Q_2}}{\dfrac{P_2 - P_1}{P_1 + P_2}} = \frac{\dfrac{10{,}000 - 20{,}000}{20{,}000 + 10{,}000}}{\dfrac{30 - 25}{25 + 30}} = \frac{33\%}{9\%} = 3.7$$

and

$$E_d = \frac{\dfrac{Q_2 - Q_1}{Q_1 + Q_2}}{\dfrac{P_2 - P_1}{P_1 + P_2}} = \frac{\dfrac{20{,}000 - 10{,}000}{10{,}000 + 20{,}000}}{\dfrac{25 - 30}{30 + 25}} = \frac{33\%}{9\%} = 3.7$$

The Total Revenue Test of Price Elasticity of Demand

As reflected in the midpoints formula, the *responsiveness* of the quantity demanded to a change in price determines the value of the elasticity coefficient. There are three possibilities: (1) the numerator is greater than the denominator, (2) the numerator is less than the denominator, and (3) the numerator equals the denominator. Exhibit 1 presents three cases that the Steel Porcupines rock band may confront.

Elastic Demand ($E_d > 1$). Suppose Steel Porcupines' demand curve is as depicted in Exhibit 1(a). Using the above midpoints formula, which drops the 2 as a divisor, if the group lowers its ticket price from $30 to $20, the quantity demanded increases from 10,000 to 30,000. Using the midpoints formula, this means that a 20 percent reduction in ticket price brings a 50 percent increase in quantity demanded. Thus, $E_d = 2.5$, and demand is **elastic.** Elastic demand is a condition in which the percentage change in quantity demanded is greater than the percentage change in price. Demand is elastic when the elasticity coefficient is greater than 1. Because the percentage change in quantity demanded is greater than the percentage change in price, the drop in price causes **total revenue** to rise. Total revenue is the total number of dollars a firm earns from the sale of a good or service, which is equal to its price multiplied by the quantity demanded. Perhaps the simplest way to tell whether demand is elastic, unitary elastic, or inelastic is to observe the response of total revenue as the price of a product changes. For example, in Exhibit 1(a), the total revenue at $30 is $300,000. The total revenue at $20 is $600,000. Compare the shaded rectangles under the demand curve, representing total revenue at each price. The gray area is an amount of total revenue unaffected by the price change. Note that the green shaded area gained at $20 per ticket ($400,000) is greater than the red shaded area lost at $30 per ticket ($100,000). This net gain of $300,000 causes the total revenue to increase by this amount when Steel Porcupines lowers the ticket price from $30 to $20.

Why would Delta Airlines cut airline fares right before the busy holiday season? Delta is betting that the demand for airline tickets is price elastic. Specifically, Delta believes that if prices are lower, the quantity of tickets demanded will more than offset the decline in price. To discover more about Delta Air Lines and its air fare strategies, visit Delta Air Lines (http://www.delta-air.com/).

Elastic demand
A condition in which the percentage change in quantity demanded is greater than the percentage change in price.

Total revenue
The total number of dollars a firm earns from the sale of a good or service, which is equal to its price multiplied by the quantity demanded.

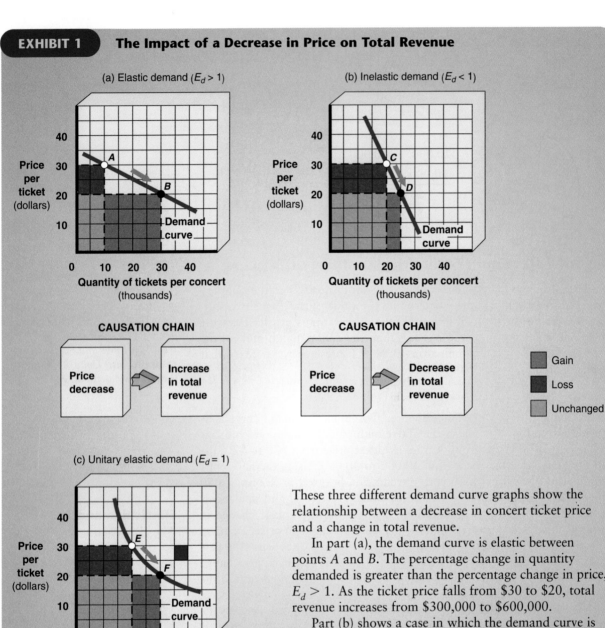

EXHIBIT 1   **The Impact of a Decrease in Price on Total Revenue**

(a) Elastic demand ($E_d > 1$)

(b) Inelastic demand ($E_d < 1$)

(c) Unitary elastic demand ($E_d = 1$)

CAUSATION CHAIN

Price decrease → Increase in total revenue

Price decrease → Decrease in total revenue

Price decrease → No change in total revenue

■ Gain
■ Loss
■ Unchanged

These three different demand curve graphs show the relationship between a decrease in concert ticket price and a change in total revenue.

In part (a), the demand curve is elastic between points *A* and *B*. The percentage change in quantity demanded is greater than the percentage change in price, $E_d > 1$. As the ticket price falls from $30 to $20, total revenue increases from $300,000 to $600,000.

Part (b) shows a case in which the demand curve is inelastic between points *C* and *D*. The percentage change in quantity demanded is less than the percentage change in price, $E_d < 1$. As the ticket price decreases over the same range, total revenue falls from $600,000 to $500,000.

Part (c) shows a unitary elastic demand curve. The percentage change in quantity demanded equals the percentage change in price between points *E* and *F*, $E_d = 1$. As the concert ticket price decreases, total revenue remains unchanged at $600,000.

Inelastic Demand ($E_d < 1$).   The demand curve in Exhibit 1(b) is inelastic. The quantity demanded is less responsive to a change in price. Here a fall in Steel Porcupines' ticket price from \$30 to \$20 causes the quantity demanded to increase by just 5,000 tickets (20,000 to 25,000 tickets). Using the midpoints formula, a 20 percent fall in the ticket price causes an 11 percent rise in the quantity demanded. This means $E_d = 0.55$ and demand is **inelastic.** Inelastic demand is a condition in which the percentage change in quantity demanded is less than the percentage change in price. Demand is inelastic when the elasticity coefficient is less than 1. When demand is inelastic, the drop in price causes total revenue to fall from \$600,000 to \$500,000. Note the net change in the shaded rectangles.

Inelastic demand
A condition in which the percentage change in quantity demanded is less than the percentage change in price.

Unitary Elastic ($E_d = 1$).   An interesting case exists when a demand curve is neither elastic nor inelastic. Exhibit 1(c) shows a demand curve for which any percentage change in price along the curve causes an exact proportional change in quantity demanded. When this situation occurs, the total amount of money spent on a good or service does not vary with changes in price. If Steel Porcupines drops the ticket price from \$30 to \$20, the quantity demanded rises from 20,000 to 30,000. Therefore, using the midpoints formula, a 20 percent decrease in price brings about a 20 percent increase in quantity demanded. If this is the case, demand is **unitary elastic ($E_d = 1$),** and the total revenue remains unchanged at \$600,000. Unitary elastic demand is defined as a condition in which the percentage change in quantity demanded is equal to the percentage change in price. Because the percentage change in price equals the percentage change in quantity, total revenue does not change regardless of changes in price.

Unitary elastic demand
A condition in which the percentage change in quantity demanded is equal to the percentage change in price.

Perfectly Elastic Demand ($E_d = \infty$).   Two extreme cases are shown in Exhibit 2. These represent the limits between which the three demand curves explained above fall. Suppose for the sake of argument that a demand curve is perfectly horizontal, as shown in Exhibit 2(a). At a price of \$20, buyers are willing to buy as many tickets as the Steel Porcupines band is willing to offer for sale. At higher prices, buyers buy nothing. For example, at \$20.01 per ticket or higher buyers will buy zero tickets. If so, $E_d = \infty$, and demand is **perfectly elastic.** Perfectly elastic demand is a condition in which a small percentage change in price brings about an infinite percentage change in quantity demanded.

Perfectly elastic demand
A condition in which a small percentage change in price brings about an infinite percentage change in quantity demanded.

Perfectly Inelastic Demand ($E_d = 0$).   Exhibit 2(b) shows the other extreme case, which is a perfectly vertical demand curve. No matter how high or low the Steel Porcupines' ticket price is, the quantity demanded is 20,000 tickets. Such a demand curve is **perfectly inelastic,** and $E_d = 0$. Perfectly inelastic demand is a condition in which the quantity demanded does not change as the price changes.

Exhibit 3 summarizes the ranges for price elasticity of demand.

Perfectly inelastic demand
A condition in which the quantity demanded does not change as the price changes.

EXHIBIT 2   **Perfectly Elastic and Perfectly Inelastic Demand**

Here two extreme demand curves for Steel Porcupines concert tickets are presented. Part (a) shows a demand curve that is a horizontal line. Such a demand curve is perfectly elastic. At $20 per ticket, Steel Porcupines can sell as many concert tickets as it wishes. At any price above $20, the quantity demanded falls from an infinite number to zero.

Part (b) shows a demand curve that is a vertical line. This demand curve is perfectly inelastic. No matter what the ticket price, the quantity demanded remains unchanged at 20,000 tickets.

Price Elasticity of Demand Variations along a Demand Curve

The price elasticity of demand for a downward-sloping straight-line demand curve varies as we move along the curve. Look at Exhibit 4, which shows a linear demand curve in part (a) and the corresponding total revenue curve in part (b). Begin at $40 on the demand curve and move down to $35, to $30, to $25, and so on. The table in Exhibit 4 lists variations in the total revenue and the elasticity coefficient (E_d) at different ticket prices. As we move down the upper segment of the demand curve, price elasticity of demand

EXHIBIT 3 Price Elasticity of Demand Terminology

Elasticity coefficient	Definition	Demand	Graph
$E_d > 1$	Percentage change in quantity demanded is greater than the percentage change in price	Elastic	
$E_d < 1$	Percentage change in quantity demanded is less than the percentage change in price	Inelastic	
$E_d = 1$	Percentage change in quantity demanded is equal to the percentage change in price	Unitary elastic	
$E_d = \infty$	Percentage change in quantity demanded is infinite in relation to the percentage change in price	Perfectly elastic	
$E_d = 0$	Quantity demanded does not change as the price changes	Perfectly inelastic	

falls, and total revenue rises. For example, measured over the price range of $35 to $30, the price elasticity of demand is 4.33, so this segment of demand is elastic ($E_d > 1$). Between these two prices, total revenue increases from $175,000 to $300,000. At $20, price elasticity is unitary elastic ($E_d = 1$), and total revenue is maximized at $400,000. As we move down the lower segment of the demand curve, price elasticity of demand falls below a value of 1.0, and total revenue falls. Over the price range of $15 to $10, for example, the price elasticity of demand is 0.45, and, therefore, this segment of demand is inelastic ($E_d < 1$). Between these two prices, total revenue decreases from $375,000 to $300,000.

Conclusion *The price elasticity of demand applies only to a specific range of prices.*

EXHIBIT 4 **The Variation in Elasticity and Total Revenue along a Hypothetical Demand Curve**

(a) Price elasticity of demand ranges

Price per ticket (dollars) — Quantity of tickets per concert (thousands)

Calculation of Total Revenue and Elasticity along a Hypothetical Demand Curve

Price	Quantity	Total revenue (thousands of dollars)	Elasticity coefficient (E_d)	Demand
$40	0	$ 0		
			15.00	Elastic
35	5	175		
			4.33	Elastic
30	10	300		
			2.20	Elastic
25	15	375		
			1.29	Elastic
20	20	400	1.00	Unitary elastic
			0.78	Inelastic
15	25	375		
			0.45	Inelastic
10	30	300		
			0.23	Inelastic
5	35	175		

(b) Total revenue curve

Total revenue (thousands of dollars) — Quantity of tickets per concert (thousands)

Part (a) shows a straight-line demand curve and its three elasticity ranges. In the $40–$20 price range, demand is elastic. As price decreases in this range, total revenue increases. At $20, demand is unitary elastic, and total revenue is at its maximum. In the $20–$5 price range, demand is inelastic. As price decreases in this range, total revenue decreases. The total revenue (*TR*) curve is plotted in part (b) to trace its relationship to price elasticity.

It is no coincidence that the demand curve in Exhibit 4(a) has elastic, unitary elastic, and inelastic segments. In fact, *any downward-sloping straight-line demand curve has ranges of all three of these types of price elasticity of demand.* As we move downward, first, there is an elastic range; second, a unitary elastic range; and, third, an inelastic range. Why? Recall that price

CHECKPOINT

Will Fliers Flock to Low Summer Fares?

USAirways is concerned over low sales and announces special cuts in its fares this summer. The New York to Los Angeles fare, for example, is reduced from $500 to $420. Does USAirways think demand is elastic, unitary elastic, or inelastic?

elasticity of demand is a ratio of percentage changes. At the upper end of the demand curve, quantities demanded are lower, and prices are higher. A change of 1 unit in quantity demanded is a large percentage change. On the other hand, a $1 price change is a relatively small percentage change. At the lower end of the curve, the situation reverses. A 1-unit change in quantity demanded is a small percentage change. A $1 price change is a relatively larger percentage change. Now pause and refer back to parts (a) and (b) of Exhibit 1. If we examine changes in price along the entire length of these demand curves, we will find elastic, unitary elastic, and inelastic segments.

Exhibit 5 summarizes the relationships among elasticity, price change, and total revenue.

EXHIBIT 5 Relationships among Elasticity, Price Change, and Total Revenue

Price elasticity of demand	Elasticity coefficient	Price	Total revenue
Elastic	$E_d > 1$	↑	↓
Elastic	$E_d > 1$	↓	↑
Unitary elastic	$E_d = 1$	↑ ↓	No change
Inelastic	$E_d < 1$	↑	↑
Inelastic	$E_d < 1$	↓	↓

Determinants of Price Elasticity of Demand

Economists have estimated price elasticity of demand for various goods and services. Exhibit 6 presents some of these estimates, and as you can see, the elasticity coefficients vary a great deal. For example, the demand for automobiles and for chinaware is elastic. On the other hand, the demand for jewelry and watches and for theater and opera tickets is inelastic. The demand for tires and tubes is approximately unitary elastic. Why do the price elasticities of demand for these products vary so much? The following factors cause these differences.

EXHIBIT 6 Estimated Price Elasticities of Demand

Item	Elasticity coefficient	
	Short run	Long run
Automobiles	1.87	2.24
Chinaware	1.54	2.55
Movies	0.87	3.67
Tires and tubes	0.86	1.19
Commuter rail fares	0.62	1.59
Jewelry and watches	0.41	0.67
Medical care	0.31	0.92
Housing	0.30	1.88
Gasoline	0.20	0.70
Theater and opera tickets	0.18	0.31
Foreign travel	0.14	1.77
Air travel	0.10	2.40

Sources: Robert Archibald and Robert Gillingham, "An Analysis of the Short-Run Consumer Demand for Gasoline Using Household Survey Data," *Review of Economics and Statistics* 62 (November 1980): 622–628; Hendrik S. Houthakker and Lester D. Taylor, *Consumer Demand in the United States: Analyses and Projections* (Cambridge, Mass: Harvard University Press, 1970): 56–149; Richard Voith, "The Long-Run Elasticity of Demand for Commuter Rail Transportation," *Journal of Urban Economics* 30 (November 1991): 360–372.

Availability of Substitutes

Coke and Pepsi are close substitutes, and the demand for each is relatively elastic. What strategies do Coca-Cola (http://www.cocacola.com/) *and Pepsi* (http://www.pepsi.com/) *use to make the demand for their products less elastic?*

By far the most important influence on price elasticity of demand is the availability of substitutes. Demand is more elastic for a good or service with close substitutes. If the price of cars rises, consumers can switch to buses, trains, bicycles, and walking. The more public transportation is available, the more responsive quantity demanded is to a change in the price of cars. When consumers have limited alternatives, the demand for a good or service is more price inelastic. If the price of tobacco rises, people addicted to it have few substitutes because not smoking is unappealing to most users.

Conclusion *The price elasticity coefficient of demand is directly related to the availability of good substitutes for a product.*

Price elasticity also depends on the market used to measure demand. For example, studies show the price elasticity of Chevrolets is greater than that of automobiles in general. Chevrolets compete with other cars sold by GM, Ford, DaimlerChrysler, Toyota, and other automakers and with buses and trains—all of which are substitutes for Chevrolets. But using the broad class of cars eliminates specific types of cars as competitors. Instead, substitutes for automobiles include buses and trains, which are also substitutes for Chevrolets. In short, there are more close substitutes for Chevrolets than there are for all cars.

Can Trade Sanctions Affect Elasticity of Demand for Cars?

Assume Congress prevents Lexus, Acura, Infiniti, Mazda 929, and other luxury Japanese cars from being sold in the United States. How would this affect the price elasticity of demand for Mercedes, BMWs, and Jaguars in the United States?

Share of Budget Spent on the Product

When the price of salt changes, consumers pay little attention. Why should they notice? The price of salt or matches can double, and this purchase will remain a small percentage of one's budget. If, however, college tuition, the price of dinners at restaurants, or housing prices double, people will look for alternatives. These goods and services account for a large part of people's budgets.

> **Conclusion** *The price elasticity coefficient of demand is directly related to the percentage of one's budget spent for a good or service.*

Adjustment to a Price Change over Time

Exhibit 6 separates the elasticity coefficients into short-run and long-run categories. As time passes, buyers can respond fully to a change in the price of a product by finding more substitutes. Consider the demand for gasoline. In the short run, people find it hard to cut back the amount they buy when the price rises sharply. They are accustomed to driving back and forth to work alone in their cars. The typical short-run response is to cut luxury travel and reduce speed on trips. If high prices persist over time, car buyers will find ways to cut back. They can buy cars with better fuel economy (more miles per gallon), form car pools, and ride buses or commuter trains. This explains why the short-run elasticity coefficient of gasoline in the exhibit is more inelastic at 0.2 than the long-run elasticity coefficient of 0.7.

> **Conclusion** *In general, the price elasticity coefficient of demand is higher the longer a price change persists.*

Other Elasticity Measures

The elasticity concept has other applications beyond calculating the price elasticity of demand. Broadly defined, it is a technique for measuring the response of one variable to changes in some other variable.

Income Elasticity of Demand

Recall from Chapter 3 that an increase in income can increase demand (shift the demand curve rightward) for a normal good or service and decrease demand (shift the demand curve leftward) for an inferior good or service. To

INTERNATIONAL ECONOMICS

Cigarette Smoking around the World

Applicable Concept: price elasticity of demand

Americans are cutting out cigarettes at a rapid rate, and the trend is going global. However, there are signs of increased smoking in poor countries and among teenagers and young women in several countries.[1] The following thumbnail reports survey the status of smoking in some countries around the world:

• *Germany.* Smoking is restricted in restaurants and banned at railway stations and on public transportation.

• *Sweden.* Smoking is banned in some public places, and no-smoking sections are required in restaurants. Smoking ads are not permitted on billboards or posters.

• *Spain.* Segregated smoking areas are designated in public buildings, and smoking is prohibited on public transportation.

• *Canada.* Smoking is prohibited in all public areas and on all flights of Canadian airlines. All cigarette advertising is banned, and high sales taxes are imposed at both the federal and the provincial levels. Cigarette taxes are used to help pay for the national health care program. One half of each pack must show graphic representations of health hazards of smoking.

• *Japan.* Smoking has become a vice of the Japanese. Smoking fits their frantic lifestyle, and most Japanese men smoke. Smoking ads are prohibited on billboards.

• *Great Britain.* The British government imposes an extra tax on high-tar and high-nicotine cigarettes.

• *European Union.* The European Parliament has approved putting graphic photos depicting the harmful effects of smoking on cigarette packs.

• *United States.* Since 1964, health warnings have been mandated on tobacco advertising, including billboards and printed advertising. In 1971, television advertising was prohibited. Most

states have banned smoking in state buildings, and the federal government has restricted smoking in federal offices and military facilities. In 1998, the Senate engaged in heated debate over proposed legislation to curb smoking by teenagers. This bill would have raised the price of cigarettes by $1.10 a pack over five years, and the tobacco industry would have paid $369 billion over the next 25 years. Opponents argued that this price increase would be a massive tax on low-income Americans that would generate huge revenues to finance additional government programs and spending. Proponents countered that the bill was not about taxes. Instead, the bill was an attack on the death march of 418,000 Americans a year who die early from tobacco-related diseases. Ultimately, the Senate was so divided on the issue that it was impossible, at least for that year, to pass a tobacco bill. In 2001, a 10-member commission created earlier by President Bill Clinton recommended a 17 cents a pack federal tax increase to pay tobacco farmers to stop growing the crop.

Income elasticity of demand

The ratio of the percentage change in the quantity demanded of a good or service to a given percentage change in income.

measure exactly how consumption responds to changes in income, economists calculate the **income elasticity of demand**. Income elasticity of demand is the ratio of the percentage change in the quantity demanded of a good or service to a given percentage change in income. We use a midpoints formula similar to the one we used for calculating price elasticity of demand:

$$E_Y = \frac{\text{percentage change in quantity demanded}}{\text{percentage change in income}}$$

Several researchers have analyzed the price elasticity of demand for cigarettes in the United States: In an article appearing in the *American Economic Review*, a model was designed to determine the short-run and long-run effects of a change in the price of cigarettes on cigarette consumption. The results of this research indicate that the demand for cigarettes is inelastic and that the responsiveness to a price change varies over time. Based on this study, a 10 percent permanent increase in the price per pack of cigarettes reduced current consumption 4 percent in the short run and 7.5 percent in the long run. Thus, the long-run price elasticity of demand is almost twice as large as the short-run price elasticity.[2]

The price elasticity of demand for cigarettes also appears to vary by education. In a study published in the *Journal of Political Economy*, less-educated adults are more responsive to price changes than better-educated adults. Individuals with less than a high school education were estimated to have a long-run price elasticity of demand of 0.60. However, individuals with more years of education were found to be unresponsive to changes in price. This finding supports the theory that less-educated people are more present oriented, or "myopic," than people with more education. Thus, less-educated individuals tend to be more influenced by current changes in the price of a pack of cigarettes.[3] Another study in 2000, confirmed that education has strong negative effects on smoking, especially for high-income individuals. The presence of young children reduces smoking, with the effect most pronounced for women.[4]

A study published in *Health Economics* estimated the relationship between cigarette smoking and price for 34,145 respondents, aged 15–29 years. The price elasticity of smoking was inelastic and varied inversely with age: 0.83 for ages 15–17; 0.52 for ages 18–20; 0.37 for ages 21–23; 0.20 for ages 24–26; and 0.09 for ages 27–29. Thus, younger people were more likely to reduce the number of cigarettes smoked in response to increased prices.[5]

ANALYZE THE ISSUE

According to the above discussion, what factors influence the price elasticity of demand for cigarettes? What other factors not mentioned in the article might also influence the price elasticity of demand for cigarettes?

[1]David Briscoe, "U.S. Cigarette Consumption Down; Worldwide Tobacco Deaths Still Up," *USA Today*, May 22, 2000, p. 5A.
[2]Gary S. Becker, Michael Grossman, and Kevin M. Murphy, "An Empirical Analysis of Cigarette Addiction," *American Economic Review* 84, no. 3 (June 1994): 396–418.
[3]Frank Chaloupka, "Rational Addictive Behavior and Cigarette Smoking," *Journal of Political Economy* 99, no. 4 (August, 1991): 722–742.
[4]Joni Hersch, "Gender, Income Levels, and the Demand for Cigarettes," *Journal of Risk and Uncertainty* 21, no. 2–3 (November 2000): 263–282.
[5]Jeffrey E Harris and Sandra W. Chan, "The Continuum of Addiction: Cigarette Smoking in Relation to Price among Americans Aged 15–29," *Health Economics* 8, no. 1 (February 1999): 81–86.

$$E_Y = \frac{\%\Delta Q}{\%\Delta Y} = \frac{\dfrac{Q_2 - Q_1}{Q_1 + Q_2}}{\dfrac{Y_2 - Y_1}{Y_1 + Y_2}}$$

Where E_Y is the income elasticity of demand coefficient, Q_1 and Q_2 represent quantities demanded before and after the income change, and Y_1 and Y_2 represent income before and after the income change. (Note that economists often use Y to represent income.)

For a *normal* good or service, the income elasticity of demand is *positive, $E_Y > 0$.* Recall that for this type of good demand and income move in the same direction. Thus, the variables change in the numerator and denominator in the same direction. For an *inferior* good or service, the reverse is true, and the income elasticity of demand is *negative, $E_Y < 0$.*

Why is the income elasticity coefficient important? Returning to our rock group example, the Steel Porcupines band needs to know the impact of a recession on ticket sales. During a downturn when consumers' incomes fall, if a rock concert is a *normal good,* the quantity of ticket sales falls. Conversely, if a rock concert is an *inferior good,* the quantity of ticket sales rises. To illustrate, suppose consumers' incomes increase from $1,000 to $1,250 per month. As a result, the quantity of tickets demanded increases from 10,000 to 15,000. Based on these data, is a rock concert a normal or an inferior good? We compute as follows:

$$E_Y = \frac{\dfrac{Q_2 - Q_1}{Q_1 + Q_2}}{\dfrac{Y_2 - Y_1}{Y_1 + Y_2}} = \frac{\dfrac{15,000 - 10,000}{10,000 + 15,000}}{\dfrac{1,250 - 1,000}{1,250 + 1,000}} = \frac{.20}{.11} = 1.8$$

Rothstein-Tauber, Inc. is one of a number of consulting firms that estimates price elasticities. You can access their Internet site at: http://www.rtimarketresearch.com/.

The computed income elasticity of demand coefficient of 1.8 summarizes the relationship between changes in rock concert ticket purchases and changes in income. First, E_Y is a positive number; therefore, a rock concert is a normal good because people buy more when their incomes rise. Second, ticket purchases are very responsive to changes in income. When income rises by 11 percent, ticket sales increase by more (20 percent).

Exhibit 7 lists estimated income elasticity of demand for selected products.

Cross-Elasticity of Demand

In Chapter 3, we learned that a change in the price of one good, say, *Y*, can cause the consumption of another good, say, *X*, to change (see prices of related goods in Exhibit 5 in Chapter 3). In Exhibit 1(b) in Chapter 4, for example, a sharp rise in the price of gasoline (a complement) caused the number of gas guzzlers purchased to decline. This responsiveness of the quantity demanded to changes in the price of some other good is estimated by the **cross-elasticity of demand.** Cross-elasticity of demand is the ratio of the percentage change in the quantity demanded of a good or service to a given percentage change in the price of another good or service. Again, we use the midpoints formula as follows to compute the cross-elasticity coefficient of demand:

Cross-elasticity of demand
The ratio of the percentage change in the quantity demanded of a good or service to a given percentage change in the price of another good or service.

$$E_c = \frac{\text{percentage change in quantity demanded of one good}}{\text{percentage change in price of another good}}$$

EXHIBIT 7 Estimated Income Elasticities of Demand

Item	Elasticity coefficient	
	Short run	Long run
Potatoes	N.A.	0.81
Furniture	2.60	0.53
Dental services	0.38	1.00
Automobiles	5.50	1.07
Physician services	0.28	1.15
Clothing	0.95	1.17
Shoes	0.90	1.50
Gasoline and oil	0.55	1.36
Jewelry and watches	1.00	1.60
Toilet articles	0.25	3.74

Sources: Hendrik S. Houthakker and Lester D. Taylor, *Consumer Demand in the United States: Analyses and Projections* (Cambridge, Mass: Harvard University Press, 1970); Dale M. Helen, "The Structure of Food Demand: Interrelatedness and Duality," *American Journal of Agricultural Economics* 64, no. 2 (May 1982): 213–221.

$$E_c = \frac{\%\Delta Q_X}{\%\Delta P_Y} = \frac{\dfrac{Q_{X_2} - Q_{X_1}}{Q_{X_1} + Q_{X_2}}}{\dfrac{P_{Y_2} - P_{Y_1}}{P_{Y_1} + P_{Y_2}}}$$

where E_c is the cross-elasticity coefficient, Q_1 and Q_2 represent quantities before and after the price of another good or service changes, and P_1 and P_2 represent the price of another good or service before and after the price change.

The cross-elasticity coefficient reveals whether a good or service is a *substitute* or a *complement*. For example, suppose Coke increases its price 10 percent, which causes consumers to buy 5 percent more Pepsi. The cross-elasticity of demand for Pepsi is a *positive* .50 (+5 percent/+10 percent). Since $E_c > 0$, suppose Coke and Pepsi are *substitutes* because the numerator and denominator variables change in the same direction. The larger the positive coefficient, the greater the substitutability between the two goods.

Now suppose there is a 50 percent increase in the price of motor oil and the quantity demanded of gasoline decreases by 10 percent. The cross-elasticity of demand for gasoline is a *negative* .20 (−10 percent/+50 percent). Since $E_c < 0$, these two goods are complements. The larger the negative coefficient, the greater the complementary relationship between the two goods. The variables in the numerator and denominator change in opposite directions.

EXHIBIT 8   **Price Elasticity of Supply**

This figure shows three supply curves. As shown in part (a), a small change in price changes the quantity supplied by an infinite amount: $E_s = \infty$. Part (b) shows the quantity supplied is unaffected by a change in price: $E_s = 0$, and supply is perfectly inelastic. In part (c), the percentage change in quantity supplied is equal to the percentage change in price: $E_s = 1$.

Price Elasticity of Supply

Price elasticity of supply
The ratio of the percentage change in the quantity supplied of a product to the percentage change in its price.

The **price elasticity of supply** closely follows the price elasticity of demand concept. Price elasticity of supply is the ratio of the percentage change in the quantity supplied of a product to the percentage change in its price. This elasticity coefficient is calculated using the following formula:

$$E_s = \frac{\text{percentage change in quantity supplied}}{\text{percentage change in price}}$$

where E_s is the price elasticity of supply coefficient. Since price and quantity supplied change in the same direction, the elasticity coefficient is a positive value. Economists use terminology corresponding to that for the elasticity of demand. Supply is *elastic* when $E_s > 1$, *unit elastic* when $E_s = 1$, *inelastic* when $E_s < 1$, *perfectly elastic* when $E_s = \infty$ and *perfectly inelastic* when $E_s = 0$. Exhibit 8 shows three of these cases.

In Chapter 8, we will explain why the time period of analysis is a primary determinant of the shape of the supply curve. More specifically, it will be shown that price elasticity of supply is greater in the long run than in the short run. Thus, the long-run supply curve will be flatter.

Exhibit 9 gives a summary of the three elasticity concepts presented in this section.

Price Elasticity and the Impact of Taxation

Who pays a tax levied on sellers of goods such as gasoline, cigarettes, and alcoholic beverages? One way to answer this question is to say that if the government places a tax on, say, gasoline, the gasoline companies pay the tax. They collect the tax when they sell gas and write the checks to the gov-

EXHIBIT 9 Summary of Other Elasticity Concepts

Type	Definition	Elasticity coefficient possibilities	Terminology
Income elasticity of demand	$\dfrac{\text{Percentage change in quantity demanded}}{\text{Percentage change in income}}$	$E_Y > 0$ $E_Y < 0$ $E_Y > 1$ $E_Y < 1$ $E_Y = 1$	Normal good Inferior good Income elastic Income inelastic Income unitary elastic
Cross-elasticity of demand	$\dfrac{\text{Percentage change in quantity demanded of one good}}{\text{Percentage change in price of another good}}$	$E_c < 0$ $E_c > 0$	Complements Substitutes
Price elasticity of supply	$\dfrac{\text{Percentage change in quantity supplied}}{\text{Percentage change in price}}$	$E_s > 1$ $E_s = 1$ $E_s < 1$ $E_s = \infty$ $E_s = 0$	Elastic Unit elastic Inelastic Perfectly elastic Perfectly inelastic

ernment for the tax. But this is not the whole story. Instead of looking simply at who writes the checks, economists use the elasticity concept to analyze who "really" pays a tax. **Tax incidence** is the share of a tax ultimately paid by consumers and sellers. In this section, we show that even though taxes are collected from sellers, buyers do not escape a share of the tax burden. The tax incidence depends on the price elasticities of demand and supply. Let's look at two examples.

Suppose the federal government decides to raise the gasoline tax $.50 per gallon. Exhibit 10 shows the impact of the tax. At E_1, the equilibrium price before the tax is $1.00 per gallon, and the equilibrium quantity is 30 million gallons per day. The effect of the tax is to shift the supply curve upward from S_1 to S_2. From the sellers' viewpoint, the cost of each gallon of gasoline increases $.50 per gallon. The effect is exactly the same as if the price of crude oil or any resource used to produce gasoline increased.

Sellers would like consumers to pay the entire amount of the tax. This would occur if consumers would pay $1.50 per gallon for the same 30 million gallons per day they purchased before the tax. But the leftward shift in supply establishes a new equilibrium at E_2. The new equilibrium price is $1.25 per gallon, and the equilibrium quantity falls to 25 million gallons per day. At E_2, the entire shaded area represents the tax revenue. The government collects $12.5 million per day, which equals the $.50 per gallon tax times the 25 million gallons sold each day. The vertical line between points E_2 and T represents the $.50 tax per gallon. Since consumers now pay $1.25 instead of $1.00 per gallon, they pay one-half of the tax. The sellers pay the remaining half of the tax. Now the sellers send $.50 to Uncle Sam and keep $.75 compared to the $1.00 per gallon they kept before the tax.

Conclusion *If the demand curve slopes downward and the supply curve slopes upward, sellers cannot raise the price by the full amount of the tax.*

Tax incidence
The share of a tax ultimately paid by consumers and sellers.

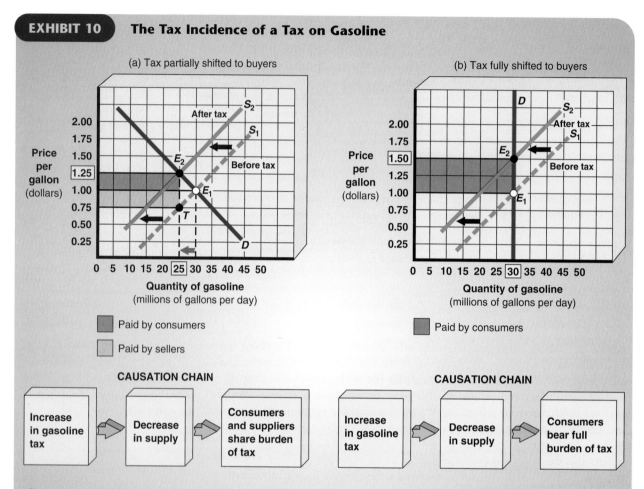

EXHIBIT 10   The Tax Incidence of a Tax on Gasoline

(a) Tax partially shifted to buyers

(b) Tax fully shifted to buyers

■ Paid by consumers

□ Paid by sellers

■ Paid by consumers

CAUSATION CHAIN

| Increase in gasoline tax | → | Decrease in supply | → | Consumers and suppliers share burden of tax |

CAUSATION CHAIN

| Increase in gasoline tax | → | Decrease in supply | → | Consumers bear full burden of tax |

In parts (a) and (b), S_1 is the supply curve before the imposition of a tax of \$.50 per gallon on gasoline. The demand curve is not affected by this tax collected from the sellers. The initial equilibrium is E_1. Before the tax, the price is \$1.00 per gallon, and 30 million gallons are bought and sold per day.

In part (a), the equilibrium price rises to \$1.25 per gallon at E_2 as a result of the tax. After the tax is paid, sellers receive only \$.75 per gallon (point T) instead of the \$1.00 they received before the tax. Thus, buyers pay \$.25 of the tax per gallon, and sellers bear the remaining \$.25. The shaded area is the total tax collected.

As shown in part (b), a tax collected from sellers can be fully shifted to buyers in the unlikely case that demand is perfectly inelastic. Since the quantity of gasoline purchased is unresponsive to a change in price, sellers receive \$1.00 per gallon before and after they pay the tax.

Part (b) of Exhibit 10 is a special case in which the market price increases by the full amount of the tax per gallon. Here the demand for gasoline is perfectly inelastic. In this case, the decrease in supply caused by the tax does not result in buyers responding by decreasing the quantity demanded. The quantity demanded is 30 million gallons per day before and after the tax. The price, however, increases by exactly the amount of tax per unit from \$1.00 to \$1.50 per gallon. After paying the tax, sellers receive a

CHECKPOINT

Can Honda Compete with Itself?

When Honda introduced the Acura to compete with European luxury cars, there was a danger that the new line would take sales away from the Accord. To make Acura more competitive with other luxury cars, suppose Honda cuts the price of Acura while the price of Accord remains unchanged. If Honda's fear has come true, will it find a negative cross-elasticity of demand, a negative income elasticity of demand, or a positive cross-elasticity of demand?

net price of $1.00 per gallon. The total tax revenue collected by the government is the shaded area. Each day $15 million is collected, which equals the $.50 per gallon tax multiplied by 30 million gallons sold each day.

For a fun little test to see if you have learned the concepts of elasticity, visit http://hadm.sph.sc.edu/Courses/ Econ/Elast/Elast.html.

Conclusion *In the case where demand is perfectly inelastic, sellers can raise the price by the full amount of a tax.*

KEY CONCEPTS

Price elasticity of demand	Inelastic demand	Perfectly inelastic demand	Cross-elasticity of demand
Elastic demand	Unitary elastic demand	Income elasticity of	Price elasticity of supply
Total revenue	Perfectly elastic demand	demand	Tax incidence

SUMMARY

- **Price elasticity of demand** is a measure of the responsiveness of the quantity demanded to a change in price. Specifically, price elasticity of demand is the ratio of the percentage change in quantity demanded to the percentage change in price.

$$E_d = \frac{\%\Delta Q}{\%\Delta P} = \frac{\dfrac{Q_2 - Q_1}{(Q_1 + Q_2)/2}}{\dfrac{P_2 - P_1}{(P_1 + P_2)/2}}$$

- **Elastic demand** occurs where there is a change of more than 1 percent in quantity demanded in response to a 1 percent change in price. Demand is elastic when the elasticity coefficient is greater than 1 and *total revenue* (price times quantity) varies inversely with the direction of the price change.

- **Inelastic demand** occurs where there is a change of less than 1 percent in quantity demanded in response to a 1 percent change in price. Demand is inelastic when the elasticity coefficient is less than 1 and total revenue varies directly with the direction of the price change.

- **Unitary elastic demand** occurs where there is a 1 percent change in quantity demanded in response to a 1 percent change in price. Demand is unitary elastic when the elasticity coefficient equals 1 and total revenue remains constant as the price changes.

- **Perfectly elastic demand** occurs when the quantity demanded declines to zero for even the slightest rise or fall in price. This is an extreme case in which the demand curve is horizontal and the elasticity coefficient equals infinity.

- **Perfectly inelastic demand** occurs when the quantity demanded does not change in response to price changes. This is an extreme case in which the demand curve is vertical and the elasticity coefficient equals zero.

- **Determinants of price elasticity of demand** include (a) the availability of substitutes, (b) the percentage of one's budget spent on the product, and (c) the length of time allowed for adjustment. Each of these factors is directly related to the elasticity coefficient.

- **Income elasticity of demand** is the percentage change in quantity demanded divided by the percentage change in income. For a *normal* good or service, income elasticity of demand is positive. For an *inferior* good or service, income elasticity of demand is negative.

- **Cross-elasticity of demand** is the percentage change in the quantity demanded of one product caused by a change in the price of another product. When the cross-elasticity of demand is negative, the two products are complements.

- **Price elasticity of supply** is a measure of the responsiveness of the quantity supplied to a change in price. Price elasticity of supply is the ratio of the percentage

change in quantity supplied to the percentage change in price.

- **Tax incidence** is the share of a tax ultimately paid by buyers and sellers. Facing a downward-sloping demand curve and an upward-sloping supply curve, sellers cannot raise the price by the full amount of the tax. If the demand curve is vertical, sellers will raise the price by the full amount of the tax.

Tax incidence of gasoline tax

SUMMARY OF CONCLUSION STATEMENTS

- The price elasticity coefficient of demand applies only to a specific range of prices.

- The price elasticity coefficient of demand is directly related to the availability of good substitutes for a product.

- The price elasticity coefficient of demand is directly related to the percentage of one's budget spent for a good or service.

- In general, the price elasticity coefficient of demand is higher the longer a price change persists.

- If the demand curve slopes downward and the supply curve slopes upward, sellers cannot raise the price by the full amount of the tax.

- In the case where demand is perfectly inelastic, sellers can raise the price by the full amount of a tax.

STUDY QUESTIONS AND PROBLEMS

1. If the price of a good or service increases and the total revenue received by the seller declines, is the demand for this good over this segment of the demand curve elastic or inelastic? Explain.

2. Suppose the price elasticity of demand for farm products is inelastic. If the federal government wants to follow a policy of increasing income for farmers, what type of programs will the government enact?

3. Suppose the price elasticity of demand for used cars is estimated to be 3. What does this mean? What will be the effect on the quantity demanded for used cars if the price rises by 10 percent?

4. Consider the following demand schedule:

Price	Quantity demanded	Elasticity coefficient
$25	20	
20	40	_____
15	60	_____
10	80	_____
5	100	_____

What is the price elasticity of demand between
a. $P = \$25$ and $P = \$20$?
b. $P = \$20$ and $P = \$15$?
c. $P = \$15$ and $P = \$10$?
d. $P = \$10$ and $P = \$5$?

5. Suppose a university raises its tuition from $3,000 to $3,500. As a result, student enrollment falls from 5,000 to 4,500. Calculate the price elasticity of demand. Is demand elastic, unitary elastic, or inelastic?

6. Will each of the following changes in price cause total revenue to increase, decrease, or remain unchanged?
a. Price falls, and demand is elastic.
b. Price rises, and demand is elastic.
c. Price falls, and demand is unitary elastic.
d. Price rises, and demand is unitary elastic.
e. Price falls, and demand is inelastic.
f. Price rises, and demand is inelastic.

7. Suppose the movie theater raises the price of popcorn 10 percent, but customers do not buy any less popcorn. What does this tell you about the price elasticity of demand? What will happen to total revenue as a result of the price increase?

8. Charles loves Mello Yello and will spend $10 per week on the product no matter what the price. What is his price elasticity of demand for Mello Yello?

9. Which of the following pairs of goods has the higher price elasticity of demand?
a. Oranges or Sunkist oranges
b. Car or salt
c. Foreign travel in the short run or foreign travel in the long run

10. The Energizer Bunny that "keeps going and going" has been a very successful ad campaign for batteries. Explain the relationship between this slogan and the firm's price elasticity of demand and total revenue.

11. Suppose the income elasticity of demand for furniture is 3.0 and the income elasticity of demand for physician services is 0.3. Compare the impact on furniture and physician services of a recession that reduces consumers' incomes by 10 percent.

12. How might you determine whether compact discs and cassettes are in competition with each other?

13. Assume the cross-elasticity of demand for car tires with respect to the price of cars is −2. What does this tell you about the relationship between car tires and cars when the price of cars rises by 10 percent?

14. Consider the following supply schedule:

Price	Quantity supplied	Elasticity coefficient
$10	50	
8	40	_____
6	30	_____
4	20	_____
2	10	_____
0	0	_____

What is the price elasticity of supply between
a. $P = \$10$ and $P = \$8$?
b. $P = \$8$ and $P = \$6$?
c. $P = \$6$ and $P = \$4$?
d. $P = \$4$ and $P = \$2$?
e. $P = \$2$ and $P = 0$?

15. Why would consumers prefer that the government tax products with elastic, rather than inelastic, demand?

16. Opponents of increasing the tax on gasoline argue that the big oil companies just pass the tax along to the consumers. Do you agree or disagree? Explain your answer.

ONLINE EXERCISES

Exercise 1

Visit a few of the major anti-tobacco groups: the American Lung Association (http://www.lungusa.org/), the tobacco Control Resource Center (http://www.tobacco.neu.edu), and Smoke-Free Kids—an initiative by the U.S. Department of Health and Human Services (http://www.cdc.gov/tobacco/sports_initiatives_splash.htm). What are these groups doing to increase the elasticity of demand for cigarettes?

Exercise 2

Does the federal government take economic concepts (such as elasticity) into consideration when it formulates energy and environmental policies? Visit the Environmental Protection Agency (EPA) and review its materials on the economy and environment (http://yosemite1.epa.gov/ee/epa/eed.nsf/pages/homepage?Opendocument). Also visit the Department of Energy, Energy Information Administration (http://www.eia.doe.gov/).

Exercise 3

Movie stars are not the only personalities that advertise products. Some rock stars offer all kinds of products for sale. Visit NSYNC's store to see what they have for sale (http://nsyncdirect.com/). What is the price elasticity of demand for the products to their customers?

Exercise 4

The Kelley Blue Book Official Guide is a major source of new and used car prices (http://www.kbb.com/). Find the new car prices for two popular cars: Honda Accord and Ford Taurus. Are the two cars closely priced? Do you think (physically similar) goods are closer substitutes when they are more closely priced than when they are less closely priced? Or do you think the issue of closeness in price is irrelevant to the degree of substitution? Explain your answer. Do you think the cross-price elasticity of demand between the Accord and Taurus is positive or negative? Explain your answer.

CHECKPOINT ANSWERS

Will Fliers Flock to Low Summer Fares?

USAirways must believe the quantity of airline tickets demanded during the summer is quite responsive to a price cut. For total revenue to rise with a price cut, the quantity demanded must increase by a larger percentage than the percentage decrease in the price. For this to occur, the price elasticity of demand must exceed 1. If you said USAirways believes demand is elastic, YOU ARE CORRECT.

Can Trade Sanctions Affect Elasticity of Demand for Cars?

Because substitutes (Japanese luxury cars) are no longer available to U.S. consumers, the quantity demanded of Mercedes, BMWs, and Jaguars in the United States would be less responsive to changes in the price for these cars. If you said the price elasticity of demand for Mercedes, BMWs, and Jaguars would become less elastic, YOU ARE CORRECT.

Can Honda Compete with Itself?

Seeing the effect of cutting the Acura's price on sales of Accords calls for cross-elasticity. Once the price of Acura is cut, Honda would calculate the change in the quantity of Accords demanded. If Acura's decrease in price causes people to buy fewer Accords, Honda is indeed competing with itself. If you said a positive cross-elasticity of demand indicates the two goods are substitutes, YOU ARE CORRECT.

PRACTICE QUIZ

For a visual explanation of the correct answers, visit the tutorial at http://tucker.swcollege.com.

1. If an increase in bus fares in Charlotte, North Carolina reduces the total revenue of the public transit system, this is evidence that demand is
   a. price elastic.
   b. price inelastic.
   c. unitary elastic.
   d. perfectly elastic.

2. Which of the following will result in an increase in total revenue?
   a. Price increases when demand is elastic.
   b. Price decreases when demand is elastic.
   c. Price increases when demand is unitary elastic.
   d. Price decreases when demand is inelastic.

3. You are on a committee that is considering ways to raise money for your city's symphony program. You would recommend increasing the price of symphony tickets only if you thought the demand curve for these tickets was
   a. inelastic.
   b. elastic.
   c. unitary elastic.
   d. perfectly elastic.

4. The price elasticity of demand for a horizontal demand curve is
   a. perfectly elastic.
   b. perfectly inelastic.
   c. unitary elastic.
   d. inelastic.
   e. elastic.

5. Suppose the quantity of steak purchased by the Jones family is 110 pounds per year when the price is $2.10 per pound and 90 pounds per year when the price is $3.90 per pound. The price elasticity of demand coefficient for this family is
   a. 0.33.
   b. 0.50.
   c. 1.00.
   d. 2.00.

6. If a 5 percent reduction in the price of a good produces a 3 percent increase in the quantity demanded, the price elasticity of demand over this range of the demand curve is
   a. elastic.
   b. perfectly elastic.
   c. unitary elastic.
   d. inelastic.
   e. perfectly inelastic.

7. A manufacturer of Beanie Babies hires an economist to study the price elasticity of demand for this product. The economist estimates that the price elasticity of demand coefficient for a range of prices close to the selling price is greater than 1. The relationship between changes in price and quantity demanded for this segment of the demand curve is
   a. elastic.
   b. inelastic.
   c. perfectly elastic.
   d. perfectly inelastic.
   e. unitary elastic.

8. A downward-sloping straight-line demand curve will have a
   a. higher price elasticity of demand coefficient along the top of the demand curve.
   b. lower price elasticity coefficient along the top of the demand curve.
   c. constant price elasticity of demand coefficient throughout the length of the demand curve.
   d. positive slope.

9. The price elasticity of demand coefficient for a good will be lower
   a. if there are few or no substitutes available.
   b. if a small portion of the budget will be spent on the good.
   c. in the short run than in the long run.
   d. if all of the above are true.

10. The income elasticity of demand for shoes is estimated to be 1.50. We can conclude that shoes
    a. have a relatively steep demand curve.
    b. have a relatively flat demand curve.
    c. are a normal good.
    d. are an inferior good.

11. To determine whether two goods are substitutes or complements, an economist would estimate the
    a. price elasticity of demand.
    b. income elasticity of demand.
    c. cross-elasticity of demand.
    d. price elasticity of supply.

12. If the government wanted to raise tax revenue and shift most of the tax burden to the sellers, it would impose a tax on a good with a
    a. steep (inelastic) demand curve and a steep (inelastic) supply curve.
    b. steep (inelastic) demand curve and a flat (elastic) supply curve.
    c. flat (perfectly elastic) demand curve and a steep (inelastic) supply curve.
    d. flat (perfectly elastic) demand curve and a flat (elastic) supply curve.

CHAPTER 6

Consumer Choice Theory

This chapter expands our understanding of demand by investigating more deeply *why* people buy goods and services. In Chapter 3, the law of demand rested on a foundation of common sense and everyday observation. When the price of a Big Mac falls, people *do* buy more, and a price rise causes people to buy less. But there is more to the story.

The focus of this chapter is the logic of consumer choice. Why does a consumer buy one bundle of goods, rather than another? Suppose someone asked why you bought a milkshake and french fries, rather than a Coke and a hot dog. You would probably answer that given the money you had to spend, the Coke and hot dog would have given you less satisfaction. In this chapter, you will transform this simple explanation into consumer choice theory and then connect this theory to the

law of demand. The chapter ends with another way to explain the demand curve, which involves effects related to income and the prices of other goods.

 In this chapter, you will learn to solve these economics puzzles:

■ Under what conditions might you be willing to pay $10,000 for a gallon of water and 1 cent for a one-carat diamond?

■ When ordering Big Macs, milkshakes, pizza, and other goods, how can you obtain the highest possible satisfaction?

■ Do white rats obey the law of demand?

From Utility to the Law of Demand

The basis of the law of demand is self-interested behavior. Consumers spend their limited budget to satisfy some want, such as listening to a compact disc or driving a new car. The motivation to consume goods and services is to gain **utility**. Utility is the satisfaction, or pleasure, that people receive from consuming a good or service. Utility is want-satisfying power "in the eye of the beholder." Just as wants differ among people, utility received from consumption varies from person to person. Fred's utility from consuming a BMW will probably differ from Maria's utility. In spite of the subjective nature of utility, this section develops in steps the derivation of a demand curve based on the utility concept.

Total Utility and Marginal Utility

Actual measurement of utility is impossible because only you know the satisfaction from consuming, say, four Big Macs in one day. But suppose we could gauge your **total utility** of consuming four Big Macs in a day. Total utility is the amount of satisfaction received from all the units of a good or service consumed. That is, the utility of the first unit consumed added to that of the second unit, and so on. What units can be used to measure total utility? Economists use a mythical unit called a *util,* which allows us to quantify our thinking about consumer behavior.

No one has invented a "utility meter," but assume we could hook such a meter to your brain. Like taking your temperature, we could read the **marginal utility** each time you eat a Big Mac. Marginal utility is the change in total utility from one additional unit of a good or service. Instead of the total pleasure from eating *X* number of Big Macs, the question is how much *extra* satisfaction the first, second, or third Big Mac gives you. For example, Exhibit 1(a) shows your marginal utility data for eating four Big Macs in a day. You munch down the first Big Mac. Ah, the util meter hits an 8. You grab another Big Mac and eat it a little more slowly. The util meter hits 4 this time. You're starting to feel full, but you eat a third Big Mac. This one gets a 2. Even though you are pretty full, there is room for one more. You eat the fourth Big Mac very slowly, and it gives you less satisfaction than any of the previous burgers. Your utility meter reads 1. This trend conforms to the **law of diminishing marginal utility**. The law of diminishing marginal utility is the principle that the extra satisfaction of a good or service declines as people consume more in a given period. Economists have found that this is a universal principle of human consumption behavior.

Exhibit 1(a) is a marginal utility, *MU,* graph. Consistent with the law of diminishing marginal utility, the *MU* curve slopes downward as you consume more Big Macs. This reflects a steady decline in the utility of each additional Big Mac consumed. If you continued to eat Big Macs, a quantity of Big Macs is eventually reached at which the marginal utility is zero. Here you say to yourself, "If I eat another bite, I'll be sick." Then if you did eat another bite after all, marginal utility would be negative. A rational person never consumes goods when the marginal utility is negative (disutility) unless he or she is paid enough to do so. In our example, we assume you are rational and will not eat a Big Mac that gives you a negative marginal utility and

Utility
The satisfaction, or pleasure, that people receive from consuming a good or service.

Total utility
The amount of satisfaction received from all the units of a good or service consumed.

Marginal utility
The change in total utility from one additional unit of a good or service.

Law of diminishing marginal utility
The principle that the extra satisfaction of a good or service declines as people consume more in a given period.

EXHIBIT 1   **Diminishing Marginal Utility and Total Utility Curves for Consuming Big Macs**

Part (a) shows that, as more Big Macs are consumed per day, the utility from each additional Big Mac declines. The utils are only imaginary because utility cannot be measured. When the marginal utility of each Big Mac consumed is summed, we obtain the total utility curve shown in part (b).

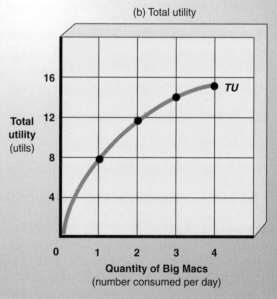

a stomachache. Also keep in mind that the *MU* curve for a good is different for different circumstances and individuals. Your *MU* curve would be much higher if you had not eaten in days. On the other hand, a vegetarian would receive no positive marginal utility from consuming a Big Mac.

Exhibit 1(b) shows how the shape of the total utility, *TU*, curve varies with marginal utility as you consume more Big Macs each day. The total utility of Big Macs increases steadily because each hamburger provides

Why Is Water Less Expensive Than Diamonds?

Applicable Concepts: total utility and marginal utility

Adam Smith posed a paradox in *The Wealth of Nations*. Water is essential to life and therefore should be of great value. On the other hand, diamonds are unessential to life, so people should value them less than water. Yet, even though water provides more utility, it is cheaper than diamonds. Smith's puzzle came to be known as the diamond-water paradox. Now you can use marginal utility analysis to explain something that baffled the father of economics.

Early economists failed to find the key to the diamond-water puzzle because they did not distinguish between marginal and total utility. Marginal utility theory was not developed until the late nineteenth century. Water is life-giving and does indeed yield much higher total utility than diamonds. However, marginal utility, and not total utility, determines the price. Water is plentiful in most of the world, so its marginal utility is low. This follows the law of diminishing marginal utility.

Jewelry-quality diamonds, on the other hand, are scarce. Because we have relatively few diamonds, the quantity of diamonds consumed is not large. As a result, the marginal utility of diamonds and the price buyers are willing to pay for them are quite high. Thus, scarcity raises marginal utility and price regardless of the size of total utility.

Exhibit 2 presents a graphical analysis that you can use to unravel the alleged paradox. Part (a) shows the marginal utility per carat you receive from each diamond consumed, and part (b) represents marginal utility per gallon of water consumed. The vertical line, *S*, in each graph is the supply of water or diamonds available per year. Since water is much more plentiful than diamonds, the supply curve for water intersects the marginal utility curve

at MU_w, which is close to zero. Conversely, the supply curve for diamonds intersects the marginal utility curve at a much higher marginal utility, MU_d. Because of the relative marginal utilities of water and diamonds, you are willing to pay much more for one more carat of a diamond than for one more gallon of water.

ANALYZE THE ISSUE

1. Can you imagine a situation in which water would be more expensive than diamonds?

2. Suppose the price per gallon of water is 1 cent and the price per carat of a diamond is $10,000. Is the total utility of diamonds 10,000 times as great as the total utility received from water?

---

additional satisfaction to the sum of all the Big Macs already consumed. However, the total utility curve becomes flatter as the marginal utility diminishes. This is because the positive pleasure per Big Mac declines, and, in turn, each Big Mac adds less to total utility as you consume more.

Consumer Equilibrium

We will now make our example of consumer choice more realistic. Let's examine how Bob Moore, a sophomore at Seaview College, might behave, given a limited budget and the choice between two goods. Suppose Bob goes to McDonald's for lunch with $8 in his pocket to spend for Big Macs and milkshakes. The price of a Big Mac is $2, and the price of a milkshake is also $2. How can Bob enjoy the maximum total utility with his limited money?

Some people claim that by visiting a Disney Resort for one day you will want "just one more day—or two more days, or even a year's worth of fun." But the law of diminishing marginal utility states that by the year's end one would probably no longer find it enjoyable. See http://www.wdisneyw.co.uk/.

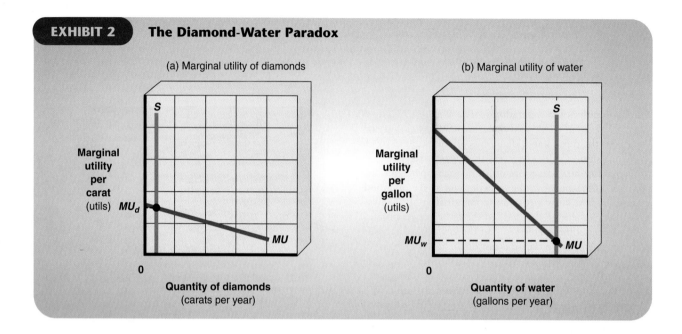

EXHIBIT 2   **The Diamond-Water Paradox**

(a) Marginal utility of diamonds

(b) Marginal utility of water

Recall from Chapter 2 the concept of *marginal analysis*. This is the method Bob uses to decide how many Big Macs and milkshakes to order. Exhibit 3 shows Bob's marginal utility for each Big Mac and milkshake consumed. The *marginal utility per dollar (MU/P)* is the ratio of the marginal utility of each good to its price. In making purchases, the key consideration is how additional satisfaction relates to price. Using marginal decision-making before giving an order, Bob compares the marginal utility of one Big Mac to the marginal utility of one milkshake. Being a rational consumer, Bob sees that spending his first $2 on a Big Mac gives more "bang for the buck." The first Big Mac gives him 4 utils per dollar, but the same $2 spent on a milkshake gives him 3 utils per dollar. Next, Bob ponders how to spend his next $2. The best buy now is a milkshake because it gives 3 utils per dollar compared to 2 utils per dollar for a second Big Mac.

Spending Bob's last $4 is a tossup. Both the second Big Mac and the second milkshake give the same 2 utils per dollar. So Bob can spend $2 for a second Big Mac and his last $2 for a second milkshake. Or he can spend $2 for a second milkshake and his last $2 for a second Big Mac. The order does not matter. Now that Bob has spent all his income, the marginal utility per dollar of the last Big Mac is equal to the marginal utility per dollar of the last milkshake.

Conclusion *If the marginal utility per last dollar spent on each good is equal and the entire budget is spent, total utility is maximized.*

To convince yourself that two Big Macs and two milkshakes do indeed maximize total utility, consider any other combination Bob could buy with $8. All others yield lower total utility. Suppose Bob were to buy three Big Macs and one milkshake. The third Big Mac adds 2 utils, but giving up the

EXHIBIT 3 Marginal Utility for Big Macs and Milkshakes (Utils per Day)

Quantity	Big
	MU
1	8
2	4
3	2
4	1

Note: The price per Big Mac and per milk

second milkshake subtracts 4 utils
Or can Bob maximize utility if he
three milkshakes? The extra utility
is less than the 4 utils he would los
this case, total utility would fall by

The above example demonstrat
sumer equilibrium. Consumer equi
ity cannot increase by spending m
spending less on another good. Sup
ginal utility of consuming Big Mac
utility of french fries, pizza, and ot
satisfaction, Bob allocates his budg
last on good B, and so on yield eq
can be restated algebraically as

$$\frac{\text{MU of good } A}{\text{price of good } A} = \frac{\text{MU}}{\text{price}}$$

The letters A, B, . . . Z indicate all
consumer with a given budget.

From Consumer Equilibriu

Understanding the law of diminish
librium provides you with a new se
Let's begin with a straightforwar
marginal utility and the demand
consuming more Big Macs and mil
sumed is less important or valua
quantity consumed increases and th
pay less per Big Mac and milkshak
conforms to the law of demand an

Consumer equilibrium
A condition in which total utility cannot increase by spending more of a given budget on one good and spending less on another good.

 A number of commercial firms, such as USADATA (http://www.usadata .com/), conduct research on con-sumer choices and preferences.

CHECKPOINT

When Dining Out, Do You Eat Smart?

Welcome to José's Hacienda! Beside each dish, the menu lists the total utility from each item. If you have $15 to spend, which meal will you order to achieve consumer equilibrium?

José's Hacienda Menu

Tacos—$3 each	Flan*—$2 each	Coke—$1 each
1 taco (99 utils)	1 flan (40 utils)	1 Coke (25 utils)
2 tacos (162 utils)	2 flans (48 utils)	2 Cokes (29 utils)
3 tacos (174 utils)	3 flans (50 utils)	3 Cokes (32 utils)

*Mexican dessert.

A more complete explanation of the law of demand combines diminishing marginal utility and consumer equilibrium. Suppose Bob reaches consumer equilibrium as follows:

$$\frac{MU \text{ of Big Mac}}{\text{price of Big Mac}} = \frac{MU \text{ of milkshake}}{\text{price of milkshake}}$$

$$\frac{4 \text{ utils}}{\$2} = \frac{4 \text{ utils}}{\$2}$$

Now suppose the price of a Big Mac falls to $1 and upsets the above equality. This changes the formula to the following:

$$\frac{MU \text{ of Big Mac}}{\text{price of Big Mac}} > \frac{MU \text{ of milkshake}}{\text{price of milkshake}}$$

$$\frac{4 \text{ utils}}{\$1} > \frac{4 \text{ utils}}{\$2}$$

Now Bob gains more utility per dollar by buying a Big Mac, rather than a milkshake. To restore maximum total utility, he spends more on Big Macs. The marginal utility of a Big Mac must fall as he buys more. At the same time, the marginal utility of a milkshake must rise as Bob buys fewer. A fall in the price of Big Macs therefore causes Bob to buy more Big Macs. Voilà! The law of demand.

Income and Substitution Effects and the Law of Demand

Since utility is not measurable, it is desirable to have an alternative explanation of demand. Economists offer the following two complementary explanations for the law of demand, which do not rely on utility.

CHECKPOINT

Does the Substitution Effect Apply to Buying a Car?

Jenny Tanaka wants to buy a new car, and the annual gasoline expense is a major consideration. Her present car gets 25 miles per gallon (mpg), and she is looking at a new car that gets 40 mpg. Jenny now drives about 12,000 miles per year and pays $1.25 per gallon of gasoline. She therefore calculates an annual gasoline consumption of 480 gallons for her 25-mpg car (12,000 miles/25 mpg) compared to 300 gallons consumed per year for the 40-mpg car (12,000 miles/40 mpg). Since driving the higher mileage car would use 180 gallons less per year, Jenny estimates the new car will save her $225 in gasoline expense per year (180 gallons × $1.25 per gallon). Suppose Jenny buys the 40-mpg car. Do you predict Jenny will have an annual gasoline savings equal to $225, less than $225, or more than $225?

Income Effect

One reason people buy more of a good when the price falls is the effect of a price change on real income. The *nominal* or *money* amount of your paycheck is simply the number of dollars you earn. On the other hand, price changes alter your *real* income. A rise in prices decreases purchasing power, and a fall in prices increases purchasing power, ceteris paribus.

Suppose your weekly nominal income is $100 and you decide to stock up on Pepsi-Cola (a normal good). If the price per quart is $1, you can afford to buy 100 quarts this week. If the price is instead $.50 per quart and the prices of other goods remain constant, you are richer because of the rise in purchasing power. As a result, you can buy 200 quarts of Pepsi-Cola without giving up any other goods or less than 200 quarts and more of other goods. As predicted by the law of demand, the lower price for Pepsi-Cola causes real income to rise and, in turn, causes the quantity demanded to rise. This relationship between changes in real income and your ability to buy goods and services is the **income effect.** The income effect is the change in quantity demanded of a good or service caused by a change in real income (purchasing power).

Income effect
The change in quantity demanded of a good or service caused by a change in real income (purchasing power).

Substitution Effect

There is another reason why the change in a good's price causes a change in the quantity demanded. This reason has to do with changing *relative prices,* that is, the price of one good compared to that of another. If the price of Pepsi falls and the price of Coke remains unchanged, Pepsi becomes a better buy. As a result, many consumers will switch from Coke and other beverages and buy Pepsi. Just as the law of demand predicts, this is an increase in quantity demanded. With the price of Pepsi lower than before, the **substitution effect** causes people to substitute Pepsi for the now relatively more expensive Coke. The substitution effect is the change in quantity demanded of a good or service caused by a change in its price relative to substitutes.

Substitution effect
The change in quantity demanded of a good or service caused by the change in its price relative to substitutes.

Testing the Law of Demand with White Rats

Applicable Concept: substitution effect

Economists often envy the controlled laboratory experiments of biologists and other scientists. In the real world, the economist is unable to observe consumer behavior without prices of other goods, expectations, and other factors changing. So it is no wonder that the idea of studying the behavior of white rats to study the law of demand is intriguing. The question was whether the consumer choice of a white rat supports the downward-sloping demand curve.

Standard laboratory rats were placed in experimental cages with two levers. If a rat pressed one lever, nonalcoholic Collins mix was the reward. Depressing the second lever rewarded the rat with root beer. It seems rats are fond of these two beverages. Each rat was given a limited "income" of lever presses per day. After, say, 300 presses, a light above the lever went out, signaling the daily budget was gone. The next day the light was turned on, and the rat was given a new income of lever presses. The "price" of each good corresponded to the number of lever pushes required to obtain one milliliter of liquid. For example, if the number of pushes per milliliter for Collins mix released increased by 10 percent, this equaled a 10 percent increase in the price of Collins mix.

The crucial test was to measure the substitution effect resulting from a change in price. As explained in the text, a change in price sets in motion both an income effect and a substitution effect. In the experiment, the price of Collins mix was lowered by decreasing the pushes per milliliter. At the same time, the price of root beer was raised by increasing the pushes per milliliter. To eliminate the income effect, the number of lever presses was raised to

compensate for loss of purchasing power. For example, if a rat purchased 4 milliliters of Collins mix per day and 11 milliliters of root beer before the price change, it would be given enough extra pushes after the price change to still purchase these quantities.

In one experiment, a male albino rat was given 300 pushes per day for two weeks, and both liquids were priced at 20 pushes per milliliter. The rat soon settled into a consistent consumption pattern of 4 milliliters of Collins mix and 11 milliliters of root beer per day. Then the experimenters made changes in prices and income. The price (pushes per milliliter) of Collins mix was cut in half, and the price of root beer was doubled. At the same time, the total income of pushes was increased just enough to allow the rat to afford its initial consumption pattern. Stated differently, the income effect was eliminated in order to focus on the substitution effect.

After two weeks of decisions under the new conditions, the rat changed its consumption pattern to 17 milliliters of Collins mix and 8 milliliters of root beer per day.

Based on the behavior of the rat described above, what do you conclude about the substitution effect and the slope of the demand curve?

Source: John H. Kagel, Raymond C. Battalio, Howard Rachlin, and Leonard Green, "Demand Curves for Animal Consumers," *Quarterly Journal of Economics* 96 (February 1981): 1–16.

Above we discussed the income and the substitution effects separately, but they are complementary explanations for the downward-sloping demand curve.

Conclusion *When the price of a normal good falls, the income effect and the substitution effect combine to cause the quantity demanded to increase.*

Some students express relief that this conclusion has no reference to the untidy word *utility*.

KEY CONCEPTS

Utility
Total utility
Marginal utility

Law of diminishing
   marginal utility
Consumer equilibrium

Income effect
Substitution effect

SUMMARY

■ **Utility** is the satisfaction or pleasure derived from consumption of a good or service. Actual measurement of utility is impossible, but economists assume it can be measured by a fictitious unit called the *util*.

■ **Total utility** is the total level of satisfaction derived from all units of a good or service consumed. *Marginal utility* is the change in total utility from a 1-unit change in the quantity of a good or service consumed.

Relationship between marginal and total utility

(a) Marginal utility

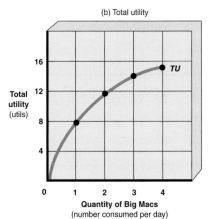

(b) Total utility

■ The **law of diminishing marginal utility** states that the marginal utility of a good or service eventually declines as consumption increases.

■ **Consumer equilibrium** is the condition of reaching the maximum level of satisfaction, given a budget, when the marginal utility per dollar spent on each good purchased is equal. Consumer equilibrium and the law of diminishing marginal utility can be used to derive a downward-sloping demand curve. When the price of a good falls, consumer equilibrium no longer holds because the marginal utility per dollar for the good rises. To restore equilibrium, the consumer must increase consumption. As the quantity demanded increases, the marginal utility falls until equilibrium is again achieved. Thus, the price falls, and the quantity demanded rises, as predicted by the law of demand.

$$\frac{MU \text{ of good } A}{\text{price of good } A} = \frac{MU \text{ of good } B}{\text{price of good } B} = \frac{MU \text{ of good } Z}{\text{price of good } Z}$$

■ The **income effect** and the **substitution effect** are complementary explanations for the law of demand. When the price changes, these effects work in combination to change the quantity demanded in the opposite directions. As the price falls, real purchasing power increases, causing an increase in the consumer's willingness and ability to purchase a good or service. This is the *income effect*. Also, as the price falls, the consumer substitutes the cheaper good for other goods that are now relatively more expensive. This is the *substitution effect*.

SUMMARY OF CONCLUSION STATEMENTS

■ If the marginal utility per last dollar spent on each good is equal and the entire budget is spent, total utility is maximized.

■ When the price of a normal good falls, the income effect and the substitution effect combine to cause the quantity demanded to increase.

STUDY QUESTIONS AND PROBLEMS

1. Does a dollar given to a rich person raise the rich person's total utility more than a dollar given to a poor person raises the poor person's total utility?

2. Do you agree with the following statement? "If you like tacos, you should consume as many as you can."

3. This week you have gone to two parties. Assume the total utility you gained from these parties is 100 utils. Then you go to a third party, and your total utility rises to 110 utils. What is the marginal utility of the third party attended per week? Given the law of diminishing marginal utility, what will happen to total utility and marginal utility when you go to a fourth party this week?

4. Suppose your marginal utility for meals at the campus cafeteria this week has fallen to zero. Explain what has happened to your total utility curve derived from consuming these meals. Now explain what will happen to total utility if you eat more meals at the cafeteria this week.

5. Suppose you consume three pounds of beef and five pounds of pork per month. The price of beef is $1.50 per pound, and pork is $2.00 per pound. Assuming you have studied economics and achieved consumer equilibrium, what is the ratio of the marginal utility of beef to the marginal utility of pork?

6. Suppose the marginal utility of a Coke is 15 utils and its price is $1. The marginal utility of a pizza is 20 utils, and its price is $2. If you buy one unit of each

good, will you achieve consumer equilibrium? If not, how can greater total utility be obtained?

7. Explain the relationship between the law of diminishing marginal utility and the law of demand.

8. Consider the table below, which lists James's marginal utility schedule for steak and hamburger meals:

Steak meals per month	Marginal utility of steak meals	Price per steak meal	Hamburger meals per month	Marginal utility of hamburger meals	Price per hamburger meal
1	20	$10	1	15	$5
2	15	10	2	8	5
3	12	10	3	6	5
4	10	10	4	4	5
5	8	10	5	2	5

Given a budget of $45, how many steak and hamburger meals will James buy per month to maximize his total utility? What is the total utility realized?

9. Using the marginal utility schedule in question 8, begin in consumer equilibrium, and assume the price per hamburger meal falls from $5 to $2 all other factors held constant. What is the total utility realized?

10. Suppose the price of a BMW falls. Explain the law of demand based on the income and substitution effects.

ONLINE EXERCISES

Exercise 1

Visit the *Journal of Applied Behavioral Analysis* (http://www.envmed.rochester.edu/wwwrap/behavior/jaba/jabahome.htm). Browse this journal for studies of animal behavior that reflects economic concepts.

Exercise 2

How many different kinds and flavors of yogurt are there? Take a look at what Dannon (http://www.dannon.com/index.html) has. Why so many flavors?

Exercise 3

Visit the Diamond Information Center at http://www .adiamondisforever.com/. What statement does this site make about the marginal utility of diamonds?

Exercise 4

What are the substitution and income effects of shopping online? Visit eBay at http://www.ebay.com/.

 CHECKPOINT ANSWERS

When Dining Out, Do You Eat Smart?

Start with 1 taco (99 marginal utils/$3, or 33 marginal utils/$1). Then order a Coke (25 marginal utils/$1). Next, order another taco (63 marginal utils/$3, or 21 marginal utils/$1). Now treat yourself to a flan (40 marginal utils/ $2, or 20 marginal utils/$1). Finish it all with a second flan (4 marginal utils/$1), another Coke (4 marginal utils/$1) and a third taco (4 marginal utils/$1). You have now spent your entire $15 budget. If you said, following the principle of consumer equilibrium, you would order 2 Cokes, 2 flans, and 3 tacos, although not a very nutritious choice, YOU ARE CORRECT.

Does the Substitution Effect Apply to Buying a Car?

Buying a higher-mpg car will reduce the cost per mile of driving relative to substitutes, such as riding a bus, train, or airplane. As the cost of driving falls, the substitution effect predicts Jenny will drive more in the 40-mpg car than the 12,000 miles she now drives per year in the 25-mpg car. The extra cost of gasoline for driving over 12,000 miles per year in the 40-mpg car must be subtracted from the $225 savings that was based on the assumption that Jenny's miles driven per year would remain unchanged when she bought the 40-mpg car. If you said Jenny will save less than $225, YOU ARE CORRECT.

PRACTICE QUIZ

For a visual explanation of the correct answers, visit the tutorial at http://tucker.swcollege.com.

1. As an individual consumes more of a given good, the marginal utility of that good to the consumer
   a. rises at an increasing rate.
   b. rises at a decreasing rate.
   c. falls.
   d. rises.

2. The amount of added utility that a consumer gains from the consumption of one more unit of a good is called
   a. incremental utility.
   b. total utility.
   c. diminishing utility.
   d. marginal utility.

3. A certain consumer buys only food and compact discs. If the quantity of food bought increases, while that of compact discs remains the same, the marginal utility of food will
   a. fall relative to the marginal utility of compact discs.
   b. rise relative to the marginal utility of compact discs.
   c. rise, but not as fast as the marginal utility of compact discs rises.
   d. fall, but not as fast as the marginal utility of compact discs falls.

4. Rational consumers will continue to consume two goods until the
   a. marginal utility per dollar's worth of the two goods is the same for the last dollar spent on each good.
   b. marginal utility is the same for each good for the last dollar spent on each good.
   c. prices of the two goods are equal for the last dollar spent on each good.
   d. prices of the two goods are unequal.

5. Assume that a person's consumption of just the right amounts of pork and chicken is in equilibrium. We can conclude that the
   a. marginal utility of pork must equal the marginal utility of chicken.
   b. price of pork must equal the price of chicken.
   c. ratio of marginal cost to price must be the same in both the pork and the chicken markets.
   d. ratio of marginal utility to price must be the same for pork and chicken.

6. Assume an individual consumes only milk and doughnuts and he/she has arranged consumption so that the last glass of milk yields 12 utils and the last doughnut 6 utils. If the price of milk is $1 per glass and the price of a doughnut is $.50, we can conclude that the
   a. consumer should consume less milk and more doughnuts.
   b. price of milk is too high relative to doughnuts.
   c. consumer should consume more milk and fewer doughnuts.
   d. consumer is in equilibrium.

7. Suppose an individual consumes pizza and cola. To reach consumer equilibrium, the individual must consume pizza and cola so that the
   a. price paid for the two goods is the same.
   b. marginal utility of the two goods is equal.
   c. ratio of marginal utility to price is the same for both goods.
   d. ratio of the marginal utility of cola to the marginal utility of pizza is 1.

8. A state of consumer equilibrium for goods consumed prevails when the
   a. marginal utility of all goods is the same for the last dollar spent for each good.
   b. marginal utility per dollar's worth of two goods is the same for the last dollar spent for each good.
   c. price of two goods is the same for the last dollar spent for each good.
   d. marginal cost per dollar spent on two goods is the same for the last dollar spent for each good.

9. The change in quantity demanded resulting from a change in purchasing power is known as the
   a. income effect.
   b. substitution effect.
   c. law of demand.
   d. consumer equilibrium effect.

10. In Exhibit 4, assume Multiplex tickets cost $6 each, video rentals cost $2 each, and bags of popcorn cost $1 each. What is the marginal utility of renting a third video?
    a. 6 utils
    b. 8 utils
    c. 10 utils
    d. 30 utils

Exhibit 4 Total Utility for Multiplex Tickets, Video Rentals, and Popcorn

Total utility from Multiplex tickets	Total utility from video rentals	Total utility from popcorn
1 movie (30 utils)	1 video (14 utils)	1 bag (8 utils)
2 movies (54 utils)	2 videos (24 utils)	2 bags (13 utils)
3 movies (72 utils)	3 videos (30 utils)	3 bags (15 utils)
4 movies (84 utils)	4 videos (32 utils)	4 bags (16 utils)

11. In Exhibit 4, assume Multiplex tickets cost $6 each, video rentals cost $2 each, and bags of popcorn cost $1 each. Suppose the consumer has $12 per week to spend on Multiplex tickets, video rentals, and popcorn. What combination of goods will give the consumer the most utility?
    a. 1 movie, 3 videos, and no popcorn
    b. 1 movie, 2 videos, and 2 bags of popcorn
    c. 1 movie, 1 video, and 4 bags of popcorn
    d. 2 movies, no videos, and no bags of popcorn

CHAPTER 7

Production Costs

S uppose you dream of owning your own company. That's right! You want to be an entrepreneur. You crave the excitement of starting your own firm and making it successful. Instead of working for someone else, you want to be your own boss. You are under no illusions; it is going to take hard work and sacrifice.

You are an electrical engineer who is an expert at designing electronic components for automatic teller machines and similar applications. So you quit your job and invest your nest egg in starting Computech (a mythical company). You lease factory space, hire employees, and purchase raw materials, and soon your company's products begin rolling off the assembly line. And then you find production cost considerations influence each decision you make in this new business venture.

The purpose of this chapter is to study production and its relationship to various types of costs. Whether your company is new and small or an international giant, understanding costs is essential for success. In this chapter and the next chapter, you will follow Computech and learn the basic principles of production and the way various types of costs vary with output.

 In this chapter, you will learn to solve these economics puzzles:

■ Why would an accountant say a firm is making a profit and an economist say it is losing money?

■ What is the difference between the short run and the long run?

■ Why have multiscreen movie theaters replaced single-screen theaters?

Costs and Profit

A basic assumption in economics is that the motivation for business decisions is profit maximization. Economists realize that managers of firms sometimes pursue other goals, such as contributing to the United Way or building an empire for the purpose of ego satisfaction. Nevertheless, the profit maximization goal has proved to be the best theory to explain why managers of firms choose a particular level of output or price. To understand profit as a driving force for business firms, we must distinguish between the way economists measure costs and the way accountants measure costs.

Explicit and Implicit Costs

Economists define the total opportunity cost of a business as the sum of **explicit costs** and **implicit costs**. Explicit costs are payments to nonowners of a firm for their resources. In our Computech example, explicit costs include the wages paid to labor, the rental charges for a plant, the cost of electricity, the cost of materials, and the cost of medical insurance. These resources are owned outside the firm and must be purchased with an actual payment to these "outsiders."

Implicit costs are the opportunity costs of using resources owned by the firm. These are opportunity costs of resources because the firm makes no actual payment to outsiders. When you started Computech, you gave up the opportunity to earn a salary as an electrical engineer for someone else's firm. When you invested your nest egg in your own enterprise, you gave up earning interest. You also used a building you own to warehouse Computech products. Although you made no payment to anyone, you gave up the opportunity to earn rental payments.

Explicit costs
Payments to nonowners of a firm for their resources.

Implicit costs
The opportunity costs of using resources owned by the firm.

Economic and Accounting Profit

In everyday use, the word *profit* is defined as follows:

$$\text{Profit} = \text{total revenue} - \text{total cost}$$

Economists call this concept *accounting profit*. This popular formula is expressed in economics as

$$\text{Accounting profit} = \text{total revenue} - \text{total explicit cost}$$

Because economic decisions include implicit as well as explicit costs, economists use the concept **economic profit** instead of accounting profit. Economic profit is total revenue minus explicit and implicit costs. Economic profit can be positive, zero, or negative (an economic loss). Expressed as an equation:

$$\text{Economic profit} = \text{total revenue} - \text{total opportunity costs}$$

or

$$\text{Economic profit} = \text{total revenue} - (\text{explicit costs} + \text{implicit costs})$$

Economic profit
Total revenue minus explicit and implicit costs.

EXHIBIT 1 Computech's Accounting versus Economic Profit

Item	Accounting profit	Economic profit
Total revenue	$500,000	$500,000
Less explicit costs:		
Wages and salaries	400,000	400,000
Materials	50,000	50,000
Interest paid	10,000	10,000
Other payments	10,000	10,000
Less implicit costs:		
Forgone salary	0	50,000
Forgone rent	0	10,000
Forgone interest	0	5,000
Equals profit	$30,000	−$35,000

Exhibit 1 illustrates the importance of the difference between accounting profit and economic profit. Computech must know how well it is doing, so you hire an accounting firm to prepare a financial report. The exhibit shows that Computech earned total revenue of $500,000 in its first year of operation. Explicit costs for wages, materials, interest, and other payments totaled $470,000. Based on standard accounting procedures, this left an accounting profit of $30,000.

If the analysis ends with accounting profit, Computech is profitable. But accounting practice overstates profit. Because implicit costs are subjective and therefore difficult to measure, accounting profit ignores implicit costs. A few examples will illustrate the importance of implicit costs. Your $50,000-a-year salary as a manager was forgone in order to spend all your time as owner of Computech. Also forgone were $10,000 in rental income and $5,000 in interest that you would have earned during the year by renting your building and putting your savings in the bank. Subtracting both explicit and implicit costs from total revenue, Computech had an economic loss of $35,000. The firm is failing to cover the opportunity costs of using its resources in the electronics industry. Thus, the firm's resources would earn a higher return if used for other alternatives.

How would you interpret a zero economic profit? It's not as bad as it sounds. Economists call this condition **normal profit**. Normal profit is the minimum profit necessary to keep a firm in operation. Zero economic profit signifies there is just enough total revenue to pay the owners for all explicit and implicit costs. Stated differently, there is no benefit from reallocating resources to another use. For example, assume an owner earns zero economic profit, including an implicit (forfeited) cost of $50,000 per year that could have been earned working for someone else. This means the owner earned as much as would have been earned in the next best employment opportunity.

Normal profit

The minimum profit necessary to keep a firm in operation. A firm that earns normal profits earns total revenue equal to its total opportunity cost.

CHECKPOINT

Should the Professor Go or Stay?

Professor Martin is considering leaving the university and opening a consulting business. For her services as a consultant, she would be paid $75,000 a year. To open this business, Professor Martin must convert a house from which she collects rent of $10,000 per year into an office and hire a secretary at a salary of $15,000 per year. Also, she must withdraw $10,000 from savings for miscellaneous expenses and forgo earning 10 percent interest per year. The university pays Professor Martin $50,000 a year. Based only on economic decision making, do you predict the professor will leave the university to start a new business?

Conclusion *Since business decision making is based on economic profit, rather than accounting profit, the word* profit *in this text always means economic profit.*

Short-Run Production Costs

Having presented the basic definitions of total cost, the next step is to study cost theory. In this section, we explore the relationship between output and cost in the short run. In the next section, the time horizon shifts to the long run.

Short Run versus Long Run

Suppose I asked you, "What is the difference between the short run and the long run?" Your answer might be that the short run is less than a year and the long run is over a year. Good guess, but wrong! Economists do not partition production decisions based on any specific number of days, months, or years. Instead, the distinction depends on the ability to vary the quantity of inputs or resources used in production. There are two types of inputs—**fixed inputs** and **variable inputs.** A fixed input is any resource for which the quantity cannot change during the period of time under consideration. For example, the physical size of a firm's plant and the production capacity of heavy machines cannot easily change within a short period of time. They must remain as fixed amounts while managers decide to vary output. In addition to fixed inputs, the firm uses *variable inputs* in the production process. A variable input is any resource for which the quantity can change during the period of time under consideration. For example, managers can hire fewer or more workers during a given year. They can also change the amount of materials and electricity used in production.

Now we can link the concepts of fixed and variable inputs to the **short run** and the **long run.** The short run is a period of time so short that there is at least one fixed input. For example, the short run is a period of time during which a firm can increase output by hiring more workers (variable input), while the size of the firm's plant (fixed input) remains unchanged. The firm's plant is the most difficult input to change quickly. The long run

Fixed input

Any resource for which the quantity cannot change during the period of time under consideration.

Variable input

Any resource for which the quantity can change during the period of time under consideration.

Short run

A period of time so short that there is at least one fixed input.

Long run

A period of time so long that all inputs are variable.

What's the Profit on That Book?

Applicable Concepts: accounting profit and economic profit

Book pricing is anything but an exact science. Determining the suggested retail price of a book is a matter of combining a mathematical formula with instinct.

"You have a basic formula—how much it costs you to make the book, the author's royalties and how much you'll spend to promote it," said publisher Roger Donald of Bantam Books. "But the formula is rarely right because you don't know how many copies it will sell. Yet you have to put a price, so you do it on the basis of your best guess."

The costs that the price must cover can be extensive. The average novel or nonfiction book costs $1.50 to $2 a copy to manufacture, although the manufacturing cost of a heavily illustrated book like an art book can reach $10 a copy. The suggested retail price must also include the cost of composition, typesetting, and jacket design as well as fixed costs like office space and editorial salaries. About 5 to 7 percent of the price pays for advertising and promotion.

In addition, bookstores and wholesalers receive an average discount off the suggested retail price of 45 to 47 percent, meaning they pay the publishers a little more than $10 for a book they can sell for almost $20. Author royalties, also based on the cover price, range from 10 to 15

percent. When all those costs are subtracted, a publisher is lucky to make $1 on a book with a cover price of $19.95. In fact, publishers rarely make money on first printings. Their profits come from subsequent printings.

ANALYZE THE ISSUE

1. Suppose Bantam Books' accounting profit for a novel is $1 per copy. Give an example of how an economist's calculation of profit would be different.

2. The above feature states that royalties paid to authors range from 10 to 15 percent of the cover price. Why don't the authors publish their own books? To simplify the analysis, assume that both the author-publisher company and Bantam Books can publish a book for the same explicit costs for typesetting, paper, warehousing, promotion, and so on.

Source: Edwin McDowell, "Publishers Experiment with Lower Prices," *New York Times,* May 8, 1989, p. D10.

---

is a period of time so long that all inputs are variable. In the long run, the firm can build new factories or purchase new machinery. New firms can enter the industry, and existing firms may leave the industry.

The Production Function

Production function

The relationship between the maximum amounts of output that a firm can produce and various quantities of inputs.

Having defined inputs, we can now describe how these inputs are transferred into outputs using a concept called a **production function**. A production function is the relationship between the maximum amounts of output a firm can produce and various quantities of inputs. An assumption of the production function model we are about to develop is that the level of technology is fixed. Technological advances would mean more output is possible from a given quantity of inputs.

Exhibit 2(a) presents a short-run production function for Eaglecrest Vineyard. The variable input is the number of workers employed per day, and each worker is presumed to have equal job skills. The acreage, amount of fertilizer, and all other inputs are assumed to be fixed; therefore, our production model is operating in the short run. Employing zero workers produces no bushels of grapes. A single worker can produce 10 bushels per day, but a lot of time is wasted when one worker picks, loads containers, and

EXHIBIT 2   **A Production Function and the Law of Diminishing Returns**

(a) Total output curve

(b) Marginal product curve

Short-Run Production Function of Eaglecrest Vineyard

(1) Labor input (number of workers per day)	(2) Total output (bushels of grapes per day)	(3) Marginal product (bushels of grapes per day) [Δ(2)/Δ(1)]
0	0	
		10
1	10	
		12
2	22	
		11
3	33	
		9
4	42	
		6
5	48	
		2
6	50	

Part (a) shows how the total output of bushels of grapes per day increases as the number of workers increases while all other inputs remain constant. This figure is a short-run production function, which relates outputs to a one-variable input while all other inputs are fixed.

Part (b) illustrates the law of diminishing returns. The first worker adds 10 bushels of grapes per day, and marginal product is 10 bushels per day. Adding a second worker adds another 12 bushels of grapes per day to total output. This is the range of increasing marginal returns. After two workers, diminishing marginal returns set in, and marginal product declines continuously.

transports the grapes to the winery. Adding a second worker raises output to 22 bushels per day because the workers divide the tasks and specialize. Adding four more workers raises total product to 50 bushels per day.

Marginal Product

Marginal product

The change in total output produced by adding one unit of a variable input, with all other inputs used being held constant.

The relationship between changes in total output and changes in labor is called the **marginal product**. Marginal product is the change in total output produced by adding one unit of a variable input, with all other inputs used being held constant. When Eaglecrest increases labor from zero to one worker, output rises from zero to 10 bushels produced per day. This increase is the result of the addition of one more worker. Therefore, the marginal product so far is 10 bushels per worker. Similar marginal product calculations generate the marginal product curve shown in Exhibit 2(b). Note that marginal product is plotted at the midpoints shown in the table because the change in total output occurs between each additional unit of labor used.

The Law of Diminishing Returns

Law of diminishing returns

The principle that beyond some point the marginal product decreases as additional units of a variable factor are added to a fixed factor.

A long-established economic law called the **law of diminishing returns** determines the shape of the marginal product curve. The law of diminishing returns states that beyond some point the marginal product decreases as additional units of a variable factor are added to a fixed factor. Because the law of diminishing returns assumes fixed inputs, this principle is a short-run, rather than a long-run, concept.

This law applies to production of both agricultural and nonagricultural products. Returning to Exhibit 2, we can identify and explain the law of diminishing returns in our Eaglecrest example. Initially, the total output curve rises quite rapidly as this firm hires the first two workers. The marginal product curve reflects the change in the total output curve because marginal product is the slope of the total output curve. As shown in Exhibit 2(b), the range from zero to two workers hired is called *increasing marginal returns*. In this range of output, the last worker adds more to total output than the previous worker.

Diminishing returns begin after the second worker is hired and the marginal product reaches its peak. Beyond two workers, diminishing returns occur, and the marginal product declines. The short-run assumption guarantees this condition. Eventually, marginal product falls because the amount of land per worker falls as more workers are added to fixed quantities of land and other inputs used to produce wine. Similar reasoning applies to the Computech example introduced in the chapter preview. Assume Computech operates with a fixed plant size and a fixed number of machines and all other inputs except the number of workers are fixed. Those in the first group of workers hired divide the most important tasks among themselves, specialize, and achieve increasing returns. Then diminishing returns begin and continue as Computech employs each additional worker. The reason is that as more workers are added, they must share fixed inputs, such as machinery. Some workers are underemployed because they are standing around waiting for a machine to become available. Also, as more workers are hired, there are fewer important tasks to perform. As a result, marginal product declines. In the extreme case, marginal product would be negative. At some number of workers, they must work with such limited floor space, machines, and other fixed inputs that they start stepping on each other's toes. No profit-seeking firm would ever hire workers with zero or negative marginal product. Chapter 11 explains the labor market in more detail and shows how Computech decides exactly how many workers to hire.

Short-Run Cost Formulas

To make production decisions in either the short run or the long run, a business must determine the costs associated with producing various levels of output. Using Computech, you will study the relationship between two "families" of short-run costs and output: first, the total cost curves and, next, the average cost curves.

Total Cost Curves

Total Fixed Cost. As production expands in the short run, costs are divided into two basic categories—**total fixed cost** and **total variable cost.** Total fixed cost consists of costs that do not vary as output varies and that must be paid even if output is zero. These are payments that the firm must make in the short run regardless of the level of output. Even if a firm, such as Computech, produces nothing, it must still pay rent, interest on loans, property taxes, and fire insurance. Fixed costs are therefore beyond management's control in the short run. The total fixed cost (*TFC*) for Computech is $100, as shown in column 2 of Exhibit 3.

Total fixed cost (*TFC*)

Costs that do not vary as output varies and that must be paid even if output is zero. These are payments that the firm must make in the short run, regardless of the level of output.

Total Variable Cost. As the firm expands from zero output, total variable cost is added to total fixed cost. Total variable cost consists of costs that are zero when output is zero and vary as output varies. These costs relate to the costs of variable inputs. Examples include wages for hourly workers, electricity, fuel, and raw materials. As a firm uses more input to produce output, its variable costs will increase. Management can control variable costs in the short run by changing the level of output. Exhibit 3 lists the total variable cost (*TVC*) for Computech in column 3.

Total variable cost (*TVC*)

Costs that are zero when output is zero and vary as output varies.

Total Cost. Given total fixed cost and total variable cost, the firm can calculate **total cost.** Total cost is the sum of total fixed cost and total variable cost at each level of output. As a formula:

$$TC = TFC + TVC$$

Total cost (*TC*) for Computech is shown in column 4 of Exhibit 3. Exhibit 4(a) uses the data in Exhibit 3 to construct graphically the relationships among total cost, total fixed cost, and total variable cost. Note that

Total cost (*TC*)

The sum of total fixed cost and total variable cost at each level of output.

EXHIBIT 3 Short-Run Cost Schedule for Computech

(1) Total product (Q)	(2) Total fixed cost (TFC)	(3) Total variable cost (TVC)	(4) Total cost (TC)	(5) Marginal cost (MC)	(6) Average fixed cost (AFC)	(7) Average variable cost (AVC)	(8) Average total cost (ATC)
0	$100	$ 0	$100		—	—	—
				$ 50			
1	100	50	150		$100	$50	$150
				34			
2	100	84	184		50	42	92
				24			
3	100	108	208		33	36	69
				19			
4	100	127	227		25	32	57
				23			
5	100	150	250		20	30	50
				30			
6	100	180	280		17	30	47
				38			
7	100	218	318		14	31	45
				48			
8	100	266	366		13	33	46
				59			
9	100	325	425		11	36	47
				75			
10	100	400	500		10	40	50
				95			
11	100	495	595		9	45	54
				117			
12	100	612	712		8	51	59

the *TVC* curve varies with the level of output and the *TFC* curve does not. The *TC* curve is simply the *TVC* curve plus the vertical distance between the *TC* and *TVC* curves, which represents *TFC*.

Average Cost Curves

In addition to total cost, firms are interested in the *per-unit cost,* or *average cost.* Average cost, like product price, is stated on a per-unit basis. The last three columns in Exhibit 3 are *average fixed cost* (AFC), *average variable cost* (AVC), and *average total cost* (ATC). These average, or per-unit, curves are also shown in Exhibit 4(b). These three concepts are defined as follows:

EXHIBIT 4   **Short-Run Cost Curves**

(a) Relationship of total cost to total variable cost and total fixed cost

(b) Relationship of marginal cost to average total cost, average variable cost, and average fixed cost

The curves in this exhibit are derived by plotting data from Exhibit 3. Part (a) shows that the total cost (*TC*) at each level of output is the sum of total variable cost (*TVC*) and total fixed cost (*TFC*). Because the *TFC* curve does not vary with output, the shape of the *TC* curve is determined by the shape of the *TVC* curve. The vertical distance between the *TC* and the *TVC* curves is *TFC*.

In part (b), the marginal cost (*MC*) curve decreases at first, then reaches a minimum, and then increases as output increases. The *MC* curve intersects both the average variable cost (*AVC*) curve and the average total cost (*ATC*) curve at the minimum point on each of these cost curves. The average fixed cost (*AFC*) curve declines continuously as output expands. *AFC* is also the difference between the *ATC* and the *AVC* curves at any quantity of output.

Average Fixed Cost. As output increases, **average fixed cost** (*AFC*) falls continuously. Average fixed cost is total fixed cost divided by the quantity of output produced. Written as a formula:

$$AFC = \frac{TFC}{Q}$$

As shown in Exhibit 4(b), the *AFC* curve approaches the horizontal axis as output expands. This is because larger output numbers divide into *TFC* and cause *AFC* to become smaller and smaller.

Average fixed cost (*AFC*)
Total fixed cost divided by the quantity of output produced.

Average variable cost (AVC)

Total variable cost divided by the quantity of output produced.

Average Variable Cost. The **average variable cost** (*AVC*) in our example forms a U-shaped curve. Average variable cost is total variable cost divided by the quantity of output produced. Written as a formula:

$$AVC = \frac{TVC}{Q}$$

The *AVC* curve is also drawn in Exhibit 4(b). At first, the *AVC* curve falls, and then after an output of 6 units per hour, the *AVC* curve rises. Thus, the *AVC* curve is U-shaped. The explanation for the shape of the *AVC* curve is given in the next section.

Average total cost (ATC)

Total cost divided by the quantity of output produced.

Average Total Cost. Average total cost (*ATC*) is sometimes referred to as *per-unit cost*. The average total cost is total cost divided by the quantity of output produced. Written as a formula:

$$ATC = AFC + AVC = \frac{TC}{Q}$$

Like the *AVC* curve, the *ATC* curve is U-shaped, as shown in Exhibit 4(b). At first, the *ATC* curve falls because its component parts—*AVC* and *AFC*—are falling. As output continues to rise, the *AVC* curve begins to rise, while the *AFC* curve falls continuously. Beyond the output of 7 units per hour, the rise in the *AVC* curve is greater than the fall in the *AFC* curve, which causes the *ATC* curve to rise in a U-shaped pattern.

Airline deregulation in the U.S. has resulted in a change in airline cost structure. Access the following site to learn how (http://www.heritage.org/library/backgrounder/bg1173es.html).

Marginal cost (MC)

The change in total cost when one additional unit of output is produced.

Marginal Cost. Marginal analysis asks how much it costs to produce an *additional* unit of output. Column 5 in Exhibit 3 is **marginal cost** (*MC*). Marginal cost is the change in total cost when one additional unit of output is produced. Stated differently, marginal cost is the ratio of the change in total cost to a one-unit change in output. Written as a formula:

$$MC = \frac{\text{change in } TC}{\text{change in } Q} = \frac{\text{change in } TVC}{\text{change in } Q}$$

Note that marginal cost can also be calculated from changes in *TVC*. This is because the only difference between total cost and total variable cost is total fixed cost. Thus, *TC* and *TVC* change by the same amount with each unit change in output. To check this relationship, look at the per-unit changes in *TC*, *TVC*, and *MC* in Exhibit 3.

Changing output by one unit at a time simplifies the marginal cost calculations in our Computech example. The marginal cost data are listed between output levels to show that marginal cost is the change in total cost as the output level changes. Exhibit 4(b) shows this marginal cost schedule graphically. In the short run, a firm's marginal cost falls initially as output expands, eventually reaches a minimum, and then rises, forming a J-shaped curve. Note that marginal cost is plotted at the midpoints because the change in cost occurs between each additional unit of output.

Exhibit 5 summarizes a firm's short-run cost relationships.

EXHIBIT 5 Short-Run Cost Formulas

Cost concept	Formula	Graph
Total cost (TC)	$TC = TFC + TVC$	
Marginal cost (MC)	$\dfrac{\text{change in } TC}{\text{change in } Q} = \dfrac{\text{change in } TVC}{\text{change in } Q}$	
Average fixed cost (AFC)	$AFC = \dfrac{TFC}{Q}$	
Average variable cost (AVC)	$AVC = \dfrac{TVC}{Q}$	
Average total cost (ATC)	$ATC = \dfrac{TC}{Q}$	

Marginal Cost Relationships

Part (b) of Exhibit 4 presents two important relationships that require explanation. First, we will explain the rule that links the marginal cost curve to the average cost curves. Second, we will return to the marginal product curve in Exhibit 2(b) and explain its connection to the marginal cost curve.

The Marginal-Average Rule

Observe that the *MC* curve in Exhibit 4(b) intersects both the *AVC* curve and the *ATC* curve at their minimum points. This is not accidental. It is a result of a relationship called the **marginal-average rule.** The marginal-average rule

Marginal-average rule
The rule that states when marginal cost is below average cost, average cost falls. When marginal cost is above average cost, average cost rises. When marginal cost equals average cost, average cost is at its minimum point.

CHECKPOINT

Did Michael Jordan Beat the Marginal-Average Rule?

Michael Jordan, formerly of the Chicago Bulls, is one of the finest players in the history of basketball. Suppose he had an average of 33 points per game over the first 10 games of the season and then scored 20, 25, 40, 50, and 20 points in the next five games. Did Michael Jordan beat the marginal-average rule?

states that when marginal cost is below average cost, average cost falls. When marginal cost is above average cost, average cost rises. When marginal cost equals average cost, average cost is at its minimum point. The marginal-average rule applies to grades, weights, and any average figure.

Perhaps the best way to understand this rule is to apply it to a noneconomic example. Suppose there are 20 students in your class and each student has a grade point average (GPA) of 4.0. The average GPA of the class is therefore 4.0. Now let another student who has a GPA of 2.0 join the class. The new average GPA of 21 students in the class falls to 3.9. The average GPA was pulled down because the *marginal* GPA of the additional student was lower than the *average* GPA of the other students. On the other hand, let's start with a class of 20 students with a 2.0 GPA and add a student who has a 4.0 GPA. In this case, the new average GPA of 21 students rises from 2.0 to 2.1. Thus, the *marginal* GPA of the last student was higher than the *average* GPA of all students in class before the addition of the new student.

Now consider the *MC* curve in part (b) of Exhibit 4. In the range of output from 0 to 6 units per hour, the *MC* curve is below the *AVC* curve, and *AVC* is falling. Beyond 6 units per hour, the *MC* curve is above *AVC*, and *AVC* is rising. Hence, the relationship between *AVC* and *MC* conforms to the marginal-average rule. It follows that the *MC* curve intersects the *AVC* curve at its lowest point. This analysis also applies to the relationship between the *MC* and *ATC* curves. Initially, the *MC* curve is lower than the *ATC* curve until it reaches its minimum, causing the *ATC* curve to fall. Beginning with 8 units of output, the *MC* curve exceeds the *ATC* curve, causing the *ATC* curve to rise.

Marginal Cost's Mirror Image

Since the *MC* curve determines the U-shape of the *AVC* and *ATC* curves, we must explain the J-shape of the *MC* curve. Exhibit 6 illustrates that the shape of the *MC* curve is the mirror reflection of the shape of the marginal product (*MP*) curve. Comparing parts (a) and (b) of Exhibit 6 gives this conclusion: *The marginal cost declines as the marginal product of a variable input rises if the wage rate is constant. Beginning at the point of diminishing returns, the marginal cost rises as the marginal product of a variable input declines.* As explained earlier in this chapter, the law of diminishing returns is the declining portion of the *MP* curve that corresponds to the rising portion of the *MC* curve.

Find law of diminishing return

| EXHIBIT 6 | The Inverse Relationship between Marginal Product and Marginal Cost |

(1)	(2)	(3)	(4)	(5)
Labor input (number of workers per day)	Total output (bushels of grapes per day)	Marginal product (bushels of grapes per day) [Δ(2)/Δ(1)]	Total cost per day [$100 × (1)]	Marginal cost [Δ(4)/(3)]
0	0		$ 0	
		10		$10.00
1	10		100	
		12		8.33
2	22		200	
		11		9.09
3	33		300	
		9		11.11
4	42		400	
		6		16.66
5	48		500	
		2		50.00
6	50		600	

Part (a) represents the marginal product of labor (*MP*) curve. At first, each additional worker hired adds more to output than does the previously hired worker, and the *MP* curve rises until a maximum is reached at two workers hired. At three workers, the law of diminishing returns sets in, and each additional worker hired adds less output than previously hired workers.

Part (b) shows the marginal cost (*MC*) curve is a U-shaped curve that is inversely related to the *MP* curve. Assuming the wage rate remains constant, as the *MP* curve rises, the *MC* curve falls. When the *MP* curve reaches a maximum at two workers, the *MC* curve is at a minimum. As diminishing returns set in and the *MP* curve falls, the *MC* curve rises.

To understand why this relationship exists, we return to the case of Eaglecrest Vineyard presented earlier in Exhibit 2. Now we again assume that labor is the only variable input and add the new important assumption that the wage rate is constant at $100 per day. When Eaglecrest moves from zero labor to hire one worker, its total output rises from zero to 10 bushels of grapes per day. As explained earlier, the marginal product is also 10 bushels, and the marginal cost is $100/10 = $10 ($\Delta TC/\Delta Q = \Delta TC/MP$). When Eaglecrest hires the second worker, total output rises by 12 bushels per day. Hiring this worker increases the firm's total cost by $100, while the marginal product rises to 12 bushels. The marginal cost of the second worker therefore falls to a minimum at $100/12 = $8.33. At this point, it is noteworthy that the minimum point on the *MC* curve corresponds to the maximum point on the *MP* curve. The third worker hired yields only 11 additional bushels of grapes per day, so marginal cost rises to $9.09. Thus, diminishing returns begin with the third worker, and the marginal cost continues to rise as more workers are hired.

Long-Run Production Costs

As explained earlier in this chapter, the long run is a time period long enough to change the quantity of all fixed inputs. A firm can, for example, build a larger or smaller factory or vary the capacity of its machinery. In this section, we will discuss how varying factory size, and *all* other inputs, in the long run affects the relationship between production and costs.

Long-Run Average Cost Curves

Suppose Computech is making its production plans for the future. Taking a long-run view of production means the firm is not locked into a small, medium-sized, or large factory. However, once a factory of any particular size is built, the firm operates in the short run because the plant becomes a fixed input.

> **Conclusion** *A firm operates in the short run when there is insufficient time to alter some fixed input. The firm plans in the long run when all inputs are variable.*

Exhibit 7 illustrates a situation in which there are only three possible factory sizes Computech might select. Short-run cost curves representing these three possible plant sizes are labeled $SRATC_s$, $SRATC_m$, and $SRATC_l$. *SR* is the abbreviation for short run, and *ATC* stands for average total cost. The subscripts *s, m,* and *l* represent small, medium, and large plant size, respectively. In the previous sections, there was no need to use SR for short run because we were discussing only short-run cost curves and not long-run cost curves.

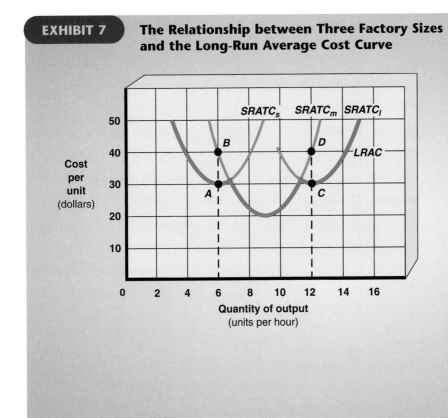

EXHIBIT 7 **The Relationship between Three Factory Sizes and the Long-Run Average Cost Curve**

Each of the three short-run *ATC* curves in the exhibit corresponds to a different plant size. Assuming these are the only three plant-size choices, a firm can choose any one of these plant sizes in the long run. For example, a young firm may operate a small plant represented by U-shaped short-run average total cost curve $SRATC_s$. As a firm matures and demand for its product expands, it can decide to build a larger factory, corresponding to either $SRATC_m$ or $SRATC_l$. The long-run average cost (*LRAC*) curve is the heavily shaded scalloped curve joining the short-run curves below their intersections.

Suppose Computech estimates that it will be producing an output level of 6 units per hour for the foreseeable future. Which plant size should the company choose? It will build the plant size represented by $SRATC_s$ because this affords a lower cost of $30 per unit (point *A*) than the factory size represented by $SRATC_m$, which has a cost of $40 per unit (point *B*).

What if production is expected to be 12 units per hour? In this case, the firm will choose the plant size represented by $SRATC_l$. At this plant size, the cost is $30 per unit (point *C*), which is lower than $40 per unit (point *D*).

Conclusion *The plant size selected by a firm in the long run depends on the expected level of production.*

Using the three short-run average cost curves shown in Exhibit 7, we can construct the firm's **long-run average cost curve** (*LRAC* curve). The long-run average cost curve traces the lowest cost per unit at which a firm can produce any level of output after the firm can build any desired plant size. The *LRAC* curve is often called the firm's planning curve. In Exhibit 7, the heavily shaded curve represents the *LRAC* curve.

Exhibit 8 shows there are actually an infinite number of possible plant sizes from which managers can choose in the long run. As the intersection points of the short-run *ATC* curves move closer and closer together, the lumps

Long-run average cost curve

The curve that traces the lowest cost per unit at which a firm can produce any level of output when the firm can build any desired plant size.

EXHIBIT 8 **The Long-Run Average Cost Curve When the Number of Factory Sizes Is Unlimited**

There are an infinite number of possible short-run *ATC* curves that correspond to different plant sizes. The long-run average cost (*LRAC*) curve is the green curve tangent to each of the possible red short-run *ATC* curves.

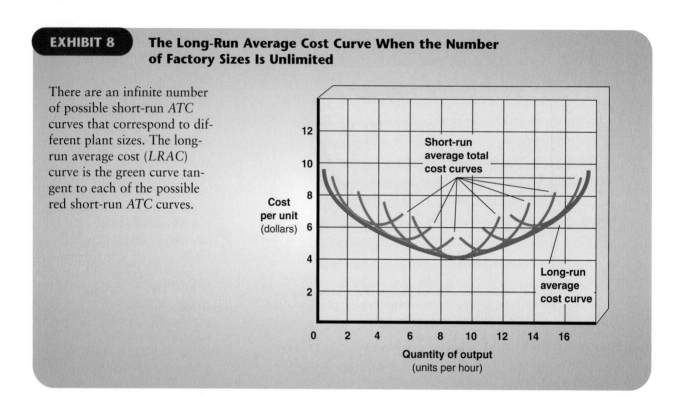

in the *LRAC* curve in Exhibit 8 disappear. With a great variety of plant sizes, the corresponding short-run *ATC* curves trace a smooth *LRAC* curve. When the *LRAC* curve falls, the tangency points are to the left of the minimum points on the short-run *ATC* curves. As the *LRAC* curve rises, the tangency points are to the right of the minimum points on the short-run *ATC* curves.

Different Scales of Production

Exhibit 8 depicted long-run average cost as a U-shaped curve. In this section, we will discuss the reasons why the *LRAC* curve first falls and then rises when output expands in the long run. In addition, we will learn that the *LRAC* curve can have a variety of shapes. Note that the law of diminishing returns is not an explanation here because in the long run there are no fixed inputs.

For simplicity, Exhibit 9 excludes possible short-run *ATC* curves that touch points along the *LRAC* curve. Typically, a young firm starts small and builds larger plants as it matures. As the scale of operation expands, the *LRAC* curve can follow three different patterns. Over the lowest range of output from zero to Q_1, the firm experiences **economies of scale**. Economies of scale exist when the long-run average cost curve declines as the firm increases output.

Economies of scale

A situation in which the long-run average cost curve declines as the firm increases output.

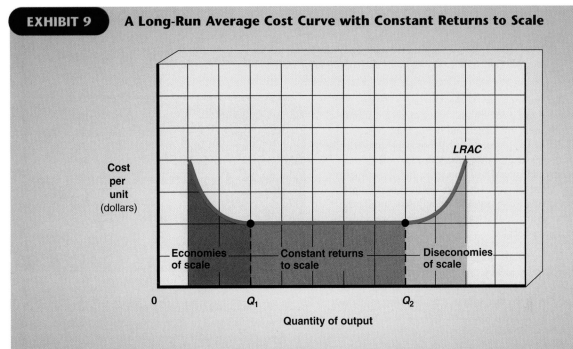

EXHIBIT 9   **A Long-Run Average Cost Curve with Constant Returns to Scale**

The long-run average cost (*LRAC*) curve illustrates a firm that experiences economies of scale until output level Q_1 is reached. Between output levels Q_1 and Q_2, the *LRAC* curve is flat, and there are constant returns to scale. Beyond output level Q_2, the firm experiences diseconomies of scale, and the *LRAC* curve rises.

There are several reasons for economies of scale. First, a larger firm can increase its *division of labor* and *use of specialization*. Adam Smith noted in *Wealth of Nations,* published in 1776, that the output of a pin factory is greater when one worker draws the wire, a second straightens it, a third cuts it, a fourth grinds the point, and a fifth makes the head of the pin. As a firm initially expands, having more workers allows managers to break a job into small tasks. Then each worker—including managers—can specialize by mastering narrowly defined tasks, rather than trying to be a jack-of-all-trades.[1] The classic example is Henry Ford's assembly line, which greatly reduced the cost of producing automobiles. Today, McDonald's trains workers at "Hamburger University"; then some workers prepare food, some specialize in taking orders, and a few workers specialize in the drive-in window operation.

Second, economies of scale result from greater *efficiency of capital.* Suppose machine *A* costs $1,000 and produces 1,000 units per day. Machine *B* costs $4,000, but it is technologically more efficient and has a capacity of 8,000 units per day. The low-output firm will find it too costly to purchase

Access information on economies of scale in the electronics industry at the following site: http://www.airborn.com.au/ab360.html.

Although McDonald's has thousands of restaurants around the world, it standardizes menus and operating procedures in these restaurants to take advantage of economies of scale. See: http://www.mcdonalds.com/.

[1]Adam Smith, *An Inquiry into the Nature and Causes of the Wealth of Nations* (1776; reprint, New York: Random House, 1937), pp. 4–6.

Invasion of the Monster Movie Theaters

Applicable Concept: economies and diseconomies of scale

A few decades ago most movie theaters had a single screen and offered just one film and few concession stand choices. Now theaters are bigger and better than ever. Megaplexes, defined as cinemas with 16 or more screens, offer several movies at the same time, espresso coffee, gourmet popcorn, Häagen-Dazs ice cream and sometimes valet parking. These megaplexes, with stadium seating providing easier viewing, have become the industry standard.

The following article illustrates the competitive advantage of economies of scale:

> The marquee at Water Tower Cinema [Gastonia, North Carolina] was bare on Wednesday—a first in the theater's more than 10-year history. The four-screen theater that in its heyday sold out its weekend movies, shut down Tuesday, leaving Gaston County again without a discount movie house. Village Twin, a 99-cent theater formerly located on U.S. 29-74, closed in the summer of 1986 because of declining attendance.

An analyst who follows the movie theater industry for First Union Capital Markets in Charlotte said the owners of second-run theaters—especially small ones—face several challenges. "In the age of megaplexes, a four-screen theater stands out on the negative side. In general we're moving to a lot more screens and a lot less theaters," Bishop Cheen

said. "If you only have four screens, you only have four reasons for a patron to leave home and spend money."[1]

Kurt Hall executive vice president of United Artists Entertainment Company, however, is concerned that diseconomies of scale will eventually set in:

> When building new theaters, United Artists is limiting its screens per site to about 15, half as many as AMC [American Multi-Cinema, Inc.]. United Artists fears that a larger megaplex won't pull in enough volume and could suffer a fate similar to Tandy Corp.'s Incredible Universe, the "big-box" electronics chain

machine *B*, so it uses machine *A*, and its average cost is $1. The large-scale firm can afford to purchase machine *B* and produce more efficiently at a per-unit cost of only $.50.

The *LRAC* curve may not turn upward and form the U-shaped cost curve in Exhibit 8. Between some levels of output, such as Q_1 and Q_2 in Exhibit 9, the *LRAC* curve no longer declines. In this range of output, the firm increases its plant size, but the *LRAC* curve remains flat. Economists call this situation **constant returns to scale**. Constant returns to scale exist when the long-run average cost curve does not change as the firm increases output. Economists believe this is the shape of the *LRAC* curve in most real-world industries. The scale of operation is important for competitive reasons. Consider a young firm producing less than output Q_1 and competing against a more established firm producing in the constant-returns-to-scale range of output. The *LRAC* curve shows that the older firm has an average cost advantage.

As a firm becomes large and expands output beyond some level, such as Q_2 in Exhibit 9, it encounters **diseconomies of scale**. Diseconomies of scale exist when the long-run average cost curve rises as the firm increases out-

Constant returns to scale

A situation in which the long-run average cost curve does not change as the firm increases output.

Diseconomies of scale

A situation in which the long-run average cost curve rises as the firm increases output.

that closed this year. Over 16 screens, the economics start to fall apart.[2]

The monster movie theaters are beginning to spring up in other countries:

Large-scale building of multiplexes—a theater with six or more screens—is in the middle of what analysts say is a 20-year drive to blanket the globe with modern theaters. Now [1999] they are rapidly taking hold in the international market, which covers everything outside North America. . . . "Multiplexes are working everywhere that they are being built," said Jack Valenti, president of the Motion Picture Assn. of America, who credits increased screen capacity overseas for Hollywood's booming foreign sales.[3]

Megaplexes are not problem free:

As moviegoers settle down in their comfortable arena seating, it's possible that the focus will be fuzzy, the picture won't be bright enough and the sound will be either too loud or too soft. For all the booming hype, and higher prices, projection at the megaplex is often less than ideal. Putting giant screens in small rooms magnifies focus problems. Projector bulbs are left to grow dim long beyond their rated lifespans. And if something goes wrong—with just one projectionist overseeing as many as 20 automated projectors—chances are no one will notice.[4]

ANALYZE THE ISSUE

1. Explain why the long-run average cost curve for movie theaters falls (economies of scale) as movie theaters add screens.

2. Explain why the long-run average cost curve for movie theaters rises (diseconomies of scale) beyond some number of screens.

[1]Audrey Y. Williams, "Cut-Rate Movie Theater Has Closed," *Charlotte Observer*, Oct. 9, 1997, p. 1A.
[2]Kevin Helliker, "Monster Movie Theaters Invade the Cinema Landscape," *Wall Street Journal*, May 13, 1997, p. B1.
[3]Robert Marich, "Multiplexes Are Being Built Overseas at a Rapid Pace," *Los Angeles Times*, Feb. 18, 1999, p. 66.
[4]Brian D. Johnson, "Movies Often Look Worse at Megaplex, Thanks to Technology Stretched to the Limit," *Maclean's*, Jan. 22, 2001, p. 30.

put. A large-scale firm becomes harder to manage. As the firm grows, the chain of command lengthens, and communication becomes more complex. People communicate through forms instead of direct conversation. The firm becomes too bureaucratic, and operations bog down in red tape. Layer upon layer of managers are paid big salaries to shuffle papers that have little or nothing to do with producing output. Consequently, it is no surprise that a firm can become too big and these management problems can cause the average cost of production to rise.

Steven Jobs, founder of Apple Computer Company, stated:

When you are growing [too big], you start adding middle management like crazy. . . . People in the middle have no understanding of the business, and because of that, they screw up communications. To them, it's just a job. The corporation ends up with mediocre people that form a layer of concrete.[2]

 Sometimes diseconomies of scale are experienced. According to the following source it has existed in U.S. public transport bus operations: http://www.publicpurpose.com/ut-us97mbecsc.htm.

[2]Deborah Wise and Catherine Harris. "Apple's New Crusade," *Business Week*, Nov. 26, 1984, p. 156.

KEY CONCEPTS

Explicit costs	Short run	Total variable cost	Marginal-average rule
Implicit costs	Long run	Total cost	Long-run average cost
Economic profit	Production function	Average fixed cost	curve
Normal profit	Marginal product	Average variable cost	Economies of scale
Fixed input	Law of diminishing returns	Average total cost	Constant returns to scale
Variable input	Total fixed cost	Marginal cost	Diseconomies of scale

SUMMARY

■ **Economic profit** is equal to total revenue minus both *explicit* and *implicit* costs. **Implicit costs** are the opportunity costs of forgone returns to resources owned by the firm. Economic profit is important for decision-making purposes because it includes implicit costs and accounting profit does not. Accounting profit equals total revenue minus explicit costs.

■ The **short run** is a time period during which a firm has at least one fixed input, such as its factory size. The **long run** for a firm is defined as a period during which all inputs are variable.

■ A **production function** is the relationship between output and inputs. Holding all other factors of production constant, the production function shows the total output as the amount of one input, such as labor, varies.

■ **Marginal product** is the change in total output caused by a one-unit change in a variable input, such as the number of workers hired. The **law of diminishing returns** states that after some level of output in the short run, each additional unit of the variable input yields smaller and smaller marginal product. This range of declining marginal product is the region of diminishing returns.

■ **Total fixed cost** consists of costs that cannot vary with the level of output such as rent for office space. Total fixed cost is the cost of inputs that do not change as the firm changes output in the short run. **Total vari-**

able cost consists of costs that vary with the level of output, such as wages. Total variable cost is the cost of variable inputs used in production. **Total cost** is the sum of total fixed cost and total variable cost.

Total cost curves

Relationship of total cost to total variable cost and total fixed cost

■ **Marginal cost** is the change in total cost associated with one additional unit of output. **Average fixed cost** is the total fixed cost divided by total output. **Average variable cost** is the total variable cost divided by total output. **Average total cost** is the total cost, or the sum of average fixed cost and average variable cost, divided by output.

■ **Marginal cost** and **marginal product** are mirror images of each other. Assuming a constant wage rate, marginal cost equals the wage rate divided by the marginal product. Increasing returns cause marginal cost to fall, and diminishing returns cause marginal cost to rise. This explains the U-shaped marginal cost curve.

Average and marginal cost curves

Marginal product

Marginal cost

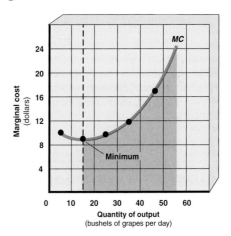

■ The **marginal-average rule** explains the relationship between marginal cost and average cost. When marginal cost is less than average cost, average cost falls. When marginal cost is greater than average cost, average cost rises. Following this rule, the marginal cost curve intersects the average variable cost curve and the average total cost curve at their minimum points.

■ The **long-run average cost curve** is a curve drawn tangent to all possible short-run average total cost curves. When the long-run average cost curve decreases as output increases, the firm experiences **economies of scale.** If the long-run average cost curve remains unchanged as output increases, the firm experiences **constant returns to scale.** If the long-run average cost curve increases as output increases, the firm experiences **diseconomies of scale.**

Long-run average cost curve

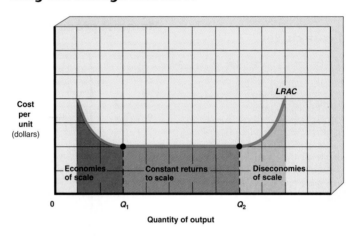

SUMMARY OF CONCLUSION STATEMENTS

■ Since business decision making is based on economic profit, rather than accounting profit, the word *profit* in this text always means economic profit.

■ The marginal cost declines as the marginal product of a variable input rises if the wage rate is constant. Beginning at the point of diminishing returns, the marginal cost rises as the marginal product of a variable input declines.

■ A firm operates in the short run when there is insufficient time to alter some fixed input. The firm plans in the long run when all inputs are variable.

■ The plant size selected by a firm in the long run depends on the expected level of production.

STUDY QUESTIONS AND PROBLEMS

1. Indicate whether each of the following is an explicit cost or an implicit cost:
   a. A manager's salary
   b. Payments to IBM for computers
   c. A salary forgone by the owner of a firm by operating his or her own company
   d. Interest forgone on a loan an owner makes to his or her own company

   e. Medical insurance payments a company makes for its employees
   f. Income forgone while going to college

2. Suppose you own a videotape rental store. List some of the fixed inputs and variable inputs you would use in operating the store.

$$AFC = AVC/Q$$
$$AVC = TVC/Q$$
$$ATC = AFC + AVC = TC/Q$$

$$MC = ATC/\Delta Q = \Delta TVC/\Delta Q$$

3. **a.** Construct the marginal product schedule for the following production function:

Labor	Total output	Marginal product
0	0	___
1	8	___
2	18	___
3	30	___
4	43	___
5	55	___
6	65	___
7	73	___
8	79	___
9	82	___
10	80	___

b. Graph the total output and marginal product curves, and identify increasing and diminishing marginal returns.

4. Consider this statement: "Total output starts falling when diminishing returns occur." Do you agree or disagree? Explain.

5. What effect might a decrease in the demand for videotape recorders have on the short-run average total cost curve for this product?

6. **a.** Construct the cost schedule (using the form below) for a firm operating in the short run.

b. Graph the average variable cost, average total cost, and marginal cost curves.

7. Explain why the average total cost curve and the average variable cost curve move closer together as output expands.

8. Ace Manufacturing produces 1,000 hammers per day. The total fixed cost for the plant is $5,000 per day, and the total variable cost is $15,000 per day. Calculate the average fixed cost, average variable cost, average total cost, and total cost at the current output level.

9. An owner of a firm estimates that the average total cost is $6.71 and the marginal cost is $6.71 at the current level of output. Explain the relationship between these marginal cost and average total cost figures.

10. What short-run effect might a decline in the demand for electronic components for bank teller machines have on Computech's average total cost curve?

11. For mathematically minded students, what is the algebraic relationship between the equation for output and the equation for marginal product in Exhibit 2? Explain the circumstances under which the long-run supply curve for an industry is a horizontal line. Next, explain the circumstances under which the long-run supply curve for an industry is an upward-sloping line.

look on notes

Total product (Q)	Total fixed cost (TFC)	Total variable cost (TVC)	Total cost (TC)	Marginal cost (MC)	Average fixed cost (AFC)	Average variable cost (AVC)	Average total cost (ATC)
0	$ 50	$ 0	$ 50	$ 0	$ 0	$ 0	$ 0
1	50	20	$ 70	20	50	20	70
2	50	35	$ 85	15	25	17.5	42
3	50	45	$ 95	5	16.	15	31
4	50	50	$100	10	12	12.	24
5	50	60	$110	20	10	12	22
6	50	80	$130	35	8	13	21
7	50	115	$165	50	7	15	22
8	50	165	$215	60	6	20.5	27.5
9	50	225	$275		5.5	25	29

ONLINE EXERCISES

Exercise 1

Visit Moviefone (http://www.moviefone.com/). Explain how movie theatres reflect both economies and dis-economies of scale.

Exercise 2

Knowledge of costs of production are a prerequisite to any firm's success. This becomes clear by visiting http://toolkit.cch.com/text/P06_7510.asp. How can some costs to a business be a combination of fixed and variable costs?

Exercise 3

The Air Transport Association of America has produced an on-line Airline Handbook that provides information on airline economics and the structure of airline costs. Access this site at: http://www.air-transport.org/Default2.asp. Click on Airline Handbook and then click on Chapter 4: Airline Economics. Summarize the major components of airline costs.

Exercise 4

In the world of information technology, increasing returns and economies of scale get a little tricky. Has the following article (http://www.useit.com/alertbox/9704b.html) confused the terms or not?

CHECKPOINT ANSWERS

Should the Professor Go or Stay?

In the consulting business, the accounting profit is $60,000. An accountant would calculate profit as the annual revenue of $75,000 less the explicit cost of $15,000 per year for the secretary's salary. However, the accountant would neglect implicit costs. Professor Martin's business venture would have implicit costs of $10,000 in forgone rent, $50,000 in forgone earnings, and $1,000 in forgone annual interest on the $10,000 taken out of savings. Her economic profit is −$1,000, calculated as the accounting profit of $60,000 less the total implicit costs of $61,000. If you said the professor will pass up the potential accounting profit and stay with the university to avoid an economic loss, YOU ARE CORRECT.

Did Michael Jordan Beat the Marginal-Average Rule?

Since Jordan's marginal points in games 11 and 12 were below his average points per game, his average points per game fell from 33 to 31. Games 13 and 14 lifted his aver-age from 31 to 33 points per game because his marginal points in both of these games exceeded his average points per game. Finally, the 20 points in game 15 again reduced his average back to 32 points per game. Thus, when Jordan's marginal points scored in a game were below his season's average points per game, his average fell. When Jordan's marginal points scored in a game were above his season's average points per game, his average rose. If you said even Michael Jordan cannot beat the marginal-average rule, YOU ARE CORRECT.

Game	Marginal points	Average points
10		33 over 10 games
11	20	32 = (33 × 10 + 20)/11 games
12	25	31 = (32 × 11 + 25)/12 games
13	40	32 = (31 × 12 + 40)/13 games
14	50	33 = (32 × 13 + 50)/14 games
15	20	32 = (33 × 14 + 20)/15 games

PRACTICE QUIZ

For a visual explanation of the correct answers, visit the tutorial at http://tucker.swcollege.com.

1. Explicit costs are payments to
   a. hourly employees.
   b. insurance companies.
   c. utility companies.
   d. all of the above.

2. Implicit costs are the opportunity costs of using the resources of
   a. outsiders.
   b. owners.
   c. banks.
   d. retained earnings.

3. Which of the following equalities is *true*?
   a. Economic profit = total revenue − accounting profit
   b. Economic profit = total revenue − explicit costs − accounting profit
   c. Economic profit = total revenue − implicit costs − explicit costs
   d. Economic profit = opportunity cost + accounting cost

4. Fixed inputs are factors of production that
   a. are determined by a firm's plant size.
   b. can be increased or decreased quickly as output changes.
   c. cannot be increased or decreased as output changes.
   d. are none of the above.

5. An example of a variable input is
   a. raw materials.
   b. energy.
   c. hourly labor.
   d. all of the above.

6. Suppose a car wash has 2 washing stations and 5 workers and is able to wash 100 cars per day. When it adds a third station, but no more workers, it is able to wash 150 cars per day. The marginal product of the third washing station is
   a. 100 cars per day.
   b. 150 cars per day.
   c. 5 cars per day.
   d. 50 cars per day.

7. If the units of variable input in a production process are 1, 2, 3, 4, and 5 and the corresponding total outputs are 10, 22, 33, 42, and 48, respectively, the marginal product of the fourth unit is
   a. 2.
   b. 6.
   c. 9.
   d. 42.

8. The total fixed cost curve is
   a. upward sloping.
   b. downward sloping.
   c. upward sloping, then downward sloping.
   d. unchanged with the level of output.

9. Assuming the marginal cost curve is a smooth U-shaped curve, the corresponding total cost curve has a(an)
   a. linear shape.
   b. S-shape.
   c. U-shape.
   d. reverse S-shape.

10. If both the marginal cost and the average variable cost curves are U-shaped, at the point of minimum average variable cost, the marginal cost must be
    a. greater than the average variable cost.
    b. less than the average variable cost.
    c. equal to the average variable cost.
    d. at its minimum.

11. Which of the following is *true* at the point where diminishing returns set in?
    a. Both marginal product and marginal cost are at a maximum.
    b. Both marginal product and marginal cost are at a minimum.
    c. Marginal product is at a maximum, and marginal cost is at a minimum.
    d. Marginal product is at a minimum, and marginal cost is at a maximum.

12. As shown in Exhibit 10, total fixed cost for the firm is
    a. zero.
    b. $250.
    c. $500.
    d. $750.
    e. $1,000.

Exhibit 10 Total Cost Curve

13. As shown in Exhibit 10, the total cost of producing 100 units of output per day is
    a. zero.
    b. $250.
    c. $500.
    d. $750.
    e. $1,000.

14. In Exhibit 10, if the total cost of producing 99 units of output per day is $475, the marginal cost of producing the 100th unit of output per day is approximately
    a. zero.
    b. $25.
    c. $475.
    d. $500.

15. Each potential short-run average total cost curve is tangent to the long-run average cost curve at
    a. the level of output that minimizes short-run average total cost.
    b. the minimum point of the average total cost curve.
    c. the minimum point of the long-run average cost curve.
    d. a single point on the short-run average total cost curve.

16. Suppose a typical firm is producing X units of output per day. Using any other plant size, the long-run average cost would increase. The firm is operating at a point at which
    a. its long-run average cost curve is at a minimum.
    b. its short-run average total cost curve is at a minimum.
    c. both a and b are true.
    d. neither a nor b is true.

17. The downward-sloping segment of the long-run average cost curve corresponds to
    a. diseconomies of scale.
    b. both economies and diseconomies of scale.
    c. the decrease in average variable costs.
    d. economies of scale.

18. Long-run diseconomies of scale exist when the
    a. short-run average total cost curve falls.
    b. long-run marginal cost curve rises.
    c. long-run average total cost curve falls.
    d. short-run average variable cost curve rises.
    e. long-run average cost curve rises.

19. Long-run constant returns to scale exist when the
    a. short-run average total cost curve is constant.
    b. long-run average cost curve rises.
    c. long-run average cost curve is flat.
    d. long-run average cost curve falls.

Market Structures

This part focuses on different types of markets, each defined by a set of characteristics that determine corresponding demand and supply conditions. Chapter 8 describes a highly competitive market consisting of an extremely large number of competing firms, and Chapter 9 explains the theory for a market with only a single seller. Between these extremes, Chapter 10 discusses two markets that have some characteristics of both competition and monopoly. The part concludes by developing labor market theory in Chapter 11.

CHAPTER 8

Perfect Competition

Ostrich farmers in Iowa, Texas, Oklahoma, and other states in the Midwest "stuck their necks out." Many invested millions of dollars converting a portion of their farms into breeding grounds for ostriches. The reason was that mating pairs of ostriches were selling for $75,000. During the late 1980s, ostrich breeders dubbed ostrich meat the low-cholesterol health treat of the 1990s, and ostrich prices rose. The high prices for ostriches fueled profit expectations, and many cattle ranchers deserted their cattle and went into the ostrich business.

Adam Smith concluded that competitive forces are like an "invisible hand" that leads people who simply pursue their own interests and, in the process, serve the interests of society. In a competitive market, when the profit potential in the ostrich business looked good, firms entered this market and started raising ostriches. Over time more and more ostrich farmers flocked to this market, and the ostrich population exploded. As a result, prices and profits tumbled, and the number of ostrich farms declined in the late 1990s. In 2001, demand increased unexpectedly because with the mad cow disease plaguing Europe, people bought alternatives to beef. Profits rose again, causing farmers to increase supply by investing in more ostriches.

This chapter combines the demand, cost of production, and marginal analysis concepts from previous chapters to explain how competitive markets determine prices, output, and profits. Here firms are small, like an ostrich ranch or an alligator farm, rather than huge, like Sears, ExxonMobil, or IBM. Other types of markets in which large and powerful firms operate are discussed in the next two chapters.

In this chapter, you will learn to solve these economics puzzles:

■ Why is the demand curve horizontal for a firm in a perfectly competitive market?

■ Why would a firm stay in business while losing money?

■ In the long run, can alligator farms earn an economic profit?

Perfect Competition

Firms sell goods and services under different market conditions, which economists call **market structures**. A market structure describes the key traits of a market, including the number of firms, the similarity of the products they sell, and the ease of entry into and exit from the market. Examination of the business sector of our economy reveals firms operating in different market structures. In this chapter and the two chapters that follow, we will study four market structures. The first is **perfect competition**, to which this entire chapter is devoted. Perfect, or pure, competition is a market structure characterized by (1) a large number of small firms, (2) a homogeneous product, and (3) very easy entry into or exit from the market. Let's discuss each of these characteristics.

Characteristics of Perfect Competition

Large Number of Small Firms. How many sellers is a large number? And how small is a small firm? Certainly, one, two, or three firms in a market would not be a large number. In fact, the exact number cannot be stated. This condition is fulfilled when each firm in a market has no significant share of total output and, therefore, no ability to affect the product's price. Each firm acts independently, rather than coordinating decisions collectively. For example, there are thousands of independent egg farmers in the United States. If any single egg farmer raises the price, the going market price for eggs is unaffected.

> **Conclusion** *The large-number-of-sellers condition is met when each firm is so small relative to the total market that no single firm can influence the market price.*

Homogeneous Product. In a perfectly competitive market, all firms produce a standardized or homogeneous product. This means the good or service of each firm is identical. Farmer Brown's wheat is identical to Farmer Jones's wheat. Buyers may believe the transportation services of one independent trucker are about the same as another's services. This assumption rules out rivalry among firms in advertising and quality differences.

> **Conclusion** *If a product is homogeneous, buyers are indifferent as to which seller's product they buy.*

Market structure

A classification system for the key traits of a market, including the number of firms, the similarity of the products they sell, and the ease of entry into and exit from the market.

Perfect competition

A market structure characterized by (1) a large number of small firms, (2) a homogenous product, and (3) very easy entry into or exit from the market. Perfect competition is also referred to as pure competition.

Very Easy Entry and Exit. Very easy entry into a market means that a new firm faces no barriers to entry. Barriers can be financial, technical, or government-imposed barriers, such as licenses, permits, and patents. Anyone who wants to try his or her hand at raising ostriches needs only a plot of land and feed.

> **Conclusion** *Perfect competition requires that resources be completely mobile to freely enter or exit a market.*

No real-world market exactly fits the three assumptions of perfect competition. The perfectly competitive market structure is a theoretical or ideal model, but some actual markets do approximate the model fairly closely. Examples include farm products markets, the stock market, and the foreign exchange market.

The Perfectly Competitive Firm as a Price Taker

For model-building purposes, suppose a firm operates in a market that conforms to all three of the requirements for perfect competition. This means that the perfectly competitive firm is a **price taker.** A price taker is a seller that has no control over the price of the product it sells. From the individual firm's perspective, the price of its products is determined by market supply and demand conditions over which the firm has no influence. Look again at the characteristics of a perfectly competitive firm: a small firm that is one among many firms, sells a homogeneous product, and is exposed to competition from new firms entering the market. These conditions make it impossible for the perfectly competitive firm to have the market power to affect the market price. Instead, the firm must adjust to or "take" the market price.

Exhibit 1 is a graphical presentation of the relationship between the market supply and demand for electronic components and the demand curve facing a firm in a perfectly competitive market. Here we will assume that the electronic components industry is perfectly competitive, keeping in mind that the real-world market does not exactly fit the model. Exhibit 1(a) shows market supply and demand curves for the quantity of output per hour. The theoretical framework for this model was explained in Chapter 4. The equilibrium price is $70 per unit, and the equilibrium quantity is 60,000 units per hour.

Because the perfectly competitive firm "takes" the equilibrium price, the individual firm's demand curve in Exhibit 1(b) is *perfectly elastic* (horizontal) at the $70 market equilibrium price. (Note the difference between the firm's units per hour and the industry's thousands of units per hour.) Recall from Chapter 5 that when a firm facing a perfectly elastic demand curve tries to raise its price one penny higher than $70, no buyer will purchase its product [Exhibit 2(a) in Chapter 5.] The reason is that many other firms are selling the same product at $70 per unit. Hence, the perfectly competitive firm will not set the price above the prevailing market price and risk selling zero output. Nor will the firm set the price below the market price because the firm can sell all it wants to at the going price; therefore, a lower price would reduce the firm's revenue.

Price taker

A seller that has no control over the price of the product it sells.

Auctions are often considered to be competitive markets. Auctions over the Internet are now quite common. For example, visit eBay (http://pages.ebay.com/) and click on Live Auctions. To see another live Internet auction, visit "ON-SALE Interactive Marketplace," a live Internet auction house offering computers and electronics (http://www.onsale.com/). For more about how auctions work, visit the Auction Marketing Institute (AMI), a nonprofit professional educational organization (http://www.auctionmarketing.org/).

EXHIBIT 1   **The Market Price and Demand for the Perfectly Competitive Firm**

In part (a), the market equilibrium price is $70 per unit. The perfectly competitive firm in part (b) is a price taker because it is so small relative to the market. At $70, the individual firm faces a horizontal demand curve, *D*. This means that the firm's demand curve is perfectly elastic. If the firm raises its price even one penny, it will sell zero output.

Short-Run Profit Maximization for a Perfectly Competitive Firm

Since the perfectly competitive firm has no control over price, what does the firm control? The firm makes only one decision—what quantity of output to produce that maximizes profit. In this section, we develop two profit maximization methods that determine the output level for a competitive firm. We begin by examining the total revenue–total cost approach for finding the profit-maximizing level of output. Next, we use marginal analysis to show another method for determining the profit-maximizing level of output. The framework for our analysis is the short run with some fixed input, such as factory size.

The Total Revenue–Total Cost Method

Exhibit 2 provides hypothetical data on output, total revenue, total cost, and profit for our typical electronic components producer—Computech. Using Computech as our example allows us to extend the data and analysis

EXHIBIT 2 Short-Run Profit Maximization Schedule for Computech as a Perfectly Competitive Firm

(1) Output (units per hour)	(2) Total revenue	(3) Total cost	(4) Profit [(2) − (3)]	(5) Marginal cost [Δ(3)/Δ(1)]	(6) Marginal revenue [Δ(2)/Δ(1)]
0	$ 0	$100	−$100		
				$ 50	
1	70	150	−80		$70
				34	
2	140	184	−44		70
				24	
3	210	208	2		70
				19	
4	280	227	53		70
				23	
5	350	250	100		70
				30	
6	420	280	140		70
				38	
7	490	318	172		70
				48	
8	560	366	194		70
				59	
9	630	425	205		70
				75	
10	700	500	200		70
				95	
11	770	595	175		70
				117	
12	840	712	128		70

presented in previous chapters. The total cost figures in column 3 are taken from Exhibit 3 in Chapter 7. Total fixed cost at zero output is $100.

Total revenue is reported in column 2 of Exhibit 2 and is computed as the product price times the quantity. In this case, we assume the market equilibrium price is $70 per unit, as determined in Exhibit 1. Because Computech is a price taker, the total revenue from selling 1 unit is $70, from selling 2 units is $140, and so on. Subtracting total cost in column 3 from total revenue in column 2 gives the total profit or loss (column 4) that the firm earns at each level of output. From zero to 2 units, the firm incurs losses, and then a *break-even point* (zero economic profit) occurs at about 3 units per hour. If the firm produces 9 units per hour, it earns the maximum profit of $205 per hour. As output expands, between 9 and 12 units of output, the firm's profit diminishes. Exhibit 3 illustrates graphically that the maximum profit occurs where the vertical distance between the total revenue and the total cost curves is at a maximum.

The Marginal Revenue Equals Marginal Cost Method

A second approach uses *marginal analysis* to determine the profit-maximizing level of output by comparing marginal revenue (marginal benefit) and marginal cost. Column 5 of Exhibit 2 gives marginal cost data calculated in

EXHIBIT 3   **Short-Run Profit Maximization Using the Total Revenue–Total Cost Method**

(a) Total revenue and total cost

This exhibit shows the profit-maximizing level of output chosen by a perfectly competitive firm, Computech. Part (a) shows the relationships among total revenue, total cost, and output, given a market price of $70 per unit. The maximum profit is earned by producing 9 units per hour. At this level of output, the vertical distance between the total revenue and the total cost curves is the greatest.

Profit maximization is also shown in part (b). The maximum profit of $205 per hour corresponds to the profit-maximizing output of 9 units per hour, represented in part (a).

(b) Profit

Marginal revenue (*MR*)

The change in total revenue from the sale of one additional unit of output.

column 5 of Exhibit 3 in Chapter 7. Recall that marginal cost is the change in total cost as the output level changes one unit. As in Exhibit 3 in Chapter 7, these marginal cost data are listed between the quantity of output line entries.

Now we introduce **marginal revenue (*MR*)**, a concept similar to marginal cost. Marginal revenue is the change in total revenue from the sale of one additional unit of output. Stated another way, marginal revenue is the ratio of the change in total revenue to a one-unit change in output. Mathematically,

$$MR = \frac{\text{change in total revenue}}{\text{one-unit change in output}}$$

As shown in Exhibit 1(b), the perfectly competitive firm faces a perfectly elastic demand curve. Because the competitive firm is a price taker, the sale of each additional unit adds to total revenue an amount equal to the price (average revenue, *TR/Q*). In our example, Computech adds $70 to its total revenue each time it sells one unit. Therefore, $70 is the marginal revenue for each additional unit of output in column 6 of Exhibit 2.

Conclusion *In perfect competition, the firm's marginal revenue equals the price that the firm views as a horizontal demand curve.*

Columns 2 and 3 in Exhibit 2 show that both total revenue and total cost rise as the level of output increases. Now compare marginal cost and marginal revenue in columns 5 and 6. As explained, marginal revenue remains equal to the price, but marginal cost follows the J-shaped pattern introduced in Exhibit 3 in Chapter 7. At first, marginal cost is below marginal revenue, and this means that producing each additional unit adds less to total cost than to total revenue. Economic profit therefore increases as output expands from zero until the output level reaches 9 units per hour. Over this output range, Computech moves from a $100 loss to a $205 profit per hour. Beyond an output level of 9 units per hour, marginal cost exceeds marginal revenue, and profit falls. This is because each additional unit of output raises total cost by more than it raises total revenue. In this case, profit falls from $205 to only $128 per hour as output increases from 9 to 12 units per hour.

Our example leads to this question: How does the firm use its marginal revenue and marginal cost curves to determine the profit-maximizing level of output? The answer is that the firm follows a guideline called the *MR = MC* rule: *The firm maximizes profit by producing the output where marginal revenue equals marginal cost.* Exhibit 4 relates the marginal revenue curve equals marginal cost curve condition to profit maximization. In Exhibit 4(a), the perfectly elastic demand is drawn at the industry-determined price of $70. The average total cost (*ATC*) curve is traced from data given earlier in column 8 of Exhibit 3 in Chapter 7. Note that Exhibit 4(a) reproduces Exhibit 4(b) in Chapter 7, except for the omission of the *AFC* curve.

EXHIBIT 4	**Short-Run Profit Maximization Using the Marginal Revenue Equals Marginal Cost Method**

(a) Price, marginal revenue, and cost per unit

(b) Profit

In addition to comparing total revenue and total cost, a firm can find the profit-maximizing level of output by comparing marginal revenue and marginal cost. As shown in part (a), profit is at a maximum where marginal revenue equals marginal cost at $70 per unit. The intersection of the marginal revenue and the marginal cost curves establishes the profit-maximizing output at 9 units per hour.

A profit curve is depicted separately in part (b) to show that the maximum profit occurs when the firm produces at the level of output corresponding to the marginal revenue equals marginal cost point.

Using marginal analysis, we can relate the $MR = MC$ rule to the same profit curve given in Exhibit 3(b), which is reproduced in Exhibit 4(b). Between 8 and 9 units of output, the MC curve is below the MR curve ($59 < $70), and the profit curve rises to its peak. Beyond 9 units of output, the MC curve is above the MR curve, and the profit curve falls. For example, between 9 and 10 units of output, marginal cost is $75, and marginal revenue is $70. Therefore, if the firm produces at 9 units of output rather than, say, 8 or 10 units of output, the MR curve equals the MC curve, and profit is maximized.

You can also calculate profit directly from Exhibit 4(a). At the profit-maximizing level of output of 9 units, the vertical distance between the demand curve and the ATC curve is the *average profit per unit*. Multiplying the average profit per unit times the quantity of output gives the profit [($70 − $47.22) × 9 = $205.22].[1] The shaded rectangle also represents the maximum profit of $205 per hour. Note that we have arrived at the same profit maximization amount ($205) derived by comparing the total revenue and the total cost curves.

Short-Run Loss Minimization for a Perfectly Competitive Firm

Because the perfectly competitive firm must take the price determined by market supply and demand forces, market conditions can change the prevailing price. When the market price drops, the firm can do nothing but adjust its output to make the best of the situation. Here only the marginal approach is used to predict output decisions of firms. Our model therefore assumes that business managers make their output decisions by comparing the *marginal* effect on profit of a *marginal* change in output.

A Perfectly Competitive Firm Facing a Short-Run Loss

Suppose a decrease in the market demand for electronic components causes the market price to fall to $35. As a result, the firm's horizontal demand curve shifts downward to the new position shown in Exhibit 5(a). In this case, there is no level of output at which the firm earns a profit because any price along the demand curve is below the ATC curve.

Since Computech cannot make a profit, what output level should it choose? The logic of the $MR = MC$ rule given in the profit maximization case applies here as well. At a price of $35, $MR = MC$ at 6 units per hour. Comparing parts (a) and (b) of Exhibit 5 shows that the firm's loss will be minimized at this level of output. The minimum loss of $70 per hour is equal to the shaded area, which is the *average loss per unit* times the quantity of output [($35 − $46.66) × 6 = −$70].

---

[1]In Exhibit 3 in Chapter 7, the average total cost figure at 9 units of output was rounded to $47. It also should be noted that there is often no level of output for which marginal revenue exactly equals marginal cost when dealing with whole units of output.

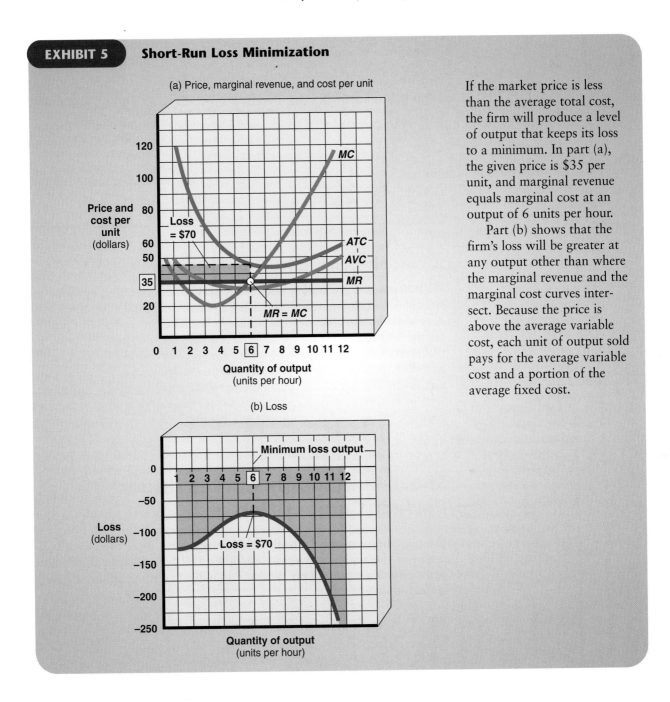

EXHIBIT 5 **Short-Run Loss Minimization**

(a) Price, marginal revenue, and cost per unit

(b) Loss

If the market price is less than the average total cost, the firm will produce a level of output that keeps its loss to a minimum. In part (a), the given price is $35 per unit, and marginal revenue equals marginal cost at an output of 6 units per hour.

Part (b) shows that the firm's loss will be greater at any output other than where the marginal revenue and the marginal cost curves intersect. Because the price is above the average variable cost, each unit of output sold pays for the average variable cost and a portion of the average fixed cost.

Note that although the price is not high enough to pay the average total cost, the price is high enough to pay the average variable cost. Each unit sold also contributes to paying a portion of the average fixed cost, which is the vertical distance between the *ATC* and the *AVC* curves. This analysis leads us to extend the *MR = MC* rule: *The firm maximizes profit or minimizes loss by producing the output where marginal revenue equals marginal cost.*

CHECKPOINT

Should Motels Offer Rooms at the Beach for Only $50 a Night?

Myrtle Beach, South Carolina, with its famous Grand Strand and Calabash seafood, is lined with virtually identical motels. Summertime rates run about $200 a night. During the winter, one can find rooms for as little as $50 a night. Assume the average fixed cost of a room per night, including insurance, taxes, and depreciation, is $50. The average guest-related cost for a room each night, including cleaning service and linens, is $45. Would these motels be better off renting rooms for $50 in the off-season or shutting down until summer?

A Perfectly Competitive Firm Shutting Down

What happens if the market price drops below the *AVC* curve, as shown in Exhibit 6? For example, if the price is $25 per unit, should Computech produce some level of output? The answer is no. The best course of action is for the firm to shut down. *If the price is below the minimum point on the* AVC *curve, each unit produced would not cover the variable cost per unit, and, therefore, operating would increase losses.* The firm is better off shutting down and producing zero output. While shut down, the firm might keep its factory, pay fixed costs, and hope for higher prices soon. If the firm does not believe market conditions will improve, it will avoid fixed costs by going out of business.

Short-Run Supply Curves Under Perfect Competition

The preceding examples provide a framework for a more complete explanation of the supply curve than was given earlier in Chapter 3. We now develop the short-run supply curve for an individual firm and then derive it for an industry.

The Perfectly Competitive Firm's Short-Run Supply Curve

Exhibit 7 reproduces the cost curves from our Computech example. Also represented in the exhibit are three possible demand curves the firm might face—MR_1, MR_2, and MR_3. As the marginal revenue curve moves upward along the marginal cost curve, the $MR = MC$ point changes.

Suppose demand for electronic components begins at a market price close to $30. Point *A* therefore corresponds to a price equal to MR_1, which equals *MC* at the lowest point on the *AVC* curve. At any lower price, the firm cuts its loss by shutting down. At a price of about $30, however, the firm produces 5.5 units per hour. Point *A* is therefore the lowest point on the individual firm's short-run supply curve.

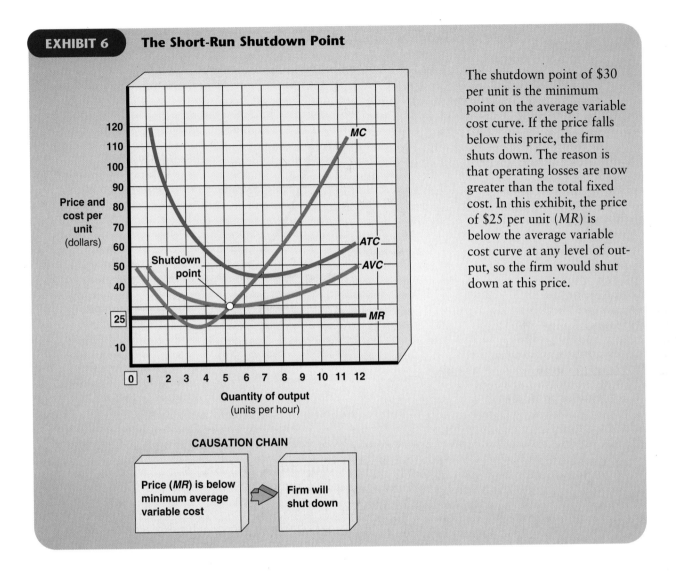

EXHIBIT 6 **The Short-Run Shutdown Point**

Price and cost per unit (dollars)

Shutdown point

MC

ATC

AVC

MR

25

Quantity of output (units per hour)

The shutdown point of $30 per unit is the minimum point on the average variable cost curve. If the price falls below this price, the firm shuts down. The reason is that operating losses are now greater than the total fixed cost. In this exhibit, the price of $25 per unit (*MR*) is below the average variable cost curve at any level of output, so the firm would shut down at this price.

CAUSATION CHAIN

| Price (*MR*) is below minimum average variable cost | → | Firm will shut down |

If the price rises to $45, represented in the exhibit by MR_2, the firm breaks even and earns a normal profit at point *B* with an output of 7 units per hour. As the marginal revenue curve rises, the firm's supply curve is traced by moving upward along its *MC* curve. At a price of $90, point *C* is reached. Now MR_3 intersects the *MC* curve at an output of 10 units per hour, and the firm earns an economic profit. If the price rises higher than $90, the firm will continue to increase the quantity supplied and increase its maximum profit.

We can now define a **perfectly competitive firm's short-run supply curve**. The perfectly competitive firm's short-run supply curve is its marginal cost curve above the minimum point on its average variable cost curve.

Perfectly competitive firm's short-run supply curve

The firm's marginal cost curve above the minimum point on its average variable cost curve.

The Firm's Short-Run Supply Curve

The exhibit shows how the short-run supply curve for Computech is derived. When the price is $30, the firm will produce 5.5 units per hour at point A. If the price rises to $45, the firm will move upward along its marginal cost curve to point B and produce 7 units per hour. At $90, the firm continues to set price equal to marginal cost, and it produces 10 units per hour. Thus, the firm's short-run supply curve is the marginal cost curve above its average variable cost curve.

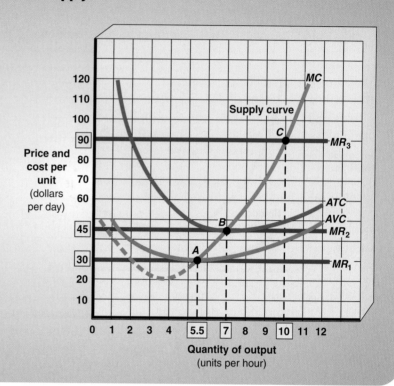

The Perfectly Competitive Industry's Short-Run Supply Curve

Perfectly competitive industry's short-run supply curve

The supply curve derived from the horizontal summation of all firms' marginal cost curves in the industry above the minimum point of each firm's average variable cost curve.

Understanding that the firm's short-run supply curve is the segment of its *MC* curve above its *AVC* curve sets the stage for derivation of the **perfectly competitive industry's short-run supply curve.** The perfectly competitive industry's short-run supply curve is the horizontal summation of the marginal cost curves of all firms in the industry above the minimum point of each firm's average variable cost curve.

In Exhibit 7 in Chapter 3, we drew a market supply curve. Now we will reconstruct this market, or industry, supply curve using more precision. Although in perfect competition there are many firms, we suppose for simplicity that the industry has only two firms, Computech and Western Computer Co. Exhibit 8 illustrates the *MC* curves for these two firms. Each firm's *MC* curve is drawn for prices above the minimum point on the *AVC* curve. At a price of $40, the quantity supplied by Computech is 7 units, and the quantity supplied by Western Computer Co. is 11 units. Now we horizontally add these two quantities and obtain one point on the industry supply curve corresponding to a price of $40 and 18 units. Following this procedure for all prices, we generate the short-run industry supply curve.

Note that the industry supply curve derived above is based on the assumption that input prices remain unchanged as output expands. In the next section, we will learn how changes in input prices affect derivation of the supply curve.

EXHIBIT 8 **Deriving the Industry Short-Run Supply Curve**

Assuming input prices remain constant as output expands, the short-run supply curve for an industry is derived by the horizontal summation of the quantities supplied at each price by all firms in the industry. In this exhibit, we assume there are only two firms in an industry. At $40, Computech supplies 7 units of output, and Western Computer Co. supplies 11 units. The quantity supplied by the industry is therefore 18 units. Other points forming the industry short-run supply curve are obtained similarly.

Short-Run Equilibrium for a Perfectly Competitive Firm

Exhibit 9 illustrates a condition of short-run equilibrium under perfect competition. Exhibit 9(a) represents the equilibrium price and cost situation for one of the many firms in an industry. As shown in the exhibit, the firm earns an economic profit in the short run by producing 9 units. Exhibit 9(b) depicts short-run equilibrium for the industry. As explained earlier, the industry supply curve is the aggregate of each firm's *MC* curve above the minimum point on the *AVC* curve. Including industry demand establishes the equilibrium price of $60 that all firms in the industry must take. The industry's equilibrium quantity supplied is 60,000 units. This state of short-run equilibrium will remain until some factor changes and causes a new equilibrium condition in the industry.

Long-Run Supply Curves Under Perfect Competition

Recall from Chapter 7 that *all* inputs are variable in the long run. Existing firms in an industry can react to profit opportunities by building larger or smaller plants, buying or selling land and equipment, or varying other inputs that are fixed in the short run. Profits also attract new firms to an industry, while losses cause some existing firms to leave the industry. As you will now see, the free entry and exit characteristic of perfect competition is a crucial determinant of the shape of the long-run supply curve.

EXHIBIT 9   **Short-Run Perfectly Competitive Equilibrium**

Short-run equilibrium occurs at point *E*. The intersection of the industry supply and demand curves shown in part (b) determines the price of $60 facing the firm shown in part (a). Given this equilibrium price, the firm represented in part (a) establishes its profit-maximizing output at 9 units per hour and earns an economic profit shown by the shaded area. Note in part (b) that the short-run industry supply curve is the horizontal summation of the marginal cost curves of all individual firms above their minimum average variable cost points.

Long-Run Equilibrium for a Perfectly Competitive Firm

As discussed in Chapter 7, in the long run a firm can change its plant size or any input used to produce a product. This means that an established firm can decide to *leave* an industry if it earns below normal profits (negative economic profits) and that new firms may *enter* an industry in which earnings of established firms exceed normal profits (positive economic profits). This process of entry and exit of firms is the key to long-run equilibrium. If there are economic profits, new firms enter the industry and shift the short-run supply curve to the right. This increase in short-run supply causes the price to fall until economic profits reach zero in the long run. On the other hand, if there are economic losses in an industry, existing firms leave, causing the short-run supply curve to shift to the left, and the price rises. This adjustment continues until economic losses are eliminated and economic profits equal zero in the long run.

Exhibit 10 shows a typical firm in long-run equilibrium. Supply and demand for the market as a whole set the equilibrium price. Thus, in the long run, the firm faces an equilibrium price of $60. Following the *MR* = *MC*

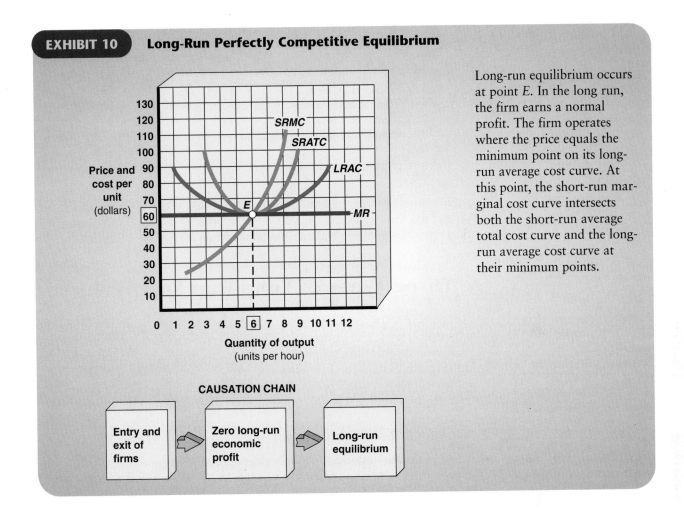

EXHIBIT 10 **Long-Run Perfectly Competitive Equilibrium**

Long-run equilibrium occurs at point *E*. In the long run, the firm earns a normal profit. The firm operates where the price equals the minimum point on its long-run average cost curve. At this point, the short-run marginal cost curve intersects both the short-run average total cost curve and the long-run average cost curve at their minimum points.

CAUSATION CHAIN

Entry and exit of firms ⇒ Zero long-run economic profit ⇒ Long-run equilibrium

rule, the firm produces an equilibrium output of 6 units per hour. At this output level, the firm earns a normal profit (zero economic profit) because marginal revenue (price) equals the minimum point on both the short-run average total cost (*SRATC*) curve and the long-run average cost (*LRAC*) curve. Given the U-shaped *LRAC* curve, the firm is producing with the optimal factory size.

With *SRMC* representing short-run marginal cost, the conditions for long-run perfectly competitive equilibrium can also be expressed as an equality:

$$P = MR = SRMC = SRATC = LRAC$$

As long as none of the variables in the above formula changes, there is no reason for a perfectly competitive firm to change its output level, factory size, or any aspect of its operation. Everything is just right! Because the typical firm is in a state of equilibrium, the industry is also at rest. Under long-run equilibrium conditions, there are neither positive economic profits to attract new firms to enter the industry nor negative economic profits to force existing firms to leave. In long-run equilibrium, maximum efficiency is achieved. The

Are You in Business for the Long Run?

You are considering building a Rent Your Own Storage Center. You are trying to decide whether to build 50 storage units at a total economic cost of $200,000, 100 storage units at a total economic cost of $300,000, or 200 storage units at a total economic cost of $700,000. If you wish to survive in the long run, which size will you choose?

adjustment process of firms moving into or out of the industry is complete, and the firms charge the lowest possible price to consumers. Next, we will discuss how the firm and industry adjust when market demand changes.

Three Types of Long-Run Supply Curves

Perfectly competitive industry's long-run supply curve

The curve that shows the quantities supplied by the industry at different equilibrium prices after firms complete their entry and exit.

There are three possibilities for a **perfectly competitive industry's long-run supply curve.** The perfectly competitive industry's long-run supply curve shows the quantities supplied by the industry at different equilibrium prices after firms complete their entry and exit. The shape of each of these long-run supply curves depends on the response of input prices as new firms enter the industry. The following sections discuss each of these three cases.

Constant-Cost Industry

Constant-cost industry

An industry in which the expansion of industry output by the entry of new firms has no effect on the individual firm's cost curve.

In a **constant-cost industry,** input prices remain constant as new firms enter or exit the industry. A constant-cost industry is an industry in which the expansion of industry output by the entry of new firms has no effect on the firm's cost curves. Exhibit 11(a) reproduces the long-run equilibrium situation from Exhibit 10.

Begin in part (b) of Exhibit 11 at the initial industry equilibrium point E_1 with short-run industry supply curve S_1 and industry demand curve D_1. Now assume the industry demand curve increases from D_1 to D_2. As a result, the industry equilibrium moves temporarily to E_2. Correspondingly, the equilibrium price rises from $60 to $80, and industry output increases from 50,000 to 70,000 units.

The short-run result for the individual firm in the industry happens this way. As shown in part (a) of Exhibit 11, the firm takes the increase in price and adjusts its output from 6 to 7 units per hour. At the higher price and output, the firm changes from earning a normal profit to making an economic profit because the new price is above its *SRATC* curve. All the other firms in the industry make the same adjustment by moving upward along their *SRMC* curves.

In perfect competition, new firms are free to enter the industry in response to a profit opportunity, and they will do so. The addition of new firms shifts the short-run supply curve rightward from S_1 to S_2. Firms will continue to enter the industry until profit is eliminated. This occurs at equilibrium point E_3, where short-run industry demand curve D_2 intersects short-run supply curve S_2. Thus, the entry of new firms has restored the ini-

EXHIBIT 11 **Long-Run Supply in a Constant-Cost Industry**

CAUSATION CHAIN

| Increase in demand sets a higher equilibrium price | ⇨ | Entry of new firms increases supply | ⇨ | Initial equilibrium price is restored | ⇨ | Perfectly elastic long-run supply curve |

Part (b) shows an industry in equilibrium at point E_1, producing 50,000 units per hour and selling them for $60 per unit. In part (a), the firm is in equilibrium, producing 6 units per hour and earning a normal profit. Then industry demand increases from D_1 to D_2, and the equilibrium price rises to $80. Industry output rises temporarily to 70,000 units per hour and the individual firm increases output to 7 units per hour. Firms are now earning an economic profit, which attracts new firms into the industry. In the long run, the entry of these firms causes the short-run supply curve to shift rightward from S_1 to S_2, the price is reestablished at $60, and a new industry equilibrium point, E_3, is established. At E_3, industry output rises to 90,000 units per hour, and the firm's output returns to 6 units per hour. Now the typical firm earns a normal profit, and new firms stop entering the industry. Connecting point E_1 to point E_3 generates the long-run supply curve.

tial equilibrium price of $60. The firm responds by moving downward along its *SRMC* curve until it once again produces 6 units and earns a normal profit.

As shown in the exhibit, the path of these changes in industry short-run equilibrium points traces a horizontal line, which is the industry's long-run supply curve.

Conclusion *The long-run supply curve in a perfectly competitive constant-cost industry is perfectly elastic.*

Now we reconsider Exhibit 11 and ask what happens when the demand curve shifts leftward from D_2 to D_1. Beginning in part (b) at point E_3, the decrease in demand causes the price to fall temporarily below $60. As a result, firms incur short-run losses, and some firms leave the industry. The exodus of firms shifts the short-run supply curve leftward from S_2 to S_1, establishing a new equilibrium at point E_1. This decrease in supply restores the equilibrium price to the initial price of $60 per unit. Once equilibrium is reestablished at E_1, there is a smaller number of firms, each earning a normal profit.

Decreasing-Cost Industry

Input prices fall as new firms enter a **decreasing-cost industry,** and output expands. A decreasing-cost industry is an industry in which the expansion of industry output by the entry of new firms decreases each individual firm's cost curve (cost curve shifts downward). For example, as production of electronic components expands, the price of computer chips may decline. The reason is that greater sales volume allows the suppliers to achieve *economies of scale* and lower their input prices to firms in the electronic component industry. Exhibit 12 illustrates the adjustment process of an increase in demand based on the assumption that our example is a decreasing-cost industry.

Conclusion *The long-run supply curve in a perfectly competitive decreasing-cost industry is downward sloping.*

Increasing-Cost Industry

In an **increasing-cost industry,** input prices rise as new firms enter the industry, and output expands. As this type of industry uses more labor and machines, the demand for greater quantities of these inputs drives up input prices. An increasing-cost industry is an industry in which the expansion of industry output by the entry of new firms increases the individual firm's cost curve (cost curve shifts upward). Suppose the electronic component disc business uses a significant proportion of all electrical engineers in the country. In this case, electrical engineering salaries will rise as firms hire more electrical engineers to expand industry output. In practice, most industries are increasing-cost industries, and, therefore, the long-run supply curve is upward sloping.

Exhibit 13 shows what happens in an increasing-cost industry when an increase in demand causes output to expand. In part (b), the industry is initially in equilibrium at point E_1. As in the previous case, the demand curve shifts rightward from D_1 to D_2, establishing a new short-run equilibrium at E_2. This movement upward along short-run industry supply curve S_1 raises the price in the short run from $60 to $80, resulting in profit for the typical firm. Once again, new firms enter the industry, and the short-run supply curve shifts rightward from S_1 to S_2. Part (a) of Exhibit 13 shows that the

Decreasing-cost industry
An industry in which the expansion of industry output by the entry of new firms decreases the individual firm's cost curve (cost curve shifts downward).

Increasing-cost industry
An industry in which the expansion of industry output by the entry of new firms increases the individual firm's cost curve (cost curve shifts upward).

Firms in increasing-cost industries, such as housing construction, in the long run encounter increased costs as output expands. To learn more about the economics of housing construction, visit the National Association of Home Builders (NAHB) (http://www.nahb.com/).

EXHIBIT 12   **Long-Run Supply in a Decreasing-Cost Industry**

CAUSATION CHAIN

Increase in demand sets a higher equilibrium price ⟹ Entry of new firms increases supply ⟹ Equilibrium price and ATC decrease ⟹ Downward-sloping long-run supply curve

The long-run supply curve for a decreasing-cost industry is downward sloping. The increase in industry demand shown in part (b) causes the price to rise to $80 in the short run. Temporarily, the individual firm illustrated in part (a) earns an economic profit. Higher profits attract new firms, and supply increases. As the industry expands, the average total cost curve for the firm shifts lower, and the firm reestablishes long-run equilibrium at the lower price of $50.

response of the firm's *SRATC* curve to the industry's expansion differs from the constant-cost industry case. In an increasing-cost industry, the firm's *SRATC* curve shifts upward from $SRATC_1$ to $SRATC_2$, corresponding to the new short-run equilibrium at point E_3. At this final equilibrium point, the price of $70 is higher than the initial price of $60. Normal profits are re-established because profits are squeezed from both the price fall and the rise in the *SRATC* curve.

The long-run industry supply curve is drawn by connecting the two long-run equilibrium points of E_1 and E_3. Equilibrium point E_2 is not a long-run equilibrium point because it is not established after the entry of new firms has restored normal profits.

EXHIBIT 13   Long-Run Supply in an Increasing-Cost Industry

CAUSATION CHAIN

| Increase in demand sets a higher equilibrium price | ⇒ | Entry of new firms increases supply | ⇒ | Equilibrium price and *ATC* increase | ⇒ | Upward-sloping long-run supply curve |

This pair of graphs derives the long-run supply curve based on the assumption that input prices rise as industry output expands. Part (b) shows that an increase in demand from D_1 to D_2 causes the price to increase in the short run from $60 to $80. The individual firm represented in part (a) earns an economic profit, and new firms enter the industry, causing an increase in industry supply from S_1 to S_2. As output expands, input prices rise and push up the firm's short-run average total cost curve from $SRATC_1$, to $SRATC_2$. As a result, a new long-run equilibrium price is established at $70, which is above the initial equilibrium price. The long-run supply curve for an increasing-cost industry is upward sloping.

Conclusion *The long-run supply curve in a perfectly competitive increasing-cost industry is upward sloping.*

Finally, given the three models presented, you may ask which is the best choice. The answer is that all three versions are possible for any given industry. Only direct observation of the industry can tell which type of industry it is.

Gators Snapping Up Profits

Applicable Concepts: short-run and long-run competitive equilibrium

In the late 1980s, many farmers who were tired of milking cows, roping steers, and slopping hogs decided to try their hands at a new animal. However, this animal could require a gun for protection while someone feeds it.

Prior to the late 1980s, alligators were on the endangered species list. Under this protection, their numbers grew so large that wandering alligators became pests in Florida neighborhoods and police were exhausted chasing them around. Consequently, the ban on hunting was removed, and shrewd entrepreneurs began seeking big profits by turning gators into farm animals. In fact, gator farming became one of Florida's fastest-growing businesses.

The gators spawned several hot industries. The lizard "look" came back into vogue, and the fashionable sported gator-skin purses, shoes, and belts. Chic didn't come cheap. In New York, gator cowboy boots sold for $1,800, and attaché cases retailed for $4,000. And you could order gator meat at trendy restaurants all along the East Coast. "Why not gator?" asked Red Lobster spokesman Dick Monroe. "Today's two-income households are looking for more variety. And they think it's neat to eat an animal that can eat them."

To meet the demand, Florida doubled the number of its licensed alligator farms compared to the previous four years when they functioned almost entirely as tourist attractions. In 1985, Florida farmers raised 37,000 gators; in 1986, that figure increased by 50 percent. Revenues soared as well. Frank Godwin, owner of Gatorland in Orlando, netted an estimated $270,000 from the 1,000 animals he harvested annually. Improved technology was applied to gator farming in order to boost profits even higher. Lawler Wells, for example, owner of Hilltop Farms in Avon Park, raised 7,000 gators in darkened hothouses that accelerated their growth.[1]

Seven years later, a 1993 article in the *Washington Post* continued the gator tale: "During the late 1980s, gator ranching was booming, and the industry was being compared to a living gold mine. People rushed into the industry. Some farmers became temporarily rich."[2]

In 1995, a *USA Today* interview with a gator hunter provided evidence of long-run equilibrium: "Armed with a pistol barrel attached to the end of an 8-foot wooden pole, alligator hunter Bill Chaplin fires his 'bankstick' and dispatches a six-footer with a single round of .44 magnum ammunition. What's in it for him? Financially, very little.

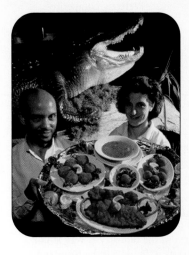

At $3.50 a pound for the meat and $45 a foot for the hide, an alligator is worth perhaps $100 a foot. After paying for skinning and processing, neither hunter nor landowner gets rich."[3]

A 2000 article in the *Dallas Morning News* provides further evidence: "Mark Glass began raising gators in 1995 south of Atlanta. He stated 'I can honestly say I haven't made any money yet, but I hope that's about to change.'"[4]

1. Draw short-run firm and industry competitive equilibriums for a perfectly competitive gator-farming industry before the number of alligator farms in Florida doubled. For simplicity, assume the gator farm is earning zero economic profit. Now show the short-run effect of an increase in demand for alligators.

2. Assuming gator farming is perfectly competitive, explain the long-run competitive equilibrium condition for the typical gator farmer and the industry as a whole.

---

[1] Ron Moreau and Penelope Wang, "Gators: Snapping Up Profits," *Newsweek,* Dec. 8, 1986, p. 68.

[2] William Booth, "Bag a Gator and Save the Species," *Washington Post,* Aug. 25, 1993, p. A1.

[3] J. Taylor Buckley, "S. Carolina Lets Hunters Go for Gators Again," *USA Today,* Sept. 21, 1995, News Section, p. A1.

[4] "More Bite for the Buck," *Dallas Morning News,* Dec. 6, 2000, p. 2A.

KEY CONCEPTS

Market structure
Perfect competition
Price taker
Marginal revenue

Perfectly competitive firm's
    short-run supply curve
Perfectly competitive
    industry's short-run
    supply curve

Perfectly competitive industry's
    long-run supply curve
Constant-cost industry
Decreasing-cost industry
Increasing-cost industry

SUMMARY

■ **Market structure** consists of three market characteristics: (1) the number of sellers, (2) the nature of the product, and (3) the ease of entry into or exit from the market.

■ **Perfect competition** is a market structure in which an individual firm cannot affect the price of the product it produces. Each firm in the industry is very small relative to the market as a whole, all the firms sell a homogeneous product, and firms are free to enter and exit the industry.

■ A **price-taker** firm in perfect competition faces a perfectly elastic demand curve. It can sell all it wishes at the market-determined price, but it will sell nothing above the given market price. This is because so many competitive firms are willing to sell the same product at the going market price.

■ The **total revenue–total cost method** is one way the firm determines the level of output that maximizes profit. Profit reaches a maximum when the vertical difference between the total revenue and the total cost curves is at a maximum.

■ The **marginal revenue equals marginal cost method** is a second approach to finding where a firm maximizes profits. **Marginal revenue** is the change in total revenue from a one-unit change in output. Marginal revenue for a perfectly competitive firm equals the market price. The *MR = MC rule* states that the firm maximizes profit or minimizes loss by producing the output where marginal revenue equals marginal cost. If the price (average revenue) is below the minimum point on the average variable cost curve, the *MR = MC* rule does not apply, and the firm shuts down to minimize its losses.

Marginal revenue equals marginal cost method

Total revenue–total cost method

- The **perfectly competitive firm's short-run supply curve** is a curve showing the relationship between the price of a product and the quantity supplied in the short run. The individual firm always produces along its marginal cost curve above its intersection with the average variable cost curve. The **perfectly competitive industry's short-run supply curve** is the horizontal summation of the short-run supply curves of all firms in the industry.

Firm's short-run supply curve

- **Long-run perfectly competitive equilibrium** occurs when the firm earns a normal profit by producing where price equals minimum long-run average cost equals minimum short-run average total cost equals short-run marginal cost.

Long-run perfectly competitive equilibrium

- In a **constant-cost industry,** total output can be expanded without an increase in the individual firm's average total cost. Because input prices remain constant, the long-run supply curve in a constant-cost industry is perfectly elastic.

- In a **decreasing-cost industry,** lower input prices result in a downward-sloping industry long-run supply curve. As industry output expands, the individual firm's average total cost curve declines (shifts downward), and the long-run equilibrium market price falls.

- In an **increasing-cost industry,** input prices rise as industry output increases. As a result, the individual firm's average total cost curve rises (shifts upward), and the industry long-run supply curve for an increasing-cost industry is upward sloping.

SUMMARY OF CONCLUSION STATEMENTS

- The large-number-of-sellers condition is met when each firm is so small relative to the total market that no single firm can influence the market price.

- If a product is homogeneous, buyers are indifferent as to which seller's product they buy.

- Perfect competition requires that resources be completely mobile to freely enter or exit a market.

- In perfect competition, the firm's marginal revenue equals the price that the firm views as a horizontal demand curve.

- In perfect competition, the firm maximizes profit or minimizes loss by producing the output where marginal revenue equals marginal cost.

- In perfect competition, if the price is below the minimum point on the *AVC* curve, each unit produced would not cover the variable cost per unit. Therefore, the firm shuts down.
- The long-run supply curve in a perfectly competitive constant-cost industry is perfectly elastic.

- The long-run supply curve in a perfectly competitive decreasing-cost industry is downward sloping.
- The long-run supply curve in a perfectly competitive increasing-cost industry is upward sloping.

STUDY QUESTIONS AND PROBLEMS

1. Explain why a perfectly competitive firm would or would not advertise.

2. Does a Kansas wheat farmer fit the perfectly competitive market structure? Explain.

3. Suppose the market equilibrium price of wheat is $2 per bushel in a perfectly competitive industry. Draw the industry supply and demand curves and the demand curve for a single wheat farmer. Explain why the wheat farmer is a price taker.

4. Assuming the market equilibrium price for wheat is $5 per bushel, draw the total revenue and the marginal revenue curves for the typical wheat farmer in the same graph. Explain how marginal revenue and price are related to the total revenue curve.

5. Consider the following cost data for a perfectly competitive firm in the short run:

Output (Q)	Total fixed cost (TFC)	Total variable cost (TVC)	Total cost (TC)	Total revenue (TR)	Profit
1	$100	$120	$___	$___	$___
2	100	200	___	___	___
3	100	290	___	___	___
4	100	430	___	___	___
5	100	590	___	___	___

If the market price is $150, how many units of output will the firm produce in order to maximize profit in the short run? Specify the amount of economic profit or loss. At what level of output does the firm break even?

6. Consider this statement: "A firm should increase output when it makes a profit." Do you agree or disagree? Explain.

7. Consider this statement: "When marginal revenue equals marginal cost, total cost equals total revenue, and the firm makes zero profit." Do you agree or disagree? Explain.

8. Consider Exhibit 14, which shows the graph of a perfectly competitive firm in the short run.
   a. If the firm's demand curve is MR_3, does the firm earn an economic profit or loss?

b. Which demand curve(s) indicates the firm incurs a loss?

c. Which demand curve(s) indicates the firm would shut down?

d. Identify the firm's short-run supply curve.

Exhibit 14 Perfectly Competitive Firm

9. Consider this statement: "The perfectly competitive firm will sell all the quantity of output consumers will buy at the prevailing market price." Do you agree or disagree? Explain your answer.

10. Suppose a perfectly competitive firm's demand curve is below its average total cost curve. Explain the conditions under which a firm continues to produce in the short run.

11. Suppose the industry equilibrium price of residential housing construction is $100 per square foot and the minimum average variable cost for a residential construction contractor is $110 per square foot. What would you advise the owner of this firm to do? Explain.

12. Suppose independent truckers operate in a perfectly competitive industry. If these firms are earning positive economic profits, what happens in the long run to the following: the price of trucking services, the industry quantity of output, the profits of trucking firms? Given these conditions, is the independent trucking industry a constant-cost, an increasing-cost, or a decreasing-cost industry?

ONLINE EXERCISES

Exercise 1

View the Economic Report of the President at http://w3 .access.gpo.gov/eop/. Click on Economic Report of the President and then scroll down to Table B-60 on page 343 and follow these steps.

1. Note the apparel and energy prices for the last 20 years.

2. Why does the price of energy fluctuate more than the price of apparel?

Exercise 2

Visit *USA Today* (http://www.usatoday.com). Click on Markets and study the Dow Jones Industrial Average fluctuation in the chart. Apply the characteristics of a perfectly competitive market structure to the stock market. Why do stock prices fluctuate so much?

Exercise 3

The dream of many people is to start their own business; to be an entrepreneur. Visit the following Internet sites and answer the following questions. *Home-Based Resource Center* (http://www.be-your-own-boss.com/) contains information about how to start and operate a home-based business. Entrepreneur's Help page (http://www.tanned feet.com/) is created by a group of corporate attorneys, financial industry professionals, business owners, and consultants who are all in their twenties or early thirties.

1. What economic factors do entrepreneurs need to consider when starting businesses?

2. How can entrepreneurs maximize the profit generated by their businesses?

3. What resources are available for entrepreneurs and small businesses?

CHECKPOINT ANSWERS

Should Motels Offer Rooms at the Beach for Only $50 a Night?

As long as price exceeds average variable cost, the motel is better off operating than shutting down. Since $50 is more than enough to cover the guest-related variable costs of $45 per room, the firm will operate. The $5 remaining after covering variable costs can be put toward the $50 of fixed costs. Were the motel to shut down, it could make no contribution to these overhead costs. If you said the Myrtle Beach motels should operate during the winter because they can get a price that exceeds their average variable cost, YOU ARE CORRECT.

Are You in Business for the Long Run?

In the long run, surviving firms will operate at the minimum of the long-run average cost curve. The average cost of 50 storage units is $4,000 ($200,000/50), the average cost of 100 storage units is $3,000 ($300,000/100), and the average cost of 200 storage units is $3,500 ($700,000/200). Of the three storage-unit quantities given, the one with the lowest average cost is closest to the minimum point on the *LRAC* curve. If you chose 100 storage units, YOU ARE CORRECT.

PRACTICE QUIZ

For a visual explanation of the correct answers, visit the tutorial at http://tucker.swcollege.com.

1. A perfectly competitive market is *not* characterized by
   a. many small firms.
   b. a great variety of different products.
   c. free entry into and exit from the market.
   d. any of the above.

2. Which of the following is a characteristic of perfect competition?
   a. Entry barriers
   b. Homogeneous products
   c. Expenditures on advertising
   d. Quality of service

3. Which of the following are the same at all levels of output under perfect competition?
   a. Marginal cost and marginal revenue
   b. Price and marginal revenue
   c. Price and marginal cost
   d. All of the above

4. If a perfectly competitive firm sells 100 units of output at a market price of $100 per unit, its marginal revenue per unit is
   a. $1.
   b. $100.
   c. more than $1, but less than $100.
   d. less than $100.

5. Short-run profit maximization for a perfectly competitive firm occurs where the firm's marginal cost equals
   a. average total cost.
   b. average variable cost.
   c. marginal revenue.
   d. all of the above.

6. A perfectly competitive firm sells its output for $100 per unit, and the minimum average variable cost is $150 per unit. The firm should
   a. increase output.
   b. decrease output, but not shut down.
   c. maintain its current rate of output.
   d. shut down.

7. A perfectly competitive firm's supply curve follows the upward sloping segment of its marginal cost curve above the
   a. average total cost curve.
   b. average variable cost curve.
   c. average fixed cost curve.
   d. average price curve.

8. Assume the price of the firm's product in Exhibit 15 is $15 per unit. The firm will produce
   a. 500 units per week.
   b. 1,000 units per week.
   c. 1,500 units per week.
   d. 2,000 units per week.
   e. 2,500 units per week.

Exhibit 15 Marginal Revenue and Cost per Unit Curves

9. In Exhibit 15, the lowest price at which the firm earns zero economic profit in the short run is
   a. $5 per unit.
   b. $10 per unit.
   c. $20 per unit.
   d. $30 per unit.

10. Assume the price of the firm's product in Exhibit 15 is $6 per unit. The firm should
    a. continue to operate because it is earning an economic profit.
    b. stay in operation for the time being even though it is incurring an economic loss.
    c. shut down temporarily.
    d. shut down permanently.

11. Assume the price of the firm's product in Exhibit 15 is $10 per unit. The maximum profit the firm earns is
    a. zero.
    b. $5,000 per week.
    c. $1,500 per week.
    d. $10,500 per week.

12. In Exhibit 15, the firm's total revenue at a price of $10 per unit pays for
    a. a portion of total variable costs.
    b. a portion of total fixed costs.
    c. none of the total fixed costs.
    d. all of the total fixed costs and total variable costs.

13. As shown in Exhibit 15, the short-run supply curve for this firm corresponds to which segment of its marginal cost curve?
    a. *A* to *D* and all points above
    b. *B* to *D* and all points above
    c. *C* to *D* and all points above
    d. *B* to *C* only

14. In long-run equilibrium, the perfectly competitive firm's price is equal to which of the following?
    a. Short-run marginal cost
    b. Minimum short-run average total cost
    c. Marginal revenue
    d. All of the above

15. In a constant-cost industry, input prices remain constant as
    a. the supply of inputs fluctuates.
    b. firms encounter diseconomies of scale.
    c. workers become more experienced.
    d. firms enter and exit the industry.

16. Suppose that, in the long run, the price of feature films rises as the movie production industry expands. We can conclude that movie production is a(an)
    a. increasing-cost industry.
    b. constant-cost industry.
    c. decreasing-cost industry.
    d. marginal-cost industry.

17. Which of the following is *true* of a perfectly competitive market?
    a. If economic profits are earned, then the price will fall over time.
    b. In long-run equilibrium, $P = MR = SRMC = SRATC = LRAC$.
    c. A constant-cost industry exists when the entry of new firms has no effect on their cost curves.
    d. All of the above are true.

CHAPTER 9

Monopoly

P laying the popular board game of Monopoly teaches some of the characteristics of monopoly theory presented in this chapter. In the game version, players win by gaining as much economic power as possible. They strive to own railroads, utilities, Boardwalk, Park Place, and other valuable real estate. Then each player tries to bankrupt opponents by having hotels that charge high prices. A player who rolls the dice and lands on another player's property has no choice—either pay the price or lose the game.

In the last chapter, we studied perfect competition, which may be viewed as the paragon of economic virtue. Why? Under perfect competition, there are many sellers, each lacking any power to influence price. Perfect competition and monopoly are polar extremes. The word *monopoly* is derived from two Greek words

meaning "single seller." A monopoly has the market power to set its price and not worry about competitors. Perhaps your college or university has only one bookstore where you can buy textbooks. If so, students are likely to pay higher prices for textbooks than they would if many sellers competed in the campus textbook market.

This chapter explains why firms do not or cannot enter a

particular market and compete with a monopolist. Then we explore some of the interesting actual monopolies around the world. We study how a monopolist determines what price to charge and how much to produce. The chapter ends with a discussion of the pros and cons of monopoly. Most of the analytical tools required here have been introduced in previous chapters.

In this chapter, you will learn to solve these economics puzzles:

■ Why doesn't the monopolist gouge consumers by charging the highest possible price?

■ How can price discrimination be fair?

■ Are medallion cabs in New York City monopolists?

The Monopoly Market Structure

The model at the opposite extreme from perfect competition is monopoly. Under **monopoly**, the consumer has a simple choice—either buy the monopolist's product or do without it. Monopoly is a market structure characterized by (1) a single seller, (2) a unique product, and (3) impossible entry into the market. Unlike perfect competition, there are no close substitutes for the monopolist's product. Monopoly, like perfect competition, corresponds only approximately to real-world industries, but it serves as a useful benchmark model. Following are brief descriptions of each monopoly characteristic.

Single Seller

In perfect competition, many firms make up the industry. In contrast, a monopoly means that a single firm *is* the industry. One firm provides the total supply of a product in a given market. Local monopolies are more common real-world approximations of the model than national or world market monopolies. For example, the campus bookstore, local telephone service, cable television company, and electric power company may be local monopolies. The only gas station in Nowhere County, Utah, and a hot dog stand at a football game are also examples of monopolies. Nationally, the U.S. Postal Service monopolizes first-class mail.

Unique Product

A unique product means there are *no close substitutes* for the monopolist's product. Thus, the monopolist faces little or no competition. In reality, however, there are few, if any, products that have no close substitutes. For example, students can buy used textbooks from sources other than the campus bookstore, and some textbooks can be purchased over the Internet. Natural gas and oil furnaces are good substitutes for electric heat. Similarly, the fax machine and e-mail are substitutes for mail service, and a satellite dish can replace your local cable television service.

Impossible Entry

In perfect competition, there are no constraints to prevent new firms from entering an industry. In the case of monopoly, extremely high barriers make it very difficult or impossible for new firms to enter an industry. Following are the three major barriers that prevent new firms from entering a market and competing with a monopolist.

Monopoly

A market structure characterized by (1) a single seller, (2) a unique product, and (3) impossible entry into the market.

Congress has granted the U.S. Postal Service (http://www.usps.com/) *the exclusive right to deliver first-class mail.*

For more than 60 years, DeBeers Consolidated Mines (http://www .debeers.com/) *has struggled to maintain a worldwide monopoly on the diamond trade. It owns most of the diamond mines in the world. See also some advertising of DeBeers' at* http://www.adcritic .com/content/debeers-cinema- anniversary.html.

The U.S. Patent and Trademark Office (http://www.uspto.gov/) *grants patents to inventors of products or processes. Visitors may also search for patents* (http://patents .uspto.gov/). *The National Association of Patent Practitioners (NAPP)* (http://www.napp.org/), *a non-profit organization, supports patent practitioners in matters relating to patent laws, their practice, and technological advances.*

Natural monopoly
An industry in which the long-run average cost of production declines throughout the entire market. As a result, a single firm can supply the entire market demand at a lower cost than two or more smaller firms.

Ownership of a Vital Resource. Sole control of the entire supply of a strategic input is one way a monopolist can prevent a newcomer from entering an industry. A famous historical example is Alcoa's monopoly of the U.S. aluminum market from the late nineteenth century until the end of World War II. The source of Alcoa's monopoly was its control of bauxite ore, which is necessary to produce aluminum. Today, it is very difficult for a new professional sports league to compete with the National Football League (NFL) and the National Basketball Association (NBA). Why? NFL and NBA teams have contracts with the best players and leases for the best stadiums and arenas.

Legal Barriers. The oldest and most effective barriers protecting a firm from potential competitors are the result of government franchises and licenses. The government permits a single firm to provide a certain product and excludes competing firms by law. For example, water and sewer service, natural gas, and cable television operate under monopoly franchises established by state and local governments. In many states, the state government runs monopoly liquor stores and lotteries. The U.S. Postal Service has a government franchise to deliver first-class mail.

Government-granted licenses restrict entry into some industries and occupations. For example, the Federal Communications Commission (FCC) must license radio and television stations. In most states, physicians, lawyers, dentists, nurses, teachers, real estate agents, barbers, taxicabs, liquor stores, funeral homes, and other professions and businesses are required to have a license.

Patents and copyrights are another form of government barrier to entry. The government grants patents to inventors, thereby legally prohibiting other firms from selling the patented product for 17 years. Copyrights give creators of literature, art, music, and movies exclusive rights to sell or license their works. The purpose behind granting patents and copyrights is to encourage innovation and new products by guaranteeing exclusive rights to profit from new ideas for a limited period.

Economies of Scale. Why might competition among firms be unsustainable so that one firm becomes a monopolist? Recall the concept of *economies of scale* from the chapter on production costs. As a result of large-scale production, the long-run average cost (*LRAC*) of production falls. This means a monopoly can emerge in time *naturally* because of the relationship between average cost and the scale of an operation. As a firm becomes larger, its cost per unit of output is lower compared to a smaller competitor. In the long run, this "survival of the fittest" cost advantage forces the smaller firms to leave the industry. Because new firms cannot hope to produce and sell output equal or close to that of the monopolist, thereby achieving the monopolist's low costs, they will not enter the industry. Thus, a monopoly can arise over time and remain dominant in an industry even though the monopolist does not own an essential resource or obtain legal barriers.

Economists call the situation in which one seller emerges in an industry because of economies of scale a **natural monopoly**. A natural monopoly is an industry in which the long-run average cost of production declines throughout the entire market. As a result, a single firm can supply the entire

INTERNATIONAL ECONOMICS

Monopolies around the World

Applicable Concept: monopoly

Interesting examples of monopolies can be found in other countries. Let's begin with a historical example. In the sixteenth through eighteenth centuries, monarchs granted monopoly rights for a variety of businesses. For example, Queen Elizabeth I in 1600 chartered the British East India Company and gave it a monopoly over England's trade with India. This company was even given the right to coin money and to make peace or war with non-Christian powers. As a result of its monopoly, the company made substantial profits from the trade in Indian cotton goods, silks, and spices. In the late 1700s, the growing power of the company and huge personal fortunes of its officers provoked more and more government control. Finally, in 1858, the company was abolished ending its trade monopoly, great power, and patronage.

"Diamonds are forever," and perhaps so is the diamond monopoly. DeBeers, a South African corporation, is close to a world monopoly. Through its Central Selling Organization (CSO) headquartered in London, DeBeers controls 80 percent of all the diamonds sold in the world. DeBeers controls the price of jewelry-quality diamonds by requiring suppliers in Russia, Australia, Congo, Botswana, Namibia, and other countries to sell their rough diamonds through DeBeers's CSO. Why do the suppliers of rough diamonds allow DeBeers to set the price and quantity of diamonds sold throughout the world? The answer is that the CSO can put any uncooperative seller out of business. All the CSO has to do is to reach into its huge stockpile of diamonds and flood the market with the type of diamonds being sold by an independent seller. As a result, the price of diamonds plummets in the competitor's market, and it ceases to sell diamonds.

Some observers believe that DeBeers's control of the market might slip in the future. Mines in Australia have become more independent, and diamonds have been found in Canada. There is also a possibility that Russia will not renew its agreement to sell diamonds through DeBeers.

Genuine caviar, the salty black delicacy, is naturally scarce because it comes from the eggs of sturgeon harvested by fisheries from the Caspian Sea near the mouth of the Volga River. After the Bolshevik revolution in 1917, a caviar monopoly was established under the control of the Soviet Ministry of Fisheries and the Paris-based Petrosian Company. The Petrosian brothers limited exports of caviar and pushed up prices to as high as $1,000 a pound for some varieties. As a result of this worldwide monopoly, both the Soviet government and the Petrosian Company earned handsome profits. It is interesting to note that the vast majority of the tons of caviar harvested each year were consumed at government banquets or sold at bargain prices to top Communist party officials.

With the fall of the Soviet Union, it was impossible for the Ministry of Fisheries to control all exports of caviar. Various former Soviet republics claimed jurisdiction and negotiated independent export contracts. Caviar export prices dropped sharply. But caviar lovers should not be too overjoyed. Today, the supply of caviar is dwindling because of overfishing and pollution of the Volga.

market demand at a lower cost than two or more smaller firms. Public utilities, such as the natural gas, water, and local telephone companies, are examples of natural monopolies. The government grants these industries an exclusive franchise in a geographic area so consumers can benefit from the cost savings that occur when one firm in an industry with significant economies of scale sells a large output. The government then regulates these monopolies to prevent exploitation.

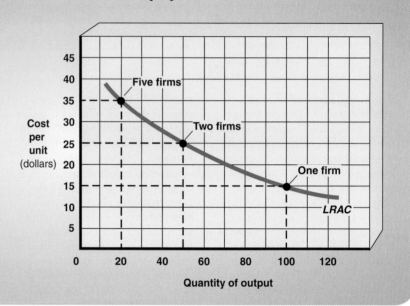

EXHIBIT 1   **Minimizing Costs in a Natural Monopoly**

In a natural monopoly, a single firm in an industry can produce at a lower cost than two or more firms. This condition occurs because the *LRAC* curve for any firm decreases over the relevant range. For example, one firm can produce 100 units at an average cost of $15 and a total cost of $1,500. Two firms in the industry can produce 100 units of output (50 units each) for a total cost of $2,500, and five firms can produce the same output for a total cost of $3,500.

Exhibit 1 depicts the *LRAC* curve for a natural monopoly. A single firm can produce 100 units at an average cost of $15 and a total cost of $1,500. If two firms each produce 50 units, the total cost rises to $2,500. With five firms producing 20 units each, the total cost rises to $3,500. In the chapter on antitrust and regulation, regulation of a natural monopoly will be explored in greater detail.

> **Conclusion** *Because of economies of scale, a single firm in an industry will produce output at a lower per-unit cost than two or more firms.*

Price and Output Decisions for a Monopolist

Price maker

A firm that faces a downward-sloping demand curve and therefore it can choose among price and output combinations along the demand curve.

A major difference between perfect competition and monopoly is the shape of the demand curve, not the shapes of the cost curves. As explained in the previous chapter, a perfectly competitive firm is a *price taker*. In contrast, the next sections explain that a monopolist is a **price maker.** A price maker is a firm that faces a downward-sloping demand curve. This means a monopolist has the ability to select the product's price. In short, a monopolist can set the price with its corresponding level of output, rather than being a helpless pawn at the mercy of the going industry price. To understand the monopolist, we again apply the marginal approach to our hypothetical electronics company—Computech.

Marginal Revenue, Total Revenue, and Price Elasticity of Demand

Suppose engineers at Computech discover an inexpensive miracle electronic device called "SAV-U-GAS" that anyone can easily attach to a car's engine. Once installed, the device raises gasoline mileage to over 100 miles per gallon. The government grants Computech a patent, and the company becomes a monopolist selling these gas-saver gizmos. Because of this barrier to entry, Computech is the only seller in the industry. Although other firms try to compete with this invention, they create poor substitutes. This means the downward-sloping demand curve for the industry and for the monopolist are identical.

Exhibit 2(a) illustrates the demand and the marginal revenue (*MR*) curves for a monopolist such as Computech. As the monopolist lowers its price to increase the quantity demanded, changes in both price and quantity affect the firm's total revenue (price times quantity), as shown graphically in Exhibit 2(b). If Computech charges $150, consumers purchase zero units, and, therefore, total revenue is zero. To sell 1 unit, Computech must lower the price to $138, and total revenue rises from zero to $138. Because the marginal revenue is the increase in total revenue that results from a 1-unit change in output, the *MR* curve at the first unit of output is $138 ($138 − 0). Thus, the price and the marginal revenue from selling 1 unit are equal at $138. To sell 2 units, the monopolist must lower the price to $125, and total revenue rises to $250. The marginal revenue of the second unit is $112 ($250 − $138). Now the marginal revenue from selling the second unit is $13 less than the price received.

As shown in Exhibit 2(a), as the monopolist lowers its price, price is greater than marginal revenue after the first unit of output. Like all marginal measurements, marginal revenue is plotted midway between the quantities.

> **Conclusion** *The demand and marginal revenue curves of the monopolist are downward sloping, in contrast to the horizontal demand and corresponding marginal revenue curves facing the perfectly competitive firm [compare Exhibit 2(a) with Exhibit 1(b) of the previous chapter].*

Starting from zero output, as the price falls, total revenue rises until it reaches a maximum at 6 units, and then it falls—tracing the "revenue hill" drawn in part (b). The explanation was presented earlier in the discussion of price elasticity of demand in Chapter 5. Recall that a straight-line demand curve has an elastic ($E_d > 1$) segment along the upper half, a unit elastic ($E_d = 1$) at the midpoint, and an inelastic ($E_d < 1$) segment along the lower half (see Exhibit 4 in Chapter 5). Recall from Chapter 5 that when $E_d > 1$, total revenue rises as the price drops, and that total revenue reaches a maximum where $E_d = 1$. When $E_d < 1$, total revenue falls as the price falls.

As shown in Exhibit 2(b), total revenue for a monopolist is related to marginal revenue. When the *MR* curve is above the quantity axis (elastic demand), total revenue is increasing. At the intersection of the *MR* curve

EXHIBIT 2 Demand, Marginal Revenue, and Total Revenue

(a) Demand and marginal revenue curves

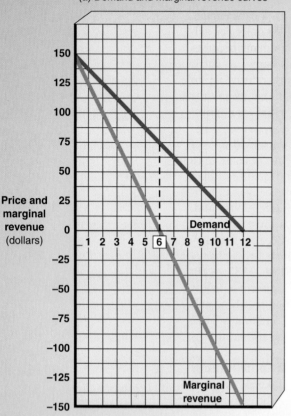

Quantity of output
(units per hour)

**Demand, Marginal Revenue, and Total Revenue
for Computech as a Monopolist**

Output per hour	Price	Total revenue	Marginal revenue
0	$150	$ 0	
			$138
1	138	138	
			112
2	125	250	
			89
3	113	339	
			61
4	100	400	
			40
5	88	440	
			10
6	75	450	0
			−9
7	63	441	
			−41
8	50	400	
			−58
9	38	342	
			−92
10	25	250	
			−107
11	13	143	
			−143
12	0	0	

(b) Total revenue curve

Quantity of output
(units per hour)

Part (a) shows the relationship between the demand and the marginal revenue curves. The *MR* curve is below the demand curve. Between zero and 6 units of output, *MR* > 0; at 6 units of output, *MR* = 0; beyond 6 units of output, *MR* < 0.

The relationship between demand and total revenue is shown in part (b). When the price is $150, total revenue is zero. When the price is set at zero, total revenue is also zero. In between these two extreme prices, the price of $75 maximizes total revenue. This price corresponds to 6 units of output, which is where the *MR* curve intersects the quantity axis, halfway between the origin and the intercept of the demand curve.

and the quantity axis (unit elastic demand), total revenue is at its maximum. When the *MR* curve is below the quantity axis, total revenue is decreasing (inelastic demand). The monopolist will never operate on the inelastic range of its demand curve that corresponds to a negative marginal revenue. The reason is that in this inelastic range the monopolist can increase total revenue by cutting output and raising price. In our example, Computech would not charge a price lower than $75 or produce an output greater than 6 units per hour. Now we turn to the question of what price the monopolist will charge to maximize profit.

In Exhibit 2(a), observe that the *MR* curve cuts the quantity axis at 6 units, which is half of 12 units. Following an easy rule helps locate the point along the quantity axis where marginal revenue equals zero: *The marginal revenue curve for a straight-line demand curve intersects the quantity axis halfway between the origin and the quantity axis intercept of the demand curve.*

Monopoly in the Short Run

Exhibit 3 reproduces the demand and marginal revenue curves from Exhibit 2 and adds cost curves. Exhibit 3(a) illustrates a situation in which Computech can earn monopoly economic profit in the short run. Like the perfectly competitive firm, a monopolist maximizes profit by producing the quantity of output where $MR = MC$ and charging the corresponding price on its demand curve. In this case, 4 units is the quantity at which $MR = MC$. As represented by point *A* on the demand curve, the price at 4 units is $100.

Point *B* represents an average total cost (*ATC*) of $75 at 4 units. Because the price is above the *ATC* curve at the $MR = MC$ output, the monopolist earns a profit of $25 per unit. At the hourly output of 4 units, total profit is $100 per hour, as shown by the shaded area.

Observe that a monopolist charges neither the highest possible price nor the revenue-maximizing price. In Exhibit 3(a), $100 is not the highest possible price. Because Computech is a *price maker,* it could have set a price above $100 and sold less output than 4 units. However, the monopolist does not maximize profit by charging the highest possible price. Any price above $100 does not correspond to the intersection of the *MR* and *MC* curves. Now note that 4 units is below the output level where *MR* intersects the quantity axis and total revenue reaches its peak. Since $MR = 0$ and $E_d = 1$ when total revenue is maximum at 6 units of output, $MC = 0$ must also hold to maximize revenue and profit at the same time. A monopolist producing with zero marginal cost is an unlikely case. Hence, the price charged to maximize profit is higher on the demand curve than the price that maximizes total revenue.

Conclusion *The monopolist always maximizes profit by producing at a price on the elastic segment of its demand curve.*

Having a monopoly does not guarantee profits. A monopolist has no protection against changes in demand conditions. If the demand curve is lower than the *ATC* curve, as shown in Exhibit 3(b), total cost exceeds total

| EXHIBIT 3 | **Profit Maximization and Loss Minimization for a Monopolist** |

Part (a) illustrates a monopolist electronics firm—Computech—maximizing profit by producing 4 units of output, which corresponds to the intersection of the marginal revenue (*MR*) and the marginal cost (*MC*) curves. The price the monopolist charges is $100, which is point *A* on the demand curve. Because $100 is above the average total cost (*ATC*) of $75 at 4 units, the monopolist earns a short-run profit of $100 per hour, represented by the shaded area.

In part (b), Computech is a monopolist minimizing short-run losses by producing 4 units of output. Here the demand curve lies below the *ATC* curve at all points. At a price of $100, the shaded area shows that total revenue is less than total cost and the loss is $100 per hour. If the demand curve shifts leftward, preventing the firm from charging a price that covers the average variable cost (*AVC*), the monopolist loses less money by shutting down.

revenue at any price charged. Because the *MR* = *MC* price of $100 (point *A*) is greater than the *AVC*, but not the *ATC*, the best Computech can do is to minimize its loss. This means the monopolist, like the perfectly competitive firm, produces in the short run where *MR* = *MC* as long as the price exceeds *AVC*. At a price of $100 (point *A*), the *ATC* is $125 (point *B*), and Computech takes a loss of $100 per hour, as represented by the shaded area ($25 × 4 units).

What if *MR* = *MC* at a price below the *AVC* for a monopolist? As under perfect competition, the monopolist will shut down. To operate would only add further to losses.

The Standard Oil Monopoly

Applicable Concept: monopoly

Oil was discovered in western Pennsylvania by Colonel Edwin L. Drake in 1859, and after the Civil War, oil wells sprang up across the landscape. Because oil was plentiful, there was cutthroat competition, and the result was low prices and profits. At this time, John D. Rockefeller, who had grown up selling eggs, was a young Cleveland produce wholesaler in his early twenties. He was doing well in produce, but realized that greater profits could be made in refining oil, where there was less competition than in drilling for oil. So, in 1869, Rockefeller borrowed all the money he could and began with two small oil refineries.

To boost his market power, Rockefeller's Standard Oil of Ohio negotiated secret agreements with the railroads. In addition to information on his competitors' shipments, Rockefeller negotiated contracts with the railroads to pay rebates not only on Standard Oil's oil shipments but also on those of its competitors. Soon Standard Oil was able to buy 21 of its 26 refining competitors in the Cleveland area. As its profits grew, Standard Oil expanded its refin-ing empire by acquiring its own oil fields, railroads, pipelines, and ships. The objective was to control oil from the oil well to the consumer. Over time, Rockefeller came to own a major part of the petroleum industry. Competitors found railroads and pipelines closed to their oil shipments. Rivals that could not be forced out of business were merged with Standard Oil.

In 1870, Standard Oil controlled only 10 percent of the oil industry in the United States. By 1880, Standard Oil controlled over 90 percent of the industry, and its oil was being shipped throughout the world. The more Standard Oil monopolized the petroleum industry, the higher its profits rose, and the greater its power to eliminate competition became. As competitors dropped out of the industry, Rockefeller became a price maker. He raised prices, and Standard Oil's profits soared. Finally, in 1911, Standard Oil was broken up under the Sherman Antitrust Act of 1890.

Monopoly in the Long Run

In perfect competition, economic profits are impossible in the long run. The entry of new firms into the industry drives the product's price down until profits reach zero. Extremely high barriers to entry, however, protect a monopolist.

> **Conclusion** *If the positions of a monopolist's demand and cost curves give it a profit and nothing disturbs these curves, the monopolist will earn profit in the long run.*

In the long run, the monopolist has great flexibility. The monopolist can alter its plant size to lower cost just as a perfectly competitive firm does. But firms such as Computech will not remain in business in the long run when losses persist—regardless of their monopoly status. Facing long-run losses, the monopolist will transfer its resources to a more profitable industry.

In reality, no monopolist can depend on barriers to protect it fully from competition in the long run. One threat is that entrepreneurs will find innovative ways to compete with a monopoly. For example, Computech must fear that firms will use their ingenuity and new electronic discoveries to develop a better and cheaper gasoline-saving device. To dampen the enthusiasm of potential rivals, one alternative for the monopolist is to sacrifice short-run profits to earn greater profits in the long run. Returning to part (a) of Exhibit 3, the monopolist might wish to charge a price below $100 and produce an output greater than 4 units per hour.

Price Discrimination

Our discussion so far has assumed the monopolist charges each customer the same price. What if Computech decides to sell identical SAV-U-GAS units for, say, $50 to truckers and $100 to everyone else? Under certain conditions, a monopolist may practice **price discrimination** to maximize profit. Price discrimination occurs when a seller charges different prices for the same product that are not justified by cost differences.

Price discrimination
The practice of a seller charging different prices for the same product that are not justified by cost differences.

Conditions for Price Discrimination

All monopolists cannot engage in price discrimination. The following three conditions must exist before a seller can price discriminate:

1. The seller must be a price maker and therefore face a downward-sloping demand curve. This means that monopoly is not the only market structure in which price discrimination may occur.

2. The seller must be able to segment the market by distinguishing between consumers willing to pay different prices. Momentarily, this separation of buyers will be shown to be based on different price elasticities of demand.

3. It must be impossible or too costly for customers to engage in **arbitrage**. Arbitrage is the practice of earning a profit by buying a good at a low price and reselling the good at a higher price. For example, suppose your campus bookstore tried to boost profits by selling textbooks at a 50 percent discount to seniors. It would not take seniors long to cut the bookstore's profits by buying textbooks at the low price, selling these texts under the list price to all students who are not seniors, and pocketing the difference. In so doing, even without knowing the word *arbitrage*, the seniors would destroy the bookstore's price discrimination scheme.

Arbitrage
The practice of earning a profit by buying a good at a low price and reselling the good at a higher price.

Although not monopolies, college and university tuition policies meet the conditions for price discrimination. First, lower tuition increases the quantity of openings demanded. Second, applicants' high school grades and SAT scores allow the admissions office to classify "consumers" with different price elasticities of demand. Students with lower grades and SAT scores have fewer substitutes, and their demand curve is less elastic than that of students with higher grades and SAT scores. If the tuition price rises at University X, few students with lower grades will be lost because they have few offers of admission from other universities. On the other hand, the loss of students with higher grades and SAT scores is greater because they have more admissions opportunities. Third, the nature of the product prevents arbitrage. A student cannot buy University X admission at one tuition price and sell it to another student for a higher price.

EXHIBIT 4 **Price Discrimination**

(a) Market for average students

(b) Market for superior students

To maximize profit, University X separates students applying for admission into two markets. The demand curve for admission of average students in part (a) is less elastic than the demand curve for admission of superior students in part (b). Profit maximization occurs when $MR = MC$ in each market. Therefore, University X sets a tuition of T_1 for average students and gives scholarships to superior students, which lowers their tuition to T_2. Using price discrimination, University X earns a greater profit than it would by charging a single price to all students.

Exhibit 4 illustrates how University X price discriminates. For simplicity, assume the marginal cost of providing education to students is constant and therefore represented by a horizontal MC curve. To maximize profit, University X follows the $MR = MC$ rule in each market. Given the different price elasticities of demand, the price at which $MR = MC$ differs for average and superior students. As a result, University X sets a higher tuition, T_1, in the average-student market, where demand is less responsive to the higher price. In the superior-student market, where demand is more responsive, these students receive scholarships, and their tuition is lower at T_2.

Is Price Discrimination Unfair?

Examples of price discrimination abound. Movie theaters offer lower prices for children than for adults. Electric utilities, which are monopolies, charge industrial users of electricity lower rates than residential users. Hotels and restaurants often give discounts to senior citizens. Airlines offer lower fares to groups of vacationers.

The typical reaction to price discrimination is that it is unfair. From the viewpoint of buyers who pay the higher prices, it is. But look at the other side of price discrimination. First, the seller is pleased because price discrimination

Why Don't Adults Pay More for Popcorn at the Movies?

At the movies, adults pay a higher ticket price than children, and each group gets a different-colored ticket. However, when adults and children go to the concession stand, both groups pay the same amount for popcorn and other snacks. Which of the following statements best explains why price discrimination stops at the ticket window? (1) The demand curve for popcorn is perfectly elastic. (2) The theater has no way to divide the buyers of popcorn based on different price elasticities of demand. (3) The theater cannot prevent resale.

increases profits. Second, many buyers benefit from price discrimination by not being excluded from purchasing the product. In Exhibit 4, price discrimination makes it possible for superior students who could not afford to pay a higher tuition to attend University X. Price discrimination also allows retired persons to enjoy hotels and restaurants they could not otherwise afford and enables more children to attend movies.

Comparing Monopoly and Perfect Competition

Now that the basics of the two extremes of perfect competition and monopoly have been presented, we can compare and evaluate these market structures. This is an important assessment because the contrast between the disadvantages of monopoly and the advantages of perfect competition is the basis for many government policies, such as antitrust laws. To keep the analysis simple, we assume the monopolist charges a single price, rather than engaging in price discrimination.

The Monopolist as a Resource Misallocator

Recall the discussion of market efficiency in Chapter 4. This condition exists when a firm charging the equilibrium price uses neither too many nor too few resources to produce a product, so there is no *market failure*. Now you can state this definition of market efficiency in terms of price and marginal cost, as follows: *A perfectly competitive firm that produces the quantity of output at which P = MC achieves an efficient allocation of resources.* This means production reaches the level of output where the price of the last unit produced matches the cost of producing it.

Exhibit 5(a) shows that a perfectly competitive firm produces the quantity of output at which $P = MC$. The price, P_c (marginal benefit), of the last unit produced equals the marginal cost of the resources used to produce it. In contrast, the monopolist shown in Exhibit 5(b) charges a price, P_m, greater than marginal cost, $P > MC$. Therefore, consumers are short-changed because the marginal benefit of the last unit produced exceeds the

EXHIBIT 5   **Comparing a Perfectly Competitive Firm and a Monopolist**

The perfectly competitive firm in part (a) sets $P = MC$ and produces Q_c output. Therefore, at the last unit of output, the marginal benefit is equal to the marginal cost of resources used to produce it. This condition means perfect competition achieves efficiency.

Part (b) shows that the monopolist produces output Q_m where $P > MC$. By so doing, consumers are shortchanged because the marginal benefit of the last unit produced exceeds the marginal cost of producing it. Under monopoly, inefficiency occurs because the monopolist underallocates resources to the production of its product. As a result, Q_m is less than Q_c.

marginal cost of producing it. Consumers want the monopolist to use more resources and produce additional units, but the monopolist restricts output to maximize profit.

Conclusion *A monopolist is characterized by inefficiency because resources are underallocated to the production of its product.*

Perfect Competition Means More Output for Less

Exhibit 6 presents a comparison of perfect competition and monopoly in the same graph. Suppose the industry begins as perfectly competitive. The market demand curve, D (equal to MR), and the market supply curve, S, establish a perfectly competitive price, P_c, and output, Q_c. Recall from Exhibit 8 in the previous chapter that the competitive industry's supply curve, S, is the horizontal sum of the marginal cost (MC) curves of all the firms in the industry.

Now let's suppose the market structure changes when one firm buys out all the competing firms and the industry becomes a monopoly. Assume further that the demand and cost curves are unaffected by this dramatic change.

EXHIBIT 6   The Impact of Monopolizing an Industry

Assume an industry is perfectly competitive, with market demand curve D and market supply curve S. The market supply curve is the horizontal summation of all the individual firms' marginal cost curves above their minimum average variable costs. The intersection of market supply and market demand establishes the equilibrium price of P_c and the equilibrium quantity of Q_c. Now assume the industry suddenly changes to a monopoly. The monopolist produces the $MR = MC$ output of Q_m, which is less than Q_c. By restricting output to Q_m, the monopolist is able to charge the higher price of P_m.

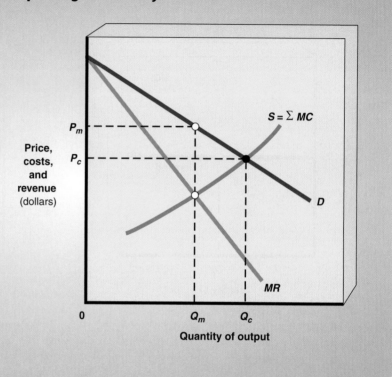

In a monopoly, the industry demand curve *is* the monopolist's demand curve. Because the single firm is a price maker, the MR curve lies below the demand curve. The industry supply curve now becomes the MC curve for the monopolist. To maximize profit, the monopolist sets $MR = MC$ by restricting the output to Q_m and raising the price to P_m.

Conclusion *Monopoly harms consumers on two fronts. The monopolist charges a higher price and produces a lower output than would result under a perfectly competitive market structure.*

The Case against and for Monopoly

So far, a strong case has been made against monopoly and in favor of perfect competition. Now it is time to pause and summarize the economist's case against monopoly:

■ A monopolist "gouges" consumers by charging a higher price than would be charged under perfect competition.

■ Because a monopolist restricts output in order to maximize profit, too few resources are used to produce the product. Stated differently, the monopolist misallocates resources by charging a price greater than

New York Taxicabs: Where Have All the Fare Flags Gone?

Applicable Concepts: perfect competition versus monopoly

In the 1920s, New York taxicabs were competitive. There was no limit on the number of taxis, and hack licenses were only $10. Cabbies could choose among three different flags to attach to their cars. A red flag cab charged a surcharge for extra passengers. A white flag signaled no surcharge for extra passengers. A green flag meant the cabbie was offering a discount fare. Price wars often erupted, and the vast majority of cabbies flew the green flags and charged bargain fares. One strategy was to fly the red flag (high rate) during rush hour and the green flag to offer discounts at off-peak times. Taxi companies also offered a variety of cabs—old, new, big, and small.

As years passed, the system changed, and currently the Taxi and Limousine Commission sets rates and imposes regulations. One law created a monopoly by requiring all cabs accepting street hails to be painted yellow and possess a medallion. That little plastic medallion on a yellow taxicab hood costs more than $250,000, and a 1937 law limits the number of medallions. On the other hand, it is illegal for cabs without medallions to cruise the streets and pick up passengers who hail them, although the law is often ignored. Nonmedallion cabs are authorized to respond only to customers who have ordered the cab in advance by phone or other means. There's no limit on the number of these cabs or what the drivers may charge.

A *New York Times* article described results of this dual system:

While today's 12,187 yellow cabs concentrate on Manhattan below 125th Street, there's a much larger fleet of radio-dispatched cars that handles business in upper Manhattan and the other boroughs. "The outer boroughs generally get better service because there's competition out there," says Edward Rogoff [professor of management at Baruch College]. "By and large, the nonmedallion cars are better vehicles with more experienced drivers who carry more insurance than the yellow cabs."[1]

In a personal interview with the author, Professor Rogoff estimated that, in general, nonmedallion vehicles charge about 25 percent less than medallion cabs.[2] How-

ever, established nonmedallion vehicle owners also want the city to make it tougher for new companies to enter the nonmedallion market. "What we want is a little monopoly help from the government," said Robert Mackle, an official of Skyline CreditRide, a cooperative of owner-drivers of black cars.[3]

In 2001, a slowdown in the economy forced nonmedallion taxicabs to become more aggressive in picking up street hails. The medallion taxicabs struck back with radio ads telling consumers not to take nonmedallion taxis because these drivers are not as qualified and trained as medallion taxi drivers.

ANALYZE THE ISSUE

Use a graph to compare the price and output of medallion yellow cabs in New York City before and after the 1920s.

---

[1] John Tierney, "You'll Wonder Where the Yellow Went," *New York Times*, July 12, 1998, Section 6, p. 18.
[2] Personal interview, 2001.
[3] Winston Williams, "Owners Bewail Flood of Cabs in New York," *New York Times*, Apr. 10, 1989, p. B1.

marginal cost. In perfectly competitive industries, price is set equal to marginal cost, and the result is an optimal allocation of resources.

- Long-run economic profit for a monopolist exceeds the zero economic profit in the long run for a perfectly competitive firm.

- To the extent that the monopolist is a rich John D. Rockefeller, for example, and consumers of oil are poor, monopoly alters the distribution of income in favor of the monopolist.

Not all economists agree that monopoly is bad. The late Joseph Schumpeter and John Kenneth Galbraith have praised monopoly power. They have argued that the rate of technological change is likely to be greater under monopoly than under perfect competition. In their view, monopoly profits afford giant monopolies the financial strength to invest in the well-equipped laboratories and skilled labor necessary to create technological change.

The counterargument is that monopolists are slow to innovate. Freedom from direct competition means the monopolist is not motivated and therefore tends to stick to the "conventional wisdom." As Nobel laureate Sir John Hicks put it, "The best of all monopoly profit is a quiet life." In short, monopoly offers the opportunity to relax a bit and not worry about the "rat race" of technological change.

What does research on this issue suggest? Not surprisingly, many attempts have been made to verify or refute the effect of market structure on technological change. Unfortunately, the results to date have been inconclusive. For all we know, a mix of large and small firms in an industry may be the optimal mix to create technological change.

KEY CONCEPTS

Monopoly
Natural monopoly

Price maker
Price discrimination

Arbitrage

SUMMARY

- **Monopoly** is a single seller facing the entire industry demand curve because it is the industry. The monopolist sells a unique product, and extremely high barriers to entry protect it from competition.

- **Barriers to entry** that prevent new firms from entering an industry are (1) ownership of an essential resource, (2) legal barriers, and (3) economies of scale. Government franchises, licenses, patents, and copyrights are the most obvious legal barriers to entry.

■ A **natural monopoly** arises because of the existence of economies of scale in which the long-run average cost (*LRAC*) curve falls as production increases. Without government restrictions, economies of scale allow a single firm to produce at a lower cost than any firm producing a smaller output. Thus, smaller firms leave the industry, new firms fear competing with the monopolist, and the result is that a monopoly emerges *naturally*.

Natural monopoly

■ A **price-maker** firm faces a downward-sloping demand curve. It therefore searches its demand curve to find the price-output combination that maximizes its profit and minimizes its loss.

■ The **marginal revenue** and demand curves are downward sloping for a monopolist. The marginal revenue curve for a monopolist is below the demand curve, and the total revenue curve reaches its maximum where marginal revenue equals zero.

■ **Price elasticity of demand** corresponds to sections of the marginal revenue curve. When *MR* is positive, price elasticity of demand is elastic, $E_d > 1$. When *MR* is equal to zero, price elasticity of demand is unit elastic, $E_d = 1$. When *MR* is negative, price elasticity of demand is inelastic, $E_d < 1$.

■ The **short-run profit-maximizing monopolist,** like the perfectly competitive firm, locates the profit-maximizing price by producing the output where the *MR* and the *MC* curves intersect. If this price is less than the average variable cost (*AVC)* curve, the monopolist shuts down to minimize losses.

Short-run monopolist

- The **long-run profit-maximizing monopolist** earns a profit because of barriers to entry. If demand and cost conditions prevent the monopolist from earning a profit, it will leave the industry.

- **Price discrimination** allows the monopolist to increase profits by charging buyers different prices, rather than a single price. Three conditions are necessary for price discrimination: (1) the demand curve must be downward sloping, (2) buyers in different markets must have different price elasticities of demand, and (3) buyers must be prevented from reselling the product at a higher price than the purchase price.

- **Monopoly disadvantages** include the following: (1) a monopolist charges a higher price and produces less output than a perfectly competitive firm, (2) resource allocation is inefficient because the monopolist produces less than if competition existed, (3) monopoly produces higher long-run profits than if competition existed, and (4) monopoly transfers income from consumers to producers to a greater degree than under perfect competition.

Price discrimination

Monopoly disadvantages

SUMMARY OF CONCLUSION STATEMENTS

- Because of economies of scale, a single firm in an industry will produce output at a lower per-unit cost than two or more firms.

- The demand and marginal revenue curves of the monopolist are downward sloping, in contrast to the horizontal demand and corresponding revenue curves facing the perfectly competitive firm.

■ The marginal revenue curve for a straight-line demand curve intersects the quantity axis halfway between the origin and the quantity axis intercepts of the demand curve.

■ The monopolist always maximizes profit by producing at a price on the elastic segment of its demand curve.

■ If the positions of a monopolist's demand and cost curves give it a profit and nothing disturbs these curves, the monopolist will earn profit in the long run.

■ A monopolist is characterized by inefficiency because resources are underallocated to the production of its product.

■ Monopoly harms consumers on two fronts. The monopolist charges a higher price and produces a lower output than would result under a perfectly competitive market structure.

STUDY QUESTIONS AND PROBLEMS

1. Using the three characteristics of monopoly, explain why each of the following is a monopolist:
   a. Local telephone company
   b. San Francisco 49ers football team
   c. U.S. Postal Service

2. Why is the demand curve facing a monopolist downward sloping whereas the demand curve facing a perfectly competitive firm is horizontal?

3. Suppose an investigator finds that the prices charged for drugs at a hospital are higher than the prices charged for the same products at drugstores in the area served by the hospital. What might the explanation for this situation be?

4. Explain why you agree or disagree with the following statements:
   a. "All monopolies are created by the government."
   b. "The monopolist charges the highest possible price."
   c. "The monopolist never takes a loss."

5. Suppose the average cost of producing a kilowatt-hour of electricity is lower for one firm than for another firm serving the same market. Without the government granting a franchise to one of these competing power companies, explain why a single seller is likely to emerge in the long run.

6. Use the following demand schedule for a monopolist to calculate total revenue and marginal revenue. For each price, indicate whether demand is elastic, unit elastic, or inelastic. Using the data from the demand schedule, graph the demand curve, the marginal revenue curve, and the total revenue curve. Identify the elastic, unit elastic, and inelastic segments along the demand curve.

Price	Quantity demanded	Total revenue	Marginal revenue	Price elasticity of demand
$5.00	0	$_____		_____
4.50	1	_____	$_____	_____
4.00	2	_____	_____	_____
3.50	3	_____	_____	_____
3.00	4	_____	_____	_____
2.50	5	_____	_____	_____
2.00	6	_____	_____	_____
1.50	7	_____	_____	_____
1.00	8	_____	_____	_____
.50	9	_____	_____	_____
0	10	_____	_____	_____

7. Make the unrealistic assumption that production is costless for the monopolist in question 6. Given the data from the above demand schedule, what price will the monopolist charge, and how much output should the firm produce? How much profit will the firm earn? When marginal cost is above zero, what will be the effect on the price and output of the monopolist?

8. Explain why a monopolist would never produce in the inelastic range of the demand curve.

9. In each of the following cases, state whether the monopolist would increase or decrease output:
   a. Marginal revenue exceeds marginal cost at the output produced.
   b. Marginal cost exceeds marginal revenue at the output produced.

10. Suppose the demand and cost curves for a monopolist are as shown in Exhibit 7 below. Explain what price the monopolist should charge and how much output it should produce.

Exhibit 7 A Monopoly in the Short Run

11. Which of the following constitute price discrimination?
    a. A department store has a 25-percent-off-the-price sale.
    b. A publisher sells economics textbooks at a lower price in North Carolina than in New York.
    c. The Japanese sell cars at higher prices in the United States than in Japan.
    d. The phone company charges higher long-distance rates during the day.

12. Suppose the candy bar industry approximates a perfectly competitive industry. Suppose also that a single firm buys all the assets of the candy bar firms and establishes a monopoly. Contrast these two market structures with respect to price, output, and allocation of resources. Draw a graph of the market demand and market supply for candy bars before and after the takeover.

ONLINE EXERCISES

Exercise 1

Visit Engagement Diamond FAQ (http://www.wam.umd.edu/~sek/wedding/mlynek.html), and select 3: From a Mine to Your Finger. How has DeBeers maintained a worldwide monopoly in diamonds?

Exercise 2

Visit your university's Internet site. If you are not sure of the address, visit http://www.universities.com/. Does your university specify admission standards at its site? Is anything said about scholarships? Does your university price discriminate?

Exercise 3

Consider the definition of a monopolist. Can the U.S. Postal Service (http://www.usps.com/) be considered a monopoly in first-class postage? Why or why not? Federal Express Corporation (http://www.fedex.com/) and United Parcel Service of America, Inc. (http://www.ups.com/) also deliver letters and packages. What has happened to the price elasticity of demand for first-class letters?

Exercise 4

Why can't two baseball teams succeed in a city like Kansas City (http://www.royals.mlb.com/NASApp/mlb/kc/homepage/kc_homepage.jsp) while both the New York Yankees (http://yankees.mlb.com/NASApp/mlb/nyy/homepage/nyy_homepage.jsp) and the New York Mets (http://www.mets.mlb.com/NASApp/mlb/nym/homepage/nym_homepage.jsp) can succeed in New York City?

CHECKPOINT ANSWER

Why Don't Adults Pay More for Popcorn at the Movies?

First, there are no other popcorn sellers in the lobby, so the theater is a price maker for popcorn and the demand curve slopes downward. Second, the theater could easily set up different lines for adults and children and charge different prices for popcorn. Third, is there a practical way to prevent resale? Does the theater want to try to stop children who resell popcorn to their parents, friends, and other adults? If you said theaters do not practice price discrimination at the concession counter because resale cannot be prevented, YOU ARE CORRECT.

PRACTICE QUIZ

For a visual explanation of the correct answers, visit the tutorial at http://tucker.swcollege.com.

1. A monopolist always faces a demand curve that is
   a. perfectly inelastic.
   b. perfectly elastic.
   c. unit elastic.
   d. the same as the market demand curve.

2. A monopolist sets the
   a. price at which marginal revenue equals zero.
   b. price that maximizes total revenue.
   c. highest possible price on its demand curve.
   d. price at which marginal revenue equals marginal cost.

3. A monopolist sets
   a. the highest possible price.
   b. a price corresponding to minimum average total cost.
   c. a price equal to marginal revenue.
   d. a price determined by the point on the demand curve corresponding to the level of output at which marginal revenue equals marginal cost.
   e. none of the above.

4. Which of the following is true for the monopolist?
   a. Economic profit is possible in the long run.
   b. Marginal revenue is less than the price charged.
   c. Profit maximizing or loss minimizing occurs when marginal revenue equals marginal cost.
   d. All of the above are true.

5. As shown in Exhibit 8, the profit-maximizing or loss-minimizing output for this monopolist is
   a. 100 units per day.
   b. 200 units per day.
   c. 300 units per day.
   d. 400 units per day.

6. As shown in Exhibit 8, this monopolist
   a. should shut down in the short run.
   b. should shut down in the long run.
   c. earns zero economic profit.
   d. earns positive economic profit.

7. To maximize profit or minimize loss, the monopolist in Exhibit 8 should set its price at
   a. $30 per unit.
   b. $25 per unit.
   c. $20 per unit.
   d. $10 per unit.
   e. $40 per unit.

8. If the monopolist in Exhibit 8 operates at the profit-maximizing output, it will earn total revenue to pay about what portion of its total fixed cost?
   a. None
   b. One-half
   c. Two-thirds
   d. All total fixed costs

9. For a monopolist to practice effective price discrimination, one necessary condition is
   a. identical demand curves among groups of buyers.
   b. differences in the price elasticity of demand among groups of buyers.
   c. a homogeneous product.
   d. none of the above.

10. What is the act of buying a commodity at a lower price and selling it at a higher price?
    a. Buying short
    b. Discounting
    c. Tariffing
    d. Arbitrage

11. Under both perfect competition and monopoly, a firm
    a. is a price taker.
    b. is a price maker.
    c. will shut down in the short run if price falls short of average total cost.
    d. always earns a pure economic profit.
    e. sets marginal cost equal to marginal revenue.

Exhibit 8 Profit Maximizing for a Monopolist

CHAPTER 10

Monopolistic Competition and Oligopoly

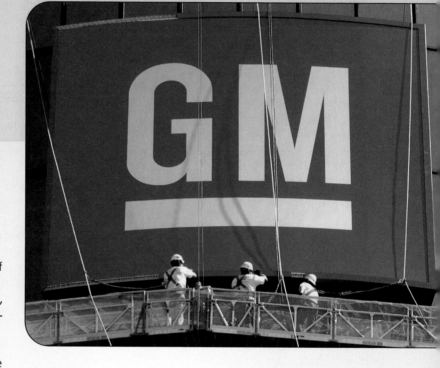

Suppose your favorite restaurant is Ivan's Oyster Bar. Ivan's does not fit either of the two extreme models studied in the previous two chapters. Instead, Ivan's characteristics are a blend of monopoly and perfect competition. For starters, like a monopolist, Ivan's demand curve is downward-sloping. This means Ivan's is a *price maker* because it can charge a higher price for seafood and lose some customers, but many loyal customers will keep coming. The reason is that Ivan's distinguishes its product from the competition by advertising, first-rate service, a great salad bar, and other attributes. In short, like a monopolist, Ivan's has a degree of *market power*, which allows it to restrict output and maximize profit. But like a perfectly competitive firm and unlike a monopolist, Ivan's is not the only place to buy a seafood dinner in town. It must share the market with many other restaurants within an hour's drive.

The small Ivan's Oyster Bars and the gigantic General Motors of the world represent most of the firms with which you deal. These firms compete in two market structures: *monopolistic competition* and *oligopoly*. Ivan's operates in the former, and General Motors belongs to the latter. The theories of perfect competition and monopoly from the previous two chapters will help you understand the impact of monopolistic competition and oligopoly market structures on the price and output decisions of real-world firms.

 In this chapter, you will learn to solve these economics puzzles:

■ Why will Ivan's Oyster Bar make zero economic profit in the long run?

■ Why do OPEC and other cartels tend to break down?

■ Are Cheerios, Rice Krispies, and other brands sold by firms in the breakfast cereal industry produced under monopolistic competition or oligopoly?

■ How does the NCAA Final Four basketball tournament use imperfect competition?

The Monopolistic Competition Market Structure

Economists define **monopolistic competition** as a market structure characterized by (1) many small sellers, (2) a differentiated product, and (3) easy market entry and exit. Monopolistic competition fits numerous real-world industries. Following is a brief explanation of each characteristic.

Many Small Sellers

Under monopolistic competition, as under perfect competition, the exact number of firms cannot be stated. Ivan's Oyster Bar, described in the chapter preview, is an example of a monopolistic competitor. Ivan assumes that his restaurant can set prices slightly higher or improve service *independently* without fear that competitors will react by changing their prices or giving better service. Thus, if any single seafood restaurant raises its price, the going market price for seafood dinners increases by a very small amount.

> **Conclusion** *The many-sellers condition is met when each firm is so small relative to the total market that its pricing decisions have a negligible effect on the market price.*

Differentiated Product

The key feature of monopolistic competition is **product differentiation.** Product differentiation is the process of creating real or apparent differences between goods and services. A differentiated product has close, but not perfect, substitutes. Although the products of each firm are highly similar, the consumer views them as somewhat different or distinct. There may be 25 seafood restaurants in a given city, but they are not all the same. They differ in location, atmosphere, quality of food, quality of service, and so on.

Product differentiation can be real or imagined. It does not matter which is correct so long as consumers believe such differences exist. For example, many customers think Ivan's has the best seafood in town even though other restaurants actually offer a similar product. The importance of this consumer viewpoint is that they are willing to pay a slightly higher price for Ivan's seafood. This gives Ivan the incentive to appear on local TV cooking shows and to buy ads showing him personally catching the seafood he serves.

> **Conclusion** *When a product is differentiated, buyers are not indifferent as to which seller's product they buy.*

Monopolistic competition
A market structure characterized by (1) many small sellers, (2) a differentiated product, and (3) easy market entry and exit.

Product differentiation
The process of creating real or apparent differences between goods and services.

How do Pepsi (http://www.pepsi.com/) and Coca-Cola (http://www.cocacola.com/) use their Web sites to differentiate their numerous soft drinks?

Nonprice competition

The situation in which a firm competes using advertising, packaging, product development, better quality, and better service, rather than lower prices.

The example of Ivan's restaurant makes it clear that under monopolistic competition rivalry centers on **nonprice competition** in addition to price competition. With nonprice competition, a firm competes using advertising, packaging, product development, better quality, and better service, rather than lower prices. Nonprice competition means there is an important distinction among monopolistic competition, perfect competition, and monopoly. Under perfect competition, there is no nonprice competition because the product is identical for all firms. Likewise, the monopolist has little incentive to engage in nonprice competition because it sells a unique product.

Easy Entry and Exit

Unlike a monopoly, firms in a monopolistically competitive market face low barriers to entry. But entry into a monopolistically competitive market is not quite as easy as entry into a perfectly competitive market. Because monopolistically competitive firms sell differentiated products, it is somewhat difficult for new firms to become established. Many persons who want to enter the seafood restaurant business can get loans, lease space, and start serving seafood without too much trouble. However, these new seafood restaurants may at first have difficulty attracting consumers because of Ivan's established reputation as the best seafood restaurant in town.

Monopolistic competition is by far the most common market structure in the United States. Examples include retail firms, such as grocery stores, hair salons, gas stations, video rental stores, diet centers, and restaurants.

The Monopolistically Competitive Firm as a Price Maker

Given the characteristics of monopolistic competition, you might think the monopolistic competitor is a *price taker*, but it is not. The primary reason is that its product is differentiated. This gives the monopolistically competitive firm, like the monopolist, limited control over its price. When the price is raised, brand loyalty ensures some customers will remain steadfast. As for a monopolist, the demand curve and the corresponding marginal revenue curve for a monopolistically competitive firm are downward sloping. But the existence of close substitutes causes the demand curve for the monopolistically competitive firm to be more elastic than the demand curve for a monopolist. When Ivan's raises its price 10 percent, the quantity of seafood dinners demanded declines, say, 30 percent. Instead, if Ivan's had a monopoly, no close substitutes would exist, and consumers would be less sensitive to price changes. As a monopolist, the same 10 percent hike might lose Ivan's only, say, 15 percent of its quantity of seafood dinners demanded.

Conclusion *The demand curve for a monopolistically competitive firm is less elastic (steeper) than for a perfectly competitive firm and more elastic (flatter) than for a monopolist.*

Advertising Pros and Cons

Before presenting the complete graphical models for monopolistic competition, let's pause to examine the topic of advertising further. As explained at the beginning of this chapter, a distinguishing feature of a monopolistically competitive firm is that it engages in nonprice competition by using expensive ads to differentiate its product. Instead of lowering the price, the firm's goal is to convince customers that its product is really different from its rivals' products. Monopolistically competitive firms are frequently running ads that feature lower prices, a higher quality of service, or new products to win customers. Ads proclaim that products make you smarter, better looking, or nicer to be around. Graphically, the firm hopes advertising will make the demand curve less elastic and shift it rightward by changing consumers' tastes in favor of its product. Profit rises when advertising increases the firm's revenue more than the cost of the advertising.

Exhibit 1 illustrates the effect of advertising on the long-run average cost (*LRAC*) curve for Yummy Frozen Yogurt. Yummy competes with It Can't Be Yogurt and five other stores in the northeastern part of town. Without advertising, the $LRAC_1$ curve represents Yummy's average cost. At the given price charged, the quantity demanded is 6,000 frozen yogurt dishes per month, and the average cost is $2 per dish (point *A*).

To increase profits in the short run, Yummy decides to advertise. Yummy knows, however, that in the long run new entrants and rising costs will shrink all yogurt stores' economic profits to zero. Then Yummy must come up with some new product to boost sales. But for now, suppose Yummy's advertising campaign is successful and demand increases. Then two short-run effects occur. One is an upward shift in the average cost curve at any level of output from $LRAC_1$ to $LRAC_2$. The vertical distance between these two curves measures the additional average fixed cost of advertising. Another effect is that the quantity demanded increases to 12,000 frozen yogurt dishes per month. Now the average cost is $1.50 at point *B* on $LRAC_2$.

So far, our story illustrates a social benefit of advertising. Look again at Exhibit 1. The increased volume of sales caused by advertising leads to *economies of scale,* explained in Chapter 7. Without advertising, Yummy operated with a lower output and a higher average cost. With advertising, the benefit to consumers from the reduction in average total cost from *A* to *B* outweighs the boost in cost per unit from advertising.

On the other hand, suppose Yummy's advertising campaign is not successful and demand remains unchanged. In this case, the quantity demanded remains at the original 6,000 frozen yogurt dishes per month, but the average total cost rises to $3.00 (point *C*). Critics of advertising argue this is the typical case and not the reduction from *A* to *B*. Instead of leading to economies of scale, advertising is self-canceling. Yummy, It Can't Be Yogurt, and other firms spend large outlays on advertising just to keep their present market share. And in the process, the cost—and therefore the price—of yogurt is increased. Moreover, the additional cost of advertising does not improve the yogurt at all. The only purpose is to persuade or mislead consumers into buying something they do not need. From society's viewpoint, the resources used in advertising could be used for schools, software, or other useful products.

EXHIBIT 1   The Effect of Advertising on Average Cost

When Yummy Frozen Yogurt increases its advertising costs to sell more yogurt, the firm's average cost curve shifts upward from $LRAC_1$ to $LRAC_2$. If advertising increases the quantity demanded from 6,000 to 12,000 dishes per month, average total cost falls from $2.00 (point A) to $1.50 (point B). However, if the extra cost of advertising fails to increase the quantity demanded, average total cost rises from $2.00 (point A) to $3.00 (point C).

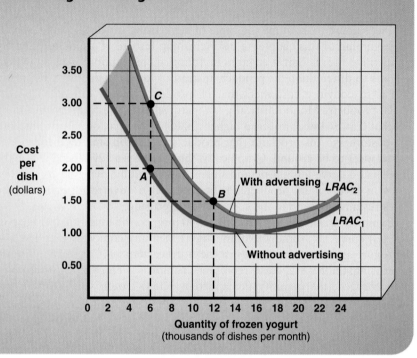

Proponents of advertising counter the argument that advertising is valueless. They argue that ads provide information. Advertising informs consumers of sales, the availability of products, and the advantages of products. Although the product costs a little more, this information saves consumers money and time. Ads also increase price competition among sellers. When Yummy offers discount coupons, other yogurt stores see these ads and respond with lower prices. Finally, consumers are rational and cannot be fooled by advertising. If a product is undesirable, customers will not buy it.

Does monopolistic competition lead to lower prices, greater output, and better-informed consumers? Or does this market structure simply raise prices and annoy customers with useless and often misleading information? This fascinating and ongoing debate is perhaps best analyzed on a case-by-case basis. In the next section, you will learn that advertising to differentiate a product is also a key characteristic of oligopoly.

Price and Output Decisions for a Monopolistically Competitive Firm

Now we are prepared to develop the short-run and long-run graphical models for monopolistic competition. In the short run, you will see that monopolistic competition resembles monopoly. In the long run, however, entry by

The Advertising Game

Applicable Concepts: advertising, barriers to entry

You are probably familiar with newspaper ads, radio or television commercials, or even Yellow Pages ads that promise legal services at very reasonable rates. Lawyers were not always free to advertise. Not until 1977 did the Supreme Court free lawyers from the disciplinary actions of local bar authorities designed to prohibit lawyers from publicizing themselves. This case involved two young Phoenix lawyers, John Bates and Van O'Steen, who had advertised their legal services in violation of the Arizona Bar's rules. The bar's position was that the "hustle of the marketplace" would "tarnish the dignified public image of the profession." The high court rejected this argument and ruled that lawyers have a constitutional right to advertise their services.

In a 1983 study, the Federal Trade Commission (FTC) surveyed 3,200 lawyers in 17 states. The FTC concluded that fees for wills, bankruptcies, uncontested divorces, and uncomplicated accident cases were 5 to 13 percent lower in cities with the least restrictions on advertising.[1] And a 1998 study by Richard J. Cebula found that advertising by lawyers raises the public's esteem for the legal profession.[2]

Another study compared prices of eyeglasses in states that had restrictions on advertising and in states that did not. The study found that in states without advertising the retail prices of eyeglasses were 25 to 40 percent higher.[3]

Critics of advertising claim that it serves as a barrier to entry against new firms. Brand loyalty allows firms to raise their prices without losing many customers. James C. Makens reported an experiment in which 150 subjects from Detroit were given two plates of turkey meat. One plate displayed an advertised brand name, and the other plate had an unknown brand. The advertised brand-name meat was preferred by 56 percent of the subjects, 34 percent preferred the unknown brand, and only 10 percent thought the two samples tasted alike. In fact, the slices of turkey meat in both samples came from the same turkey.[4]

In 1967, William Comanor and Thomas Wilson investigated the link between advertising expenditures and profits in 40 industries. The authors of the study reached the following conclusion:

It is evident that advertising is a highly profitable activity. Industries with high advertising outlays earn, on the average, a profit rate which exceeds that of other industries by nearly four percentage points. This differential represents a 50 percent increase in profit rates. It is likely, moreover, that much of this profit

rate differential is accounted for by the entry barriers created by advertising expenditures and by the resulting achievement of market power.[5]

Other economists claim that advertising is not a barrier to entry. In fact, a study by Yale Brozen found that advertising allows new entrants to penetrate markets dominated by long-established firms. Advertising gives new competitors a chance to introduce their products and win customers from their entrenched rivals.[6]

Finally, a study compared differences in the information content of women's magazine advertisements between market economies, such as Great Britain and France, and transition economies, such as Russia and the Czech Republic. The market economies focused much more on lifestyle content compared to significantly more product-related information ads in the transition economies.[7]

ANALYZE THE ISSUE

Advertising is tasteless, offensive, and a waste of resources; therefore, all advertising should be banned. Give three arguments against this idea.

---

[1] Ruth Marcus, "Practicing Law in the Advertising Age," *Washington Post,* June 30, 1987, p. A6.

[2] Richard J. Cebula, "Does Advertising Adversely Influence the Image of Lawyers in the United States?" *Journal of Legal Studies* 27 (June 1998): 503–516.

[3] Lee Benham, "The Effect of Advertising on the Price of Eyeglasses," *Journal of Law and Economics* 15, No. 2 (1972): 337–352.

[4] James C. Makens, "Effect of Brand Preferences upon Consumers' Perceived Taste of Turkey Meat," *Journal of Applied Psychology* 49 (Nov. 4, 1965): 261–263.

[5] William Comanor and Thomas Wilson, "Advertising, Market Structure, and Performance," *Review of Economics and Statistics* 49 (Nov. 1967): 437. Further evidence of this view is presented in William Comanor and Thomas Wilson, *Advertising and Market Power* (Cambridge, Mass.: Harvard University Press, 1974).

[6] Yale Brozen, "Entry Barriers: Advertising and Product Differentiation," in *Industrial Concentration: The New Learning,* ed. Harvey J. Goldschmid, H. Michael Mann, and J. Fred Weston, (Boston: Little, Brown, 1974): 115–137.

[7] Erica Van Herpen, et al., "The Information Content of Magazine Advertising in Market and Transition Economies," *Journal of Consumer Policy* 23, No. 3 (Sept. 2000): 257–283.

EXHIBIT 2   A Monopolistically Competitive Firm in the Short Run

Ivan's Oyster Bar is a monopolistically competitive firm that maximizes short-run profit by producing the output where marginal revenue equals marginal cost. At an output of 600 seafood dinners per week, the price of $18 per dinner is dictated by the firm's demand curve. Given the firm's costs, output, and prices, Ivan's will earn a weekly short-run profit of $1,800.

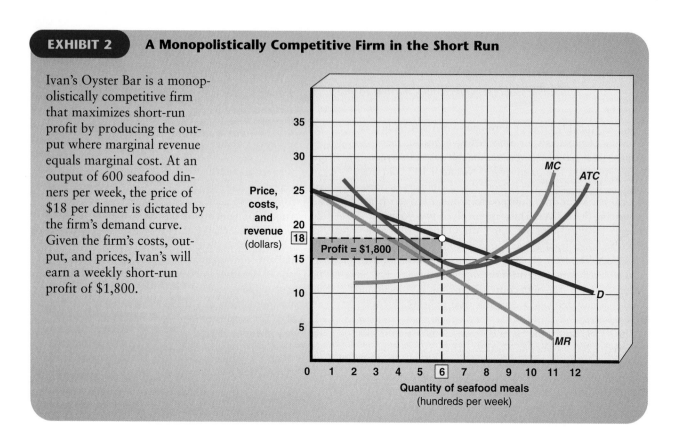

new firms leads to a more competitive market structure. This section presents a graphical analysis that shows why a monopolistically competitive firm is part perfectly competitive and part monopolistic.

Monopolistic Competition in the Short Run

Exhibit 2 shows the short-run equilibrium position for Ivan's Oyster Bar—a typical firm under monopolistic competition. As explained earlier, the demand curve slopes downward because customers believe, rightly or wrongly, that Ivan's product is a little better than its competitors' products. Customers like Ivan's family atmosphere, location, and quality of service. These nonprice factors differentiate Ivan's product and allow the restaurant to raise the price of sautéed alligator, shrimp, and oysters at least slightly without losing many sales.

Like the monopolist, the monopolistically competitive firm maximizes short-run profit by following the *MR = MC* rule. In this case, the marginal cost (*MC*) and the marginal revenue (*MR*) curves intersect at an output of 600 seafood meals per week. The price per meal of $18 is the point on the demand curve corresponding to this level of output. Because the price exceeds the average total cost (*ATC*) of $15 per meal, Ivan's earns a short-run weekly economic profit of $1,800. As under monopoly, if the price equals the *ATC* curve, the firm earns a short-run normal profit. If the price is below the *ATC* curve, the firm suffers a short-run loss, and if the price is below the average variable cost (*AVC*) curve, the firm shuts down.

Monopolistic Competition in the Long Run

The monopolistically competitive firm, unlike a monopolist, will not earn an economic profit in the long run. Rather, like a perfect competitor, the monopolistically competitive firm earns only a normal profit (that is, zero economic profit) in the long run. The reason is that short-run profits and easy entry attract new firms into the industry. When Ivan's Oyster Bar earns a short-run profit, as shown in Exhibit 2, two things happen. First, Ivan's demand curve shifts downward as some of each seafood restaurant's market share is taken away by new firms seeking profit. Second, Ivan's—and other seafood restaurants as well—tries to recapture market share by advertising, improving its decor, and utilizing other forms of nonprice competition. As a result, long-run average costs increase, and the firm's *LRAC* curve shifts upward.

The combination of the leftward shift in the firm's demand curve and the upward shift in its *LRAC* curve continues in the long run until the monopolistic competitive firm earns zero or normal economic profit. The result is the long-run equilibrium condition shown in Exhibit 3. At a price of $17 per meal, the demand curve is tangent to the *LRAC* curve at the *MR = MC* output of 500 meals per week. Once long-run equilibrium is achieved in a monopolistically competitive industry, there is no incentive for new firms to enter or established firms to leave.

While small video rental stores were forced to close due to cable television and satellite technologies, Blockbuster Video has been able to increase its market share. See http://blockbuster.com/.

Comparing Monopolistic Competition and Perfect Competition

Some economists argue that the long-run equilibrium condition for a monopolistically competitive firm, as shown in Exhibit 3, results in poor economic performance. Other economists contend that the benefits of a monopolistically competitive industry outweigh the costs. In this section, we again use the standard of perfect competition to understand both sides of this debate.

The Monopolistic Competitor as a Resource Misallocator

Like a monopolist, the monopolistically competitive firm fails the efficiency test. As shown in Exhibit 3, under monopolistic competition, Ivan's charges a price that exceeds the marginal cost. Thus, the value to consumers of the last meal produced is greater than the cost of producing it. Ivan's could devote more resources and produce more seafood dinners. To sell this additional output, Ivan's must move downward along its demand curve by reducing the $17 price per meal. As a result, customers would purchase the additional benefits of consuming more seafood meals. However, Ivan's uses less resources and restricts output to 500 seafood meals per week in order to maximize profits where *MR = MC*.

EXHIBIT 3   **A Monopolistically Competitive Firm in the Long Run**

In the long run, the entry of new seafood restaurants decreases the demand for Ivan's seafood. In addition, Ivan's shifts its average cost curve upward by increasing advertising and other expenses in order to compete against new entrants. In the long run, the firm earns zero economic profit at a price of $17 per seafood meal and produces an *MR* = *MC* output of 500 meals per week.

Monopolistic Competition Means Less Output for More

Exhibit 4(a) reproduces the long-run condition from Exhibit 3. Exhibit 4(b) assumes that the seafood restaurant market is perfectly competitive. Recall from Chapter 8 that the characteristics of perfect competition include the condition that customers perceive seafood meals as *homogeneous* and, as a result, no firms engage in advertising. Because we now assume for the sake of argument that Ivan's product is identical to all other seafood restaurants, Ivan's becomes a *price taker*. In this case, the industry's long-run supply and demand curves set an equilibrium price of $16 per meal. Consequently, Ivan's faces a horizontal demand curve with the price equal to marginal revenue. Also recall from Chapter 8 that long-run equilibrium for a perfectly competitive firm is established by the entry of new firms until the minimum point of $16 per meal on the firm's *LRAC* curve equals the price (*MR* and *MC*). Stated as a formula:

$$P = MR = MC = LRAC$$

A comparison of parts (a) and (b) of Exhibit 4 reveals two important points. First, both the monopolistic competitor and the perfect competitor earn zero economic profit in the long run. Second, the long-run equilibrium output of the monopolistically competitive firm is to the left of the mini-

EXHIBIT 4

A Comparison of Monopolistic Competition and Perfect Competition in the Long Run

(a) Monopolistic competition

(b) Perfect competition

In part (a), Ivan's Oyster Bar is a monopolistically competitive firm that sets its price at $17 per seafood meal and produces 500 meals per week. As a monopolistic competitor, Ivan's earns zero economic profit in the long run and does not produce at the lowest point on its *LRAC* curve.

Under conditions of perfect competition in part (b), Ivan's becomes a price taker, rather than a price maker. Here the firm faces a flat demand curve at a price of $16 per seafood meal. The output is 800 meals per week, which corresponds to the lowest point on the *LRAC* curve. Therefore, the price is lower, and the excess capacity of 300 meals per week is utilized when Ivan's operates as a perfectly competitive firm, rather than as a monopolistically competitive firm.

mum point on the *LRAC* curve and the price exceeds *MC*. Like a monopolist, the monopolistically competitive firm therefore charges a higher price and produces less output than a perfectly competitive firm.

In our example, Ivan's would charge $1 less per meal and produce 300 more seafood meals per week in a perfectly competitive market. The extra 300 meals not produced are *excess capacity*, which represents underutilized resources. The criticism of monopolistic competition, then, is that there are too many firms producing too little output at inflated prices and wasting society's resources in the process. For example, on many nights, there are not enough customers for all the restaurants in town. Servers, cooks, tables, and other resources are therefore underutilized. With fewer firms, each would produce a greater output at a lower price and with a lower average cost.

Opinions vary concerning whether the benefits of monopolistic competition exceed the costs. Having many seafood restaurants offers consumers more choice and variety of output. Having Ivan's Oyster Bar and many

Strong frequent flier programs help major airlines dominate in the market and keep small airlines from expanding their market share. Check on the frequent flier programs offered by Delta at http://www.delta-air.com/index.html, *or United at* http://www.ual.com/.

Oligopoly

A market structure characterized by (1) few sellers, (2) either a homogeneous or a differentiated product, and (3) difficult market entry.

Mutual interdependence

A condition in which an action by one firm may cause a reaction from other firms.

similar competitors gives consumers extra quality and service options. If you do not like Ivan's sautéed alligator, you may be able to find another restaurant that serves this dish. Also, having many restaurants in a market saves consumers valuable time. Chances are that you will not shed crocodile tears because the travel time required to enjoy an alligator meal is lower.

The Oligopoly Market Structure

Now we turn to oligopoly, an imperfectly competitive market structure in which a few large firms dominate the market. Many manufacturing industries, such as steel, aluminum, automobiles, aircraft, drugs, and tobacco, are best described as oligopolistic. This is the "big business" market structure, in which firms aggressively compete by bombarding us with advertising on television and filling our mailboxes with junk mail.

Economists define an **oligopoly** as a market structure characterized by (1) few sellers, (2) either a homogeneous or a differentiated product, and (3) difficult market entry. Like monopolistic competition, oligopoly is found in real-world industries. Let's examine each characteristic.

Few Sellers

Oligopoly is competition "among the few." Here we refer to the "Big Three" or "Big Four" to mean that three or four firms dominate an industry. But what does "a few" firms really mean? Does this mean at least 2, but less than 10? As with other market structures, there is no specific number of firms that must dominate an industry before it is an oligopoly. Basically, an oligopoly is a consequence of **mutual interdependence**. Mutual interdependence is a condition in which an action by one firm may cause a reaction from other firms. Stated another way, a market structure with a few powerful firms makes it easier for oligopolists to collude. The large number of firms under perfect competition or monopolistic competition and the absence of other firms in monopoly rule out mutual interdependence and collusion in these market structures.

When General Motors (GM) considers a price hike or a style change, it must predict how Ford and DaimlerChrysler will change their prices and styling in response. Therefore, the decisions under oligopoly are more complex than under perfect competition, monopoly, and monopolistic competition.

Conclusion *The few-sellers condition is met when these few firms are so large relative to the total market that they can affect the market price.*

Homogeneous or Differentiated Product

Under oligopoly, firms can produce either a homogeneous or a differentiated product. The steel produced by USX is identical to the steel from Republic Steel. The oil sold by Saudi Arabia is identical to the oil from Iran. Similarly, zinc, copper, and aluminum are standardized products. But cars produced by the major automakers are differentiated products. Tires, detergents, and breakfast cereals are also differentiated products sold in oligopolies.

Conclusion *Buyers in an oligopoly may or may not be indifferent as to which seller's product they buy.*

Difficult Entry

Similar to monopoly, formidable barriers to entry in an oligopoly protect firms from new entrants. These barriers include exclusive financial requirements, control over an essential resource, patent rights, and other legal barriers. But the most significant barrier to entry in an oligopoly is *economies of scale*. For example, larger automakers achieve lower average total costs than those incurred by smaller automakers. Consequently, the U.S. auto industry has moved over time from more than 60 firms to only 2 major U.S. owned firms.

Price and Output Decisions for an Oligopolist

Mutual interdependence among firms in an oligopoly makes this market structure more difficult to analyze than perfect competition, monopoly, or monopolistic competition. The price-output decision of an oligopolist is not simply a matter of charging the price where $MR = MC$. Making price and output decisions in an oligopoly is like playing a game of chess. One player's move depends on the anticipated reactions of the opposing player. One player thinks, "If I move my rook here, my opponent might move her knight there." Likewise, a firm in an oligopoly can make many different possible reactions to the price, nonprice, and output changes of another firm. Consequently, there are different oligopoly models because no single model can cover all cases. The following is a discussion of four well-known oligopoly models: (1) nonprice competition, (2) the kinked demand curve, (3) price leadership, and (4) the cartel.

Nonprice Competition

Major oligopolists often compete using advertising and product differentiation. Instead of "slugging it out" with price cuts, oligopolists may try to capture business away from their rivals through better advertising campaigns and improved products. This model of behavior explains why advertising expenditures often are large in the cigarette, soft drink, athletic shoe, and automobile industries. It also explains why the research and development (R&D) function is so important to oligopolists. For example, much engineering effort is aimed largely at developing new products and improving existing products.

Why might oligopolists compete through nonprice competition, rather than price competition? The answer is that each oligopolist perceives that its rival will easily and quickly match any price reduction. On the other hand, it is much more difficult to combat a clever and/or important product improvement.

The Kinked Demand Curve

Unlike other market structures, different assumptions define different models for any given oligopolistic industry. Over time, the "rules of the game" change, and a new model becomes the best predictor of the behavior of oligopolists. We begin with the **kinked demand curve**. The strange shape of this curve explains why prices in an oligopolistic market selling cars change far less often than prices in a perfectly competitive market selling wheat.

The kinked demand curve is a demand curve facing an oligopolist that assumes rivals will match a price decrease, but ignore a price increase. Without collusion, the kinked demand curve exists because management tacitly believes that the competition will not be "undersold." On the other hand, a price hike by one firm allows competitors to capture its share of the market. Oligopolistic firms must make pricing decisions, so they are *price makers,* rather than price takers. But as we will soon see in the kinked demand model, the high degree of interdependence among oligopolists restricts their pricing discretion.

In Exhibit 5, a kinked demand curve is drawn for Tucker Motor Company, which we assume competes with GM, Ford, and DaimlerChrysler in the automobile market. (I suggest you check out the movie titled *Tucker* at your video rental store.) The current price per car is $15,000, and the quantity demanded at this price is 3 million Tucker cars per year. Tucker's management assumes that if it raises its price even slightly above $15,000, the other automakers *will not follow* with higher prices. This price gap between the Tucker and other cars would drive many of Tucker's customers over to its rivals. The segment of the demand curve above $15,000 is therefore relatively flat. Stated differently, above the "kink" in the demand curve, demand is relatively elastic.

If Tucker raises the price to, say, $17,250 at point *X*, this price hike cuts Tucker's quantity demanded to 1.5 million cars per year. Since raising its price is ill-advised, management can consider a price reduction strategy. Suppose Tucker cuts the price of its cars to $12,250 at point *Y*. The model shows that Tucker gains few customers and the quantity demanded rises only slightly to 3.2 million cars per year. The reason for such a small sales boost is that other automakers also cut their prices so that each firm can keep its initial market share. However, the lower price does attract some new buyers who could not afford a car at the higher price. The segment of the demand curve below the kink is therefore relatively steep. Here demand is less elastic, meaning the quantity demanded is not very responsive to a price drop.

Given the kinked demand curve facing the oligopolist, management fears the worst and is afraid to raise or lower the price of its product. Under this model of oligopoly, the price established at the kink changes very infrequently. Price rigidity is eliminated only after large cost increases or decreases force a new kinked demand curve with a new higher or lower price at the kink.

Economists continue to debate the importance of the kinked demand model. Critics challenge the theory on theoretical and empirical grounds. On a theoretical level, there is no explanation for how the original price at the kink was determined. On empirical grounds, studies of certain oligopolistic industries fail to find price stickiness. On the other hand, widespread use of price lists in catalogs that remain fixed for a long time is consistent with kinked demand theory. In any case, the kinked demand theory does not provide a complete explanation of price and output decisions.

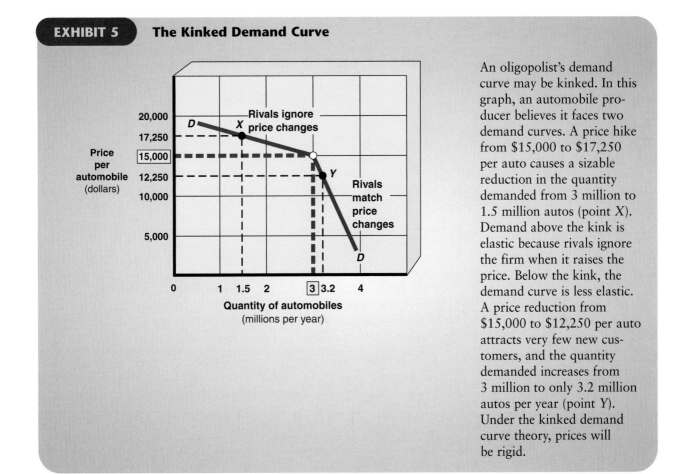

EXHIBIT 5　　**The Kinked Demand Curve**

An oligopolist's demand curve may be kinked. In this graph, an automobile producer believes it faces two demand curves. A price hike from $15,000 to $17,250 per auto causes a sizable reduction in the quantity demanded from 3 million to 1.5 million autos (point *X*). Demand above the kink is elastic because rivals ignore the firm when it raises the price. Below the kink, the demand curve is less elastic. A price reduction from $15,000 to $12,250 per auto attracts very few new customers, and the quantity demanded increases from 3 million to only 3.2 million autos per year (point *Y*). Under the kinked demand curve theory, prices will be rigid.

Price Leadership

Without formal agreement, firms can play a game of follow-the-leader that economists call **price leadership.** Price leadership is a pricing strategy in which a dominant firm sets the price for an industry and the other firms follow. Following this tactic, firms in an industry simply match the price of perhaps, but not necessarily, the biggest firm. For example, suppose GM initiates a price increase per car. Reacting to this price hike, other automakers quickly follow the leader's example and boost the price of their cars by an equal amount. Price leadership is not uncommon. In addition to GM, USX Corporation (steel), Alcoa (aluminum), DuPont (nylon), R. J. Reynolds (cigarettes), Goodyear Tire and Rubber (tires), and American Tobacco (cigarettes) are other examples of price leaders in U.S. industries.

Price leadership

A pricing strategy in which a dominant firm sets the price for an industry and the other firms follow.

The Cartel

The price leadership model assumes that firms do not collude to avoid price competition. Instead, firms avoid price wars by informally playing by the established pricing rules. Another way to avoid price wars is for oligopolists to agree to a peace treaty. Instead of allowing mutual interdependence to lead to rivalry, firms openly or secretly conspire to form a monopoly called

INTERNATIONAL ECONOMICS

Major Cartels in Global Markets

Applicable Concept: cartel

Cartels flourished in Germany and other European countries in the first half of the twentieth century. Many had international memberships. After World War II, European countries passed laws against such restrictive trade practices. The following are some of the most important cartels today:

• *Organization of Petroleum Exporting Countries (OPEC).* OPEC was created by Iran, Iraq, Kuwait, Saudi Arabia, and Venezuela in Baghdad in 1960. Today, OPEC's membership consists of 12 countries that control about 80 percent of the world's oil reserves. Cartels are anticonsumer. OPEC's objective is to set oil pro-

duction quotas for its members and, in turn, influence global prices of oil and gasoline. In the future, OPEC may become weaker if Russia competes with it. Russia possesses the world's largest oil reserves and may soon obtain Western technology necessary for efficient oil production.

• *International Telephone Cartel (CCITT).* The world's least-known, and perhaps most effective, cartel is known by its French acronym, CCITT. This cartel is based in Switzerland and sets the minimum price you pay for an international telephone call. As a result, rates for international calls are much higher than compet-

itive long-distance telephone rates in the United States. In fact, often 95 percent of the charge for an international call placed by AT&T, MCI, Sprint, and other U.S. telephone companies is remitted through the CCITT.

• *International Airline Cartel (IATA).* Most of the world's international airlines belong to the IATA. This cartel controls access to airports, fixes airline rates, and promotes mutual objectives for its members. The market power of the IATA may decline as more nations follow the example of the United States and reduce protection and regulation of airlines.

Cartel

A group of firms that formally agree to control the price and the output of a product.

OPEC is one of the most successful cartels in history. See their site at http://www.opec.org/.

a **cartel.** A cartel is a group of firms that formally agree to control the price and the output of a product. The goal of a cartel is to reap monopoly profits by replacing competition with cooperation. Cartels are illegal in the United States, but not in other nations. The best-known cartel is the Organization of Petroleum Exporting Countries (OPEC). The members of OPEC divide crude oil output among themselves according to quotas openly agreed upon at meetings of the OPEC oil ministries. Saudi Arabia is the largest producer and has the largest quota. The International Economics feature provides a brief summary of some of today's major global cartels.

Using Exhibit 6, we can demonstrate how a cartel works and why keeping members from cheating is a problem. Our analysis begins before oil-producing firms have formed a cartel. Assume each firm has the same cost curve shown in the exhibit. Price wars have driven each firm to charge $30 a barrel, which is equal to the minimum point on its *LRAC* curve. Because oil is a standardized product, as under perfect competition, each firm fears raising its price because it will lose all its customers. Thus, the typical firm is in long-run competitive equilibrium at a price of $30 per barrel ($MR_1$), producing 6 million barrels per day. In this condition, economic profits are zero, and the firms decide to organize a meeting of all oil producers to establish a cartel.

Now assume the cartel is formed and each firm agrees to reduce its output to 4 million barrels per day and charge $45 per barrel. If no firms cheat,

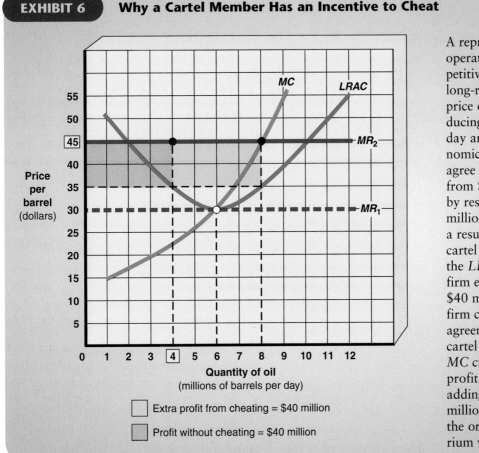

EXHIBIT 6   Why a Cartel Member Has an Incentive to Cheat

☐ Extra profit from cheating = $40 million

☐ Profit without cheating = $40 million

A representative oil producer operating in a perfectly competitive industry would be in long-run equilibrium at a price of $30 per barrel, producing 6 million barrels per day and making zero economic profit. A cartel can agree to raise the price of oil from $30 to $45 per barrel by restricting the firm to 4 million barrels per day. As a result of this quota, the cartel price is above $35 on the *LRAC* curve, and the firm earns a daily profit of $40 million. However, if the firm cheats on the cartel agreement, it will set the cartel price equal to the *MC* curve and earn a total profit of $80 million by adding an additional $40 million. If all firms cheat, the original long-run equilibrium will be reestablished.

each firm faces a higher horizontal demand curve, represented by MR_2. At the cartel price, each firm earns an economic profit of $40 million, rather than a normal profit. But what if one firm decides to cheat on the cartel agreement by stepping up its output while other firms stick to their quotas? Output corresponding to the point at which $MR_2 = MC$ is 8 million barrels per day. If a cheating firm expands its output to this level, it can double its profit by earning an extra $40 million. Of course, if all firms cheat and the cartel breaks up, the price and output of each firm returns to the initial levels, and economic profit again falls to zero.

An Evaluation of Oligopoly

Oligopoly is much more difficult to evaluate than other market structures. None of the models just presented gives a definite answer to the question of efficiency under oligopoly. Depending on the assumptions made, an oligopolist can behave much like a perfectly competitive firm or more like a monopoly. Nevertheless, let's assume some likely changes that occur if a

CHECKPOINT

Which Model Fits the Cereal Aisle?

As you walk along the cereal aisle, notice the many different cereals on the shelf. For example, you will probably see General Mills' Wheaties, Total, and Cheerios; Kellogg's Corn Flakes, Cracklin' Oat Bran, Frosted Flakes, and Rice Krispies; Quaker Cap'n Crunch and 100% Natural; and Post's Super Golden Crisp, to name only a few. There are many different brands of the same product—cereal—on the shelves. Each brand is slightly different from the others. Is the breakfast cereal industry's market structure monopolistic competition or oligopoly?

---

perfectly competitive industry is suddenly turned into an oligopoly selling a differentiated product.

First, the price charged for the product will be higher than under perfect competition. The smaller the number of firms in an oligopoly and the more difficult it is to enter the industry, the higher the oligopoly price will be in comparison to the perfectly competitive price.

Second, an oligopoly is likely to spend money on advertising, product differentiation, and other forms of nonprice competition. These expenditures can shift the demand curve to the right. As a result, both price and output may be higher under oligopoly than under perfect competition.

Third, in the long run, a perfectly competitive firm earns zero economic profit. The oligopolist, however, can earn a higher profit because it is more difficult for competitors to enter the industry.

Review of the Four Market Structures

Now that we have completed the discussion of perfect competition, monopoly, monopolistic competition, and oligopoly, you are prepared to compare these four market structures. Exhibit 7 summarizes the characteristics and gives examples of each market structure.

EXHIBIT 7 Comparison of Market Structures

Market structure	Number of sellers	Type of product	Entry condition	Examples
Perfect competition	Large	Homogeneous	Very easy	Agriculture*
Monopoly	One	Unique	Impossible	Public utilities
Monopolistic competition	Many	Differentiated	Easy	Retail trade
Oligopoly	Few	Homogeneous or differentiated	Difficult	Auto, steel, oil

*In the absence of government intervention.

An Economist Goes to the Final Four

Applicable Concepts: oligopoly and cartel

Many fascinating markets functioned during the Men's Final Four basketball tournament in April of 1992, and as an industrial organization economist, I observed them with great interest.

The competition began shortly after we got off the plane at the Minneapolis Airport. A group of high school students was giving away huge inflatable plastic hands with index fingers sticking up in the air. They were imprinted with the Pepsi Cola slogan and logo and your choice of a Final Four team. And the group was giving away free cans of Pepsi. Uh huh! The latest battle in the Great Cola Wars was on, but this was just the beginning.

Giant inflatable "cans" of Coke and Pepsi appeared all over downtown Minneapolis—on the sidewalks, on top of gas stations—not to mention that entire sides of three-story buildings were painted Coca-Cola red and white with the 64 NCAA basketball finalists and all the winners listed, bracket by bracket, just as they appeared in the newspaper. And on Sunday, following the first-round games, painters were three stories up on scaffolding, filling in the Coke sign's brackets for the final two teams, Duke and Michigan, in school colors no less. This was competition between showboating industry giants—a spectacular example of differentiated oligopoly. . . .

Then there were the hotels, which by joining a centralized booking service became a cartel. The first hotel that I booked had raised its normal price by 75 percent for the weekend. Others did the same. I later found a national chain motel that had not joined in the feeding frenzy. It charged a modest price, but it was well out into the suburbs. Still, by Saturday afternoon it was filled with Final Four fans.

Fortunately, I did not have the same problem with the airline, rental car company, or restaurants. Normal rates for transportation prevailed. National market-oriented

companies either do not want to bother with adjusting prices for local high-demand special events, or they do not wish to alienate their regular customers by taking advantage of the situation.

ANALYZE THE ISSUE

1. The author says that the Coke-Pepsi competition was an example of "differentiated oligopoly." What does he mean? In what ways were the soda giants differentiating their products?

2. Why didn't national companies adjust their prices in the face of increased Final Four demand?

Source: Michael Stoller, "An Economist Goes to the Final Four," *Margin* 8 (Spring 1993): 48–49.

KEY CONCEPTS

Monopolistic competition	Nonprice competition	Mutual interdependence	Price leadership
Product differentiation	Oligopoly	Kinked demand curve	Cartel

SUMMARY

■ **Monopolistic competition** is a market structure characterized by (1) many small sellers, (2) a differentiated product, and (3) easy market entry and exit. Given these characteristics, firms in monopolistic competition have a negligible effect on the market price.

■ **Product differentiation** is a key characteristic of monopolistic competition. It is the process of creating real or apparent differences between products.

■ **Nonprice competition** includes advertising, packaging, product development, better quality, and better service. Under monopolistic competition and oligopoly, firms may compete using nonprice competition, rather than price competition.

■ **Short-run equilibrium for a monopolistic competitor** can yield economic losses, zero economic profits, or economic profits. In the long run, monopolistic competitors make zero economic profits.

Short-run equilibrium for a monopolistic competitor

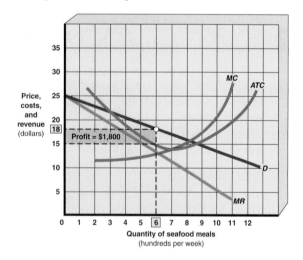

Quantity of seafood meals
(hundreds per week)

■ **Comparing monopolistic competition with perfect competition,** we find that the monopolistically competitive firm does not achieve allocative efficiency, charges a higher price, restricts output, and does not produce where average costs are at a minimum.

Comparison of monopolistic and perfect competition

(a) Monopolistic competition

Quantity of seafood meals
(hundreds per week)

(b) Perfect competition

Quantity of seafood meals
(hundreds per week)

■ **Oligopoly** is a market structure characterized by (1) few sellers, (2) a homogeneous or a differentiated product, and (3) difficult market entry. Oligopolies are **mutually interdependent** because an action by one firm may cause a reaction from other firms.

- The **nonprice competition model** is a theory that might explain oligopolistic behavior. Under this theory, firms use advertising and product differentiation, rather than price reductions, to compete.
- The **kinked demand curve** model explains why prices may be rigid in an oligopoly. The kink is established because an oligopolist assumes that rivals will match a price decrease, but ignore a price increase.

Kinked demand curve

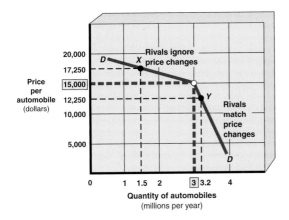

- **Price leadership** is another theory of pricing behavior under oligopoly. When a dominant firm in an industry raises or lowers price, other firms follow suit.

- A **cartel** is a formal agreement among firms to set prices and output quotas. The goal is to maximize profits, but firms have an incentive to cheat, which is a constant threat to a cartel.

Cartel

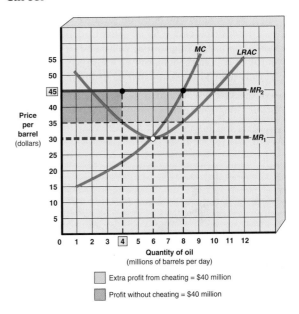

- **Comparing oligopoly with perfect competition,** we find that the oligopolist allocates resources inefficiently, charges a higher price, and restricts output so that price may exceed average cost.

SUMMARY OF CONCLUSION STATEMENTS

- The many-sellers condition is met when each firm is so small relative to the total market that each firm's pricing decisions have a negligible effect on the market price.
- When a product is differentiated, buyers are not indifferent as to which seller's product they buy.
- The demand curve for a monopolistically competitive firm is less elastic (steeper) than for a perfectly competitive firm and more elastic (flatter) than for a monopolist.

- The few-sellers condition is met when these few firms are so large relative to the total market that they can affect the market price.
- Buyers in an oligopoly may or may not be indifferent as to which seller's product they buy.

STUDY QUESTIONS AND PROBLEMS

1. Compare the monopolistically competitive firm's demand curve to those of a perfect competitor and a monopolist.

2. Suppose the minimum point on the *LRAC* curve of a soft drink firm's cola is $1 per liter. Under conditions of monopolistic competition, will the price of a liter bottle of cola in the long run be above $1, equal to $1, less than $1, or impossible to determine?

3. Exhibit 8 represents a monopolistically competitive firm in long-run equilibrium.

Exhibit 8

a. Which price represents the long-run equilibrium price?

b. Which quantity represents the long-run equilibrium output?

c. At which quantity is the *LRAC* curve at its minimum?

d. Is the long-run equilibrium price greater than, less than, or equal to the marginal cost of producing the equilibrium output?

4. Consider this statement: "Because price equals long-run average cost and profits are zero, a monopolistically competitive firm is efficient." Do you agree or disagree? Explain.

5. Assuming identical long-run cost curves, draw two graphs, and indicate the price and output that result in the long run under monopolistic competition and perfect competition. Evaluate the differences between these two market structures.

6. Draw a graph that shows how advertising affects a firm's *ATC* curve. Explain how advertising can lead to lower prices in a monopolistically competitive industry.

7. List four goods or services that you have purchased that were produced by an oligopolist. Why are these industries oligopolistic, rather than monopolistically competitive?

8. Why is mutual interdependence important under oligopoly, but not so important under perfect competition, monopoly, or monopolistic competition?

9. Suppose the jeans industry is an oligopoly in which each firm sells its own distinctive brand of jeans. Each firm believes its rivals will not follow its price increases, but will follow its price cuts. Explain the demand curve facing each firm. Given this demand curve, does this mean that firms in the jeans industry do or do not compete against one another?

10. What might be a general distinction between oligopolists that advertise and those that do not?

11. Suppose IBM raised the price of its printers, but Hewlett-Packard (the largest seller) refused to follow. Two years later IBM cut its price, and Hewlett-Packard retaliated with an even deeper price cut, which IBM was forced to match. For the next five years, Hewlett-Packard raised its prices five times, and each time IBM followed suit within 24 hours. Does the pricing behavior of these computer industry firms follow the cartel model or the price leadership model? Why?

12. Evaluate the following statement: "A cartel will put an end to price war, which is a barbaric form of competition that benefits no one."

ONLINE EXERCISES

Exercise 1

Visit Irin Reports (http://www.irin.com/) and follow these steps:

1. Click on Annual Reports and look up the annual reports of IBM Corporation and Apple Computers, Inc.

2. Explain how IBM and Apple have partial monopolies and yet they compete with each other.

3. Explain why IBM and Apple spend such a large amount of money on sales and marketing (see their income statements).

Exercise 2

Facial tissues, according to some analysts, are a product with low consumer loyalty. What is Kimberly-Clark (http://www.kimberly-clark.com/), maker of Kleenex, doing to increase product differentiation and brand loyalty?

Exercise 3

How does DaimlerChrysler (http://www.chrysler.com/) use the Internet to advertise its products? Is DaimlerChrysler different from General Motors (http://www.gm.com/) or Ford (http://www.ford.com/)? Are these companies operating within a monopolistically competitive or oligopolistic market environment?

Exercise 4

Why does Morton International produce many different types of table salt (http://www.mortonsalt.com/prod/prflprod.htm)?

CHECKPOINT ANSWER

Which Model Fits the Cereal Aisle?

The fact that there is a differentiated product does not necessarily mean that many firms are competing along the cereal aisle. The different cereals listed in this example are produced by only four companies: General Mills, Kellogg's, Quaker Oats, and Post. In fact, there are relatively few firms in the cereal industry, so even though they sell a differentiated product, the market structure cannot be monopolistic competition. If you said the cereal industry is an oligopoly, YOU ARE CORRECT.

PRACTICE QUIZ

For a visual explanation of the correct answers, visit the tutorial at http://tucker.swcollege.com.

1. An industry with many small sellers, a differentiated product, and easy entry would *best* be described as which of the following?
   a. Oligopoly
   b. Monopolistic competition
   c. Perfect competition
   d. Monopoly

2. Which of the following industries is the *best* example of monopolistic competition?
   a. Wheat
   b. Restaurant
   c. Automobile
   d. Water service

3. Which of the following is *not* a characteristic of monopolistic competition?
   a. A large number of small firms
   b. A differentiated product
   c. Easy market entry
   d. A homogeneous product

4. A monopolistically competitive firm will
   a. maximize profits by producing where *MR = MC.*
   b. probably not earn an economic profit in the long run.
   c. shut down if price is less than average variable cost.
   d. do all of the above.

5. The theory of monopolistic competition predicts that in long-run equilibrium a monopolistically competitive firm will
   a. produce the output level at which price equals long-run marginal cost.
   b. operate at minimum long-run average cost.
   c. overutilize its insufficient capacity.
   d. produce the output level at which price equals long-run average cost.

6. A monopolistically competitive firm is inefficient because the firm
   a. earns positive economic profit in the long run.
   b. is producing at an output where marginal cost equals price.
   c. is not maximizing its profit.
   d. produces an output where average total cost is not minimum.

7. A monopolistically competitive firm in the long run earns the same economic profit as a
   a. perfectly competitive firm.
   b. monopolist.
   c. cartel.
   d. none of the above.

8. One possible effect of advertising on a firm's long-run average cost curve is to
   a. raise the curve.
   b. lower the curve.
   c. shift the curve rightward.
   d. shift the curve leftward.

9. Monopolistic competition is an inefficient market structure because
   a. firms earn zero profit in the long run.
   b. marginal cost is less than price in the long run.
   c. a wider variety of products is available compared to perfect competition.
   d. all of the above.

10. The "Big Three" U.S. automobile industry is described as a(an)
    a. monopoly.
    b. perfect competition.
    c. monopolistic competition.
    d. oligopoly.

11. The cigarette industry in the United States is described as a(an)
    a. monopoly.
    b. perfect competition.
    c. monopolistic competition.
    d. oligopoly.

12. A characteristic of an oligopoly is
    a. mutual interdependence in pricing decisions.
    b. easy market entry.
    c. both a and b.
    d. neither a nor b.

13. The kinked demand curve theory attempts to explain why an oligopolistic firm
    a. has relatively large advertising expenditures.
    b. fails to invest in research and development (R&D).
    c. infrequently changes its price.
    d. engages in excessive brand proliferation.

14. According to the kinked demand curve theory, when one firm raises its price, other firms will
    a. also raise their prices.
    b. refuse to follow.
    c. increase their advertising expenditures.
    d. exit the industry.

15. Which of the following is evidence that OPEC is a cartel?
    a. Agreement on price and output quotas by oil ministries
    b. Ability to raise prices regardless of demand
    c. Mutual interdependence in pricing and output decisions
    d. Ability to completely control entry

CHAPTER 11

Labor Markets

In 2000, champion golfer Tiger Woods earned the impressive figure of $53 million, but talk show host Oprah Winfrey did even better. She earned $250 million. While one headline reports a sports team signed their star player to a contract paying $10 million annually, another cites a recent survey showing chief executive officers (CEOs) of large corporations are paid an average annual salary of $40 million. The president of the United States is paid $400,000 per year. The worker with a college degree or more earns an average of $60,000. The average high school graduate earns less than $35,000, while many others, including college students, toil for the minimum wage.

How are earnings determined? What accounts for the wide differences in earnings? This chapter provides answers by explaining different types of labor markets that determine workers' compensation and the quantity of workers firms hire. Understanding hiring decisions is indeed a key to understanding why some become rich and famous by playing baseball— a kid's game—while other workers might be exploited by firms with labor market power.

The chapter begins with development of a competitive labor market in which no single buyer or seller can influence the price (wage rate) of labor. The chapter concludes with a discussion of power. As in the product markets, labor market determinations are affected by market power. Power on the side of either unions or employers can alter wage and employment outcomes. For example, the chapter explains how unions affect wages and examines trends in union membership around the world.

In this chapter, you will learn to solve these economics puzzles:

■ What determines the wage rate an employer pays?

■ How do labor unions influence wages and employment?

■ Does the NCAA exploit college athletes?

The Labor Market under Perfect Competition

In Chapters 8–10, you studied the price and quantity determinations of goods and services produced by firms operating under different market structures—perfect competition, monopoly, oligopoly, and monopolistic competition. As you have learned, market structure affects the price and the quantity of a good or service sold by firms to consumers. Similarly, as this chapter will demonstrate, the price (wage rate) paid to labor and the quantity of labor hired by firms are influenced by whether or not the labor market is competitive.

Recall from Chapter 8 that we assumed the hypothetical firm called Computech produces and sells electronic units for bank teller machines in a perfectly competitive market. Here we also assume Computech hires workers in a perfectly competitive labor market. In a perfectly competitive labor market, there are many sellers and buyers of labor services. Consequently, wages and salaries are determined by the intersection of the demand for labor and the supply of labor.

The Demand for Labor

How many workers should Computech hire? To answer this question, Computech must know how much workers contribute to its output. Column 1 of Exhibit 1 lists possible numbers of workers Computech might hire per day, and as discussed earlier in Chapter 7 on production costs, column 2 shows the total output per day. One worker would produce 5 units per day, 2 workers together would produce 9 units per day, and so on. Note that columns 1 and 2 constitute a *production function* as represented earlier in Exhibit 2(a) in Chapter 7. Column 3 lists the additional output from hiring each worker. The first worker hired would add 5 units of output per day, the second would produce an additional 4 units (total product of 9 − 5 units produced), and so on. Recall from Chapter 7 that the additional output from hiring another unit of labor is defined as the *marginal product of labor* [see Exhibit 2(b) in Chapter 7]. Consistent with the *law of diminishing returns*, the marginal product falls as the firm hires more workers.[1]

---

[1]Recall from Chapter 7 that marginal product may increase with the addition of more labor at low rates of output due to specialization and division of labor. Then, as output expands in the short run, the law of diminishing returns will cause marginal product to decrease.

EXHIBIT 1 Computech's Demand for Labor

Points	(1) Labor input (workers per day)	(2) Total output (units per day)	(3) Marginal product (units per day)	(4) Product Price	(5) Marginal revenue product [(3) × (4)]
	0	0	—	$70	—
A	1	5	5	70	$350
B	2	9	4	70	280
C	3	12	3	70	210
D	4	14	2	70	140
E	5	15	1	70	70

The next step in Computech's hiring decision is to convert marginal product into dollars by calculating the **marginal revenue product (*MRP*)**, which is the increase in a firm's total revenue resulting from hiring an additional unit of labor or other variable resource. Stated simply, *MRP* is the dollar value of worker productivity. It is the extra revenue a firm earns from selling the output of an extra worker. Returning to Exhibit 1 in Chapter 8 on perfect competition, suppose the market equilibrium price per unit is $70. Because Computech operates in a perfectly competitive market, the firm can sell any quantity of its product at the $70 market determined price. Given this situation, the first unit of labor contributes an *MRP* of $350 per day to revenue ($70 per unit times the 5 units of output). Column 5 of Exhibit 1 lists the *MRP* of each additional worker hired.

Marginal revenue product (*MRP*)
The increase in a firm's total revenue resulting from hiring an additional unit of labor or other variable resource.

Conclusion *A perfectly competitive firm's marginal revenue product is equal to the marginal product of its labor times the price of its product. Expressed as a formula:* MRP = P × MP.

Now assuming all other inputs are fixed, Computech can derive its **demand curve for labor,** which conforms to the law of demand explained in Chapter 3. The demand curve for labor is a curve showing the different quantities of labor employers are willing to hire at different wage rates. It is equal to the *MRP* of labor. The *MRP* numbers from Exhibit 1 are duplicated in Exhibit 2. As shown in the exhibit, the price of labor in terms of daily wages is measured on the vertical axis. The quantity of workers Computech will hire per day at each wage rate is measured on the horizontal axis. The demand curve for labor is downward sloping: As the wage rate falls, Computech will hire more workers per day. If the wage rate is above $350 (point *A*), Computech will hire no workers because the cost of a worker is more than the dollar value of any worker's contribution to total

Demand curve for labor
A curve showing the different quantities of labor employers are willing to hire at different wage rates in a given time period, ceteris paribus. It is equal to the marginal revenue product of labor.

EXHIBIT 2 Computech's Demand Curve for Labor

Computech's downward-sloping demand curve for labor is derived from the marginal revenue product (*MRP*) of labor, which declines as additional workers are hired. The *MRP* is the change in total revenue that results from hiring one more worker (see Exhibit 1). At point *B*, Computech pays $280 per day and finds it profitable to pay this wage to 2 workers because each worker's *MRP* equals or exceeds the wage rate. If Computech pays a lower wage rate of $140 per day at point *D*, it is not profitable for the firm to hire the fifth worker because this worker's *MRP* of $70 is below the wage rate of $140 per day. At a wage rate of $70, the fifth worker would be hired.

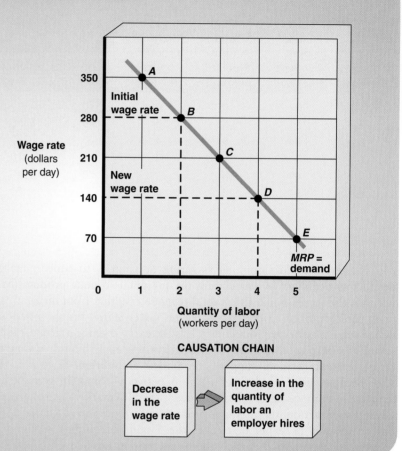

revenue (*MRP*). But what happens if Computech pays each worker $280 per day? At point *B*, Computech finds it profitable to hire 2 workers because the *MRP* of the first worker is greater than the wage rate (extra cost) and the second worker's *MRP* equals the wage rate. If the wage rate is $140 per day at point *D*, Computech will find it profitable to hire 4 workers. In this case, Computech will not hire the fifth worker. Why? The fifth worker contributes an *MRP* of $70 to total revenue (point *E*), but this amount is below the wage rate paid of $140. Consequently, Computech cannot maximize profits by hiring the fifth worker because it would be adding more to costs than to revenue. Specifically, Computech would lose $70 per day by hiring the fifth worker. At a wage rate of $70, however, the fifth worker would be hired.

Conclusion *A firm hires additional workers up to the point where the* MRP *equals the wage rate.*

Each firm in the market has a demand for labor based on its *MRP* data. Summing these individual demand curves for labor provides the market demand curve for labor in the electronic components industry. Another important point must be made. The demand for labor is called **derived demand.** The derived demand for labor and other factors of production depends on the consumer demand for the final goods and services the factors produce. If consumers are not willing to purchase products requiring electronic components, such as bank teller machines, there is no *MRP*, and firms will hire no workers to make electronic components for them. On the other hand, if customer demand for bank teller machines soars, the price of units rises, and the *MRP* of firms in the electronic components industry also rises. The result is a rightward shift in the market demand curve for labor.

Derived demand

The demand for labor and other factors of production that depends on the consumer demand for the final goods and services the factors produce.

The Supply of Labor

The **supply curve of labor** is also consistent with the law of supply discussed in Chapter 3. The supply curve of labor shows the different quantities of labor workers are willing to offer employers at different wage rates. Summing the individual supply curves of labor for firms producing electronic units for bank teller machines provides the market supply curve of labor. As shown in Exhibit 3, as the wage rate rises, more workers are willing to supply their labor. Each point indicates the wage rate that must be paid to attract the corresponding number of workers. At point *A*, 20,000 workers offer their services to the industry for $140 per day. At the higher wage rate of $280 per day (point *B*), the quantity of labor supplied is 40,000 workers. More people are willing to work at higher wage rates because the incentive of earning more compensates for the opportunity cost of leisure time. Higher wages also attract workers from other industries that require similar skills, but have lower wage rates.

Ignoring differences in wage scales, why might the supply of less-skilled workers (carpenters) be greater than that of more skilled workers (physicians)? The explanation for this difference is the **human capital** required to perform various occupations. Human capital is the accumulation of education, training, experience, and health that enables a worker to enter an occupation and be productive. Less human capital is required to be a carpenter than a physician. Therefore, many people are qualified, and the supply of carpenters is larger than the supply of physicians.

Supply curve of labor

A curve showing the different quantities of labor workers are willing to offer employers at different wage rates in a given time period, ceteris paribus.

Human capital

The accumulation of education, training, experience, and health that enables a worker to enter an occupation and be productive.

The Equilibrium Wage Rate

Wage rates are determined in perfectly competitive markets by the interaction of labor supply and demand. The equilibrium wage rate for the entire electronic components market, shown in Exhibit 4(a), is $210 per day. This wage rate clears the market because the quantity of 30,000 workers demanded equals the quantity of 30,000 workers who are willing to supply their labor services at that wage rate. In a competitive labor market, no single worker can set his or her wage above the equilibrium wage. Such a worker fears not being hired because there are so many workers who will work for $210 per day. Similarly, so many firms are hiring labor that a single

For an in-depth analysis of the minimum wage visit the Economic Policy Institute at http://www.epinet.org/ *and click on "minimum wage."*

EXHIBIT 3   The Market Supply Curve of Labor

The upward-sloping supply curve of labor for the electronic components industry indicates that a direct relationship exists between the wage rate and the quantity of labor supplied. At point A, 20,000 workers are willing to work for $140 per day in this market. If the wage rate rises to $280 per day, 40,000 workers will supply their services to the electronic components labor market.

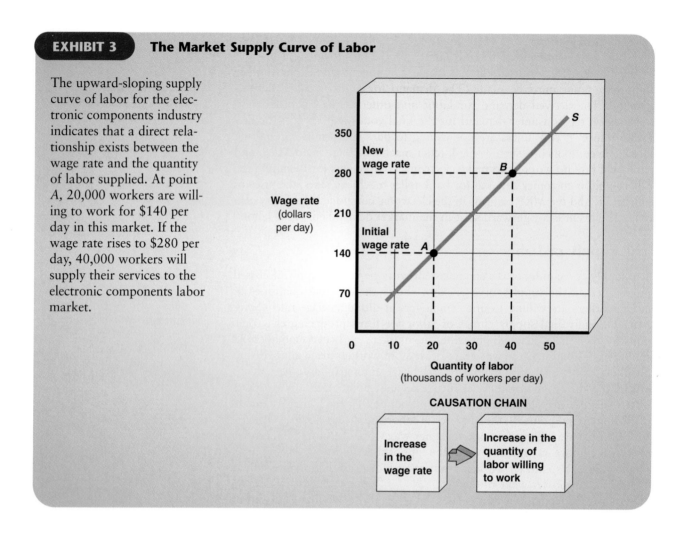

CAUSATION CHAIN

Increase in the wage rate → Increase in the quantity of labor willing to work

firm cannot influence the wage by paying workers more or less than the prevailing wage. Hence, a wage rate above $210 per day would create a surplus of workers seeking employment (unemployment) in the electronic components market, and a wage rate below $210 per day would cause a shortage.

Although the supply curve of labor is upward sloping for the electronic components market, this is not the case for an individual firm, such as Computech shown in Exhibit 4(b). Because a competitive labor market assumes that each firm is too small to influence the wage rate, Computech is a "wage taker" and therefore pays the market determined wage rate of $210 per day regardless of the quantity of labor it employs. For this reason, the labor supply to Computech is represented by a horizontal line at the equilibrium wage rate. Given this wage rate of $210 per day, Computech then hires labor up to the equilibrium point, *E,* where the wage rate equals the third worker's marginal revenue product.

EXHIBIT 4   **A Competitive Labor Market Determines the Firm's Equilibrium Wage**

(a) Electronic components labor market

(b) Computech

In part (a), the intersection of the supply of and the demand for labor curves determines the equilibrium wage rate of $210 per day in the electronic components industry. Part (b) illustrates that a single firm, such as Computech, is a "wage taker." The firm can hire all the workers it wants at this equilibrium wage, so its supply curve, *S*, is a horizontal line. Computech chooses to hire 3 workers, where the firm's demand curve for labor intersects its supply curve of labor.

Labor Unions

The perfectly competitive model does not apply to workers who belong to unions. Unions arose because workers recognized that acting together gave them more bargaining power than acting individually and being at the mercy of their employers. Some of the biggest unions are the Teamsters, United Auto Workers, National Education Association, and American Federation of Government Employees. Primary objectives of unions are to improve working conditions and raise the wages of union members above the level that would exist in a competitive labor market. To raise wages, unions use three basic strategies: (1) increase the demand for labor, (2) decrease the supply of labor, and (3) exert power to force employers to pay a wage rate above the equilibrium wage rate.

The American Federation of Musicians (http://www.afm.org) *is a trade union, the UAW* (http://www.uaw.org) *is an industrial union, the American Federation of Teachers* (http://www.aft.org) *is a public employee union, and the ABA* (http://www.abanet.org) *is an employee organization.*

Unions Increase the Demand for Labor

Now suppose the workers form a union. One way to increase wages is to use a method called *featherbedding*. This means the union forces firms to hire more workers than are required or to impose work rules that reduce output

EXHIBIT 5   A Union Causes an Increase in the Demand Curve for Labor

A union shifts the demand curve for labor rightward from D_1 to D_2 by featherbedding or other devices. As a result, the equilibrium wage rate increases from $210 per day at point E_1 to $280 per day at point E_2, and employment rises from 30,000 to 40,000 workers.

Wage rate (dollars per day)

Quantity of labor (thousands of workers per day)

CAUSATION CHAIN

| Union featherbeds | → | Increase in the demand for labor | → | Increase in wage rate and employment |

---

per worker. Another approach is to boost domestic demand for labor by decreasing competition from other nations. For example, the union might lobby Congress to protect the U.S. electronic parts industry against competition from Japan. Another approach might be to advertise and try to convince the public to "Look for the Union Label." Effective advertising would boost the demand for electronic products with union-made components and, in turn, the demand for union labor because it is *derived demand.*

Exhibit 5 shows how union power can be used to increase the demand curve for labor. This exhibit reproduces the labor market for electronic components workers from Exhibit 4(a). Begin at equilibrium point E_1, with the wage rate of $210 per day paid to each of 30,000 workers. Then the union causes the demand curve for labor to increase from D_1 to D_2. At the new equilibrium point, E_2, firms hire an additional 10,000 workers and pay each worker an extra $70 per day.

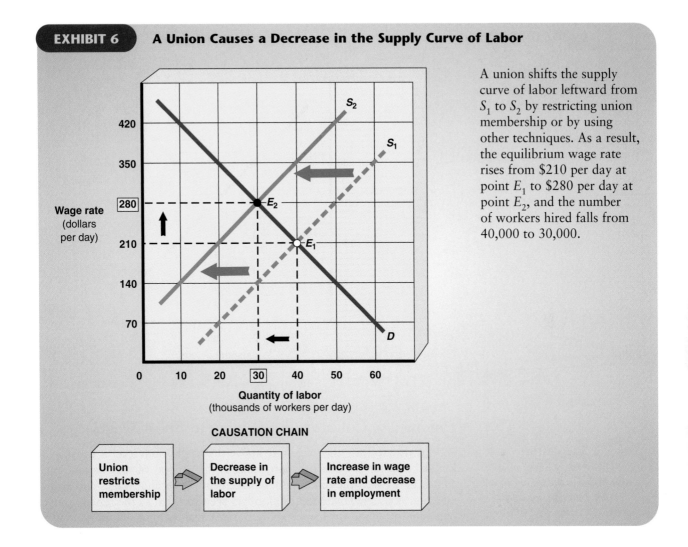

EXHIBIT 6 **A Union Causes a Decrease in the Supply Curve of Labor**

A union shifts the supply curve of labor leftward from S_1 to S_2 by restricting union membership or by using other techniques. As a result, the equilibrium wage rate rises from $210 per day at point E_1 to $280 per day at point E_2, and the number of workers hired falls from 40,000 to 30,000.

CAUSATION CHAIN

| Union restricts membership | ⇒ | Decrease in the supply of labor | ⇒ | Increase in wage rate and decrease in employment |

Unions Decrease the Supply of Labor

Exhibit 6 shows another way unions can use their power to increase the wage rate of their members—by restricting the supply of labor. Now suppose the labor market is in equilibrium at point E_1, with 40,000 workers making electronic units and earning $210 per day. Then the union uses its power to shift the supply curve of labor leftward from S_1 to S_2 by, say, requiring a longer apprenticeship, charging higher fees, or using some other device designed to reduce union membership. For example, the union might lobby for legislation to reduce immigration or to shorten working hours. As a result of these union actions, the equilibrium wage rate rises to $280 per day at point E_2, and employment is artificially reduced to 30,000 workers. It should be noted that self-serving practices of unions to limit the labor supply and raise wages can be disguised as standards of professionalism such as those required by the American Medical Association and the American Bar Association, teacher certification requirements, Ph.D. requirements for university faculty, and so on.

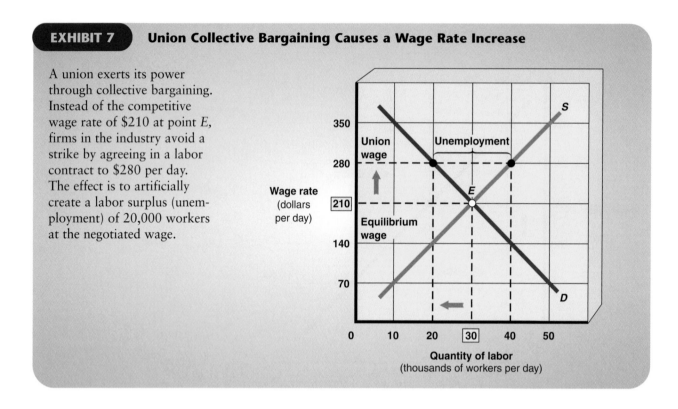

EXHIBIT 7   Union Collective Bargaining Causes a Wage Rate Increase

A union exerts its power through collective bargaining. Instead of the competitive wage rate of $210 at point *E*, firms in the industry avoid a strike by agreeing in a labor contract to $280 per day. The effect is to artificially create a labor surplus (unemployment) of 20,000 workers at the negotiated wage.

Unions Use Collective Bargaining to Boost Wages

Collective bargaining

The process of negotiating labor contracts between the union and management concerning wages and working conditions.

Visit the AFL-CIO (http://www.aflcio.org/ home.htm) *for the latest in the union movement.*

A third way to raise the wage rate above the equilibrium level is to use **collective bargaining.** Collective bargaining is the process of negotiating labor contracts between the union and management concerning wages and working conditions. By law, once a union has been certified as the representative of a majority of the workers, employers must deal with the union. If employers deny union demands, the union can strike and reduce profits until the firms agree to a higher wage rate.

The result of collective bargaining is shown in Exhibit 7. Again, we return to the situation depicted for the electronic components market in Exhibit 4(a). At the equilibrium wage rate of $210 per day (point *E*), there is no surplus or shortage of workers. Then the industry is unionized, and a collective bargaining agreement takes effect in which firms agree to pay the union wage rate of $280 per day. At the higher wage rate, employment falls from 30,000 to 20,000 workers. However, 40,000 workers wish to work for $280 per day, so there is a surplus of 20,000 unemployed workers in the industry. How might firms react to a situation in which they hire fewer workers and pay higher wages? Employers might respond by substituting capital for labor or by transferring operations overseas, where labor costs are lower than in the United States.

Finally, there are several factors that can cause either the demand curve for labor or the supply curve of labor to shift. Exhibit 8 provides a list of these factors.

> **EXHIBIT 8 Factors Causing Changes in Labor Demand and Labor Supply**
>
> | Changes in labor demand | Changes in labor supply |
> | --- | --- |
> | 1. Unions | 1. Unions |
> | 2. Prices of substitute inputs | 2. Demographic trends |
> | 3. Technology | 3. Expectations of future income |
> | 4. Demand for final products | 4. Changes in immigration laws |
> | 5. Marginal product of labor | 5. Education and training |

Union Membership around the World

How important are unions as measured by the percentage of the labor force that belongs to a union? Let's start during the Great Depression, when millions of people were out of work and union membership was relatively low (see Exhibit 9). To boost employment and earnings, President Franklin D. Roosevelt's National Industrial Recovery Act (NIRA) of 1933 established the right of employees to bargain collectively with their employers, but the act was declared unconstitutional by the Supreme Court in 1935. However, the 1935 National Labor Relations Act (NLRA), known as the Wagner Act, incorporated the labor provisions of the NIRA. The Wagner Act guaranteed workers the right to form unions and to engage in collective bargaining. The combined impact of this legislation and the production demands of World War II created a surge in union membership between 1935 and 1945.

Since World War II, union power has declined. Union membership has fallen from about 35 percent in 1945 to about 14 percent today. Since 1983, union membership of public sector workers grew slightly from 36.7 percent to 37.3 in 1999. On the other hand, union membership for private-sector workers has declined significantly from 16.5 percent to 9.4 percent over the same period of time.

Exhibit 10 shows the unionization rates in other countries. While in Sweden and Denmark nearly all workers belong to a union, union membership in the United States is far below that of other industrialized countries.

Employer Power

So far labor markets have been explained with employees possessing varying degrees of power to influence wage rates and employment while employers were competitive with no market power. However, significant power can exist on the employer side of the labor market. The extreme case occurs in a **monopsony**. Monopsony is a labor market in which a single firm hires labor. For example, a single textile mill, mining company, or housing contractor might be the only buyer of labor in a particular market. The classical phrase for this situation is the "company town," where for miles around a small

Monopsony
A labor market in which a single firm hires labor.

EXHIBIT 9   U.S. Union Membership, 1930–1999

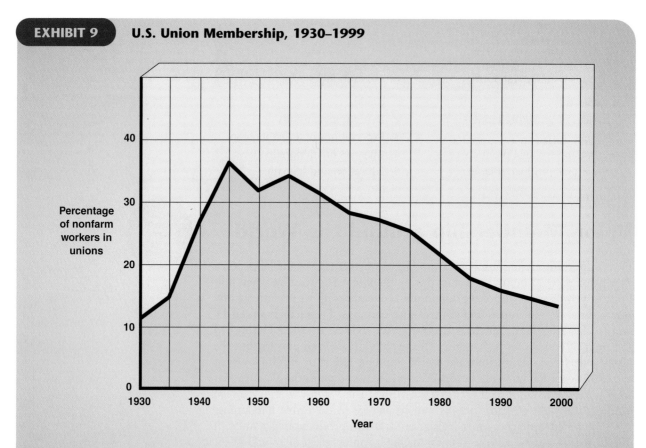

As a percentage of nonfarm workers, union membership in the United States grew most rapidly during the decade 1935–1945. Since its peak in 1945, union membership as a percentage of the labor force has fallen to about the level in 1935.

Source: *Statistical Abstract of the United States,* http://www.census.gov/prod/www/statistical-abstract-us.html, Table 712.

town everyone's livelihood depends on a single employer. The reason for the monopsony is the absence of other firms in the area competing for relatively immobile labor—because workers must acquire new skills to find work outside the company town market. Even if a firm doesn't dominate a local labor market, it may have monopsony power over certain types of labor. A hospital, for example, may be the only large employer of nurses in a local market, and therefore it has monopsony power.

Marginal Factor Cost

This chapter began by assuming Computech operated in a competitive labor market in which no single employer in the electronic components market had any direct influence on the market wage rate. Recall from Exhibit 4 that Computech is a wage taker. More precisely, Computech hires the quan-

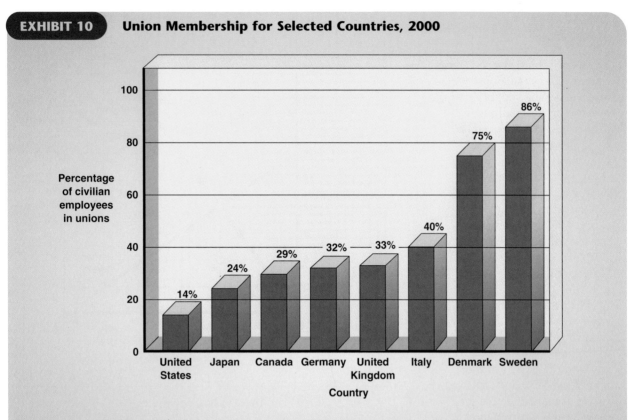

EXHIBIT 10 **Union Membership for Selected Countries, 2000**

Percentage of civilian employees in unions

United States	14%
Japan	24%
Canada	29%
Germany	32%
United Kingdom	33%
Italy	40%
Denmark	75%
Sweden	86%

Country

Union membership as a percentage of the civilian labor force in Sweden and Denmark is far above that of the United States. The unionization rates of other industrialized countries, such as Italy, the United Kingdom, Germany, Canada, and Japan, are also higher than the rate in the United States.

Source: U.S. Department of Labor, Bureau of International Labor Affairs, *Foreign Labor Trends 2000,* published by country.

tity of labor at the prevailing labor market equilibrium wage rate, which is determined by the point where the firm's downward-sloping *MRP* curve (demand curve for labor) intersects the horizontal supply curve of labor. The equilibrium wage rate is established by a competitive labor market beyond Computech's power to control.

Now we visit the isolated small town of Plainsville and find General Griffin's, which is a monopsonist producing turkeys. As shown in Exhibit 11, the supply of labor curve facing the monopsonist is upward sloping, rather than horizontal. The reason is that General Griffin's is the only firm hiring workers in Plainsville and it therefore faces the industry, or entire, supply curve of labor in the Plainsville labor market. This situation compares to that of the monopolist, which faces the industry demand curve for a particular product. As a result, the monopolist in a product market cannot

EXHIBIT 11   **A Monopsonist Determines Its Wage Rate**

The monopsonist, General Griffin's, faces the industry upward-sloping supply curve of labor in the small town of Plainsville. As the wage rate rises, all workers must be paid the same higher wage. As a result, the change in total wage cost (marginal factor cost in column 4) exceeds the wage paid to the last worker (column 1). The *MFC* curve therefore lies above the supply curve of labor.

The demand curve for labor is the marginal revenue product (*MRP*) or the worth to the monopsonist of each worker it hires. The intersection of the *MFC* and *MRP* curves at point *E* determines that General Griffin's hires 2 workers per hour. Because this firm has a monopsony in the Plainsville labor market, it can pay $6 per hour at point *B* on the supply curve of labor, which is enough to attract 2 workers. However, the worker is exploited because the *MRP* at point *E* for the second worker is $12 per hour, and the wage rate is only $6. In a competitive labor market, the equilibrium would be point *C*, paying a higher wage and employing more workers.

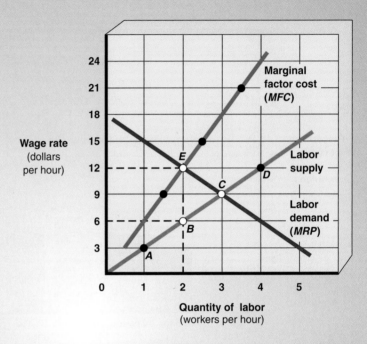

Points	(1) Wage rate (per hour)	(2) Labor input (workers per hour)	(3) Total wage cost (per hour) [(1) × (2)]	(4) Marginal factor cost (*MFC*) [Δ(3)/Δ(2)]
	$ 0	0	$ 0	
				$ 3
A	3	1	3	
				9
B	6	2	12	
				15
C	9	3	27	
				21
D	12	4	48	

CHECKPOINT

Can the Minimum Wage Create Jobs?

In Chapter 4, Exhibit 5 explained that the effect of the minimum wage in a competitive labor market is to decrease the number of unskilled workers employed. Assume the minimum wage is $9, and consider the effect on the monopsonist represented in Exhibit 11. This means by law the monopsonist cannot hire a worker for a lower wage. Contrary to the case of perfect competition, can the minimum wage increase the number of persons working in the case of monopsony? Explain your answer using Exhibit 11.

sell an additional unit of a good without lowering the price, and the marginal revenue curve falls below the demand curve. For the monopsonist, a distinction exists between the supply curve of labor and the **marginal factor cost (*MFC*)** curve. Marginal factor cost is the additional total cost resulting from a one-unit increase in the quantity of a factor. Note that the *MFC* curve starts above the bottom of the supply curve of labor and then rises above it. The *MFC* points are plotted at the midpoints because the change in total wage cost occurs between each additional unit of labor. Having made this observation, relax and take a deep breath; then we will proceed to the nuts and bolts of monopsonist theory.

If General Griffin's pays $3 per hour at point *A* on the upward-sloping supply curve of labor in Plainsville, only 1 worker will be willing to be hired. If the monopsonist wants to hire more labor, it must offer higher wages. If the firm raises its wage offer to $6 per hour for each worker (point *B*), the quantity of labor supplied increases to 2 workers per hour. In the exhibit, the total wage cost per hour in column 3 is computed by multiplying the wage rate per hour in column 1 times the number of workers per hour in column 2. At point *A*, the total wage cost per hour is $3, which equals the wage rate. At point *B*, the total wage cost per hour rises to $12, and *MFC* is greater than the wage rate of $6 per hour. The explanation is that all workers are assumed to perform the same job. Consequently, the first worker will demand to be paid the same wage rate as the second worker hired at the higher wage rate. Stated differently, General Griffin's must pay a higher wage to each additional worker, as well as all previously hired workers. If General Griffin's attempts to pay different wage rates for the same job, worker morale will deteriorate causing labor unrest. Comparing points *A* through *D* confirms that *MFC* is greater than the wage rate for a monopsonist, much like the monopolist's price, which is greater than the marginal revenue.

> **Conclusion** *Because the monopsonist can hire additional workers only by raising the wage rate for all workers, the marginal factor cost exceeds the wage rate.*

Marginal factor cost (*MFC*)
The additional total cost resulting from a one-unit increase in the quantity of a factor.

CHECKPOINT

If You Don't Like It Mickey, Take Your Bat and Go Home

Mickey Mantle told of his salary negotiations in his autobiography *The Mick*. After winning baseball's Triple Crown in 1955, his salary increased from about $85,000 to $100,000. The next season he raised his batting average even higher, and the Yankee team owner offered him a pay cut. What is the most likely explanation for the owner's behavior—an increase in the supply of star baseball players, owner monopsony power, or the owner's desire that Mantle find another team?

Monopsonistic Equilibrium

For more on the NCAA, visit it Web site at http://www.ncaa.org.

How many workers will General Griffin's hire? To answer this question requires the demand curve for labor that traces labor's marginal revenue product (*MRP*), explained earlier in this chapter. Recall that *MRP* reflects the value or contribution of each additional worker because *MRP* is the increase in total revenue produced by hiring each additional worker. Also, as explained in Chapter 8, the profit-maximizing producer selects the level of output where marginal revenue equals marginal cost. Similarly, *the monopsonist in the labor market hires the quantity of labor at which the marginal revenue product of labor equals its marginal factor cost.*

In Exhibit 11, General Griffin's will follow the *MRP* = *MFC* rule by hiring 2 workers, determined by the intersection of the *MRP* and *MFC* curves at point *E*. But pay special attention to this point: The monopsonist is a "wage maker." It has labor market power and does not have to pay $12 per hour, which equals the contribution of the second worker measured by his or her *MRP*. Instead of paying workers what their services are worth, the monopsonist follows the supply curve of labor, selects point *B*, and pays $6 per hour, rather than $12 per hour. Since $6 per hour is all the firm must pay to attract and hire 2 workers, the monopsonist can exploit labor by paying less than its marginal revenue product.

One alternative for labor facing a powerful employer is to organize a powerful union and engage in collective bargaining. Totally successful collective bargaining by a labor union could raise the wage rate from $6 per hour at point *B* to $12 per hour at point *E*. General Griffin's will resist the union's demands and offer a lower wage closer to point *B*. Thus, points *B* and *E* represent the boundaries of a potential final settlement. What the negotiated final equilibrium wage rate will be depends on the tactics and resources of the negotiating parties.

Finally, suppose the monopsony is broken up into a large number of small firms. Recall from earlier in this chapter that in competitive labor markets additional workers are hired to the point where the wage rate is equal to *MRP*. In this case, the supply curve of labor intersects the *MRP* (demand) curve at point *C*, and more workers would be hired with $9 per hour paid to each worker.

Conclusion *A monopsonist hires fewer workers and pays a lower wage than a firm in a competitive labor market.*

Should College Athletes Be Paid?

Applicable Concept: monopsony

It was perfect football weather on a beautiful autumn Saturday at Nebraska State's stadium. There was a hush in the crowd of 80,000 as the clock showed 5 seconds left in the game and the scoreboard read Home 26 Visitor 30. The Screaming Eagles were playing the Fighting Irish, and the season was on the line. With time running out, the Eagles' All-American quarterback, Joe Wyoming, launched a desperation pass from his 45-yard line. The pass hit the extended fingers of a wide receiver who leaped over three defenders at the Irish 25-yard line and then ran into the end zone all alone. The home crowd roared with the joy of ecstasy after staring defeat in the face.

So the season had been in the hands of Joe Wyoming, who received a full scholarship, which cost the university more than $40,000 over four years. Because Joe led the Eagles to victory over Notre Dame, the team played in the Sugar Bowl, which paid Nebraska State $5 million for the appearance. In addition, next year's ticket sales, alumni contributions, and trademark licensing boosted revenues $10 million, while applications for admission to the university increased sharply.

Economist John Leonard argues that college athletes are clearly underpaid because players cannot be paid salaries under National Collegiate Athletic Association (NCAA) rules. His study estimated that a star college football player who is named to an All-American team generates a marginal revenue product of $100,000 per year for the university. Yet, that athlete is paid only $10,000 per year.

In Chapter 10, a cartel was explained as a group of firms that use a collusive agreement to act as a monopoly. NCAA regulations serve as a collusive agreement among colleges and universities to act as a monopsony and hire the services of college-bound athletes. Just like an output or sellers' cartel, such as the Organization of Petroleum Exporting Countries (OPEC), the NCAA must enforce the rules against cheaters.

Because this agreement holds players' wages far below their marginal revenue product, the gap creates an incentive for schools to offer "illegal" inducements of cars, money, clothes, and trips to attract good players. Such cheating benefits the college athletes whose wages are raised closer to their marginal revenue products. The school that is not caught benefits by recruiting better players, achieving athletic success, and receiving greater sports revenue. The other schools that follow the rules must depend on the NCAA to punish cheaters by taking away TV appearances, tournament play, bowl invitations, and scholarships.

ANALYZE THE ISSUE

Do you favor paying college athletes salaries determined by a competitive labor market, rather than an NCAA agreement? Explain.

KEY CONCEPTS

Marginal revenue product
　(*MRP*)
Demand curve for labor

Derived demand
Supply curve of labor
Human capital

Collective bargaining
Monopsony

Marginal factor cost
　(*MFC*)

SUMMARY

- **Marginal revenue product** (*MRP*) is determined by a worker's contribution to a firm's total revenue. Algebraically, the marginal revenue product equals the price of the product times the worker's marginal product: $MRP = P \times MP$.

- The **demand curve for labor** shows the quantities of labor a firm is willing to hire at different prices of labor. The marginal revenue product (*MRP*) of labor curve is the firm's demand curve for labor. Summing individual demand for labor curves gives the market demand curve for labor.

Demand curve for labor

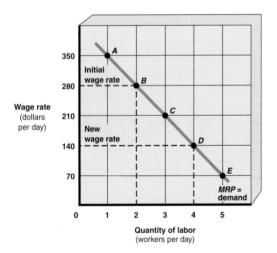

- **Derived demand** means that a firm demands labor because labor is productive. Changes in consumer demand for a product cause changes in the demand for labor and for other resources used to make the product.

- The **supply curve of labor** shows the quantities of workers willing to work at different prices of labor. The market supply curve of labor is derived by adding the individual supply curves of labor.

Supply curve of labor

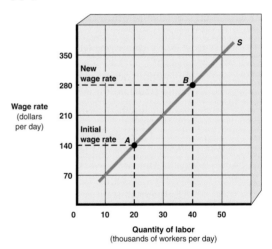

- **Human capital** is the accumulated investment people make in education, training, experience, and health in order to make themselves more productive. One explanation for earnings differences is differences in human capital.

- **Collective bargaining** is the process through which a union and management negotiate a labor contract.

- **Monopsony** is a labor market in which a single firm hires labor. Because the monopsonist faces the industry supply curve of labor and each worker is paid the same wage, changes in total wage cost exceed the wage rate necessary to hire each additional worker. As a result, the **marginal factor cost (*MFC*)** of labor curve, which measures changes in total wage cost per worker, lies above the supply curve of labor. The monopsonist's wage rate and quantity of labor are determined where the *MFC* equals *MRP*. Since at this point the worker's *MRP* is greater than the wage paid, the monopsonist exploits the workers.

Monopsony

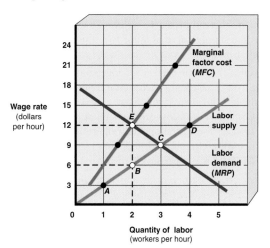

SUMMARY OF CONCLUSION STATEMENTS

- A perfectly competitive firm's marginal revenue product is equal to the marginal product of its labor times the price of its product. Expressed as a formula: $MRP = P \times MP$.
- A firm hires additional workers up to the point where the *MRP* equals the wage rate.

- Because the monopsonist can hire additional workers only by raising the wage rate for all workers, the marginal factor cost exceeds the wage rate.
- A monopsonist hires fewer workers and pays a lower wage than a firm in a competitive labor market.

STUDY QUESTIONS AND PROBLEMS

1. Consider this statement: "Workers demand jobs, and employers supply jobs." Do you agree or disagree? Explain.

2. The Zippy Paper Company has no control over either the price of paper or the wage it pays its workers. The following table shows the relationship between the number of workers Zippy hires and total output:

Labor input (workers per day)	Total output (boxes of paper per day)
0	0
1	15
2	27
3	36
4	43
5	48
6	51

If the selling price is $10 per box, answer the following questions:
   a. What is the marginal revenue product (*MRP*) of each worker?
   b. How many workers will Zippy hire if the wage rate is $100 per day?
   c. How many workers will Zippy hire if the wage rate is $75 per day?
   d. Assume the wage rate is $75 per day and the price of a box of paper is $20. How many workers will Zippy hire?

3. Assume the Grand Slam Baseball Store sells $100 worth of baseball cards each day, with 1 employee operating the store. The owner decides to hire a second worker, and the 2 workers together sell $150 worth of baseball cards. What is the second worker's marginal revenue product (*MRP*)? If the price per card sold is $5, what is the second worker's marginal product (*MP*)?

4. What is the relationship between the marginal revenue product (*MRP*) and the demand curve for labor?

5. The market supply curve of labor is upward sloping, but the supply curve of labor for a single firm is horizontal. Explain why.

6. Assume the labor market for loggers is perfectly competitive. How would each of the following events influence the wage rate loggers are paid?
   a. Consumers boycott products made with wood.
   b. Loggers form a union that requires longer apprenticeships, charges high fees, and uses other devices designed to reduce union membership.

7. How does a human capital investment in education increase your lifetime earnings?

8. Suppose states pass laws requiring public school teachers to have a master's degree in order to retain their teaching certificates. What effect would this legislation have on the labor market for teachers?

9. Use the data in question 2, and assume the equilibrium wage rate is $90 per day, determined in a perfectly competitive labor market. Now explain the impact of a union-negotiated collective bargaining agreement that changes the wage rate to $100 per day.

10. Some economists argue that the American Medical Association and the American Bar Association create an effect on labor markets similar to that of a labor union. Do you agree?

11. The Jacksonville Jaguars is an expansion professional football team in the National Football League (NFL). NFL draft and employment rules create monopsony power for each member club. In 1995, the Jaguars were in the process of hiring players. Using the following hypothetical table of data, construct a graph to determine the number of quarterbacks the Jaguars hired and the salary paid to each quarterback. Assuming the labor market is competitive, what are the number of quarterbacks hired and the salary paid each?

(1) Salary (thousands of dollars)	(2) Number of quarterbacks	(3) Total cost of quarterbacks (thousands of dollars)	(4) Marginal factor cost (*MFC*) (thousands of dollars)	(5) Marginal revenue product (*MRP*) (thousands of dollars)
$ 0	0	$ 0	—	—
100	1	100	$100	$700
200	2	400	300	600
300	3	900	500	500
400	4	1,600	700	400
500	5	2,500	900	300

ONLINE EXERCISES

Exercise 1

Visit the Economic Policy Institute (http://www.epinet .org/) and click on "wage and income trends." What has happened to wages for workers over time?

Exercise 2

Visit Business Cycle Indicators Home Page (http://www .globalexposure.com) and select Wages/Labor. Then choose Index of average hourly compensation and Index of real average hourly compensation for the last 10 years. Compare these graphs.

Exercise 3

Visit GPO Gate, Catalog of Economic Report of the President (http://www.gpo.ucop.edu/catalog/erp99_appen_b .html). Select Table B-36, civilian employment and unemployment by sex and age, and follow these steps:

1. Compute the civilian population male and female employment ratio, and graph this data for the last 10 years.

2. Explain the trend in these data.

Exercise 4

America's Labor Market Information System (ALMIS), a program sponsored by the Employment and Training Administration (ETA) at the U.S. Department of Labor, offers on-line labor market information (http://almis.dws .state.ut.us/). Review the national projections for the occupation of our choice. What are the projections for the occupation of your choice in the state in which you currently reside?

CHECKPOINT ANSWERS

Can the Minimum Wage Create Jobs?

The minimum wage of $9 corresponds to point *C* in Exhibit 11. At this point, the labor supply and labor demand (*MRP*) curves intersect. Thus, the effect of the minimum wage is to force the monopsonist to operate at the equilibrium that would be established in a competitive labor market. If you said under monopsony the minimum wage could raise the wage rate and create additional employment, YOU ARE CORRECT.

If You Don't Like It Mickey, Take Your Bat and Go Home

Baseball players had no free-agent rights in the 1950s. If Mantle did not like the salary offer, his only choice was to go back to his home in Oklahoma. Faced with that alternative, he accepted the salary cut. If you said each owner achieved monopsony power by prohibiting players from going to another team, YOU ARE CORRECT.

PRACTICE QUIZ

For a visual explanation of the correct answers, visit the tutorial at http://tucker.swcollege.com.

1. Marginal revenue product measures the increase in
   a. output resulting from one more unit of labor.
   b. total revenue resulting from one more unit of output.
   c. revenue per unit from one more unit of output.
   d. total revenue resulting from one more unit of labor.

2. Troll Corporation sells dolls for $10 each in a market that is perfectly competitive. Increasing the number of workers from 100 to 101 would cause output to rise from 500 to 510 dolls per day. Troll should hire the 101st worker only when the wage is
   a. $100 or less per day.
   b. more than $100 per day.
   c. $5.10 or less per day.
   d. none of the above.

3. Derived demand for labor depends on the
   a. cost of factors of production used in the product.
   b. market supply curve of labor.
   c. consumer demand for the final goods produced by labor.
   d. firm's total revenue less economic profit.

4. If demand for a product falls, the demand curve for labor used to produce the product will
   a. shift leftward.
   b. shift rightward.
   c. shift upward.
   d. remain unchanged.

5. The owner of a restaurant will hire waiters if the
   a. additional labor's pay is close to the minimum wage.
   b. marginal product is at the maximum.
   c. additional work of the employees adds more to total revenue than to costs.
   d. waiters do not belong to a union.

6. In a perfectly competitive market, the demand curve for labor
   a. slopes upward.
   b. slopes downward because of diminishing marginal productivity.
   c. is perfectly elastic at the equilibrium wage rate.
   d. is described by all of the above.

7. A union can influence the equilibrium wage rate by
   a. featherbedding.
   b. requiring longer apprenticeships.
   c. favoring trade restrictions on foreign products.
   d. all of the above.
   e. none of the above.

8. In which of the following market structures is the firm *not* a price taker in the factor market?
   a. Oligopoly
   b. Monopsony
   c. Monopoly
   d. Perfect competition

9. The extra cost of obtaining each additional unit of a factor of production is called the marginal
   a. physical product.
   b. revenue product.
   c. factor cost.
   d. implicit cost.

10. A monopsonist's marginal factor cost (MFC) curve lies above its supply curve because the firm must
    a. increase the price of its product to sell more.
    b. lower the price of its product to sell more.
    c. increase the wage rate to hire more labor.
    d. lower the wage rate to hire more labor.

11. To maximize profits, a monopsonist will hire the quantity of labor to the point where the marginal factor cost is equal to
    a. marginal physical product.
    b. marginal revenue product.
    c. total revenue product.
    d. any of the above.

12. BigBiz, a local monopolist, currently hires 50 workers and pays them $6 per hour. To attract an additional worker to its labor force, BigBiz would have to raise the wage rate to $6.25 per hour. What is BigBiz's marginal factor cost?
    a. $6.25 per hour
    b. $12.50 per hour
    c. $18.75 per hour
    d. $20.00 per hour

13. Suppose a firm can hire 100 workers at $8.00 per hour, but must pay $8.05 per hour to hire 101 workers. Marginal factor cost (MFC) for the 101st worker is approximately equal to
    a. $8.00.
    b. $8.05.
    c. $13.05.
    d. $13.00.

14. A monopsonist in equilibrium has a marginal revenue product of $10 per worker hour. Its equilibrium wage rate must be
    a. less than $10.
    b. equal to $10.
    c. greater than $10.
    d. equal to $5.

4

Microeconomic Policy Issues

These three chapters apply micro principles learned in previous chapters to explore policy issues concerning some important economic topics. The first chapter in this part extends the theory of labor market into an examination of actual data on income and poverty. The second chapter mixes politics and economic theory to discuss interesting topics such as the Microsoft case and the deregulation of energy. The third chapter takes a closer look at ways to deal with externalities such as pollution permits, which are actually traded on the Chicago Board of Trade.

CHAPTER 12

Income Distribution, Poverty, and Discrimination

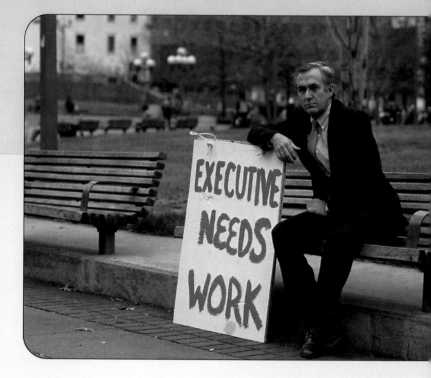

The previous chapter examined how variations in wages are determined in competitive and monopsonistic labor markets. These labor supply and demand models do not give the complete picture of labor markets. In this chapter, however, we turn our attention to the distribution of income, poverty, and discrimination, which are important topics related to labor market wage decisions.

The chapter begins by exploring the controversial issue of how the total family income "pie" is cut into various size "slices" or shares for different groups of families. You will examine government data that indicate the trend over the years in the share of income for the richest fifth of the population and the poorest fifth. Here the hotly contested issue of whether the "rich got richer" at the expense of the poor is addressed. In addition, the inequality of income in the United States is compared to that of other countries.

Poverty is an unhappy consequence of an unequal income distribution. Eighteenth-century English poet and essayist Samuel Johnson stated "a decent provision for the poor is the true test of civilization." Former President Bill Clinton campaigned in 1992 on a pledge to "end welfare as we know it," and in 1996 the president signed a bipartisan landmark bill to reform welfare. Today, the consequences of this law are being felt throughout the nation. Another purpose of this chapter is to define poverty and ask what can be done about it.

The chapter concludes with the subject of discrimination, which is one possible explanation for unequal income distribution and poverty. Here you will apply the supply and demand model to explain why women earn less on average than men and African Americans earn less than whites.

In this chapter, you will learn to solve these economics puzzles:

■ Could the rich become richer and other income groups also become better off?

■ How can a negative income tax solve the welfare controversy?

■ What is the effect on labor markets of laws that protect women from jobs deemed "too strenuous" or "too dangerous"?

The Distribution of Income

One function of labor markets is to determine the *distribution of income*—that is, how wages and salaries are divided among members of society. Recall from Chapter 2 that the For Whom question is one of the three basic questions that any economic system must answer. Here we study the For Whom question in more detail.

Trends in Income Distribution

One way to analyze the distribution of income in the United States is illustrated in Exhibit 1. In column 1 of this exhibit, families are divided into six groups according to the percentage of the total annual money income they received. The remaining columns of the table give the percentages of the total money income for each of the six groups in selected years since 1929. These data reveal changes in the distribution of income among families over time. For example, families with income in the top 5 percent in 1929 earned about 10 percent more of the total income pie than they did in 2000. Otherwise, the distribution of income has not fluctuated greatly since 1947. However, there is concern that since 1970 the percentage of income received by

The U.S. Bureau of the Census provides current and historical data on income distribution at http://www .census.gov/hhes/www/income .html.

EXHIBIT 1 The Division of the Total Annual Money Income among Families, 1929–2000						
Percentage of families	**1929**	**1947**	**1970**	**1980**	**1990**	**2000**
Lowest fifth	3.5%	5.0%	5.5%	5.1%	4.6%	4.3%
Second-lowest fifth	9.0	11.9	12.2	11.5	10.8	9.8
Middle fifth	13.8	17.0	17.6	17.5	16.6	15.5
Second-highest fifth	19.3	23.1	23.8	24.3	23.8	23.0
Highest fifth	54.4	43.0	40.9	41.6	44.3	47.4
Highest 5%	30.0	17.5	15.6	15.3	17.4	20.8

Source: U.S. Bureau of the Census, http://www.census.gov/hhes/income/histinc/incfamdet .html Table F-2.

EXHIBIT 2 Median Money Income of Families, 2000

Characteristic	Median income*
All families	$50,891
Families headed by a male	37,523
Families headed by a female	25,787
Families with head aged 25–34 years	45,890
Families with head aged 65 years and over	32,854
Families headed by person with less than 9th grade education	24,964
Families with head high school graduate	44,248
Families with head attaining Bachelor's degree	77,244

*Fifty percent of families earn less than the median income and 50 percent earn more.
Source: U.S. Bureau of the Census, http://www.census.gov/hhes/income/histinc/incfamdet.html, Tables F-7, F-11, and F-18.

families in the lowest 20 percent group has fallen, while the income percentages received by the families in the highest fifth and the highest 5 percent have risen.

As shown in Exhibit 1, there is an unequal distribution of income among families. Why didn't each fifth of the families receive 20 percent of the total income? There are many reasons. For example, Exhibit 2 reveals that families headed by a college graduate fare better than those headed by an individual with less education. Recall from the previous chapter that human capital refers to education and skills that increase a worker's productivity. Workers with a greater investment in human capital are likely to be worth more to an employer. Data in this exhibit also indicate that families headed by a male generally earn more than those headed by a female.

Equality versus Efficiency

Because the data presented in Exhibits 1 and 2 show that an unequal distribution of income exists in the United States, the normative question to be debated concerns the pros and cons of a more equal income distribution. Those who favor greater equality fear the link between the rich and political power. The wealthy may well use their money to influence national policies that benefit the rich. It is also argued that income inequality results in unequal opportunities for various groups. For example, children of the poor cannot obtain a college education, and, therefore, their underutilized productive capacity is a waste of human capital. The poor are also unable to afford health care, and this condition is a national concern.

Advocates of income inequality pose this question. Suppose you had your choice to live in egalitarian society *A*, where every person earns $40,000 a year, or society *B*, where 20 percent earn $100,000 and 80 percent earn $30,000. You would choose society *B* because the incentive to earn more and live better is worth the risk of earning less and living worse. After all, why is the average income higher in society *B*? The answer is that income inequality gives people an incentive to be productive. In contrast, people in society *A* lack such motivation because everyone earns the same income. Those who favor equality of income believe that critics ignore the nonmonetary incentives, such as pride in one's work and nation, that can motivate people.

A frequently debated topic concerning income inequality is whether the "rich got richer" during the 1980s and 1990s. As we observed earlier, the data in Exhibit 1 reveal that the percentages of total income received by the highest 5 percent and the highest fifth did increase, while the percentages received by each of the fifths below the highest decreased slightly.

Conclusion *Measured by distribution of family money income, the richest families did become a little richer and the rest of the family groups a little poorer during the 1980s and the 1990s.*

It is important to note that simply observing changes in income distribution over time does not tell the whole story. Exhibit 3 traces real median family income, adjusted for rising prices, for the period 1980–2000. This measure indicates the trend of the average level of income received by all groups. Generally, the trend for real median income since the 1980s was upward. This means the size of the income "pie" grew, and, therefore, the sizes of all the slices grew larger. However, consistent with the distribution data, the relative share of the pie for those with the biggest slice got slightly larger. Beginning in 1990, real median income fell steadily until 1993, but since then it has risen to a new high in 2000.

The Lorenz Curve

The distribution of income data presented in Exhibit 1 can be represented by the **Lorenz curve.** The Lorenz curve is a graph of the actual cumulative distribution of income compared to a perfectly equal cumulative distribution of income. This curve is a primary tool for measuring income distribution developed in 1905 by statistician M. O. Lorenz. Look at the hypothetical Lorenz curve in Exhibit 4. The vertical axis measures the *cumulative* percentage of family income, and the horizontal axis measures the *cumulative* percentage of families from poorest to richest. Starting at the lower left-hand corner on the graph, 0 families earned 0 percent of the cumulative percentage of money income. At the upper right-hand corner on the graph, 100 percent of the families earned 100 percent of the cumulative percentage of money income. The combination of other total family–total money income points between 0 and 100 percent forms the Lorenz curve.

Reading along the horizontal axis, each fifth (20 percent) of the cumulative percentage of families corresponds to its cumulative share of income earned measured along the curve. At point *A*, the lowest 20 percent of families receive 10 percent of total or cumulative income. To read this, go from the 20 percent point on the horizontal axis up to point *A* on the Lorenz curve. Then draw a horizontal line to the vertical axis, and read that it intersects this axis at 10 percent. Point B is interpreted as the lowest 40 percent of families earn 10 percent plus 15 percent, which equals a cumulative

Lorenz curve

A graph of the actual cumulative distribution of income compared to a perfectly equal cumulative distribution of income.

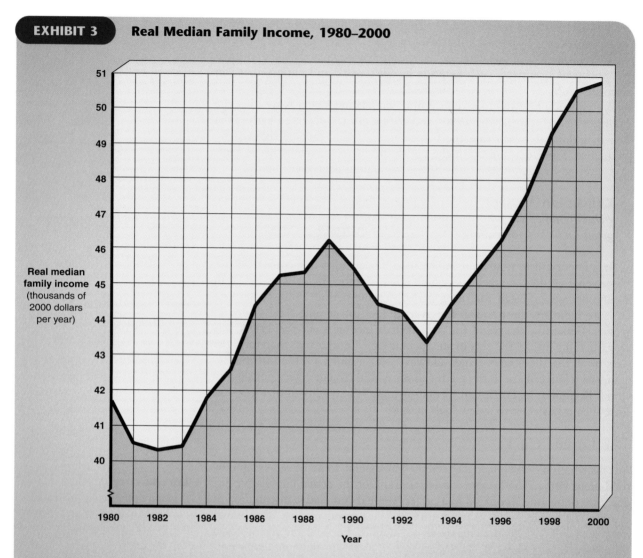

EXHIBIT 3   **Real Median Family Income, 1980–2000**

Real median income measures the income adjusted for inflation received by all families in the United States. Fifty percent of families earn less and 50 percent earn more than the median income. This measure fell and rose during the early 1980s, but the trend was generally upward since the 1980s. Between 1982 and 1989, real median income increased by 13 percent. Beginning in 1990, real median income fell steadily until 1993, but since then it has risen to a new high in 2000.

Source: U.S. Bureau of the Census, http://www.census.gov/hhes/income/histinc/indfamdet.html, Table F-7.

share of 25 percent. Similarly, point *C* is the cumulative share earned by the lowest 60 percent of families, which equals 40 percent. Finally, point *D* is a bit tricky to interpret. At this point, the lowest 80 percent of families receive about 62 percent of total income. And here is the twist. You must interpret that the richest 20 percent of families earn 38 percent of income (100 percent − 62 percent).

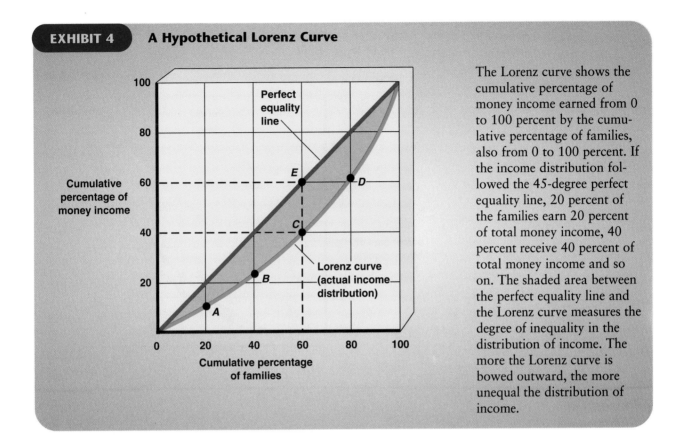

EXHIBIT 4   **A Hypothetical Lorenz Curve**

The Lorenz curve shows the cumulative percentage of money income earned from 0 to 100 percent by the cumulative percentage of families, also from 0 to 100 percent. If the income distribution followed the 45-degree perfect equality line, 20 percent of the families earn 20 percent of total money income, 40 percent receive 40 percent of total money income and so on. The shaded area between the perfect equality line and the Lorenz curve measures the degree of inequality in the distribution of income. The more the Lorenz curve is bowed outward, the more unequal the distribution of income.

We now turn to the 45-degree line above the Lorenz curve that cuts the box in half. This line represents perfect equality: 20 percent of the families receive 20 percent of total income, 40 percent of the families receive 40 percent of total income, and so on. The distance of the Lorenz curve from the perfect equality line is therefore a measure of unequal income distribution. The gap between points *C* and *E*, for example, indicates that 60 percent of families earn 20 percent less of total income than required for perfect equality. Similar measurements generate the shaded area between the Lorenz curve and the perfect equality line. Thus, the shaded area is a measure of the degree of income inequality for our hypothetical data. A larger shaded area would mean greater income inequality, and the shape of the Lorenz curve would become more bowed outward. A smaller shaded area would represent a more equal income distribution, and the Lorenz curve would be a flatter curve.

It is very important to note that there are limitations associated with using money income statistics. Such data are not adjusted for government-provided food stamps, medical care, housing, or other goods and services. Money income also reflects income before taxes and does not measure unreported income or wealth. Still, used carefully, the Lorenz curve is a convenient tool for visualizing the degree of income inequality.

EXHIBIT 5   **Lorenz Curves for Family Income Distribution in the United States, 1929 and 2000**

Since 1929, the Lorenz curve has shifted somewhat inward toward the perfect equality line. Thus, there has been a reduction in the inequality of distribution of family money income over these years.

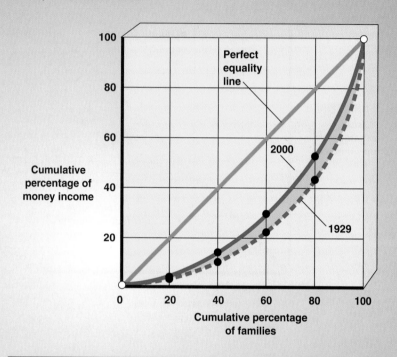

Percentage of families	1929		2000	
	Percentage share	Cumulative share	Percentage share	Cumulative share
Lowest fifth	3.5%	3.5%	4.3%	4.3%
Second-lowest fifth	9.0	12.5	9.8	14.1
Middle fifth	13.8	26.3	15.5	29.6
Second-highest fifth	19.3	45.6	23.0	52.6
Highest fifth	54.4	100.0	47.4	100.0

Income Distribution Trend in the United States

In Exhibit 1, we looked at income distributions for selected years between 1929 and 2000. What can we conclude from these data using the Lorenz curve? Has the overall income distribution become more or less equal? The table in Exhibit 5 restates the income share data for 1929 and 2000 from Exhibit 1, and the cumulative percentage shares of families of quintiles are calculated from the percentage shares.

Exhibit 5 suggests that overall money income distribution has changed little over the period. In the exhibit, there is only a small shaded area between the 1929 and 2000 Lorenz curves. However, the share of income received by the highest fifth of families fell from 54 percent in 1929 to 47 percent in 2000.

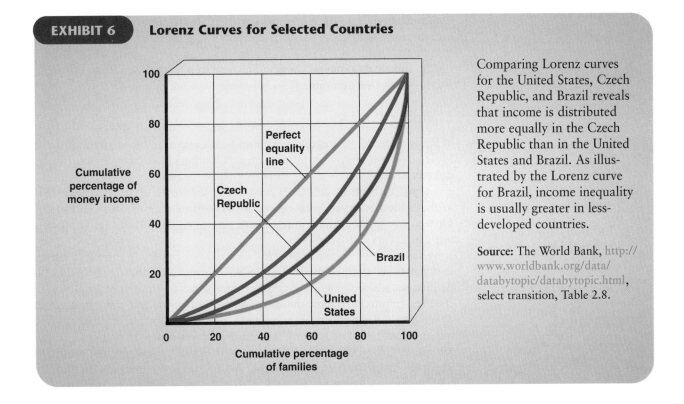

EXHIBIT 6 **Lorenz Curves for Selected Countries**

(Graph: Cumulative percentage of money income on vertical axis (0 to 100); Cumulative percentage of families on horizontal axis (0 to 100). Curves shown for Perfect equality line, Czech Republic, Brazil, and United States.)

Comparing Lorenz curves for the United States, Czech Republic, and Brazil reveals that income is distributed more equally in the Czech Republic than in the United States and Brazil. As illustrated by the Lorenz curve for Brazil, income inequality is usually greater in less-developed countries.

Source: The World Bank, http://www.worldbank.org/data/databytopic/databytopic.html, select transition, Table 2.8.

Conclusion *The Lorenz curve has shifted only slightly inward and therefore closer to the perfect equality line between 1929 and 2000.*

International Comparisons of Income Distribution

How does the distribution of income in the United States compare with that of other countries? Exhibit 6 presents separate Lorenz curves for the United States, the Czech Republic, and Brazil. This exhibit indicates that the degree of income inequality in the United States exceeds that of the Czech Republic. On the other hand, income distribution is more equal in the United States than in Brazil, In general, the distribution of income in developed nations, such as the United States, Germany, Italy, and Sweden, is more equal than in developing nations, such as Brazil, Mexico, and Zimbabwe.

Poverty

Having discussed the broader question of how the degree of income distribution inequality is measured, we now turn the spotlight on the fiercely debated issue of poverty. We are all disturbed by homelessness and hungry children. How can poverty exist in a nation of abundance such as the

The U.S. Bureau of the Census provides current and historical data on, and information addressing, poverty at http://www.census.gov/hhes/www/poverty.html.

United States? Can economists offer useful ideas to reform and improve our current welfare system? Most of the nation agrees that the welfare system must periodically undergo reforms to reduce poverty, cut welfare dependency, and save taxpayers money. The first step to understanding the problem is to ask this question: Who is poor?

Defining Poverty

What is poverty? Is it eating pork and beans when others are eating steak? Or is poverty a family having one car when others have two or more? Is the poverty standard only a matter of normative arguments? Indeed, the term *poverty* is difficult to define. A person whose income is comparatively low in the United States may be viewed as well off in a less-developed country. Or what we in the United States regard as poverty today might have seemed a life of luxury 200 years ago.

There are two views of poverty. One defines poverty in *absolute* terms, and the other defines poverty in *relative* terms. Absolute poverty can be defined as a dollar figure that represents some level of income per year required to purchase some minimum amount of goods and services essential to meeting a person's or a family's basic needs. In contrast, relative poverty might be defined as a level of income that places a person or family in the lowest, say, 20 percent of all persons or families receiving incomes. An unequal distribution of income guarantees that some persons or families will occupy in relative terms the bottom rung of the income ladder. The U.S. government first established an official definition of the **poverty line** in 1964. The poverty line is the level of income below which a person or a family is considered poor. The poverty line is defined in absolute terms: It is based on the cost of a minimal diet multiplied by three because low-income families spend about one-third of their income on food. In 1964, the poverty income level for a family of four was $3,000 ($1,000 for food × 3). Since 1969, the poverty line figure has been adjusted upward each year for inflation. In 1988, for example, the official poverty income level was $12,092 or below for a family of four. In 2000, a family of four needed an income of $17,761 to clear the poverty threshold.

Exhibit 7(a) shows the percentage of all persons in the U.S. population below the poverty level, beginning with 1959. The poverty rate for all persons was on a downward trend until the early 1980s when the trend reversed. From 1980 to 1995, the percentage remained between 13 and 14 percent until the rate dropped to 11 percent in 2000. This was the lowest level in more than a quarter century. The exhibit also gives an idea of poverty levels by race for selected years. First, as shown by comparing parts (b) and (c), the percentage of blacks below the poverty line remained almost three times the percentage of whites between 1970 and 1995. Second, the percentages for blacks declined in the 1990s while the percentage for whites changed very little.

The poverty rate shown in Exhibit 7 has two major problems. First, this percentage gives no indication of how poor the people included are. A person with an income $1 below the poverty line counts, and so does a person whose income is $5,000 below the threshold. Second, the poverty rate is computed by comparing a family's census cash income from all sources to the poverty line. Cash income includes cash payments from Social Security,

Poverty line

The level of income below which a person or a family is considered to be poor.

EXHIBIT 7   **Persons below the Poverty Level as a Percentage of the U.S. Population, 1959–2000**

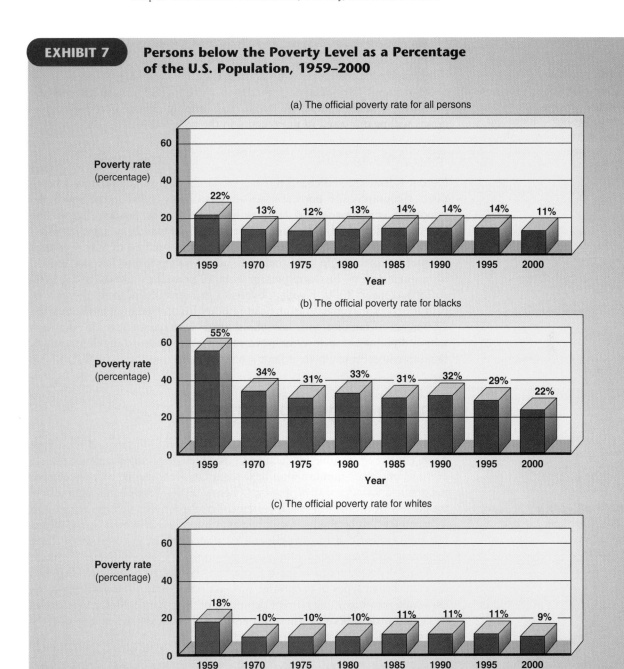

(a) The official poverty rate for all persons

(b) The official poverty rate for blacks

(c) The official poverty rate for whites

In part (a), the official poverty rate for all persons declined sharply between 1959 and the 1970s. After 1980, the poverty rate rose slightly and then fell in 2000. Comparison of parts (b) and (c) reveals that the poverty rate for blacks fell sharply between 1959 and 1970, but since then it has remained almost three times the poverty rate of whites until 2000.

Source: U.S. Bureau of the Census, *Poverty in the United States: 2000,* http://www.census.gov/hhes/www/poverty .html, Table B-1.

In-kind transfers

Government payments in the form of goods and services, rather than cash, including such government programs as food stamps, Medicaid, and housing.

unemployment compensation, and Temporary Assistance to Needy Families (TANF). Cash income for the poor does not include noncash transfers, called **in-kind transfers.** In-kind transfers are government payments in the form of goods and services, rather than cash, including such government programs as food stamps, Medicaid, and housing. These antipoverty programs will be discussed in more detail in the next section.

Who Are the Poor?

Exhibit 8 lists selected characteristics of families below the poverty level in 2000. Geographically, poor families are most likely to live in the South. An important characteristic of families living below the poverty line in the United States is family structure. The poverty rate was 20 percent for families headed by women with no husband present compared to only 5 percent for married couples. In fact, there has been a sharp rise in families headed by women with no husband present from 10 percent of all families in 1960 to 18 percent in 2000. Finally, poverty is greatly influenced by the lack of educational achievement of the head of household. As shown in the exhibit, 23 percent of families with household heads who have not received a high school diploma are below the poverty line compared to only 2 percent of families whose heads have at least a bachelor's degree.

Antipoverty Programs

The government has a number of programs specifically designed to aid the poor. The groups eligible for such assistance include disabled persons, elderly persons, and poor families with dependent children. People become eligible for public assistance if their income is below certain levels as measured by a **means test.** A means test is a requirement that a family's income not exceed a certain level to be eligible for public assistance. People who pass the means test may be *entitled* to government assistance. Thus, government welfare programs are often called *entitlement programs.*

Federal programs to assist the poor in the United States are classified into two broad types of programs: *cash* assistance and *in-kind transfers.* As explained previously, the current definition of the poverty threshold excludes in-kind transfers because these programs did not exist when the poverty rate measure was adopted over three decades ago.

Means test

A requirement that a family's income not exceed a certain level to be eligible for public assistance.

Cash Transfer Programs

The following are major government programs that alleviate poverty by providing eligible persons with cash payments needed to purchase food, shelter, clothing, and other basic needs.

Social Security (OASDHI). The technical name for our gigantic social insurance program is Old Age, Survivors, and Disability Health Insurance, or OASDHI. Under the Social Security Act passed in 1935, each worker must pay a payroll tax matched in equal amount by his or her employer. Look at

EXHIBIT 8 Characteristics of U.S. Persons and Families below the 2000 Poverty Level

Characteristic	Percentage below the poverty line
Region	
South	13%
West	12
Northeast	10
Midwest	9
Type of Family	
Headed by married couple	5
Headed by male, no wife	10
Headed by female, no husband	20
Education of Household Head	
No high school diploma	23
High school diploma, no college	10
Bachelor's degree or more	2

Source: U.S. Bureau of the Census, *Poverty in the United States: 2000*; http://www.census.gov/hhes/www/poverty.html, Table A; and *Statistical Abstract of the United States, 2000*, http://www.census.gov/prod/www/statistical-abstract-us.html, Table 761, p. 479.

your paycheck, and you will find this deduction under FICA, which stands for Federal Insurance Contribution Act. Most of this money is used to pay current benefit recipients, and the remainder goes into the Social Security Trust Fund. Workers may retire between ages 65 and 67 (depending on year of birth) with full benefits or at age 62 with reduced benefits. If a wage earner dies, Social Security provides payments to survivors, including spouse and children until about 18 years of age (age 21 if they are in school). In addition, payments are made to disabled workers.

Radical changes in policy are being debated. Since the creation of Social Security in 1935, money paid into the program has been invested exclusively in interest-bearing government securities, mainly long-term bonds. But the United States could obtain a higher return on investment and increase retirement savings for the baby-boom generation by channeling some of the money into the stock market, where stocks generally outperform bonds by a significant margin.

Although the Social Security Trust Fund now takes in more money in taxes and interest than it pays out in benefits, the program will not be able to pay all the benefits received by the baby-boom generation because, under the latest estimates, the trust fund will be depleted in 2041. Another reform idea is to create an investment account for each person covered by Social

Security. The government would require workers to contribute a small amount each year beyond their current level of payroll taxes. These accounts would be held by the Social Security system, but individuals would be free to choose stock index funds, bond index funds, or some combination of these options. When a person retires, money accumulated in the account would be paid out in the form of an annuity, supplementing regular Social Security benefits.

Unemployment Compensation. **Unemployment compensation** is a government insurance program that pays income for a short time period to unemployed workers. This unemployment insurance is financed by a payroll tax on employers, which varies by state and according to the size of the firm's payroll. This means nothing is deducted from employees' paychecks for unemployment insurance. Although the federal government largely collects the taxes and funds this program, it is administered by the states. Any insured worker who becomes unemployed, and did not just quit his or her job, can become eligible for benefit payments after a short waiting period of usually one week.

Temporary Assistance to Needy Families (TANF). TANF gives states broad discretion to determine eligibility and benefit levels. However, families may not receive benefits for longer than 60 months. Unwed teenage parents must stay in school and live at home, and people convicted of drug-related felonies are banned from receiving TANF or Food Stamp benefits. In addition, non-working adults must participate in community service within two months of receiving benefits, and must find work within two years. Parents with children under age 1 are exempt from the work requirements (under age 6 if child care is not available).

In-Kind Transfers

The following are important government in-kind transfer programs that raise the standard of living for the poor.

Food Stamps. The food stamp program began in 1964 as a federally financed program that is administered by state governments. The government issues coupons to the poor, who use them like money at the grocery store. The grocer cashes the stamps at a local bank, which redeems them at face value from the government. The cash value of stamps issued varies with the eligible recipient's income and family size. The food stamp program has become a major part of the welfare system in the United States.

Medicaid. This is the largest in-kind transfer program. Medicaid provides medical services to eligible poor under age 65 who pass a means test. TANF families qualify for Medicaid in all states.

Housing Assistance. Federal and state governments have a number of different programs to provide affordable housing for poor people. The federal agency overseeing most of these programs is the Department of Housing

Unemployment compensation

The government insurance program that pays income for a short time period to unemployed workers.

The Social Security Administration manages SSI benefits, the Administration for Children and Families manages TANF, and HUD sponsors low-income housing assistance. Visit their sites at http://www.ssa.gov, http://www.acf.dhhs.gov, *and* http://www.hud.gov, *respectively.*

and Urban Development (HUD). These programs include housing projects owned and operated by the government and subsidies to assist people who rent private housing. In both cases, recipients pay less than the market value for apartments and therefore receive an in-kind transfer.

Welfare Criticisms

The majority of objections to welfare can be classified into the following major criticisms:

- *Work Disincentives.* Critics have argued because welfare provides income that is easier to obtain than by working, the poor are often induced to reduce their work effort. In fact, the more a recipient earns from a job, the fewer the benefits he or she receives. Moreover, the taxes to finance welfare payments have some disincentive effects on the work effort of taxpayers. Taxes reduce take-home pay and thus reduce the reward for work.

- *Inefficiencies.* Critics have charged that the huge welfare bureaucracy in Washington, D.C., and throughout the nation results in more money in the pockets of bureaucrats than in the pockets of the poor. This major criticism was expressed by economics professor Thomas Sowell as follows:

  The amount necessary to lift every man, woman, and child in America above the poverty line has been calculated, and it is one-third of what is in fact spent on poverty programs. Clearly, much of the transfer ends up in the pockets of highly paid administrators, consultants, and staff as well as higher income recipients of benefits from programs advertised as antipoverty efforts.[1]

- *Inequities.* Today, many critics argue that poor persons with equal needs receive different benefits. For example, a needy family in California might receive welfare benefits twice as great as those received by a needy family of the same size in South Carolina. The reason is that benefits under TANF and Medicaid are essentially controlled by the states.

Finally, as we will see in the next section of this chapter, Congress attempted to meet some of these criticisms when it passed the Welfare Reform Act of 1996.

Reform Proposals

Although there have been numerous reform proposals, the various ideas can be classified into two broad approaches. First, the negative income tax system offers a major transformation of the entire patchwork of welfare programs. Second, workfare, which was included in the 1996 welfare bill, is a piecemeal approach, rather than a radical transformation.

What types of welfare reforms are necessary? The Urban Institute has some ideas (http://www.urban.org/ news/focus/focus_welfare.html). *What do you think?*

---

[1]Thomas Sowell, *Markets and Minorities* (New York: Basic Books, 1981), p.122.

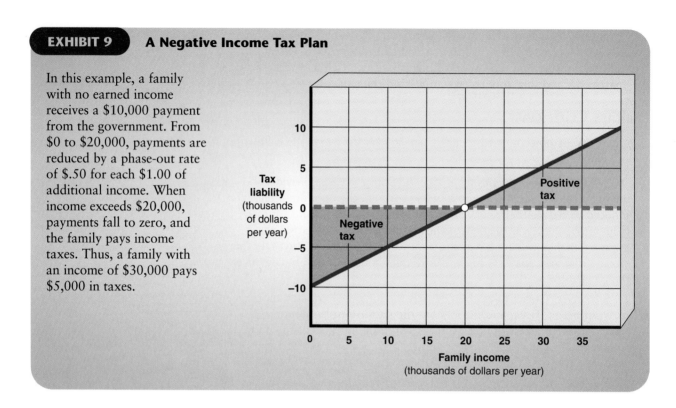

EXHIBIT 9   **A Negative Income Tax Plan**

In this example, a family with no earned income receives a $10,000 payment from the government. From $0 to $20,000, payments are reduced by a phase-out rate of $.50 for each $1.00 of additional income. When income exceeds $20,000, payments fall to zero, and the family pays income taxes. Thus, a family with an income of $30,000 pays $5,000 in taxes.

Negative Income Tax

Negative income tax (NIT)
A plan under which families below a certain break-even level of income would receive cash payments that decrease as their incomes increase.

The idea of a **negative income tax** (**NIT**) was first advanced by the prominent economist Milton Friedman in the early 1960s to reduce work disincentives and welfare bureaucracy while providing for the poor. The NIT is a plan under which families below a certain break-even level of income would receive cash payments that decrease as their incomes increase. A NIT system would combine all cash and in-kind transfer welfare programs into a single program administered by a single agency.

Exhibit 9 illustrates how a negative income tax might work. A low-income family of four receives a cash payment until it reaches a *break-even income* at $20,000 per year, where the family neither receives a payment nor pays income taxes. Above $20,000, the family pays income taxes. For example, a family with an income of $30,000 pays $5,000 in taxes, while a family with an income of $10,000 is paid an NIT subsidy of $5,000. A family with zero income is paid an NIT payment of $10,000. Thus, the government pays families an amount that varies inversely (negatively) with income.

Conclusion *The negative income tax is the reverse of a positive income tax system, in which people pay the government an amount that varies directly with their income.*

The basic idea behind the NIT system is simple: families with incomes above the break-even income finance payments to families with incomes below the break-even income. Begin at zero income in the exhibit, and assume the

Pulling on the Strings of the Welfare Safety Net

Applicable Concept: welfare reform

Although, the jury is still out on welfare reform, there are signs of success. The percentage of the U.S. population on welfare has fallen sharply since 1996.[1] The following is a sampling of articles describing results of the new welfare scheme under the Personal Responsibility and Work Opportunity Act of 1996:

• As reported in the *Washington Post*, Los Angeles County provides a striking example of different welfare reform efforts over time. In the 1980s, Los Angeles County tested a welfare overhaul aimed at providing education and job training so recipients could qualify for better jobs. At the end of the first year, there was no significant impact. After the welfare reform act in 1996, independent researchers found that 43 percent of poor families who were required to participate in the city's new welfare reform program with work requirements got jobs, while only 32 percent of families randomly selected to remain in the traditional welfare program did. This represents an increase of one-third over the old welfare program. The typical welfare family subject to the new reform initiatives earned $1,286 in the first six months of the program, while "control group" families earned $879, a difference of 46 percent. The study covered the period from 1996 to 1997.[2]

• A *New York Times* article reported the impact on minorities in 1998:

As the welfare rolls continued to plunge, white, black and Hispanic recipients left welfare at unprecedented rates. But the disproportionately large exodus of whites altered the racial balance in a program long rife with racial conflict and stereotypes, according to figures that were compiled in an analysis of recent state data by the New York Times.

The legacy of those stereotypes makes the discussion of race and welfare an unusually sensitive one. In the past, advocates and scholars have taken pains to note there were more white families on welfare than black. But that is no longer the case. Blacks now outnumber whites. The Hispanic share of the rolls is growing fastest. And black and Hispanic recipients combined outnumber whites by about two to one. In addition, the remaining caseload is increasingly concentrated in large cities. Some analysts warn that the growing racial and urban imbalance could erode political support for welfare, especially when times turn tight. More immediately, the changing demographics suggest that states may need new strategies as they serve those left behind, like recipients who do not speak English.[3]

• Another *New York Times* article describes requests to charities:

Ms. Olessi Montano said the Y.W.C.A. had seen a "dramatic increase" in the number of families asking for shelter in the past few months, and the $30,000 yearly grant used to house them had already run out. The demand for food and clothing is outpacing the supply, she added. "It's bogus to say the welfare rolls are down and people are moving into jobs," Ms. Olessi Montano said. "That's not true. The need for services is growing by the minute." Treva Woung, program director for St. Rocco's Shelter in Newark, said she had seen a 50 percent increase in homeless single mothers who have been evicted from or denied state-subsidized housing. The shelter has beds for 60 women and children.[4]

• The Associated Press reports in 2001 on the federal block grants:

Welfare reform has created a "welfare windfall" for states. Because the welfare rolls have fallen so fast, the states have had to spend less on welfare, which means they have billions of dollars in federal block grants left unspent. This frees up state money for schools, tax cuts, roads, and buildings rather than the poor.[5]

ANALYZE THE ISSUE

The current approach to welfare reform is to cut the growth of welfare by shifting control from the federal government to the states. The idea is that because state and local officials are closer to the people, welfare programs will improve. Analyze the results presented above based on work disincentives, inefficiencies, and inequities.

[1]U.S. Department of Health and Human Services, http://www .acf.dhhs.gov/news/welfare/index.htm, select U.S. Welfare Caseload Tables.
[2]Judith Havemann, "Welfare Reform Success Cited in L.A.," *Washington Post*, Aug. 20, 1998, p. A1.
[3]Jason Depule, "Shrinking Welfare Rolls Leave Record High Share of Minorities," *New York Times*, July 27, 1998, sec. A, p. 1.
[4]"As Welfare Rolls Drop, Requests to Charities Rise," *New York Times*, Aug. 18, 1998, p. B-5.
[5]Associated Press, "States Using Federal Welfare Dollars to Replace State Spending," MSNBC, June 4, 2001.

CHECKPOINT

Does a Negative Income Tax Discourage Work?

Under a negative income system, people who work receive reduced payments from the government. Even worse, beyond the break-even income, workers must pay taxes. This means there is no basis in an NIT system to argue that the poor will have an incentive to work. Explain why you agree or disagree. (Hint: Construct a table using Exhibit 9 and consider after-tax income.)

income guarantee is set at the poverty income threshold of $10,000. Beyond the guaranteed-minimum income of $10,000, government payments are reduced by, say, $.50 for each $1.00 earned. This rate, called the *phase-out rate,* determines the cash transfers to low-income families until the break-even income is reached.

The NIT system offers several potential advantages. First, the bureaucratic costs would be cut because an NIT program could be administered by a single agency. Second, poor people would not suffer the stigma of repeatedly standing in lines at the welfare office or using food stamps in the grocery store. Third, many economists argue that individuals are rational and know best how to spend their money. Thus, a cash subsidy is preferable to an in-kind transfer.

After years of discussion and study, the NIT has not gained wide support except among many economists. The NIT system is perceived as a political liability because voters perceive it as a "giveaway" of taxpayers' money. These critics believe in-kind welfare is preferable to cash assistance. When a recipient is given food stamps or a housing subsidy, he or she acquires food and housing, rather than, say, buying drugs and gambling. NIT proponents point out, however, that some food stamps are sold illegally for cash, which is used to buy drugs, alcohol, or whatever. Finally, a concern is that a generous guaranteed-minimum income paid in cash might create a disincentive to work, rather than an incentive to work.

Workfare

The 1996 welfare reform bill titled the *Personal Reponsibility and Work Opportunity Act* set a lifetime limit of five years of welfare benefits per family and gave the states block grants to run welfare programs. To overcome the disincentive to work characteristic of earlier welfare programs, the current approach is to increase the work performed by welfare recipients and encourage their participation in job-training programs. To keep their benefits, welfare recipients must perform some work activities within two years of receiving welfare or risk losing benefits. This idea is called workfare. Workfare programs require able-bodied adults to work for the local government or any available private-sector employer in order to be eligible for welfare benefits. The paramount question thus becomes how to create jobs for welfare recipients. A large public job plan would be costly and politically unpopular, especially among public employees who fear losing their jobs.

EXHIBIT 10   Labor Markets without and with Racial Discrimination

(a) Market without discrimination

(b) Market with discrimination

In part (a), there is no labor market discrimination against blacks. In this case, the equilibrium wage for all labor is $245 per day. Under discrimination in part (b), the labor demand and labor supply curves for white and black workers differ. As a result, the equilibrium wage rate for whites, $280, is higher than that for blacks, $210.

Another option is for the government to pay employers to hire welfare recipients. A variation on this idea is for the government to hire personnel firms that would earn a fee for each person placed in a job.

There are potential problems with providing subsidies for companies that hire welfare recipients. One problem is that subsidies can stigmatize welfare recipients and reduce their long-term employment prospects. Another potential problem is that subsidies could be a windfall payment to employers for hiring people who would have been hired without the subsidies. Finally, there is a displacement problem because a subsidized welfare-recipient worker can take the job of an unsubsidized worker who has never received welfare benefits.

Discrimination

Poverty and discrimination in the workplace are related. Nonwhites and females earn less income when employer prejudice prevents them from receiving job opportunities. Discrimination also occurs when nonwhites and females earn less, but do basically the same work as whites and males. Exhibit 10 uses labor market theory to explain how discrimination can cause the equilibrium wage to be lower for nonwhites than for whites.

CHECKPOINT

Should the Law Protect Women?

Do you want women serving in combat, mining coal, and building skyscrapers? Some states have enacted laws that protect women by keeping them out of jobs deemed "too strenuous" or "too dangerous." Would the likely effect of such laws be to decrease wages in male-dominated occupations, increase wages in female-intensive occupations, or decrease wages in female-intensive occupations?

Exhibit 10(a) assumes that employers do not discriminate. This means employers hire workers regardless of race—that is, on the basis of their contribution to revenue (their *MRP*s). Hence, the intersection of the market demand curve, *D*, and the market supply curve, *S*, determines the equilibrium wage rate of $245 per day paid by nondiscriminating employers. The total number of black and white workers hired is 14,000 workers.

Now assume for the sake of argument that employers do practice job discrimination against black workers. The result, shown in Exhibit 10(b), is two different labor markets—one for whites and one for blacks. Because discrimination exists, the demand curve for labor for blacks is to the left of the demand curve for labor for whites, reflecting unjustified restricted employment practices. The supply curve of labor for blacks is also to the left of the supply curve of labor for whites because there are fewer blacks seeking employment than whites.

Given the differences in the labor market demand and supply curves, the equilibrium wage rate for whites of $280 is higher than the $210 paid to blacks. Comparison of these wage rates with the labor market equilibrium wage rate of $245 reveals that the effect of discrimination is to change the relative wages of white and black workers. Whites earn a higher wage rate than they would earn in a labor market that did not favor hiring them. Conversely, the black wage rate is lower as a result of discrimination.

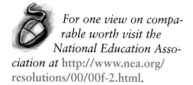

For one view on comparable worth visit the National Education Association at http://www.nea.org/resolutions/00/00f-2.html.

Comparable Worth

A controversial public policy aimed at eliminating labor market pay inequities is a concept called **comparable worth**. Comparable worth is the principle that employees who work for the same employer must be paid the same wages when their jobs, even if different, require similar levels of education, training, experience, and responsibility. Comparable worth is a nonmarket wage-setting remedy to the situation where jobs dominated by women pay less than jobs dominated by men. Because women's work is alleged to be undervalued, the solution is equal pay for jobs evaluated as having "comparable worth" according to point scores assigned to different jobs. In essence, comparable worth replaces labor-market-determined wages with bureaucratic judgments about the valuation of different jobs. For example, compensation paid to an elevator inspector and a nurse can be computed based on quantitative scores in a job-rating scheme. If the jobs' point totals are equal, the average elevator inspector and nurse must be paid equally by law.

Comparable worth

The principle that employees who work for the same employer must be paid the same wage when their jobs, even if different, require similar levels of education, training, experience, and responsibility. A nonmarket wage-setting process is used to evaluate and compensate jobs according to point scores assigned to different jobs.

Is a Librarian Worth the Same Wage as an Electrician?

Applicable Concept: comparable worth

Few women are typically listed in *Forbes* ranking of the nation's top 100 chief executive officers by compensation. On average, women earn only about 75 percent as much as men in spite of laws against pay discrimination. Discrimination in wages and employment on the basis of sex was made illegal by two federal laws. In 1963, Congress passed the Equal Pay Act (EPA), which outlawed pay discrimination between men and women doing substantially the same job. This does not mean that unequal pay for the same work cannot exist, but if it does, the differential must be due to factors other than gender. These factors might include a seniority system, a merit system, or a system that measures earnings by quantity or quality of production.

Comparable worth laws have been passed in several states, Canada, Great Britain, and Australia. Proponents of comparable worth argue that the equal-pay-for-equal-work idea has failed. They observe that the pay is lower in female-dominated occupations and argue that female productivity and experience receive less reward in these jobs than do male productivity and experience in male-dominated jobs. In short, they maintain that women crowd into secretarial work, nursing, and retail sales because of discrimination against women. The increased supply of female labor in these crowded professions lowers the prevailing wage.

Comparable-worth advocates urge the courts to interpret such labor market inequalities as a violation of the sex-discrimination provisions of Title VII of the Civil Rights Act of 1964. This law defines discriminatory practices more broadly than does the EPA. Title VII makes it unlawful to discriminate on the basis of race, sex, or national origin in classifying, assigning, or promoting employees; in extending or assigning facilities; in providing training, retraining, or apprenticeships; or in implementing any other terms, conditions, or privileges of employment.

If the courts accept comparable worth and expand the scope of Title VII, they will not consider whether employers intentionally pay less for "women's jobs," but only whether the employers are in compliance with an established rating scheme. The best-known case occurred in 1983, when the American Federation of State, County, and Municipal Employees won the first federal court case against the state of Washington. The state was found guilty of wage discrimination against women because it had not followed its comparable-worth point system. To comply with Title VII, the court ordered Washington to upgrade nearly 15,000 female employees and award back pay estimated to cost $377 million. The decision was

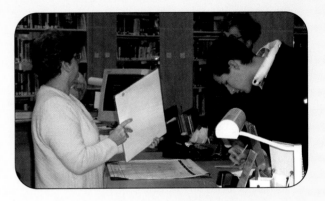

appealed to higher courts, and the union ultimately lost the case.

Quantitative job evaluations are not new, although their use is the cornerstone of the comparable-worth movement. In the Washington case, independent consultants gave a registered nurse more points than a computer systems analyst, and truck drivers received fewer points than clerks. In another case, job consultants studied the Minnesota job classification system and assigned point values to 762 state job classes. According to the point system, male-dominated jobs often paid more than female-dominated jobs even though the female jobs had greater "worth." The Minnesota Task Force on Pay Equity then recommended to the legislature that it raise the "underpaid" female job classes, rather than lower the "overpaid" male job classes.

A *Los Angeles Times* article reported on recent enforcement of the EPA: In 2000, there was a sharp rise in complaints of sex discrimination to the Equal Employment Opportunity Commission (EEOC). Settlement of these cases amounted to nearly $23 million to recover back wages.[1]

ANALYZE THE ISSUE

Suppose the consultants use a job-scoring system and determine that the wage rate for a secretary is $50 per hour, while the competitive labor market wage rate is $10 per hour. What would be the effect of such a comparable-worth law?

[1]Lisa Girion, "Wage Gap Continues to Vex Women," *Los Angeles Times,* Feb. 11, 2001, p. W1.

KEY CONCEPTS

Lorenz curve	In-kind transfers	Unemployment	Negative income tax
Poverty line	Means test	compensation	Comparable worth

SUMMARY

■ The **Lorenz curve** is a measure of inequality of income. Since 1947, the share of money income for each fifth of families ranked according to their income has been quite stable. Also, the degree of income inequality among families in the United States has changed little since 1929. During the 1980s and 1990s, the richest families did become richer; however, the median income of all groups increased.

Lorenz curve

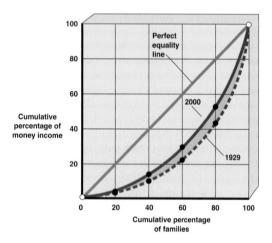

■ The **poverty line** is a level of cash income below which a family is classified as poor. The poverty income threshold is three times the cost of a minimal diet for a family. Today, about 11 percent of the U.S. population is officially classified as poor.

■ **In-kind transfers** are payments to the poor in the form of goods and services, rather than cash. Calculation of the poverty line counts only cash income. In-kind transfers, such as food stamps, Medicaid, and housing, do not count as income for families classified as officially poor. Government cash transfers counted in the poverty line include payments from Social Security, unemployment compensation, and Temporary Assistance to Needy Families.

■ **Welfare criticisms** include three major arguments: (1) Welfare reduces the incentive to work for the poor and taxpayers. (2) Welfare is inefficient because much of the money covers administrative costs, rather than providing benefits for the poor. (3) Because many antipoverty programs are controlled by the state, welfare benefits vary widely.

■ The **negative income tax** is a plan to guarantee a certain amount of income for all families. As a low-income family earns income, government payments (negative income tax) are phased out. After reaching a break-even income, families become taxpayers instead of being on the welfare rolls.

Negative income tax

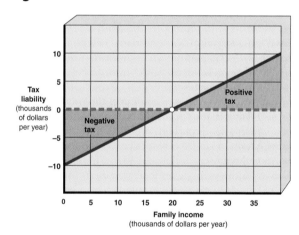

■ **Comparable worth** is the theory that workers in jobs determined to be of equal value by means of point totals should be paid equally. Instead of allowing labor markets to set wages, independent consultants award points to different jobs on the basis of such criteria as knowledge, experience, and working conditions.

SUMMARY OF CONCLUSION STATEMENTS

- Measured by distribution of family money income, the richest families did become a little richer and the rest of the family groups a little poorer since the 1980s.

- The Lorenz curve has shifted only slightly inward and therefore closer to the perfect equality line between 1929 and 2000.

- The negative income tax is the reverse of a positive income tax system, in which people pay the government an amount that varies directly with their income.

STUDY QUESTIONS AND PROBLEMS

1. The following table contains data on the distribution of income in the countries of Alpha and Beta:

	Alpha		Beta	
Percentage of families	Percentage share	Cumulative share	Percentage share	Cumulative share
Lowest fifth	17.7%	_____	9.0%	_____
Second-lowest fifth	19.9	_____	14.2	_____
Middle fifth	20.4	_____	17.5	_____
Second-highest fifth	20.7	_____	21.9	_____
Highest fifth	21.3	_____	37.4	_____

   a. Compute the cumulative distribution of income for each country.
   b. Construct the Lorenz curve for each country.
   c. For which country is the distribution of income more equal?

2. Suppose each family in the United States earned an equal money income. What would be the effect?

3. Explain the difference between poverty defined absolutely and poverty defined relatively. Which definition is the basis of the poverty line?

4. Calculate the official poverty threshold annual income for a family of four. Assume the minimally acceptable diet is estimated to be $5 per person per day and the minimum wage is $5 per hour. Will a head of a family of four earn the poverty threshold you have calculated?

5. What are in-kind transfers? Give examples. How are in-kind transfers considered in determining whether a family is below the poverty income threshold?

6. Would free health care reduce poverty, as measured by the government? Would free public housing, day care, and job training for the poor reduce the poverty rate? Explain.

7. What percentage of families in the United States was classified as poor in the 1990s? Which demographic groups have higher poverty rates?

8. List the major government cash assistance and in-kind transfer programs to assist the poor. Which of the programs are not exclusively for the poor?

9. What are three major criticisms of welfare?

10. Assume the government implements a negative income tax plan with a guaranteed-minimum income of $5,000 and a phase-out rate for payments of 50 percent. Provide the missing data in the following table:

A Negative Income Tax Plan

Family income	Negative tax	Total after-tax income
$ 0	_____	_____
2,000	_____	_____
4,000	_____	_____
6,000	_____	_____
8,000	_____	_____
10,000	_____	_____

11. Critics of welfare argue that the role of government should be to break down legal barriers to employment, rather than using programs that directly provide cash or goods and services. For example, advocates of this approach would remove laws mandating minimum wages, comparable worth, union power, professional licensing, and other restrictive practices. Do you agree or disagree? Why?

ONLINE EXERCISES

Exercise 1

Sometimes we hear of references to different socio-economic classes. According to the Electronic Policy Network (http://epn.org/faq/index1.html#class) what are the definitions of low, middle, and upper class in terms of dollars per year of income?

Exercise 2

Visit the U.S. Census Bureau (http://www.census.gov/ftp/pub/hhes/income/histinc/f02.html), and compare the income distribution in the United States over time. What can account for the change?

Exercise 3

Visit the U.S. Census Bureau (http://www.census.gov/ftp/pub/hhes/income/dewb94/index.html). Click on "Moving Up and Down the Income Ladder." What are some of the causes of poverty?

Exercise 4

Visit the Heritage Foundation (http://www.heritage.org/library/cda/cda99-07.html) and observe the first graph that displays U.S. Census data describing the distribution of income in the United States in 1997. According to the Heritage Foundation how could this data misrepresent income distribution? Do you agree?

CHECKPOINT ANSWERS

Does a Negative Income Tax Discourage Work?

The following table is interpreted from Exhibit 9. Even though payments from the government decrease, total after-tax income increases from the combination of the income earned and the negative tax. After the break-even income of $20,000, total after-tax income continues to rise. If you said the NIT system assumes the poor are rational people who are motivated to earn more total after-tax income by working, YOU ARE CORRECT.

A Negative Income Tax Return

Family income	Negative tax	Positive tax	Total after-tax income
$ 0	$10,000	$ 0	$10,000
5,000	7,000	0	12,000
10,000	5,000	0	15,000
15,000	2,500	0	17,500
20,000	0	0	20,000
25,000	0	−2,500	22,500
30,000	0	−5,000	25,000
35,000	0	−7,500	27,500

Should the Law Protect Women?

A law that limits women's access to certain occupations results in their crowding into the remaining occupations. The obstacles facing women in male-dominated occupations artificially restrict competition with men. If you said the increased labor supply in female-intensive occupations decreases their wages, while the decreased labor supply in male-intensive occupations increases wages for males, YOU ARE CORRECT.

PRACTICE QUIZ

For a visual explanation of the correct answers, visit the tutorial at http://tucker.swcollege.com.

1. In 2000, the wealthiest 5 percent of all U.S. families earned what percentage of total annual money income among families?
   a. More than 20 percent
   b. Less than 10 percent
   c. More than 25 percent
   d. More than 50 percent

2. A figure that measures the relationship between the cumulative percentage of money income on the vertical axis and the cumulative percentage of families on the horizontal axis is called the
   a. family-income curve.
   b. Washington curve.
   c. Lorenz curve.
   d. Gini curve.

Exhibit 11 Lorenz Curve

3. As shown in Exhibit 11, the perfect equality line is drawn between points
   a. W and Y along the curve.
   b. X and Z.
   c. W and Y along the straight line.
   d. W and X.

4. As shown in Exhibit 11, 20 percent of families earned a cumulative share of about _____ percent of income.
   a. 5
   b. 10
   c. 30
   d. 50

5. As shown in Exhibit 11, 40 percent of families earned a cumulative share of about _____ percent of income.
   a. 5
   b. 15
   c. 30
   d. 50

6. Since 1929, the overall family income distribution in the United States has become
   a. much more unequal.
   b. much less unequal.
   c. slightly more unequal.
   d. slightly more equal.

7. Comparing the family income distributions of the United States, the Czech Republic, and Brazil, the conclusion is that income is distributed
   a. most equally in Brazil.
   b. most equally in the United States.
   c. about the same in all three countries.
   d. most equally in the Czech Republic.

8. To establish the poverty line that divides poor and nonpoor families, the government
   a. multiplies the cost of a minimal diet by three.
   b. multiplies the cost of a minimal diet by five.
   c. adds 50 percent to the cost of a minimal diet.
   d. adds 100 percent to the cost of a minimal diet.

9. The poverty line
   a. is defined as one-half average family income.
   b. includes in-kind transfers.
   c. includes Medicaid benefits.
   d. has been attacked for overstating poverty.

10. Which of the following is an in-kind transfer?
    a. Social Security payments
    b. Unemployment compensation
    c. Food stamps
    d. Welfare payments

11. Which of the following is a cash assistance (not an in-kind transfer) program?
    a. Temporary Assistance to Needy Families (TANF)
    b. Medicare
    c. Medicaid
    d. Food stamps

12. The negative income tax (NIT) is a plan under which families
    a. above a level of income pay no tax.
    b. pay the same tax rate except for the poor.
    c. below a level of income pay no tax.
    d. below a level of income receive a cash payment.

13. Which of the following might decrease the supply curve of labor?
    a. Discrimination against blacks
    b. Discrimination against women
    c. Difficult licensing requirements
    d. All of the above

CHAPTER 13

Antitrust and Regulation

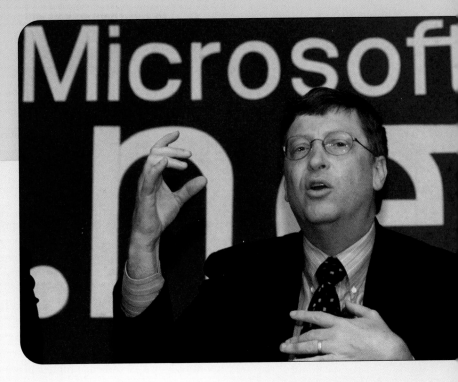

P eople of the same trade seldom meet together, even for merriment and diversion, but the conversation ends in a conspiracy against the public, or in some contrivance to raise prices.[1]

—*Adam Smith*

As soon as Microsoft dominated the personal computer software industry, Bill Gates, its founder, was charged by the government with anticompetitive business practices. Meanwhile, the media compared the case to John D. Rockefeller's Standard Oil monopoly and the robber barons of the 1890s. In the past, antitrust laws have been successfully used against the nation's largest corporations. This threat of the high legal costs of defending against an antitrust

[1]Adam Smith, *An Inquiry into the Nature and Causes of the Wealth of Nations* (1776; reprint, New York: Random House, The Modern Library, 1937), p. 128.

suit serve as a powerful deterrent, discouraging monopolies from engaging in unfair actions intended to eliminate rivals. Here you will explore and form opinions on the Microsoft case, the Standard Oil case, and other major antitrust cases. In addition, this chapter compares antitrust laws in the United States to antitrust laws of other countries.

When antitrust policy is successful, consumers benefit from lower prices and more output.

As you study antitrust policy in this chapter, you will learn that antitrust is somewhat of an art form, blended from economic theory and politics—perhaps more politics than economic theory. Interestingly, certain industries are exempt from antitrust legislation: labor unions, professional baseball teams, public utilities, public transit companies, schools, hospitals, and suppliers of military equipment.

The second half of this chapter turns to government regulation, which affects virtually every business and consumer. Our food is regulated, toys are regulated, airline safety is regulated, and most industries must deal with some form of regulation. What are the reasons for regulation, and what are its consequences? The explanation begins with a brief survey of regulation in the United States. Although government regulation remains pervasive, a deregulation movement began in the late 1970s to reduce regulation in industries such as transportation and telecommunications. Deregulation in the electricity industry began in 1992. In 2001, the power shortages in California provoked debate on the issue of regulation versus deregulation in this industry. In the last section, we discuss the rationale for three different types of regulation justified on the basis of market failure.

In this chapter, you will learn to solve these economics puzzles:

■ Can universities and colleges improve education by engaging in price-fixing?

■ Why can the California energy crisis be characterized as the "perfect storm"?

■ Why doesn't the water company or electric company compete?

■ Why is market failure an economic rationale for regulation?

Antitrust

Trust

A combination or cartel consisting of firms that place their assets in the custody of a board of trustees.

Before the Civil War, industries were populated by small firms, and few economic problems were caused by monopoly. After the Civil War, during the rapid industrialization of the 1870s and 1880s, the railroads and telegraph linked diverse regions of the country and enabled firms to expand into national markets. To gain more control of expanding industries, many competing companies merged or formed a **trust**. A trust is a combination or cartel consisting of firms that place their assets in the custody of a board of trustees. The trust allows firms that have not actually merged to form a cartel or cohesive group of firms that controls an industry in order to charge monopoly prices and earn higher profits. The long list of trusts formed during this period included the iron trust, sugar trust, copper trust, steel trust, coal trust, oil trust, tobacco trust, and even the paper-bag trust. The organizers of many of these trusts became widely known as *robber barons* because they exploited and bullied anyone in their way.

During the last decades of the nineteenth century, many trusts used various tactics to avoid competition. Recall from Chapter 9 on monopoly that Standard Oil acquired oil fields, railroads, pipelines, and ships and then denied access to rivals. Thus, competing firms had to merge with Standard Oil or go out of business. With the competition eliminated, John D. Rockefeller, the best-known so-called robber baron, raised Standard Oil's prices and limited production, and consumers suffered along with Standard Oil's competitors.

Another anticompetitive strategy used by the industrial giants was **predatory pricing**. Predatory pricing is the practice of one or more firms temporarily reducing prices in order to eliminate competition and then raise prices. Often trusts would sell a product below cost until their weaker competitors were unable to withstand mounting losses and were forced from the industry. Perhaps even more alarming, some trusts resorted to political corruption. For example, the railroad and petroleum trusts employed corrupt legislators and judges to gain a competitive edge.

By the end of the nineteenth century, the threat of continuing economic and political abuses created a public opinion quite hostile to big business. Newspapers regularly printed news of the trusts' questionable business practices. The numerous and politically influential farmers blamed the trusts for the high railroad charges that were making farming unprofitable. Consumers and labor unions also raised their voices against monopoly power. The influence of the trusts was discussed constantly in the halls of Congress. In 1888, both major political parties added antimonopoly planks to their campaign platforms. Hatred and distrust of the centralization of economic and political power originated in the Jeffersonian tradition of the United States. Against this background of populist (pro-people) fear of big business and its political power, Congress passed laws aimed at preventing firms from engaging in anticompetitive activities.

The following is a brief description of the major antitrust legislation that constitutes basic antitrust law.

The Sherman Act

The first antitrust law was the **Sherman Act.** The Sherman Act of 1890 is the federal antitrust law that prohibits monopolization and conspiracies to restrain trade. Today, this act remains the cornerstone of antitrust policy in the United States. It has two main provisions:

Section 1: Every contract, combination in the form of trust or otherwise, or conspiracy in restraint of trade or commerce among the several States, or with foreign nations, is hereby declared to be illegal. . . .

Section 2: Every person who shall monopolize, or attempt to monopolize, or combine or conspire with any other person or persons, to monopolize any part of the trade or commerce among the several States, or with foreign nations, shall be deemed guilty of a misdemeanor, and, on conviction thereof, shall be punished by a fine not exceeding five thousand dollars, or by imprisonment not exceeding one year, or by both said punishments, in the discretion of the court.[2]

In response to the public outcry, Congress intended to craft this law with sweeping language against the trusts. But what does the Sherman Act really say? It is unclear exactly which business practices constitute a "restraint of trade" and therefore a violation of the law. As a result of the extremely

Predatory pricing

The practice of one or more firms temporarily reducing prices in order to eliminate competition and then raising prices.

Sherman Act

The federal antitrust law enacted in 1890 that prohibits monopolization and conspiracies to restrain trade.

 For a complete text of the Sherman Act, the Clayton Act, and other antitrust legislation, visit the U.S. Department of Justice website at http://www.usdoj.gov/atr/foia/divisionmanual/ch2.htm.

---

[2]In 1974, the act was amended so that violations would be treated as felonies.

vague language, there were numerous court battles, and the act was ineffective for years. For example, the federal government did not win its first notable cases against Standard Oil and American Tobacco until 1911.

The serious consequences of violations of the Sherman Act are reflected in the more recent case of Archer Daniels Midland Company (ADM). In 1995, this agribusiness giant pleaded guilty to price-fixing involving lysine and citric acid. It paid a $100 million fine. In 1998, a federal jury convicted three past and present executives of conspiring with competitors to fix the prices of these products. They faced a maximum three-year prison sentence and at least a $350,000 fine.

The Clayton Act

Clayton Act

A 1914 amendment that strengthens the Sherman Act by making it illegal for firms to engage in certain anticompetitive business practices.

As explained above, the Sherman Act was initially proving to be little more than a legislative mandate for the courts to spell out the meaning of antitrust laws. To define anticompetitive acts more precisely, Congress passed the **Clayton Act.** The Clayton Act of 1914 is an amendment that strengthened the Sherman Act by making it illegal for firms to engage in certain anticompetitive business practices. Under this act, the following business practices are illegal with the important controversial condition that the effect of these practices must be to "substantially lessen competition or tend to create a monopoly":

1. *Price Discrimination.* A firm charges different customers different prices for the same product where the price differences are not related to cost differences. (Recall the discussion of this topic in the chapter on monopoly.)

2. *Exclusive Dealing.* A manufacturer requires a retailer to sign an agreement stipulating the condition that the retailer will not carry any rival products of the manufacturer.

3. *Tying Contracts.* The seller of one product requires the buyer to purchase some other product(s). For example, movie distributors cannot force theaters to purchase projection rights to a blockbuster movie only on the condition that they pay for a bundle of films with much less box office potential.

4. *Stock Acquisition of Competing Companies.* One firm buys the stock of a competing firm.

5. *Interlocking Directorates.* The directors of one company serve on the board of directors of another company in the same industry. Interlocking directorates are illegal whether or not the effect may be to "substantially lessen competition."

Although more specific than the Sherman Act, the Clayton Act is also vague. The key question is, Exactly when does a situation or action "substantially lessen competition"? To this day, the task of interpreting this ambiguous phrase remains with the courts, and the interpretation changes over time.

The Federal Trade Commission Act

Since the federal government faced a growing antitrust responsibility in the early 1900s, an agency was needed to investigate alleged anticompetitive practices and reach judgments. The **Federal Trade Commission Act** was enacted for this purpose. The Federal Trade Commission Act of 1914 established the Federal Trade Commission (FTC) to investigate unfair competitive practices of firms. This act contains perhaps the most general language of any antitrust act. It declares illegal "unfair methods of competition in commerce." The act established a five-member commission appointed by the president to determine the exact meaning of "unfair methods." Today, the FTC is concerned primarily with (1) enforcing consumer protection legislation, (2) prohibiting deceptive advertising, and (3) preventing collusion. When a complaint is filed with the FTC, the commission investigates. If there is a violation, the FTC can negotiate a settlement, issue a cease-and-desist order, or initiate a lawsuit.

Federal Trade Commission Act

The federal act that in 1914 established the Federal Trade Commission (FTC) to investigate unfair competitive practices of firms.

 For more information about the Federal Trade Commission, visit its website at http://www.ftc.gov/.

The Robinson-Patman Act

The Clayton Act has been amended twice. Although price discrimination became illegal under the Clayton Act, that section was not widely enforced at first. This situation changed with the passage of the **Robinson-Patman Act.** The Robinson-Patman Act of 1936 is an amendment to the Clayton Act that strengthens the Clayton Act against price discrimination. The Robinson-Patman Act is complex and controversial. Its basic purpose is to prevent large sellers from offering different prices to different buyers where the effect is to harm even a single small firm. In fact, the Robinson-Patman Act is often called the "Chain Store Act" because this act is an outgrowth of the competition between small independent sellers and chain stores that developed after World War I.

The Robinson-Patman Act encourages lawsuits by small independent firms because it broadens the list of illegal price discrimination practices. The Robinson-Patman Act, for example, makes it illegal for a firm to offer quantity discounts, free advertising, or promotional allowances to one buyer if the firm does not offer the same concessions to all buyers. Be careful to note that the prohibition on price discrimination in the Robinson-Patman Act is limited to situations where the effect is to "substantially lessen competition or tend to create a monopoly." The first You're the Economist offers the opportunity to debate issues concerning this act.

Robinson-Patman Act

A 1936 amendment to the Clayton Act that strengthens the Clayton Act against price discrimination.

 Additional information on the Robinson-Patman Act can be found at the following Internet address: http://www.lawmall.com/rpa/.

The Celler-Kefauver Act

Prior to 1950, the U.S. Supreme Court interpreted the Sherman Act as prohibiting mergers between competing firms by stock acquisition, but not prohibiting mergers by the sale of physical assets (plant, equipment, and so on). The **Celler-Kefauver Act** was the second amendment to the Clayton Act, and it was enacted to address this problem. The Celler-Kefauver Act of 1950 is an amendment to the Clayton Act that prohibits one firm from

Celler-Kefauver Act

A 1950 amendment to the Clayton Act that prohibits one firm from merging with a competitor by purchasing its physical assets if the effect is to substantially lessen competition.

EXHIBIT 1 Summary of Major Antitrust Laws

Law (date enacted)	Key provisions
Sherman Act (1890)	Prohibits interstate price fixing and other conspiracies and combinations that restrain trade and attempt to monopolize.
Clayton Act (1914)	Bolsters and clarifies the Sherman Act by prohibiting specific business practices, including exclusive dealing, tying contracts, stock acquisition of competitors, and interlocking directorates.
Federal Trade Commission Act (1914)	Established an agency (the FTC) to help enforce antitrust laws by investigating unfair and deceptive business practices.
Robinson-Patman Act (1936)	Amends the Clayton Act by broadening the list of illegal price discrimination practices to include quantity discounts, free advertising, and promotional allowances offered to large buyers and not to small buyers. The Robinson-Patman Act is often called the "Chain Store Act."
Celler-Kefauver Act (1950)	Amends the Clayton Act by closing the loophole that permitted a firm to merge by buying the assets of a rival, rather than by stock acquisition, as outlawed in the original Clayton Act. The Celler-Kefauver Act is often called the "Antimerger Act."

merging with a competitor by purchasing its physical assets if the effect is to substantially lessen competition. Consequently, this act is sometimes called the "Antimerger Act" because it closed the loophole in the Clayton Act and thereby prohibited anticompetitive mergers, which were the target of the original Clayton Act.

The five major antitrust laws are summarized in Exhibit 1.

Key Antitrust Cases

An excellent source of antitrust information is found at the following Internet address: http://www .antitrust.org/.

Antitrust policy can be compared to baseball or other sports. The House and Senate of the U.S. Congress set the "rules of the game" for antitrust cases, just as the American and National Leagues set the rules of baseball. For example, the rules of baseball say that a player hitting a homer must run from first base to home base, rather than from third base to home base. Similarly, the Sherman Act forbids monopolization through predatory pricing by businesses. This brings us to the role of the umpire. After a game, a Little League player asked the first base umpire, "What do you call when the runner and the ball reach first base at exactly the same time?" The umpire replied, "There's no such thing as a tie. It's always the way I call it." That's how it is with court decisions on antitrust laws, and, just like many of the umpire's calls, all the courts' decisions are not "crowd pleasers." With this point in mind, let's look at some important "calls" of courts on antitrust cases.

Is Utah Pie's Slice of the Pie Too Small?

Applicable Concept: Robinson-Patman Act

In the 1950s, the market for frozen dessert pies was small, but growing. The Salt Lake City market was supplied by distant plants in California that were owned by Carnation, Continental Baking, and Pet Milk. Until 1957, these three firms accounted for almost all the frozen fruit pies sold in the Salt Lake City market.

The Utah Pie Company had been baking dessert pies in Salt Lake City and selling them fresh for 30 years. This family-owned-and-operated business entered the frozen pie market in 1957. It was immediately successful and grabbed a huge share of the Salt Lake City market. During the relevant years, the market shares of the various competitors were as follows:

	1958	1959	1960	1961
Utah Pie	67%	34%	46%	45%
Pet	16	36	28	29
Carnation	10	9	12	9
Continental	1	3	2	8
All others	6	19	13	8

Utah Pie's strategy for penetrating the market was to set its prices below those of its competitors. Due to its immediate success, it built a new plant in 1958. Its local plants gave Utah Pie a locational advantage over its competitors. For most of the time in question, Utah Pie's prices were the lowest in the Salt Lake City market. The incumbent firms, of course, responded to Utah Pie's entry and lower prices by reducing their own prices. As a result, all the larger firms sold frozen pies in Salt Lake City at prices lower than those charged for pies of like grade and quality in other geographic markets considerably closer to their California plants.

Utah Pie sued these three firms, claiming price discrimination. Ultimately, the case was reviewed by the Supreme Court [in 1967], which took a dim view of such pricing behavior: "Sellers may not sell like goods to different purchasers at different prices if the result may be to injure competition in either the sellers' or the buyers' market unless such discriminations are justified as permitted by the Act." Consequently, the Supreme Court found the defendants guilty of price discrimination. Inasmuch as no competitors had been forced from the market, it appears that price discrimination does not have to have an obviously predatory impact to be ruled illegal. All the Court saw in this case was a pattern of falling prices. It feared that such a pattern could result in a lessening of competition if one or more competitors fell out of the market.

ANALYZE THE ISSUE

Utah Pie sued its three outside competitors under the Robinson-Patman Act. Some have criticized this case because it is an example of the type of bizarre result that can be produced by antitrust policy. Do you agree? Explain.

Source: David L. Kaserman and John W. Mayo, *Government and Business: The Economics of Antitrust and Regulation* (Fort Worth: Dryden Press, 1995), p. 282.

For excellent summaries of numerous key antitrust cases, visit an Internet site maintained by Anthony D. Becker at: http://www.stolaf.edu/people/becker.

The Standard Oil Case (1911)

The Theodore Roosevelt administration took action to break up Standard Oil under the Sherman Act. After 10 years of litigation, the Supreme Court ruled in 1911 that Standard Oil had achieved its monopoly position in the oil refining industry through illegal business practices. John D. Rockefeller's trust had used railroad rebates, discounts, espionage, control of supplies to rivals, and predatory pricing to gain a monopoly. The remedy was for the Standard Oil Trust to be broken into competing companies: Standard Oil of New York became Mobil, Standard Oil of California became Chevron, Standard Oil of Indiana became Amoco, and Standard Oil of New Jersey became Exxon.

The Standard Oil Trust case established a standard for antitrust rulings. The Supreme Court ruled that (1) Standard Oil was a monopoly with a 90 percent share of the refined-oil market and (2) Standard Oil achieved its monopoly through illegal business behavior intended to exclude rivals. The Court stated that point (2) was critical to its decision but not point (1). This doctrine became known as the **rule of reason.** The rule of reason is the antitrust doctrine that the existence of monopoly alone is not illegal unless the monopoly engages in illegal business practices. Stated differently, monopoly *per se* is not illegal. Thus, "big is not necessarily bad." Standard Oil and other dominant firms would be broken up not merely because of their dominance, but also because of their abusive behavior.

Rule of reason

The antitrust doctrine that the existence of monopoly alone is not illegal unless the monopoly engages in illegal business practices.

Between 1911 and 1920, the rule of reason was also applied in breaking up the American Tobacco Trust and other trusts. In 1920, the Supreme Court also applied the rule of reason when it decided that U.S. Steel was not guilty under the Sherman Act. Although U.S. Steel controlled almost 75 percent of the domestic iron and steel industry, the Supreme Court ruled that it is not *size* that violates the law. Since there was no evidence of unfair pricing practices, U.S. Steel was a "good citizen" not in violation of the Sherman Act.

The Alcoa Case (1945)

Thirty-four years after the Standard Oil case, the courts did a "flip flop" on the rule of reason. In 1940, the Aluminum Company of America (Alcoa) was the only producer of aluminum in the United States. Alcoa's monopoly was primarily the result of its patents and its ownership of a unique resource, bauxite. Moreover, Alcoa kept its prices low to avoid competition and prosecution, behaving as a "good citizen" despite its size. A federal appeals court ruled that Alcoa had violated the Sherman Act and declared:

> *Having proved that Alcoa had a monopoly of the domestic ingot market the government had gone far enough. . . .Congress did not condone "good trusts" and condemn "bad" ones; it forbade all.*[3]

---

[3]*U.S. v. Aluminum Co. of America,* 148 F.2d 416 (2d Cir. 1945).

With the Alcoa decision, the courts turned from "big is not necessarily bad" to "big is bad." The rule of reason was transformed into the **per se rule.** The per se rule is the antitrust doctrine that the existence of monopoly alone is illegal regardless of whether or not the monopoly engages in illegal business practices. Instead of judgments based on the performance of a monopoly, antitrust policy in the United States was switched by the court's interpretation to judgments based solely on the market structure. Interestingly, the court's solution was not to break up Alcoa. Instead, the federal government subsidized its competitors. War plants were sold at bargain prices to Reynolds Aluminum and Kaiser Aluminum, and later more rivals entered the aluminum industry.

Per se rule

The antitrust doctrine that the existence of monopoly alone is illegal, regardless of whether or not the monopoly engages in illegal business practices.

The IBM Case (1982)

In 1969, the U.S. Department of Justice brought antitrust action against IBM because of its dominance in the mainframe computer market. The government argued that IBM had a 72 percent share of the electronic digital computing industry. IBM argued that the relevant market was broader and included programmable calculators and other information-processing products. After 13 years of litigation, IBM had spent over $100 million on its defense and had constructed an entire building to store case documents. Finally, in 1982, the government dropped the case. One reason was that Digital Equipment, Apple Computer, and Japanese companies were competing with IBM. Another reason illustrates the mix of politics and antitrust policy. In 1982, Ronald Reagan was president, and he believed in a much less restrictive interpretation of antitrust laws. In any event, the IBM case represented a shift in the general sentiment among those enforcing the antitrust laws from the per se rule back to the rule of reason.

The AT&T Case (1982)

In 1978, the U.S. Department of Justice brought an antitrust suit against AT&T and the Bell System. The issue was complicated. At this time, AT&T was a *natural monopoly* regulated by the government. (Regulation of a natural monopoly will be explained later in this chapter; see Exhibit 5.) The government allowed AT&T to have a monopoly in long-distance and local telephone service and in the production of telephones. The Federal Communications Commission (FCC) regulated long-distance rates, and state utility commissioners regulated local rates. What was the objective of giving one company the exclusive right to telephone services in the United States? In order to provide everyone with low-cost local services, the regulatory commissions set AT&T local charges low and AT&T long-distance rates high to cover the lower local rates.

In the 1970s, advances in technology changed the nature of the long-distance telephone industry. Telephone service was no longer a natural monopoly because fiber optics and satellites made cable connections obsolete. Competitors developed, and the government alleged that these rivals were being charged unfairly high fees for access to AT&T's local telephone lines.

On the same day the IBM case ended in 1982, AT&T and the Department of Justice announced this case was settled. AT&T ("Ma Bell") divested itself of 22 local companies ("Baby Bells"), but retained its long-distance telephone service, its research facilities (Bell Laboratories), and its manufacturing facilities (Western Electric Company). As a result, local companies became regulated monopolies in their areas, and local phone rates rose sharply. In nationwide long-distance telephone service, AT&T's competition with MCI and Sprint lowered the price of long-distance telephone service. Moreover, individual customers became responsible for buying their own phones, rather than using only AT&T phones. The result has been a highly competitive market, offering a wide range of phone prices and a wide variety of phones.

The MIT Case (1992)

For years, the presidents of many of the nation's top universities—Cornell, Harvard, Yale, Columbia, Brown, Princeton, University of Pennsylvania, Dartmouth, and MIT—attended annual meetings to discuss tuition, faculty salaries, and financial aid packages. After such meetings, these schools often adjusted tuition charges, salary increases, and even fees for room and board. For example, one year Dartmouth planned to raise faculty salaries by 8.5 percent. The other schools wanted to hold the line at 6.5 percent, so Dartmouth was persuaded to cave in. At other meetings, the group's goal was to make sure each student who applied to more than one of the schools would be offered the same financial aid. At another meeting, Harvard and Yale accused Princeton of offering excessively generous scholarships to top students.

The U.S. Justice Department investigated and charged the eight Ivy League universities and MIT with an illegal conspiracy to fix prices. The eight Ivy League schools settled the case with a consent degree. This agreement required these schools to cease colluding on tuition, salaries, and financial aid in the future, and, in return, none of the schools admitted guilt for a price conspiracy. MIT refused to sign the consent order and pursued the case all the way to the Supreme Court. In 1992, the Court ruled MIT had violated antitrust laws and concluded that students and parents have the right to compare prices when choosing a university.

The Microsoft Case (2001)

Microsoft Corporation dominates the computer software industry with about a 90 percent share of the personal computer operating system software and Internet browser markets. District Judge Thomas Jackson generally agreed with the Justice Department and 19 states and ruled that the software giant had violated the Sherman Act. He stated that Microsoft had tied its Windows operating systems at zero price (predatory pricing) to its Internet Explorer browser in order to eliminate competition and establish a monopoly in the browser market. The Justice Department claimed that Microsoft required computer manufacturers to agree, as a condition for receiving licenses to install Windows, not to remove Internet Explorer and not to provide prominent display of rival browsers.

CHECKPOINT

Does Price-Fixing Improve Your Education?

Price-fixing agreements are among the monopolistic restraint-of-trade practices prohibited by Section One of the Sherman Act. The Supreme Court has concluded that no formal agreement is necessary for proof of conspiracy. Instead, conspiracy may be inferred from the acts of the accused even if the consequences might be considered socially desirable. The presidents of the universities charged with price-fixing in the MIT case defended their business practices with the argument that they openly met to fix prices in order to improve education. With tuition and amount of financial aid fixed, students and parents will choose their university on the basis of academic quality alone. Consider the discussion of pricing strategies for an oligopoly discussed in Chapter 10. Can you give the presidents a better argument for their defense?

Bill Gates disputes the charges and claims the government is interfering with Microsoft's right to create new products that benefit consumers. Gates stated "The goal of competition is this thing called low prices. In the software business, power goes up while prices come down. In extreme cases, you actually get free products."

The remedies discussed include both conduct and structural remedies. A conduct remedy is a judicial instruction against engaging in specific behavior. For example, Microsoft could be required to include major rival browsers with its browser. Bill Gates likens this to "requiring Coca-Cola to include three cans of Pepsi in every six-pack it sells." Moreover, Microsoft claims that integrating Internet Explorer with Windows is one product and not tying. In short, no one using the Windows operating system needs a separate browser.

A structural remedy is a "surgical fix" aimed at permanently altering the company so substantially that further violations are not possible. For example, Microsoft could be split into three companies. One company would have operating systems, such as Windows. A second company could have applications, such as Word, Excel, and PowerPoint. The third company would get Internet Explorer and related Internet business. A major concern with this remedy is that a three-headed monopoly monster might destroy innovation and a seamless transition between Windows and other software applications. The fear is that prices might rise and software will become much more complicated.

In 2001, a federal appeals court nullified Judge Jackson's ruling, but it ruled that Microsoft did violate antitrust law to protect a monopoly for its Windows operating system. However, the court ruled the government had failed to prove Microsoft illegally attempted to monopolize the Internet browser market. In response, Microsoft announced that it would allow personal computer manufacturers to continue adding icons of other technology companies to Microsoft's operating system. As this text is written, this antitrust case remains highly controversial and the outcome is uncertain.

Finally, the major antitrust cases are summarized in Exhibit 2.

EXHIBIT 2 Summary of Major Antitrust Cases

Case (date)	Key provision
Standard Oil (1911)	This case established the rule of reason, allowing a monopoly unless it engages in illegal practices.
Alcoa (1945)	This case overturned the rule of reason and established the per se rule, under which all monopolies are illegal.
IBM (1982)	The government dropped its case after 13 years and shifted antitrust policy back to the rule of reason.
AT&T (1982)	Technology made this government-regulated natural monopoly obsolete, and AT&T was found guilty of anticompetitive pricing.
MIT (1992)	Eight Ivy League schools agreed to stop colluding to fix prices, and MIT was found guilty of price-fixing while attending open meetings.
Microsoft (2001)	This case charged Microsoft with predatory pricing by tying its monopoly in Windows to its Internet Explorer browser.

Mergers and International Antitrust Policy

The decades of the 1980s and 1990s were characterized by a wave of mergers. Mergers are a concern to antitrust regulators because firms can avoid charges of price-fixing by merging into one firm. The antitrust policy toward mergers depends on the type of merger and its likely effect on the relevant market.

Types of Mergers

Horizontal merger

A merger of firms that compete in the same market.

A **horizontal merger** is a merger of firms that compete in the same market. The mergers of Coca-Cola and PepsiCo., Ford Motor Company and General Motors, and Anheuser-Busch and Coors would be hypothetical examples of horizontal mergers. Horizontal mergers raise a "red flag" because they decrease competition in a market. For example, in 1986, the government blocked the proposed merger between Coca-Cola and Seven-Up.

Vertical merger

A vertical merger is a merger of a firm with its suppliers.

A **vertical merger** is a merger of a firm with its suppliers. This type of merger is between companies at different stages of a production process. Hypothetical examples of vertical mergers would be General Motors merging with a major tire company and Ford Motor Company merging with a large number of car dealerships. Although the government often challenges vertical mergers, international competition has reduced antitrust scrutiny of vertical mergers. If this type of merger lowers costs by eliminating unnecessary supplier charges, U.S. firms will be more competitive in world markets.

A **conglomerate merger** is a merger between firms in unrelated markets. Suppose an insurance company buys a computer software company or a cigarette company merges with a hotel chain. Actual examples are Philip Morris merging with Miller Brewing Company and General Motors merging with Electronic Data Systems Corporation. No antitrust action was taken to prevent these mergers because the products of the two firms were considered to be unrelated. Conglomerate mergers are generally allowed because they do not significantly decrease competition.

Conglomerate merger

A merger between firms in unrelated markets.

Antitrust Policies in Other Countries

Early antitrust laws were aimed at the domestic economy with little concern for international competitiveness. Because of the internationalization of competition in recent decades, some economists call for a relaxation of antitrust laws to allow firms to merge and compete more effectively in the world economy. Other economists disagree and argue that strong antitrust laws are necessary because small firms create most jobs and innovations.

One reason firms in other countries are so competitive with U.S. firms is that other countries' antitrust laws are weak in comparison to U.S. antitrust laws. For example, no other country breaks up companies for antitrust violations. There are two basic explanations. First, most other countries have smaller populations than the United States. Because other countries have fewer potential customers, they view the international market as the target and design weak antitrust laws accordingly. Stated differently, other countries must sell their products internationally in order to achieve economies of scale and be competitive.

Second, other countries have weak antitrust laws based on their culture and history. In the United States, there is a strong belief in Adam Smith's individualistic competition among small firms. This "big is bad" ideology is the foundation of U.S. antitrust laws, but this belief is not prevalent in other countries. In other countries, "big is better," and in countries such as Japan and Germany, government and business work together to compete internationally. In contrast, there is a general mistrust of big government working directly with big businesses in the United States. Exhibit 3 provides brief descriptions of antitrust policies in various countries.

Regulation

The same distrust of big business that is the basis of antitrust laws also led to the evolution of regulation and federal regulatory agencies in the United States. The regulatory process in the United States has gone through several phases. In the first phase, from 1887 to the Great Depression, the railroads were the primary target. During the 1930s, the Great Depression created a favorable environment in which regulation spread to the communications, financial, and other industries. After 1970, regulation increased steadily in the areas of health, safety, and the environment until the 1980s, when a deregulation movement began and continues to have momentum in the early 2000s.

EXHIBIT 3 Summary of Antitrust Policies around the World	
Country	**Antitrust policy**
Germany	Cartels are allowed and encouraged. The Federal Cartel Office is relatively small, and it has the authority to force price decreases if it determines a cartel has abused its power.
Britain	The British Monopoly Commission has the power to recommend structured changes, but it seldom does so. The commission, however, has reduced prices in some industries.
France	France has encouraged large-scale mergers. The Commission on Competition is very weak and often approves mergers.
European Union (EU)	The EU's antitrust laws officially took precedence over member nations' laws in 1992. The EU prohibits all agreements that have the effect of preventing, restraining, or distorting competition within the EU.
Japan	Antitrust policies allow for cartel-like structures called *keiretsus*. *Keiretsus* links together companies, customers, suppliers, banks, and government agencies. Japan has a Fair Trade Commission that operates like the U.S. FTC. The Fair Trade Commission is weak and subordinated to Japan's pro-cartel Ministry of International Trade and Industry (MITI). We will discuss the MITI in more detail in the chapter on economies in transition.

Historical Origins of Regulation

The Early Years. The railroads came under regulation in the late nineteenth century as a result of their unfair pricing practices. At this time in history, railroads faced little competition from other carriers, so there was little to prevent railroads from overcharging. Railroads also practiced price discrimination against isolated rural customers by charging them higher rates for short hauls than they charged city customers for long hauls. In 1887, the Interstate Commerce Commission (ICC) was established to regulate rail prices and to cut the costs of rail transportation by reducing duplicate trains, depots, and tracks.

The Great Depression Era. During the 1930s, regulation was extended to other industries. The Food and Drug Administration (FDA) was established in 1931 to oversee the safety of food and drugs. All surface transportation, including trucks, barges, and oil pipelines, came to be regulated by the ICC. The Civil Aeronautics Board (CAB) was created in 1938 to regulate air travel, and the Federal Communications Commission (FCC) was established in 1934 to regulate telephones, telegraphs, and broadcasting industries. In 1934, as a result of the stock market crash of 1929, the Securities and Exchange Commission (SEC) was created to combat fraud and malpractice in the securities industry.

The Health, Safety, and Environment Era. The Occupational Safety and Health Administration (OSHA) was created in 1970 to reduce the incidence of injury and death in the workplace. This agency cites and fines employers who violate safety and health rules. In the same year, the Environmental

Protection Agency (EPA) was established to set and enforce pollution standards. In 1972, the Consumer Product Safety Commission (CPSC) was established to protect the public against injury from unsafe products. The CPSC has the power to ban the sale of hazardous products.

The Deregulation Trend. In the 1970s, the higher production costs resulting from regulation generated widespread dissatisfaction with government regulation. The result was a movement toward **deregulation** in the late 1970s and 1980s. Deregulation is the elimination or phasing out of government restrictions on economic activity. Initially, the major thrust of deregulation was in the transportation and telecommunications industries. The *Airline Deregulation Act of 1978* removed regulated airfares and restrictions against competition in air travel markets. The *Staggers Rail Act of 1980* deregulated the railroads, and the *Motor Carrier Act of 1982* deregulated bus transportation. The Civil Aeronautics Board (CAB), established in 1938 to regulate airline fares and air routes, was abolished in 1984. The You're the Economist at the end of the chapter examines the effects on the airline industry.

Deregulation
The elimination or phasing out of government restrictions on economic activity.

In telecommunications, the most important case was the deregulation and dismantling of AT&T. As explained above, technological innovations made competition in telecommunications possible, and, as a result of an antitrust lawsuit, AT&T was broken up and forced to compete with MCI, Sprint, and other companies for long-distance service. In 1996, a telecommunications bill was passed that is making changes in U.S. telecommunications. This bill deregulated cable television rates, while allowing local and long-distance telephone companies and cable companies to compete. This bill also required television manufacturers to equip new sets with a computer chip to block shows parents do not wish their children to watch.

For nearly 100 years electricity was a regulated industry in the United States. Privately held utility companies obtained the right to operate a monopoly in exchange for government regulations that set rates and capped profits. In 1992, Congress started the deregulation movement for power companies when it approved the *Energy Policy Act,* which opened competition at the wholesale level. In 2001, 24 states and the District of Columbia have approved deregulation plans. However, it will take time before we will know if alarm over the California power shortage will create a deregulation backlash (see You're the Economist on electricity deregulation).

The principal functions of the federal regulatory agencies discussed above are summarized in Exhibit 4.

Three Cases for Government Regulation

Government regulation involves political, social, and economic factors, and the general justification for regulation is to protect the public. In this section, we examine three basic situations in which regulation is often imposed: (1) natural monopoly, (2) externalities, and (3) imperfect information. In

EXHIBIT 4 Federal Regulatory Agencies

Agency	Year created	Function
Interstate Commerce Commission (ICC)	1887*	Regulated interstate ground transportation, including the railroad, trucking, bus, and water carrier industries.
Food and Drug Administration (FDA)	1931	Protects the health of the nation against impure and unsafe foods, drugs, and cosmetics. Develops policy regarding labeling of all drugs.
Securities and Exchange Commission (SEC)	1934	Provides for complete financial disclosure and protects investors in stock and other securities against fraud.
Federal Communications Commission (FCC)	1934	Regulates television, radio, telephone, and telegraph services; satellite transmissions; and cable TV.
Civil Aeronautics Board (CAB)	1938†	Regulated airline fares and routes.
Occupational Safety and Health Administration (OSHA)	1970	Enforces rules in cases involving safety and health violations in the workplace.
Environmental Protection Agency (EPA)	1970	Regulates pollution in the areas of air, water, waste, noise, radiation, and toxic substances.
Consumer Product Safety Commission (CPSC)	1972	Protects the public against unreasonable risks of injury from consumer products.

*Abolished in 1995.
†Abolished in 1984.

each of these cases, the argument in favor of regulation is *market failure.* Recall from Chapter 4 that market failure is a situation in which the market operating on its own fails to lead to an efficient allocation of resources.

Natural Monopoly

The objective of antitrust policy is to create a level playing field for competing firms. Depending on the case, antitrust policy can result in breaking up a monopoly, preventing formation of a monopoly, and/or punishing anticompetitive business practices of a monopoly. But, what happens when it is inefficient for more than one company to operate in a particular market? Stated another way, creation of a level playing field for competitors may not be in the best interest of economic efficiency. This situation exists in a *natural monopoly.* As explained earlier in Exhibit 1 in Chapter 9 on monopoly, a natural monopoly is an industry in which long-run average cost is minimized when only one firm serves the market. Recall that the services of such public utilities as local telephone, gas, electric, cable TV, and water companies are natural monopolies subject to government regulation. To avoid abuse of this type of monopoly, the prices or rates these public utilities can charge are determined by a federal, state, or local regulatory commission or board.

Exhibit 5 illustrates the demand curve, long-run marginal cost curve, and long-run average cost curve for a natural monopoly in the cable TV market—say, Vision Cable. Because of *economies of scale,* the long-run

EXHIBIT 5   **A Regulated Monopoly**

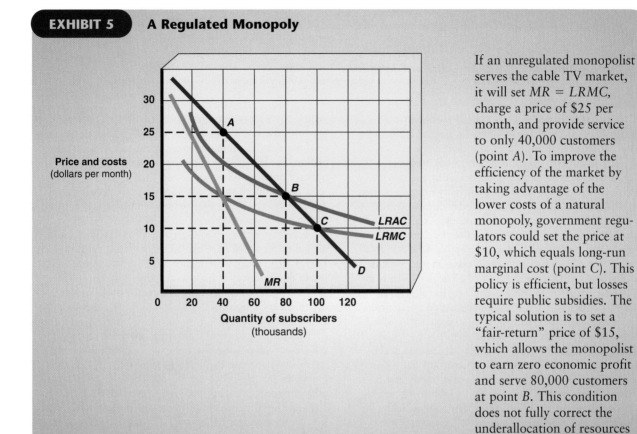

If an unregulated monopolist serves the cable TV market, it will set $MR = LRMC$, charge a price of $25 per month, and provide service to only 40,000 customers (point A). To improve the efficiency of the market by taking advantage of the lower costs of a natural monopoly, government regulators could set the price at $10, which equals long-run marginal cost (point C). This policy is efficient, but losses require public subsidies. The typical solution is to set a "fair-return" price of $15, which allows the monopolist to earn zero economic profit and serve 80,000 customers at point B. This condition does not fully correct the underallocation of resources caused by an unregulated natural monopoly.

average cost (*LRAC*) curve is negatively sloped. Following the *marginal-average rule* explained in Chapter 7, the long-run marginal cost (*LRMC*) curve is below the falling *LRAC* curve. Given this condition, the firm's demand curve intersects the *LRAC* curve at a quantity of 80,000 subscribers and a cost of $15 per month equal to the price (point B). Suppose this output is divided equally between Vision Cable and another cable company. As discussed earlier in Exhibit 1 of Chapter 9, the result of competition between cable television companies is that the cost per subscriber is much higher—and even higher if output is divided among more than two cable companies.

To take advantage of the lower cost, the policy prescription is to create a cable TV market served by only one producer—Vision Cable. The policy problem now is how to keep this unregulated natural monopoly from enjoying a substantial monopoly profit. Instead of providing services for 80,000 customers, Vision Cable will service only 40,000 customers by following the $MR = MC$ rule to maximize profits. The price that corresponds to this output is $25 per month at point A. Because the profit-maximizing

Is Electricity Deregulation a Mistake?

Applicable Concepts: regulation and deregulation

The most recent candidate for deregulation is electricity. Electricity has been treated as a natural monopoly and regulated for many years. But recent technological changes in energy production allow efficient production on a small scale. The latest technology uses natural gas turbines to generate electricity on a scale comparable to a jet engine. Small-scale generation raises the possibility of competition. In addition to technology, there are other forces pushing for deregulation. For example, customers in a high-priced state such as California point to the lower prices paid by nearby states, such as in Washington State. With deregulation, Californians anticipate benefiting from the purchase of cheap hydroelectric power from the Pacific Northwest.

The United States has been watching the experience of other countries that have already deregulated electricity, such as Great Britain. Their sobering experience foreshadows the ongoing problems in California. In a deregulated electricity market, there is a "spot market" in which the price of electricity is determined each hour (or half-hour in Great Britain). The price depends upon supply and demand. Unfortunately, there is considerable evidence that electricity suppliers in Great Britain have withheld supplies artificially so as to force up the price. California is now pursuing similar accusations against out-of-state suppliers.

In the United States, several states have introduced their own approaches to deregulation. California, Pennsylvania, New York, and Texas, for example, are at various stages of deregulation. The California experience actually started smoothly. Then, in the Summer of 1999, California began to experience some problems and they arrived in force in the summer of 2000. During that summer, and even into the following fall and winter, Californians received almost daily warnings of possible blackouts and brownouts. Following are features of the California approach to deregulation that economists believe contributed to their troubles:[1]

- California required its electric utilities to sell their power plants and buy electricity on the spot market.
- California utilities were not permitted to sign long-term contracts with electricity generators, reinforcing the utilities' reliance on the spot market.
- California capped retail rates.

The stage was set for a special set of events that can be called the "perfect storm."[2] During a heat wave in the summer of 2000, demand soared as customers turned on their air conditioners. California utilities had no choice but to buy on the spot market as prices soared 10-fold over their normal levels. Customer rates were capped, so consumer decisions did not reflect what the utilities were paying for electricity. In turn, utilities could not cover their

costs. The utilities quickly found themselves facing bankruptcy. Spot rates continued to climb. Duke Power Company of North Carolina has stated that 80 percent of its spot price was a premium to cover the risk of selling to California utilities that might not repay. Adding to the upward pressure on prices were a drought in the Northwest that reduced the availability of hydroelectric power and natural gas prices that soared as the demand for gas turbine generation skyrocketed.

Faced with this crisis, Governor Gray Davis of California called for more price caps. He convinced the Federal Energy Regulatory Commission (FERC) to cap wholesale prices during hours of highest demand. But, as explained in Chapter 4, price ceilings cause shortages, and California began a daily regime of blackouts and brownouts despite calls for conservation.

Only time will tell if California reforms its deregulatory approach or abandons deregulation. In the interim, its utilities can now sign long-term contracts for electric power. In fact, as of November 2001, there is now a surplus of electricity due to long-term contracts![3] The state has gone heavily into debt to purchase electricity transmission lines, and rates have increased, in some cases as much as 80 percent. Nevertheless, retail rates have not been deregulated. If they were, customers would see the highest prices on hot summer days and would conserve most when conservation is most needed. California is encouraging the construction of additional generating capacity. However, the state will have to consider environmental sacrifices to keep production costs down. The crucial question for California is whether its citizens believe it is in their long-term best interest to let the market work subject to the laws of supply and demand.

ANALYZE THE ISSUE

California's energy crisis has been characterized as the "perfect storm" because so many events came together simultaneously to cause the crisis. A storm need not be fatal if one is well prepared. To what extent did California contribute to its own crisis?

---

[1] George Passantino, Deputy Director of Reason Public Policy Institute, http://www.rppi.org/electricity/ebrief011001.html.

[2] *The Perfect Storm* is the title of a book and later a movie based on a true story of a unique set of weather conditions that caused a fishing boat to sink.

[3] "California Now Faces Power Surplus: Long-term contracts lock in high process; demand has fallen," by Karen Gaudetter, Associated Press, November 22, 2001.

CHECKPOINT

Why Doesn't the Water Company Compete?

The local water company is considered to be a natural monopoly, and the government prohibits other firms from competing with it. If a natural monopoly can produce water at a lower price than other firms, then why would the government protect the water company from competitors?

---

price exceeds the *LRAC* curve, monopoly pricing creates too high a price and too small an output. Stated differently, the result is an inefficient cable TV market, in which there is an underallocation of resources to produce cable TV service.

For the cable television market to be efficient, regulators must set a price ceiling at $10 per month, which is equal to long-run marginal cost at point *C* on the demand curve. This pricing strategy follows the competitive principle of **marginal cost pricing.** Marginal cost pricing is a system of pricing in which the price charged equals the marginal cost of the last unit produced. At a price of $10, Vision Cable suffers a loss because although the price covers long-run marginal cost, the price is not high enough to cover long-run average cost. This means the firm can survive in the long run only if the government subsidizes the loss.

What to do? Is there an option that does not require taxpayers' money? Yes! In practice, regulatory commissions have relaxed the objective of efficiency and have focused on establishing a "fair-return" price to be charged by the monopolist. In Exhibit 5, the commission would establish the fair-return price at $15 per month at point *B,* where the demand curve intersects the *LRAC* curve. Because the price ceiling equals long-run average cost, Vision Cable earns zero economic profit and serves 80,000 customers in the long run. However, remember from the chapter on production costs that in economics cost includes a normal profit, which is just enough to keep the firm in the cable industry.

Marginal cost pricing
A system of pricing in which the price charged equals the marginal cost of the last unit produced.

> **Conclusion** *Government regulators can achieve efficiency for a natural monopoly by setting a price ceiling equal to the intersection of the demand and the marginal cost curves, but this policy results in losses. An alternative is to set a price ceiling, called the fair-return price, that yields a normal profit, but is somewhat inefficient.*

Externalities

The case of pollution was treated in detail in Exhibit 7(a) in Chapter 4. To refresh your memory, recall that the individual firm in a competitive market has no incentive to eliminate pollution voluntarily. Pollution is an *external cost* imposed on *third parties* who neither produce nor consume a good. Pollution causes polluting firms to overproduce, while causing firms that pay the cost of cleaning up the pollution to under produce. Therefore, expenditures on pollution control would place firms at a competitive disadvantage with respect to firms that do not pay the cost of controlling pollution. If society wants less pollution, this type of market failure justifies government regulation from, say, the EPA. The exact nature of the regulation, however, may take a variety of forms, ranging from direct controls requiring specific pollution-control equipment to taxation.

Without repeating the explanation given in Exhibit 7(b) in Chapter 4, note that the *external benefits* of a good, such as a vaccination, can lead to underproduction of the good. Again, regulation is necessary if society is to respond to externalities. In this case, the government solution can take various forms, including requiring consumption or providing special subsidies.

Imperfect Information

In some cases, consumers lack important information about a product, and they cannot make rational decisions. Without complete and reliable information, consumers may be unaware of the dangers of unsafe drugs, hazardous chemicals, and defective products. The source of imperfect information about products may be company errors. Much worse, companies may be able to boost sales by withholding valuable information about a problem with their products.

Let's consider a hypothetical case in which an unsafe Tucker Motors (TM) truck is sold. Suppose the safety defect is a gas tank that is located too close to the side of the truck. As a result, another vehicle can crash into the side of the TM truck and hit the gas tank. Such an accident can cause a deadly explosion. Assume further that TM is aware of this safety problem, but the cost of recalling and fixing the trucks exceeds the estimated cost of lawsuits caused by the defective gas tanks. The market incentive is therefore for TM to withhold knowledge of this defect from uninformed consumers.

Exhibit 6 illustrates this case. With consumers unaware of the defect, the interaction of the supply and demand curves for TM trucks yields an equilibrium at E_1, with 100,000 trucks being sold per year at a price of $15,000 per truck. Next, suppose the Consumer Product Safety Commission (CPSC) exposes the problem, and the media report stories about crash victims who have been severely burned and killed by the flames from the exploding gas tanks in TM trucks. Once the consuming public is aware of the defect, consumers' preferences for TM trucks change, and the demand curve decreases from D_1 to D_2. The result is a new equilibrium at E_2, with 75,000 TM trucks being sold per year at a price of $10,000 per truck. In other words, this case is an application of market supply and demand analysis as presented in Chapter 4.

Conclusion *Deficient information on unsafe products can cause consumers to overconsume a product.*

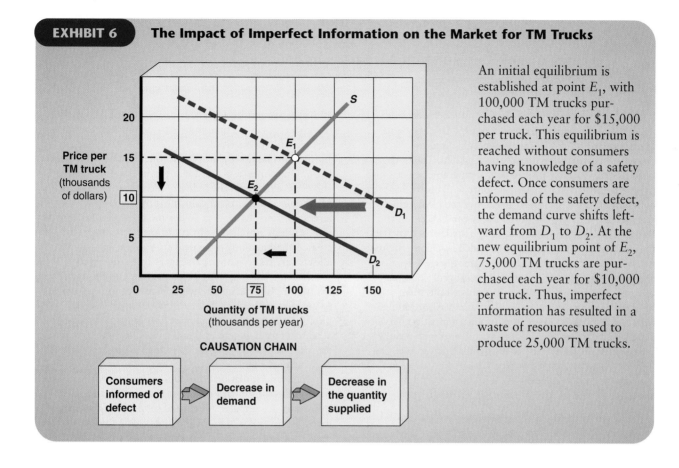

EXHIBIT 6   **The Impact of Imperfect Information on the Market for TM Trucks**

An initial equilibrium is established at point E_1, with 100,000 TM trucks purchased each year for $15,000 per truck. This equilibrium is reached without consumers having knowledge of a safety defect. Once consumers are informed of the safety defect, the demand curve shifts leftward from D_1 to D_2. At the new equilibrium point of E_2, 75,000 TM trucks are purchased each year for $10,000 per truck. Thus, imperfect information has resulted in a waste of resources used to produce 25,000 TM trucks.

In the TM truck example, resources were used to produce 25,000 trucks that consumers would not purchase when given complete information. These resources were misallocated because they could have been used to produce other goods and services. The solution is for government to prevent companies from making false or deceptive claims by gathering and disseminating accurate information to consumers. This is the rationale for the safety testing of cars, EPA mileage ratings on cars, and warning labels on cigarettes. In extreme cases, a product may be deemed too unsafe, and it is outlawed from sale. Others disagree with this view and argue that the government should only provide information. Once consumers have sufficient information, they should be free to choose.

Does Airline Deregulation Mean Friendlier Skies?

Applicable Concept: regulation versus deregulation

A much publicized case of deregulation achievement is the airline industry. Under regulation by the Civil Aeronautics Board (CAB), airfare competition and the incentive to control costs were reduced or eliminated. The CAB set both fares and routes for carriers. Unable to compete with price, the carriers could compete only with costly nonprice competition, such as advertising. Once the CAB authorized a carrier to provide service between two cities, the frequency of service remained unregulated. When carriers purchased fleets of planes and provided too many flights for their protected routes, profits were squeezed because the percentage of seats filled with passengers (load factor) fell, and the average cost rose. Carriers would then attempt to boost profits by lobbying the CAB for higher fares. In addition to eliminating price competition between established carriers, the CAB restricted entrants into the industry. From 1938 until 1977, the CAB never awarded a major route to any new airline.

Successful deregulation of an industry would be expected to provide the following three results:

- The average price of the service falls.
- The volume and variety of services rise.
- New firms enter the industry, and other firms fail and exit the industry.

The Airline Deregulation Act of 1978 provided these results by changing the structure and business behavior of the airline industry. Although the Federal Aviation Administration (FAA) would still regulate the safety of air service, the CAB was eliminated under this act in 1984, and price competition produced the expected results of lower fares and greater quantity of service. Revenue per passenger mile of airline travel declined 16 percent from 1978 to 1990 on an inflation-adjusted basis, saving consumers billions of dollars in lower fares. Over this same period, the fall in fares contributed to a doubling of passenger miles flown per year from 227 billion to 458 billion. Since 1990, fares adjusted for inflation have continued to fall, and passenger miles flown rose to 620 billion in 1998. After the barrier to entry was removed, the number of carriers increased sharply between 1978 and 1980 from 37 to 214. Since 1980, many carriers, such as the "few frills" People Express, exited the industry, and by 1998, the number of carriers dropped to 97.[1] As a result of the

attack of September 11, 2001, on the United States, there is a concern, (at the time this text was written) that many airlines will not survive.

The airline deregulatory movement is not without criticism. One concern is that lots of airlines went "belly up," and these exits from the industry increased the percentage of all domestic air travel controlled by the industry's largest carriers. Moreover, under the pressure of competition, carriers searched for ways to cut costs, and they created the hub-and-spoke delivery system. This system allows carriers to gather passengers from the "spoke" routes using smaller, less efficient planes and fly them from the hub in fully occupied, bigger planes at lower cost. Many carriers have gained near monopoly power in "hub" airports. These dominant hub carriers can control access to terminal gates, takeoff time slots, baggage service, and they can charge smaller lines high rates for using these airport rights.

Today, deregulation continues to exert downward pressure on fares. Low-fare tickets, cyberfares, and frequent flyer miles are popular. Quality of service is higher measured by fewer consumer complaints today than in the regulation era—although complaints rose sharply in 1999 and growing market concentration is a concern.[2] Should the airlines remain deregulated or return to a government-enforced cartel? Defenders of deregulation argue that growth of market concentration and its abuses can be controlled by enforcing antitrust laws and allowing international competition.

ANALYZE THE ISSUE

Prior to deregulation, critics argued that airline safety would suffer. Instead, although the Federal Aviation Administration's budget was cut following deregulation, the accident rate involving fatalities has fallen. Give a rationale for why the critics' prediction did not come to pass.

---

[1]*Statistical Abstract of the United States, 2000*, http://www.census.gov/prod/ www/statistical-abstract-us.html, Table 1067, p. 651 and Table 1076, p. 655.
[2]Ibid., Table 1075, p. 654.

KEY CONCEPTS

Trust
Predatory pricing
Sherman Act of 1890
Clayton Act of 1914
Federal Trade Commission
   Act of 1914

Robinson-Patman Act
   of 1936
Celler-Kefauver Act of
   1950
Rule of reason

Per se rule
Horizontal merger
Vertical merger
Conglomerate merger

Deregulation
Marginal cost pricing

SUMMARY

- A **trust** is a cartel that places the assets of competing companies in the custody of a board of trustees. During the last decades of the nineteenth century, trusts engaged in anticompetitive strategies to eliminate competition and raise prices, such as *predatory pricing*.

- The **Sherman Act of 1890** and the **Clayton Act of 1914** are the two most important antitrust laws. The Sherman Act marked the first attempt of the U.S. government to outlaw monopolizing behavior. Because this act was vague, the Clayton Act was passed to define anticompetitive behavior more precisely. The Clayton Act prohibited (1) price discrimination, (2) exclusive dealing, (3) tying contracts, (4) stock acquisition of competing companies, and (5) interlocking directorates.

- The **Federal Trade Commission Act of 1914** established the Federal Trade Commission (FTC) to investigate unfair competitive practices of firms.

- The **Robinson-Patman Act of 1936** strengthened the Clayton Act by prohibiting certain forms of price discrimination. This law is called the "Chain Store Act" because it was aimed at large retail chain stores that were obtaining volume discounts.

- The **Celler-Kefauver Act of 1950** strengthened the Clayton Act by declaring illegal the acquisition of the assets of one firm by another firm if the effect is to lessen competition.

- The **rule of reason** and the **per se rule** are the two main doctrines the courts have used in interpreting antitrust law. Under the rule of reason, monopolists were not subject to prosecution unless they acted in an anticompetitive manner. A court decision in the Alcoa case of 1945 replaced the rule of reason with the per se rule, which states that the mere existence of monopoly is illegal. Today, the trend is in favor of dominant firms because of international competition.

- A **horizontal merger** is a merger of two competing firms. A **vertical merger** is a merger of two firms where one produces an input used by the other firm. A **conglomerate merger** is a merger of two firms producing unrelated products.

- **Deregulation** is a movement that began in the late 1970s and 1980s to eliminate regulations primarily in the transportation and telecommunications industries. Today, the movement to further deregulate electric utilities is being questioned.

- **Marginal cost pricing** is a competitive pricing strategy for a regulated natural monopoly. Using this approach, regulators set the monopolist's price equal to its marginal cost. Another method is for regulators to establish a fair-return price equal to long-run average cost and the monopolist earns zero economic profit. Regulation of a natural monopoly is justified on the basis of market failure. Two other cases based on market failure include externalities and imperfect information.

Marginal cost pricing

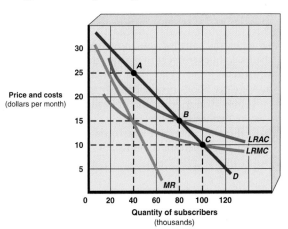

SUMMARY OF CONCLUSION STATEMENTS

- Government regulators can achieve efficiency for a natural monopoly by setting a price ceiling equal to the intersection of the demand and the marginal cost curves, but this policy results in losses. An alternative is to set a price ceiling, called the fair-return price that yields a normal profit, but is somewhat inefficient.

- Deficient information on unsafe products can cause consumers to overconsume a product.

STUDY QUESTIONS AND PROBLEMS

1. Describe the major provisions of the Sherman Act and the Clayton Act. Who is responsible for enforcing these laws?

2. Two business practices outlawed by the Clayton Act are tying contracts and interlocking directorates. Explain the difference in the conditions required for these two practices to be a violation of this antitrust law.

3. Distinguish between the Robinson-Patman Act of 1936 and the Celler-Kefauver Act of 1950.

4. Using cases presented in the text, explain the issue in the courts' interpretation of "monopoly versus monopolizing."

5. A controversy in many antitrust court cases involves the definition of the relevant market for a firm's product. How would you argue in the Alcoa case that the government's claim of the firm's high market share was in error?

6. In the MIT case, which students are harmed by the Ivy League schools' coordination of scholarship policy? Professional baseball is exempt from antitrust laws. Should colleges and universities also be exempt from antitrust laws?

7. Based on the antitrust laws, how would you expect the federal government to react to the following situations?
   a. A college bookstore deliberately reduces prices until its only rival is driven out of business. The bookstore then raises its prices.
   b. Real estate firms meet in an open meeting and agree to charge 6 percent commissions on sales.

   c. Microsoft merges with WordPerfect by a stock acquisition.
   d. A small tax preparation company merges with a regional grocery store chain.

8. Based on the cases discussed in this text, is the following statement correct? "The antitrust laws in reality deal less with monopolies than with oligopolies."

9. Assume a regulatory agency is given authority over prices and entry conditions for a given industry. Also assume the agency decides to allow new entry, as the CAB actually did before deregulation, only when it is proven to be "necessary." Would this condition be expected to favor (a) existing regulated firms, (b) new entrants, or (c) consumers? Explain.

10. Exhibit 7 represents a natural monopolist.

Exhibit 7

a. If the monopolist is not regulated, what price will it charge, and what quantity will it produce?

b. If the monopolist is required to use marginal cost pricing, what price will it charge, and what quantity will it produce? Why will the monopolist stay in business?

c. Assume regulators set a fair-return price at P_b. Why would the monopolist stay in business?

11. Assume a natural monopolist is required to use marginal cost pricing and a government subsidy covers the loss. What problems might be associated with a public subsidy?

12. Do you agree that "cost does not really matter" as a principle for safety regulation, or do you believe that the cost of a safety device must be justified on the basis of the value of human life protected from a hazard?

 ONLINE EXERCISES

Exercise 1

Visit Antitrust Guidelines (http://www.usdoj.gov/atr/ public/guidelines/guidelin.htm). Under International Operations select Antitrust Enforcement Guidelines for International Operations. Explain how these guidelines may allow a monopoly.

Exercise 2

Visit GPO Gate, Catalog for Economic Report of the President (http://www.gpo.ucop.edu/catalog/erp97.html), and select Chapter 6, Refining the Role of Government in the U.S. Market Economy. Scroll down and browse The Telecommunications Act of 1996.

Exercise 3

Visit http://www.antitrust.org/news/mergers.html. Read about recent mergers. Summarize a particular case.

Exercise 4

Go to the Department of Justice website at http://www .usdoj.gov/01whatsnew/01_3.html. Choose the first DOJ Hot Topic, and write a brief report on the latest in antitrust enforcement.

CHECKPOINT ANSWERS

Does Price-Fixing Improve Your Education?

Accepting the schools' argument that they improve quality by price-fixing makes no more sense than allowing General Motors, Ford, DaimlerChrysler, and Japanese automakers to fix prices in order to improve quality. However, there is often a thin line between price-fixing and price leadership. Price leadership is not illegal as long as the price followers are not coerced. If you said price leadership is defendable and price fixing is not, YOU ARE CORRECT.

Why Doesn't the Water Company Compete?

Suppose new firms are allowed to compete with the water company, which is a natural monopolist. The concern is that the rivals will be outcompeted. New water companies must build plants, dig up the streets, and lay new water pipes and duplicate other resources in the same neighborhood. Because the competitors cannot produce water at a lower cost, they will leave the industry, and the resources used to compete with the natural monopolist will be wasted. If you said the government is not protecting the natural monopolist from competition so much as it is protecting against inefficient competitors wasting resources, YOU ARE CORRECT.

PRACTICE QUIZ

For a visual explanation of the correct answers, visit the tutorial at http://www.tucker.swcollege.com.

1. Which of the following is illegal under the Sherman Act?
   a. Attempts to monopolize
   b. Price-fixing
   c. Formation of cartels
   d. All of the above are illegal.

2. Officers of five large building-materials companies meet and agree that none of them will submit bids on government contracts lower than an agreed-upon level. This is an example of
   a. price-fixing.
   b. vertical restriction.
   c. a tying contract.
   d. an interlocking directorate.

3. A fabric shop cannot sell Singer sewing machines if it also sells other brands of sewing machines. This is an example of
   a. a resale price maintenance.
   b. territorial restrictions.
   c. a tying agreement.
   d. exclusive dealing.

4. Under the Clayton Act, horizontal mergers by stock acquisition were
   a. not considered.
   b. illegal if they could be shown to lessen competition.
   c. illegal under any circumstances.
   d. legal if they could be shown to lessen competition.

5. Under the Clayton Act, which of the following was illegal even if it was *not* shown to lessen competition substantially?
   a. Price discrimination
   b. Tying contracts
   c. Horizontal mergers by stock acquisition
   d. Interlocking directorates

6. The importance of the Federal Trade Commission Act of 1914 is that it
   a. set up an independent antitrust agency with the power to investigate complaints.
   b. strengthened the law against mergers.
   c. strengthened the law against price discrimination.
   d. did none of the above.

7. Which of the following is concerned primarily with price discrimination?
   a. Sherman Act
   b. Clayton Act
   c. Robinson-Patman Act
   d. Celler-Kefauver Act

8. Which of the following is concerned primarily with mergers?
   a. Sherman Act
   b. Clayton Act
   c. Robinson-Patman Act
   d. Celler-Kefauver Act

9. The Utah Pie case was brought under which of the following laws?
   a. Sherman Act
   b. Federal Trade Commission Act
   c. Robinson-Patman Act
   d. Celler-Kefauver Act

10. Although U.S. Steel controlled nearly 75 percent of the domestic iron and steel industry, in 1920 the Supreme Court ruled that the firm was *not* in violation of the Sherman Act because there was no evidence of abusive behavior. What antitrust doctrine was the Court applying in this case?
    a. The rule of reason
    b. The per se rule
    c. The marginal cost pricing rule
    d. The natural monopoly rule

11. In which antitrust case did the courts first apply the per se rule to determine whether a firm was in violation of the Sherman Act?
    a. Standard Oil case
    b. Alcoa case
    c. IBM case
    d. MIT case

12. The Interstate Commerce Commission (ICC) was established in
    a. 1887.
    b. 1890.
    c. 1929.
    d. 1933.

13. Today, the Civil Aeronautics Board (CAB) regulates
    a. airline ticket prices.
    b. airline routes.
    c. airline safety.
    d. all of the above.
    e. none of the above; the CAB was abolished in 1984.

14. Which of the following provides the basis for regulation?
    a. Natural monopoly
    b. Externalities
    c. Imperfect information
    d. All of the above

15. Consider a regulated natural monopoly. If the regulatory commission wants to establish a fair-return price, then it should set a price ceiling where the demand curve crosses the monopoly's long-run
    a. marginal revenue curve.
    b. average revenue curve.
    c. marginal cost curve.
    d. average cost curve.

CHAPTER 14

Environmental Economics

The United States is the envy of many of the world's citizens for its quality of life. Americans can choose from an almost unlimited number of goods and services. When it comes to transportation, for example, the typical family may own two or three cars. This same family may own touring bikes, mountain bikes, and hybrids that incorporate features of each. Some U.S. citizens own boats, and others own jet-skis. Those in colder climates may get around on snow-skis, snowshoes, or snowmobiles. Some families even own their own planes. The choice of what to buy in the United States is a private decision. I will choose a snowmobile over snowshoes if I want to travel fast and am willing to spend the money. I will choose a jet-ski over a kayak if I find high-speed travel more exciting than paddling along quietly. While my choice is private, my decision has consequences for others.

My jet-ski may create waves that threaten to tip your kayak. The noise I make may spoil your desire for peace and quiet. It may also scare wildlife. And the fuel I use to power the jet-ski not only adds to fuel consumption, but can contribute to water pollution. Engine exhausts may even make a small contribution to carbon emissions, which may contribute to global warming. Within the next 50 years, some fear that global warming could cause melting of the polar ice caps, resulting in rising ocean levels and massive

flooding of coastal areas throughout the world, as well as climate shifts that could render today's farms tomorrow's deserts.

Up to this point, the competitive market has been shown to be the best engine to generate what consumers want at the lowest possible price. Yet the unbridled use of many of these goods, from jet-skis and snowmobiles to Coke cans and cigarettes, may not be the best choice for society or the planet. Competitive markets work well when producers and consumers consider all costs in their decisions. But for some goods and services, decision makers fail to include the cost to others of their decision, such as revving the jet-ski or snowmobile to the detriment of others or throwing the Coke can or cigarette butt out the car window. While these are local problems, other problems are global in scale, such as carbon emissions from gasoline-burning engines that many believe cause global warming. This chapter will begin by showing why competitive markets may fail to sufficiently protect the environment. First, we will see that competitive markets result in market failure by producing "too much pollution." Then we will see how we might correct the market failure. Finally, we will consider the pros and cons of government intervention to improve our environment.

In this chapter, you will learn to solve these economics puzzles:

■ Why do competitive markets produce too many hogs and charge too low a price for those hogs?

■ How can government legislation, taxes, and permits help society achieve its environmental goals?

■ Can government intervention actually reduce environmental quality?

Competitive Markets and Environmental Efficiency

While society values goods and services produced in markets, it also values air, water, and other environmental amenities. Air and water are shared resources that generally are not priced in the marketplace. The end result is that markets often treat these resources as if they were free, resulting in their overuse. Competitive markets, which are the ideal in efficiently allocating many goods and services, fail to achieve preferred levels of output when they treat valuable resources such as air and water as if they were free.

The competitive market has been shown in earlier chapters to achieve *economic efficiency*. This efficiency exists when the price to consumers, reflecting marginal benefit, equals marginal cost. Consumers, such as jet-ski buyers, consider purchase price, styling, and performance features, such as speed, when comparing models. Producers choose what type of jet-ski to make based on profit maximization. Assuming perfect competition, profit maximization occurs where price equals marginal cost.

Private benefits and costs

Benefits and costs to the decision maker, ignoring benefits and costs to third parties. Third parties are people outside the market transaction who are affected by the product.

Buyers and sellers consider only their personal or **private benefits and costs.** Private benefits and costs are benefits and costs to the decision maker, ignoring benefits and costs to third parties. Third parties are people outside the market transaction who are affected by the product. As explained in Chapter 4, benefits and costs to third parties are known by a variety of names, including third-party effects, spillovers, and most commonly *external benefits and costs* or *externalities*. Recall that externalities are benefits or costs that are not considered by market buyers and sellers. Noise pollution is an externality that affects third parties not powering jet-skis.

Other externalities that degrade the environment include sulfur emissions from coal-burning electric power plants and the emission of chlorofluorocarbons (CFCs), associated with aerosol sprays and air conditioners. Sulfur emissions are widely thought to contribute to acid rain, resulting in tree deaths and fish kills. CFCs may be linked to a hole in the atmosphere's ozone layer, which increases the chance of skin cancer from the sun's ultraviolet rays.

Everyday externalities include the secondhand effects of cigarette smoke on the health of nonsmokers as well as cigarette butts tossed out of car windows, farmers' use of pesticides that wash into soil and water with detrimental health effects, and even noise from your next-door neighbor who is having a loud party while you are trying to study for an economics exam. Externalities can be positive as well as negative. You benefit from your classmate's decision to get a flu vaccine.

When externalities are present, competitive markets are not likely to achieve economic efficiency. In competitive markets, price, which reflects marginal private benefit, equals marginal private cost. Efficiency for society requires consideration of both private and **social benefits and costs.** Social benefits are the sum of benefits to everyone in society, including both benefits and external benefits. Social costs are the sum of costs to everyone in society, including both private costs and external costs. The condition for economic efficiency occurs when each unit of a good that is produced creates at least as much benefit to society as it does social cost. As a society, we do not want to produce any units of a good that creates more in additional social cost than it does in extra social benefit. In other words, we do not want our scarce resources used up on items that will not enhance our collective well-being. A succinct way of stating this condition for maximizing social welfare is to produce units of any good up to the point where

Social benefits and costs
The sum of benefits to everyone in society, including both private benefits and external benefits. Social costs are the sum of costs to everyone in society, including both private costs and external costs.

marginal social benefit = marginal social cost

Environmental regulations force market participants to include externalities in their decision making. For example, United States regulations prohibit the use of CFCs in air conditioners, aerosol cans, and other products. Although regulations like the ban on CFCs reduce emissions, they are not necessarily the most efficient approach to achieving less pollution.

Alternative approaches emphasize setting a goal without mandating the technology to achieve the goal. For example, one approach allows businesses that wish to expand in areas with high levels of pollution an alternative to reducing factory pollution to meet air quality regulations. Instead of reducing their own emissions, they can pay another party to offset emissions to meet the regulation. It may be cheaper for the company to pay someone else to reduce emissions than to achieve an in-house reduction. We discuss this approach in more detail later in the chapter in the section on Emissions Trading.

Private and Social Costs

When a producer of jet-skis or any other product chooses a production method, the producer is motivated by profit maximization. To maximize profit, the firm must choose the most efficient, least costly production method. Production costs include the costs of capital, labor, natural resources (such as land or energy), and entrepreneurship. External costs to others, such as pollution, are not included in production costs because the firm considers only its private costs. Social costs include private costs and external costs.

Competition and External Costs

Suppose considerable amounts of carbon emissions are produced by consumers using gasoline-powered lawn mowers. To reduce pollution, the manufacturer must redesign the engine. Also, suppose there is a lawn-mower manufacturer, GreenAcres, that considers social costs. It will choose a different production method for lower emission lawn mowers. This production method for lower emission lawn mowers must have a higher cost than the method used by other, more polluting lawn mowers produced by other firms. If this were not the case, other companies would already be using this method.

In a perfectly competitive market, consumers perceive all products as identical. While there may be exceptions, the typical consumer will pay no more for an environmentally friendly GreenAcres mower than for other lawn mowers. In the short run, GreenAcres will earn less than other firms because its costs are higher. In the long run, GreenAcres will lose money and eventually go out of business. Only the lowest-cost firms will survive in the long run. Since price exactly equals private average (and marginal) cost in the long run, average cost for the environmentally conscious company will lie above price, resulting in losses and eventual exit from the industry.

Exhibit 1(a) compares the typical and the "green" lawn mower companies in the short run. Exhibit 1(b) compares the two companies in the long run. The typical company chooses the lowest-cost method of production considering *private cost* only. Its marginal private cost and average private cost are shown as *MPC* and *APC*, respectively. The "green" company chooses the production method that has the lowest marginal and average *social cost*, shown as *MSC* and *ASC*, respectively. In the short run, *MSC* lies above *MPC*, so the "green" company produces less. In the long run, *ASC* lies above *APC*, so the "green" company loses money and eventually exits the industry.

Competitive Market Inefficiency When Externalities Exist

In competition, only firms that choose the lowest-cost method of production will survive. Firms that choose higher-cost methods will lose money and eventually exit the industry. There is no room for GreenAcres or any firm that does not minimize cost.

Rewarding firms that ignore externalities while punishing firms that recognize externalities is not socially efficient. Efficiency requires that price reflect marginal social benefit and equal marginal social cost. Competition results in a price that reflects marginal private benefit and equals marginal private cost. Efficiency requires that all relevant opportunity costs be included in marginal social cost, while competition forces firms to consider only private costs if they are to survive. If they are allowed to, competitive firms will ignore harmful by-products of their products, such as pollution, global warming, and congestion.

EXHIBIT 1 **A Comparison of Costs for Typical and "Green" Firms**

(a) Short-run marginal cost

(b) Long-run average cost

A "green" firm has higher costs in both the short run and the long run. The typical firm considers only private costs, as shown by *MPC* (marginal private cost) in part (a) and *APC* (long-run average private cost) in part (b). The "green" firm includes both private and external costs, shown by *MSC* (marginal social cost) in part (a) and *ASC* (average social cost) in part (b). These curves reflect social costs. In the short run, price in a competitive industry equals marginal private cost. The "green" firm produces a smaller quantity than the competitive firm. In the long run, price equals minimum long-run average private cost in a competitive industry. Minimum cost for the "green" firm is above price, so the "green" firm loses money and eventually leaves the industry.

Exhibit 2 shows lawn mower market equilibrium in a competitive market of traditional firms compared to a market of environmentally sensitive "green" firms. Competitive industry supply, S_P, sums the *marginal private costs* of "typical" individual firms that ignore externalities, while "green" industry supply, S_S, sums the *marginal social costs* of GreenAcres and other firms that recognize external costs in their engine design.

When externalities are present, competition leads to a lower price and a larger quantity than the socially efficient point (also see Exhibit 7(a) in Chapter 4). By ignoring external costs, competitive firms produce "too much," and the market equilibrium price is "too low," compared to a socially efficient industry. Competition leads to too many lawn mowers bought and sold because neither the buyers nor the sellers take into account the external cost of lawn mower engines that release emissions when used. When there are external costs, the efficient point is at the intersection of the demand curve and the social supply curve, S_S.

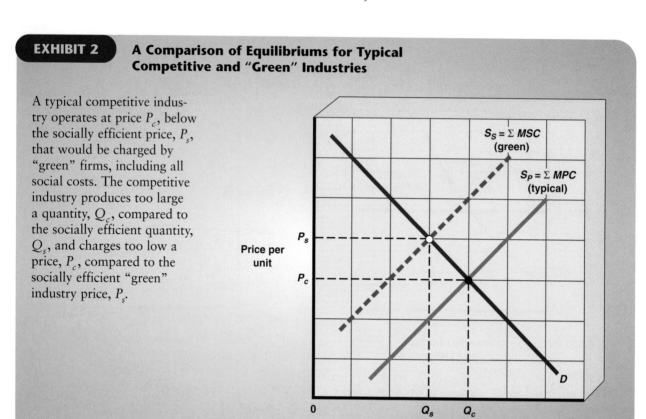

EXHIBIT 2   **A Comparison of Equilibriums for Typical Competitive and "Green" Industries**

A typical competitive industry operates at price P_c, below the socially efficient price, P_s, that would be charged by "green" firms, including all social costs. The competitive industry produces too large a quantity, Q_c, compared to the socially efficient quantity, Q_s, and charges too low a price, P_c, compared to the socially efficient "green" industry price, P_s.

From society's point of view, the efficient outcome is an equilibrium point of Q_s lawn mowers sold at price P_s. Associated with this outcome is a smaller quantity of pollution than at the competitive equilibrium. The quantity of pollution associated with quantity Q_s of lawn mowers is the efficient quantity of pollution.

If left to the competitive market, profit-maximizing producers would have no reason to reduce emissions. Emissions reductions, if they occurred at all, would be only an unintended by-product of technological change. For example, if manufacturers substitute a smaller engine so as to reduce lawn mower fuel use, the smaller engine would emit fewer pollutants. The emissions reduction is a by-product of the market reward for a more fuel-efficient mower, which consumers want and are willing to pay for. For emissions reduction to be worthwhile in its own right in a competitive market, it is necessary that consumers be willing to pay for a lower emission mower.

Why won't consumers offer more for a cleaner mower, just as they might for a more fuel-efficient one? First, consider choosing between two mowers that are identical except that one mower uses one gallon of gas per acre, while the other uses two gallons per acre. You will be willing to pay more for the first mower because you will get to keep the full monetary benefit of reduced fuel purchases.

Now suppose you must choose between two identical mowers except that the "green" mower emits only half as much pollution as the other one. The typical consumer will not be willing to pay more for the "green" mower because individually he or she will get only a negligible benefit. Benefits will extend to everyone, in the form of cleaner air and reduced global warming. Furthermore, if others buy "green" mowers, you will get the benefits whether or not you purchase a low-emission machine. You are better off being a *free rider*. Recall from the definition of a public good in Chapter 4 that a free rider is someone who enjoys benefits without paying the cost. You will get the same benefit of cleaner air whether or not you buy the clean mower. So you will choose to be a free rider and pay nothing for cleaner air, rather than paying extra to get a low-emission machine and still breathing the same cleaner air.

The end result is that no one buys a low-emission mower. Each individual chooses to free-ride, hoping to benefit from others who choose the "green" model. Once again, competitive markets are unlikely to be efficient.

Efficient Quantity of Pollution

The efficient production level for society is where marginal social benefit equals marginal social cost. The efficient amount of pollution is the amount generated at the socially efficient output level. It is of utmost importance to recognize that the efficient quantity of pollution is not zero. Zero pollution would require zero lawn mowers. Unless society is willing to abandon the American ideal of a neatly trimmed emerald green lawn, there will continue to be lawn mowers. Nor is it likely that many Americans will return to manual push mowers that do not require fuel, but are slower and take more strength than gasoline-engine mowers.

Visit the Global Network of Environmental Technology at http://www.gnet.org/ *to discover global information on environmental technologies.*

Other alternatives to consider are reduced-emission or emission-free lawn mowers, such as electric mowers. For a parallel situation, consider alternatives to conventional gasoline-engine automobiles. Alternatives are solar and electric vehicles, as well as other transport modes, such as bus, rail, and bicycle. Solar cars powered by photovoltaic cells and hydrogen-powered cars are among the virtually emission-free alternatives. But a fundamental concept in economics is that there are tradeoffs. Currently, the cost of solar and hydrogen cars is too high given society's willingness to pay for reduced emissions. Performance may suffer as well; solar cars, for example, are slower and less able to climb mountainous terrain than gasoline-powered cars.

Achieving Environmental Efficiency

Competitive markets fail to produce the socially efficient quantity when there are externalities. Externalities are a cause of **market failure**. As explained in Chapter 4, market failure occurs when the private market fails to produce society's preferred outcome.

Market failure
A situation in which market equilibrium results in too few or too many resources used in the production of a good or service.

When there is market failure, we must consider alternatives to the market to achieve efficiency. Government has a potential role when market failure occurs. Just as government can apply antitrust laws when an industry is not competitive, government can apply environmental laws when an industry ignores external costs. Not only are many cars required to have catalytic converters, but also many states require annual inspections to make sure the converters are working properly (and also to check that consumers have not removed the converters in order to improve gas mileage!).

In the environmental arena, as in other areas of government intervention, there is always the possibility of **government failure**. Government failure occurs when the government fails to correct market failure. Government officials may fail to achieve an efficient outcome either by doing too little about pollution or by doing too much.

Government failure

Government intervention or lack of intervention that fails to correct market failure.

Government officials motivated to keep their jobs may be influenced by large campaign contributors as well as voter desires. A Michigan legislator is likely to be sympathetic to the concerns of the auto industry and will also be aware of the autoworker layoffs and unemployment that accompany reduced car production. The official may be less motivated by externalities that are borne by third parties who do not vote in Michigan. On the other hand, a New York legislator may support an overly strict emissions standard for automobiles. New York voters benefit from cleaner air and are less concerned about auto-industry job losses.

Much of the effort of environmental economists has gone toward improving the odds that government will help, rather than hinder, environmental goals. Economists generally favor **incentive-based regulations** over **command-and-control regulations**. Incentive-based (IB) regulations set an environmental goal, but are flexible as to how buyers and sellers achieve the goal. Incentive-based regulations can make it profitable for firms to reduce emissions. Command-and-control (CAC) regulations set an environmental goal and also dictate how the goal will be achieved. Firms unable to meet the goal are penalized, and those that exceed it are not rewarded.

Incentive-based regulations

Government regulations that set an environmental goal, but are flexible as to how buyers and sellers achieve the goal.

The advantage of IB over CAC regulations is comparable to the advantages of a market system over those of a command system. Market systems are more efficient because they allow gains from comparative advantage. Businesses can pursue those activities where they have low opportunity costs. Similarly, allowing firms to choose how to achieve environmental goals encourages firms that can improve at low cost to reduce emissions more than firms less able to achieve lower emissions.

Command-and-control regulations

Government regulations that set an environmental goal and dictate how the goal will be achieved.

Efficiency gains from IB regulations compared to those from CAC regulations are both short run and long run. In the short run, allowing firms to choose how they will reduce emissions is more efficient than prescribing a single approach because firms incur different opportunity costs to lower emissions. In the long run, firms have an incentive to further reduce emissions by improving their technology. It is possible, though unlikely, that CAC regulations will be as efficient as IB regulations in the short run, just as it is possible, though unlikely, that a command system will happen to choose the lowest cost method of production. In the long run, however, command systems do not encourage innovative technology. There is no reward for improving, only a penalty for not meeting the standard. Let's consider how CAC and IB regulations reduce auto emissions.

Command-and-Control Regulations

In the 1970s, the U.S. government mandated the use of catalytic converters to reduce auto pollutants. The converter results in reduced hydrocarbon emissions associated with the burning of gasoline. While the catalytic converter undoubtedly reduces pollution, it suffers from several inefficiencies.

First, the requirement that cars have catalytic converters is uniform throughout the country. The marginal car in a high-pollution region, such as Los Angeles, has a much higher external cost than the same car driven across the prairies of Kansas. Efficiency calls for stricter regulations in automobile-intensive regions, such as Los Angeles. Second, there may be other technologies that can achieve the same reduced emissions at a lower cost. Finally, automakers have little incentive to invest in better future technology because the regulations require the firm to meet, but not beat, the standard.

A more subtle inefficiency is that CAC regulations may act as a barrier to entry to other firms, both domestic and international. The U.S. auto industry initially resisted environmental controls, knowing that controls would drive up costs. Foreign manufacturers, such as the Japanese automakers, already met the proposed U.S. standards, but achieved their goal with a different technology. Catalytic converters put the Japanese at a temporary cost disadvantage. Japanese cars were required to have catalytic converters even though they already met the air quality standard.

Another example of CAC is the use of Corporate Average Fuel Economy (CAFÉ) standards. These oft-discussed standards would require each automaker to achieve a minimum number of miles per gallon (mpg) for its fleet. For example, Ford's cars might be required to achieve 27 mpg. The last time this standard was imposed, Ford and other manufacturers invented minivans and sport utility vehicles (SUVs), which were classified as trucks and therefore were not subject to the standard. Since then, consumers have shifted to minivans and SUVs despite their lower fuel efficiency. In the end, Ford met the higher fuel standard, while the average mpg of vehicles actually on the road decreased!

Incentive-Based Regulations

Effluent Taxes. The simplest type of incentive-based (IB) regulation is an effluent tax. An effluent tax is a tax on the pollutant. If car manufacturers face a tax that depends on emissions, they can no longer ignore externalities. They now consider the tax, based on emissions, along with private resource costs. Exhibit 3 shows how an effluent tax can achieve efficiency.

A less direct way of reducing pollutants is a gasoline tax. By increasing the price of gasoline to car owners, the tax results in a smaller quantity demanded of gasoline and gasoline emissions. Over time, consumers faced with high gasoline prices seek more fuel-efficient cars, lowering emissions even more.

Taxes can achieve efficiency directly or indirectly and can be placed on buyers or sellers. Although the tax approach may appear simple in theory, some important practical difficulties limit the use of pollution taxes. First, how do we measure external cost? There is no market that buys and sells air

Visit the government's Environmental Protection Agency (EPA) at http://www.epa.gov/ to discover more about its role in our economy.

Effluent tax

A tax on the pollutant.

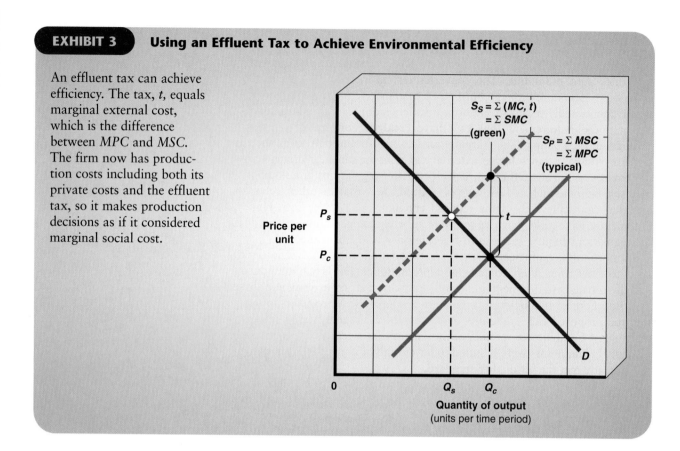

Using an Effluent Tax to Achieve Environmental Efficiency

An effluent tax can achieve efficiency. The tax, *t*, equals marginal external cost, which is the difference between *MPC* and *MSC*. The firm now has production costs including both its private costs and the effluent tax, so it makes production decisions as if it considered marginal social cost.

$S_S = \Sigma\,(MC, t)$
$= \Sigma\,SMC$
(green)

$S_P = \Sigma\,MSC$
$= \Sigma\,MPC$
(typical)

Price per unit

P_s

P_c

t

D

0   Q_s Q_c

Quantity of output
(units per time period)

pollution or global warming. So the tax is at best an approximation of external cost. Second, studies that have attempted to measure external cost find it to be quite large, requiring a substantial tax. It is widely thought that the price of a gallon of gasoline would have to increase by $1 to approximate the external costs of auto emissions. Such a $1 tax, added to the approximately 40 cents in gasoline taxes that are already imposed to pay for roads, would be unpopular with voters and as a consequence unattractive to politicians.

Emissions Trading. What if there was a market in which air pollution or global warming could be traded? As a result of the 1990 amendments to the Clean Air Act, there are markets for **emissions trading**. Emissions trading allows firms to buy and sell the right to pollute. The most active market so far is for sulfur emissions. Sulfur dioxide causes increased rain acidity. Acid rain can cause damage to lakes, trees, and even cars.

There are markets for air pollution rights. A firm that wishes to build new factories that would add to pollution in an already polluted area may have to find *offsets* before it can relocate. An offset is a reduction in an existing pollution source that offsets a new pollution source. One offset, for example, is the state of Maryland which allows new or expanding factories to buy up automobile "clunkers." Under this program, the factory offers to pay $500 to owners of cars that are at least 16 years old. The factory scraps

Emissions trading

Firms buying and selling the right to pollute.

the old clunkers, thereby offsetting its new source of pollution. The clunker approach makes use of the fact that a small percentage of cars are responsible for a disproportionate share of pollution.

To set up trading for lawn mower or car emissions, the government could require manufacturers to buy permits for each unit of emissions. In the short run, firms would include the cost of permits along with private costs as a component of price. Price would increase most for the dirtiest machines. In the long run, firms would have an incentive to build cleaner products. Firms with the cleanest fleet would need the fewest permits and might even profit by selling permits to companies that cannot improve as quickly. Whereas GreenAcres' lawn mowers would go out of business in an unfettered competitive industry, the company would now be in position to succeed.

A simple example can demonstrate the cost savings of an IB approach, such as emissions trading, compared to a CAC approach. Suppose two coal-fired electric plants each emit 100 tons of sulfur into the air. Plant A can reduce sulfur at a constant cost of $100/ton, while plant B can do so at a cost of $200/ton. The Environmental Protection Agency (EPA) announces that it wishes to cut sulfur emissions in half. Under CAC regulations, each plant will reduce its emissions to 50 tons—a reduction of 100 tons. The cost to plant A is $100/ton $\times$ (50 tons) = $5,000. The cost to plant B is $200/ton $\times$ (50 tons) = $10,000. The total cost to society of achieving a 100-unit reduction in sulfur emissions is $15,000.

Now suppose the EPA announces that it will give away 100 emissions permits, 50 to plant A and 50 to plant B. Each plant now is allowed to emit 50 units of sulfur. If the two plants do nothing more, each will have to reduce emissions from 100 to 50 tons, and each will do so at the same cost as with CAC regulations. However, there is a lower cost solution. Plant A is willing to sell its 50 permits at any price above $100/ton because it can reduce its emissions in-house for $100/ton. Plant B is willing to buy emissions permits at any price below $200/ton, the marginal cost of reducing its own emissions. Both plants can gain by plant A selling an additional 50 permits to plant B at a price between $100 and $200.

Suppose they agree to a price of $150/ton. Plant A now finds it profitable to eliminate all its emissions. Its marginal cost of reducing emissions is $100/ton. By reducing its emissions to zero, Plant A no longer needs any permits. It can sell its 50 permits for $150/ton, making a profit of $50 per ton by reducing its emissions (at a cost of $100/ton) and selling its 50 permits to Plant B (at a gain of $150/ton). In turn, plant B finds it cheaper to buy permits for $150/ton than to reduce emissions at a cost of $200/ton.

In sum, the net cost to reduce emissions by 100 tons for Plant A is $100/ton $\times$ (100 tons) − $150/ton $\times$ (50 tons) = $2,500. The cost to plant B, now that it no longer reduces emissions, is $150/ton $\times$ (50 tons) = $7,500. The cost to society of achieving a 100-unit reduction in emissions is $10,000—$5,000 less than under the original CAC method.

The real world helps us see problems that textbook theory does not always reveal. Emissions trading has the theoretical potential to achieve environmental goals at the lowest cost, but, so far, real-world trading has fallen short of efficiency. There are a number of obstacles to efficient trading, some minor and some major.

New-source bias

Bias that occurs when regulations provide an incentive to keep assets past the efficient point.

Taking the factory and clunker example, one minor problem is a **new-source bias.** A new-source bias occurs when regulations provide an incentive to keep assets past the efficient point. A firm faced with the need to find offsets if it builds a new factory may stick with an older and dirtier factory, rather than paying for offsets. If there were no offset program, it might have been economical to retire the old factory in favor of a less-polluting new factory. But if the new factory cannot meet the air quality standard without offsets, the lowest-cost solution becomes extending the life of the old plant. Electric utilities are also finding it worthwhile to continue to operate old coal-fired plants that are exempt from stringent regulations that can only be met by newer technology. There also may be a type of free-rider problem. Car owners about to junk their 15-year-old clunkers for $25 may keep them another year if a firm might be willing to pay $500 for them. These minor problems are just growing pains of emissions trading, and future emissions markets will find ways to reduce these undesirable outcomes.

The major problems will be harder to overcome. These include small numbers of buyers or sellers, imperfect information about the value of a permit, and concerns about permit value in the future. Firms will trade actively only if trading is a better alternative than other alternatives. Some firms may shut down or perhaps relocate in other countries where permits are not needed. Nevertheless, emissions trading is probably here to stay. The government may initiate emissions trading by distributing permits according to production or pollution over a designated period, or it may sell permits through an auction to the highest bidders. Buyers may be electric utilities, or they may be environmentalists. Environmentalists can achieve pollution reduction by outbidding utilities and then refusing to sell permits to utilities, forcing the utilities to reduce pollution.

Consider the World Resource Institute's view on incentive-based approaches to environmental stewardship (http://www.wri.org/wri/ incentives/summ_background.html).

The Chicago Board of Trade, or "Smog" Exchange, allows trading in pollution permits much like trading on the New York Stock Exchange. Companies are required to own a permit for each unit of emissions. Clean companies need fewer permits and offer to sell their extra permits on the exchange. Dirty companies need additional permits and are buyers on the exchange. They will only buy if the permit price is less than what it would cost them to reduce pollution by one more unit. Sellers of permits will charge at least what it costs them to reduce pollution by one more unit.

Exhibit 4 shows the price of sulfur dioxide allowances since trading began in 1994 up to August 2000. Prices dropped steeply over the first year and a half of trading, from almost $150 per permit to only $75. Then permit prices climbed steeply to about $200 by August 1999 before dropping again to the current level of about $150 one year later. The steep climb was in anticipation of the greater demand for allowances beginning in the year 2000, when a second phase of the emissions trading program began. In the second phase, additional utilities that were not included in Phase I now had to meet emissions requirements. One explanation of the subsequent drop in price was an announcement by the EPA that they were interested in phasing out the use of high-sulfur coal for electric power generation in the Midwest.

There is concern that the benefits of emissions trading will be diminished by lack of trading and opposition to the idea of creating a market for pollution rights. There is even a revival of interest in command-and-control regu-

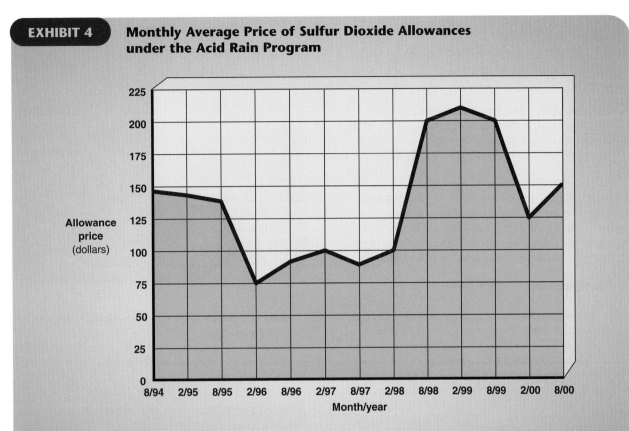

EXHIBIT 4   **Monthly Average Price of Sulfur Dioxide Allowances under the Acid Rain Program**

The Chicago Board of Trade allows trading in pollution permits much like trading on the New York Stock Exchange. This figure shows the sulfur dioxide allowance prices reported by brokerage firms and Fieldston Publications' market survey.

Source: Allowance Prices, http://www.epa.gov/airmarkt/trading/so2market/prices.html.

lation. If the government happens to pick the right approach and rewards cleaner technology, some economists favor CAC over the imperfect emissions trading to date. For example, there are supporters of California's approach to reducing auto emissions. California is considering a requirement that by the year 2003 10 percent of the cars sold within California must be emissions free. The mandate is likely to be met with electric vehicles (EVs).

Critics of the California approach first point out that EVs are not emissions free if they require electricity from a power plant. Certainly, power plants also pollute, although there may be an advantage to transferring pollution away from the most densely populated areas. EVs powered by photovoltaic cells (PVCs) that use solar energy are closer to being emissions free, but there is still pollution in the PVC production process. Perhaps the greatest drawback to EVs is their poor performance to date. They suffer from poor acceleration, limited range, and limited ability to climb hills. Critics maintain that inferior products continue to be the legacy of CAC approaches.

Does Emissions Trading Work?

Applicable Concepts: emissions trading, command-and-control regulation

March 26, 2000—The *New York Times* reports on a General Accounting Office study that found sulfur levels in Adirondack waterways have dropped substantially in recent years. However, the study also found that nitrogen levels have risen dramatically.

Sulfur levels decreased in 92 percent of the lakes examined. Nitrogen levels rose in 48 of 52 of the lakes tested despite the fact that the amount of nitrogen deposited during the 1990s was fairly stable. The study attributed the rising waterway nitrogen levels to a decline in the ability of forests and soils in the Adirondacks to neutralize nitrogen.

The falling sulfur levels are consistent with a U.S. Geological Survey study, reported in 1997, that found that sulfur deposition declined measurably in most regions in the eastern U.S. immediately after the 1995 imposition of sulfur dioxide emission limits on large emission sources. Electric power companies took advantage of the sulfur program's market-based flexibility and cut sulfur emissions to levels below allowed limits every year since 1995.

While many officials have focused on emissions from coal-fired power plants as the likely cause of the nitrogen increase in New York, acid rain experts are pointing to automobile emissions as a large contributor to the nitrogen problem.

Faulting midwestern power plants for the nitrogen increases, New York legislators have introduced federal legislation to cut nitrogen emissions to 50 percent below reductions mandated by the 1990 amendments to the Clean Air Act. However, many scientists are skeptical that a further reduction in emissions from power plants will solve the problem in the Adirondacks.

Gary Lovett of the Institute of Ecosystem Studies says that he agrees further power plant emissions reductions are necessary. However, he and others believe that the problem will not be solved without tackling the thorny problem of automobile emissions.

Acid rain occurs when sulfur and nitrogen emitted into the atmosphere by the burning of fossil fuels react with moisture in the atmosphere to create nitric and sulfuric acid. The acid then falls to earth in the form of acid rain, snow, or fog.

ANALYZE THE ISSUE

1. What has been the primary benefit of emissions trading?

2. Why do investigators believe nitrogen levels have risen?

3. How could emissions trading be expanded to further reduce sulfur emissions and at the same time reduce nitrogen levels?

Source: Environmental Financial Products, "Acid Rain Progress Mixed: Sulfur in NY Water Declines, NO_x Rising," http://www.envifi.com/Clips/acid_rain.htm. Reprinted by permission.

Much of the public seems more comfortable with controls and rules than with prices and trading. There are a number of possible explanations for the public's view. First, people have difficulty accepting that any pollution is efficient. Nobody wants to think about a higher risk of cancer due to a leak from a nuclear power plant.

Another possible reason for the public's view is a mistrust of experts. People were told by experts that nuclear power would be safe, that hazardous waste disposal sites would not leak, and that people living near oil tanks would not have higher risks of cancer. When outcomes differ from what experts promise, the public favors safety over efficiency. No one wants to take a chance on illness or death if the experts are wrong again. And yet would you give up your car or favor a law that set the speed limit at 20 miles per hour? These laws might increase safety, but they would certainly be inefficient.

Government and Environmental Efficiency

Market failure is likely for products with external costs. To achieve efficiency, buyers and sellers must consider external costs. Government has the power to establish laws, taxes, or permit systems so that market participants pay for external costs.

Although government policy can potentially improve efficiency, there is no guarantee. The countries that emerged from the Soviet Union, where government played a far more dominant role than in the United States, have environmental problems that dwarf those in the United States. In these countries, air and water quality borders on ecocide, with high rates of illness due to environmental degradation. The Chernobyl disaster, in which a nuclear plant malfunctioned and released radioactivity, has caused thousands of premature deaths. In China, another nation where the government plays a major role in the economy, the Beijing weather report frequently calls for "smoky" skies.

In the United States, large numbers of U.S. Department of Defense sites are among the biggest environmental challenges. Hazardous wastes from the production of weapons are now leaking in burial sites including Oak Ridge, Tennessee, and Richland, Washington. The U.S. Forest Service frequently permits lumber companies to harvest trees from national forests at subsidized prices. Government environmental officials have even gone to jail for illegally meeting with industry representatives to weaken environmental regulations. And government has tended to ignore the cost to firms of complying with hundreds of thousands of pages of environmental legislation—a set of regulations more voluminous than the U.S. Tax Code. For all these reasons, as well as the widespread dissatisfaction with government in general, there is concern about the effectiveness of government policy in achieving environmental goals. Government officials may pursue self-interest, which could favor polluting industries over societal interests as a whole, especially if industry executives are major campaign contributors.

Ronald Coase, an economist at the University of Chicago and the winner of the 1991 Nobel Prize in economics, was among the first to caution against the assumption that government intervention in the environmental arena would improve upon private-sector environmental performance. In his famous 1960 paper, "The Problem of Social Cost," he even questioned the fundamental assumption of market failure. According to the **Coase Theorem**, the private sector could achieve social efficiency with minimal government intervention. The role of the government should be limited to the legal establishment of property rights, with environmental disputes resolved in court. The Coase Theorem is the proposition that private market negotiations can achieve social efficiency regardless of the initial definition of property rights.

Coase Theorem

The proposition that private market negotiations can achieve social efficiency regardless of the initial definition of property rights.

EXHIBIT 5 Choosing the Efficient Amounts of Spark-Emitting Trains and Farm Crops

Number of trains	Total railroad profit	Marginal railroad profit	Number of crops	Total farm profit	Marginal farm profit
0	$ 0		10.5	$105	
		$20			$ −5
1	20		10	100	
		20			−10
2	40		9	90	
		20			−20
3	60		7	70	
		20			−30
4	80		4	40	
		20			−40
5	100		0	0	

One example is a case of a train throwing off sparks and occasionally burning a farmer's crops. Exhibit 5 shows railroad profits increasing and farm profits decreasing as more trains run.

Each train has an external cost. Emitted sparks can cause fires, which reduce the farmer's crops. If the railroad ignores external cost, it appears that the railroad would choose to run 5 trains so as to maximize profit, leaving the farmer with no crops. It also appears that to protect the farmer, there should be a law requiring the railroad to find a spark-free technology.

Suppose the courts establish a law that farmers have the right to spark-free trains. How could the railroad meet this tougher environmental standard? The railroad could change to a new, higher-cost technology. The cost must be higher, or the railroad would have chosen this environmentally friendly technology in the first place. If the cost is too high, the railroad might go out of business or relocate its tracks away from farms. Alternatively, it may be less expensive to offer the farmer money for any burned crops.

If the trains continue to throw off sparks, the first train will reduce the farmer's profits by $5 and will add $20 to the railroad's profits. The two parties will be able to negotiate a deal, with the farmer receiving a payment of between $5 and $20 from the railroad. What about a second train? This train will add another $20 to railroad profits, but will reduce farm profits by $10. Again, the farmer will permit the railroad to run a second train as long as the railroad pays the farmer at least $10. If a third train runs, marginal social benefit will equal marginal social cost. Society will benefit from more train service, but will lose from fewer crops. The third train will be marginally worthwhile, but additional trains will not run. The fourth train will add $20 to railroad profits, but will reduce farm profit by $30. The railroad will lose money if it runs the fourth train. By clearly establishing the farmer's right to spark-free trains, the number of trains will be decreased from 5 to 3 trains.

Notice that the farmer will be better off if he or she allows sparks as long as the railroad compensates the farmer for damage than if the government requires a spark-free technology. The farmer earns $105 when there are no sparks. With sparks, the farmer will earn at least $105, receiving

CHECKPOINT

Is It Efficient to Buy Odor-Reducing Technology If You Live Next to a Hog Farm?

You live next door to a hog farm. It is estimated that the smell from the hog farm reduces the value of your home by $7,000. For $5,000, it is possible to purchase technology that reduces the hog smell by half, so your house value would decrease by only $3,500. Assuming the hog farm has the property right to locate next door and that it is not required to reduce the hog smell, what will you do? Will you do nothing or buy the new technology?

---

between $5 and $20 for permitting the first train, at least $10 (and possibly as much as $20) for permitting the second train, and another $20 for the third train. With three trains, the farmer will still earn $70 from crops, for a total of at least $105.

This outcome is similar to the government solutions examined earlier. Efficiency leads to the efficient amount of pollution, which is typically not zero. No sparks may mean no trains. But Coase asks, why assume that society is best served by assuming the railroad is the polluter and the farmer the victim? In the 1800s, sparking engines may have been the best available technology, and an occasional fire may have been a natural consequence.

So consider the outcome if property rights to produce sparks are given to the railroads so that trains are allowed to throw off sparks. If the farmer does nothing, the railroad will run five trains, and the farmer will end up with no crops and no profit. The farmer will increase profit by $40 if only four trains run. Since the fifth train will add only $20 to railroad profit, the farmer can afford to pay as much as $40 (or as little as $20) to stop the fifth train. Similarly, the farmer will gain $30 by stopping the fourth train, more than enough to pay the railroad for forgoing $20 in profit. Once again, negotiations will stop at three trains, the efficient number.

This example demonstrates the Coase Theorem: As long as the courts clearly establish property rights, markets may achieve social efficiency *regardless of the initial assignment of property rights.* Coase's great contribution was to focus attention on property rights, a focus that led to the emissions-trading approach that allows firms to negotiate by buying and selling the right to pollute. But Coase argues for an even more limited role for government. In his view, the government should establish courts and then let markets negotiate.

Coase was instrumental in raising concern about government solutions. It might then seem a simple step to accept his claim that private markets would efficiently resolve environmental problems. In actuality, only a small number of environmental problems readily qualify for Coase Theorem solutions.

First, there are no **transactions costs** in the Coase Theorem. Transactions costs are the costs of negotiating and enforcing a contract. Turning to the courts is a costly process, in terms of both time and money. And dealing with the source of the externality has its own costs. Have you ever tried to negotiate with a noisy neighbor at 2 A.M.? However, there are also transactions

Transaction costs
The costs of negotiating and enforcing a contract.

INTERNATIONAL ECONOMICS

Should the United States Abandon the Global Environment Treaty?

Applicable Concepts: externalities, free-rider problem

SYDNEY, Australia, March 29, 2001—Britain and Australia have joined Japan in expressing serious concern at a U.S. decision to abandon a 1997 Kyoto environmental treaty against global warming. They have called on the U.S. to reconsider its position after White House spokesman Ari Fleischer said on Wednesday that the United States had effectively abandoned the treaty it earlier signed. "It is not in the United States' economic best interest," Fleischer said, adding that U.S. President George W. Bush has been "unequivocal" on the matter. Former president Bill Clinton signed the treaty in 1998, but the U.S. Senate has not yet ratified it.

Low Point in World Environment History

The United States emits about 30 percent of the world's greenhouse gases, according to Australia's Environment Minister Robert Hill. It is also the world's largest single economy and is seen to be best equipped to tackle the problem of global warming. The U.S. "cannot easily walk away from that responsibility," Hill said. "The Kyoto protocol wouldn't work without the United States," Hill told reporters. "That would mean that the agreement of developed countries to cut greenhouse gases which was made in 1997 would have failed."

Australian senator Bob Brown said the U.S. position on the treaty was "a low point in world environment history."

Britain: Decision Almost Unthinkable

Scientists widely believe that greenhouse gas emissions—which result mostly from burning coal and oil—trap heat in the earth's atmosphere. The climatic result is said to contribute to global warming which can cause disastrous weather changes. Britain has labeled Bush's decision to abandon the Kyoto treaty as "almost unthinkable." Global warming is "the most dangerous and fearful challenge to humanity over the next 100 years," said British environment minister Michael Meacher in a BBC television interview. Meacher said the U.S. decision was "extremely serious" and an "issue of transatlantic, global and foreign policy."

The decision has dealt a blow to European hopes of salvaging the pact which seeks to limit industrial-nation emissions of greenhouse gases thought to cause global warming. The EU [European Union] said last week [March, 2001] that the global warming issue was an integral part U.S.-EU relations.

U.S. Argument

U.S. President George W. Bush opposes the Kyoto pact because it does not also bind developing nations to curb emissions. Bush also believes the costs outweigh the benefits, Fleischer said. A Cabinet-level review of global warming issues has been ordered to develop a U.S. response to the issue, the

---

costs associated with government solutions. So Coasean negotiations may be preferable to government intervention even where there are substantial private transactions costs.

Second, there are no *income effects* in the Coase Theorem. As explained in the chapter on consumer theory, income effects are present when income changes affect purchasing patterns. Some parties may not be able to afford the efficient solution. A small farmer is unlikely to have enough money to pay for fewer trains, and you might not have enough money to convince your neighbor to turn down the volume.

Third, Coase assumes there are only two parties in the negotiation. Externalities are typically third-party problems, and there may be many third par-

White House spokesman added. U.S. officials said Washington would work with other countries on alternatives to the pact and that it was not considering formally "unsigning" the treaty.

An official said Washington currently plans to attend last-ditch talks on the treaty in Bonn, Germany, next July. Australia hopes the U.S. position is just part of a policy review of the Bush administration which came into office in January. "I understand their desire to review their whole energy policy and that is not unreasonable for a new administration," Hill said. Earlier this month, Japan voiced "regret" over Bush's decision not to impose mandatory carbon dioxide emission reductions at electrical power plants. "Japan has been urging the United States, which emits the largest amount of carbon dioxide, to ratify the Kyoto protocol," government spokesman Yasuo Fukuda said. Japan said the decision could undermine the global

environmental treaty to reduce by 5.2 percent major industrialized nations' emissions by 2012, below 1990 levels.

Race with Time

Australian Environmental Minister Robert Hill said he would urge the United States to stay engaged in the fight against global warming. "Time is against us, we are already starting to experience the consequences of climate change." Australia, a carbon-intensive economy, said it would continue to reduce its greenhouse gases under the Kyoto protocol, regardless of the U.S. stance. Australia is on track to meet its greenhouse emissions target by 2010, Hill said. The country aims to reduce its greenhouse emissions to eight percent above 1990 levels by 2010. "Climate change threatens Australia's economy, its future lifestyle and security and could completely remove some Pacific and Indian Ocean island neighbors from existence," Senator Brown said.

ANALYZE THE ISSUE

1. Do free-rider problems make global agreements such as the Kyoto protocol more difficult to achieve?

2. Why does President Bush cite the exemption of developing countries from emissions limitations as a reason to oppose the treaty?

3. Why do you think the Kyoto agreement does not require developing nations to curb their emissions?

Source: "Alarm after U.S. Abandons Environmental Treaty," http://www .cnn.com/2001/WORLD/asiapcf/ auspac/03/28/kyoto.protocol/. Reprinted by permission.

ties. Do all the farmers get together to negotiate with the railroad, and do all the neighbors get together to reduce noise from the party? With many parties, there is once again a **free-rider problem.** If noise levels decrease, I get the benefit whether or not I contribute to the negotiations. So why contribute? Stated as a concept, if some individuals benefit, while others pay, the free-rider problem is that few will be willing to pay for improvement of the environment or other public goods. As a result, these goods are underproduced.

In sum, neither government nor the markets can be asserted to be the best solution. On balance, though, the effort to work toward improved government solutions seems worthwhile, given the outcome for the environment of purely self-interested markets.

Free-rider problem

The problem that if some individuals benefit, while others pay, few will be willing to pay for the improvement of the environment or other public goods. As a result, these goods are underproduced.

KEY CONCEPTS

Private benefits and costs
Social benefits and costs
Market failure
Government failure

Incentive-based regulations
Command-and-control
  regulations

Effluent tax
Emissions trading
New-source bias

Coase Theorem
Transactions costs
Free-rider problem

SUMMARY

- **Externalities** are benefits or costs that fall on third parties who are neither buyers nor sellers. Pollution is a negative externality or external cost that is a by-product of many industrial production processes.

- **Market failure** is present when the market produces a socially inefficient outcome. One instance is when there are externalities. All firms, including competitive firms, consider private costs, but disregard external costs, in making decisions.

- **Government failure** occurs when public-sector actions or lack of actions move us away from desired outcomes, such as efficiency. Government officials seeking campaign contributions and votes may choose environmental measures that favor wealthy contributors over society's best interests.

- **Command-and-control regulations** occur when the government dictates the approach to achieving an environmental goal. Command-and-control regulations are generally inefficient on three grounds: they do not distinguish between high- and low-pollution areas, they do not allow firms to choose lower cost

technologies that could achieve the environmental standard, and they do not encourage investment in improved technology to lower future emissions.

- **Incentive-based regulations** build on markets to achieve environmental efficiency. Effluent taxes are taxes that reflect external costs. Emissions trading allows firms to buy and sell the "right to pollute."

- The **Coase Theorem** maintains that markets can be efficient in the presence of externalities with minimal government intervention. Even in the presence of externalities, markets may produce efficient outcomes so long as property rights are clearly established.

- **Transactions costs, income effects,** and **free-rider problems** are obstacles to achieving environmental efficiency through markets. Transactions costs are the costs of negotiating an agreement, income effects are present when limited income prevents one party from being able to afford the efficient solution, and free-rider problems are present when participants are better off hiding than revealing their willingness to pay for an environmental improvement.

STUDY QUESTIONS AND PROBLEMS

1. Compare price and quantity in a competitive industry to those of a "green" industry for a product generating pollution.

2. Suppose a car sells for $20,000 in a market with no pollution restrictions. Will the car sell for more than $20,000, less than $20,000, or $20,000 when there are pollution restrictions? Explain.

3. You are considering whether to buy one house for $100,000 or another identical house located near high-voltage electric power lines for $90,000. Assume that it has been established that living near high-voltage lines increases the risk of cancer due to electromagnetic fields (EMFs). If you choose the $90,000 house, is the radiation from EMFs an externality? Explain.

4. Restaurants have observed that large parties (eight or more) leave a lower average tip than smaller parties. Identify the effect—which also makes it more difficult to reach global environmental agreements—responsible for this phenomenon.

5. Suppose your instructor gives eight homework assignments during the semester. She indicates that anyone who does not turn in all eight assignments will automatically fail the course. Is this an example of a command-and-control or an incentive-based regulation? Explain any inefficiencies of your instructor's approach.

6. Environmentalists in Tennessee brought suit against the Champion Paper Company of North Carolina for polluting the Pigeon River, which flows from North Carolina into eastern Tennessee. Tennessee claimed that the coffee-colored water smelled bad and would not support fishing or swimming. Environmentalists requested that the river be restored to its pristine state, whereby water quality is restored to the level before the coming of industry. The Environmental Protection Agency heard the suit and applied an efficiency standard. Is pristine water an efficiency standard? Explain.

7. Draw a graph to demonstrate your answer to question 6.

8. California is considering a requirement that 2 percent of its car fleet be emissions-free by the year 2003. This mandate has spurred electric vehicle research. Such vehicles could be powered by photovoltaic cells or by batteries that are recharged using an electric outlet. Would you agree that it is correct to conclude that electric vehicles that use electric outlets are emissions-free? What about electric vehicles powered by photovoltaic cells?

9. Explain why consumers would not be willing to pay the full costs of a less-polluting car in the absence of government regulations.

10. Evaluate the following statement: "When products pollute, government solutions are more efficient than market solutions."

11. Provide an example of a market where you think the Coase Theorem applies. Explain why you think the market satisfies assumptions regarding transactions costs, income effects, and free riders.

12. In a study of ranching laws in the 1800s, an economic researcher found that as the laws restricted the ability of cattle to roam freely, agricultural output increased. Do this researcher's results support the Coase Theorem? Explain.

13. If we are to take action against global warming, we must reduce carbon emissions. Explain how to reduce carbon emissions using
a. command-and-control regulation.
b. an effluent tax.
c. emissions trading.

14. A global agreement known as the Montreal Protocol led to the phase-out of chlorofluorocarbons (CFCs), chemical compounds found in aerosol cans and refrigerants. CFCs may have contributed to the hole in the ozone layer. With a diminished ozone layer, there is an increased chance of skin cancer. Explain the effect of this agreement on the price of deodorants and air conditioners. Also, is a ban on CFCs an efficient approach to the ozone hole problem?

ONLINE EXERCISES

Exercise 1

Consider the global warming problem by visiting the Environmental Protection Agency's Internet site at http://www .epa.gov/globalwarming/. What are the causes and consequences of global warming? How serious is it?

Exercise 2

Visit GPO Catalog for the President (http://www.gpo .ucop.edu/catalog/erp97.html). Select Chapter 6, Refining the Role of Government in the U.S. Market Economy. Scroll down and browse the section titled Markets, Governments, and Complementarity.

Exercise 3

Visit NTIS Environmental Home Page (http://www.ntis .gov/products/environment.htm), and browse Environmental Topics.

Exercise 4

Visit the Environmental Protection Agency's website at http://www.epa.gov/epahome/press.htm. Click on the region you live in to see current press releases and media advisories. Choose one of these topics, and write a brief report.

CHECKPOINT ANSWER

Is It Efficient to Buy Odor-Reducing Technology If You Live Next to a Hog Farm?

It is not efficient to purchase the new odor-reducing technology. It would cost $5,000, but would increase your house value by only $3,500. It is not efficient to cut the odor by half if the market will not compensate you suffi-ciently for reduced hog odors. If your only options are to do nothing or to buy the new technology and you said to do nothing, YOU ARE CORRECT. (A third option is to pay the hog farm to locate elsewhere. You would be willing to pay up to $7,000 to avoid the $7,000 lost due to the smell of the nearby farm.)

PRACTICE QUIZ

For a visual explanation of the correct answers, visit the tutorial at http://tucker.swcollege.com.

1. Recently, the city of New Orleans discovered chemical compounds in its drinking water that may cause cancer. Since New Orleans's drinking water comes from the Mississippi River, the source of these chemicals is the waste discharges of industrial plants upstream from New Orleans. This is an example of
   a. an external cost imposed on the citizens of New Orleans by the industrial plants upstream.
   b. a market failure where the market price of the output of these industrial plants does not fully reflect the social cost of producing these goods.
   c. an externality where the marginal social costs of producing these industrial goods differ from the marginal private costs.
   d. all of the above.

2. A government policy that charges steel firms a fee per ton of steel produced (an "effluent charge") where the fee is determined by the amount of pollutants discharged into the air or water will lead to
   a. a decrease in the market equilibrium quantity of steel produced.
   b. a decrease in the market equilibrium price of steel.
   c. an increase in the market equilibrium price of steel.
   d. the results in parts a and b.
   e. the results in parts a and c.

3. Social costs are
   a. the full resource costs of an economic activity.
   b. usually less than private costs.
   c. the costs of an economic activity borne by the producer.
   d. all of the above.

4. As a general rule, if pollution costs are external, firms will produce
   a. too much of a polluting good.
   b. too little of a polluting good.
   c. an optimal amount of a polluting good.
   d. an amount that cannot be determined without additional information.

5. Many economists would argue that
   a. the optimal amount of pollution is greater than zero.
   b. all pollution should be eliminated.
   c. the market mechanism can handle pollution without any government intervention.
   d. central planning is the most efficient way to eliminate pollution.

6. Which of the following used marketable pollution permits as an incentive for reducing pollution?
   a. Clean Air Act of 1970
   b. Comprehensive Environmental Response, Compensation, and Liability Act of 1980
   c. Clean Air Act amendments of 1990
   d. Water Quality and Improvement Act of 1970

7. The disposable diaper industry is perfectly competitive. Which of the following is true?
   a. Since the industry is perfectly competitive, price and quantity are at the socially efficient levels.
   b. Competitive price is higher and competitive quantity lower than the socially efficient point.
   c. Competitive price is higher and competitive quantity higher than the socially efficient point.
   d. Competitive price is lower and competitive quantity higher than the socially efficient point.

8. An example of the command-and-control approach to environmental policy is
   a. placing a tax on high-sulfur coal to reduce its use and the corresponding sulfur emissions (which contribute to acid rain).
   b. requiring electric utilities to install scrubbers to reduce sulfur dioxide emissions (which contribute to acid rain).
   c. allowing coal producers to buy and sell permits to allow sulfur emissions.
   d. allowing individuals to sue coal producers if sulfur emissions exceed a government-set standard.

9. The profit-maximizing firm in Exhibit 6 creates water and air pollution as a consequence of producing its output of beef cattle. If pollution costs are borne by third parties, the firm will maximize economic profit by choosing to
   a. voluntarily incur costs to reduce its pollution.
   b. produce at output rate Q_3.
   c. produce at output rate Q_2.
   d. produce at output rate Q_4.

10. Use Exhibit 6 to complete the following: To maximize social welfare, the firm should produce at output rate
   a. Q_1.
   b. Q_2.
   c. Q_3.
   d. Q_4.

Exhibit 6

11. As shown in Exhibit 7, if Orville has the property right to fly over Wilbur's house, but Wilbur is allowed to negotiate with Orville on the number of flights, what will be the number of flights?
   a. 2
   b. 3
   c. 4
   d. 5

Exhibit 7 Impact of Flights on House Value

Number of flights	Total profits	Marginal profits	Value of Wilbur's house
1	$10,000	$10,000	$100,000
2	18,000	8,000	95,000
3	24,000	6,000	90,000
4	28,000	4,000	85,000
5	30,000	2,000	80,000

12. As shown in Exhibit 7, if Wilbur has the property right to have no planes flying over his house, but Orville is allowed to negotiate with Wilbur, what will be the number of fights?
   a. 2
   b. 3
   c. 4
   d. 5

13. As shown in Exhibit 7, at the socially efficient number of flights, what will be the market value of Orville's house?
   a. $100,000
   b. $95,000
   c. $90,000
   d. $85,000

Macroeconomic Fundamentals

The three chapters in this part explain key measures of how well the macroeconomy is performing. Knowledge of this material is vital to the discussion of macro theory and policy in the next part. The first chapter in this part explains GDP computation. The next chapter begins by teaching how to measure business cycles and concludes with an examination of unemployment. The final chapter in this part explores the measurement and consequences of inflation.

CHAPTER 15

Gross Domestic Product

M easuring the performance of the economy is an important part of life. Suppose one candidate for president of the United States proclaims that the economy's performance is the best in a generation, and the opposing presidential candidate argues that the economy could perform better. Which statistics would you seek to tell how well the economy is doing? The answer requires understanding some of the nuts and bolts of *national income accounting*. National income accounting is the system used to measure the aggregate income and expenditures for a nation. Despite certain limitations, the national income accounting system provides a valuable indicator of an economy's performance. For example, you can visit the Internet and check the annual *Economic Report of the President* to compare the size or growth of

the U.S. economy between 2000 and 2001 or other years.

Prior to the Great Depression, there were no national accounting procedures for estimating the data required to assess the economy's performance. To provide accounting methodologies for macro data, the late economist Simon Kuznets published a small report in 1934 titled *National Income, 1929–32*. For his pioneering work, Kuznets, the "father of GDP," earned the

1971 Nobel Prize in economics. Today, thanks in large part to Kuznets, most countries use common national accounting methods. National income accounting serves a nation similar to the manner in which accounting serves a business or household. In each case, accounting methodology is vital for identifying economic problems and formulating plans for achieving goals.

In this chapter, you will learn to solve these economics puzzles:

■ Why doesn't economic growth include increases in spending for welfare, Social Security, and unemployment programs?

■ Can one newscaster report that the economy grew, while another reports that for the same year the economy declined, and both reports be correct?

■ How is the calculation of national output affected by environmental damage?

Gross Domestic Product

The most widely reported measure throughout the world of a nation's economic performance is **gross domestic product (GDP)**, which is the market value of all final goods and services produced in a nation during a period of time, usually a year. GDP therefore excludes production abroad by U.S. businesses. Beginning in November 1991, the U.S. Department of Commerce switched emphasis to gross domestic product from **gross national product (GNP)**, which is the market value of all final goods and services produced by a nation's residents, no matter where they are located. For example, GNP includes General Motors' earnings on its foreign operations, and GDP does not. On the other hand, GNP excludes Toyota's profits from its Camry car plant in Kentucky, and GDP does not. In short, the main reason for the emphasis on GDP is to reflect the reality that the United States is becoming increasingly more integrated into the global economy. Actually, GDP and GNP do not differ greatly for the United States. For example, in 2000, our GNP was about 0.1 percent less than our GDP.

Why is GDP important? One advantage of GDP is that it avoids the "apples and oranges" measurement problem. If an economy produces 10 apples one year and 10 oranges the next, can we say that the value of output has changed in any way? To answer this question, we must attach price tags in order to evaluate the relative monetary value of apples and oranges to society. This is the reason GDP measures value using dollars, rather than listing the number of cars, heart transplants, legal cases, toothbrushes, and tanks produced. Instead, the market-determined dollar value establishes the monetary importance of production. In GDP calculations, "money talks." That is, GDP relies on markets to establish the relative value of goods and services.

GDP also requires that we give the following two points special attention: (1) GDP counts only new domestic production, and (2) it counts only final goods.

GDP Counts Only New Domestic Production

National income accountants calculating GDP carefully exclude transactions in two major areas: secondhand transactions and nonproductive financial transactions.

Gross domestic product (GDP)

The market value of all final goods and services produced in a nation during a period of time, usually a year.

Gross national product (GNP)

The market value of all final goods and services produced by a nation's residents, no matter where they are located.

The Bureau of Economic Analysis (BEA) (http://www.bea.doc.gov/), *an agency of the Department of Commerce, is the nation's economic accountant, preparing data on all components of GDP. The BEA also provides a rich source of international and regional data, among other information.*

Secondhand Transactions. *Current* GDP does not include the sale of a used car or the sale of a home constructed some years ago. Such transactions are merely exchanges of previously produced goods and not *current* production of new goods that add to the existing stock of cars and homes. However, the sales commission on a used car or a home produced in another GDP period counts in current GDP because the salesperson performed a service during the present period of time.

Nonproductive Financial Transactions. GDP does not count purely private or public financial transactions, such as giving private gifts, buying and selling stocks and bonds, and making **transfer payments.** A transfer payment is a government payment to individuals not in exchange for goods or services currently produced. Welfare, Social Security, veterans' benefits, and unemployment benefits are transfer payments. These transactions are considered nonproductive because they do not represent production of any new or *current* output. Similarly, stock market transactions represent only the exchange of certificates of ownership (stocks) or indebtedness (bonds) and not actual new production.

GDP Counts Only Final Goods

The popular press usually defines GDP as simply "the value of all goods and services produced." This is technically incorrect because GDP counts only **final goods,** which are finished goods and services produced for the ultimate user. Including all goods and services produced would inflate GDP by *double counting* (counting many items more than once). In order to count only final goods and avoid overstating GDP, national income accountants must take care not to include **intermediate goods.** Intermediate goods are goods and services used as inputs for the production of final goods. Stated differently, intermediate goods are not produced for consumption by the ultimate user.

Suppose a wholesale distributor sells glass to an automaker. This transaction is not included in GDP. The glass is an intermediate good used in the production of cars. When a customer buys a new car from the car dealer, the value of the glass is included in the car's selling price, which is the value of a final good counted in GDP. Let's consider another example. A wholesale distributor sells glass to a hardware store. GDP does not include this transaction because the hardware store is not the final user. When a customer buys the glass from the hardware store to repair a broken window, the final purchase price of the glass is added to GDP as a consumer expenditure.

Measuring GDP

GDP is like an enormous puzzle with many pieces to fit together, including markets for products, markets for resources, consumers spending and earning money, and businesses spending and earning money. How can one fit all these puzzle pieces together? One way to understand how all these concepts fit together is to use a simple macroeconomic model called the **circular flow model.** The circular flow model shows the flow of products from businesses

---

Transfer payment
A government payment to individuals not in exchange for goods or services currently produced.

Final goods
Finished goods and services produced for the ultimate user.

Intermediate goods
Goods and services used as inputs for the production of final goods.

The Dismal Scientist (http://www.dismal.com/ dismal/default.asp) *is an economic news and analysis service, part of which is devoted to the GDP.*

Circular flow model
A diagram showing the flow of products from businesses to households and the flow of resources from households to businesses. In exchange for these resources, money payments flow between businesses and households.

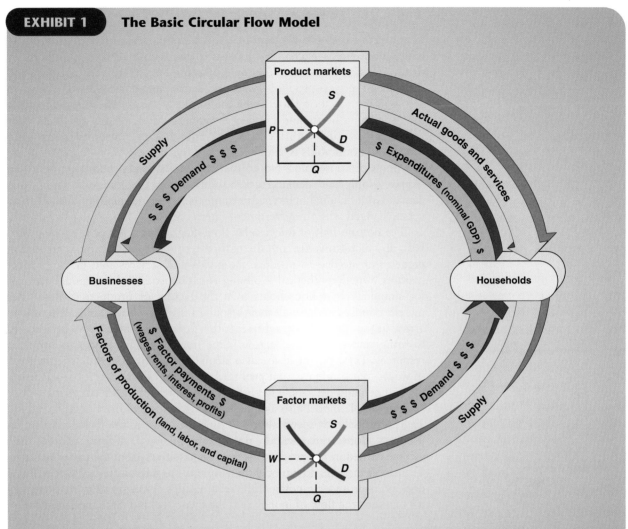

EXHIBIT 1   **The Basic Circular Flow Model**

In this simple economy, households spend all their income in the upper loop and demand consumer goods and services from businesses. Businesses seek profits by supplying goods and services to households through the product markets. Prices and quantities in individual markets are determined by the market supply and demand model. In the factor markets in the lower loop, resources (land, labor, and capital) are owned by households and supplied to businesses that demand these factors in return for money payments. The forces of supply and demand determine the returns to the factors, for example, wages and the quantity of labor supplied. Overall, goods and services flow clockwise, and the corresponding payments flow counterclockwise.

to households and the flow of resources from households to businesses. In exchange for these resources, money payments flow between businesses and households. Exhibit 1 shows the circular flow in a hypothetical economy with no government, no financial markets, and no foreign trade. In this ultra-simple pure market economy, only the households and the businesses make decisions.

The Circular Flow Model

The upper half of the diagram in Exhibit 1 represents *product markets,* in which households exchange money for goods and services produced by firms. The *supply* arrow in the top loop represents all finished products and the value of services produced, sold, and delivered to consumers. The *demand* arrow in the top loop shows why the businesses make this effort to satisfy the consuming households. When consumers decide to buy products, they are actually voting with their dollars. This flow of consumption expenditures from households is sales revenues to businesses and expenses from the viewpoint of households. Notice that the box labeled *product markets* contains a supply and demand graph. This means the forces of supply and demand in individual markets determine the price and quantity of each product exchanged without government interference.

The bottom half of the circular flow diagram consists of the *factor markets,* in which firms *demand* the natural resources, labor, capital, and entrepreneurship needed to produce the goods and services sold in the product markets. Our hypothetical economy is capitalistic, and the model assumes for simplicity that households own the factors of production. Businesses therefore must purchase all their resources from the households. The *supply* arrow in the bottom loop represents this flow of resources from households to firms, and the *demand* arrow is the flow of money payments for these resources. These payments are also income earned by households in the form of wages, rents, interest, and profits. As in the product markets, market supply and demand determine the price and quantity of factor payments.

Our simple model also assumes all households live from hand to mouth. That is, households spend all the income they earn in the factor markets on products. Households therefore do not save. Likewise, all firms spend all their income earned in the product markets on resources from the factor markets. The simple circular flow model therefore fails to mirror the real world. But it does aid your understanding of the relationships among product markets, factor markets, the flow of money, and the theory behind GDP measurement.

Flow versus Stock

Flow

A flow is a rate of change in a quantity during a given time period, such as dollars per year. For example, income and consumption are flows that occur per week, per month, or per year.

Stock

A quantity measured at one point in time. For example, an inventory of goods or the amount of money in a checking account.

The arrows in Exhibit 1 are **flows,** rather than **stocks.** A flow is a rate of change in a quantity during a given time period. Changes in the amount of steel produced per month, the number of computer games purchased per day, the amount of income earned per year, and the number of gallons of water pouring into a bathtub per minute are examples of flows. Flows are always measured in units per time period, such as tons per month, billions of dollars per year, or gallons per hour. A stock is a quantity measured at one point in time. An inventory of goods, the amount of money in a checking account, and the amount of water in a bathtub are examples of stocks. Stocks are measured in tons, dollars, gallons, and so on at a given point in time.

The important point is this: *All measurements in the circular flow model are rates of change (flows) and tell us nothing about the total amounts (stocks) of goods, services, money, or anything in the economy.* Consumption expenditures, business production, wages, rents, interest payments, and profits are *flows* of money for newly produced products or resources that affect the level of *stocks* not shown in the model.

EXHIBIT 2 Gross Domestic Product Using the Expenditure Approach, 2000

National income account		Amount (billions of dollars)	Percentage of GDP
Personal consumption expenditures (C)		$6,728	68%
Durable goods	$ 820		
Nondurable goods	1,989		
Services	3,919		
Gross private domestic investment (I)		1,768	18
Fixed investment	1,718		
Change in business inventories	50		
Government consumption expenditures and gross investment (G)		1,741	18
Federal	590		
State and local	1,151		
Net exports of goods and services (X − M)		−364	−4
Exports (X)	1,103		
Imports (M)	1,467		
Gross domestic product		$9,873	100%

Source: Survey of Current Business, http://www.bea.doc.gov/bea/dn/nipaweb/PopularTables.asp, Table 1.1.

The Expenditure Approach

How does the government actually calculate GDP? One way national income accountants calculate GDP is to use the **expenditure approach** to measure total spending flowing through product markets in the circular flow diagram. The expenditure approach measures GDP by adding all the spending for final goods during a period of time. Exhibit 2 shows 2000 GDP using the expenditure approach, which breaks down expenditures into four components. The data in this exhibit show that all production in the U.S. economy is ultimately purchased by spending from households, businesses, government, or foreigners. Let's discuss each of these expenditure categories.

Personal Consumption Expenditures (C)

The largest component of GDP in 2000 was $6,728 billion for *personal consumption expenditures,* represented by the letter C. Personal consumption expenditures comprise total spending by households for durable goods, nondurable goods, and services. Durable goods include items such as automobiles, appliances, and furniture because they last longer than one year. Food, clothing, soap, and gasoline are examples of nondurables, because

Expenditure approach
The national income accounting method that measures GDP by adding all the spending for final goods during a period of time.

they are considered used up or consumed in less than a year. Services, which is the largest category, include recreation, legal advice, medical treatment, education, and any transaction not in the form of a tangible object.

Gross Private Domestic Investment (I)

In 2000, $1,768 billion was spent for what is officially called *gross private domestic investment* (I). This national account includes "gross" (all) "private" (not government) "domestic" (not foreign) spending by businesses for investment. Gross private domestic investment is the sum of two components: (1) *fixed investment* expenditures for newly produced capital goods, such as commercial and residential structures, machinery, equipment, and tools; and (2) change in *business inventories,* which is the net change in spending for unsold finished goods and raw materials. Note that gross private domestic investment is simply the national income accounting category for "investment," defined in Chapter 2. The only difference is that investment in Exhibit 4 in Chapter 2 was in physical capital, rather than the dollar value of capital.

Now we will take a closer look at gross private domestic investment. Note that national accountants include the rental value of newly constructed residential housing in the $1,718 billion spent for fixed investment. A new factory, warehouse, or robot is surely a form of investment, but why include residential housing as business investment, rather than consumption by households? The debatable answer is that a new home is considered investment because it provides services in the future that the owner can rent for financial return. For this reason, all newly produced housing is considered investment whether the owner rents or occupies the property.

Finally, the $50 billion change in business inventories means this amount of net dollar value of unsold finished goods and raw materials was added to the stock of inventories during 2000. A decline in inventories would reduce GDP because households consumed more production than firms produced during this year. When businesses have more on their shelves this year than last, more new production has taken place than has been consumed during this year.

Government Consumption Expenditures and Gross Investment (G)

This category includes the value of goods and services government purchases measured by their costs. For example, spending for police and state university professors enters the GDP accounts at the prices the government pays for them. In addition, the government spends for investment additions to its stock of capital, such as tanks, schools, highways, bridges, and government buildings. In 2000, federal, state, and local government consumption expenditures and gross investment (G) were $1,741 billion. As the figures in Exhibit 2 reveal, consumption expenditures and gross investment of state and local governments far exceeded those of the federal government. It is important to understand that consumption expenditures and gross investment exclude *transfer payments* because, as explained at the beginning of the chapter, they do not represent newly produced goods and services. Instead, transfer payments are paid to those entitled to Social Security benefits, veterans' benefits, welfare, unemployment compensation, and benefits from other programs.

Net Exports $(X - M)$

The last GDP expenditure account is *net exports,* expressed in the formula $(X - M)$. *Exports (X)* are expenditures by foreigners for U.S. domestic goods. *Imports (M)* are the dollar amount of our purchases of Japanese automobiles, French wine, and other goods produced abroad. Because we are using expenditures for U.S. output to measure GDP, one might ask why imports are subtracted from exports. The answer is the result of how the government actually collects data from which GDP is computed. Spending for imports is not subtracted when spending data for consumption, investment, and government consumption are reported. These three components of GDP therefore overstate the value of expenditures for U.S.-produced products.

Consider the data collected to compute consumption (C). In reality, personal consumption expenditures reported to the U.S. Department of Commerce include expenditures for both domestically produced and imported goods and services. For example, automobile dealers report to the government that consumers purchased a given dollar amount of new cars during 2000, but they are not required to separate their figures between sales of U.S. cars and sales of foreign cars. Because GDP measures only domestic economic activity, sales of foreign goods must be removed. Subtracting imports in the net exports category removes all sales of foreign goods, including new foreign cars, from consumption (C) and likewise from investment (I) and government consumption expenditures (G).

The overstatement of 2000 GDP expenditures is corrected by subtracting $1,467 billion in imports from $1,103 billion in exports to obtain net exports of −$364 billion, which is about 4 percent of GDP. The negative sign indicates that the United States is spending more dollars to purchase foreign products than it is receiving from the rest of the world for U.S. goods. The effect of a negative net exports figure is to reduce U.S. GDP when it is subtracted from the consumption, investment, and government components. Prior to the early 1980s, the United States was a consistent net exporter, selling more goods and services to the rest of the world than we purchased from them. Since 1983, the United States has been a net importer. International trade is discussed in more detail in the last section of the text.

A Formula for GDP

Using the expenditure approach, GDP is expressed mathematically in billions of dollars as

$$GDP = C + I + G + (X - M)$$

For 2000 (see Exhibit 2),

$$\$9,873 = \$6,728 + \$1,768 + \$1,741 + (\$1,103 - \$1,467)$$

This simple equation plays a central role in macroeconomics. It is the basis for analyzing macro problems and formulating macro policy. When economists study the macro economy, they can apply this equation to predict the behavior of the major sectors of the economy: consumption (C) is spending by households, investment (I) is spending by firms, government consumption expenditures and gross investment (G) is spending by the government, and net exports (X − M) is net spending by foreigners.

The Income Approach

Income approach

The national income account method that measures GDP by adding all incomes, including compensation of employees, rents, net interest, and profits.

The second, somewhat more complex approach to measuring GDP is the **income approach.** The income approach measures GDP by adding all the incomes earned by households in exchange for the factors of production during a period of time. Both the expenditure approach and the income approach yield identical GDP calculations. As shown in the basic circular flow model, each dollar of expenditure paid by households to businesses in the product markets means a dollar of income flows to households through the factor markets as a payment for the land, labor, and capital required to produce the product. Using the income approach, GDP is expressed as follows:

$$\textbf{GDP} = \textbf{compensation of employees} + \textbf{rents} + \textbf{profits} \\ + \textbf{ net interest} + \textbf{nonincome adjustments}$$

In practice, it is necessary to add two nonincome figures to factor payments, which complicates the income approach. These nonincome accounts are (1) capital consumption allowance and (2) indirect business taxes. Exhibit 3 presents actual 2000 GDP calculated following the income approach, and then each component is discussed in turn.

Compensation of Employees

Employees' compensation is the largest of the national income accounts. About 58 percent of GDP in 2000 ($5,715 billion) was income earned from wages, salaries, and certain supplements paid by firms and government to suppliers of labor. Since labor services play such an important role in production, it is not surprising that employee compensation represents the largest share of the GDP income pie. The supplements consist of employer taxes for Social Security and unemployment insurance. Also included are fringe benefits from a variety of private health insurance and pension plans.

Rental Income of Persons

The smallest source of income is from rent and royalties received by property owners who permit others to use their assets during a time period. For example, this category includes house and apartment rents received by landlords. In 2000, $142 billion was earned in rental income.

The Economic Report of the President (http://www.gpo.ucop.edu/catalog/erp99.html) *includes data discussed in this chapter.*

EXHIBIT 3 Gross Domestic Product Using the Income Approach, 2000			
National income account		Amount (billions of dollars)	Percentage of GDP
Compensation of employees		$5,715	58%
Wages and salaries	$4,837		
Supplements	878		
Rental income of persons		142	1
Profits		1,591	16
Proprietors' income	715		
Corporate profits	876		
Net interest		533	6
Nonincome adjustments		1,892	
Depreciation	1,254		19
Indirect business taxes	638		
Gross domestic product (GDP)		$9,873	100%

Source: Survey of Current Business, http://www.bea.doc.gov/bea/dn/nipaweb/ PopularTables.asp, Tables 1.9 and 1.14.

Profits

Proprietors' Income. All forms of income earned by unincorporated businesses totaled $715 billion in 2000. Self-employed proprietorships and partnerships simultaneously own their businesses and pay themselves for labor services to their firms.

Corporate Profits. This income category includes all income earned by the stockholders of corporations regardless of whether stockholders receive it. The $876 billion of corporate profits in 2000 was the sum of three sources: (1) dividends, (2) undistributed corporate profits (retained earnings for expanding plant and equipment), and (3) corporate income taxes. Thus, corporate profits using the income approach are "before taxes."

Net Interest

Households both receive and pay interest. Persons who make loans to businesses earn interest income. Suppose you purchase a bond issued by General Motors. When General Motors pays interest on its bonds, the interest payments are included in the national income accounts. Households also receive interest from savings accounts and certificates of deposit. On the other hand, households borrow money and pay interest on, for example, credit cards, installment loans, and mortgage loans. The net interest of $533 billion in 2000 is the difference between interest income earned and interest payments.

CHECKPOINT

How Much Does Mario Add to GDP?

Mario works part-time at Pizza Hut and earns an annual wage plus tips of $15,000. He sold 4,000 pizzas at $10 per pizza during the year. He was unemployed part of the year, so he received unemployment compensation of $3,000. During the past year, Mario bought a used car for $1,000. Using the expenditure approach, how much has Mario contributed to GDP?

Nonincome Adjustments

Compensation of employees, rental income of persons, profits, and net interest are all forms of national income. Do not confuse these items with the following two nonincome items. To reconcile GDP and the national income accounts, the following two adjustments are made.

Depreciation. The first nonincome adjustment is officially called the *consumption of fixed capital*. Consumption of fixed capital is an estimate of the depreciation of capital. This somewhat imposing term is simply an allowance for the portion of capital worn out producing GDP. Over time, capital goods, such as buildings, machines, and equipment, wear out and become less valuable. Depreciation (capital consumption allowance) is therefore a portion of GDP that is not available for income payments. Because it is impossible to measure depreciation accurately, an estimate is entered. In 2000, $1,254 billion was the estimated amount of GDP attributable to depreciation during the year.

Indirect business taxes

Taxes levied as a percentage of the prices of goods sold and therefore collected as part of the firm's revenue. Firms treat such taxes as production costs. Examples include general sales taxes, excise taxes, and customs duties.

Indirect Business Taxes. The second adjustment reported in Exhibit 3 is $638 billion collected by government in the form of **indirect business taxes.** Indirect business taxes are levied as a percentage of the prices of goods sold and therefore become part of the revenue received by firms. Firms treat such taxes as production costs. These taxes include sales taxes, federal excise taxes, license fees, business property taxes, and customs duties. Indirect taxes are not income payments to suppliers of resources. Instead, firms collect indirect taxes and send these funds to the government. Suppose you purchased a new automobile for $20,000, including a $1,000 federal excise tax and state sales tax. These taxes are included in the price, but are not income for individuals. Because indirect tax revenues are not reported in the income accounts, they are added as a separate nonincome account.

Exhibit 4 presents the conceptual frameworks of the expenditure and income approaches to computing GDP.

GDPs in Other Countries

Exhibit 5 compares GDPs for selected countries in 2000. The United States had the world's highest GDP; U.S. GDP, for example, was more than twice Japan's GDP and about 17 times Mexico's GDP in 2000.

EXHIBIT 4 Expenditure and Income Approaches to GDP

Expenditure approach		Income approach
Consumption (*C*) expenditures by households plus		Compensation of employees plus
Investment (*I*) expenditures by businesses plus	= GDP =	Rents plus
Government consumption expenditures and gross investment (*G*) plus		Profits plus
Net export (*X* − *M*) expenditures by foreign economies		Net interest plus Nonincome adjustments

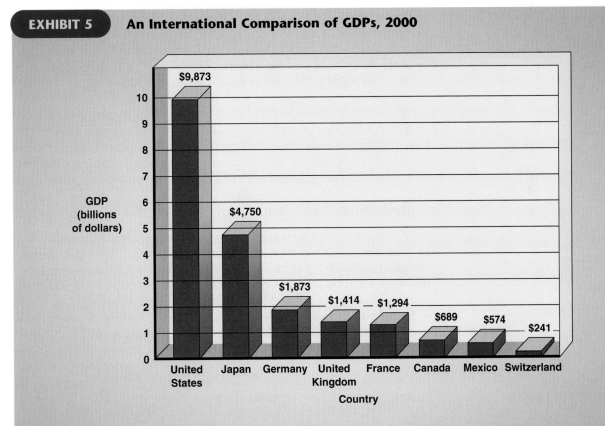

EXHIBIT 5   An International Comparison of GDPs, 2000

This exhibit shows GDPs in 2000 for selected countries. The United States had the world's highest GDP. Japan's GDP, for example, was about half the size of U.S. GDP.

Source: *Organization for Economic Cooperation and Development,* http://www.oecd.org/std/gdp.htm.

GDP Shortcomings

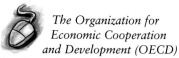 *The Organization for Economic Cooperation and Development (OECD) is a forum for monitoring economic trends in its 25 member countries, which include the United States, the United Kingdom, and Japan. Visit the OECD at* http:// www.oecd.org/.

For various reasons, GDP omits certain measures of overall economic well-being. Because GDP is the basis of government economic policies, there is concern that GDP may be giving us a false impression of the nation's material well being. GDP is a less-than-perfect measure of the nation's economic pulse because it excludes the following factors.

Nonmarket Transactions

Because GDP counts only market transactions, it excludes certain unpaid activities, such as homemaker production, child rearing, and do-it-yourself home repairs and services. For example, if you take your dirty clothes to the laundry, GDP increases by the amount of the cleaning bill paid. But GDP ignores the value of laundering these same clothes if you wash them yourself at home.

There are two reasons for excluding nonmarket activities from GDP. First, it would be extremely imprecise to attempt to collect data and assign a dollar value to services people provide for themselves or others without compensation. Second, it is difficult to decide which nonmarket activities to exclude and which ones to include. Perhaps repairing your own roof, painting your own house, and repairing your own car should be included. Now consider the value of washing your car. GDP does include the price of cleaning your car if you purchase it at a car wash, so it could be argued that GDP should include the value of you washing your car at home.

The issue of unpaid, do-it-yourself activities affects comparisons of the GDPs of different nations. One reason some less-developed nations have lower GDPs than major industrialized nations is that a greater proportion of people in less-developed nations farm, clean, make repairs, and perform other tasks for their families rather than hiring someone else to do the work.

Distribution, Kind, and Quality of Products

GDP is blind to whether a small fraction of the population consumes most of a country's GDP or consumption is evenly divided. GDP also wears a blindfold with respect to the quality and kinds of goods and services that make up a nation's GDP. Consider the fictional economies of Zuba and Econa. Zuba has a GDP of $2,000 billion, and Econa has a GDP of $1,000 billion. At first glance, Zuba appears to possess superior economic well-being. However, Zuba's GDP consists of only military goods, and Econa's products include computers, tractors, wheat, milk, houses, and other consumer items. Moreover, assume the majority of the people of Zuba could care less about the output of military goods and would be happier if the country produced more consumer goods.

> **Conclusion** *GDP is a quantitative, rather than a qualitative, measure of the output of goods and services.*

Neglect of Leisure Time

The wealthier a nation becomes, in general, the more leisure time its citizens can afford. Rather than working longer hours, workers often choose to increase their time for recreation and travel. During the twentieth century, the length of the typical workweek in the United States declined steadily from about 50 hours in 1900 to about 34 hours in 2000.[1]

> **Conclusion** *It can be argued that GDP understates national well-being because no allowance is made for people working fewer hours than they once did.*

The Underground Economy

Illegal gambling, prostitution, loan-sharking, illegal guns, and illegal drugs are goods and services that meet all the requirements for GDP. They are final products with a value determined in markets, but GDP does not include unreported criminal activities. The "underground" economy also includes tax evasion. One way to avoid paying taxes on a legal activity is to trade or barter goods and services, rather than selling them. One person fixes a neighbor's car in return for baby-sitting services, and the value of the exchange is unreported. Other individuals and businesses make legal sales for cash and do not report the income earned to the Internal Revenue Service.

Estimates of the size of this subterranean economy vary. Some studies by economists estimate the size of the underground sector is between 9 and 13 percent of GDP.[2] This range of estimates is slightly less than the estimated size of the underground economy in most European countries.

> **Conclusion** *If the underground economy is sizable, GDP will understate an economy's performance.*

Economic Bads

More production means a larger GDP regardless of the level of pollution created in the process. Recall from Chapter 4 the discussion of *negative externalities,* such as pollution caused by steel mills, chemical plants, and cigarettes. Air, water, and noise pollution are *economic bads* that impose costs on society not reflected in private market prices and quantities bought and sold. When a polluting company sells its product, this transaction increases GDP. However, critics of GDP argue that it fails to account for the diminished quality of life from the "bads" not reported in GDP.

---

[1] *Economic Report of the President, 2001,* http://w3.access.gpo.gov/eop/, Table B-47.
[2] James Sproule, "The Other Path: Why Are Your Neighbors Paying in Cash?" *The Wall Street Journal Europe,* Feb. 28, 2001, p. 8.

Is GDP a False Beacon Steering Us into the Rocks?

Applicable Concept: national income accounting "goods" and "bads"

Suppose a factory in your community has been dumping hazardous wastes into the local water supply and people develop cancer and other illnesses from drinking polluted water. The Environmental Protection Agency (EPA) discovers this pollution and, under the federal "Superfund" law, orders a cleanup and a fine for the damages. The company defends itself against the EPA by hiring lawyers and experts and takes the case to court. After years of trial, the company loses the case and has to pay for the cleanup and damages.

In terms of GDP, an amazing "good" result occurs: the primary measure of national economic output, GDP, increases. GDP counts the millions of dollars spent to clean up the water supply. GDP even includes the health care expenses of anyone who develops cancer or other illnesses caused by drinking polluted water. GDP also includes the money spent by the company on lawyers and experts to defend itself against the EPA. And GDP includes the money spent by the EPA to regulate the polluting company.

Now consider what happens when trees are cut down and oil and minerals are used to produce houses, cars, and other goods. The value of the wood, oil, and minerals is an intermediate good implicitly computed in GDP because the value of the final goods is explicitly computed in GDP. Using scarce resources to produce goods and services therefore raises GDP and is considered a "good" result. On the other hand, don't we lose the value of trees, oil, and minerals in the production process, so isn't this a "bad" result?

The Bureau of Economic Analysis (BEA) is an agency of the U.S. Department of Commerce. The BEA is the nation's economic accountant, and it publishes the *Survey of Current Business,* which is the source of GDP data cited throughout this text. Critics have called for a new measure designed to estimate the kinds of damage described above. These new accounts would adjust for changes in air and water quality and depletion of oil and minerals. These accounts would also adjust for changes in the stock of

renewable natural resources, such as forests and fish stocks. In addition, accounts should be created to measure global warming and destruction of the ozone layer.

As explained in this chapter, a dollar estimate of capital depreciation is subtracted from GDP to compute net domestic product (NDP). The argument here is that a dollar estimate of the damage to the environment should also be subtracted. To ignore measuring such environmental problems, critics argue, threatens future generations. In short, conventional GDP perpetuates a false dichotomy between economic growth and environmental protection.

Critics of this approach argue that assigning a dollar value to environmental damage and resource depletion requires a methodology that is extremely subjective and complex. Nevertheless, national income accountants have not ignored these criticisms, and the National Academy of Sciences has reviewed BEA proposals on how to account on interactions between the environment and the economy.

ANALYZE THE ISSUE

Suppose a nuclear power plant disaster occurs. How could GDP be a "false beacon" in this case?

Other National Accounts

In addition to GDP, the media often report several other national accounts because they are necessary for studying the macro economy. We now take a brief look at each.

Net Domestic Product (NDP)

It can be argued that depreciation should be subtracted from GDP. Recall that GDP is not entirely a measure of newly produced output because it includes an estimated value of capital goods required to replace those worn out in the production process. The measurement designed to correct this deficiency is **net domestic product (NDP)**, which is the gross domestic product minus depreciation of the capital worn out in producing output. Stated as a formula:

$$NDP = GDP - depreciation (consumption of fixed capital)$$

Consumption of fixed capital is the official government term for an estimate of the depreciation of capital. This somewhat imposing term is simply an allowance for the portion of capital worn out producing GDP. Over time, capital goods, such as buildings, machines, and equipment, wear out and become less valuable. Because it is impossible to measure depreciation accurately, an estimate is entered. In 2000, $1,259 billion was the estimated amount of GDP attributable to depreciation during the year. Exhibit 6 shows the actual calculation of NDP from GDP in 2000. Exhibit 7 illustrates the transition from GDP to NDP and three other measures of national income.

National Income (NI)

Suppose we are interested in how much income is *earned* by households who are the suppliers of resources. The figure that measures the total flow of payments to the owners of the factors of production is **national income (NI)**. National income is the total income earned by resource owners, including wages, rents, interest, and profits. One way to compute national income is to add compensation of employees, rents, profits, and net interest

Net domestic product (NDP)

Gross domestic product minus depreciation of the capital worn out in producing output.

National income (NI)

The total income earned by resource owners, including wages, rents, interest, and profits.

EXHIBIT 6	Net Domestic Product Calculated from Gross Domestic Product, 2000	
		Amount (billions of dollars)
Gross domestic product (GDP)		$9,873
Depreciation		−1,254
Net domestic product (NDP)		$8,619

Source: Survey of Current Business, http://www.bea.doc.gov/bea/dn/nipaweb/PopularTables.asp, Table 1.9.

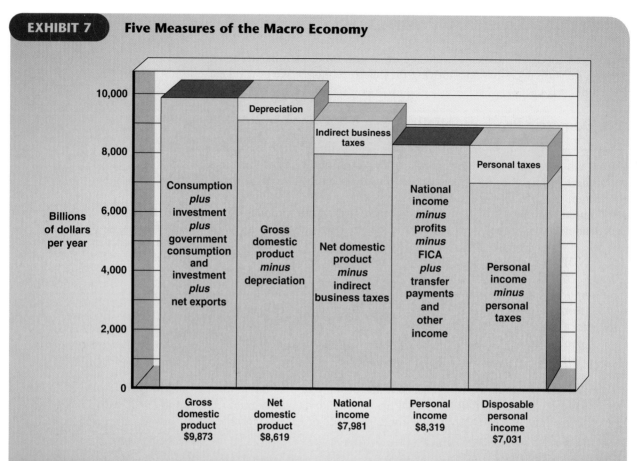

EXHIBIT 7 **Five Measures of the Macro Economy**

The five bars show five major measurements of the U.S. macro economy in 2000 in billions of dollars. Beginning with gross domestic product, depreciation is subtracted to obtain net domestic product. Removing indirect business taxes yields national income. Next, personal income equals national income minus corporate profits and contributions for Social Security insurance (FICA payments) plus transfer payments, and other income. Subtracting personal taxes from personal income yields disposable personal income.

using the income approach demonstrated in Exhibit 3. A simpler method is to use the following formula:

$$NI = NDP - \text{indirect business taxes}$$

As Exhibit 8 shows, national income equals NDP minus *indirect business taxes*. As defined earlier in this chapter, indirect business taxes include sales taxes, federal excise taxes, license fees, business property taxes, and customs duties. Indirect taxes are not income payments to suppliers of resources. Instead, firms collect indirect business taxes and send these funds to the government.

Because indirect business taxes are included in the price, but are not income for individuals, they must be subtracted from NDP to determine NI. Exhibit 8 derives 2000 NI from NDP.

EXHIBIT 8 National Income Calculated from Net Domestic Product, 2000

	Amount (billions of dollars)
Net domestic product (NDP)	$8,619
Indirect business taxes	−638
National income (NI)	$7,981

Source: Survey of Current Business, http://www.bea.doc.gov/bea/dn/nipaweb/PopularTables.asp, Table 1.9.

Personal Income (PI)

National income measures the total amount of money *earned,* but determining the amount of income actually *received* by households (not businesses) requires a measurement of **personal income (PI)**. Personal income is the total income received by households that is available for consumption, saving, and payment of personal taxes. Suppose we want to measure the total amount of money individuals receive that they can use to consume products, save, and pay taxes. National income is not the appropriate measure for two reasons. First, NI excludes transfer payments, which constitute income that can be spent, saved, or used to pay taxes. Second, NI includes corporate profits, but stockholders do not receive all these profits. A portion of corporate profits is paid in corporate taxes. Also, retained earnings are not distributed to stockholders, but are channeled back into business operations.

Exhibit 7 illustrates the relationship between personal income and national income, and Exhibit 9 gives the figures for 2000. National income accountants adjust national income by subtracting corporate profits and payroll taxes for Social Security (FICA deductions). Next, *transfer payments* and other income individuals receive from net interest and dividends are added. The net result is the personal income received by households, in 2000 amounted to $8,319 billion.

Personal income (PI)
The total income received by households that is available for consumption, saving, and payment of personal taxes.

Disposable Personal Income (DI)

One final measure of national income is shown at the far right of Exhibit 7. **Disposable personal income (DI)** is the amount of income that households actually have to spend or save after payment of personal taxes. Disposable or *after-tax* income (DI) is equal to personal income minus personal taxes paid to federal, state, and local governments. Personal taxes consist of personal income taxes, personal property taxes, and inheritance taxes. As tabulated in Exhibit 10, disposable personal income in 2000 was $7,031 billion.

Disposable personal income (DI)
The amount of income that households actually have to spend or save after payment of personal taxes.

Changing Nominal GDP to Real GDP

So far, GDP has been expressed as **nominal GDP**. Nominal GDP is the value of all final goods based on the prices existing during the time period of production. Nominal GDP is also referred to as *current-dollar* or *money GDP.*

Nominal GDP
The value of all final goods based on the prices existing during the time period of production.

EXHIBIT 9 Personal Income Calculated from National Income, 2000

	Amount (billions of dollars)
National income (NI)	$7,981
Corporate profits	−876
Contributions for Social Security (FICA)	−701
Transfer payments and other income	1,915
Personal income (PI)	$8,319

Source: Survey of Current Business, http://www.bea.doc.gov/bea/dn/nipaweb/ PopularTables.asp, Table 1.9.

Nominal GDP grows in three ways: First, output rises, and prices remain unchanged. Second, prices rise, and output is constant. Third, in the typical case, both output and prices rise. The problem, then, is how to adjust GDP so it reflects only changes in output and not changes in prices. This adjusted GDP allows meaningful comparisons over time when prices are changing.

Changing prices can have a huge impact on how we compare dollar figures. Suppose a newspaper headline reports that a film entitled *The History of Economic Thought* is the most popular movie of all time. You ask how could this be? What about *Gone with the Wind*? Reading the article reveals that this claim is based on the nominal measure of gross box-office receipts. This gives a recent movie with higher ticket prices an advantage over a movie released in 1939 when the average ticket price was only 25 cents. A better measure of popularity would be to compare "real" box office receipts by multiplying actual attendance figures for each movie by a base year movie price.

Real GDP

The value of all final goods produced during a given time period based on the prices existing in a selected base year.

Measuring the difference between changes in output and changes in the price level involves making an important distinction between nominal GDP and **real GDP.** Real GDP is the value of all final goods produced during a given time period based on the prices existing in a selected base year. The U.S. Department of Commerce currently uses 1996 as the base year.

EXHIBIT 10 Disposable Personal Income Calculated from Personal Income, 2000

	Amount (billions of dollars)
Personal income (PI)	$8,319
Personal taxes	−1,288
Disposable personal income (DI)	$7,031

Source: Survey of Current Business, http://www.bea.doc.gov/bea/dn/nipaweb/ PopularTables.asp, Table 2.1.

The GDP Chain Price Index

The most broadly based measure used to take the changes-in-the-price-level "air" out of the nominal GDP "balloon" and compute real GDP is officially called the **GDP chain price index.** The GDP chain price index is a measure that compares changes in the prices of all final goods produced during a given time period relative to the prices of those goods in a base year. The GDP chain price index is a broad "deflator" index calculated by a complex chain-weighted geometric series. It is highly inclusive because it measures not only price changes of consumer goods, but also price changes of business investment, government consumption expenditures, exports, and imports. Do not confuse the GDP chain price index with the *consumer price index (CPI),* which is widely reported in the news media. The CPI is a different index, measuring only consumer prices, which we will discuss in the chapter on inflation.

GDP chain price index
A measure that compares changes in the prices of all final goods during a given year to the prices of those goods in a base year.

Now it's time to see how it works. We begin with the following conversion equation:

$$\text{real GDP} = \frac{\text{nominal GDP}}{\text{GDP chain price index}} \times 100$$

Using 1996 as the base year, suppose you are given the 2000 nominal GDP of $9,873 billion and the 2000 GDP chain price deflator of 107.04. To calculate 2000 real GDP, use the above formula as follows:

$$\$9,224 \text{ billion} = \frac{\$9,873 \text{ billion}}{107.04} \times 100$$

Exhibit 11 shows actual U.S. nominal GDP, real GDP, and the GDP chain price index computations for selected years. Column 1 reports nominal GDP,

EXHIBIT 11 Nominal GDP, Real GDP, and the GDP Chain Price Index for Selected Years

Year	(1) Nominal GDP (billions of dollars)	(2) Real GDP (billions of 1996 dollars)	(3) GDP chain price index (1996 = 100)
1960	$ 527	$2,377	22.18
1970	1,040	3,578	29.06
1980	2,796	4,901	57.05
1990	5,803	6,708	86.51
1992	6,319	6,880	91.85
1994	7,054	7,348	96.00
1996	7,813	7,813	100.00
1997	8,318	8,159	101.95
1998	8,781	8,509	103.20
2000	9,873	9,224	107.04

Source: Survey of Current Business, http://www.bea.doc.gov/bea/dn/nipaweb/ PopularTables.asp, Tables 1.1, 1.2 and 7.1.

EXHIBIT 12   **Changes in Real GDP and Nominal GDP, 1985–2000**

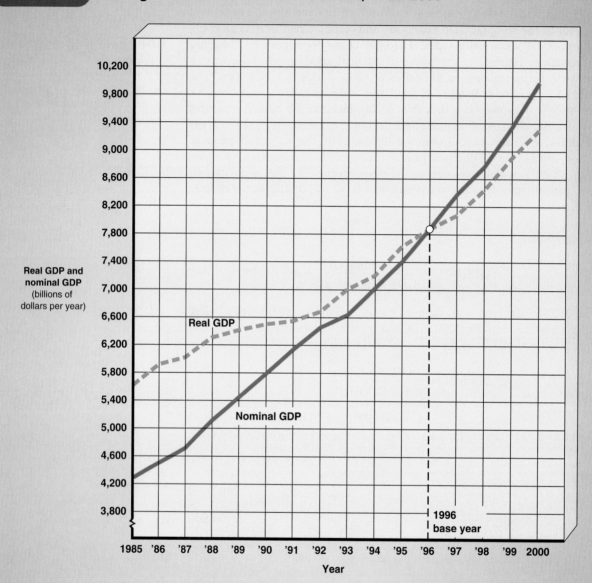

Each year's real GDP reflects output valued at 1996 base-year prices, but nominal GDP is annual output valued at prices prevailing during the current year. The intersection of real and nominal GDP occurs in 1996 because in the base year both nominal GDP and real GDP measure the same output at 1996 prices. Note that the nominal GDP curve has risen more sharply than the real GDP curve since 1985 as a result of inflation included in the nominal figures.

Source: *Survey of Current Business,* http://www.bea.doc.gov/bea/dn/nipaweb/PopularTables.asp, Tables 1.1 and 1.2.

CHECKPOINT

Is the Economy Up or Down?

One person reports, "GDP rose this year by 8.3 percent." Another says, "GDP fell by 0.6 percent." Can both reports be right?

---

column 2 gives real GDP figures for these years, and column 3 lists corresponding GDP chain price indexes. Notice that the GDP chain price index exceeds 100 in years beyond 1996. This means that prices, on average, have risen since 1996, causing the real purchasing power of the dollar to fall. In years before 1996, the GDP chain price index is less than 100, which means the real purchasing power of the dollar was higher relative to the 1996 base year. At the base year of 1996, nominal and real GDP are identical, and the GDP price index equals 100.

Exhibit 12 traces real GDP and nominal GDP for the economy since 1985. Note that nominal GDP usually grows faster than real GDP. For example, if we calculate the economy's growth rate in nominal GDP between 1997 and 1998, we find it was 5.7 percent. If instead we calculate real GDP growth between the same years, we find the growth rate was 4.4 percent. You must therefore pay attention to which GDP is being used in an analysis.

KEY CONCEPTS

Gross domestic product (GDP)	Intermediate goods	Indirect business taxes	Disposable personal income (DI)
Gross national product (GNP)	Circular flow model	Net domestic product (NDP)	Nominal GDP
Transfer payment	Flow	National income (NI)	Real GDP
Final goods	Stock	Personal income (PI)	GDP chain price index
	Expenditure approach		
	Income approach		

SUMMARY

- **Gross domestic product (GDP)** is the most widely used measure of a nation's economic performance. GDP is the market value of all **final goods** produced in the United States during a period of time regardless of who owns the factors of production. Secondhand and financial transactions are not counted in GDP. To avoid double counting, GDP also does not include **intermediate goods.** GDP is calculated by either the expenditure approach or the income approach.

- **Gross national product (GNP)** is the market value of final goods and services produced by U.S. residents, no

matter where they are located. To reflect the increasing integration of the United States into the global economy, the U.S. Department of Commerce changed its emphasis to GDP in 1991.

- The **circular flow model** is a diagram representing the flow of products and resources between businesses and households in exchange for money payments. **Flows** must be distinguished from **stocks.** Flows are measured in units per time period—for example, dollars per year. Stocks are quantities that exist at a given point in time measured in dollars.

Circular flow model

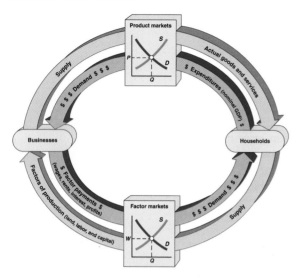

- The **expenditure approach** sums the four major spending components of GDP: consumption, investment, government, and net exports. Algebraically, GDP = $C + I + G + (X - M)$, where X equals foreign spending for domestic exports and M equals domestic spending for foreign products.

- The **income approach** sums the major income components of GDP, consisting of compensation of employees, rents, profits, net interest, and nonincome expenses for depreciation and **indirect business taxes.** Indirect business taxes are levied as a percentage of product prices and include sales taxes, excise taxes, and customs duties.

- **Net domestic product** (NDP) is GDP minus depreciation.

- **National income** (NI) is total income *earned* by households and is calculated as NDP minus indirect business taxes.

- **Personal income (PI)** is the total income *received* by households and is calculated as NI minus corporate taxes and Social Security taxes plus transfer payments, net interest, and dividends.

- **Disposable personal income (DI)** is personal income minus personal taxes. DI is the amount of income a household has available to consume or save.

Measures of the macro economy

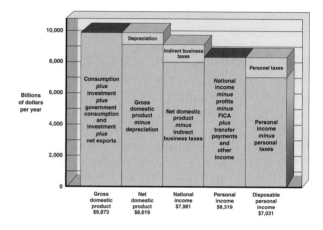

- **Nominal GDP** measures all final goods and services produced in a given time period, valued at the prices existing during the time period of production.

- **Real GDP** measures all final goods and services produced in a given time period, valued at the prices existing in a base year.

- The **GDP chain price index** is a broad price index used to convert nominal GDP to real GDP. The GDP chain price index measures changes in the prices of consumer goods, business investment, government spending, exports, and imports. Real GDP is computed by dividing nominal GDP for year X by year X's GDP chain price index and then multiplying the result by 100.

SUMMARY OF CONCLUSION STATEMENTS

- GDP is a quantitative, rather than a qualitative, measure of the output of goods and services.

- It can be argued that GDP understates national well-being because no allowance is made for people working fewer hours than they once did.

- If the underground economy is sizeable, GDP will understate an economy's performance.

STUDY QUESTIONS AND PROBLEMS

1. Which of the following are final goods or services, and which are intermediate goods or services?
   a. A haircut purchased from a barber
   b. A new automobile
   c. An oil filter purchased in a new automobile
   d. Crude oil

2. Using the basic circular flow model, explain why the value of businesses' output of goods and services equals the income of households.

3. A small economy produced the following final goods and services during a given month: 3 million pounds of food, 50,000 shirts, 20 houses, 50,000 hours of medical services, 1 automobile plant, and 2 tanks. Calculate the value of this output at the following market prices:
   - $1 per pound of food
   - $20 per shirt
   - $50,000 per house
   - $20 per hour of medical services
   - $1 million per automobile plant
   - $500,000 per tank

4. An economy produces final goods and services with a market value of $5,000 billion in a given year, but only $4,500 billion worth of goods and services is sold to domestic or foreign buyers. Is this nation's GDP $5,000 billion or $4,500 billion? Explain your answer.

5. Explain why a new forklift sold for use in a warehouse is a final good even though it is fixed investment (capital) used to produce other goods. Is there a double-counting problem if this sale is added to GDP?

6. Explain why the government consumption expenditures *(G)* component of GDP falls short of actual government expenditures.

7. Explain how net exports affect the U.S. economy. Describe both positive and negative impacts on GDP. Why do national income accountants use net exports to compute GDP, rather than simply adding exports to the other expenditure components of GDP?

8. Suppose the following are data for a given year from the annual *Economic Report of the President*. Calculate GDP, using the expenditure and the income approaches.

	Amount (billions of dollars)
Corporate profits	$ 305
Consumption of fixed capital	479
Gross private domestic investment	716
Personal taxes	565
Personal saving	120
Government consumption expenditures	924
Imports	547
Net interest	337
Compensation of employees	2,648
Rental income	19
Exports	427
Personal consumption expenditures	2,966
Dividends	87
Indirect business taxes	370
Contributions for Social Security (FICA)	394
Transfer payments	543
Proprietors' income	328

9. Using the data in question 8, compute net domestic product (NDP) by making the required subtraction from GDP. Explain why NDP might be a better measure of economic performance than GDP.

10. Again using the data from question 8, determine national income (NI) by making the required subtractions from GDP. Next, derive personal income (PI) from national income (NI). Then make the required adjustments to PI to obtain disposable personal income (DI).

11. Suppose U.S. nominal GDP increases from $5,000 billion in 1999 to $5,500 billion in 2000. Can you conclude that these figures present a misleading measure of economic growth? What alternative method would provide a more accurate measure of the rate of growth?

12. Which of the following are counted in this year's GDP? Explain your answer in each case.
    a. Flashy Car Company sold a used car.
    b. Juanita Jones cooked meals for her family.

c. IBM paid interest on its bonds.
d. José Suarez purchased 100 shares of IBM stock.
e. Bob Smith received a welfare payment.
f. Carriage Realty earned a brokerage commission for selling a previously owned house.
g. The government makes interest payments to persons holding government bonds.

h. Air and water pollution increase.
i. Gambling is legalized in all states.
j. A retired worker receives a Social Security payment.

13. Explain why comparing the GDPs of various nations might not tell you which nations are better off.

 ONLINE EXERCISES

Exercise 1

Visit World Factbook (http://www.odci.gov/cia/publications/factbook/). Choose the United States. Scroll down to Economy, and note the GDP composition by sector for the United States. What is your conclusion?

Exercise 2

Review the recent summary of national economic conditions available through the Federal Reserve Board at http://www.federalreserve.gov and click on "Beige Book." Is the national economy healthy? Why or why not? Click on the Federal Reserve District City for your Federal Reserve district. Is the economy in your district healthy? Why or why not?

Exercise 3

Go to the Bureau of Economic Analysis News Releases at http://www.bea.doc.gov/bea/rels.htm. Scroll down and click on Gross Domestic Product. How much has real GDP changed in the last quarter of the year?

Exercise 4

Go to the Bureau of Economic Analysis News Releases at http://www.bea.doc.gov/bea/dn1.htm. Scroll down to Table 1. What are the components of GDP?

 CHECKPOINT ANSWERS

How Much Does Mario Add to GDP?

Measuring GDP by the expenditure approach, Mario's output production is worth $40,000 because consumers purchased 4,000 pizzas at $10 each. Transfer payments and purchases of goods produced in other years are excluded from GDP. The $3,000 in unemployment compensation received and the $1,000 spent for a used car are therefore not counted in GDP. Mario's income of $15,000 is also not counted using the expenditure approach. If you said, using the expenditure approach to measure GDP, Mario contributed $40,000 to GDP, YOU ARE CORRECT.

Is the Economy Up or Down?

Between 1973 and 1974, for example, nominal GDP rose from $1,385 to $1,501 billion—an 8.3 percent increase. During the same period, real GDP fell from $4,123 to $4,099 billion—a 0.6 percent decrease. If you said both reports can be correct because of the difference between nominal and real GDP, YOU ARE CORRECT.

PRACTICE QUIZ

For a visual explanation of the correct answers, visit the tutorial at http://tucker.swcollege.com.

1. The dollar value of all final goods and services produced within the borders of a nation is
   a. GNP deflator.
   b. gross national product.
   c. net domestic product.
   d. gross domestic product.

2. Based on the circular flow model, money flows from businesses to households in
   a. factor markets.
   b. product markets.
   c. neither factor nor product markets.
   d. both factor and product markets.

3. The circular flow model does not include which of the following?
   a. The quantity of shoes in inventory on January 1
   b. The total wages paid per month
   c. The percentage of profits paid out as dividends each year
   d. The total profits earned per year in the U.S. economy

4. The expenditure approach measures GDP by adding all the expenditures for final goods made by
   a. households.
   b. businesses.
   c. government.
   d. foreigners.
   e. all of the above.

5. GDP is a less-than-perfect measure of the nation's economic pulse because it
   a. excludes nonmarket transactions.
   b. does not measure the quality of goods and services.
   c. does not report illegal transactions.
   d. all of the above are true.

6. Subtracting an allowance for depreciation of fixed capital from gross domestic product yields
   a. real GDP.
   b. nominal GDP.
   c. national income.
   d. net domestic product.

7. Adding all incomes earned by households from the sale of resources yields
   a. intermediate goods.
   b. indirect business taxes.
   c. national income.
   d. personal income.

8. Personal income equals disposable income plus
   a. personal savings.
   b. transfer payments.
   c. dividend payments.
   d. personal taxes.

9. Disposable personal income
   a. is the income people spend for personal items such as homes and cars.
   b. includes transfer payments.
   c. excludes transfer payments.
   d. includes personal taxes.

10. Which of the following statements is true?
    a. National income is total income *earned* by households whereas personal income is total income *received* by households.
    b. Disposable personal income equals personal income minus personal taxes.
    c. The expenditure approach and the income approach yield the same GDP figure.
    d. All of the above are true.

11. Gross domestic product data that reflect actual prices as they exist in a given year are expressed in terms of
    a. fixed dollars.
    b. current dollars.
    c. constant dollars.
    d. real dollars.

12. The GDP chain price index is
    a. widely reported in the news.
    b. broadly based.
    c. adjusted for government spending.
    d. a measure of changes in consumer prices.

13. Which of the following statements is true?
    a. The inclusion of intermediate goods and services in GDP calculations would underestimate our nation's production level.
    b. The expenditure approach sums the compensation of employees, rents, profits, net interest, and nonincome expenses for depreciation and indirect business taxes.
    c. Real GDP has been adjusted for changes in the general level of prices due to inflation or deflation.
    d. Real GDP equals nominal GDP multiplied by the GDP deflator.

A Four-Sector Circular Flow Model

Sound the trumpets! This exhibit is going to put all the puzzle pieces together. Exhibit A-1 presents a more complex circular flow model by adding three sectors: financial markets, government, and foreign markets. In addition to the spending of households for the output of firms shown in the simplified model in Exhibit 1, these additions add three *leakages* from the amount of income paid to households. First, part of households' income is saved. Second, part of it is taxed. Third, part of the income is spent on imports. On the other hand, this model includes three sources of spending *injections* for firms' output besides spending from households. First, firms purchase new plants, equipment, and inventories (investment) from other firms. Second, government consumption expenditures are for goods and services from firms. Third, foreigners purchase exports from the firms.

Conclusion *The dollar value of all output is sold when the dollar value of leakages from the income flow (savings, taxes, imports) equals the dollar value of injections of spending (investment, government, exports).*

EXHIBIT A-1   The Circular Flow Model of an Open Economy

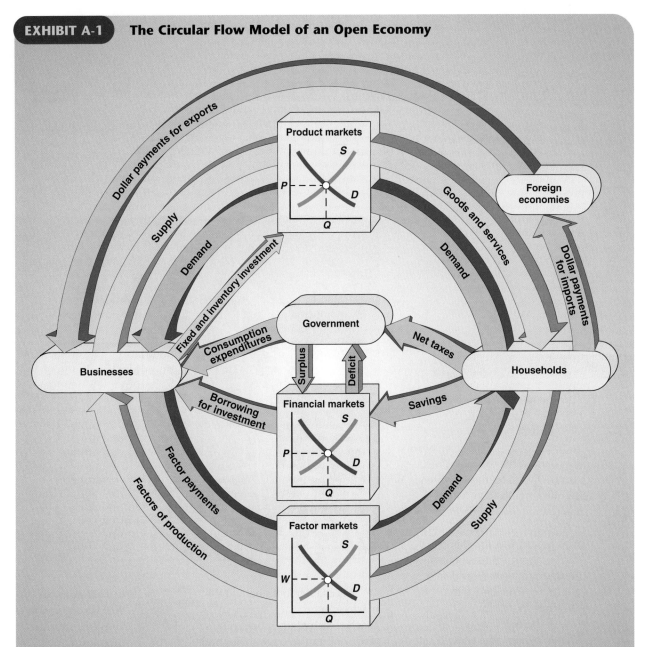

This exhibit presents a circular flow model for an economy, such as the United States, that engages in international trade. The theoretical model includes links between the product and factor markets in the domestic economy and the financial markets, government, and foreign economies. To simplify the model, only dollar payments are shown for the foreign sector.

CHAPTER 16

Business Cycles and Unemployment

The headline in the morning newspaper reads, "The Economy Busts." Later in the day, a radio announcer begins the news by saying, "The unemployment rate increased for the fourth consecutive month." On television, the evening news broadcasts an interview with several economists who predict that the slump will last for another three months. Next, a presidential candidate appears on the screen and says, "It's time for change." The growth rate of the economy and the unemployment rate are headline-catching news. Indeed, these measures of macroeconomic instability are important because they affect your future. When real GDP rises and the economy "booms," jobs are more plentiful. A fall in real GDP means a "bust" in that the economy forces some firms into bankruptcy and workers lose their jobs. Not being able to find a job when you want one is a painful experience not easily forgotten.

This chapter looks behind the macro economy at a story that touches each of us. It begins by discussing the business cycle. How are the expansions and contractions of business cycles measured? And what causes the business-cycle roller coaster? Finally, you will learn what the types of unemployment are, what "full employment" is, and what the monetary, nonmonetary, and demographic costs of unemployment are.

In this chapter, you will learn to solve these economics puzzles:

■ What is the difference between a recession and a depression?

■ Is a worker who has given up searching for work counted as unemployed?

■ Can an economy produce more output than its potential?

The Business-Cycle Roller Coaster

A central concern of macroeconomics is the upswings and downswings in the level of real output called the **business cycle.** The business cycle consists of alternating periods of economic growth and contraction. Business cycles are inherent in market economies. A key measure of cycles is the rise and fall in real GDP, which mirror changes in employment and other key measures of the macro economy. Recall from the previous chapter that changes in real GDP measure changes in the value of national output, while ignoring changes in the price level.

The Four Phases of the Business Cycle

Exhibit 1(a) illustrates a theoretical business cycle. Although business cycles vary in duration and intensity, each cycle is divided into four phases: **peak, recession, trough,** and **recovery.** The business cycle looks like a roller coaster. It begins at a peak, drops to a bottom, climbs steeply, and then reaches another peak. Once the trough is reached, the upswing starts again. Although forecasters cannot precisely predict the phases of a cycle, the economy is always operating along one of these phases. Over time, there has been a long-term upward trend with shorter-term cyclical fluctuations around the long-run trend.

Two *peaks* are illustrated in Exhibit 1(a). At each of these peaks, the economy is close to or at full employment. That is, as explained in Chapter 2, the economy is operating near its production possibilities curve, and real GDP is at its highest level relative to recent years. A macro setback called a *recession* or *contraction* follows each peak. A recession is a downturn in the business cycle during which real GDP declines. During a recession, the economy is functioning inside its production possibilities curve. A general rule-of-thumb is that a recession is at least two consecutive quarters (six months) in which there is a decline in real GDP. During a prolonged recession, business profits fall, the percentage of the workforce without jobs rises, and production capacity is underutilized.

The *trough* is where the level of real GDP "bottoms out." At the trough, unemployment and idle productive capacity are at their highest levels relative to recent years. The length of time between the peak and the trough is the duration of the recession. Since the end of World War II, recessions in the United States have averaged 11 months. As shown in Exhibit 2, the last recession lasted nine months, from July 1990 to April 1991. The percentage decline in real GDP was 1.2 percent, and the national unemployment rate hit 7.1 percent.

What is the difference between *recession* and *depression*? According to the old saying: "A recession is when your neighbor loses his or her job, and a depression is when you lose your job!" This one-liner is close to the true distinction between these two concepts. As explained earlier, economists use *recession* to refer to any decline in real GDP lasting at least six months, so why not use the term *Great Recession*? Because no subsequent recession has approached the prolonged severity of the Great Depression of the early 1930s, the term *depression* is primarily a historical reference to this extremely deep and long recession. The Great Depression is discussed at the end of this chapter and in the chapter on monetary policy.

Business cycle

Alternating periods of economic growth and contraction, which can be measured by changes in real GDP.

Peak

The phase of the business cycle in which real GDP reaches its maximum after rising during a recovery.

Recession

A downturn in the business cycle during which real GDP declines; also called a contraction.

Trough

The phase of the business cycle in which real GDP reaches its minimum after falling during a recession.

Recovery

An upturn in the business cycle during which real GDP rises; also called an expansion.

 Visit the National Bureau of Economic Research (http://www.nber.org/cycles.html) *for a history of U.S. business cycle expansions and contractions in the United States.*

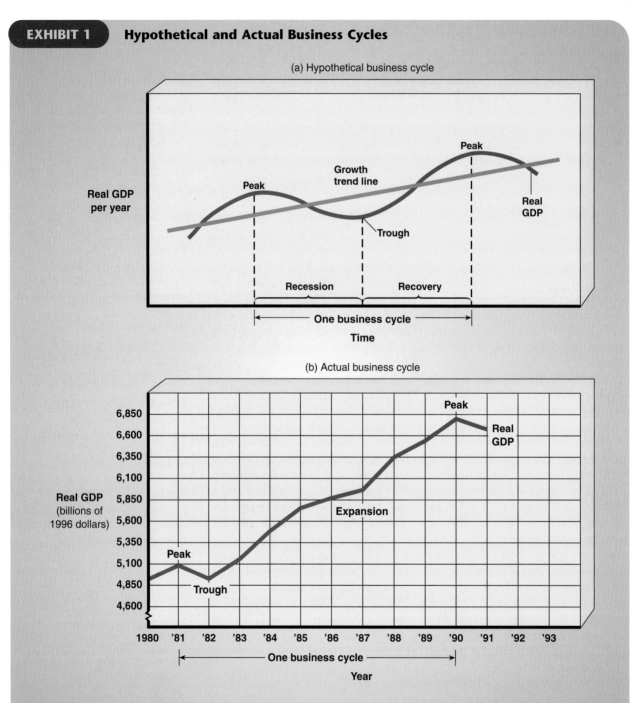

EXHIBIT 1   **Hypothetical and Actual Business Cycles**

(a) Hypothetical business cycle

(b) Actual business cycle

Part (a) illustrates a hypothetical business cycle consisting of four phases: peak, recession, trough, and recovery. These fluctuations of real GDP can be measured by a growth trend line, which shows that over time real GDP has trended upward. In reality, the fluctuations are not so clearly defined as those in this graph.

Part (b) illustrates actual ups and downs of the business cycle. The U.S. economy experienced a short upswing in 1981. After a recession during 1981–1982, a strong upswing continued until another recession during 1990–1991.

Source: *Survey of Current Business,* http://www.bea.doc.gov/bea/dn/nipaweb/PopularTables.asp, Table 1.2.

EXHIBIT 2 Severity of Post–World War II Recessions

Recession dates	Duration (months)	Percentage change in real GDP	Peak unemployment rate
Nov. 1948–Oct. 1949	11	−2.0%	7.9%
July 1953–May 1954	10	−3.0	6.1
Aug. 1957–Apr. 1958	8	−3.5	7.5
Apr. 1960–Feb. 1961	10	−1.0	7.1
Dec. 1969–Nov. 1970	11	−1.1	6.1
Nov. 1973–Mar. 1975	16	−4.3	9.0
Jan. 1980–July 1980	6	−2.4	7.8
July 1981–Nov. 1982	16	−3.4	10.8
July 1990–March 1991	8	−1.2	7.1
March 2001– . . .			
Average	10	−2.5	7.7

Source: Stephen McNees, "The 1990–91 Recession in Historical Perspective," *New England Economic Review* 2 (Jan./Feb. 1992): 4–5, Table 1. Updated by author.

The trough is both bad news and good news. It is simultaneously the bottom of the "valley" of the downturn and the foot of the "hill" of improving economic conditions called a *recovery* or *expansion*. Recovery is an upturn in the business cycle during which real GDP rises. During the recovery phase of the cycle, profits generally improve, real GDP increases, and employment moves toward full employment.

Exhibit 1(b) illustrates an actual business cycle by plotting the movement of real GDP in the United States from 1980 to 1991. The cycle indicates that real GDP reached a peak in 1981 and then experienced a recession between 1981 and 1982. The economy's trough occurred in 1982, and a strong recovery phase lasted until a second peak in 1990.

Exhibit 3 traces annual real GDP since the last recession ending in 1991, shown in Exhibit 1(b). This expansion is the longest in U.S. history. The previous longest expansion in U.S. history lasted more than eight years from February 1961 through December 1969 (106 months). A major reason for this recent record-breaking economic expansion is the new economy. As discussed previously in Chapter 2, widespread technological change has greatly reduced the time and effort required to produce goods and services. As this text is written in 2001, the National Bureau of Economic Research determined that the U.S. economy entered a recession in March; therefore, the longest expansion in U.S. history was 10 years.

Finally, we will now expand the definition of **economic growth** given in Chapter 2. Economic growth is an expansion in national output measured by the annual percentage increase in a nation's real GDP. The growth trend line in the hypothetical model in Exhibit 1(a) illustrates that over time our real GDP tends to rise. This general, long-term upward trend in real GDP persists in spite of the peaks, recessions, troughs, and recoveries. As shown by the dashed line in Exhibit 4, since 1929 real GDP in the United States has grown at an average annual rate of about 3 percent. This annual change

Economic growth
An expansion in national output measured by the annual percentage increase in a nation's real GDP.

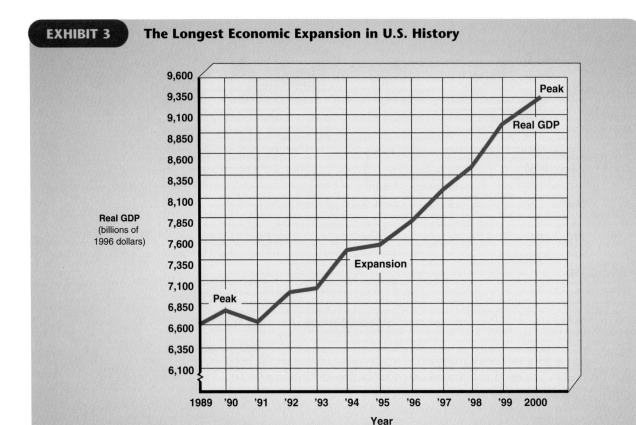

| EXHIBIT 3 | The Longest Economic Expansion in U.S. History |

The exhibit shows the movement in real GDP since the last recession ended in 1991, as shown in Exhibit 1(b). This expansion is the longest in U.S. history, and it ended in March 2001. The previous longest expansion in U.S. history lasted more than eight years from February 1961 through December 1969 (106 months).

Source: *Survey of Current Business,* http://www.bea.doc.gov/bea/dn/nipaweb/PopularTables.asp, Table 1.2.

may seem small, but about 3 percent annual growth will lead to a doubling of real GDP in only 24 years. One of our challenging policy goals is to maintain or increase that growth rate.

> **Conclusion** *We value economic growth as one of our nation's economic goals because it increases our standard of living—it creates a bigger "economic pie."*

Closer examination of Exhibit 4 reveals that the growth path of the U.S. economy over time is not a smooth, rising trend, but instead a series of year-to-year variations in real GDP growth. In some years, such as 1997 through 2000, the economy experienced above-average growth. And in other years, such as 1991, the economy slipped below the zero growth line. Note that the annual growth for the 1991 recession year was negative and therefore dipped below the zero growth line.

However, the economy entered the recovery phase in 1992, and the growth rate reached 3.0 percent. In 2000, the growth rate was 4.1 percent.

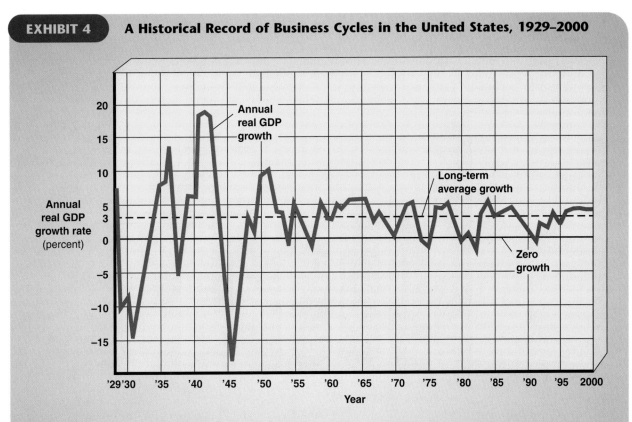

EXHIBIT 4 **A Historical Record of Business Cycles in the United States, 1929–2000**

Real GDP has increased at an average annual growth rate of about 3 percent since 1929. Above-average annual growth rates have alternated with below-average annual growth rates. During a recession year, such as 1991, the annual growth rate is negative and therefore below the zero growth line. The economy entered the recovery phase in 1992, and the growth rate reached 3.0 percent. In 2000, the growth rate was 4.1 percent.

Source: *Survey of Current Business,* http://www.bea.doc.gov/bea/dn/nipaweb/PopularTables.asp, Table S-1.

Real GDP Growth Rates in Other Countries

Exhibit 5 presents real GDP growth rates for selected countries in 2000. Mexico, Canada, the United States, France, Germany, and the United Kingdom experienced real GDP growth of 3 percent or more. On the other hand, Italy had a 2.9 percent growth rate, and Japan experienced a 1.5 percent growth rate.

Business-Cycle Indicators

In addition to changes in real GDP, the media often report several other macro variables that measure business activity, which are published by the U.S. Department of Commerce in *Business Conditions Digest*. These economic *indicator* variables are classified in three categories: leading indicators, coincident indicators, and lagging indicators. Exhibit 6 lists the variables corresponding to each indicator series.

The Index of Leading Indicators can be accessed at http://www.conference-board.org/. *Descriptions of recent revisions in this index can be found at* http://www.tcb-indicators.org/.

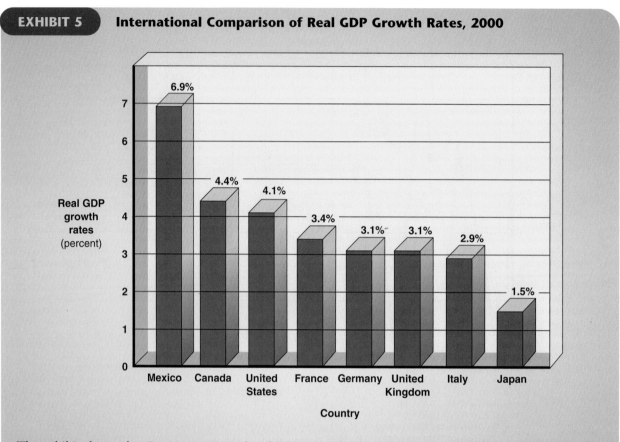

EXHIBIT 5   **International Comparison of Real GDP Growth Rates, 2000**

The exhibit shows that Japan experienced real GDP growth of 1.5 percent in 2000. In contrast, Mexico, the United States, and other Western industrialized countries had higher growth rates for the year. The United States had a growth rate of 4.1 percent.

Source: *Survey of Current Business,* International Perspectives, http://www.bea.doc.gov/bea/pubs.htm, Table H.

Leading indicators

Variables that change before real GDP changes.

The government's chief forecasting gauge for business cycles is the index of **leading indicators.** Leading indicators are variables that change before real GDP changes. This index captures the headlines when there is concern over swings in the economy. The first set of 10 variables in Exhibit 6 is used to forecast the business cycle months in advance. For example, a slump looming ahead is signaled when declines exceed advances in the components of the leading indicators data series. But beware! The leading indicators may rise for two consecutive months and then fall for the next three consecutive months. Economists are therefore cautious and wait for the leading indicators to move in a new direction for several months before forecasting a change in the cycle.

Is a recession near? The Conference Board's Consumer Confidence Index is often reported in the news as a key measure of the economy's health. It is based on a survey of 5,000 households who are asked their expectations of how well the economy will perform over the next six months. Prolonged consumer pessimism can result in less consumer spending and contribute to

EXHIBIT 6 Business-Cycle Indicators

Leading indicators	
Average workweek	New building permits
Unemployment claims	Stock prices
New consumer goods orders	Money supply
Delayed deliveries	Interest rates
New orders for plant and equipment	Consumer expectations

Coincident indicators	Lagging indicators
Nonagricultural payrolls	Unemployment rate
Personal income minus transfer payments	Duration of unemployment rate
Industrial production	Labor cost per unit of output
Manufacturing and trade sales	Consumer price index for services
	Commercial and industrial loans
	Consumer credit to personal income ratio
	Prime rate

slowing economic growth. Stated differently, persistent consumer pessimism can result in lower personal consumption expenditures (C) and business investment (I) because businesses reduce investment when consumers purchases of their products fall. As this text is written in 2001, the attack on the United States has contributed to further erosion in consumer confidence and a recession.

The second data series of variables listed in Exhibit 6 are four **coincident indicators.** Coincident indicators are variables that change at the same time that real GDP changes. For example, as real GDP rises, economists expect employment, personal income, industrial production, and sales to rise.

The third group of variables listed in Exhibit 6 are **lagging indicators.** Lagging indicators are seven variables that change after real GDP changes. For example, the duration of unemployment is a lagging indicator. As real GDP increases, the average time workers remain unemployed does not fall until some months after the beginning of the recovery.

Coincident indicators
Variables that change at the same time that real GDP changes.

Lagging indicators
Variables that change after real GDP changes.

Total Spending and the Business Cycle

The uneven historical pattern of economic growth for the U.S. economy gives rise to the following question: What causes business cycles? The theory generally accepted by economists today is that changes in total or aggregate expenditures are the cause of variations in real GDP. Recall from the previous chapter that aggregate expenditures refer to total spending for

CHECKPOINT

Where Are We on the Business-Cycle Roller Coaster?

Suppose the economy has been in a recession and everyone is asking when the economy will recover. To find an answer to the state of the economy's health, a television reporter interviews Terrence Asaud, a local car dealer. Asaud says, "I do not see any recovery. The third quarter of this year we sold more cars than the second quarter, but sales in these two quarters were far below the first quarter." Is Mr. Asaud correct? Are his observations consistent with the peak, recession, trough, or recovery phase of the business cycle?

final goods by households, businesses, government, and foreign buyers. Expressed as a formula: $GDP = C + I + G + (X - M)$.

Why do changes in total spending cause the level of GDP to change? Stated simply, if total spending increases, businesses find it profitable to increase output. When firms increase production, they use more land, labor, and capital. Hence, increased spending leads to economic growth in output, employment, and incomes. When total spending falls, businesses find it profitable to produce a lower volume of goods and avoid unsold accumulating inventory. In this case, output, employment, and incomes fall. These cutbacks, in turn, can lead to recession.

The situation just described assumes the economy is operating below full employment. Once the economy reaches full employment, increases in total spending have no impact on real GDP. Further spending in this case will simply pull up the price level and "inflate" nominal GDP.

In subsequent chapters, much more will be explained about the causes of business cycles. Using aggregate demand and supply curves, you will learn to analyze why changes occur in national output, unemployment, and the price level.

Unemployment

Since the abyss of the Great Depression, a major economic goal of the United States has been to achieve a high level of employment. The *Employment Act of 1946* declared it the responsibility of the federal government to use all practical means consistent with free competitive enterprise to create conditions under which all able individuals who are willing to work and seeking work will be afforded useful employment opportunities. Later, Congress amended this act with the *Full Employment and Balanced Growth Act of 1978*, which established specific goals for unemployment and the level of prices.

Each month the Bureau of Labor Statistics (BLS) of the U.S. Department of Labor, in conjunction with the Bureau of the Census, conducts a survey of a random sample of about 60,000 households in the United States. Each member of the household who is 16 years of age or older is asked whether he or she is employed or unemployed. If a person works at least 1 hour per week for pay or at least 15 hours per week as an unpaid worker in a family

The Bureau of Labor Statistics (BLS), an agency within the Department of Labor, is the principal fact-finding agency for the federal government in the field of labor economics and statistics. Visit the BLS (http://stats.bls.gov/).

business, he or she is counted as employed. If the person is not employed, the question then is whether or not he or she has looked for work in the last month. If so, the person is said to be unemployed. Based on its survey data, the BLS publishes the **unemployment rate** and other employment-related statistics monthly.

The unemployment rate is the percentage of people in the **civilian labor force** who are without jobs and are actively seeking jobs. But who is actually counted as an unemployed worker, and which people belong to the labor force? Certainly, all people without jobs are not classified as unemployed. Babies, full-time students, and retired persons are not counted as unemployed. Likewise, individuals who are ill or severely disabled are not included as unemployed. And there are other groups not counted.

Turn to Exhibit 7. The *civilian labor force* is the number of people 16 years of age and over who are either employed or unemployed, excluding members of the armed forces and other groups listed in the "persons not in labor force" category. Based on survey data, the BLS computes the *civilian unemployment rate,* using the following formula:

$$\text{unemployment rate} = \frac{\text{unemployed}}{\text{civilian labor force}} \times 100$$

In 2000, the unemployment rate was

$$4.0\% = \frac{5.7 \text{ million persons}}{140.9 \text{ million persons}} \times 100$$

Exhibit 8 charts a historical record of the U.S. unemployment rate since 1929. Note that the highest unemployment rate reached was 25 percent in 1933 during the Great Depression. At the other extreme, the lowest unemployment rate we have attained was 1.2 percent in 1944.

Unemployment in Other Countries

Exhibit 9 shows that none of the selected major industrial countries had a lower unemployment rate than the United States in 2000. Germany, France, and Italy, for example, had unemployment rates over twice the rate of the United States.

Unemployment Rate Criticism

The unemployment rate is criticized for both understating and overstating the "true" unemployment rate. An example of *overstating* the unemployment rate occurs when respondents to the BLS survey falsely report they are seeking employment. The motivation may be that their eligibility for unemployment compensation or welfare benefits depends on actively pursuing a job. Or possibly an individual is "employed" in illegal activities.

The other side of the coin is that the official definition of unemployment *understates* the unemployment rate by not counting so-called **discouraged workers.** A discouraged worker is a person who wants to work, but has given up searching for work because he or she believes there will be no job

---

Unemployment rate
The percentage of people in the labor force who are without jobs and are actively seeking jobs.

Civilian labor force
The number of people 16 years of age and older who are employed or who are actively seeking a job; excluding armed forces, homemakers, discouraged workers, and other persons not in the labor force.

Discouraged worker
A person who wants to work, but who has given up searching for work because he or she believes there will be no job offers.

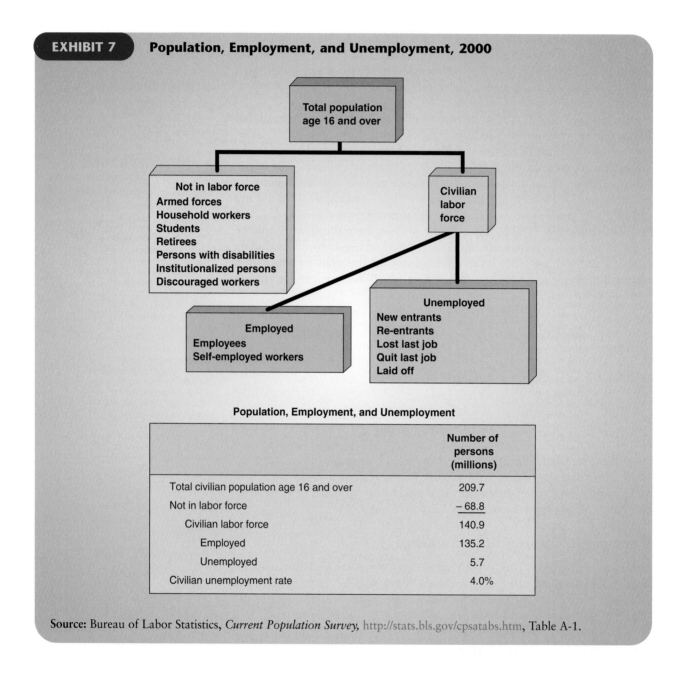

EXHIBIT 7   Population, Employment, and Unemployment, 2000

Population, Employment, and Unemployment

	Number of persons (millions)
Total civilian population age 16 and over	209.7
Not in labor force	− 68.8
Civilian labor force	140.9
Employed	135.2
Unemployed	5.7
Civilian unemployment rate	4.0%

Source: Bureau of Labor Statistics, *Current Population Survey,* http://stats.bls.gov/cpsatabs.htm, Table A-1.

offers. After repeated rejections, discouraged workers often turn to their families, friends, and public welfare for support. The BLS counts a discouraged worker as anyone who has looked for work within the last six months, but is no longer actively looking. The BLS simply includes discouraged workers in the "not in labor force" category listed in Exhibit 7. Because the number of discouraged workers rises during a recession, the underestimation of the official unemployment rate increases during a downturn.

EXHIBIT 8	The U.S. Unemployment Rate, 1929–2000

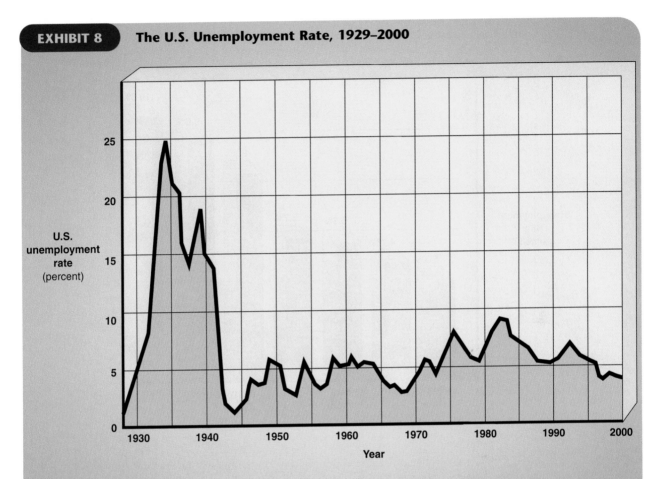

The exhibit shows fluctuations in the civilian unemployment rate since 1929. The unemployment rate reached a high point of 25 percent in 1933 during the Great Depression. The lowest unemployment rate of 1.2 percent was achieved during World War II in 1944. In 2000, the unemployment rate was 4.0 percent.

Source: *Economic Report of the President, 2001,* http://w3.access/gpo.gov/eop/, Table B-35.

Another example of *understating* the unemployment rate occurs because the official BLS data include all part-time workers as fully employed. These workers are actually partially employed, and many would work full time if they could find full-time employment.

Finally, the unemployment statistics do not measure *underemployment.* If jobs are scarce and a college graduate takes a job not requiring his or her level of skills, a human resource is underutilized. Or suppose an employer cuts an employee's hours of work from 40 to 20 per week. Such losses of work potential are greater during a recession, but are not reflected in the unemployment rate.

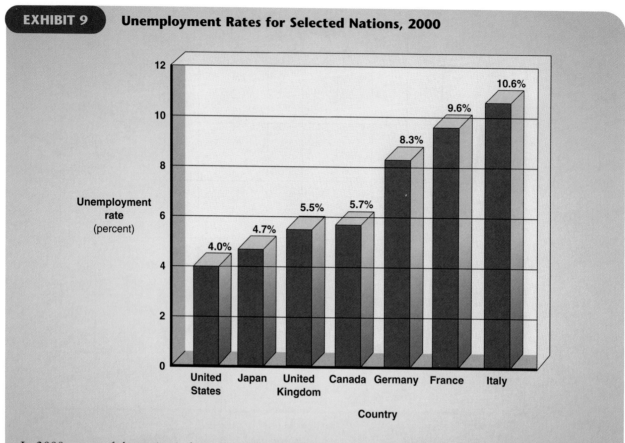

EXHIBIT 9   **Unemployment Rates for Selected Nations, 2000**

In 2000, none of the major industrialized nations shown had a lower unemployment rate than the United States. The unemployment rates of France, Germany, and Italy were more than twice as high as the U.S. rate.

Source: *Economic Report of the President, 2001,* http://w3.access.gpo.gov/eop/, Table B-109.

Types of Unemployment

The unemployment rate is determined by three different types of unemployment: *frictional, structural,* and *cyclical.* Understanding these conceptual categories of unemployment aids in understanding and formulating policies to ease the burden of unemployment. In fact, each type of unemployment requires a different policy prescription to reduce it.

Frictional Unemployment

For some unemployed workers, the absence of a job is only temporary. At any given time, some people with marketable skills are fired, and others voluntarily quit jobs to accept or look for new ones. And there are always young people who leave school and search for their first job. Workers in some industries, such as construction, experience short periods of unemployment between projects, and temporary layoffs are common. Other workers are seasonally unemployed. For example, ski resort workers will be employed in the winter, but not in the summer, and certain crops are harvested "in season." Because jobs requiring their skills are available once the unemployed and the job vacancies are matched, such workers are considered "between jobs." This type of unemployment is called **frictional unemployment,** and it is not of great concern. Frictional unemployment is unemployment caused by the normal search time required by workers with marketable skills who are changing jobs, initially entering the labor force, or re-entering the labor force. The cause of frictional unemployment is either the transition time to a new job or the lack of information required to match a job applicant immediately with a job vacancy. For this reason, frictional unemployment is sometimes called *transitional unemployment* or *search unemployment.*

The fact that job market information is imperfect influences frictional unemployment in the economy. Because it takes time to search for the information required to match employer and employees, some workers will always be frictionally unemployed. Frictional unemployment is therefore a normal condition in an economic system permitting freedom of job choice. Improved methods of distributing job information through job listings on the Internet help unemployed workers find jobs more quickly and reduce frictional unemployment.

Structural Unemployment

Unlike frictional unemployment, **structural unemployment** is not a short-term situation. Instead, it is long-term, or possibly permanent, unemployment resulting from the nonexistence of jobs for unemployed workers. Structural unemployment is unemployment caused by a mismatch of the skills of workers out of work and the skills required for existing job opportunities. Note that changing jobs and lack of job information are *not* problems for frictionally unemployed workers. Unlike frictionally unemployed workers who have marketable skills, structurally unemployed workers require additional education or retraining. Changes in the structure of the economy create the following three cases of structural unemployment.

First, workers might face joblessness because they lack the education or the job-related skills to perform available jobs. This type of structural unemployment particularly affects teenagers and minority groups, but other groups of workers can be affected as well. For example, environmental concerns, such as protecting the spotted owl by restricting trees from being cut, cost some loggers their jobs. Reducing such structural unemployment requires retraining loggers for new jobs as, say, forest rangers. Another example involves the "peace dividend" from the reduction in defense spending after a war. This situation creates structural unemployment for discharged military personnel who require retraining for, say, teaching, nursing, or police jobs.

Second, the consuming public may decide to increase the demand for Mazda RX-7s and decrease the demand for Chevrolet Corvettes. This shift in demand would cause U.S. auto workers who lose their jobs in Bowling

Frictional unemployment
Unemployment caused by the normal search time required by workers with marketable skills who are changing jobs, initially entering the labor force, re-entering the labor force, or seasonally unemployed.

Structural unemployment
Unemployment caused by a mismatch of the skills of workers out of work and the skills required for existing job opportunities.

 When workers lose their jobs for no fault of their own, they may be eligible for unemployment compensation. For information on unemployment compensation visit the Legal Information Institute (http://www.law.cornell.edu/topics/unemployment_compensation.html).

What Kind of Unemployment Did the Invention of the Wheel Cause?

Did the invention of the wheel cause frictional, structural, or cyclical unemployment?

Green, Kentucky, to become structurally unemployed. To regain employment, these unemployed autoworkers must retrain and find job openings in other industries, for example, manufacturing IBM computer printers in North Carolina.

Third, implementation of the latest technology may also increase the pool of structural unemployment in a particular industry and region. For example, the U.S. textile industry, located primarily in the South, can fight less expensive foreign textile imports by installing modern machinery. This new capital may replace textile workers. But suppose these unemployed textile workers do not wish to move to a new location where new types of jobs are available. The costs of moving, fear of the unknown, and family ties are understandable reasons for reluctance to move, and, instead, the workers become structurally unemployed.

There are many causes of structural unemployment, including poor schools, new products, new technology, foreign competition, geographic differences, restricted entry into jobs, and shifts in government priorities. Because of the numerous sources of mismatching between skills and jobs, economists consider a certain level of structural unemployment inevitable. Public and private programs that train employees to fill existing job openings decrease structural unemployment. Conversely, one of the concerns about the minimum wage is that it may contribute to structural unemployment. In Exhibit 5 of Chapter 4, we demonstrated that a minimum wage legislated above the equilibrium wage causes unemployment. One approach intended to offset such undesirable effects of the minimum wage is a subminimum wage paid during a training period to give employers an incentive to hire unskilled workers.

Cyclical Unemployment

Cyclical unemployment

Unemployment caused by the lack of jobs during a recession.

Cyclical unemployment is directly attributable to the lack of jobs caused by the business cycle. Cyclical unemployment is unemployment caused by the lack of jobs during a recession. When real GDP falls, companies close, jobs disappear, and workers scramble for fewer available jobs. Similar to the game of musical chairs, there are not enough chairs (jobs) for the number of players (workers) in the game.

The Great Depression is a dramatic example of cyclical unemployment. There was a sudden decline in consumption, investment, government consumption expenditures, and net exports. As a result of this striking fall in real GDP, the unemployment rate rose to about 25 percent (see Exhibit 8). Now notice what happened to the unemployment rate when real GDP rose sharply during World War II. To smooth out these swings in unemployment, a focus of macroeconomic policy is to moderate cyclical unemployment.

Is It a Machine's World?

Applicable Concept: types of unemployment

In the late 1980s, an article described a recurring labor market situation:

People looking for job security have rarely chosen the music industry. But these days, musicians say, competition from machines has removed what little stability there was. Modern machines can effectively duplicate string sections, drummers and even horn sections, so with the exception of concerts, the jobs available to live musicians are growing fewer by the day. . . .

It is not the first time that technology has thrown a wrench into musical careers. When talking pictures helped usher in the death of vaudeville, and again, when recorded music replaced live music in radio station studios, the market for musicians took a beating from which it never fully recovered. . . . The musicians' plight is not getting universal sympathy. Some industry insiders say that the current job problems are an inevitable price of progress, and that musicians should update their skills to deal with the new instruments. . . .

But others insist that more than musicians' livelihood is at stake. Mr. Glasel, [Musicians' Union] Local 802's president, warns that unbridled computerization of music could eventually threaten the quality of music. Jobs for trumpet players, for instance, have dropped precipitously since the synthesizer managed a fair approximation of the trumpet. And without trumpet players, he asked, "where is the next generation going to get its Dizzy Gillespie?"[1]

And lawn-mowing jobs beware! AutoMower, a programmable robot that looks like a vacuum cleaner without a handle, can trim the yard, and it is now available for sale. Ditto for checkout cashiers. A 2001 article in *USA Today* reports that the self-checkout scanner is on its way. It's being tested across the nation in grocery supermarkets.

Self-scan stations look like conventional checkouts, but it's the shopper alone who unloads, scans all grocery items, including bags of produce, and then pays. A "snappy" electronic voice completes the transactions saying "Have a nice day and thank you for shopping at . . ." The self-checkout technology offers customers shorter waits in line, but what will be the impact on the number of checkout jobs? Only time will tell.[2]

ANALYZE THE ISSUE

1. Are the musicians experiencing frictional, structural, or cyclical unemployment? Explain.

2. What solution would you propose for the trumpet players mentioned above?

---

[1]James S. Newton, "A Death Knell Sounds for Musical Jobs," *New York Times,* Mar. 1, 1987, sec. 3, p. 9.
[2]Lorrie Grant, "Now, Harried Shoppers Can Take Control at Supermarkets," *USA Today,* June 7, 2001, pp. 1–2A.

The Goal of Full Employment

In this section, we take a closer look at the meaning of **full employment.** Because both frictional and structural unemployment are present in good and bad times, *full employment* does not mean "zero percent unemployment." Full employment is the situation in which an economy operates at an unemployment rate equal to the sum of the frictional and structural unemployment rates. Full employment therefore is the rate of unemployment that exists without cyclical unemployment.

Full employment

The situation in which an economy operates at an unemployment rate equal to the sum of the frictional and structural unemployment rates.

Unfortunately, economists cannot state with certainty what percentages of the labor force are frictionally and structurally unemployed at any point in time. In practice, therefore, full employment is difficult to define. Moreover, the full-employment rate of unemployment, or natural rate of unemployment, changes over time. In the 1960s, 4 percent unemployment was generally considered to represent full employment. In the 1980s, the accepted rate was 6 percent, and, currently, the consensus among economists is that the natural rate is close to 5 percent.

Several reasons are given for why full employment is not fixed. One reason is that between the early 1960s and the early 1980s, the participation of women and teenagers in the labor force increased. This change in the labor force composition increased the full-employment rate of unemployment because both women and young workers (under age 25) typically experience higher unemployment rates than men. Another frequently cited and controversial reason for the rise in the full-employment rate of unemployment is that larger unemployment compensation payments, food stamps, welfare, and Social Security benefits from the government make unemployment less painful. In the 1990s, the natural rate of unemployment declined somewhat because the entry of females and teenagers into the labor force slowed. Also, the baby-boom generation has aged, and middle-aged workers have lower unemployment rates.

The GDP Gap

GDP gap

The difference between full-employment real GDP and actual real GDP.

When people in an economy are unemployed, society forfeits the production of goods and services. To determine the dollar value of how much society loses if the economy fails to reach the natural rate of unemployment, economists estimate the **GDP gap**. The GDP gap is the difference between full-employment real GDP and actual real GDP. The level of GDP that could be produced at full employment is also called *potential real GDP*. Because the GDP gap is estimated on the basis of the difference between GDP at the full-employment rate of unemployment and GDP at the actual unemployment rate, the GDP gap measures the cost of cyclical unemployment. Expressed as a formula:

$$\text{GDP gap} \;=\; \text{potential real GDP} \;-\; \text{actual real GDP}$$

Exhibit 10 shows the size of the GDP gap (in 1996 prices) from 1990 to 2000, based on potential real GDP and actual real GDP for each of these years. When the two lines in the figure cross, the economy is performing at its peak. During the early 1970s, the stimulus of the Vietnam War created overtime work, and the economy produced a GDP gap in which actual real GDP exceeded potential real GDP (negative GDP gap). During the 1990–1991 recession, the economy operated below its potential (positive GDP gap), and society lost billions of dollars in potential real GDP. After 1991, the economy operated below its potential until after 1996 when the economy operated above its potential with a continuously widening negative GDP gap.

EXHIBIT 10   **Potential and Actual GDP, 1990–2000**

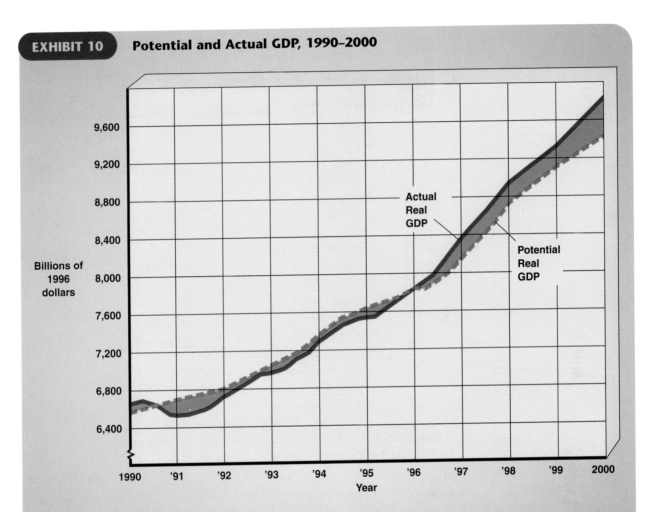

The GDP gap is the difference between potential real GDP and actual real GDP. Because potential real GDP is based on full employment, a positive GDP gap measures the cost of cyclical unemployment in terms of real GDP. A negative GDP gap measures a boom in the economy when workers are employed overtime. Since 1996, the U.S. economy has experienced a continuously widening negative GDP gap.

Sources: Economagic, http://www.economagic.com/; *OECD Economic Outlook*, December 2000, http://www .sourceoecd.org/content/html/index.htm, Annex Table 11, and *Survey of Current Business*, http://www.bea.doc .gov/bea/dm1.htm, Table 1.2.

Conclusion *The gap between actual and potential real GDP measures the monetary losses of real goods and services to the nation from operating at less than full employment.*

Nonmonetary and Demographic Consequences of Unemployment

The burden of unemployment is more than the loss of potential output measured by the GDP gap. Unemployment also has nonmonetary costs. Some people endure unemployment pretty well because they have substantial savings to

EXHIBIT 11 Civilian Unemployment Rates by Selected Demographic Groups, 2000

Demographic group	Unemployment rate (percent)
Overall	4.0%
Sex	
Male	3.9
Female	4.1
Race	
White	3.5
Black	7.6
Teenagers (16–19 years old)	
All	13.1
White males	12.3
Black males	26.4
White females	10.4
Black females	23.0
Education (25 years and over)	
Less than high school diploma	6.4
High school graduates	3.5
College graduates	1.7

Source: U.S. Bureau of Labor Statistics, *Current Population Survey,* http://stats.bls.gov/cpsatabs.htm, Table A-3.

The Employment and Training Administration of the U.S. Department of Labor has made projections of occupational employment growth for all states (http://www.doleta.gov/regions/). *One of the most important uses of the projections is to help individuals make informed career decisions.*

draw on, but others sink into despair. Without work, many people lose their feeling of worth. A person's self-image suffers when he or she cannot support a family and be a valuable member of society. Research has associated high unemployment with suicides, crime, mental illness, heart attacks, and other maladies. Moreover, severe unemployment causes despair, family breakups, and political unrest.

Various labor market groups share the impact of unemployment unequally. Exhibit 11 presents the unemployment rates experienced by selected demographic groups. In 2000, the overall unemployment rate was 4.0 percent, but the figures in the exhibit reveal the unequal burden by race, age, and educational attainment. First, note that the unemployment rates for males and females were almost equal. Second, the unemployment rate for blacks was roughly twice that for whites. Third, teenagers experienced a high unemployment rate because they are new entrants to the workforce who have little employment experience, high quit rates, and little job mobility. Again, race is a strong factor, and the unemployment rate for black teenagers was more than twice that for white teenagers. Among the explanations are discrimination; the concentration of blacks in the inner city, where job opportunities for less skilled (blue-collar) workers are inadequate; and the minimum-wage law.

Brother Can You Spare a Dime?

Applicable Concept: human costs of unemployment

The unemployment rate does not measure the full impact of unemployment on individuals. Prolonged unemployment not only means lost wages, but it also impairs health and social relationships. The United States fought its most monstrous battle against unemployment during the Great Depression of the 1930s. Return to Exhibit 8 and note that the unemployment rate stayed at 20 percent or more from 1932 through 1935. In 1933, it reached almost 25 percent of the civilian labor force; that is about one out of every four people who wanted to work could not. This meant 16 million Americans were out of work when our country's population was less than half its present size.[1] For comparison, at the low point of the 1990–1991 recession, about 10 million Americans were officially unemployed.

But these statistics tell only part of the horror story. Millions of workers were "discouraged workers" who had simply given up looking for work because there was no work available, and these people were not counted. People were standing in line for soup kitchens, selling apples on the street, and living in cardboard shacks. "Brother can you spare a dime?" was a common greeting. Some people jumped out of windows, and others roamed the country trying valiantly to survive. John Steinbeck's great novel *The Grapes of Wrath* described millions of midwesterners who drove in caravans to California after being wiped out by drought in what became known as the Dust Bowl.

A 1992 study estimated the frightening impact of sustained unemployment not reflected in official unemployment data. Mary Merva, a University of Utah economist, co-authored a study of unemployment in 30 selected big cities from 1976 to 1990. This research found that a 1 percentage point increase in the national unemployment rate resulted in

- 6.7 percent more murders,
- 3.1 percent more deaths from stroke,
- 5.6 percent more fatal heart disease, and
- 3.9 percent increase in suicides.[2]

Although these estimates are subject to statistical qualifications, they underscore the notion that prolonged unemployment poses a real danger to many individuals. As people change their behavior in the face of layoffs, cutbacks, or a sudden drop in net worth, more and more Americans find themselves clinically depressed.

---

[1]U.S. Bureau of the Census, *Historical Statistics of the United States, Colonial Times to 1957* (Washington, D.C.: U.S. Government Printing Office, 1960), Series D 46–47, p. 73.
[2]Robert Davis, "Recession's Cost: Lives," *USA Today,* News, Oct. 16, 1992, p. 1A.

Finally, comparison of the unemployment rates in 2000 by educational attainment reveals the importance of education as an insurance policy against unemployment. Firms are much less likely to lay off a higher-skilled worker with a college education, in whom they have a greater investment in terms of training and salaries, than a worker with only a high school diploma.

KEY CONCEPTS

Business cycle	Economic growth	Unemployment rate	Structural unemployment
Peak	Leading indicators	Civilian labor force	Cyclical unemployment
Recession	Coincident indicators	Discouraged worker	Full employment
Trough	Lagging indicators	Frictional unemployment	GDP gap
Recovery			

SUMMARY

- **Business cycles** are recurrent rises and falls in real GDP over a period of years. Business cycles vary greatly in duration and intensity. A cycle consists of four phases: peak, recession, trough, and recovery. The generally accepted theory today is that changes in the forces of demand and supply cause business cycles. A **recession** is officially defined as at least two consecutive quarters of real GDP decline. A **trough** is the turning point in national output between recession and recovery. During a **recovery,** there is an upturn in the business cycle during which real GDP rises.

Hypothetical business cycle

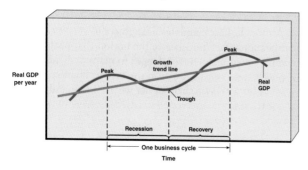

- **Economic growth** is measured by the annual percentage change in real GDP in a nation. The long-term average annual growth rate in the United States is 3 percent.

- **Leading, coincident,** and **lagging indicators** are economic variables that change before, at the same time as, and after changes in real GDP, respectively.

- The **unemployment rate** is the ratio of the number of unemployed to the number in the civilian labor force

multiplied by 100. The nation's **civilian labor force** consists of people who are employed plus those who are out of work, but seeking employment.

- **Discouraged workers** are a reason critics say the unemployment rate is *understated.* Discouraged workers are persons who want to work, but have given up searching for work. Another criticism of the unemployment rate is that it *overstates* unemployment because respondents can falsely report they are seeking a job.

- **Frictional, structural,** and **cyclical unemployment** are different types of unemployment. **Frictional unemployment,** including seasonal unemployment, results when workers are seeking new jobs that exist. The problem is that imperfect information prevents matching the applicants with the available jobs. **Structural unemployment** is unemployment caused by factors in the economy, including lack of skills, changes in product demand, and technological change. **Cyclical unemployment** is unemployment resulting from insufficient aggregate demand.

- **Full employment** occurs when the unemployment rate is equal to the total of the frictional and structural unemployment rates. Currently, the full-employment rate of unemployment (natural rate of unemployment) in the United States is considered to be close to 5 percent. At this rate of unemployment, the economy is producing at its maximum potential.

- The **GDP gap** is the difference between full employment, or potential, real GDP and actual real GDP. Therefore, the GDP gap measures the loss of output due to cyclical unemployment.

SUMMARY OF CONCLUSION STATEMENTS

- We value economic growth as one of our nation's economic goals because it increases our standard of living—it creates a bigger "economic pie."

- The gap between actual and potential real GDP measures the monetary losses of real goods and services to the nation from operating at less than full employment.

STUDY QUESTIONS AND PROBLEMS

1. What is the basic cause of the business cycle?

2. Following are real GDP figures for 10 quarters:

Quarterly Real GDP (billions of dollars)

Quarter	Real GDP (billions of dollars)	Quarter	Real GDP (billions of dollars)
1	$400	6	$ 500
2	500	7	800
3	300	8	900
4	200	9	1,000
5	300	10	500

Plot these data points, and identify the four phases of the business cycle. Give a theory that may explain the cause of the observed business cycle. What are some of the consequences of a prolonged decline in real GDP? Is the decline in real GDP from $1,000 billion to $500 billion a recession?

3. In a given year, there are 10 million unemployed workers and 120 million employed workers in the economy. Excluding members of the armed forces and persons in institutions, and assuming these figures include only civilian workers, calculate the civilian unemployment rate.

4. Describe the relevant criteria that government statisticians use to determine whether a person is "unemployed."

5. How has the official unemployment rate been criticized for overestimating and underestimating unemployment?

6. Why is frictional unemployment inevitable in an economy characterized by imperfect job information?

7. How does structural unemployment differ from cyclical unemployment?

8. Is it reasonable to expect the unemployment rate to fall to zero for an economy? What is the relationship of frictional, structural, and cyclical unemployment to the full-employment rate of unemployment, or the natural rate of unemployment?

9. In the 1960s, economists used 4 percent as their approximation for the natural rate of unemployment. Currently, full employment is on the order of 5 percent unemployment. What is the major factor accounting for this rise?

10. Speculate on why teenage unemployment rates exceed those for the overall labor force.

11. Explain the GDP gap.

ONLINE EXERCISES

Exercise 1

Visit the Economic Statistics Briefing Room (http://www.whitehouse.gov/fsbr/esbr.html), and select Output. Study the real GDP data by clicking on the chart icon and the Table of GDP data. Make an economic forecast for the next year.

Exercise 2

Visit "Business Cycle Indicators" (http://www.concentric.net/~netlink/bci/whatBCI.html). What is the difference between leading, lagging and coincident economic indicators? What are the 16 distinct categories of economic indicators?

Exercise 3

Visit the Bureau of Labor Statistics state unemployment figures (http://www.bls.gov/news.release/laus.t03.htm) and follow these steps:

1. What is the unemployment rate in your state?

2. Compare your state's unemployment with that for the nation as a whole (http://www.bls.gov/cps/). What might account for the difference?

Exercise 4

Visit Indicators on Unemployment (http://www.un.org/Depts/unsd/social/unempl.htm). Compare the U.S. unemployment rate to the unemployment rate of other countries.

CHECKPOINT ANSWERS

Where Are We on the Business-Cycle Roller Coaster?

The car dealer's sales in the first quarter conformed to the recession phase of the business cycle, and those in the second quarter to the trough. Then car sales in the third quarter were below those in the first quarter, but the increase over the second quarter indicated a recovery. If you said real GDP during a recovery can be lower than real GDP during a recession, YOU ARE CORRECT.

What Kind of Unemployment Did the Invention of the Wheel Cause?

The invention of the wheel represented a new technology for primitive people. Even in the primitive era, many workers who transported goods lost their jobs to the more efficient cart with wheels. If you said the invention of the wheel caused structural unemployment, YOU ARE CORRECT.

PRACTICE QUIZ

For a visual explanation of the correct answers, visit the tutorial at http://tucker.swcollege.com.

1. The phases of a business cycle are
   a. upswing and downswing.
   b. full employment and unemployment.
   c. peak, recession, trough, and recovery.
   d. full employment, depression, expansion, and plateau.

2. The phase of a business cycle during which real GDP reaches its minimum level is the
   a. recession.
   b. depression.
   c. recovery.
   d. trough.

3. Which of the following is *not* a variable in the index of leading indicators?
   a. New consumer goods orders
   b. Delayed deliveries
   c. New businesses formed
   d. Prime rate

4. Which of the following is a coincident indicator?
   a. Personal income
   b. Industrial production
   c. Manufacturing and trade sales
   d. All of the above

5. The labor force consists of all persons
   a. 21 years of age and older.
   b. 21 years of age and older who are working.
   c. 16 years of age and older.
   d. 16 years of age and older who are working or actively seeking work.

6. People who are not working will be counted as employed if they are
   a. on vacation.
   b. absent from their job because of bad weather.
   c. absent from their job because of a labor dispute.
   d. all of the above.

7. The number of people officially unemployed is *not* the same as the number of people who can't find a job because
   a. people who have jobs continue to look for better ones.
   b. the armed forces are included.
   c. discouraged workers are not counted.
   d. of all of the above.

8. Frictional unemployment applies to
   a. workers with skills not required for existing jobs.
   b. short periods of unemployment needed to match jobs and job seekers.

   c. people who spend long periods of time out of work.
   d. unemployment related to the ups and downs of the business cycle.

9. Structural unemployment is caused by
   a. shifts in the economy that make certain job skills obsolete.
   b. temporary layoffs in industries such as construction.
   c. the impact of the business cycle on job opportunities.
   d. short-term changes in the economy.

10. Unemployment that is due to a recession is
    a. involuntary unemployment.
    b. frictional unemployment.
    c. structural unemployment.
    d. cyclical unemployment.

11. The sum of the frictional and structural unemployment rates is equal to the
    a. potential unemployment rate.
    b. actual unemployment rate.
    c. cyclical unemployment rate.
    d. full-employment rate.

12. Which of the following statements is *true*?
    a. The four phases of the business cycle, in order, are peak, recovery, trough, and recession.
    b. When unemployment is rising, then real GDP is rising.
    c. The economic problem typically associated with a recovery is rising unemployment.
    d. Full employment exists in an economy when the unemployment rate equals the sum of the frictional and structural unemployment rates.

13. Which of the following groups typically has the highest unemployment rate?
    a. White men and women as a group
    b. African American men and women as a group
    c. Teenagers as a group
    d. Persons who completed high school

14. Which of the following statements is *true*?
    a. The GDP gap is the difference between full-employment real GDP and actual real GDP.
    b. We desire economic growth because it increases the nation's real GDP.
    c. Economic growth is measured by the annual percentage increase in a nation's real GDP.
    d. Discouraged workers are a reason critics say the unemployment rate is understated.
    e. All of the above are true.

CHAPTER 17

Inflation

In addition to the goals of full employment and economic growth discussed in the previous chapter, keeping prices stable is one of the most important economic goals facing a nation. In the United States, the Great Depression of the 1930s produced profound changes in our lives. Similarly, the "Great Inflation" of the 1970s and early 1980s left memories of the miseries of inflation. Concern that inflation would again become a major problem persists even though the rate of inflation since 1992 has averaged less than 3 percent. In fact, every American president since Franklin Roosevelt has resolved to keep the price level stable. Politicians are aware that as with high unemployment, voters are quick to blame any administration that fails to keep inflation under control.

This chapter explains what inflation is. You will study how the government actually measures changes in the price level and computes the rate of inflation. The chapter concludes with a discussion of the consequences and root causes of inflation. It explains who the winners are and who the losers are. For example, you will see what happened in Bolivia when the inflation rate reached 116,000 percent. After studying this chapter, you will have a much clearer understanding of why inflation is so feared.

In this chapter, you will learn to solve these economics puzzles:

■ What is the inflation rate of your college education?

■ Can a person's income fall even though he or she received a raise?

■ Can an interest rate be negative?

■ Does inflation harm everyone equally?

Meaning and Measurement of Inflation

After World War II, a 12-ounce bottle of Pepsi sold for 5 cents. Nowadays, a 12-ounce can of Pepsi sells for more than 10 times that much. This is not **inflation.** Inflation is an increase in the *general* (average) price level of goods and services in the economy. Inflation's opposite is **deflation.** Deflation is a decrease in the *general* (average) price level of goods and services in the economy. Note that inflation does not mean that *all* prices of *all* products in the economy rise during a given period of time. For example, the annual percentage change in the average overall price level during the 1970s reached double digits, but the prices of pocket calculators and digital watches actually declined. The reason that the average price level rose in the 1970s was that the rising prices of Pepsi, houses, and other goods outweighed the falling prices of pocket calculators, digital watches, and other goods.

Conclusion *Inflation is an increase in the overall average level of prices and not an increase in the price of any specific product.*

The Consumer Price Index

The most widely reported measure of inflation is the **consumer price index (CPI)**, which measures changes in the average price of consumer goods and services. The CPI is sometimes called the *cost-of-living index.* It includes only consumer goods and services in order to determine how rising prices affect the income of consumers. Unlike the *GDP chain price index,* explained in the previous chapter on GDP, the CPI does not consider items purchased by businesses and government.

The Bureau of Labor Statistics (BLS) of the U.S. Department of Labor prepares the CPI. Each month the bureau's "price collectors" contact retail stores, homeowners, and tenants in selected cities throughout the United States. Based on these monthly inquiries, the BLS records average prices for a "market basket" of different items purchased by the typical *urban* family. These items are included under the following categories: food and beverage, housing, apparel and upkeep, transportation, medical care, entertainment, and other goods and services. Exhibit 1 presents a more detailed breakdown of these categories and shows the relative importance of each as a percentage of total expenditures. The survey reveals, for example, that 40.0 cents out of each consumer dollar are spent for housing and 17.6 cents for transportation. The composition of the market basket generally remains unchanged from one period to the next, so the CPI is called a *fixed-weight price index.* If 40 percent of consumer spending was on housing in 1982–1984, the assumption is that 40 percent of spending is still spent on housing in, say, 2000. Over time, the composition of items in the CPI has changed. For example, revisions have added personal computers, VCRs, compact disc players, and videocassette rentals. The base period is changed roughly every 10 years.

Inflation
An increase in the general (average) price level of goods and services in the economy.

Deflation
A decrease in the general (average) price level of goods and services in the economy.

Consumer price index (CPI)
An index that measures changes in the average prices of consumer goods and services.

 The Bureau of Labor Statistics provides data on Consumer Price Indexes (http://www.bls.gov/data/top20.htm). *Also, there are a variety of different price indexes from which inflation can be calculated. These indexes can be accessed through the Economic Statistics Briefing Room* (http://www.whitehouse.gov/news/fsbr.html).

EXHIBIT 1 Composition of the Consumer Price Index

Category		Percentage
All items		100.0%
Food and beverage		16.2
At home	9.6	
Away from home	5.6	
Alcoholic beverages	1.0	
Housing		40.0
Shelter	30.3	
Fuels and utilities	5.1	
Furnishings	4.6	
Apparel		4.4
Transportation		17.6
New and used vehicles	7.5	
Gasoline, parts, and maintenance	8.7	
Public transportation	1.4	
Medical care		5.8
Commodities	1.2	
Services	4.6	
Recreation		5.9
Education and communication		5.3
Education	2.8	
Communication	2.5	
Other goods and services		4.8

Source: Bureau of Labor Statistics, http://stats.bls.gov/cpihome.htm, December 2000, Table 1.

How the CPI Is Computed

Exhibit 2 illustrates the basic idea behind the CPI and shows how this price index measures inflation. Suppose, in 1982, a typical family in the United States lived a very meager existence and purchased a market basket of only hamburgers, gasoline, and jeans. Column 1 shows the quantity purchased for each of these items, and column 2 lists the corresponding average selling price. Multiplying the price times the quantity gives the market basket cost in column 3 of each consumer product purchased in 1982. The total cost paid by our typical family for the market basket, based on 1982 prices and quantities purchased, is $245.

Fourteen years later it is 1996, and we wish to know the impact of rising prices on consumer purchases. To calculate the CPI, we determine the cost of the *same* market basket, valued at 1996 *current-year prices,* and compare this to the cost at 1982 base-year prices. A **base year** is a year chosen as a reference point for comparison with some earlier or later year. Expressed as a general formula:

Base year

A year chosen as a reference point for comparison with some earlier or later year.

EXHIBIT 2 Consumer Price Index for a Simple Economy

Products in consumers' market basket	(1) 1982 quantity purchased	(2) 1982 price	(3) Market basket cost in 1982 [(1) × (2)]	(4) 1996 price	(5) Market basket cost in 1996 [(1) × (4)]
Hamburgers	50	$ .80	$ 40	$ 1.00	$ 50
Gallons of gasoline	250	.70	175	.90	225
Jeans	2	15.00	30	30.00	60
			Total 1982 cost = $245		Total 1996 cost = $335

$$1996 \text{ CPI} = \frac{1996 \text{ market basket cost}}{1982 \text{ market basket cost}} \times 100$$

$$1996 \text{ CPI} = \frac{\$335}{\$245} \times 100 = 136.7$$

$$\text{CPI} = \frac{\text{cost of the market basket of products at current-year (1996) prices}}{\text{cost of the same market basket of products at base-year (1982) prices}} \times 100$$

As shown in Exhibit 2, the 1996 cost for our market basket example is calculated by multiplying the 1996 price for each item in column 4 times the 1982 quantity purchased in column 1. Column 5 lists the result for each item in the market basket, and the total market basket cost in 1996 is $335. The CPI value of 136.7 is computed in Exhibit 2 as the ratio of the current 1996 cost of the market basket ($335) to the cost of the same market basket in the 1982 base year ($245) multiplied by 100.

The value of the CPI in the base year is always 100 because the numerator and the denominator of the CPI formula are the same in the base year. Currently, the CPI uses 1982–1984 spending patterns as its base year. Once the BLS selects the base year and uses the market basket technique to generate the CPI numbers, the annual *inflation rate* is computed as the percentage change in the official CPI from one year to the next. Mathematically,

$$\frac{\text{annual rate}}{\text{of inflation}} = \frac{\text{CPI in given year} - \text{CPI in previous year}}{\text{CPI in previous year}} \times 100$$

Exhibit 3 lists actual CPI data as it is reported in the *Economic Report of the President*. You can use the above formula and calculate the inflation rate for any given year using the base year of (1982–1984 = 100). In 2000, for example, the CPI was 172.2, while in 1999, it was 166.6. The rate of inflation for 2000 is computed as follows:

$$3.4\% = \frac{172.2 - 166.6}{166.6} \times 100$$

EXHIBIT 3 Consumer Price Indexes and Inflation Rates, Selected Years

Year	CPI	Inflation rate
1931	15.2	—
1932	13.7	−9.9%
1979	72.6	—
1980	82.4	13.5
1990	130.7	—
1991	136.2	4.2
1992	140.3	3.0
1999	166.6	—
2000	172.2	3.4

Sources: Economic Report of the President, 2001, http://www.access.gpo.gov/eop/, **Table B-62;** and **Bureau of Labor Statistics,** ftp://ftp.bls.gov/pub/special.requests/cpi/cpiai.txt.

Disinflation

A reduction in the rate of inflation.

The negative inflation rate for 1932 was deflation, and the 13.5 percent inflation rate for 1980 illustrates a relatively high rate in recent U.S. history. The fall in the inflation rate from 4.2 percent to 3.0 percent between 1991 and 1992 was **disinflation.** Disinflation is a reduction in the rate of inflation. Disinflation does not mean that prices are falling; rather, it means that the rate of increases in prices is falling.

History of U.S. Inflation Rates

Exhibit 4 shows how prices have changed in the United States since 1929, as measured by annual changes in the CPI. During the early years of the Great Depression, the nation experienced *deflation,* and the CPI declined at almost a double-digit rate. In contrast, the CPI reached a double-digit inflation rate during and immediately following World War II. After 1950, the inflation rate generally remained below 3 percent until the inflationary pressures from the Vietnam War in the late 1960s. In fact, the average inflation rate between 1950 and 1968 was only 2 percent. Then the inflation rate climbed to more than 10 percent in 1974, 1979, 1980, and 1981, reaching a high of 13.5 percent in 1980. During the 1973–1982 period, the average annual inflation rate was 8.8 percent. Following the 1981–1982 recession, the annual inflation rate moderated, and averaged 3.3 percent between 1983 and 2000. In 2000, the inflation rate was 3.4 percent. Note that between 1980 and 1983 and 1990 through 1992 the rate of inflation declined, meaning that disinflation occurred.

Consumer Price Index Criticisms

Just as there is criticism of the unemployment rate, the CPI is not a perfect measure of inflation, and it has been the subject of much public debate. There are three reasons for this criticism:

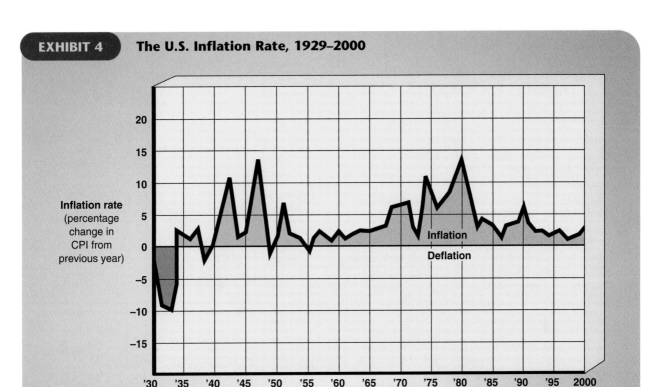

EXHIBIT 4   **The U.S. Inflation Rate, 1929–2000**

During the Great Depression, the economy experienced deflation as prices plunged. During and immediately after World War II, the annual rate of inflation reached the double-digit level. After 1950, and until the inflationary pressures from the Vietnam War in the late 1960s, the inflation rate was generally below 3 percent. During the 1950–1968 period, the average inflation rate was only 2 percent. In contrast, the inflation rate climbed sharply to an average of 7.6 percent between 1969 and 1982. Since 1983, inflation has moderated and has averaged 3.3 percent annually. In 2000, the inflation rate was 3.4 percent.

Source: Bureau of Labor Statistics, ftp://ftp.bls.gov/pub/special.requests/cpi/cpiai.txt.

1. Changes in the CPI are based on a typical basket of products purchased that does not match the actual market basket purchased by many consumers. Suppose you spend your nominal annual income entirely on lemonade, hot dogs, and jeans. During this year, the inflation rate is 5 percent, but assume the prices of lemonade, hot dogs, and jeans actually fall. In this case, your real income will rise, and the official inflation rate based on the CPI will *overstate* the impact of inflation on your standard of living. Retired persons, for example, buy a bundle of products that differs from that of the "typical" family. Because retired persons purchase proportionally more medical services than the typical family, the inflation rate may understate the impact of inflation on older persons.

Does It Cost More to Laugh?

Applicable Concept: consumer price index

Are we paying bigger bucks for smaller yuks? Or is it a lower fee for more glee? Is there a bone to pick with the price of rubber chickens? Is the price of Groucho glasses raising eyebrows, the cost of *Mad* magazine driving you mad, and, well, you get the idea.

Malcolm Kushner, an attorney-turned-humor consultant based in Santa Cruz, California, developed an index based on a compilation of leading humor indicators to measure price changes in things that make us laugh. Kushner created the cost-of-laughing index to track how trends in laughter affect the bottom line. He is a humor consultant who advises corporate leaders on making humor work for business professionals. For example, humor can make executives better public speakers, and laughter reduces stress and can even cure illnesses. Kushner believes humor is America's greatest asset, and his consulting business gets a lot of publicity from publication of the index. His latest book, *Public Speaking for Dummies and Leading with Laughter,* provides six audiocassettes of U.S. presidents successfully using humor. To combat rising humor costs, Kushner has established a Web site at http://www .kushnergroup.com. It organizes links to databases of funny quotes, anecdotes, one-liners, and other material for business speakers and writers.

The exhibit with the Groucho face traces annual percentage changes in the cost of laughing that Kushner has reported to the media. On an annual basis, the inflation rate for laughing did a belly flop from 4.4 percent in 1995 to 3 percent in 1996, where it has remained almost flat as a pancake through 2001.

Closer examination of the cost-of-laughing index over the years gives both happy and sad faces. The good news in 2001 is that the price of rubber chickens fell, but the bad news is that the price of a dancing chicken rose. The

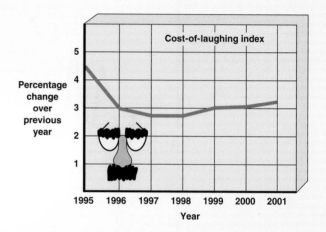

major reason for more expensive humor is the price of writing a half-hour television situation comedy. Just like the CPI, Kushner's index has been criticized. Note that the fee for writing a TV sitcom dominates the index. Kushner responds to this issue by saying, "Well, I wanted the index to be truly national. The fact that this price dominates the index reflects that TV comedy shows dominate our national culture. If you can laugh for free at a sitcom, you don't need to buy a rubber chicken or go to a comedy club."

ANALYZE THE ISSUE

No question here. This one is just for fun.

---

2. The BLS has difficulty adjusting the CPI for changes in *quality*. Compare a personal computer made in the past with a new personal computer. The new computer may cost somewhat more, but it is much better than the old computer. A portion of the price increase therefore reflects better quality instead of simply a higher price for the same item. If the quality of items improves, increases in the CPI *overstate* inflation. Similarly, deteriorating quality *understates* inflation. The BLS attempts to make adjustments for quality changes in automobiles, electronic equipment, and other products in the market basket, but these adjustments are difficult to determine accurately.

Cost-of-Laughing Index

Item	1998	1999	2000	2001
Rubber chicken[1]	$66.00	$60.00	$60.00	$48.00
Groucho glasses[1]	15.00	15.00	15.00	15.00
Poo-poo cushion[1]	6.00	6.00	5.40	5.40
Mad magazine[2]	2.50	2.50	2.99	2.99
Singing telegrams[3]				
Pink gorilla	75.00	75.00	85.00	85.00
Dancing chicken	65.00	75.00	75.00	85.00
Fee for writing a TV sitcom[4]	11,891.00	12,248.00	12,615.00	13,025.00
Comedy clubs[5]				
Atlanta: The Punch Line	15.00	14.00	14.00	18.15
Chicago: Second City	16.00	16.00	15.00	17.00
Denver: Comedy Club	8.00	10.00	11.00	15.00
Houston: Laff Stop	10.00	10.00	12.50	12.50
Indianapolis: Crackers Comedy	10.00	10.00	10.00	10.00
Los Angeles: Laugh Factory	10.00	10.00	12.00	12.00
New York: Comic Strip	12.00	12.00	14.00	15.00
Pittsburgh: The Funny Bone	11.00	11.00	12.00	12.00
San Francisco: Punch Line	12.00	12.00	15.00	15.00
Seattle: Comedy Underground	10.00	10.00	10.00	10.00
TOTAL COST OF HUMOR BASKET	$12,234.50	$12,596.50	$12,983.89	$13,403.04
ANNUAL INFLATION RATE	2.9%	3.0%	3.0%	3.2%

[1] One dozen wholesale from Franco-American Novelty Company, Long Island City, New York.
[2] April issue.
[3] Available from Bellygrams, Manhattan, New York.
[4] Minimum fee under Writers Guild of America basic agreement.
[5] Admission on Saturday night.
Source: Data provided by Malcolm Kushner.

3. The use of a single base-year market basket ignores the law of demand. If the price of a product rises, consumers purchase substitutes, and a smaller quantity is demanded. Suppose orange growers suffer from severe frosts and the supply of oranges decreases. Consequently, the price of oranges increases sharply. According to the *law of demand,* consumers will decrease the quantity demanded of oranges and substitute consumption of, say, apples for oranges. Because the market basket does not automatically change by reducing the percentage or weight of oranges and increasing the percentage of apples, the CPI will *overstate*

CHECKPOINT

The College Education Price Index

Suppose your *market basket* for a college education consisted of only the four items listed in the following table:

Item	2000	2001
Tuition and fees[1]	$2,500	$2,600
Room and board[2]	6,000	6,200
Books[3]	1,000	1,200
Soft drinks[4]	150	200

[1]Tuition for two semesters.
[2]Payment for nine months.
[3]Twenty books of 800 pages with full color.
[4]Three hundred 12-ounce Coca-Colas.

Using 2000 as your base year, what is the percentage change in the college education price index in 2001?

the impact of higher prices for oranges on the price level. To deal with this *substitution* bias problem, the BLS takes annual surveys to keep up with changing consumption patterns and correct for the fixed market basket limitations of the CPI.

Consequences of Inflation

We will now turn from measuring inflation to examining its effects on people's income and wealth. Why should inflation cause concern? As you will learn in this section, inflation is feared because it can significantly alter one's standard of living. You will see that inflation can create winners, who enjoy a larger slice of the national income pie, and losers, who receive a smaller slice as a result of inflation.

Inflation Shrinks Income

Economist Arthur Okun once stated, "This society is built on implicit and explicit contracts. . . . They are linked to the idea that the dollar means something. If you cannot depend on the value of the dollar, this system is undermined. People will constantly feel they've been fooled and cheated."[1] When prices rise, people worry whether the rise in their income will keep pace with inflation. And the more quickly prices rise, the more people suffer from the stresses of inflation and its uncertainties.

---

[1]"How Inflation Threatens the Fabric of U.S. Society," *Business Week,* May 22, 1978, p. 118.

Inflation tends to reduce your standard of living through declines in the purchasing power of money. The greater the rate of inflation, the greater the decline in the quantity of goods we can purchase with a given **nominal income,** or *money income.* Nominal income is the actual number of dollars received over a period of time. The source of income can be wages, salary, rent, dividends, interest, or pensions.

Nominal income does not measure your real purchasing power. Finding out if you are better or worse off over time requires converting nominal income to **real income.** Real income is the actual number of dollars received (nominal income) adjusted for changes in the CPI. Real income measures the amount of goods and services that can be purchased with one's nominal income. If the CPI increases and your nominal income remains the same, your real income (purchasing power) falls. In short, if your nominal income fails to keep pace with inflation, your standard of living falls. Suppose your nominal income in 1999 is $40,000 and the 1999 CPI value is 166.6. Your real income relative to a base year is:

Nominal income
The actual number of dollars received over a period of time.

Real income
The actual number of dollars received (nominal income) adjusted for changes in the CPI.

$$\text{real income} = \frac{\text{nominal income}}{\text{CPI (as decimal, or CPI/100)}}$$

$$\text{1999 real income} = \frac{\$40,000}{1.67} = \$23,952$$

Now assume your nominal income rises in 2000 by 10 percent, from $40,000 to $44,000, and the CPI increases by 3.4 percent, from 166.6 to 172.2. Thus, you earn more money, but how much better off are you? To answer this question, you must compute your 2000 real income as follows:

$$\text{2000 real income} = \frac{\$44,000}{1.72} = \$25,581$$

Using the preceding two computed real-income figures, the percentage change in real income between 1999 and 2000 was 6.8 percent ($1,629/ $23,952 × 100). This means that your standard of living has risen because you have an extra $1,629 to spend on movies, clothes, or travel. Even though the general price level has risen, your purchasing power has increased because the percentage rise in nominal income more than offsets the rate of inflation. Instead of precisely calculating this relationship, a good approximation can be obtained through the following simple formula:

Percentage change in real income	**=**	Percentage change in nominal income	**—**	Percentage change in CPI

Based on the examples given above, you can see why inflation can be a redistribution mechanism.

Conclusion *People whose nominal incomes rise faster than the rate of inflation gain purchasing power, while people whose nominal incomes do not keep pace with inflation lose.*

Inflation and Wealth

Wealth
The value of the stock of assets owned at some point in time.

Why worry about inflation? Because inflation erodes the purchasing power of assets. Visit http://www.fundselect.com/html/Inflation01.html.

Income is one measure of economic well-being, and **wealth** is another. Income is a flow of money earned by selling factors of production. Wealth is the value of the stock of assets owned at some point in time. Wealth includes real estate, stocks, bonds, bank accounts, life insurance policies, cash, and automobiles. A person can have a high income and little wealth, or great wealth and little income.

Inflation can benefit holders of wealth because the value of assets tends to increase as prices rise. Consider a home purchased in 1980 for $100,000. By the early 2000s, this home might sell for $200,000, largely as a result of inflation. Thus, people who own forms of wealth that can increase in value faster than the inflation rate, such as real estate, are often winners.

On the other hand, the impact of inflation on wealth penalizes people without it. Consider younger couples wishing to purchase a home. As prices rise, it becomes more difficult for them to buy a home or acquire other assets.

Inflation and the Real Interest Rate

Nominal interest rate
The actual rate of interest without adjustment for the inflation rate.

Real interest rate
The nominal rate of interest minus the inflation rate.

Borrowers and savers may be winners or losers, depending on the rate of inflation. Understanding how this might happen requires making a distinction between the **nominal interest rate** and the **real interest rate.** The nominal interest rate is the actual rate of interest earned over a period of time. The nominal interest rate, for example, is the interest rate specified on a loan or savings account. If you borrow $10,000 from a bank at a 10 percent annual interest rate for five years, this is more accurately called a 10 percent annual nominal interest rate. Similarly, a $10,000 certificate of deposit that yields 10 percent annual interest is said to have a 10 percent annual nominal interest rate.

The real interest rate is the nominal interest rate minus the inflation rate. The occurrence of inflation means that the real rate of interest will be less than the nominal rate. Suppose the inflation rate during the year is 5 percent. This means that a 10 percent annual nominal interest rate paid on a $10,000 loan amounts to a 5 percent *real interest rate* and a certificate of deposit that yields 10 percent annual nominal interest also earns 5 percent *real interest.*

For another perspective on real interest rates, see the Internet site maintained by Financial Pipeline (http://www.finpipe.com/rintrate.htm).

To understand how inflation can make those who borrow winners, suppose you receive a one-year loan from your parents to start a business. Earning a profit is not your parents' motive, and they know you will repay the loan. Their only concern is that you replace the decline in purchasing power of the money they loaned you. Both you and your parents anticipate the inflation rate will be 5 percent during the year, so the loan is made and you agree to repay the principal plus the 5 percent to offset inflation. In short, both parties assume payment of a zero real interest rate (the 5 percent nominal interest rate minus the 5 percent rate of inflation). Now consider what happens if the inflation rate is actually 10 percent during the year of the loan. The clear unintentional winner is you, the debtor, because your creditor parents are paid the principal plus 5 percent interest, but their purchasing power still falls by 5 percent because the actual inflation rate is 10 percent. Stated differently, instead of zero, the real interest rate paid on the loan was −5 percent (the 5 percent nominal interest rate minus the 10 percent rate of inflation). In real terms, your parents paid you to borrow from them.

During the late 1970s, the rate of inflation rose frequently. This forced mortgage lenders to protect themselves against declining real interest rates on their loans by offering adjustable-rate mortgages (ARMs) in addition to conventional fixed-rate mortgages.

A nest egg in the form of a savings account set aside for a rainy day is also affected by inflation. For example, if the interest rate on a one-year $10,000 certificate of deposit is 5 percent and the inflation rate is zero (5 percent real interest rate), the certificate holder will earn a 5 percent return on his or her savings. If the inflation rate exceeds the nominal rate of interest, the real interest rate is negative, and the saver is hurt because the interest earned does not keep pace with the inflation rate. This is the reason: Suppose, after one year, the saver withdraws the original $10,000 plus the $500 interest earned, and the inflation rate during the year has been 10 percent. The real value of $10,500 is only $9,545 ($10,500/1.1).

Finally, it is important to note that the nominal interest rate is never negative, but the real interest rate can be either positive or negative.

Conclusion *When the real rate of interest is negative, lenders and savers lose because interest earned does not keep up with the inflation rate.*

Demand-Pull and Cost-Push Inflation

Economists distinguish between two basic types of inflation, depending on whether it originates from the buyers' or the sellers' side of the market. The analysis presented in this section returns to the cause-and-effect relationship between total spending and the business cycle discussed in the previous chapter.

Demand-Pull Inflation

Perhaps the most familiar type of inflation is **demand-pull inflation,** which is a rise in the general price level resulting from an excess of total spending (demand). Demand-pull inflation is often expressed as "too much money chasing too few goods." When sellers are unable to supply all the goods and services buyers demand, sellers respond by raising prices. In short, the general price level in the economy is "pulled up" by the pressure from buyers' total expenditures.

Demand-pull inflation occurs at or close to full employment, when the economy is operating at or near full capacity. Recall that at full employment all but the frictionally and structurally unemployed are working and earning income. Therefore, total, or aggregate, demand for goods and services is high. Businesses find it profitable to expand their plants and production to

Demand-pull inflation
A rise in the general price level resulting from an excess of total spending (demand).

meet the buyers' demand, but cannot in the short run. As a result, national output remains fixed, and prices rise as buyers try to outbid one another for the available supply of goods and services. If total spending subsides, so will the pressure on the available supply of products, and prices will not rise as rapidly or may even fall.

A word of caution: Consumers may not be the only villain in the demand-pull story. Recall that total aggregate spending includes consumer spending (C), business investment (I), government spending (G), and net exports $(X - M)$. Even foreigners may contribute to inflation by bidding up the price of U.S. exports.

Cost-Push Inflation

Cost-push inflation

An increase in the general price level resulting from an increase in the cost of production.

An excess of total spending is not the only possible explanation for rising prices. In 1979, for example, the Organization of Petroleum Exporting Countries (OPEC) sharply increased the price of oil. This action meant a significant increase in the cost of producing goods and services. The result was **cost-push inflation**. Cost-push inflation is a rise in the general price level resulting from an increase in the cost of production.

The source of cost-push inflation is not always such a dramatic event as an OPEC price hike. Any increased costs to businesses are a potential source of cost-push inflation. This means that upward pressure on prices may be caused by cost increases for labor, raw materials, construction, equipment, borrowing, and so on. Businesses can also contribute to cost-push inflation by raising prices to increase profits.

The influence of *expectations* on both demand-pull and cost-push inflation is an important consideration. Suppose buyers see prices rise and believe they should purchase that new house or car today before these items cost much more tomorrow. At or near full employment, this demand-pull results in a rise in prices. On the suppliers' side, firms might expect their production costs to rise in the future, so they raise prices in anticipation of the higher costs. The result is cost-push inflation.

Here you should take note of a coming attraction. The chapter on aggregate demand and supply develops a modern macro model that you can use to analyze with more precision the factors that determine national output, employment, and the price level. In particular, the last section of this chapter applies the aggregate demand and supply model to the concepts of demand-pull and cost-push inflation.

Inflation in Other Countries

Inflation is not a distinctly American phenomenon. Exhibit 5 reveals that inflation rates vary widely among nations. In 2000, Turkey and Zimbabwe, for example, experienced very high rates of inflation. In contrast, the United Kingdom, the United States, and France had modest inflation rates.

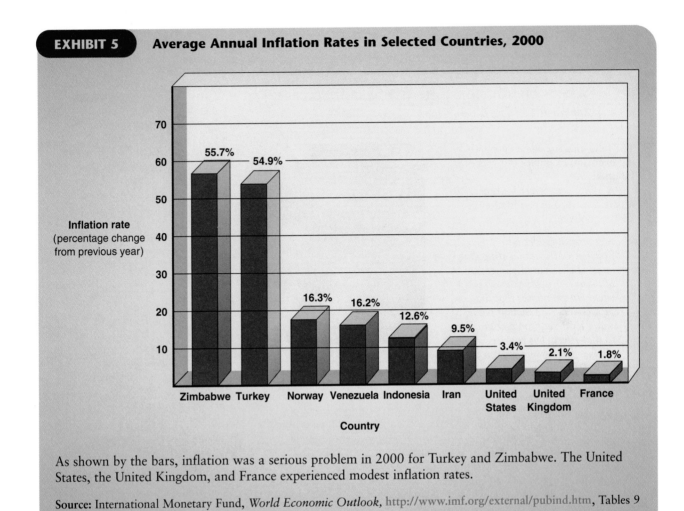

EXHIBIT 5 — **Average Annual Inflation Rates in Selected Countries, 2000**

As shown by the bars, inflation was a serious problem in 2000 for Turkey and Zimbabwe. The United States, the United Kingdom, and France experienced modest inflation rates.

Source: International Monetary Fund, *World Economic Outlook*, http://www.imf.org/external/pubind.htm, Tables 9 and 12.

Inflation on a Rampage

Some people must carry a large stack of money to pay for a chocolate bar because of the disastrous consequences of **hyperinflation.** Hyperinflation is an extremely rapid rise in the general price level. There is no consensus on when a particular rate of inflation becomes "hyper." However, most economists would agree that an inflation rate of about 100 percent per year or more is hyperinflation. Runaway inflation is conducive to rapid and violent social and political change stemming from four causes.

First, individuals and businesses develop an *inflation psychosis,* causing them to buy quickly today in order to avoid paying even more tomorrow. Everyone feels pressure to spend earnings before their purchasing power deteriorates. No matter whether you are paid once, twice, or any number of times per day, you will be eager to spend it immediately.

Hyperinflation
An extremely rapid rise in the general price level.

Read more about some interesting episodes of hyperinflation around the world (http://www.sjsu.edu/faculty/watkins/hyper.htm).

INTERNATIONAL ECONOMICS

When the Inflation Rate Is 116,000 Percent, Prices Change by the Hour

Applicable Concept: hyperinflation

The following are some outstanding historical examples of hyperinflation.

A 1985 *Wall Street Journal* article described hyperinflation in La Paz, Bolivia:

A courier stumbles into Banco Boliviano Americano, struggling under the weight of a huge bag of money he is carrying on his back. He announces that the sack contains 32 million pesos, and a teller slaps on a notation to that effect. The courier pitches the bag into a corner. "We don't bother counting the money anymore," explains Max Lowes Stah, a loan officer standing nearby. "We take the client's word for what's in the bag." Pointing to the courier's load, he says, "That's a small deposit." At that moment the 32 million pesos—enough bills to stuff a mail sack—were worth only $500. Today, less than two weeks later, they are worth at least $180 less. Life's like that with quadruple-digit inflation. . . .

Prices go up by the day, the hour or the customer. If the pace continues all year it would mean an annual rate of 116,000 percent. The 1,000-peso bill, the most commonly used, costs more to print than it purchases. To purchase an average-size television set with 1,000 peso bills, customers have to haul money weighing more than 68 pounds into the showroom. Inflation makes use of credit cards impossible here, and merchants generally can't take checks, either. Restaurant owners often covered their menus with cellophane and

changed prices several times daily using a dry-erase marker.[1]

In 1989, inflation in Argentina was about 3,500 percent; 2,500 percent in Peru; 1,200 percent in Brazil; 1,400 percent in Bulgaria, and 200 percent in Poland.

A 1993 Associated Press article reported a rate of inflation in the billions for Belgrade, Yugoslavia:

The number Wednesday was 286,125,293,792. It was not the day's winning lottery figures nor the number of miles to the Hubble space telescope. It was the latest calculation of Yugoslavia's nearly incalculable inflation rate. . . . To cover the costs of war and pay off the unemployed, the government has resorted to indiscriminately printing money. That has rendered the national currency, the dinar, practically worthless. . . . "Look at the prices," Spomenka Magas, 39, a homemaker said in disgust, "I cannot count all the zeroes anymore."[2]

A 2001 *Newsweek* article made the following observation:

Hyperinflation is the worst economic malady that can

befall a nation, wiping out the value of money, savings, assets, and thus work. It is worse even than a deep recession. Hyperinflation robs you of what you have now (savings), whereas a recession robs you of what you might have had (higher standards of living if the economy had grown). That's why it so often toppled governments and produced revolution. Recall that it was not the Great Depression that brought the Nazis to power in Germany but rather hyperinflation, which destroyed the middle class of that country by making its savings worthless.[3]

ANALYZE THE ISSUE

1. Can you relate inflation psychosis to these excerpts? Give an example of a debtor-lender relationship that is jeopardized by hyperinflation.

2. Explain why the workers in Bolivia were striking even though wages rose at an annual rate of 1,500 percent. Do you see any connection between hyperinflation and the political system?

[1]Sonia L. Nazario, "When Inflation Rate Is 116,000 Percent, Prices Change by the Hour," *Wall Street Journal*, Feb. 7, 1985, p. 1.
[2]Slobodan Lekic, "Belgrade Puts Rate of Inflation in Billions," *Charlotte Observer*, Dec. 2, 1993, p. 24A.
[3]Fareed Zakaria, "Is This the End of Inflation? Turkey's Currency Crisis May Be the Last Battle in the Global War Against Hyperinflation," *Newsweek*, Mar. 19, 2001, p. 38.

Second, huge unanticipated inflation jeopardizes debtor-lender contracts, such as credit cards, home mortgages, life insurance policies, pensions, bonds, and other forms of savings. For example, if nominal interest rates rise unexpectedly in response to higher inflation, borrowers find it more difficult to make their monthly payments.

Third, hyperinflation sets a **wage-price spiral** in motion. A wage-price spiral occurs in a series of steps when increases in nominal wage rates are passed on in higher prices, which, in turn, result in even higher nominal wage rates and prices. A wage-price spiral continues when management believes it can boost prices faster than the rise in labor costs. As the cost of living moves higher, however, labor must again demand even higher wage increases. Each round yields higher and higher prices as wages and prices chase each other in an upward spiral.

Fourth, because the future rate of inflation is difficult or impossible to anticipate, people turn to more speculative investments that might yield higher financial returns. To hedge against the high losses of purchasing power from hyperinflation, funds flow into gold, silver, stamps, jewels, art, antiques, and other currencies, rather than new factories, machinery, and technological research, which expand an economy's production possibilities curve.

History reveals numerous hyperinflation examples. One of the most famous occurred during the 1920s in the German Weimar Republic. Faced with huge World War I reparations payments, the Weimar government simply printed money to pay its bills. By late 1923, the annual inflation rate in Germany had reached 35,000 percent per month. Prices rose frequently, sometimes increasing in minutes, and German currency became so worthless that it was used as kindling for stoves. No one was willing to make new loans, and credit markets collapsed. Wealth was redistributed as those who were heavily in debt easily paid their debts and people's savings were wiped out.

Finally, hyperinflation is invariably the result of a government's ill-advised decision to increase a country's money supply. Moreover, hyperinflation is not a historical relic, as illustrated in the previous International Economics article.

Wage-price spiral

A situation that occurs when increases in nominal wage rates are passed on in higher prices, which, in turn, result in even higher nominal wage rates and prices.

KEY CONCEPTS

Inflation	Base year	Wealth	Cost-push inflation
Deflation	Disinflation	Nominal interest rate	Hyperinflation
Consumer price index (CPI)	Nominal income	Real interest rate	Wage-price spiral
	Real income	Demand-pull inflation	

SUMMARY

- **Inflation** is an increase in the general (average) price level of goods and services in the economy.

- The **consumer price index** (CPI) is the most widely known price-level index. It measures the cost of purchasing a market basket of goods and services by a typical household during a time period relative to the cost of the same bundle during a base year. The annual rate of inflation is computed using the following formula:

  annual rate of inflation =

  $$\frac{\text{CPI in given year} - \text{CPI in previous year}}{\text{CPI in previous year}} \times 100$$

- **Deflation** is a decrease in the general level of prices. During the early years of the Great Depression, there was deflation, and the CPI declined at about a double-digit rate.

- **Disinflation** is a reduction in the inflation rate. This does not mean that prices were falling, but only that the inflation rate fell.

- The **inflation rate** determined by the CPI is criticized because (1) it is not representative, (2) it incorrectly adjusts for quality changes, (3) it ignores the relationship between price changes and the importance of items in the market basket.

- **Nominal income** is income measured in actual money amounts. Measuring your purchasing power requires converting nominal income into **real income**, which is nominal income adjusted for inflation.

- The **real interest rate** is the *nominal interest rate* adjusted for inflation. If real interest rates are negative, lenders incur losses.

- **Demand-pull inflation** is caused by pressure on prices originating from the buyers' side of the market. In contrast, **cost-push inflation** is caused by pressure on prices originating from the sellers' side of the market.

- **Hyperinflation** can seriously disrupt an economy by causing inflation psychosis, credit market collapses, a wage-price spiral, and speculation. A **wage-price spiral** occurs when increases in nominal wages cause higher prices, which, in turn, cause higher wages and prices.

SUMMARY OF CONCLUSION STATEMENTS

- Inflation is an increase in the overall average level of prices and not an increase in the price of any specific product.

- People whose nominal incomes rise faster than the rate of inflation gain purchasing power, while people whose nominal incomes do not keep pace with inflation lose.

- When the real rate of interest is negative, lenders and savers lose because interest earned does not keep up with the inflation rate.

STUDY QUESTIONS AND PROBLEMS

1. Consider this statement: "When the price of a good or service rises, the inflation rate rises." Do you agree or disagree? Explain.

2. Suppose, in the 1982 base year, a typical market basket purchased by an urban family cost $250. In 2001, the same market basket cost $1,000. What is the consumer price index (CPI) for 2001? If the same market basket cost $950 in 2000, what was the 2001 annual rate of inflation?

3. What are four criticisms of the CPI?

4. Suppose you earned $100,000 per year in 2001. Using 1982 as the base year, calculate your real 2001 income measured in 1982 dollars, assuming the CPI is 200 in 2001.

5. Explain how a person's purchasing power can decline in a given year even though he or she received a salary increase.

6. Who loses from inflation? Who wins from inflation?

7. Suppose you borrow $100 from a bank at 5 percent interest for one year and the inflation rate that year is 10 percent. Was this loan advantageous to you or to the bank?

8. Suppose the annual nominal rate of interest on a bank certificate of deposit is 12 percent. What would be the effect of an inflation rate of 13 percent?

9. Describe the likely impact on the income of each of the following individuals if the inflation rate is 10 percent per year:

a. Social Security recipient
b. Welfare recipient
c. UAW auto worker
d. Federal income taxpayer
e. Self-employed owner of a small restaurant

10. When the economy approaches full employment, why does demand-pull inflation become a problem?

11. How does demand-pull inflation differ from cost-push inflation?

12. Explain this statement: "If everyone expects inflation to occur, it will."

ONLINE EXERCISES

Exercise 1

Visit Economy at a Glance (http://www.bls.gov/eag/eag.us.htm), and follow these steps:

1. After Employment Cost Index, click the corresponding stairstep bar graph icon, and study the graph for percentage change in wages and salaries and benefit costs.

2. After Consumer Price Index, click the corresponding stairstep bar graph icon, and study the percentage change in the CPI.

Compare the two graphs since 1988.

Exercise 2

Go to http://www.homefair.com/calc/salcalc.html, and calculate the cost of living difference between your hometown and a city you might want to live in. What is the difference in real income between these two cities?

Exercise 3

Visit the Dismal Scientist, a company that provides economic data, analysis, and forecasts on the Internet (http://www.dismal.com/dismal/default.asp). Click on "forecasts," and request annual forecasts for prices. Is the inflation rate expected to move up or down?

CHECKPOINT ANSWER

The College Education Price Index

$$\frac{\text{2000 college education}}{\text{price index}} = \frac{\text{market basket cost at 2000 prices}}{\text{market basket cost at base-year (2000) prices}} \times 100 = \frac{\$9,650}{\$9,650} = 100$$

$$\frac{\text{2001 college education}}{\text{price index}} = \frac{\text{market basket cost at 2001 prices}}{\text{market basket cost at base-year (2000) prices}} \times 100 = \frac{\$10,200}{\$9,650} = 105.7$$

$$\frac{\text{Percentage change in price}}{\text{level of college education}} = \frac{105.7 - 100}{100} \times 100 = 5.7\%$$

If you said the price of a college education increased 5.7 percent in 2001, YOU ARE CORRECT.

PRACTICE QUIZ

For a visual explanation of the correct answers, visit the tutorial at http://tucker.swcollege.com.

1. Inflation is
   a. an increase in the general price level.
   b. not a concern during war.
   c. a result of high unemployment.
   d. an increase in the relative price level.

2. If the consumer price index in Year X was 300 and the CPI in Year Y was 315, the rate of inflation was
   a. 5 percent.
   b. 15 percent.
   c. 25 percent.
   d. 315 percent.

3. Consider an economy with only two goods: bread and wine. In 1982, the typical family bought 4 loaves of bread at 50 cents per loaf and 2 bottles of wine for $9 per bottle. In 2001, bread cost 75 cents per loaf, and wine cost $10 per bottle. The CPI for 2001 (using a 1982 base year) is
   a. 100.
   b. 115.
   c. 126.
   d. 130.

Exhibit 6 Consumer Price Index

Year	Consumer price index
1	100
2	110
3	115
4	120
5	125

4. As shown in Exhibit 6, the rate of inflation for Year 2 is
   a. 5 percent.
   b. 10 percent.
   c. 20 percent.
   d. 25 percent.

5. As shown in Exhibit 6, the rate of inflation for Year 5 is
   a. 4.2 percent.
   b. 5 percent.
   c. 20 percent.
   d. 25 percent.

6. Deflation is a(an)
   a. increase in most prices.
   b. decrease in the general price level.
   c. situation that has never occurred in U.S. history.
   d. decrease in the inflation rate.

7. Which of the following would overstate the consumer price index?
   a. Substitution bias
   b. Improving quality of products
   c. Neither a nor b
   d. Both a and b

8. Suppose a typical automobile tire cost $50 in the base year and had a useful life of 40,000 miles. Ten years later, the typical automobile tire cost $75 and had a useful life of 75,000 miles. If no adjustment is made for mileage, the CPI would
   a. underestimate inflation between the two years.
   b. overestimate inflation between the two years.
   c. accurately measure inflation between the two years.
   d. not measure inflation in this case.

9. When the inflation rate rises, the purchasing power of nominal income
   a. remains unchanged.
   b. decreases.
   c. increases.
   d. changes by the inflation rate minus one.

10. Last year the Harrison family earned $50,000. This year their income is $52,000. In an economy with an inflation rate of 5 percent, which of the following is correct?
    a. The Harrisons' nominal income and real income have both risen.
    b. The Harrisons' nominal income and real income have both fallen.
    c. The Harrisons' nominal income has fallen, and their real income has risen.
    d. The Harrisons' nominal income has risen, and their real income has fallen.

11. If the nominal rate of interest is less than the inflation rate,
    a. lenders win.
    b. savers win.
    c. the real interest rate is negative.
    d. the economy is at full employment.

12. Demand-pull inflation is caused by
    a. monopoly power.
    b. energy cost increases.
    c. tax increases.
    d. full employment.

13. Cost-push inflation is due to
    a. excess total spending.
    b. too much money chasing too few goods.
    c. resource cost increases.
    d. the economy operating at full employment.

PART 6

Macroeconomic Theory and Policy

This part begins with two chapters that present a theoretical model originating in a book published in 1936 by British economist John Maynard Keynes. The purpose of the Keynesian model is to understand the causes and cures of the Great Depression. The next chapter explains another theoretical macro model based on aggregate demand and aggregate supply. The following chapter discusses the federal government's taxing and spending policies, and the next chapter explains actual data measures of government spending and taxation patterns. The part concludes with a chapter on hotly debated topics: federal deficits, surpluses, and the national debt.

CHAPTER 18

The Keynesian Model

In U.S. history, the 1920s are known as the "Roaring 20s." It was a time of optimism and prosperity. Between 1920 and 1929, real GDP rose by 42 percent. Stock prices soared year after year and made many investors rich. As business boomed, companies invested in new factories, and the U.S. economy was a job-creating machine. People bought fine clothes, had parties, and danced the popular Charleston. Then the business cycle took an abrupt downturn on October 29, 1929, Black Thursday. The most severe recession in recent U.S. history had begun. During the Great Depression, stock prices fell. Wages fell. Real output fell. Banks failed. Businesses closed their doors, and the unemployment rate soared to 25 percent. Men would fight over a job, sell apples on the corner to survive, and walk the streets in bewilderment.

The misery of the Great Depression created a revolution in economic thought. Prior to the Great Depression, economists recognized that over the years business downturns would interrupt the nation's prosperity, but they believed these episodes were temporary. They argued that in a short time the price system would automatically restore an economy to full employment without government intervention.

Why didn't the economy self-correct to its 1929 level of real output? What went wrong? The stage was set for a new idea offered by British econo-mist **John Maynard Keynes** (pronounced "canes"). Keynes argued that the economy was not self-correcting and therefore could indeed remain below full employment indefinitely because of inadequate aggregate spending. Keynes's work not only explained the crash, but also offered cures requiring the government to play an active role in the economy.

Whether or not economists agree with Keynes's ideas, this great economist still influences macroeconomics today. This chapter begins with a discussion of classical economic theory before Keynes. Then you will learn what determines the level of consumption and investment expenditures. Finally, these components form a simple Keynesian model.

In this chapter, you will learn to solve these economics puzzles:

- Why did economists believe the Great Depression was impossible?

- What are the components of the Keynesian Cross?

■ Why did Keynes believe that "animal spirits" and government policy were important to maintain full employment?

John Maynard Keynes

British economist (1883–1946) whose influential work offered an explanation of the Great Depression and suggested, as a cure, that the government should play an active role in the economy.

Introducing Classical Theory and the Keynesian Revolution

Prior to the Great Depression of the 1930s, a group of economists known as the **classical economists** dominated economic thinking.[1] The founder of the classical school of economics was Adam Smith (discussed in the chapter on economies in transition). Macroeconomics had not developed as a separate economic theory, and classical economics was therefore based primarily on microeconomic market equilibrium theory. The classical school of economics was mainstream economics from the 1770s to the Great Depression era. The classical economists believed in the *laissez-faire* "leave it alone" theory that our economy was self-regulating and would correct itself without government interference. The classical economists believed, as you studied in Chapter 4, that the forces of supply and demand naturally achieve full employment in the economy because flexible prices (including wages and interest rates) in competitive markets bring all markets to equilibrium. After a temporary adjustment period, markets always clear because firms sell all goods and services offered for sale. In short, recessions would naturally cure themselves because the capitalistic price system would automatically restore full employment. The classical model is explained in more detail in the chapter on aggregate demand and supply.

> **Conclusion** *The classical economists believed that a continuing depression is impossible because markets eliminate persistent shortages or surpluses.*

The simple idea known as **Say's Law**, developed in the early 1800s by *Jean Baptiste Say*, convinced classical economists that a prolonged depression was impossible. Say's Law is the theory that supply creates its own demand. Say's Law was the cornerstone of classical economics. Simply put, this theory states that long-term underspending is impossible because the

Classical economists

A group of economists whose theory dominated economic thinking from the 1770s to the Great Depression. They believed recessions would naturally cure themselves because the price system would automatically restore full employment.

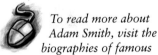

To read more about Adam Smith, visit the biographies of famous Edinburghers, maintained by the city of Edinburgh, Scotland, where Adam Smith was born (http://www.ebs.hw.ac.uk/EDC/edinburghers/biographies.html).

Say's Law

The theory that supply creates its own demand.

---

[1]The classical economists included Adam Smith, J. B. Say, David Ricardo, John Stuart Mill, Thomas Malthus, Alfred Marshall, and others.

production of goods and services (supply) generates an equal amount of total spending (demand) for these goods and services. Recall the circular flow model explained in the chapter on GDP. Suppose a firm produces $1 worth of bread in the product market. This supply decision creates $1 of income to the household sector through the factor markets. In other words, Say's Law is a theory that a glut of unsold products causing workers to lose their jobs is a temporary problem because there is just the right amount of income in the economy to purchase all products without layoffs.

Conclusion *In the classical view, unemployment is the result of a short-lived adjustment period in which wages and prices decline or people voluntarily choose not to work. Thus, there is a natural tendency for the economy to restore full employment over time.*

In 1936, seven years after the beginning of the Great Depression and three years before the beginning of World War II, John Maynard Keynes published *The General Theory of Employment, Interest, and Money.*[2] Keynes wrote in a time of great uncertainty and instability. In his book, Keynes, a Cambridge University economist, challenged the baffled classical economists by turning Say's Law upside down. Keynesian theory argues that "demand creates its own supply." Keynes explained that *aggregate expenditures (demand)* can be forever inadequate for an economy to achieve full employment. Aggregate expenditures are the sum of consumption (C), investment (I), government spending (G), and net exports (X − M). Aggregate expenditures are also known as *aggregate spending* and *aggregate demand*. Recall from the chapter on GDP that you learned that C, I, G, and (X − M) are national accounting categories used to calculate GDP following the expenditures approach. The remainder of this chapter is devoted to Keynes's theory for the determination of consumption and investment expenditures. The government and net exports expenditure components are developed in the next chapter.

The Consumption Function

What determines your family's spending for food, clothing, automobiles, education, and other consumer goods and services? According to Keynes, the most important factor is disposable income (personal income to spend after taxes; see Exhibit 9 in the chapter on GDP). Keynes argued it is a fundamental psychological law that if take-home pay increases, consumers increase their spending and saving. Keynes's focus on the relationship between consumption and disposable income is represented by the **consumption function**. The consumption function shows the amount households spend for goods and services at different levels of disposable income. Recall from Exhibit 2 in the chapter on GDP that consumption is the largest single component of aggregate expenditures.

Consumption function

The graph or table that shows the amount households spend for goods and services at different levels of disposable income.

---

[2]John Maynard Keynes, *The General Theory of Employment, Interest, and Money* (New York: Harcourt, Brace, and World, 1936).

EXHIBIT 1 Consumption Function ($Y_d = C + S$)

(1) Real disposable income (Y_d)	(2) Consumption (C)	(3) Saving (S)
$ 0	$1.00	-$1.00
1.00	1.75	-0.75
2.00	2.50	-0.50
3.00	3.25	-0.25
4.00	4.00	0
5.00	4.75	0.25
6.00	5.50	0.50
7.00	6.25	0.75
8.00	7.00	1.00

Note: All amounts are in trillions of dollars per year.

Exhibit 1 provides data on real disposable income (Y_d) in column 1, consumption (C) in column 2, and saving (S) in column 3 for a hypothetical economy. Since households spend each dollar of real disposable income either for consumption or for saving, the formula for saving is

$$S = Y_d - C$$

From the above equation, it follows that

$$Y_d = C + S$$

Exhibit 2 charts the consumption function using the real disposable income and consumption data given in columns 1 and 2 in Exhibit 1. At low levels of disposable income, households spend more on consumer goods and services than they earn during the year. If annual real disposable income is any level below $4 trillion, households **dissave**. Dissaving is the amount by which personal consumption expenditures exceed disposable income. Negative saving or dissaving is financed by drawing down previously accumulated financial assets, such as savings accounts, stocks, and bonds, or by borrowing. At a real disposable income of $2 trillion per year, for example, families spend $2.5 trillion and thereby dissave $.5 trillion.

Note that if disposable income is zero, consumption expenditures will be $1 trillion of **autonomous consumption**. Autonomous consumption is consumption that is independent of the level of disposable income. It is the amount of consumption expenditures that occur even when disposable income is zero. In the event disposable income is zero, households will dissave to satisfy basic consumption needs.

Dissaving
The amount by which personal consumption expenditures exceed disposable income.

Autonomous consumption
Consumption that is independent of the level of disposable income.

The exhibit shows the consumption function for a hypothetical economy. The break-even income is $4 trillion real disposable income, where households spend each dollar of real disposable income, $C = Y_d$, and savings are zero. Below $4 trillion, households spend more than their real disposable income by borrowing or withdrawing from past savings. Above the break-even income, households spend less than their real disposable income, and saving occurs. The marginal propensity to consume (*MPC*) is 0.75 because the slope of the consumption schedule shows that for each dollar increase in income (ΔY_d), consumption increases (ΔC) by 75 cents, and the remaining 25 cents is saved.

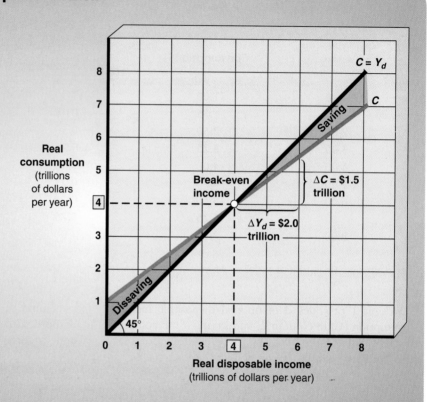

Exhibit 2 represents dissaving as the vertical distance below the consumption function to the *45-degree line.* The 45-degree line is a geometric construct that makes it easier to identify the *break-even* or *no-saving income,* which equates aggregate real disposable income measured on the horizontal axis and consumption on the vertical axis. In our example, $C = Y_d$ at $4 trillion, where households spend every dollar earned and saving is therefore zero.

The consumption function has a positive slope because consumption spending increases with real disposable income. At higher levels beyond the break-even income, households earn more income than they wish to spend, and a portion of income is **saved.** Saving is the part of disposable income households do not spend for consumer goods and services. In Exhibit 2, positive saving is the vertical distance above the consumption function to the 45-degree line. For example, at a disposable income of $8 trillion, households save $1 trillion.

Saving

The part of disposable income households do not spend for consumer goods and services.

Marginal Propensities to Consume and Save

Keynes argued that as income grows, so does consumption, but by less than income. This crucial concept is called the **marginal propensity to consume** (**MPC**). The marginal propensity to consume is the change in consumption resulting from a given change in real disposable income. Stated differently, the MPC is the ratio of the change in consumption (ΔC) to the change in real disposable income (ΔY_d). The Greek letter Δ (delta) means "a change in." Mathematically,

$$MPC = \frac{\text{change in consumption}}{\text{change in real disposable income}} = \frac{\Delta C}{\Delta Y_d}$$

Marginal propensity to consume (MPC)

The change in consumption resulting from a given change in real disposable income.

Exhibit 3 reproduces and expands the data from Exhibit 1. As shown in column 4 of Exhibit 3, the MPC is 0.75. This means for every dollar increase (decrease) in disposable income (ΔY_d), consumption (ΔC) increases (decreases) 75 cents. In each model developed throughout this text, we assume the MPC is constant for all income levels. In our numerical example, real disposable income rises by $1 trillion between each level of income listed in column 1 of Exhibit 3, and consumption rises by $.75 trillion. Mathematically,

For a look at actual data showing the relationship between per capita income and personal consumption expenditures visit http://infoplease.lycos .com/ipa/A0104550.html.

$$MPC = \frac{\Delta C}{\Delta Y_d} = \frac{\$.75 \text{ trillion}}{\$1 \text{ trillion}} = 0.75$$

EXHIBIT 3 Consumption, Saving, *MPC*, and *MPS* Data

(1) Real disposable income (Y_d)	(2) Consumption (C)	(3) Saving (S)	(4) Marginal propensity to consume (MPC) [$\Delta C/\Delta Y_d$ or $\Delta 2/\Delta 1$]	(5) Marginal propensity to save (MPS) [$\Delta S/\Delta Y_d$ or $\Delta 3/\Delta 1$]
$ 0	$1.00	−$1.00	—	—
1.00	1.75	−0.75	0.75	0.25
2.00	2.50	−0.50	0.75	0.25
3.00	3.25	−0.25	0.75	0.25
4.00	4.00	0	0.75	0.25
5.00	4.75	0.25	0.75	0.25
6.00	5.50	0.50	0.75	0.25
7.00	6.25	0.75	0.75	0.25
8.00	7.00	1.00	0.75	0.25

Note: All amounts are in trillions of dollars per year.

Marginal propensity to save (MPS)

The change in saving resulting from a given change in real disposable income.

What do households do with an extra dollar of real disposable income if they do not spend it? They save it. The **marginal propensity to save (MPS)** is the change in savings resulting from a given change in real disposable income. That is, the MPS is the ratio of the change in saving (ΔS) to the change in real disposable income (ΔY_d). Mathematically,

$$MPS = \frac{\text{change in saving}}{\text{change in real disposable income}} = \frac{\Delta S}{\Delta Y_d}$$

The *MPS* given in column 5 of Exhibit 3 is 0.25. Each dollar increase (decrease) in disposable income (ΔY_d) yields a rise (fall) of 25 cents in the amount of savings (ΔS). Mathematically,

$$MPS = \frac{\Delta S}{\Delta Y_d} = \frac{\$.25 \text{ trillion}}{\$1 \text{ trillion}} = 0.25$$

As derived previously, $Y_d = C + S$, so it follows that $\Delta C + \Delta S = \Delta Y_d$. Dividing both sides of this equation by ΔY_d yields

$$\frac{\Delta C}{\Delta Y_d} + \frac{\Delta S}{\Delta Y_d} = \frac{\Delta Y_d}{\Delta Y_d}$$

or

$$MPC + MPS = 1$$

In our example, $0.75 + 0.25 = 1$, which means any change in real disposable income is divided between changes in consumption and changes in saving. Hence, if you know the *MPC*, you can calculate the *MPS* and vice versa.

In addition to the consumption function, Exhibit 2 shows a graphic representation of the *MPC*. The *MPC* (slope) of the consumption function, *C*, between $4 trillion and $6 trillion is measured by dividing $\Delta C = \$1.5$ trillion (the rise) by $\Delta Y_d = \$2.0$ trillion (the run). Since the *MPC* is constant, the ratio $\Delta C/\Delta Y_d$ between any two levels of real disposable income is 0.75. As a formula:

$$\text{slope of consumption function} = \frac{\text{rise}}{\text{run}} = \frac{\Delta C}{\Delta Y_d} = \frac{\$1.5 \text{ trillion}}{\$2.0 \text{ trillion}} = 0.75$$

The points along the consumption function, *C*, in Exhibit 2 can be expressed by the following equation:

$$C = a + bY_d$$

CHECKPOINT

What's Your *MPC*?

As your income increases over time, your marginal propensity to consume (*MPC*) can remain constant, or it can change. Would you expect your *MPC* to increase, decrease, or remain constant as your income increases throughout your career?

where *a* is autonomous consumption and *b* is the *MPC*, which falls between 0 and 1. Keynes used this basic equation to derive consumption (*C*), and it is called the Keynesian consumption function.

Using this equation,

$$C = \$1 \text{ trillion} + 0.75Y_d$$

For example, at $Y_d = \$4$ trillion,

$$C = \$1 \text{ trillion} + 0.75(\$4 \text{ trillion})$$
$$C = \$4 \text{ trillion}$$

Note that only at $4 trillion real disposable income does consumption equal this amount, as represented by the intersection of the *C* line and the 45-degree line. To demonstrate the relationship between the *MPC* and various levels of consumption, Exhibit 4 shows two consumption functions that have the same autonomous consumption of $1 trillion, but each has a different slope. C_1 has an *MPC* of 0.50, and C_2 has a larger *MPC* of 0.75. Thus, the higher the marginal propensity to consume, the steeper the consumption function.

The key conclusion drawn from this analysis so far is this: *There is a direct relationship between changes in real disposable income and changes in consumption.* For example, suppose there is an income-tax cut. As a result, real disposable income (Y_d) increases and, in turn, induces an upward movement along the consumption function. An income-tax hike, on the other hand, reduces real disposable income and causes a downward movement along the consumption function.

A Historical Consumption Function

Exhibit 5 provides evidence that supports Keynes's theoretical consumption function. Note the use of the 45-degree line again. During the Great Depression, families spent more than their real disposable income, and dissaving occurred. As a result, people were forced to dip into their savings or borrow. As real disposable income increased after the Great Depression, the level of personal consumption spending increased, and households continued to save a portion of their real disposable income.

EXHIBIT 4   **Consumption Functions for Two Marginal Propensities to Consume**

The *MPC* is the slope of the consumption function. Here two consumption functions are shown for *MPC*s of 0.50 and 0.75. The autonomous consumption of $1 trillion is the same for each consumption function. The higher the *MPC*, the steeper the consumption function.

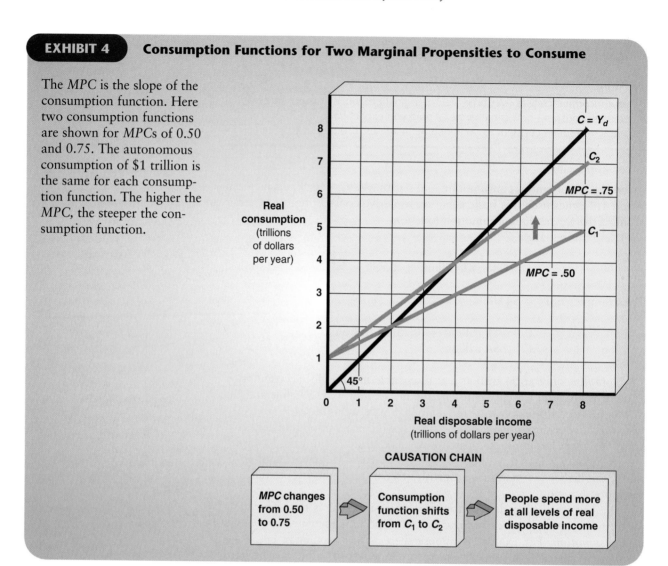

CAUSATION CHAIN

MPC changes from 0.50 to 0.75 ⇒ Consumption function shifts from C_1 to C_2 ⇒ People spend more at all levels of real disposable income

Reasons the Consumption Function Shifts

Just as nonprice factors in the market supply and demand model, such as consumer tastes and income, shift the demand curve, changes in certain *nonincome* factors cause the consumption function to shift.

Conclusion *A change in real disposable income is the sole cause of a movement along the consumption function. A shift or relocation in the consumption schedule occurs when a factor other than real disposable income changes.*

| EXHIBIT 5 | U.S. Personal Consumption and Disposable Income, 1933–2000 |

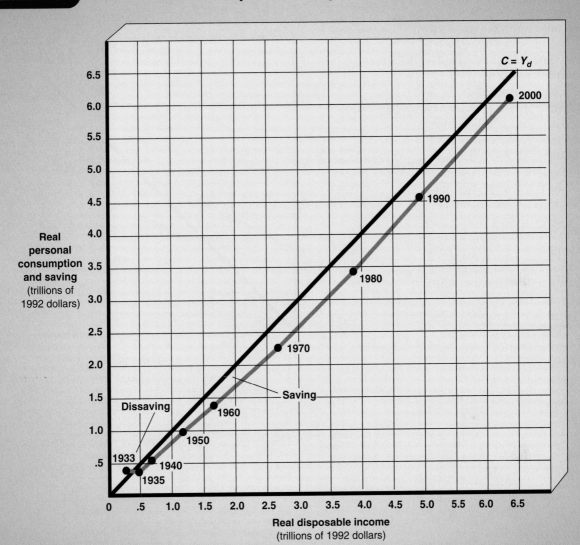

Keynes argued that a fundamental psychological law exists whereby real disposable income strongly influences real consumption. Actual data on real personal consumption expenditures and real disposable income are consistent with Keynes's theory.

Source: *Survey of Current Business,* http://www.bea.doc.gov/bea/dnl.htm, Tables 1.2, 2A, and 4.

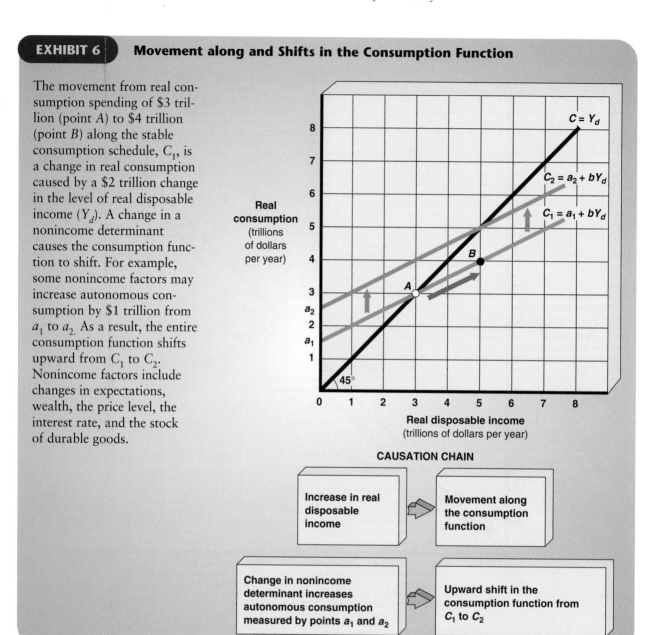

EXHIBIT 6   **Movement along and Shifts in the Consumption Function**

The movement from real consumption spending of $3 trillion (point A) to $4 trillion (point B) along the stable consumption schedule, C_1, is a change in real consumption caused by a $2 trillion change in the level of real disposable income (Y_d). A change in a nonincome determinant causes the consumption function to shift. For example, some nonincome factors may increase autonomous consumption by $1 trillion from a_1 to a_2. As a result, the entire consumption function shifts upward from C_1 to C_2. Nonincome factors include changes in expectations, wealth, the price level, the interest rate, and the stock of durable goods.

CAUSATION CHAIN

| Increase in real disposable income | ⇨ | Movement along the consumption function |
| Change in nonincome determinant increases autonomous consumption measured by points a_1 and a_2 | ⇨ | Upward shift in the consumption function from C_1 to C_2 |

Exhibit 6 illustrates this difference in terminology. The sole cause of the change in consumption spending from $3 trillion (point A) to $4 trillion (point B) along the stable consumption schedule, C_1, is a $2 trillion change in the level of real disposable income. A change in a nonincome determinant, on the other hand, can cause the consumption schedule to shift upward from $C_1 = a_1 + bY_d$ to $C_2 = a_2 + bY_d$. As a result, households spend an extra $1 trillion $(a_2 - a_1)$ at each point along C_2. This means that the level of autonomous consumption has increased by $1 trillion from $1.5 trillion to $2.5 trillion because of some influence other than current Y_d. Nonincome variables that can shift the consumption schedule include expectations, wealth, the price level, the interest rate, and the stock of durable goods.

Expectations

Consumer expectations are optimistic or pessimistic views of the future which can change consumption spending in the present. Expectations may involve the future inflation rate, the likelihood of becoming unemployed, the likelihood of receiving higher income, or the future shortage of products resulting from a war or other circumstances. Suppose households believe prices will be much higher next year and buy now, rather than paying more in the future. The effect of such expectations would be to trigger current spending and shift the consumption schedule upward. The anticipation of a recession and fears about losing jobs would make families more tightfisted in their current spending. This means an autonomous decrease in consumption, and the consumption function shifts downward.

What is the current status of consumer confidence (a measure of consumer expectations), as well as many other measures of interest to macroeconomic observers? Visit USA Today's "Economic Track" to find out (http://www.usatoday .com/money/economy/econ0017 .htm).

Wealth

Holding all other factors constant, the more wealth households accumulate, the more they spend at any current level of disposable income, causing the consumption function to shift upward. The dramatic stock market crash of 1929 sharply decreased the financial wealth of many families in the United States and was a significant factor in the depressed consumption of the 1930s. Wealth owned by households includes both *real* assets, such as homes, automobiles, and VCRs, and *financial* assets, including cash, savings accounts, stocks, bonds, insurance policies, and pensions. Changes in prices of stocks, real estate, and other assets affect the value of wealth and, in turn, can shift the nation's consumption function.

The Price Level

Any change in the general price level shifts the consumption schedule by reducing or enlarging the *purchasing power* of financial assets (wealth) with fixed nominal value. Suppose you own a $100,000 government bond or certificate of deposit. If the price level increases by, say, 10 percent, this same financial asset will buy approximately 10 percent less. Once the real value of financial wealth falls, families are poorer and spend less at any level of current disposable income. As a result, the consumption function shifts downward. The next chapter discusses this phenomenon in more detail.

The Interest Rate

The consumption schedule includes the option of borrowing to finance spending. A lower rate of interest on loans encourages consumers to borrow more, and a higher interest rate discourages consumer indebtedness. If interest rates fall, households may use more credit to finance consumer purchases. The result is a shift upward in the consumption schedule.

Stock of Durable Goods

When World War II ended, Americans had pent-up demand for many durable goods. During the war, automobiles, washing machines, refrigerators, and other goods were not produced. Consumption exploded after the war ended as people rushed out to make purchases and satisfy their long wish lists. This massive buying spree caused an upward shift in the consumption function.

Investment Expenditures

According to Keynes, changes in the private-sector components of aggregate expenditures (personal consumption and investment spending) are the major cause of the business cycle. And the more volatile of these two components is investment spending. Possibly the explanation is that changes in nonincome determinants of personal consumption tend to offset each other. Or maybe people are simply reluctant to change their personal consumption habits. Whatever the reason for the stability of personal consumption, Exhibit 7 demonstrates this point. Over the years, the annual growth rate of real investment has indeed fluctuated much more than real personal consumption. Recall from Exhibit 2 in the chapter on GDP that investment expenditures (gross private domestic investment) consist of spending on newly produced nonresidential structures, such as factories, and equipment and on changes in inventories and residential structures.

The Investment Demand Curve

The classical economists believed that the interest rate alone determines the level of investment spending. Keynes disputed this idea. Instead, Keynes argued that expectations of future profits are the primary factor in determining investment and the interest rate is the financing cost of any investment proposal.

Using a micro example to illustrate the investment decision-making process, suppose a consulting firm plans to purchase a new computer program for $1,000 that will be obsolete in a year. It anticipates that the new software will increase the firm's revenue by $1,100. Thus, assuming no taxes and other expenses exist, the expected rate of return or profit is 10 percent.

Now consider the impact of the cost of borrowing funds to finance the software investment. If the interest rate is less than 10 percent, the business will earn a profit, so it will make the investment expenditure to buy the computer program. On the other hand, a rate of interest higher than 10 percent means the software investment will be a loss, so this project will not be undertaken.

Investment demand curve

The curve that shows the amount businesses spend for investment goods at different possible rates of interest.

Understanding a single firm's investment decision from a micro perspective allows us to develop the **investment demand curve** from the macro vantage point. The investment demand curve shows the amount businesses spend for investment goods at different possible rates of interest. Exhibit 8 expresses the interest rate as annual percentages on the vertical axis. As shown in part (a), changes in the interest rate generate movements along the firm's investment demand curve. If the interest rate falls from, say, 12 percent at point *A* to 8 percent at point *B*, an additional $5 million of real investment spending occurs because *marginal* planned projects become profitable. Stated another way, as a result of this fall in the rate of interest, the firm's real investment increases from $5 million to $10 million.

The relationship among the expected rate of profit, the interest rate, and investment follows this investment rule: *Businesses will undertake all planned investment projects for which the expected rate of profit equals or exceeds the interest rate.*

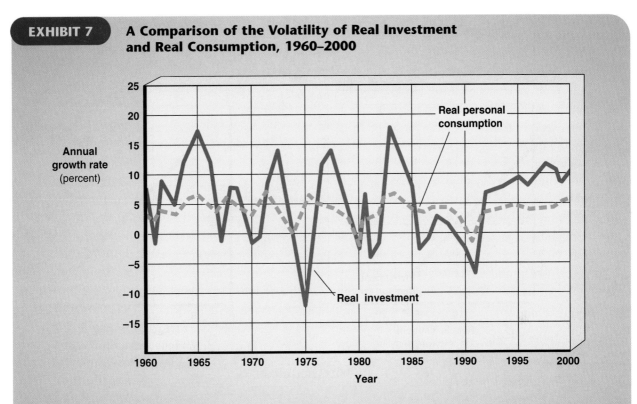

| EXHIBIT 7 | A Comparison of the Volatility of Real Investment and Real Consumption, 1960–2000 |

Real investment spending is highly volatile compared to real personal consumption. The data for the past 40 years confirm that the annual growth rate of real investment (gross private domestic investment) fluctuates much more than the annual growth rate of real personal consumption.

Sources: *Economic Report of the President, 2001*, http://w3.access.gpo.gov/eop/, Table B-4; and *Survey of Current Business*, http://www.bea.doc.gov/bea/dn1.htm, Table S-1.

Why Investment Demand Is Unstable

Why did Keynes view investment spending as so susceptible to ups and downs? The reason is there are several volatile determinants that cause the investment demand curve to be quite unstable. In short, any factor that decreases the expected rate of profit shifts the investment demand curve downward and thereby lowers the investment component of real GDP. As shown in Exhibit 8(b), the initial investment demand curve, I_1, has shifted rightward to I_2, and at an interest rate of 8 percent, $5 million of additional investment spending occurs between points *B* and *C*. The next sections discuss major factors that can shift the investment demand curve.

The Conference Board's Consumer Research Center provides a quarterly report tracking business executives' expectations. Visit http://www .conference-board.org/products/ c-consumer.cfm.

Expectations

Keynes argued that swings in "animal spirits" cause volatile investment expenditures. Translated, this means businesspersons are quite susceptible to moods of optimism and pessimism about future economic conditions. Their expectations about the future translate into estimates of future sales,

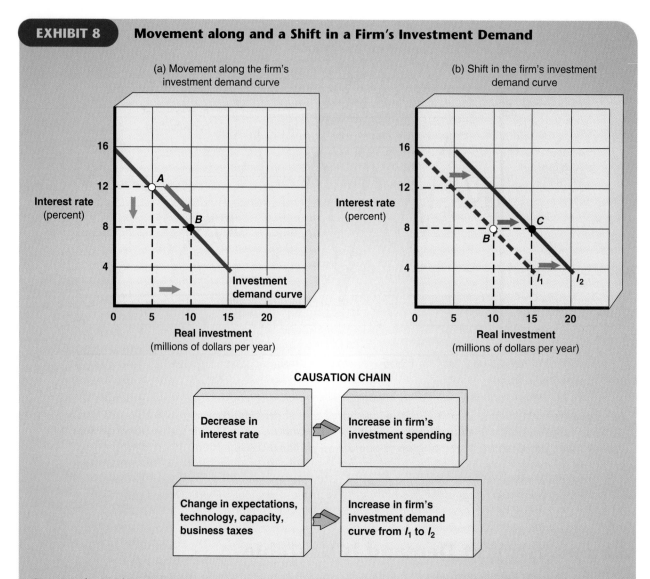

EXHIBIT 8   **Movement along and a Shift in a Firm's Investment Demand**

(a) Movement along the firm's investment demand curve

Interest rate (percent)

Investment demand curve

Real investment (millions of dollars per year)

(b) Shift in the firm's investment demand curve

Interest rate (percent)

Real investment (millions of dollars per year)

CAUSATION CHAIN

Decrease in interest rate → Increase in firm's investment spending

Change in expectations, technology, capacity, business taxes → Increase in firm's investment demand curve from I_1 to I_2

Part (a) shows that investment spending by a hypothetical business firm depends on the interest rate. Ceteris paribus, lowering the interest rate from 12 percent at point *A* to 8 percent at point *B* increases the quantity of real investment purchases from $5 million to $10 million during the year.

Keynes argued that investment spending is unstable because a change in volatile factors, such as expectations, technological change, capacity utilization, and business taxes, can shift the location of the investment demand curve. As shown in part (b), the initial investment demand, I_1, has shifted rightward to I_2, and at an interest rate of 8 percent, $5 million in additional investment spending occurs between points *B* and *C*.

future costs, and future profitability of investment projects. These forecasts involve a clouded crystal ball, requiring a degree of intuition or normative analysis. There are always so many ever-changing factors, such as government spending and tax policies, world events, population growth, and stock market conditions, that make forecasting difficult and ever changing.

When a wave of pessimism becomes pervasive, businesspeople reduce their expectations for profitability at each rate of interest. Such a pessimistic attitude can become contagious and shift the investment demand curve leftward. This was the case during the Great Depression, when the outlook was dismal. At other times, businesspersons become very optimistic and revise upward their expected rate of profit for investment at each interest rate. If so, the investment demand curve shifts upward. Thus, Keynes viewed changes in business confidence (expectations) as a major cause of volatility in investment spending.

Technological Change

Technological progress includes the introduction of new products and new ways of doing things. Robots, personal computers, fax machines, cellular phones, the Internet, and similar new inventions provide less costly ways of production. New technologies create a flurry of investment spending as firms buy the latest innovations in order to improve their production capabilities, thereby causing the investment demand curve to shift upward.

Capacity Utilization

During the Great Depression, many businesses operated at less than 50 percent of capacity. Capacity is defined as the maximum possible output of a firm or industry. Since much of the nation's capital stock stood idle, firms had little incentive to buy more. As a result, the investment demand curve shifted far to the left. Conversely, firms may be operating their plants at a high rate of capacity utilization, and the outlook for sales growth is optimistic. In this case, there is pressure on firms to invest in new investment projects, and the investment demand curve shifts to the right.

Business Taxes

As explained earlier, changes in income taxes on individuals affect disposable income and the level of consumption. Similarly, taxes on business firms can shift the investment demand curve. Business decisions, in reality, depend on the expected *after-tax* rate of profit. An increase in business taxes therefore would lower profitability and shift the investment demand curve to the left. On the other hand, the U.S. government may wish to encourage investment by allowing, say, a *tax credit* for new investment. A 10 percent *investment tax credit* means that if ExxonMobil decides to invest $10 million in a new plant, the corporation's tax bill to the IRS will be cut by $1 million. The effect of this tax policy is that the government increases the profitability of new investment projects by 10 percent and the investment demand curve shifts to the right.

Investment as an Autonomous Expenditure

Autonomous expenditure

Spending that does not vary with the current level of disposable income.

Assuming none of the above factors changes in the short run, Keynes argued investment spending is an **autonomous expenditure.** An autonomous expenditure is spending that does not vary with the current level of disposable income. Stated simply, autonomous expenditures in the Keynesian model remain a fixed amount regardless of the level of disposable income. Exhibit 9 shows how the rate of interest determines the aggregate level of autonomous investment for all firms in an economy regardless of or external to the level of real disposable income. In part(a), at an interest rate of 8 percent, *all* businesses together spend $1 trillion for capital goods and inventory. Part (b) shows that this $1 trillion is the amount of real investment spending, no matter what the level of real disposable income. If the rate of interest is lower, investment increases, and the horizontal investment demand curve shifts vertically upward. A higher rate of interest discourages investment and shifts the horizontal investment demand curve vertically downward.

The Aggregate Expenditures Function

Aggregate expenditures function (*AE*)

The function that represents total spending in an economy at a given level of real disposable income.

You will now use what you have learned about consumption and investment to develop a basic Keynesian model. To keep the analysis simple, visualize a simple economy with no government sector (no taxes or government spending) and no foreign trade (net exports). Moreover, the marginal propensity to consume is 0.50, so each dollar increase in disposable income leads to an increase in consumption of 50 cents. As shown previously in Exhibit 9, investment spending depends on the expected rate of profit and interest rate and is $1 trillion regardless of the level of real disposable income.

A little drum roll please! Now we are ready to finish this chapter by tying concepts together and pointing the spotlight on an important model necessary to understand Keynes's cure for the Great Depression. The table in Exhibit 10 gives various levels of real disposable income in column 1 and corresponding levels of consumption and investment in columns 2 and 3, respectively. The relationship between real disposable income and the sum of *C* + *I* listed in column 4 is called the **aggregate expenditures function (*AE*).** The aggregate expenditures function is the total spending in an economy at a given level of real disposable income. The *AE* function is derived graphically in Exhibit 10 by summing the consumption function (*C*) and the investment demand curve (*I*) on the vertical axis at each level of disposable income on the horizontal axis. Note that the *C* and the *C* + *I* functions are parallel. The slope of the consumption function is determined by the *MPC,* as explained earlier in Exhibit 2. Then the autonomous investment of $1 trillion is added at each level of real disposable income. As a result, the consumption function, *C,* shifts vertically by $1 trillion to become the *AE* function.

The aggregate expenditures function is sometimes called the *Keynesian Cross.* Note in Exhibit 10 that the *AE* line begins above the 45-degree line and then *crosses* it at $6 trillion of real disposable income. The *AE* line rep-

EXHIBIT 9   **The Aggregate Investment Demand and Autonomous Investment Demand Curves**

(a) Aggregate investment demand curve

(b) Aggregate autonomous investment curve

In part (a), the level of real investment for all firms in an economy is determined by the investment rule that all investment projects for which the expected rate of profit equals or exceeds the interest rate will be undertaken. If the interest rate is 8 percent, real autonomous investment will be $1 trillion, shown as point *A* on the investment demand curve, *I*.

In part (b) of the exhibit, autonomous real investment expenditures are shown to be independent of the level of real disposable income per year. This means firms will spend $1 trillion regardless of the level of real disposable income per year.

resents only private-sector spending in our hypothetical economy. For example, if real disposable income is $1 trillion per year, then consumers spend $2.5 trillion per year, businesses spend $1 trillion for investment, and *AE* = $3.5 trillion. This means the *AE* line is above the 45-degree line and a condition of dissaving exists. As a result, the aggregate spending exceeds aggregate income by $2.5 trillion. Instead, if real disposable income is $8 trillion per year and investment remains fixed at $1 trillion, the *AE* line is below the 45-degree line. This means aggregate spending is $1 trillion less than real disposable income. At $6 trillion of real disposable income per year, the economy is in macro equilibrium because aggregate income equals aggregate spending by households and firms.

EXHIBIT 10   **Aggregate Expenditures Function Data**

The aggregate expenditures function (*AE*) for a hypothetical economy begins with the consumption function (*C*). Then we add the investment demand curve (*I*) to obtain the *AE* function (*C* + *I*). Note that the *C* and *C* + *I* lines are parallel. Because *I* is assumed to be an autonomous expenditure of $1 trillion, the slope of the *C* + *I* function equals the slope (*MPC*) of the consumption function (*C*). At $6 trillion of real disposable income per year, aggregate income equals consumption plus investment, and the economy is in equilibrium.

(1) Real disposable income (Y_d)	(2) Consumption (C)	(3) Investment (I)	(4) Aggregate expenditures (AE) [(C + I) or (2) + (3)]
$0	$2.0	$1	$3.0
1	2.5	1	3.5
2	3.0	1	4.0
3	3.5	1	4.5
4	4.0	1	5.0
5	4.5	1	5.5
6	5.0	1	6.0
7	5.5	1	6.5
8	6.0	1	7.0

Note: All amounts are in trillions of dollars per year.

Does a Stock Market Crash Affect the Economy?

Applicable Concept: aggregate expenditures function

The stock market soared during the "Roaring 20s," and then, on October 29, 1929, the market crashed. The Dow Jones average of industrial stock prices fell 37 points, a 12.7 percent drop. Over the years, much debate has occurred over whether the 1929 crash was merely a symptom or a major cause of the downturn. Evidence exists that the 1929 crash only reflected an economic decline already in progress. Between August and October 1929, production fell at an annual rate of 20 percent, and personal income fell at an annual rate of 5 percent.

The argument over the impact of a stock market crash on the economy was renewed on October 19, 1987, when America's stock exchanges suffered one of their worst single-day losses ever. The Dow Jones Industrial Average fell 23 percent for a whopping loss of $500 billion in the value of outstanding stocks in a single day. Economists, stock analysts, and government officials are still debating the causes and consequences of "Black Monday." As a result of the September attack on the United States in 2001, the stock market suffered its worst one-week loss since the Great Depression. In the immediate aftermath, equities losses were an extraordinary $1.2 trillion in value.

Stock market plunges are often widely reported in the news. One result of these plunges is that many Americans feel poorer because of the threat to their life's savings. In only a few hours, spectacular paper losses reduce the wealth that people are counting on to purchase homes, automobiles, college tuition, or retirement. Although not all U.S. households own stock, everyone fears the Wall Street roller coaster will affect their jobs and income. If a stock market crash leads to a recession, it would cause layoffs or cuts in profit-sharing and pension funds.

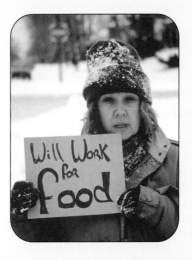

Businesses fear that many families will postpone buying major consumer items in case they need their cash to tide them over the difficult economic times ahead. Reluctance of consumers to spend would lower demand, and, in turn, prices and profits would fall. Falling sales and anxiety about a recession may lead many executives to postpone modernization plans. Rather than buying new factories and equipment, which help reduce costs, businesses would continue with used plants and machinery. This would mean less private investment spending and lower employment, output, and income for the overall economy.

ANALYZE THE ISSUE

Immediately following the attack on the United States on September 11, 2001, the stock market plunged, and many observers predicted a recession. Using the consumption and investment functions, explain their prediction.

KEY CONCEPTS

John Maynard Keynes
Classical economists
Say's Law
Consumption function
Dissaving

Autonomous consumption
Saving
Marginal propensity to
    consume (*MPC*)

Marginal propensity to
    save (*MPS*)
Investment demand curve

Autonomous expenditure
Aggregate expenditures
    function (*AE*)

SUMMARY

- **Say's Law** is the classical theory that "supply creates its own demand" and therefore the Great Depression was impossible. Say's Law is the theory that the value of production generates an equal amount of income and, in turn, total spending. The classical economists rejected the argument that underconsumption is possible because they believed flexible prices, wages, and interest rates would soon establish a balance between supply and demand.

- **John Maynard Keynes** rejected the classical theory that the economy self-corrects in the long run to full employment. The key in Keynesian theory is aggregate demand, rather than the classicals' focus on aggregate supply. Unless aggregate spending is adequate, the economy can experience prolonged and severe unemployment.

- The **consumption function** (**C**) is determined by changes in the level of disposable income. **Autonomous consumption** is consumption that occurs even if disposable income equals zero. Changes in such nonincome determinants as expectations, wealth, the price level, interest rates, and the stock of durable goods can cause shifts in the consumption function.

Consumption function

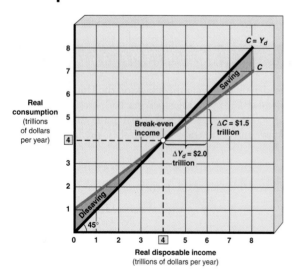

- The **marginal propensity to consume** (**MPC**) is the change in consumption associated with a given change in disposable income. The *MPC* tells how much of an additional dollar of disposable income households will spend for consumption.

- The **marginal propensity to save** (**MPS**) is the change in saving associated with a given change in disposable income. The *MPS* measures how much of an additional dollar of disposable income households will save.

- The **investment demand curve** (**I**) shows the amount businesses spend for investment goods at different possible rates of interest. The determinants of this schedule are the expected rate of profit and rate of interest. Shifts in the investment demand curve result from changes in expectations, technology, capacity utilization, and business taxes.

- An **autonomous expenditure** is spending that does not vary with the current level of disposable income. The Keynesian model applies this simplifying assumption to investment. As a result, the investment demand curve is a fixed amount determined by the rate of profit and the interest rate.

- The **aggregate expenditures function** (**AE**) shows the total spending in an economy at a given level of disposable income. Assuming investment spending is autonomous, the slope of the *AE* function is determined by the *MPC*.

Aggregate expenditures function

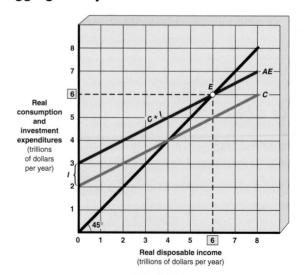

SUMMARY OF CONCLUSION STATEMENTS

- The classical economists believed that a continuing depression is impossible because markets eliminate persistent shortages or surpluses.

- In the classical view, unemployment is the result of a short-lived adjustment period in which wages and prices decline or people voluntarily choose not to work. Thus, there is a natural tendency for the economy to restore full employment over time.

- There is a direct relationship between changes in real disposable income and changes in consumption.

- A change in real disposable income is the sole cause of a movement along the consumption function. A shift or relocation in the consumption schedule occurs when a factor other than real disposable income changes.

- Businesses will undertake all planned investment projects for which the expected rate of profits equals or exceeds the interest rate.

STUDY QUESTIONS AND PROBLEMS

1. Explain how the classical economists concluded that Say's Law is valid and long-term unemployment impossible.

2. Use the consumption function data below to answer the following questions:

Keynesian Consumption Function (billions of dollars per year)

Real disposable income	Consumption	Saving	MPC	MPS
$100	$150	$___	___	___
200	200	___	___	___
300	250	___	___	___
400	300	___	___	___
500	350	___	___	___

a. Calculate the saving schedule.
b. Determine the marginal propensities to consume (*MPC*) and save (*MPS*).
c. Determine the break-even income.
d. What is the relationship between the *MPC* and the *MPS*?

3. Explain why the *MPC* and the *MPS* must always add up to one.

4. How do households "dissave"?

5. Explain how each of the following affects the consumption function:
a. The expectation is that a prolonged recession will occur in the next year.
b. Stock prices rise sharply.
c. The price level rises by 10 percent.
d. The interest rate on consumer loans rises sharply.
e. Income taxes increase.

6. Your college is considering investing $1 million to add 10,000 seats to its football stadium. The athletic department forecasts it can sell all these extra seats each game for a ticket price of $20 per seat, and the team plays six home games per year. If the school can borrow at an interest rate of 14 percent, should the school undertake this project? What would happen if the school expected a losing season and could sell tickets for only half of the 10,000 seats?

7. Why is the investment demand curve less stable than the consumption and saving functions? What are the basic determinants that can shift the investment demand curve?

8. Suppose most business executives expect a slowdown in the economy. How might this situation affect the economy?

9. The levels of real disposable income and aggregate expenditures for a two-sector economy (consumption and investment) are given in the following table:

   a. Construct a graph of the aggregate expenditures function (*AE*).

   b. Determine the autonomous consumption, *MPC*, and *MPS* for this hypothetical economy.

   c. What is the equilibrium level of real disposable income?

   d. What will happen to the equilibrium level of real disposable income if there is an increase in autonomous investment?

Real disposable income (trillions of dollars per year)	Aggregate expenditures (trillions of dollars per year)
$0	$3.00
1	3.25
2	3.50
3	3.75
4	4.00
5	4.25
6	4.50
7	4.75
8	5.00

ONLINE EXERCISES

Exercise 1

Visit http://www.blupete.com/Literature/Biographies/Philosophy/Keynes.htm. Briefly describe the life of John Maynard Keynes.

Exercise 2

Visit GPO Gate, Catalog for Economic Report of the President (http://www.gpo.ucop.edu/catalog/erp99_appen_b.html), and follow these steps:

1. Select Tables B-2 and B-31. What percentage of real GDP is real disposable personal income?

2. Select Tables B-2 and B-31. Compute aggregate expenditures for 1997 and compare to real disposable income. Was the economy operating above or below equilibrium?

Exercise 3

Read the article found in the Christian Science Monitor at this Internet site (http://www.csmonitor.com/durable/1998/02/04/opin/opin.2.html) concerning savings in the United States and answer the following questions:

1. What is the advantage of a high savings rate for a nation?

2. What are the disadvantages?

3. What long-term problem might a nation face with a low savings rate?

CHECKPOINT ANSWER

What's Your *MPC*?

Early in your career when your income is relatively low, you are likely to spend your entire income, and perhaps even dissave, just to afford necessities. During this stage of your life, your *MPC* will be close to 1. As your income increases and you have purchased the necessities, addi-tional income can go to luxuries. If you become wealthier, you have a higher marginal propensity to save and consequently a lower marginal propensity to consume. If you said your *MPC* will probably decrease as your income increases, YOU ARE CORRECT.

PRACTICE QUIZ

For a visual explanation of the correct answers, visit the tutorial at http://tucker.swcollege.com.

1. The French classical economist Jean-Baptiste Say transformed the equality of production and spending into a law that can be expressed as follows:
   a. The invisible hand creates its own supply.
   b. Wages always fall to the subsistence level.
   c. Supply creates its own demand.
   d. Aggregate output does not always equal consumption.

2. Autonomous consumption is
   a. positively related to the level of consumption.
   b. negatively related to the level of consumption.
   c. positively related to the level of disposable income.
   d. independent of the level of disposable income.

3. The consumption function represents the relationship between consumer expenditures and
   a. interest rates.
   b. saving.
   c. the price level.
   d. disposable income.

4. John Maynard Keynes's proposition that a dollar increase in disposable income will increase consumption, but by less than the increase in disposable income, implies a marginal propensity to consume that is
   a. greater than or equal to one.
   b. equal to one.
   c. less than one, but greater than zero.
   d. negative.

5. Above the break-even disposable income for the consumption function, which of the following occurs?
   a. Dissaving
   b. Saving
   c. Neither a nor b
   d. Both a and b

6. Which of the following changes produces an upward shift in the consumption function?
   a. An increase in consumer wealth
   b. A decrease in consumer wealth
   c. A decrease in autonomous consumption
   d. Both b and c

7. An upward shift in the consumption schedule, other things being equal, could be caused by households
   a. becoming optimistic about the state of the economy.
   b. becoming pessimistic about the state of the economy.
   c. expecting future income and wealth to decline.
   d. doing none of the above.

8. The investment demand curve represents the relationship between business spending for investment goods and
   a. GDP.
   b. interest rates.
   c. disposable income.
   d. saving.

9. Which of the following changes produces a leftward shift in the investment demand curve?
   a. A wave of optimism about future profitability
   b. Technological change
   c. High plant capacity utilization
   d. Increase in business taxes

10. The aggregate expenditures function (*AE*) represents which of the following?
    a. The consumption function only
    b. Autonomous consumption only
    c. The investment demand curve only
    d. All three of the above combined
    e. A combination of a and c

Exhibit 11 Aggregate Expenditures Function

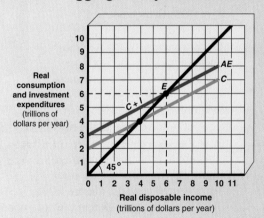

11. In Exhibit 11, what is the households' marginal propensity to consume *(MPC)*?
    a. 0.50
    b. 0.67
    c. 0.75
    d. 0.80

12. In Exhibit 11, aggregate disposable income will equal consumption plus investment (aggregate expenditures), and the economy will be in equilibrium when real disposable income is
    a. $2.33 trillion.
    b. $3 trillion.
    c. $6 trillion.
    d. $10 trillion.

CHAPTER 19

The Keynesian Model in Action

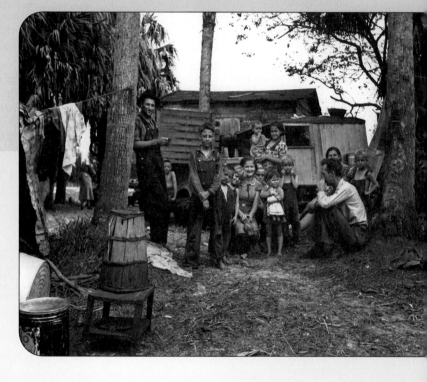

I n 1935, George Bernard Shaw received a letter from John Maynard Keynes, which stated, "I believe myself to be writing a book (*The General Theory*) on economic theory which will largely revolutionize—not, I suppose, at once but in the course of the next ten years—the way the world thinks about economic problems." Indeed, Keynes's macroeconomic theory offered powerful ideas whose time had come during the Great Depression. Building on the foundation of the previous chapter, Keynes conceived the economy as driven by aggregate demand that can be separated and analyzed under the individual components of consumption (C), investment (I), government spending (G), and net exports (X − M).

You must keep in mind that during the Great Depression era, plants had idle capacity and

unemployment was massive. Under these conditions, inflation was not the problem. The Keynesian model therefore generally ignores price level changes and focuses instead on the determination of full-employment output achieved by changes in aggregate expenditures.

Like adding icing to a cake, this chapter begins by adding government spending and international trade to the aggregate expenditures line in the Keynesian

model developed in the previous chapter. Next, you will learn how the economy gravitates to an equilibrium where aggregate expenditures equal aggregate output. And you will look at the link between the equilibrium output and the level of employment in an economy. The analysis will make it clear why Keynes argued there is no self-correction mechanism that eventually moves the nation to the full-employment equilibrium output.

Finally, you will understand one of Keynes's most powerful ideas—the spending multiplier. At the very heart of Keynesian theory is the concept that an initial increase in aggregate spending of $1 in an economy can increase equilibrium output by more than $1. Thus, Keynesian economics offers a cure for an economy in deep recession: government policies that expand aggregate demand, raise national output, create jobs, and restore full employment.

In this chapter, you will learn to solve these economics puzzles:

■ Why did Keynes reject the classical theory that "supply creates its own demand"?

■ Why does Keynes argue that the government should adopt active policies, rather than allowing the price system to prevail?

■ Can the Keynesian model explain an ice cream war?

Adding Government and International Trade to the Keynesian Model

In this chapter, we continue our study of the simple economy begun in the previous chapter (Exhibit 10). Consumption and investment are not the only forms of spending. As shown earlier in the chapter on GDP (Exhibit 2), consumption and investment represent 86 percent of total spending, while government spending and net exports constitute the remaining 14 percent of GDP.

Government Spending

Government spending is the second largest component of aggregate expenditures in the United States. Like investment, government spending can be considered an autonomous expenditure. The reasoning is that government spending is primarily the result of a political decision made independent of the level of national output.

Exhibit 1(a) shows hypothetical government spending as a horizontal line labeled G at $1 trillion. If government officials increase government spending, the G line shifts upward to G_1, and reduced government spending shifts the G line downward to G_2. The amount of the shift is equal to the amount of change in government spending.

Here we must pause to take special note of the change from real disposable income to real GDP on the horizontal axis of the graph. Does it make a difference? No, it makes little difference. In the previous chapter, real disposable income was used, following the theory Keynes himself developed. However, it is important to connect aggregate output and income measures. Recall from Exhibit 7 in the chapter on GDP the adjustments required to convert GDP into disposable income (Y_d). As it turns out, real disposable income is a sizable portion of real GDP. Over the last decade, real disposable income, on average, has consistently been about 70 percent of real GDP. If we

The federal government's Office of Management and Budget provides information on the government's spending and tax collections (http://w3.access.gpo.gov/ usbudget/fy1999/index.html).

EXHIBIT 1 — Autonomous Government Spending and Net Exports Curves

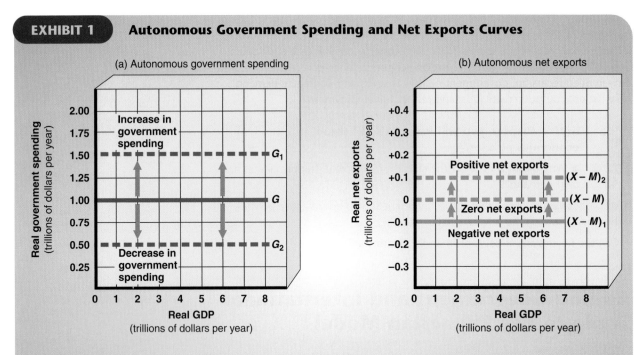

In part (a), government spending (G) is assumed to be determined by the political decision-making process. The autonomous government spending line, G, is therefore a horizontal line indicating that government spending is independent of the level of real GDP. An increase in government spending shifts G upward to G_1. A decrease shifts G downward to G_2.

Part (b) also shows that net exports are assumed to be independent of the level of GDP. Horizontal line $(X - M)_1$ is negative because imports exceed exports. If exports equal imports, then the net exports line shifts upward to $(X - M)$. If exports exceed imports, the net exports line is represented by a positive net exports line, $(X - M)_2$.

Visit the Foreign Trade Division of the U.S. Census Bureau (http://www.census.gov/ftp/pub/foreign-trade/www/). If you click on "Top Trading Partners," you can see the major countries for which the United States is running trade deficits and trade surpluses.

are willing to assume that real disposable income remains the same high proportion of real GDP each year, then we can substitute real GDP for real disposable income in the Keynesian model. Changes in real GDP therefore reflect changes in both real national output and real disposable income.

Net Exports

Like investment and government spending, exports and imports can be treated as autonomous expenditures unaffected by a nation's domestic level of real GDP. Economic conditions in the countries that buy U.S. products affect the level of our exports. On the other hand, the level of imports purchased by U.S. citizens is influenced by economic conditions in the United States. As shown in Exhibit 1(b), net exports, $(X - M)$, can be positive, zero, or negative. The level of net exports or $(X - M)$ line is horizontal because net exports are assumed to be independent of the level of real GDP. Since for many years the value of imports we have purchased from foreigners has exceeded the value of exports we have been selling them, the model

EXHIBIT 2 Equilibrium and Disequilibrium Levels of Employment, Output, and Income							
(1)	(2)	(3)	(4)	(5)	(6)	(7)	(8)
Aggregate output and income (real GDP) (Y)	Consumption (C)	Investment (I)	Government (G)	Net exports (X − M)	Aggregate expenditures (AE)	Unplanned inventory investment depletion (−) or accumulation (+)	Direction of real GDP and employment
$ 0	$0.6	$1	$1	$−.1	2.5	$−2.5	Increase
1.0	1.1	1	1	−.1	3.0	−2.0	Increase
2.0	1.6	1	1	−.1	3.5	−1.5	Increase
3.0	2.1	1	1	−.1	4.0	−1.0	Increase
4.0	2.6	1	1	−.1	4.5	−0.5	Increase
5.0	3.1	1	1	−.1	5.0	0	Equilibrium
6.0	3.6	1	1	−.1	5.5	+0.5	Decrease
7.0	4.1	1	1	−.1	6.0	+1.0	Decrease
8.0	4.6	1	1	−.1	6.5	+1.5	Decrease

Note: All amounts are in trillions of dollars per year.

assumes net exports are negative at line $(X − M)_1$. If exports and imports are equal, the net exports line shifts upward to zero at line $(X − M)$. If exports exceed imports, the positive $(X − M)$ line shifts farther upward to line $(X − M)_2$.

The Aggregate Expenditures–Output Model

Keynes countered classical theory by developing an alternative theory that explained how a depressed economy can be stuck forever in a below-full-employment equilibrium without adequate aggregate expenditures. In this section, a simple Keynesian model is developed to explain what Keynes meant by his famous saying, "In the long run, we are all dead."

Tabular Analysis of Keynesian Equilibrium

Exhibit 2 presents data to illustrate the relationship among employment, aggregate output and income, and aggregate expenditures for our hypothetical economy. GDP (Y) is listed in column 1, consumption (C) is listed in column 2, and investment (I) in column 3 is an autonomous expenditure of $1 trillion from Exhibit 9(b) in the previous chapter. Government spending (G) in column 4 is also an autonomous expenditure of $1 trillion from Exhibit 1(a), and net exports $(X − M)$ in column 5 are taken from Exhibit 1(b). The aggregate expenditures function (AE) in column 6 is the sum of the $C + I + G + (X − M)$ components of aggregate expenditures in columns 2 through 5.

Examination of the levels of real GDP in column 1 and the levels of aggregate expenditures in column 6 indicate that an equality exists only at the $5 trillion level of real GDP.

Conclusion *At the equilibrium level of real GDP, the total value of goods and services produced (aggregate output and income, Y) is precisely equal to the total spending for these goods and services (aggregate expenditures, AE).*

All output levels other than $5 trillion are unsustainable macro-disequilibrium levels. Consider what happens if businesses employ only enough workers to produce an output of $1 trillion real GDP. Business managers expect total spending to equal aggregate output at this level of production, but this does not happen. At the level of $1 trillion, aggregate expenditures of $3 trillion exceed aggregate output by an *unplanned inventory investment depletion* of $2 trillion, listed in column 7. Firms respond to this happy state of affairs by hiring more workers, expanding output, and generating additional aggregate income. As a result of this process, the economy moves toward the equilibrium of $5 trillion real GDP. Thus, the pressure of empty shelves and warehouses drives our hypothetical economy to create jobs and reduce the unemployment rate (not explicitly shown in the model).

The reverse is true for all levels of real GDP above the $5 trillion equilibrium level. Now suppose firms hire more workers and aggregate output is $7 trillion real GDP. At the real GDP disequilibrium level of $7 trillion, *unplanned inventory investment accumulation* occurs because aggregate expenditures of $6 trillion are insufficient to purchase $7 trillion of output. The result is that unwanted inventories worth $1 trillion remain unsold on the shelves and in the warehouses of business firms. Producers react to this undesirable condition by cutting the rate of output and employment. In this case, real GDP declines toward the equilibrium level of $5 trillion, jobs are lost, and unemployment rises.

Conclusion *Aggregate expenditures in Keynesian economics pull aggregate output either higher or lower toward equilibrium in the economy as opposed to the classical view that aggregate output generates an equal amount of aggregate spending.*

Graphic Analysis of Keynesian Equilibrium

The tabular analysis of Keynesian theory can be presented graphically. Using the data from Exhibit 2, Exhibit 3 presents a graph measuring real aggregate expenditures on the *y*-axis and real GDP on the *x*-axis. Exhibit 3 illustrates the **aggregate expenditures–output model**. The aggregate expenditure–output model determines the equilibrium level of real GDP by the intersection of the aggregate expenditures and aggregate output (and income) curves. The 45-degree line now takes on a special significance. Each point along this line is equidistant from the horizontal and the vertical axes. Therefore, each point reflects a *possible* equilibrium between real GDP aggregate output (*Y*) and aggregate expenditures (*AE*). Note that the *AE* line indicates aggregate expenditures along a line less steep than the 45-degree line. This is because the slope of the *AE* line is determined by the marginal propensity to consume (*MPC*),

Aggregate expenditures–output model

The model that determines the equilibrium level of real GDP by the intersection of the aggregate expenditures and aggregate output (and income) curves.

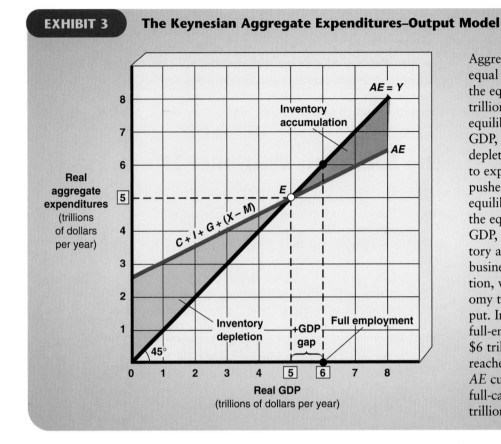

EXHIBIT 3   **The Keynesian Aggregate Expenditures–Output Model**

Aggregate expenditures (*AE*) equal aggregate output (*Y*) at the equilibrium level of $5 trillion real GDP. Below the equilibrium level of real GDP, an undesired inventory depletion causes businesses to expand production, which pushes the economy toward equilibrium output. Above the equilibrium level of real GDP, an unintended inventory accumulation causes businesses to reduce production, which pushes the economy toward equilibrium output. In Keynesian theory, the full-employment output of $6 trillion real GDP can be reached only by shifting the *AE* curve upward until the full-capacity output of $6 trillion real GDP is reached.

which is less than 1. Aggregate expenditures equal aggregate output at the $5 trillion real GDP level, and any other level of output is unstable. If businesses produce at some output level that is higher than equilibrium GDP, such as $7 trillion real GDP, the vertical distance between the 45-degree equilibrium and the *AE* lines measures an undesired inventory accumulation of $1 trillion. This leads businesses to reduce employment, and production drops downward until the economy reaches equilibrium at $5 trillion. You may have already recognized that the difference of $1 trillion between the equilibrium output (actual GDP) at point *E* and the full-employment output (potential GDP) is a positive *GDP gap*, discussed in the chapter on business cycles and unemployment (see Exhibit 10).

Now consider the case in which businesses hire only enough workers to produce aggregate output where the *AE* line is above the 45-degree equilibrium line. Since aggregate expenditures exceed aggregate output, businesses sell more than they currently produce, which depletes their inventories. Business managers react to this excess aggregate demand condition by hiring more workers and expanding production, causing movement upward along the *AE* function toward the equilibrium level of $5 trillion real GDP.

Now it's time to pause, take a deep breath, and appreciate what you have been studying so diligently. It's a powerful idea! Exhibit 3 illustrates the basic explanation offered by Keynes for the Great Depression: *Once an equilibrium is established between aggregate expenditures and aggregate output, there is no tendency for the economy to change even when equilibrium is well below full employment, as pre-Keynesian economists believed.* The solution Keynes offered Western economies facing the Great Depression is to shift the *AE* line upward until the full-employment equilibrium is reached. Otherwise, prolonged unemployment persists indefinitely, and the economy never self-corrects. We now turn to the key idea behind changes in aggregate spending to stabilize the macro economy.

The Spending Multiplier Effect

Changes in aggregate expenditures in the Keynesian model make things happen. The crux of Keynesian macroeconomic policy depends on a change in aggregate expenditures, which is multiplied or amplified by rounds of spending and respending throughout the economy. Exhibit 4 is an enlarged version of Exhibit 3. Our analysis begins at the initial equilibrium of $5 trillion real GDP (point *E*), which is below the full-employment output level of $6 trillion real GDP. Now let's assume the government decides to increase government spending by $.5 trillion. An increase in autonomous government spending of $.5 trillion per year shifts the aggregate expenditures curve *vertically* upward by this amount from point *E* on AE_1 to point *a* on AE_2. This means, at the initial output of $5 trillion real GDP, aggregate demand expands by $.5 trillion to $5.5 trillion. The initial expansion of spending causes inventories (not shown in the graph) to decline by $.5 trillion because aggregate spending of $5.5 trillion exceeds aggregate output of $5.0 trillion real GDP. Firms respond by stepping up output by $.5 trillion real GDP per year to replace inventories. The exhibit shows this by the move from point *a* to point *b*. Now the marginal propensity to consume enters the picture. Assuming the *MPC* is 0.50, the expansion of output from $5 trillion to $5.5 trillion puts an extra $500 billion of income into the pockets of workers. Given the *MPC* of 0.50, these workers increase spending on goods and services by $250 billion (movement from point *b* to point *c*). This expansion of consumer spending again causes inventories to decline and output, in turn, to expand by $250 billion, represented by the distance between point *c* and point *d*. This again puts extra income into workers' pockets, of which $125 billion (the distance between points *d* and *e*) is spent (*MPC* × Δ*Y* = 0.50 × $250 billion = $125 billion).

This process of spending-output-spending continues through an infinite number of rounds until output reaches the new equilibrium level of $6 trillion per year at point E_1. Thus, an initial expansion of government spending of $.5 trillion expanded equilibrium output by $1 trillion, which is twice the magnitude of the increase in government spending. Hence, the **spending multiplier** is 2. The spending multiplier is the ratio of the change in real GDP to the initial change in any component of aggregate expenditures, including consumption, investment, government spending, and net exports. The formula to compute the amount of change in government spending or other aggregate expenditures required to shift equilibrium aggregate output is

Spending multiplier

The ratio of the change in real GDP to an initial change in any component of aggregate expenditures, including consumption, investment, government spending, and net exports. As a formula, the spending multiplier equals 1/(1 − MPC) or 1/MPS.

$$\text{spending multiplier} = \frac{\text{change in equilibrium output}}{\textit{initial} \text{ change in aggregate expenditures}}$$

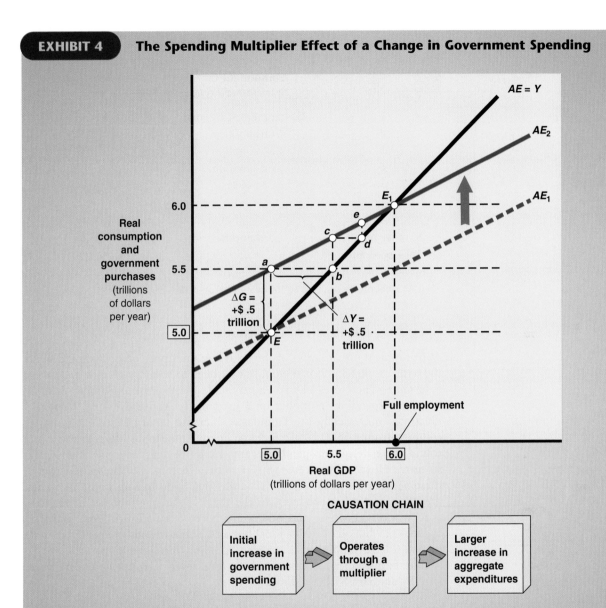

EXHIBIT 4   **The Spending Multiplier Effect of a Change in Government Spending**

CAUSATION CHAIN

| Initial increase in government spending | → | Operates through a multiplier | → | Larger increase in aggregate expenditures |

This graph is an enlargement of the spending multiplier process beginning at the point where the economy is in equilibrium at $5 trillion. Then an initial increase of $500 billion in government spending shifts the aggregate expenditures line up vertically from AE_1 to AE_2. A new equilibrium is restored after all spending-output-spending rounds are complete at point E_1 with a full-employment output of $6 trillion. Thus, the $500 billion initial increase in government spending has caused a $1 trillion increase in real GDP, and the value of the multiplier is 2.

In the example presented in Exhibit 4, the spending multiplier is computed as

$$\text{spending multiplier} = \frac{\Delta Y}{\Delta G} = \frac{\$1,000 \text{ billion}}{\$500 \text{ billion}} = 2$$

EXHIBIT 5 Spending Multiplier Effect

Round	Component of total spending	New consumption spending
1	Government spending	$ 500
2	Consumption	250
3	Consumption	125
4	Consumption	63
—	—	—
—	—	—
—	—	—
All other rounds	Consumption	62
Total spending		$1,000

Note: All amounts are rounded to the nearest billion dollars per year.

Spending Multiplier Arithmetic

The graphical presentation of the spending multiplier process should make the basic mechanics clear to you, but we need to be more specific and derive a formula. Therefore, let's pause to tackle the task of explaining in more detail the spending multiplier of 2 used in the above example. Exhibit 5 illustrates numerically the cumulative increase in aggregate expenditures resulting from a $500 billion increase in government spending. In the initial round, the government spends this amount for bridges, national defense, and so forth. Households receive this amount of income. In the second round, these households spend $250 billion (0.50 × $500 billion) on houses, cars, groceries, and other products. In the third round, the incomes of realtors, auto workers, grocers, and others are boosted by $250 billion, and they spend $125 billion (0.50 × $250 billion). These rounds of spending create income for respending in a downward spiral throughout the economy in smaller and smaller amounts until the total level of aggregate expenditures rises by an extra $1,000 billion.

> **Conclusion** *Any initial change in spending by the government, households, or firms creates a chain reaction of further spending, which causes a greater cumulative change in aggregate demand.*

You might recognize from algebra that the spending multiplier effect is a process based on an infinite geometric series. The formula for the sum of such a series of numbers is the initial number times $1/(1 - r)$, where r is the ratio that relates the numbers. Using this formula, the sum (total spending) is calculated as $500 billion $(\Delta G) \times [1/(1 - 0.50)] = \$1,000$ billion. By simply defining r in the infinite series formula as *MPC*, the spending multiplier for aggregate demand is expressed as

$$\text{spending multiplier} = \frac{1}{1 - MPC}$$

EXHIBIT 6 Relationship between MPC, MPS, and the Spending Multiplier

(1) Marginal propensity to consume (MPC)	(2) Marginal propensity to save (MPS)	(3) Spending multiplier
.90	.10	10
.80	.20	5
.75	.25	4
.67	.33	3
.50	.50	2
.33	.67	1.5

Applying this formula to our example:

$$\text{spending multiplier} = \frac{1}{1 - 0.50} = \frac{1}{0.50} = 2$$

Recall from the previous chapter that $MPC + MPS = 1$ and therefore $MPS = 1 - MPC$. Hence, the above multiplier formula can be rewritten as

$$\text{spending multiplier} = \frac{1}{MPS}$$

Applying the multiplier formula to our example:

$$\text{spending multiplier} = \frac{1}{MPS} = \frac{1}{1 - .50} = 2$$

Since *MPS* and *MPC* are related, the size of the multiplier depends on the size of the *MPC*. What will the result be if people spend 80 percent or 33 percent of each dollar of income instead of 50 percent? If the *MPC* increases (decreases), consumers spend a larger (smaller) share of each additional dollar of output/income in each round, and the size of the multiplier increases (decreases). Exhibit 6 lists several sizes of the multiplier for different values of *MPC* and *MPS*. Economists use real-world macroeconomic data to estimate a more complex multiplier than the simple multiplier formula developed in this chapter. Their estimates of the real-world *MPC* range from 0.80 to 0.90. An *MPC* of 0.50 is used in the above examples for simplicity.

Recessionary and Inflationary Gaps

The multiplier is important in the Keynesian model because it means that the initial change in aggregate expenditures results in an amplified change in the equilibrium level of real GDP. Such inherent instability can mean bad or

CHECKPOINT

Full-Employment Output, Where Are You?

Suppose the U.S. economy is in equilibrium at $3 trillion real GDP ($3,000 billion) with a recessionary gap. Given an *MPC* of 0.50, the government estimates that a tax cut of $200 billion is just enough to restore full employment. What is the full-employment real GDP target?

good news for an economy. The bad news occurs, for example, when the multiplier amplifies small declines in total spending from, say, consumer and business manager pessimism into downturns in national output, income, and employment. The good news is that, in theory, macroeconomic policy can manage, or manipulate, the economy's performance by a relatively small initial change in aggregate expenditures.

Recessionary Gap

Using Government Spending to Close a Recessionary Gap.   Consider the aggregate expenditures function AE_1 in Exhibit 7. Beginning at point E_1, this hypothetical economy's initial equilibrium level is $4 trillion real GDP. The *MPC* is 0.50, and the spending multiplier is therefore 2. The full-employment output is $6 trillion real GDP, which means the economy faces a positive GDP gap of $2 trillion. Along the vertical line at the full-employment output level, look at the segment between point a on the initial AE_1 line and point E_2 on the AE_2 line, which is labeled a **recessionary gap**. A recessionary gap is the amount by which aggregate expenditures fall short of the amount required to achieve full-employment equilibrium. In our example, the recessionary gap is $1 trillion. What is the importance of the recessionary gap? The recessionary gap is the initial increase in autonomous spending required to trigger the multiplier, shift the aggregate expenditures function upward from AE_1 to AE_2, and eliminate the positive GDP gap. Stated as an expression,

Recessionary gap

The amount by which the aggregate expenditures curve must be increased to achieve full-employment equilibrium.

initial increase in autonomous expenditures $\times$ spending multiplier
= increase in equilibrium output

Using the data in our example,

$1 trillion $\times$ 2 = $2 trillion

We now turn to the important question of how to inject an additional $1 trillion spending into the economy, cause AE_1 to shift upward to AE_2, and thereby increase the equilibrium output from $4 trillion to $6 trillion real GDP. Under Keynesian theory, when market forces do not automatically do the job, then the central government should take aggressive action and adopt policies that boost autonomous spending [C, I, G, or $(X - M)$] by an amount equal to the recessionary gap.

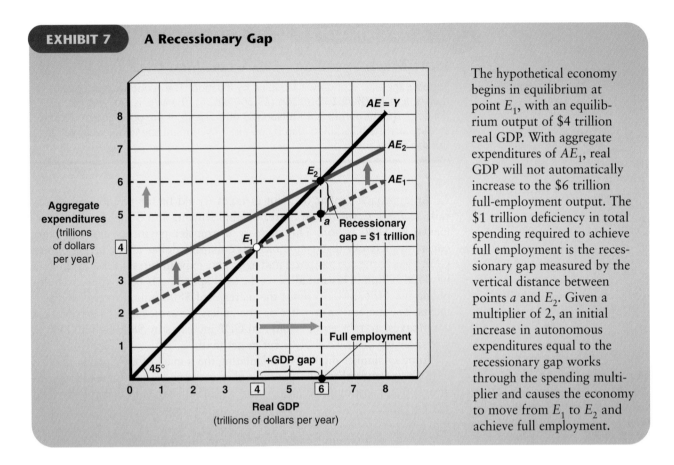

EXHIBIT 7   **A Recessionary Gap**

The hypothetical economy begins in equilibrium at point E_1, with an equilibrium output of $4 trillion real GDP. With aggregate expenditures of AE_1, real GDP will not automatically increase to the $6 trillion full-employment output. The $1 trillion deficiency in total spending required to achieve full employment is the recessionary gap measured by the vertical distance between points a and E_2. Given a multiplier of 2, an initial increase in autonomous expenditures equal to the recessionary gap works through the spending multiplier and causes the economy to move from E_1 to E_2 and achieve full employment.

Using a Tax Cut to Close a Recessionary Gap.   Instead of increasing government spending, let's assume the government decides to cut taxes to close the positive GDP gap in Exhibit 7. This is an option we have not yet discussed in the context of the aggregate expenditures–output model, and it requires special consideration. The government may consider changes in two types of taxes: autonomous taxes and income taxes. For simplicity, here the analysis is confined to the simpler concept of autonomous taxes, such as property taxes, which are independent of the levels of real output and income.

Suppose in Exhibit 7 the government reduces autonomous taxes by $800 billion. Would this tax cut be enough to restore full employment? Since real disposable income rises at every level of GDP, so does consumption at all levels of real GDP. As a result, the consumption function and, in turn, the aggregate expenditures function shifts upward, but not by the full amount of the tax cut. Since the MPC is 0.50, this means households spend only $400 billion of the additional $800 billion of disposable income from the tax cut. The remaining $400 billion of the tax cut is added to savings. Hence, after multiplying the tax cut by the MPC, the result of the tax cut is computed as above. That is, in this case, the increase in equilibrium real GDP is $400 billion × 2 = $800 billion. Since GDP would increase only from $4 trillion to $4.8 trillion, the economy would operate below the full-employment real GDP of $6 trillion.

CHECKPOINT

How Much Spending Must Uncle Sam Cut?

Suppose the U.S. economy is troubled by inflation. The economy is in equilibrium at a real GDP of $3.5 trillion ($3,500 billion), the *MPC* is .90, and the full-employment output is $3 trillion ($3,000 billion). If the government decides to eliminate the inflationary gap by cutting government spending, what will be the size of the cut?

An approach similar to a cut in taxes would be for the government to raise *transfer payments* (welfare, unemployment, and Social Security payments) by $800 billion. This increase in transfer payments, holding taxes constant, increases disposable income dollar-for-dollar at each level of real GDP. Hence, the consumption and aggregate expenditures lines shift upward by $400 billion. This initial boost in total spending is computed by multiplying the *MPC* of 0.50 times the increase of $800 billion in transfer payments. The increase in transfer payments has the same effect as an identical cut in taxes, and the equilibrium real GDP increases by $800 billion. Hence, a transfer payment is simply a cut in net taxes.

Another simpler method of calculating the impact of a change in taxes is to use a **tax multiplier**. The tax multiplier is the change in aggregate expenditures (total spending) resulting from an initial change in taxes. Expressed as a formula:

> **Tax multiplier**
>
> *The change in aggregate expenditures (total spending) resulting from an initial change in taxes. As a formula, the tax multiplier equals 1 − spending multiplier.*

$$\text{tax multiplier} = 1 - \text{spending multiplier}$$

After you calculate the tax multiplier, multiply your answer by the amount of the tax increase or decrease in order to determine the change in aggregate expenditures. Expressed as a formula:

$$\text{change in taxes } (\Delta T) \times \text{ tax multiplier}$$
$$= \text{ change in aggregate expenditures}$$

Returning to the example shown in Exhibit 7, suppose we wish to calculate the tax cut required to increase real GDP by $2 trillion from $4 trillion to $6 trillion and achieve full employment. Using the tax multiplier formula:

$$\text{tax multiplier} = 1 - 2 = -1$$
$$\Delta T \times (-1) = \$2 \text{ trillion}$$
$$\Delta T = -\$2 \text{ trillion}$$

Therefore, in this hypothetical economy, a $2 trillion tax cut will increase GDP by the $2 trillion required to achieve full employment.

Inflationary Gap

> **Inflationary gap**
>
> *The amount by which the aggregate expenditures curve must be decreased to achieve full-employment equilibrium.*

Under other circumstances, an **inflationary gap** may burden an economy. An inflationary gap is the amount by which aggregate expenditures exceed the amount required to achieve full-employment equilibrium. In Exhibit 8, the inflationary gap of $1 trillion is the vertical distance between point *a* on

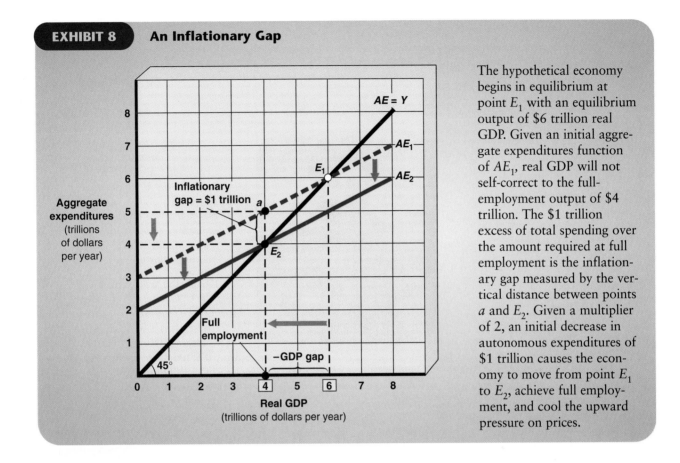

EXHIBIT 8 **An Inflationary Gap**

The hypothetical economy begins in equilibrium at point E_1 with an equilibrium output of $6 trillion real GDP. Given an initial aggregate expenditures function of AE_1, real GDP will not self-correct to the full-employment output of $4 trillion. The $1 trillion excess of total spending over the amount required at full employment is the inflationary gap measured by the vertical distance between points a and E_2. Given a multiplier of 2, an initial decrease in autonomous expenditures of $1 trillion causes the economy to move from point E_1 to E_2, achieve full employment, and cool the upward pressure on prices.

the initial AE_1 line and point E_2 on the AE_2 line. Since the economy can produce only $4 trillion in real output, this excess aggregate demand puts upward pressure on prices as buyers compete for this limited real output. If aggregate spending declines from AE_1 to AE_2, the economy moves from an equilibrium of $6 trillion at point E_1 to the full-employment equilibrium of $4 trillion at point E_2, and the inflationary pressure cools.

Again, the Keynesian prescription is for the central government to take aggressive action and adopt policies that reduce autonomous spending [C, I, G, or $(X - M)$] by an amount equal to the inflationary gap. Note from the analysis in the previous section that the government could cut government consumption expenditures or use a tax hike or a cut in transfer payments to reduce consumption. Stated as an expression,

initial decrease in autonomous expenditures $\times$ spending multiplier
= decrease in equilibrium output

In our example, the *MPC* is 0.50, so the multiplier is 2. The actual real GDP of $6 trillion is greater than the potential real GDP of $4 trillion, so the negative real GDP gap is −$2 trillion. Hence,

$$-\$1 \text{ trillion} \times 2 = -\$2 \text{ trillion}$$

INTERNATIONAL ECONOMICS

The Great Ice Cream War

Applicable Concept: aggregate expenditures–output model

The following *Wall Street Journal* article provides a rare insight into the politics of international trade, and the Analyze the Issue connects trade policy to the macro model developed in this chapter:

> *While many people relish American-made ice cream with deliberately foreign-sounding names, few people realize that the U.S. government declared war on ice cream imports by restricting them to less than one-tenth of one percent of U.S. consumption. With quotas so low and transportation costs high, few countries bothered to ship any ice cream at all to the United States. For example, in 1988 the United States exported hundreds of thousands of gallons of ice cream to Canada, yet Canadian ice cream was banned from the United States. Only 576 gallons was imported from New Zealand and 12 gallons from Denmark. This was not enough ice cream to stock a large grocery store on a summer Saturday.*
>
> *The U.S. ice cream quotas dated back to December 31, 1970, when President Nixon decreed that future ice cream*

> *imports could not exceed 431,330 gallons a year. Why? That year, according to Deputy Secretary of Agriculture Ann Veneman, testifying before the ITC [U.S. International Trade Commission], the U.S. was hit with a "flood of imports." This so-called "flood" amounted to barely 1% of U.S. ice cream consumption.*
>
> *How did Mr. Nixon decide to limit imports to exactly 431,330 gallons a year? Section 22 of the Agriculture Adjustment Act allowed the U.S. government to protect domestic price-support programs by restricting imports to 50 percent of the annual*

> *average imports for a representative period. Ice cream imports did not begin until 1969, so the U.S. government chose 1969 and the two previous years with no ice cream imports in order to calculate a low annual average import quota for this product.*

Finally, the article concluded that the U.S. government probably spent more than $1,000 in administrative expenses for each gallon of ice cream imported into the United States. The article's author concludes: "International trade disputes are rapidly degenerating into a full employment program for government bureaucrats."

ANALYZE THE ISSUE

Assume the U.S. economy is in an inflationary gap condition. Use the Keynesian aggregate expenditures–output model to explain why increasing U.S. exports and restricting imports is or is not a desirable policy.

Source: James Bovard, "The Great Ice Cream War," *Wall Street Journal*, Sept. 6, 1989, p. A18.

KEY CONCEPTS

Aggregate expenditures–
   output model

Spending multiplier
Recessionary gap

Tax multiplier
Inflationary gap

SUMMARY

- The **Keynesian theory** argues that the economy is inherently unstable and may require government intervention to control aggregate expenditures and restore full employment. If we assume that real disposable income remains the same high proportion of real GDP, then we can substitute real GDP for real disposable income in the Keynesian model. **Government spending** and **net exports** can be treated as autonomous expenditures in the Keynesian model. **Net exports** are the only component of aggregate expenditures that changes from a positive to a negative value as real GDP rises. Both exports and imports are determined by foreign or domestic income, tastes, trade restrictions, and exchange rates.

Government spending

Net exports

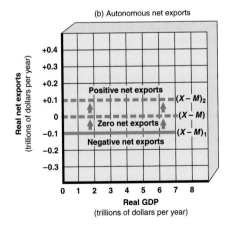

- The **Keynesian aggregate expenditures–output model** determines the equilibrium level of real GDP by the intersection of the aggregate expenditures and the aggregate output and income curves. Each equilibrium level in the economy is associated with a level of employment and corresponding unemployment rate. Aggregate expenditures and real GDP are equal, graphically, where the $AE = C + I + G + (X - M)$ line intersects the 45-degree line. At any output greater or less than the equilibrium real GDP, unintended inventory investment pressures businesses to alter aggregate output and income until equilibrium at full-employment real GDP is restored.

Keynesian aggregate expenditures–output model

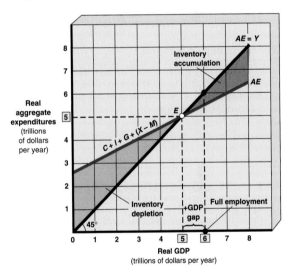

- The **spending multiplier** is the ratio of the change in equilibrium output to the initial change in any of the components of aggregate expenditures. Algebraically, the multiplier is the reciprocal of the marginal propensity to save. The multiplier effect causes the equilibrium level of real GDP to change by several times the initial change in spending.

- A **recessionary gap** is the amount by which aggregate expenditures fall short of the amount necessary for the economy to operate at full-employment real GDP. To eliminate a positive GDP gap, the Keynesian solution is to increase autonomous spending by an amount equal to the recessionary gap and operate through the multiplier to increase equilibrium output and income.

Recessionary gap

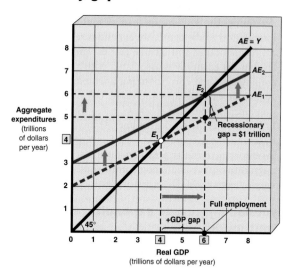

- The **tax multiplier** is the multiplier by which an initial change in taxes changes aggregate demand (total spending) after an infinite number of spending cycles. Expressed as a formula, the tax multiplier = 1 − spending multiplier.

- An **inflationary gap** is the amount by which aggregate expenditures exceed the amount necessary to establish full-employment equilibrium and indicates upward pressure on prices. To eliminate a negative GDP gap, the Keynesian solution is to decrease autonomous spending by an amount equal to the inflationary gap and operate through the multiplier to decrease equilibrium output and income.

Inflationary gap

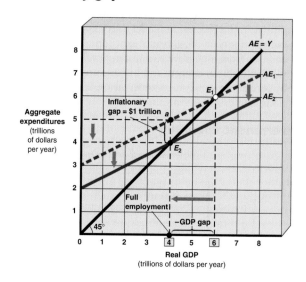

SUMMARY OF CONCLUSION STATEMENTS

- At the equilibrium level of real GDP, the total value of goods and services produced (aggregate output and income, Y) is precisely equal to the total spending for these goods and services (aggregate expenditures, *AE*).

- Aggregate expenditures in Keynesian economics pull aggregate output either higher or lower toward equilibrium in the economy as opposed to the classical view that aggregate output generates an equal amount of aggregate spending.

- Any initial change in spending by the government, households, or firms creates a chain reaction of further spending, which causes a greater cumulative change in aggregate demand.

STUDY QUESTIONS AND PROBLEMS

1. Assume the level of autonomous investment is $100 billion and aggregate expenditures equal consumption and investment. Based on the table below, answer the following questions.
   a. Fill in the unplanned inventory column.

   b. Determine the *MPC* and *MPS*.
   c. If this economy employs a labor force of 40 million, what will happen to this level of employment? Explain and identify the equilibrium level of output.

Employment, Output, Consumption, and Unplanned Inventory

Possible levels of employment (millions of workers)	Real GDP (output) equals disposable income (billions of dollars)	Consumption (billions of dollars)	Unplanned inventory (billions of dollars)
40	$325	$300	$_____
45	375	325	_____
50	425	350	_____
55	475	375	_____
60	525	400	_____
65	575	425	_____
70	625	450	_____

2. Using the data given in question 1, what is the impact of adding net exports? Let imports equal $75 billion, and assume exports equal $50 billion. What is the equilibrium level of employment and output?

3. Explain the determination of the equilibrium real GDP by drawing an abstract graph of the aggregate expenditures–output model. Label the aggregate expenditures line *AE* and the aggregate output line *AO*. Explain why the interaction of *AE* and *AO* determines the Keynesian equilibrium level of real GDP.

4. Use the aggregate expenditures–output model to demonstrate the multiplier effect.

5. How are changes in the *MPC*, changes in the *MPS*, and the size of the multiplier related? Answer the following questions:
   a. What is the multiplier if the *MPC* is 0? 0.33? 0.90?
   b. Suppose the equilibrium real GDP is $100 billion and the *MPC* is 4/5. How much will the equilibrium output change if businesses increase their level of investment by $10 billion?
   c. Using the data given in question (b), what will be the change in equilibrium real GDP if the *MPC* equals 2/3?

6. Assume the *MPC* is 0.90 and autonomous investment increases by $500 billion. What will be the impact on real GDP?

7. Suppose autonomous investment increases by $100 billion and the *MPC* is 0.75.
   a. Use the following table to compute four rounds of the spending multiplier effect:
   b. Use the spending multiplier formula to compute the final cumulative impact on aggregate spending.

Round	Components of total spending	New consumption spending (billions of dollars)
1	Investment	$_____
2	Consumption	$_____
3	Consumption	$_____
4	Consumption	$_____
	Total spending	$_____

8. First, use the data given in question 1, and assume the level of autonomous investment is $50 billion. If the full-employment level of output is $525 billion, what is the equilibrium level of output and employment? Does a recessionary gap or an inflationary gap exist? Second, assume the level of autonomous investment is $150 billion. What is the equilibrium level of output and employment? Does a recessionary gap or an inflationary gap exist? Explain the consequences of an inflationary gap using the aggregate expenditures–output model.

9. Assume an economy's *MPC* is 0.75 and there is a recessionary gap of $100 billion. How much must government spending increase to eliminate the gap. Instead of increasing government spending by the amount you calculate, what would be the effect of the government cutting taxes by this amount?

10. Suppose the government wishes to eliminate an inflationary gap of $100 billion and the *MPC* is 0.50. How much must the government cut its spending? Instead of decreasing government spending by the amount you calculate, what would be the effect of the government increasing taxes by this amount?

ONLINE EXERCISES

Exercise 1

Visit "Economagic.com Economic Time Series Page" at http://www.economagic.com/popular.htm and follow these steps:

1. Select Real Personal Consumption Expenditures.

2. Explain how the observed trend in personal consumption expenditures since 1990 affected the Keynesian aggregate expenditures-output model.

Exercise 2

Browse The World's Economic Outlook (http://www .theatlantic.com/unbound/flashbks/budget/keynesf.htm). This influential article concerning U.S. fiscal policy provides a sample of Keynes's writings.

Exercise 3

Visit the Economic Statistics Briefing Room (http://www .whitehouse.gov/fsbr/international.html), and determine the change in the United States's trade balance. What impact will this have on the U.S. National economy?

Exercise 4

Why do so many cities and vacations spots advertise themselves like this web site http://www.seerockcity.com/? What economic concept is at play as more people visit the site?

CHECKPOINT ANSWERS

Full-Employment Output, Where Are You?

A tax cut of $200 billion boosts consumer income by this amount. Since the *MPC* is 0.50, consumers will spend $100 billion of the tax cut and save the remaining $100 billion. To compute the impact of the rise in consumption (ΔC) on real GDP (ΔY), use this formula:

$$\Delta C \times multiplier = \Delta Y$$

where

$$multiplier = \frac{1}{MPS} = \frac{1}{1 - MPC} = \frac{1}{1 - 0.50} = 2$$

Thus,

$$\$100 \text{ billion} \times 2 = \$200 \text{ billion}$$

The increase in real GDP from the tax cut equals $200 billion, which is added to the initial equilibrium real GDP of $3 trillion to achieve full-employment output. If you said the full-employment real GDP is $3.2 trillion, YOU ARE CORRECT.

How Much Spending Must Uncle Sam Cut?

The negative GDP gap is $500 billion real GDP. To calculate the size of the government spending cut (ΔG) required to decrease real GDP (ΔY) by $500 billion, use this formula:

$$\Delta G \times multiplier = -\Delta Y$$

where

$$multiplier = \frac{1}{MPS} = \frac{1}{1 - MPC} = \frac{1}{1 - 0.90} = 10$$

Thus,

$$\Delta G = \frac{-\Delta Y}{multiplier} = \frac{-\$500 \text{ billion}}{10} = -\$50 \text{ billion}$$

If you said the size of the cut in government spending is $50 billion, YOU ARE CORRECT.

PRACTICE QUIZ

For a visual explanation of the correct answers, visit the tutorial at http://tucker.swcollege.com.

1. The net exports line can be
   a. positive.
   b. negative.
   c. zero.
   d. any of the above.

2. There will be unplanned inventory investment accumulation when
   a. aggregate output (real GDP) equals aggregate expenditures.
   b. aggregate output (real GDP) exceeds aggregate expenditures.
   c. aggregate expenditures exceed aggregate output (real GDP).
   d. firms increase output.

3. John Maynard Keynes proposed that the multiplier effect can correct an economic depression. Based on this theory, an increase in equilibrium output would be created by an initial
   a. increase in investment.
   b. increase in government spending.
   c. decrease in government spending.
   d. both a and b.
   e. both a and c.

4. The spending multiplier is defined as
   a. 1/(1 − marginal propensity to consume).
   b. 1/(marginal propensity to consume).
   c. 1/(1 − marginal propensity to save).
   d. 1/(marginal propensity to consume + marginal propensity to save).

5. If the value of the marginal propensity to consume (*MPC*) is 0.50, the value of the spending multiplier is
   a. .5.
   b. 1.
   c. 2.
   d. 5.

6. If the marginal propensity to consume (*MPC*) is 0.80, the value of the spending multiplier is
   a. 2.
   b. 5.
   c. 8.
   d. 10.

7. If the marginal propensity to consume (*MPC*) is 0.75, a $50 billion decrease in government spending would cause equilibrium output to
   a. increase by $50 billion.
   b. decrease by $50 billion.
   c. increase by $200 billion.
   d. decrease by $200 billion.

8. If the marginal propensity to consume (*MPC*) is 0.90, a $100 billion increase in planned investment expenditure, other things being equal, will cause an increase in equilibrium output of
   a. $90 billion.
   b. $100 billion.
   c. $900 billion.
   d. $1,000 billion.

9. Keynes's criticism of the classical theory was that the Great Depression would not correct itself. The multiplier effect would restore an economy to full employment if
   a. government were to follow a "least government is the best government" policy.
   b. government taxes were increased.
   c. government spending were increased.
   d. government spending were decreased.

10. The equilibrium level of real GDP is $1,000 billion, the full-employment level of real GDP is $1,250 billion, and the marginal propensity to consume (*MPC*) is 0.60. The full-employment target can be reached if government spending is
    a. increased by $60 billion.
    b. increased by $100 billion.
    c. increased by $250 billion.
    d. held constant.

11. In Exhibit 9, the spending multiplier for this economy is equal to
    a. 1⅔.
    b. 2½.
    c. 3.
    d. 5.

Exhibit 9 Keynesian Aggregate Expenditures–Output Model When the *MPC* Is 3/5

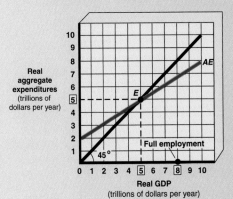

12. To close the recessionary gap and achieve full-employment real GDP as shown in Exhibit 9, the government should increase spending by
   a. $1.0 trillion.
   b. $1.2 trillion.
   c. $2.0 trillion.
   d. $2.5 trillion.

13. To close the recessionary gap and achieve full-employment real GDP shown in Exhibit 9, the government should cut taxes by
   a. $.60 trillion.
   b. $1 trillion.
   c. $2 trillion.
   d. $3 trillion.

CHAPTER 20

Aggregate Demand and Supply

A s explained in the previous two chapters, before British economist John Maynard Keynes, classical economic theory argued that the economy would bounce back to full employment as long as prices and wages were flexible. As the unemployment rate soared and persisted during the Great Depression, Keynes formulated a new theory with new policy implications. Instead of a wait-and-see policy until markets self-correct the economy, Keynes argued that policymakers must take action to influence aggregate spending through changes in government spending. The prescription for the Great Depression was simple: Increase government spending and jobs will be created.

Although Keynes was not concerned with the problem of inflation, his theory has implications for fighting demand-pull inflation. In this case, the government must cut spending or increase taxes to reduce aggregate demand.

In this chapter, you will use aggregate demand and supply analysis to study the business cycle. The chapter opens with a presentation of the aggregate demand curve and then the aggregate supply curve. Once these concepts are developed,

the analysis shows why modern macroeconomics teaches that shifts in aggregate supply or aggregate demand can influence the price level, the equilibrium level of real GDP, and employment. You will probably return to this chapter often because it provides the basic tools with which to organize your thinking about the macro economy.

In this chapter, you will learn to solve these economics puzzles:

■ Why does the aggregate supply curve have three different segments?

■ Would the greenhouse effect cause inflation, unemployment, or both?

■ Was John Maynard Keynes's prescription for the Great Depression right?

The Aggregate Demand Curve

Aggregate demand curve (AD)

The curve that shows the level of real GDP purchased by house-holds, businesses, government, and foreigners (net exports) at different possible price levels during a time period, ceteris paribus.

Here we view the collective demand for *all* goods and services, rather than the *market* demand for a particular good or service. Exhibit 1 shows the **aggregate demand (AD) curve,** which slopes downward and to the right for a given year. The aggregate demand curve shows the level of real GDP purchased by households, businesses, government, and foreigners (net exports) at different possible price levels during a time period, ceteris paribus. The aggregate demand curve shows us the total dollar amount of goods and services that will be demanded in the economy at various price levels. As for

---

EXHIBIT 1   **The Aggregate Demand Curve**

The aggregate demand curve (*AD*) shows the relationship between the price level and the level of real GDP, other things being equal. The lower the price level, the larger the GDP demanded by households, businesses, government, and foreigners. If the price level is 150 at point *A*, a real GDP of $4 trillion is demanded. If the price level is 100 at point *B*, the real GDP demanded increases to $6 trillion.

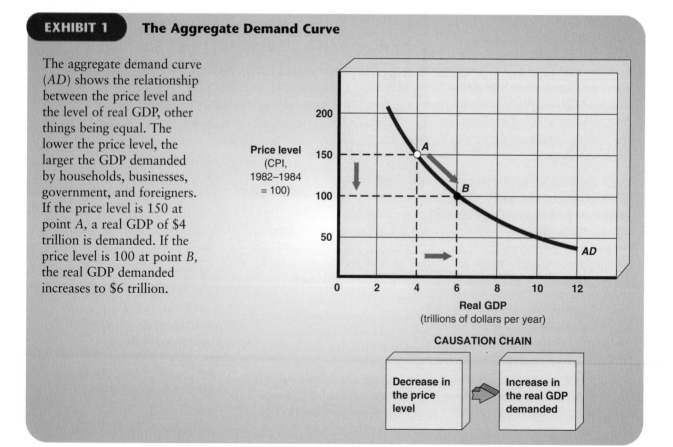

the demand curve for an individual market, other factors remaining constant, the lower the economywide price level, the greater the aggregate quantity demanded for real goods and services.

The downward slope of the aggregate demand curve shows that at a given level of aggregate income, people buy more goods and services at a lower average price level. While the horizontal axis in the market supply and demand model measures *physical* units, such as a bushel of wheat, the horizontal axis in the aggregate demand and supply model measures the value of *final* goods and services included in real GDP. Note that the horizontal axis represents the quantity of aggregate production demanded, measured in base-year dollars. The vertical axis is an *index* of the overall price level, such as the GDP deflator or the CPI, rather than the price per bushel of wheat. As shown in Exhibit 1, if the price level measured by the CPI is 150 at point *A*, a real GDP of $4 trillion is demanded in, say, 2000. If the price level is 100 at point *B*, a real GDP of $6 trillion is demanded.

Although the aggregate demand curve looks like a market demand curve, these concepts are different. As we move along a market demand curve, the price of related goods is assumed to be constant. But when we deal with changes in the general or average price level in an economy, this assumption is meaningless because we are using a market basket measure for *all* goods and services.

> **Conclusion** *The aggregate demand curve and the demand curve are not the same concepts.*

Reasons for the Aggregate Demand Curve's Shape

The reasons for the downward slope of an aggregate demand curve include the *real balances* or *wealth effect,* the *interest-rate effect,* and the *net exports effect.*

Real Balances Effect

Recall from the discussion in the chapter on inflation that cash, checking deposits, savings accounts, and certificates of deposit are examples of financial assets whose real value changes with the price level. If prices are falling, households are more willing and able to spend. Suppose you have $1,000 in a checking account with which to buy 10 weeks' worth of groceries. If prices fall by 20 percent, $1,000 will now buy enough groceries for 12 weeks. This rise in real wealth may make you more willing and able to purchase a new VCR out of current income.

For current wealth and income data, visit the Economic Statistics Briefing Room (http://www.whitehouse.gov/fsbr/income.html).

> **Conclusion** *Consumers spend more on goods and services when lower prices make their dollars more valuable. Therefore, the real value of money is measured by the quantity of goods and services each dollar buys.*

When inflation reduces the real value of fixed-value financial assets held by households, the result is lower consumption, and real GDP falls. The effect of the change in the price level on real consumption spending is called the **real balances** or **wealth effect.** The real balances or wealth effect is the impact on total spending (real GDP) caused by the inverse relationship between the price level and the real value of financial assets with fixed nominal value.

Interest-Rate Effect

A second reason why the aggregate demand curve is downward sloping involves the **interest-rate effect.** The interest-rate effect is the impact on total spending (real GDP) caused by the direct relationship between the price level and the interest rate. A key assumption of the aggregate demand curve is that the supply of money available for borrowing remains fixed. A high price level means people must take more dollars from their wallets and checking accounts in order to purchase goods and services. At a higher price level, the demand for borrowed money to buy products also increases and results in higher cost of borrowing, that is, interest rates. Rising interest rates discourage households from borrowing to purchase homes, cars, and other consumer products. Similarly, at higher interest rates, businesses cut investment projects because the higher cost of borrowing diminishes the profitability of these investments. Thus, assuming fixed credit, an increase in the price level translates through higher interest rates into a lower real GDP.

Net Exports Effect

Whether American-made goods have lower prices than foreign goods is another important factor in determining the aggregate demand curve. A higher domestic price level tends to make U.S. goods more expensive compared to foreign goods, and imports rise because consumers substitute imported goods for domestic goods. An increase in the price of U.S. goods in foreign markets also causes U.S. exports to decline. Consequently, a rise in the domestic price level of an economy tends to increase imports, decrease exports, and thereby reduce the net exports component of real GDP. This condition is the **net exports effect.** The net exports effect is the impact on total spending (real GDP) caused by the inverse relationship between the price level and the net exports of an economy.

Exhibit 2 summarizes the three effects that explain why the aggregate demand curve in Exhibit 1 is downward sloping.

Nonprice-Level Determinants of Aggregate Demand

As was the case with individual demand curves, we must distinguish between *changes in real GDP demanded,* caused by changes in the price level, and *changes in aggregate demand,* caused by changes in one or more of the *nonprice-level determinants.* Once the ceteris paribus assumption is relaxed, changes in variables other than the price level cause a change in the location of the aggre-

Real balances or **wealth effect**

The impact on total spending (real GDP) caused by the inverse relationship between the price level and the real value of financial assets with fixed nominal value.

Interest-rate effect

The impact on total spending (real GDP) caused by the direct relationship between the price level and the interest rate.

Net exports effect

The impact on total spending (real GDP) caused by the inverse relationship between the price level and the net exports of an economy.

For current international trade data, visit the Economic Statistics Briefing Room (http://www.whitehouse.gov/fsbr/international.html) *and the Census Bureau* (http://www.census.gov/ftp/pub/indicator/www/ustrade.html).

EXHIBIT 2 Why the Aggregate Demand Curve Is Downward Sloping

Effect	Causation chain
Real balances effect	Price level decreases → Purchasing power rises → Wealth rises → Consumers buy more goods → Real GDP demanded increases
Interest-rate effect	Price level decreases → Purchasing power rises → Demand for fixed supply of credit falls → Interest rates fall → Businesses and households borrow and buy more goods → Real GDP demanded increases
Net exports effect	Price level decreases → U.S. goods become less expensive than foreign goods → Americans and foreigners buy more U.S. goods → Exports rise and imports fall → Real GDP demanded increases

gate demand curve. Nonprice-level determinants include the consumption (C), investment (I), government spending (G), and net exports ($X - M$) components of aggregate expenditures explained in the chapter on GDP.

Conclusion *Any change in aggregate expenditures shifts the aggregate demand curve.*

Exhibit 3 illustrates the link between an increase in expenditures and an increase in aggregate demand. Begin at point A on aggregate demand curve AD_1, with a price level of 100 and a real GDP of $6 trillion. Assume the price level remains constant at 100 and the aggregate demand curve increases from AD_1 to AD_2. Consequently, the level of real GDP rises from $6 trillion (point A) to $8 trillion (point B) at the price level of 100. The cause might be that consumers have become more optimistic about the future and their consumption expenditures (C) have risen. Or possibly an increase in business optimism has increased profit expectations, and the level of investment (I) has risen because businesses are spending more for plants and equipment. The same increase in aggregate demand could also have been caused by a boost in government spending (G) or a rise in net exports ($X - M$). A swing to pessimistic expectations by consumers or firms will cause the aggregate demand curve to shift leftward. A leftward shift in the aggregate demand curve may also be caused by a decrease in government spending or net exports.

For current and historical data on production and consumer as well as producer prices, visit the Economic Statistics Briefing Room (http://www.whitehouse.gov/fsbr/production.html and http://www.whitehouse.gov/fsbr/prices.html, respectively).

The Aggregate Supply Curve

Just as we must distinguish between the *aggregate* demand and *market* demand curves, the theory for a *market* supply curve does not apply directly to the *aggregate* supply curve. Keeping this condition in mind, we can define the **aggregate supply (AS) curve** as the curve that shows the level of real

Aggregate supply curve (AS)

The curve that shows the level of real GDP produced at different possible price levels during a time period, ceteris paribus.

A Shift in the Aggregate Demand Curve

At the price level of 100, the real GDP level is $6 trillion at point *A* on AD_1. An increase in one of the nonprice-level determinants of consumption (*C*), investment (*I*), government spending (*G*), or net exports (*X* − *M*) causes the level of real GDP to rise to $8 trillion at point *B* on AD_2. Because this effect occurs at any price level, an increase in aggregate expenditures shifts the *AD* curve rightward. Conversely, a decrease in aggregate expenditures shifts the *AD* curve leftward.

Price level (CPI, 1982–1984 = 100)

Real GDP (trillions of dollars per year)

CAUSATION CHAIN

Increase in nonprice-level determinants: *C, I, G, (X − M)* ⟹ Increase in the aggregate demand curve

GDP produced at different possible price levels during a time period, ceteris paribus. Stated simply, the aggregate supply curve shows us the total dollar amount of goods and services produced in an economy at various price levels. Given this general definition, we must pause to discuss two opposing views—the Keynesian horizontal aggregate supply curve and the classical vertical aggregate supply curve.

Keynesian View of Aggregate Supply

In 1936, John Maynard Keynes published *The General Theory of Employment, Interest, and Money*. In this book, Keynes argued that price and wage inflexibility means that unemployment can be a prolonged affair. Unless an economy trapped in a depression or severe recession is rescued by an increase in aggregate demand, full employment will not be achieved. This Keynesian prediction calls for government to intervene and actively manage aggregate demand to avoid a depression or recession.

Why did Keynes assume that product prices and wages were fixed? During a deep recession or depression, there are many idle resources in the economy. Consequently, producers are willing to sell additional output at current prices because there are no shortages to put upward pressure on

EXHIBIT 4   **The Keynesian Horizontal Aggregate Supply Curve**

CAUSATION CHAIN

| Government spending (G) increases | ⇨ | Aggregate demand increases and the economy moves from E₁ to E₂ | ⇨ | Price level remains constant, while real GDP and employment rise |

The increase in aggregate demand from AD_1 to AD_2 causes a new equilibrium at E_2. Given the Keynesian assumption of a fixed price level, changes in aggregate demand cause changes in real GDP along the horizontal portion of the aggregate supply curve, AS. Keynesian theory argues that only shifts in aggregate demand possess the ability to restore a depressed economy to the full-employment output of $10 trillion.

prices. Moreover, the supply of unemployed workers willing to work for the prevailing wage rate diminishes the power of workers to increase their wages, and union contracts prevent lowering wage rates. Given the Keynesian assumption of fixed or rigid product prices and wages, changes in the aggregate demand curve cause changes in real GDP along a horizontal aggregate supply curve. In short, Keynesian theory argues that only shifts in aggregate demand possess the ability to revitalize a depressed economy.

Exhibit 4 portrays the core of Keynesian theory. We begin at equilibrium E_1, with a fixed price level of 100. Given aggregate demand schedule AD_1, the equilibrium level of real GDP is $6 trillion. Now government spending (G) increases, causing aggregate demand to rise from AD_1 to AD_2 and equilibrium to shift from E_1 to E_2 along the horizontal aggregate supply curve, AS. At E_2, the economy moves to $8 trillion, which is closer to the full-employment GDP of $10 trillion.

Conclusion *When the aggregate supply curve is horizontal and an economy is below full employment, the only effects of an increase in aggregate demand are increases in real GDP and employment, while the price level does not change. Stated simply, the Keynesian view is that "demand creates its own supply."*

Classical View of Aggregate Supply

Prior to the Great Depression, a group of economists known as the *classical economists* dominated economic thinking. The founder of the classical school of economics was Adam Smith. Exhibit 5 uses the aggregate demand and supply model to illustrate the classical view that the aggregate supply curve, *AS*, is a vertical line at the full-employment output of $10 trillion. The vertical shape of the classical aggregate supply curve is based on two assumptions. First, the economy normally operates at its full-employment output level. Second, the price level of products and production costs change by the same percentage, that is, proportionally, in order to maintain a full-employment level of output. This classical theory of flexible prices and wages is at odds with the Keynesian concept of sticky (inflexible) prices and wages.

Exhibit 5 illustrates why classical economists believe a market economy automatically self-corrects to full employment. Following the classical scenario, the economy is initially in equilibrium at E_1, the price level is 150, real output is at its full-employment level of $10 trillion, and aggregate demand curve AD_1 traces total spending. Now suppose private spending falls because households and businesses are pessimistic about economic conditions. This condition causes AD_1 to shift leftward to AD_2. At a price level of 150, the immediate effect is that aggregate output exceeds aggregate spending by $2 trillion ($E_1$ to E'), and unexpected inventory accumulation occurs. To eliminate unsold inventories resulting from the decrease in aggregate demand, business firms temporarily cut back on production and reduce the price level from 150 to 100.

At E', the decline in aggregate output in response to the surplus also affects prices in the factor markets. The result of the economy moving from point E_1 to E', there is a decrease in the demand for labor, natural resources, and other inputs used to produce products. This surplus condition in the factor markets means that some workers who are willing to work are laid off and compete with those who still have jobs by reducing their wage demands. Owners of natural resources and capital likewise cut their prices.

How can the classical economists believe that prices and wages are completely flexible? The answer is contained in the *real balances effect*, explained earlier. When businesses reduce the price level from 150 to 100, the cost of living falls by the same proportion. Once the price level falls by 33 percent, a nominal or money wage rate of, say, $21 per hour will purchase 33 percent more groceries after the fall in product prices than it would before the fall. Workers will therefore accept a pay cut of 33 percent, or $7 per hour. Any worker who refuses the lower wage rate of $14 per hour is replaced by an unemployed worker willing to accept the going rate.

Exhibit 5 shows an economywide proportional fall in prices and wages by the movement downward along AD_2 from E' to a new equilibrium at E_2. At E_2, the economy has self-corrected through downwardly flexible prices

EXHIBIT 5　　**The Classical Vertical Aggregate Supply Curve**

CAUSATION CHAIN

| Aggregate demand decreases at full employment and the economy moves from E_1 to E' | At E' unemployment and a surplus of unsold goods and services cause cuts in prices and wages | The economy moves from E' to E_2, where full employment is restored |

Classical theory teaches that prices and wages quickly adjust to keep the economy operating at its full-employment output of $10 trillion. A decline in aggregate demand from AD_1 to AD_2 will temporarily cause a surplus of $2 trillion, the distance from E' to E_1. Businesses respond by cutting the price level from 150 to 100. As a result, consumers increase their purchases because of the real balances or wealth effect, and wages adjust downward. Thus, classical economists predict the economy is self-correcting and will restore full employment at point E_2. E_1 and E_2 therefore represent points along a classical vertical aggregate supply curve, *AS*.

and wages to its full-employment level of $10 trillion worth of real GDP at the lower price level of 100. E_1 and E_2 therefore represent points along a classical vertical aggregate supply curve, *AS*.

Conclusion *When the aggregate supply curve is vertical at the full-employment GDP, the only effect over time of a change in aggregate demand is a change in the price level. Stated simply, the classical view is that "supply creates its own demand."*[1]

---

[1]This quotation is known as Say's Law, named after French classical economist Jean Baptiste Say (1767–1832).

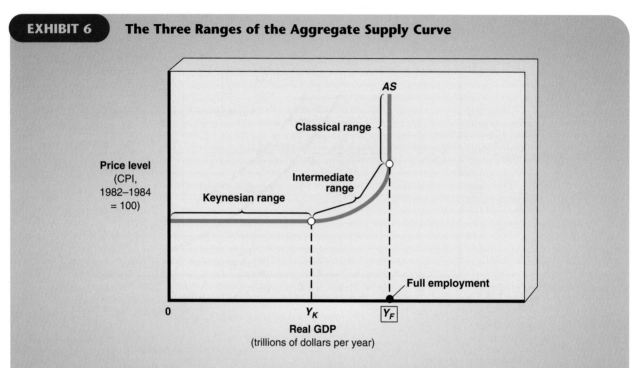

EXHIBIT 6   **The Three Ranges of the Aggregate Supply Curve**

The aggregate supply curve shows the relationship between the price level and the level of real GDP supplied. It consists of three distinct ranges: (1) a Keynesian range between 0 and Y_K, where the price level is constant for an economy in severe recession; (2) an intermediate range between Y_K and Y_F, where both the price level and the level of real GDP vary as an economy approaches full employment; and (3) a classical range where the price level can vary, while the level of real GDP remains constant at the full-employment level of output, Y_F.

Keynesian range

The horizontal segment of the aggregate supply curve, which represents an economy in a severe recession.

Intermediate range

The rising segment of the aggregate supply curve, which represents an economy as it approaches full-employment output.

Classical range

The vertical segment of the aggregate supply curve, which represents an economy at full-employment output.

Although Keynes himself did not use the *AD-AS* model, we can use Exhibit 5 to distinguish between Keynes's view and the classical theory of flexible prices and wages. Keynes believed that once the demand curve has shifted from AD_1 to AD_2, the surplus—the distance from E' to E_1—will persist because he rejected price-wage downward flexibility. The economy therefore will remain at the less-than-full-employment output of $8 trillion until the aggregate demand curve shifts rightward and returns to its initial position at AD_1.

Three Ranges of the Aggregate Supply Curve

Having studied the polar theories of the classical economists and Keynes, we will now discuss an eclectic or general view of how the shape of the aggregate supply curve varies as real GDP expands or contracts. The aggregate supply curve, *AS,* in Exhibit 6 has three quite distinct ranges or segments, labeled (1) **Keynesian range,** (2) **intermediate range,** and (3) **classical range.**

EXHIBIT 7 **The Aggregate Demand and Aggregate Supply Model**

Macroeconomic equilibrium occurs where the aggregate demand curve, *AD*, and the aggregate supply curve, *AS*, intersect. In this case, equilibrium, *E*, is located at the far end of the Keynesian range, where the price level is 100 and the equilibrium output is $6 trillion. In macroeconomic equilibrium, businesses neither overestimate nor underestimate the real GDP demanded at the prevailing price level.

The Keynesian range is the horizontal segment of the aggregate supply curve, which represents an economy in a severe recession. In Exhibit 6, below real GDP Y_K, the price level remains constant as the level of real GDP rises. Between Y_K and the full-employment output of Y_F, the price level rises as the real GDP level rises. The intermediate range is the rising segment of the aggregate supply curve, which represents an economy approaching full-employment output. Finally, at Y_F, the level of real GDP remains constant, and only the price level rises. The classical range is the vertical segment of the aggregate supply curve, which represents an economy at full-employment output. We will now examine the rationale for each of these three quite distinct ranges.

Aggregate Demand and Aggregate Supply Macroeconomic Equilibrium

In Exhibit 7, the *macroeconomic equilibrium* level of real GDP corresponding to the point of equality, *E*, is $6 trillion, and the equilibrium price level is 100. This is the unique combination of price level and output level that equates how much people want to buy with the amount businesses want to produce and sell. Because the entire real GDP value of final products is bought and sold at the price level of 100, there is no upward or downward pressure for the macroeconomic equilibrium to change. Note that the economy shown in Exhibit 7 is operating on the edge of the Keynesian range, with a GDP gap of $4 trillion.

Suppose that in Exhibit 7 the level of output on the *AS* curve is below $6 trillion and the *AD* curve remains fixed. At a price level of 100, the real GDP demanded exceeds the real GDP supplied. Under such circumstances, businesses cannot fill orders quickly enough, and inventories are drawn down unexpectedly. Business managers react by hiring more workers and producing more output. Because the economy is operating in the Keynesian range, the price level remains constant at 100. The opposite scenario occurs if the level of real GDP supplied on the *AS* curve exceeds the real GDP in the intermediate range between $6 trillion and $10 trillion. In this output segment, the price level is between 100 and 200, and businesses face sales that are less than expected. In this case, unintended inventories of unsold goods pile up on the shelves, and management will lay off workers, cut back on production, and reduce prices.

This adjustment process continues until the equilibrium price level and output level are reached at point *E* and there is no upward or downward pressure for the price level to change. Here the production decisions of sellers in the economy equal the total spending decisions of buyers during the given period of time.

Conclusion *At macroeconomic equilibrium, sellers neither overestimate nor underestimate the real GDP demanded at the prevailing price level.*

Changes in the *AD-AS* Macroeconomic Equilibrium

One explanation of the business cycle is that the aggregate demand curve moves along a stationary aggregate supply curve. The next step in our analysis therefore is to *shift* the aggregate demand curve along the three ranges of the aggregate supply curve and observe the impact on the real GDP and the price level. As the macroeconomic equilibrium changes, the economy experiences more or fewer problems with inflation and unemployment.

Keynesian Range

Keynes's macroeconomic theory offered a powerful solution to the Great Depression. Keynes perceived the economy as driven by aggregate demand, and Exhibit 8(a) demonstrates this theory with hypothetical data. The range of real GDP below $6 trillion is consistent with Keynesian price and wage inflexibility. Assume the economy is in equilibrium at E_1, with a price level of 100 and a real GDP of $4 trillion. In this case, the economy is in recession far below the full-employment GDP of $10 trillion. The Keynesian prescription for a recession is to increase aggregate demand until the economy achieves full employment. Because the aggregate supply curve is horizontal in the Keynesian range, "demand creates its own supply." Suppose demand shifts rightward from AD_1 to AD_2 and a new equilibrium is established at E_2. Even at the higher real GDP level of $6 trillion, the price level remains at 100. Stated differently, aggregate output can expand throughout this range without raising prices. This is because, in the Keynesian range, substantial idle production capacity (including property and unemployed workers competing for available jobs) can be put to work at existing prices.

Conclusion *As aggregate demand increases in the Keynesian range, the price level remains constant as real GDP expands.*

EXHIBIT 8 **Effects of Increases in Aggregate Demand**

(a) Increasing demand in the Keynesian range

(b) Increasing demand in the intermediate range

(c) Increasing demand in the classical range

The effect of a rightward shift in the aggregate demand curve on the price and output levels depends on the range of the aggregate supply curve in which the shift occurs. In part (a), an increase in aggregate demand causing the equilibrium to change from E_1 to E_2 in the Keynesian range will increase real GDP from $4 trillion to $6 trillion, but the price level will remain unchanged at 100.

In part (b), an increase in aggregate demand causing the equilibrium to change from E_3 to E_4 in the intermediate range will increase real GDP from $6 trillion to $8 trillion, and the price level will rise from 100 to 125.

In part (c), an increase in aggregate demand causing the equilibrium to change from E_5 to E_6 in the classical range will increase the price level from 150 to 200, but real GDP will not increase beyond the full-employment level of $10 trillion.

Intermediate Range

The intermediate range in Exhibit 8(b) is between $6 trillion and $10 trillion worth of real GDP. As output increases in the range of the aggregate supply curve near the full-employment level of output, the considerable slack in the economy disappears. Assume an economy is initially in equilibrium at E_3 and aggregate demand increases from AD_3 to AD_4. As a result, the level of real GDP rises from $6 trillion to $8 trillion, and the price level rises from 100 to 125. In this output range, several factors contribute to inflation. First, *bottlenecks* (obstacles to output flow) develop when some firms have no unused capacity and other firms operate below full capacity. Suppose the steel industry is operating at full capacity and cannot fill all its orders for steel. An inadequate supply of one resource, such as steel, can hold up auto production even though the auto industry is operating well below capacity. Consequently, the bottleneck causes firms to raise the price of steel and, in turn, autos. Second, a shortage of certain labor skills while firms are earning higher profits causes businesses to expect that labor will exert its power to obtain sizable wage increases, so businesses raise prices. Wage demands are more difficult to reject when the economy is prospering because businesses fear workers will change jobs or strike. Besides, businesses believe higher prices can be passed on to consumers quite easily because consumers expect higher prices as output expands to near full capacity. Third, as the economy approaches full employment, firms must use less productive workers and less efficient machinery. This inefficiency creates higher production costs, which are passed on to consumers in the form of higher prices.

> **Conclusion** *In the intermediate range, increases in aggregate demand increase both the price level and the real GDP.*

Classical Range

While inflation resulting from an outward shift in aggregate demand was no problem in the Keynesian range and only a minor problem in the intermediate range, it becomes a serious problem in the classical or vertical range.

> **Conclusion** *Once the economy reaches full-employment output in the classical range, additional increases in aggregate demand merely cause inflation, rather than more real GDP.*

Assume the economy shown in Exhibit 8(c) is in equilibrium at E_5, which intersects AS at the full-capacity output. Now suppose aggregate demand shifts rightward from AD_5 to AD_6. Because the aggregate supply curve AS is vertical at $10 trillion, this increase in the aggregate demand curve boosts the price level from 150 to 200, but fails to expand real GDP. The explanation is that once the economy operates at capacity, businesses raise their prices in order to ration fully employed resources to those willing to pay the highest prices.

In summary, the *AD-AS* model presented in this chapter is a combination of the conflicting assumptions of the Keynesian and the classical theories separated by an intermediate range, which fits neither extreme precisely.

Be forewarned that in later chapters you will encounter a continuing great controversy over the shape of the aggregate supply curve. Modern-day classical economists believe the entire aggregate supply curve is steep or vertical. On the other hand, Keynesian economists contend that the aggregate supply curve is much flatter or horizontal.

Nonprice-Level Determinants of Aggregate Supply

Our discussion so far has explained changes in real GDP supplied resulting from changes in the aggregate demand curve, given a stationary aggregate supply curve. Now we consider a stationary aggregate demand curve and changes in the aggregate supply curve caused by changes in one or more of the *nonprice-level determinants*. The nonprice-level factors affecting aggregate supply include resource prices (domestic and imported), technological change, taxes, subsidies, and regulations. Note that each of these factors affects production costs. At a given price level, the profit businesses make at any level of real GDP depends on production costs. If costs change, firms respond by changing their output. Lower production costs shift the aggregate supply curve rightward, indicating greater real GDP is supplied at any price level. Conversely, higher production costs shift the aggregate supply curve leftward, meaning less real GDP is supplied at any price level.

Exhibit 9 represents a supply-side explanation of the business cycle, in contrast to the demand-side case presented in Exhibit 8. (Note that for simplicity the aggregate supply curve can be drawn using only the intermediate segment.) The economy begins in equilibrium at point E_1, with real GDP at $7 trillion and the price level at 175. Then suppose labor unions become less powerful and their weaker bargaining position causes the wage rate to fall. With lower labor costs per unit of output, businesses seek to increase profits by expanding production at any price level. Hence, the aggregate supply curve shifts rightward from AS_1 to AS_2, and equilibrium changes from E_1 to E_2. As a result, real GDP increases $1 trillion, and the price level decreases from 175 to 150. Changes in other nonprice-level factors also cause an increase in aggregate supply. Lower oil prices, greater entrepreneurship, lower taxes, and reduced government regulation are other examples of conditions that lower production costs and therefore cause a rightward shift of the aggregate supply curve.

What kinds of events might raise production costs and shift the aggregate supply curve leftward? Perhaps there is war in the Persian Gulf or the Organization of Petroleum Exporting Countries (OPEC) disrupts supplies of oil, and higher energy prices spread throughout the economy. Under such a "supply shock," businesses decrease their output at any price level in response to higher production costs per unit. Similarly, larger-than-expected wage increases, higher taxes to protect the environment (see Exhibit 7 in Chapter 4), or greater government regulation would increase production costs and therefore shift the aggregate supply curve leftward. A leftward shift in the aggregate supply curve is discussed further in the next section.

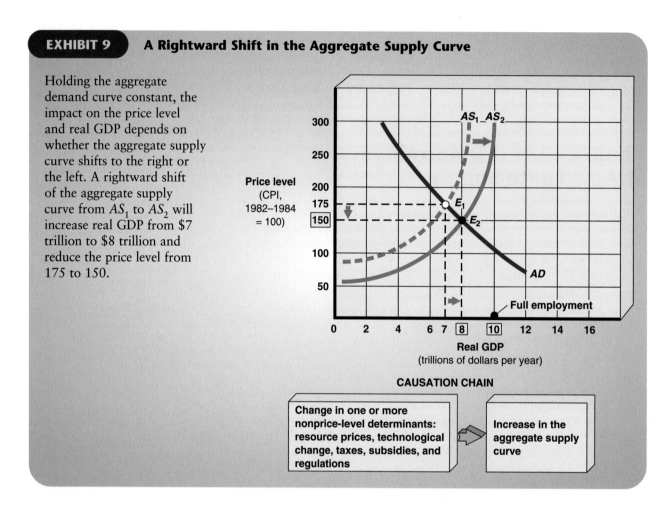

EXHIBIT 9   **A Rightward Shift in the Aggregate Supply Curve**

Holding the aggregate demand curve constant, the impact on the price level and real GDP depends on whether the aggregate supply curve shifts to the right or the left. A rightward shift of the aggregate supply curve from AS_1 to AS_2 will increase real GDP from $7 trillion to $8 trillion and reduce the price level from 175 to 150.

CAUSATION CHAIN

Change in one or more nonprice-level determinants: resource prices, technological change, taxes, subsidies, and regulations	⇨	Increase in the aggregate supply curve

Exhibit 10 summarizes the nonprice-level determinants of aggregate demand and supply for further study and review. In the chapter on monetary policy, you will learn how changes in the supply of money in the economy can also shift the aggregate demand curve and influence macroeconomic performance.

Cost-Push and Demand-Pull Inflation Revisited

We now apply the aggregate demand and aggregate supply model to the two types of inflation introduced in the chapter on inflation. This section begins with a historical example of *cost-push inflation* caused by a decrease in the aggregate supply curve. Next, another historical example illustrates *demand-pull inflation,* caused by an increase in the aggregate demand curve.

During the late 1970s and early 1980s, the U.S. economy experienced **stagflation.** Stagflation is the condition that occurs when an economy experiences the twin maladies of high unemployment and rapid inflation simul-

Stagflation

The condition that occurs when an economy experiences the twin maladies of high unemployment and rapid inflation simultaneously.

EXHIBIT 10 Summary of the Nonprice-Level Determinants of Aggregate Demand and Aggregate Supply

Nonprice-level determinants of aggregate demand (total spending)	Nonprice-level determinants of aggregate supply
1. Consumption (C) 2. Investment (I) 3. Government spending (G) 4. Net exports (X − M)	1. Resource prices (domestic and imported) 2. Taxes 3. Technological change 4. Subsidies 5. Regulation

---

taneously. How could this happen? The dramatic increase in the price of imported oil in 1973–1974 was a villain explained by a *cost-push inflation* scenario. Cost-push inflation, defined in terms of our macro model, is a rise in the price level resulting from a decrease in the aggregate supply curve while the aggregate demand curve remains fixed. As a result of cost-push inflation, real output and employment decrease.

Exhibit 11(a) uses actual data to show how a leftward shift in the aggregate supply curve can cause stagflation. In this exhibit, aggregate demand curve AD and aggregate supply curve AS_{73} represent the U.S. economy in 1973. Equilibrium was at point E_1, with the price level (CPI) at 44.4 and real GDP at $4,123 billion. Then, in 1974, the impact of a major supply shock shifted the aggregate supply curve leftward from AS_{73} to AS_{74}. The explanation for this shock was the oil embargo instituted by OPEC in retaliation for U.S. support of Israel in its war with the Arabs. Assuming a stable aggregate demand curve between 1973 and 1974, the punch from the energy shock resulted in a new equilibrium at point E_2, with the 1974 CPI at 49.3. The inflation rate for 1974 was therefore 11 percent {[(49.3 − 44.4)/44.4] × 100}. Real GDP fell from $4,123 billion in 1973 to $4,099 billion in 1974, and the unemployment rate (not shown directly in the exhibit) climbed from 4.9 percent to 5.6 percent between these two years.[2]

In contrast, an outward shift in the aggregate demand curve can result in *demand-pull inflation*. Demand-pull inflation, in terms of our macro model, is a rise in the price level resulting from an increase in the aggregate demand curve while the aggregate supply curve remains fixed. Again, we can use aggregate demand and supply analysis and actual data to explain demand-pull inflation. In 1965, when the unemployment rate of 4.5 percent was close to the 4 percent natural rate of unemployment, real government spending increased sharply to fight the Vietnam War without a tax increase (an income tax surcharge was enacted in 1968). Inflation jumped sharply from 1.6 percent in 1965 to 2.9 percent rate in 1966.

 The National Bureau of Economic Research (NBER) (http://www.nber.org/) *measures business cycle expansions and contractions* (http://www.nber.org/cycles.html). *The Bureau of Economic Analysis provides current and historical data for real GDP* (http://www.bea.doc.gov/bea/dn1.htm) *and the Bureau of Labor Statistics provides current and historical unemployment data* (http://www.bls.gov/cps).

---

[2]*Economic Report of the President, 2001,* http://w3.access.gpo.gov/eop, Tables B-2, B-35, B-62 and 64.

EXHIBIT 11   Cost-Push and Demand-Pull Inflation

Parts (a) and (b) illustrate the distinction between cost-push inflation and demand-pull inflation. Cost-push inflation is inflation that results from a decrease in the aggregate supply curve. In part (a), higher oil prices in 1973 caused the aggregate supply curve to shift leftward from AS_{73} to AS_{74}. As a result, real GDP fell from $4,123 billion to $4,099 billion, and the price level (CPI) rose from 44.4 to 49.3. This combination of higher price level and lower real output is called stagflation.

As shown in part (b), demand-pull inflation is inflation that results from an increase in aggregate demand beyond the Keynesian range of output. Government spending increased to fight the Vietnam War without a tax increase, causing the aggregate demand curve to shift rightward from AD_{65} to AD_{66}. Consequently, real GDP rose from $3,028 billion to $3,227 billion, and the price level (CPI) rose from 31.5 to 32.4.

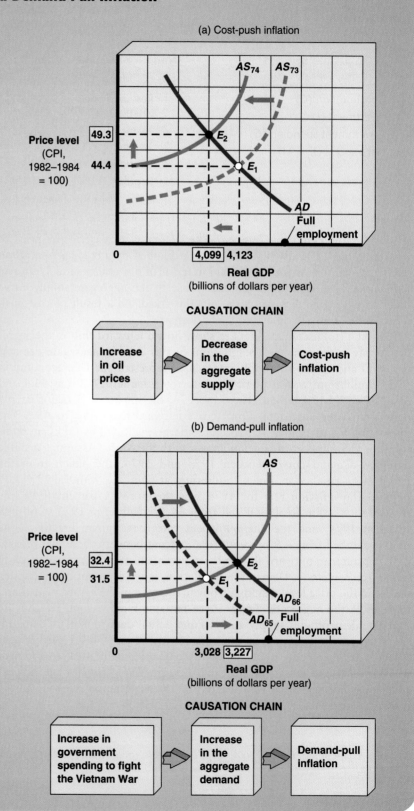

(a) Cost-push inflation

CAUSATION CHAIN

Increase in oil prices → Decrease in the aggregate supply → Cost-push inflation

(b) Demand-pull inflation

CAUSATION CHAIN

Increase in government spending to fight the Vietnam War → Increase in the aggregate demand → Demand-pull inflation

CHECKPOINT

Would the Greenhouse Effect Cause Inflation, Unemployment, or Both?

You are the chair of the President's Council of Economic Advisers. There has been an extremely hot and dry summer due to a climatic change known as the greenhouse effect. As a result, crop production has fallen drastically. The president calls you to the White House to discuss the impact on the economy. Would you explain to the president that a sharp drop in U.S. crop production would cause inflation, unemployment, or both?

Exhibit 11(b) illustrates what happened to the economy between 1965 and 1966. Suppose the economy began operating in 1965 at E_1, which is in the intermediate output range. The impact of the increase in military spending shifted the aggregate demand curve from AD_{65} to AD_{66}, and the economy moved upward along the aggregate supply curve until it reached E_2. Holding the aggregate supply curve constant, the *AD-AS* model predicts that increasing aggregate demand at near full employment causes demand-pull inflation. As shown in Exhibit 11(b), real GDP increased from $3,028 billion to $3,227 billion, and the CPI rose from 31.5 to 32.4. Thus, the inflation rate for 1966 was 2.9 percent {[(32.4 − 31.5)/31.5] × 100}. Corresponding to the rise in real output, the unemployment rate of 4.5 percent in 1965 fell to 3.8 percent in 1966.[3]

In summary, the aggregate supply and aggregate demand curves shift in different directions for various reasons in a given time period. These shifts in the aggregate supply and aggregate demand curves cause upswings and downswings in real GDP—the business cycle. A leftward shift in the aggregate demand curve, for example, can cause a recession. Whereas, a rightward shift of the aggregate demand curve can cause real GDP and employment to rise, and the economy recovers. A leftward shift in the aggregate supply curve can cause a downswing, and a rightward shift might cause an upswing.

Conclusion *The business cycle is a result of shifts in the aggregate demand and aggregate supply curves.*

---

[3]Ibid.

Was John Maynard Keynes Right?

Applicable Concept: aggregate demand and aggregate supply analysis

In *The General Theory of Employment, Interest, and Money*, Keynes wrote:

> The ideas of economists and political philosophers, both when they are right and when they are wrong, are more powerful than is commonly understood. Indeed the world is ruled by little else. Practical men, who believe themselves to be quite exempt from any intellectual influences, are usually the slaves of some defunct economist. Madmen in authority, who hear voices in the air, are distilling their frenzy from some academic scribbler of a few years back. . . . There are not many who are influenced by new theories after they are twenty-five or thirty years of age, so that the ideas which civil servants and politicians and even agitators apply to current events are not likely to be the newest.[1]

Keynes (1883–1946) is regarded as the father of modern macroeconomics. He was the son of an eminent English economist, John Neville Keynes, who was a lecturer in economics and logic at Cambridge University. Keynes was educated at Eton and Cambridge in mathematics and probability theory, but ultimately selected the field of economics and accepted a lectureship in economics at Cambridge.

Keynes was a many-faceted man who was an honored and supremely successful member of the British academic, financial, and political upper class. For example, Keynes amassed a $2 million personal fortune by speculating in stocks, international currencies, and commodities. (Use CPI index numbers to compute the equivalent amount in today's dollars.) In addition to making a huge fortune for himself, Keynes served as a trustee of King's College and built its endowment from 30,000 to 380,000 pounds.

Keynes was a prolific scholar who is best remembered for *The General Theory,* published in 1936. This work made a convincing attack on the classical theory that capitalism would self-correct from a severe recession. Keynes based his model on the belief that increasing aggregate demand will achieve full employment, while prices and wages remain inflexible. Moreover, his bold policy prescription was for the government to raise its spending and/or reduce taxes in order to increase the economy's aggregate demand curve and put the unemployed back to work.

---

[1]J. M. Keynes, *The General Theory of Employment, Interest, and Money* (London: Macmillan, 1936), p. 383.

Was Keynes correct? Based on the following data, use the aggregate demand and aggregate supply model to explain Keynes's theory that increases in aggregate demand propel an economy toward full employment.

Price Level, Real GDP, and Unemployment Rate, 1933–1941

Year	CPI (1982–1984 = 100)	Real GDP (billions of 1996 dollars)	Unemployment rate (percent)
1933	13.0	$ 603	24.9%
1939	13.9	903	17.2
1940	14.0	980	14.6
1941	14.7	1,148	9.9

Sources: Bureau of Labor Statistics, ftp://ftp.bls.gov/pub/special .requests/cpi/cpiai.txt; *Survey of Current Business,* http://www .bea.doc.gov/bea/dn1.htm, GDP and Other Major NIPA Series, Table 2A; and *Economic Report of the President, 2001,* http:// w3.access.gpo.gov/eop/, Table B-35.

KEY CONCEPTS

Aggregate demand curve (*AD*)

Real balances or wealth effect

Interest-rate effect

Net exports effect

Aggregate supply curve (*AS*)

Keynesian range

Intermediate range

Classical range

Stagflation

SUMMARY

■ The **aggregate demand curve** shows the level of real GDP purchased in the economy at different price levels during a period of time.

■ **Reasons why the aggregate demand curve is downward sloping** include the following three effects: (1) The **real balances** or **wealth effect** is the impact on real GDP caused by the inverse relationship between the purchasing power of fixed-value financial assets and inflation, which causes a shift in the consumption schedule. (2) The **interest-rate effect** assumes a fixed money supply; therefore, inflation increases the demand for money. As the demand for money increases, the interest rate rises, causing consumption and investment spending to fall. (3) The **net exports effect** is the impact on real GDP caused by the inverse relationship between net exports and inflation. An increase in the U.S. price level tends to reduce U.S. exports and increase imports, and vice versa.

Shift in the aggregate demand curve

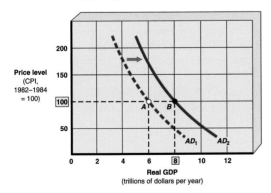

The **aggregate supply curve** shows the level of real GDP that an economy will produce at different possible price levels. The shape of the aggregate supply curve depends on the flexibility of prices and wages as real GDP expands and contracts. The aggregate supply curve has three ranges: (1) The **Keynesian range** of the curve is horizontal because neither the price level nor

production costs will increase or decrease when there is substantial unemployment in the economy. (2) In the **intermediate range,** both prices and costs rise as real GDP rises toward full employment. Prices and production costs rise because of bottlenecks, the stronger bargaining power of labor, and the utilization of less-productive workers and capital. (3) The **classical range** is the vertical segment of the aggregate supply curve. It coincides with the full-employment output. Because output is at its maximum, increases in aggregate demand will only cause a rise in the price level.

Aggregate supply curve

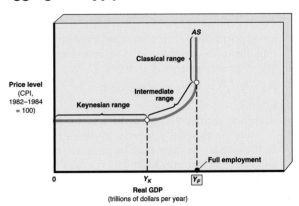

■ **Aggregate demand and aggregate supply analysis** determines the equilibrium price level and the equilibrium real GDP by the intersection of the aggregate demand and the aggregate supply curves. In macroeconomic equilibrium, businesses neither overestimate nor underestimate the real GDP demanded at the prevailing price level.

■ **Stagflation** exists when an economy experiences inflation and unemployment simultaneously. Holding aggregate demand constant, a decrease in aggregate supply results in the unhealthy condition of a rise in the price level and a fall in real GDP and employment.

■ **Cost-push inflation** is inflation that results from a decrease in the aggregate supply curve while the aggregate demand curve remains fixed. Cost-push inflation is undesirable because it is accompanied by declines in both real GDP and employment.

■ **Demand-pull inflation** is inflation that results from an increase in aggregate demand in both the classical and the intermediate ranges of the aggregate supply curve, while aggregate supply is fixed.

Cost-push inflation

Demand-pull inflation

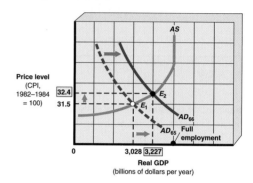

SUMMARY OF CONCLUSION STATEMENTS

■ The aggregate demand curve and the demand curve are not the same concepts.

■ Consumers spend more on goods and services because lower prices make their dollars more valuable. Therefore, the real value of money is measured by the quantity of goods and services each dollar buys.

■ Any change in aggregate expenditures shifts the aggregate demand curve.

■ When the aggregate supply curve is horizontal and an economy is below full employment, the only effects of an increase in aggregate demand are increases in real GDP and employment, while the price level does not change. Stated simply, the Keynesian view is that "demand creates its own supply."

■ When the aggregate supply curve is vertical at the full-employment GDP, the only effect over time of a change in aggregate demand is a change in the price level. Stated simply, the classical view is that "supply creates its own demand."

■ At macroeconomic equilibrium, sellers neither overestimate nor underestimate the real GDP demanded at the prevailing price level.

■ As aggregate demand increases in the Keynesian range, the price level remains constant as real GDP expands.

■ In the intermediate range, increases in aggregate demand increase both the price level and the real GDP.

■ Once the economy reaches full-employment output in the classical range, additional increases in aggregate demand merely cause inflation, rather than more real GDP.

■ The business cycle is a result of shifts in the aggregate demand and aggregate supply curves.

STUDY QUESTIONS AND PROBLEMS

1. Explain why the aggregate demand curve is downward sloping. How does your explanation differ from the reasons behind the downward-sloping demand curve for an individual product?

2. Explain the theory of the classical economists that flexible prices and wages ensure that the economy operates at full employment.

3. In which direction would each of the following changes in conditions cause the aggregate demand curve to shift? Explain your answers.
   a. Consumers expect an economic downturn.
   b. A new U.S. president is elected, and the profit expectations of business executives rise.
   c. The federal government increases spending for highways, bridges, and other infrastructure.
   d. The United States increases exports of wheat and other crops to Russia, Ukraine, and other former Soviet republics.

4. Identify the three ranges of the aggregate supply curve. Explain the impact of an increase in aggregate demand in each segment.

5. Consider this statement: "Equilibrium GDP is the same as full employment." Do you agree or disagree? Explain.

6. Assume the aggregate demand and the aggregate supply curves intersect at a price level of 100. Explain the effect of a shift in the price level to 120 and to 50.

7. In which direction would each of the following changes in conditions cause the aggregate supply curve to shift? Explain your answers.
   a. The price of gasoline increases because of a catastrophic oil spill in Alaska.
   b. Labor unions and all other workers agree to a cut in wages to stimulate the economy.

c. Power companies switch to solar power, and the price of electricity falls.
   d. The federal government increases the excise tax on gasoline in order to finance a deficit.

8. Assume an economy operates in the intermediate range of its aggregate supply curve. State the direction of shift for the aggregate demand or aggregate supply curves for each of the following changes in conditions. What is the effect on the price level? On real GDP? On employment?
   a. The price of crude oil rises significantly.
   b. Spending on national defense doubles.
   c. The costs of imported goods increase.
   d. An improvement in technology raises labor productivity.

9. What shifts in aggregate supply or aggregate demand would cause each of the following conditions for an economy?
   a. The price level rises, and real GDP rises.
   b. The price level falls, and real GDP rises.
   c. The price level falls, and real GDP falls.
   d. The price level rises, and real GDP falls.
   e. The price level falls, and real GDP remains the same.
   f. The price level remains the same, and real GDP rises.

10. Explain cost-push inflation verbally and graphically, using aggregate demand and aggregate supply analysis. Assess the impact on the price level, real GDP, and employment.

11. Explain demand-pull inflation graphically using aggregate demand and supply analysis. Assess the impact on the price level, real GDP, and employment.

ONLINE EXERCISES

Exercise 1

Go to the Economic Statistics Briefing Room (http://www.whitehouse.gov/fsbr/output.html).

1. What has happened to gross domestic product in the last year?

2. What changes in aggregate demand and/or aggregate supply could have caused these changes?

Exercise 2

Visit the Bureau of Labor Statistics to find the latest consumer price index measurements (http://www.bls.gov/cpi). Under "Data," click on "Table Containing History of CPI-U U.S. All Items Indexes and Annual Percent Changes from 1913 to Present."

1. What has happened to the inflation rate in the last year?

2. Given your answers to part 1 and Exercise 1 above, now what can you conclude has happened to aggregate demand and/or aggregate supply in order to have created these changes in output (GDP) and prices?

Exercise 3

Visit the Federal Reserve Bank of Minneapolis, which publishes historical CPI measurements, with corresponding inflation rates (http://woodrow.mpls.frb.fed.us/economy/calc/hist1913.html). Scroll down and look at what has happened to changes in the inflation rates in the last 10 years.

1. What changes in aggregate demand and/or aggregate supply could have caused these changes in the inflation rate?

2. Is there a difference between a change in aggregate demand and a change in aggregate supply in terms of the impact each has on the output (GDP) and therefore the employment level?

3. Is the change in aggregate demand or the change in aggregate supply most likely responsible for the change in the inflation rate in the last 10 years? Why?

Exercise 4

Visit the Organization for Economic Cooperation and Development (OECD) (http://www1.oecd.org/std/mei.htm), and select Country Graphs, which compares macroeconomic performance of nations around the world. What changes in aggregate demand and/or aggregate supply would be required to bring about these changes in these nations' economies?

 CHECKPOINT ANSWER

Would the Greenhouse Effect Cause Inflation, Unemployment, or Both?

A drop in food production reduces aggregate supply. The decrease in aggregate supply causes the economy to contract, while prices rise. In addition to the OPEC oil embargo between 1972 and 1974, worldwide weather conditions destroyed crops and contributed to the supply shock that caused stagflation in the U.S. economy. If you said that a severe greenhouse effect would cause both higher unemployment and inflation, YOU ARE CORRECT.

PRACTICE QUIZ

For a visual explanation of the correct answers, visit the tutorial at http://tucker.swcollege.com.

1. The aggregate demand curve is defined as the
   a. net national product.
   b. sum of wages, rent, interest, and profits.
   c. real GDP purchased at different possible price levels.
   d. total dollar value of household expectations.

2. When the supply of credit is fixed, an increase in the price level stimulates the demand for credit, which, in turn, reduces consumption and investment spending. This effect is called the
   a. real balances effect.
   b. interest-rate effect.
   c. net exports effect.
   d. substitution effect.

3. The real balances effect occurs because a higher price level reduces the real value of people's
   a. financial assets.
   b. wages.
   c. unpaid debt.
   d. physical investments.

4. The net exports effect is the inverse relationship between net exports and the _____ of an economy.
   a. real GDP
   b. GDP deflator
   c. price level
   d. consumption spending

5. Which of the following will shift the aggregate demand curve to the left?
   a. An increase in exports
   b. An increase in investment
   c. An increase in government spending
   d. A decrease in government spending

6. Which of the following will *not* shift the aggregate demand curve to the left?
   a. Consumers become more optimistic about the future.
   b. Government spending decreases.
   c. Business optimism decreases.
   d. Consumers become pessimistic about the future.

7. The popular theory prior to the Great Depression that the economy will automatically adjust to achieve full employment is
   a. supply-side economics.
   b. Keynesian economics.
   c. classical economics.
   d. mercantilism.

8. Classical economists believed that the
   a. price system was stable.
   b. goal of full employment was impossible.
   c. price system automatically adjusts the economy to full employment in the long run.
   d. government should attempt to restore full employment.

9. Which of the following is *not* a range on the eclectic or general view of the aggregate supply curve?
   a. Classical range
   b. Keynesian range
   c. Intermediate range
   d. Monetary range

10. Macroeconomic equilibrium occurs when
    a. aggregate supply exceeds aggregate demand.
    b. the economy is at full employment.
    c. aggregate demand equals aggregate supply.
    d. aggregate demand equals the average price level.

11. Along the classical or vertical range of the aggregate supply curve, a decrease in the aggregate demand curve will decrease
    a. both the price level and real GDP.
    b. only real GDP.
    c. only the price level.
    d. neither real GDP nor the price level.

12. Other factors held constant, a decrease in resource prices will shift the aggregate
    a. demand curve leftward.
    b. demand curve rightward.
    c. supply curve leftward.
    d. supply curve rightward.

13. Assuming a fixed aggregate demand curve, a leftward shift in the aggregate supply curve causes a(an)
    a. increase in the price level and a decrease in real GDP.
    b. increase in the price level and an increase in real GDP.
    c. decrease in the price level and a decrease in real GDP.
    d. decrease in the price level and an increase in real GDP.

14. An increase in the price level caused by a rightward shift of the aggregate demand curve is called
    a. cost-push inflation.
    b. supply shock inflation.
    c. demand shock inflation.
    d. demand-pull inflation.

15. Suppose workers become pessimistic about their future employment, which causes them to save more and spend less. If the economy is on the intermediate range of the aggregate supply curve, then
    a. both real GDP and the price level will fall.
    b. real GDP will fall and the price level will rise.
    c. real GDP will rise and the price level will fall.
    d. both real GDP and the price level will rise.

The Self-Correcting Aggregate Demand and Supply Model

It can be argued that the economy is self-regulating. This means that over time the economy will move itself to full-employment equilibrium. Stated differently, this classical theory is based on the assumption that the economy might ebb and flow around it, but full employment is the normal condition for the economy regardless of gyrations in the price level. To understand this adjustment process, the *AD-AS* model presented in the chapter must be extended into a more complex model called the self-correcting *AD-AS* model. First, a distinction will be made between the short-run and long-run aggregate supply curves. Indeed, one of the most controversial areas of macroeconomics is the shape of the aggregate supply curve and the reasons for that shape. Second, we will explain long-run equilibrium using the self-correcting *AD-AS* model. Third, the appendix concludes by using the self-correcting *AD-AS* model to explain short run and long run adjustments to changes in aggregate demand.

Short-run aggregate supply curve (SRAS)

The curve that shows the level of real GDP produced at different possible price levels during a time period in which nominal incomes do not change in response to changes in the price level.

Why the Short-Run Aggregate Supply Curve Is Upward Sloping

Exhibit A-1(a) shows the **short-run aggregate supply curve (*SRAS*),** which does not have either the perfectly flat Keynesian segment or the perfectly vertical classical segment developed in Exhibit 6 of the chapter. The short-run supply curve shows the level of real GDP produced at different possible price levels during a time period in which nominal wages and salaries (incomes) do not change in response to changes in the price level. Recall from the chapter on inflation that

$$\text{real income} = \frac{\text{nominal income}}{\text{CPI (as decimal)}}$$

As explained by this formula, a rise in the price level measured by the CPI decreases real income and a fall in the price level increases real income. Given the definition of the short-run aggregate supply curve, there are two reasons why one can assume nominal wages and salaries remain fixed in spite of changes in the price level:

1. *Incomplete knowledge.* Workers may be unaware in a short period of time that a change in the price level has changed their real incomes. Consequently, they do not adjust their wage and salary demands according to changes in their real incomes.

2. *Fixed-wage contracts.* Unionized employees, for example, have nominal wages stated in their contracts. Also, many professionals receive set salaries for a year. In these cases, nominal incomes remain constant for a given time period regardless of changes in the price level.

Given the assumption that changes in the prices of goods and services measured by the CPI do not in a short period of time cause changes in nominal wages, let's examine Exhibit A-1 (a) and explain the *SRAS* curve's upward-sloping shape. Begin at point *A* with a CPI of 100 and observe that the economy is operating at the full-employment real GDP of $8 trillion. Also assume that labor contracts are based on this expected price level. Now suppose the price level unexpectedly increases from 100 to 150 at point *B*. At higher prices for products, firms' revenues increase, and with nominal wages and salaries fixed, profits rise. In response, firms increase output from $8 trillion to $12 trillion, and the economy operates beyond its full-employment output. This occurs because firms increase work-hours and they train and hire homemakers, retirees, and unemployed workers who were not profitable at or below full-employment real GDP.

Now return to point *A* and assume the CPI falls to 50 at point *C*. In this case, the prices firms receive for their products drop while nominal wages and salaries remain fixed. As a result, firms' revenues and profits fall, and they reduce output from $8 trillion to $4 trillion real GDP. Correspondingly, employment (not shown explicitly in the model) falls below full employment.

Conclusion *The upward-sloping shape of the short-run aggregate supply curve is the result of fixed nominal wages and salaries as the price level changes.*

Long-run aggregate supply curve (*LRAS*)

The curve that shows the level of real GDP produced at different possible price levels during a time period in which nominal incomes change by the same percentage as the price level changes.

Why the Long-Run Aggregate Supply Curve Is Vertical

The **long-run aggregate supply curve** (*LRAS*) is presented in Exhibit A-1(b). The long-run aggregate supply curve shows the level of real GDP produced at different possible price levels during a time period in which nominal incomes change by the same percentage as the price level changes. Like the classical vertical segment of the aggregate supply curve developed in Exhibit 6 of the chapter, the long-run aggregate supply curve is vertical at full-employment real GDP.

To understand why the long-run aggregate supply curve is vertical requires the assumption that sufficient time has elapsed for labor contracts to expire, so that nominal wages and salaries can be renegotiated. Stated another way, over a long enough time, workers will calculate changes in their real incomes and obtain increases in their nominal incomes to adjust proportionately to changes in purchasing power. Suppose the CPI is 100 (or in decimal 1.0) at point *A* in Exhibit 1-A(b) and the average nominal wage is $10 per hour. This means the average real wage is also $10 ($10 nominal wage divided by 1.0). But if the CPI rises to 150 at point *B*, the $10 average real wage falls to $6.67 ($10/1.5). In the long run, workers will demand and receive a new nominal wage of $15, returning their real wage to $10 ($15/1.5). Thus, both the CPI (rise from 100 to 150) and the nominal wage (rise from $10 to $15) changed by the same rate of 50 percent, and the economy moved from point *A* to *B* upward along the long-run aggregate supply curve. Note that because both the prices of products measured by the CPI and the nominal wage rise by the same percentage, profit margins remain unchanged in real terms, and firms have no incentive to produce either more or less than the full-employment real GDP of $8 trillion. And since this same adjustment process occurs between any two price levels along *LRAS*, the curve is vertical.

> **Conclusion** *The vertical shape of the long-run aggregate supply curve is the result of nominal wages and salaries eventually changing by the same percentage as the price level changes.*

Equilibrium in the Self-Correcting *AD-AS* Model

Exhibit A-2 combines aggregate demand with the short-run and long-run aggregate supply curves from the previous exhibit to form the self-correcting *AD-AS* model. Equilibrium in the model occurs at point *E* where the economy's aggregate demand curve (*AD*) intersects the vertical long-run aggregate supply curve (*LRAS*) and the short-run aggregate supply curve (*SRAS*). In long-run equilibrium, the economy's price level is 100, and full-employment real GDP is $8 trillion.

EXHIBIT A-1   **Aggregate Supply Curves**

The short-run aggregate supply curve in part (a) is based on the assumption that nominal wages and salaries are fixed based on an expected price level of 100 and full-employment real GDP of $8 trillion. An increase in the price level from 100 to 150 increases profits, real GDP, and employment, moving the economy from point A to point B. A decrease in the price level from 100 to 50 decreases profits, real GDP, and employment, moving the economy from point A to point C.

The long-run aggregate supply curve in part (b) is vertical at full-employment real GDP. For example, if the price level rises from 100 at point A to 150 at point B, workers now have enough time to renegotiate higher nominal incomes by a percentage equal to the percentage increase in the price level. This flexible adjustment means that real incomes and profits remain unchanged, and the economy continues to operate at full-employment real GDP.

The Impact of an Increase in Aggregate Demand

Now you're ready for some actions and reactions using the model. Suppose that, beginning at point E_1 in Exhibit A-3, a change in a nonprice determinant (summarized in Exhibit 10 in the chapter) causes an increase in aggregate demand from AD_1 to AD_2. For example, the shift could be the result of an increase in consumption spending (C), government spending (G), or business investment (I) or greater demand for U.S. exports. Regardless of the cause, the short-run effect is for the economy to move upward along $SRAS_{100}$ to the intersection with AD_2 at the temporary or short-run equilibrium point E_2 with a price level of 150. Recall that nominal incomes in the short run are fixed. Faced with higher demand, firms raise prices for products, and, since the price of labor remains unchanged, firms earn higher

---

EXHIBIT A-2   **Self-Correcting *AD-AS* Model**

The short-run aggregate supply curve (*SRAS*) is based on an expected price level of 100. Point *E* shows that this equilibrium price level occurs at the intersection of the aggregate demand curve *AD*, *SRAS*, and the long-run aggregate supply curve (*LRAS*).

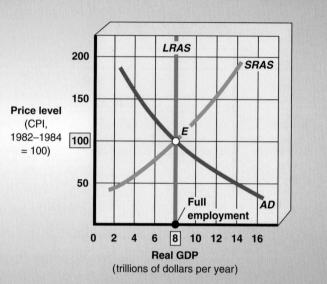

---

profits and increase employment. As a result, real GDP for a short period of time increases above the full-employment real GDP of $8 trillion to $12 trillion real GDP. However, the economy cannot produce in excess of full employment forever. What forces are at work to bring real GDP back to full-employment real GDP?

Assume time passes and labor contracts expire. The next step in the transition process at E_2 is that workers begin demanding nominal income increases that will eventually bring their real incomes back to the same real incomes established initially at E_1. These increases in nominal incomes shift the short-run aggregate supply curve leftward, which causes an upward movement along AD_2. One of the succession of possible intermediate adjustment short-run supply curves along AD_2 is $SRAS_{150}$. This short-run intermediate adjustment is based upon an expected price level of 150 determined by the intersection of $SRAS_{150}$ and *LRAS*. Although short-run aggregate supply curve $SRAS_{150}$ intersects AD_2 at E_3, the adjustment to the increase in aggregate demand is not yet complete. Workers negotiated increases in nominal incomes based upon an expected price level of 150, but the leftward shift of the short-run aggregate supply curve raised the price level to about 175 at E_3. Workers must therefore negotiate another round of higher nominal incomes to restore their purchasing power. This process continues until long-run equilibrium is restored at E_4, and here the adjustment process ends.

The long-run forecast for the price level at full employment is now 200 at point E_4. $SRAS_{100}$ has shifted leftward to $SRAS_{200}$, which intersects *LRAS* at point E_4. As a result of the shift in the short-run aggregate supply curve from E_2 to E_4 and the corresponding increase in nominal incomes, firms' profits are cut, and they react by raising product prices, reducing employment, and reducing output. At E_4, the economy has self-adjusted to

EXHIBIT A-3   **Adjustments to an Increase in Aggregate Demand**

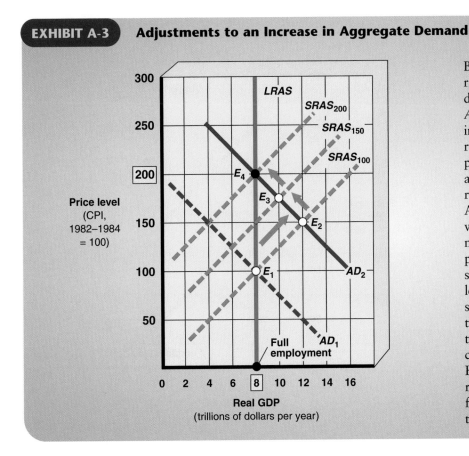

Beginning at long-run equilibrium E_1, the aggregate demand curve increases from AD_1 to AD_2. Since nominal incomes are fixed in the short run, firms raise product prices, earn higher profits, and expand output to short-run equilibrium point E_2. After enough time passes, workers increase their nominal incomes to restore their purchasing power, and the short-run supply curve shifts leftward along AD_2 to a transitional point such as E_3. As the economy moves from E_2 to E_4, profits fall and firms cut output and employment. Eventually, long-run equilibrium is reached at E_4 with full employment restored by the self-correction process.

both short-run and long-run equilibrium at a price level of 200 and full-employment real GDP of $8 trillion. If there are no further shifts in aggregate demand, the economy will remain at E_4 indefinitely. Note that nominal income is higher at point E_4 than it was originally at point E_1, but real wages and salaries remain unchanged as explained in Exhibit A-1(b).

Conclusion *An increase in aggregate demand in the long run causes the short-run aggregate supply curve to shift leftward because nominal incomes rise and the economy self corrects to a higher price level at full-employment real GDP.*

The Impact of a Decrease in Aggregate Demand

Point E_1 in Exhibit A-4 begins where the sequence of events described in the previous section ends. Now let's see what happens when the aggregate demand curve decreases from AD_1 to AD_2. The reason might be that a wave of pessimism from a stock market crash causes consumers to cut back on their spending and firms postpone buying new factories and equipment. As a result, firms find their sales and profits have declined, and they react

EXHIBIT A-4   Adjustments to a Decrease in Aggregate Demand

Assume the economy is initially at long-run equilibrium point E_1 and aggregate demand decreases from AD_1 to AD_2. Nominal incomes in the short run are fixed based on an expected price level of 200. In response to the fall in aggregate demand, firms' profits decline, and they cut output and employment. As a result, the economy moves downward along $SRAS_{200}$ to temporary equilibrium at E_2. When workers lower their nominal incomes because of competition from unemployed workers, the aggregate supply curve shifts downward to an intermediate point such as E_3. As workers decrease their nominal incomes based on the new long-run expected price level of 150 at point E_3, profits rise, and firms increase output and employment. In the long run, the short-run aggregate supply curve continues to automatically adjust downward along AD_2 until it again returns to long-run equilibrium at E_4.

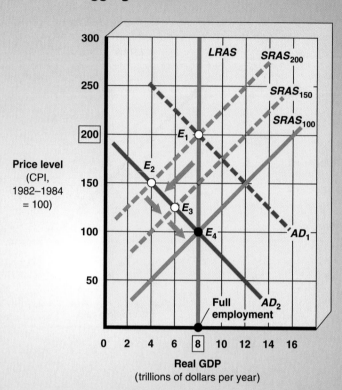

by cutting product prices, output, and employment. Workers' nominal incomes remain fixed in the short run with contracts negotiated based on an expected price level of 200. The result of this situation is that the economy moves downward along $SRAS_{200}$ from point E_1 to short-run equilibrium point E_2. Here the price level falls from 200 to 150, and real GDP has fallen from $8 trillion to $4 trillion.

At E_2, the economy is in a serious recession, and after, say, a year, workers will accept lower nominal wages and salaries when their contracts are renewed in order to keep their jobs in a time of poor profits and competition from unemployed workers. This willingness to accept lower nominal incomes is made easier by the realization that lower prices for goods means it costs less to maintain the workers' standard of living. As workers make a series of downward adjustments in nominal incomes, the short-run aggregate supply curve moves downward along AD_2 toward E_4. $SRAS_{150}$ illustrates one possible intermediate position corresponding to the long-run expected price level of 150 determined by the intersection of $SRAS_{150}$ and $LRAS$. However, like E_2, E_3 is not the point of long-run equilibrium. Workers negotiated decreases in nominal increases based upon an expected price level of 150, but the rightward shift of the short-run aggregate supply curve lowered the price level to about 125 at E_3. Under pressure of unemployed workers who will work for still lower real wages and salaries, workers will continue this process of adjusting their nominal incomes lower until $SRAS_{150}$ shifts rightward to point E_4.

Eventually, the long-run expected full-employment price level returns to 100 at point E_4 where the economy has self-corrected to long-run full-employment equilibrium. The result of this adjustment downward along AD_2 between E_2 and E_4 is that lower nominal incomes raise profits and firms respond by lowering prices of products, increasing employment, and increasing output so that real GDP increases from $4 trillion to $8 trillion. Unless aggregate demand changes, the economy will be stable at E_4 indefinitely. Finally, observe that average nominal income has decreased by the same percentage between points E_1 and E_4 as the percentage decline in the price level. Therefore real incomes are unaffected as explained in Exhibit A-1(b).

Conclusion *A decrease in aggregate demand in the long run causes the short-run aggregate supply curve to shift rightward because nominal incomes fall and the economy self corrects to a lower price level at full-employment real GDP.*

KEY CONCEPTS

Short-run aggregate supply curve (SRAS)   Long-run aggregate supply curve (LRAS)

SUMMARY OF CONCLUSION STATEMENTS

- The upward-sloping shape of the short-run aggregate supply curve is the result of fixed nominal wages and salaries as the price level changes.

- The vertical shape of the long-run aggregate supply curve is the result of nominal wages and salaries eventually changing by the same percentage as the price level changes.

- An increase in aggregate demand in the long run causes the short-run aggregate supply curve to shift leftward because nominal incomes rise and the economy self corrects to a higher price level at full-employment real GDP.

- A decrease in aggregate demand in the long run causes the short-run aggregate supply curve to shift rightward because nominal incomes fall and the economy self corrects to a lower price level at full-employment real GDP.

CHAPTER 21

Fiscal Policy

I n the early 1980s, under President Ronald Reagan, the federal government reduced personal income tax rates. The goal was to expand aggregate demand and boost national output and employment in order to end the recession of 1980–1981. During the 1996 presidential campaign, one of President Bill Clinton's programs was to stimulate economic growth by boosting government spending on long-term investment. This investment program included highways, bridges, fiber-optic communications networks, and education. In 2001, President George W. Bush proposed and signed into law a tax cut in order to stimulate the economy which appeared to be faltering.

Reagan's and Bush's tax cuts and Clinton's investment spending program are examples of **fiscal policy,** which is one of the major issues that touches everyone's life.

Fiscal policy is the use of government spending and taxes to influence the nation's output, employment, and price level. Federal government spending policies affect Social Security benefits, price supports for dairy farmers, and employment in the defense industry. Tax policies can change the amount of your paycheck and therefore influence whether you purchase a car or attend college.

Using fiscal policy to influence the performance of the economy

has been an important idea since the Keynesian revolution of the 1930s. This chapter removes the political veil and looks at fiscal policy from the viewpoint of two opposing economic theories.

First, you will study Keynesian demand-side fiscal policies that "fine-tune" aggregate demand so that the economy grows and achieves full employment with a higher price level. Second, you will study supply-side fiscal policy, which gained prominence during the Reagan administration. Supply-siders view aggregate supply as far more important than aggregate demand. Their fiscal policy prescription is to increase aggregate supply so that the economy grows and achieves full employment with a lower price level.

In this chapter, you will learn to solve these economics puzzles:

■ Does an increase in government spending or a tax cut of equal amount provide the greater stimulus to economic growth?

■ Can Congress fight a recession without taking any action?

■ Why did Ronald Reagan think the federal government could increase tax revenues by cutting taxes?

Fiscal policy
The use of government spending and taxes to influence the nation's spending, employment, and price level.

Discretionary Fiscal Policy

Here we begin where the previous chapter left off, that is, discussing the use of **discretionary fiscal policy,** as Keynes advocated, to influence the economy's performance. Discretionary fiscal policy is the deliberate use of changes in government spending or taxes to alter aggregate demand and stabilize the economy. Exhibit 1 lists three basic types of discretionary fiscal policies and the corresponding ways in which the government can pursue each of these options. The first column of the table shows that the government can choose to increase aggregate demand by following an *expansionary* fiscal policy. The second column lists *contractionary* fiscal policy options the government can use to restrain aggregate demand.

Discretionary fiscal policy
The deliberate use of changes in government spending or taxes to alter aggregate demand and stabilize the economy.

Increasing Government Spending to Combat a Recession

Suppose the U.S. economy represented in Exhibit 2 has fallen into recession at equilibrium point E_1, where aggregate demand curve AD_1 intersects the aggregate supply curve, *AS*, in the near-full-employment range. (Note that for simplicity the aggregate demand and aggregate supply curves are drawn here as straight lines.) The price level measured by the CPI is 150, and a real GDP gap of $100 billion exists below the full-employment output of $6.1 trillion real GDP. As explained in the previous chapter (Exhibit 5), one approach the president and Congress can follow is provided by classical

The White House's Economic Statistics Briefing Room has current data on prices (http://www.whitehouse .gov/fsbr/prices.html). The Bureau of Labor Statistics (BLS) maintains data on unemployment (http:// stats.bls.gov/cps/home.htm), among other data and survey results. The Federal Reserve Bank of St. Louis's FRED (Federal Reserve Economic Data) database (http://www.stls.frb.org/fred/) provides historical U.S. economic and financial data, including quarterly GDP data since 1959 (http://www .stls.frb.org/fred/data/gdp.html).

EXHIBIT 1 Discretionary Fiscal Policies

Expansionary fiscal policy	Contractionary fiscal policy
Increase government spending	Decrease government spending
Decrease taxes	Increase taxes
Increase government spending and taxes equally	Decrease government spending and taxes equally

| EXHIBIT 2 | Using Government Spending to Combat a Recession |

The economy in this exhibit is in recession at equilibrium point E_1 on the intermediate range of the aggregate supply curve, AS. The price level is 150, with an output level of $6 trillion real GDP. To reach the full-employment output of $6.1 trillion in real GDP, the aggregate demand curve must be shifted to the right by $200 billion real GDP, measured by the horizontal distance between point E_1 on curve AD_1 and point X on curve AD_2. The necessary increase in aggregate demand from AD_1 to AD_2 can be accomplished by increased government spending. Given a spending multiplier of 4, a $50 billion increase in government spending brings about the required $200 billion rightward shift in the aggregate demand curve, and equilibrium in the economy changes from E_1 to E_2. Note that the equilibrium real GDP changes by $100 billion and not by the full amount by which the aggregate demand curve shifts horizontally.

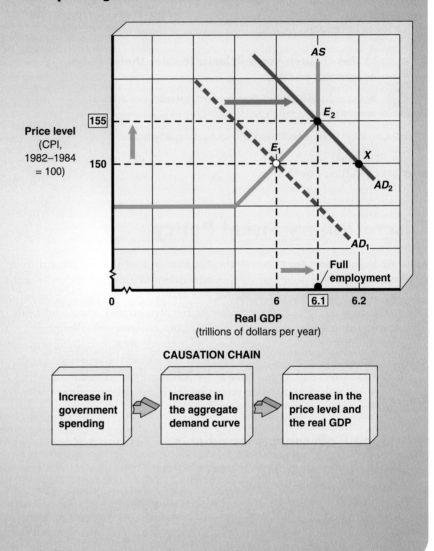

theory. The classical economists' prescription is to wait because the economy will self-correct to full employment in the long run by adjusting downward along AD_1. But election time is approaching, so there is political pressure to do something about the recession now. Besides, recall Keynes's famous statement, "In the long run, we are all dead." Hence, policymakers follow Keynesian economics and decide to shift the aggregate demand curve rightward from AD_1 to AD_2 and thereby cure the recession.

How can the federal government do this? In theory, any increase in consumption (C), investment (I), or net exports ($X - M$) can spur aggregate demand. But these spending boosts are not directly under the government's control as is government spending (G). After all, there is always a long wish list of spending proposals for federal highways, health care, education, environmental programs, and so forth. Rather than crossing their fingers and waiting for things to happen in the long run, suppose members of Congress gladly increase government spending to boost employment now.

But just how much new government spending is required? Note that the economy is operating $100 billion below its full-employment output, but the horizontal distance between AD_1 and AD_2 is $200 billion. This gap between AD_1 and AD_2 is indicated by the dotted line between points E_1 and X. This means that the aggregate demand curve must be shifted to the right by $200 billion. But it is not necessary to increase government spending by this amount. Recall from the Keynesian model in action chapter that the formula to compute the amount of additional government spending required to shift the aggregate demand curve rightward and establish a new full-employment real GDP equilibrium is as follows:

initial change in government spending (ΔG) × spending multiplier = change in aggregate demand (total spending)

The **spending multiplier** (*SM*) in the formula amplifies the amount of new government spending. As defined in the Keynesian model in action chapter, the spending multiplier is the change in aggregate demand (total spending) resulting from an initial change in any component of aggregate demand, including consumption, investment, government spending, and net exports. Expressed as a formula, $SM = 1/(1 - MPC)$ or $SM = 1/MPS$ (recall that *MPC* stands for marginal propensity to consume and *MPS* for marginal propensity to save). Assume the *MPC* is 0.75 and therefore the value for the spending multiplier in our example is 4. Given this information, our problem is solved mathematically as

$$\Delta G \times 4 = \$200 \text{ billion}$$
$$\Delta G = \$50 \text{ billion}$$

Thus, it takes $50 billion worth of new government spending to shift the aggregate demand curve to the right by $200 billion. As described in the previous chapter (Exhibit 6), bottlenecks occur throughout the upward-sloping range of the *AS* curve. This means prices rise as production increases in response to greater aggregate demand. Returning to Exhibit 2, you can see that $50 billion worth of new government spending shifts aggregate demand from AD_1 to AD_2. As a result, firms increase output upward along the aggregate supply curve, *AS*, and total spending moves upward along aggregate demand curve AD_2. This adjustment mechanism moves the economy to a new equilibrium at E_2, with full employment, a higher price level of 155, and a real GDP of $6.1 trillion per year. At point E_2, the economy experiences *demand-pull inflation*. And here is the important point: Although the aggregate demand curve has increased by $200 billion, the equilibrium real GDP has increased by only $100 billion, from $6 to $6.1 trillion.

Conclusion *In the intermediate segment of the aggregate supply curve, the equilibrium real GDP changes by less than the change in government spending times the spending multiplier.*

Spending multiplier (*SM*)
The ratio of the change in real GDP to an initial change in any component of aggregate expenditures, including consumption, investment, government spending, and net exports. As a formula, spending multiplier equals $1/(1 - MPC)$ or $1/MPS$.

The National Bureau of Economic Research (NBER) measures U.S. business cycle expansions and contractions (http://www.nber.org/).

Cutting Taxes to Combat a Recession

Another expansionary fiscal policy intended to increase aggregate demand and restore full employment calls for the government to cut taxes. Let's return to point E_1 in Exhibit 2. As before, the problem is to shift the aggregate demand curve to the right by $200 billion. But this time, instead of a $50 billion increase in government spending, assume Congress votes a $50 billion tax cut. How does this cut in taxes affect aggregate demand? First, *disposable personal income* (take-home pay) increases by $50 billion—the amount of the tax reduction. Second, once again assuming the MPC is 0.75, the increase in disposable personal income induces new consumption spending of $38 billion (0.75 × $50 billion). Thus, a cut in taxes triggers a multiplier process similar to, but smaller than, the spending multiplier.

Exhibit 3 demonstrates that a tax reduction adds less to aggregate demand than does an equal increase in government spending. Column 1 reproduces the effect of increasing government spending by $50 billion, and column 2 gives for comparison the effect of lowering taxes by $50 billion. Note that the only difference between increasing government spending and cutting taxes by the same amount is the impact in the initial round. The reason is that a tax cut injects zero new spending into the economy because the government has purchased no new goods and services. The effect of a tax reduction in round 2 is that people spend a portion of the $50 billion boost in after-tax income from the tax cut introduced in round 1. Subsequent rounds in the tax multiplier chain generate a cumulative increase in consumption expenditures that totals $150 billion. Comparing the total changes in aggregate demand in columns 1 and 2 of Exhibit 3 leads to the following:

> **Conclusion** *A tax cut has a smaller multiplier effect on aggregate demand than an equal increase in government spending.*

Tax multiplier

The change in aggregate demand (total spending) resulting from an initial change in taxes. As a formula, tax multiplier equals 1 − spending multiplier.

The **tax multiplier,** presented earlier in the chapter on the Keynesian model in action, can be computed by using a formula and the information from column 2 of Exhibit 3. The tax multiplier is the change in aggregate demand (total spending) resulting from an initial change in taxes. Mathematically, the tax multiplier is given by this formula:

$$\text{tax multiplier} = 1 - \text{spending multiplier}$$

Returning to Exhibit 2, the tax multiplier formula can be used to see how large a tax cut is needed to shift the aggregate demand curve rightward by $200 billion and restore full employment. Applying the formula given above and a spending multiplier of 4 yields a tax multiplier of −3. Note the sign of the tax multiplier is always negative. Thus, a $66.6 billion tax cut is needed to shift the aggregate demand curve rightward by $200 billion and restore full-employment equilibrium at point E_2. Mathematically,

$$\text{change in taxes } (\Delta T) \times \text{ tax multiplier} = \text{change in aggregate demand}$$
$$\Delta T \times -3 = \$200 \text{ billion}$$
$$\Delta T = -\$66.6 \text{ billion}$$

EXHIBIT 3 Comparison of the Spending and Tax Multipliers

Round	Component of total spending	Increase in aggregate demand from	
		(1) A $50 billion increase in government spending $(+\Delta G)$	(2) A $50 billion cut in taxes $(-\Delta T)$
1	Government spending	$ 50	$ 0
2	Consumption	38	38
3	Consumption	29	29
4	Consumption	22	22
.	.	.	.
.	.	.	.
.	.	.	.
All other rounds	Consumption	61	61
	Total spending	$200	$150

Note: All amounts are rounded to the nearest billion dollars per year.

A word of warning concerning the above analysis: in reality, the assumption that the *MPC* remains unchanged in response to a tax cut may be invalid. In 1964, Congress enacted President Kennedy's tax-cut proposal. The tax multiplier worked, and consumer spending lifted the economy out of a recession. On the other hand, in 1975, President Gerald Ford persuaded Congress to reduce income taxes to help increase aggregate demand during a recession. This time, however, the size of the tax multiplier fell because consumers reduced their *MPC*. The reason was that people saved much of the tax cut, rather than spending it. As a result, the anticipated boost to aggregate demand did not materialize.

As this text was being written in 2001, the United States faced the possibility that the longest economic expansion in U.S. history might not continue. Early in 2001, President Bush and Congress agreed to send out about $40 billion in tax rebates and phase in new lower marginal rates in coming years (see the schedule in the next chapter). Again, the key to success depends on the size of the *MPC* and in turn the tax multiplier. What proportion of the tax cut will be spent for consumption? In this case, the effects were complicated by the economic ramifications of the attack on the United States on September 11, which were not fully known when this book went to press. Also, a recession began in March 2001 and ended the expansion.

Using Fiscal Policy to Combat Inflation

So far, Keynesian expansionary fiscal policy, born of the Great Depression, has been presented as the cure for an economic downturn. Contractionary fiscal policy, on the other hand, can serve in the fight against inflation. Exhibit 4 shows an economy operating at point E_1 on the classical range of the aggregate supply curve, *AS*. Hence, this economy is producing the full-employment output of $6.1 trillion real GDP, and the price level is 160. In this situation, any increase in aggregate demand only causes inflation, while real GDP remains unchanged.

Suppose Congress and the president decide to use fiscal policy to reduce the CPI from 160 to 155 because they fear the wrath of voters suffering from the consequences of inflation. Although a fall in consumption, investment, or net exports might do the job, Congress and the president may be unwilling to wait and may instead prefer taking direct action by cutting government spending. Given a marginal propensity to consume of 0.75, the spending multiplier is 4. As shown by the horizontal distance between point E_1 on AD_1 and point E' on AD_2 in Exhibit 4, aggregate demand must be decreased by $100 billion in order to shift the aggregate demand curve from AD_1 to AD_2 and establish equilibrium at E_2, with a price level of 155. Mathematically,

$$\Delta G \times 4 = -\$100 \text{ billion}$$
$$\Delta G = -\$25 \text{ billion}$$

Using the above formula, a $25 billion cut in real government spending would cause a $100 billion decrease in the aggregate demand curve from AD_1 to AD_2. The result is a temporary excess aggregate supply of $100 billion, measured by the distance from E' to E_1. As explained in Exhibit 5 of the previous chapter, the economy follows classical theory and moves downward along AD_2 to a new equilibrium at E_2. Consequently, inflation cools with no change in the full-employment real GDP.

Another approach to the inflation problem would be for Congress and the president to raise taxes. Although tax increases are often considered political suicide, let's suppose Congress calculates just the correct amount of a tax hike required to reduce aggregate demand by $100 billion. Assuming a spending multiplier of 4, the tax multiplier is -3. Therefore, a $33.3 billion tax hike provides the necessary $100 billion leftward shift in the aggregate demand curve from AD_1 to AD_2. As a result, the desired equilibrium change from E_1 to E_2 is achieved, and the price level drops from 160 to 155 at the full-employment output of $6.1 trillion. Mathematically,

$$\Delta T \times -3 = -\$100 \text{ billion}$$
$$\Delta T = -\$33.3 \text{ billion}$$

The Balanced Budget Multiplier

The analysis of Keynesian discretionary fiscal policy presented in the previous section supposes the federal government selects a change in *either* government spending or taxes as a remedy for recession or inflation. However,

EXHIBIT 4   **Using Fiscal Policy to Combat Inflation**

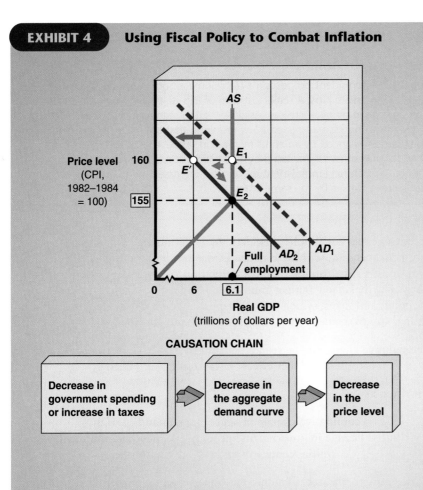

CAUSATION CHAIN

| Decrease in government spending or increase in taxes | → | Decrease in the aggregate demand curve | → | Decrease in the price level |

The economy in this exhibit is in equilibrium at point E_1 on the classical range of the aggregate supply curve, *AS*. The price level is 160, and the economy is operating at the full-employment output of $6.1 trillion real GDP. To reduce the price level to 155, the aggregate demand curve must be shifted to the left by $100 billion, measured by the horizontal distance between point E_1 on curve AD_1 and point E' on curve AD_2. One way this can be done is by decreasing government spending. With *MPC* equal to 0.75, and therefore a spending multiplier of 4, a $25 billion decrease in government spending results in the needed $100 billion leftward shift in the aggregate demand curve. As a result, the economy reaches equilibrium at point E_2, and the price level falls from 160 to 155, while real output remains unchanged at full capacity.

An identical decrease in the aggregate demand curve can be obtained by a hike in taxes. A $33.3 billion tax increase works through a multiplier of 3 and provides the needed $100 billion decrease in the aggregate demand curve from AD_1 to AD_2.

CHECKPOINT

Walking the Balanced Budget Tightrope

Suppose the president proposes a $16 billion economic stimulus package intended to create jobs. A major criticism of this new spending proposal is that it is not matched by tax increases. Assume the U.S. economy is below full employment and Congress has passed a law requiring that any increase in spending be matched or balanced by an equal increase in taxes. The *MPC* is 0.75, and aggregate demand must be increased by $20 billion to reach full employment. Will the economy reach full employment if Congress increases spending by $16 billion and increases taxes by the same amount?

Balanced budget multiplier

An equal change in government spending and taxes, which changes aggregate demand by the amount of the change in government spending.

a controversial fiscal policy requires the government to match or "balance" any new spending with new taxes. Understanding the impact on the economy of this fiscal policy requires derivation of the **balanced budget multiplier.** The balanced budget multiplier is an equal change in government spending and taxes, which changes aggregate demand by the amount of the change in government spending. Expressed as a formula,

cumulative change in aggregate demand (ΔAD) = government spending multiplier effect + tax multiplier effect

rewritten as

**cumulative change in aggregate demand (ΔAD) =
(initial change in government spending × spending multiplier) +
(initial change in taxes × tax multiplier)**

To see how the balanced budget multiplier works, suppose Congress enacts a $1 billion increase in government spending for highways and finances these purchases with a $1 billion increase in gasoline taxes. Mathematically,

$$\Delta AD = \left(\$1 \text{ billion} \times \frac{1}{1 - MPC}\right) + \left(\$1 \text{ billion} \times 1 - \frac{1}{1 - MPC}\right)$$

$$= \left(\$1 \text{ billion} \times \frac{1}{1 - 0.75}\right) + \left(\$1 \text{ billion} \times 1 - \frac{1}{1 - 0.75}\right)$$

$$= (\$1 \text{ billion} \times 4) + (\$1 \text{ billion} \times -3)$$

$$= \$4 \text{ billion} - \$3 \text{ billion}$$

$$= \$1 \text{ billion}$$

Hence, the balanced budget multiplier is always equal to 1, and the cumulative change in aggregate demand is $1 billion—*the amount of the initial change in government spending.*

Conclusion *Regardless of the* MPC, *the net effect on the economy of an equal initial increase (decrease) in government spending and taxes is an increase (decrease) in aggregate demand equal to the initial increase (decrease) in government spending.*

Automatic Stabilizers

Unlike discretionary fiscal policy, **automatic stabilizers** are policy tools built into the federal budget that help fight unemployment and inflation, while spending and tax laws remain unchanged. Automatic stabilizers are federal expenditures and tax revenues that automatically change levels in order to stabilize an economic expansion or contraction. Automatic stabilizers are sometimes referred to as *nondiscretionary fiscal policy.* Exhibit 5 illustrates the influence of automatic stabilizers on the economy. The downward-sloping line, *G,* represents federal government expenditures, including such *transfer payments* as unemployment compensation and welfare. This line falls as real GDP rises. When the economy expands, unemployment falls, and government spending for unemployment compensation, welfare, and other transfer payments decreases. During a downturn, people lose their jobs, and government spending automatically increases because unemployed individuals become eligible for unemployment compensation and other transfer payments.

The direct relationship between tax revenues and real GDP is shown by the upward-sloping line, *T.* During an expansion, jobs are created, unemployment falls, and workers earn more income and therefore pay more taxes. Thus, income tax collections automatically vary directly with the growth in real GDP.

We begin the analysis of automatic stabilizers with a balanced federal budget. Federal spending, *G,* is equal to tax collection, *T,* and the economy is in equilibrium at $6 trillion real GDP. Now assume consumer optimism soars and a spending spree increases the consumption component (*C*) of total spending. As a result, the economy moves to a new equilibrium at $8 trillion real GDP. The rise in real GDP creates more jobs and higher tax collections. Consequently, taxes rise to $1,000 billion on line *T,* and the vertical distance between lines *T* and *G* represents a federal **budget surplus** of $500 billion. A budget surplus occurs when government revenues exceed government expenditures in a given time period.

Now begin again with the economy at $6 trillion in Exhibit 5, and let's change the scenario. Assume that business managers lower their profit expectations. Their revised outlook causes business executives to become pessimistic, so they cut investment spending (*I*), causing aggregate demand to decline. The corresponding decline in real GDP from $6 trillion to $4 trillion causes tax revenues to fall from $1,000 billion to $500 billion on line *T.* The combined effect of the fall in spending and taxes creates a **budget deficit.** A budget deficit occurs when government expenditures exceed government revenues in a given time period. The vertical distance between lines *G* and *T* at $4 trillion real GDP illustrates a federal budget deficit of $500 billion.

The key feature of automatic stabilization is that it "leans against the prevailing wind." In short, changes in federal spending and taxes moderate changes in aggregate demand. When the economy expands, the fall in government spending for transfer payments and the rise in the level of taxes result in a budget surplus. As the budget surplus grows, people send more money to Washington, which applies braking power against further increases in real GDP. When the economy contracts, the rise in government spending for transfer payments and the fall in the level of taxes yield a budget deficit.

Automatic stabilizers
Federal expenditures and tax revenues that automatically change levels in order to stabilize an economic expansion or contraction; sometimes referred to as nondiscretionary fiscal policy.

Budget surplus
A budget in which government revenues exceed government expenditures in a given time period.

Budget deficit
A budget in which government expenditures exceed government revenues in a given time period.

EXHIBIT 5   **Automatic Stabilizers**

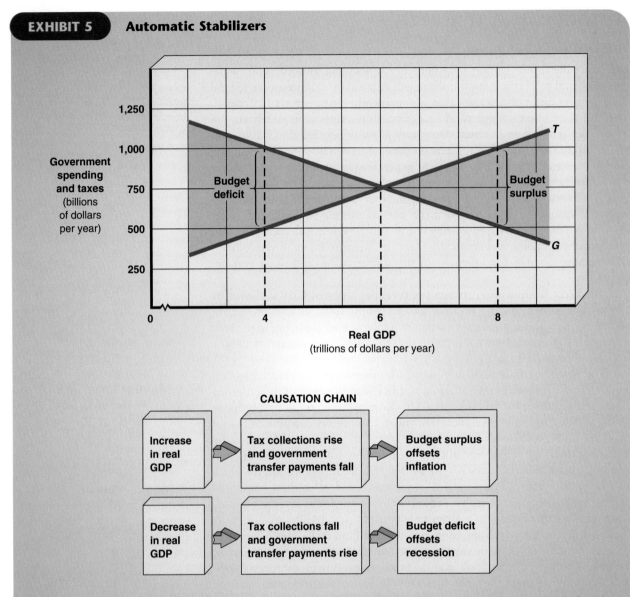

CAUSATION CHAIN

| Increase in real GDP | → | Tax collections rise and government transfer payments fall | → | Budget surplus offsets inflation |

| Decrease in real GDP | → | Tax collections fall and government transfer payments rise | → | Budget deficit offsets recession |

Federal government spending varies inversely with real GDP and is represented by the downward-sloping line, G. Taxes, in contrast, vary directly with real GDP and are represented by the upward-sloping line, T. This means government spending for welfare and other transfer payments declines and tax collections rise as real GDP rises. Thus, if real GDP falls below $6 trillion, the budget deficit rises automatically. The size of the budget deficit is shown by the vertical distance between lines G and T. This budget deficit assists in offsetting a recession because it stimulates aggregate demand. Conversely, when real GDP rises above $6 trillion, a federal budget surplus increases automatically and assists in offsetting inflation.

As the budget deficit grows, people receive more money from Washington to spend, which decelerates further decreases in real GDP.

Conclusion *Automatic stabilizers assist in offsetting a recession when real GDP falls and in offsetting inflation when real GDP expands.*

Supply-Side Fiscal Policy

The focus so far has been on fiscal policy that affects the macro economy solely through the impact of government spending and taxation on aggregate demand. Supply-side economists, whose intellectual roots are in classical economics, argue that *stagflation* in the 1970s was the result of the federal government's failure to follow the theories of **supply-side fiscal policy.** Supply-side fiscal policy emphasizes government policies that increase aggregate supply in order to achieve long-run growth in real output, full employment, and a lower price level. Supply-side policies became an active economic idea with the election of Ronald Reagan as president in 1980. As discussed in the previous chapter, the U.S. economy in the 1970s experienced high rates of both inflation and unemployment. Stagflation aroused concern about the ability of the U.S. economy to generate long-term advances in the standard of living. This set the stage for a new macroeconomic policy.

Suppose the economy is initially at E_1 in Exhibit 6(a), with a CPI of 150 and an output of $4 trillion real GDP. The economy is experiencing high unemployment, so the goal is to achieve full employment by increasing real GDP to $6 trillion. As described earlier in this chapter, the federal government might follow Keynesian expansionary fiscal policy and shift the aggregate demand curve rightward from AD_1 to AD_2. Higher government spending or lower taxes operate through the multiplier effect and cause this increase in aggregate demand. The good news from such a demand-side fiscal policy prescription is that the economy moves toward full employment, but the bad news is that the price level rises. In this case, *demand-pull inflation* would cause the price level to rise from 150 to 200.

Exhibit 6(b) represents the supply-siders' alternative to Keynesian fiscal policy. Again, suppose the economy is initially in equilibrium at E_1. Supply-side economists argue that the federal government should adopt policies that shift the aggregate supply curve rightward from AS_1 to AS_2. An increase in aggregate supply would move the economy to E_2 and achieve the full-employment level of real GDP. Under supply-side theory, there is an additional bonus to full employment. Instead of rising as in Exhibit 6(a), the price level in Exhibit 6(b) falls from 150 to 100. Comparing the two graphs in Exhibit 6, you can see that the supply-siders have a better theoretical case than proponents of demand-side fiscal policy when both inflation and unemployment are concerns.

Note the causation chain under each graph in Exhibit 6. The demand-side fiscal policy options are from column 1 of Exhibit 1 in this chapter, and the supply-side policy alternatives are reproduced from Exhibit 9 in the previous chapter. For supply-side economics to be effective, the government must implement policies that increase the total output that firms produce at each possible price level. An increase in aggregate supply can be accomplished

Supply-side fiscal policy
A fiscal policy that emphasizes government policies that increase aggregate supply in order to achieve long-run growth in real output, full employment, and a lower price level.

David Stockman, President Reagan's director of the Office of Management and Budget, played a major role in creating a fiscal policy based on supply-side economic theory. An interesting article concerning Stockman, written by William Greider, appeared in the Atlantic Monthly *in December 1981* (http://www.theatlantic.com/ unbound/flashbks/classics/ stockman.htm).

EXHIBIT 6   Keynesian Demand-Side versus Supply-Side Effects

In part (a), assume an economy begins in equilibrium at point E_1, with a price level of 150 and a real GDP of $4 trillion. To boost real output and employment, Keynesian economists prescribe that the federal government raise government spending or cut taxes. By following such demand-side policies, the policy-makers work through the multiplier effect and shift the aggregate demand curve from AD_1 to AD_2. As a result, the equilibrium changes to E_2, where real GDP rises to $6 trillion, but the price level also rises to 200. Hence, full employment has been achieved at the expense of higher inflation.

The initial situation for the economy at point E_1 in part (b) is identical to that shown in part (a). However, supply-siders offer a different fiscal policy prescription than the Keynesians. Using some combination of cuts in resource prices, technological advances, tax cuts, subsidies, and regulation reduction, supply-side fiscal policy shifts the aggregate supply curve from AS_1 to AS_2. As a result, the equilibrium in the economy changes to E_2, and real GDP increases to $6 trillion, just as in part (a). The advantage of the supply-side versus the demand-side stimulus is that the price level falls to 100, rather than rising to 200.

by some combination of cuts in resource prices, technological advances, subsidies, and reductions in government taxes and government regulations.

Although a laundry list of supply-side policies was advocated during the Reagan administration, the most familiar policy action taken was the tax cuts implemented in 1981. By reducing tax rates on wages and profits, the Reagan administration sought to increase the aggregate supply of goods and services at any price level. However, tax cuts are a Keynesian policy intended to increase aggregate demand, so supply-siders must have a different view of the impact of tax cuts on the economy. To explain these different views of

EXHIBIT 7 **How Supply-Side Fiscal Policies Affect Labor Markets**

Begin with equilibrium in the labor market at point E_1. Here the intersection of the labor supply and demand curves determines a wage rate of W_1 and L_1 hours of labor per year. By lowering tax rates, supply-side fiscal policies increase net after-tax earnings. This extra incentive causes workers to provide additional hours of labor per year. As a result, the labor supply curve increases and establishes a new equilibrium at point E_2. The new wage rate paid by employers falls to W_2, and they use more labor hours per year, L_2.

tax cuts, let's begin by stating that both Keynesians and supply-siders agree that tax cuts increase disposable personal income. In Keynesian economics, this boost in disposable personal income works through the *tax multiplier* to increase aggregate demand, as shown earlier in Exhibit 3. Supply-side economists argue instead that changes in disposable income affect the incentive to supply work, save, and invest.

Consider how a supply-side tax cut influences the labor market. Suppose supply and demand in the labor market are initially in equilibrium at point E_1 in Exhibit 7. Before a cut in personal income tax rates, the equilibrium hourly wage rate is W_1, and workers supply L_1 hours of labor per year at this wage rate. When the tax rates are cut, supply-side theory predicts the labor supply curve will shift rightward and establish a new equilibrium at E_2. The rationale is that an increase in the after-tax wage rate gives workers the incentive to work more hours per year. Those in the labor force will want to work longer hours and take fewer vacations. And because Uncle Sam takes a smaller bite out of workers' paychecks, many of those not already in the labor force will now supply their labor. As a result of the increase in the labor supply curve, the price of labor falls to W_2 per hour, and the equilibrium number of labor hours increases to L_2.

Supply-side tax cuts of the early 1980s also provided tax breaks that subsidized business investment. Tax credits were available for new equipment and plants and for research and development to encourage technological advances. The idea here was to increase the nation's productive capacity by increasing the quantity and quality of capital. Consequently, the aggregate supply curve would shift rightward because businesses have an extra after-tax profit incentive to invest and produce more at each price level.

The Bureau of Labor Statistics (BLS) (http://www.bls.gov/) *is the primary source of labor, unemployment, and survey data for the federal government. The BLS also publishes the* Occupational Outlook Handbook (http://www.bls.gov/oco/), *which provides job descriptions, working conditions, training and educational requirements, and similar information on various jobs.*

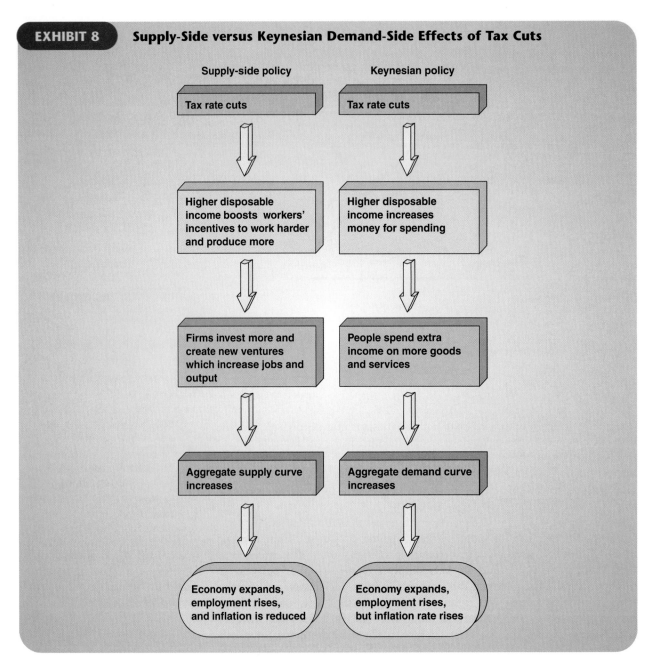

EXHIBIT 8   **Supply-Side versus Keynesian Demand-Side Effects of Tax Cuts**

The idea of using tax cuts to shift the aggregate supply curve outward is controversial. Despite its logic, the Keynesians argue that the magnitude of any rightward shift in aggregate supply is likely to be small and occur only in the long run. They point out that it takes many years before tax cuts for business generate any change in actual plants and equipment or technological advances. Moreover, individuals can accept tax cuts with a "thank you, Uncle Sam" and not work longer or harder. Meanwhile, unless a reduction in government spending offsets tax cuts, the effect will be a Keynesian increase in the aggregate demand curve and a higher price level. Exhibit 8 summarizes the important distinction between the supply-side and Keynesian theories on tax cut policy.

The Laffer Curve

Applicable Concept: supply-side fiscal policy

Supply-side economics became popular during the presidential campaign of 1980. This fiscal policy prescription gained prominence after supply-side economist Arthur Laffer, using a paper napkin, explained what has come to be known as the Laffer curve to a journalist at a restaurant in Washington, D.C. The Laffer curve is a graph depicting the relationship between tax rates and total tax revenues. As shown in the graph, the hypothetical Laffer curve can be drawn with the federal tax rate on the horizontal axis and tax revenue on the vertical axis. The idea behind this curve is that the federal tax rate affects the incentive for people to work, save, invest, and produce, which, in turn, influences tax revenue. As the tax rate climbs, Laffer and other supply-siders argue that the erosion of incentives shrinks national income and total tax collections.

Here is how the Laffer curve works. Suppose the federal government sets the federal income tax rate at zero (point A). At a zero income tax rate, people have the maximum incentive to produce, and optimum national income will be earned, but there is zero tax revenue for Uncle Sam. Now assume the federal government sets the income tax rate at the opposite extreme of 100 percent (point D). At a 100 percent confiscating income tax rate, people have no reason to work, produce, and earn income. People seek ways to reduce their tax liabilities by engaging in unreported or underground transactions or by not working at all. As a result, no tax revenue is collected by the Internal Revenue Service. Because the government confiscates all reported income, however, the incentive to work and produce is much less at a 100 percent tax rate than at a zero percent tax rate.

Because the federal government does not want to collect zero tax revenue, Congress sets the federal income tax rate between zero and 100 percent. Assuming that the income tax rate is related to tax revenue as depicted in the graph, maximum tax revenue, R_{max}, is collected at a tax rate of T_{max} (point B). Laffer argued that the federal income tax rate of T (point C) in 1981 exceeded T_{max} and the result would be tax revenue of R, which is below R_{max}. In Laffer's view, reducing the federal income tax rate leads

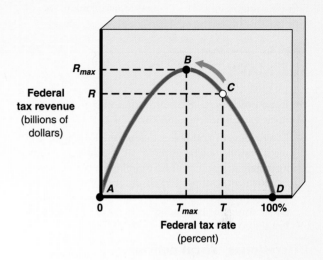

to an increase in tax revenue because people would increase their work effort, saving, and investment and would reduce their attempts to avoid paying taxes. Thus, Laffer curve policy argued that a cut in federal income tax rates would unleash economic activity and boost tax revenues needed to reduce the federal budget deficit. President Reagan's belief in the Laffer curve was a major reason why he thought that the federal government could cut personal income tax rates and still balance the federal budget.

The Laffer curve remains a controversial part of supply-side economics. There is still considerable uncertainty about the shape of the Laffer curve and at what point, B, C, or otherwise along the curve, the U.S. economy is operating. Thus, the existence and the usefulness of the Laffer curve are a matter of dispute.

ANALYZE THE ISSUE

Compare the common perception of how a tax rate cut affects tax revenues with economist Laffer's theory.

KEY CONCEPTS

Fiscal policy	Tax multiplier	Budget surplus	Supply-side fiscal policy
Discretionary fiscal policy	Balanced budget multiplier	Budget deficit	Laffer curve
Spending multiplier (*SM*)	Automatic stabilizers		

SUMMARY

- **Fiscal policy** is the use of government spending and taxes to stabilize the economy.

- **Discretionary fiscal policy** follows the Keynesian argument that the federal government should manipulate aggregate demand in order to influence the output, employment, and price levels in the economy. Discretionary fiscal policy requires new legislation to change either government spending or taxes in order to stabilize the economy.

Discretionary fiscal policies

Expansionary fiscal policy	Contractionary fiscal policy
Increase government spending	Decrease government spending
Decrease taxes	Increase taxes
Increase government spending and taxes equally	Decrease government spending and taxes equally

- **Expansionary fiscal policy** is a deliberate increase in government spending, a deliberate decrease in taxes, or some combination of these two options.

- **Contractionary fiscal policy** is a deliberate decrease in government spending, a deliberate increase in taxes, or some combination of these two options. Using either expansionary or contractionary fiscal policy, the government can shift the aggregate demand curve in order to combat recession, cool inflation, or achieve other macroeconomic goals.

- The **tax multiplier** is the multiplier by which an initial change in taxes changes aggregate demand (total spending) after an infinite number of spending cycles. Expressed as a formula, the tax multiplier = 1 − spending multiplier.

- A **balanced budget multiplier** is not neutral. A dollar of government spending increases real GDP more than a dollar cut in taxes. Thus, even though the government does not spend more than it collects in taxes, it is still stimulating the economy.

- **Combating recession and inflation** can be accomplished by changing government spending or taxes. The total change in aggregate demand from a change in government spending is equal to the change in government spending times the spending multiplier. The total change in aggregate demand from a change in taxes is equal to the change in taxes times the tax multiplier.

Combating recession

Combating inflation

- A **budget surplus** occurs when government revenues exceed government expenditures. A **budget deficit** occurs when government expenditures exceed government revenues.

- **Automatic stabilizers** are changes in taxes and government spending that occur automatically in response to changes in the level of real GDP. The business cycle therefore creates braking power: A *budget surplus* slows down an expanding economy. A *budget deficit* reverses a downturn in the economy.

Automatic stabilizers

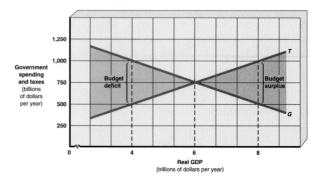

■ According to **supply-side fiscal policy**, lower taxes encourage work, saving, and investment, which shift the aggregate supply curve rightward. As a result, output and employment increase without inflation.

■ The **Laffer curve** represents the relationship between the income tax rate and the amount of income tax revenue collected by the government.

SUMMARY OF CONCLUSION STATEMENTS

■ In the intermediate segment of the aggregate supply curve, the equilibrium real GDP changes by less than the change in government spending times the spending multiplier.

■ A tax cut has a smaller multiplier effect on aggregate demand than an equal increase in government spending.

■ Regardless of the *MPC*, the net effect on the economy of an equal initial increase (decrease) in government spending and taxes is an increase (decrease) in aggregate demand equal to the initial increase (decrease) in government spending.

■ Automatic stabilizers assist in offsetting a recession when real GDP falls and in offsetting inflation when real GDP expands.

STUDY QUESTIONS AND PROBLEMS

1. Explain how discretionary fiscal policy fights recession and inflation.

2. How does each of the following affect the aggregate demand curve?
   a. Government spending increases.
   b. The amount of taxes collected decreases.

3. In each of the following cases, explain whether the fiscal policy is expansionary, contractionary, or neutral.
   a. The government decreases government spending.
   b. The government increases taxes.
   c. The government increases spending and taxes by an equal amount.

4. Why does a reduction in taxes have a smaller multiplier effect than an increase in government spending of an equal amount?

5. Suppose you are an economic adviser to the president and the economy needs a real GDP increase of $500 billion to reach full-employment equilibrium. If the marginal propensity to consume (*MPC*) is 0.75 and you are a Keynesian, by how much do you believe Congress must increase government spending in order to restore the economy to full employment?

6. Consider an economy that is operating at the full-employment level of real GDP. Assuming the *MPC* is 0.90, predict the effect on the economy of a $50 billion increase in government spending balanced by a $50 billion increase in taxes.

7. Why is a $100 billion increase in government spending for goods and services more expansionary than a $100 billion decrease in taxes?

8. What is the difference between discretionary fiscal policy and automatic stabilizers? How are federal budget surpluses and deficits affected by the business cycle?

9. Assume you are a supply-side economist who is an adviser to the president. If the economy is in recession, what would your fiscal policy prescription be?

10. Suppose Congress enacts a tax reform law and the average federal tax rate drops from 30 percent to 20 percent. Researchers investigate the impact of the tax cut and find that the income subject to the tax increases from $600 billion to $800 billion. The theoretical explanation is that workers have increased their work effort in response to the incentive of lower taxes. Is this a movement along the downward-sloping or the upward-sloping portion of the Laffer curve?

11. Indicate how each of the following would change either the aggregate demand curve or the aggregate supply curve:
    a. Expansionary fiscal policy
    b. Contractionary fiscal policy
    c. Supply-side economics
    d. Demand-pull inflation
    e. Cost-push inflation

ONLINE EXERCISES

Exercise 1

Visit the National Bureau of Economic Research (http://www.nber.org/cycles.html) and view the duration in months for contractions (recessions) experienced in the United States.

1. What has happened to the duration of time in which contractions have been experienced in the United States in the post World War II (post 1945) era?

2. What do you think could account for this change?

3. What should government do with fiscal policy to combat a recession (a contraction)?

Exercise 2

Identify a liberal argument in favor of increased government spending at the Center on Budget and Policy Priorities at http://www.cbpp.org/. Identify a conservative argument against increased government spending at the National Center for Policy Analysis at http://www.ncpa.org.

Exercise 3

Go to a Web site maintained by Professor Kailash Khandke (http://www.furman.edu/~kkhandke/fall98/keyn2f97.htm). Work through several simulations.

CHECKPOINT ANSWER

Walking the Balanced Budget Tightrope

A $16 billion increase in government spending increases aggregate demand by $64 billion [government spending increase × spending multiplier, where the spending multiplier = $1/(1 - MPC) = 1/.25 = 4$]. On the other hand, a $16 billion increase in taxes reduces aggregate demand by $48 billion (tax cut × tax multiplier, where the tax multiplier = 1 − spending multiplier = 1 − 4 = −3). Thus, the net effect of the spending multiplier and the tax multiplier is an increase in aggregate demand of $16 billion. If you said Congress has missed its goal of a $20 billion boost in aggregate demand by $4 billion and has not restored full employment, YOU ARE CORRECT.

PRACTICE QUIZ

For a visual explanation of the correct answers, visit the tutorial at http://tucker.swcollege.com.

1. Contractionary fiscal policy is deliberate government action to influence aggregate demand and the level of real GDP through
   a. expanding and contracting the money supply.
   b. encouraging business to expand or contract investment.
   c. regulating net exports.
   d. decreasing government spending or increasing taxes.

2. The spending multiplier is defined as
   a. 1/(1 − marginal propensity to consume).
   b. 1/(marginal propensity to consume).
   c. 1/(1 − marginal propensity to save).
   d. 1/(marginal propensity to consume + marginal propensity to save).

3. If the marginal propensity to consume (*MPC*) is 0.60, the value of the spending multiplier is
   a. 0.4.
   b. 0.6.
   c. 1.5.
   d. 2.5.

4. Assume the economy is in recession and real GDP is below full employment. The marginal propensity to consume (*MPC*) is 0.80, and the government increases spending by $500 billion. As a result, aggregate demand will rise by
   a. zero.
   b. $2,500 billion.
   c. more than $2,500 billion.
   d. less than $2,500 billion.

5. Mathematically, the value of the tax multiplier in terms of the marginal propensity to consume (*MPC*) is given by the formula
   a. $MPC − 1$.
   b. $(MPC − 1)/MPC$.
   c. $1/MPC$.
   d. $1 − [1/(1 − MPC)]$.

6. Assume the marginal propensity to consume (*MPC*) is 0.75 and the government increases taxes by $250 billion. The aggregate demand curve will shift to the
   a. left by $1,000 billion.
   b. right by $1,000 billion.
   c. left by $750 billion.
   d. right by $750 billion.

7. If no fiscal policy changes are made, suppose the current aggregate demand curve will shift horizontally by $1,000 billion and cause inflation. If the marginal propensity to consume (*MPC*) is 0.80, federal policymakers could follow Keynesian economics and restrain inflation by
   a. decreasing government spending by $200 billion.
   b. decreasing taxes by $100 billion.
   c. decreasing taxes by $1,000 billion.
   d. decreasing government spending by $1,000 billion.

8. If no fiscal policy changes are implemented, suppose the future aggregate demand curve will exceed the current aggregate demand curve by $500 billion at any level of prices. Assuming the marginal propensity to consume (*MPC*) is 0.80, this increase in aggregate demand could be prevented by
   a. increasing government spending by $500 billion.
   b. increasing government spending by $140 billion.
   c. decreasing taxes by $40 billion.
   d. increasing taxes by $125 billion.

9. Suppose inflation is a threat because the current aggregate demand curve will increase by $600 billion at any price level. If the marginal propensity to consume (*MPC*) is 0.75, federal policymakers could follow Keynesian economics and restrain inflation by
   a. decreasing taxes by $600 billion.
   b. decreasing transfer payments by $200 billion.
   c. increasing taxes by $200 billion.
   d. increasing government spending by $150 billion.

10. If no fiscal policy changes are implemented, suppose the future aggregate demand curve will shift and exceed the current aggregate demand curve by $900 billion at any level of prices. Assuming the marginal propensity to consume (*MPC*) is 0.90, this increase in aggregate demand could be prevented by
    a. increasing government spending by $500 billion.
    b. increasing government spending by $140 billion.
    c. decreasing taxes by $40 billion.
    d. increasing taxes by $100 billion.

11. Which of the following is *not* an automatic stabilizer?
    a. Defense spending
    b. Unemployment compensation benefits
    c. Personal income taxes
    d. Welfare payments

12. Supply-side economics is most closely associated with
    a. Karl Marx.
    b. John Maynard Keynes.
    c. Milton Friedman.
    d. Ronald Reagan.

13. Which of the following statements is true?
    a. A reduction in tax rates along the downward-sloping portion of the Laffer curve would increase tax revenues.
    b. According to supply-side fiscal policy, lower tax rates would shift the aggregate demand curve to the right, expanding the economy and creating some inflation.
    c. The presence of automatic stabilizers tends to destabilize the economy.
    d. To combat inflation, Keynesians recommend lower taxes and greater government spending.

CHAPTER 22
The Public Sector

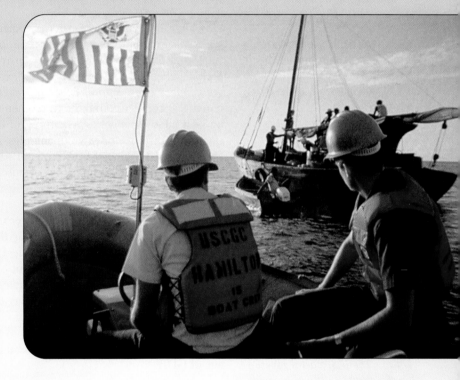

I n the early 1980s, President Ronald Reagan adopted the Laffer theory that the federal government could cut tax rates and increase tax revenues. Critics said the result would be lower tax revenues. In the late 1990s, President Bill Clinton said cutting taxes was not a good idea because ensuring the integrity of Social Security should come first. During the 2000 Republican presidential primary campaign, Steve Forbes continued his attempt to win support for a flat tax. In 2001, newly elected President George W. Bush signed a tax cut into law that featured phased-in changes in the marginal tax rates.

These events illustrate the persistent real-world controversy surrounding fiscal policy. The previous chapter presented the theory behind fiscal policy, and in this chapter, you will examine the practice of fiscal policy. Here the facts of taxation and government

expenditures are clearly presented and placed in perspective. You can check, for example, the trend in federal taxes during the Reagan, George Bush, Clinton, and George W. Bush years and compare the tax burden in the United States to that in other countries. Here you will also discover why the government uses different types of taxes and tax rates.

The final section of the chapter addresses the word of caution given in Chapter 4. Recall at the conclusion of the discussion of

public goods that government intervention might fail to correct alleged market failures. Because the purpose of this chapter is to examine and challenge the economic role of the public sector, you will learn a theory called *public choice,* which examines public-sector decisions of politicians, government bureaucrats, voters, and special-interest groups. This theory explains why many people seek ways to privatize government programs by turning them over to the private sector.

In this chapter, you will learn to solve these economics puzzles:

■ How does the tax burden in the United States compare to other countries?

■ How does the Social Security tax favor the upper-income worker?

■ Is a flat tax fair?

■ Should we replace the income tax with a national sales tax or a flat tax?

Government Size and Growth

How big is the public sector in the United States? If we look at Exhibit 1, we see total **government expenditures** or **outlays**—including those of federal, state, and local governments—as a percentage of GDP for the 1929–2000 period. When we refer to *government expenditures,* we refer to more than the *government consumption expenditures and investment* (G) account used by national income accountants to calculate GDP (see Exhibit 2 in the chapter on GDP). Government expenditures, or outlays, equal government consumption expenditures and investment plus *transfer payments.* Recall from the chapter on GDP that the government national income account (G) includes federal government spending for defense, highways, and education. Transfer payments, not in (G), include payments to persons entitled to welfare, Social Security, and unemployment benefits.

As shown in Exhibit 1, total government expenditures skyrocketed as a percentage of GDP during World War II and then took a sharp plunge, but not to previous peacetime levels. Since 1950, total government expenditures grew from about one-quarter to about one-third of GDP between 1975 and 1995. In 2000, total government outlays fell to about 30 percent of GDP. The other side of the coin is that today the private sector's share of national output is approximately 70 percent of GDP. Note that since the 1960s, state and local governments expenditures have generally increased as a percentage of GDP. Beginning in the 1990s, federal outlays have decreased as a percentage of GDP.

Government Expenditures Patterns

Exhibit 2 shows program categories for federal government expenditures for the years 1970 and 2000. It may be surprising that the largest category by far in the federal budget for 2000 was a functional category called *income security.* "Security" because these payments provide income to the elderly or disadvantaged, including Social Security, Medicare, unemployment compensation, public assistance (welfare), federal retirement, and disability benefits. These entitlements are transfer payments in the form of either direct cash payments or in-kind transfers that redistribute income among persons.

The second largest category of federal government expenditures in 2000 was national defense. Note that the percentage of the federal budget spent for defense declined from 40 percent in 1970 to 16 percent in 2000, while income security ("safety net") expenditures grew from 22 percent in 1970

Government expenditures
Federal, state, and local government outlays for goods and services, including transfer payments.

The U.S. federal government's Office of Management and Budget provides much valuable information about the government's budget (http://www.gpo.gov/usbudget/index.html)*, especially if you select "A Citizen's Guide to the Federal Budget." It describes what a budget is, where the money goes and comes from, the major steps in the budget process and provides other easy-to-read and -understand information. See also "Budget Explorer-The Complete U.S. Federal Budget" at* http://www.kowaldesign.com/budget/.

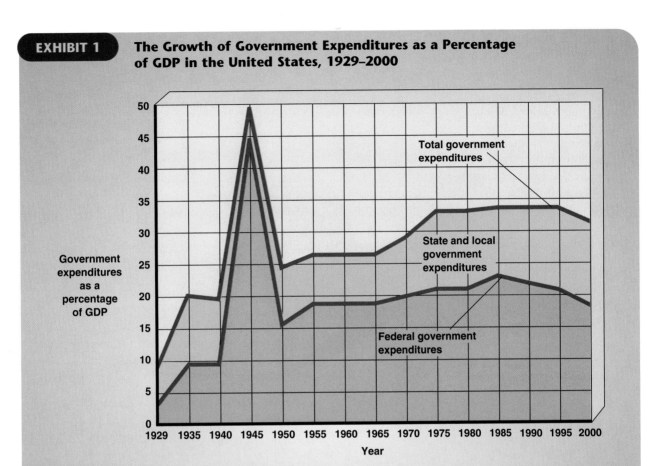

| EXHIBIT 1 | The Growth of Government Expenditures as a Percentage of GDP in the United States, 1929–2000 |

The graph shows the growth of the federal, state, and local governments as measured by government expenditures for goods and services as a percentage of GDP since 1929. There was a dramatic rise in expenditures during World War II and a dramatic fall after the war, but not to previous peacetime levels. Taking account of all government outlays, including transfer payments, the government sector has grown from about one-quarter of GDP in 1950 to about one-third between 1975 and 1995. In 2000, total government expenditures dropped to 30 percent of GDP. Since the 1960s, state and local government expenditures have generally increased as a percentage of GDP. In the late 1990s, federal outlays decreased as a percentage of GDP.

Sources: *Economic Report of the President, 2001,* http://w3.access.gpo.gov/eop/, Tables B-1, B-79, B-85, and B-86; and *Survey of Current Business,* GDP and Other Major NIPA Series, 1929–2000, http://www.bea.doc.gov/bea/dn1 .htm, Table 1.

to 48 percent in 2000. Hence, with a boost from an end to the Cold War, the dominant trend in federal government spending between 1970 and 2000 was an increase in the redistribution-of-income role of the federal government and a decrease in the portion of the budget spent for defense.

Federal expenditures for net interest on the federal debt was in third place in 2000. Net interest paid is the interest paid on federal government borrowing minus the interest earned on federal government loans. This category has grown from 9 percent of the budget in 1970 to 12.5 percent in

---

EXHIBIT 2 **Federal Expenditures, 1970 and 2000**

Between 1970 and 2000, income security became the largest category of federal expenditures. During the same period, national defense declined from the largest spending category to the second largest. Net interest on the federal debt has grown from 9 percent of the budget in 1970 to 12.5 percent in 2000. Therefore, income security and net interest payments combined accounted for 60.5 percent of federal outlays in 2000.

Sources: *Economic Report of the President, 1975,* Table C-65; and *2001,* http://w3.access.gpo.gov/eop/, Table B-81.

(a) 1970 expenditures

(b) 2000 expenditures

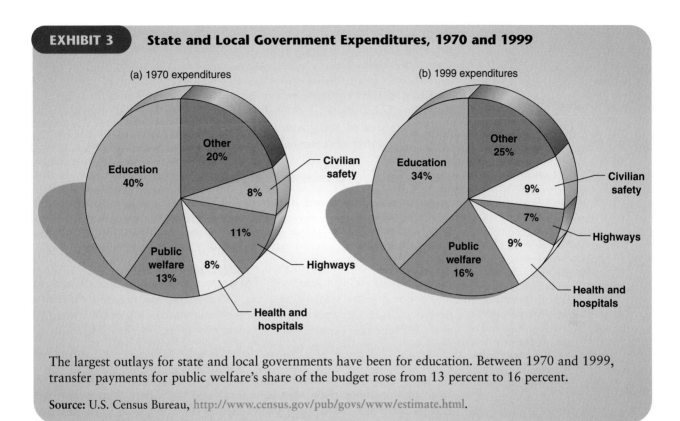

EXHIBIT 3   **State and Local Government Expenditures, 1970 and 1999**

(a) 1970 expenditures

(b) 1999 expenditures

The largest outlays for state and local governments have been for education. Between 1970 and 1999, transfer payments for public welfare's share of the budget rose from 13 percent to 16 percent.

Source: U.S. Census Bureau, http://www.census.gov/pub/govs/www/estimate.html.

2000. Thus, the federal government spent about the same proportion of the budget on financing its debt as on education and health. In 2000, income security and interest payments combined accounted for a whopping 60.5 percent of federal expenditures.

Exhibit 3 shows the degree to which the consolidated expenditures of all state and local governments differ from the spending pattern of the federal government. By far, the largest priority in state and local government budgets has been education. Nevertheless, outlays for education declined from 40 percent of total expenditures to 34 percent between 1970 and 1999. During the same period, transfer payments for public welfare rose from 13 percent of expenditures to 16 percent. The proportion of the total budget spent for highways declined, while the portions spent on health and hospitals and for civilian safety (fire, police, and corrections) remained about the same.

The relative shares of total public-sector expenditures by level of government are also of interest. In 2000, the federal government spent $1,814 billion, and state and local governments spent $1,171 billion, representing 61 percent and 39 percent, respectively, of total government expenditures in the economy. The federal government was not always the champion spender in the public sector. Prior to World War II, state and local government expenditures exceeded federal expenditures.

Finally, you need to be aware that the size and the growth of government are measured several ways. We could study *absolute* government spending or compare the growth of spending after adjusting for inflation. Still another technique is to measure the proportion of the population that the public sector employs. Using any of these measurements confirms the conclusion shown in Exhibit 1.

> **Conclusion** *The government's share of total economic activity has generally increased since World War II ended in 1945. Most of the growth in combined government expenditures as a percentage of GDP reflects rapidly growing federal government transfer programs.*

Financing Government Budgets

Where do government units obtain the funds to finance their outlays? Exhibit 4 tells the story for the three levels of government. Beginning with the federal government, we find the largest revenue source in 2000 was *individual income taxes* (50 percent), followed by *social insurance taxes* (32 percent), which include payroll taxes paid by employers and employees for Social Security, workers' compensation, and unemployment insurance. The third best revenue getter was, perhaps surprisingly, *corporate income taxes* (10 percent). An *excise tax* is a sales tax on the purchase of a particular good or service. Excise taxes contributed 3 percent of total tax receipts. The "Other" category includes receipts from such taxes as customs duties, estate taxes, and gift taxes.

Exhibit 4 also shows the consolidated receipts for all state and local governments for comparison with federal tax sources. There is quite a difference between the sources of receipts. At the state and local levels, the two largest sources of receipts were *sales taxes* (26 percent) and *property taxes* (20 percent). *Corporate income taxes* and *individual income taxes* contributed a combined 20 percent of tax receipts to state and local governments' treasuries. Death and gift taxes, motor vehicle licenses, and other miscellaneous sources provided the remainder of the total receipts.

The Tax Burden

Before turning our attention in the next section to the criteria for selecting which tax to impose, we must ask how burdensome overall taxation in the United States is. It may surprise you to learn that by international standards U.S. citizens are among the most lightly taxed people in the industrialized world. Exhibit 5 reveals that in 2000 the tax collector was clearly much more heavy-handed in most other advanced industrial countries when we compare the fraction of GDP paid in taxes. The Swedes, French, Germans, and Japanese for example, pay far higher taxes as a percentage of GDP than Americans. It should be noted that countries that tax more heavily also are expected to provide more public services—especially medical care—compared to the United States.

Another way to study the burden of taxation in the United States is to observe how it has changed over time. Exhibit 6 charts the growth of taxes as a percentage of GDP in the United States since 1929. Federal, state, and local taxes have climbed from about 11 percent of GDP in 1929 to their highest level of close to 33 percent in 2000. The exhibit also shows that the

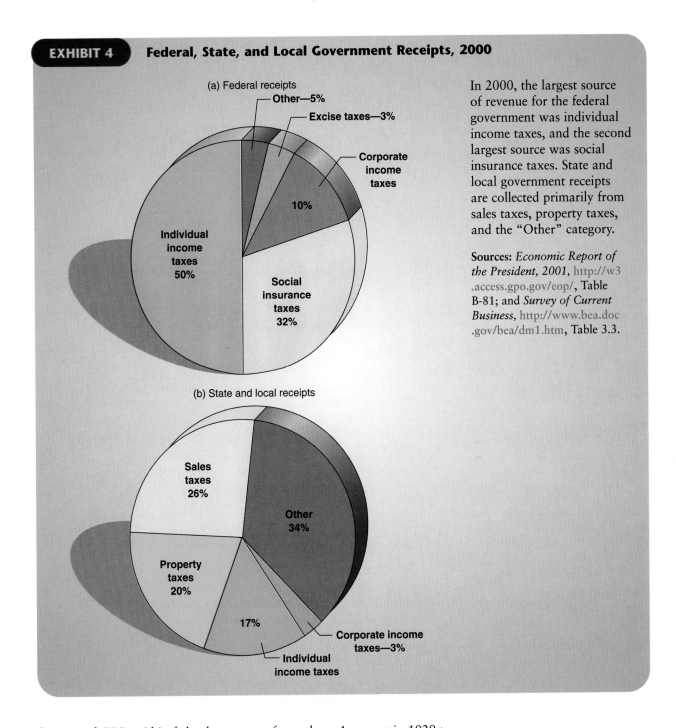

EXHIBIT 4   **Federal, State, and Local Government Receipts, 2000**

(a) Federal receipts

Other—5%

Excise taxes—3%

Corporate income taxes

10%

Individual income taxes 50%

Social insurance taxes 32%

In 2000, the largest source of revenue for the federal government was individual income taxes, and the second largest source was social insurance taxes. State and local government receipts are collected primarily from sales taxes, property taxes, and the "Other" category.

Sources: *Economic Report of the President, 2001,* http://w3 .access.gpo.gov/eop/, Table B-81; and *Survey of Current Business,* http://www.bea.doc .gov/bea/dm1.htm, Table 3.3.

(b) State and local receipts

Sales taxes 26%

Other 34%

Property taxes 20%

17%

Corporate income taxes—3%

Individual income taxes

fraction of GDP paid in federal taxes rose from about 4 percent in 1929 to over 20 percent during World War II and has since remained fairly constant, generally in the 17 to 20 percent range. In 2000, federal taxes as a percentage of GDP rose to a post–World War II high of 20.6 percent. The ratio of state and local taxes to GDP exceeded the ratio for the federal government until the beginning of World War II, but the federal government became by far the greater tax collector during and after the war. However, there has

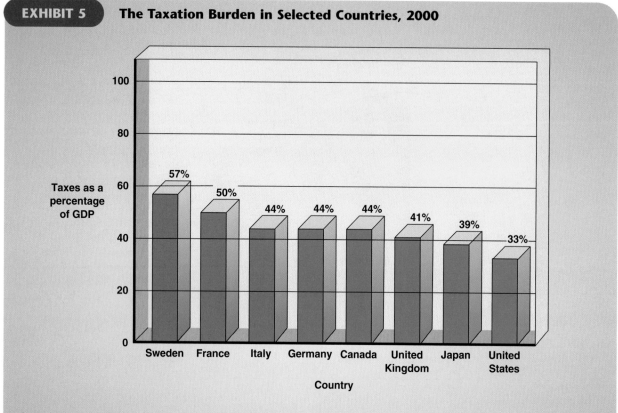

EXHIBIT 5   **The Taxation Burden in Selected Countries, 2000**

Americans were more lightly taxed in 2000 than the citizens of other advanced industrial countries. For example, the Swedes, French, Italians, Germans, Canadians, British, and Japanese paid higher taxes as a percentage of GDP.

Source: *OECD Economic Outlook*, June 2001, http://www.sourceoecd.org/content/html/index.htm, Annex Table 29.

The fiscal policy of the federal government manipulates, among other variables, the taxes Americans pay in order to influence variables in the economy. Visit "The Digital Daily," an electronic publication of the Internal Revenue Service (http://www.irs.ustreas.gov/prod/cover.html), *to see the latest changes in the federal government's tax policy (it may be helpful to look within "Tax Info for You"). Who might benefit from these changes? What effect might these changes have on the economy?*

been a significant postwar upward trend in the fraction of GDP paid as taxes to state and local governments. In 1945, this fraction was 5.1 percent, and in 1960, it was 8.1 percent. By 2000, the figure had climbed to about 12.6 percent.

The Art of Taxation

Jean Baptiste Colbert, finance minister to King Louis XIV of France, once said, "The art of taxation consists of so plucking the goose as to obtain the largest amount of feathers while promoting the smallest amount of hissing." Each year with great zeal members of Congress and other policymakers debate various ways of raising revenue without causing too much "hissing."

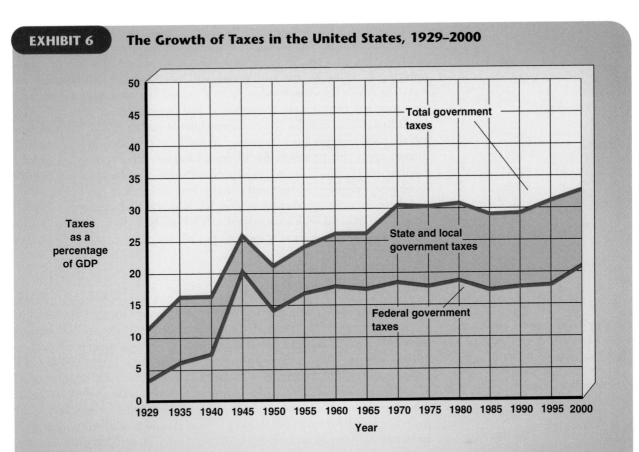

EXHIBIT 6 **The Growth of Taxes in the United States, 1929–2000**

The graph shows the growth in federal, state, and local government taxes as a percentage of GDP since 1929. Total government taxes climbed from about 11 percent of GDP in 1929 to the 25 percent range in the 1960s and thereafter rose to their highest level of about 33 percent in 2000. Between 1960 and 1995, federal taxes accounted for a fairly constant fraction of GDP. State and local taxes, however, have comprised an ever-increasing percentage of GDP since the 1950s. In 2000, federal taxes as a percentage of GDP rose to about 21 percent.

Sources: *Economic Report of the President, 2001,* http://w3.access.gpo.gov/eop/, Tables B-1, B-79, B-85, and B-86; and *Survey of Current Business,* GDP and Other Major NIPA Series, 1929–2000, http://www.bea.doc.gov/bea/dn1.htm, Table 1.

As you will learn, the task is difficult because each kind of tax has a different characteristic. Government must decide which tax is "appropriate" based on two basic philosophies of fairness—benefits received and ability to pay.

The Benefits-Received Principle

What standard or guideline can we use to be sure everyone pays his or her "fair" share of taxes? One possibility is the **benefits-received principle** of taxation, which is the concept that those who benefit from government expenditures should pay the taxes that finance their benefits. The gasoline tax is

Benefits-received principle
The concept that those who benefit from government expenditures should pay the taxes that finance their benefits.

an example of a tax that follows the *benefits-received principle*. The number of gallons of gasoline bought is a measure of the amount of highway services used, and the more gallons purchased, the greater the tax paid. Applying benefit-cost analysis, voters will only approve additional highways for which the benefits they receive exceed the costs in gasoline taxes they must pay for highway construction and repairs.

Although the benefits-received principle of taxation is applicable to a private good like gasoline, the nature of *public goods* often makes it impossible to apply this principle. Recall from Chapter 4 that national defense is a public good, which users collectively consume. So how can we separate those who benefit from national defense and make them pay? We cannot, and there are other goods and services for which the benefits-received principle is inconsistent with societal goals. It would be foolish, for example, to ask families receiving food stamps to pay all the taxes required to finance their welfare benefits.

The Ability-to-Pay Principle

Ability-to-pay principle
The concept that those who have higher incomes can afford to pay a greater proportion of their income in taxes, regardless of benefits received.

A second popular principle of taxation sharply contrasts with the benefits-received principle. The **ability-to-pay principle** of taxation is the concept that those who have higher incomes can afford to pay a greater proportion of their income in taxes regardless of benefits received. Under this tax philosophy, the rich may send their children to private schools or use private hospitals, but they should bear a heavier tax burden because they are better able to pay. How could there possibly be a problem with such an approach? An individual who earns $200,000 per year should pay X more taxes than an individual who earns only $10,000 per year. The difficulty lies in determining exactly how much more the higher-income individual should pay in taxes to ensure that he or she is paying a "fair" amount. Unfortunately, no scientific method can measure precisely what one's "ability" to pay taxes means in dollars or percentage of income. Nevertheless, in the U.S. economy, the ability-to-pay principle dominates the benefits-received principle.

Progressive, Regressive, and Proportional Taxes

As we have seen, governments raise revenues from various taxes, such as income taxes, sales taxes, excise taxes, and property taxes. For purposes of analysis, economists classify each of these taxes into three types of taxation—*progressive, regressive,* and *proportional.* The focus of these three classifications is the relationship between changes in the tax rates and increases or decreases in income. Income is the tax base because people pay taxes out of income even though a tax is levied on property, such as land, buildings, automobiles, or furniture.

Progressive tax
A tax that charges a higher percentage of income as income rises.

Progressive Taxes. Following the ability-to-pay principle, individual and corporate income taxes are **progressive taxes.** A progressive tax charges a higher percentage of income as income rises. For example, if a person earning $10,000 a year paid $1,500 in taxes, the *average* tax rate is 15 percent. If another person earned $100,000 a year and paid $28,000 in taxes, the average tax rate is 28 percent. This tax rate progressivity is the principle

EXHIBIT 7 Federal Individual Income Tax Rate Schedule for a Single Taxpayer, 2000

(1) Taxable income		(2)	(3) Average tax rate	(4) Change in taxable	(5) Change	(6) Marginal tax rate
Over	Not over	Tax*	[(2)/(1)]	income	in tax	[(5)/(4)]
$ 0	$ 26,250	$ 3,937	15%	$ 26,250	$ 3,937	15.0%
26,250	63,550	14,381	23	37,300	10,444	28.0
63,550	132,600	35,787	27	69,050	25,343	31.0
132,600	288,350	91,857	32	155,750	56,070	36.0
288,350	—	—	—	—	—	39.6

*Tax calculated at the top of the taxable income brackets.

Source: Internal Revenue Service, Publication 17, *Your Federal Income Tax, 2000,*
http://www.irs.ustreas.gov/prod/forms_pubs/index.html, Tax Rate Schedules, p. 266.

behind the federal and state income tax systems. Exhibit 7 illustrates the progressive nature of the federal income tax for a single person filing a 2000 tax return in 2001.

Column 1 of Exhibit 7 lists the *taxable income* tax brackets. Taxable income is gross income minus the personal exemption and the standard deduction. Since 1990, the personal exemption and the standard deduction have been subject to adjustment for inflation. This follows the action taken in 1985 to "index" the tax brackets so inflation does not push taxpayers into higher tax brackets.

Column 2 shows the tax bill that a taxpayer at the upper income of each of the four lowest taxable income brackets must pay, and the figures in column 3 are the corresponding **average tax rates.** The average tax rate is the tax divided by the income:

Average tax rate
The tax divided by the income.

$$\text{average tax rate} = \frac{\text{total tax due}}{\text{total taxable income}}$$

Thus, at a taxable income of $26,250, the average tax rate is 15 percent ($3,937 divided by $26,250), and at $63,550, it is 23 percent ($14,381 divided by $63,550). A taxable income of over $288,350 is included to represent the upper-income bracket. As these figures indicate, our federal individual income tax is a progressive tax because the average tax rate rises as income increases.

Another key tax rate measure is the **marginal tax rate,** which is the fraction of additional income paid in taxes. The marginal tax rate formula is expressed as:

Marginal tax rate
The fraction of additional income paid in taxes.

$$\text{marginal tax rate} = \frac{\text{change in taxes due}}{\text{change in taxable income}}$$

EXHIBIT 8 New Federal Income Tax Rate Schedules

2000	2001	2002 & 2003	2004 & 2005	2006 & later
15.0%	15.0%	10.0%	10.0%	10.0%
28.0	27.5	27.0	26.0	25.0
31.0	30.5	30.0	29.0	28.0
36.0	35.5	35.0	34.0	33.0
39.6	39.1	38.6	37.6	35.0

Column 6 in Exhibit 7 computes the marginal tax rate for each federal tax bracket in the table. You can comprehend the marginal tax rate by observing in column 1 that when taxable income rises from zero to $26,250 in the lowest tax bracket, the taxpayer's tax rises from zero to $3,937. Column 4 reports this change in taxable income, and column 5 shows the change in the tax. The marginal tax rate in column 6 is therefore 15 percent ($3,937 divided by $26,250). Apply the same analysis when taxable income increases by $37,300 from $26,250 to $63,550 in the next bracket. An additional $10,444 is added to the $3,937 tax bill, so the marginal tax rate on this extra income is 28 percent ($10,444 divided by $37,300). A similar computation provides the marginal tax rate for the remaining taxable income. The marginal tax rate is important because it determines how much a taxpayer's tax bill changes as his or her income rises or falls within each tax bracket.

The tax on individual income is the main source of revenue for most industrial countries. In the United States, the Supreme Court declared the personal income tax unconstitutional in 1895. This changed in 1913 when the states ratified the Sixteenth Amendment to the Constitution, granting Congress the power to levy taxes on income. The federal income tax was an inconsequential source of revenue until World War II, but since then it has remained a major source. Currently, 41 states have income taxes, and it may be that personal income taxes will become an increasingly important source of state and local revenues in years to come.

The bulk of the tax cut plan passed in 2001 centers on a reduction of income tax rates to be phased in over coming years as shown in Exhibit 8. Note that a new 10 percent marginal tax rate has replaced the 15 percent rate. Also, all these tax cuts are scheduled to expire on December 31, 2010, unless Congress extends the law.

Regressive tax

A tax that charges a lower percentage of income as income rises.

Regressive Taxes.   A tax can also be a **regressive tax.** A regressive tax charges a lower percentage of income as income rises. Suppose Mutt, who is earning $10,000 a year, pays a tax of $5,000, and Jeff, who earns $100,000 a year, pays $10,000 in taxes. Although Jeff pays twice the absolute amount, this would be regressive taxation because the richer Jeff paid an average tax rate of 10 percent and the poorer Mutt suffered a 50 percent tax bite. Such a tax runs afoul of the ability-to-pay principle of taxation.

We will now demonstrate that sales and excise taxes are regressive taxes. Assume that there is a 5 percent sales tax on all purchases and that the Jones family earned $80,000 during the last year, while the Jefferson family earned $20,000. A sales tax is regressive because the richer Jones family will spend a smaller portion of their income to buy food, clothing, and other consumption items. The Joneses, with an $80,000 income, can afford to spend $40,000 on groceries and clothes and save the rest, while the Jeffersons, with a $20,000 income, spend their entire income to feed and clothe their family. Because each family pays a 5 percent sales tax, the lower-income Jeffersons pay sales taxes of $1,000 (.05 × $20,000), or 1/20 of their income. The higher-income Joneses, on the other hand, pay sales taxes of $2,000 (.05 × $40,000), or only 1/40 of their income. Although the richer Jones family pays twice the amount of sales tax to the tax collector, the sales tax is regressive because their average tax rate is lower than the Jefferson family's tax rate.

In practice, an example of a regressive tax is the Social Security payroll tax, FICA. The payroll tax works like this: A fixed percentage of 12.4 percent is levied on each worker's earnings. The tax is divided equally between employers and employees. This means that an employee with a gross monthly wage of, say, $1,000 will have $62 (6.2 percent of $1,000) deducted from his or her check by the employer. In turn, the employer adds $62 and sends $124 to the government.

Payroll taxes are regressive for two reasons. First, only wages and salaries are subject to this tax, while other sources of income, such as interest and dividends, are not. Because wealthy individuals typically receive a larger portion of their income from sources other than wages and salaries than do lower-income individuals, the wealthy pay a smaller fraction of their total income in payroll taxes. Second, earnings above a certain level are exempt from the Social Security tax. Thus, the *marginal tax rate* above a given threshold level is zero. In 2000, this level was $76,200 for wage and salary income subject to Social Security tax. Hence, any additional dollars earned above this figure add no additional taxes, and the average tax rate falls. On the other hand, there is no wage base limit for the Medicare tax.

Finally, property taxes are also considered regressive for two reasons. First, property owners add this tax to the rent paid by tenants who generally are lower income persons. Second, property taxes are a higher percentage of income for poor families than rich families because the poor spend a much greater proportion of their incomes for housing.

Proportional Taxes. There continues to be considerable interest in simplifying the federal progressive income tax by substituting a **proportional tax**— also called a *flat tax*. A proportional tax charges the same percentage of income, regardless of the size of income. For example, one way to reform the federal tax system would be to eliminate all deductions, exemptions, and loopholes and simply apply the same tax rate, say, 17 percent of income to everyone. This would avoid the "hissing" from taxpayers, who would no longer require legions of accountants and lawyers to file their tax returns. Actually, most flat-tax proposals are not truly proportional because they exempt income below some level and are therefore somewhat progressive. Also, it is debatable that a 17 percent flat tax would raise enough revenue.

Proportional tax
A tax that charges the same percentage of income regardless of the size of income. Also called a flat-tax rate *or simply a* flat tax.

Is It Time to Trash the 1040s?

Applicable Concepts: flat tax and national sales tax

Two controversial fundamental tax reform ideas are often hot news topics. One proposal is the flat tax discussed earlier in this chapter, and the other is a national sales tax. The flat tax is favored by House Majority Leader Dick Armey (R-Texas) and Steve Forbes, a former candidate for the Republican presidential nomination. It would grant a personal exemption of about $30,000 for a typical family and then tax income above this amount at 17 percent with no deductions. Their argument is that a flat tax would allow people to file their tax returns on a postcard and reduce the number of tax cheats. In short, the primary purpose of a flat tax is to generate more economic efficiency and growth.

The flat-tax plan described above creates serious political problems by eliminating taxes on income from dividends, interest, capital gains, and inheritances. Also, eliminating deductions and credits would face strong opposition from the public. For example, eliminating the mortgage-interest deduction and exemptions for health care and charity would be a difficult political battle. And there is the fairness question. People at the lower end of the current system of five progressive rates could face a tax increase while upper-income people would get the biggest tax break. The counterargument is that under the current tax system many millionaires pay nothing because they shelter their income. Under a flat-tax scheme, they would lose deductions and credits.

A national retail sales tax is favored by House Ways and Means Committee Chairman Bill Archer (R-Texas) and Senator Richard Lugar (R-Indiana). This tax would eliminate the income tax entirely (personal and corporate) and tax only consumer purchases at about 15 percent. Like the flat tax, loopholes would be eliminated, and tax collection would become so simple that the federal government could save billions of dollars by cutting or eliminating the IRS. Taxpayers would save because they no longer need to hire accountants and lawyers to prepare their complicated tax returns.

Critics of a national sales tax doubt it would raise enough money at 15 percent to finance the federal govern-

ment. Also, retail businesses would have the added burden of being tax collectors for the federal government, and the IRS would still be required to ensure that these taxes are collected on billions of sales transactions. Moreover, huge price increases from the national sales tax would lead to "black market" transactions. The counterargument is that this problem would be no worse than current income tax evasion.

Finally, a sales tax is a regressive tax because the poor spend a greater share of their income on food, housing, and life's necessities. To offset this problem, sales tax advocates propose subsidies up to some level of income, such as the poverty line.

ANALYZE THE ISSUE

Assume the federal government replaces the federal income tax with a national sales tax placed on all consumption expenditures. Analyze the impact of this tax change on taxation efficiency and equity. Note that the federal government already collects a nationwide consumption tax through excise taxes on gasoline, liquor, and tobacco.

Let's look at whether the flat tax satisfies the benefits-received principle and the ability-to-pay principle. First, the flat tax does not necessarily relate to the benefits received from any particular government goods or services. Second, consider a 17 percent tax that collects $17,000 from Ms. "Rich," who is earning $100,000 a year, and $1,700 from Mr. "Poor," who is earning $10,000 a year. Both taxpayers pay the same proportional 17 percent of their incomes, but the $1,700 tax is thought to represent a much greater sacrifice to Mr. Poor than does the $17,000 tax paid by Ms. Rich. After paying her taxes, Ms. Rich can still live comfortably, but Mr. Poor complains that he desperately needed the $1,700 to buy groceries for his family. To be fair, one can argue that the $17,000 paid by Ms. Rich is not enough, based on the ability-to-pay principle.

Reforming the Tax System

Over the years, Congress has enacted reforms of the federal tax system. The major *goal* of the Tax Reform Act of 1986, for example, was to improve the efficiency and the equity of the income tax by changing tax rates and closing loopholes. This revision marked the first time Congress has completely rewritten the Federal Tax Code since 1954. This law removed millions of households from the tax rolls by roughly doubling the personal exemption allowed for each taxpayer and his or her dependents. Before the tax law changed, there were 15 marginal tax brackets for individuals, ranging from 11 to 50 percent. The Tax Reform Act of 1986 reduced the number of tax brackets to only four. Since 1993, as demonstrated earlier in Exhibit 7, there have been five tax brackets. Most taxpayers are in the 15 percent bracket, meaning that their taxes rise by only 15 cents for each extra dollar they earn. The loss in tax revenue that resulted from lowering the individual tax rates was offset by raising taxes on corporations and closing numerous tax loopholes. Consistent with the two key taxation objectives, the intention of this major revision of the federal income tax law was to improve efficiency and to make the system fairer by shifting more of the tax burden to corporations.

Public Choice Theory

James Buchanan, who won the 1986 Nobel Prize in economics, is the founder of a body of economic literature called **public choice theory**. Public choice theory is the analysis of the government's decision-making process for allocating resources. Assuming private-market failure is the reason for government intervention in markets, the theory of public choice considers how well the government performs when it replaces or regulates a private market. Rather than operating as the market mechanism to allocate resources, the government is a nonmarket, political decision-making force. Instead of behaving as private-interest buyers or sellers in the marketplace, actors in the political system have complex incentives in their roles as elected officials, bureaucrats, special-interest lobbyists, and voters.

    Buchanan and other public choice theorists raise the fundamental issue of how well a democratic society can make efficient economic decisions. The basic principle of public choice theory is that politicians follow their

Public choice theory

The analysis of the government's decision-making process for allocating resources.

own self-interest and seek to maximize their reelection chances, rather than promoting the best interests of society. Thus, a major contribution of Buchanan has been to link self-interest motivation to government officials just as Adam Smith earlier applied the pursuit of self-interest as the motivation for consumers and producers. In short, individuals in any government agency or institution will act analogously to their private-sector counterparts; they will give first priority to improving their own earnings, working conditions, and status, rather than to being altruistic.

Given this introduction to the subject, let's consider a few public choice theories that explain why the public sector, like the private sector, may also "fail."

Majority-Rule Problem

Benefit-cost analysis

The comparison of the additional rewards and costs of an economic alternative.

To evaluate choices, economists often use a technique called **benefit-cost analysis.** Benefit-cost analysis is the comparison of the additional rewards and costs of an economic alternative. If a firm is considering producing a new product, its benefit ("carrots") will be the extra revenue earned from selling the product. The firm's cost ("sticks") is the opportunity cost of using resources to make the product. How many units of the product should the firm manufacture?

> **Conclusion** *Rationally, a profit-maximizing firm follows the marginal rule and produces additional units so long as the marginal benefit exceeds the marginal cost.*

The basic rule of benefit-cost analysis is that undertaking a program whose cost exceeds its benefit is an inefficient waste of resources. In the competitive market system, undertaking projects that yield benefits greater than their costs is a sure bet. In the long run, any firm that does not follow the benefit-cost rule will either go out of business or switch to producing products that yield benefits equal to or greater than their costs. Majority-rule voting, however, can result in the approval of projects whose costs outweigh their benefits. Exhibit 9 illustrates how an inefficient economic decision can result from the ballot box.

As shown in Exhibit 9, suppose Bob, Juan, and Theresa are the only voters in a mini-society that is considering whether to add two publicly financed park projects, *A* and *B*. The total cost to taxpayers of either park project is $300, and the marginal cost of park *A* or park *B* to each taxpayer is an additional tax of $100 (columns 2 and 5). Next, assume each taxpayer determines his or her additional dollar value derived from the benefits of park projects *A* and *B* (columns 3 and 6). Assuming each person applies marginal analysis, each will follow the *marginal rule* and vote for a project only if his or her benefit exceeds the cost of the $100 tax. Consider park project *A*. This project is worth $0 to Bob, $101 to Juan, and $101 to Theresa, and this means two Yes votes and one No vote: The majority votes for park *A* (column 4). This decision would not happen in the business world. The Disney Company, for example, would rationally reject such a project because the total of all consumers' marginal benefits is only $202, which is less than its $300 marginal cost.

EXHIBIT 9 Majority-Rule Benefit-Cost Analysis of Two Park Projects

(1) Voter	Park Project A			Park Project B		
	(2) Marginal cost (taxes)	(3) Marginal benefit	(4) Vote	(5) Marginal cost (taxes)	(6) Marginal benefit	(7) Vote
Bob	$100	$ 0	No	$100	$ 90	No
Juan	100	101	Yes	100	90	No
Theresa	100	101	Yes	100	301	Yes
Total	$300	$202	Passes	$300	$481	Fails

The important point here is that majority-rule voting can make the correct benefit-cost marginal analysis, but it can also lead to a rejection of projects with marginal total benefits that exceed marginal costs. Suppose park project *B* costs $300 as well, and Bob's benefits are $90, Juan's $90, and Theresa's $301 (column 6). The total of all marginal benefits from constructing park *B* is $481, and this project would be undertaken in a private-sector market. But because only Theresa's benefits exceed the marginal $100 tax, park project *B* in the political arena receives only one Yes vote against two No votes and fails.

Why is there a distinction between political majority voting and benefit-cost analysis? The reason is that dollars can measure the intensity of voter preferences and "one-person, one-vote" does not. A count of ballots can determine whether a proposal passes or fails, but this count may not be proportional to the dollar strength of benefits among the individual voters.

Special-Interest-Group Effect

In addition to benefit-cost errors from majority voting, special-interest groups can create government support for programs with costs outweighing their benefits. The *special-interest effect* occurs when the government approves programs that benefit only a small group within society, but society as a whole pays the costs. The influence of special-interest groups is indeed a constant problem for effective government because the benefits of government programs to certain small groups are great and the costs are relatively insignificant to each taxpayer. For example, let's assume the benefits of support prices for dairy farmers are $10 million. Because of the size of these benefits to dairy farmers, this special-interest group can well afford to hire professional lobbyists and donate a million dollars or so to the reelection campaigns of politicians voting for dairy price supports.

In addition to the incentive of financial support from special interests, politicians can also engage in *logrolling*. Logrolling is the political practice of trading votes of support for legislated programs. Politician *A* says to politician *B*, "You vote for my dairy price support bill, and I will vote for your tobacco price support bill."

But who pays for these large benefits to special-interest groups? Taxpayers do, of course, but the extra tax burden per taxpayer is very low. Although Congress may enact a $20 million program to favor, say, a few defense contractors, this expenditure costs 100 million taxpayers only 20 cents per taxpayer. Because in a free society it is relatively easy to organize special-interest constituencies and lobby politicians to spread the cost, it is little wonder that spending programs are popular. Moreover, the small cost of each pet program per taxpayer means there is little reward for a single voter to learn the details of the many special-interest legislation proposals.

Rational Voter Ignorance

Politicians, appointed officials, and bureaucrats constitute the supply side of the political marketplace. The demand side of the political market consists of special-interest groups and voters who are subject to what economists call **rational ignorance.** Rational ignorance is a voter's decision that the benefit of becoming informed about an issue is not worth the cost. A frequent charge in elections is that the candidates are not talking about the issues. One explanation is that the candidates realize that a sizable portion of the voters will make a calculated decision not to judge them based on in-depth knowledge of their positions on a wide range of issues. Instead of going to the trouble of reading position papers and doing research, many voters choose their candidate based simply on party affiliation or on how the candidate appears on television. This approach is rational if the perceived extra effort required to be better informed exceeds the marginal benefit of knowing more about the candidate.

The principle of rational ignorance also explains why eligible voters fail to vote on election day. A popular explanation is that low voter participation results from apathy among potential voters, but the decision can be an exercise in practical benefit-cost analysis. Nonvoters presumably perceive that the opportunity cost of going to the polls outweighs the benefit gained from any of the candidates or issues on the ballot. Moreover, nonvoters perceive that one extra vote is unlikely to change the outcome.

Public choice theorists argue that one reason benefits are difficult to measure is that the voter confronts an *indivisible* public service. In a grocery store, the consumer can decide to spend so much on apples, oranges, and other *divisible* items, but voting involves candidates who take stands on many issues. The point is that voting does not allow the voter to pick and choose among the candidate's good and bad positions. Most voters, in short, must "buy" a confusing mixture of "wants" and "unwants" that are difficult to interpret as a benefit.

Bureaucratic Inefficiency

The bureaucracy is the body of nonelected officials and administrators who operate government agencies. As government grows, one of the concerns is that the bureaucracy may become more powerful than the executive, legislative, and judicial branches. Public choice theory also considers how bureaucratic behavior affects economic decision making. One principle is that the government bureaucracy tends to be inefficient because of the absence of the profit motive.

Rational ignorance

The voter's choice to remain uninformed because the marginal cost of obtaining information is higher than the marginal benefit from knowing it.

CHECKPOINT

What Does Public Choice Say about a Budget Deficit?

Contrary to the current situation of the federal government spending less than it collects in taxes (discussed in the next chapter), James Buchanan predicted years ago that growing government deficits would be inevitable. He maintained that government officials would increase spending for their constituents in order to gain votes. Furthermore, politicians would shy away from tax increases for fear of alienating voters. The net effect would be deficits. Was Buchanan's prediction based on the rational ignorance effect, government inefficiency, or the shortsightedness effect?

What happens when a government agency performs poorly? First, there is no competition from other producers to take away market share. There are no shareholders demanding reform when profits are falling because taxpayers are a poor substitute for stockholder pressure. Second, the typical government response each year is to request a larger budget. Without profits as a measure of performance, the tendency is to use the size of an agency's budget and staff as an indicator of success. In brief, the basic incentive structure of government agencies encourages inefficient management because, unlike the market system, there is a lack of incentive to be cost-conscious or creative. Instead, the hallmark of the bureaucrat is to be extremely cautious and make all decisions "by the book." Such behavior may maximize prestige and security, but it usually fails to minimize costs.

Shortsightedness Effect

Finally, it can be argued that democracy has a bias toward programs offering clear benefits and hidden costs. The reason is that political officeholders must run for reelection after a relatively short period of two or four years. Given this reality, politicians tend to favor proposals providing immediate benefits, with future generations paying most of the costs. Conversely, they reject programs that have easily identifiable short-run high costs, but offer benefits only after a decade. Hence, the essence of the hidden costs bias or *shortsightedness effect* is that both voters and politicians suffer from a short time horizon. Such a myopic view of either future costs or future benefits can cause an irrational acceptance of a program even though long-run costs exceed short-run benefits or an irrational rejection of a program with long-run benefits that outweigh short-run costs.

KEY CONCEPTS

Government expenditures	Progressive tax	Regressive tax	Benefit-cost analysis
Benefits-received principle	Average tax rate	Proportional or flat tax	Rational ignorance
Ability-to-pay principle	Marginal tax rate	Public choice theory	

SUMMARY

- **Government expenditures,** including transfer payments, have grown from about one-quarter of GDP in 1950 to about one-third of GDP beginning in the 1970s. In the late 1990s, federal outlays decreased as a percentage of GDP to about 30 percent of GDP in 2000.

Government expenditures

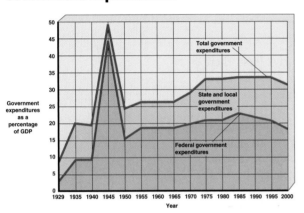

- **Federal tax revenues** are collected primarily from individual income taxes and social insurance taxes, while **state and local government tax revenues** consist primarily of sales and property taxes.

Federal tax revenues

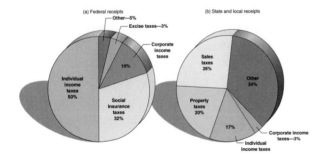

- **Total tax revenues** have climbed from about 11 percent of GDP in 1929 to their highest level of 33 percent in 2000. Since 1960, federal taxes have remained a fairly constant fraction of GDP. State and local taxes, however, have generally increased as a percentage of GDP since the 1950s. In 2000, federal tax revenues were 20.6 percent of GDP, and state and local taxes were 12.6 percent.

Total tax revenues

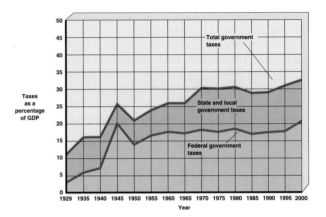

- The **taxation burden,** measured by taxes as a percentage of GDP, is lighter in the United States than in many other advanced industrial countries.

Taxation burden

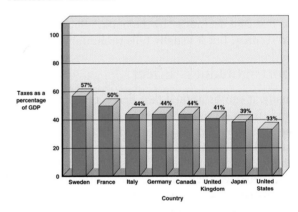

- The **benefits-received principle** and the **ability-to-pay principle** are two basic philosophies of taxation fairness. The gasoline tax is a classic example of the benefits-received principle because users of the highways pay the gasoline tax. Progressive income taxes follow the ability-to-pay principle because there is a direct relationship between the average tax rate and income size. Sales, excise, property, and flat-rate taxes violate this principle because each results in a greater burden on the poor than on the rich.

■ **Public choice theory** reveals the government's decision-making process. For example, government failure can occur for any of the following reasons: (1) majority voting may not follow benefit-cost analysis; (2) special-interest groups can obtain large benefits and spread their costs over many taxpayers; (3) rational voter ignorance means a sizable portion of the voters will decide not to make informed judgments; (4) bureaucratic behavior may not lead to cost-effective decisions; and (5) politicians suffer from a short time horizon, leading to a bias toward hiding the costs of programs.

SUMMARY OF CONCLUSION STATEMENTS

■ The government's share of total economic activity has generally increased since World War II ended in 1945. Most of the growth in combined government expenditures as a percentage of GDP reflects rapidly growing federal government transfer programs.

■ Rationally, a profit-maximizing firm follows the marginal rule and produces additional units so long as the marginal benefit exceeds the marginal cost.

STUDY QUESTIONS AND PROBLEMS

1. Explain why U.S. federal, state, and local expenditures or outlays account for about 30 percent of GDP, but total government spending (G in GDP accounts) is only about 20 percent of GDP.

2. Identify the major differences between federal government outlays and spending by state and local governments.

3. What are the primary tax revenue sources at the federal, state, and local levels of government?

4. Which of the following taxes satisfy the benefits-received principle, and which satisfy the ability-to-pay principle?
   a. Gasoline tax
   b. Federal income tax
   c. Tax on Social Security benefits

5. What is the difference between the marginal tax rate and the average tax rate?

6. Explain why a 5 percent sales tax on gasoline is regressive.

7. Ms. Jones has a taxable income of $30,000, and she must pay $3,000. Mr. Smith has a taxable income of $60,000. How much tax must Mr. Smith pay for the tax system to be
   a. progressive?
   b. regressive?
   c. proportional?

8. Explain why each of the following taxes is progressive or regressive:
   a. A $1 per pack federal excise tax on cigarettes
   b. The federal individual income tax
   c. The federal payroll tax

9. Complete the following table, which describes the sales tax paid by individuals at various income levels. Indicate whether the tax is progressive, proportional, or regressive.

Income	Total spending	Sales tax paid	Sales tax paid as a percentage of income
$ 1,000	$ 1,000	$ 100	_____%
5,000	3,500	350	_____
10,000	6,000	600	_____
100,000	40,000	4,000	_____

10. Calculate the average and the marginal tax rates in the following table, and indicate whether the tax is progressive, proportional, or regressive. What observation can you make concerning the relationship between marginal and average tax rates?

Income	Tax paid	Average tax rate	Marginal tax rate
$ 0	$ 0	0%	0%
100	10	____	____
200	30	____	____
300	60	____	____
400	100	____	____
500	150	____	____

11. Compare "dollar voting" in private markets with "majority voting" in the political decision-making system.

ONLINE EXERCISES

Exercise 1

Visit the federal government's Office of Management and Budget (http://www.gpo.gov/usbudget/index.html). Select A Citizen's Guide to the Federal Budget and then select What Is The Budget?

1. What is the budget?

2. How much is government spending as a share of GDP?

Exercise 2

Visit the federal government's Office of Management and Budget (http://www.gpo.gov/usbudget/index.html). Select A Citizen's Guide to the Federal Budget and then select How Does the Government Create a Budget? Describe the major steps in the budget process.

Exercise 3

Visit the federal government's Office of Management and Budget (http://www.gpo.gov/usbudget/index.html). Select A Citizen's Guide to the Federal Budget and then select Where the Money Comes From—and Where it Goes. Where does the money come from?

Exercise 4

Visit the President's Office of Management and Budget (http://www.whitehouse.gov/omb/) and click on Budget Information and then A Citizen's Guide to the Federal Budget, Budget of the United States Government for the current fiscal year. How is the federal government currently allocating its expenditures? That is, what is the number one spending item? Number two? etc.

CHECKPOINT ANSWER

What Does Public Choice Say about a Budget Deficit?

The government uses the deficit to finance clear short-term benefits with little attention to long-term consequences. If you said public choice predicts that government officials will emphasize near-term benefits so as to gain votes (the shortsightedness effect), YOU ARE CORRECT.

PRACTICE QUIZ

For a visual explanation of the correct answers, visit the tutorial at http://tucker.swcollege.com.

1. From 1975 to 1995, total government expenditures as a percentage of GDP in the United States
   a. fell by half.
   b. remained fairly constant.
   c. grew from one-fourth to one-half.
   d. grew from one-quarter to one-third.

2. Which of the following accounted for the second largest percentage of total federal government expenditures in 2000?
   a. Income security
   b. National defense
   c. Interest on the national debt
   d. Education and health

3. Which of the following contributed the second largest percentage of total state and local government revenues in 2000 (excluding "other category")?
   a. Corporate income taxes
   b. Sales and excise taxes
   c. Individual income taxes
   d. Property taxes

4. Which of the following countries devotes about the same percentage of its GDP to taxes as the United States?
   a. Sweden
   b. Italy
   c. United Kingdom
   d. Japan

5. "The poor should not pay income taxes." This statement reflects which of the following principles of taxation?
   a. Fairness of contribution
   b. Benefits-received
   c. Inexpensive-to-collect
   d. Ability-to-pay

6. Some cities finance their airports with a departure tax: every person leaving the city by plane is charged a small fixed dollar amount that is used to help pay for building and running the airport. The departure tax follows the
   a. benefits-received principle.
   b. ability-to-pay principle.
   c. flat-rate principle.
   d. public-choice principle.

7. Which of the following statements is *true*?
   a. The most important source of tax revenue for the federal government is individual income taxes.
   b. The most important source of tax revenue for state and local governments is sales taxes.
   c. The second most important source of revenue for local governments is local property taxes.

d. The taxation burden, measured by taxes as a percentage of GDP, is lighter in the United States than in most other advanced industrial countries.
   e. All of the above are true.

8. Which of the following statements is *true*?
   a. A sales tax on food is a regressive tax.
   b. The largest source of federal government tax revenue is individual income taxes.
   c. The largest source of state and local government tax revenue is sales taxes.
   d. All of the above are true.

9. A tax that is structured so that people with higher incomes pay a larger percentage of their income for the tax than do people with smaller incomes is called a(an)
   a. income tax.
   b. regressive tax.
   c. property tax.
   d. progressive tax.

10. Generally, most economists feel that a _____ type of income tax is a fairer way to raise government revenue than a sales tax.
    a. regressive
    b. proportional
    c. flat-rate
    d. progressive

11. The federal personal income tax is an example of a(an)
    a. excise tax.
    b. proportional tax.
    c. progressive tax.
    d. regressive tax.

12. A 5 percent sales tax on food is an example of a
    a. flat tax.
    b. progressive tax.
    c. proportional tax.
    d. regressive tax.

13. Margaret pays a local income tax of 2 percent regardless of the size of her income. This tax is
    a. proportional.
    b. regressive.
    c. progressive.
    d. a mix of a and b.

14. Which of the following statements relating to public choice is *true*?
    a. A low voter turnout may result when voters perceive that the marginal cost of voting exceeds its marginal benefit.
    b. If the marginal cost of voting exceeds its marginal benefit, the vote is unimportant.
    c. Special-interest groups always cause the will of a majority to be imposed on a minority.
    d. All of the above are true.

CHAPTER 23

Federal Deficits, Surpluses, and the National Debt

The U.S. government has been in the red almost continuously since the Revolutionary War forced the Continental Congress to borrow money. The only exception was a brief interlude more than a century and a half ago when our government was debt-free. In December 1834, President Andrew Jackson proudly reported to Congress what he considered to be a major accomplishment of his administration. By New Year's Day of 1835, the federal government would succeed in paying off the national debt. It was Jackson's second term as president. Since the close of the War of 1812, the country had experienced tremendous growth, and revenues flowed into the U.S. Treasury from import tariffs and the sale of public land. By early 1836, the nation had been out of debt for two years, and there was a budget surplus of $37 million. The dilemma in those days was how to use the surplus.

In 1836, Congress simply decided to divide all but $5 million of the surplus among the states. Then the financial panic of 1837 caused the government to plunge into debt again, where it remains today and for the foreseeable future.

Unlike Andrew Jackson, Abraham Lincoln in his 1864 Annual Message to Congress expressed no concern for paying off the national debt. Lincoln stated:

The great advantage of citizens being creditors as well as debtors, with relation to the public debt, is obvious. Men can readily perceive that they cannot be much oppressed by a debt which they owe to themselves.

Today, the national debt continues to be a lightning rod for controversy, and federal government borrowing to cover its budget deficits has accumulated a national debt approaching $6 trillion. To the average citizen, this is an incomprehensible amount of money for even the government to owe. Perhaps the best way to picture this sea of red ink is that your individual share is about $20,000. On the other hand, the good news is that the Congressional Budget Office predicts trillions of dollars in surpluses over the next 10 years—a projection that has ignited a heated public policy debate over how to use the windfall. In this chapter, we will discuss this watershed event and related issues.

In this chapter, you will learn to solve these economics puzzles:

- Can Uncle Sam go bankrupt?
- How does the national debt of the United States compare to the debt of other countries?
- Are we passing the debt burden to our children?
- Who owns the national debt?

The Federal Budget Balancing Act

What will happen next? Like a high-wire performer swinging one way and then another while the crowd below gazes transfixed, the public in the late 1990s watched the federal budget sway from deficit to surplus. As you learned in the preceding chapter, a federal budget deficit occurs whenever the government spends more than it collects in taxes. The accumulation of these budget deficits over the years is the origin of the national debt. When the federal government has a surplus in its budget, some or all of the surplus can be used to retire the national debt, and it decreases. Here you will take a closer look at the actual budgetary process that creates and finances our national debt.

The Federal Budgetary Process

In theory, Keynesian discretionary fiscal policy requires that legislation be enacted to change government spending or taxes in order to shift the aggregate demand curve represented in the *AD-AS* model. In practice, the federal budgetary process, which determines the level of spending and taxation, is not so orderly. The annual "battle of the budget" on Capitol Hill involves political decisions on how much the government plans to spend and where the money will come from to finance these outlays. Wrangling takes place between all sorts of camps: the president versus Congress, Republicans versus Democrats, national security versus economic equality, price stability versus full employment, health care versus tax cuts and so on. Given the complexities of world events, special-interest groups, volatile public opinion, and political ambitions that complicate the budget process, it is no wonder actual fiscal policy often ignores textbook macroeconomics.

The U.S. federal government's Office of Management and Budget provides much valuable information about the government's budget (http://www.gpo.gov/usbudget/index.html), *especially if you select "A Citizen's Guide to the Federal Budget." It describes what a budget is, where the money goes and comes from, the major steps in the budget process and provides other easy-to-read and -understand information.*

The following brief look at the federal budgetary process shows how Congress and the president make federal spending and tax decisions each year:

Stage 1. Formation of the budget.   Between February and December, federal agencies develop and submit their budget requests for the upcoming fiscal year to the Office of Management and Budget (OMB). (The government's fiscal year begins on October 1 and ends on September 30, so the budgetary process begins in the preceding calendar year.) The Pentagon argues for more defense spending, the Department of Transportation for more highway funds, and so on. The OMB reviews each agency's request. After receiving advice from the president, officials from cabinet departments, the Council of Economic Advisers, (CEA), and the Treasury, the OMB compiles all the proposals into a budget recommendation. Applying the administration's goals, the OMB sends the proposed budget to the president by December.

Stage 2. Presidential budget submission.   In January, nine months before the new fiscal year begins on October 1, the president submits the proposed budget to Congress. The official title is *The Budget of the United States.* This unveiling of the administration's budget is always big news. Does the president recommend that less money be spent for defense and more for education? Is there an increase in the Social Security payroll tax or the income tax? And how large is the national debt? Is there a budget deficit or a budget surplus?

Stage 3. Budget resolution.   After the president submits the budget in January, Congress takes the lead in the budgetary process. The president's budget now becomes the starting point for congressional consideration. The Congressional Budget Office (CBO) employs a professional staff who advise Congress on the budget much the way the OMB advises the president. The CBO analyzes the budget by February and reports its evaluation at budget committee hearings in both the House of Representatives and the Senate. After debate, in May Congress approves an overall budget outline called the *budget resolution,* which sets target levels for spending, tax revenues, and the budget deficit or surplus.

Stage 4. Budget passed.   Throughout the summer, and supposedly ending October 1, Congress and the president debate while congressional committees and subcommittees prepare specific spending and tax law bills. The budget resolution is supposed to guide the spending and revenue decisions of these committees. After Congress passes, and the president signs, the spending and revenue bills, the federal government has its actual budget for spending and tax collection.

As summarized in Exhibit 1, the budgetary process seems orderly enough, but in practice it does not work so smoothly. The process can, and often does, go astray. One problem is that Congress does not necessarily follow its own rules. The budget bills are not always passed on time, and when that happens, the fiscal year starts without a budget. Then federal agencies

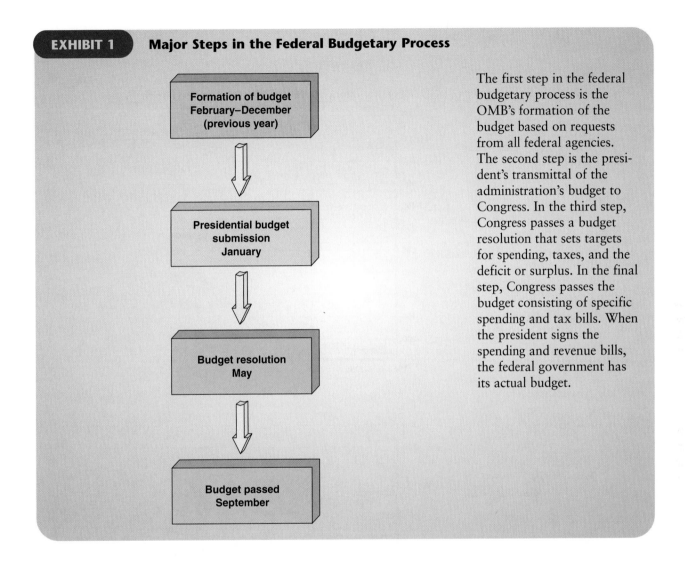

EXHIBIT 1   **Major Steps in the Federal Budgetary Process**

Formation of budget
February–December
(previous year)

Presidential budget
submission
January

Budget resolution
May

Budget passed
September

The first step in the federal budgetary process is the OMB's formation of the budget based on requests from all federal agencies. The second step is the president's transmittal of the administration's budget to Congress. In the third step, Congress passes a budget resolution that sets targets for spending, taxes, and the deficit or surplus. In the final step, Congress passes the budget consisting of specific spending and tax bills. When the president signs the spending and revenue bills, the federal government has its actual budget.

must operate on the basis of *continuing resolutions,* which means each agency operates as it did the previous year until spending bills are approved. In some years, Congress even fails to pass a continuing resolution, and the federal government must shut down and workers stay home until Congress approves the necessary funds.

Financing the National Debt

When the federal government must borrow more money each year to finance a deficit, the deficit adds to the accumulated national debt. Exhibit 2 reveals that since 1960 the federal government has most often operated with a budget deficit. Exhibit 2(a) shows the growth of federal expenditures (spending for final goods and services plus transfer payments) and tax revenues, and Exhibit 2(b) traces the corresponding budget surpluses or deficits. Note that between 1960 and 1997 a deficit occurred each year except 1969. Beginning

EXHIBIT 2

U.S. Federal Budget Expenditures, Revenues, and Budget Surpluses or Deficits, 1960–2000

Part (a) shows that until 1992 federal expenditures (including transfer payments) grew faster than federal tax revenues, causing deficits to increase rapidly. After 1992, this trend reversed, and the result was growing budget surpluses since 1998.

Part (b) shows that prior to 1998 the U.S. government was in surplus only in 1969. For much of the 1960s, the federal government was close to a balanced budget. During the early 1980s, however, federal budget deficits grew sharply. After 1992, budget deficits declined, and from 1998 to 2000 there were sharply rising budget surpluses.

Source: *Economic Report of the President, 2001,* http://w3.access.gpo.gov/eop/, Table B-78.

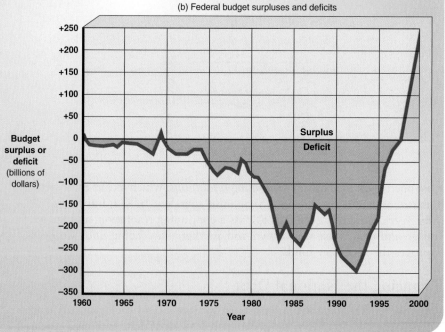

in the early 1980s, the magnitude of the deficits increased sharply. After 1992, this trend reversed, and budget deficits declined sharply until a budget surplus occurred in 1998 and then surpluses continued to grow sharply through 2000.

When the government overspends, the U.S. Treasury must borrow to finance the difference between expenditures and revenues. The U.S. Treasury borrows by selling Treasury bills (T-bills), notes, and bonds promising to make specified interest payments and to repay the loaned funds on a given date. These government securities are IOUs of the federal government. They are considered a safe haven for idle funds and are purchased by Federal Reserve banks, government agencies, private banks, corporations, individual U.S. citizens, and foreigners. If you own a U.S. government savings bond, for example, you have loaned your funds to the federal government. The stock of these federal government IOUs accumulated over the years is called the *gross public debt, federal debt,* or **national debt.** The national debt is the total amount owed by the federal government to owners of government securities.

Note that the national debt does not include state and local governments' debt. Conversely, as stated above, the national debt does include U.S. Treasury securities purchased by various federal agencies, such as the Social Security trust fund. Currently, the Social Security trust fund collects more in taxes than it pays out in retirement benefits, and it lends the extra money to the federal government for spending. In fact, budget surpluses would be significantly lower without federal government borrowing from this trust fund. If we subtract the portion of the national debt held by all government agencies (what the federal government owes to itself), we can compute the **net public debt.** Beware! Confusion sometimes occurs when the media use the term *public debt* without specifying whether the reference is to "gross" or "net" public debt.

In prior years—when deficits occurred continuously and as Treasury securities came due, the Treasury would issue larger amounts of new securities, resulting in greater national debt and interest payments. How might the U.S. Treasury use money from budget surpluses to reduce the national debt? When Treasury securities mature, the Treasury could issue smaller amounts of new securities. Proponents of using the surpluses to pay down the national debt argue that the benefits are that the federal government would have lower interest payments and greater borrowing capacity reserved for the future.

Deficit Elimination during the 1990s

In the 1992 presidential election, Ross Perot, the wealthy independent candidate, compared the national debt to the "crazy aunt in the basement that nobody wanted to talk about." Bill Clinton's campaign staff kept a sign on the wall saying, "It's the economy, stupid." After the election, President Clinton proposed his deficit reduction plan, which called for higher taxes and less government spending.

National debt

The total amount owed by the federal government to owners of government securities.

Net public debt

National debt minus all government interagency borrowing.

 The Bureau of the Public Debt (http://www .publicdebt.treas.gov/) *publishes data and other information about federal budget deficits and the public debt.*

In 1993, Congress passed the Deficit Reduction Act, which increased tax revenues. This act took into account the ability-to-pay principle by increasing the highest marginal tax rate for individuals and raising the corporate income tax rate. It also increased the federal tax on gasoline. A gasoline tax offers the extra benefit of reducing the quantity of energy demanded and conforms to the benefits-received principle. However, a gasoline tax suffers from the problem of being regressive.

Restraint on federal spending began with the 1990 Budget Enforcement Act (BEA), which set spending caps on three broad areas of discretionary spending. The BEA also required that any proposal to increase spending or decrease tax revenues over agreed limits had to be offset by an equal amount of tax revenue increases or new spending cuts. The spending caps are not totally rigid. They can be raised to reflect any spending that both the president and Congress designate for emergency purposes, such as national disasters and military conflicts. Critics argue that "emergency" spending is a loophole that threatens surpluses because exactly what qualifies as an emergency is not defined. The Balanced Budget Act of 1997 continued mandatory limits on spending and taxes.

The spending caps combined with tax increases and a growing high-employment economy transformed federal budget deficits into surpluses during the late 1990s. Exhibit 3 shows federal expenditures and revenues expressed as a percentage of GDP. The difference between these two curves represents the federal deficit, also expressed as a percentage of GDP. Since 1992, federal government expenditures as a percentage of GDP have declined to about 18 percent of GDP. Over the same years, federal government tax revenues as a percentage of GDP have crept steadily upward to just over 20 percent of GDP. The results are federal surpluses since 1998.

The crucial question is how long federal expenditures can remain roughly equal to tax revenues. As pointed out in the previous chapter, tax revenues as a percentage of GDP are above the level reached during World War II. Let's assume that tax revenues remain constant at the current relatively high level. The problem is that in about a decade members of the so-called baby-boom generation will start turning 65, and they will require higher medical care expenditures, paid for mostly by the federal Medicare program. As these federal government expenditure pressures build from the retirement of the baby-boomers, the concern is that federal deficits will reappear and rise sharply.

Debt Ceiling

Debt ceiling

A legislated legal limit on the national debt.

Another method for curbing the national debt is the **debt ceiling.** A debt ceiling is a legislated legal limit on the national debt. This means that the federal government cannot legally allow a budget deficit to raise the national debt beyond the ceiling. It works like the credit limit on your charge card. When you reach the limit, you cannot charge any more and you must pay cash. When the federal government hits the debt limit, it cannot borrow any more to supplement its cash from taxes and other sources.

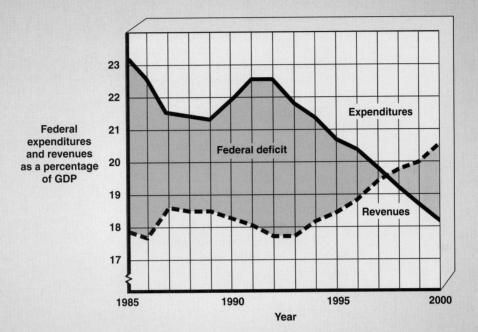

Federal Expenditures, Revenues, and Deficits as a Percentage of GDP, 1985–2000

The difference between federal expenditures and revenues expressed as a percentage of GDP is the federal deficit, also expressed as a percentage of GDP. Since 1992, federal government expenditures have consistently declined to about 18 percent of GDP, while federal government tax revenues have risen steadily to over 20 percent of GDP. The results are federal surpluses since 1998.

Source: *Economic Report of the President, 2001*, http://w3.access.gpo.gov/eop/, Table B-79.

What usually happens when the budget pushes against the debt ceiling is that the ceiling is raised to accommodate the budget deficit. Raising the debt ceiling often provokes a fiery political debate over government spending. Failure to raise the debt ceiling means no money for the government to pay its bills, meet its payroll, or pay interest due on the present debt. In 1990, Congress rejected President George Bush's spending plan, and the government shut down throughout the three-day Columbus Day weekend. Most workers were off for the holiday, and few government agencies were affected. In 1995 and 1996, however, a deadlock between President Clinton and the Republican Congress over a short-term spending bill caused the government to shut down for several weeks.

Why Worry Over the National Debt?

One critic of government spending is the Cato Institute (http://www.cato .org/), *a public policy research foundation.*

You have already seen in Exhibit 2(b) that federal deficits grew sharply between 1980 and 1992. As shown in Exhibit 4(a), the result is that the national debt also rose sharply. The national debt was about $1 trillion in 1980. In 1986, the national debt broke the $2 trillion mark, and the $3 trillion barrier was breached in late 1989. The $4 trillion mark was passed in 1992, and the $5 trillion mark was crossed in 1995. In 2000, we were at about the $6 trillion milestone.

What are two major causes of rising national debt? Observe in Exhibit 4(a) the increase in the debt during World War II. In wartime, the government must increase military expenditures sharply and escalate the national debt. Recession also causes the national debt to rise dramatically. In cyclical downturns like the 1930s, 1974–1975, 1981–1982, and 1990–1991, the debt rose rapidly because a decline in real GDP automatically increases the budget deficit from lower tax collections and greater spending for unemployment compensation and welfare.

Politicians and nonpoliticians alike often speak of the gloom and doom of the national debt. Should we lose sleep over it? To find out, we'll consider three controversial questions.

1. Can Uncle Sam Go Bankrupt?

Reasons to Worry.   If households and firms persistently operate in the red, as the federal government does, they will sooner or later go bankrupt. How long can the national debt continue to rise before the U.S. government is broke?

Reasons Not to Worry.   Whether private or public debt is the issue, debt must be judged relative to the debtor's ability to repay the principal and interest on the debt. Exhibit 4(b) shows that the national debt as a percentage of GDP is lower today than at the end of World War II. In 1945, public debt was about 120 percent of GDP, and by 1980 the ratio of debt to GDP had fallen to 33 percent. This means the debt grew considerably slower than GDP between 1945 and 1980. Since 1980, however, the trend reversed, and the debt grew faster than GDP. Between 1980 and 1995, the national debt grew from 33 percent to 66 percent of GDP. Still the United States was not bankrupt in 1945, and it is much farther from going bankrupt today. Moreover, the ratio today is back to its level of the late 1950s, and it decreased to 56 percent in 2000.

There is an even more important point: Uncle Sam never has to pay off the national debt. At the maturity date on a government security, the U.S. Treasury has the constitutional authority to collect taxes levied by Congress, print money, or refinance its obligations. Suppose the government decides not to raise taxes or cause inflation by simply printing money, so it refinances the debt. When a $1 million government bond comes due, as described earlier in this chapter, the U.S. Treasury can simply "roll over" the debt. This financial trade expression means a borrower (here the federal government) pays off its $1 million bond that reaches maturity by issuing a new $1 million bond. In short, the federal government refinances its debt by

EXHIBIT 4   **The National Debt, 1930–2000**

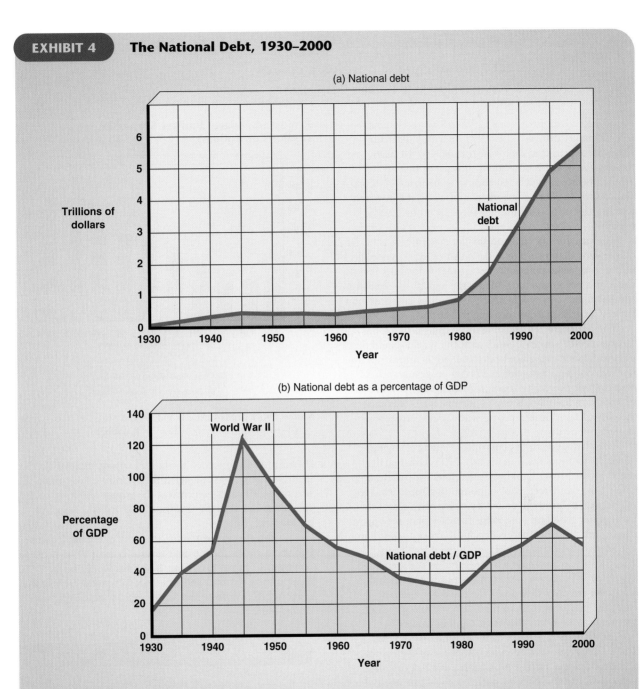

In part (a), we see that the federal debt has skyrocketed since 1980. A concern is that sooner or later the U.S. government will be bankrupt. The counterargument is shown in part (b). The national debt as a percentage of GDP has declined since the end of World War II, when it reached a peak of about 120 percent. Between 1980 and 1995, the federal debt as a percentage of GDP increased, but in recent years, the ratio has fallen back to its level of the late 1950s. It was 56 percent in 2000.

Sources: *Economic Report of the President, 2001,* http://w3.access.gpo.gov/eop/, Tables B-78 and B-1; and *Survey of Current Business,* GDP and Other Major NIPA Series 1929–2000, http://www.bea.doc.gov/bea/dn1.htm, Table 1.

The Great Federal Budget Surplus Debate

Applicable Concept: federal budget surplus

It took 29 contentious years (1969–1998) to eliminate federal budget deficits. After 1999, federal budget surpluses were projected each year for the next 10 years, and the revision of these projections upward or downward aroused nearly as much controversy as deficits did in previous years. In short, the hotly contested debate involved whether the surplus should be saved, spent, or devoted to tax cuts.

The case for tax cuts and smaller government is based on the view that a surplus is the result of excess tax collections. Proponents point out that current federal tax revenues as a percentage of GDP are the highest in a century. Moreover, tax cuts would spur the economy and prevent future Congresses from spending the surplus.

The argument for spending the surplus is based on "unmet needs." Instead of tax cuts, the surplus could be used to finance spending for defense, public infrastructure, research and development, and social programs such as education or prescription drugs. Also, a large proportion of American households pay no income taxes. Tax cuts therefore do not benefit people who are not prosperous enough to pay taxes.

The alternative to tax cuts and spending is paying down the national debt. In his July 1999 semiannual report to the Senate Banking Committee, Federal Reserve Chairman Alan Greenspan supported this approach. He said Congress faced the quandary of trying to establish fiscal policy based on long-range forecasts that may prove inaccurate. "If the Congress decides to move forward and put into place significant tax cuts in the future years," he said, "I think it also has to be prepared to cut spending significantly in the event that the forecasts on which they are based are proved wrong." On the other hand, he said, using the budget surplus to fund "irrevocable spending programs" would be "the worst of all outcomes."

Testifying before the Senate Budget Committee in 2001, Greenspan seemed more convinced of the accuracy of federal budget surplus projections, and he generally supported, without endorsement, both tax cuts and reducing the national debt. Greenspan also suggested that the proposed tax bill include provisions that would limit the tax cuts if specified targets for the budget surplus or debt reduction were not met. (These provisions were not included in the 2001 tax bill.)

The outcome of the debate in 1999 was that Congress passed a $792 billion tax cut spread over 10 years. The central element of this bill was a phased-in 1 percentage point reduction in all marginal tax rates for individuals.

Projected Federal Budget Surpluses (billions of dollars)

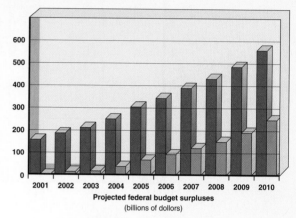

Projected federal budget surpluses
(billions of dollars)

■ Includes Social Security trust fund
▫ Excludes Social Security trust fund

Source: Office of Management and Budget, http://w3.access.gpo.gov/usbudget/index.html, August 2001, Table 18.

President Clinton vetoed the bill. However, in 2001 President George W. Bush signed a $1.35 trillion bill cutting taxes over 10 years, which was the largest and most widespread tax cut since the 1980s, during Ronald Reagan's presidency.

As this text is written in 2001, the projected federal budget surpluses for the next several years may be revised downward or even disappear. If so, this would be the result of new tax cuts and emergency spending to help the economy recover from the September 11 attack on the United States.

ANALYZE THE ISSUE

1. Refer to Exhibit 6 of the chapter on fiscal policy. Using demand-side and supply-side fiscal policy theories, explain how a tax cut could either increase or decrease the price level.

2. Using the Laffer curve discussed in the You're the Economist in the chapter on fiscal policy, explain how proponents could claim the tax cut would increase tax revenues.

CHECKPOINT

What's Behind the National Debt?

Suppose the federal government has balanced budgets each year and the entire national debt comes due. How could the federal government pay off the national debt without refinancing, raising taxes, or printing money?

replacing old bonds with new bonds. This means that just as a matured bond issued by General Motors can be refinanced by issuing new bonds and the debt continues, the federal government never has to pay off the national debt. These debts can be rolled over forever, provided bond buyers have faith in General Motors and Uncle Sam.

International Perspective on National Debt

Exhibit 5 provides an international perspective on the national debt. This figure shows the ratio of national debt to GDP for several industrialized nations. The United Kingdom has a lower debt in relation to GDP than the United States. Italy and Japan, on the other hand, have national-debt-to-GDP ratios twice as large as the U.S. ratio.

2. Are We Passing the Debt Burden to Our Children?

Reasons to Worry. The fear is that interest payments to finance the national debt will swallow an enormous helping of the federal government's budget pie. This means future generations will pay more of their tax dollars to the government's creditors and have less to spend for highways, health care, defense, and other public sector programs. Exhibit 6 shows net interest payments as a percentage of GDP. The net interest payment was only about 1.5 percent of GDP right after World War II, but it increased dramatically after the mid-1970s to more than 3 percent in the mid-1980s. In 2000, the interest payment burden declined to 2.2 percent.

Reasons Not to Worry. The burden of the national debt on present and future generations depends on who owns the accumulated national debt. Stated more precisely, the burden of the debt depends on whether it is held internally or externally. The bulk of the public debt is **internal national debt.** Internal national debt is the portion of the national debt owed to a nation's own citizens. Internal debt financing is viewed as "we owe it to ourselves." One U.S. citizen buys a government security and lends Uncle Sam the money to pay the interest and principal on a maturing government security held by another U.S. citizen. Although this redistribution of income and wealth does indeed favor bondholders, who are typically upper-income individuals, transferring dollars between U.S. citizens does not alter the overall purchasing power in the U.S. economy.

Internal national debt
The portion of the national debt owed to a nation's own citizens.

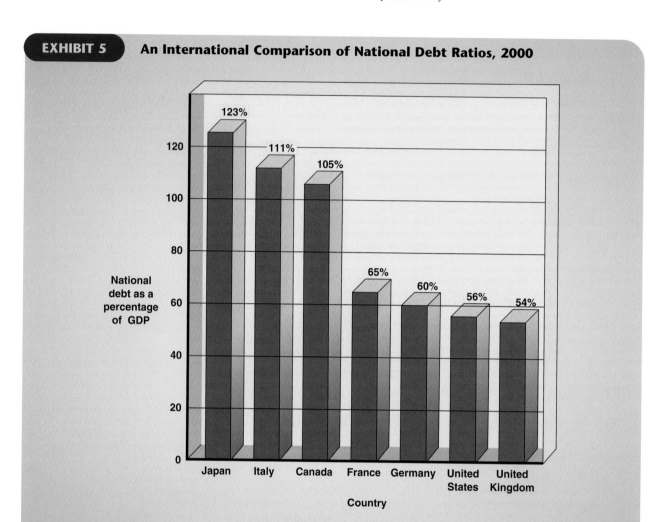

EXHIBIT 5   **An International Comparison of National Debt Ratios, 2000**

This exhibit shows the ratios of national debt to GDP in 2000 for selected industrialized countries. Japan, Italy, Canada, France, and Germany have higher debt/GDP ratios than the United States.

Source: Organization for Economic Cooperation and Development, *Economic Outlook,* June 2001, http://www.sourceoecd.org/content/html/index.htm, Annex Table 34.

External national debt

The portion of the national debt owed to foreign citizens.

Those on the "not to worry" side of this issue also concede that an **external national debt** is a concern. External national debt is the portion of the national debt owed to foreign citizens. Financing the external national debt means interest and principal payments are transfers of money from U.S. citizens to other nations. If foreign governments, banks, corporations, and individual investors hold part of the national debt, the "we owe it to ourselves" argument is weakened. Exhibit 7 shows who owns the securities the U.S. Treasury has issued. In 2000, foreigners owned 21 percent of the total national debt. About 49 percent was held by the federal, state, and local governments, primarily by federal agencies such as the U.S. Treasury, the Social Security Administration, and Federal Reserve banks. The Federal

EXHIBIT 6	**Federal Net Interest as a Percentage of GDP, 1940–2000**

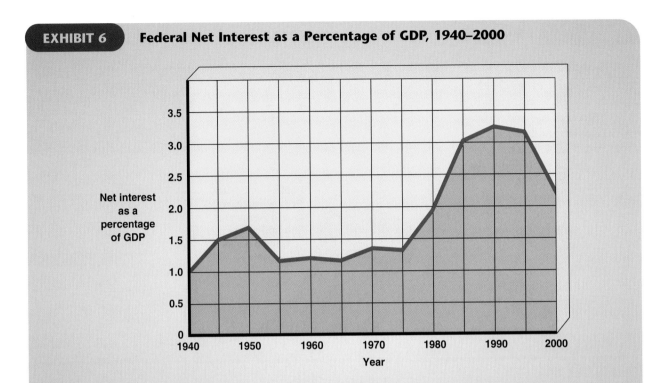

Some fear that interest payments on the national debt will swallow an enormous portion of the federal budget. The exhibit shows that the net interest payment as a proportion of GDP was only about 1.5 percent right after World War II. In the 1980s and early 1990s, however, the interest rate burden increased dramatically. Since 1995, it has declined to 2.2 percent in 2000.

Source: *Economic Report of the President, 2001,* http://w3.access.gpo.gov/eop/, Tables B-1 and B-80.

Reserve is an independent government agency explained in the next chapter. The private sector, consisting of individuals, banks, corporations, and insurance companies, held 30 percent of the national debt. The debt held by the private sector and government entities constitutes the internal national debt.

Although approximately 79 percent of the national debt is internal, the 21 percent of total U.S. debt that is external debt is not necessarily undesirable. Foreign investment in the United States supplements domestic saving. Borrowing from abroad can prevent the higher interest rates that would exist if the U.S. Treasury relied only on domestic savers to purchase federal government securities. A lower interest rate increases U.S. investment and consumer spending, causing the aggregate demand curve to shift rightward.

If we do not need to worry about shifting the burden to future generations, can the current generation escape the debt burden? The answer is *No*. During World War II, for example, the United States operated at full employment along its *production possibilities curve*. As illustrated earlier in Exhibit 1 of Chapter 2, the people at that time in history were forced to trade off consumer goods production for military goods production. Because massive

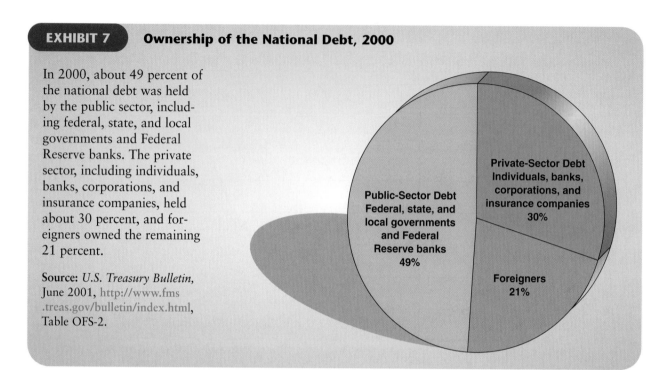

EXHIBIT 7   **Ownership of the National Debt, 2000**

In 2000, about 49 percent of the national debt was held by the public sector, including federal, state, and local governments and Federal Reserve banks. The private sector, including individuals, banks, corporations, and insurance companies, held about 30 percent, and foreigners owned the remaining 21 percent.

Source: *U.S. Treasury Bulletin,* June 2001, http://www.fms .treas.gov/bulletin/index.html, Table OFS-2.

Private-Sector Debt Individuals, banks, corporations, and insurance companies
30%

Public-Sector Debt Federal, state, and local governments and Federal Reserve banks
49%

Foreigners
21%

amounts of resources were diverted to fight World War II, people at that time were forced to give up private consumption of houses, cars, refrigerators, and so on. After the war was over, resources were again devoted to producing more consumer goods and fewer military goods. The same analysis can be used today. At full employment, the burden of the national debt on the current generation is the opportunity cost of private-sector goods forgone because land, labor, and capital are used to produce public-sector goods.

In other words, the burden of the national debt is incurred when production takes place; it is not postponed until the debt is paid by future generations. When the debt comes due in the future, the government can simply refinance the debt and redistribute money from one group of citizens to another. This redistribution of income does not cause a reallocation of resources away from consumer goods and services in favor of government programs.

3. Does Government Borrowing Crowd Out Private-Sector Spending?

Crowding-out effect

A reduction in private-sector spending as a result of federal budget deficits financed by U.S. Treasury borrowing. When federal government borrowing increases interest rates, the result is lower consumption by households and lower investment spending by businesses.

Reasons to Worry. Critics of Keynesian fiscal policy believe that government spending financed by borrowing designed to boost aggregate demand has little, if any, effect on growth of real GDP. The reason is that the **crowding-out effect** dampens the stimulus to aggregate demand from increased federal government spending. The crowding-out effect is a reduction in private-sector spending as a result of higher interest rates caused by U.S. Treasury borrowing (selling securities) to finance government spending. For example, suppose the federal government spends and borrows, rather than collecting taxes, to finance new health care programs. In this case, the size of the national debt rises, and interest rates are pushed up in loan markets. Higher interest rates occur because the federal government competes with private borrowers for available savings, and less credit is available to consumers and business borrowers. The result of this crowding-out effect is lower consumption ($-\Delta C$) and business investment ($-\Delta I$), which offset the boost in aggregate demand ($+\Delta AD$) from increased government spending ($+\Delta G$) operating through the spending multiplier.

The crowding-out effect contradicts the theory explained in the previous Reasons Not to Worry section that future generations do not bear some of today's debt burden. Recall from Chapter 2 that current investment spending increases living standards in the future by shifting the production possibilities curve outward (Exhibit 4 in Chapter 2). If federal borrowing crowds out private investment in plants and equipment, future generations will have a smaller possible productive capacity.

The *AD-AS* model will help you understand the crowding-out concept. Exhibit 8 reproduces the situation in which government spending is used to combat a recession, depicted earlier in Exhibit 2 of the chapter on fiscal policy. Begin at E_1, with an equilibrium GDP of $4 trillion, and assume the government increases its spending and uses the spending multiplier to shift the aggregate demand curve rightward from AD_1 to AD_2. Following Keynesian theory, there is zero crowding out, and the economy achieves full employment at equilibrium point E_2, corresponding to real GDP of $8 trillion. Critics of Keynesian theory, however, argue that crowding out occurs. The result of expansionary fiscal policy is not E_2, but some equilibrium point along the *AS* line between E_1 and E_2. For example, a fall in private expenditures might partially offset the government spending stimulus. With incomplete crowding out, the aggregate demand curve increases only to AD_2' because of the decline in consumption and investment. The economy therefore moves to E_2' at a real GDP of $6 trillion and does not achieve full employment at E_2. Or crowding out can completely offset the multiplier effect of increased government spending. The fall in private expenditures by consumers and businesses can result in no change in aggregate demand curve AD_1. In this case, the economy remains at E_1, with unemployment unaffected by expansionary policy. Meanwhile, the deficit required to finance extra government spending increases the national debt.

Reasons Not to Worry. The crowding-out effect is controversial. Keynesian economists counter critics by saying that any crowding-out effect is small or nonexistent. Instead, at below full-employment real GDP, their counterargument is the **crowding-in effect.** For example, government capital spending for highways, dams, universities, and infrastructure financed by borrowing might offset any decline in private investment. Another Keynesian argument is that consumers and businesspersons may believe that federal spending is "just what the doctor ordered" for an ailing economy. Federal borrowing incurred to finance the new spending would boost consumption and therefore increase aggregate demand. The reason is because holders of Treasury bills, notes, and bonds feel richer. As a result of their greater wealth, consumers

Crowding-in effect
An increase in private-sector spending as a result of federal budget deficits financed by U.S. Treasury borrowing. At less than full employment, consumers hold more Treasury securities, and this additional wealth causes them to spend more. Businesses' investment spending increases because of optimistic profit expectations.

EXHIBIT 8   **Zero, Partial, and Complete Crowding Out**

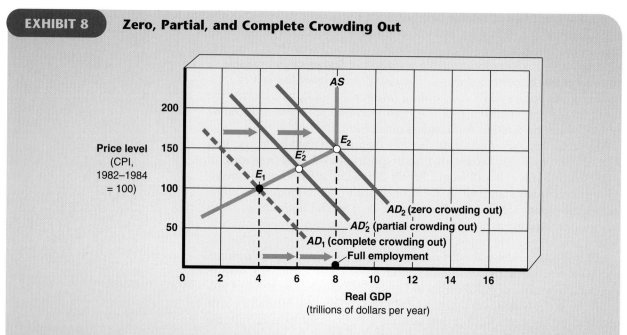

Beginning at equilibrium E_1, the federal government borrows to finance a deficit created by expansionary fiscal policy. Keynesian theory predicts zero crowding out, which means that an increase in government spending operates through the spending multiplier to shift aggregate demand from AD_1 to AD_2. If crowding out is zero, consumption and investment spending are unaffected by the increase in government spending financed by borrowing. Partial crowding out occurs when a decrease in private spending partially offsets the multiplier effect from an increase in deficit-financed government spending. Partial crowding out results in a shift only from AD_1 to AD_2' and an equilibrium at E_2', rather than E_2. If crowding out is complete, a decrease in private spending completely offsets the increase in government spending financed by debt. In this case, the aggregate demand curve remains at AD_1, and the economy remains at E_1.

spend more now and plan to spend more in the future. Such a blush of optimism may also raise the profit expectations of business managers, and they may increase investment spending. The effect of increased private-sector spending could nullify some or all of the crowding-out effect, which would otherwise offset the boost in aggregate demand from increased government spending. Hence, as explained in the graphical analysis in Exhibit 8, the spending multiplier shifts the aggregate demand curve from AD_1 to AD_2, with zero crowding out.

Finally, both sides of the debate agree that complete crowding out occurs in one situation. Suppose the economy is operating at full employment (point E_2). This is comparable to being on the economy's production possibilities curve. If the government shifts the aggregate demand curve rightward by increasing spending or tax cuts, the result will be higher prices and a replacement of private-sector output with public-sector output.

Conclusion *Crowding out is complete if the economy is at full employment, but debatable at less than full employment.*

How Real Is the National Debt?

Applicable Concept: national debt

Perhaps federal budget deficits and the national debt that results are really not so large and threatening. For years, the late Professor Robert Eisner, past president of the American Economic Association, fought conventional wisdom on this subject.[1] Eisner argued that we should use real rather than nominal increases in the national debt to report deficits. Suppose the national debt is $5 trillion and the price level increases by 3 percent in a given year. The nominal value of the national debt therefore falls by $150 billion. Stated differently, holders of Treasury securities would have to buy $150 billion in newly issued government securities to replace the value eroded by inflation. According to Eisner, this $150 billion real-value inflation adjustment to the national debt should be subtracted from an actual federal budget deficit for the year. Let's say the deficit reported by government statisticians is $200 billion. Using Eisner's "new accounting," the real deficit is only $50 billion ($200 billion official deficit − $150 billion inflation adjustment). The reported deficit (change in nominal debt) is positive because it injects this value of Treasury security assets to security holders to finance government spending. The amount of inflation adjustment is negative because it is a loss of Treasury security asset values from higher prices.

Eisner disapproved of budget surpluses. He said: "The government running a surplus, whether 'reserved' for Social Security or anything else, means taking more in taxes than it gives the public in outlays. That should please nobody, neither liberals looking for more public investment nor conservatives who want business and households to have more freedom to make their own private spending decisions."[2]

Eisner also warned that current federal rules of accounting are an economic policy disaster. Private businesses, as well as state and local governments, use two budgets. One is the *operating budget,* which includes salaries, interest payments, and other current expenses. The second type of budget, called a *capital budget,* includes spending for investment items, such as machines, buildings, and roads. Expenditures on the capital budget may be paid for by long-term borrowing.

The federal government does not use a capital budget. Capital budgeting allows spreading the cost of long-lasting assets over future years. For example, the federal budget makes no distinction between the rental cost of a federal office building and the cost of constructing a new federal office building to replace rented office space. However, interest payments on borrowing for a new building provide the benefit of a long-lasting asset that offsets rent payments. Suppose a $200 billion deficit is reported. If a capital budgeting system were utilized, the public would see that most federal borrowing really finances assets yielding long-term benefits. In short, proponents of a capital budget believe the public's focus should be on the operating budget, which gives a truer measure of the deficit or surplus. Opponents of changing the accounting rules argue that controversial expenditures would be placed in the capital budget to manipulate the size of the deficit or surplus in the operating budget for political reasons.

Finally, some economists argue for other numerical adjustments that show the federal deficit or surplus is really not as it seems. They say it is not the federal deficit or surplus that really matters, but the combined deficits or surpluses of federal, state, and local governments. When state and local governments run budget surpluses, these surpluses are a source of saving in financial markets that adds to federal surpluses or offsets federal borrowing to finance its deficit.

1. Do households make a distinction between spending for current expenses and spending for capital expenses? Compare borrowing $1,000 to take a vacation in Hawaii to borrowing $80,000 to buy a condominium and move out of your rented apartment.

2. Critics of "new accounting" for federal borrowing argue that it does not matter what the government spends the money for. What matters is the total amount that the government spends minus taxes collected. Explain this viewpoint.

---

[1]Robert Eisner, *The Great Deficit Scare* (New York: Century Foundation Press, 1997).

[2]Robert Eisner, "Jeers for the Budget Surplus," *Wall Street Journal,* Feb. 17, 1998, p. A22.

KEY CONCEPTS

National debt	Internal national debt	Crowding-out effect
Net public debt	External national debt	Crowding-in effect
Debt ceiling		

SUMMARY

■ The **national debt** is the dollar amount that the federal government owes holders of government securities. It is the cumulative sum of past deficits. The U.S. Treasury issues government securities to finance the deficits. The debt has increased sharply since 1980.

National debt

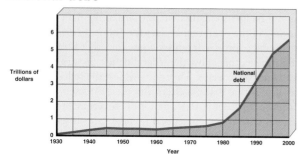

■ The **net public debt** is the national debt minus all government interagency borrowing. It is the debt that the federal government owes to itself.

■ A **debt ceiling** is a method used to restrict the growth of the national debt.

■ **Internal national debt** is the percentage of the national debt a nation owes to its own citizens. In 2000, about 79 percent of the national debt was internally held by individuals, banks, corporations, insurance companies, and government entities. The "we owe it to ourselves" argument over the debt is that U.S. citizens own the bulk of the U.S. national debt. **External national debt** is a burden because it is the portion of the national debt a nation owes to foreigners. The interest paid on external debt transfers purchasing power to other nations. In 2000, approximately 21 percent of the national debt was external.

Internal and external national debt

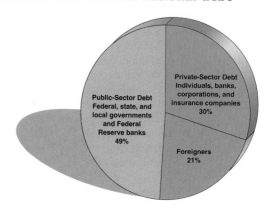

■ The **burden of debt debate** involves controversial questions:

a. **Can Uncle Sam Go Bankrupt?** The national debt is a lower percentage of GDP today than at the end of World War II. The U.S. government will not go bankrupt because it never has to pay off its debt. When government securities mature, the U.S. Treasury can refinance, or roll over, the debt by issuing new securities.

b. **Are We Passing the Debt Burden to Our Children?** One side of this argument is that the debt is mostly internal, so financing the debt only involves exchanging old bonds for new bonds among U.S. citizens. The burden of the debt falls only on the current generation when the tradeoff between public-sector goods and private-sector goods along the production possibilities curve occurs. In short, when resources are used to make missiles today, citizens are forced to give up, say, airplane production in the current period and not later. The counterargument is that there is a sizable external national debt that transfers purchasing power to foreigners.

c. **Does Government Borrowing Crowd Out Private-Sector Spending?** The **crowding-out effect** is a burden of the national debt that occurs when the government borrows to finance its deficit, causing the interest rate to rise. As the interest rate rises, consumption and business investment fall. Keynesian theory assumes zero crowding out when the federal government increases spending in order to shift the aggregate demand curve rightward. If crowding out occurs, reduced private spending offsets the multiplier effect of increased government spending. As a result, the expected magnitude of the rightward shift in the aggregate demand curve is partially or completely offset.

Opponents believe in the **crowding-in effect**. In this view, government capital spending for highways, dams, universities, and infrastructure offsets any decline in business investment from crowding

out. Deficits can also boost consumption because holders of the government securities used to finance the debt feel wealthier and spend more. Also, businesses' profit expectations rise because of the additional fiscal stimulus, so business investment increases.

Zero, partial, and complete crowding out

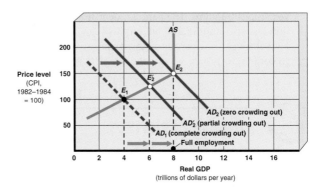

SUMMARY OF CONCLUSION STATEMENTS

- Crowding out is complete if the economy is at full employment, but debatable at less than full employment.

STUDY QUESTIONS AND PROBLEMS

1. Explain the relationship between budget deficits and the national debt.

2. Discuss various ways of measuring the size of the national debt.

3. Explain this statement: "The national debt is like taking money out of your left pocket and putting it into your right pocket."

4. Explain this statement: "The most unlikely problem of the national debt is that the government will go bankrupt."

5. Suppose the percentage of the federal debt owned by foreigners increases sharply. Would this trend concern you? Why or why not?

6. Explain the theory that crowding out can weaken or nullify the effect of expansionary fiscal policy financed by federal government borrowing.

7. Suppose the federal government has no national debt and spends $100 billion, while raising only $50 billion in taxes.
   a. What amount of government bonds will the U.S. Treasury issue to finance the deficit?

b. Next year, assume tax revenues remain at $50 billion. If the government pays a 10 percent rate of interest, add the debt-servicing interest payment to the government's $100 billion expenditure for goods and services the second year.

c. For the second year, compute the deficit, the amount of new debt issued, and the new national debt.

8. Suppose the media report that the federal deficit this year is $200 billion. The national debt was $5,000 billion last year and $5,200 billion this year. The price level this year is 3 percent higher than it was last year. According to Eisner, what is the real deficit?

9. During the presidential campaign of 1932 in the depth of the Great Depression, candidates Herbert Hoover and Franklin D. Roosevelt both advocated reducing the budget deficit, using tax hikes and/or expenditure reductions. Evaluate this fiscal policy.

10. Consider this statement: "Our grandchildren may not suffer the entire burden of a federal deficit." Do you agree or disagree? Explain.

11. Suppose you are the economic policy adviser to the president and he or she asks for your recommendation to eliminate a federal deficit. What would you recommend?

ONLINE EXERCISES

Exercise 1

Visit The Public Debt to the Penny (http://www .publicdebt.treas.gov/opd/opdpenny.htm). What is the latest amount of the national debt?

Exercise 2

Visit Interest Expense on the Public Debt (http://www .publicdebt.treas.gov/opd/opdint.htm). What is the latest interest paid to finance the national debt?

Exercise 3

Visit CCER National Budget Simulation (http://garnet .berkeley.edu:3333/budget/budget.html). Make the budget cuts you would choose to balance the federal budget.

Exercise 4

Visit The Concord Coalition (http://www.concordcoalition .org/). What is your share of the national debt (assume a population of 268 million)? Choose What's New, and read about the latest issue discussed.

CHECKPOINT ANSWER

What's Behind the National Debt?

Every item owned by the federal government, including the White House, office buildings, tanks, and computers, is an asset standing behind the national debt. If you said the assets of the federal government could be sold to pay off the national debt, YOU ARE CORRECT.

PRACTICE QUIZ

For a visual explanation of the correct answers, visit the tutorial at http://tucker.swcollege.com.

1. During the late 1990s, federal government budget deficits
   a. were completely removed.
   b. dropped significantly from a high of $300 billion.
   c. remained fairly stable at about $150 billion per year.
   d. exceeded $200 billion in each year.

2. The federal government finances a budget by
   a. taxing businesses and households.
   b. selling Treasury securities.
   c. printing more money.
   d. reducing its purchases of goods and services.

3. In 2000, the national debt was approximately
   a. $60 billion.
   b. $600 billion.
   c. $6 trillion.
   d. $5 trillion.

4. The national debt
   a. was about six times larger in 2000 than 1980.
   b. doubled between 1980 and 2000.
   c. stayed at approximately the same amount between 1980 and 2000.
   d. was four times larger in 2000 than it was in 1980.

5. Which of the following countries has the smallest national debt as a percentage of GDP?
   a. Italy
   b. Canada
   c. United Kingdom
   d. Japan
   e. France

6. Which of the following is *false*?
   a. The national debt's size decreased steadily after World War II until 1980 and then increased sharply each year.
   b. The national debt increases in size whenever the federal government has a budget surplus.
   c. The national debt is currently about the same size as it was during World War II.
   d. All of the above are false.

7. In 2000, how much of the U.S. national debt was owed to foreigners?
   a. About 2.5 percent
   b. About 21 percent
   c. About 31 percent
   d. About 59 percent

8. Which of the following owns a portion of the national debt?
   a. Federal, state, and local governments
   b. Private U.S. citizens
   c. Banks
   d. Foreigners
   e. All of the above

9. The portion of the U.S. national debt held by foreigners
   a. represents a burden because it transfers purchasing power from U.S. taxpayers to other countries.
   b. is an accounting entry that represents no real burden.
   c. decreased as a proportion of the total debt during the 1980s.
   d. has been constant for many decades.

10. Which of the following statements about crowding out is *true*?
    a. It is caused by a budget surplus.
    b. It is not caused by a budget deficit.
    c. It cannot completely offset the multiplier effect of deficit government spending.
    d. It affects interest rates and, in turn, consumption and investment spending.

11. Which of the following statements about crowding out is *true*?
    a. It can completely offset the multiplier.
    b. It is caused by a budget deficit.
    c. It is not caused by a budget surplus.
    d. All of the above are true.

Money, Banking, and Monetary Policy

S tudents often find the material in these chapters the most interesting in their principles course because the topic is *money*. The first chapter begins the discussion of money with basic definitions and a description of the Federal Reserve System. The next chapter explains how the banking system and the Federal Reserve influence the supply of money. The following chapter compares different macroeconomic theories, and the final chapter explores additional macro theories based on expectations.

CHAPTER 24

Money and the Federal Reserve System

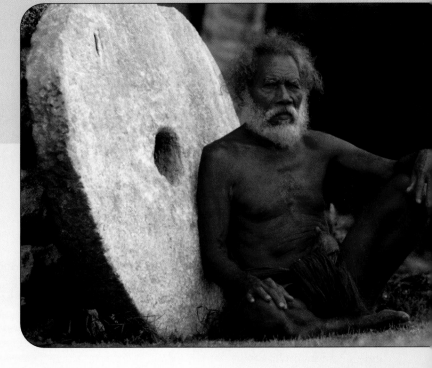

A s the lyrics of the old song go, "Money makes the world go round, the world go round, the world go round." Recall the circular flow model presented in the chapter on GDP. Households exchange *money* for goods and services in the product markets, and firms exchange *money* for resources in the factor markets. In short, money affects the way an economy works. In the chapter on aggregate demand and supply and the chapter on fiscal policy presented earlier in the text, the *AD-AS* model was developed without explicitly discussing money. In this chapter, and throughout Part 7, money takes center stage.

Exactly what is money? The answer may surprise you. Imagine yourself on the small South Pacific island of Yap. You are surrounded by exotic fowl, crystal-clear lagoons, delicious fruits, and sunny skies. Now suppose while leisurely

strolling along the beach one evening, you suddenly discover a beautiful bamboo hut for sale. As you will discover in this chapter, to pay for your dream hut, you must roll a 5-foot-diameter stone to the area of the island designated as the "bank."

We begin our discussion of money with the three functions money serves. Next, we identify the components of three different definitions of the money supply used in the United States. The

remainder of the chapter describes the organization and services of the Federal Reserve System, our nation's central bank. Beginning in this chapter and in the next three chapters, you will learn how the Federal Reserve System controls the stock of money in the economy. Then, using the *AD-AS* model, you will learn how variations in the stock of money in the economy affect total spending, unemployment, and prices.

In this chapter, you will learn to solve these economics puzzles:

- Why do nations use money?
- Is "plastic money" really money?
- What does a Federal Reserve bank do?

What Makes Money *Money?*

Can exchange occur in an economy without money? It certainly can, using a trading system called **barter.** Barter is the direct exchange of one good for another good, rather than for money. The problem with barter is that it requires a *coincidence of wants*. Imagine for a moment that dollars and coins are worthless. Farmer Brown needs shoes, so he takes his bushels of wheat to the shoe store and offers to barter wheat for shoes. Unfortunately, the store owner refuses to barter because she wants to trade shoes for pencils, toothpaste, and coffee. Undaunted, Farmer Brown spends more time and effort to find Mr. Jones, who has pencils, toothpaste, and coffee he will trade for bushels of wheat. Although Farmer Brown's luck has improved, he and Mr. Jones must agree on the terms of exchange. Exactly how many pounds of coffee, for example, is a bushel of wheat worth? Assuming this exchange is worked out, Farmer Brown must spend more time returning to the shoe store and negotiating the terms of an exchange of pencils, coffee, and toothpaste for shoes.

Barter
The direct exchange of one good for another good, rather than for money.

> **Conclusion** *The use of money simplifies and therefore increases market transactions. Money also prevents wasting time that can be devoted to production, thereby promoting economic growth by increasing a nation's production possibilities.*

The Three Functions of Money

Suppose citizens of the planet of Starcom want to replace their barter system and must decide what to use for money. Assuming this planet is fortunate enough to have economists, they would explain that anything, regardless of its value, can serve as money if it conforms to the following definition. **Money is anything that serves as a medium of exchange, unit of account, and store of value.** Money is not limited to dimes, quarters, and dollar bills. Notice that "anything" meeting the three tests is a candidate to serve as money. This explains why precious metals, beaver skins, wampum (shells strung in belts), and cigarettes have all served as money. Let's discuss each of the three functions money serves.

Money
Anything that serves as a medium of exchange, unit of account, and store of value.

Money as a Medium of Exchange. In a simple society, barter is a way for participants to exchange goods and services in order to satisfy wants. Barter, however, requires wasting time in the process of exchange that people could use for productive work. If the goal is to increase the volume of transactions and live in a modern economy, the most important function of money is to

For a look at the history of money, visit History of Money from Ancient Times to the Present Day (http://www.ex.ac.uk/~RDavies/arian/llyfr.html).

Medium of exchange

The primary function of money to be widely accepted in exchange for goods and services.

serve as a **medium of exchange.** Medium of exchange is the primary function of money to be widely accepted in exchange for goods and services. Money removes the problem of coincidence of wants because everyone is willing to accept money in payment, rather than goods and services. You give up two $20 bills in exchange for a ticket to see a rock concert. Because money serves as generalized purchasing power, all in society know that no one will refuse to trade their products for money. In short, money increases trade by providing a much more convenient method of exchange than a cumbersome barter system.

Money as a Unit of Account. How does a wheat farmer know whether a bushel of wheat is worth one, two, or more pairs of shoes? How does a family compare its income to expenses or a business know whether it is making a profit? Government must be able to measure tax revenues collected and program expenditures made. And GDP is the *money* value of final goods and services used to compare the national output of the United States to, say, Japan. In each of these examples, money serves as a **unit of account.** Without money, we face the difficult task of, say, pricing sausage pizzas in terms of other goods. Unit of account is the function of money to provide a common measurement of the relative value of goods and services. Without dollars, there is no common denominator. We must therefore decide if one sausage pizza equals a box of pencils, 20 oranges, one quart of oil, and so forth. Now let's compare the value of two items using money. If the price of one sausage pizza is $10 and the price of a movie ticket is $5, then one sausage pizza equals two movie tickets. In the United States, the monetary unit is the dollar; in Japan, it is the yen; Mexico has its peso; and so on.

Unit of account

The function of money to provide a common measurement of the relative value of goods and services.

Money as a Store of Value. Can you save shrimp for months and then exchange them for some product? You could, but not without the extra expense of freezing the shrimp. Money, on the other hand, serves as a **store of value** in exchange for some item in the future. Store of value is the ability of money to hold value over time. You can bury money in your backyard or store it under your mattress for months or years and not worry about it spoiling. Stated differently, money allows us to synchronize our income more precisely with expenditures. However, recall from the chapter on inflation that hyperinflation can destroy money's store-of-value function and, in turn, its medium-of-exchange function.

Store of value

The ability of money to hold value over time.

Conclusion *Money is a useful mechanism for transforming income in the present into future purchases.*

The key property of money is that it is completely *liquid.* This means that money is immediately available to spend in exchange for goods and services without any additional expense. Money is more liquid than real assets (real estate or gold) or paper assets (stocks or bonds). These assets also serve as stores of value, but liquidating (selling) them often involves expenses, such as brokerage fees, and time delays.

The Atlanta Federal Reserve publishes an online brochure about U.S. money entitled "Fundamental Facts about U.S. Money" (http://www.frbatlanta.org/publica/brochure/fundfac/money.htm).

CHECKPOINT

Are Debit Cards Money?

Debit cards are used to pay for purchases, and the money is automatically deducted from the user's bank account. Are debit cards money?

Conclusion *Money is the most liquid form of wealth because it can be spent directly in the marketplace.*

Are Credit Cards Money?

It is an understandable misconception that credit cards, such as Visa, Master-Card, and American Express, are "plastic money." Let's test credit cards for the three functions of money. First, because credit cards are widely accepted, they serve as a means of payment in an exchange for goods or services.

Second, the credit card statement, and not the card itself, serves as a unit of account. One of the advantages of credit cards is that you receive a statement listing the exact price in dollars paid for each item you charged. Your credit card statement clearly records the dollar amount you spent for gasoline, a dinner, or a trip.

But credit cards clearly fail to meet the store-of-value criterion and are therefore *not* money. The word *credit* means receiving money today to buy products in return for a promise to pay in the future. A credit card represents only a prearranged short-term loan up to a certain limit. If the credit card company goes out of business or for any reason decides not to honor your card, it is worthless. Hence, credit cards do not store value and are *not* money. If credit cards were money, you would be indifferent between receiving $1,000 in cash and an equal dollar increase in your credit limit.

Other Desirable Properties of Money

Once something has passed the three basic requirements to serve as money, there are additional hurdles to clear. First, an important consideration is *scarcity*. Money must be scarce, but not too scarce. Sand, for example, could theoretically serve as money, but sand is a poor choice because people can easily gather a bucketful to pay their bills. A Picasso painting would also be undesirable as money. Because there are so few for circulation, people must resort to barter.

Counterfeiting threatens the scarcity of money. Advances in computer graphics, scanners, and color copiers were allowing counterfeiters to win their ongoing battle with the U.S. Secret Service (an agency of the Treasury Department). In response, new bills were issued with a polymer security thread running through them. The larger off-center portraits on the bills allow for a watermark next to the portrait that is visible from both sides against a light. A new $1 coin has also been issued.

The Atlanta Federal Reserve informs one about how to spot counterfeit money (http://www.frbatlanta.org/publica/brochure/fundfac/money.htm).

Fixed Assets, or: Why a Loan in Yap Is Hard to Roll Over

Applicable Concept: functions of money

YAP, Micronesia—On this tiny South Pacific island, life is easy and the currency is hard. . . . [T]he currency is solid as a rock. In fact, it is rock. Limestone to be precise.

For nearly 2,000 years the Yapese have used large stone wheels to pay for major purchases, such as land, canoes and permission to marry. Yap is a U.S. trust territory, and the dollar is used in grocery stores and gas stations. But reliance on stone money . . . continues.

Buying property with stones is "much easier than buying it with U.S. dollars," says John Chodad, who recently purchased a building lot with a 30-inch stone wheel. "We don't know the value of the U.S. dollar."

Stone wheels don't make good pocket money, so for small transactions, Yapese use other forms of currency, such as beer. . . .

Besides stone wheels and beer, the Yapese sometimes spend gaw, consisting of necklaces of stone beads strung together around a whale's tooth. They also can buy things with yar, a currency made from large seashells, but these are small changes.

The people of Yap have been using stone money ever since a Yapese warrior named Anagumang first brought the huge stones over from limestone caverns on neighboring Palau, some 1,500 to 2,000 years ago. Inspired by the moon, he fashioned the stone into large circles. The rest is history.

Yapese lean the stone wheels against their houses or prop up rows of them in village "banks." Most of the stones are 2 1/2 to 5 feet in diameter, but some are as much as 12 feet across. Each has a hole in the center so it can be slipped onto the trunk of a fallen betel-nut tree and carried. It takes 20 men to lift some wheels.

By custom, the stones are worthless when broken. You never hear people on Yap musing about wanting a piece of the rock. Rather than risk a broken stone—or back—Yapese tend to leave the larger stones where they are and make a mental accounting that the ownership has been transferred. . . .

The worth of stone money doesn't depend on size. Instead, the pieces are valued by how hard it was to get them here. . . .

There are some decided advantages to using massive stones for money. They are immune to black-market trading, for one thing, and they pose formidable obstacles to pickpockets. . . .

ANALYZE THE ISSUE

1. Explain how Yap's large stones pass the three tests in the definition of money.

2. Briefly discuss Yap's large stones in terms of other desirable properties of money.

Source: Art Pine, "Fixed Assets, Or: Why a Loan in Yap Is Hard to Roll Over," *Wall Street Journal*, Mar. 29, 1984, p. 1. Reprinted by permission.

Conclusion *The supply of money must be great enough to meet ordinary transaction needs, but not be so plentiful that it becomes worthless.*

Second, money should be *portable* and *divisible*. That is, people should be able to reach into their pockets and make change to buy items at various prices. Statues of George Washington might be attractive money, but they would be difficult to carry and make change. Finally, money must be *uniform*. An ounce of gold is an ounce of gold. The quality differences of beaver skins and seashells, on the other hand, complicate using these items for money. Each exchange would involve the extra trouble of buyers and sellers arguing over which skins or shells are better or worse.

What Stands Behind Our Money?

Historically, early forms of money played two roles. If, for example, a ruler declared beans as money, you could spend them or sell them in the marketplace. Precious metals, tobacco, cows, and other tangible goods are examples of **commodity money**. Commodity money is anything that serves as money while having market value in other uses. This means that money itself has intrinsic worth (the market value of the material). For example, money can be pure gold or silver, both of which are valuable for nonmoney uses, such as making jewelry and serving other industrial purposes.

Commodity money
Anything that serves as money while having market value in other uses.

Today, the United States's paper money and coins are no longer backed by gold or silver. Our paper money was exchangeable for gold or silver until 1934. As a result of the Great Depression, people rapidly tried to get rid of their paper money. The U.S. Treasury's stock of gold dropped so low that Congress passed a law in 1934 that prevented anyone from exchanging gold for $5 and larger bills. Later, in 1963, Congress removed the right to exchange $1 bills for silver. And in the mid-1960s, zinc, copper, and nickel replaced silver in coins.

The important consideration for money is acceptability. The acceptability of a dollar is due in no small degree to the fact that Uncle Sam decrees it to be **fiat money**. Fiat money is money accepted by law and not because of its redeemability or intrinsic value. A dollar bill contains only about three cents worth of paper, printing inks, and other materials. A quarter contains maybe 10 cents worth of nickel and copper. Pull out a bill and look at it closely. In the upper left corner on the front side is small print that proclaims, "THIS NOTE IS LEGAL TENDER FOR ALL DEBTS, PUBLIC AND PRIVATE." This means that your paper money is fiat money and cannot be refused as payment for a debt. Also notice that nowhere on the note is there any promise to redeem it for gold, silver, or anything else.

Fiat money
Money accepted by law and not because of its redeemability or intrinsic value.

Conclusion *Whether or not an item will serve as money does not depend on its own market value or the backing of precious metal.*

The Three Money Supply Definitions

Now that you understand the basic definition of money, we turn to exactly what constitutes the money supply of the U.S. economy. There is disagreement over the answer to this question because some economists define the money supply more narrowly than others. The following sections examine the methods used to measure the money supply, officially called M1, M2, and M3.

M1: The Most Narrowly Defined Money Supply

M1 is the narrowest definition of the money supply. This money definition measures purchasing power immediately available to the public without borrowing or having to give notice. Specifically, M1 measures the currency, traveler's checks, and checkable deposits held by the public at a given time, such

M1
The narrowest definition of the money supply. It includes currency, traveler's checks, and checkable deposits.

History of Money in the Colonies

The early colonists left behind their well-developed money system in Europe. North American Indians accepted wampum as money. These are beads of polished shells strung in belts. Soon, a group of settlers learned to counterfeit wampum, and it lost its value. This meant that the main method of trading with the Indians was to barter. Later, trade developed with the West Indies, and Spanish coins called "pieces of eight" were circulated widely. Colonists often cut these coins into pieces to make change. Half of a coin became known as "four bits." A quarter part of the coin was referred to as "two bits." The first English colony to mint its own coins was Massachusetts in 1652. A striking pine tree was engraved on these coins called shillings. Other coins such as a sixpence and threepence were also produced at a mint in Boston. Several other colonies followed by authorizing their own coin issues.

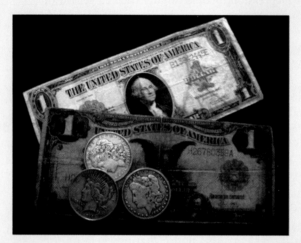

The first national coin of the United States was issued in 1787, when Congress approved a one-cent copper coin. One side was decorated with a chain of 13 links encircling the words, "We Are One." The other side had a sundial, the noonday sun, and the word "fugo," meaning "time flies." Later, this coin became known as the Franklin cent although there is no evidence that Benjamin Franklin played any role in its design.

In 1792, Congress established a mint in Philadelphia. It manufactured copper cents and half-cents about the size of today's quarters and nickels. In 1794, silver half-dimes and half-dollars increased the variety of available coins. The next year gold eagles ($10) and half-eagles ($5) appeared. The motto "E Pluribus Unum" ("out of many, one") was first used on the half-eagle in 1795. The next year America's first quarters and dimes were issued.

The first paper money in the Americas was printed in 1690. Massachusetts soldiers returned to the colony from fighting the French in Quebec, where they had tried a siege of the city which failed. The colony had no precious metal to pay the soldiers. Hundreds of soldiers threatened mutiny, and the colony decided it must issue bills of credit, which were simply pieces of paper promising to pay the soldiers. Other colonies followed this example and printed their own paper money. Soon, paper money became widely circulated.

In 1775, the need to finance the American Revolution forced the Continental Congress to issue paper money, but so much was issued that it rapidly lost its value. Later George Washington said, "A wagon load of money will scarcely purchase a wagon load of provisions"—a statement that gave rise to the phrase "not worth a continental."

as a given day, month, or year. M1 does not include the money held by the government, Federal Reserve banks, or depository institutions. Expressed as a formula:

$$M1 = \text{currency} + \text{traveler's checks} + \text{checkable deposits}$$

Exhibit 1 shows the components of M1 and other money supply definitions based on daily averages during January 2000.

EXHIBIT 1   **Definitions of the Money Supply, 2000**

Each of the three pie charts represents the money supply in January 2000. M1, the most narrowly defined money supply, is equal to currency (coins and paper money) in circulation plus traveler's checks plus checkable deposits in financial institutions. M2 is a more broadly defined money supply, equal to M1 plus noncheckable savings deposits and small time deposits of less than $100,000. M3 is the most broadly defined money supply, equal to M2 plus large time deposits of $100,000 or more.

Source: *Economic Report of the President, 2001,* http://w3 .access.gpo.gov/eop/, Tables 69 and 70.

Currency
$524 billion

Traveler's checks and checkable deposits
$595 billion

47%

53%

M1 = $1,119 billion

M1 = 24%

Savings deposits
$2,588 billion

21%

55%

Small time deposits
$962 billion

M2 = $4,669 billion

Large time deposits
$1,869 billion

29%

M2 = 71%

M3 = $6,538 billion

Currency.   **Currency** includes coins and paper money, officially called Federal Reserve notes that the public holds for immediate spending. The purpose of currency is to enable us to make small purchases. Currency represents 47 percent of M1.

Currency
Money, including coins and paper money.

Checkable deposits

The total of checking account balances in financial institutions convertible to currency "on demand" by writing a check without advance notice.

Checkable Deposits. Most "big ticket" purchases are paid for with checks or credit cards (which are not money), rather than currency. Checks eliminate trips to the bank, and they are safer than cash. If lost or stolen, checks and credit cards can be replaced at little cost—money cannot. Exhibit 1 shows that the largest share of M1 consists of **checkable deposits.** Checkable deposits are the total of checking account balances in financial institutions that are convertible to currency "on demand" by writing a check without advance notice. A checking account balance is a bookkeeping entry, often called a *demand deposit* because it can be converted into cash "on demand." Before the 1980s, only commercial banks could legally provide demand deposits. However, the law changed with the passage of the Depository Institutions Deregulation and Monetary Control Act of 1980. (This act will be discussed later in the chapter.) Today, checking accounts are available from many different financial institutions, such as savings and loan associations, credit unions, and mutual savings banks. For example, many people hold deposits in negotiable order of withdrawal (NOW) accounts or automatic transfer of savings (ATS) accounts, which serve as interest-bearing checking accounts. NOW and ATS accounts permit depositors to spend their deposits without a trip to the bank to withdraw funds. In January 2000, 53 percent of M1 was in traveler's checks and checkable deposits.

M2: Adding Near Monies to M1

M2

The definition of the money supply that equals M1 plus near monies, such as savings deposits and small time deposits of less than $100,000.

M2 is a broader measure of the money supply because it equals M1 plus *near money.* M1 is considered by many economists to be too narrow because it does not include near money accounts that can be used to purchase goods and services. These include passbook savings accounts, money market mutual funds, and time deposits of less than $100,000. Near monies are interest-bearing deposits easily converted into spendable funds. Written as a formula:

$$\text{M2} \;=\; \text{M1} \;+\; \text{near monies}$$

rewritten as

M2 = M1 + savings deposits + small time deposits of less than $100,000

Savings Deposits. As shown in Exhibit 1, M1 was about one-fourth of M2 in January 2000, and *savings deposits* constituted 55 percent of M2. Savings deposits are interest-bearing accounts that can be easily withdrawn. These deposits include passbook savings accounts, money market mutual funds, and other types of interest-bearing deposits with commercial banks, mutual savings banks, savings and loan associations, and credit unions.

Small Time Deposits. There is a distinction between a *checkable deposit* and a *time deposit.* A time deposit is an interest-bearing account in a financial institution that requires a withdrawal notice or must remain on deposit for a specified period unless an early withdrawal penalty is paid. Certificates of deposit are deposits for a specified time, with a penalty charged for early withdrawal. Where is the line drawn between a small and a large time deposit? The answer is that time deposits of less than $100,000 are "small" and therefore are included in M2. As shown in Exhibit 1, small time deposits were 21 percent of M2 in January 2000.

M3: Adding Large Time Deposits to M2

M3 is the measure of the money supply that equals M2 plus large time deposits. The "large" time deposits included in M3 are any CDs with a value of $100,000 or more. Expressed as a formula:

$$M3 \ = \ M2 \ + \ \textbf{large time deposits of \$100,000 or more}$$

As Exhibit 1 shows, large time deposits were 29 percent of M3, and M2 constituted the remaining 71 percent in January 2000.

The differences in the sizes of M1, M2, and M3 are substantial. As reported under each pie chart in Exhibit 1, M1 = $1,119 billion, M2 = $4,669 billion, and M3 = $6,538 billion. Here you might ask why M2 and M3 include the savings and time deposits excluded from M1. The traditional reason is that these accounts are less liquid than the items included in the narrow definition of money. Although savings accounts, time deposits, and many other assets can be transformed into cash without much difficulty, currency plus traveler's checks plus checkable deposits constitute the public's most immediately spendable forms of money.

Conclusion *M1 is more liquid than M2 or M3.*

To simplify the discussion throughout the remainder of this text, we will be referring to M1 when we discuss the money supply. However, one can argue that M2, M3, or another measurement of the money supply may be the best definition. Actually, the boundary lines for any definition of money are somewhat arbitrary.

The Federal Reserve System

Who controls the money supply in the United States? The answer is the **Federal Reserve System,** popularly called the Fed. The Fed is the central banker for the nation and provides banking services to commercial banks, other financial institutions, and the federal government. The Fed regulates, supervises, and is responsible for policies concerning money. Congress and the president consult with the Fed to control the size of the money supply and thereby influence the economy's performance.

Every major nation has a central bank. These central banks include, for example, the Bank of England, the Bank of Japan, and the European Central Bank. The movement in the United States to establish a central banking

M3
The definition of the money supply that equals M2 plus large time deposits of $100,000 or more.

The Federal Reserve (http://www.federal reserve.gov/releases/ H6/hist/) *maintains current and historical data on M1, M2, and M3 money.*

Federal Reserve System
The 12 central banks that service banks and other financial institutions within each of the Federal Reserve districts; popularly called the Fed.

The Federal Reserve (http://www.federal reserve.gov/) *issues the money we use to buy our favorite goods and services.*

system gained strength as a series of bank failures resulted in The Panic of 1907. In that year, stock prices fell, many businesses and banks failed, and millions of depositors lost their savings. The prescription for preventing financial panic was for the government to establish more centralized control over banks. This desire for more safety in banking led to the creation of the Federal Reserve System by the Federal Reserve Act of 1913 during the administration of President Woodrow Wilson. No longer would the supply of money in the economy be determined by individual banks.

The Fed's Organizational Chart

The *Federal Reserve System* is an independent agency of the federal government. Congress is responsible for overseeing the Fed, but does not interfere with its day-to-day decisions. The chair of the Fed reports to Congress twice each year and often coordinates its actions with the U.S. Treasury and the president. Although the Fed enjoys independent status, its independence can be revoked. If the Fed pursues policies contrary to the interests of the nation, Congress can abolish the Fed.

The Federal Reserve System consists of 12 central banks that service banks and other financial institutions within each of the Federal Reserve districts. Each Federal Reserve bank serves as a central banker for the private banks in its region. The United States is the only nation in the world to have 12 separate regional banks instead of a single central bank. In fact, the Fed's structure is the result of a compromise between the traditionalists, who favored a single central bank, and the populists, who distrusted concentration of financial power in the hands of a few. In addition, there are 25 Federal Reserve branch banks located throughout the country. The map in Exhibit 2 shows the 12 Federal Reserve districts.

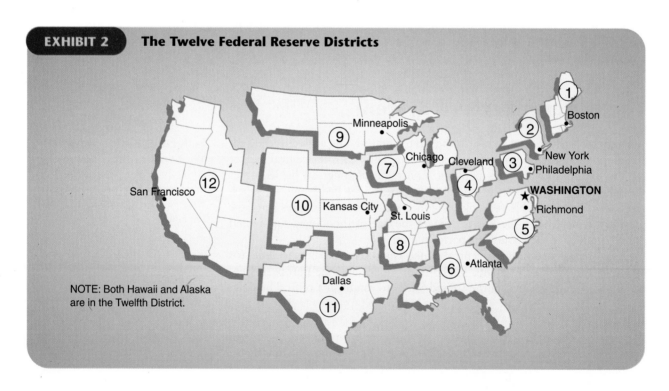

EXHIBIT 2   The Twelve Federal Reserve Districts

NOTE: Both Hawaii and Alaska are in the Twelfth District.

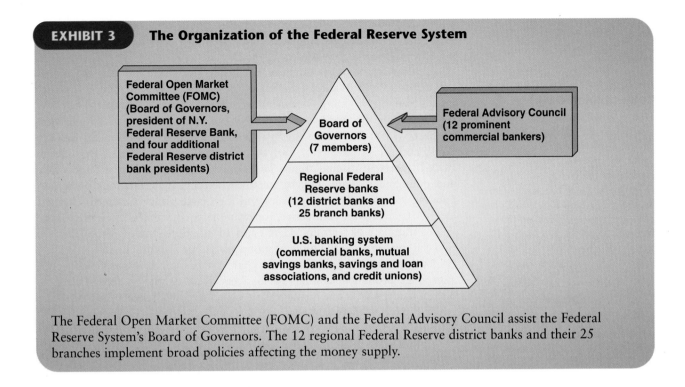

EXHIBIT 3 **The Organization of the Federal Reserve System**

Federal Open Market Committee (FOMC) (Board of Governors, president of N.Y. Federal Reserve Bank, and four additional Federal Reserve district bank presidents)

Board of Governors (7 members)

Federal Advisory Council (12 prominent commercial bankers)

Regional Federal Reserve banks (12 district banks and 25 branch banks)

U.S. banking system (commercial banks, mutual savings banks, savings and loan associations, and credit unions)

The Federal Open Market Committee (FOMC) and the Federal Advisory Council assist the Federal Reserve System's Board of Governors. The 12 regional Federal Reserve district banks and their 25 branches implement broad policies affecting the money supply.

The organizational chart of the Federal Reserve System, given in Exhibit 3, shows that the **Board of Governors,** located in Washington, D.C., administers the system. The Board of Governors is made up of seven members, appointed by the president and confirmed by the U.S. Senate, who serve for one nonrenewable 14-year term. Their responsibility is to supervise and control the money supply and the banking system of the United States. Fourteen-year terms for Fed governors create autonomy and insulate the Fed from short-term politics. These terms are staggered so one term expires every two years. This staggering of terms prevents a president from stacking the board with members favoring the incumbent party's political interests. A president usually makes two appointments in a one-term presidency and four appointments in a two-term presidency. The president designates one member of the Board of Governors to serve as chair for a four-year term. The chair is the principal spokesperson for the Fed and has considerable power over policy decisions. In fact, it is often argued that the Fed's chair is the most powerful individual in the United States next to the president. The current chair is Alan Greenspan, who was originally appointed by President Reagan in 1987, reappointed by President George Bush, and reappointed twice by President Clinton.

The Federal Reserve System receives no funding from Congress. This creates financial autonomy for the Fed by removing the fear of congressional review of its budget. Then where does the Fed get funds to operate? Recall from Exhibit 7 of the previous chapter that the Fed holds government securities issued by the U.S. Treasury. The Fed earns interest income from the government securities it holds and the loans it makes to depository institutions. Because the Fed returns any profits to the Treasury, it is motivated to adopt policies to promote the economy's well-being, rather than earning a

Board of Governors of the Federal Reserve System
The seven members appointed by the president and confirmed by the U.S. Senate who serve for one nonrenewable 14-year term. Their responsibility is to supervise and control the money supply and the banking system of the United States.

Federal Open Market Committee (FOMC)

The Federal Reserve's committee that directs the buying and selling of U.S. Government securities, which are major instruments for controlling the money supply. The FOMC consists of the seven members of the Federal Reserve's Board of Governors, the president of the New York Federal Reserve Bank, and the presidents of four other Federal Reserve district banks.

profit. Moreover, the Board of Governors does not take orders from the president or any other politician. Thus, the Board of Governors is the independent, self-supporting authority of the Federal Reserve System.

On the left side of the organizational chart in Exhibit 3 is the very important **Federal Open Market Committee (FOMC)**. The FOMC directs the buying and selling of U.S. government securities, which are major instruments for controlling the money supply. The FOMC consists of the seven members of the Board of Governors, the president of the New York Federal Reserve Bank, and the presidents of four other Federal Reserve district banks. The FOMC meets to discuss trends in inflation, unemployment, growth rates, and other macro data. FOMC members express their opinions on implementing various monetary policies and then issue policy statements known as *FOMC directives*. A directive, for example, might set the operation of the Fed to stimulate or restrain M1 in order to influence employment. The next two chapters explain the tools of monetary policy in more detail.

As shown on the right side of the chart, the *Federal Advisory Council* consists of 12 prominent commercial bankers. Each of the 12 Federal Reserve district banks selects one member each year. The council meets periodically to advise the Board of Governors.

Finally, at the bottom of the organizational chart is the remainder of the Federal Reserve System, consisting of only about 3,000 of the approximately 8,000 commercial banks in the United States. Although these 3,000 Fed member banks represent only about one-third of U.S. banks, they have about 70 percent of all U.S. bank deposits. A sure sign of Fed membership is the word *National* in a bank's name. The U.S. comptroller of the currency charters national banks, and they are required to be Fed members. Banks that do not have "National" in their title can also be Fed members. States can also charter banks, and these state banks have the option of joining the Federal Reserve. Less than 20 percent of state banks choose to join the Fed.

Nonmember depository institutions, including many commercial banks, savings and loan associations (S&Ls), savings banks, and credit unions, are not official members of the Fed team. They are, however, influenced by and depend on the Fed for a variety of services, which we will now discuss.

What a Federal Reserve Bank Does

The Federal Reserve (http://www.federal reserve.gov/pf/pf.htm) *describes its purposes and functions.*

The typical bank customer never enters the doors of a Federal Reserve district bank or one of its branch banks. The reason is that the Fed does not offer the public checking accounts, savings accounts, or any of the services provided by commercial banks. Instead, the Federal Reserve serves as a "banker's bank." Following are brief descriptions of some of the principal functions of the Federal Reserve.

Controlling the Money Supply

The primary role of the Fed is to control the nation's money supply. The mechanics of Fed control over the money supply are explained in the next two chapters. To most people, this is a wondrously mysterious process. So that you do not suffer in complete suspense, here is a sneak preview: The Fed has three policy tools or levers it can use to change the stock of money in the banking system. The potential macro outcome of changes in the money supply is to affect total spending and therefore real GDP, employment, and the price level.

Clearing Checks

Because most people and businesses use checks to pay for goods and services, check clearing is an important function. Suppose you live in Virginia and have a checking account with a bank in that state. While on vacation in California, you purchase tickets to Disneyland with a check for $100. Disneyland accepts your check and then deposits it in its business checking account in a California bank. This bank must collect payment for your check and does so by giving the check to the Federal Reserve bank in San Francisco. From there, your check is sent to the Federal Reserve bank in Richmond. At each stop along its journey, the check earns a black stamp mark on the back. Finally, the process ends when $100 is subtracted from your personal checking account. Banks in which checks are deposited have their Fed accounts credited, and banks on which checks are written have their accounts debited. The Fed clearinghouse process is much speedier than depending on the movement of a check between commercial banks.

Supervising and Regulating Banks

The Fed examines banks' books, sets limits for loans, and approves bank mergers and works with the **Federal Deposit Insurance Corporation (FDIC)**. The FDIC is a government agency established by Congress in 1933 to insure commercial bank deposits up to a specified limit. Congress created the FDIC in response to the huge number of bank failures during the Great Depression and set the insurance limit at $25,000. If the government provides a safety net, people are less likely to panic and withdraw their funds from banks during a period of economic uncertainty. When deposits are insured and a bank fails, the government stands ready to pay depositors or transfers their deposits to a solvent bank. Banks that are members of the Fed are members of the FDIC. State agencies supervise state-chartered banks that are not members of either the Federal Reserve System or the FDIC. Today, the FDIC insures customers' deposits up to $100,000 per bank account.

Federal Deposit Insurance Corporation (FDIC)
A government agency established in 1933 to insure commercial bank deposits up to a specified limit.

For more information about the FDIC, visit its website (http://www .fdic.gov/).

Maintaining and Circulating Currency

Note that the Fed does *not* print currency—it *maintains and circulates* money. All Federal Reserve notes are printed at the Bureau of Engraving and Printing's facilities in Washington, D.C., and Fort Worth, Texas. The Treasury mints and issues all coins. Coins are made at U.S. mints located in Philadelphia and Denver. The bureau and the mints ship new notes and coins to the Federal Reserve banks for circulation. Much of this money is printed or minted simply to replace worn-out bills and coins. Another use of new currency is to meet public demand. Suppose it is the holiday season and banks need more paper money and coins to meet their customers' shopping needs. The Federal Reserve must be ready to ship extra money from its large vaults by armored truck.

Protecting Consumers

Since 1968, the Federal Reserve has issued several consumer protection regulations. Perhaps the most important is the *Equal Credit Opportunity Act*, which prohibits discrimination based on race, color, sex, marital status, religion, or national origin in the extension of credit. It also gives married women the right to establish credit histories in their own names. The Federal Reserve receives and tries to resolve consumer complaints against banks.

Maintaining Federal Government Checking Accounts and Gold

The Fed is also Uncle Sam's bank. The U.S. Treasury has the Fed handle its checking account. From this account, the federal government pays for such expenses as federal employees' salaries, Social Security, tax refunds, veterans' benefits, defense, and highways.

Finally, it is interesting to note that the New York Federal Reserve District Bank holds one of the oldest forms of money—*gold*. This gold belongs mainly to foreign governments and is one of the largest accumulations of this precious metal in the world. Viewing a federal reserve bank's vault is not something that most tourists typically have on their list of things to do, but I strongly recommend this tour.

The gold vault at the New York Federal Reserve Bank is nearly half the length of a football field and filled with steel and concrete walls several yards thick. Most cells contain the gold of only one nation, and only a few bank employees know the identities of the owners. When trade occurs between two countries, payment between the parties can be made by transferring gold bars from one compartment to another. Note that the Fed and the monetary system of the Yapese have a similarity. Recall from the International Economics box that in Yap large stone wheels are not moved; rather they just change ownership.

The U.S. Banking Revolution

Prior to the 1980s, the U.S. banking system was simpler. It consisted of many commercial banks authorized by law to offer checking accounts. Then there were the other financial institutions, the so-called thrifts, which include S&Ls, mutual savings banks, and credit unions. The thrifts by law were permitted to accept only savings deposits with no checking privileges. The commercial banks, on the other hand, could not pay interest on checkable deposits. Moreover, a "maximum interest rate allowed by law" limited competition among commercial banks and other financial institutions. As will be explained momentarily, this relatively tranquil U.S. banking structure changed dramatically, and the stage was set for a fascinating banking "horror story."

The Monetary Control Act of 1980

Monetary Control Act

A law, formally titled the Depository Institutions Deregulation and Monetary Control Act of 1980, that gave the Federal Reserve System greater control over nonmember banks and made all financial institutions more competitive.

A significant law affecting the U.S. banking system is the Depository Institutions Deregulation and Monetary Control Act of 1980, commonly called the **Monetary Control Act.** This law gave the Federal Reserve System greater control over nonmember banks and made all financial institutions more competitive. The act's major provisions are the following.

1. The authority of the Fed over nonmember depository institutions was increased. Prior to the Monetary Control Act, only about 6,000 of the 15,000 banks in the United States were members of the Fed and subject to its direct control. Under the new provisions, the Federal Reserve sets uniform reserve requirements for *all* commercial banks, including state and national banks, S&Ls, and credit unions with checking accounts.

2. All depository institutions are able to borrow loan reserves from Federal Reserve banks. This practice, called *discounting,* will be explained in the next chapter. Banks also have access to check clearing and other services of the Fed.

3. The act allows commercial banks, thrifts, money market mutual funds, stock brokerage firms, and retailers to offer a wide variety of banking services. For example, commercial banks and other financial institutions can pay unrestricted interest rates on checking accounts. Also, S&Ls and other financial institutions can offer checking accounts. Federal credit unions are authorized to make residential real estate loans, and other major corporations can offer traditional banking services.

4. The Monetary Control Act eliminated all interest rate ceilings. Before this act, S&Ls were allowed to pay depositors a slightly higher interest rate on passbook savings deposits than those paid by commercial banks. The Monetary Control Act removed this advantage of S&Ls over other financial institutions competing for depositors.

Finally, the movement toward deregulation, which blurred the distinctions between financial institutions, continued. In 1999, the *Financial Services Modernization Act* was signed into law. This sweeping measure lifted Depression-era barriers and allows banks, securities firms and insurance companies to merge and sell each other's products.

The Savings and Loan Crisis

The savings and loan crisis of the 1980s and early 1990s has been called the worst U.S. financial crisis since the Great Depression. After the Monetary Control Act removed interest rate ceilings on deposits, competition for customers forced S&Ls to pay higher interest rates on short-term deposits. Unlike the banks, however, S&Ls were earning their income from long-term mortgages at fixed interest rates below the rate required to keep or attract new deposits. The resulting losses enticed the S&Ls to forsake home mortgage loans, which they knew best, and seek high-interest, but riskier, commercial and consumer loans. Unfortunately, these risky higher-interest loans resulted in defaults and more losses. If conditions were not bad enough, lower oil prices depressed the oil-based state economies in Texas, Louisiana, and Oklahoma.

The *Federal Savings and Loan Insurance Corporation (FSLIC)* was the agency that insured deposits in S&Ls, similar to the FDIC for banks. The magnitude of the losses exceeded the insurance fund's ability to pay depositors, and Congress placed the FSLIC's deposit-insurance fund under the FDIC's control. To close or sell ailing S&Ls and protect depositors, Congress

The Wreck of Lincoln Savings and Loan

Applicable Concept: deposit insurance

The case of Lincoln Savings and Loan is a classic example that illustrates some of the causes of the most recent U.S. financial crisis. In 1984, the Securities and Exchange Commission charged Charles Keating, Jr., with fraud in an Ohio loan scam, but regulators later allowed him to buy Lincoln Savings and Loan in California. Keating hired a staff to carry out his wishes and paid them well. His top executives and relatives made millions, and secretaries were paid over $50,000 per year. Keating was also generous with politicians in Washington, D.C. Allegedly, five U.S. senators received $1.5 million in campaign contributions from Keating to influence regulators.

Where did Keating's money come from? It came from Lincoln Savings depositors and, ultimately, from taxpayers because the federal government insures deposits of failed S&Ls. When Keating took over Lincoln, it was a healthy S&L with assets of $1.1 billion. But because of deregulation mandated by the Monetary Control Act and other legislation and the lack of enforcement of regulations under the new laws, many S&Ls plunged into high-risk, but potentially highly profitable, ventures. Keating therefore took Lincoln out of sound home mortgage loans and into speculation in Arizona hotels costing $500,000 per room to build, raw land for golf courses, shopping centers, junk bonds, and currency futures.

In 1987, after it was already too late, California regulators became alarmed at the way Lincoln operated and asked the FBI and the FSLIC to take over Lincoln. Keating responded by contacting his friends in Washington, and the regulatory process moved at a snail's pace. Years passed before the government finally closed Lincoln and informed the public their deposits were not safe in this S&L. During the time regulators were deciding what action to take, it is estimated that Lincoln cost taxpayers another $1 billion. Ultimately, the collapse of Lincoln cost U.S. taxpayers about $3 billion, making it the most expensive S&L failure of all.

Keating and other S&L entrepreneurs say they did nothing wrong. After all, Congress and federal regulators encouraged—or did not discourage—S&Ls to compete by borrowing funds at high interest rates and making risky, but potentially highly profitable, investments. If oil prices

and land values fall unexpectedly and loans fail, this is simply the way a market economy works and not the fault of risk-prone wheeler-dealers like Keating.

In 1993, a federal judge sentenced Keating to 12 1/2 years in prison for swindling small investors. The sentence ran concurrently with a 10-year state prison sentence. The judge also ordered Keating to pay $122.4 million in restitution to the government for losses caused by sham property sales. However, the government has been unable to locate any significant assets.

ANALYZE THE ISSUE

Critics of federal banking policy argue that deposit insurance is a key reason for banking failures. The banks enjoy a "heads I win, tails the government loses" proposition. Several possible reforms of deposit insurance have been suggested. For example, the $100,000 limit on insured deposits could be reduced or eliminated. Do you think a change in deposit insurance would prevent future Lincoln Savings and Loan–type bankruptcies?

enacted the Financial Institutions Reform, Recovery, and Enforcement Act of 1989 (FIRREA), better known as the Thrift Bailout Bill. One provision of this act required thrifts to invest a higher minimum percentage of their assets in long-term housing loans and to divest themselves of certain risky assets.

Another provision created the Resolution Trust Corporation (RTC) to carry out a massive federal bailout of failed institutions. The RTC bought the assets and deposits of failed S&Ls and sold them to offset the cost borne by taxpayers. The RTC closed in 1995, and the ultimate cost to taxpayers totaled over $300 billion!

KEY CONCEPTS

Barter	Commodity money	Federal Reserve System	Federal Deposit Insurance
Money	Fiat money	Board of Governors	Corporation (FDIC)
Medium of exchange	M1, M2, M3	Federal Open Market	Monetary Control Act
Unit of account	Currency	Committee (FOMC)	
Store of value	Checkable deposits		

SUMMARY

- **Money** can be anything that meets these three tests. Money must serve as (1) a medium of exchange, (2) a unit of account, and (3) a store of value. Money facilitates more efficient exchange than barter. Other desirable properties of money include scarcity, portability, divisibility, and uniformity.

- **Medium of exchange** is the most important function of money. This means that money is widely accepted in payment for goods and services.

- **Unit of account** is another important function of money. Money is used to measure relative values by serving as a common yardstick for valuing goods and services.

- **Store of value** is the ability of money to hold its value over time. Money is said to be highly *liquid*, which means it is readily usable in exchange.

- **Credit cards** are not money. Credit cards represent a short-term loan and therefore fail as a store of value.

- **Commodity money** is money that has a marketable value, such as gold and silver. Today, the United States uses *fiat money*, which must be accepted by law, but is not convertible into gold, silver, or any commodity.

- **M1** is the narrowest definition of money, which equals currency plus traveler's checks plus checkable deposits. **M2** is a broader definition of money, which equals M1 plus *near monies*, such as savings deposits and small time deposits. **M3** is an even broader definition of money, which equals M2 plus large time deposits of more than $100,000 or more.

Definitions of money supply (M1, M2, and M3)

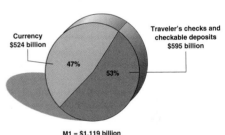

Currency $524 billion

Traveler's checks and checkable deposits $595 billion

47% 53%

M1 = $1,119 billion

M1 = 24%

Savings deposits $2,588 billion

21% 55%

Small time deposits $962 billion

M2 = $4,669 billion

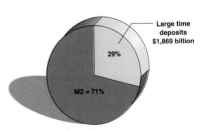

Large time deposits $1,869 billion

29%

M2 = 71%

M3 = $6,538 billion

- The **Federal Reserve System,** our central bank, was established in 1913. The Fed consists of 12 Federal Reserve district banks with 25 branches. The *Board of Governors* is the Fed's governing body. The *Federal Open Market Committee (FOMC)* directs the buying and selling of U.S. government securities, which is a key method of controlling the money supply.

- **Basic Federal Reserve bank functions** are (1) controlling the money supply, (2) clearing checks, (3) supervising and regulating banking, (4) maintaining and circulating currency, (5) protecting consumers, and (6) maintaining the federal government's checking accounts and gold.

- The **Monetary Control Act of 1980** revolutionized U.S. banking by expanding the authority of the Federal Reserve System to all financial institutions. In addition, this law increased competition by blurring the distinction among commercial banks, thrift institutions, and even nonfinancial institutions.

SUMMARY OF CONCLUSION STATEMENTS

- The use of money simplifies and therefore increases market transactions. Money also prevents wasting time that can be devoted to production, thereby promoting economic growth by increasing a nation's production possibilities.

- Money is a useful mechanism for transforming income in the present into future purchases.

- Money is the most liquid form of wealth because it can be spent directly in the marketplace.

- The supply of money must be great enough to meet ordinary transaction needs, but not be so plentiful that it becomes worthless.

- Whether or not an item will serve as money does not depend on its own market value or the backing of precious metal.

- M1 is more liquid than M2 or M3.

STUDY QUESTIONS AND PROBLEMS

1. Discuss this statement: "A man with a million dollars who is lost in the desert learns the meaning of money."

2. Could each of the following items potentially serve as money? Consider each as (1) a medium of exchange, (2) a unit of account, and (3) a store of value.
   a. Visa credit card
   b. Federal Reserve note
   c. Dog
   d. Beer mug

3. Consider each of the items in question 2 in terms of scarcity, portability, divisibility, and uniformity.

4. What backs the U.S. dollar? Include the distinction between commodity money and fiat money in your answer.

5. What are the components of the most narrowly defined money supply in the United States?

6. Distinguish between M1 and M2. What are near monies?

7. What is the major purpose of the Federal Reserve System? What is the major responsibility of the Board of Governors and the Federal Open Market Committee?

8. Should the Fed be independent or a government agency?

9. Which banks must be insured by the FDIC? Which banks can choose not to be insured by the FDIC?

10. Briefly discuss the importance of the Depository Institutions Deregulation and Monetary Control Act of 1980.

ONLINE EXERCISES

Exercise 1

Browse The History of Money (http://woodrow.mpls.frb .fed.us/econed/curric/history.html). Whose picture was on the $10,000 bill?

Exercise 2

Visit the Federal Reserve Board Testimony and Speeches (http://www.federalreserve.gov/s-t.htm) and click on Testimony of Federal Reserve Officials. Review the most recent testimony by Chairman Alan Greenspan.

Exercise 3

Think about the credit card applications you receive in the mail, or visit MasterCard (http://www.mastercard.com/). Is it clear from these advertisements that credit cards are not money?

Exercise 4

Go to The Federal Reserve (http://www.federalreserve .gov/releases/H6/hist/) data on M1, M2, and M3 money. What are the current measures of M1, M2 and M3 in recent months?

CHECKPOINT ANSWER

Are Debit Cards Money?

Debit cards serve as a means of payment, and debit card statements serve as a unit of account. Finally, unlike credit cards, debit cards serve as a store of value because they are not an extension of credit. If you said debit cards are money because they serve all three functions required for money, YOU ARE CORRECT.

PRACTICE QUIZ

For a visual explanation of the correct answers, visit the tutorial at http://tucker.swcollege.com.

1. Which of the following is a problem with barter?
   a. Individuals will not exchange goods.
   b. Individuals' wants must coincide in order for there to be exchange.
   c. Goods can be exchanged, but services cannot.
   d. None of the above is a problem.

2. Which of the following is *not* a characteristic of money?
   a. It provides a way to measure the relative value of goods and services.
   b. It is always backed by something of high intrinsic value such as gold or silver.
   c. It is generally acceptable as a medium of exchange.
   d. It allows for saving and borrowing.

3. Which of the following is a *not* a store of value?
   a. Dollar.
   b. Money market mutual fund share
   c. Checking account balance
   d. Credit card

4. The easier it is to convert an asset directly into goods and services without loss, the
   a. less secure it is.
   b. more secure it is.
   c. more liquid it is.
   d. less liquid it is.

5. M1 refers to
   a. the most narrowly defined money supply.
   b. currency held by the public plus checking account balances and traveler's checks.
   c. the smallest dollar amount of the money supply definitions.
   d. all of the above.

6. The M1 definition of the money supply includes
   a. coins and currency in circulation.
   b. coins and currency in circulation, checkable deposits, and traveler's checks.
   c. Federal Reserve notes, gold certificates, and checkable deposits.
   d. Federal Reserve notes and bank loans.

7. Which of the following items is *not* included when computing M1?
   a. Coins in circulation
   b. Currency in circulation

   c. Savings accounts
   d. Checking account entries

8. Which one of the following is part of the M2 definition of the money supply, but not part of M1?
   a. Traveler's checks
   b. Currency held in banks
   c. Currency in circulation
   d. Money market mutual fund shares

9. Which of the following is *not* part of M1?
   a. Checking accounts
   b. Coins
   c. Credit cards
   d. Traveler's checks
   e. Paper currency.

10. Which definition of the money supply includes credit cards, or "plastic money"?
    a. M1
    b. M2
    c. M3
    d. All of the above
    e. None of the above

11. Which of these institutions has the responsibility to control the money supply?
    a. Commercial banks
    b. Congress
    c. U.S. Treasury Department
    d. Federal Reserve System

12. Which of the following is *not* one of the functions of the Federal Reserve?
    a. Clearing checks
    b. Printing currency
    c. Supervising and regulating banks
    d. Controlling the money supply

13. Which of the following is in charge of the buying and selling of government securities by the Fed?
    a. The president
    b. Federal Open Market Committee (FOMC)
    c. Congress
    d. None of the above

14. The major protection against sudden mass attempts to withdraw cash from banks is the
    a. Federal Reserve.
    b. Consumer Protection Act.
    c. deposit insurance provided by the FDIC.
    d. gold and silver backing the dollar.

CHAPTER 25

Money Creation

It has been said that the most important person in Washington, D.C., is the chair of the Federal Reserve because he or she can influence the money supply and therefore the performance of the economy. This chapter builds on your knowledge of money and the Federal Reserve System gained in the previous chapter. You will discover that the Federal Reserve (the Fed) and the banks work together to determine the money supply. The chapter begins with a brief history of the evolution of banking. Then we examine the mechanics of how banks create money in a simplified system. This remarkable process depends on the ability of banks to amplify checkable deposits by generating a spiral of new loans and, in turn, deposits for new spending in the economy. Finally, the Fed's toolkit swings open, and we discuss the three tools used by the Fed to change the money supply.

A common misconception is that banks (including savings and loans and other depository institutions) accept deposits and make loans, and that's about the end of the story. But there is another very important chapter to tell. Banking transactions expand or contract the money supply. Without minting coins or using the printing presses to make paper money, your local bank and other banks can create money; that is, banks can increase the money supply (M1).

The reason people do not understand money creation is that they think the federal government controls the money supply by turning the printing presses on and off. As explained in the previous chapter, this notion is only partly true because money consists primarily of bookkeeping entries, rather than pieces of paper and coins. Consequently, writing checks, using an automatic teller machine, and getting a loan affect the size of the checkable deposits component of the money supply.

In this chapter, you will learn to solve these economics puzzles:

■ Exactly how is money created in the economy? That is, how does the money supply increase?

■ What are the major tools the Federal Reserve uses to control the supply of money?

■ Why is there nothing "federal" about the federal funds rate?

Money Creation Begins

To explore banking on the Internet, visit Wells Fargo bank (http://www .wellsfargo.com/), or visit Providian bank (http://www.providian .com/). There are several online publications providing research and analysis of financial institutions like American Banker *(http://www.americanbanker.com/ PSUser/) and* ABA Banking Journal *(http://www.banking.com/aba/).*

In the Middle Ages, gold was the money of choice in most European nations. One of the problems with gold is that it is a heavy commodity, which makes it difficult to use in transactions or to hide from thieves. The medieval solution was to keep it safely deposited with the people who worked with gold, called *goldsmiths*. This demand for their services inspired goldsmith entrepreneurs to become the founders of modern-day banking.

The goldsmiths sat on their benches with ledgers close by and recorded the amounts of gold placed in their vaults. In fact, the word *bank* is derived from the Italian word for bench, which is *banco*. After assessing the purity of the gold, a goldsmith issued a receipt to the customer for the amount of gold deposited. In return, the goldsmith collected a service charge, just as you pay today for services at your bank. Anyone who possessed the receipt and presented it to the goldsmith could make a withdrawal for the amount of gold written on the receipt.

With these gold receipts in circulation, people began paying their debts with these pieces of paper, rather than actually exchanging gold. Thus, goldsmith receipts became paper money. At first, the goldsmiths were very conservative and issued receipts exactly equal to the amount of gold stored in their vaults. However, some shrewd goldsmiths observed that net withdrawals in any period were only a *fraction* of all the gold "on reserve." This observation produced a powerful idea. Goldsmiths discovered that they could make loans for more gold than they actually held in their vaults. As a result, goldsmiths made extra profit from interest on loans, and borrowers had more money for spending in their hands.

How a Single Bank Creates Money

Fractional reserve banking
A system in which banks keep only a percentage of their deposits on reserve as vault cash and deposits at the Fed.

The medieval goldsmiths were the first to practice **fractional reserve banking**. Modern fractional reserve banking is a system in which banks keep only a percentage of their deposits on reserve as vault cash and deposits at the Fed. In a 100 percent reserve banking system, banks would be unable to create money by making loans. However, as you will learn momentarily, holding less than 100 percent on reserve allows banks to make loans and, in turn, to create money in the economy.

TYPICAL BANK Balance Sheet 1

Assets		Liabilities	
Required reserves	$ 5 million	Checkable deposits	$50 million
Excess reserves	0		
Loans	45 million		
Total	$50 million	Total	$50 million

Note: The Fed requires the bank to keep 10 percent of its checkable deposits in reserves. Holding $5 million in required reserves, the bank has zero excess reserves and $45 million in loans to earn profit.

Banker Bookkeeping

We begin our exploration of how the fractional reserve banking system operates in the United States by looking at the balance sheet of a single bank, Typical Bank. A balance sheet is a statement of the assets and liabilities of a bank at a given point in time. Balance sheets are called *T-accounts*. The hypothetical T-account of Typical Bank in Balance Sheet 1 lists only major categories and omits details to keep things simple.

On the right side of the balance sheet are the bank's *liabilities*. Liabilities are the amounts the bank owes to others. In our example, the only liabilities are *checkable deposits*, or demand deposits. Note that checkable deposits are assets on the customers' personal balance sheets, but they are debt obligations of Typical Bank. If a depositor writes a check against his or her checking account, the bank must pay this amount. Therefore, checkable deposits are liabilities to the bank.

On the left side of the balance sheet, we see Typical Bank's *assets*. Assets are amounts the bank owns. In our example, these assets consist of **required reserves**, *excess reserves*, and *loans*. Required reserves are the minimum balance that the Fed requires a bank to hold in vault cash or on deposit with the Fed. Note that the Fed is a Scrooge and pays no interest on reserves held with the Fed. And because reserves earn no return, Typical Bank will maximize profits by trying to keep only the minimum amount possible in required reserves.

The **required reserve ratio** determines the minimum required reserves. The required reserve ratio is the percentage of deposits that the Fed requires a bank to hold in vault cash or on deposit with the Fed. Here we assume that the Fed's required reserve ratio is 10 percent. Thus, the bank must have required reserves of $5 million (10 percent of $50 million). This leaves Typical Bank with $45 million in loans that provide profit to the bank.

Exhibit 1 shows that the actual required reserve ratio depends on the level of a bank's checkable deposits. Note that the Fed requires a lower percentage for a smaller bank. In the real world, Typical Bank's required reserve ratio would be 3 percent if its checkable deposits were at or below $42.8 million. Above $42.8 million in checkable deposits, the required reserve ratio is 10 percent.

Required reserves

The minimum balance that the Fed requires a bank to hold in vault cash or on deposit with the Fed.

Required reserve ratio

The percentage of deposits that the Fed requires a bank to hold in vault cash or on deposit with the Fed.

EXHIBIT 1 Required Reserve Ratio of the Federal Reserve

Type of deposit	Required reserve ratio
Checkable deposits	
0–$42.8 million	3%
Over $42.8 million	10

Source: *Federal Reserve Bulletin,* March 2001, Table 1.15, p. A8.

Excess reserves

Potential loan balances held in vault cash or on deposit with the Fed in excess of required reserves.

Typical Bank has zero **excess reserves** so far in our analysis. Excess reserves are potential loan balances held in vault cash or on deposit with the Fed in excess of required reserves. We will see shortly that excess reserves play a starring role in the banking system's ability to change the money supply. The relationship between reserves accounts can be expressed as follows:

$$\text{total reserves} = \text{required reserves} + \text{excess reserves}$$

or

$$\text{excess reserves} = \text{total reserves} - \text{required reserves}$$

The final entry on the asset side of Typical Bank's balance sheet is loans, which are interest-earning assets of the bank. Loans are bank assets because they represent outstanding credit payable to the bank. In a fractional reserve banking system, the bank uses balances not held in reserves to earn income. In our example, loan officers have written loans totaling $45 million. Finally, note that Typical Bank's assets equal its liabilities. As you will see momentarily, any change on one side of the T-account must be accompanied by an equal amount of change on the other side of the balance sheet.

Step One: Accepting a New Deposit

You are now prepared to see how a bank creates money. Assume the required reserve ratio is 10 percent and one of Best National Bank's depositors, Brad Rich, takes $100,000 in cash from under his mattress and deposits it in his checking account. Balance Sheet 2 records this change by increasing the bank's checkable deposits on the liability side by $100,000. Brad's deposit is a liability of the bank because Brad could change his mind and withdraw his money. On the asset side, Brad's deposit increases assets because the bank has an extra $90,000 to lend after setting aside the proper amount of required reserves. Balance Sheet 2 shows that total reserves are divided between required reserves of $10,000 (10 percent of the deposit) and excess reserves of $90,000 (90 percent of the deposit). Thus, the bank's assets and liabilities remain equal when Brad makes his deposit.

Before proceeding, we must pause to make an important point. Depositing coins or paper currency in a bank has no initial effect on the money supply (M1). Recall from the previous chapter that M1 includes currency in cir-

BEST NATIONAL BANK	Balance Sheet 2		
Assets	**Liabilities**		**Change in M1**
Required reserves +$ 10,000	Brad Rich account +$100,000		0
Excess reserves + 90,000			
Total $100,000	Total	$100,000	

Step 1: Brad Rich deposits $100,000 in cash, which increases checkable deposits. The Fed requires the bank to keep 10 percent of its new deposit in required reserves, so this account is credited with $10,000. The remaining 90 percent is excess reserves of $90,000. There is no effect on the money supply.

culation. Therefore, the transfer of $100,000 in cash from the mattress to the bank creates no money because M1 already counts this amount. Moreover, the money supply would *not* have increased had Brad Rich's initial $100,000 deposit been a check written on another bank. In this case, an increase in the assets and liabilities of Best National Bank by $100,000 would simply decrease the assets and liabilities of the other bank by $100,000. Recall that M1 also includes checkable deposits.

Conclusion *Transferring currency to a bank and moving deposits from one bank to another do not affect the money supply (M1).*

Step Two: Making a Loan

So far, M1 has not changed, as shown in Balance Sheet 2, because Brad has simply taken $100,000 in currency and transferred it to a checkable deposit. Stated differently, the public holds the same $100,000 for spending, and only the composition has changed from cash to a checkable deposit. In step two, the actual money creation process occurs. The profit motive provides the incentive for bank officials not to let $90,000 from a new deposit sit languishing in excess reserves. Instead, Best National Bank is eager to make loans and earn a profit by charging interest. Suppose, coincidentally, that Connie Jones walks in with a big smile, asking for a $90,000 loan to purchase equipment for her health spa. Connie has a fine credit record, so the bank accepts Connie's note (IOU) agreeing to repay the loan. As shown in Balance Sheet 3, three entries on the assets side have changed. First, the loan to Connie Jones boosts the loans account to $90,000. Second, the bank must increase required reserves by $9,000 because of the $90,000 increase in checkable deposits on the liabilities side. (Recall that required reserves are 10 percent of checkable deposits.) Third, transferring $9,000 from excess reserves to required reserves reduces the bank's excess reserves from $90,000 to $81,000. Total reserves remain at $100,000 in both Balance Sheet 2 and Balance Sheet 3.

The corresponding entry on the liabilities side of the balance sheet is the bread and butter of money creation. Checkable deposits have increased by

The Federal Deposit Insurance Corporation (FDIC) educates the public about banks, banking, and the FDIC (http://www.fdic.gov/).

BEST NATIONAL BANK Balance Sheet 3				
Assets		**Liabilities**		**Change in M1**
Required reserves	$ 19,000	Brad Rich account	$100,000	
Excess reserves	81,000	Connie Jones account	+90,000	$90,000
Loans	+90,000			
Total	$190,000	Total	$190,000	

Step 2: The bank loans Connie Jones $90,000 by crediting her checking account with this amount. A corresponding $90,000 balance is added to the loan account. The result is an increase in the money supply of $90,000.

$90,000 to $190,000. The reason is that the bank issued a check in Connie's name drawn on a checking account in the bank. Thus, Best National Bank has performed money magic with this transaction. Look what happened to the $100,000 deposited by Brad Rich. It has generated a new $90,000 *loan*, which promptly added this amount to checkable deposits and therefore increased the money supply by $90,000.

> **Conclusion** *When a bank makes a loan, it creates deposits, and the money supply increases by the amount of the loan because the money supply includes checkable deposits.*

Before proceeding further, you need to pause and take a breath. After resting, take particular notice of the impact of these transactions on the money supply. In step one, Brad's initial deposit did not change M1. But in step two, M1 increased by $90,000 when Best National Bank created money out of thin air by making the loan to Connie Jones. Now Connie has more money in her checking account than she did before, and no one else has less. Connie can now use this money to buy goods and services.

Step Three: Clearing the Loan Check

Now Connie Jones can use her new money to purchase equipment for her spa. Suppose Connie buys equipment for her business from Better Health Spa and writes a check for $90,000 drawn on Best National Bank. The owner of Better Health Spa then deposits the check in the firm's account at Yazoo National Bank. Yazoo National will send the check to its Federal Reserve district bank for collection. Recall that each bank maintains reserves at the Fed. The Fed clears the check by debiting the reserve account of Best National Bank and crediting the reserve account of Yazoo National Bank. The Fed then returns the check to Best National Bank, and this bank reduces Connie Jones's checking account by $90,000. As shown in Balance Sheet 4, Connie Jones's checking account falls to zero, and Best National Bank's liabilities are reduced by $90,000. On the asset side of the balance sheet, required reserves decrease by $9,000, and excess reserves return to

BEST NATIONAL BANK　Balance Sheet 4

Assets		Liabilities		Change in M1
Required reserves	$ 10,000	Brad Rich account	$100,000	0
Excess reserves	0	Connie Jones account	0	
Loan	90,000			
Total	$100,000	Total	$100,000	

Step 3: Connie Jones pays Better Health Spa with a $90,000 check drawn on Best National Bank. Better Health Spa deposits the check in Yazoo National Bank, which collects from Best National Bank. The result is a debit to Connie's account and her bank's reserves accounts.

zero. Now that all the dust has settled, Best National Bank has required reserves of $10,000 and an IOU for $90,000. Note that this check-clearing process in step three has no effect on M1. The $90,000 increase in M1 created by Best National Bank's loan to Connie remains on deposit at Yazoo National Bank in Better Health Spa's checking account.

Finally, if Brad Rich withdraws $100,000 in cash from Best National Bank, the process described above operates in reverse. The result is a $90,000 decline (destruction) in the money supply.

Multiplier Expansion of Money by the Banking System

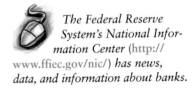

The Federal Reserve System's National Information Center (http://www.ffiec.gov/nic/) *has news, data, and information about banks.*

The process of money creation (loans) does not stop at the doors of Best National Bank. Just like the spending multiplier from the chapter on fiscal policy, there is a money multiplier process. Let's continue our story by following the effect on Yazoo National after Better Health Spa deposits $90,000 from Connie Jones. As shown in Balance Sheet 5, Yazoo National's checkable deposits increase by $90,000. Given a required reserve ratio of 10 percent, Yazoo National Bank must keep $9,000 in required reserves, and the remaining $81,000 go into excess reserves.

Yazoo National's loan officer now has $81,000 in additional excess reserves to lend and thus create additional checkable deposits, excess reserves, and eventually loans in other banks. Exhibit 2 presents the expansion of the money supply created when Brad Rich makes his initial $100,000 deposit and then banks make loans that are deposited in other banks.

In Exhibit 2, we see that, lo and behold, an initial deposit of $100,000 in Best National Bank can eventually create a $900,000 increase in the money supply (M1). This is because Brad Rich's initial $100,000 deposit eventually

YAZOO NATIONAL BANK Balance Sheet 5			
Assets		**Liabilities**	
Required reserves	+$ 9,000	Better Health Spa account	+$90,000
Excess reserves	+ 81,000		
Total	$90,000	Total	$90,000

Note: Given a required reserve ratio of 10 percent, Better Health Spa's deposit of $90,000 from Connie Jones creates $81,000 in additional excess reserves that the bank can lend and thus create additional checkable deposits.

creates total excess reserves of $900,000, which are available for new loans and, in turn, new deposits in different banks. As this process continues, each bank accepts smaller and smaller increases in checkable deposits because 10 percent of each deposit is held as required reserves. As shown in Exhibit 2, the banking system as a whole can create new checkable deposits of $900,000, equal to the total of newly created excess reserves in individual banks. Note that the initial $100,000 was from cash already counted in M1 and so it is not counted in the expansion of the money supply.

The Money Multiplier

Money multiplier

The maximum change in the money supply (checkable deposits) due to an initial change in the excess reserves banks hold. The money multiplier is equal to 1 divided by the required reserve ratio.

Fortunately, we do not need to calculate all the individual bank transactions listed in Exhibit 2 in order to derive the change in the money supply initiated by a deposit or withdrawal. Instead, we can use the **money multiplier,** or *deposit multiplier.* The money multiplier gives the *maximum* change in the money supply (checkable deposits) due to an initial change in the excess reserves held by banks.[1] The money multiplier is equal to 1 divided by the required reserve ratio. Expressed as a formula:

$$\text{money multiplier} = \frac{1}{\text{required reserve ratio}}$$

The actual change in the money supply is computed by the following formula:

actual money supply change = **initial change in excess reserves (ER) × money multiplier (MM)**

Symbolically and using the data in Exhibit 2,

$$\Delta M1 = \Delta ER \times MM$$
$$\$900,000 = \$90,000 \times 10$$

---

[1]The money multiplier (*MM*) is the sum of the infinite geometric progression $1 + (1 - r) + (1 - r)^2 + (1 - r)^3 + \cdots + (1 - r)\infty$, where r equals the required reserve ratio.

EXHIBIT 2 Expansion of the Money Supply

Round	Bank	Increase in checkable deposits	Increase in required reserves	Increase in excess reserves
1	Best National Bank	$ 100,000	$ 10,000	$ 90,000
2	Yazoo National Bank	90,000	9,000	81,000
3	Bank A	81,000	8,100	72,900
4	Bank B	72,900	7,290	65,610
5	Bank C	65,610	6,561	59,049
6	Bank D	59,049	5,905	53,144
7	Bank E	53,144	5,314	47,830
.	.	.	.	.
.	.	.	.	.
.	.	.	.	.
Total	All other banks	478,297	47,830	430,467
	Total increase	$1,000,000	$100,000	$900,000

Note: A $100,000 cash deposit in Best National Bank creates $900,000 in new deposits in other banks. Each round creates excess reserves, which are loaned to a customer who deposits the loan check in another bank in the next round.

The Real-World Money Multiplier

In reality, for several reasons, the size of the money multiplier can be considerably smaller than our handy little formula indicates. First, Connie Jones, or any customer along the money creation process, can decide to put a portion of the loan in her pocket, rather than writing a check to Better Health Spa for the full amount of the loan. Money outside the banking system in someone's wallet or purse or underneath the mattress is a cash leakage, which reduces the value of the money multiplier.

Second, the size of the money multiplier falls when banks do not use all their excess reserves to make loans. Perhaps some banks anticipate large deposit account withdrawals and prepare for them by holding excess reserves. Or some banks can hold excess reserves because they lack enough "worthy" loan applications. When banks decide for whatever reason to retain excess reserves, the money multiplier will be smaller.

How Monetary Policy Creates Money

The previous chapter explained that the principal function of the Fed is to control the money supply, using three policy tools or levers. The Fed's use of these tools to influence the economy is more precisely called **monetary policy**. Monetary policy is the Federal Reserve's use of open market operations, changes in the discount rate, and changes in the required reserve ratio to change the money supply (M1). Using these three tools or levers of monetary policy, the Fed can limit and expand deposit creation by the banks and thereby change the money supply.

Monetary policy
The Federal Reserve's use of open market operations, changes in the discount rate, and changes in the required reserve ratio to change the money supply (M1).

Federal Reserve System	Balance Sheet 6 July 25, 2001 (billions of dollars)		
Assets		**Liabilities**	
U.S. government securities	$536	Federal Reserve notes	$571
Loans to banks	1	Deposits	35
Other assets	94	Other liabilities and net worth	25
Total assets	$631	Total liabilities and net worth	$631

Source: Federal Reserve Board, *Factors Affecting Reserve Balances,* http://www.federalreserve.gov/releases/.

Open Market Operations

You have seen how decisions of the public—including those of Brad Rich, Connie Jones, and Better Health Spa—worked through the banking system and increased M1. In this section, you will build on this foundation by learning how the Fed can expand or contract the money supply. We begin with the aggregated Balance Sheet 6 of the 12 Federal Reserve banks of the Federal Reserve System. Total assets of the Fed on July 25, 2001, were $631 billion. The majority of these assets ($536 billion) were held in U.S. government securities in the form of Treasury bills, Treasury notes, and Treasury bonds. Loans to banks were only $1 billion, which amounted to a small percentage of assets. This contrasts with commercial banks, which hold most of their assets in loans. Finally, the other assets of the Fed include coins, cash items in the process of collection, bank property, and foreign currencies.

The major liability of the Fed was $571 billion worth of Federal Reserve notes—paper currency. This is in contrast to the major liability of commercial banks, which is checkable deposits. As explained in the previous chapter, the Fed issues, but does not actually print, Federal Reserve notes. Instead, the Fed decides how much to issue and then calls the Bureau of Engraving and Printing to order new batches of $10, $20, $50, and $100 bills, which the Fed sends to the banks in armored trucks.

Another important liability of the Fed is the deposits of banks and the U.S. Treasury. The Fed therefore serves as a bank for these banks and the Treasury. Note that these bank deposits include the required reserve deposits discussed at the beginning of the chapter. On July 25, 2001, total liabilities and net worth equaled total assets of $631 billion. Again, some details of the balance sheet are intentionally omitted.

Recall the Federal Open Market Committee (FOMC) introduced in the previous chapter. The FOMC, as its name implies, determines the money supply through **open market operations.** Open market operations are the buying and selling of government securities by the Federal Reserve System. The New York Federal Reserve Bank's trading desk executes these orders.

Open market operations

The buying and selling of government securities by the Federal Reserve System.

FEDERAL RESERVE BANK   Balance Sheet 7

Assets	Liabilities	Initial change in M1
U.S. Government securities +$100,000	Reserves of Best National Bank +$100,000	+$100,000

Note: To increase the money supply, the Fed conducted open market operations by purchasing $100,000 in government securities. The Fed pays a securities dealer with a Fed check, which the dealer deposits in its bank. The initial change in the money supply is an increase of $100,000.

Suppose the FOMC decides to increase the money supply and instructs the New York Fed trading desk to *buy* $100,000 worth of 90-day U.S. Treasury bills (called T-bills).[2]

The Fed contacts securities dealers in the private sector for competitive bids. Suppose the Fed accepts the lowest bid, buys $100,000 worth of T-bills, and pays the dealer with a check drawn against itself. As shown in Balance Sheet 7, the Fed's assets increase by $100,000 worth of U.S. government IOUs. Once the securities dealer deposits the Fed's check in the firm's account at Best National Bank, the bank will send the $100,000 check back to the Fed. When the Fed receives the check, it will increase Best National's reserves account at the Fed by this amount. The Fed therefore increases its liabilities by $100,000, and M1 increases immediately by $100,000 because the security dealer's checking account increases at Best National Bank. Like a magician waving a magic wand, the Fed has created new money: The initial $100,000 checkable deposit and excess reserves for loans. Given a 10 percent reserve requirement, Best National Bank's required reserves increase by $10,000, and its excess reserves increase by $90,000. Therefore, the money supply will potentially increase by $1 million [the $100,000 initial increase in M1 when the Fed buys the security multiplied by the money multiplier of 10 (1/0.10)]. Note that unlike the example shown previously in Exhibit 2 involving an initial $100,000 cash deposit already counted in M1, the initial deposit was created by the Fed and therefore not already counted in M1. Expressed as a formula:

actual money supply change = initial checkable deposit (C⌐
+ (initial change in ⟨
× money multiplier)

$$\Delta M1 = \Delta CD + (\Delta ER \times MM)$$

$$\$1,000,000 = \$100,000 + (\$90,000 \times 10)$$

---

[2]The U.S. Treasury issues T-bills in minimum denominations of $10,000. These n obligations of the federal government mature in three months, six months, or one yea. used to finance the budget deficit, as explained in the chapter on this topic. The Treasu 3-month bills at weekly auctions and six-month and one-year bills less often.

FEDERAL RESERVE BANK Balance Sheet 8

Assets		Liabilities		Initial change in M1
U.S. government securities	−$100,000	Reserves of Best National Bank	−$100,000	−$100,000

Note: To decrease the money supply, the Fed conducted open market operations by selling $100,000 in government securities. The Fed accepts a securities dealer's check drawn on the dealer's bank. The initial change in the money supply is a decrease of $100,000.

The process goes into reverse if the FOMC directs the New York Fed trading desk to *sell* U.S. government securities for the Fed's portfolio. As shown in Balance Sheet 8, the goal of the Fed is to decrease the money supply by selling, say, $100,000 in Treasury bonds from the asset side of its balance sheet. In this case, the Fed accepts the best offer from a securities dealer. Again, assume the securities dealer's $100,000 check payable to the Fed is written on the firm's account with Best National Bank. When the Fed accepts the check, it reduces the reserves recorded on the liabilities side of Balance Sheet 8, and Best National Bank reduces the checkable account of the securities dealer. By subtracting $100,000 from Best National Bank's reserves, the Fed decreases M1 initially by $100,000. Again, the Fed has waved its magic wand and extinguished money in the banking system. Given a 10 percent reserve requirement, the money supply can potentially fall by $1 million (the $100,000 initial decrease in M1 when the Fed sells the security multiplied by the money multiplier of 10).

Another way to study open market operations is to look at a typical day at the trading desk, located at the Federal Reserve Bank of New York. The manager of the trading desk starts the day by studying estimates of excess reserves in the banking system. If excess reserves are low, few banks have funds to lend. High excess reserves mean many banks can make loans. After collecting this and other data, the manager looks at the directive from the FOMC and formulates the day's "game plan." Then the manager makes conference calls to several members of the FOMC for approval. With their blessing, the manager has traders in the trading room call dealers who trade in government securities for price quotations. The open market operation has two alternative objectives: *A purchase of government securities by the Fed injects reserves into the banking system and increases the money supply. A sale of government securities by the Fed reduces reserves in the banking system and decreases the money supply.*

Exhibit 3 illustrates the Federal Reserve's open market operations.

The Discount Rate

So far, money creation in the banking system depends on excess reserves acquired from new checkable deposits. Actually, the Fed itself provides another option for banks to obtain reserves through its *discount window.* This is a department within each of the Federal Reserve district banks and

EXHIBIT 3   Open Market Operations

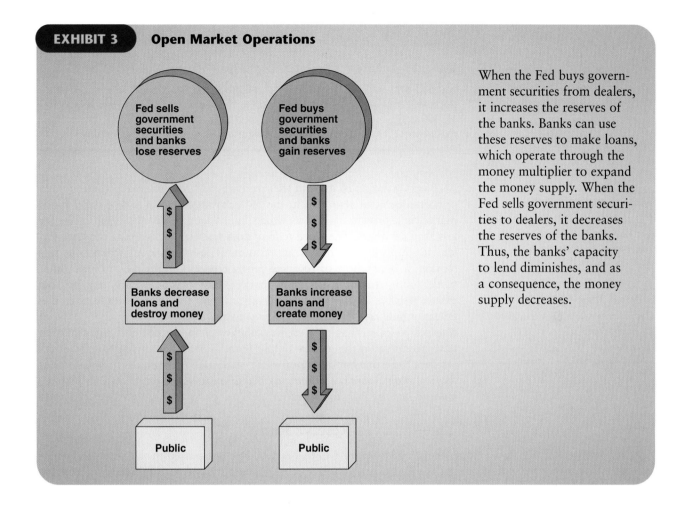

When the Fed buys government securities from dealers, it increases the reserves of the banks. Banks can use these reserves to make loans, which operate through the money multiplier to expand the money supply. When the Fed sells government securities to dealers, it decreases the reserves of the banks. Thus, the banks' capacity to lend diminishes, and as a consequence, the money supply decreases.

not an actual window. Suppose Best National Bank has no excess reserves and Brad Rich does not walk in with a deposit. Also assume the Fed does not purchase government securities and pay a dealer with a check deposited in Best National Bank. Now enter Connie Jones, who asks for a loan. In this situation, the bank has no money to lend, but it can borrow reserves from the Fed for a short period and pay the **discount rate.** The discount rate is the interest rate the Fed charges on loans of reserves to banks. All banks and other depository institutions have the privilege of occasionally borrowing at the Fed to cover reserve deficiencies. Changes in the discount rate often signal the Fed's monetary policy direction and therefore can affect the public's expectations about the economy. A lower discount rate encourages banks to borrow reserves and make loans.

Discount rate
The interest rate the Fed charges on loans of reserves to banks.

Conclusion *A higher discount rate discourages banks from borrowing reserves and making loans. If the Fed wants to expand the money supply, it reduces the discount rate. If the objective is to contract the money supply, the Fed raises the discount rate.*

CHECKPOINT

Who Has More Dollar Creation Power?

You find a $1,000 bill hidden beneath the floorboards in your house and decide to deposit it in your checking account. On the same day, the Fed decides to buy $1,000 in government securities from your bank. Assuming a 10 percent reserve requirement, which of these actions creates more money in the economy?

Federal funds market

A private market in which banks lend reserves to each other for less than 24 hours.

Federal funds rate

The interest rate banks charge for overnight loans of reserves to other banks.

Read more about the required reserve ratio at the Federal Reserve (http://www.federalreserve.gov/pf/pf.htm) *and click on The Implementation of Monetary Policy.*

Banks wanting to expand their reserves in order to seek profitable loan opportunities can also turn to the **federal funds market.** The federal funds market is a private market in which banks lend reserves to each other for less than 24 hours. The word *federal* does not mean it is a government market. It simply means this is an economywide or national market. In this market, a bank short of reserves can borrow some reserves from another bank. Using the interbank loan market, Best National Bank can borrow excess reserves from Yazoo National and pay the **federal funds rate.** The federal funds rate is the interest rate banks charge for overnight loans of reserves to other banks. Reserves borrowed in the federal funds market have no effect on the money supply because such borrowing simply moves reserves from one bank to another. Special note: *Most banks borrow money to meet their reserve requirements primarily through the federal funds market and not the discount window.*

The Required Reserve Ratio

Under the Monetary Control Act of 1980 discussed in the preceding chapter, the Fed can set reserve requirements by law for all banks and savings and loan associations. By changing the required reserve ratio, the Fed can change banks' excess reserves and therefore banks' lending ability. This is potentially an extremely powerful policy lever. Recall that the money multiplier equals 1 divided by the required reserve ratio. Suppose the Fed is concerned about inflation, so it wants to restrain the money supply and thereby dampen aggregate demand in the economy. If the Fed increases the required reserve ratio, the effect is to reduce excess reserves and generate a smaller change in the money supply because the money supply multiplier is smaller. For example, a required reserve ratio of 10 percent yields a money multiplier of 10 (1/0.10). If the Fed increases the ratio to 20 percent, the money multiplier falls to 5 (1/0.20).

> **Conclusion** *There is an inverse relationship between the size of the required reserve ratio and the money multiplier.*

Raising the required reserve ratio can sharply reduce the lending power of banks. Consider an initial increase in excess reserves of $10 billion in the banking system when the required reserve ratio is 10 percent. The potential value of loans (deposits) is $100 billion ($10 billion of excess reserves × 10). Now assume the Fed raises the required reserve ratio to 20 percent. The potential value of loans (deposits) falls to $50 billion ($10 billion of excess reserves × 5).

EXHIBIT 4 The Effect of Monetary Policy Tools on the Money Supply

Fed's monetary policy action	Mechanism	Change in the money supply
Open market operations purchase	Reserves increase	Increases
Open market operations sale	Reserves decrease	Decreases
Discount rate decreases	Borrowing reserves becomes cheaper	Increases
Discount rate increases	Borrowing reserves becomes costlier	Decreases
Required reserve ratio decreases	Money multiplier increases	Increases
Required reserve ratio increases	Money multiplier decreases	Decreases

Conclusion *If the Fed wishes to increase the money supply, it decreases the required reserve ratio. If the objective is to decrease the money supply, the Fed increases the required reserve ratio. In reality, changing the required reserve ratio is considered a heavy-handed approach, and thus it is an infrequently used tool of monetary policy.*

Exhibit 4 presents a summary of the impact of monetary policy tools.

The Fed used all three of its monetary policy tools to increase the money supply and battle the 1990–1991 recession. In the fall of 1990, the Fed recognized the economy was slipping into a recession, so it purchased federal securities to inject new reserves into the banking system. The discount rate was lowered eight times between the end of 1990 and early 1992. In early 1992, the reserve requirement on demand deposits was also lowered from 12 percent to 10 percent. Despite the power of the Fed to conduct monetary policy, it faces difficulties when it tries to jump-start the economy, as the next section explains.

Monetary Policy Shortcomings

Monetary policy, like fiscal policy, has its limitations. The Fed's control over the money supply is imperfect for the following reasons.

Money Multiplier Inaccuracy

If the Fed is to manage the money supply, it must know the size of the money multiplier so that it can forecast the increase in the money supply resulting from a change in excess reserves. The value of the money multiplier, however, can be uncertain and subject to decisions independent of the Fed. As explained earlier in the chapter, the public's decision to hold cash and the willingness of banks to make loans affect the total expansion from an initial change in excess reserves. These decisions vary with conditions of prosperity and recession. When the business cycle is in an upturn, banks are very willing to use their excess reserves for making loans, and the money supply expands. During a downturn, bankers are less willing to use their excess reserves for making loans, and the money supply tends to contract.

Nonbanks

Nonbanks provide financial services, but do not offer checkable deposits included in M1. Nonbanks are not directly under the Fed's jurisdiction. Insurance companies, pension funds, brokerage houses, finance companies, and other corporations hold large amounts of funds and make loans with the potential to offset changes in the money supply. For example, customers turned down for a loan at their bank can turn to Household Finance Corporation, or another finance company, for cash.

Which Money Definition Should the Fed Control?

As discussed in the previous chapter, there are different definitions of the money supply. What if the Fed masterfully controls M1, but the public transfers more of its deposits to M2? For example, banks can pay higher interest and attract more customers to invest in certificates of deposits. Consequently, the Fed might respond by focusing on M2 instead of M1. In fact, in recent years, the Fed has focused more on M2 because it has become more closely correlated with changes in the GDP than M1.

Lags in Monetary Policy versus Fiscal Policy

Fiscal policy does not happen instantaneously, and neither does monetary policy. As with fiscal policy, monetary policy is subject to time lags. First, an *inside lag* exists between the time a policy change is needed and the time the Fed identifies the problem and decides which policy tool to use. The inside lag is fairly short because financial data are available daily, data on inflation and unemployment monthly, and data on real GDP within three months. Once the Fed has the data, it can quickly decide which policy changes are needed and make appropriate adjustments. The inside lag for monetary policy is shorter than for fiscal policy because fiscal policy is the result of a long political budget process.

Second, there is an *outside lag* between the time a policy decision is made and the time the policy change has its effect on the economy. This lag refers to the length of time it takes the money multiplier or spending multiplier to have its full effect on aggregate demand and, in turn, employment, the price level, and real GDP.

Now it's time to answer an important question: Who is the hare and who is the tortoise in the race to the finish line of stabilizing the economy? In the popular version of this story, the hare is much faster, but goofs off along the way and eventually loses to the tortoise at the finish line. In our economics story, however, the Fed is the hare and wins easily over fiscal policy (the tortoise). Although the computer model estimates differ widely, the total lag (inside plus outside lags) for monetary policy can be 3 to 12 months. In contrast, the total lag for fiscal policy is not less than a year, and a total lag of three years is quite possible.

How Does the FOMC Really Work?

Applicable Concept: monetary policy

The Federal Open Market Committee (FOMC), which is the Fed's most powerful monetary policy-making group, meets eight times a year at the Federal Reserve in Washington, D.C. Often it seems that the whole world is watching for the results. Prior to the meeting, board members are given three books prepared by the Fed staff. The "Green Book" forecasts aggregate demand and various prices based on a variety of equations and the assumptions that monetary policy does or does not change. A "Blue Book" might discuss as many as three monetary policy options, the rationale for each option, and the impact of each option on the economy. There is also a "Beige Book" published eight times per year that gathers anecdotal information on current economic conditions obtained from interviews with key businesspersons, economists, bankers, and other sources.

The meeting begins at precisely 9:00 A.M. with a discussion of foreign currency operations and domestic open market operations illustrated with colorful graphics. Next, the staff presents their analysis of recent developments and forecast for the economy laid out in the Green Book. Then each board member around the impressive 27-foot oval mahogany table expresses their views about the analyses, except for Alan Greenspan who chooses not to participate in this round. Now, it's coffee time and everyone relaxes beneath a 23-foot ceiling with a 1,000-pound chandelier.

After the coffee break, the staff discusses each policy option from the Blue Book without recommending a particular option. Generally, three options are presented. Option A is always a decline in interest rates, Option B is always no change in interest rates, and Option C is always an increase. After the staff presentation, board members politely discuss the policy options, but with an important difference. In this policy round, Alan Greenspan goes first. He leads the discussion and advocates a policy decision. After other board members express their views, the chairman summarizes the consensus and reads a draft of the Directive to be voted upon. The Directive gives instructions to the Fed's staff on how to conduct open market operations until the next FOMC meeting. For example, the New York Fed's trading desk may be instructed to increase the money supply in the range of 1 to 5 percent and lower interest rates by buying 90-day U.S. Treasury bills. After discussion, board members vote on the Directive, with the chairman voting first and the decision going to the majority. The chairman is always expected to be on the winning side.

The Directive is sent to the New York Fed's trading desk, and soon about four dozen bond dealers receive the Fed's call. If there is a change in policy, it will be announced at 2:15 that afternoon. To maintain confidentiality, minutes of the meeting will become available the Thursday following the next meeting. A full transcript of the meeting will not be available for five years.

The Fed now communicates its changes in monetary policy by announcing changes in its targets for the federal funds rate. Recall that the Fed does not set this interest rate, but it can influence the rate through open market operations. If the Fed buys bonds, the supply of excess reserves in the banking system increases, and the rate falls. If the Fed sells bonds, the supply of excess reserves in the banking system decreases, and the rate increases. As a result, interest rates in general are influenced. In 2001 as this text was being written, the Fed was fighting against a recession. To accomplish this goal, the Fed cut the federal funds rate ten times, the most since the last recession in the early 1990s. The next chapter explains in more detail the link between changes in the interest rate and changes in other key macro measures.

ANALYZE THE ISSUE

What happened at the last FOMC meeting? Would you like to send the Fed your comments on monetary policy? Visit http://www.federalreserve.gov/fomc/default.htm. To experience an FOMC meeting, visit http://www.ny.frb.org/pihome/educator/fomcsim.html.

Source: Laurence H. Meyer, "Come with Me to the FOMC," April 2, 1998, http://www.federalreserve.gov/.

KEY CONCEPTS

Fractional reserve banking
Required reserves
Excess reserves

Required reserve ratio
Money multiplier
Monetary policy

Open market operations
Discount rate

Federal funds market
Federal funds rate

SUMMARY

- **Fractional reserve banking,** the basis of banking today, originated with the goldsmiths in the Middle Ages. Because depository institutions (banks) are not required to keep all their deposits in vault cash or with the Federal Reserve, banks create money by making loans.

- **Required reserves** are the minimum balance that the Fed requires a bank to hold in vault cash or on deposit with the Fed. The percentage of deposits that must be held as required reserves is called the **required reserve ratio.**

- **Excess reserves** exist when a bank has more reserves than required. Excess reserves allow a bank to create money by exchanging loans for deposits. The money supply is reduced when excess reserves are reduced and loans are repaid.

- The **money multiplier** is used to calculate the maximum change (positive or negative) in checkable deposits (money supply) due to a change in excess reserves. As a formula:

$$\text{money multiplier} = \frac{1}{\text{required reserve ratio}}$$

The actual change is computed as

money multiplier $\times$ initial change in excess reserves = money supply change

- **Monetary policy** is action taken by the Fed to change the money supply. The Fed uses three basic tools: (1) *open market operations,* (2) *changes in the discount rate,* and (3) *changes in the required reserve ratio.*

- **Open market operations** are the buying and selling of government securities by the Fed through its trading desk at the New York Federal Reserve Bank. **Buying government securities** creates extra bank reserves and loans, thereby *expanding* the money supply. **Selling government securities** reduces bank reserves and loans, thereby *contracting* the money supply.

Open market operations

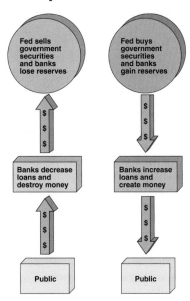

- **Changes in the discount rate** occur when the Fed changes the rate of interest it charges on loans of reserves to banks. Lowering the discount rate makes it easier for banks to borrow reserves from the Fed and expands the money supply. Raising the discount rate discourages banks from borrowing reserves from the Fed and contracts the money supply.

- **Changes in the required reserve ratio** and the size of the money multiplier are *inversely* related. Thus, if the Fed decreases the required reserve ratio, the money multiplier and money supply increase. If the Fed increases the required reserve ratio, the money multiplier and money supply decrease.

- **Monetary policy limitations** include the following: (1) The money multiplier can vary. (2) Nonbanks, such as insurance companies, and finance companies, can offer loans and other financial services not directly under the Fed's control. (3) The Fed might control M1, but the public can shift funds to M2, M3, or another money supply definition. (4) Time lags occur.

SUMMARY OF CONCLUSION STATEMENTS

- Transferring currency to a bank and moving deposits from one bank to another do not affect the money supply (M1).

- When a bank makes a loan, it creates deposits, and the money supply increases by the amount of the loan because the money supply includes checkable deposits.

- The open market operation has two alternative objectives: A purchase of government securities by the Fed injects reserves into the banking system and increases the money supply. A sale of government securities by the Fed reduces reserves in the banking system and decreases the money supply.

- A higher discount rate discourages banks from borrowing reserves and making loans. If the Fed wants to expand the money supply, it reduces the discount rate. If the objective is to contract the money supply, the Fed raises the discount rate.

- There is an inverse relationship between the size of the required reserve ratio and the money multiplier.

- If the Fed wishes to increase the money supply, it decreases the required reserve ratio. If the objective is to decrease the money supply, the Fed increases the required reserve ratio. In reality, changing the required reserve ratio is considered a heavy-handed approach, and thus it is an infrequently used tool of monetary policy.

STUDY QUESTIONS AND PROBLEMS

1. Relate Shakespeare's admonition "Neither a borrower nor a lender be" to the goldsmiths' evolutionary use of fractional reserve banking.

2. If you deposit a $20 bill into a checking account and your bank has a 10 percent reserve requirement, by how much will the bank's excess reserves rise?

3. Consider this statement: "Banks do not create money because this is the Fed's responsibility." Do you agree or disagree? Explain.

4. In what form does a bank hold its required reserves? Assume the Fed has a 20 percent required reserve ratio. What amount of checkable deposits can be supported by $10 million in required reserves?

5. Suppose you deposit your paycheck drawn on another bank. Explain the impact on the money supply.

6. Suppose you remove $1,000 from under your mattress and deposit it in First National Bank. Using a balance sheet, show the impact of your deposit on the bank's assets and liabilities. If the required reserve ratio is 10 percent, what is the maximum amount the bank can loan from this deposit?

7. Suppose it is the holiday season and you withdraw $1,000 from your account at First National Bank to purchase presents. Using a balance sheet, show the impact on this bank's assets and liabilities. If the required reserve ratio is 20 percent, what is the impact on the bank's loans?

8. Suppose the Federal Reserve's trading desk buys $500,000 in T-bills from a securities dealer who then deposits the Fed's check in Best National Bank. Use a balance sheet to show the impact on the bank's loans. Consider the money multiplier and assume the required reserve ratio is 10 percent. What is the maximum increase in the money supply that can result from this open market transaction?

9. Assume the required reserve ratio is 10 percent and a bank's excess reserves are $50 million. Explain why checkable deposits resulting from new loans based on excess reserves are not likely to generate the maximum of $500 million.

10. Briefly describe the effect on the money supply of the following monetary policies:
    a. The Fed purchases $20 million worth of U.S. Treasury bonds.
    b. The Fed increases the discount rate.
    c. The Fed decreases the discount rate.
    d. The Fed sells $40 million worth of U.S. T-bills.
    e. The Fed decreases the required reserve ratio.

11. What are some problems faced by the Fed in controlling the money supply?

ONLINE EXERCISES

Exercise 1

In order to study the Fed's monetary policy tools, follow these steps:

1. Review Open Market Operations (http://www.ny.frb .org/pihome/fedpoint/fed32.html).
2. Review the federal funds rate (http://www .federalreserve.gov/fomc/default.htm).
3. Review the Reserve Requirements (http://www.ny.frb .org/pihome/fedpoint/fed45.html).

Exercise 2

Visit the Federal Reserve (http://www.federalreserve .gov/releases/H15/data.htm) and follow these steps:

1. Scroll down to Bank Prime Loan which indicates the prime interest rate (the interest rates bank charge their most credit-worthy customers) and click on Monthly and observe the movement in the prime rate over the last few months.

2. Now Click on Discount Window Borrowing and Monthly. Observe the movement in the discount rate over the last few months.
3. Is there a relationship between the change in the prime lending rate and the discount rate? Why?

Exercise 3

Visit the Federal Reserve Bank of Kansas City's interactive web site (http://www.kc.frb.org/fed101/index.cfm) and explore FED101.

Exercise 4

Visit a cyberspace bank, such as Centura Bank (http:// www.centura.com/sfnb/sfnb_welcome.cfm). How are its services different from those of your local bank? Also review the Office of Thrift Supervision (OTS) materials on electronic banking (http://www.ots.treas.gov/main .cfm?catNumber=3&catParent=0). The OTS regulates federally chartered savings and loans.

CHECKPOINT ANSWER

Who Has More Dollar Creation Power?

Your action adds $1,000 to your bank's liabilities. Also, assets in the form of required reserves increase by $100 (.10 × $1,000). This means excess reserves increase by $900, allowing the bank to make this amount of new loans. When the Fed buys $1,000 in government securities, the bank again receives $1,000 in reserves. But the

Fed's transaction does not change the bank's liabilities; therefore, the full $1,000 can go into loans. Comparing the effect on the total money supply, the money multiplier effect shows a $9,000 addition to the money supply from your action and a $10,000 addition from the Fed's action. If you said the Fed's action creates more money, YOU ARE CORRECT.

PRACTICE QUIZ

For a visual explanation of the correct answers, visit the tutorial at http://tucker.swcollege.com.

1. If a bank has total deposits of $100,000 with $10,000 set aside to meet reserve requirements of the Fed, its required reserve ratio is
   a. $10,000.
   b. 10 percent.
   c. 0.1 percent.
   d. 1 percent.

2. Assume a simplified banking system in which all banks are subject to a uniform required reserve ratio of 30 percent and checkable deposits are the only form of money. A bank that receives a new deposit of $10,000 is able to extend new loans up to a maximum of
   a. $3,000.
   b. $7,000.
   c. $10,000.
   d. $30,000.

3. The Best National Bank operates with a 10 percent required reserve ratio. One day a depositor withdraws $400 from his or her checking account at the bank. As a result, the bank's excess reserves
   a. fall by $400.
   b. fall by $360.
   c. rise by $40.
   d. rise by $400.

4. If an increase of $100 in excess reserves in a simplified banking system can lead to a total expansion in bank deposits of $400, the required reserve ratio must be
   a. 40 percent.
   b. 400 percent.
   c. 25 percent.
   d. 4 percent.
   e. 2.5 percent.

5. In a simplified banking system in which all banks are subject to a 25 percent required reserve ratio, a $1,000 open market sale by the Fed would cause the money supply to
   a. increase by $1,000.
   b. decrease by $1,000.
   c. decrease by $4,000.
   d. increase by $4,000.

6. In a simplified banking system in which all banks are subject to a 20 percent required reserve ratio, a $1,000 open market purchase by the Fed would cause the money supply to
   a. increase by $100.
   b. decrease by $200.
   c. decrease by $5,000.
   d. increase by $5,000.

7. The cost to a member bank of borrowing from the Federal Reserve is measured by the
   a. reserve requirement.
   b. price of securities in the open market.
   c. discount rate.
   d. yield on government bonds.

Exhibit 5 Balance Sheet of Best National Bank

Assets		Liabilities	
Required reserves	$_____	Checkable deposits	$100,000
Excess reserves			
Loans	80,000		_____
Total	$100,000	Total	$100,000

8. The required reserve ratio in Exhibit 5 is
   a. 10 percent.
   b. 15 percent.
   c. 20 percent.
   d. 25 percent.

9. If the bank in Exhibit 5 received $100,000 in new deposits, its new required reserves would be
   a. $10,000.
   b. $20,000.
   c. $30,000.
   d. $40,000.

10. Suppose Brad Jones deposits $1,000 in the bank shown in Exhibit 5. The result would be
    a. a $200 increase in excess reserves.
    b. a $200 increase in required reserves.
    c. a $1,200 increase in required reserves.
    d. zero change in required reserves.

11. If all banks in the system were identical to Best National Bank in Exhibit 5, the money multiplier would be
    a. 5.
    b. 10.
    c. 15.
    d. 20.

12. Assume all banks in the system are identical to Best National Bank in Exhibit 5. A $1,000 open market sale by the Fed would
    a. expand the money supply by $1,000.
    b. expand the money supply by $15,000.
    c. contract the money supply by $1,000.
    d. contract the money supply by $5,000.

CHAPTER 26

Monetary Policy

Vladimir Lenin, the first Communist leader of the Soviet Union, once said the best way to destroy a nation is to destroy its money. Adolf Hitler had the same idea. During World War II, he planned to counterfeit British currency and drop it from planes flying over England. Both cases illustrate that it matters how much money is in circulation. A sudden increase in the quantity of money can render a nation's money valueless. As a consequence, people must resort to barter and waste time making direct exchanges of goods and services, rather than being productive.

The previous two chapters provided the prerequisites for understanding the market for money. You have learned three definitions for the money supply, how the banking system creates money, and how the Fed can control the money supply. Here you will begin by studying the demand for and the supply of money and how they interact to determine the rate of interest. Then we add to this story by linking changes in the money supply to the aggregate demand and aggregate supply model. Using this tool of analysis, you will understand how changes in the demand for money affect interest rates and, in turn, real GDP, employment, and prices.

The first half of this chapter explores how Keynesian economists view the relationship between monetary policy and the economy. The second half of the chapter presents the opposing view of the monetarists. This debate is a clash between two radically different perspectives over the channels through which monetary policy influences the economy. This ideologically charged confrontation is important to the United States's future and is still far from resolved. The chapter concludes with a You're the Economist that allows you to apply the Keynesian and monetarist views to the Great Depression.

In this chapter, you will learn to solve these economics puzzles:

■ Why do people wish to hold money balances?

■ What is a monetary policy transmission mechanism?

■ Why would a Nobel Laureate economist suggest replacing the Federal Reserve with an intelligent horse?

The Keynesian View of the Role of Money

The Demand for Money

Why do people hold (demand) currency and checkable deposits (M1), rather than putting their money to work in stocks, bonds, real estate, or other nonmoney forms of wealth? Because money yields no direct return, people (including businesses) who hold cash or checking account balances incur an *opportunity cost* of forgone interest or profits on the amount of money held. So what are the benefits of holding money? Why would people hold money and thereby forgo earning interest payments? John Maynard Keynes, in his 1936 work entitled *The General Theory of Employment, Interest, and Money,* gave three important motives for doing so: transactions demand, precautionary demand, and speculative demand.

Transactions Demand for Money.   The first motive to hold money is the **transactions demand.** The transactions demand for money is the stock of money people hold to pay everyday predictable expenses. The desire to have "walking around money" to make quick and easy purchases is the principal reason for holding money. Students, for example, have a good idea of how much money they will spend on rent, groceries, utilities, gasoline, and other routine purchases. A business can also predict its payroll, utility bill, supply bills, and other routine expenses. Without enough cash, the public must suffer forgone interest and possibly withdrawal penalties as a result of converting their stocks, bonds, or certificates of deposit into currency or checkable deposits in order to make transactions.

Precautionary Demand for Money.   In addition to holding money for ordinary expected purchases, people have a second motive to hold money, called the **precautionary demand.** The precautionary demand for money is the stock of money people hold to pay unpredictable expenses. This is the "mattress money" people hold to guard against those proverbial rainy days. For example, your car might break down, or your income may drop unexpectedly.

Transactions demand for money
The stock of money people hold to pay everyday predictable expenses.

Precautionary demand for money
The stock of money people hold to pay unpredictable expenses.

Speculative demand for money

The stock of money people hold to take advantage of expected future changes in the price of bonds, stocks, or other nonmoney financial assets.

Demand for money curve

A curve representing the quantity of money that people hold at different possible interest rates, ceteris paribus.

The Bank Rate Monitor (http://www.bankrate .com/brm/default.asp) *surveys more than 2,500 financial institutions to provide information on bank interest rates. Also the Federal Reserve maintains current and historical data on interest rates* (http://www.federalreserve.gov/ releases/H15/data.htm). *For example, one can observe the prime rate (or "Bank prime loan" as it is called at this Fed website), which is really a proxy for "the" interest rate.*

Similarly, a business might experience unexpected repair expenses or lower-than-anticipated cash receipts from sales. Because of unforeseen events that could prevent people from paying their bills on time, people hold precautionary balances. This affords the peace of mind that unexpected payments can be made without having to cash in interest-bearing financial assets or to borrow.

Speculative Demand for Money. The third motive for holding money is the **speculative demand.** The speculative demand for money is the stock of money people hold to take advantage of expected future changes in the price of bonds, stocks, or other nonmoney financial assets. In addition to the transactions and precautionary motives, individuals and businesses demand "betting money" to speculate, or guess, whether the prices of alternative assets will rise or fall. This desire to take advantage of profit-making opportunities when the prices of nonmoney assets fall is the driving force behind the speculative demand. When the interest rate is high, people buy, say, IBM 30-year bonds because the opportunity cost of holding money is the high forgone interest earned on these nonmoney assets. When the interest rate is low, people hold more money because there is less opportunity cost in forgone interest earned on investing in bonds. Suppose the interest rate on IBM 30-year bonds is low. If so, people decide to hold more of their money in the bank and *speculate* that soon the interest rate will climb higher.

> **Conclusion** *As the interest rate falls, the opportunity cost of holding money falls, and people increase their speculative balances.*

The Demand for Money Curve. The three motives for holding money combine to create a **demand for money curve,** which represents the quantity of money that people hold at different possible interest rates, ceteris paribus. As shown in Exhibit 1, people increase their money balances when interest rates fall. The reason is that many people move their money out of, for example, money market mutual funds and into checkable deposits (M1).

> **Conclusion** *There is an inverse relationship between the quantity of money demanded and the interest rate.*

What determines the shape of the demand for money curve? Let's start with the transactions and the precautionary demands for money. These money balances are computed as a given proportion of real GDP. Suppose real GDP is $5,000 billion and people wish to hold, say, 10 percent for transactions and precautionary purposes. This means the first $500 billion read along the horizontal axis in Exhibit 1 are held to make purchases and handle unforeseen events.

Now consider the impact of changes in the interest rate on the speculative demand for money. As the interest rate falls, people add larger speculative balances to their transactions and precautionary balances. For example, when the rate is 8 percent per year, the total quantity of money demanded at point A is $1,000 billion, of which $500 billion are speculative balances. If the interest rate is 4 percent, the total quantity of money demanded increases

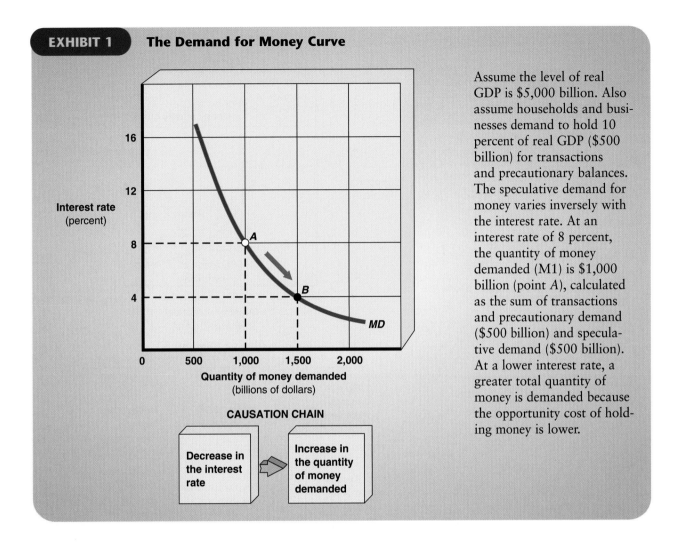

EXHIBIT 1 **The Demand for Money Curve**

Assume the level of real GDP is $5,000 billion. Also assume households and businesses demand to hold 10 percent of real GDP ($500 billion) for transactions and precautionary balances. The speculative demand for money varies inversely with the interest rate. At an interest rate of 8 percent, the quantity of money demanded (M1) is $1,000 billion (point *A*), calculated as the sum of transactions and precautionary demand ($500 billion) and speculative demand ($500 billion). At a lower interest rate, a greater total quantity of money is demanded because the opportunity cost of holding money is lower.

to $1,500 billion at point *B*, of which $1,000 billion are speculative balances. Therefore, the demand for money curve, labeled *MD*, looks much like any other demand curve.

Conclusion *The speculative demand for money at possible interest rates gives the demand for money curve its downward slope.*

The Equilibrium Interest Rate

We are now ready to form the money market and determine the equilibrium interest rate by putting the demand for money and the supply of money together. In Exhibit 2, the money demand curve *(MD)* is identical to that in Exhibit 1. The supply of money curve *(MS)* is a vertical line because the $1,000 billion quantity of money supplied does not respond to changes in the interest rate. The reason is that our model assumes the Fed has used its tools to set the money supply at this quantity of money regardless of the interest rate.

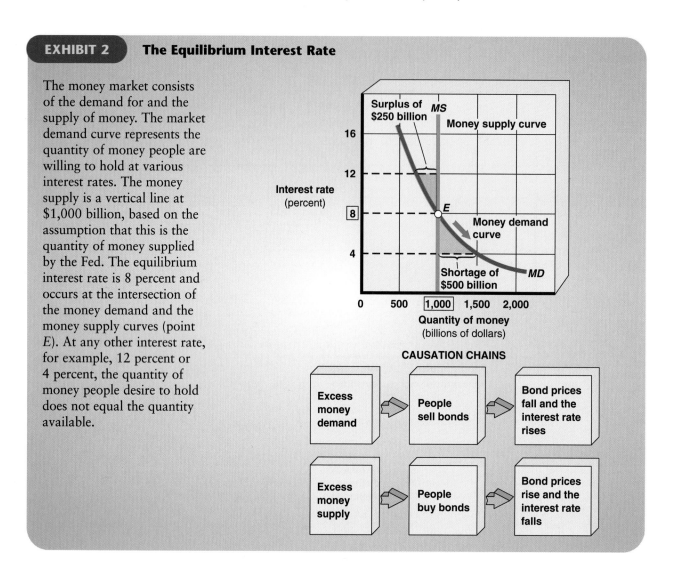

EXHIBIT 2   **The Equilibrium Interest Rate**

The money market consists of the demand for and the supply of money. The market demand curve represents the quantity of money people are willing to hold at various interest rates. The money supply is a vertical line at $1,000 billion, based on the assumption that this is the quantity of money supplied by the Fed. The equilibrium interest rate is 8 percent and occurs at the intersection of the money demand and the money supply curves (point *E*). At any other interest rate, for example, 12 percent or 4 percent, the quantity of money people desire to hold does not equal the quantity available.

At point *E*, the equilibrium interest rate is 8 percent, determined by the intersection of the demand for money curve and the vertical supply of money curve. People wish to hold exactly the amount of money in circulation, and, therefore, neither upward nor downward pressure on the interest rate exists.

Excess Quantity of Money Demanded.   Suppose the interest rate in Exhibit 2 is 4 percent instead of 8 percent. Such a low opportunity cost of money means that people desire to hold a greater quantity of money than the quantity supplied. To eliminate this shortage of $500 billion, individuals and businesses adjust their asset portfolios. They seek more money by selling their bonds or other nonmoney assets. When many sell or try to sell their bonds, there is an increase in the supply of bonds for sale. Consequently, the price of bonds falls, and the interest rate rises. This rise in the interest rate ceases at the equilibrium interest rate of 8 percent because people are content with their portfolios of money and bonds at point *E*.

Here we need to pause and look at an example to understand what is happening. Suppose IBM pays 4 percent on its $1,000 30-year bonds. This means IBM pays a bondholder $40 in interest each year and promises to repay the original $1,000 price (face amount) at the end of 30 years. However, a holder of these bonds can sell them before maturity at a market-determined price. If bondholders desire to hold more money than is supplied, they will sell more of these bonds. Then the increase in the supply of bonds causes the price of bonds to fall to, say, $500. As a result, the interest rate rises to 8 percent ($40/$500).

Excess Quantity of Money Supplied.   The story reverses for any rate of interest above 8 percent. Let's say the interest rate is 12 percent. In this case, people are holding more money than they wish. Stated differently, they wish to hold less money than is currently in circulation. For instance, the quantity of money demanded would be $250 billion less than the quantity supplied. To correct this imbalance, people will move out of cash and checkable deposits by buying bonds. This increase in the demand for bonds will drive up the price of bonds and lower the interest rate. As the interest rate falls, the quantity of money demanded increases as people become more willing to hold money. Finally, the money market reaches equilibrium at point *E*, and people are content with their mix of money and bonds.

> **Conclusion** *There is an inverse relationship between bond prices and the interest rate that enables the money market to achieve equilibrium.*

How Monetary Policy Affects the Interest Rate

Assuming a stationary demand for money, the equilibrium rate of interest changes in response to changes in monetary policy. As we learned in Exhibit 4 of the previous chapter, the Federal Reserve can alter the money supply through open market operations, changes in the required reserve ratio, or changes in the discount rate. In this section, you will see that the Fed's power to change the money supply can also alter the equilibrium rate of interest.

Increasing the Money Supply.   Exhibit 3(a) shows how increasing the money supply will cause the equilibrium rate of interest to fall. Our analysis begins at point E_1, with the money supply at $1,000 billion, which is equal to the quantity of money demanded, and with the equilibrium interest rate at 12 percent. Now suppose the Fed increases the money supply to $1,500 billion by buying government securities in the open market. The impact of the Fed's expansionary monetary policy is to create a $500 billion surplus of money at the prevailing 12 percent interest rate.

How will people react to this excess money in their pockets or checking accounts? Money becomes a "hot potato," and people buy bonds. The rush to purchase bonds drives the price of bonds higher and the interest rate lower. As the interest rate falls, people are *willing* to hold larger money balances. Or, stated differently, the quantity of money demanded increases until the new equilibrium at E_2 is reached. At the lower interest rate of 8 percent, the opportunity cost of holding money is also lower, and the imbalance between the money demand and the money supply curves disappears.

The Federal Reserve must first determine the state of the economy before deciding what to do, if anything, to the money supply. The Federal Reserve publishes a summary of economic conditions by Federal Reserve district and sector in its Beige Book (simply click on Beige Book at http://www.federalreserve.gov/*).*

*Browse the New York Fed's Fedpoints (*http://www.ny.frb.org/pihome/fedpoint/*—in particular, those that address how the Federal Reserve controls the money supply: "Reserve Requirements" (*http://www.ny.frb.org/pihome/fedpoint/fed45.html*), federal funds rate (*http://www.federalreserve.gov/fomc/default.htm*), and "Open Market Operations" (*http://www.ny.frb.org/pihome/fedpoint/fed32.html*).*

EXHIBIT 3   The Effect of Changes in the Money Supply

In part (a), the Federal Reserve increases the money supply from $1,000 billion ($MS_1$) to $1,500 billion ($MS_2$). At the initial interest rate of 12 percent (point E_1), there is an excess of $500 billion beyond the amount people wish to hold. They react by buying bonds, and the interest rate falls until it reaches a new lower equilibrium interest rate at 8 percent (point E_2).

The reverse happens in part (b). The Fed decreases the money supply from $1,500 billion ($MS_1$) to $1,000 billion ($MS_2$). Beginning at 8 percent (point E_1), people wish to hold $500 billion more than is available. This shortage disappears when people sell their bonds. As the price of bonds falls, the interest rate rises to the new higher equilibrium interest rate of 12 percent at point E_2.

Decreasing the Money Supply. Exhibit 3(b) illustrates how the Fed can put upward pressure on the interest rate with contractionary monetary policy. Beginning at point E_1, the money market is in equilibrium at an interest rate of 8 percent. This time the Fed shrinks the money supply by selling government securities through its trading desk, by raising the required reserve ratio, or by raising the discount rate. As a result, the money supply decreases from $1,500 billion to $1,000 billion. At the initial equilibrium interest rate of 8 percent, this decrease in the money supply causes a shortage of $500 billion.

Individuals and businesses wish to hold more money than is available. How can the public put more money in their pockets and checking accounts?

CHECKPOINT

What Does the Money Supply Curve Look Like When the Fed Targets an Interest Rate?

Suppose the Fed has a policy of adjusting the money supply to achieve interest rate targets. For example, the Fed might set a 10 percent target interest rate. If an increase in the demand for money boosts the interest rate above 10 percent, the Fed adjusts the money supply until the 10 percent interest rate is restored. Under such a monetary policy, is the supply of money curve vertical, horizontal, or upward sloping with respect to interest rates?

They can sell their bonds for cash. This selling pressure lowers bond prices, causing the rate of interest to rise. At point E_2, the upward pressure on the interest rate stops. Once the equilibrium interest rate reaches 12 percent, people willingly hold the $1,000 billion money supply.

How Monetary Policy Affects Prices, Output, and Employment

The next step in our journey is to understand how monetary policy alters the macroeconomy. Here you should pause and study Exhibit 4. This exhibit illustrates the causation chain linking monetary policy and economic performance.

> **Conclusion** *In the Keynesian model, changes in the supply of money affect interest rates. In turn, interest rates affect investment spending, aggregate demand, and, finally, real GDP, employment, and prices.*

The Impact of Monetary Policy Using the *AD-AS* Model. How do changes in the rate of interest affect aggregate demand? Begin with Exhibit 5(a), which is identical to Exhibit 3(a) and represents the money market. As explained earlier, we assume that the Fed increases the money supply from $1,000 billion ($MS_1$) to $1,500 billion ($MS_2$) and the equilibrium interest rate falls from 12 percent to 8 percent. In part (b), we can see that the falling rate of interest causes an increase in the quantity of investment spending from $800 billion to $850 billion per year. Stated another way, there is a movement downward along the *investment demand curve (I)*, which you recall from the chapter on GDP is a component of total spending or aggregate demand. The investment demand curve shows the amount businesses spend for investment goods at different possible interest rates.

The classical economists believed that the interest rate alone determines the level of investment spending. Keynes disputed this idea. Instead, Keynes argued that the expectation of future profits is the primary factor determining investment and the interest rate is the financing cost of any investment proposal. Using a micro example to illustrate the investment decision-making process, suppose a consulting firm plans to purchase a new computer program for $1,000 that will be obsolete in a year. The firm anticipates the new software will increase its revenue by $1,100. Thus, assuming that no taxes and other expenses exist, the expected rate of return or profit is 10 percent.

The Federal Reserve exercises monetary control over the economy in part through its open market operations. You can view the minutes from recent Open Market Committee meetings (http://www.federalreserve.gov/fomc/).

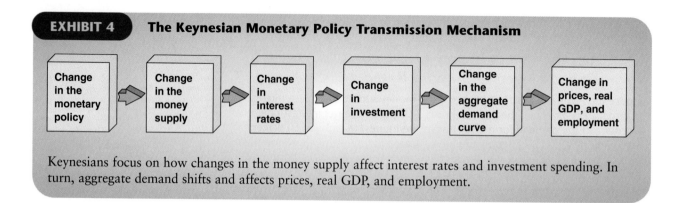

EXHIBIT 4   **The Keynesian Monetary Policy Transmission Mechanism**

Change in the monetary policy ⇒ Change in the money supply ⇒ Change in interest rates ⇒ Change in investment ⇒ Change in the aggregate demand curve ⇒ Change in prices, real GDP, and employment

Keynesians focus on how changes in the money supply affect interest rates and investment spending. In turn, aggregate demand shifts and affects prices, real GDP, and employment.

Now consider the impact of the cost of borrowing funds to finance the software investment. If the interest rate is less than 10 percent, the business will earn a profit, and it will make the investment expenditure to obtain the computer program. On the other hand, a rate of interest higher than 10 percent means the software investment will be a loss, so this purchase will not be made. The expected rate of profit–interest rate–investment relationship follows this rule: *Businesses will undertake all investment projects for which the expected rate of profit equals or exceeds the interest rate.*

In Exhibit 5(c), we use the fiscal policy aggregate demand and aggregate supply analysis developed earlier. Begin at point E_1, with a real GDP per year of $6 trillion and a price level of 150. Now consider the link to the change in the money supply.

The increase in investment resulting from the fall in the interest rate works through the *spending multiplier* and shifts the aggregate demand curve rightward from AD_1 to AD_2. At the new equilibrium point, E_2, the level of real GDP rises from $6 trillion to $6.1 trillion, and full employment is achieved. In addition, the price level rises from 150 to 155. Exhibit 5(a) also demonstrates the effect of a contractionary monetary policy. In this case, the money supply shifts inward from MS_2 to MS_1, causing the equilibrium rate of interest to rise from 8 percent to 12 percent. The Fed's "tight" money policy causes the level of investment spending to fall from $850 billion to $800 billion, which, in turn, decreases the equilibrium level of real GDP per year from $6.1 trillion to $6 trillion. As a result, the unemployment rate rises, and the inflation rate falls because the price level falls from 155 to 150.

The Monetarist View of the Role of Money

The Monetarist Transmission Mechanism

Monetarism

The theory that changes in the money supply directly determine changes in prices, real GDP, and employment.

Monetarists believe Keynesians suffer from the delusion that monetary policy operates only indirectly, causing changes in the interest rate before affecting aggregate demand and then prices, real GDP, and employment. The opposing school of economic thought, called **monetarism**, challenges this view. Monetarism is the theory that changes in the money supply directly

EXHIBIT 5   **The Effect of Expansionary Monetary Policy on Aggregate Demand**

(a) Money market

(b) Investment demand curve

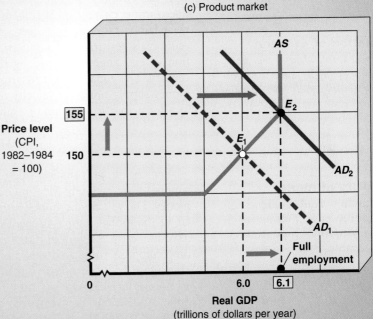

(c) Product market

In part (a), the money supply is initially MS_1, and the equilibrium rate of interest is 12 percent. The equilibrium point in the money market changes from E_1 to E_2 when the Fed increases the money supply to MS_2. This causes the quantity of money people wish to hold to increase from $1,000 billion to $1,500 billion, and a new lower equilibrium interest rate is established at 8 percent.

The fall in the rate of interest shown in part (b) causes a movement downward along the investment demand curve from point A to point B. Thus, the quantity of investment spending per year increases from $800 billion to $850 billion.

In part (c), the investment component of the aggregate demand curve increases, causing this curve to shift outward from AD_1 to AD_2. As a result, the aggregate demand and supply equilibrium in the product market changes from E_1 to E_2, and the real GDP gap is eliminated. The price level also changes from 150 to 155.

EXHIBIT 6   **The Monetarist Monetary Policy Transmission Mechanism**

Monetarists emphasize that changes in the money supply directly cause changes in the aggregate demand curve and thereby changes in prices, real GDP, and employment.

Change in the monetary policy → Change in the money supply → Change in the aggregate demand curve → Change in prices, real GDP, and employment

determine changes in prices, real GDP, and employment. Exhibit 6 illustrates the monetarist transmission mechanism. Comparison of this figure with Exhibit 4 shows that the monetarist model omits the Keynesian interest rate–investment linkage.

The Equation of Exchange. Monetarists put the spotlight on the money supply. They argue that to predict the condition of the economy, you simply look at the money supply. If it expands too much, higher rates of inflation will be the forecast. If it contracts too much, unemployment lines will lengthen. Monetarism has its intellectual roots in classical economics, introduced in the chapter on aggregate demand and supply. Monetarists proudly wear laissez faire on their sleeves and believe the price system is the macro economy's best friend. To understand monetarism, we begin with the **equation of exchange** developed by the classical economists in the nineteenth century. The equation of exchange is an accounting identity that states the money supply times the velocity of money equals total spending. Expressed as a formula, the equation of exchange is written as

$$MV = PQ$$

Equation of exchange

An accounting identity that states the money supply times the velocity of money equals total spending.

Let's begin with the left side of the equation ($M \times V$). M is the money supply (more precisely M1) in circulation, and V represents the **velocity of money.** The velocity of money is the average number of times per year a dollar of the money supply is spent on final goods and services. Assume you have one crisp $20 bill and this is the only money in an ultrasimple economy. Suppose you spend this money on a pizza and soda at Zeno's Pizza Hut. Once Mr. Zeno puts your money in his pocket, he decides to buy an economics book and learn how the views of Keynesians and monetarists differ. And so, Mr. Zeno buys the book at the Wise Professor Book Store for exactly $20. At this point, both Mr. Zeno and Ms. Wise have sold $20 worth of goods. Thus, a single $20 bill has financed $40 worth of total spending. And as long as this $20 bill passes from hand to hand during, say, one year, the value of sales will increase. For example, assume the $20 travels from hand to hand 5 times. This means the velocity of money is 5, and the equation of exchange is expressed as

Velocity of money

The average number of times per year a dollar of the money supply is spent on final goods and services.

$$\$20 \times 5 = \$100$$

The equation of exchange is an *identity*—true by definition—that expresses the fact that the value of what people spend is equal to, or exchanged for, what they buy. What people buy is nominal GDP, or ($P \times Q$). Recall that nominal, or money, GDP is equal to the average selling price during the year (P) multiplied by the quantity of actual output of final goods and services (Q). In our simple economy, total spending equals $100. Note that the identity between MV and PQ does not say what happens to either P or Q if MV increases. Although we know by how much the total value of output (PQ) increases, we do not know whether the price level (P) or the quantity of output (Q) or both increase.

Consider a more realistic example. Suppose that nominal GDP last year was $5 trillion and M1 was $1 trillion. How many times did each dollar of the money supply have to be spent to generate this level of total spending in the economy? Using the equation of exchange,

$$M \times V = P \times Q$$
$$\$1 \text{ trillion} \times V = \$5 \text{ trillion}$$
$$V = 5$$

Thus, each dollar was spent an average of 5 times per year.

The Quantity Theory of Money. The equation of exchange is converted from an *identity* to a *theory* by making certain assumptions. The classical economists became the forerunners of modern-day monetarists by arguing that the velocity of money (V) and real output (Q) are fairly constant. The classical economists viewed V as constant because people's habits of holding a certain quantity of money, and therefore the number of times a dollar is spent, are slow to change. Recall from the chapter on aggregate demand and supply that classical economists believed in price and wage flexibility. Hence, they believed the economy would automatically adjust to long-run full-employment output (Q).

Because V and Q are constant by assumption, we have one of the oldest theories of inflation, called the **quantity theory of money**. The quantity theory of money states that changes in the money supply are directly related to changes in the price level. Monetary policy based on the quantity theory of money therefore impacts directly on the price level. To illustrate, we will modify the equation of exchange by putting a bar ($^{—}$) over V and over Q to indicate they are fixed or constant in value:

Quantity theory of money
The theory that changes in the money supply are directly related to changes in the price level.

$$M \times \overline{V} = P \times \overline{Q}$$

What if the money supply doubles? The price level also doubles. Or if the Fed cuts the money supply in half, then the price level is also cut in half. Meanwhile, real output of goods and services, Q, remains unchanged.

Conclusion *According to the quantity of money theory, any change in the money supply must lead to a proportional change in the price level.*

In short, monetarists say the cause of inflation is "too much money chasing too few goods." The quantity theory of money denies any role for nonmonetary factors, such as supply shocks from a hike in oil prices, which cause cost-push inflation [see Exhibit 11(a) in the chapter on aggregate demand and supply]. Moreover, this theory ignores the impact of fiscal policy changes in taxation and spending on the price level.

What do the data reveal about the link between changes in the money supply and changes in the rate of inflation? Exhibit 7 shows this relationship between 1990 and 2000. Inspection of these data seems to indicate a loose direct relationship between changes in M1 and the rate of inflation. Between 1992 and 1996, growth in the money supply declined, and the inflation rate generally declined from 1992 until 1998. And in 1998 and 1999, both the money supply and the inflation rate increased. For other years in the exhibit, this relationship does not exist.

Modern Monetarism. Today's monetarists have changed the assumptions of the classical quantity theory of money. The evidence indicates that velocity is not constant and the economy does not always operate at full employment. Although M and P are correlated, they do not change proportionally. *Monetarists argue that although velocity is not unchanging, it is nevertheless predictable.* Suppose the predicted velocity of money is 5 and the money supply increases by $100 billion this year. Monetarists would predict that nominal GDP will increase by about $500 billion ($\Delta M \times \hat{V}$). [The circumflex (^) indicates velocity is predicted.] If the economy is far below full employment, most of the rise in total spending will be in real output. If the economy is near full employment, much of the increase will be in rising prices.

Monetarists refute the Keynesian view that the rate of interest is so important. Instead, the monetarist view is often expressed in the famous single-minded statement that "money does matter." Instead of working through the rate of interest to affect investment and, in turn, the economy, changes in the money supply directly determine economic performance.

> **Conclusion** *To avoid inflation and unemployment, the monetarists' prescription is to be sure that the money supply is at the proper level.*

Fixed Money Target. Monetarism gained credibility in the late 1950s and 1960s, led by Professor Milton Friedman at the University of Chicago. The monetarists have an answer for how we make sure the economy grows at the right rate. Instead of risking policy errors, the answer is to forget about the rate of interest and follow steady, predictable monetary policy. Recall from the chapter on money creation that there are limitations on the Fed's ability to control the money supply because of the independent actions of households, firms, banks, and the U.S. Treasury. Monetarists would stop the Fed from tinkering with the money supply, missing the target, and making the economy worse, rather than better. Instead, they say the money supply should expand at the same rate as the potential growth rate in real GDP. That is, it should increase somewhere between 3 percent and 5 percent per year. The Fed should therefore pick a rate and stick to it, even if unexpected changes in velocity cause short periods of inflation or unemployment. This

Money Supply Growth versus the Inflation Rate, 1990–2000

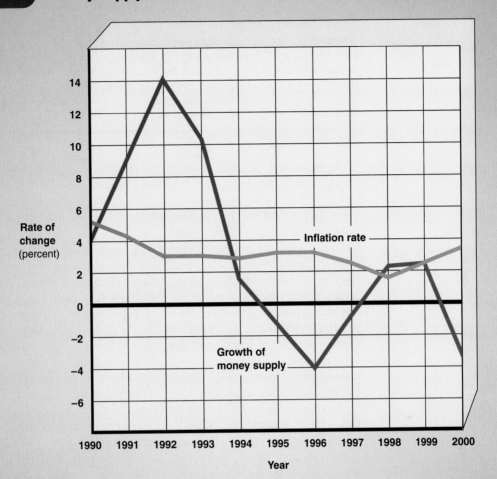

The exhibit shows the relationship between the inflation rate and the percentage change in the money supply measured by M1. From 1992 to 1996 and in 1998 and 1999, there appears to be a generally direct relationship between these two key macroeconomic variables. During these periods of time, changes in the growth of M1 seem to be loosely related to changes in the rate of inflation. In other years, this relationship does not exist.

Sources: Bureau of Labor Statistics, ftp://ftp.bls.gov/pub/special.requests/cpi/cpiai.txt; *Economic Report of the President, 2001,* http://w3.access.gpo.gov/eop/, Table 69; and Federal Reserve Board, http://www.federalreserve.gov/releases/H6/hist/h6hist1.txt.

is called following a *monetary rule.* Monetarists argue that their "straitjacket" approach would reduce the intensity and duration of unemployment and inflation by eliminating the monetarists' public enemy number one—the Fed's discretion to change the money supply. A Keynesian once summarized the fixed money supply approach as "Don't do something, just stand there."

CHECKPOINT

A Horse of Which Color?

A famous economist once proposed replacing the Fed with an intelligent horse. Each New Year's Day, the horse would stand in front of Fed headquarters to answer monetary policy questions. Reporters would ask, "What is going to happen to the money supply this year?" The horse would tap its hoof four times, and the next day headlines would read "Fed to Once Again Increase the Money Supply 4 Percent." Is this famous economist a Keynesian or a monetarist?

Conclusion *Monetarists advocate that the Federal Reserve increase the money supply by a constant percentage each year.*

How Stable Is Velocity?   How stable, or predictable, is the velocity of money? This is a critical question in the Keynesian-monetarist debate. Keynesians do not accept the monetarists' argument that over long periods of time velocity is stable and predictable. Hence, a change in the money supply can lead to a much larger or smaller change in GDP than the monetarists would predict. As shown in Exhibit 8, Keynesians are quick to point out the turbulent variations in velocity. Beginning in 1930 velocity fell from 3.5 to less than 2 in the mid-1940s. In the early 1980s, velocity peaked at slightly less than 7 and then gyrated up and down during the 1980s. Monetarists counter by pointing to the evidence that between 1946 and 1981 and between 1992 and 2000, velocity generally rose at a quite predictable or steady annual rate. This, they say, is a fairly predictable long-run trend.

Keynesians focus on short-run variations in V that accompany any long-run velocity growth rate. They therefore argue that following a monetary rule is folly. Suppose the money supply increases at a constant rate, but velocity is greater than expected. This means that total spending will be greater than predicted, causing inflation. Lower-than-predicted velocity results in unemployment because the economy expands too little. The Keynesians believe that the Federal Reserve must be free to change the money supply to offset unexpected changes in velocity. Monetarists counter that the Fed *cannot* predict short-run variations in V, so its "quick-fix" changes in the money supply will often be wrong. This is why monetarists advocate that the Fed follow a monetary rule. Keynesians are willing to accept occasional policy errors and reject this idea in favor of maintaining Fed flexibility to change the money supply in order to affect interest rates, aggregate demand, and the economy.

A Comparison of Macroeconomic Views

By now, your head is probably spinning with dueling schools of economic thought. The debate among the classicals, Keynesians, and monetarists can be quite confusing. This chapter has presented differences in monetary policy among these schools. To refresh your memory and complete the discussion, this section presents a brief review of key differences in fiscal policy

EXHIBIT 8   **The Velocity of Money, 1930–2000**

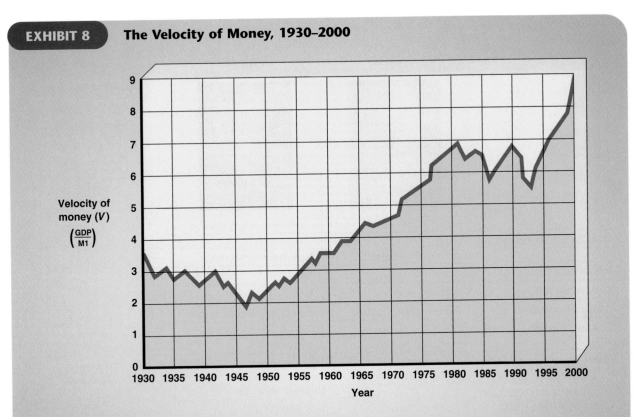

The velocity of money (*V*) equals GDP divided by the supply of money (M1). Keynesians argue that velocity is not stable. For example, velocity fell from 3.5 in 1930 to less than 2 in the mid-1940s. During the 1980s, velocity became quite unpredictable. Monetarists believe velocity is stable over the long term and point to the periods between 1946 and 1981 and between 1992 and 2000. During these years, velocity rose at a relatively constant annual rate.

Sources: *Economic Report of the President, 2001,* http://w3.access.gpo.gov/eop/, Tables B-1 and B-69; and *Survey of Current Business,* http://www.bea.doc.gov/bea/dn1.htm, Table 1.1.

introduced in earlier chapters. Exhibit 9 gives a thumbnail summary of the key differences among the three camps. Note the similarity between the classical and the monetarist schools.

Classical Economics

As discussed in the chapter on aggregate demand and supply, the dominant school of economic thought before the Great Depression was classical economics. The basic theory of the classical economists, introduced by Adam Smith in *The Wealth of Nations,* was that a market-directed economy will automatically correct itself to full employment. Consequently, there is no need for fiscal policy designed to restore full employment.

Recall that a key assumption of classical theory is that, given time to adjust, prices and wages will decrease to ensure the economy operates at full

EXHIBIT 9 Comparison of Macroeconomic Theories

Issue	Classical	Keynesian	Monetarist
	Adam Smith	John Maynard Keynes	Milton Friedman
Stability of economy	Stable in long run at full employment	Inherently unstable at less than full employment	Stable in long run at full employment
Price-wage flexibility	Yes	No	Yes
Velocity of money	Stable	Unstable	Predictable
Cause of inflation	Excess money supply	Excess aggregate demand	Excess money supply
Causes of unemployment	Short-run price and wage adjustment	Inadequate aggregate demand	Short-run price and wage adjustment
Effect of monetary policy	Changes aggregate demand and prices	Changes interest rate, which changes investment and real GDP	Changes aggregate demand and prices
Effect of fiscal policy	Not necessary	Spending multiplier changes aggregate demand	No effect because of crowding-out effect

employment. A decrease in the aggregate demand curve causes a temporary surplus, which, in turn, causes businesses to cut prices, and, in turn, causes more goods to be purchased because of the real balances effect. As a result, wages adjust downward, and employment rises. Classical economists therefore view the economy as operating in the long run along a vertical aggregate supply curve originating at the full-employment real GDP.

Keynesian Economics

The Great Depression challenged the classical prescription to wait until markets adjust and full employment is automatically restored. As the unemployment rate rose to 24.9 percent in 1933, people asked how long it would take for the market mechanism to adjust. John Maynard Keynes responded with this famous saying, "In the long run we are all dead." Keynes and his book, *The General Theory,* attacked classical theory and in the process revolutionized macroeconomic thought.

For a critique of monetarism visit http://www .huppi.com/kangaroo/ L-chimonetarism.htm.

As explained in the chapter on fiscal policy, using fiscal policy to affect aggregate demand is a cornerstone of Keynesian economics. While Keynesians believe monetary policy is often not very powerful, especially during a downturn, they regard fiscal policy as their "top banana." However, Keynesians recognize that one of the potential problems of fiscal policy is the *crowding-out effect*. As shown earlier in Exhibit 8 of the chapter on federal deficits and the national debt, financing a federal deficit by borrowing competes with private borrowers for funds. Given a fixed money supply, the extra demand from the federal government to finance its deficit causes the interest rate to rise. As a result, businesses cut back on investment spending and offset the expected increase in aggregate demand. The Keynesian view, however, is that the investment demand curve is not very sensitive to changes in the interest rate and therefore only a relatively small amount of investment spending will be crowded out. Thus, the decline in investment only slightly counteracts or offsets an increase in aggregate demand created by a deficit.

Conclusion *Keynesians view the shape of the investment demand curve as rather steep or vertical, so the crowding-out effect is insignificant.*

Monetarism

Monetarists are iconoclasts because they attack the belief in the ability of either the Fed or the federal government to stabilize the economy. They argue that fiscal policy is an essentially useless tool that has little or no impact on output or employment because of a total crowding-out effect. Suppose the money supply remains fixed and the federal government borrows to finance its deficit. The intended goal is to increase aggregate demand and restore full employment. According to the monetarists, financing the deficit will drive up the interest rate and crowd out a substantial, not a small, amount of investment spending. The reason is that the monetarists view the investment demand curve is sensitive to changes in the interest rate; therefore, greater amounts of investment spending will be crowded out. As a result, the net effect is no increase in aggregate demand and no reduction in unemployment.

Conclusion *Monetarists view the shape of the investment demand curve as less steep or more flat, so the crowding-out effect is significant.*

Although the monetarists do not trust the Federal Reserve to use discretionary monetary policy, they are quick to point out that only money is important. Changes in the money supply, the basic lever of monetary policy, have a powerful impact. Instead of ineffectual government deficit spending to cure unemployment, an increase in the money supply would definitely stimulate the economy based on the quantity theory of money. In short, changes in the money supply directly result in changes in real GDP.

Monetary Policy during the Great Depression

Applicable Concept: Keynesians versus monetarists

Monetarists and Keynesians still debate the causes of the Great Depression. Monetarists Milton Friedman and Anna Schwartz, in their book *A Monetary History of the United States,* argued that the Great Depression was caused by the decline in the money supply, as shown in Exhibit 10(a). The accompanying parts (b), (c), and (d) present changes in the price level, real GDP, and unemployment rate.

During the 1920s, the money supply expanded steadily, and prices were generally stable. In response to the great stock market crash of 1929, bank failures, falling real GDP, and rising unemployment, the Fed changed its monetary policy. Through the Great Depression years from 1929 to 1933, M1 declined by 27 percent. Assuming velocity is relatively constant, how will a sharp reduction in the quantity of money in circulation affect the economy? Monetarists predict a reduction in prices, output, and employment. As Exhibit 10(b) shows, the price level declined by 24 percent between 1929 and 1933. In addition to deflation, Exhibit 10(c) shows that real GDP was 27 percent lower in 1933 than in 1929. Unemployment rose from 3.2 percent in 1929 to 24.9 percent in 1933.

Friedman and Schwartz argued that the ineptness of the Fed's monetary policy during the Great Depression caused the trough in the business cycle to be more severe and sustained. As proof, let's look at the period after 1933. The money supply grew and was followed closely by an increase in prices, real GDP, and employment.

The Great Depression was indeed not the Fed's finest hour. In the initial phase of the contraction, foreign banks were fearful and withdrew large amounts of their gold from U.S. banks. To stop the outflow of gold to other countries, the Fed raised the discount rate in 1931. As a result, banks borrowed less of their required reserves from the Fed's discount window, and the money supply fell. Later the discount rate fell, but only after the economy was deeper into the Great Depression.

What should the Fed have done? Friedman and Schwartz argued that the Fed should not have waited until 1931 to use open market operations to increase the money

supply. Thus, they concluded that the Fed was to blame for not pursuing an expansionary policy, which would have reduced the severity and duration of the contraction.

Finally, although the emphasis here is monetary policy, it should be noted that both monetary and fiscal policies worsened the situation. President Herbert Hoover attempted to balance the budget, rather than using expansionary fiscal policy.

ANALYZE THE ISSUE

1. Explain why monetarists believe the Fed should have expanded the money supply during the Great Depression.

2. The Keynesians challenge the Friedman-Schwartz monetarists' monetary policy cure for the Great Depression. Use the *AD-AS* model to explain the Keynesian view. (Hint: Your answer must include the investment demand curve.)

Source: Milton Friedman and Anna J. Schwartz, *A Monetary History of the United States, 1867–1960* (Princeton, N.J.: Princeton University Press, 1963).

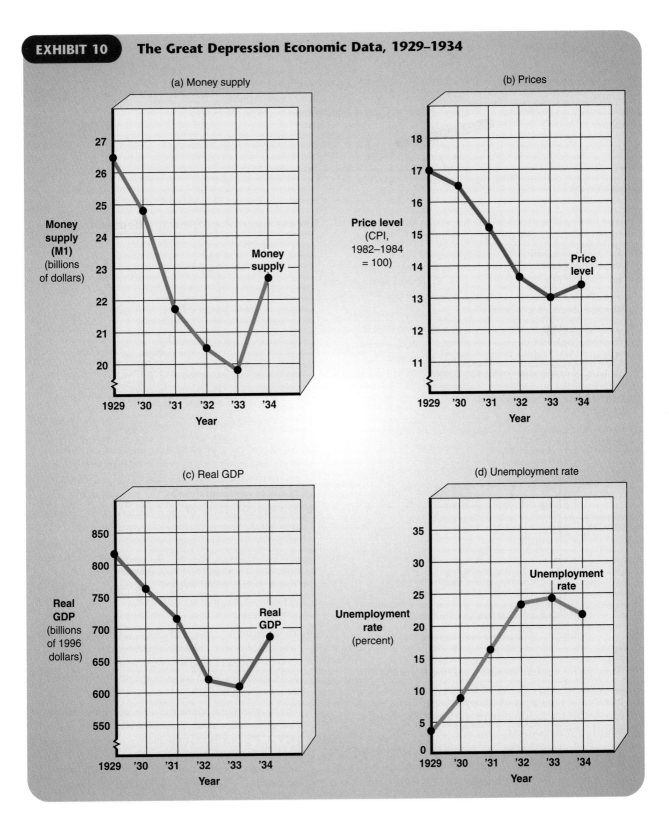

EXHIBIT 10 **The Great Depression Economic Data, 1929–1934**

(a) Money supply

(b) Prices

(c) Real GDP

(d) Unemployment rate

KEY CONCEPTS

Transactions demand for money

Precautionary demand for money

Speculative demand for money

Demand for money curve

Monetarism

Equation of exchange

Velocity of money

Quantity theory of money

SUMMARY

■ The **demand for money** in the Keynesian view consists of three reasons why people hold money: (1) **Transactions demand** is money held to pay for everyday predictable expenses. (2) **Precautionary demand** is money held to pay unpredictable expenses. (3) **Speculative demand** is money held to take advantage of price changes in nonmoney assets.

■ The **demand for money curve** shows the quantity of money people wish to hold at various rates of interest. As the interest rate rises, the quantity of money demanded is less than when the interest rate is lower.

Demand for money curve

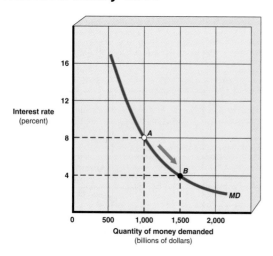

■ The **equilibrium interest rate** is determined in the money market by the intersection of the demand for money and the supply of money curves. The money supply (M1), which is determined by the Fed, is represented by a vertical line.

■ An **excess quantity of money demanded** causes households and businesses to increase their money balances by selling bonds. This causes the price of bonds to fall, thus driving up the interest rate.

Excess quantity of money demanded

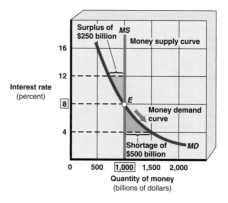

■ An **excess quantity of money supplied** causes households and businesses to reduce their money balances by purchasing bonds. The effect is to cause the price of bonds to rise, and, thereby, the rate of interest falls.

■ The **Keynesian view of the monetary policy transmission mechanism** operates as follows: First, the Fed uses its policy tools to change the money supply. Second, changes in the money supply change the equilibrium interest rate, which affects investment spending. Finally, a change in investment changes aggregate demand and determines the level of prices, real GDP, and employment.

■ **Monetarism** is the simpler view that changes in monetary policy directly change aggregate demand and thereby prices, real GDP, and employment. Thus, monetarists focus on the money supply, rather than on the rate of interest.

■ The **equation of exchange** is an accounting identity that is the foundation of monetarism. The equation ($MV = PQ$) states that the money supply multiplied by the **velocity of money** is equal to the price level multiplied by real output. The velocity of money is the number of times each dollar is spent during a year. Keynesians view velocity as volatile, but monetarists disagree.

■ The **quantity theory of money** is a monetarist argument that the velocity of money (*V*) and the output (*Q*) variables in the equation of exchange are relatively constant. Given this assumption, changes in the money supply yield proportionate changes in the price level. The monetarist solution to inept Fed tinkering with the money supply that causes inflation or recession is to have the Fed simply pick a rate of growth in the money supply that is consistent with real GDP growth and stick to it.

■ **Keynesians' and monetarists' views on fiscal policy** are also different. Keynesians believe the investment demand curve is relatively vertical, and monetarists view it as relatively flat. Monetarists assert that the *crowding-out effect* is large and therefore fiscal policy is ineffective. Keynesians argue that the crowding-out effect is small and that fiscal policy is effective.

SUMMARY OF CONCLUSION STATEMENTS

■ As the interest rate falls, the opportunity cost of holding money falls, and people increase their speculative balances.

■ There is an inverse relationship between the quantity of money demanded and the interest rate.

■ The speculative demand for money at possible interest rates gives the demand for money curve its downward slope.

■ There is an inverse relationship between bond prices and the interest rate that enables the money market to achieve equilibrium.

■ In the Keynesian model, changes in the supply of money affect interest rates. In turn, interest rates affect investment spending, aggregate demand, and, finally, real GDP, employment, and prices.

■ According to the quantity of money theory, any change in the money supply must lead to a proportional change in the price level.

■ To avoid inflation and unemployment, the monetarists' prescription is to be sure that the money supply is at the proper level.

■ Monetarists advocate that the Federal Reserve increase the money supply by a constant percentage each year.

■ Keynesians view the shape of the investment demand curve as rather steep or vertical, so the crowding-out effect is insignificant.

■ Monetarists view the shape of the investment demand curve as less steep or more flat, so the crowding-out effect is significant.

STUDY QUESTIONS AND PROBLEMS

1. How much money do you keep in cash or checkable deposits on a typical day? Under the following conditions, would you increase or decrease your demand for money? Also identify whether the condition affects your transactions demand, precautionary demand, or speculative demand.
   a. Your salary doubles.
   b. The rate of interest on bonds and other assets falls.
   c. An automatic teller machine (ATM) is installed next door, and you have a card.
   d. Bond prices are expected to rise.
   e. You are paid each week, instead of monthly.

2. What are the basic motives for the transactions demand, precautionary demand, and speculative demand? Explain how these three demands are combined in a graph to show the total demand for money.

3. Suppose a bond pays annual interest of $80. Compute the interest rate per year that a bondholder can earn if the bond has a face value of $800, $1,000, and $2,000. State the conclusion drawn from your calculations.

Exhibit 11 Money Market

Interest rate (percent)	Demand for money (billions of dollars)	Supply of money (billions of dollars)
8%	$100	$200
6	200	200
4	300	200
2	400	200

4. Using the above demand and supply schedule for money, do the following:
   a. Graph the demand for and the supply of money curves.
   b. Determine the equilibrium interest rate.
   c. Suppose the Fed increases the money supply by $100 billion. Show the effect in your graph, and describe the money market adjustment process to a new equilibrium interest rate. What is the new equilibrium rate of interest?

5. Assume you are the chair of the Federal Reserve Board of Governors and the condition of the economy is as shown in Exhibit 5. Assume you are a Keynesian, and start at point E_1 in the money market and the product market. State the likely direction of change in the price level, real GDP, and employment caused by each of the following monetary policies:
   a. The Fed makes an open market sale of government bonds.

b. The Fed reduces the required reserve ratio.
   c. The Fed increases the discount rate.

6. "A monetarist investigator might say that the sewer flow of 6,000 gallons an hour consisted of an average of 200 gallons in the sewer at any one time with a complete turnover of the water 30 times every hour."[1] Interpret this statement using the equation of exchange.

7. What is the quantity theory of money, and what does each term in the equation represent?

8. Exhibit 6 shows the monetarist monetary policy transmission mechanism. Assume the economy is in a recession. At each arrow, identify a reason why the transmission process could fail.

9. Explain the difference between the Keynesian and the monetarist views on how an increase in the money supply causes inflation.

10. Based on the quantity theory of money, what would be the impact of increasing the money supply by 25 percent?

11. Suppose the investment demand curve is a vertical line. Given this condition, would the Keynesian or the monetarist view of the impact of monetary policy on investment spending be correct?

12. Why is the shape of the aggregate supply curve important to the Keynesian-monetarist controversy? (Hint: Review Exhibit 6 in the chapter on aggregate demand and supply.)

ONLINE EXERCISES

Exercise 1

To analyze monetary policy, follow these steps:

1. Visit the Federal Reserve (http://www.federalreserve.gov/releases/) and find H.6 and click on Historical Data and then Table 1. Observe what happened to M2 (the money supply) during 1990–1993.

2. Return to the Federal Reserve at http://www.federalreserve.gov/releases/H15/data.htm. Find Bank Prime Loan and click on Monthly and observe what happened to the bank prime loan interest rate during 1990–1993.

3. The Federal Reserve publishes data on investment in capital (plant and equipment). Visit the Fed's site at

http://www.federalreserve.gov/releases/G17/ipdisk/gvp.sa and scroll down to Equipment, Total. What generally happened to investment (business spending on equipment) from 1990–1993?

4. Visit the Federal Reserve Bank of Saint Louis at http://www.stls.frb.org/fred/data/gdp/gdpc96 and observe what happened to real GDP during 1990–1993.

5. Visit Economagic, http://www.economagic.com/ and observe what happened to the GDP implicit price deflator, one measure of inflation, during 1990–1993.

6. Using the aggregate demand and supply model, explain how monetary policy affected an economic recovery after 1991.

---

[1]Werner Sichel and Peter Eckstein, *Basic Economic Concepts* (Chicago: Rand McNally, 1974), p. 344.

Exercise 2

In order to analyze monetary policy, follow these steps:

1. Visit the Federal Reserve (http://www.federalreserve.gov/releases/) and find H.6 and click on Historical Data and then Table 1. Observe what happened to M2 (the money supply) during 1990–1993.

2. Return to the Federal Reserve at http://www.federalreserve.gov/releases/H15/data.htm. Find discount window borrowing and click on Monthly. Observe what happened to the discount rate during 1990–1993.

3. Review Reserve Requirements (http://www.ny.frb.org/pihome/fedpoint/fed45.html). Under the section titled Reserve Requirements and Monetary Policy, find the April 1992 change in the reserve requirement.

4. Based on the evidence given in the steps above, was the Fed's monetary policy expansionary or contractionary? Compare this monetary policy to policy illustrated in Exhibit 10(a) of the text.

Exercise 3

Experience a Federal Open Market Committee meeting through a simulation (http://www.ny.frb.org/pihome/educator/fomcsim.html) created by the New York Federal Reserve Bank.

Exercise 4

To ensure that Congress knows what the Federal Reserve is doing, the chairman of the Federal Reserve must make a semiannual report on economic conditions and the conduct of monetary policy (http://www.federalreserve.gov/boarddocs/hh/). This report is commonly known as the Humphrey-Hawkins testimony, named for the federal statute that requires it. What are the concluding comments of the latest testimony by the chairman of the Federal Reserve?

CHECKPOINT ANSWERS

What Does the Money Supply Look Like When the Fed Targets an Interest Rate?

In Exhibit 12, consider the effect of a shift in the money demand curve from MD_1 to MD_2 when the Fed follows an interest rate target of 10 percent. The initial effects are an excess demand for money and upward pressure on the rate of interest. Because the Fed sets the interest rate target at 10 percent, it will increase the money supply along the money supply curve, *MS*, and establish a new equilibrium at E_2. At the new equilibrium, the money supply has increased from \$800 billion to \$850 billion, and the interest rate is unchanged at 10 percent. Therefore, the money supply curve is traced by an infinite number of possible equilibrium points along the *MS* curve. If you said the money supply curve is horizontal when the Fed sets an interest rate target, YOU ARE CORRECT.

A Horse of Which Color?

The famous economist is Milton Friedman, who favors a monetary rule for the Fed. The horse is a sarcastic way of rejecting Keynesian activist policies that destabilize the economy. Friedman even argues that the Board of Governors of the Federal Reserve System should announce the growth rate for the money supply each year and must resign if the target is missed. If you said the economist is a monetarist, YOU ARE CORRECT.

Exhibit 12

PRACTICE QUIZ

For a visual explanation of the correct answers, visit the tutorial at http://tucker.swcollege.com.

1. Keynes gave which of the following as a motive for people holding money?
   a. Transactions demand
   b. Speculative demand
   c. Precautionary demand
   d. All of the above

2. A decrease in the interest rate, other things being equal, causes a(an)
   a. upward movement along the demand curve for money.
   b. downward movement along the demand curve for money.
   c. rightward shift of the demand curve for money.
   d. leftward shift of the demand curve for money.

3. Assume the demand for money curve is stationary and the Fed increases the money supply. The result is that people
   a. increase the supply of bonds, thus driving up the interest rate.
   b. increase the supply of bonds, thus driving down the interest rate.
   c. increase the demand for bonds, thus driving up the interest rate.
   d. increase the demand for bonds, thus driving down the interest rate.

4. Assume the demand for money curve is fixed and the Fed decreases the money supply. The result is a temporary
   a. excess quantity of money demanded.
   b. excess quantity of money supplied.
   c. increase in the price of bonds.
   d. increase in the demand for bonds.

5. Assume the demand for money curve is fixed and the Fed increases the money supply. The result is that the price of bonds
   a. rises.
   b. remains unchanged.

   c. falls.
   d. None of the above occurs.

6. Using the aggregate supply and demand model, assume the economy is in equilibrium on the intermediate portion of the aggregate supply curve. A decrease in the money supply will decrease the price level and
   a. lower both the interest rate and real GDP.
   b. raise both the interest rate and real GDP.
   c. lower the interest rate and raise real GDP.
   d. raise the interest rate and lower real GDP.

7. Based on the equation of exchange, the money supply in the economy is calculated as
   a. $M = V/PQ$.
   b. $M = V(PQ)$.
   c. $MV = PQ$.
   d. $M = PQ - V$.

8. The V in the equation of exchange represents the
   a. variation in GDP.
   b. variation in the CPI.
   c. variation in real GDP.
   d. the average number of times per year a dollar is spent on final goods and services.

9. Which of the following is *not* an issue in the Keynesian-monetarist debate?
   a. The importance of monetary versus fiscal policy
   b. The importance of a change in the money supply
   c. The importance of the crowding-out effect
   d. All of the above

10. Keynesians reject the influence of monetary policy on the economy. One argument supporting this Keynesian view is that the
    a. money demand curve is horizontal at any interest rate.
    b. aggregate demand curve is nearly flat.
    c. investment demand curve is nearly vertical.
    d. money demand curve is vertical.

Exhibit 13 Money Market Demand and Supply Curves

11. Starting from an equilibrium at E_1 in Exhibit 13, a rightward shift of the money supply curve from MS_1 to MS_2 would cause an excess
    a. demand for money, leading people to sell bonds.
    b. supply of money, leading people to buy bonds.
    c. supply of money, leading people to sell bonds.
    d. demand for money, leading people to buy bonds.

12. Beginning from an equilibrium at E_2 in Exhibit 13, a decrease in the money supply from $600 billion to $400 billion causes people to
    a. sell bonds and drive the price of bonds down.
    b. buy bonds and drive the price of bonds up.
    c. buy bonds and drive the price of bonds down.
    d. sell bonds and drive the price of bonds up.

CHAPTER 27

The Phillips Curve and Expectations Theory

This chapter explores the Phillips curve, expectations theory, and incomes policies (wage and price controls). The Phillips curve traces the relationship between two of the greatest problems of economies everywhere—inflation and unemployment. One of the most fascinating puzzles in economics is whether or not a stable tradeoff exists between these two economic evils. If true, policymakers face a dilemma described by the old saying "Inside each solution there is another problem looking to work its way out." If policymakers reduce the unemployment rate, the inflation rate worsens. Or, if they reduce the inflation rate, the unemployment rate rises. In the 1960s, most economists and policymakers thought the way to achieve a particular inflation-unemployment point on the Phillips curve menu was to use Keynesian demand-management policies.

Just as the reality of the Great Depression refuted classical theory, the Great Stagflations of the 1970s and early 1980s challenged the Phillips curve and Keynesian policies. To explain how varying rates of inflation can occur at the same rate of unemployment, we explore two competing ways of thinking called *adaptive expectations* and *rational expectations*. Both of these theories are attacks on the Keynesians who urge the government to interfere with the market economy in order to achieve full employment.

The chapter begins with a discussion of the Phillips curve and why both expectations camps believe there is no permanent inflation-unemployment tradeoff. In the last part of this chapter, you will see what happens when policymakers fight inflation using policies to control wages and prices (incomes), rather than monetary and fiscal policies.

In this chapter, you will learn to solve these economics puzzles:

■ Why might expansionary fiscal and monetary policies be useless in the long run?

■ If the Fed is independent, why would the money supply increase before a presidential election?

■ Can economic theory explain pop quizzes?

■ Can wearing a button reduce inflation?

The Phillips Curve

In a celebrated article published in 1958, Australian economist A.W. Phillips of the London School of Economics plotted data on unemployment rates and the rate of change in wage rates between 1861 and 1957 in the United Kingdom.[1] Phillips showed there was a remarkably stable inverse relationship between changes in money wages and the unemployment rate. Economists have since extended this concept to the following definition of the **Phillips curve**. The Phillips curve is a curve showing an inverse relationship between the inflation rate and the unemployment rate. The reason it is acceptable to use the inflation rate, rather than the change in wages, is that wages are the main component of prices. At low rates of unemployment, labor has the market power to push up wages and, in turn, prices. When many workers are pounding the pavement eager for jobs, labor lacks bargaining power to ask for raises. As a result, the upward pressure on prices eases.

Phillips curve
A curve showing an inverse relationship between the inflation rate and the unemployment rate.

The Phillips Curve in Theory

Exhibit 1 shows the relationship between the *AD-AS* model developed earlier and the Phillips curve. In part (a), we assume that the aggregate supply curve, *AS*, is stationary. Thus, points *A–D* represent possible equilibrium points depending on the location of the aggregate demand curve. As the aggregate demand curve increases from AD_1 to AD_4, real GDP rises from $6.0 trillion to $6.6 trillion, more workers are employed, and the price level (CPI) rises from 100 to 112. The astute reader will recognize from the chapter on aggregate demand and supply that we are discussing *demand-pull inflation.*

The inverse relationship between the price level and unemployment in part (a) determines the shape of the Phillips curve in part (b). Points *A–D* in both figures correspond. If the economy operates at point *A*, the annual rate of inflation is zero, and the unemployment rate is 8 percent.

Try The Inflation Calculator (http://www .westegg.com/inflation/), *which will adjust any amount of money for inflation.*

---

[1]A.W. Phillips, "The Relation between Unemployment and the Rate of Change in Money Wage Rates in the United Kingdom, 1861–1957," *Economica* 25 (November 1958): 283–299.

EXHIBIT 1 **The Theoretical Relationship between Changes in Aggregate Demand and the Phillips Curve**

In part (a), the aggregate demand curve shifts upward, while the aggregate supply curve remains stationary. The result is a series of equilibrium points *A–D*. As aggregate demand rises along the *AS* curve, the price level (CPI), real GDP, and employment increase. Points *A–D* in parts (a) and (b) correspond. An increase in aggregate demand from AD_1 to AD_4 causes the unemployment rate to fall, but the inflation rate rises. Thus, the increase in aggregate demand results in a movement upward along the Phillips curve.

If the economy is at point *B*, the annual rate of inflation is 4 percent, and the unemployment rate is 5 percent. Similarly, points *C* and *D* correspond in both graphs. Note that below point *A* the price level is below 100 and the economy experiences deflation. The conclusion drawn from Exhibit 1: *Changes in aggregate demand cause a movement along a stationary Phillips curve.*

The Phillips Curve in Practice

So far so good. If the world works this way, policymakers must choose from a menu of inflation rate and unemployment rate combinations along the Phillips curve. Do we want *X* percent less unemployment with an opportunity cost of *Y* percent more inflation? Early studies verified the Phillips curve for the U.S. economy in the 1960s. As shown in Exhibit 2, the data fit the Phillips curve very well. Based on this evidence, most economists, including Nobel Laureates Paul Samuelson and Robert Solow of MIT, believed the Phillips curve was stable. Policymakers might choose low inflation and high unemployment, as in 1961. Or they may prefer higher inflation and lower unemployment, as, for example, in 1969. And the most popular way in the 1960s to reach a particular point on the Phillips curve was to "fine tune" the economy using Keynesian demand-management policies.

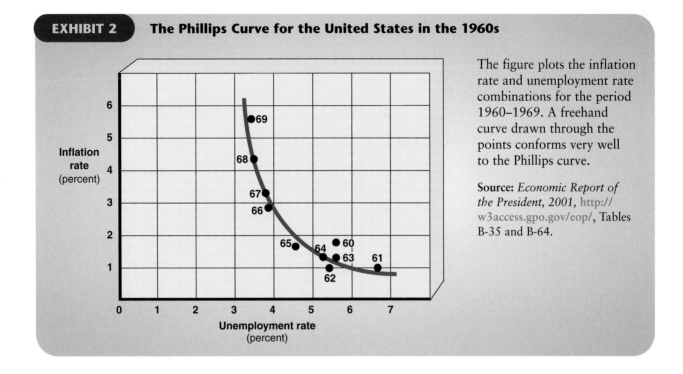

EXHIBIT 2   **The Phillips Curve for the United States in the 1960s**

The figure plots the inflation rate and unemployment rate combinations for the period 1960–1969. A freehand curve drawn through the points conforms very well to the Phillips curve.

Source: *Economic Report of the President, 2001,* http://w3access.gpo.gov/eop/, Tables B-35 and B-64.

Then, just as policymakers and economists became comfortable with the Phillips curve, the dream turned into a nightmare. As shown in Exhibit 3, the points for 1970–2000 show the Phillips curve in chaos. The pattern disappeared, and many points moved far above and to the right of the 1960s data. At higher unemployment rates, the corresponding inflation rate was much higher than the Phillips curve predicted. For example, look at the years 1975, 1979, 1980, and 1981. These data reflect bouts with stagflation, which occurred in the 1970s and early 1980s. Recall from Exhibit 11(a) in the chapter on aggregate demand and supply that *cost-push inflation* is the result of a leftward shift of the aggregate supply curve. In the Great Stagflations of 1973–1974 and 1979–1980, the influence of such "supply shocks" as soaring oil prices pushed up production costs and shifted the economy's aggregate supply curve inward. Thus, the Phillips curve theory was in shambles as the nation simultaneously experienced both high inflation and high unemployment. Policymakers therefore turned their focus from the Phillips curve, based on tradeoffs, to a "misery index," which added the inflation and unemployment rates.

The Long-Run Phillips Curve

The simple idea of a stable tradeoff between unemployment and inflation was an overnight sensation in the 1960s. By the early 1970s, the Phillips curve was becoming a "has-been." Since Keynesian demand-management policies generate the curve, it will come as no surprise that monetarist opponents such

EXHIBIT 3   Inflation and Unemployment Rates for the United States, 1970–2000

After the 1960s, the Phillips curve became unstable. Clearly, many points have been established upward and to the right. The inflation rate therefore can be much higher at any unemployment rate than the Phillips curve of the 1960s predicted.

Source: Bureau of Labor Statistics, ftp://ftp.bls.gov/pub/special.requests/cpi/cpiai.txt and http://stats.bls.gov/webapps/legacy/cpsatab1.htm, Table A-1.

as Milton Friedman and Edmund S. Phelps always believed the Phillips curve was just a transitory, short-run relationship. In the mid-1960s, they suggested that the unemployment rate and the rate of inflation are unrelated in the long run. As shown in Exhibit 4, the challengers argued that after a few years the Phillips curve is a vertical line. As explained below, this monetarist view is also debatable.

Natural Rate Hypothesis

If the Phillips curve is vertical in the long run, there are profound implications for macroeconomic policy. Expansionary monetary and fiscal policies can at best produce a short-lived lowering of unemployment. This is the so-called **natural rate hypothesis.** The natural rate hypothesis argues that the economy will self-correct to the natural rate of unemployment. The long-run Phillips curve is therefore a vertical line at the natural rate of unemployment. Recall from the chapter on business cycles and unemployment that the natural rate of unemployment, or the full-employment unemployment rate, is equal to the sum of the frictional and structural unemployment rates. In

Natural rate hypothesis

The hypothesis that argues the economy will self-correct to the natural rate of unemployment. The long-run Phillips curve is therefore a vertical line at the natural rate of unemployment.

Exhibit 4, the natural rate of unemployment is 6 percent. Two versions of expectations theory explain the natural rate model. We begin our analysis using *adaptive expectations theory* and then turn to the more recent *rational expectations theory*.

Adaptive Expectations Theory

To explain the reasoning behind the natural rate hypothesis, let us begin in Exhibit 4 with the economy operating at point *A*, with a 3 percent inflation rate and a 6 percent unemployment rate. Assume the inflation rate has been 3 percent in recent years and this trend is expected to continue. Based on this recent 3 percent rise in the CPI, collective bargaining agreements call for hourly nominal or money wages of $10.00 this year and $10.30 next year. Now suppose an election is approaching and the president and Congress strive to make voters happy by reducing the unemployment rate to 4 percent. Or perhaps policymakers incorrectly believe 4 percent is the natural rate of unemployment. Regardless of the reason to reach this goal, suppose the new expansionary fiscal policy shifts the aggregate demand curve upward along the aggregate supply curve and the economy moves unexpectedly from point *A* this year to point *B* the next year.

Keynesians declare "mission accomplished" when the economy moves up short-run Phillips curve PC_1 from point *A* to point *B*. This unexpected change brings good news to businesses. Based on an expected inflation rate of 3 percent, employers agreed to pay real wages of $10.00 at point *B*. However, if the inflation rate rises unexpectedly to 6 percent, real wages fall to $9.72 as prices rise.[2] With cheaper labor costs in real terms, profits increase, more workers are hired, real GDP expands, and the unemployment rate drops to 4 percent.

So far, Keynesians and monetarists agree that policymakers and businesses are running the race like the hare and the workers are acting like the tortoise. But monetarists do not believe workers are caught flat-footed as time passes. Workers soon realize that higher prices have eroded their purchasing power. Consequently, they demand an extra 3 percent raise in the nominal wage rate so that their real wages can be restored to the level prior to the unexpected rise in the inflation rate from 3 to 6 percent. When workers get their raise to offset the higher cost of living, business profits decline, and some workers are laid off until the unemployment rate returns to 6 percent at point *C*. At point *C*, the unemployment rate is right back where it began before the government unsystematically changed its fiscal policy, but the inflation rate has risen from 3 to 6 percent. Keynesians, on the other hand, believe nominal wages are fixed because workers do not demand and get an extra 3 percent rise in nominal wages. In the Keynesian view, demand stimulus reduced unemployment in exchange for the higher inflation rate, and the economy remains at point *B* and does not automatically move in time to point *C*.

One estimate of how consumers and producers view the economic future is The Consumer Confidence Survey and Business Executives' Expectations, published by the Conference Board's Consumer Research Center (CRC) (http://www.conference-board.org/products/c-consumer.cfm).

---

[2]Assume the price level at point *A* is 100 and the price level rises to 106 at point *B*. The real wage is computed as the nominal wage multiplied by the initial price level divided by the new price level. Thus, the real wage rate at point *B* is equal to $10.30 × (100/106) = $9.72. If the price level had risen to 103 as expected, the real wage at point *B* would equal $10.30 × (100/103) = $10.00.

EXHIBIT 4   **The Short-Run and Long-Run Phillips Curves**

Beginning at point *A*, the economy is operating at the 6 percent natural rate of unemployment. The actual and anticipated inflation rates are 3 percent. An increase in aggregate demand temporarily causes the inflation rate to rise to 6 percent. Under adaptive expectations theory, real wages fall, profits rise, and more workers are employed. The unemployment rate falls to 4 percent, and the economy moves along the short-run Phillips curve PC_1 to point *B*. Over time, workers demand and get nominal wage rate hikes, and profits fall. Workers lose their jobs, and the unemployment rate returns to 6 percent at point *C* on the short-run Phillips curve PC_2. This process will repeat each time expansionary policy attempts to reduce unemployment below the natural rate. The long-run Phillips curve is therefore a vertical line at the natural rate of unemployment. This suggests that Keynesian expansionary policies create only inflation over time.

Under rational expectations theory, workers do not rely only on recent experience. They adjust their nominal wages quickly in proportion to changes in prices. Expansionary policy will move the economy directly upward along the long-run Phillips curve.

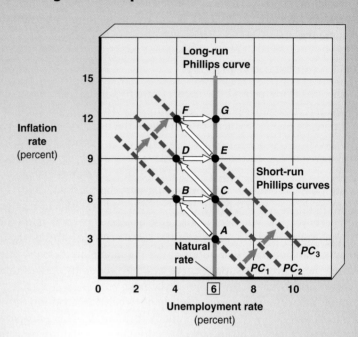

CAUSATION CHAINS

Short-run adaptive expectations theory

Long-run adaptive expectations theory

Rational expectations theory

Our story describes a *wage-price spiral*, defined in the chapter on inflation, and we need a theory to explain how people form their inflationary expectations. The reason the economy moved from point *A* to point *B* is based on **adaptive expectations theory.** Adaptive expectations theory is the concept that people believe the best indicator of the future is recent information. As a result, people persistently underestimate inflation when it is accelerating and overestimate it while it is slowing down. Adaptive expectations theory assumes ignorance of future events, including changes in fiscal and monetary policies. People learn from recent experience and gradually adjust their anticipated inflation rate to the actual inflation rate. This means that at point *C* workers expect a higher rate of inflation at any unemployment rate because last year the actual rate of inflation was 6 percent. Unions therefore expect a 6 percent rate of inflation and are no longer satisfied with a contract with less than a 6 percent increase in the nominal wage rate, since anything less would mean a cut in real wages. Thus, workers *adapt* their expectations to 6 percent instead of 3 percent, and the short-run Phillips curve shifts outward from PC_1 to PC_2 in Exhibit 4. In other words, the economy moves from point *A* to point *C* on the vertical long-run Phillips curve. If policymakers follow a contractionary policy, adaptive expectations operate in reverse, and the inflation rate declines (see You're the Economist: The Political Business Cycle).

Suppose policymakers figure it worked last time, so why not try it again. So they take another stab at creating jobs by stimulating aggregate demand. This time the economy will ride up the new short-run Phillips curve PC_2 from point *C* to point *D*, and the whole process will repeat. When the actual inflation rate rises from 6 to 9 percent, nominal wage increases will be a step slow in catching up with price hikes. In time, workers will demand and get a nominal wage hike, which restores their real wage rate, and the economy will reach point *E*. Faced with the new short-run Phillips curve PC_3, the government will cause an inflation rate of 12 percent at point *F* if it persists in trying to achieve 4 percent unemployment. Eventually, nominal wages will rise (reducing profits), some workers will lose their jobs, and the economy will move from point *F* to point *G*.

Conclusion *According to adaptive expectations theory, expansionary monetary and fiscal policies to reduce the unemployment rate are useless in the long run. After a short-run reduction in unemployment, the economy will self-correct to the natural rate of unemployment, but at a higher inflation rate. Thus, there is no long-run tradeoff between inflation and unemployment.*

The Long-Run Phillips Curve and the Labor Market

We are now able to give one explanation for the tendency of the inflation-unemployment points shown earlier in Exhibit 3 to shift upward to the right in the 1970s and early 1980s. Demand stimulus policies in the 1960s caught people by surprise, and there was a movement upward along a short-run Phillips curve. As inflation worsened during the 1970s and the early 1980s, adaptive expectations caused the short-run Phillips curves to shift outward. As the inflation rate dropped sharply during the late 1980s,

Adaptive expectations theory
The concept that people believe the best indicator of the future is recent information. As a result, people persistently underestimate inflation when it is accelerating and overestimate it while it is slowing down.

The Bureau of Labor Statistics maintains statistics and information from its monthly report of households, called the Current Population Survey (http://www.bls.gov/cps/). *Included is a Labor Department report on how the government measures unemployment* (http://www.bls.gov/cps/cps_htgm.htm). *The Department of Labor also provides a number of employment-related programs, such as America's Job Bank* (http://www.AJB.dni.us/) *and Welfare to Work* (http://wtw.doleta.gov/).

The Political Business Cycle

Applicable Concept: adaptive expectations

The basic ideal of Keynesian economics is that the government uses monetary and fiscal policies to stabilize the economy. On the other hand, the government may be diabolical and deliberately cause business cycles. The **political business cycle** is therefore Keynesianism in reverse. A political business cycle is a business cycle caused by policymakers to improve politicians' reelection chances.

A basic assumption of the political business cycle model is that democratic government causes business cycles. This theory views politics as by nature a short-run game. The rational self-interest goal of politicians is to maximize votes today and worry about tomorrow when tomorrow comes. This means a politician who faces an election must act now and not later. Voters are also short-sighted and want good news now, rather than promises of long-term solutions. If people want jobs, for example, the politicians who seek reelection will use expansionary policies to create jobs. The political process will therefore gladly force a lower unemployment rate now in exchange for a higher inflation rate in the future. The politician who commits the sin of truth and tells the voters a "quick fix" is harmful will probably taste defeat.

Given the realities of politics, politicians may find it easier to let the Fed stimulate the economy. Expansionary fiscal policy requires Congress to approve tax cuts or spending increases. Since members of Congress belong to opposing parties, each side has an incentive to prevent the other party from taking credit for legislation. Even if a bill eventually passes, it may be too late for the election. Fiscal policy takes considerable time to implement and actually affect the economy and, in turn, the voters.

If the Fed is independent, why would the Fed be willing to create the political business cycle? Recall that the president appoints the Fed chairperson and members of the Board of Governors. Thus, the Fed is a semiseparate branch of government and often wishes to avoid conflict with Congress or the president. If the Fed is willing to stimulate aggregate demand before an election, incumbent politicians will benefit at the expense of their opponents. Once the election is over, the Fed will slow down the economy to reduce the inflation rate. Then the concern becomes recession until the next election looms and the Fed stimulates the economy again. Meanwhile, politicians can blame the Fed for driving up prices or starting the downturn.

Exhibit 5 reveals that the money supply has generally been on the rise before presidential elections. In 1964, 1968, 1972, 1976, 1988, and 1992, the money supply rose before the presidential election and then fell after the presidential election. The 1980, 1984, 1996, and 2000 elections are exceptions.

ANALYZE THE ISSUE

Based on adaptive expectations theory, assume an expansionary monetary policy has moved the economy to point C in Exhibit 4. Now suppose the election is over and inflation concerns policymakers, so the Fed applies the brakes to monetary policy. Use this diagram to explain the short-run and long-run effects of a contractionary monetary policy.

Political business cycle

A business cycle caused by policymakers to improve politicians' reelection chances.

people's inflationary expectations adapted in the downward direction, and the short-run Phillips curve shifted inward. Moreover, as discussed in the chapter on business cycles and unemployment, it is estimated that the *natural rate of unemployment* increased from the 1960s to the 1980s. Recall that the natural rate of unemployment is the full-employment unemployment rate at which the economy operates at capacity (potential GDP). This means the vertical long-run Phillips curve intersecting each short-run Phillips curve shifted to the right. As explained in the chapter on business cycles and unemployment, the explanation in part is because women and teenagers became a larger percentage of the labor force and these groups of workers often experience higher rates of unemployment. It is also argued

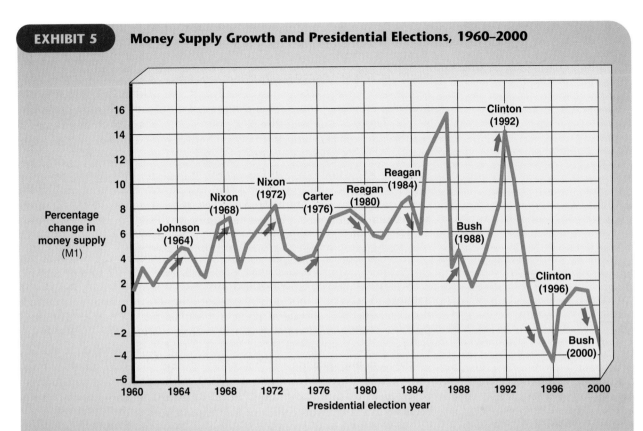

EXHIBIT 5   **Money Supply Growth and Presidential Elections, 1960–2000**

Since 1960, the money supply has often increased prior to presidential elections. The 1980, 1984, 1996, and 2000 elections are exceptions.

Sources: *Economic Report of the President, 2001,* http://w3/access.gpo/eop/, Table B-69; and Federal Reserve Board, http://www.federalreserve.gov/releases/H6/hist/h6hist1.txt.

that the following measures might reduce the natural rate of unemployment: revising unemployment compensation, changing the minimum wage law, providing better education and training, improving information on available jobs, removing discrimination, and reducing the monopoly power of unions and businesses.

The Theory of Rational Expectations

Whether expectations are formed "adaptively" or "rationally" is a hotly contested debate among economists. In the mid-1970s, Robert Lucas of the University of Chicago (1995 Nobel Laureate) is generally credited with introducing the **theory of rational expectations,** which is the competing view that adaptive expectations theory is too simplistic. Rational expectations theory is the belief that people use all available information to predict the

Rational expectations theory

The belief that people use all available information to predict the future, including future monetary and fiscal policies. Systematic and predictable macroeconomic policies can therefore be negated when businesses and workers anticipate the effects of these policies on the economy.

future, including future monetary and fiscal policies. Systematic and predictable macroeconomic policies can therefore be negated when businesses and workers anticipate the effects of these policies on the economy. According to the rational expectations hypothesis, people do not simply think inflation will be about the same next year as last year. Although everyone's crystal ball is clouded, people are intelligent and informed on how the economy works. They not only consider past price changes, but also how changes in the federal deficit or money supply will affect inflation next year. Suppose businesses and workers predict that a surge in the money supply or a tax cut will raise the actual inflation rate to, say, 6 percent. They will immediately raise their expectations of the inflation rate to 6 percent even though the most recent rate of inflation was 3 percent. In short, rational expectationists believe that both nominal wages and prices are flexible.

Let's reconsider the case in which the government is trying to reduce the unemployment rate. Begin at point *A* in Exhibit 4, and suppose policymakers strive to reduce unemployment, using new expansionary policies to stimulate demand. Under rational expectations theory, workers are not caught napping. Workers will not simply wait until the actual inflation rate exceeds the expected inflation rate at point *B* and then ask for a raise. Although they may lack formal training in forecasting, workers are quite sophisticated in understanding the macro economy. They watch news on television, check economic data on the Internet, and read the *Wall Street Journal, Time,* the local newspapers, and AFL-CIO publications for information on government policies and future changes in prices. When new information becomes available, workers revise their expectations.

Changes in the consumer price index (CPI)—a measure of the average change in prices paid by urban consumers for a fixed market basket of goods and services—is a standard measure of inflation. The Bureau of Labor Statistics provides current and historical data on the CPI (http://www.bls.gov/cpi/).

Since workers wisely use all relevant information to predict future changes, they anticipate that the aggregate demand curve is going to shift rightward, causing a rise in the price level and a fall in real wages. They know that unless they get wage hikes to match the price increases, they will be losers. Consequently, workers rationally raise their nominal wage demands so that no gap between the actual and expected rates of inflation occurs. In fact, many collective bargaining agreements contain escalator clauses, providing automatic nominal wage increases as the price level rises. Assuming that workers correctly anticipate the inflation rate, real wages remain unchanged because nominal wages and prices rise proportionately. This means the temporary increase in profits, real GDP, and employment does *not* happen as predicted by adaptive expectationists. In short, rational expectationists refute the short-run Phillips curves drawn in Exhibit 4. There would be, for example, no decrease in unemployment from 6 percent (point *A*) to 4 percent (point *B*). Instead, the only movement in the inflation rate is directly from 3 percent (point *A*) to 6 percent (point *C*). This means higher anticipated inflation is added without delay to current nominal wages and prices, which generates a vertical Phillips curve along such points as *A, C, E,* and *G.* Thus, we have one startling conclusion: *According to rational expectations theory, systematic and predictable expansionary monetary and fiscal policies used to reduce unemployment are not only useless, but also harmful because the only result is higher inflation.*

CHECKPOINT

Does Rational Expectations Theory Work in the Classroom?

An economics professor is considering improving class attendance and preparation by giving pop quizzes. Two approaches are being considered. If rational expectations theory operates in the classroom, should the professor give pop quizzes on days when homework is due or keep it a secret and give pop quizzes randomly?

On the brighter side, rational expectations theory argues that a credible "stay the course" contractionary fiscal and monetary policy can quickly cool inflation without increasing unemployment. Suppose the economy is at the natural rate of unemployment and the Fed decreases the money supply to lower the rate of inflation. Workers analyze available information on the future impact of the Fed's action from AFL-CIO economists and other sources. They are convinced that policymakers are committed to decreasing aggregate demand until the price level recedes. Armed with this analysis, workers are not surprised, and they reduce their nominal wages as prices fall. In this case, there is no short-run Phillips curve. Contrary to adaptive expectations, inflation can be cured without recession, since workers are not caught off-guard.

Keynesians reject rational expectations theory because they argue that prices and wages are "sticky" downward (see Exhibit 4 of the chapter on aggregate demand and supply). On the other hand, the classical economists believed that the economy automatically adjusts after short-run delays to full employment in the long run. But in the rational expectations model, not so! There is no short run. Nevertheless, because the theory of rational expectations is similar to the self-correction model of the classical economists, rational expectationists are called *new classical* economists. Thus, we have another conclusion: *According to rational expectations theory, if people are not surprised by monetary and fiscal policy changes, the economy's self-correction mechanism will restore the natural rate of unemployment. Preannounced, stable policies to achieve low and constant money supply growth and a balanced federal budget are therefore the best way to lower the inflation rate.*

Applying the *AD-AS* Model to the Great Expectations Debate

The distinction between adaptive expectations and rational expectations can be analyzed using the aggregate demand–aggregate supply model presented in Exhibit 6. Assume the economy is currently in equilibrium at point E_1, with a full-employment output of $6 trillion. Now suppose the Fed pursues

EXHIBIT 6 **Adaptive Expectations versus Rational Expectations**

Suppose policymakers use expansionary policies to increase the aggregate demand curve from AD_1 to AD_2. Adaptive expectations theory argues that labor adjusts nominal wages sluggishly. As a result, the path of the economy is E_1–E_2–E_3 with a temporary increase in real GDP to $6.5 trillion and lower unemployment at point E_2. The theory of rational expectations is the competing view that the expansionary policy used to increase the aggregate demand curve from AD_1 to AD_2 is anticipated. Workers anticipate that the price level (CPI) will rise to 110, so they increase their nominal wages without a period of adjustment. As a result, the aggregate supply curve shifts from $SRAS_1$ to $SRAS_2$, causing the economy to move directly from equilibrium point E_1 to point E_3. The result of Keynesian expansionary policies under both theories is that inflation becomes worse and there is no effect on real GDP or employment.

an expansionary monetary policy designed to create jobs and further reduce unemployment. Hence, the aggregate demand curve shifts rightward from AD_1 to AD_2 along the short-run aggregate supply curve $SRAS_1$. Based on adaptive expectations theory, a monetarist urges the Fed to leave the economy alone. The monetarist's prediction is that the economy moves from equilibrium at E_1 to E_2, causing real GDP to rise from the potential GDP of $6 trillion to the GDP of $6.5 trillion. Recall from Exhibit 8 of the chapter on business cycles and unemployment that this condition in the economy is a negative GDP gap of $0.5 trillion. In addition, the price level (CPI) increases from 100 to 105. Eventually, at equilibrium E_2, with unemployment below the natural rate, workers are no longer "caught off-guard" and demand higher nominal wages to offset the rise in prices. As a result, production costs rise, causing the short-run aggregate supply curve to shift leftward from $SRAS_1$ to $SRAS_2$; therefore, a new equilibrium is established at E_3. This response drives up the unemployment rate to the natural rate as real output returns to the initial level of $6 trillion. However, Fed activism has not had a neutral effect on the price level because it has risen from the initial level of 100 to 110. The monetarist's prediction is therefore higher inflation and no impact on employment and real GDP in the long run.

A rational expectationist sees events differently. Most people are not "fooled." They are able to rationally predict the consequences of expansionary monetary policies. People anticipate that the economy will move from point E_1 to point E_3, the price level will rise from 100 to 110, and real GDP will not change. Consequently, businesses and workers do not stumble around in the dark, unable to see what the actual inflation rate is going to be. They know, or *anticipate*, that the inflation rate is going to rise 10 percent, and they react immediately by raising prices and wages 10 percent. Since prices and wages increase quickly and proportionately, rational expectations theory predicts a direct path of change in the economy's equilibrium from E_1 to E_3. Stated differently, if firms and workers formulate expectations rationally, any impact of stimulative monetary policy is nullified. Under rational expectations theory, only *unanticipated* or *surprise* policies can influence output and employment.

If workers foresee inflation and prevent erosion of their real wages by demanding and receiving nominal wage raises in advance, aggregate supply is the vertical curve, *LRAS*. When real wages remain unchanged, there is no incentive for businesses to alter production as prices rise. If rational expectations theory is correct, the economy does not enjoy the short-lived pleasure of lower unemployment predicted by adaptive expectations theory at point E_2.

Incomes Policy

Suppose we accept the power of unions and businesses to raise wages and prices as inevitable. Let's also assume Milton Friedman is correct that discretionary monetary and fiscal policies are useless or counterproductive. Then what approach is left to fight inflation? There is another way, used in the past, which is a collection of regulatory policies called **incomes policies**. Incomes policies are federal government policies designed to affect the real incomes of workers by controlling nominal wages and prices. Such policies include presidential jawboning, wage-price guidelines, and wage-price controls.

Incomes policies
Federal government policies designed to affect the real incomes of workers by controlling nominal wages and prices. Such policies include presidential jawboning, wage-price guidelines, and wage-price controls.

Presidential Jawboning

The mildest form of incomes policies is **jawboning.** Jawboning is oratory intended to pressure unions and businesses to reduce wage and price increases. The government attempts to prevent or roll back wage and price

Jawboning
Oratory intended to pressure unions and businesses to reduce wage and price increases.

hikes by appealing to labor and business leaders. The most spectacular success with this technique occurred in 1962. President John F. Kennedy called major U.S. steel manufacturers and convinced them to rescind their price increases. But President Kennedy jawboned with a club in hand. He threatened to sell government stockpiles of steel at lower prices. The president also informed the firms that those failing to cooperate would lose government contracts to firms that would lower prices. President Lyndon Johnson followed Kennedy's example and jawboned even more. Then there was the "Blow the Whistle" program under President Richard Nixon. An official agency was established to monitor unwarranted price increases and publicly announce violators of the national interest.

Most economists argue that firms raise prices when changes in demand or cost make it profitable to do so. Jawboning may do a little good for a while, but over time it is a blunt weapon against inflation.

Wage and Price Guidelines

Wage and price guidelines
Voluntary standards set by the government for "permissible" wage and price increases.

A more formal policy to cool down the inflation rate is **wage and price guidelines.** Wage and price guidelines are voluntary standards set by the government for "permissible" wage and price increases. The Truman and Eisenhower administrations made unsystematic attempts to discourage business and labor from raising prices and wages. But the first systematic wage and price guideline program was initiated in the Kennedy administration, this approach was also used during the Johnson and Carter administrations. For example, the Carter administration asked labor unions to limit their wage increases to 7 percent. Violators were identified in hopes that adverse publicity would force the unions to comply. Without any enforcement mechanism, the dominant view among economists is that guidelines accomplish little against self-interest.

Wage and Price Controls

Wage and price controls
Legal restrictions on wage and price increases. Violations can result in fines and imprisonment.

When guidelines have the force of law, the economy moves to a mandatory system of **wage and price controls.** Wage and price controls are legal restrictions on wage and price increases. Violations can result in fines and imprisonment. Once people believe wages and prices are under control by law, the good news is that they expect lower prices. The bad news is that controls are government interference with market supply and demand.

As discussed in Chapter 4, a ceiling price established below the equilibrium price will cause shortages in markets (see Exhibit 4 in Chapter 4). This usually means rationing of such scarce items as gasoline. When price is not allowed to serve as the rationing device, consumers must incur higher opportunity costs by waiting in long lines for gasoline. This happened in 1979, when the government imposed a price ceiling on gasoline. Another rationing device is government ration coupons that give the right to buy a good. Ration coupons were used for many goods during World War II. Shortages also lead to *black markets,* which are illegal markets for goods at unregulated prices. To enforce the system requires a government bureaucracy at taxpayers' expense.

CHECKPOINT

Can Wage and Price Controls Cure Stagflation?

Suppose war in the Persian Gulf destroyed much of the world's oil reserves. As a result, the U.S. economy is experiencing a bout of stagflation. You are a member of Congress, and a bill is introduced to fight the problems of high inflation and high unemployment by imposing wage and price controls. Using the *AD-AS* model, will you vote in favor of controls to cure stagflation by freezing the price level? [Hint: Look at Exhibit 4 of Chapter 4 and Exhibit 11(a) in the chapter on aggregate demand and supply.]

Long lines for products, ration coupons, and black markets are not popular. This explains why wage and price controls appear primarily during war and rarely in peacetime. The United States has imposed wage and price controls during World War II, the Korean War, and, most recently, during the Nixon administration. President Nixon hoped to combat high inflationary expectations built up during the Vietnam War. The inflation rate from 1969 to 1971 averaged 5.2 percent, an alarming rate in those days. The plan was to control inflation and then fight unemployment, which averaged 4.8 percent over the same period. The first phase of the attack was a 90-day freeze on wages and prices in August 1971. A 15-member Pay Board and a 7-member Price Commission administered the controls. For three months businesses could not raise prices, wages were frozen, and landlords could not charge higher rents. The intent was to give inflationary expectations a shock treatment. Then the freeze lifted, and wage and price controls were established to limit increases between 1971 and 1974. The bottom line is that in 1971 the inflation rate was 4.4 percent. In 1973, the inflation rate climbed to 6.2 percent. When the experiment with controls ended in 1974, the inflation rate rose to 11 percent. During the same period, the unemployment rate remained between 5 and 6 percent. Obviously, controls did not slay the inflation dragon although some economists have argued that controls made the dragon less fierce.

In 1968, the Council of Economic Advisers eloquently stated the opinion of most economists on wage and price controls:

> *While such controls may be necessary under conditions of an all-out war,*
> *it would be folly to consider them as a solution to inflationary pressures*
> *that accompany high employment under any other circumstance. . . .*
> *Although such controls may be unfortunately popular when they are in*
> *effect, the appeal quickly disappears once people live under them.*[3]

The majority view is that controls destroy the efficient allocation of resources provided by the price system and intrude on economic freedom. Defenders of controls believe this is a small price to pay.

---

[3]*Annual Report of the Council of Economic Advisers* (Washington, D.C.: Government Printing Office, 1968), p. 119.

EXHIBIT 7 How Different Macroeconomic Models Cure Inflation

School of thought
Monetarism

Milton Friedman

Inflation prescription:
Monetarists see the cause of inflation as "too much money chasing too few goods," based on the quantity of money theory ($MV = PQ$). To cure inflation, they would cut the money supply and force the Fed to stick to a fixed money supply growth rate. In the short run, the unemployment rate will rise, but in the long run, it self-corrects to the natural rate.

School of thought
Keynesianism

John Maynard Keynes

Inflation prescription:
Keynesians believe in using contractionary fiscal and monetary policies to cool an overheated economy. To decrease aggregate demand, they advocate that the government use tax hikes and/or spending cuts. The Fed should reduce the money supply and cause the rate of interest to rise. The opportunity cost of reducing inflation is greater unemployment. Keynesians also believe that incomes policies are effective.

School of thought
Supply-side economics

Arthur Laffer

Inflation prescription:
Supply-siders view the cause of inflation as "not enough goods." Their approach is to increase aggregate supply by cuts in marginal tax rates, government regulations, and import barriers. The effect provides incentives to work, invest, and expand production capacity. Thus, both the inflation rate and the unemployment rate fall.

School of thought
New classic school

Robert Lucas

Inflation prescription:
The theory of rational expectations asserts that the public must be convinced that policymakers will stick to restrictive and persistent fiscal and monetary policies. If policymakers have credibility, the inflation rate will be anticipated and quickly fall without a rise in unemployment.

How Different Macroeconomic Theories Attack Inflation

Robert Lucas, a winner of the Nobel Prize in Economics, is often associated with the theory of rational expectations. Who is the latest Nobel laureate in economics? Find out at http://www.nobel.se/.

If incomes policies do not cure an overheated economy during peacetime, policymakers must decide which macroeconomic school "hat" to wear. Exhibit 7 gives a brief description of how four basic macroeconomic models deal with inflation. Recall the monetarist view presented in the previous chapter and supply-side economics explained in the chapter on fiscal policy.

Ford's Whip Inflation Now (WIN) Button

Applicable Concept: incomes policies

The most interesting historical artifact of the fight against inflation is gathering dust in the White House attic. In October 1974, President Gerald Ford proposed the "WIN" button to a joint session of Congress. The idea was that Americans would wear their "Whip Inflation Now" buttons, and this would break the wage-price spiral. The WIN button represented an appeal to patriotism that would discourage businesses and labor from raising prices and wages.

The logical question is, What circumstances drove the president of the United States to use a button against inflation? We will begin the story in 1971, when the Nixon administration approved wage and price controls to cool inflationary expectations. Beginning in 1972, bad crops caused food prices to soar, and the OPEC oil embargo boosted the price of crude oil. These supply shocks boosted the inflation rate from 3.2 percent in 1972 to 6.2 percent in 1973. Clearly, the wage and price control program was falling apart before controls ended in 1974.

Following the demand-management prescription against inflation, the Fed raised the discount rate in late 1973. Federal Reserve Chair Arthur Burns stated that the Fed must follow a contractionary monetary policy for years to come. Despite the Fed's restrictive policy, the inflation rate rose to an annual rate of about 14 percent in early 1974. By late 1974, the unemployment rate had risen to 6 percent, but policymakers remained committed to anti-inflation policies. The Fed raised the discount rate again in the fall of 1974, and President Ford called an economic summit meeting. The outcome of the summit was a resolve to stick to the battle plan and beat inflation before turning to the worsening unemployment problem. Aiming for public support, President Ford unveiled the WIN button, accompanied by a tax surcharge and federal spending ceiling proposals. While the fight against inflation preoccupied policymakers, the unemployment rate rose from 5.6 percent in 1974 to 8.5 percent in 1975. The percentage change in real GDP between 1974 and 1975 was −0.6 percent, and recession suddenly replaced inflation as the

number one enemy. In response, Congress approved a $22.8 billion tax cut bill in 1975, and the Fed increased the money supply. In 1974, the inflation rate was 11.0 percent, and in 1975, the inflation rate was still at the high rate of 9.1 percent.

What caused this puzzling twist in stabilization policy to deal with stagflation? Many economists explain this turn of events by the absence of a conceptual framework to understand the effects of supply shocks on the aggregate supply curve. Instead, policymakers tried to shift the aggregate demand curve back and forth while asking people to wear a WIN button.

ANALYZE THE ISSUE

Assume the economy is in equilibrium at full employment and the public anticipates restrictive monetary and fiscal policies, including WIN buttons, which decrease aggregate demand in order to combat inflation. Use the *AD-AS* model depicted in Exhibit 6 to explain the new classical predictions of the impact on the price level, real GDP, and the unemployment rate.

KEY CONCEPTS

Phillips curve	Political business cycle	Jawboning
Natural rate hypothesis	Rational expectations	Wage and price guidelines
Adaptive expectations	theory	Wage and price controls
theory	Incomes policies	

SUMMARY

■ The **Phillips curve** shows a stable inverse relationship between the inflation rate and the unemployment rate. If policymakers reduce inflation, unemployment increases, and vice versa. During the 1960s, the curve closely fitted inflation and unemployment rates in the United States. Since 1970, the Phillips curve has not conformed to the stable inflation-unemployment trade-off pattern of the 1960s.

The Phillips Curve for the United States

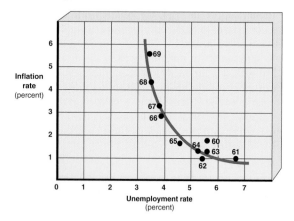

■ The **natural rate hypothesis** argues that the economy self-corrects to the natural rate of unemployment. Over time, changes in the rate of inflation are fully anticipated, and prices and wages rise or fall proportionately. As a result, the long-run Phillips curve is a vertical line at the natural rate of unemployment. Thus, Keynesian demand-management policies ultimately cause only higher or lower inflation, and the natural rate of unemployment remains unchanged.

■ **Adaptive expectations theory** is the proposition that people base their economic forecasts on recent past information, rather than future information. Once the government causes the inflation rate to rise or fall, people adapt their inflationary expectations to the current inflation rate. The result is a short-run Phillips curve that intersects the vertical long-run Phillips curve. Over time, the economy self-corrects to the natural rate of unemployment.

■ The **political business cycle** is a business cycle created by the incentive for politicians to manipulate the economy to get reelected. Using expansionary policies, officeholders can stimulate the economy before the election. Unemployment falls, and the price level rises. After the election, the strategy is to contract the economy to fight inflation and unemployment rises.

■ **Rational expectations theory** argues that it is naive to believe that people change their inflationary expectations based only on the current inflation rate. Rational expectationists belong to the new classical school. Assuming the impact of government policy is predictable, people immediately anticipate higher or lower inflation. Workers quickly change their nominal wages as businesses change prices. Consequently, inflation worsens or improves, and unemployment remains unchanged at the natural rate. Thus, there is no short-run Phillips curve, and the vertical long-run Phillips curve is identical to adaptive expectations theory.

■ **Incomes policies** are a variety of federal government programs aimed at directly controlling wages and prices. Incomes policies include jawboning, wage-price guidelines, and wage-price controls. Over time, incomes policies tend to be ineffective.

■ **Wage and price controls** are legal restrictions on wages and prices. Most economists do not favor wage and price controls in peacetime. Such controls are expensive to administer, destroy efficiency, and intrude on economic freedom.

SUMMARY OF CONCLUSION STATEMENTS

- Changes in aggregate demand cause a movement along a stationary Phillips curve.

- According to adaptive expectations theory, expansionary monetary and fiscal policies to reduce the unemployment rate are useless in the long run. After a short-run reduction in unemployment, the economy will self-correct to the natural rate of unemployment, but at a higher inflation rate. Thus, there is no long-run tradeoff between inflation and unemployment.

- According to rational expectations theory, systematic and predictable expansionary monetary and fiscal policies used to reduce unemployment are not only useless, but also harmful because the only result is higher inflation.

- According to rational expectations theory, if people are not surprised by monetary and fiscal policy changes, the economy's self-correction mechanism will restore the natural rate of unemployment. Preannounced, stable policies to achieve low and constant money supply growth and a balanced federal budget are therefore the best way to lower the inflation rate.

STUDY QUESTIONS AND PROBLEMS

1. What is a Phillips curve? Assuming the economy's aggregate supply curve is stable, how would an increase in aggregate demand affect the unemployment rate and the inflation rate?

2. What were the inflation rate and the unemployment rate last year? Do these rates lie on a Phillips curve?

3. What happened in the 1970s and early 1980s to cast doubt on the Phillips curve?

4. Suppose you flipped an honest coin 10 times and heads came up 8 times. You are about to toss the coin another 10 times. Using adaptive expectations, how many heads do you expect? Based on rational expectations, how many heads do you expect?

5. According to adaptive expectations, what happens to the inflation rate and the unemployment rate in the following situations?
   a. Initially, the economy is operating at the natural rate of 6 percent unemployment. The anticipated rate of inflation is 6 percent, and the actual rate is also 6 percent.
   b. In the next period, there is an unexpected rise in the inflation rate to 10 percent.
   c. In the next period, there is an unexpected rise in the inflation rate to 12 percent.

6. Explain what happens under adaptive expectations theory when monetary and fiscal policymakers use expansionary policy to achieve an unemployment rate below the natural rate.

7. Keynesians believe monetary and fiscal policymakers should stabilize the business cycle. Compare the political business cycle to Keynesian policy objectives.

8. Use Exhibit 8 to answer the questions below.

Exhibit 8

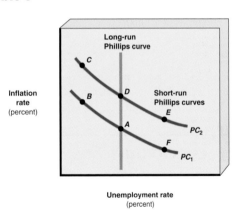

a. Which points represent the natural unemployment rate?
b. Which points represent an unemployment rate below the natural unemployment rate?
c. Which points represent an unemployment rate above the natural unemployment rate?
d. Explain points A and D on the graph.
e. Explain points B and C on the graph.
f. Explain points E and F on the graph.
g. Why is curve PC_2 to the right of curve PC_1?

9. Based on rational expectations theory, what happens to the inflation rate and the unemployment rate in the following situations?

a. Initially, the economy is operating at the natural rate of 4 percent unemployment, and the inflation rate is also 4 percent. People correctly anticipate that an increase in the money supply will increase the inflation rate to 6 percent next year.

b. In the next period, people correctly forecast that a tax cut will cause the inflation rate to rise to 8 percent.

c. In the next period, they anticipate that the Fed's hike in the discount rate will cause the inflation rate to fall to 4 percent.

ONLINE EXERCISES

Exercise 1

Visit the Cleveland Federal Reserve (http://www.clev.frb.org/research/jul96et/charts/monpol2a.htm). What is the relationship between unemployment and inflation for 1960-1998 in the United States? Does this support or refute the existence of a Phillips Curve?

Exercise 2

Visit the National Center for Policy Analysis (http://www.ncpa.org/pd/economy/pd062000f.html). According to this article, what may have happened to the Phillips Curve in the 1990s? Could it have shifted inward to the left? What may have caused this?

Exercise 3

For each of the last several months, review the level of unemployment in the United States and the current con-

sumer price index (http://www.bls.gov/eag/eag.us.htm). Next review the prime interest rate over the same months, as published by the Federal Reserve (http://www.federalreserve.gov/releases/H15/data/m/prime.txt). Does the natural-rate hypothesis seem to hold? Has the Federal Reserve raised or lowered interest rates in line with this hypothesis?

Exercise 4

The Conference Board (http://www.tcb-indicators.org/), and the National Bureau of Economic Research (http://www.nber.org) publish and maintain data on business cycle indicators. What do you expect to happen to our economy in the future?

CHECKPOINT ANSWERS

Does Rational Expectations Theory Work in the Classroom?

Under rational expectations, if the students know what is going to happen, they will use this information to negate the policy. If pop quizzes are given on the same day homework is due, the rational student will be certain to attend class on those days and take cuts on other class days. If quizzes are random, quiz dates are unknown, so there is always a chance that missing a class may mean missing a quiz. If you said the professor will keep pop quizzes a secret and give them randomly, YOU ARE CORRECT.

Can Wage and Price Controls Cure Stagflation?

Assume the economy begins in equilibrium at E_1 in Exhibit 9 and an oil shock causes the economy to move to a new equilibrium at E_2. Without wage and price controls, the price level increases from 150 to 200, and real GDP decreases from $4 trillion to $3 trillion. Now assume laws keep the price level frozen at 150. This means firms cannot raise prices to meet higher costs, so under controls they are forced to lay off more workers and cut production even further. The economy's equilibrium moves from E_2 to E_3, and real GDP is $2 trillion, rather than $3 trillion, causing unemployment to climb even higher.

Using wage and price controls to fight inflation would cause an even more severe decrease in real GDP; therefore, unemployment is greater than otherwise would be the case. If you voted *no* on the wage and price controls bill because they cause greater shortages and a deeper recession, YOU ARE CORRECT.

Exhibit 9

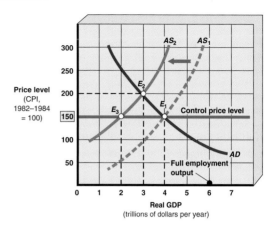

PRACTICE QUIZ

For a visual explanation of the correct answers, visit the tutorial at http://tucker.swcollege.com.

1. The Phillips curve depicts the relationship between the
   a. unemployment rate and the change in GDP.
   b. inflation rate and the interest rate.
   c. level of investment spending and the interest rate.
   d. inflation rate and the unemployment rate.

2. A difficulty in using the Phillips curve as a policy menu is the
   a. fact that the natural rate of unemployment does not exist.
   b. fact that the curve would not remain in one position.
   c. difficulty deciding between monetary and fiscal policies.
   d. fact that Democrats choose one point on the curve and Republicans choose another point.

3. Since the 1970s, the
   a. Phillips curve has not been stable.
   b. inflation rate and the unemployment rate have been about equal.
   c. Phillips curve has proven to be a reliable model to guide public policy.
   d. relationship between the inflation rate and the unemployment rate moved in a counterclockwise direction.

4. According to the natural rate hypothesis,
   a. the Phillips curve is quite flat, so that a large reduction in employment can be achieved without inflation.
   b. workers only adapt their wage demands to inflation after a considerable time lag.
   c. the Phillips curve is vertical in the long run at full employment.
   d. workers cannot anticipate the inflationary effects of expansionary public policies.

5. Adaptive expectations theory
   a. argues that the best indicator of the future is recent information.
   b. underestimates inflation when it is accelerating.
   c. overestimates inflation when it is slowing down.
   d. does none of the above.
   e. does all of the above.

6. The conclusion of adaptive expectations theory is that expansionary monetary and fiscal policies intended to reduce the unemployment rate are
   a. effective in the long run.
   b. effective in the short run.

   c. unnecessary and cause inflation in the long run.
   d. necessary and reduce inflation in the long run.

7. Most macroeconomic policy changes, say the rational expectations theorists, are
   a. unpredictable.
   b. predictable.
   c. slow to take place.
   d. irrational.

8. Rational expectations theorists advise the federal government to
   a. change policy often.
   b. pursue stable policies.
   c. do the opposite of what the public expects.
   d. ignore future economic predictions.

Exhibit 10 Short-Run and Long-Run Phillips Curves

9. Suppose the government shown in Exhibit 10 uses contractionary monetary policy to reduce inflation from 9 to 6 percent. If people have *adaptive* expectations, then
   a. the economy will remain stuck at point E_1.
   b. the natural rate will permanently increase to 8 percent.
   c. unemployment will rise to 8 percent in the short run.
   d. unemployment will remain at 6 percent as the inflation rate falls.

10. Suppose the government shown in Exhibit 10 uses contractionary monetary policy to reduce inflation from 9 to 6 percent. If people have *rational* expectations, then
    a. the economy will remain stuck at point E_1.
    b. the natural rate will permanently increase to 8 percent.
    c. unemployment will rise to 8 percent in the short run.
    d. unemployment will remain at 6 percent as the inflation rate falls.

11. Voluntary wage-price restraints are known as
    a. wage-price controls.
    b. price rollbacks.
    c. wage-price guidelines.
    d. anti-inflation commitments.

12. Which of the following government policies is an incomes policy?
    a. A reduction in welfare expenditures
    b. The publication of a list of guidelines suggesting maximum wage and price increases
    c. An increase in the money supply
    d. All of the above

The International Economy

The final part of this text is devoted to global topics. The first chapter explains the importance of free trade and the mechanics of trade bookkeeping and exchange rates. The second chapter takes a historical look at the theoretical debate over capitalism and the transition of Cuba, Russia, and China toward this system. The last chapter provides comparisons of advanced and developing countries.

CHAPTER 28

International Trade and Finance

J ust imagine your life without world trade. For openers, you would not eat bananas from Honduras or chocolate from Nigerian cocoa beans. Nor would you sip French wine, Colombian coffee, or Indian tea. Also forget about driving a Japanese motorcycle or automobile. In addition, you could not buy Italian sweaters and most VCRs, televisions, fax machines, and personal computers because they are foreign made. Taking your vacation in Paris would also be ruled out if there were no world trade. And the list goes on and on, so the point is clear. World trade is important because it gives consumers more power by expanding their choices. Today, the speed of transportation and communication means producers must compete on a global basis for the favor of consumers.

In Pat Buchanan's campaigns for president in 1996 and 2000, his America First theme sparked debate over foreign trade protectionism. And regardless of whether it was a 1999 World Trade Organization (WTO) meeting in Seattle or a G-8 summit meeting in 2001, global trade talks were faced with turmoil in the streets as thousands of demonstrators protested "new world order" trading rules, while

police were forced to break up the demonstrations.

The first part of this chapter explains the theoretical reason why countries should specialize in producing certain goods and then trade them for imports. Also, you will study arguments for and against the United States protecting itself from "unfair" trade practices by other countries. In the second part of the chapter, you will learn how nations pay each other for world trade. Here you will explore international bookkeeping and discover how supply and demand forces determine that, for instance, 1 dollar is worth 100 yen.

In this chapter, you will learn to solve these economics puzzles:

■ How does Babe Ruth's decision not to become a pitcher illustrate an important principle in international trade?

■ Is there a valid argument for trade protectionism?

■ Should the United States return to the gold standard?

Why Nations Need Trade

Exhibit 1 reveals which regions are our major trading partners. Leading U.S. exports are chemicals, machinery, airplanes, and computers. Major imports include cars, trucks, petroleum, electronics, and clothing. Why does a nation even bother to trade with the rest of the world? Does it seem strange for the United States to import goods it could produce for itself? Indeed, why doesn't the United States become self-sufficient by growing all its own food (including bananas, sugar, and coffee), making all its own cars, and prohibiting sales of all foreign goods? This section explains why specialization and trade are a nation's keys to a higher standard of living.

The Production Possibilities Curve Revisited

Consider a world with only two countries—the United States and Japan. To keep the illustration simple, also assume *both* countries produce only two goods—grain and steel. Accordingly, we can construct in Exhibit 2 a *production possibilities curve* for each country. We will also set aside the *law of increasing opportunity costs,* explained in Chapter 2, and assume workers are equally suited to producing grain or steel. This assumption transforms the bowed-out shape of the production possibilities curve into a straight line.

Comparing parts (a) and (b) of Exhibit 2 shows that the United States can produce more grain than Japan. If the United States devotes all its resources to this purpose, 100 tons of grain are produced per day, represented by point *A* in Exhibit 2(a). The maximum grain production of Japan, on the other hand, is only 40 tons per day because Japan has less labor, land, and other factors of production than the United States. This capability is represented by point *D* in Exhibit 2(b).

Now consider the capacities of the two countries for producing steel. If all their respective resources are devoted to this output, the United States produces 50 tons per day (point *C*), and Japan produces only 40 tons per day (point *F*). Again, the greater potential maximum steel output of the United States reflects its greater resources. Both countries are also capable of producing other combinations of grain and steel along their respective production possibilities curves, such as point *B* for the United States and point *E* for Japan.

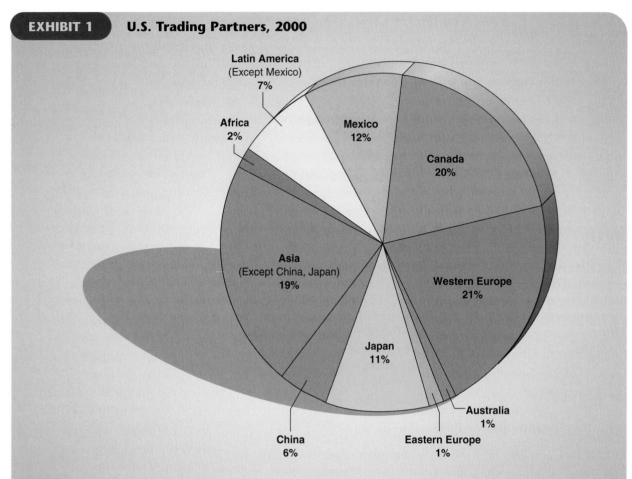

EXHIBIT 1   **U.S. Trading Partners, 2000**

In 2000, Latin America (including Mexico) and Canada accounted for 39 percent of U.S. trade (exports and imports). Asia (including China and Japan) and Western Europe accounted for another 57 percent. Trade with Africa, Eastern Europe, and Australia was relatively small.

Source: Office of Trade and Economic Analysis, http://www.ita.doc.gov/td/industry/otea/usfth.tabcon.html, Tables 6 and 7.

The World Trade Organization (WTO) (http://www.wto.org/) *provides data and analysis on international trade.*

Specialization without Trade

Assuming no world trade, the production possibilities curve for each country also defines its *consumption possibilities*. Stated another way, we assume that both countries are *self-sufficient* because without imports they must consume only the combination chosen along their production possibilities curve. Under the assumption of self-sufficiency, suppose the United States prefers to produce and consume 60 tons of grain and 20 tons of steel per day (point *B*). Also assume Japan chooses to produce and consume 30 tons of grain and 10 tons of steel (point *E*). Exhibit 3 lists data corresponding to points *B* and *E* and shows that the total world output is 90 tons of grain and 30 tons of steel.

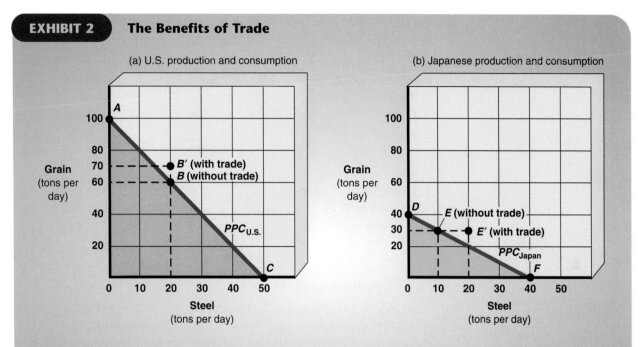

EXHIBIT 2 **The Benefits of Trade**

(a) U.S. production and consumption

(b) Japanese production and consumption

As shown in part (a), assume the United States chooses point *B* on its production possibilities curve, $PPC_{U.S.}$. Without trade, the United States produces and consumes 60 tons of grain and 20 tons of steel. In part (b), assume Japan also operates along its production possibilities curve, PPC_{Japan}, at point *E*. Without trade, Japan produces and consumes 30 tons of grain and 10 tons of steel.

Now assume the United States specializes in producing grain at point *A* and imports 20 tons of Japanese steel in exchange for 30 tons of grain. Through specialization and trade, the United States moves to consumption possibility point *B'*, outside its production possibilities curve. Japan also moves to a higher standard of living at consumption possibility point *E'*, outside its production possibilities curve.

Now suppose the United States specializes by producing and consuming at point *A*, rather than point *B*. Suppose also that Japan specializes by producing and consuming at point *F*, rather than point *E*. As shown in Exhibit 3, specialization in each country increases total world output per day by 10 tons of grain and 10 tons of steel. Because this extra world output has the potential for making both countries better off, why wouldn't the United States and Japan specialize and produce at points *A* and *F*, respectively? The reason is that although production at these points is clearly possible, neither country wants to consume these combinations of output. The United States prefers to consume less grain and more steel at point *B* compared to point *A*. Japan, on the other hand, prefers to consume more grain and less steel at point *E*, rather than point *F*.

Conclusion *When countries specialize, total world output increases, and, therefore, the potential for greater total world consumption also increases.*

EXHIBIT 3 Effect of Specialization on World Output

	Grain production (tons per day)	Steel production (tons per day)
Before specialization		
United States (at point *B*)	60	20
Japan (at point *E*)	30	10
Total world output	90	30
After specialization		
United States (at point *A*)	100	0
Japan (at point *F*)	0	40
Total world output	100	40

Specialization with Trade

Now let's return to Exhibit 2 and demonstrate how world trade benefits countries. Suppose the United States agrees to specialize in grain production at point *A* and to import 20 tons of Japanese steel in exchange for 30 tons of its grain output. Does the United States gain from trade? The answer is Yes. At point *A*, the United States produces 100 tons of grain per day. Subtracting the 30 tons of grain traded to Japan leaves the United States with 70 tons of its own grain production to consume. In return for grain, Japan unloads 20 tons of steel on U.S. shores. Hence, specialization and trade allow the United States to move from point *A* to point *B'*, which is a consumption possibility *outside* its production possibilities curve in Exhibit 2(a). At point *B'*, the United States consumes the same amount of steel and 10 more tons of grain compared to point *B* (without trade).

Japan also has an incentive to specialize by moving its production mix from point *E* to point *F*. With trade, Japan's consumption would be at point *E'*. At point *E'*, Japan has as much grain to consume as it had at point *E*, plus 10 more tons of steel. After trading 20 tons of the 40 tons of steel produced at point *F* for grain, Japan can still consume 20 tons of steel from its production, rather than only 10 tons of steel at point *E*. Thus, point *E'* is a consumption possibility that lies *outside* Japan's production possibilities curve.

Conclusion *International trade allows a country to consume a combination of goods that exceeds its production possibilities curve.*

Comparative and Absolute Advantage

Why did the United States decide to produce and export grain instead of steel? Why did Japan choose to produce steel, rather than grain? Here you study the economic principle that determines specialization and trade.

Comparative Advantage

Engaging in world trade permits countries to escape the prison of their own production possibilities curves by producing bread, cars, or whatever goods they make best. The decision of the United States to specialize in and export grain and the decision of Japan to specialize in and export steel are based on **comparative advantage.** Comparative advantage is the ability of a country to produce a good at a lower opportunity cost than another country. Continuing our earlier example, we can calculate opportunity costs for the two countries and use comparative advantage to determine which country should specialize in grain and which in steel. For the United States, the opportunity cost of producing 50 tons of steel is 100 tons of grain not produced, so 1 ton of steel costs 2 tons of grain. For Japan, the opportunity cost of producing 40 tons of steel is 40 tons of grain, or 1 ton of steel costs 1 ton of grain. Japan's steel is therefore cheaper in terms of grain forgone. This means Japan has a comparative advantage in steel production because it must give up less grain to produce steel than the United States. Stated differently, the opportunity cost of steel production is lower in Japan than in the United States.

The other side of the coin is to measure the cost of grain in terms of steel. For the United States, 1 ton of grain costs ½ ton of steel. For Japan, 1 ton of grain costs 1 ton of steel. The United States has a comparative advantage in grain because its opportunity cost in terms of steel forgone is lower. Thus, the United States should specialize in grain because it is more efficient in grain production. Japan, on the other hand, is relatively more efficient at producing steel and should specialize in this product.

> **Conclusion** *Comparative advantage refers to the relative opportunity costs between countries of producing the same goods. World output and consumption are maximized when each country specializes in producing and trading goods for which it has a comparative advantage.*

Absolute Advantage

So far, a country's production and international trade decisions depend on comparing what a country gives up to produce more of a good. It is important to note that comparative advantage is based on opportunity costs regardless of the absolute costs of resources used in production. We have not considered how much labor, land, or capital either the United States or Japan uses to produce a ton of grain or steel. For example, Japan might have an **absolute advantage** in producing *both* grain and steel. Absolute advantage is the ability of a country to produce a good using fewer resources than another country. In our example, Japan might use fewer resources per ton to produce grain and steel than the United States. Maybe the Japanese work harder or are more skilled. In short, the Japanese may be more productive producers, but their absolute advantage does not matter in specialization and world trade decisions. If the United States has a comparative advantage in grain, it should specialize in grain even if Japan can produce both grain and steel with fewer resources.

Comparative advantage
The ability of a country to produce a good at a lower opportunity cost than another country.

The U.S. Department of Commerce, International Trade Administration (http://www.ita.doc.gov/), *provides a wealth of information concerning international trade.*

Absolute advantage
The ability of a country to produce a good using fewer resources than another country.

CHECKPOINT

Do Nations with an Advantage Always Trade?

Comparing labor productivity, suppose the United States has an absolute advantage over Italy in the production of calculators and towels. In the United States, a worker can produce 4 calculators or 400 towels in 10 hours. In Italy, a worker can produce 1 calculator or 100 towels in the same time. Under these conditions, are specialization and trade advantageous?

Perhaps a different example will clarify the difference between absolute advantage and comparative advantage. When Babe Ruth played for the New York Yankees, he was the best hitter and the best pitcher on the team. In other words, he had an *absolute advantage* in both hitting and throwing the baseball. For example, Babe Ruth could produce the same home runs as any other teammate with fewer times at bat. The problem was that if he pitched, he would bat fewer times because pitchers need rest after pitching. The coaches decided that the Babe had a *comparative advantage* in hitting. Other pitchers on the team could pitch almost as well as the Babe, but no one could touch his hitting. In terms of opportunity costs, the Yankees would lose fewer games if the Babe specialized in hitting.

Free Trade versus Protectionism

Free trade
The flow of goods between countries without restrictions or special taxes.

In theory, international trade should be based on comparative advantage and **free trade.** Free trade is the flow of goods between countries without restrictions or special taxes. In practice, despite the advice of economists, every nation protects its own domestic producers to some degree from foreign competition. Behind these barriers to trade are people whose jobs and incomes are threatened, so they clamor to the government for **protectionism.** Protectionism is the government's use of embargoes, tariffs, quotas, and other restrictions to protect domestic producers from foreign competition.

Protectionism
The government's use of embargoes, tariffs, quotas, and other restrictions to protect domestic producers from foreign competition.

Embargo

Embargoes are the strongest limit on trade. An embargo is a law that bars trade with another country. For example, the United States and other nations in the world imposed an arms embargo on Iraq in response to Iraq's invasion of Kuwait in 1990. The United States also maintains embargoes against Cuba and Libya.

Embargo
A law that bars trade with another country.

Tariff

Tariff
A tax on an import.

Tariffs are the most popular and visible measures used to discourage trade. A tariff is a tax on an import. Tariffs are also called customs duties. The current U.S. tariff code specifies tariffs on nearly 70 percent of U.S. imports. A tariff can be based on weight, volume, or number of units, or it can be *ad* *valorem* (figured as a percentage of the price). The average U.S. tariff is less than 5 percent, but individual tariffs vary widely. Tariffs are imposed to reduce imports by raising import prices and to generate revenues for the U.S. Treasury.

During the worldwide depression of the 1930s, when one nation raised its tariffs to protect its industries, other nations retaliated by raising their tariffs. Under the Smoot-Hawley tariffs of the 1930s, the average tariff in the United States was an unbelievable 59 percent. In 1947, most of the world's industrialized nations mutually agreed to end the tariff wars by signing the *General Agreement on Tariffs and Trade (GATT)*. Since then, GATT nations have met periodically to negotiate lower tariff rates. GATT agreements have significantly reduced tariffs over the years among member nations. In the 1994 *Uruguay round,* member nations signed a GATT agreement that decreased tariffs and reduced other trade barriers. The most divisive element of this agreement was the creation in 1995 of the Geneva-based World Trade Organization (WTO) to enforce rulings in global trade disputes. The WTO has more than 130 members and a standing appellate body to render final decisions regarding disputes between WTO members. Critics fear that the WTO might be far more likely to rule in favor of other countries in their trade disputes with the United States. Some people argue that the WTO is unaccountable and these critics reject free trade and globalization. In 1999, thousands of protesters poured into downtown Seattle and disrupted a WTO conference for three days. Police were forced to use tear gas, pepper spray and rubber bullets to break up the demonstrations.

Quota

Another way to limit foreign competition is to impose a **quota**. A quota is a limit on the quantity of a good that may be imported in a given time period. For example, the United States may allow 10 million tons of sugar to be imported over a one-year period. Once this quantity is reached, no more sugar can be imported for the year. About 12 percent of U.S. imports are subject to import quotas. Examples include import quotas on sugar, dairy products, textiles, steel, and even ice cream. Quotas can limit imports from all foreign suppliers or from specific countries. Quotas, like all barriers to trade, invite nations to retaliate with more measures to restrict trade. In addition to embargoes, tariffs, and quotas, some nations use more subtle measures to discourage trade. For example, some countries set up an overwhelming number of bureaucratic steps that must be taken in order to import a product.

Arguments for Protection

Free trade provides consumers with lower prices and larger quantities of goods from which to choose. Thus, removing import barriers might save each family a few hundred dollars a year. The problem, however, is that imports could cost some workers their jobs and thousands of dollars per year from lost income. Thus, it is no wonder that, in spite of the greater

The U.S. International Trade Commission (ITC) (http://www.usitc.gov/), *the Office of the U.S. Trade Representative* (http://www.ustr.gov/), *and the U.S. Department of State* (http://www.state.gov/www/issues/economic/trade_reports/) *issues reports on foreign trade barriers and unfair trade practices. The Bureau of Export Administration* (http://www.bxa.doc.gov/) *administers export control policies, issues export licenses, and prosecutes violators.*

Quota
A limit on the quantity of a good that may be imported in a given time period.

total benefits to consumers, trade barriers exist. The reason is primarily because workers and owners from import-competing firms have more at stake than consumers, so they go to Washington and lobby for protection. The following are some of the most popular arguments for protection. These arguments have strong political or emotional appeal, but weak support from economists.

Infant Industry Argument

The infant industry argument, as the name suggests, is that a new domestic industry needs protection because it is not yet ready to compete with established foreign competitors. An infant industry is in a formative stage and must bear high start-up costs to train an entire workforce, develop new technology, establish marketing channels, and reach economies of scale. With time to grow and protection, an infant industry can reduce costs and "catch up" with established foreign firms.

Economists ask where one draws the arbitrary line between an "infant" and a "grown-up" industry. It is also difficult to make a convincing case for protecting an infant industry in a developed country, such as the United States, where industries are well established. The infant industry argument, however, may have some validity for less-developed countries. Yet, even for these countries, there is a danger. Once protection is granted, the new industry will not experience the competitive pressures necessary to encourage reasonably quick growth and participation in world trade. Also, once an industry is given protection, it is difficult to take it away.

National Security Argument

Another common argument is that defense-related industries must be protected with embargoes, tariffs, and quotas to ensure national security. By protecting critical defense industries, a nation will not be dependent on foreign countries for the essential defense-related goods it needs to defend itself in wartime. The national defense argument has been used to protect a long list of industries, including petrochemicals, munitions, steel, and rubber.

This argument gained validity during the War of 1812. Great Britain, the main trading partner of the United States, became an enemy that blockaded our coast. Today, this argument makes less sense for the United States. The government stockpiles missiles, sophisticated electronics, petroleum, and most goods needed in wartime. These stockpiles prepare the Pentagon to fight a limited war, such as the 1991 Gulf War. In an all-out nuclear war, there would be little time to worry about strategic supplies.

Employment Argument

The employment argument suggests that restricting imports increases domestic jobs in protected industries. According to this protectionist argument, the sale of an imported good comes at the expense of its domestically produced counterpart. Lower domestic output therefore leads to higher domestic unemployment than would otherwise be the case.

INTERNATIONAL ECONOMICS

World Trade Slips on Banana Peel

Applicable Concept: protectionism

Growing bananas for European markets was a multibillion-dollar bright spot for Latin America's struggling economies. In fact, about half of this region's banana exports traditionally were sold to Europe. Then, in 1993, the European Union (EU) adopted a package of quotas and tariffs aimed at cutting Europe's banana imports from Latin America. The purpose of these restrictions was to give trade preference to 66 banana-growing former colonies of European nations in Africa, the Caribbean, and the Pacific. Ignored was the fact that growers in Latin America grow higher-quality bananas at half the cost of EU-favored growers because of their low labor costs and flat tropical land near port cities.[1]

In 1999, the World Trade Organization (WTO) ruled that the EU was discriminating in favor of European companies importing the fruit and imposed $191.4 million per year in punitive tariffs on European goods. This was the first time in the four years the WTO had been in existence that such retaliation had been approved, and only the second time going back to its predecessor, the General Agreement on Tariffs and Trade. When the EU failed to comply with the WTO findings, the United States enforced

its WTO rights by imposing increased duties on EU imports including goods ranging from cashmere sweaters and Italian handbags to sheep's milk cheese, British biscuits, and German coffeemakers. The effect of the U.S. sanctions was to double the wholesale price of these items. Denmark and the Netherlands were exempt from the U.S. tariffs because they were the only nations that voted against the EU banana rules.

Critics charged that the United States was pushing the case for political reasons. American companies, including Chiquita Brands International and Dole Food Company, grow their bananas mostly in Latin America. With America's trade deficit running at a record level, U.S. trade experts also argued that the United States had little

choice but to act against the EU for failing to abide by the WTO's ruling. Moreover, with increasing voices in the United States questioning the wisdom of international trade and globalization, it was important that the WTO prove that it can arbitrate these disputes.

In 2001, it appears that the banana dispute may be resolved. The EU agreed to take steps to increase market access for U.S. banana distributors, and the United States lifted its retaliatory duties on EU products. The agreement also provides that the United States can reimpose the duties if the EU does not complete its phased-in reductions in restrictions on banana imports.[2]

ANALYZE THE ISSUE

Make an argument in favor of the European import restrictions. Make an argument against this plan.

---

[1]James Brooke, "Forbidden Fruit in Europe: Latin Bananas Face Hurdles," *New York Times*, April 5, 1993, p. A1.
[2]"U.S. Lifts Sanctions in Banana War," *The Food Institute Report*, July 9, 2001, p. 9.

It is true that protectionism can increase output and save jobs in some industries at home. Ignored, however, are the higher prices paid by consumers because protectionism reduces competition between domestic goods and imported goods. In addition, there are employment reduction effects to consider. For example, suppose a strict quota is imposed on steel imported into our nation. Reduced foreign competition allows U.S. steelmakers to charge higher prices for their steel. As a result, prices rise and sales fall for cars and other products using steel, causing production and employment to fall in these industries. Thus, the import quota on steel may save jobs in the steel industry but at the expense of more jobs lost in the steel-consuming industries. Also, by selling U.S. imports, foreigners earn dollars that they can use to buy U.S. exports. Import quotas cause foreigners to have fewer dollars to spend on U.S. exports, resulting in a decrease in employment in U.S. export industries. In short, protectionism might cause a net reduction in the nation's total employment.

Cheap Foreign Labor Argument

Another popular claim is the cheap labor argument. It goes something like this: "How can we compete with such unfair competition? Labor costs $10 an hour in the United States, and firms in many developing countries pay only $1 an hour. Without protection, U.S. wages will be driven down, and our standard of living will fall."

A major flaw in this argument is that it neglects the reason for the difference in the wage rates between countries. A U.S. worker has more education, training, capital, and access to advanced technology. Therefore, if U.S. workers produce more output per hour than workers in another country, U.S. workers will earn higher wages without a competitive disadvantage. Suppose textile workers in the United States are paid $10 per hour. If a U.S. worker takes 1 hour to produce a rug, the labor cost per rug is $10. Now suppose a worker in India earns $1 per hour, but requires 20 hours to produce a rug. In this case, the labor cost per rug is $20. Although the wage rate is 10 times higher in the United States, U.S. productivity is 20 times higher because a U.S. worker can produce 20 rugs in 20 hours, while the worker in India produces only 1 rug in the same amount of time.

Sometimes U.S. companies move their operations to foreign countries where labor is cheaper. Such moves are not always successful because the savings from paying foreign workers a lower wage rate are offset by lower productivity. Other disadvantages of foreign operations include greater transportation costs to U.S. markets and political instability.

Free Trade Agreements

Read more about NAFTA (http://www-tech.mit.edu/Bulletins/nafta.html).

The trend in recent years has been for nations to negotiate a reduction in trade barriers. In 1993, Congress approved the *North American Free Trade Agreement (NAFTA)*, which linked the United States to its first- and third-largest trading partners, Canada and Mexico. Under NAFTA, which became effective January 1, 1994, tariffs will be phased out over 15 years, and other

Birth of the Euro

In 1958, several European nations formed a Common Market to eliminate trade restrictions among member countries. The Common Market called for gradual removal of tariffs and import quotas on goods traded among member nations. Later the name was changed to the European Economic Community (EEC). The EEC, now called the European Union (EU), also established a common system of tariffs for imports from nonmember nations and created common policies for economic matters of joint concern, such as agriculture and transportation. The EU now comprises 15 western European nations: Austria, Belgium, Denmark, Finland, France, Germany, Greece, Ireland, Italy, Luxembourg, the Netherlands, Portugal, Spain, Sweden, and the United Kingdom.

In 1999, 11 European countries followed the United States as an example and united in the *European Monetary Union, (EMU)*. The United Kingdom, Denmark, and Sweden have not joined the EMU. In the United States, 50 states are linked with a common currency, and the Federal Reserve serves as the central bank by conducting monetary policy for the nation. Among the states, trade, labor, and investment enjoy freedom of movement. Under the EMU, members will replace their national currencies in 2002 with a single currency—

the euro. The objective is to remove exchange rate fluctuations that impede cross-border transactions. This is why the U.S. Congress created a national currency in 1863 to replace state and private bank currencies.

The EMU faces many unanswered questions. Unlike the United States, the 12 member nations do not share a common language or governments. This makes maintaining common macro policies difficult. France, for example, might seek to control inflation, while Germany has reducing unemployment as its highest priority.

Coordinating monetary policy among EMU nations is also difficult. Although the EMU has a new *European Central Bank* with sole authority over the supply of euros, the central banks of member nations are still functioning. But these national central banks will operate similar to the district banks of the Federal Reserve System in the United States. Only time will tell whether EMU nations will perform better with a single currency rather than separate national currencies. It is possible that the euro could become a strong alternative to the U.S. dollar as a key currency for the global financial systems.

impediments to trade and investment are being eliminated among the three nations. For example, elimination of Mexican duties allows the United States to supply Mexico with more U.S. goods and to boost U.S. jobs. On the other hand, NAFTA is expected to raise Mexico's wages and standard of living. As a result, the number of unauthorized Mexican immigrants to the United States should decline. Note that NAFTA made no changes in restrictions on labor movement and workers must enter under a limited immigration quota or illegally. The success of NAFTA remains controversial. At the conclusion of this chapter, we will use data to examine its impact.

The United States and other countries are considering other free trade agreements. In Europe, 15 nations have joined the *European Union (EU),* which is dedicated to removing all trade barriers within Europe and thereby creating a single European economy almost as large as the U.S. economy. In addition, a new currency, the *euro,* is replacing marks, francs, lire, and other member currencies.

The *Asian Pacific Economic Cooperation (APEC)* was formed in 1989 and today consists of 21 nations, including China, Hong Kong, Russia, Taiwan, and Mexico. This organization is based on a nonbinding agreement to reduce trade barriers between member nations.

Critics are concerned that regional free trade accords will make global agreements increasingly difficult to achieve. Some fear that trading blocs may erect new barriers, creating "Fortress North America," "Fortress Europe," and similar impediments to the worldwide reduction of trade barriers.

The Balance of Payments

When trade occurs between the United States and other nations, many types of financial transactions are recorded in a summary called the **balance of payments.** The balance of payments is a bookkeeping record of all the international transactions between a country and other countries during a given period of time. This summary records the value of a nation's spending inflows and outflows made by individuals, firms, and governments. Exhibit 4 presents a simplified U.S. balance of payments for 2000.

Note the pluses and minuses in the table. A transaction that is a payment to the United States is entered as a positive amount. A payment by the United States to another country is entered with a minus sign. As our discussion unfolds, you will learn that the balance of payments provides much useful information.

Current Account

The first section of the balance of payments is the *current account,* which includes, as the name implies, trade in currently produced goods and services. The most widely reported and largest part of the current account is the **balance of trade.** The balance of trade is the value of a nation's goods imports subtracted from its goods exports. As shown in Exhibit 4, the United States had a *balance of trade deficit* of $452 billion in 2000. A trade deficit occurs when the value of a country's imports of goods (not services) exceeds the value of its exports of goods. When a nation has a trade deficit, it is called an *unfavorable balance of trade* because more is spent for imports than is earned from exports. Recall that net exports can have a positive (favorable) or negative (unfavorable) effect on GDP = C + I + G + (X − M).

Exhibit 5 charts the annual balance of trade for the United States from 1975 through 2000. Observe that the United States experienced a *balance of trade surplus* in 1975. A trade surplus arises when the value of a country's merchandise exports is greater than the value of its merchandise imports. This is called a *favorable balance of trade* because the United States earned

Balance of payments

A bookkeeping record of all the international transactions between a country and other countries during a given time period.

Balance of trade

The value of a nation's goods imports subtracted from its goods exports.

United States Foreign Trade Developments (http://www.ita.doc.gov/ td/industry/otea/), *published by the International Trade Administration, includes a monthly analysis of U.S. trade balances (click on Monthly Trade Update).*

EXHIBIT 4 U.S. Balance of Payments, 2000 (billions of dollars)

Type of transaction	
Current account	
1. Goods exports	$ +772
2. Goods imports	−1,224
Trade balance (lines 1–2)	−452
3. Service exports	+293
4. Service imports	−217
5. Investment income (net)	−15
6. Unilateral transfers (net)	−54
Current account balance (lines 1–6)	$ −445
Capital account	
7. U.S. capital inflow	$ +1,024
8. U.S. capital outflow	−580
Capital account balance (lines 7–8)	+444
9. Statistical discrepancy	+1
Net balance (lines 1–9)	$ 0

Source: Survey of Current Business, U.S. International Transactions, http://www.bea.doc.gov/bea/rels.htm.

more from exports than it spent for imports. Since 1975, however, sizable trade deficits have occurred. These trade deficits have attracted much attention because in part they reflect the popularity of foreign goods and the lack of competitiveness for goods "Made in U.S.A."

Because of the Asian financial crisis that began in 1997 with effects continuing to 2000, Asian consumers and businesses could afford to buy fewer U.S. products, and U.S. exports to Asia fell. Moreover, Asian products were cheaper and U.S. imports rose. The reasons were the declining value of the region's currencies compared to the dollar (discussed later in this chapter) and the price cuts by Asian businesses desperate for cash to pay their debts. This situation contributed to the sharp increase in the trade deficit beginning in 1997.

Lines 3–6 of the current account in Exhibit 4 list ways other than goods to move dollars back and forth between the United States and other countries. For example, a Japanese tourist who pays a hotel bill in Hawaii buys an export of services, which is a plus or credit to our current account (line 3). Similarly, an American visitor to foreign lands buys an import of services, which is a minus or debit to our services and therefore a minus to our current account (line 4). Income flowing back from U.S. investments abroad, such as plants, real estate, and securities, is a payment for use of the services of U.S. capital. Foreign countries also receive income flowing from the services of their capital owned in the United States. In 2000, line 5 of the table reports a net flow of −$15 billion to the United States.

EXHIBIT 5   **U.S. Balance of Trade, 1975–2000**

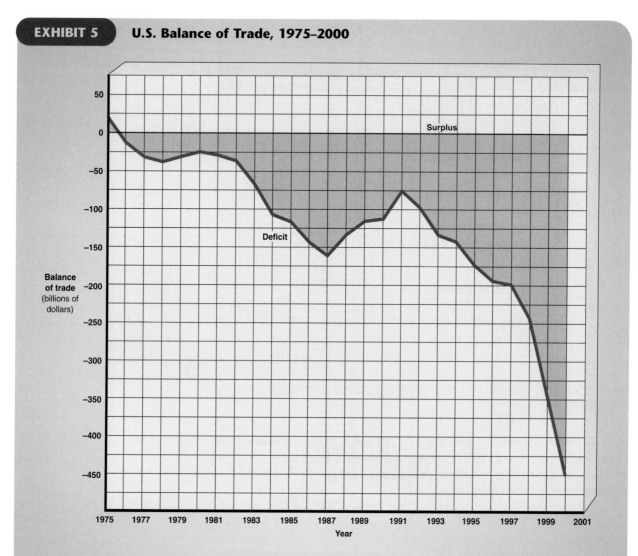

Since 1975, the United States has experienced trade deficits, in which the value of goods imports has exceeded the value of exports. These goods trade deficits attract much attention because in part they reflect the popularity of foreign goods in the United States. The Asian financial crisis contributed to the sharp increase in the trade deficit beginning in 1997.

Source: Office of Trade & Economic Analysis, http://www.ita.doc.gov/td/industry/otea/usfth/tcbcon.html, Table 1.

Finally, we consider line 6, unilateral transfers. This category includes gifts made by our government, charitable organizations, or private individuals to other governments or private parties elsewhere in the world. For example, this item includes U.S. foreign aid to other nations. Similar unilateral transfers into the United States must be subtracted to determine the *net* unilateral transfers. Net unilateral transfers for the United States were −$54 billion in 2000.

Adding lines 1–6 gives the current account balance deficit of −$445 billion in 2000. This deficit means that foreigners sent us more goods and services than we sent to them. Because the current account balance includes *both* goods and services, it is a broader measure than the trade balance. Since 1982, the trend in the current account balance has followed the swing into the red shown by the trade balance in Exhibit 5.

Capital Account

The second section of the balance of payments is the *capital account,* which records payment flows for financial capital, such as stocks, bonds, government securities, and real estate. For example, when Japanese investors buy U.S. Treasury bills, Rockefeller Center, or farmland in Hawaii, there is an inflow of dollars into the United States. As Exhibit 4 shows, foreigners made payments of $1,024 billion to our capital account (line 7). This exceeded the $580 billion outflow from the United States to purchase foreign-owned financial capital.

An important feature of the capital account is that the United States finances any deficit in its current account through this account. The capital account balance in 2000 was $444 billion. This surplus indicates that there was more foreign investment in U.S. assets than U.S. investment in foreign assets during this year.

> **Conclusion** *A current account deficit is financed by a capital account surplus.*

The current account deficit should equal the capital account surplus, but line 9 in the exhibit reveals that the balance of payments is not perfect. The capital account balance does not exactly offset the current account balance. Hence, a credit amount is simply recorded as a statistical discrepancy; therefore, the balance of payments always balances, or equals zero.

The International Debt of the United States

If each nation's balance of payments is always zero, why is there so much talk about a U.S. balance of payments problem? The problem is with the *composition* of the balance of payments. Suppose the United States runs a $400 billion deficit in its current account. This means that the current account deficit must be financed by a net annual capital inflow in the capital account of $400 billion. That is, foreign lenders, such as banks and businesses, must purchase U.S. assets and grant loans to the United States that on balance equal $400 billion. For example, a Japanese bank could buy U.S. Treasury bonds. Recall from Exhibit 7 in the chapter on federal deficits and the national debt that this portion of the national debt owed to lenders outside the United States is called *external debt.*

In 1984, the United States became a net debtor for the first time in about 70 years. This means that investments in the United States accumulated by foreigners—stocks, bonds, real estate, and so forth—exceeded the stock of

The World Bank (http://www.worldbank .org/) *maintains data on international debt.*

CHECKPOINT

Should Everyone Keep a Balance of Payments?

Nations keep balances of payments and calculate accounts such as their merchandise trade deficit or surplus. If nations need these accounts, the 50 states should also maintain balances of payments to manage their economies. Or should they? What about cities?

The Pacific Exchange Rate Service (http:// pacific.commerce.ubc .ca/xr/) *provides a list of all the currencies of the world and the countries' exchange rate arrangements. Also, the Federal Reserve publishes current and historical exchange rates* (http://www .federalreserve.gov/releases/ *and select Foreign Exchange Rates), and the Interactive Currency Table* (http://www.xe.net/currency/table .htm), *by Xenon Laboratories, provides exchange rate values and foreign exchange rate conversions.*

foreign assets owned by the United States. In fact, during the decade of the 1980s, the United States moved from being the world's largest creditor nation to being the largest debtor nation.

The concern over continuing trade deficits and the rising international debt that accompanies them is that the United States is artificially enjoying a higher standard of living. When the United States continues to purchase more goods and services abroad than it exports, it might find itself "enjoying now and paying later." Suppose the Japanese and other foreigners decide not to make new U.S. investments and loans. In this case, the United States will be forced to eliminate its trade deficit by bringing exports and imports into balance. In fact, if other countries not only refuse to provide new capital inflows, but also decide to liquidate their investments, the United States would be forced to run a trade surplus. Stated differently, we would be forced to tighten our belts and accept a lower standard of living. A change in foreign willingness to purchase U.S. assets also affects the international value of the dollar—the topic to which we now turn.

Exchange Rates

Exchange rate

The number of units of one nation's currency that equals one unit of another nation's currency.

Each transaction recorded in the balance of payments requires an exchange of one country's currency for that of another. Suppose you buy a Japanese car made in Japan, say, a Mazda. Mazda wants to be paid in yen and not dollars, so dollars must be traded for yen. On the other hand, suppose Pink Panther Airline Company in France purchases an airplane from Boeing in the United States. Pink Panther has francs to pay the bill, but Boeing wants dollars. Consequently, francs must be exchanged for dollars.

The critical question for Mazda, Pink Panther, Boeing, and everyone involved in world trade is "What is the **exchange rate**?" The exchange rate is the number of units of one nation's currency that equals one unit of another nation's currency. For example, assume 1.81 dollars can be exchanged for 1 British pound. This means the exchange rate is 1.81 dollars = 1 pound. Alternatively, the exchange rate can be expressed as a reciprocal. Dividing 1 British pound by 1.81 dollars gives 0.552 pounds per dollar. Now suppose you are visiting England and want to buy a T-shirt with a price tag of 10 pounds. Knowing the exchange rate tells you the T-shirt costs $18.10 (10 pounds × $1.81/pound).

Conclusion *An exchange rate can be expressed as a reciprocal.*

We now turn to how an exchange rate is determined.

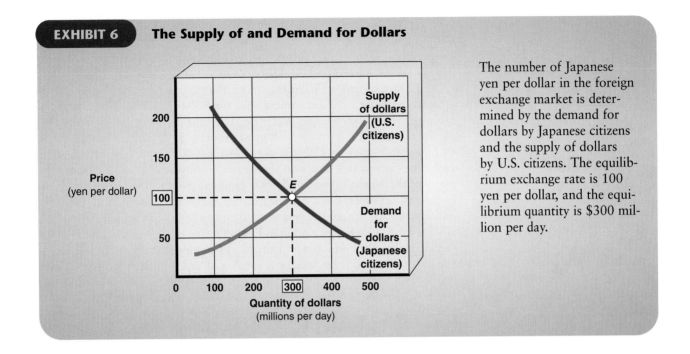

EXHIBIT 6 **The Supply of and Demand for Dollars**

The number of Japanese yen per dollar in the foreign exchange market is determined by the demand for dollars by Japanese citizens and the supply of dollars by U.S. citizens. The equilibrium exchange rate is 100 yen per dollar, and the equilibrium quantity is $300 million per day.

Supply and Demand for Foreign Exchange

The exchange rate for dollars, or any nation's currency, is determined by international forces of supply and demand. For example, consider the exchange rate of yen to dollars, shown in Exhibit 6. Like the price and the quantity of any good traded in markets, the quantity of dollars exchanged is measured on the horizontal axis, and the price per unit is measured on the vertical axis. In this case, the price per unit is the value of the U.S. dollar expressed as the number of yen per dollar.

The demand for dollars in the world currency market comes from Japanese individuals, corporations, and governments that want to buy U.S. exports. Because the Japanese buyers must pay for U.S. exports with dollars, they *demand* to exchange their yen for dollars. As expected, the demand curve for dollars or any foreign currency is downward sloping. A decline in the number of yen per dollar means that one yen buys a larger portion of a dollar. This means U.S. goods and investment opportunities are less expensive to Japanese buyers because they must pay fewer yen for each dollar. Thus, as the yen price of dollars decreases, the quantity of dollars demanded by the Japanese to purchase Fords, stocks, land, and other U.S. products and investments increases. For example, suppose a CD recording of the hottest rock group has a $20 price tag. If the exchange rate is 200 yen to the dollar, a Japanese importer would pay 4,000 yen. If the price of dollars to Japanese buyers falls to 100 yen each, the same $20 CD will cost Japanese importers only 2,000 yen. This lower price causes Japanese buyers to increase their orders, which, in turn, increases the quantity of dollars demanded.

The supply curve of dollars is upward sloping. This curve shows the amount of dollars offered for exchange at various yen prices per dollar in the world currency exchange market. Similar to the demand for dollars, the supply of dollars in this market flows from individuals, corporations, and governments in the United States that want to buy Mazdas, stocks, land, and other products and investments from Japan. Because U.S. citizens must pay for the Japanese goods and services in yen, they must exchange dollars for yen. An example will illustrate why the supply curve of dollars slopes upward. Suppose a Nikon camera sells for 100,000 yen in Tokyo and the exchange rate is 100 yen per dollar or .01 dollar per yen ($1/100 yen). This means the camera costs an American tourist $1,000. Now assume the exchange rate rises to 250 yen per dollar or .004 dollar per yen ($1/250 yen). The camera will now cost the American buyer only $400. Because the prices of the Nikon camera and other Japanese products fall when the number of yen per dollar rises, Americans respond by purchasing more Japanese imports, which, in turn, increases the quantity of dollars supplied.

The foreign exchange market in Exhibit 6 is in equilibrium at an exchange rate of 100 yen for $1. As you learned in Chapter 3, if the exchange rate is above equilibrium, there will be a surplus of dollars in the world currency market. Citizens of the United States are supplying more dollars than the Japanese demand, and the exchange rate falls. On the other hand, below equilibrium, there will be a shortage of dollars in the world currency market. In this case, the Japanese are demanding more dollars than Americans supply, and the exchange rate rises.

Shifts in Supply and Demand for Foreign Exchange

For most of the years between World War II and 1971, currency exchange rates were *fixed*. Exchange rates were based primarily on gold. For example, the German mark was fixed at about 25 cents. The dollar was worth 1/35 of an ounce of gold, and 4 German marks were worth 1/35 of an ounce of gold. Therefore, 1 dollar equaled 4 marks, or 25 cents equaled 1 mark. In 1971, Western nations agreed to stop fixing their exchange rates and to allow their currencies to *float* according to the forces of supply and demand. Exhibit 7 illustrates that these rates can fluctuate widely. For example, in 1980, 1 dollar was worth about 230 Japanese yen. After gyrating up and down over the years, the exchange rate hit a postwar low of 94 yen per dollar in 1995. In 2000, the exchange rate was about 108 yen per dollar.

Recall from Chapter 3 that the equilibrium price for products changes in response to shifts in the supply and demand curves. The same supply and demand analysis applies to equilibrium exchange rates for foreign currency. There are four important sources of shifts in the supply and demand curves for foreign exchange. Let's consider each in turn.

Tastes and Preferences.   Exhibit 8(a) illustrates one important factor that causes the demand for foreign currencies to shift. Suppose the Japanese lose their "taste" for tobacco, U.S. government bonds, and other U.S. products and investment opportunities. This decline in the popularity of U.S. products in Japan decreases the demand for dollars at each possible exchange rate, and the demand curve shifts leftward from D_1 to D_2. This change causes the equilibrium exchange rate to fall from 150 yen to the dollar at E_1 to 100 yen to the dollar at E_2. Because the number of yen to the dollar declines, the dollar is said to *depreciate* or become *weaker*. **Depreciation of currency** is a fall in the price of one currency relative to another.

Depreciation of currency

A fall in the price of one currency relative to another.

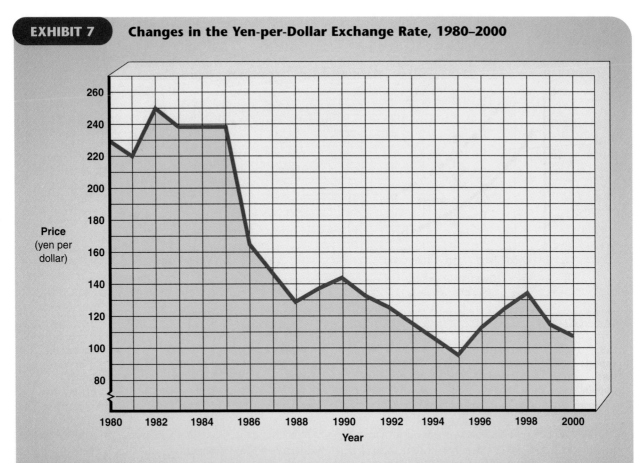

| EXHIBIT 7 | Changes in the Yen-per-Dollar Exchange Rate, 1980–2000 |

Today, most economies are on a system of flexible exchange rates. As the demand and supply curves for currencies change, exchange rates change. In 1980, 1 dollar was worth about 230 Japanese yen. By 1995, the exchange rate had dropped to 94 yen per dollar.

Sources: *Economic Report of the President, 2001,* http://w3.access.gpo.gov/eop/, Table B-110; and Federal Reserve Board, http://www.federalreserve.gov/releases/g5a/current/.

What happens to the exchange rate if the "Buy American" idea changes our tastes and the demand for Japanese imports decreases? In this case, U.S. citizens supply fewer dollars at any possible exchange rate, and the supply curve in Exhibit 8(b) shifts leftward from S_1 to S_2. As a result, the equilibrium exchange rate rises from 100 yen to the dollar at E_1 to 150 yen to the dollar at E_2. Because the number of yen per dollar rises, the dollar is said to *appreciate* or become *stronger*. **Appreciation of currency** is a rise in the price of one currency relative to another.

Relative Incomes.   Assume income in the United States rises, while income in Japan remains unchanged. As a result, U.S. citizens buy more domestic products and more Japanese imports. The results are a rightward shift in the supply curve for dollars and a decrease in the equilibrium exchange rate.

Appreciation of currency
A rise in the price of one currency relative to another.

EXHIBIT 8 — **Changes in the Supply and Demand Curves for Dollars**

(a) Decrease in demand

(b) Decrease in supply

CAUSATION CHAIN

| U.S. exports less popular | ⟹ | Decrease in the demand for dollars | ⟹ | Value of the dollar falls (dollar depreciates) |

CAUSATION CHAIN

| Japanese imports less popular | ⟹ | Decrease in the supply of dollars | ⟹ | Value of the dollar rises (dollar appreciates) |

In part (a), U.S. exports become less popular in Japan. This change in tastes for U.S. products and investments decreases the demand for dollars, and the demand curve shifts leftward from D_1 to D_2. As a result, the equilibrium exchange rate falls from 150 yen to the dollar at E_1 to 100 yen to the dollar at E_2.

Part (b) assumes U.S. citizens are influenced by the "Buy American" idea. In this case, our demand for Japanese imports decreases, and U.S. citizens supply fewer dollars to the foreign currency market. The result is that the supply curve shifts leftward from S_1 to S_2, and the equilibrium exchange rate rises from 100 yen per dollar at E_1 to 150 yen per dollar at E_2.

Paradoxically, growth of U.S. income leads to the dollar depreciating or becoming weaker, against the Japanese yen.

Conclusion *An expansion in relative U.S. income causes a depreciation of the dollar.*

Relative Price Levels.   Now we consider a more complex case, in which a change in a factor causes a change in both the supply and the demand curves for dollars. Assume the foreign exchange rate begins in equilibrium at 100 yen per dollar, as shown at point E_1 in Exhibit 9. Now assume the price level increases in Japan, but remains constant in the United States. The Japanese therefore want to buy more U.S. exports because they have become cheaper relative to Japanese products. This willingness of the Japanese to buy U.S. goods and services shifts the demand curve for dollars rightward from D_1 to D_2. In addition, U.S. products are cheaper for U.S. citizens compared to Japanese imports. As a result, the willingness to import from Japan is reduced

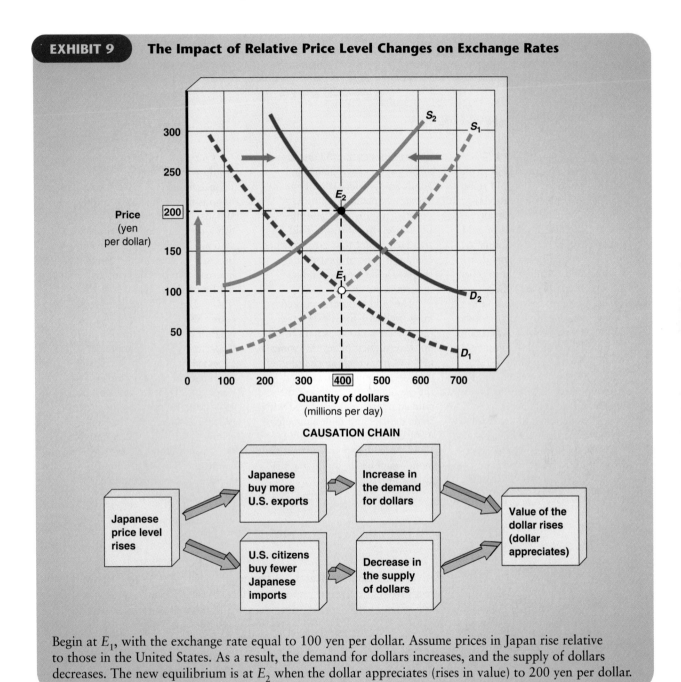

EXHIBIT 9   **The Impact of Relative Price Level Changes on Exchange Rates**

CAUSATION CHAIN

Begin at E_1, with the exchange rate equal to 100 yen per dollar. Assume prices in Japan rise relative to those in the United States. As a result, the demand for dollars increases, and the supply of dollars decreases. The new equilibrium is at E_2 when the dollar appreciates (rises in value) to 200 yen per dollar.

at each exchange rate, which means the supply curve of dollars decreases from S_1 to S_2. The result of the shifts in both the demand and the supply curves for dollars is to establish a new equilibrium at point E_2, and the exchange rate reaches 200 yen per dollar.

Conclusion *A rise in a trading partner's relative price level causes the dollar to appreciate.*

INTERNATIONAL ECONOMICS

Return to the Gold Standard?

Applicable Concept: exchange rates

From the 1870s until the 1930s, most industrial countries were on the gold standard. The gold standard served as an international monetary system in which currencies were defined in terms of gold. Under the gold standard, a nation with a balance of payments deficit was required to ship gold to other nations to finance the deficit. Hence, a large excess of imports over exports meant a corresponding outflow of gold from a nation. As a result, that nation's money supply decreased, which, in turn, reduced the aggregate demand for goods and services. Lower domestic demand led to falling prices, lower production, and fewer jobs. In contrast, a nation with a balance of payments surplus would experience an inflow of gold and the opposite effects. In this case, the

nation's money supply increased, and its aggregate demand for goods and services rose. Higher aggregate spending, in turn, boosted employment and the price level. In short, the gold standard meant that governments could not control their money supplies and thereby conduct monetary policy.

The gold standard worked fairly well as a fixed exchange rate system so long as nations did not face sudden or severe swings in flows from their stocks of gold. The Great Depression marked the beginning of the end of the gold standard. Nations faced with trade deficits and high unemployment began going off the gold standard, rather than contract their money supplies by following the gold standard.

Once the Allies felt certain they would win World War II, the finance ministers of Western nations met in 1944 at Bretton Woods, New Hampshire, to establish a new international monetary system. The new system was based on fixed exchange rates and an international central bank called the International Monetary Fund (IMF). The IMF made loans to countries faced with short-term balance of payments problems. Under this system, nations were expected to maintain fixed exchange rates within a narrow range. In the 1960s and early 1970s, the Bretton Woods system became strained as conditions changed. In the 1960s, inflation rates in the United States rose relative to those in other countries, causing U.S. exports to become

Relative Real Interest Rates.   Changes in relative real (inflation-adjusted) interest rates can have an important effect on the exchange rate. Suppose real interest rates in the United States rise, while those in Japan remain constant. To take advantage of more attractive yields, Japanese investors buy an increased amount of bonds and other interest-bearing securities issued by private and government borrowers in the United States. This change increases the demand for dollars, which increases the equilibrium exchange rate of yen to the dollar, causing the dollar to appreciate (or the yen to depreciate).

There can also be an effect on the supply of dollars. When real interest rates rise in the United States, our citizens purchase fewer Japanese securities. Hence, they offer fewer dollars at each possible exchange rate, and the supply curve for dollars shifts leftward. As a result, the equilibrium exchange rate increases, and the dollar appreciates from changes in both the demand for and the supply of dollars.

more expensive and U.S. imports to become less expensive. This situation increased the supply of dollars abroad and caused an increasing surplus of dollars, thus putting downward pressure on the exchange rate. Monetary authorities in the United States worried that central banks would demand gold for their dollars, the U.S. gold stock would diminish sharply, and the declining money supply would adversely affect the economy.

Something had to give, and it did. In August 1971, President Richard Nixon announced that the United States would no longer honor its obligation to sell gold at $35 an ounce. By 1973, the gold standard was dead, and most of our trading partners were letting the forces of supply and demand determine exchange rates.

Today, some people advocate returning to the gold standard. These gold buffs do not trust the government to control the money supply without the discipline of a gold standard. They argue that if governments have the freedom to print money, political pressures will sooner or later cause them to increase the money supply too much and let inflation rage.

One argument against the gold standard is that no one can control the supply of gold. Big gold discoveries can cause inflation and have done so in the past. On the other hand, slow growth in the stock of mined gold can lead to slow economic growth and a loss of jobs. Governments therefore are unlikely to return to the gold standard because it would mean turning

monetary policy over to uncontrollable swings in the stock of gold.

ANALYZE THE ISSUE

Return to Exhibit 6, and assume the equilibrium exchange rate is 150 yen per dollar and the equilibrium quantity is 300 million dollars. Redraw this figure, and place a horizontal line through the equilibrium exchange rate to represent a fixed exchange rate. Now use this figure to explain why a country would abandon the gold standard.

The Impact of Exchange Rate Fluctuations

Now it is time to stop for a minute, take a breath, and draw some important conclusions. As you have just learned, exchange rates between most major currencies are flexible. Instead of being pegged to gold or another fixed standard, their value is determined by the laws of supply and demand. Consequently, shifts in supply and demand create a weaker or a stronger dollar. But it should be noted that exchange rates do not fluctuate with total freedom. Governments often buy and sell currencies to prevent wide swings in exchange rates.

In summary, the strength or weakness of any nation's currency has a profound impact on its economy.

Conclusion *When the dollar is weak or depreciates, U.S. goods and services cost foreign consumers less, so they buy more U.S. exports. At the same time, a weak dollar means foreign goods and services cost U.S. consumers more, so they buy fewer imports.*

EXHIBIT 10 U.S. Trade Balances with Mexico, 1993–2000

Year	U.S. exports to Mexico (billions of dollars)	U.S. imports from Mexico (billions of dollars)	Exchange rate: pesos per dollar	U.S. trade surplus (+) or deficit (−) (billions of dollars)
1993	$ 42	$ 40	3.12	$+2
1994	51	50	3.39	+1
1995	46	62	6.45	−16
1996	57	74	7.60	−18
1997	71	87	7.92	−15
1998	79	95	9.15	−16
1999	87	110	9.55	−23
2000	112	136	9.46	−24

Sources: Office of Trade and Economic Analysis, http://www.ita.doc.gov/industry/otea/usfth/tabcon.html, Tables 6 and 7; and Federal Reserve Board, http://www.federalreserve.gov/releases/G5A/current/.

A weak dollar is therefore a "mixed blessing." Ironically, a weak dollar makes U.S. producers happy because they can sell their less expensive exports to foreign buyers. As export sales rise, jobs are created in the United States. On the other hand, a weak dollar makes foreign producers and domestic consumers unhappy because the prices of Japanese cars, French wine, and Italian shoes are higher. As U.S. imports fall, jobs are lost in foreign countries.

A strong dollar is also a "mixed blessing."

Conclusion *When the dollar is strong or appreciates, U.S. goods and services cost foreign consumers more, so they buy fewer U.S. exports. At the same time, a strong dollar means foreign goods and services cost U.S. consumers less, so they buy more foreign imports.*

A strong dollar therefore makes our major trading partners happy because the prices of Japanese cars, French wine, and Italian shoes are lower. A strong dollar, contrary to the implication of the term, makes U.S. producers unhappy because their exports are more expensive and related jobs decline. Conversely, a strong dollar makes foreign producers happy because the prices of their goods and services are lower, causing U.S. imports to rise.

Finally, as promised earlier in this chapter, we return to the discussion of NAFTA in order to illustrate the impact of this free trade agreement and the effect of a strong dollar. Recall that in January 1994, NAFTA began a 15-year gradual phaseout of tariffs and other trade barriers. Exhibit 10 provides trade data for the United States and Mexico for the years surrounding NAFTA. As the exhibit shows, both exports and imports of goods increased sharply after NAFTA. On the other hand, a small trade surplus of $2 billion in 1993 turned into a huge trade deficit of $24 billion in 2000.

Before blaming this trade deficit entirely on NAFTA, you must note that the exchange rate rose from 3.12 pesos per dollar to 9.46. Prior to the peso's devaluation in 1995, Mexicans sold more goods to U.S. markets, and they earned more money to spend on goods from U.S. factories. Since 1995, however, the strong dollar put the price of U.S. goods out of reach for many Mexican consumers, so U.S. exports to Mexico have been lower than with a weaker dollar. At the same time, Mexican goods became less expensive for U.S. consumers, and U.S. imports from Mexico have risen.

KEY CONCEPTS

Comparative advantage	Protectionism	Quota	Exchange rate
Absolute advantage	Embargo	Balance of payments	Depreciation of currency
Free trade	Tariff	Balance of trade	Appreciation of currency

SUMMARY

- **Comparative advantage** is a principle that allows nations to gain from trade. Comparative advantage means that each nation *specializes* in a product for which its opportunity cost is lower in terms of the production of another product and then nations trade. When nations follow this principle, they gain. The reason is that world output increases and each nation ends up with a higher standard of living by consuming more goods and services than would be possible without specialization and trade.

- **Free trade** benefits a nation as a whole, but individuals may lose jobs and incomes from the competition from foreign goods and services.

- **Protectionism** is a government's use of embargoes, tariffs, quotas, and other methods to impose barriers intended to both reduce imports and protect particular domestic industries. Embargoes prohibit the import or export of particular goods. Tariffs discourage imports by making them more expensive. Quotas limit the quantity of imports or exports of certain goods. These trade barriers often result primarily from domestic groups that exert political pressure on government in order to gain from these barriers.

Comparative advantage

- The **balance of payments** is a summary bookkeeping record of all the international transactions a country makes during a year. It is divided into different accounts, including the **current account**, the **capital account**, and the **statistical discrepancy**. The current account summarizes all transactions in currently produced goods and services. The overall balance of payments is always zero after an adjustment for the statistical discrepancy.

- The **balance of trade** measures only goods (not services) that a nation exports and imports. A balance of trade can be in deficit or in surplus. The balance of trade is the most widely reported and largest part of the current account. Since 1975, the United States has experienced balance of trade deficits.

Balance of trade

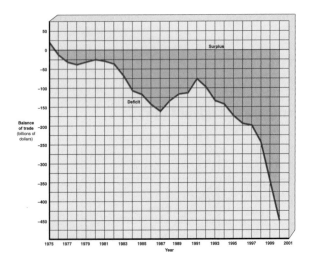

- An **exchange rate** is the price of one nation's currency in terms of another nation's currency. Foreigners who wish to purchase U.S. goods, services, and financial assets demand dollars. The supply of dollars reflects the desire of U.S. citizens to purchase foreign goods, services, and financial assets. The intersection of the supply and demand curves for dollars determines the number of units of a foreign currency per dollar.

Exchange rate

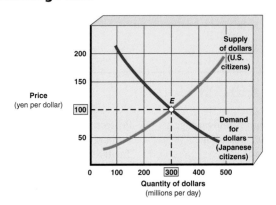

- **Shifts in supply and demand for foreign exchange** result from changes in such factors as tastes, relative price levels, relative real interest rates, and relative income levels.

- **Depreciation of currency** occurs when one currency becomes worth fewer units of another currency. If a currency depreciates, it becomes weaker. Depreciation of a nation's currency increases its exports and decreases its imports.

- **Appreciation of currency** occurs when one currency becomes worth more units of another currency. If a currency appreciates, it becomes stronger. Appreciation of a nation's currency decreases its exports and increases its imports.

SUMMARY OF CONCLUSION STATEMENTS

- When countries specialize, total world output increases, and, therefore, the potential for greater total world consumption also increases.

- International trade allows a country to consume a combination of goods that exceeds its production possibilities curve.

- Comparative advantage refers to the relative opportunity costs between countries of producing the same goods. World output and consumption are maximized when each country specializes in producing and trading goods for which it has a comparative advantage.

- A current account deficit is financed by a capital account surplus.

- An exchange rate can be expressed as a reciprocal.

- An expansion in relative U.S. income causes a depreciation of the dollar.

■ A rise in a trading partner's relative price level causes the dollar to appreciate.

■ When the dollar is weak or depreciates, U.S. goods and services cost foreign consumers less, so they buy more U.S. exports. At the same time, a weak dollar means foreign goods and services cost U.S. consumers more, so they buy fewer imports.

■ When the dollar is strong or appreciates, U.S. goods and services cost foreign consumers more, so they buy fewer U.S. exports. At the same time, a strong dollar means foreign goods and services cost U.S. consumers less, so they buy more foreign imports.

STUDY QUESTIONS AND PROBLEMS

1. The countries of Alpha and Beta produce diamonds and pearls. The production possibilities schedule below describes their potential output in tons per year:

Points on production possibilities curve	Alpha		Beta	
	Diamonds	Pearls	Diamonds	Pearls
A	150	0	90	0
B	100	25	60	60
C	50	50	30	120
D	0	75	0	180

Using the data in the table, answer the following questions:
a. What is the opportunity cost of diamonds for each country?
b. What is the opportunity cost of pearls for each country?
c. In which good does Alpha have a comparative advantage?
d. In which good does Beta have a comparative advantage?
e. Suppose Alpha is producing and consuming at point *B* on its production possibilities curve and Beta is producing and consuming at point *C* on its production possibilities curve. Use a table such as Exhibit 3 to explain why both nations would benefit if they specialize.
f. Draw a graph, and use it to explain how Alpha and Beta benefit if they specialize and Alpha agrees to trade 50 tons of diamonds to Beta and Alpha receives 50 tons of pearls in exchange.

2. Bill can paint either two walls or one window frame in one hour. In the same time, Frank can paint either three walls or two window frames. To minimize the time spent painting, who should specialize in painting walls, and who should specialize in painting window frames?

3. Consider this statement: "The principles of specialization and trade according to comparative advantage among nations also apply to states in the United States." Do you agree or disagree? Explain.

4. Would the U.S. government gain any advantage from using tariffs or quotas to restrict imports?

5. Suppose the United States passed a law stating that we would not purchase imports from any country that imposed any trade restrictions on our exports. Who would benefit and who would lose from such retaliation?

6. Now consider question 5 in terms of the law's impact on domestic producers that export goods. Does this policy adversely affect domestic producers that export goods?

7. Consider this statement: "Unrestricted foreign trade costs domestic jobs." Do you agree or disagree? Explain.

8. Do you support a constitutional amendment to prohibit the federal government from imposing any trade barriers, such as tariffs and quotas, except in case of war or national emergency? Why or why not?

9. Discuss this statement: "Because each nation's balance of payments equals zero, it follows that there is actually no significance to a balance of payments deficit or surplus."

10. For each of the following situations, indicate the direction of the shift in the supply or the demand curve for dollars, the factor causing the change, and the resulting movement of the equilibrium exchange rate for the dollar in terms of foreign currency:
a. American-made cars become more popular overseas.
b. The United States experiences a recession, while other nations enjoy economic growth.
c. Inflation rates accelerate in the United States, while inflation rates remain constant in other nations.
d. Real interest rates in the United States rise, while real interest rates abroad remain constant.

e. The Japanese put quotas and high tariffs on all imports from the United States.

f. Tourism from the United States increases sharply because of a fare war among airlines.

11. The following table summarizes the supply and the demand for euros:

	U.S. dollars per euro				
	$.05	$.10	$.15	$.20	$.25
Quantity demanded (per day)	500	400	300	200	100
Quantity supplied (per day)	100	200	300	400	500

Using the table:

a. Graph the supply and demand curves for euros.

b. Determine the equilibrium exchange rate.

c. Determine what the effect of a fixed exchange rate at $.10 per euro would be.

ONLINE EXERCISES

Exercise 1

Visit the Center for the Study of Western Hemispheric Trade (CSWHT) Tracking U.S. Trade Index (http://www.lanic.utexas.edu/cswht/tradeindex/). What change has occurred between the United States and its NAFTA trading partners since November 1995?

Exercise 2

Visit the Office of Trade and Economic Analysis (http://www.ita.doc.gov/td/industry/otea/), and follow these steps:

1. Select U.S. Foreign Trade Highlights. Under U.S. Aggregate Foreign Trade Data, 1997 & Prior Years, choose Tables 9, 12, and 13. Which are the three top total U.S. trading partners? For the latest year reported, which country has the greatest trade surplus and trade deficit with the United States?

2. Click the Back button to return to the original site. Select U.S. Industry & Trade Outlook. Under Historical Tables, click on *tables*. Under Outlook Trends Table, choose Computers & Peripherals, and compare U.S. imports to exports of computers.

3. Click the Back button to return to the original site, and select State Export Data. Under Export Markets For Each State Ranked by 1997 Export Value, choose your state. What are the top three national export markets for your state? What has happened to your state's exports to these countries?

Exercise 3

Visit the Federal Reserve (http://www.federalreserve.gov/releases/H10/hist/) and select Japan. Observe the exchange rate value of the Yen for a single dollar from 1990 to the present. What could have caused this change?

Exercise 4

Visit the Universal Currency Converter (http://www.xe.net/currency/). How much is the U.S. dollar currently worth in terms of the U.K. pound? What about the Japanese yen?

CHECKPOINT ANSWERS

Do Nations with an Advantage Always Trade?

In the United States, the opportunity cost of producing 1 calculator is 100 towels. In Italy, the opportunity cost of producing 1 calculator is 100 towels. If you said, because the opportunity cost is the same for each nation, specialization and trade would not boost total output, and therefore Italy would not trade these products, YOU ARE CORRECT.

Should Everyone Keep a Balance of Payments?

The principal purpose of the balance of payments is to keep track of payments of national currencies. Because states and cities within the same nation use the same national currency, payments for goods and services traded between these parties do not represent a loss (outflow) or gain (inflow). If you said only nations need to use the balance of payments to account for flows of foreign currency across national boundaries, YOU ARE CORRECT.

PRACTICE QUIZ

For a visual explanation of the correct answers, visit the tutorial at http://tucker.swcollege.com.

1. With trade, the production possibilities for two nations lie
   a. outside their consumption possibilities.
   b. inside their consumption possibilities.
   c. at a point equal to the world production possibilities curve.
   d. none of the above.

2. Free trade theory suggests that when trade takes place,
   a. both nations will be worse off.
   b. one nation must gain at the other nation's expense.
   c. both nations will be better off.
   d. one nation will gain and the other nation will be neither better nor worse off.

3. Which of the following is *true* when two countries specialize according to their comparative advantage?
   a. It is possible to increase their total output of all goods.
   b. It is possible to increase their total output of some goods only if both countries are industrialized.
   c. One country is likely to gain from trade, while the other loses.
   d. None of the above is true.

4. According to the theory of comparative advantage, a country should produce and
   a. import goods in which it has an absolute advantage.
   b. export goods in which it has an absolute advantage.
   c. import goods in which it has a comparative advantage.
   d. export goods in which it has a comparative advantage.

Exhibit 11 Potatoes and Wheat Output (tons per hour)

Country	Potatoes	Wheat
United States	1	3
Ireland	1	2

5. In Exhibit 11, which country has the comparative advantage in the production of potatoes?
   a. The United States because it requires fewer resources to produce potatoes.
   b. The United States because it has the lower opportunity cost of potatoes.
   c. Ireland because it requires fewer resources to produce potatoes.
   d. Ireland because it has the lower opportunity cost of potatoes.

6. In Exhibit 11, the opportunity cost of wheat is
   a. ⅓ ton of potatoes in the United States and ½ ton of potatoes in Ireland.
   b. 2 tons of potatoes in the United States and 1½ tons of potatoes in Ireland.
   c. 8 tons of potatoes in the United States and 4 tons of potatoes in Ireland.
   d. ½ ton of potatoes in the United States and ⅔ ton of potatoes in Ireland.

7. In Exhibit 11, the opportunity cost of potatoes is
   a. ½ ton of wheat in the United States and ⅔ ton of wheat in Ireland.
   b. 2 tons of wheat in the United States and 1½ tons of wheat in Ireland.
   c. 16 tons of wheat in the United States and 6 tons of wheat in Ireland.
   d. 3 tons of wheat in the United States and 2 tons of wheat in Ireland.

8. If the countries in Exhibit 11 follow the principle of comparative advantage, the United States should
   a. buy all of its potatoes from Ireland.
   b. buy all of its wheat from Ireland.
   c. buy all of its potatoes and wheat from Ireland.
   d. produce both potatoes and wheat and not trade with Ireland.

9. A tariff increases
   a. the quantity of imports.
   b. the ability of foreign goods to compete with domestic goods.
   c. the prices of imports to domestic buyers.
   d. all of the above.

10. The infant industry argument for protectionism is based on which of the following views?
    a. Foreign buyers will absorb all of the output of domestic producers in a new industry.
    b. The growth of an industry that is new to a nation will be too rapid unless trade restrictions are imposed.
    c. Firms in a newly developing domestic industry will have difficulty growing if they face strong competition from established foreign firms.
    d. It is based on none of the above.

11. The figure that results when goods imports are subtracted from goods exports is
    a. the capital account balance.
    b. the balance of trade.
    c. the current account balance.
    d. always less than zero.

12. Which of the following international accounts records payments for exports and imports of goods, military transactions, foreign travel, investment income, and foreign gifts?
    a. The capital account
    b. The merchandise account
    c. The current account
    d. The official reserve account

13. Which of the following international accounts records the purchase and sale of financial assets and real estate between the United States and other nations?
    a. The balance of trade account
    b. The current account
    c. The capital account
    d. The balance of payments account

14. If a Japanese radio priced at 2,000 yen can be purchased for $10, the exchange rate is
    a. 200 yen per dollar.
    b. 20 yen per dollar.
    c. 20 dollars per yen.
    d. none of the above.

15. The United States
    a. was on a fixed exchange rate system prior to late 1971, but now is on a flexible exchange rate system.
    b. has been on a fixed exchange rate system since 1945.
    c. has been on a flexible exchange rate system since 1945.
    d. was on a flexible exchange rate system prior to late 1983, but now is on a fixed exchange rate system.

16. Suppose the exchange rate changes so that fewer Japanese yen are required to buy a dollar. We would conclude that
    a. the Japanese yen has depreciated in value.
    b. U.S. citizens will buy fewer Japanese imports.
    c. Japanese will demand fewer U.S. exports.
    d. none of the above will occur.

17. Which of the following would cause a decrease in the demand for euros by those holding U.S. dollars?
    a. Inflation in France, but not in the United States
    b. Inflation in the United States, but not in France
    c. An increase in the real rate of interest on investments in France above the real rate of interest on investments in the United States
    d. None of the above

18. An increase in the equilibrium price of a nation's money could be caused by a(an)
    a. decrease in the supply of the money.
    b. decrease in the demand for the money.
    c. increase in the supply of the money.
    d. increase in the quantity of money demanded.

19. If the dollar appreciates (becomes stronger), this causes
    a. the relative price of U.S. goods to increase for foreigners.
    b. the relative price of foreign goods to decrease for Americans.
    c. U.S. exports to fall and U.S. imports to rise.
    d. a balance of trade deficit for the United States.
    e. all of the above to occur.

20. Which of the following would cause the U.S. dollar to depreciate against the Japanese yen?
    a. Greater popularity of U.S. exports in Japan
    b. A higher price level in Japan
    c. Higher real interest rates in the United States
    d. Higher incomes in the United States

CHAPTER 29

Economies in Transition

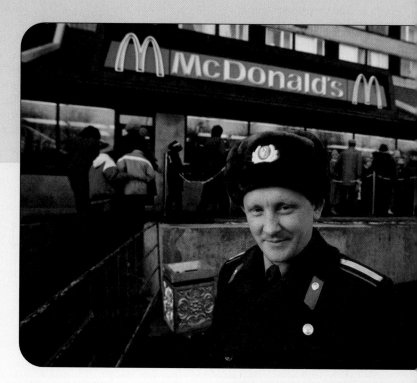

> The inherent vice of capitalism is the unequal sharing of blessings. The inherent virtue of communism is the equal sharing of miseries.
> —*Winston Churchill*

The rapid emergence of the market system in Russia, China, and other communist countries continues to fascinate us. Newspapers and periodicals report the astonishing news that leaders of countries that used to be devoted followers of Marxist ideology now say they believe that capitalism, private property, and profit are ideas superior to the communist system. McDonald's joint venture in Moscow personifies this transformation toward a market system and the failure of communism. Today, Russia and other countries continue to experience economic crisis during their restructuring, but the commitment to free-market reforms remains. What caused this astonishing turn of events?

To understand how the pieces of the global economic puzzle fit together, this chapter begins with a discussion of the three basic types of economies. Then you will examine the pros and cons of the "isms"—capitalism, socialism, and communism. Here you will explore the worldwide clash between the ideas of Adam Smith and Karl Marx and study their current influence on economic systems. Finally, you will examine economic reforms in Cuba, Russia, and China. The chapter concludes with a look at the Japanese "malaise."

In this chapter, you will learn to solve these economics puzzles:

■ Why did drivers in the former Soviet Union remove the windshield wipers and side mirrors whenever they parked their cars?

■ What did Adam Smith mean when he said that an "invisible hand" promotes the public interest?

■ If the Soviet Union was foolish to run its economy on five-year plans, why do universities, businesses, and governments in a capitalistic economy plan?

Basic Types of Economic Systems

An **economic system** consists of the organizations and methods used to determine what goods and services are produced, how they are produced, and for whom they are produced. As explained earlier in Chapter 2, scarcity forces each economic system to decide what combination of goods to produce, how to produce such goods, and who gets the output once produced. The decision-making process involves interaction among many aspects of a nation's culture, such as its laws, form of government, ethics, religions, and customs. Economist Robert L. Heilbroner established a simple way to look at the basic methods that society can employ. Each economic system can be classified into one of three basic types: (1) *traditional*, (2) *command*, and (3) *market*.

Economic system
The organization and methods used to determine what goods and services are produced, how they are produced, and for whom they are produced.

The Traditional Economy

Why does England have a king or queen? Tradition is the answer. Historically, the **traditional economy** has been a common system for making economic decisions. The traditional economy is a system that answers the What, How, and For Whom questions the way they have always been answered. People in this type of society learn that copying the previous generation allows them to feel accepted. Anyone who changes ways of doing things asks for trouble from others. This is because people in such a society believe that what was good yesterday, and years ago, must still be a good idea today.

Traditional systems are used by primitive tribes, the Ainu of Japan, the native people of Brazil's rain forest, and the Amish of Pennsylvania. In these societies, the way past generations decided what crops are planted, how they are harvested, and to whom they are distributed remains unchanged today. People perform their jobs in the manner established by their ancestors. The Amish are well known for rejecting tractors and using horse-drawn plows. Interestingly, the Amish reject Social Security because their society voluntarily redistributes wealth to members who are needy.

Traditional economy
A system that answers the What, How, and For Whom questions the way they always have been answered.

The Traditional Economy's Strengths and Weaknesses

The benefit of the traditional approach is that it minimizes friction among members because relatively little is disputed. Consequently, people in this system may cooperate more freely with one another. In today's industrial world, the Amish and other traditional economies appear very satisfied with their relatively uncomplicated systems. However, critics argue that the traditional system restricts individual initiative and therefore does not lead to the production of advanced goods, new technology, and economic growth.

The Command Economy

In a **command economy,** a dictator or group of central planners makes economic decisions for society. In this system, the What, How, and For Whom questions are answered by central authority. The former Soviet Union in the past and Cuba today are examples of nations with command economies using national economic plans implemented through powerful government committees. Politically selected committees decide on everything, including

Command economy
A system that answers the What, How, and For Whom questions by central authority.

The International Monetary Fund (http://www .imf.org/) *provides information about economies around the globe.*

the number, color, size, quality, and price of autos, brooms, sweaters, and tanks. The state owns the factors of production and dictates answers to the three basic economic questions. The authorities might decide to produce modern weapons instead of schools, or they might decide to devote resources to building huge monuments like the pyramids, built by the rulers of ancient Egypt to honor their dead kings and queens.

In the old Soviet economy, for example, the three basic economic questions were answered by a central planning agency called the *Gosplan*. The Gosplan set production quotas and prices for farms, factories, mines, housing construction, medical care, and other producing units. What should the cows be fed? If it is hay, how much land can be used to grow it? How much milk should the cows give? How many people will be dairy farmers? What wages should a dairy farmer earn? Should milk be given to everyone, to a few, or to any persons chosen by the leaders? The Gosplan tried to make all these decisions. Today, in Russia and the former Soviet republics, the Gosplan is a distant memory of the discarded Soviet command system.

We can represent the command economy by the pyramid shown in Exhibit 1. At the top of the pyramid is a supremely powerful group of central planners, such as the old Soviet Gosplan. That agency established production targets and prices for goods and services. Then the Gosplan transmitted this information to a second layer of specialized state planning agencies. One of these specialized government bureaucracies purchased raw materials, another agency established fashion trends, another set prices, and another government bureaucracy made decisions based on employment and wages.

Production objectives were transmitted from the upper authority layers to the individual producing units, represented by the third layer of the pyramid in Exhibit 1. These producers supplied goods and services to the consumers, as commanded by the central authorities. The bottom portion of the pyramid illustrates the distribution, according to the master plan, of output to consuming units of individuals and households.

The Command Economy's Strengths and Weaknesses

Believe it or not, the command system can be defended. Proponents argue that economic change occurs much faster than in a traditional economy. This is one reason those dissatisfied with a traditional society might advocate establishment of a command system. The central authorities can ignore custom and order new ways of doing things. Another reason for adopting a command economy is the controversial belief that the government will provide economic security and equity. It is alleged that central authorities ensure that everyone is provided food, clothing, shelter, and medical care regardless of their ability to contribute to society.

The absolute power of central authorities to make right decisions is also the power to be absolutely wrong. Often the planners do not set production goals accurately, and either shortages or surpluses of goods and services are the result. For example, at one point the planners miscalculated and produced too few windshield wipers and side mirrors for Soviet cars. Faced with shortages of these parts, Soviet drivers removed windshield wipers and side mirrors whenever they parked their cars to prevent theft. On the other hand,

EXHIBIT 1 **The Command Economy Pyramid**

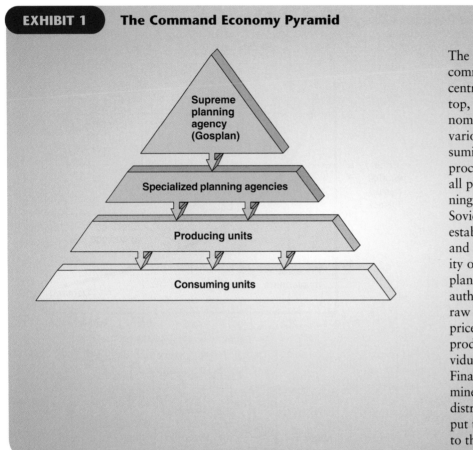

Supreme
planning
agency
(Gosplan)

Specialized planning agencies

Producing units

Consuming units

The principal feature of a command economy is the central planning board at the top, which transmits economic decisions down to the various producing and consuming units below. This process begins with an overall plan from a supreme planning board, such as the old Soviet Gosplan. The Gosplan established production targets and was the ultimate authority over a layer of specialized planning agencies, which authorized capital expansion, raw material purchases, prices, wages, and any other production decisions for individual producing units. Finally, the factories, farms, mines, and other producers distributed the specified output to consumers according to the approved master plan.

the Gosplan allocated some collective farms far more fertilizer than they could use. To receive the same amount of fertilizer again the next year, farmers simply burned the excess fertilizer. As a result of such decision-making errors, people waited in long lines or stole goods. How does any decision-making group really know how many windshield wipers to produce each year and how much workers making them should earn?

Because profit is not the motive of producers in a command economy, quality and variety of goods also suffer. If the Gosplan ordered a state enterprise to produce 400,000 side mirrors for cars, for example, producers had little incentive to make the extra effort required to create a quality product in a variety of styles. The easiest way to meet the goal was to produce a low-quality product in one style regardless of consumer demand.

Exhibit 2 illustrates how the pricing policy of central planners causes shortages. The demand curve for side mirrors conforms to the law of demand. At lower prices in rubles, the quantity demanded increases. The supply curve is fixed at 400,000 side mirrors because it is set by the central planners and is therefore unresponsive to price variations.

Suppose one of the principal goals of the command economy is to keep the price low. To reach this goal, the central planners set the price of side mirrors at 20 rubles, which is below the equilibrium price of 40 rubles. At

EXHIBIT 2   **Central Planners Fixing Prices**

The central planners' goal is to keep prices low, so they set the price of a side mirror for a car at 20 rubles, which is below the market-determined equilibrium price of 40 rubles. At the set price, however, the quantity demanded is 800,000 side mirrors per year, and the quantity supplied is 400,000 per year. Thus, the shortage at the government-established price is 400,000 side mirrors per year. As a result, long lines form to buy side mirrors, and black markets appear.

CAUSATION CHAIN

Planners set quantity supplied ⇒ Planners set the price of mirrors below equilibrium ⇒ Shortage of mirrors

20 rubles, more people can afford a side mirror compared to the equilibrium price set by an uncontrolled marketplace. The consequence of this lower price set by the planners is a shortage. The quantity demanded at 20 rubles is 800,000 side mirrors, and the quantity supplied is only 400,000 mirrors. Thus, the model explains why side mirrors disappeared from stores long before many who were willing to buy them could do so.

The same graphical analysis applies to centrally planned rental prices for apartments. The central planners in the former Soviet Union set rents below the equilibrium rental prices for apartments. As the model predicts, low rents resulted in a shortage of housing. Meanwhile, the planners promised that improvements in housing would come in time.

Conclusion *When central planners set prices below equilibrium for goods and services, they create shortages, which mean long lines, empty shelves, and black markets.*[1]

[1]Recall from Exhibit 4 of Chapter 4 that a black market is an illegal market that emerges when a price ceiling is imposed in a free market.

The Market Economy and the Ideas of Adam Smith

In a **market economy,** neither customs nor a single person or group of central planners answers the three basic economic questions facing society. The market economy is an economic system that answers the What, How, and For Whom questions using prices determined by the interaction of the forces of supply and demand. One of the first people to explain the power of a market economy was the Scottish economist Adam Smith. In the same year that the American colonies declared their political independence, Smith's *An Inquiry into the Nature and Causes of the Wealth of Nations* presented the blueprint for employing markets to improve economic performance. Smith spent over 10 years observing the real world and writing about how nations could best improve their material well-being. He concluded that the answer was to use free markets because this mechanism provides the incentive for everyone to follow his or her *self-interest.*

Adam Smith is the *father of modern economics.* He intended to write a book that would influence popular opinion, and unlike many famous works, his book was an immediate success. The basic philosophy of his book is "the best government is the least government." This belief is known as *laissez-faire,* a French expression meaning "allow to act." As Smith stated, the role of the government should be limited to providing national defense, providing education, maintaining infrastructure, enforcing contracts, and little else. Smith also advocated free trade among nations and rejected the idea that nations should impose trade barriers.

During Smith's lifetime, European nations such as England, France, and Spain intervened to control economic activities. In *The Wealth of Nations,* Smith argued that economic freedoms are "natural rights" necessary for the dignity of humankind. He believed that free competition among people who follow their self-interest would best benefit society because markets free of government interference produce the greatest output of goods and services possible. As noted above, Smith was an advocate of free international trade and asked the question implied in the full title of his book: Why are some nations richer than others? He explained that the source of any nation's wealth is not really the amount of gold or silver it owns. This was an idea popular during Smith's time called *mercantilism.* Instead, he argued that it is the ability of people to produce products and trade in free markets that creates a nation's wealth.

The importance of a market is that it harnesses the power of self-interest to answer the What, How, and For Whom questions. Without central planning, markets coordinate the actions of millions of consumers and producers. Smith said that the market economy seemed to be controlled by an **invisible hand.** The invisible hand is a phrase that expresses the belief that the best interests of a society are served when individual consumers and producers compete to achieve their own private interests. Guided by an invisible hand, producers must compete with one another to win consumers' money. The *profit motive* in a competitive marketplace provides profits as a reward for efficient producers, while losses punish inefficient producers. Smith saw profit as the necessary driving force in an individualistic market system. The profit motive leads the butcher, the baker, and other producers to answer the What, How, and For Whom questions at the lowest prices. Consumers also

Market economy

An economic system that answers the What, How, and For Whom questions using prices determined by the interaction of the forces of supply and demand.

 For a short and well-written discussion of the life and works of Adam Smith, visit http://www.efr .hw.ac.uk/EDC/edinburghers/ adam-smith.html.

Invisible hand

A phrase that expresses the belief that the best interests of a society are served when individual consumers and producers compete to achieve their own private interests.

compete with one another to purchase the best goods at the lowest price. Competition automatically regulates the economy and provides more goods and services than a system in which government attempts to accomplish the same task in the *public interest*. In Smith's own words:

> *Every individual necessarily labours to render the annual revenue of the society as great as he can. He generally, indeed, neither intends to promote the public interest, nor knows how much he is promoting it. By . . . directing that industry in such a manner as its produce may be of the greatest value, he intends only his own gain, and he is in this, as in many other cases, led by an* invisible hand *to promote an end which was no part of his intention. Nor is it always the worse for the society that it was no part of it. By pursuing his own interest he frequently promotes that of the society more effectually than when he really intends to promote it.*[2]

The Market Economy's Strengths and Weaknesses

In a market system, if consumers want Beanie Babies, they can buy them because sellers seek to profit from the sale of Beanie Babies. No single person or central planning board makes a formal decision to shift resources and tell firms how to produce what many might view as a frivolous product. Because no central body or set of customs interferes, the market system provides a wide variety of goods and services that buyers and sellers exchange at the lowest prices.

> **Conclusion** *A market economy answers the What to produce and How to produce questions very effectively.*

Those who attack the market economy point out the market failure problems of lack of competition, externalities, public goods, and income inequality, discussed in Chapter 4. For example, critics contend that competition among buyers and sellers results in people who are very wealthy and people who are very poor. In a market economy, output is divided in favor of people who earn higher incomes and own property. Some people will dine on caviar in a fine restaurant, while others will wander the street and beg for food and shelter. Supporters of the market system argue that this inequality of income must exist to give people incentives or rewards for the value of their contributions to others.

The Mixed Economy

In the real world, no nation is a pure traditional, command, or market economy. Even primitive tribes employ a few markets in their system. For example, members of a tribe may exchange shells for animal skins. In China, the government allows many private shops and farms to operate in free markets. Although the United States is best described as a market economy, there is also a blend of the other two systems. As mentioned earlier, the Amish oper-

---

[2]Adam Smith, *An Inquiry into the Nature and Causes of the Wealth of Nations* (1776; reprint, New York: Random House, 1937), p. 423.

INTERNATIONAL ECONOMICS

Choosing a System

Applicable Concept: basic types of economic systems

Suppose we discover life on a new planet and the chief of their society learns of the successful economy of the United States and summons an economic adviser to learn the secret.

Sitting at the head of a huge oval table, the chief addresses the adviser seated at the other end saying, "Our economic system depends on tradition and command. It works, but not nearly so well as the U.S. economy. Our men and women lead a highly tradition-bound way of life. Men farm and hunt as their forefathers. Women work only in the home and care for children following the role approved by their elders. There is no confusion over how things are done, and there is no chaos over what work, or what output will be produced. People are simply assigned jobs by their leaders and told how much to produce. Likewise, people are told to work on community projects for our national benefit. If anyone refuses to follow instructions, they are shunned or banished. Tell me, how could there possibly be a better way to organize our economy?"

The adviser confidently responds, "Yes, there is definitely a better way. Replace tradition and command systems with the 'invisible hand' of the market

system. This idea was explained long ago by a scholar named Adam Smith, the father of modern economics."

The chief is puzzled. "I have never heard of Adam Smith or the market economy. In a nutshell, explain to me how it differs from our system."

"Very well," says the adviser. "In a market economy, each person is allowed to decide for himself or herself what to do based on price signals."

The chief is horrified and takes umbrage. "But what happens when they do not choose correctly? Let's talk about something specific, like computer production. Unless we designate people to make computers, how do we know the right number will select this job? What if women want to work in this industry? Who decides how much these workers should be paid and how many computers should be produced to satisfy the demand for them?"

"You may rest assured," says the adviser. "Using prices determined in markets free from intervention will answer all your questions better than if leaders try to control everything."

The chief interrupts triumphantly. "Do you really expect me to believe that without instructions from the

leaders, too few or too many products will not be bought and sold?"

"Ah, exactly!" the adviser quickly answers. "The market will automatically do all these wonderful things. People will be more motivated by their own rational self-interest than by tradition or central authority. In short, the system runs itself."

"The economy runs without my leaders' directions!" says the chief. "That's absurd and you have wasted my time. I thought you had a meaningful proposal. Good day."

ANALYZE THE ISSUE

1. Describe how a traditional or a command system would make employment and production decisions compared to a market system.

2. Why might the leader find a market system inconceivable? Is it possible for economic activities not based on self-interest to take place in a market economy?

Source: Adapted from Robert L. Heilbroner, *The Making of Economic Society,* 5th ed. (Englewood Cliffs, N.J.: Prentice-Hall, 1993), pp. 12–13.

ate a well-known traditional economy in our nation. The draft during wartime is an example of a command economy in which the government obtains involuntary labor. In addition, taxes "commanded" from taxpayers fund government programs, such as national defense and Social Security. If the economic systems of most nations do not perfectly fit one of the basic definitions, what term best describes their economies? A more appropriate description is

Mixed economy

An economic system that answers the What, How, and For Whom questions through a mixture of traditional, command, and market systems.

that most countries employ a blend of the basic types of economic systems, broadly called a **mixed economy**. A mixed economy is a system that answers the What, How, and For Whom questions through a mixture of traditional, command, and market systems.

The traditional, command, and market economies can exist in a wide variety of political situations. For instance, the United States and Japan are politically "free" societies in which the market system flourishes. But China uses the market system to a limited degree in spite of its lack of political freedom. Moreover, some of the Western democracies engage in central economic planning. French officials representing government, business, and labor meet annually to discuss economic goals for industry for the next five-year period, but compliance is voluntary. In Japan, a government agency called the *Ministry for International Trade and Industry (MITI)* engages in long-term planning. One of the goals of the MITI is to encourage exports so that Japan can earn the foreign currencies it needs to pay for oil and other resources.

The "Isms"

What type of economic system will a society choose to answer the What, How, and For Whom questions? We could call most economies "mixed," but this would be too imprecise. In the real world, economic systems are labeled with various forms of the popular "isms"—capitalism, socialism, and communism, which are based on the basic types of systems.

Capitalism

Capitalism

An economic system characterized by private ownership of resources and markets.

The popular term for the market economy discussed previously is capitalism. **Capitalism** is an economic system characterized by private ownership of resources and markets. *Capitalism* is also called the *free enterprise system*. Regardless of its political system, a capitalist economic system must possess two characteristics: (1) private ownership of resources and (2) decentralized decision making using markets.

Private Ownership.   Ownership of resources determines to a great degree who makes the What, How, and For Whom decisions. In a capitalist system, resources are primarily *privately* owned and controlled by individuals and firms, rather than having property rights *publicly* held by government on behalf of society. In the United States, most capital resources are privately owned, but the term *capitalism* is somewhat confusing because it stresses private ownership of factories, raw materials, farms, and other forms of *capital* even though public ownership of land exists as well.

Consumer sovereignty

The freedom of consumers to cast their dollar votes to buy, or not to buy, at prices determined in competitive markets.

Decentralized Decision Making.   This characteristic of capitalism allows buyers and sellers to exchange goods in markets without government involvement. A capitalist system operates on the principle of **consumer sovereignty**. Consumer sovereignty is the freedom of consumers to cast their dollar votes to buy, or not to buy, at prices determined in competitive markets. As a result, consumer spending determines what goods and services firms produce. In a capitalist system, most allocative decisions are coordinated by consumers and producers interacting through markets and making their own decisions guided by Adam Smith's invisible hand.

In the real world, many U.S. markets are not perfectly open or free markets with the consumer as sovereign. For example, consumers cannot buy illegal drugs or body organs. In Chapter 4, you learned that the U.S. government sets minimum prices (support prices) for wheat, milk, cheese, and other products. These markets are free only if the market price is above the support price. Similarly, the minimum wage law forces employers to pay a wage above some dollar amount per hour regardless of market conditions.

Conclusion *No nation in the world precisely fits the two criteria for capitalism; however, the United States comes close.*

Capitalism's Strengths and Weaknesses

One of the major strengths of capitalism is its capacity to achieve *economic efficiency* because competition and the profit motive force production at the lowest cost. Another strength of pure capitalism is *economic freedom* because economic power is widely dispersed. Individual consumers, producers, and workers are free to make decisions based on their own self-interest. Economist Milton Friedman makes a related point: Private ownership limits the political power of government to deny goods, services, or jobs to their political adversaries.

Critics of capitalism cite several shortcomings. First, capitalism tends toward an unequal distribution of income. This inequality of income among citizens results for several reasons. Private ownership of capital and the other factors of production can cause these factors to become concentrated in the hands of a few individuals or firms. Also, people do not have equal labor skills, and the marketplace rewards those with greater skills. These inequalities may be perpetuated because the rich can provide better education, legal aid, political platforms, and wealth to their heirs. Second, pure capitalism is criticized for its failure to protect the environment. The pursuit of profit and self-interest can take precedence over damage or pollution to the air, rivers, lakes, and streams. In Chapter 4, recall the graphical model used to illustrate the socially unacceptable impact of producers who pollute the environment.

Socialism

The idea of socialism has existed for thousands of years. Its basis is the command system. **Socialism** is an economic system characterized by government ownership of resources and centralized decision making. Socialism is also called *command socialism*. Under socialism, a command system owns and controls in the *public interest* the major industries, such as steel, electricity, and agriculture. However, some free markets can exist in farming, retail trade, and certain service areas. Just as no pure capitalist system exists in the real world, none of the socialist countries in the world today practices pure socialism. In fact, there are as many variants of socialism as there are countries called socialist.

Socialism
An economic system characterized by government ownership of resources and centralized decision making.

Before discussing socialism further, you must realize socialism is an economic system, and that politics should not be confused with economics. Great Britain, France, and Italy have representative democracies, but many of their major industries are or have been nationalized. In the United States, the federal government owns and operates the Tennessee Valley Authority, the National Aeronautics and Space Administration (NASA), and the U.S. Postal Service, while at the same time allowing private utilities and mail service firms to operate.

The Ideas of Karl Marx

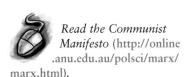

Read the Communist Manifesto (http://online .anu.edu.au/polsci/marx/ marx.html).

In spite of the transition to capitalism in Russia and Eastern Europe, socialism still prevails in China, Cuba, and many less-developed countries. The theory for socialism and *communism* can be traced to Karl Marx. Marx was a nineteenth-century German philosopher, revolutionary, and economist. Unlike other economists of the time who were followers of Adam Smith, Marx rejected the concept of a society operating through private interest and profit.

Karl Marx was born in Germany, the son of a lawyer. He was an outstanding student at Berlin University. In 1841, after receiving a doctorate in philosophy, he turned to journalism. In 1843, Marx married the daughter of a wealthy family and moved to Paris, but his political activities forced him to leave Paris for England. From the age of 31, he lived and wrote his books in London. In London, Marx lived an impoverished life while he and his lifelong friend Friedrich Engels wrote the *Communist Manifesto*, published in 1848. A massive work followed, titled *Das Kapital*, which was published in three volumes in 1867, 1884, and 1885.

These two works made Karl Marx the most influential economist in the history of socialism. In fact, he devoted his entire life to a revolt against capitalism. As Marx read *The Wealth of Nations*, he saw profits as unjust payments to owners of firms—the capitalists. Marx predicted that the market system would destroy itself because wealthy owners would go too far and exploit workers as unrelenting greed for profits would lead these wealthy owners to pay starvation wages. Moreover, the owners would force laborers to work in unsafe conditions, and many would not have a job at all.

Marx believed that private ownership and exploitation would produce a nation driven by a class struggle between a few "haves" and many "have-nots." As he stated in the *Communist Manifesto,* "The history of all existing society is the history of class struggle. Freeman and slave, patrician and plebeian, lord and serf, guildmaster and journeyman, in a word, oppressor and oppressed."[3] In Marx's vision, capitalists were the modern-day oppressors, and the workers were the oppressed proletariat. Someday, Marx predicted, the workers would rise up in a spontaneous bloody revolution against a system benefiting only the owners of capital. Marx believed **communism** to be the ideal system, which would evolve in stages from capitalism through socialism. Communism is a stateless, classless economic system in which all the factors of production are owned by the workers and people share in production according to their needs. This is the highest form of socialism toward which the revolution should strive.

Communism

A stateless, classless economic system in which all the factors of production are owned by the workers and people share in production according to their needs. In Marx's view, this is the highest form of socialism toward which the revolution should strive.

---

[3]Karl Marx and Friedrich Engels, *The Communist Manifesto* (New York: International Press, 1848), p. 31.

Under communism, no private property exists to encourage self-interest. There is no struggle between classes of people, and everyone cooperates. In fact, there is no reason to commit crime, and police, lawyers, and courts are unnecessary. Strangely, Marx surpassed Adam Smith in advocating a system with little central government. Marx believed that those who work hard, or are more skilled, will be public spirited. Any "haves" will give voluntarily to "have-nots" until everyone has exactly the same material well-being. In Marx's own words, people would be motivated by the principle "from each according to his ability, to each according to his need." World peace would evolve as nation after nation accepted cooperation and rejected profits and competition. Under the idealized society of communism, there would be no state. No central authority would be necessary to pursue the interests of the people.

Today, we call the economic systems that formerly existed in the Soviet Union, and Eastern Europe, and still exist in China, Cuba, and other countries *communist*. However, the definition for *socialism* given in this chapter more accurately describes their real-world economic systems. Actually, no nation has achieved the ideal communist society described by Marx, nor has capitalism self-destructed as he predicted. The 1917 communist revolution in Russia did not fit Marx's theory. At that time, Russia was an underdeveloped country, rather than an industrial country filled with greedy capitalists who exploited workers.

Characteristics of Socialism

Regardless of a society's political system, a socialist economy has two basic characteristics: (1) public ownership and (2) centralized decision making.

Public Ownership.   Under socialism, the government owns most of the factors of production, including factories, farms, mines, and natural resources. Agriculture in the old Soviet Union illustrates how even this real-world socialist country deviated from total public ownership. In the Soviet Union, there were three rather distinct forms of agriculture: state farms, collective farms, and private plots. In both the state-farm and the collective-farm sectors, central planning authorities determined prices and outputs. In contrast, the government allowed those holding small private plots on peasant farms to operate primarily in free markets that determined price and output levels. Reforms now allow farmers to buy land, tractors, trucks, and other resources from the state. If these reforms continue, they will dramatically end the collectivization of agriculture begun under Josef Stalin.

Centralized Decision Making.   Instead of the pursuit of *private interest,* the motivation of pure socialism is the *public interest* of the whole society. For instance, a factory manager cannot decide to raise or lower prices to obtain maximum profits for the factory. Regardless of inventory levels or the opportunity to raise prices, the planners will not permit this action. Instead of exploiting the ups and downs of the market, the goal of the socialist system is to make centralized decisions that protect workers and consumers from decentralized market decisions. Critics argue that the main objective of this centralization is to perpetuate the personal dictatorships of leaders such as Stalin in the old Soviet Union and Fidel Castro in Cuba.

CHECKPOINT

To Plan or Not to Plan—That Is the Question

You make plans. You planned to go to college. You plan which career to follow. You plan to get married, and so on. Businesses plan. They plan to hire employees, expand their plants, increase profits, and so forth. Because individuals and businesses plan in a market economy, there is really no difference between our system and a command economy. Or is there?

Before the open market reforms, Soviet planners altered earnings to attract workers into certain occupations and achieve planned goals. For example, if space projects needed more engineers, then the state raised the earnings of engineers until the target number of people entered the engineering profession.

As shown earlier in Exhibit 2, central planners in the Soviet Union also manipulated consumer prices. If consumers desired more cars than were available, the authorities increased the price of cars. If people wished to purchase less of an item than was available, then planners lowered prices. The problem is that this decision process took time. And while the market awaited its orders from the Soviet planners, excess inventories of some items accumulated, and consumers stood in line for cheap products that never seemed to be available. There was an old Soviet saying, "If you see a line, get in it. Whatever it is, it's scarce, and you will not see it tomorrow."

The Soviet factory system did not adhere completely to the command system. The government rewarded successful managers with bonuses that could be substantial. Better apartments, nice vacations, and medals were incentives for outstanding performance. Under economic reforms, plant managers now make decisions based on profitability instead of centralized controls.

Socialism's Strengths and Weaknesses

Proponents of the socialism model argue that this system is superior in achieving an equitable distribution of income. This is because government ownership of capital and other resources prevents a few individuals or groups from acquiring a disproportionate share of the nation's wealth. Also, supporters argue that rapid economic growth is achieved when planners have the power to direct more resources to producing capital goods and fewer resources to producing consumer goods (see Exhibit 4 of Chapter 2).

National goals may seem to be easily formulated and pursued under state directives, but there are problems. For example, proponents of such an economy can claim there is no unemployment because the government assigns all workers a job and allocates resources to complete their production goals. However, economic inefficiency results because the government often uses many workers to perform work requiring only one or two workers. Critics also point out that the absence of the profit motive discourages entrepreneurship and innovation and thus suppresses economic growth.

Socialism is particularly vulnerable to the charge that it ignores the goal of economic freedom and instead creates a privileged class of government bureaucrats who assume the role of "capitalists." Central planners are the

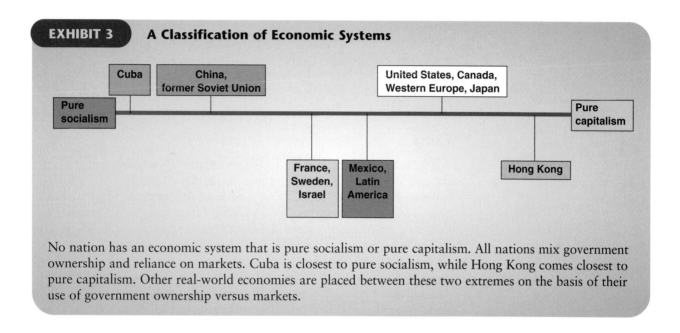

EXHIBIT 3 **A Classification of Economic Systems**

No nation has an economic system that is pure socialism or pure capitalism. All nations mix government ownership and reliance on markets. Cuba is closest to pure socialism, while Hong Kong comes closest to pure capitalism. Other real-world economies are placed between these two extremes on the basis of their use of government ownership versus markets.

key translators of information about consumer preferences and production capabilities flowing to millions of economic units. This complex and cumbersome process is subject to errors and a lack of responsiveness to the wants of the majority of the population. Critics also question whether the distribution of income under socialism is more equitable than under capitalism. In the socialist system, "perks" for government officials, nepotism, and the illegal use of markets create disparities in income.

Comparing Economic Systems

In reality, all nations operate economic systems that blend capitalism and socialism. Exhibit 3 presents a continuum that attempts to place countries between the two extremes of pure socialism on the left and pure capitalism on the right. Economies characterized by a high degree of both private ownership and market allocation are closest to pure capitalism. Hong Kong (now part of China), Japan, the United States, and Canada fall at the capitalism end of the line. Conversely, economies characterized by much government ownership of resources and central planning are closest to pure socialism. Although the outcome of reforms is unclear in Russia, the former Soviet republics, and China, at present these economies and Cuba fall close to the pure socialism end of the spectrum.

To learn more about any country and its economy, visit The World Factbook, a comprehensive publication of the U.S. Central Intelligence Agency (CIA) (http://www.cia.gov/cia/publications/factbook/index.html).

Economies in Transition

By the early 1990s, the centrally planned economies in the old Soviet Union and Eastern Europe had collapsed. After more than 70 years in the Soviet Union and over 40 years in Eastern Europe and China, the failed communist economies made a startling switch to embrace capitalism. Faced with severe shortages of food, housing, cars, and other consumer goods, communism could no longer claim better living standards for its citizens. The following is a brief discussion of reforms aimed at introducing market power into the economic systems of Cuba, Russia, and China. This section concludes with a discussion of Japan's financial crisis.

Cuba

Today, Cuba remains wedded to the communist system. Nevertheless, the collapse of Soviet bloc aid coupled with the effects of the U.S. trade embargo have forced Fidel Castro, a die-hard Marxist, to reluctantly adopt limited free-market reforms. To earn foreign exchange, the dollar has been legalized, and the Cuban government has poured capital into tourism by building several new state-owned hotels and restoring historic sections of Havana. Cuba has also set up quasi-state enterprises that accept only hard currency. Since few Cubans have dollars or other hard currency, many are earning it by turning to illegal schemes, such as driving gypsy cabs, engaging in prostitution, or selling Cuba's famous cigars and coffee on the black market. Other Cubans have abandoned state jobs and opened small businesses under these new rules. However, these small-scale businesses cannot employ anyone beyond the family of the owner. Also, spare rooms in houses can be rented, and artisans can sell their work to tourists. In addition, state farm enterprises have been broken into worker-owned units, and the government allows farmers to sell produce leftover after they have met the state's quota. As a result, more food and a greater variety of food are becoming available.

In spite of the private enterprise reforms, Cuba remains essentially a communist system. The vast majority of workers receive low state salaries in pesos and rations of staples. Profits from hotels and shops go directly into the central bank and help finance Castro's government. The state also discourages private enterprises by taxing them heavily on expected earnings, rather than on actual sales. In addition, there are highly restrictive regulations. For example, restaurants in Havana are limited to 12 seats and cannot expand regardless of demand.

In 2000, the United States introduced a new five-point program which provides an expansion of cash transfers, direct mail service, and the sale of food to nongovernment entities. These measures are intended to help the Cuban people without strengthening the Cuban government.

Russia

In 1991, communist rule ended in Russia. To function efficiently, markets must offer incentives, so workers, the public, and even foreign investors were permitted to buy state property. This meant individuals could own the factors of production and earn profits. Such market incentives are a dagger thrust into the heart of a system previously devoted to rejecting capitalism.

A key reform for Russia was to allow supply and demand to set higher prices for basic consumer goods. As shown earlier in Exhibit 2, without central planners, when prices rise to their equilibrium level, the quantity supplied increases and the quantity demanded decreases. At the beginning of 1992, the Russian government removed direct government price controls on most market goods. As the model predicts, average prices rose, leaping 1,735 percent in 1992, and a greater variety of goods started appearing on the shelves. Although workers had to pay more for basic consumer goods, they could at least find goods to buy.

Since 1992, Russia has created an independent central bank and implemented anti-inflationary monetary policies. As a result, the inflation rate fell to 15 percent in 1997. Nevertheless, Russia continued to face financial crisis. In the late spring of 1998, its stock market crashed, payment on its foreign debt was suspended, and the ruble was devalued. In 1999, Russia proposed that its commercial bank creditors agree to a significant reduction of the $31 billion debt owed to them as part of a restructuring agreement. In 2000, the inflation rate was 21 percent, and too often companies do not pay their bills, wages, or taxes. The entrepreneurial spirit is in an embryonic stage, and corruption is a frequent way of life. Although Russia is far from a successful market economy, the nation is struggling to achieve an amazing economic transition. Under President Vladimir Putin, elected in 2000, there is a "window of opportunity" to create a dynamic economy embracing capitalism.

The People's Republic of China

Unlike Russia, China has sought economic reform under the direction of its Communist Party. Fundamental economic reforms occurred in China after the death of Mao Tse Tung in 1976. Much of this reform was due to the leadership of Deng Xiaoping. Mao was devoted to the egalitarian ideal of communist ideology. Thoughts of self-interest were counterrevolutionary, and photographs of Marx, Lenin, and Mao hung on every street corner and in every office and factory. Deng shifted priorities by increasing production of consumer goods and raising wages of workers so they could buy more of these goods. International trade also expanded from less than 1 percent of U.S. trade in 1975 to 6 percent of U.S. merchandise trade in 2000.

To make China an industrial power in the twenty-first century, Chinese planners introduced a two-tier system for industry and agriculture in 1978. Each farm and state enterprise was given a contract to produce a quota. Any amount produced over the quota could be sold in an open market. Also, the Chinese government encouraged the formation of nonstate enterprises owned jointly by managers and their workforces and special economic zones open to foreign investment. In other words, a blend of capitalism and socialism would provide the incentives needed to increase output. As Deng Xiaoping explained, "It doesn't matter whether the cat is black or white as long as it catches mice." These reforms worked, leading to huge increases in farm and industrial output in the 1980s. In fact, some peasant farmers became some of the wealthiest people in China. After Deng's death in the mid-1990s, leadership of China passed to President Jian Zemin, who continues the policy of free-market reforms. Today, forests of glossy skyscrapers, expressways, upscale apartments, and shopping malls in Beijing, Shanghai, and other cities attest to the market-oriented reforms begun years ago. (See *International Economics: China Seeks Free-Market Revolution.*)

The Japanese Ministry of International Trade and Industry (http://www.jwindow.net/GOV/CABINET/MITI/home.html), *the Japan External Trade Organization* (http://www.jetro.go.jp/top/index.html), *and the Japan Economic Foundation* (http://www.jef.or.jp/en/index.html) *provide news and information about Japanese trade and the Japanese economy.*

INTERNATIONAL ECONOMICS

China Seeks Free-Market Revolution

Applicable Concept: comparative economic systems

For more than 2,000 years, China had a "self-reliance" policy that caused its economy to lag far behind advanced economies. In 1978, China adopted new economic reforms that are continuing to transform one of the poorest economies in the world into one of the fastest growing.

Under the reform system, households operate in a mixed world of state controls and free markets. A two-track pricing system still exists for some key goods and services, such as coal, petroleum, steel, transportation, and agriculture. The rural economy is central to China's economic reforms. In the past, farmers worked collectively in people's communes. The government told the farmers what to produce and how much to produce. They could sell their products only to the state at a price fixed by the government, rather than in markets. A so-called household contract responsibility system was created as a reform to

assign land owned by the state to farmers. The farmers must pay an annual share of profits to the government, and the state does not cover losses. Farmers, however, have the authority to decide what to produce and the price at which to sell in open markets. As a result, both farmers and consumers are noticeably better off because everyone can find and afford more food.

As farming productivity rose sharply, fewer farmers were needed to work on the land, and this sur-

plus labor moved into emerging township and village nonstate enterprises. These enterprises were mostly in light industry and owned collectively by townships or villages. As a result, the composition of rural output changed. When the reforms began in the late 1970s, farming accounted for 70 percent of the total rural output and industry for 20 percent. By 1993, industry's share had jumped to more than 40 percent.[1] Overall, the structure of the economy has changed. In 1976, agriculture accounted for 33 percent of GDP; by 2000, its share had fallen to 17 percent.[2]

A 1993 article in the *Boston Globe* provides an interesting observation on China's economic transformation:

> *Stuffing the genie back into the bottle might prove difficult. The flood of money has created a bubble, particularly in stocks and property, making some*

The Japanese "Malaise"

The postwar transformation of the Japanese economy has been a remarkable success story. In 1950, Japan was starting to recover from the devastation of World War II, and its per capita GDP was one-eighth that of the United States. In the 1950s, "Made in Japan" meant cheap and poor-quality products. By the 1990s, "Made in Japan" meant top-quality, high-tech products, probably at the lowest price, and Japan's per capita GDP exceeded that of the United States. This rapid economic growth happened in a country that has a land area smaller than California and a population half as large as that of the United States. Moreover, Japan lacks many natural resources, so it must import almost all of its oil and other important minerals.

Many factors contributed to the success of Japan's capitalist economy. First, Japanese workers are very loyal to the firms that employ them. One *people in China very rich, very fast.* The China Daily, *China's official English-language newspaper, recently heralded the existence of 1 million millionaires. . . . These millionaires, many of whom just five years ago were still wearing Mao outfits and following the party's socialist dictates, now sport stylish Western-style suits with the label ostentatiously left on the cuff.*[3]

A 2001 *Time* article describes a change in China's population:

Carol Yang is convinced she has it all. Her mother isn't so sure. True, Yang has a job at an international public relations firm and is married to a loving husband. But Yang doesn't have any children, and her mother worries about that. "She thinks that I'm not a complete woman if I don't have kids," says Yang, 33, a

manager in Shanghai. "But I tell her that times have changed and that children are no longer the measure of a successful woman."

Yang's attitude should hearten China's controversial womb police, who have spent two decades attempting to control the nation's population by fining citizens with more than one child. They have succeeded remarkably well. Today the average Chinese woman has two children, compared with six 30 years ago. "For all the bad press, China has achieved the impossible," says Sven Burmester, the U.N. Population Fund representative in Beijing. "The country has solved its population problem." In fact, China's population will actually start declining in 2042, according to U.N. projections.[4]

ANALYZE THE ISSUE

1. Why would China abandon the goal of income equality and shift from a centrally planned to a more market-oriented economy?

2. Which groups in China are likely to resist the reforms?

---

[1]Liguang Wu, "Economic Reform in China: Retrospect," *Senior Economist,* Nov. 1993, pp. 3–5.
[2]World Bank Group, *Country at a Glance,* http://www.worldbank.org/ html/estdr/regions/htm.
[3]Maggie Farley, "China's Economic Boom Energizing Inflation," *Boston Globe,* Aug. 13, 1993, p. 1A.
[4]"China's Lifestyle Choice: Changes to the Famous One-Child Policy Miss the Point," *Time,* Aug. 6, 2001, p. 32.

---

reason for this is a strong tradition that emphasizes loyalty for both employers and employees. Another reason, although changing, is that most major Japanese corporations provide lifetime employment to age 55, when mandatory retirement occurs. A worker cannot be discharged except for criminal acts, excessive absenteeism, or other misconduct. This job security means employees have an incentive to strive for the long-run success of their firm. Another reason for worker loyalty is labor-management cooperation. In Japan, unions often support wage reductions in order to avoid layoffs during periods of weak demand for their company's product. Other areas of labor-management cooperation include ways to improve product quality, work schedules, and company plans. For example, workers form *quality circles* to exchange suggestions for improving performance.

Second, taxes as a percentage of GDP are lower in Japan than in other industrialized nations except the United States. As a result of low tax rates, people have a strong incentive to engage in entrepreneurship and make the Japanese economy grow rapidly. It should also be noted that there are many reasons for Japan's lower taxes. One reason often given is that Japan has been protected by the U.S. defense shield and therefore spends little on its military.

Third, the savings and investment rates of Japan are higher than those of other economies. The Japanese people save about 15 percent of their disposable income compared to only about 2 percent for the United States. One explanation for the high Japanese saving rate is Japan's very limited social insurance system. Therefore, workers must save for their retirement. Also, Japan gives tax credits to encourage saving. Similarly, corporations channel the major share of their profits into investment.

Fourth, Japan has an industrial policy that combines government and businesses in joint ventures. The MITI, discussed earlier in this chapter, is an example of how the Japanese government actively follows policies to help certain industries to be profitable in international trade.

The average annual growth rate of real GDP for Japan during 1967–1976 was 7.0 percent, compared with 4.2 percent during 1977–1992, 1.6 percent for 1993–1997, and −0.9 percent between 1998 and 2000. Why the slowdown? Observers credit Japan's high growth rate in the past to its ability to utilize the technology developed by more advanced countries. Now the technology gap is closed, and Japanese manufacturing is no more modern than other competing nations.

In the late 1990s, Japan experienced severe economic problems. A collapse in real estate and other asset prices created a massive debt problem for the Japanese financial system. Instead of quickly establishing a system for disposing of bad loans, government and bank officials delayed. Cutbacks in lending by Japanese banks led to a credit crunch that contributed to recession in Japan and the rest of Asia. Japan's financial crisis, its worst recession since World War II, and a slide in the yen triggered devaluations of other nations' currencies. U.S. exports to Japan fell, and fears about economic and political turmoil in Asia caused the Dow Jones Industrial Average of the U.S. stock market to drop.

Legislation was passed in Japan to deal with the financial sector problems. To support this effort and recapitalize the banking system, the government made available an unprecedented sum of public funds, amounting to about 12 percent of GDP. In 2001, Prime Minister Junichiro Koizumi's Liberal Democratic Party secured a landslide victory. Koizumi's reforms center on fiscal austerity and on breaking down the intense and hugely expensive bonds of collusion between politicians and big business.

KEY CONCEPTS

Economic system
Traditional economy
Command economy

Market economy
Invisible hand
Mixed economy

Capitalism
Consumer sovereignty

Socialism
Communism

SUMMARY

- An **economic system** is the set of established procedures by which a society answers the What, How, and For Whom to produce questions.

- **Three basic types of economic systems** are the traditional, command, and market systems. The **traditional system** is based on decisions made according to custom, and the **command system,** shown in the figure below, answers the three economic questions through some powerful central authority. In contrast, the **market system** uses the impersonal mechanism of the interaction of buyers and sellers through markets to answer the What, How, and For Whom questions.

Command economy

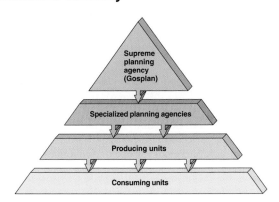

- **Capitalism** is an economic system in which the factors of production are privately owned and economic choices are made by consumers and firms in markets. As prescribed by Adam Smith, government plays an extremely limited role, and self-interest is the driving force, held in check, or regulated, by competition.

- **Consumer sovereignty** is the determination by consumers of the types and quantities of products that are produced in an economy.

- **Socialism** is an economic system in which the government owns the factors of production. The central authorities make the myriad of society's economic decisions according to a national plan. The collective good, or public interest, is the intended guiding force behind the central planners' decisions.

- **Communism** is an economic system envisioned by Karl Marx to be an ideal society in which the workers own all the factors of production. Marx believed that workers who worked hard would be public spirited and would voluntarily redistribute income to those who are less productive. Such a communist nation described by Marx does not exist.

SUMMARY OF CONCLUSION STATEMENTS

- When central planners set prices below equilibrium for goods and services, they create shortages, which mean long lines, empty shelves, and black markets.

- A market economy answers the What to produce and How to produce questions very effectively.

- No nation in the world fits precisely the two criteria for capitalism; however, the United States comes close.

STUDY QUESTIONS AND PROBLEMS

1. Give an example of how a nation's culture affects its economic system.

2. Explain the advantages and the disadvantages of any two of the three basic types of economic systems.

3. Suppose a national program of free housing for the elderly is paid for by a sizable increase in income taxes. Explain a tradeoff that might occur between economic security and efficiency.

4. "The schools are not in the business of pleasing parents and students, and they cannot be allowed to set their own agendas. Their agendas are set by politicians, administrators, and various constituencies that hold the keys to political power. The public system is built to see to it that the schools do what their govern-

ment wants them to do—that they conform to the higher-order values their governors seek to impose."[4] Relate this statement to Exhibit 1.

5. Suppose you are a farmer. Explain why you would be motivated to work in traditional, command, and market economies.

6. Karl Marx believed the market system was doomed. Why do you think he was right or wrong?

7. If all real-world economies are mixed economies, why is the U.S. economy described as capitalist, while the Cuban economy is described as communist?

8. Suppose you are a factory manager. Describe how you might reach production goals under a system of pure capitalism and under a system of pure socialism.

ONLINE EXERCISES

Exercise 1

Browse Capitalism: Frequently Asked Questions (http://www.ocf.berkeley.edu/~shadab/). Select topics of interest. For example, select How is democracy related to capitalism? Or choose Is socialism ideal?

Exercise 2

Browse The Adam Smith Institute (http://www.adamsmith.org/) and Karl Marx (http://www.anu.edu.au/polsci/marx/marx.html).

Exercise 3

Visit Financial Times Home Page (http://www.usa.ft.com/) and undertake a Search for "transition economies."

Select an article that describes how transition economies are progressing.

Exercise 4

Visit the United Nations' Division for Economic Analysis and Projections (DEAP) (http://www.unece.org/ead/ead_h.htm), part of the United Nations Economic Commission for Europe (UN/ECE). After reading the text of this home page, select Publications, and browse an article under Economic Survey of Europe or Economic Bulletin for Europe.

---

[4]John Chubb and Terry More, *Politics, Markets, and the Nation's Public Schools* (Washington, D.C.: Brookings Institution, 1990), p. 38.

CHECKPOINT ANSWER

To Plan or Not to Plan—That Is the Question

When an individual or a business plans in a market economy, other individuals are free to make and follow their own plans. Suppose Hewlett-Packard decides to produce X number of laserjet printers and sell them at a certain price. The decision does not prohibit IBM from producing Y number of laserjet printers and selling them for less than Hewlett-Packard's printers. If either firm makes a mistake, only that firm suffers, and other industries are for the most part unaffected. Under a command system, a central economic plan would be made for all laserjet printer manufacturers. If the central planners order the wrong quantity or quality, there could be major harm to other industries and society. If you said there is a major difference between individual planning and central planning for all society, YOU ARE CORRECT.

PRACTICE QUIZ

For a visual explanation of the correct answers, visit the tutorial at http://tucker.swcollege.com.

1. The economic system in which all of the basic decisions are made through a centralized authority, such as a government agency, is termed a
   a. market economy.
   b. capitalistic economy.
   c. command economy.
   d. traditional economy.

2. Command economies typically suffer from
   a. unemployment, but not underemployment.
   b. neither unemployment nor underemployment.
   c. both unemployment and underemployment.
   d. underemployment, but not unemployment.

3. Adam Smith stated that the role of government in society should be to
   a. provide defense.
   b. enforce contracts.
   c. do absolutely nothing.
   d. do both (a) and (b).

4. When making economic decisions, Adam Smith urged society to
   a. follow the principle of self interest.
   b. follow the principle of public interest.
   c. transfer wealth according to need.
   d. provide equal income for all citizens.

5. The doctrine of laissez faire
   a. advocates an economic system with extensive government intervention and little individual decision making.
   b. was advocated by Adam Smith in his book *The Wealth of Nations*.
   c. was advocated by Karl Marx in his book *Das Kapital*.
   d. is described by none of the above.

6. In Adam Smith's competitive market economy, the question of what goods to produce is determined by the
   a. "invisible hand" of the price system.
   b. "invisible hand" of government.
   c. "visible hand" of public interest.
   d. "visible hand" of laws and regulations.

7. Adam Smith wrote that the
   a. economic problems of eighteenth-century England were caused by free markets.
   b. government should control the economy with an "invisible hand."
   c. pursuit of private self interest promotes the public interest in a market economy.
   d. public or collective interest is not promoted by people pursuing their self interest.

8. Adam Smith, in his book *The Wealth of Nations,* advocated
   a. socialism.
   b. an economy guided by an "invisible hand."
   c. government control of the "invisible hand."
   d. the adoption of mercantilism.

9. The economic system in which private individuals own the factors of production is
   a. a planned economy.
   b. capitalism.
   c. collectivism.
   d. socialism.

10. Which of the following is *not* a basic characteristic of capitalism?
    a. Economic decisions occur in markets.
    b. Factors of production are privately owned.
    c. Income is distributed on the basis of need.
    d. Businesses make their own product and price decisions.

11. According to Karl Marx, under capitalism,
    a. profits would be shared fairly.
    b. incomes would be distributed equally.
    c. workers would be exploited and revolt against owners of capital.
    d. workers would actually own the factors of production.

12. Karl Marx predicted which of the following?
    a. The market system would self-destruct.
    b. The "haves" would revolt against the "have-nots."
    c. The wealthy were entitled to profits as their reward for risk taking.
    d. None of the above.

13. How many nations in the world today operate totally according to Karl Marx's theory of communism?
    a. None
    b. Several
    c. Only the United States
    d. Many

14. In Marx's ideal communist society, the state
    a. actively promotes income equality.
    b. follows the doctrine of laissez faire.
    c. owns resources and conducts planning.
    d. does not exist.

15. Karl Marx was a(an)
    a. nineteenth-century German philosopher.
    b. eighteenth-century Russian economist.
    c. fourteenth-century Polish banker.
    d. nineteenth-century Russian journalist.

CHAPTER 30

Growth and the Less-Developed Countries

How would your life be different if you lived in Rwanda, Somalia, or Haiti instead of the United States? It is unlikely that someone in your family would have a telephone or a car. You surely would not own a personal computer or a compact disc player. You would not have new clothes and be enrolled in a college or university studying economics. You would not be going out to restaurants or movies. You would be fortunate to have shoes and one full meal each day. You would receive little or no medical care and live in unsanitary surroundings. Hunger, disease, and squalor would engulf you. In fact, the World Bank estimates that over 3 billion people in the world survive on no more than $2 per day.

It is exceedingly difficult for Americans to grasp the fact that one-half of the world's population lives on such a meager subsistence level. This brings us to this chapter's important task of unraveling the secrets of economic growth and development. Why do some countries prosper while others decline?

At different times in history, Egypt, China, Italy, and Greece were highly developed by the standards of their time. On the other hand, at one time the United States was a struggling, relatively poor country on the path to becoming a rich country. There were three stages: First, there was the agricultural stage. Then came the manufacturing stage, when industries such as railroads, steel, and automobiles were driving forces toward economic growth. And, finally, there has been a shift toward service industries. This is the U.S. success story, but it is not the only road countries can follow to lift themselves from the misery of poverty.

In this chapter, you will learn to solve these economics puzzles:

■ Is there a difference between economic growth and economic development?

■ Why are some countries rich and others poor?

■ Is trade a better "engine of growth" than foreign aid and loans?

Comparing Developed and Less-Developed Countries

The World Bank (http://www.worldbank/org/) *and the United Nations* (http://www.un.org/) *provide comprehensive information about different countries and their economies, including GDP per capita.*

There is income disparity among family groups within the United States and other nations. In this section, the great inequality of income between the families of nations will be used to classify groups of rich versus poor nations.

Classifying Countries by GDP per Capita

There are more than 180 countries in the world. Exhibit 1 shows the World Bank's ranking of selected countries from high to low **GDP per capita.** GDP per capita is the value of final goods produced (GDP) divided by the total population. Although any system of defining rich versus poor countries is arbitrary, GDP per capita or average GDP is a fundamental measure of a country's economic well-being. At the top of the income ladder are 26 developed countries called the **industrially advanced countries (IACs).** Industrially advanced countries are high-income nations that have market economies based on large stocks of technologically advanced capital and well-educated labor. The United States, Canada, Australia, New Zealand, Japan, and most of the countries of Western Europe are IACs. Excluded from the IACs are countries with high incomes, whose economies are based on oil under the sand, and not on widespread industrial development. The United Arab Emirates is an example of such a country.

GDP per capita

The value of final goods produced (GDP) divided by the total population.

Industrially advanced countries (IACs)

High-income nations that have market economies based on large stocks of technologically advanced capital and well-educated labor. The United States, Canada, Australia, New Zealand, Japan, and most of the countries of Western Europe are IACs.

Less-developed countries (LDCs)

Nations without large stocks of technologically advanced capital and well-educated labor. LDCs are economies based on agriculture, such as most countries of Africa, Asia, and Latin America.

Countries of the world other than IACs are classified as underdeveloped or **less-developed countries (LDCs).** Less-developed countries are nations without large stocks of technologically advanced capital and well-educated labor. LDCs are economies based on agriculture, such as most countries of Africa, Asia, and Latin America. Three-fourths of the world's population, consisting of about 150 countries, live in LDCs and share widespread poverty.

A closer examination of Exhibit 1 reveals that the differences in living standards between the IACs and LDCs are enormous. For example, the GDP per capita in the United States was $34,005 greater than the average income in Ethiopia. Stated differently, the 2000 average income in the United States was about 375 times larger than the average income in Ethiopia ($34,096/$91 = 375). What a difference! Imagine trying to live on only $91 for a year in the United States. You probably would not survive.

Exhibit 2 compares GDP per capita for IACs to LDCs by regions of the world for 2000. The average citizen in the IACs enjoyed an income of $24,044, which was 53 times that of the average citizen in South Asia ($24,044/$458 = 53). The exhibit also reveals that the greatest concentra-

EXHIBIT 1 Annual GDP per Capita for Selected Countries, 2000

Country	GDP per capita	Country	GDP per capita
Industrially Advanced Countries (IACs)			
Luxembourg	$43,625	United Kingdom	$24,244
Switzerland	35,655	France	24,010
Japan	34,426	Hong Kong	24,000
Norway	34,130	Canada	20,613
United States	34,096	Australia	20,563
Denmark	32,834	Singapore	20,460
Sweden	26,899	Italy	20,317
Austria	25,733	Israel	17,259
Germany	25,507	Spain	14,912
Netherlands	25,049	New Zealand	14,677
Finland	25,038	Portugal	11,344
Ireland	24,632	Greece	11,250
Belgium	24,299	South Korea	8,554
Less-Developed Countries (LDCs)			
Mexico	$4,797	Russia	$1,264
Hungary	4,738	Morocco	1,161
Chile	4,464	Indonesia	628
Poland	4,024	Ukraine	626
Panama	3,403	Haiti	578
Brazil	3,063	Georgia	538
Turkey	3,015	Pakistan	419
South Africa	2,999	Vietnam	364
Thailand	1,993	Rwanda	265
Romania	1,569	Mozambique	207
Jordan	1,493	Ethiopia	91
Paraguay	1,385		

Source: Countrywatch.com, http://cnn.countrywatch.com/cnn_globrank.asp?TP=NUMERIC&TBL=NUMERICCER.

tions of world poverty are located in the rural areas of South Asia and Sub-Saharan Africa. The East Asia and Pacific regions have many countries characterized by bleak and pervasive poverty, but there are notable exceptions, nicknamed the "Four Tigers" of East Asia—Hong Kong, Singapore, South Korea, and Taiwan. These Pacific Rim countries are newly industrialized countries which we discuss at the end of this chapter.

Problems with GDP per Capita Comparisons

There are problems associated with using GDP per capita to compare rich versus poor countries, however. First, there is a measurement problem because each country tabulates GDP with differing degrees of accuracy. LDCs in

---

EXHIBIT 2   **Average GDP per Capita for IACs and LDCs by Region, 2000**

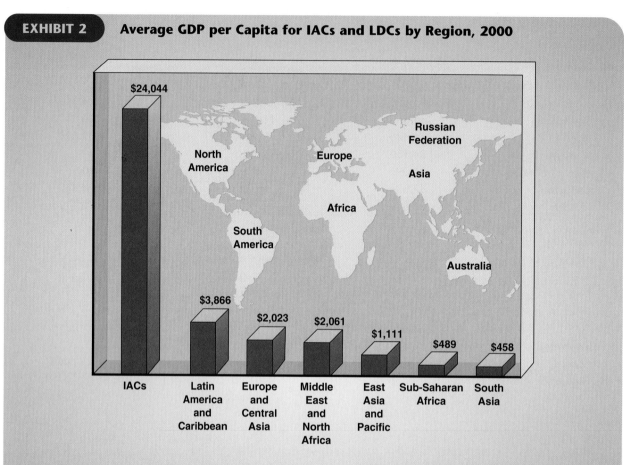

This exhibit shows average GDP per capita by regions of the world for 2000. The differences between the rich industrially advanced countries (IACs) and the poor less-developed countries (LDCs) in the various regions of the world are enormous. For example, the average citizen in the IACs had an income 53 times that of the average citizen in the LDCs of South Asia.

Source: World Bank Group, *Country at a Glance,* http://www.worldbank.org/data/countrydata/countrydata.html, Table 1.

---

general do not use sophisticated methods of gathering and processing GDP and population data. For example, in countries whose economies are based largely on agriculture, a family is more likely to produce goods and services outside the price system. In LDCs, families often grow their own food, make their own clothes, and build their own homes. Estimating the value of this output at market prices is difficult.

Conclusion *LDCs' GDP per capita is subject to greater measurement errors than data for IACs.*

Second, GDP per capita comparisons among countries can be misleading because they ignore the relative income distribution. Some countries have very high per capita incomes, yet most of the income goes to just a few wealthy families. The United Arab Emirates' GDP per capita is greater than that of several IACs. However, the United Arab Emirates earns its income from oil exports, and its income is actually distributed disproportionately to a relatively small number of wealthy families.

Conclusion *GDP per capita comparisons among nations can be misleading because GDP per capita does not measure income distribution.*

Third, GDP per capita comparisons among nations are subject to conversion problems. Making these data comparisons requires converting one nation's currency, say, Japan's yen, into a common currency, the U.S. dollar. Because, as explained in the chapter on international trade and finance, the value of a country's currency can rise or fall for many reasons, the true value of a nation's output can be distorted. For example, one government might maintain an artificially high exchange rate and another government might not during a given year.

Conclusion *A conversion problem may widen or narrow the GDP per capita gap between nations because the fluctuations in exchange rates do not reflect actual differences in the value of goods and services produced.*

Finally, there is a purchasing power parity problem. For example, in 2000, the GDP per capita of Japan ($34,426) exceeded that of the United States ($34,096). Based only on these data, one would conclude that the typical Japanese consumer is better off than the average American consumer. A visitor to Japan, however, quickly observes that the typical Japanese consumer is less well off than the average American. The reason is that despite Japan's higher average income, Japan has a higher average cost of living. For example, a very modest home in Tokyo's suburbs costs over $1 million.

The International Monetary Fund (IMF), discussed at the end of this chapter, has prepared revised estimates of GDP per capita using purchasing power comparisons, rather than exchange rates, to convert unadjusted GDP per capita data into U.S. dollars. Using this method, the LDCs often look better relative to the IACs.

Conclusion *Differences in purchasing power that affect living standards can alter the interpretation of international comparisons of GDP per capita.*

Quality-of-Life Measures of Development

GDP per capita measures market transactions, but this measure does not give a complete picture of differences in living standards among nations. Exhibit 3 presents other selected socioeconomic indicators of the quality of life. These are variables such as life expectancy at birth, literacy rate, child malnutrition rate, and per capita energy consumption.

Take a close look at the statistics in Exhibit 3. These data reflect the dimensions of poverty in many of the LDCs. For example, a person born in the United States has a life expectancy that is 30 years longer than a person born

EXHIBIT 3 Quality-of-Life Indicators for Selected Countries

Country	(1) GDP per capita, 2000	(2) Life expectancy at birth (years), 2000	(3) Literacy rate, 2000[1]	(4) Malnutrition as percent of children under 5, 2000	(5) Per capita energy consumption, 1998[2]
Japan	$34,426	81	99%	—	4,035
United States	34,096	77	97	1%	7,937
Bolivia	1,025	62	85	8	581
China	803	70	84	9	830
India	431	63	57	45	486
Bangladesh	274	61	41	56	159
Mozambique	207	47	40	26	405

[1]Percentage age 15 and over who can read and write.
[2]Kilograms of oil equivalent

Sources: **World Bank Group,** http://www.worldbank.org/data/countrydata/countrydata.html; *The World Factbook,* http://www.odci.gov/cia/publications/factbook/indexgeo.html and **Countrywatch.com,** http://cnn.countrywatch.com/cnn_globrank.asp?TP=NUMERIC&TBL=NUMERICCER.

in Mozambique, and the percentage of malnourished children under five years old is dramatically higher in Mozambique. Per capita energy consumption measures the use of nonhuman energy to perform work. In IACs, most work is done by machines, and in LDCs, virtually all work is done by people. The average American uses 7,937 kilograms of (oil-equivalent) energy per year, while the average person in Mozambique uses only 405 kilograms.

How good an indicator of the quality of life is GDP per capita? Exhibit 3 reflects the principle that no measure is perfect. China, for example, has a GDP per capita much less than for Bolivia. Yet the life expectancy, literacy rate, child malnutrition rate, and per capita energy consumption either favor China or are almost the same as those for Bolivia. In this case, using GDP per capita alone to compare standards of living is misleading. However, the data do confirm this conclusion: *In general, GDP per capita is highly correlated with alternative measures of quality of life.*

Economic Growth and Development around the World

Read the World Bank's World Development Report (http://www.worldbank.org/).

Economic growth and development are major goals of IACs and LDCs. People all over the world strive for a higher quality of life for their generation and future generations. However, growth is closer to a life-or-death situation for many LDCs, such as Haiti, Rwanda, and Somalia.

Economic growth and economic development are somewhat different, but related, concepts. As shown in Exhibit 4, recall from Chapter 2 that economic growth is the ability of an economy to produce greater levels of output, represented by an outward shift of its production possibilities curve (*PPC*). Thus, economic growth is defined on a *quantitative* basis using the percentage change in GDP per capita. When a nation's GDP rises more rapidly than its population, GDP per capita rises, and the nation experi-

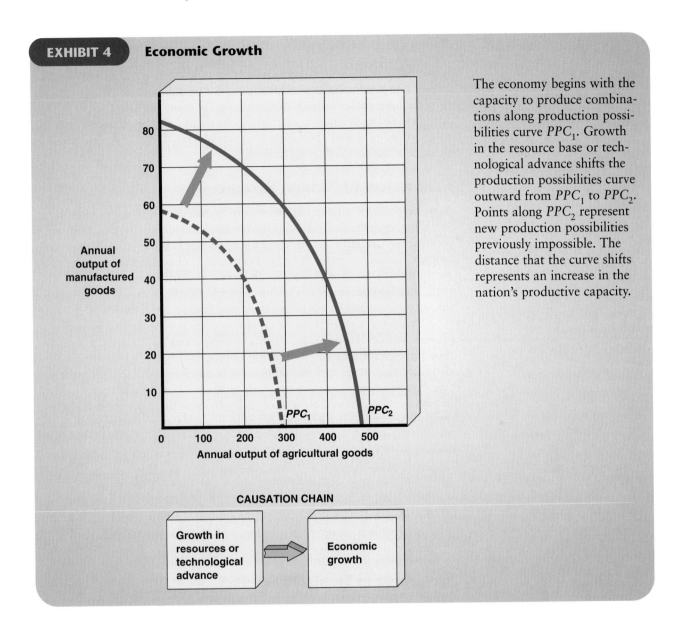

EXHIBIT 4   **Economic Growth**

Annual output of manufactured goods

PPC₁ PPC₂

Annual output of agricultural goods

The economy begins with the capacity to produce combinations along production possibilities curve PPC_1. Growth in the resource base or technological advance shifts the production possibilities curve outward from PPC_1 to PPC_2. Points along PPC_2 represent new production possibilities previously impossible. The distance that the curve shifts represents an increase in the nation's productive capacity.

CAUSATION CHAIN

Growth in resources or technological advance → Economic growth

ences economic growth. Conversely, if GDP expands less than the population of a nation, GDP per capita falls, and the nation experiences negative economic growth.

Economic development is a broader concept that is more *qualitative* in nature. Economic development encompasses improvement in the quality of life, including economic growth in the production of goods and services. In short, continuous economic growth is necessary for economic development, but economic growth is not the only consideration. For example, as explained earlier, GDP per capita does not measure the distribution of income or the political environment that provides the legal, monetary, education, and transportation structures necessary for economic growth.

Economic growth and development involve a complex process that is determined by several interrelated factors. Like the performance of an NBA basketball team, success depends on the joint effort of team players, and one or two weak players can greatly reduce overall performance. However, there is no precise formula for winning. If your team has a player like Michael Jordan, it can win even with a few weak players. The remainder of this section examines the key factors, or players, that operate together to produce a nation's economic well-being.

Endowment of Natural Resources

Most of the LDCs have comparatively limited bases of natural resources, including mineral deposits and arable land resources. In these countries, most of the available land is used for agricultural production, and clearing tropical forests to obtain more land can cause soil erosion. Also, tropical climates prevail in Central and South America, Africa, the Indian subcontinent, and Southeast Asia. The hot, humid climate in these regions is conducive to weed and insect infestations that plague agriculture.

Although a narrow base of resources does pose a barrier to economic growth and development, no single conclusion can be drawn. For example, how have countries like Hong Kong, Japan, and Israel achieved high standards of living in spite of limited natural resource bases? Each of these countries has practically no minerals, little fertile land, and no domestic sources of energy. Nonetheless, these economies have become prosperous. In contrast, Argentina, Venezuela, and Brazil have abundant fertile land and minerals. Yet these and other countries have been growing slowly or not at all. Venezuela, for example, is one of the most oil-rich countries in the world. Ghana, Kenya, and Bolivia are also resource-rich countries that are poor, with little or no economic growth.

> **Conclusion** *Natural resource endowment can promote economic growth, but a country can develop without a large natural resource base.*

Investment in Human Resources

A low level of human capital can also present a barrier to economic growth and development. Recall that human capital is the education, training, experience, and health that improve the knowledge and skills of workers to produce goods and services. In most of the LDCs, investment in human capital is much less than in the IACs. Look back at Column 3 in Exhibit 3. Consider how the literacy rate falls for the poorer countries. As the literacy rate falls, so does the ability to educate the labor force and create a basic foundation for economic growth. In fact, often the skills of workers in the poor countries are suited primarily to agriculture, rather than being appropriate for a wide range of industries and economic growth. Further complicating matters is a "brain drain" problem because the best educated and trained workers of poor countries pursue their education in wealthier countries. Column 2 of Exhibit 3 also gives a measure of health among countries with

CHECKPOINT

Does Rapid Growth Mean a Country Is Catching Up?

Suppose country Alpha has a production possibilities curve closer to the origin than the curve for country Beta. Now assume Alpha experiences a 3 percent growth rate in GDP for 10 years and Beta experiences a 6 percent growth rate in GDP for 10 years. At the end of five years, which of the following is the best prediction for the standard of living? (1) Alpha's residents are better off. (2) Beta's residents are better off. (3) Which country's residents are better off cannot be determined.

varying levels of GDP per capita. As the GDP per capita falls, the life expectancy at birth falls. Thus, richer countries have the advantage of a more educated and healthier workforce.

Conclusion *Investment in human capital generally results in increases in GDP per capita.*

Thus far, the discussion has been about the quality of labor. We must also talk about the quantity of labor because productivity is related to both the quality and the quantity of labor. Overpopulation is a problem for LDCs. In a nutshell, here is why: Other factors held constant, population (labor force) growth can increase a country's GDP. Yet rapid population growth can convert an expanding GDP into a GDP per capita that is stagnant, slow growing, or negative. Stated another way, there is no gain if an increase in output is more than matched by an increase in the number of mouths that must be fed. Suppose the GDP of an LDC grows at, say, 3 percent per year. If there is no growth in population, GDP per capita also grows at 3 percent per year. But what if the population also grows at 3 percent per year? The result is that GDP per capita remains unchanged. If the population growth is instead only 1 percent per year, GDP per capita rises 2 percent per year. Obstacles to population control are great and include strong religious and sociocultural arguments against birth control programs.

Conclusion *Rapid population growth combined with low human capital investment explains why many countries are LDCs.*

Exhibit 5 presents data that support the relationship between high population growth and low GDP per capita growth. The table classifies selected countries by GDP per capita growth rate and then lists the corresponding annual population growth rates between 1994 and 2000. Although these data do not include all countries in the world, several points can be made. First, the average growth rate of GDP per capita for IACs in the exhibit is 5.0 percent per year. This output growth rate was achieved with a very low average population growth rate of 0.54 percent. Second, the LDCs experienced GDP per capita growth rates that are below the average rate for the IACs. In fact, in each of these poorer countries, the annual GDP per capita

EXHIBIT 5 Annual Growth Rates for Selected Countries		
Country	**(1) GDP per capita growth 2000**	**(2) Population growth 1994–2000**
Industrially Advanced Countries (IACs)		
Ireland	9.5%	1.0%
Sweden	3.9	0.2
Spain	4.0	0.1
Greece	3.8	0.2
United States	4.0	1.2
Less-Developed Countries (LDCs)		
Solomon Island	−16.5	3.1
Zimbabwe	−7.3	2.6
Congo, Dem. Rep.	−7.1	3.0
New Guinea	−4.4	2.7
Paraguay	−2.8	2.6

Source: World Bank Group, *Country at a Glance Tables,* http://www.worldbank.org/data/countrydata/countrydata.html.

growth rate was negative. If this trend continues, these LDCs will never close their standard-of-living gap with the rest of the world. Third, the negative output growth rate of the LDCs in the exhibit was combined with a relatively higher average annual population growth rate of 2.8 percent.

Conclusion *Nations that grow slowly or experience declines in GDP per capita will fail to catch up with the IACs' standard of living.*

Accumulation of Capital

It did not take long for Robinson Crusoe on a deserted island to invest in a net in order to catch more fish than he could catch with his hands. Similarly, farmers working with modern tractors can cultivate more acres than farmers working with horse-drawn plows. Recall from Chapter 1 that capital in economics means factories, tractors, trucks, roads, computers, irrigation systems, electricity-generating facilities, and other human-made goods used to produce goods and services.

LDCs suffer from a critical shortage of capital. A family in Somalia owns little in the way of tools except a wooden plow. To make matters worse, roads are terrible, there are few plants generating electricity, and telephone lines are scarce. As shown in Exhibit 6, recall from Chapter 2 that a high-investment country can shift its production possibilities curve outward, but investment in capital goods is not a "free lunch." When more resources are used to produce more factories and machines, there is an opportunity cost of fewer resources available for the production of current consumer goods. This means that LDCs are often caught in a **vicious circle of poverty.** A vicious

Vicious circle of poverty
The trap in which countries are poor because they cannot afford to save and invest, but they cannot save and invest because they are poor.

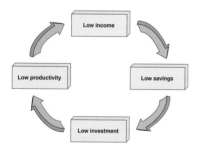

EXHIBIT 6	**Alpha's and Beta's Present and Future Production Possibilities Curves**

In part (a), each year Alpha produces only enough capital (K_a) to replace existing capital that is worn out. Without greater capital and assuming other resources remain fixed, Alpha is unable to shift its production possibilities curve outward. In part (b), each year Beta produces K_b capital, which is more than the amount required to replenish its depreciated capital. In 2010, this expanded capital provides Beta with the extra production capacity to shift its production possibilities curve to the right. If Beta chooses point B on its curve, it has the production capacity to increase the amount of consumer goods from C_b to C_c without producing fewer capital goods.

circle of poverty is the trap in which countries are poor and cannot afford to save. And low savings translate into low investment. Low investment results in low productivity, which, in turn, keeps incomes low. Any savings that do exist among higher-income persons in poor LDCs are often invested in IACs. This phenomenon is often called "capital flight." These wealthy individuals are afraid to save in their own country because of the threat that their government may be overthrown and their savings could be lost.

The United States and other nations have attempted to provide LDCs with foreign aid so that they might grow. These countries desperately need more factories and **infrastructure**. Infrastructure is capital goods usually provided by the government, including highways, bridges, waste and water systems, and airports. Unfortunately, the amount of capital given to the LDCs is relatively small, and, as explained above, workers in the LDCs lack the skills necessary to use the most modern forms of capital. More specifically, LDCs face a major obstacle to capital accumulation because of the lack of entrepreneurs to assume the risks of capital formation.

Infrastructure

Capital goods usually provided by the government, including highways, bridges, waste and water systems, and airports.

Conclusion *There is a significant positive relationship between investment and economic growth and development.*

Technological Progress

As explained earlier in Chapter 2, holding natural resources, labor, and capital constant, advancing the body of knowledge applied to production shifts the production possibilities curve of a country. In fact, technological advances have been at the heart of economic growth and development in recent history. During the last 250 years, brainpower has discovered new power-driven machines, advanced communication devices, new energy sources, and countless ways to produce more output with the same resources. How have innovative products improved your productivity? Consider—to name just a few products—the impact of CD-ROMs, fax machines, VCRs, personal computers, word-processing software, video cameras, and the Internet. In contrast, in many poor countries, waterwheels still bring water to the surface, cloth is woven on handlooms, and ox carts are the major means of transportation. Consequently, large inputs of human effort are used relative to capital resources.

The United States and other IACs have provided the world with an abundant accumulation of technological knowledge that might be adopted by those LDCs without the resources to undertake the required cost of research and development. However, the results of this transfer process have been mixed. Pacific Rim countries, such as Hong Kong, Singapore, Taiwan, South Korea, and Japan, have surely achieved rapid growth in part from the benefit of technological borrowing. Currently, Russia and other Eastern European nations are attempting to apply existing technological knowledge to boost their rates of growth.

The other side of the coin is that much available technology is not suited to LDCs. The old saying "You need to learn to walk before you can run" often applies to the LDCs. For example, the small farms of most LDCs are not suited for much of the agricultural technology developed for IACs' large farms. And how many factories in the LDCs are ready to use the most modern robotics in the production process? Stated differently, LDCs need appropriate technology, rather than necessarily the latest technology.

> **Conclusion** *Many LDCs continue to experience low growth rates even though IACs provide advanced technologies for them to emulate.*

Political Environment

To learn more about any country and its economy, visit The World Factbook (http://www.odci.gov/cia/ publications/factbook/index.html). *Select Country Listing and then any country of your choice.*

The discussion above leads to the generalization that in order for LDCs to achieve economic growth and development, they must wisely use natural resources, invest in human and physical capital, and adopt advanced technology. This list of policies is not complete. LDC governments must also create a political environment favorable to economic growth. All too often a large part of the problem in poor countries is the wasting of resources as a result of war and political instability. Political leaders must not be corrupt and/or incompetent. Instead of following policies that favor a small elite ruling class, LDC governments must adopt appropriate domestic and international economic policies, discussed under the following three headings of law and order, infrastructure, and international trade.

Law and Order.   A basic governmental function is to establish domestic law and order. This function includes many areas, such as a stable legal system, stable money and prices, competitive markets, and private ownership of property. In particular, expropriation of private property rights among LDCs is a barrier to growth. Well-defined private property rights have fostered economic growth in the IACs because this institutional policy has encouraged an entrepreneurial class. Private ownership provides individuals with the incentive to save money and invest in businesses. A stable political environment that ensures private ownership of profits also provides an incentive for individuals in other countries to invest in developing poor countries.

Infrastructure.   Assuming an LDC government maintains law and order and the price system is used to allocate goods and services, it is vital that wise decisions be made concerning infrastructure. Indeed, many of the greatest problems of LDCs concern inadequate infrastructure. Without such public goods as roads, schools, bridges, and public health and sanitation services, poor countries are unable to generate the substantial external benefits that are an important ingredient in economic growth and development. From the viewpoint of individual firms, infrastructure must be provided by government because these public goods projects would be too costly for a firm to undertake.

International Trade.   In general, LDCs can benefit from an expanding volume of trade. For example, this is the theory behind the North American Free Trade Agreement (NAFTA) and the General Agreement on Tariffs and Trade (GATT), discussed in the chapter on international trade and finance. As explained earlier in this chapter, policies such as tariffs and quotas restrain international trade and thereby inhibit economic growth and development. These trade policies are antigrowth because they restrict the ability of people in one country to trade with people in other countries. Similarly, a country that fixes the exchange rate of its own currency above the market-determined exchange rate makes that country's exports less attractive to foreigners. This means, in turn, that domestic citizens sell less of their goods to foreigners and earn less foreign currency with which to buy imports.

Read more about GATT (http://iisd1.iisd.ca/ trade/wto/gatt.htm) and NAFTA (http://www-tech.mit .edu/Bulletins/nafta.html).

Conclusion *Exchange rate controls artificially set by government above the market exchange rates reduce the volume of both exports and imports (international trade).*

Exhibit 7 summarizes the key factors explained above that determine the economic growth and development of countries. Analysis of this exhibit reveals that economic growth and development are the result of a multidimensional process. This means that it is difficult for countries to break the poverty barrier because they must follow various avenues and improve many factors in order to gain increased economic well-being. But it is important to remember that lack of one or more key factors, such as natural resources, does not necessarily keep an LDC in the trap of underdevelopment.

EXHIBIT 7 **Key Categories That Determine Economic Growth and Development**

There are five basic categories that interact to determine the economic growth and development of countries: natural resources, human resources, capital, technological progress, and the political environment. The exhibit also indicates important factors that influence investment in human resources, capital, technological advances, and the political environment. LDCs are faced with a formidable task. Since economic growth and development are multidimensional, LDCs must improve many factors in order to achieve economic progress.

Conclusion *There is no single strategy for economic growth and development.*

The Helping Hand of Advanced Countries

How can poor countries escape the vicious circle of poverty? Low GDP per capita leads to low savings and investment, which lead, in turn, to low growth. Although there is no easy way for poor countries to become richer, the United States and other advanced countries can be an instrument of growth. The necessary savings can come from the LDCs' own domestic savings, or it can come from foreign external sources that include foreign private investment, foreign aid, and foreign loans.

Exhibit 8 illustrates how external funds can shift a country's production possibilities curve outward. Here you should look back and review Exhibit 6.

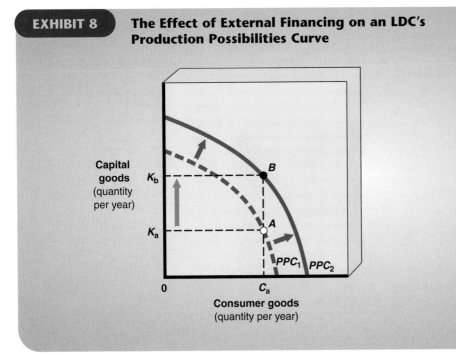

EXHIBIT 8   **The Effect of External Financing on an LDC's Production Possibilities Curve**

The poor country of Alpha is initially operating at point A on production possibilities curve PPC_1, with only enough capital (K_a) to replace depreciation. If C_a is the consumption level of subsistence, Alpha's economy cannot grow by reducing consumption. An inflow of external funds from abroad permits the LDC to increase its capital from K_a to K_b without reducing its consumption (C_a), and its production possibilities curve shifts outward to PPC_2.

Suppose country Alpha is trapped in poverty and produces only enough capital (K_a) to replace the existing capital being worn out. Alpha's consumption level is at C_a, corresponding to point A on production possibilities curve PPC_1, Because C_a is at the subsistence level, Alpha cannot save and invest by substituting current consumption for capital and move upward along PPC_1. This inability to increase capital means Alpha cannot use internal sources of funds to increase its production possibilities curve in the future. There is a way out of the trap using external sources. Now assume Alpha receives an inflow of funds from abroad and buys capital goods that increase its rate of investment from K_a to K_b. At K_b, the rate of capital formation exceeds the value of capital depreciated, and Alpha's production possibilities curve shifts rightward to PPC_2. Economic growth made possible by external investment means Alpha can achieve economic growth without reducing its consumption level (C_a) at point B on PPC_2.

Foreign Private Investment

Many countries' development benefits from private-sector foreign investment from private investors. For example, Microsoft might finance construction of a plant in the Philippines to manufacture software, or Bank of America may make loans to the government of Haiti. These large multinational corporations and commercial banks supply scarce capital to the LDCs. A multinational corporation is a firm with headquarters in one country and one or more branch plants in other countries. Multinational firms often seek new investment opportunities in LDCs because these poor countries offer

INTERNATIONAL ECONOMICS

Hong Kong: A Crouching Pacific Rim Tiger

Applicable Concept: newly industrialized countries

As the map shows, the Pacific Rim countries are located along an arc extending from Japan and South Korea in the north to New Zealand in the south. The Four Tigers of East Asia are Hong Kong, Singapore, South Korea, and Taiwan. These "miracle economies" have often experienced higher economic growth rates, lower inflation rates, and lower unemployment rates than many long-established advanced countries. For example, as shown on the map, the average growth rates in real GDP from 1983 to 1992 ranged from 7.8 percent (South Korea) to 6.4 percent (Hong Kong) compared to 3.4 percent for the United States and 3.9 percent for Japan. In addition to the Four Tigers, China, Malaysia, Indonesia, Thailand, and Vietnam have been high-growth economies. The Asian financial crisis, however, beginning in 1997 with effects continuing to 1999, resulted in economic turmoil and lower growth or recession for these countries. In 1998, Hong Kong was in a deep recession with a GDP growth rate of −5.3 percent.

Prior to the Asian financial crisis, Hong Kong was a great success story. When Adam Smith published his famous book, *The Wealth of Nations,* in 1776, Hong Kong was little more than a small barren rock island almost void of natural resources except fish. Today, Hong Kong is a bustling model of free enterprise in spite of the fact that

seven million people are crowded into only about 400 square miles—one of the highest population densities in the world.

What is the reason for Hong Kong's success? Following the doctrine of Adam Smith, this economy is a paragon of laissez faire. Hong Kong has among the lowest individual and corporate income tax rates in the world and almost no legal restrictions on business. It has no capital gains tax, no interest tax, no sales tax, and no withholding tax. Hong Kong has become the largest banking center in the Pacific region after Tokyo. International trade is also largely unrestricted, and Hong Kong depends to a large extent on trade through its magnificent harbor for its economic success. Tariffs on imported goods are low, and Hong Kong is known as a safe-haven warehouse and trading center, with little or no interference from the government.

Hong Kong has proven that industrious people and entrepreneurs working hard on a crowded island with minimum regulations and open trade can improve their living standard without natural resources. Nevertheless, Hong Kong faces economic and political uncertainty. Under a 99-year lease signed in 1898, the United Kingdom transferred Hong Kong to the People's Republic of China in 1997. Will China allow Hong Kong to continue to follow Adam Smith's laissez-faire philosophy and return to high growth rates, or will Hong Kong change direction? It is anyone's guess. In 1999, Hong Kong's growth rate improved to 3.0 percent, and it reached 10.5 percent in 2000. This recovery was largely the result of trade with the Chinese mainland. And Hong Kong Disney is scheduled to open in 2005. So, as this text is written in 2001, it appears that this Asian tiger is "crouched" to leap forward and roar again.

ANALYZE THE ISSUE

One of the keys to Hong Kong's success is its free trade policy. Why is this so important for a developing country? What would be the effect of Hong Kong attempting to protect its domestic industries by raising tariffs and following other protectionist trade policies?

Singapore
GDP per capita: $20,460
GDP growth rate: 1983–1992: 7.0%,
    2000: 9.9%
People: 4.0 million
Land: 240 square miles
Literacy: 92%

Hong Kong
GDP per capita: $24,000
GDP growth rate: 1983–1992: 6.4%,
    2000: 10.5%
People: 6.8 million
Land: 390 square miles
Literacy: 93%

Taiwan
GDP per capita: $13,845
GDP growth rate: 1983–1992: 8.5%,
    2000: 6.0%
People: 22.3 million
Land: 14,000 square miles
Literacy: 94%

South Korea
GDP per capita: $8,554
GDP growth rate: 1983–1992: 8.7%,
    2000: 8.8%
People: 47.3 million
Land: 38,000 square miles
Literacy: 98%

abundant supplies of low-wage labor and raw materials. But the political environment in the LDCs must be conducive to investment. Multinational corporations often become the largest employers, largest taxpayers, and largest exporters in the LDCs.

Foreign Aid

About 1 percent of the U.S. federal budget is spent on **foreign aid.** Foreign aid is the transfer of money or resources from one government to another for which no repayment is required. These transfers may be made as out-right grants, technical assistance, or food supplies. Foreign aid flows from country to country through governments and voluntary agencies, such as the Red Cross, CARE, and Church World Relief. The United States distributes most of its official development assistance through the **Agency for International Development (AID),** established in 1961. The Agency for International Development is the agency of the U.S. State Department that is in charge of U.S. aid to foreign countries.

Learn more about the Agency for International Development (http://www .info.usaid.gov/).

Foreign aid
The transfer of money or resources from one government to another for which no repayment is required.

Agency for International Development (AID)
The agency of the U.S. State Department that is in charge of U.S. aid to foreign countries.

One reason that countries like the United States provide foreign aid to LDCs is the belief that it is a moral responsibility of richer countries to share wealth with poorer countries. A second reason is that it is in the best economic interest of the IACs to help the LDCs. When these countries become more prosperous, the IACs have more markets for their exports, and thereby all countries benefit from trade.

The LDCs often complain that foreign aid has too many economic and political strings attached. Loans are often offered on a "take it or leave it" basis, tied to policies other than basic trade policies, such as human rights, politics, or the military. Consequently, many LDCs argue for "trade, not aid." If the IACs would simply buy more goods from the LDCs, the LDCs could use their gains in export earnings to purchase more capital and other resources needed for growth. Many people in the United States feel that most foreign aid is a waste of money because it is misused by the recipient countries. This belief has caused Congress to grow increasingly reluctant to send taxpayers' money abroad except in the clearest cases of need or for reasons of national security.

Foreign Loans

A third source of external funds that can be used to finance domestic investment is loans from abroad. Governments, international organizations, and private banks all make loans to LDCs. Like foreign private investment and foreign aid, loans give LDCs the opportunity to shift their production possibilities curves outward. There are various types of loan sources for LDCs. Bilateral loans are made directly from one country to another. The principal agent for official U.S. bilateral loans is the U.S. Agency for International Development, introduced earlier.

One prominent multilateral lending agency is the **World Bank.** The 184-member World Bank is the lending agency affiliated with the United Nations that makes long-term low-interest loans and provides technical assistance to less-developed countries. Loans are made only after a planning period lasting a year or more. The World Bank was established in 1944 by major nations meeting in Bretton Woods, New Hampshire. Its first charge was to assist postwar reconstruction. Today, the World Bank is located in Washington, D.C., and its main purpose is to channel funds from rich countries to poor countries. The World Bank makes "last resort" loans to LDCs to finance basic infrastructure projects, such as dams, irrigation systems, and transportation facilities, for which private financing is not available. In addition, the World Bank helps LDCs get loans from private lenders by insuring the loans. Thus, the poor countries are able to complete projects and use the economic returns to pay off the lender with interest.

The World Bank is not the only multilateral lending agency making loans to LDCs. The World Bank's partner institution is the **International Monetary Fund (IMF).** The International Monetary Fund is the lending agency that makes short-term conditional low-interest loans to developing countries. The IMF was also established at Bretton Woods in 1944. The purpose of the IMF is to help countries overcome short-run financial difficulties. Typically, the IMF makes conditional loans that require the debtor countries

Visit the International Monetary Fund (http://www.imf.org/).

World Bank
The lending agency that makes long-term low-interest loans and provides technical assistance to less-developed countries.

International Monetary Fund (IMF)
The lending agency that makes short-term conditional low-interest loans to developing countries.

CHECKPOINT

Is the Minimum Wage an Antipoverty Solution for Poor Countries?

Imagine you are an economic adviser to the president of a poor LDC. The president is seeking policies to promote economic growth and a higher standard of living for citizens of this country. You are asked whether adopting a minimum wage equal to the average of the IACs' average hourly wages would achieve these goals. Recall the discussion of the minimum wage from Chapter 4 and evaluate this policy.

to implement fiscal and monetary policies that will alleviate balance-of-payments problems. The 184-member IMF is not a charitable institution. It operates like a credit union with funding quotas that earn interest on the loans. The United States is the IMF's largest shareholder, and thus it has effective veto power over IMF decisions.

In recent years, the IMF has performed a major role in providing short-term loans to developing countries and to economies making the transition to capitalism. In the late 1990s, the IMF provided multibillion-dollar bailouts to Russia, several Asian countries, Brazil, and other countries experiencing economic turmoil. Critics argue that as long as governments believe the IMF will bail them out, they will fail to correct their own problems. IMF supporters counter that if the IMF does not intervene, troubled economies will default on outstanding loans and cause a worldwide ripple effect. Critics respond that a flood of low-cost short-term loans from the IMF encourages bad government policies and excessive risk taking by banks. Consequently, a bailout in a crisis generates new financial crises and reduces world economic growth.

Finally, private banks also engage in lending to LDCs. Until the 1970s, LDCs borrowed primarily from the World Bank and foreign governments. In the 1970s, private banks began to lend to both governments and private firms in LDCs. During the 1980s, the news was full of stories that some U.S. banks had made so many risky loans to LDCs that default on these loans would lead to the failure of one major U.S. bank after another. As the story goes, "If you can't repay the bank for your car loan, you're in trouble. If a government can't repay the bank a billion dollars, the bank's in trouble."

In the late 1980s, the debt crisis was avoided by (1) writing off some of the loans, (2) lowering the interest rate of remaining loans, and (3) lending LDCs more money to pay interest on their debt. The U.S. government, other Western governments, and the IMF were active in these solutions. Was this a case of "throwing good money after bad" because many loans would never be repaid? The answer is No. Easing the debt burden salvaged some payments and was in the best interest of both rich and poor countries because a fresh start encouraged trade. Nevertheless, the huge outstanding debts of some of the LDCs (especially Mexico, Argentina, Chile, and Brazil) make another debt crisis a lingering possibility.

KEY CONCEPTS

GDP per capita
Industrially advanced
   countries (IACs)
Less-developed countries
   (LDCs)

Vicious circle of poverty
Infrastructure
Foreign aid
Agency for International
   Development (AID)

World Bank
International Monetary
   Fund (IMF)

SUMMARY

- **GDP per capita** provides a general index of a country's standard of living. Countries with low GDP per capita and slow growth in GDP per capita are less able to satisfy basic needs for food, shelter, clothing, education, and health.

- **Industrially advanced countries (IACs)** are countries in which GDP per capita is high and output is produced by technologically advanced capital. Countries that have high incomes without widespread industrial development, such as the oil-rich Arab countries, are not included in the IAC list.

- **Less-developed countries (LDCs)** are countries with low production per person. In these countries, output is produced without large amounts of technologically advanced capital and well-educated labor. The LDCs account for about three-fourths of the world's population.

- The **Four Tigers of the Pacific Rim** are Hong Kong, Singapore, South Korea, and Taiwan. These newly industrialized countries have achieved high growth rates and standards of living.

- **GDP per capita comparisons** are subject to four problems: (1) The accuracy of LDC data is questionable, (2) GDP per capita ignores the degree of income distribution, (3) changes in exchange rates affect GDP per capita gaps between countries, and (4) there is no adjustment for cost-of-living differences between countries.

- **Economic growth** and **economic development** are related, but somewhat different, concepts. Economic growth is measured quantitatively by GDP per capita, while economic development is a broader concept. In addition to GDP per capita, economic development includes quality-of-life measures, such as life expectancy at birth, adult literacy rate, and per capita energy consumption. Economic growth and development are the result of a complex process that is determined by five major factors: (1) natural resources, (2) human resources, (3) capital, (4) technological progress, and (5) the political environment. There is no single correct strategy for economic development, and a lack of strength in one or more of the five areas does not prevent growth.

- The **vicious circle of poverty** is a trap in which an LDC is too poor to save and therefore it cannot invest and shift its production possibilities curve outward. As a result, the LDC remains poor. One way for a poor country to gain savings, invest, and grow is to use funds from external sources such as foreign private investment, foreign aid, and foreign loans. Borrowing by many LDCs led to the debt crisis of the 1980s, which was resolved by writing off and restructuring the loans.

SUMMARY OF CONCLUSION STATEMENTS

- LDCs' GDP per capita is subject to greater measurement errors than data for IACs.

- GDP per capita comparisons among nations can be misleading because GDP per capita does not measure income distribution.

- A conversion problem may widen or narrow the GDP per capita gap between nations because the fluctuations in exchange rates do not reflect actual differences in the value of goods and services produced.

- Differences in purchasing power that affect living standards can alter the interpretation of international comparisons of GDP per capita.

- In general, GDP per capita is highly correlated with alternative measures of quality of life.

- Natural resource endowment can promote economic growth, but a country can develop without a large natural resource base.

- Investment in human capital generally results in increases in GDP per capita.

- Rapid population growth combined with low human capital investment explains why many countries are LDCs.

- Nations that grow slowly or experience declines in GDP per capita will fail to catch up with the IACs' standard of living.

- There is a significant positive relationship between investment and economic growth and development.

- Many LDCs continue to experience low growth rates even though IACs provide advanced technologies for them to emulate.

- Exchange rate controls artificially set by government above the market exchange rates reduce the volume of both exports and imports (international trade).

- There is no single strategy for economic growth and development.

STUDY QUESTIONS AND PROBLEMS

1. What is the difference between industrially advanced countries (IACs) and less-developed countries (LDCs)? List five IACs and five LDCs.

2. Explain why GDP per capita comparisons among nations are not a perfect measure of differences in economic well-being.

3. Assume you are given the following data for country Alpha and country Beta:

Country	GDP per capita
Alpha	$15,000
Beta	25,000

    a. Based on the GDP per capita data given above, which country would you prefer to live in?

    b. Now assume you are given the following additional quality-of-life data. In which country would you prefer to reside?

Country	Life expectancy at birth (years)	Daily per capita calorie supply	Per capita energy consumption*
Alpha	75	2,500	4,000
Beta	60	3,000	3,000

*Kilograms of oil equivalent.

4. What is the difference between economic development and economic growth? Give examples of how each of these concepts can be measured.

5. Do you agree with the argument that the rich nations are getting richer and the poor nations are getting poorer? Is this an oversimplification? Explain.

6. Explain why it is so difficult for poor LDCs to generate investment in capital in order to increase productivity and growth and therefore improve their standard of living.

7. Why is the quest for economic growth and development complicated?

8. Which of the following is associated with a high or low level of economic growth and development:

	High	Low
a. Overpopulation	_____	_____
b. Highly skilled labor	_____	_____
c. High savings rate	_____	_____
d. Political stability	_____	_____
e. Low capital accumulation	_____	_____
f. Advanced technology	_____	_____
g. Highly developed infrastructure	_____	_____
h. High proportion of agriculture	_____	_____
i. High degree of income inequality	_____	_____

9. Without external financing from foreign private investment, foreign aid, and foreign loans, poor countries are caught in the vicious circle of poverty. Explain. How does external financing help poor countries achieve economic growth and development?

10. What are some of the problems for LDCs of accepting foreign aid?

11. Why would an LDC argue for "trade, not aid"?

12. Explain the differences among the Agency for International Development (AID), the World Bank, and the International Monetary Fund (IMF).

ONLINE EXERCISES

Exercise 1

Visit Handbook of International Statistics (http://www
.odci.gov/cia/publications/hies97/toc.htm), and follow
these steps:

1. Select Economic Profile and Tables 2 and 4. Compare
   the economic profiles of OECD countries to those of
   newly industrializing economies.

2. Select Aggregate Trends and Table 10. Compare
   defense expenditures among nations.

3. Select Independent Republics of the Former Soviet
   Union and Table 26. Compare economic and social
   indicators among the republics of the former Soviet
   Union.

4. Select Foreign Trade and Aid and Table 117. Compare new industrializing economies' trade with the
   United States.

5. Select Environmental Topics and Table 132. Compare
   carbon dioxide emissions among nations.

Exercise 2

Visit the World Bank Group, and select the latest World
Development Report (http://www.worldbank.org/).

Exercise 3

Visit the World Bank Group, and browse Regions and
Countries (http://www.worldbank.org/html/extdr/
regions.htm). Select a country, and read a brief.

Exercise 4

Visit the World Bank Group (http://www.worldbank.org),
and browse Development Topics.

Exercise 5

Visit the United Nations Social Indicators (http://www
.un.org/Depts/unsd/social), and select Income and Economic Activity. Compare per capita GDP among countries. Also compare male and female economic activity
rates for different countries.

CHECKPOINT ANSWERS

Does Rapid Growth Mean a Country Is Catching Up?

GDP growth alone does not measure the standard of living. You must also consider population. Even though
Beta experienced a greater GDP growth rate, its GDP per
capita might be less than Alpha's because its population
growth rate is greater. Of course, the reverse is also possible, but without population data, we cannot say. If you
said which country's people are better off cannot be determined because the GDP must be divided by the population
to measure the average standard of living, YOU ARE
CORRECT.

Is the Minimum Wage an Antipoverty Solution for Poor Countries?

An important source of foreign investment for LDCs is
multinational corporations that locate plants and other
facilities in these countries. LDCs compete with each other
for the economic growth and development benefits that
these multinational corporations can provide. For an LDC
to win the competition, it must offer political stability,
adequate infrastructure, a favorable business climate, and
a cheap labor force. If you said you would not support the
president's proposal to raise the minimum wage because it
would place the LDC at a competitive disadvantage in the
labor market, thereby reducing foreign private investment
and growth, YOU ARE CORRECT.

PRACTICE QUIZ

For a visual explanation of the correct answers, visit the tutorial at http://tucker.swcollege.com.

1. An LDC is defined as a country
   a. without large stocks of advanced capital.
   b. without well-educated labor.
   c. with low GDP per capita.
   d. that is described by all of the above.

2. According to the definition given in the text, which of the following is *not an LDC?*
   a. India
   b. Egypt
   c. China
   d. Ireland

3. Which of the following is true when making GDP per capita comparisons among nations?
   a. The GDP per capita is subject to greater measurement errors for LDCs compared to IACs.
   b. The GDP per capita does not measure income distribution.
   c. The GDP per capita is subject to fluctuations from changes in exchange rates.
   d. All of the above are true.

4. LDCs are characterized by
   a. high life expectancy.
   b. high adult literacy.
   c. high malnutrition.
   d. all of the above.
   e. none of the above.

5. According to the classification in the text, which of the following is *not an IAC?*
   a. United Arab Emirates
   b. Israel
   c. Hong Kong
   d. Greece

6. When the government fixes the exchange rate above market exchange rates,
   a. international trade falls.
   b. the infrastructure improves.
   c. real GDP per capita rises.
   d. the vicious circle of poverty is broken.

7. Which of the following statements is *true?*
   a. An LDC is a country with a low GDP per capita, low levels of capital, and uneducated workers.
   b. The vicious circle of poverty exists because GDP must rise before people can save and invest.
   c. LDCs are characterized by rapid population growth and low levels of investment in human capital.
   d. All of the above are true.

8. An outward shift of the production possibilities curve represents
   a. economic growth.
   b. a decline in economic development.
   c. a decrease in human capital.
   d. a decrease in resources.

9. Which of the following problems do LDCs face?
   a. Low per capita income and high GDP growth rate
   b. Low population growth and low per capita income
   c. Rapid population growth and low human capital
   d. Low per capita income and high saving rate

10. Which of the following best defines the vicious circle of poverty?
    a. The GDP per capita must rise before people can save and invest.
    b. People cannot save while capital accumulates.
    c. Increased GDP per capita relates to lower population growth.
    d. Poverty, saving, and investment are related like a circle.

11. Which of the following is infrastructure?
    a. International Harvester tractor plant
    b. Waste and water system provided by government
    c. USAirWays airplane
    d. Service of postal workers

12. Economic growth and development in LDCs are low because many of them lack
    a. capital investment.
    b. technological progress.
    c. a favorable political environment.
    d. all of the above.
    e. none of the above.

13. Which of the following makes short-term conditional low-interest loans to developing countries?
    a. Agency for International Development (AID)
    b. World Bank
    c. International Monetary Fund (IMF)
    d. New International Economic Order (NIEO)

14. Which of the following makes long-term low-interest loans to less-developed countries?
    a. Agency for International Development (AID)
    b. New International Economic Order (NIEO)
    c. International Monetary Fund (IMF)
    d. World Bank.

Answers to Odd-Numbered Study Questions and Problems

Chapter 1 Introducing the Economic Way of Thinking

1. A poor nation with many people who lack food, clothing, and shelter certainly experiences wants beyond the availability of goods and services to satisfy these unfulfilled wants. On the other hand, no wealthy nation has all the resources necessary to produce everything everyone in the nation wishes to have. Even if you had $1 million and were completely satisfied with your share of goods and services, other desires would be unfulfilled. There is never enough time to accomplish all the things that you can imagine would be worthwhile.

3. a. capital

5. a. microeconomic issue
   b. macroeconomic issue
   c. microeconomic issue
   d. macroeconomic issue

7. The real world is full of complexities that make it difficult to understand and predict the relationships between variables. For example, the relationship between changes in the price of gasoline and changes in consumption of gasoline requires abstraction from the reality that such variables as the fuel economy of cars and weather conditions often change at the same time as the price of gasoline.

9. The two events are associated, and the first event (cut in military spending) is the cause of the second event (higher unemployment in the defense industry). The point is that association does not necessarily mean causation, but it might.

11. d. statement of normative economics

Appendix to Chapter 1 Applying Graphs to Economics

1. a. The probability of living is *inversely* related to age. This model could be affected by improvements in diet, better health care, reductions in hazards to health in the workplace, or changes in the speed limit.

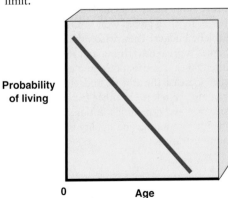

b. Annual income and years of formal education are *directly* related. This relationship might be influenced by changes in such human characteristics as intelligence, motivation, ability, and family background. An example of an institutional change that could affect this relationship over a number of years is the draft.

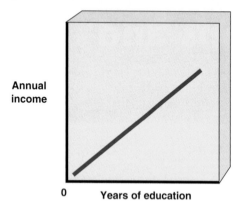

c. Inches of snow and sales of bathing suits are *inversely* related. The weather forecast and the price of travel to sunny vacation spots can affect this relationship.

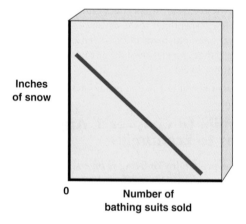

d. Most alumni and students will argue that the number of football games won is *directly* related to the athletic budget. They reason that winning football games is great advertising and results in increased attendance, contributions, and enrollment that, in turn increase the athletic budget. Success in football can also be related to other factors, such as school size, age and type of institution, number and income of alumni, and quality of the faculty and administrators.

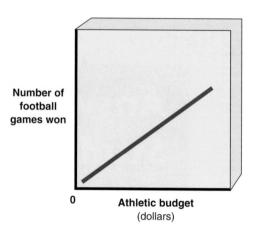

Chapter 2 Production Possibilities, Opportunity Cost, and Economic Growth

1. Because the wants of individuals and society exceed the goods and services available to satisfy these desires, choices must be made. The consumption possibilities of an individual with a fixed income are limited, and as a result, additional consumption of one item necessarily precludes an expenditure on another next best choice. The forgone alternative is called the opportunity cost, and this concept also applies to societal decisions. If society allocates resources to the production of guns, then those same resources cannot be used at the same time to make butter.

3. Regardless of the price of a lunch, economic resources—land, labor, and capital—are used to produce the lunch. These scarce resources are no longer available to produce other goods and services.

5. Using marginal analysis, students weigh the benefits of attending college against the costs. There is an incentive to attend college when the benefits (improved job opportunities, income, intellectual improvement, social life, and so on) outweigh the opportunity costs.

7.

Flowerboxes	Opportunity cost (pies forgone)
0	
1	4 (30 − 26)
2	5 (26 − 21)
3	6 (21 − 15)
4	7 (15 − 8)
5	8 (8 − 0)

9. Movements along the curve are efficient points and conform to the well-known "free lunch" statement. However, inefficient points are exceptions because it is possible to produce more of one output without producing less of another output.

11.

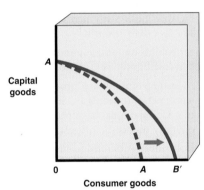

Chapter 3 Market Demand and Supply

1. If people buy a good or service because they associate higher quality with higher price, this is a violation of the ceteris paribus assumption. An increase in the quantity demanded results only from a decrease in price. Quality and other nonprice determinants of demand, such as tastes and preferences and the price of related goods, are held constant in the model.

3. a. Demand for cars decreases: oil and cars are *complements*.
   b. Demand for insulation increases: oil and home insulation are *substitutes*.
   c. Demand for coal increases: oil and coal are *substitutes*.
   d. Demand for tires decreases: oil and tires are *complements*.

5. One reason that the demand curve for word processing software shifted to the right might be that people

desire new, higher-quality output features. The supply curve can shift to the right when new technology makes it possible to offer more software for sale at different prices.

7. a. Demand shifts to the right.
   b. Supply shifts to the left.
   c. Supply shifts to the right.
   d. Demand shifts to the right.
   e. Demand shifts to the right.
   f. Supply of corn shifts to the left.

9. a. The supply of CD players shifts rightward.
   b. The demand for CD players is unaffected.
   c. The equilibrium price falls, and the equilibrium quantity increases.
   d. The demand for CDs increases because of the fall in the price of CD players (a complementary good).

11. The number of seats (quantity supplied) remains constant, but the demand curve shifts because tastes and preferences change according to the importance of each game. Although demand changes, the price is a fixed amount, and to manage a shortage, colleges and universities use amount of contributions, number of years as a contributor, or some other rationing device.

Chapter 4 Markets in Action

1.

a. The equilibrium price is $1.50 per gallon, and the equilibrium quantity is 300 million gallons per month. The price system will restore the market's $1.50 per gallon price because either a surplus will drive prices down or a shortage will drive prices up.

b. The support price results in a persistent surplus of 200 million gallons of milk per month, which the government purchases with taxpayers' money. Consequently, taxpayers who do not drink milk are still paying for milk. The purpose of the support price is to bolster the incomes of dairy farmers.

c. The ceiling price will result in a persistent shortage of 200 million gallons of milk per month, but 200 million gallons are purchased by consumers at the low price of $1.00 per gallon. The shortage places a burden on the government to ration milk in order to be fair and to prevent black markets. The government's goal is to keep the price of milk below the equilibrium price of $1.50 per gallon, which would be set by a free market.

3. The labor market can be divided into two separate markets, one for skilled union workers and one for unskilled workers. If the minimum wage is above the equilibrium wage rate and is raised, the effect will be to increase the demand for, and the wage of, skilled union workers because the two groups are substitutes.

5. The equilibrium price rises.

7. The government can reduce emissions by (a) regulations that require smoke-abatement equipment or (b) pollution taxes that shift supply leftward.

9. Pure public goods are not produced in sufficient quantities by private markets because there is no feasible method to exclude free riders.

Chapter 5 Price Elasticity of Demand and Supply

1. Demand is elastic because the percentage change in quantity was greater than the percentage change in price.

3. If the price of used cars is raised 1 percent, the quantity demanded will fall 3 percent. If the price is raised 10 percent, the quantity demanded will fall 30 percent.

5.
$$E_d = \frac{\%\Delta Q}{\%\Delta P} = \frac{\dfrac{4,500 - 5,000}{5,000 + 4,500}}{\dfrac{3,500 - 3,000}{3,000 + 3,500}} = \frac{\dfrac{1}{19}}{\dfrac{1}{13}} = 0.68$$

The price elasticity of demand for the university is inelastic.

7. Demand for popcorn is perfectly inelastic, and total revenue will increase.

9. a. Sunkist oranges
   b. car
   c. foreign travel in the long run

11. Furniture sales fall by 30 percent and physician services by only 3 percent. Thus, the demand for physician services is much less responsive to a reduction in income than the demand for furniture.

13. The negative number tells you car tires are complements. If the price of cars rises by 10 percent, the quantity demanded of car tires falls by 20 percent.

15. As the demand for a product becomes more inelastic, the greater the amount of a tax on this product that sellers can pass on to consumers by raising the product's price.

Chapter 6 Consumer Choice Theory

1. Utility is a subjective concept, and, therefore, this statement may or may not be true.

3. Marginal utility is 10 utils. When you attend the fourth party, total utility will increase, but marginal utility will be less than 10 utils.

5. In consumer equilibrium, the marginal utility ratio is 3/4, which is equal to the price ratio.

7. As people consume more of any product, eventually the satisfaction per unit decreases. Since the marginal utility from additional units falls, people will not buy a greater quantity unless the price falls.

9. The initial consumer equilibrium is as follows:

$$\frac{MU \text{ of steak meal}}{Price \text{ of steak meal}} = \frac{MU \text{ of hamburger meal}}{Price \text{ of hamburger meal}}$$

$$\frac{12 \text{ utils}}{\$10} = \frac{3 \text{ utils}}{\$5}$$

The marginal utility per dollar for each good equals 1.2. If the price of a hamburger meal falls to $2, this equality no longer holds. Now the marginal utility per dollar for a hamburger meal becomes higher at 1.5 (3 utils/$2). James can now increase his total utility by purchasing more hamburger meals per month. Given the law of diminishing returns, the marginal utility of hamburger meals falls until consumer equilibrium is restored.

Chapter 7 Production Costs

1. a. explicit cost
   b. explicit cost
   c. implicit cost
   d. implicit cost
   e. explicit cost
   f. implicit cost

3. a.

Labor	Marginal product
1	8
2	10
3	12
4	13
5	12
6	10
7	8
8	6
9	3
10	−2

b.

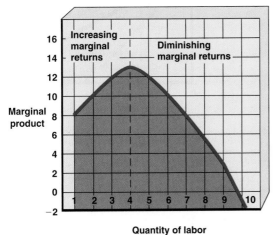

5. None. The position of a firm's short-run average total cost curve is not related to the demand curve.

7. The *ATC* and *AVC* curves converge as output expands because *ATC* = *AVC* + *AFC*. As output increases, *AFC* declines, so most of *ATC* is therefore *AVC*.

9. The average total cost–marginal cost rule states that when the marginal cost is below the average total

cost, the addition to total cost is below the average total cost, and the average total cost falls. When the marginal cost is greater than the average total cost, the average total cost rises. In this case, the average total cost is at a minimum because it is equal to the marginal cost.

11. The marginal product for any number of workers is the slope of the total output curve. The marginal product is the derivative of the total output curve *dTO/dQ*, where *TO* is the total output and *Q* is the number of workers.

Chapter 8 Perfect Competition

1. A perfectly competitive firm will not advertise. Because all firms in the industry sell the same product, there is no reason for customers to be influenced by ads into buying one firm's product, rather than another firm's product.

3.

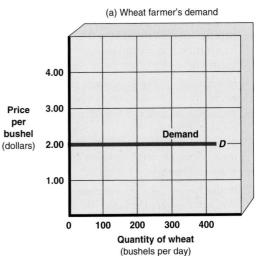

A single wheat farmer is a price taker facing a perfectly elastic demand curve because in perfect competition one seller has no control over its price. The reason is that each wheat farmer is one among many, sells a homogeneous product, and must compete with any new farmer entering the wheat market.

5. At a price of $150, the firm produces 4 units and earns an economic profit of $70 ($TR - TC = $600 - 530). The firm breaks even at an output of 2 units.

7. This statement is incorrect. A firm can earn maximum profit (or minimum loss) when marginal revenue equals marginal cost. The confusion is between the "marginal" and the "total" concepts. Marginal cost is the change in total cost from one additional unit of output, and marginal revenue is the change in total revenue from one additional unit of output.

9. The statement is incorrect. The perfectly competitive firm must consider both its marginal revenue and its marginal cost. Instead of trying to sell all the quantity of output possible, the firm will sell the quantity where $MR = MC$ because beyond this level of output the firm earns less profit.

11. Advise the residential contractor to shut down because the market price exceeds the average variable cost and the firm cannot cover its operating costs.

Chapter 9 Monopoly

1. Each market is served by a single firm providing a unique product. There are no close substitutes for local telephone service, professional football in San Francisco, and first-class mail service. A government franchise imposes a legal barrier to potential competitors in the telephone and first-class mail services. An NFL franchise grants monopoly power to its members in most geographic areas.

3. The reason may be that the hospital has monopoly power because it is the only hospital in the area and patients have no choice. On the other hand, there may be many drugstores competing to sell drugs, and this keeps prices lower than those charged by the hospital.

5. In a natural monopoly, a single seller can produce electricity at a lower cost because the $LRAC$ curve declines. One firm can therefore sell electricity at a cheaper price and drive its competitor out of business over time. Another possibility would be for two competing firms to merge and earn greater profit by lowering cost further.

7. In this special case, sales maximization and profit maximization are the same. The monopolist should charge $2.50 per unit, produce 5 units of output, and earn $12.50 in profit. When the marginal cost curve is not equal to zero, the monopolist's $MR = MC$ output is less than 5 units, the price is higher than $2.50 per unit, and profit is below $12.50.

9. a. increase output
   b. decrease output

11. a. not price discrimination
    b. price discrimination
    c. not price discrimination if justified by a transportation cost difference
    d. price discrimination

Chapter 10 Monopolistic Competition and Oligopoly

1. The monopolistically competitive firm's demand curve is less elastic (steeper) than a perfectly competitive firm's demand curve, but more elastic (flatter) than a monopolist's demand curve.

3. a. P_1
   b. Q_1
   c. Q_3
   d. greater than the marginal cost ($B > A$)

5.

Because $P_{mc} > MC$, the monopolistically competitive firm fails to achieve allocative efficiency. The monopolistically competitive firm is also inefficient because it charges a higher price and produces less output than under perfect competition. The perfectly competitive firm sets P_{pc} equal to MC and produces a level of output corresponding to the minimum point on the $LRAC$ curve.

7. Answers might include automobiles, airline travel, personal computers, and cigarettes. An oligopoly differs from monopolistic competition by having few sellers, rather than many sellers; either a homogeneous or a differentiated product, rather than all differentiated products; and difficult entry rather than easy entry.

9. Any maverick jeans firm that raises or lowers its price will earn less profits. Therefore, firms in the jeans industry face a kinked demand curve, and prices remain rigid. Although firms do not engage in price competition, they can engage in nonprice competition. Each firm can use advertising and style to market its brand-name product.

11. The pricing behavior follows the price leadership model. The price leader is Hewlett-Packard, which is the largest and most dominant firm in the computer printer industry. After a price war, IBM followed each of Hewlett-Packard's price hikes.

Chapter 11 Labor Markets

1. This statement is incorrect. Workers supply their labor to employers. Demand refers to the quantity of labor employers hire at various wage rates based on the marginal revenue product of labor.

3. The MRP of the second worker is this person's contribution to total revenue, which is $50 ($150 − $100). Because $MRP = P \times MP$ and $MP = MRP/P$, the second worker's marginal product (MP) is 10 ($50/$5).

5. The firm in a perfectly competitive labor market is a price taker. Because a single firm buys the labor of a relatively small portion of workers in an industry, it can hire additional workers and not drive up the wage rate. For the industry, however, all firms must offer higher wages to attract workers from other industries.

7. Students investing in education are increasing their human capital. A student with greater human capital increases his or her marginal product. At a given product price, the MRP is higher, and firms find it profitable to hire the better educated worker and pay higher wages.

9. At a wage rate of $90 per day, Zippy Paper Company hires 3 workers because each worker's MRP exceeds

or equals the wage rate. Setting the wage rate at $100 per day causes Zippy Paper Company to cut employment from 3 to 2 workers because the third worker's MRP is $10 below the union-caused wage rate of $100 per day.

11. As shown in the exhibit below, for a monopsony, the optimum quantity of labor is 3 quarterbacks, determined at point A, where the MFC curve intersects the MRP curve. However, the team can attract and hire 3 quarterbacks for an annual salary of $300,000 each at point B on the supply of labor curve, rather than paying a quarterback's contribution to the team's revenues (MRP), which is $500,000 per year at point A. In a competitive labor market, the Jacksonville Jaguars hire 4 quarterbacks and pay each $400,000 per year.

Chapter 12 Income Distribution, Poverty, and Discrimination

1. a.

	Alpha		Beta	
Percentage of families	**Percentage share**	**Cumulative share**	**Percentage share**	**Cumulative share**
Lowest fifth	17.7%	17.7%	9.0%	9.0%
Second-lowest fifth	19.9	37.6	14.2	23.2
Middle fifth	20.4	58.0	17.5	40.7
Second-highest fifth	20.7	78.7	21.9	62.6
Highest fifth	21.3	100.0	37.4	100.0

b.

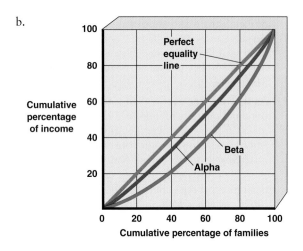

c. Because the Lorenz curve for Alpha is closest to the perfect equality line, Alpha's distribution of income is more equal compared to Beta.

3. Absolute poverty is defined as a dollar figure that represents some level of income per year required to purchase some minimum amount of goods and services essential to meeting a person's or a family's basic needs. Relative poverty is defined as a level of income required to place a person or family in, say, the lowest 20 percent among all persons or families receiving incomes. The poverty line is based on the absolute definition.

5. In-kind transfers are payments in the form of goods and services, rather than cash. Examples include such government programs as food stamps, Medicaid, and housing. Noncash income is not counted in a family's income to determine whether the family's income is below the poverty line.

7. The percentage of families in the United States classified as poor in early 2000 was about 12 percent. Poor families are more likely to live in the South. The age, race, and education of the head of the family are also important characteristics of poor families.

9. The three major criticisms are that welfare (1) reduces the work incentive, (2) is inefficient because the programs cost too much to administer, and (3) treats poor persons with the same needs unequally because the states pay different benefits.

11. This is an opinion question. To agree, you assume that markets are perfectly competitive and discrimination is therefore unprofitable. To disagree, you can argue that in reality labor markets will never be perfectly competitive and the government must therefore address the institutional causes of poverty.

Chapter 13 Antitrust and Regulation

1. The Sherman Act outlaws price-fixing or anticompetitive practices designed to eliminate rivals. The Clayton Act clarifies the Sherman Act by outlawing specific business practices, including price discrimination, exclusive dealing, tying contracts, stock acquisition, and interlocking directorates. The U.S. Department of Justice and Federal Trade Commission (FTC) are responsible for enforcing these laws. Private firms can also bring suit against other firms under these laws.

3. Both the Robinson-Patman Act and the Celler-Kefauver Act were amendments to close loopholes in the Clayton Act. The Robinson-Patman Act expanded the list of illegal price discrimination practices to include quantity discounting, free advertising, and promotional allowances offered that "substantially lessen competition or tend to create a monopoly." The Celler-Kefauver Act closed the loophole in the Clayton Act whereby competing firms could merge by asset acquisition (not outlawed in the Clayton Act), rather than by acquiring stock (outlawed in the Clayton Act).

5. In fact, Alcoa argued that metals such as copper and steel are substitutes for aluminum. Therefore, the relevant industry to compute market share was the metals industry and not the aluminum industry. If the court had chosen the U.S. metals industry as the relevant industry, Alcoa would not have a monopoly.

7. a. The federal government will charge the bookstore with predatory pricing in order to monopolize its college market for books, which is a violation of the Sherman Act.
   b. The federal government will charge the real estate firms with collusion to fix prices, which is a violation of the Sherman Act.
   c. The federal government will charge a violation of the Clayton Act because the combined market share of this horizontal merger would substantially lessen competition in the word processing market.
   d. The federal government will not charge a violation because this is a conglomerate merger between firms in unrelated industries.

9. The "necessary" condition would be expected to favor existing regulated firms by eliminating or greatly restricting competition and raising prices. The existing regulated firms are better organized politically than either new competitors or consumers. While consumers favor competition and lower prices, regulators would be expected to interpret "necessary" to mean that the service provided by existing firms is sufficient without new firms.

11. Although a public subsidy achieves efficiency, marginal-cost pricing is usually unpopular with

voters, who must provide the monopolist with public funds. Moreover, a public subsidy gives the monopolist a disincentive to minimize costs.

Chapter 14 Environmental Economics

1. A competitive industry selling a pollution-generating product will charge a lower price and sell a larger quantity than would be the case for a "green" industry. The competitive industry has lower costs because it fails to include external costs. Lower costs allow a lower price. A lower price leads to a larger quantity demanded and sold.

3. If you choose the $90,000 house, the EMF radiation is *not* an externality. An externality is a third-party effect, whereby buyers and sellers of a product ignore the spillover effects of their transaction. In this case, the market reflects the risk of cancer, with the seller accepting a lower price and the buyer saving $10,000 to reflect the cancer risk.

   Houses have many characteristics that influence their price, including number of rooms, location, nearby schools, and environmental amenities. If you are willing to buy a house near a nuclear plant, or near EMF, you, the buyer, bear the consequences, not a third party.

5. An instructor who automatically flunks students who do not turn in all homework assignments is exhibiting command-and-control. She is dictating the production process for achieving knowledge. The inefficiencies are that students may turn in poorly done assignments or may copy assignments and that some students may understand the material without doing the homework or may have an alternative production method, such as the use of computer software, to achieve knowledge. The instructor's method is particularly inefficient if her assignments are busywork and do not really help the students to achieve knowledge.

7.

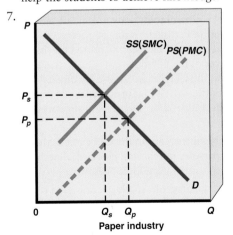

Paper industry

At Q_p, pollution from paper production leads to coffee-colored rivers. At socially efficient Q_s, there is less pollution, and rivers are less polluted. The rivers are unlikely to be pristine, which requires no production at all.

9. Consumers will share in the benefits of cleaner air if any individual buys a less polluting car. Since they enjoy the same benefit whether they pay extra or their neighbor pays extra for a cleaner car, they will let the neighbor buy the cleaner car. Of course, since their neighbor uses the same reasoning, no one ends up paying extra to buy a cleaner car.

11. Convincing examples should be sent to the author of the text. It is very difficult to find markets where the transactions costs of reaching an agreement are near zero. It is also difficult to find two-party situations, since most pollution spills over to many individuals. With many individuals involved, the free-rider problem arises, as a given individual wants to benefit from pollution agreements, but let others bear the cost. There can often be income effects, as fighting pollution may take a large amount of one's income. Candidates for markets where the Coase Theorem might apply include convincing your neighbor to leash her dog (you might help finance invisible fencing), enforcing laws concerning the fencing of cattle, and settling disputes when one builder interferes with the views of existing homes.

13. a. Command-and-control would dictate the use of an alternative technology with lower carbon emissions.
    b. An effluent tax would place a tax on carbon emissions so that firms could no longer ignore these costs. In turn, prices of carbon-emitting products would increase, and quantities would decrease.
    c. Permits would be issued giving the right to emit carbon. The number of permits would equal the socially efficient emissions level. Firms would be allowed to buy or sell these permits. Firms with higher marginal costs of emissions abatement would buy permits, while firms that could reduce emissions at a lower cost would profit from selling permits.

Chapter 15 Gross Domestic Product

1. a. final service
   b. final good
   c. intermediate good
   d. intermediate good

3. 3 million pounds of food

× $1 per pound	=	$3 million
50,000 shirts × $20 per shirt	=	1 million
20 houses × $50,000 per house	=	1 million
50,000 hours of medical services × $20 per hour	=	1 million
1 automobile plant × $1 million per plant	=	1 million
2 tanks × $500,000 per tank	=	1 million
Total value of output	=	$8 million

5. Capital is not excluded from being a final good. A final good is a finished good purchased by an ultimate user and not for resale. The ultimate user is the warehouse, so the sale would be included in GDP and there would be no double-counting problem.

7. Using the expenditure approach, net exports are exports minus imports. If the expenditures by foreigners for U.S. products exceeds the expenditures by U.S. citizens for foreign products, net exports will be a positive contribution to GDP. If foreigners spend less for U.S. products than U.S. citizens spend for foreign products, GDP is reduced. Net exports are used by national income accountants because actual consumption, investment, and government spending figures reported to the U.S. Department of Commerce do not exclude the amount of expenditures for imports.

9. NDP = GDP − depreciation

$4,007 = $4,486 − $479

The depreciation charge is not a measure of newly produced output. It is an estimate, subject to error, of the value of capital worn out in the production of final goods and services. Errors in the capital consumption allowance overstate or understate GDP.

11. When the price level is rising, nominal GDP overstates the rate of change. Dividing nominal GDP by the GDP chain price index results in real GDP by removing the distortion from inflation. Comparison of the 2000 real GDP and the 1999 real GDP reflects only changes in the market value of all final products and not changes in the price level.

13. GDP does not tell the mix of output in two nations, say, between military and consumer goods. GDP also does not reveal whether GDP is more equally distributed in one nation compared to another.

Chapter 16 Business Cycles and Unemployment

1. The generally accepted theory of business cycles is that they are the result of changes in the level of total spending, or aggregate demand. Total spending includes spending for final goods by households, businesses, government, and foreign buyers. Expressed as a formula, GDP = C + I + G + (X − M).

3. $$\text{Civilian unemployment rate} = \frac{\text{unemployed}}{\text{civilian labor force}} \times 100$$

where the civilian labor force = unemployed + employed. Therefore,

$$7.7\% = \frac{10 \text{ million persons}}{130 \text{ million persons}} \times 100$$

5. The official unemployment rate is overstated when respondents to the BLS falsely report that they are seeking employment. The unemployment rate is understated when *discouraged workers* who want to work have given up searching for a job.

7. Structural unemployment occurs when those seeking jobs do not possess the skills necessary to fill the available jobs. Cyclical unemployment is caused by deficient total spending.

9. The increasing participation of women and teenagers in the labor force has increased the rate of unemployment. Women take more time out of the labor force than do men for childbearing and child rearing.

11. The GDP gap is the difference between potential real GDP and actual real GDP. Because potential real GDP is estimated on the basis of the full-employment rate of unemployment, the GDP gap measures the cost of *cyclical* unemployment in terms of real GDP.

Chapter 17 Inflation

1. This statement is incorrect. The price of a single good or service can rise while the average price of all goods and services falls. In short, the inflation rate rises when the average price of consumer goods and services rises.

3. First, the CPI is based on a typical market basket purchased by the urban family. Any group not buying the same market basket, such as retired persons, is not experiencing the price changes measured by changes in the CPI. Second, the CPI does not reflect changes in taxes. Third, the CPI fails to adjust for quality changes. Fourth, the CPI ignores the law of demand and the substitution effect as prices of products change.

5. If the percentage increase in the CPI exceeds the salary increase, a person's purchasing power declines in a given year.

7. The loan is advantageous to you because the real interest rate is −5 percent (5 percent nominal interest rate minus 10 percent inflation). In one year, you must repay $105. If prices rise by 10 percent during the year, the real value of the $105 will be only $95.

Therefore, you have borrowed $100 worth of purchasing power and are repaying $95 worth of purchasing power.

9. a. Social Security payments are adjusted for CPI changes.
   b. Welfare payments are adjusted for CPI changes.
   c. UAW auto workers have a cost-of-living adjustment (COLA), which adjusts nominal wages for changes in the CPI.
   d. Federal income taxpayers are protected against "bracket creep" caused by changes in the CPI.
   e. Self-employed business owners are not protected against changes in the CPI.

11. Demand-pull inflation is caused by an excess of total or aggregate spending in the economy. Cost-push inflation is caused by increasing production costs that force prices upward. Cost-push inflation may also be caused by businesses raising prices to increase profits.

Chapter 18 The Keynesian Model

1. Classical economists argued that underconsumption and unemployment could not exist in the long run because of price-wage flexibility. Unsold merchandise would force firms to compete and lower product prices, and unemployed workers would accept a lower wage rate.

3. Consumers have only two options for any extra disposable income they receive. The *MPC* and *MPS* must add up to one because the portion of extra income that is not spent must be saved.

5. a. The consumption schedule downshifts, and the saving schedule downshifts.
   b. The consumption schedule downshifts, and the saving schedule downshifts.
   c. The consumption schedule downshifts, and the saving schedule upshifts.
   d. The consumption schedule downshifts, and the saving schedule downshifts.
   e. Both the consumption and the saving schedules downshift.

7. Changes in the nonincome determinants of the consumption and saving schedules tend to offset each other, and people are reluctant to change their consumption and saving habits. On the other hand, Keynes considered the volatility of businesses' decisions to invest as a major cause of the business cycle. The potentially unstable determinants of investment spending include expectations, technological change, the stock of capital goods, and business taxes.

9. a.

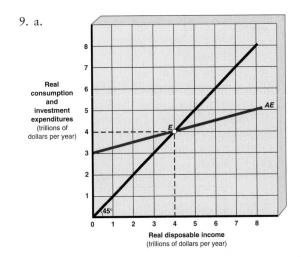

b. The autonomous consumption is $3 trillion, and the *MPC* = 0.25. Note that each $1 trillion increase in real disposable income results in a $0.25 trillion increase in aggregate expenditures. Since *MPS* = (1 − *MPC*), *MPS* = (1 − 0.25) = 0.75.

c. The equilibrium level of real disposable income equals $4 trillion where the *AE* line intersects the 45° line.

d. An increase in autonomous investment adds new spending by businesses at each level of aggregate spending. The *AE* line would therefore shift upward, and the equilibrium level of real disposable income increases.

Chapter 19 The Keynesian Model in Action

1. **Employment, Output, Consumption, and Unplanned Inventory**

Possible levels of employment (millions)	Real GDP (output) equals disposable income (billions of dollars)	Consumption (billions of dollars)	Unplanned inventory (billions of dollars)
40	325	300	−75
45	375	325	−50
50	425	350	−25
55	475	375	0
60	525	400	25
65	575	425	50
70	625	450	75

a. Answers are given in the above table.

b.
$$MPC = \frac{\text{change in consumption}}{\text{change in disposable income}}$$

$$= \frac{\$25 \text{ billion}}{\$50 \text{ billion}} = \frac{1}{2} = 0.50$$

since $MPS = 1 - MPC = 1 - 0.50 = 0.50$

c. At an employment level of 40 million workers, $75 million in unplanned inventory investment encourages businesses to expand output, and GDP increases toward the equilibrium real GDP of $475 billion.

3.

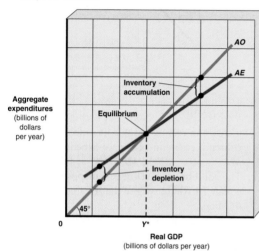

Aggregate expenditures (billions of dollars per year)

Real GDP (billions of dollars per year)

The aggregate expenditures (AE) line intersects the aggregate output (AO) line at the equilibrium level of real GDP, Y^*. Below Y^*, an unplanned inventory depletion causes businesses to expand output, which pushes the economy toward equilibrium output. Above Y^*, an unintended inventory accumulation pushes the economy toward Y^* by pressuring businesses to reduce production.

5.
$$\text{Multiplier} = \frac{1}{1 - MPC} = \frac{1}{MPS}$$

The greater the MPC, the smaller the MPS and the greater the size of the multiplier.

a. 1, 1.5, 10
b. $Y = M \times I = 5 \times \$10 \text{ billion} = \$50 \text{ billion}$
c. $Y = M \times I = 3 \times \$10 \text{ billion} = \$30 \text{ billion}$

7. a.

Round	Components of total spending	New consumption spending (billions of dollars)
1	Investment	$100
2	Consumption	75
3	Consumption	56
4	Consumption	42
	Total spending	$273

b. The spending multiplier is

$$\frac{1}{(1 - MPC)} = \frac{1}{(1 - 0.75)} = \frac{1}{0.25} = 4$$

Therefore, change in investment spending × spending multiplier = change in aggregate spending ($100 billion × 4 = $400 billion).

Note: This problem demonstrates how useful the spending multiplier formula is because it avoids working through individual steps in the multiplier process.

9.
$$\text{Spending multiplier} = \frac{\text{change in GDP}}{\text{change in government spending}} = \frac{\Delta Y}{\Delta G}$$

Since $MPC = 0.75$,

$$\text{Spending multiplier} = \frac{1}{(1 - MPC)} = \frac{1}{0.25} = 4$$

rewritten as

$$4 = \frac{\$100 \text{ billion}}{\Delta G}$$

Therefore,

$$\Delta G = \frac{\$100 \text{ billion}}{4} = \$25 \text{ billion}$$

Given the MPC is 0.75, this means households spend only $18.75 billion of the additional $25 billion of disposable income from the tax cut. Therefore,

$$\Delta C \times \text{spending multiplier} = \text{change in GDP}$$
$$\$18.75 \text{ billion} \times 4 = \$75 \text{ billion}$$

Because GDP must increase by $100 billion, a tax cut of $25 billion would not be enough to restore full-employment GDP.

Chapter 20 Aggregate Demand and Supply

1. There are three reasons why the aggregate demand curve is downward sloping:

   a. The *real balances* or *wealth effect* means that a lower price level increases the purchasing power of money and other financial assets. The result is an upward shift in consumption, which increases the quantity of real goods and services demanded.

   b. The *interest-rate effect* assumes a fixed money supply, and, therefore, a lower price level reduces the demand for borrowing and the interest rate. The lower rate of interest increases spending for consumption and investment.

   c. The *net exports effect* encourages foreign customers to buy more of an economy's domestic exports relative to its domestic purchases of imports when the price level falls. An increase in net exports increases aggregate expenditures.

Rationales for the downward-sloping demand curve for an individual market are the income effect, the substitution effect, and the law of diminishing marginal utility, which are quite different from the three effects that determine the aggregate demand curve.

3. a. A leftward shift occurs because of a decrease in the consumption schedule.
   b. A rightward shift occurs because of an increase in autonomous investment spending.
   c. A rightward shift occurs because of an increase in government spending.
   d. A rightward shift occurs because of an increase in net exports.

5. This statement may not be correct. The equilibrium GDP is not necessarily the same as the full-employment GDP. Equilibrium GDP refers to the equality between the aggregate demand and the aggregate supply curves, which does not necessarily equal the full capacity of the economy to produce goods and services.

7. a. leftward
   b. rightward
   c. rightward
   d. leftward

9. a. Aggregate demand increases.
   b. Aggregate supply increases.
   c. Aggregate demand decreases.
   d. Aggregate supply decreases.
   e. Aggregate demand decreases along the classical range.
   f. Aggregate demand increases along the Keynesian range.

11. Assuming the aggregate supply curve remains constant, a rightward shift of the aggregate demand curve from AD_1 to AD_2 in the upward-sloping or the vertical range of the aggregate supply curve causes the price level to rise from P_1 to P_2. In addition to demand-pull inflation, the level of real GDP increases from Q_1 to Q_2 and provides the economy with new jobs. In the classical range, inflation is the only undesirable result, and real GDP remains unaffected at Q_2.

Chapter 21 Fiscal Policy

1. *Expansionary* fiscal policy refers to increasing government spending and/or decreasing taxes in order to increase aggregate demand and eliminate a GDP gap. *Contractionary* fiscal policy is designed to cool inflation by decreasing aggregate demand. This result is accomplished by decreasing government spending and/or increasing taxes.

3. a. contractionary fiscal policy
   b. contractionary fiscal policy
   c. expansionary fiscal policy

5. The spending multiplier is
$$\frac{1}{1 - MPC} = \frac{1}{0.25} = \frac{1}{1/4} = 4$$
The spending multiplier (M) times the change in government spending (ΔG) equals the change in aggregate demand (ΔAD). Therefore,
$$\Delta G \times M = \Delta AD$$
$$\Delta G \times 4 = \$500 \text{ billion}$$
$$\Delta G = \$125 \text{ billion}$$
The government must increase government spending by $125 billion in order to eliminate the GDP gap.

7. The tax multiplier equals the spending multiplier minus one. Thus, the impact of the expansion in government spending exceeds the impact of an equal amount of tax cut.

9. As a supply-side economist, you would argue that the location of the aggregate supply curve is related to the tax rates. Ceteris paribus, if the tax rates are cut, there will be strong incentives for workers to supply more work, households to save more, and businesses to invest more in capital goods. Thus, cutting tax rates shifts the aggregate supply curve rightward, the level of real GDP rises, and the price level falls.

11. a. rightward shift in the aggregate demand curve
    b. leftward shift in the aggregate demand curve
    c. rightward shift in the aggregate supply curve
    d. rightward shift in the aggregate demand curve
    e. leftward shift in the aggregate supply curve

Chapter 22 The Public Sector

1. Transfer payments account for the difference between total government expenditures, or outlays, and total government spending. Transfers do not "use up" resources; they reallocate purchasing power by collecting taxes from one group and paying benefits to other groups.

3. The primary sources are individual income taxes at the federal level, sales and excise taxes at the state level, and property taxes at the local level.

5. The marginal tax rate is the percentage of additional income paid in taxes. The average tax rate is the amount of taxes paid as a percentage of income.

7. a. more than $6,000
   b. less than $6,000
   c. $6,000

9. Sales tax paid as a percentage of income:

   10%

   7%

   6%

   4%

   Because the sales tax paid as a percentage of income falls as income rises, the tax is regressive.

11. A profit-maximizing firm follows the marginal rule that units will be produced so long as the marginal benefit exceeds or equals the marginal cost. Dollars can measure the intensity of benefits in relation to costs. A "one-person, one-vote" system does not necessarily measure benefits in proportion to the dollar value of benefits among individual voters. Thus, a majority of voters can approve projects for which costs exceed benefits and reject projects for which benefits exceed costs.

Chapter 23 Federal Deficits, Surpluses, and the National Debt

1. The national debt is the sum of past federal budget deficits. When budget deficits are large, the national debt increases at a rapid rate. When budget deficits are small, the national debt increases at a lower rate.

3. The statement makes the argument that most of the debt is internal national debt that one U.S. citizen owes to another U.S. citizen. Suppose the federal government finances a deficit by having the Treasury sell government bonds to one group of U.S. citizens, thereby increasing the national debt. When the bonds mature, the government can pay the interest and principal by issuing new government bonds (rolling over the debt) to another group of U.S. citizens. This argument ignores the income distribution problem that results because interest payments go largely to those who are better off.

5. When the government makes interest payments on internally held debt, the money remains in the hands of U.S. citizens. External debt is very different. Repayment of interest and principal to foreigners withdraws purchasing power from U.S. citizens in favor of citizens abroad.

7. a. In year one, the federal deficit begins at $50 billion, and the U.S. Treasury issues $50 billion worth of bonds to finance the deficit.
   b. The next year the federal government must pay interest of $5 billion to service the debt ($50 billion bonds × .10 interest rate). Adding the interest payment to the $100 billion spent for goods and services yields a $105 billion expenditure in year two.
   c. For the second year, the deficit is $55 billion ($105 billion in expenditures −$50 billion in taxes), and the U.S. Treasury borrows this amount by issuing new bonds. The new national debt is $105 billion, consisting of the $50 billion in bonds issued in the first year and the $55 billion in bonds issued in the second year.

9. During a depression, tax hikes and/or expenditure cuts would only reduce aggregate demand and, in turn, real GDP, jobs, and income. Because the economy is operating in the Keynesian segment of the aggregate demand curve, this fiscal policy would have no impact on the price level.

11. This answer should be logical and supported by a thoughtful explanation.

Chapter 24 Money and the Federal Reserve System

1. Money is worthless in and of itself. The value of money is to serve as a medium of exchange, a unit of account, and a store of value.

3. a. The quantity of credit cards can be controlled. Credit cards are portable, divisible, and uniform in quality.
   b. The quantity of Federal Reserve notes is controlled by the U.S. government. These notes are portable, divisible, and uniform in quality.
   c. The quantity of dogs is difficult to control. Dogs are not very portable or divisible, and they are certainly not uniform.
   d. The quantity of beer mugs can be controlled. Beer mugs are not very portable or divisible, but they could be made fairly uniform.

5. The narrowest definition of money in the United States is M1. M1 = currency (coins plus paper bills) + traveler's checks + checkable deposits.

7. The Fed's most important function is to regulate the U.S. money supply. The *Board of Governors* is composed of seven persons who have the responsibility to supervise and control the money supply and the U.S. banking system. The *Federal Open Market Committee (FOMC)* controls the money supply by directing the buying and selling of U.S. government securities.

9. Banks that belong to the Fed must join the FDIC. Banks chartered by the states may affiliate with the FDIC. There are relatively few nonmember noninsured state banks.

Chapter 25 Money Creation

1. At first, the goldsmiths followed Shakespeare's advice and gave receipts only for gold on deposit in their vaults. They then realized that at any given time new deposits were coming in that could offset old deposits people were drawing down. The conclusion is that banking does not require a 100 percent required reserve ratio. Therefore, loans can be made, which stimulate the economy.

3. Banks can and do create money by granting loans to borrowers. These loans are deposited in customers' checking accounts, and, therefore, banks are participants in the money supply creation process.

5. There is no impact on the money supply. A check deposited in bank A, drawn on bank B, increases deposits, reserves, and lending at bank A. However, bank B experiences an equal reduction in deposits, reserves, and lending.

7. **First National Bank**
   Balance Sheet

Assets		Liabilities	
Reserves	−$1,000	Checkable deposits	−$1,000
Required	−$100		
Excess	−$900		
Total assets	−$1,000	Total liabilities	−$1,000

Negative excess reserves mean that loans must be reduced by $1,000.

9. Some customers may hold cash, rather than writing a check for the full amount of the loan. Some banks may hold excess reserves, rather than using these funds to make loans.

11. The decision of the public to hold cash and the willingness of banks to use excess reserves for loans affect the money multiplier. Variations in the money multiplier can cause unexpected changes in the money supply. Nonbanks can make loans and offer other financial services that are not under the direct control of the Federal Reserve. Finally, the public can decide to transfer funds from M1 to M2 or other definitions of the money supply.

Chapter 26 Monetary Policy

1. a. Transactions and precautionary balances increase.
   b. Speculative balances decrease.
   c. Transactions and precautionary balances decrease.
   d. Speculative balances increase.
   e. Transactions and precautionary balances decrease.

3.

Bond price	Interest rate
$ 800	10%
1,000	8
2,000	4

There is an inverse relationship between the price of a bond and the interest rate.

5. a. The price level declines slightly. Real GDP and employment fall substantially.
   b. The price level, real GDP, and employment rise.
   c. The price level declines slightly. Real GDP and employment fall substantially.

7. In the monetarist view, the velocity of money, V, and the output, Q, variables in the equation of exchange are constant. Therefore, the quantity theory of money is stated as

$$M \times V = P \times Q$$

Given this equation, changes in the money supply, M1, yield proportionate changes in the price level, P.

9. In the Keynesian view, an increase in the money supply decreases the interest rate and causes investment spending, which increases aggregate demand through the multiplier effect and causes demand-pull inflation. In the monetarist view, money supply growth gives people more money to spend. This direct increase in aggregate demand causes demand-pull inflation.

11. Under such conditions, the Keynesian view is correct. The Fed would have no influence on investment because changes in the interest rate failed to alter the quantity of investment goods demanded.

Chapter 27 The Phillips Curve and Expectations Theory

1. The Phillips curve is an inverse relationship between the inflation rate and the unemployment rate. The increase in aggregate demand would cause the inflation rate to increase and the unemployment rate to decrease.

3. In the 1970s and early 1980s, the economy experienced supply shocks from skyrocketing oil and food prices. The result was a leftward shift in the aggregate supply curve and stagflation.

5. a. The inflation rate is 6 percent, and the unemployment rate is 6 percent.

b. The inflation rate rises to 10 percent, and the employment rate falls in the short run. In the long run, the unemployment rate returns to 6 percent.

c. The inflation rate rises to 12 percent, and the unemployment rate falls in the short run. In the long run, the unemployment rate returns to 6 percent.

7. The economy is stimulated prior to an election, and there is a boom. After the election, the strategy is to contract the economy, causing recession until the next election approaches. Thus, political policies are counter to Keynesian policies because political policies cause the business cycle instead of stabilizing it.

9. a. Both prices and nominal wages will rise immediately, causing the inflation rate to rise from 4 percent to 6 percent. The unemployment rate remains unchanged at the 4 percent natural rate.

b. Both prices and nominal wages will rise immediately, causing the inflation rate to rise from 6 percent to 8 percent. The unemployment rate remains unchanged at the 4 percent natural rate.

c. Both prices and nominal wages will fall immediately, causing the inflation rate to fall from 8 percent to 4 percent. The unemployment rate remains unchanged at the 4 percent natural rate.

Chapter 28 International Trade and Finance

1. a. In Alpha, the opportunity cost of producing 1 ton of diamonds is ½ ton of pearls. In Beta, the opportunity cost of producing 1 ton of diamonds is 2 tons of pearls.

b. In Alpha, the opportunity cost of producing 1 ton of pearls is 2 tons of diamonds. In Beta, the opportunity cost of producing 1 ton of pearls is ½ ton of diamonds.

c. Because Alpha can produce diamonds at a lower opportunity cost than Beta can, Alpha has a comparative advantage in the production of diamonds.

d. Because Beta can produce pearls at a lower opportunity cost than Alpha can, Beta has a comparative advantage in the production of pearls.

e.

	Diamonds (tons per year)	Pearls (tons per year)
Before specialization		
Alpha (at point *B*)	100	25
Beta (at point *C*)	30	120
Total output	130	145
After specialization		
Alpha (at point *A*)	150	0
Beta (at point *D*)	0	180
Total output	150	180

As shown in the table, specialization in each country increases total world output per year by 20 tons of diamonds and 35 tons of pearls.

f.

(a) Alpha

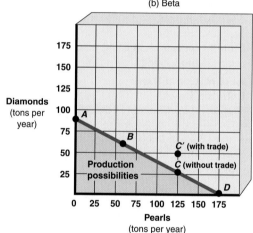

(b) Beta

Without trade, Alpha produces and consumes 100 tons of diamonds and 25 tons of pearls at point *B* on its production possibilities curve. Without trade, Beta produces and consumes 30 tons of diamonds and 120 tons of pearls (point *C*). Now assume Alpha specializes in producing diamonds at point *A* and imports 50 tons of pearls in exchange for 50 tons of diamonds. Through specialization and trade, Alpha moves its consumption possibility to point *B'*, outside its production possibilities curve.

3. The principle of specialization and trade according to comparative advantage applies to both nations and states in the United States. For example, Florida grows oranges, and Idaho grows potatoes. Trade between these states, just like trade among nations, increases the consumption possibilities.

5. U.S. industries (and their workers) that compete with restricted imports would benefit. Consumers would lose from the reduced supply of imported goods from which to choose and from higher prices for domestic products, resulting from lack of competition from imports.

7. Although some domestic jobs may be lost, new ones are created by international trade. Stated differently, the economy as a whole gains when nations specialize and trade according to the law of comparative advantage, but imports will cost jobs in some specific industries.

9. Although each nation's balance of payments equals zero, its current and capital account balances usually do not equal zero. For example, a current account deficit means a nation purchased more in imports than it sold in exports. On the other hand, this nation's capital account must have a surplus to offset the current account deficit. This means that foreigners are buying more domestic capital (capital inflow) than domestic citizens are buying foreign capital (capital outflow). Thus, net ownership of domestic capital stock is in favor of foreigners.

11. a.

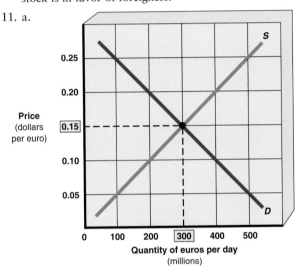

b. $0.15 per euro
c. An excess quantity of 200 million euros would be demanded.

Chapter 29 Economies in Transition

1. Americans prefer large cars and canned soup. Europeans predominantly buy small cars and dry soup. The role of women and minorities in the workplace is an excellent example of how culture relates to the labor factor of production.

3. Such a program would provide additional economic security for the elderly, but higher taxes could reduce the incentive to work, and economic efficiency might be reduced.

5. In a traditional agricultural system, a benefit would be that members of society would cooperate by helping to build barns, harvest, and so on. Under the command system, worrying about errors and crop failures would be minimized because the state makes the decisions and everyone in society has a basic income. In a market economy, a bumper crop would mean large profits and the capacity to improve one's standard of living.

7. Because most economies are mixed systems, this term is too broad to be very descriptive. The terms *capitalism* and *communism* are more definitive concerning the role of private ownership, market allocations, and decentralized decision making. Embracing a market-oriented system means a transfer of power from the command bureaucracy to consumers. Markets are incompatible with the principle that citizens are supposed to be concerned with the collective interest.

Chapter 30 Growth and the Less-Developed Countries

1. The difference between IACs and LDCs is based on GDP per capita. This classification is somewhat arbitrary. A country with a high GDP per capita and narrow industrial development based on oil, such as the United Arab Emirates, is excluded from the IAC list. There are 26 countries listed in the text as IACs, including Switzerland, Japan, the United States, Singapore, and Hong Kong. The following countries are considered to be LDCs: Argentina, Mexico, South Africa, Jordan, and Bangladesh.

3. a. Based only on GDP per capita, you would conclude that Alpha is a better place to live because this country produces a greater output of goods and services per person.
   b. Based on the additional evidence, you would change your mind and prefer to live in Beta because the quality-of-life data indicate a higher standard of living in this country.

5. As shown in Exhibit 5, the average growth rate of GDP per capita for an IAC was about 4 percent per year. Over the same period of time, the GDP per capita growth rate for LDCs was negative. This evidence is consistent with the argument. The argument is oversimplified because there is considerable diversity among the LDCs. For example, Mexico had a GDP per capita growth rate of 5.4 percent in 2000, which was greater than many IACs.

7. Economic growth and development are complicated because there is no single prescription that a country can follow. The text presents a multidimensional model with five basic categories: natural resources, human resources, capital, technological progress, and political environment. Because an LDC is weak in one or more of the key factors, such as natural resources, does not necessarily mean that the LDC cannot achieve economic success.

9. Because they are poor countries with low GDP per capita, they lack domestic savings to invest in capital; and lacking investment, they remain poor. The rich in these poor countries often put their savings abroad because of the fear of political instability. An inflow of external funds from abroad permits the LDC to increase its capital without reducing its consumption and to shift its production possibilities curve outward.

11. Poor countries are too poor to save enough to finance domestic capital formation. International trade is a way LDCs can generate savings from abroad. Exports provide the LDCs with foreign exchange to pay for imports of capital stock that is necessary for economic growth and development.

Practice Quiz Answers

CHAPTER 1 Introducing the Economic Way of Thinking

1. c   2. d   3. c   4. c   5. a   6. a   7. a   8. a   9. a
10. c   11. a   12. b

APPENDIX TO CHAPTER 1 Applying Graphs to Economics

1. d   2. d   3. a   4. d   5. d   6. c   7. c   8. c   9. d
10. d   11. d   12. b

CHAPTER 2 Production Possibilities, Opportunity Cost, and Economic Growth

1. c   2. a   3. c   4. c   5. b   6. c   7. c   8. e   9. a
10. c   11. b

CHAPTER 3 Market Demand and Supply

1. e   2. a   3. b   4. b   5. a   6. b   7. c   8. b   9. c
10. b   11. c   12. c   13. d   14. d   15. c   16. d   17. d
18. c

CHAPTER 4 Markets in Action

1. a   2. a   3. c   4. d   5. d   6. d   7. c   8. b   9. a
10. b   11. c   12. a

CHAPTER 5   Price Elasticity of Demand and Supply

1. a   2. b   3. a   4. a   5. a   6. d   7. a   8. a   9. d
10. c   11. c   12. c

CHAPTER 6   Consumer Choice Theory

1. c   2. d   3. a   4. a   5. d   6. d   7. c   8. b   9. a
10. a   11. b

CHAPTER 7   Production Costs

1. d   2. b   3. c   4. c   5. d   6. d   7. c   8. d   9. d
10. c   11. c   12. b   13. c   14. b   15. d   16. c   17. d
18. e   19. c

CHAPTER 8   Perfect Competition

1. b   2. b   3. b   4. b   5. c   6. d   7. b   8. d   9. b
10. b   11. a   12. d   13. b   14. d   15. d   16. a   17. d

CHAPTER 9   Monopoly

1. d   2. d   3. d   4. d   5. b   6. d   7. b   8. d   9. b
10. d   11. e

CHAPTER 10   Monopolistic Competition and Oligopoly

1. b   2. b   3. d   4. d   5. d   6. d   7. a   8. a   9. b
10. d   11. d   12. a   13. c   14. b   15. a

CHAPTER 11   Labor Markets

1. d   2. a   3. c   4. a   5. c   6. b   7. d   8. b   9. c
10. c   11. b   12. c   13. c   14. a

CHAPTER 12   Income Distribution, Poverty, and Discrimination

1. a   2. c   3. c   4. a   5. b   6. d   7. d   8. a   9. d
10. c   11. a   12. d   13. d

CHAPTER 13   Antitrust and Regulation

1. d   2. a   3. d   4. b   5. d   6. a   7. c   8. d   9. c
10. a   11. b   12. a   13. e   14. d   15. d

CHAPTER 14   Environmental Economics

1. d   2. e   3. a   4. a   5. a   6. c   7. d   8. b   9. d
10. b   11. b   12. b   13. c

CHAPTER 15   Gross Domestic Product

1. d   2. a   3. a   4. e   5. d   6. d   7. c   8. d   9. b
10. d   11. b   12. b   13. c

CHAPTER 16   Business Cycles and Unemployment

1. c   2. d   3. d   4. d   5. d   6. d   7. c   8. b   9. a
10. d   11. d   12. d   13. c   14. e

CHAPTER 17   Inflation

1. a   2. a   3. b   4. b   5. a   6. b   7. d   8. b   9. b
10. d   11. c   12. d   13. c

CHAPTER 18   The Keynesian Model

1. c   2. d   3. d   4. c   5. b   6. a   7. a   8. b   9. d
10. d   11. b   12. c

CHAPTER 19   The Keynesian Model in Action

1. d   2. b   3. d   4. a   5. c   6. b   7. d   8. d   9. c
10. b   11. b   12. c

CHAPTER 20   Aggregate Demand and Supply

1. c   2. b   3. a   4. c   5. d   6. a   7. c   8. c   9. d
10. c   11. c   12. d   13. a   14. d   15. a

CHAPTER 21   Fiscal Policy

1. d   2. a   3. d   4. b   5. d   6. c   7. a   8. d   9. c
10. d   11. a   12. d   13. a

CHAPTER 22   The Public Sector

1. b   2. b   3. d   4. d   5. d   6. a   7. e   8. d   9. d
10. d   11. c   12. d   13. a   14. a

CHAPTER 23   Federal Deficits, Surpluses, and the National Debt

1. a   2. b   3. c   4. a   5. c   6. d   7. b   8. e   9. a
10. d   11. d

CHAPTER 24   Money and the Federal Reserve System

1. b   2. b   3. d   4. c   5. d   6. b   7. c   8. d   9. c
10. e   11. d   12. b   13. b   14. c

CHAPTER 25   Money Creation

1. b   2. b   3. b   4. c   5. c   6. d   7. c   8. c   9. b
10. b   11. a   12. d

CHAPTER 26   Monetary Policy

1. d   2. b   3. d   4. a   5. a   6. d   7. c   8. d   9. d
10. c   11. b   12. a

CHAPTER 27   The Phillips Curve and Expectations Theory

1. d   2. b   3. a   4. c   5. e   6. c   7. b   8. c   9. c
10. d   11. c   12. b

CHAPTER 28   International Trade and Finance

1. b   2. c   3. a   4. d   5. d   6. a   7. d   8. a   9. c
10. c   11. b   12. c   13. c   14. a   15. a   16. b   17. a
18. a   19. e   20. d

CHAPTER 29   Economies in Transition

1. c   2. d   3. d   4. a   5. b   6. a   7. c   8. b   9. b
10. c   11. c   12. a   13. a   14. d   15. a

CHAPTER 30   Growth and the Less-Developed Countries

1. d   2. d   3. d   4. e   5. a   6. a   7. d   8. a   9. c
10. a   11. b   12. d   13. c   14. d

United States Gross Domestic Product and Related Statistics

United States Gross Domestic Product (in billions of dollars) and Related Statistics

	1929	1930	1931	1932	1933	1934	1935	1936	1937	1938
1. Gross domestic product	103.7	91.3	76.6	58.8	56.4	66.0	73.3	83.7	91.9	86.1
2. Personal consumption expenditures	77.5	70.2	60.7	48.7	45.9	51.5	55.9	62.2	66.8	64.2
3. Gross private domestic investment	16.5	10.8	5.9	1.3	1.7	3.7	6.7	8.6	12.2	7.1
4. Government consumption expenditures and gross investment	9.4	10.0	9.9	8.8	8.7	10.6	10.9	13.1	12.8	13.8
5. Net exports	0.4	0.3	0.0	0.0	0.1	0.3	-0.2	-0.2	0.0	0.9
6. Net domestic product	94.4	82.1	68.0	51.2	49.2	58.4	65.6	75.8	83.1	76.9
7. National income	86.8	75.6	60.4	43.9	41.4	50.2	57.9	65.8	74.0	67.4
8. Personal income	85.3	76.5	65.5	50.0	46.9	53.8	60.5	68.8	74.3	68.6
9. Disposable personal income	83.2	74.6	64.2	49.1	45.9	52.7	59.2	67.3	72.2	66.5
10. Real gross domestic product (in 1996 dollars)	822.2	751.5	703.6	611.8	603.3	668.3	728.3	822.5	865.8	835.6
11. Percent change in real GDP	—	-8.6	-6.4	-13.0	-1.4	10.8	9.0	12.9	5.3	-3.5
12. Consumer price index (1982–84 = 100)	17.1	16.7	15.2	13.7	13.0	13.4	13.7	13.9	14.4	14.1
13. Rate of inflation (percent)	0.0	-2.3	-9.0	-9.9	-5.1	3.1	2.2	1.5	3.6	-2.1
14. Civilian unemployment rate (percent)	3.2	8.7	15.9	23.6	24.9	21.7	20.1	16.9	14.3	19.0
15. Supply of money, M1 (in billions of dollars)	26.4	24.9	21.9	20.3	19.8	22.7	27.0	30.9	29.1	31.7
16. Percent change in M1	0.0	-5.7	-12.0	-7.3	-2.5	14.7	18.9	14.4	-5.8	8.9
17. Prime rate charged by banks	6.0	6.0	5.0	4.0	4.0	1.5	1.5	1.5	1.5	1.5
18. Federal budget surplus or deficit (in billions of dollars)	0.7	0.7	-0.5	-2.7	-2.6	-3.6	-2.8	-4.3	-2.2	-1.0
19. Federal debt (in billions of dollars)	16.9	16.2	16.8	19.5	22.5	27.1	28.7	33.8	36.4	37.2

United States Gross Domestic Product (in billions of dollars) and Related Statistics (continued)

	1939	1940	1941	1942	1943	1944	1945	1946	1947	1948
1. Gross domestic product	92.0	101.3	126.7	161.8	198.4	219.7	223.0	222.3	244.4	269.6
2. Personal consumption expenditures	67.2	71.2	81.0	88.9	99.7	108.5	119.8	144.2	162.3	175.4
3. Gross private domestic investment	9.3	13.6	18.1	10.4	6.1	7.8	10.8	31.1	35.0	48.1
4. Government consumption expenditures and gross investment	14.7	15.1	26.6	62.8	94.9	105.5	93.2	39.8	36.4	40.6
5. Net exports	0.8	1.4	1.0	−0.3	−2.4	−2.2	−0.9	7.1	10.8	5.4
6. Net domestic product	82.9	91.8	115.6	148.1	182.0	200.3	202.1	198.7	218.3	241.5
7. National income	72.9	81.1	104.3	137.6	171.4	184.3	183.3	182.3	198.6	223.3
8. Personal income	73.1	78.6	96.3	123.8	152.4	166.3	171.9	179.5	192.1	211.1
9. Disposable personal income	71.4	76.7	93.8	118.7	135.4	148.3	152.1	162.0	172.1	191.6
10. Real gross domestic product (in 1996 dollars)	903.5	980.7	1,148.8	1,360.0	1,583.7	1,714.1	1,693.3	1,505.5	1,495.1	1,560.0
11. Percent change in real GDP	8.1	8.5	17.1	18.4	16.5	8.2	−1.2	−11.1	−.7	4.3
12. Consumer price index (1982–84 = 100)	13.9	14.0	14.7	16.3	17.3	17.6	18.0	19.5	22.3	24.1
13. Rate of inflation (percent)	−1.4	0.7	5.0	10.9	6.1	1.7	2.3	8.3	14.4	8.1
14. Civilian unemployment rate (percent)	17.2	14.6	9.9	4.7	1.9	1.2	1.9	3.9	3.9	3.8
15. Supply of money, M1 (in billions of dollars)	36.0	41.9	48.2	62.6	79.9	90.7	102.4	107.6	112.2	110.7
16. Percent change in M1	11.9	16.4	15.0	29.9	27.6	13.5	12.9	5.1	4.3	−1.3
17. Prime rate charged by banks	1.5	1.5	1.5	1.5	1.5	1.5	1.5	1.5	1.8	2.0
18. Federal budget surplus or deficit (in billions of dollars)	−2.8	−2.9	−4.9	−20.5	−54.6	−47.6	−47.6	−15.9	4.0	11.8
19. Federal debt (in billions of dollars)	48.2	50.7	57.5	79.2	142.6	204.1	260.1	271.0	257.1	252.0

United States Gross Domestic Product (in billions of dollars) and Related Statistics (continued)

	1949	1950	1951	1952	1953	1954	1955	1956	1957	1958
1. Gross domestic product	267.7	294.3	339.5	358.6	379.9	381.1	415.2	438.0	461.5	467.9
2. Personal consumption expenditures	178.8	192.7	208.6	219.7	233.4	240.5	259.0	271.9	287.0	296.6
3. Gross private domestic investment	36.9	54.1	60.2	54.0	56.4	53.8	69.0	72.0	70.5	64.5
4. Government consumption expenditures and gross investment	46.8	46.9	68.3	83.9	90.8	86.5	86.8	91.8	100.1	106.5
5. Net exports	5.2	0.7	2.4	1.0	−0.8	0.3	0.4	2.3	4.0	0.4
6. Net domestic product	238.8	264.6	305.9	322.4	341.4	340.6	372.4	390.7	410.4	415.2
7. National income	216.7	241.0	278.7	293.3	308.2	308.4	338.5	358.7	375.0	377.3
8. Personal income	208.2	229.9	258.7	276.1	292.9	295.2	316.8	340.0	359.3	370.0
9. Disposable personal income	191.1	210.6	231.2	243.6	258.8	264.5	283.4	302.8	319.7	330.8
10. Real gross domestic product (in 1996 dollars)	1,550.9	1,686.6	1,815.1	1,887.3	1,973.9	1,960.5	2,099.5	2,141.1	2,183.9	2,162.8
11. Percent change in real GDP	−0.6	8.7	7.6	4.0	4.6	−0.7	7.1	2.0	2.0	−1.0
12. Consumer price index (1982–84 = 100)	23.8	24.1	26.0	26.5	26.7	26.9	26.8	27.2	28.1	28.9
13. Rate of inflation (percent)	−1.2	1.3	7.9	1.9	0.8	0.7	−0.4	1.5	3.3	2.8
14. Civilian unemployment rate (percent)	5.9	5.3	3.3	3.0	2.9	5.5	4.4	4.1	4.3	6.8
15. Supply of money, M1 (in billions of dollars)	110.1	115.3	122.0	126.4	128.2	131.8	134.6	136.5	135.5	140.8
16. Percent change in M1	−0.5	4.7	5.8	3.6	1.4	2.8	2.1	1.4	−0.7	3.9
17. Prime rate charged by banks	2.0	2.0	2.6	3.0	3.2	3.1	3.2	3.8	4.2	3.8
18. Federal budget surplus or deficit (in billions of dollars)	0.6	−3.1	6.1	−1.5	−6.5	−1.2	−3.0	3.9	3.4	−2.8
19. Federal debt (in billions of dollars)	252.6	256.9	255.3	259.1	266.0	270.8	274.4	272.7	272.3	279.7

United States Gross Domestic Product (in billions of dollars) and Related Statistics (continued)

	1959	1960	1961	1962	1963	1964	1965	1966	1967	1968
1. Gross domestic product	507.4	527.4	545.7	586.5	618.7	664.4	720.1	789.3	834.1	911.5
2. Personal consumption expenditures	318.1	332.3	342.7	363.8	383.1	411.7	444.3	481.8	508.7	558.7
3. Gross private domestic investment	78.5	78.9	78.2	88.1	93.8	102.1	118.2	131.3	128.6	141.2
4. Government consumption expenditures and gross investment	112.5	113.8	121.5	132.2	138.5	145.1	153.7	174.3	195.3	212.8
5. Net exports	−1.7	2.4	3.4	2.4	3.3	5.5	3.9	1.9	1.4	−1.3
6. Net domestic product	452.6	470.4	487.1	525.5	555.1	597.8	649.3	712.7	751.0	820.6
7. National income	411.5	427.5	442.5	477.1	504.4	542.1	589.6	646.7	681.7	743.6
8. Personal income	394.0	412.7	430.3	457.9	481.0	515.8	557.4	606.4	650.4	714.5
9. Disposable personal income	351.2	366.2	382.4	405.6	425.8	463.0	498.9	539.1	576.2	626.2
10. Real gross domestic product (in 1996 dollars)	2,319.0	2,376.7	2,432.0	2,578.9	2,690.4	2,846.5	3,028.5	3,227.5	3,308.3	3,466.1
11. Percent change in real GDP	7.2	2.5	2.3	6.0	4.3	5.8	6.4	6.6	2.5	4.8
12. Consumer price index (1982–84 = 100)	29.1	29.6	29.9	30.2	30.6	31.0	31.5	32.4	33.4	34.8
13. Rate of inflation (percent)	0.7	1.7	1.0	1.0	1.3	1.3	1.6	2.9	3.1	4.2
14. Civilian unemployment rate (percent)	5.5	5.5	6.7	5.5	5.7	5.2	4.5	3.8	3.8	3.6
15. Supply of money, M1 (in billions of dollars)	140.0	140.7	145.2	147.8	153.3	160.3	167.8	172.0	183.3	197.4
16. Percent change in M1	−1.2	0.5	3.2	1.8	3.7	4.6	4.7	2.5	6.6	7.7
17. Prime rate charged by banks	4.5	4.8	4.5	4.5	4.5	4.5	4.5	5.6	5.6	6.3
18. Federal budget surplus or deficit (in billions of dollars)	−12.8	0.3	−3.3	−7.1	−4.8	−5.9	−1.4	−3.7	−8.6	−25.2
19. Federal debt (in billions of dollars)	287.5	290.5	292.6	302.9	310.3	316.1	322.3	328.5	340.4	368.7

United States Gross Domestic Product (in billions of dollars) and Related Statistics (continued)

	1969	1970	1971	1972	1973	1974	1975	1976	1977	1978
1. Gross domestic product	985.3	1,039.7	1,128.6	1,240.4	1,385.5	1,501.0	1,635.2	1,823.9	2,031.4	2,295.9
2. Personal consumption expenditures	605.5	648.9	702.4	770.7	852.5	932.4	1,030.3	1,149.8	1,278.4	1,430.4
3. Gross private domestic investment	156.4	152.4	178.2	207.6	244.5	249.4	230.2	292.0	361.3	436.0
4. Government consumption expenditures and gross investment	224.6	237.1	251.0	270.1	287.9	322.4	361.1	384.5	415.3	455.6
5. Net exports	-1.2	1.2	-3.0	-8.0	0.6	-3.1	13.6	-2.3	-23.7	-26.1
6. Net domestic product	885.6	930.6	1,009.7	1,109.5	1,242.6	1,336.2	1,444.2	1,615.0	1,799.8	2,034.4
7. National income	802.7	837.5	903.9	1,000.4	1,127.4	1,211.9	1,302.2	1,456.4	1,635.8	1,860.2
8. Personal income	780.8	841.1	905.1	994.3	1,113.4	1,225.6	1,331.7	1,475.4	1,637.1	1,848.3
9. Disposable personal income	675.0	736.5	801.7	868.6	979.0	1,072.3	1,181.4	1,299.9	1,436.0	1,614.8
10. Real gross domestic product (in 1996 dollars)	3,571.4	3,578.0	3,697.7	3,898.4	4,123.4	4,099.0	4,084.4	4,311.7	4,511.8	4,760.6
11. Percent change in real GDP	3.0	0.2	3.3	5.4	5.8	-0.6	-0.4	5.6	4.6	5.5
12. Consumer price index (1982-84 = 100)	36.7	38.8	40.5	41.8	44.4	49.3	53.8	56.9	60.6	65.2
13. Rate of inflation (percent)	5.5	5.7	4.4	3.2	6.2	11.0	9.1	5.8	6.5	7.6
14. Civilian unemployment rate (percent)	3.5	4.9	5.9	5.6	4.9	5.6	8.5	7.7	7.1	6.1
15. Supply of money, M1 (in billions of dollars)	203.9	214.3	228.2	249.1	262.7	274.0	286.8	305.9	330.5	356.9
16. Percent change in M1	3.3	5.1	6.5	9.2	5.5	4.3	4.7	6.7	8.0	8.0
17. Prime rate charged by banks	8.0	7.9	5.7	5.3	8.0	10.8	7.9	6.8	6.8	9.1
18. Federal budget surplus or deficit (in billions of dollars)	3.2	-2.8	-23.0	-23.4	-14.9	-6.1	-53.2	-73.7	-53.7	-59.2
19. Federal debt (in billions of dollars)	365.8	380.9	408.2	435.9	466.3	483.9	541.9	629.0	706.4	776.6

United States Gross Domestic Product (in billions of dollars) and Related Statistics (continued)

	1979	1980	1981	1982	1983	1984	1985	1986	1987	1988
1. Gross domestic product	2,566.4	2,795.6	3,131.3	3,259.2	3,534.9	3,932.7	4,213.0	4,452.9	4,742.5	5,108.3
2. Personal consumption expenditures	1,596.3	1,762.9	1,944.2	2,079.3	2,286.4	2,498.4	2,712.6	2,895.2	3,105.3	3,356.6
3. Gross private domestic investment	490.6	477.9	570.8	516.1	564.2	735.5	736.3	747.2	781.5	821.1
4. Government consumption expenditures and gross investment	503.5	569.7	631.4	684.4	735.9	800.8	878.3	942.3	997.9	1,036.9
5. Net exports	−24.0	−14.9	−15.0	−20.5	−51.7	−102.0	−114.2	−131.9	−142.3	−106.3
6. Net domestic product	2,266.0	2,450.3	2,736.5	2,822.8	3,078.8	3,450.4	3,696.5	3,901.3	4,156.4	4,480.9
7. National income	2,075.6	2,243.0	2,497.1	2,603.0	2,796.5	3,162.3	3,380.4	3,525.8	3,803.4	4,151.1
8. Personal income	2,081.5	2,323.9	2,599.4	2,768.4	2,946.9	3,274.8	3,515.0	3,712.4	3,962.5	4,272.1
9. Disposable personal income	1,808.2	2,019.8	2,247.9	2,406.8	2,586.0	2,887.6	3,086.5	3,262.5	3,459.5	3,752.4
10. Real gross domestic product (in 1996 dollars)	4,912.1	4,900.9	5,021.0	4,919.3	5,132.3	5,505.2	5,717.1	5,912.4	6,113.3	6,368.4
11. Percent change in real GDP	3.2	−0.2	2.5	−2.0	4.3	7.3	3.8	3.4	3.4	4.2
12. Consumer price index (1982–84 = 100)	72.6	82.4	90.9	96.5	99.6	103.9	107.6	109.6	113.6	118.3
13. Rate of inflation (percent)	11.3	13.5	10.3	6.2	3.2	4.3	3.6	1.9	3.6	4.1
14. Civilian unemployment rate (percent)	5.8	7.1	7.6	9.7	9.6	7.5	7.2	7.0	6.2	5.5
15. Supply of money, M1 (in billions of dollars)	381.4	408.1	436.2	474.3	520.8	551.2	619.3	724.2	749.6	786.3
16. Percent change in M1	6.9	7.0	6.9	8.7	9.8	5.9	12.4	16.9	3.5	4.9
17. Prime rate charged by banks	12.7	15.3	18.9	14.9	10.8	12.0	9.9	8.3	8.2	9.3
18. Federal budget surplus or deficit (in billions of dollars)	−40.7	−73.8	−79.0	−128.0	−207.8	−185.4	−212.3	−221.2	−149.8	−155.2
19. Federal debt (in billions of dollars)	829.5	909.1	994.8	1,137.3	1,371.7	1,564.7	1,817.5	2,120.6	2,346.1	2,601.3

United States Gross Domestic Product (in billions of dollars) and Related Statistics (continued)

	1989	1990	1991	1992	1993	1994	1995	1996	1997	1998
1. Gross domestic product	5,489.1	5,803.2	5,986.2	6,318.9	6,642.3	7,054.3	7,400.5	7,813.2	8,318.4	8,781.5
2. Personal consumption expenditures	3,596.7	3,831.5	3,971.2	4,209.7	4,454.7	4,716.4	4,969.0	5,237.5	5,529.3	5,856.0
3. Gross private domestic investment	872.9	861.7	800.2	866.6	955.1	1,097.1	1,143.8	1,242.7	1,390.5	1,538.7
4. Government consumption expenditures and gross investment	1,100.2	1,181.4	1,235.5	1,270.5	1,293.0	1,327.9	1,372.0	1,421.9	1,487.9	1,538.5
5. Net exports	−80.7	−71.4	−20.7	−27.9	−60.5	−87.1	−84.3	−89.0	−89.3	−151.7
6. Net domestic product	4,811.8	5,092.0	5,238.2	5,531.5	5,829.5	6,179.4	6,488.8	6,857.0	7,305.0	7,709.5
7. National income	4,392.1	4,642.1	4,756.6	4,994.9	5,251.9	5,556.8	5,876.7	6,210.4	6,618.4	7,041.4
8. Personal income	4,599.8	4,903.2	5,085.4	5,390.4	5,610.0	5,888.0	6,200.9	6,547.4	6,937.0	7,426.0
9. Disposable personal income	4,016.3	4,293.6	4,4474.8	4,754.6	4,935.3	5,165.4	5,422.6	5,677.7	5,968.2	6,355.6
10. Real gross domestic product (in 1996 dollars)	6,591.8	6,707.9	6,676.4	6,880.0	7,062.6	7,347.7	7,543.8	7,813.2	8,159.5	8,508.9
11. Percent change in real GDP	3.5	1.8	−0.5	3.0	2.7	4.0	2.7	3.6	4.4	4.3
12. Consumer price index (1982–84 = 100)	124.0	130.7	136.2	140.3	144.5	148.2	152.4	156.9	160.5	163.0
13. Rate of inflation (percent)	4.8	5.4	4.2	3.0	3.0	2.6	2.8	3.0	2.3	1.6
14. Civilian unemployment rate (percent)	5.3	5.6	6.8	7.5	6.9	6.1	5.6	5.4	4.9	4.5
15. Supply of money, M1 (in billions of dollars)	792.5	824.4	896.3	1,024.3	1,129.7	1,150.1	1,126.8	1,081.1	1,073.9	1,097.0
16. Percent change in M1	0.8	4.0	8.7	14.3	10.3	1.8	−2.0	−4.1	−0.7	2.2
17. Prime rate charged by banks	10.9	10.0	8.5	6.3	6.0	7.2	8.8	8.3	8.4	8.4
18. Federal budget surplus or deficit (in billions of dollars)	−152.5	−221.2	−269.4	−290.4	−255.1	−203.3	−164.0	−107.5	−22.0	69.2
19. Federal debt (in billions of dollars)	2,868.0	3,206.6	3,598.5	4,002.1	4,351.4	4,643.7	4,921.0	5,181.9	5,369.7	5,478.7

United States Gross Domestic Product (in billions of dollars) and Related Statistics (continued)

	1999	2000
1. Gross domestic product	9,268.6	9,872.9
2. Personal consumption expenditures	6,250.2	6,728.4
3. Gross private domestic investment	1,636.7	1,767.5
4. Government consumption expenditures and gross investment	1,632.5	1,741.0
5. Net exports	−250.9	−364.0
6. Net domestic product	8,117.2	8,631.7
7. National income	7,462.1	7,980.9
8. Personal income	7,777.3	8,312.2
9. Disposable personal income	6,618.0	7,031.0
10. Real gross domestic product (in 1996 dollars)	8,856.5	9,224.0
11. Percent change in real GDP	4.1	4.1
12. Consumer price index (1982–84 = 100)	166.6	172.2
13. Rate of inflation (percent)	2.2	3.4
14. Civilian unemployment rate (percent)	4.2	4.0
15. Supply of money, M1 (in billions of dollars)	1,124.8	1,088.2
16. Percent change in M1	2.3	−3.2
17. Prime rate charged by banks	8.0	9.2
18. Federal budget surplus or deficit (in billions of dollars)	124.4	236.0
19. Federal debt (in billions of dollars)	5,606.1	5,629.0

Source: Survey of Current Business, Federal Reserve Bulletin, and *Economic Report of the President.*

Glossary

A

Ability-to-pay principle The concept that those who have higher incomes can afford to pay a greater proportion of their income in taxes, regardless of benefits received. (Chapter 22)

Absolute advantage The ability of a country to produce a good using fewer resources than another country. (Chapter 28)

Adaptive expectations theory The concept that people believe the best indicator of the future is recent information. As a result, people persistently underestimate inflation when it is accelerating and overestimate it while it is slowing down. (Chapter 27)

Agency for International Development (AID) The agency of the U.S. State Department that is in charge of U.S. aid to foreign countries. (Chapter 30)

Aggregate demand curve (AD) The curve that shows the level of real gross domestic product (GDP) purchased by households, businesses, government, and foreigners (net exports) at different possible price levels during a time period, ceteris paribus. (Chapter 20)

Aggregate expenditures function (AE) The function that represents total spending in an economy at a given level of real disposable income. (Chapter 18)

Aggregate expenditures–output model The model that determines the equilibrium level of real GDP by the intersection of the aggregate expenditures and aggregate output (and income) curves. (Chapter 19)

Aggregate supply curve (AS) The curve that shows the level of real GDP produced at different possible price levels during a time period, ceteris paribus. (Chapter 20)

Appreciation of currency A rise in the price of one currency relative to another. (Chapter 28)

Arbitrage The practice of earning a profit by buying a good at a low price and reselling the good at a higher price. (Chapter 9)

Automatic stabilizers Federal expenditures and tax revenues that automatically change levels in order to stabilize an economic expansion or contraction; sometimes referred to as *nondiscretionary fiscal policy.* (Chapter 21)

Autonomous consumption Consumption that is independent of the level of disposable income. (Chapter 18)

Autonomous expenditure Spending that does not vary with the current level of disposable income. (Chapter 18)

Average fixed cost (AFC) Total fixed cost divided by the quantity of output produced. (Chapter 7)

Average tax rate The tax divided by the income. (Chapter 22)

Average total cost (ATC) Total cost divided by the quantity of output produced. (Chapter 7)

Average variable cost (AVC) Total variable cost divided by the quantity of output produced. (Chapter 7)

B

Balance of payments A bookkeeping record of all the international transactions between a country and other countries during a given period of time. (Chapter 28)

Balance of trade The value of a nation's goods imports subtracted from its goods exports. (Chapter 28)

Balanced budget multiplier An equal change in government spending and taxes, which changes aggregate demand by the amount of the change in government spending. (Chapter 21)

Barter The direct exchange of one good for another good, rather than for money. (Chapter 24)

Base year A year chosen as a reference point for comparison with some earlier or later year. (Chapter 17)

Benefit-cost analysis The comparison of the additional rewards and costs of an economic alternative. (Chapter 22)

Benefits-received principle The concept that those who benefit from government expenditures should pay the taxes that finance their benefits. (Chapter 22)

Board of Governors of the Federal Reserve System The seven members appointed by the president and confirmed by the U.S. Senate who serve for one nonrenewable 14-year term. Their responsibility is to supervise and control the money supply and the banking system of the United States. (Chapter 24)

Budget deficit A budget in which government expenditures exceed government revenues in a given time period. (Chapter 21)

Budget line A line that represents all combinations of two goods that a consumer can purchase with a fixed income given the price of each good.

Budget surplus A budget in which government revenues exceed government expenditures in a given time period. (Chapter 21)

Business cycle Alternating periods of economic growth and contraction, which can be measured by changes in real GDP. (Chapter 16)

C

Capital The physical plants, machinery, and equipment used to produce other goods. Capital goods are human-made goods that do not directly satisfy human wants. (Chapter 1)

Capitalism An economic system characterized by private ownership of resources and markets. (Chapter 29)

Cartel A group of firms that formally agree to control the price and the output of a product. (Chapter 10)

Celler-Kefauver Act A 1950 amendment to the Clayton Act that prohibits one firm from merging with a competitor by purchasing its physical assets if the effect is to substantially lessen competition. (Chapter 13)

Ceteris paribus A Latin phrase that means that while certain variables change, "all other things remain unchanged." (Chapter 1)

Change in demand An increase or a decrease in the quantity demanded at each possible price. An increase in demand is a rightward shift in the entire demand curve. A decrease in demand is a leftward shift in the entire demand curve. (Chapter 3)

Change in quantity demanded A movement between points along a stationary demand curve, ceteris paribus. (Chapter 3)

Change in quantity supplied A movement between points along a stationary supply curve, ceteris paribus. (Chapter 3)

Change in supply An increase or a decrease in the quantity supplied at each possible price. An increase in supply is a rightward shift in the entire supply curve. A decrease in supply is a leftward shift in the entire supply curve. (Chapter 3)

Checkable deposits The total of checking account balances in financial institutions convertible to currency "on demand" by writing a check without advance notice. (Chapter 24)

Circular flow model A diagram showing the flow of products from businesses to households and the flow of resources from households to businesses. In exchange for these resources, money payments flow between businesses and households. (Chapter 15)

Civilian labor force The number of people 16 years of age and older who are employed, or who are actively seeking a job; excluding armed forces, homemakers, discouraged workers, and other persons not in the labor force. (Chapter 16)

Classical economists A group of economists whose theory dominated economic thinking from the 1770s to the Great Depression. They believed recessions would naturally cure themselves because the price system would automatically restore full employment. (Chapter 18)

Classical range The vertical segment of the aggregate supply curve, which represents an economy at full-employment output. (Chapter 20)

Clayton Act A 1914 amendment that strengthens the Sherman Act by making it illegal for firms to engage in certain anticompetitive business practices. (Chapter 13)

Coase Theorem The proposition that private market negotiations would achieve social efficiency regardless of the initial definition of property rights. (Chapter 14)

Coincident indicators Variables that change at the same time that real GDP changes. (Chapter 16)

Collective bargaining The process of negotiations between the union and management over wages and working conditions. (Chapter 11)

Command-and-control regulations Government regulations that set an environmental goal and dictate how the goal will be achieved. (Chapter 14)

Command economy A system that answers the What, How, and For Whom questions by central authority. (Chapter 29)

Commodity money Anything that serves as money while having market value in other uses. (Chapter 24)

Communism A stateless, classless economic system in which all the factors of production are owned by the workers and people share in production according to their needs. In Marx's view, this is the highest form of socialism toward which the revolution should strive. (Chapter 29)

Comparable worth The principle that employees who work for the same employer must be paid the same wage when their jobs, even if different, require similar levels of education, training, experience, and responsibility. A nonmarket wage-setting process is used to evaluate and compensate jobs according to point scores assigned to different jobs. (Chapter 12)

Comparative advantage The ability of a country to produce a good at a lower opportunity cost than another country. (Chapter 28)

Complementary good A good that is jointly consumed with another good. As a result, there is an inverse relationship between a price change for one good and the demand for its "go together" good. (Chapter 3)

Conglomerate merger A merger between firms in unrelated markets. (Chapter 13)

Constant-cost industry An industry in which the expansion of industry output by the entry of new firms has no effect on the individual firm's cost curve. (Chapter 8)

Constant returns to scale A situation in which the long-run average cost curve does not change as the firm increases output. (Chapter 7)

Consumer equilibrium A condition in which total utility cannot increase by spending more of a given budget on one good and spending less on another good. (Chapter 6)

Consumer price index (CPI) An index that measures changes in the average prices of consumer goods and services. (Chapter 17)

Consumer sovereignty The freedom of consumers to cast their dollar votes to buy, or not to buy, at prices determined in competitive markets. (Chapter 29)

Consumption function The graph or table that shows the amount households spend for goods and services at different levels of disposable income. (Chapter 18)

Cost-push inflation A rise in the general price level resulting from an increase in the cost of production. (Chapter 17)

Cross-elasticity of demand The ratio of the percentage change in quantity demanded for a good or service to a given percentage change in the price of another good or service. (Chapter 5)

Crowding-in effect An increase in private-sector spending as a result of federal budget deficits financed by U.S. Treasury borrowing. At less than full employment, consumers hold more Treasury securities, and this additional wealth causes them to spend more. Business investment spending increases because of optimistic profit expectations. (Chapter 23)

Crowding-out effect A reduction in private-sector spending as a result of federal budget deficits financed by U.S. Treasury borrowing. When federal government borrowing increases interest rates, the result is lower consumption by households and lower investment spending by businesses. (Chapter 23)

Currency Money, including coins and paper money. (Chapter 24)

Cyclical unemployment Unemployment caused by the lack of jobs during a recession. (Chapter 16)

D

Debt ceiling A legislated legal limit on the national debt. (Chapter 23)

Decreasing-cost industry An industry in which the expansion of industry output by the entry of new firms decreases the individual firm's cost curves (cost curve shifts downward). (Chapter 8)

Deflation A decrease in the general (average) price level of goods and services in the economy. (Chapter 17)

Demand A curve or schedule showing the various quantities of a product consumers are willing to purchase at possible prices during a specified period of time, ceteris paribus. (Chapter 3)

Demand curve for labor A curve showing the different quantities of labor employers are willing to hire at different wage rates in a given time period, ceteris paribus. It is equal to the marginal revenue product of labor. (Chapter 11)

Demand for money curve A curve representing the quantity of money that people hold at different possible interest rates, ceteris paribus. (Chapter 26)

Demand-pull inflation A rise in the general price level resulting from an excess of total spending (demand). (Chapter 17)

Depreciation of currency A fall in the price of one currency relative to another. (Chapter 28)

Deregulation The elimination or phasing out of government restrictions on economic activity. (Chapter 13)

Derived demand The demand for labor and other factors of production that depends on the consumer demand for the final goods and services the factors produce. (Chapter 11)

Direct relationship A positive association between two variables. When one variable increases, the other variable increases, and when one variable decreases, the other variable decreases. (Chapter 1)

Discount rate The interest rate the Fed charges on loans of reserves to banks. (Chapter 25)

Discouraged worker A person who wants to work, but who has given up searching for work because he or she believes there will be no job offers. (Chapter 16)

Discretionary fiscal policy The deliberate use of changes in government spending or taxes to alter aggregate demand and stabilize the economy. (Chapter 21)

Diseconomies of scale A situation in which the long-run average cost curve rises as the firm increases output. (Chapter 7)

Disinflation A reduction in the rate of inflation. (Chapter 17)

Disposable personal income (*DI*) The amount of income that households actually have to spend or save after payment of personal taxes. (Chapter 15)

Dissaving The amount by which personal consumption expenditures exceed disposable income. (Chapter 18)

E

Economic growth The ability of an economy to produce greater levels of output, represented by an outward shift of its production possibilities curve. Economic growth is measured by the annual percentage increase in a nation's real GDP. (Chapters 2 and 16)

Economic profit Total revenue minus explicit and implicit costs. (Chapter 7)

Economic system The organizations and methods used to determine what goods and services are produced, how they are produced, and for whom they are produced. (Chapter 29)

Economics The study of how society chooses to allocate its scarce resources to the production of goods and services in order to satisfy unlimited wants. (Chapter 1)

Economies of scale A situation in which the long-run average cost curve declines as the firm increases output. (Chapter 7)

Effluent tax A tax on a pollutant. (Chapter 14)

Elastic demand A condition in which the percentage change in quantity demanded is greater than the percentage change in price. (Chapter 5)

Embargo A law that bars trade with another country. (Chapter 28)

Emissions trading Trading that allows firms to buy and sell the right to pollute. (Chapter 14)

Entrepreneurship The creative ability of individuals to seek profits by combining resources to produce innovative products. (Chapter 1)

Equation of exchange An accounting identity that states the money supply times the velocity of money equals total spending. (Chapter 26)

Equilibrium A market condition that occurs at any price where the quantity demanded and the quantity supplied are equal. (Chapter 3)

Excess reserves Potential loan balances held in vault cash or on deposit with the Fed in excess of required reserves. (Chapter 25)

Exchange rate The number of units of one nation's currency that equals one unit of another nation's currency. (Chapter 28)

Expenditure approach The national income accounting method that measures GDP by adding all the spending for final goods during a period of time. (Chapter 15)

Explicit costs Payments to nonowners of a firm for their resources. (Chapter 7)

External national debt The portion of the national debt owed to foreign citizens. (Chapter 23)

Externality A cost or benefit imposed on people other than the consumers and producers of a good or service. (Chapter 4)

F

Federal Deposit Insurance Corporation (FDIC) A government agency established in 1933 to insure commercial bank deposits up to a specified limit. (Chapter 24)

Federal funds market A private market in which banks lend reserves to each other for less than 24 hours. (Chapter 25)

Federal funds rate The interest rate banks charge for overnight loans of reserves to other banks. (Chapter 25)

Federal Open Market Committee (FOMC) The Federal Reserve's committee that directs the buying and selling of U.S. government securities, which are major instruments for controlling the money supply. The FOMC consists of the seven members of the Federal Reserve's Board of Governors, the president of the New York Federal Reserve Bank, and the presidents of four other Federal Reserve district banks. (Chapter 24)

Federal Reserve System The 12 central banks that service banks and other financial institutions within each of the Federal Reserve districts; popularly called the Fed. (Chapter 24)

Federal Trade Commission Act The federal act that in 1914 established the Federal Trade Commission (FTC) to investigate unfair competitive practices of firms. (Chapter 13)

Fiat money Money accepted by law and not because of its redeemability or intrinsic value. (Chapter 24)

Final goods Finished goods and services produced for the ultimate user. (Chapter 15)

Fiscal policy The use of government spending and taxes to influence the nation's output, employment, and price level. (Chapter 21)

Fixed input Any resource for which the quantity cannot change during the period of time under consideration. (Chapter 7)

Flow A measurement in units per time period such as dollars per year. For example, income and consumption are flows that occur per week, per month, or per year. (Chapter 15)

Foreign aid The transfer of money or resources from one government to another for which no repayment is required. (Chapter 30)

Fractional reserve banking A system in which banks keep only a percentage of their deposits on reserve as vault cash and deposits at the Fed. (Chapter 25)

Free-rider problem The problem that if some individuals benefit, while others pay, few will be willing to pay for improvement of the environment or other public goods. As a result, these goods are under-produced. (Chapter 14)

Free trade The flow of goods between countries without restrictions or special taxes. (Chapter 28)

Frictional unemployment Unemployment caused by the normal search time required by workers with marketable skills who are changing jobs, initially entering the labor force, reentering the labor force, or seasonally unemployed. (Chapter 16)

Full employment The situation in which an economy operates at an unemployment rate equal to the sum of the frictional and structural unemployment rates. (Chapter 16)

G

GDP chain price index A measure that compares changes in the prices of all final goods during a given year to the prices of those goods in a base year. (Chapter 15)

GDP gap The difference between full-employment real GDP and actual real GDP. (Chapter 16)

GDP per capita The value of final goods produced (GDP) divided by the total population. (Chapter 30)

Government expenditures Federal, state, and local government outlays for goods and services, including transfer payments. (Chapter 22)

Government failure Government intervention that fails to correct market failure. (Chapter 14)

Gross domestic product (GDP) The market value of all final goods and services produced in a nation during a period of time, usually a year. (Chapter 15)

Gross national product (GNP) The market value of all final goods and services produced by a nation's residents no matter where they are located. (Chapter 15)

H

Horizontal merger A merger of firms that compete in the same market. (Chapter 13)

Human capital The accumulation of education, training, experience, and health that enables a worker to enter an occupation and be productive. (Chapter 11)

Hyperinflation An extremely rapid rise in the general price level. (Chapter 17)

I

Implicit costs The opportunity costs of using resources owned by the firm. (Chapter 7)

In-kind transfers Government payments in the form of goods and services, rather than cash, including such government programs as food stamps, Medicaid, and housing. (Chapter 12)

Incentive-based regulations Government regulations that set an environmental goal, but are flexible as to how buyers and sellers achieve the goal. (Chapter 14)

Income approach The national income accounting method that measures GDP by adding all incomes, including compensation of employees, rents, net interest, and profits. (Chapter 15)

Income effect The change in quantity demanded of a good or service caused by a change in real income (purchasing power). (Chapter 6)

Income elasticity of demand The ratio of the percentage change in quantity demanded for a good or service to a given percentage change in income. (Chapter 5)

Incomes policies Federal government policies designed to affect the real incomes of workers by controlling nominal wages and prices. Such policies include presidential jawboning, wage-price guidelines, and wage-price controls. (Chapter 27)

Increasing-cost industry An industry in which the expansion of industry output by the entry of new firms increases the individual firm's cost curves (cost curve shifts upward). (Chapter 8)

Independent relationship A zero association between two variables. When one variable changes, the other variable remains unchanged. (Chapter 1)

Indifference curve A curve that represents various combinations of two goods that provide equal total utility.

Indifference map A number of indifference curves for a given consumer and two goods.

Indirect business taxes Taxes levied as a percentage of the prices of goods sold and therefore collected as part of the firm's revenue. Firms treat such taxes as production costs. Examples include general sales taxes, exicse taxes, and customs duties. (Chapter 15)

Industrially advanced countries (IACs) High-income nations that have market economies based on large stocks of technologically advanced capital and well-educated labor. The United States, Canada, Australia, New Zealand, Japan, and most of the countries of Western Europe are IACs. (Chapter 30)

Inelastic demand A condition in which the percentage change in quantity demanded is less than the percentage change in price. (Chapter 5)

Inferior good Any good for which there is an inverse relationship between changes in income and its demand curve. (Chapter 3)

Inflation An increase in the general (average) price level of goods and services in the economy. (Chapter 17)

Inflationary gap The amount by which aggregate expenditures exceed the amount required to achieve full-employment equilibrium. (Chapter 19)

Infrastructure Capital goods usually provided by the government, including highways, bridges, waste and water systems, and airports. (Chapter 30)

Interest-rate effect The impact on total spending (real GDP) caused by the direct relationship between the price level and the interest rate. (Chapter 20)

Intermediate goods Goods and services used as inputs for the production of final goods. (Chapter 15)

Intermediate range The rising segment of the aggregate supply curve, which represents an economy as it approaches full-employment output. (Chapter 20)

Internal national debt The portion of the national debt owed to a nation's own citizens. (Chapter 23)

International Monetary Fund (IMF) The lending agency that makes short-term conditional low-interest loans to developing countries. (Chapter 30)

Inverse relationship A negative association between two variables. When one variable increases, the other variable decreases, and when one variable decreases, the other variable increases. (Chapter 1)

Investment The accumulation of capital, such as factories, machines, and inventories, that is used to produce goods and services. (Chapter 2)

Investment demand curve The graph that shows the amount businesses spend for investment goods at different possible rates of interest. (Chapter 18)

Invisible hand A phrase that expresses the belief that the best interests of a society are served when individual consumers and producers compete to achieve their own private interests. (Chapter 29)

J

Jawboning Oratory intended to pressure unions and businesses to reduce wage and price increases. (Chapter 27)

K

Keynesian range The horizontal segment of the aggregate supply curve, which represents an economy in a severe recession. (Chapter 20)

Kinked demand curve A demand curve facing an oligopolist that assumes rivals will match a price decrease, but ignore a price increase. (Chapter 10)

L

Labor The mental and physical capacity of workers to produce goods and services. (Chapter 1)

Laffer curve A graph depicting the relationship between tax rates and total tax revenues. (Chapter 21)

Lagging indicators Variables that change after real GDP changes. (Chapter 16)

Land A shorthand expression for any natural resource provided by nature. (Chapter 1)

Law of demand The principle that there is an inverse relationship between the price of a good and the quantity buyers are willing to purchase in a defined time period, ceteris paribus. (Chapter 3)

Law of diminishing marginal utility The principle that the extra satisfaction of a good or service declines as people consume more in a given period. (Chapter 6)

Law of diminishing returns The principle that beyond some point the marginal product decreases as additional units of a variable factor are added to a fixed factor. (Chapter 7)

Law of increasing opportunity costs The principle that the opportunity cost increases as production of one output expands. (Chapter 2)

Law of supply The principle that there is a direct relationship between the price of a good and the quantity sellers are willing and able to offer for sale in a defined time period, ceteris paribus. (Chapter 3)

Leading indicators Variables that change before real GDP changes. (Chapter 16)

Less-developed countries (LDCs) Nations without large stocks of technologically advanced capital and well-educated labor. LDCs are economies based on agriculture, such as most countries of Africa, Asia, and Latin America. (Chapter 30)

Long run A period of time so long that all inputs are variable. (Chapter 7)

Long-run average cost curve The curve that traces the lowest cost per unit at which a firm can produce any level of output when the firm can build a plant of any desired plant size. (Chapter 7)

Lorenz curve A graph of the actual cumulative distribution of income compared to a perfectly equal cumulative distribution of income. (Chapter 12)

M

M1 The narrowest definition of the money supply. It includes currency, traveler's checks, and checkable deposits. (Chapter 24)

M2 The definition of the money supply that equals M1 plus near monies, such as savings deposits and small time deposits of less than $100,000. (Chapter 24)

M3 The definition of the money supply that equals M2 plus large time deposits of $100,000 or more. (Chapter 24)

Macroeconomics The branch of economics that studies decision making for the economy as a whole. (Chapter 1)

Marginal analysis An examination of the effects of additions to or subtractions from a current situation. (Chapter 2)

Marginal-average rule The rule that states when marginal cost is below average cost, average cost falls. When marginal cost is above average cost, average cost rises. When marginal cost equals average cost, average cost is at its minimum point. (Chapter 7)

Marginal cost The change in total cost when one additional unit of output is produced. (Chapter 7)

Marginal cost pricing A system of pricing in which the price charged equals the marginal cost of the last unit produced. (Chapter 13)

Marginal factor cost (MFC) The additional total cost resulting from a one-unit increase in the quantity of a factor. (Chapter 11)

Marginal product The change in total output produced by adding one unit of a variable input, with all other inputs used being held constant. (Chapter 7)

Marginal propensity to consume (MPC) The change in consumption spending resulting from a given change in income. (Chapter 18)

Marginal propensity to save (MPS) The fraction of any change in real disposable income that households save. (Chapter 18)

Marginal rate of substitution The rate at which the consumer is willing to substitute one good for another good without a change in total utility.

Marginal revenue The change in total revenue from the sale of one additional unit of output. (Chapter 8)

Marginal revenue product (MRP) The increase in a firm's total revenue resulting from hiring an additional unit of labor or other variable resource. (Chapter 11)

Marginal tax rate The fraction of additional income paid in taxes. (Chapter 22)

Marginal utility The change in total utility from one additional unit of a good or service. (Chapter 6)

Market Any arrangement in which buyers and sellers interact to determine the price and quantity of goods and services exchanged. (Chapter 3)

Market economy An economic system that answers the What, How, and For Whom questions using prices determined by the interaction of the forces of supply and demand. (Chapter 29)

Market failure A situation in which market equilibrium results in too few or too many resources used in the production of a good or service. This inefficiency may justify government intervention. (Chapters 4 and 14)

Market structure A classification system for the key traits of a market, including the number of firms, the similarity of the products they sell, and the ease of entry into and exit from the market. (Chapter 8)

Means test A requirement that a family's income not exceed a certain level to be eligible for public assistance. (Chapter 12)

Medium of exchange The primary function of money to be widely accepted in exchange for goods and services. (Chapter 24)

Microeconomics The branch of economics that studies decision making by a single individual, household, firm, industry, or level of government. (Chapter 1)

Mixed economy An economic system than answers the What, How, and For Whom questions through a mixture of traditional, command, and market systems. (Chapter 29)

Model A simplified description of reality used to understand and predict the relationship between variables. (Chapter 1)

Monetarism The theory that changes in the money supply directly determine changes in prices, real GDP, and employment. (Chapter 26)

Monetary Control Act A law, formally titled the Depository Institutions Deregulation and Monetary Control Act of 1980, that gives the Federal Reserve System greater control over nonmember banks and makes all financial institutions more competitive. (Chapter 24)

Monetary policy The Federal Reserve's use of open market operations, changes in the discount rate, and changes in the required reserve ratio to change the money supply (M1). (Chapter 25)

Money Anything that serves as a medium of exchange, unit of account, and store of value. (Chapter 24)

Money multiplier The maximum change in the money supply (checkable deposits) due to an initial change in the excess reserves banks hold. The money multiplier is equal to 1 divided by the required reserve ratio. (Chapter 25)

Monopolistic competition A market structure characterized by (1) many small sellers, (2) a differentiated product, and (3) easy market entry and exit. (Chapter 10)

Monopoly A market structure characterized by (1) a single seller, (2) a unique product, and (3) impossible entry into the market. (Chapter 9)

Monopsony A labor market in which a single firm hires labor. (Chapter 11)

Mutual interdependence A condition in which an action by one firm may cause a reaction from other firms. (Chapter 10)

N

National debt The total amount owed by the federal government to owners of government securities. (Chapter 23)

National income (NI) The total income earned by resource owners, including wages, rents, interest, and profits. (Chapter 15)

Natural monopoly An industry in which the long-run average cost of production declines throughout the entire market. As a result, a single firm can supply the entire market demand at a lower cost than two or more smaller firms. (Chapter 9)

Natural rate hypothesis The hypothesis that the economy will self-correct to the natural rate of unemployment. The long-run Phillips curve is therefore a vertical line at the natural rate of unemployment. (Chapter 27)

Negative income tax (NIT) A plan under which families below a certain break-even level of income would receive cash payments that decrease as their incomes increase. (Chapter 12)

Net domestic product (NDP) The gross domestic product minus depreciation of capital worn out in producing output. (Chapter 15)

Net exports effect The impact on total spending (real GDP) caused by the inverse relationship between the price level and the net exports of an economy. (Chapter 20)

Net public debt National debt minus all government interagency borrowing. (Chapter 23)

New economy Economic growth resulting from technological advances that make businesses and workers more productive. (Chapter 2)

New-source bias Bias that occurs when there is an incentive to keep assets past the efficient point, as a result of regulations. (Chapter 14)

Nominal GDP The value of all final goods based on the prices existing during the time period of production. (Chapter 15)

Nominal income The actual number of dollars received over a period of time. (Chapter 17)

Nominal interest rate The actual rate of interest earned over a period of time. (Chapter 17)

Nonprice competition The situation in which a firm competes using advertising, packaging, product development, better quality, and better service, rather than lower prices. (Chapter 10)

Normal good Any good for which there is a direct relationship between changes in income and its demand curve. (Chapter 3)

Normal profit The minimum profit necessary to keep a firm in operation. A firm that earns normal profit earns total revenue equal to its total opportunity cost. (Chapter 7)

Normative economics An analysis based on value judgment. (Chapter 1)

O

Oligopoly A market structure characterized by (1) few sellers, (2) either a homogeneous or a differentiated product, and (3) difficult market entry. (Chapter 10)

Open market operations The buying and selling of government securities by the Federal Reserve System. (Chapter 25)

Opportunity cost The best alternative sacrificed for a chosen alternative. (Chapter 2)

P

Peak The phase of the business cycle in which real GDP reaches its maximum after rising during a recovery. (Chapter 16)

Per se rule The antitrust doctrine that the existence of monopoly alone is illegal, regardless of whether or not the monopoly engages in illegal business practices. (Chapter 13)

Perfect competition A market structure characterized by (1) a large number of small firms, (2) a homogeneous product, and (3) very easy entry into or exit from the market. Perfect competition is also referred to as *pure competition.* (Chapter 8)

Perfectly competitive firm's short-run supply curve The firm's marginal cost curve above the minimum point on its average variable cost curve. (Chapter 8)

Perfectly competitive industry's long-run supply curve The curve that shows the quantities supplied by the industry at different equilibrium prices after firms complete their entry and exit. (Chapter 8)

Perfectly competitive industry's short-run supply curve The supply curve derived from the horizontal summation of the marginal cost curves of all firms in the industry above the minimum point of each firm's average variable cost curve. (Chapter 8)

Perfectly elastic demand A condition in which a small percentage change in price brings about an infinite percentage change in quantity demanded. (Chapter 5)

Perfectly inelastic demand A condition in which the quantity demanded does not change as the price changes. (Chapter 5)

Personal income (PI) The total income received by households that is available for consumption, saving, and payment of personal taxes. (Chapter 15)

Phillips curve A curve showing an inverse relationship between the inflation rate and the unemployment rate. (Chapter 27)

Political business cycle A business cycle caused by policymakers to improve politicians' reelection chances. (Chapter 27)

Positive economics An analysis limited to statements that are verifiable. (Chapter 1)

Poverty line The level of income below which a person or a family is considered to be poor. (Chapter 12)

Precautionary demand for money The stock of money people hold to pay unpredictable expenses. (Chapter 26)

Predatory pricing The practice of one or more firms temporarily reducing prices in order to eliminate competition and then raising prices. (Chapter 13)

Price ceiling A legally established maximum price a seller can charge. (Chapter 4)

Price discrimination The practice of a seller charging different prices for the same product not justified by cost differences. (Chapter 9)

Price elasticity of demand The ratio of the percentage change in the quantity demanded of a product to a percentage change in its price. (Chapter 5)

Price elasticity of supply The ratio of the percentage change in the quantity supplied of a product to the percentage change in its price. (Chapter 5)

Price floor A legally established minimum price a seller can be paid. (Chapter 4)

Price leadership A pricing strategy in which a dominant firm sets the price for an industry and the other firms follow. (Chapter 10)

Price maker A firm that faces a downward-sloping demand curve and therefore it can choose among price and output combinations along the demand curve. (Chapter 9)

Price system A mechanism that uses the forces of supply and demand to create an equilibrium through rising and falling prices. (Chapter 3)

Price taker A seller that has no control over the price of the product it sells. (Chapter 8)

Private benefits and costs Benefits and costs to the decision maker, ignoring benefits and costs to third parties. Third parties are people outside the market transaction who are affected by the product. (Chapter 14)

Product differentiation The process of creating real or apparent differences between goods and services. (Chapter 10)

Production function The relationship between the maximum amounts of output that a firm can produce and various quantities of inputs. (Chapter 7)

Production possibilities curve A curve that shows the maximum combinations of two outputs an economy can produce in a given period of time with its available resources and technology. (Chapter 2)

Progressive tax A tax that charges a higher percentage of income as income rises. (Chapter 22)

Proportional tax A tax that charges the same percentage of income, regardless of the size of income. Also called a *flat-rate tax* or simply a *flat tax.* (Chapter 22)

Protectionism The government's use of embargoes, tariffs, quotas, and other restrictions to protect domestic producers from foreign competition. (Chapter 28)

Public choice theory The analysis of the government's decision-making process for allocating resources. (Chapter 22)

Public good A good or service that, once produced, has two properties: (1) users collectively consume benefits, and (2) there is no way to bar people who do not pay (free riders) from consuming the good or service. (Chapter 4)

Q

Quantity theory of money The theory that changes in the money supply are directly related to changes in the price level. (Chapter 26)

Quota A limit on the quantity of a good that may be imported in a given time period. (Chapter 28)

R

Rational expectations theory The belief that people use all available information to predict the future, including future monetary and fiscal policies. Systematic and predictable macroeconomic policies can therefore be negated when businesses and workers anticipate the effects of these policies on the economy. (Chapter 27)

Rational ignorance The voter's choice to remain uninformed because the marginal cost of obtaining information is higher than the marginal benefit from knowing it. (Chapter 22)

Real balances or wealth effect The impact on total spending (real GDP) caused by the inverse relationship between the price level and the real value of financial assets with fixed nominal value. (Chapter 20)

Real GDP The value of all final goods produced during a given time period based on the prices existing in a selected base year. (Chapter 15)

Real income The actual number of dollars received (nominal income) adjusted for changes in the CPI. (Chapter 17)

Real interest rate The nominal rate of interest minus the inflation rate. (Chapter 17)

Recession A downturn in the business cycle during which real GDP declines; also called a *contraction*. (Chapter 16)

Recessionary gap The amount by which aggregate expenditures fall short of the amount required to achieve full-employment equilibrium. (Chapter 19)

Recovery An upturn in the business cycle during which real GDP rises; also called an *expansion*. (Chapter 16)

Regressive tax A tax that charges a lower percentage of income as income rises. (Chapter 22)

Required reserve ratio The percentage of deposits that the Federal Reserve requires a bank to hold in vault cash or on deposit with the Fed. (Chapter 25)

Required reserves The minimum balance that the Federal Reserve requires a bank to hold in vault cash or on deposit with the Fed. (Chapter 25)

Resources The basic categories of inputs used to produce goods and services. Resources are also called *factors of production*. Economists divide resources into three categories: land, labor, and capital. (Chapter 1)

Robinson-Patman Act A 1936 amendment to the Clayton Act that strengthens the Clayton Act against price discrimination. (Chapter 13)

Rule of reason The antitrust doctrine that the existence of monopoly alone is not illegal unless the monopoly engages in illegal business practices. (Chapter 13)

S

Saving The part of disposable income households do not spend for consumer goods and services. (Chapter 18)

Say's Law The theory that supply creates its own demand. (Chapter 18)

Scarcity The condition in which human wants are forever greater than the available supply of time, goods, and resources. (Chapter 1)

Sherman Act The federal antitrust law enacted in 1890 that prohibits monopolization and conspiracies to restrain trade. (Chapter 13)

Short run A period of time so short that there is at least one fixed input. (Chapter 7)

Shortage A market condition existing at any price where the quantity supplied is less than the quantity demanded. (Chapter 3)

Slope The ratio of the change in the variable on the vertical axis (the rise or fall) to the change in the variable on the horizontal axis (the run). (Chapter 1)

Social benefits and costs The sum of benefits to everyone in society, including both private benefits and external benefits. Social costs are the sum of costs to everyone in society, including both private costs and external costs. (Chapter 14)

Socialism An economic system characterized by government ownership of resources and centralized decision making. (Chapter 29)

Speculative demand for money The stock of money people hold to take advantage of expected future changes in the price of bonds, stocks, or other nonmoney financial assets. (Chapter 26)

Spending multiplier The ratio of the change in real GDP to an initial change in any component of aggregate expenditures, including consumption, investment, government spending, and net exports. As a formula, the spending multiplier equals $1/(1 - MPC)$ or $1/MPS$. (Chapter 19)

Stagflation The condition that occurs when an economy experiences the twin maladies of high unemployment and rapid inflation simultaneously. (Chapter 20)

Stock A quantity measured at one point in time. For example, an inventory or the amount of money in a checking account. (Chapter 15)

Store of value The ability of money to hold value over time. (Chapter 24)

Structural unemployment Unemployment caused by a mismatch of the skills of workers out of work and the skills required for existing job opportunities. (Chapter 16)

Substitute good A good that competes with another good for consumer purchases. As a result, there is a direct relationship between a price change for one good and the demand for its "competitor" good. (Chapter 3)

Substitution effect The change in quantity demanded of a good or service caused by a change in its price relative to substitutes. (Chapter 6)

Supply A curve or schedule showing the various quantities of a product sellers are willing to produce and offer for sale at possible prices during a specified period of time, ceteris paribus. (Chapter 3)

Supply curve of labor A curve showing the different quantities of labor workers are willing to offer employers at different wage rates in a given time period, ceteris paribus. (Chapter 11)

Supply-side fiscal policy A fiscal policy that emphasizes government policies that increase aggregate supply in order to achieve long-run growth in real output, full employment, and a lower price level. (Chapter 21)

Surplus A market condition existing at any price where the quantity supplied is greater than the quantity demanded. (Chapter 3)

T

Tariff A tax on an import. (Chapter 28)

Tax incidence The share of a tax ultimately paid by consumers and sellers. (Chapter 5)

Tax multiplier The change in aggregate demand (total spending) resulting from an initial change in taxes. As a formula, the tax multiplier equals $1 -$ spending multiplier. (Chapter 21)

Technology The body of knowledge applied to how goods are produced. (Chapter 2)

Total cost (TC) The sum of total fixed cost and total variable cost at each level of output. (Chapter 7)

Total fixed cost (TFC) Costs that do not vary as output varies and that must be paid even if output is zero. These are payments that the firm must make in the short run, regardless of the level of output. (Chapter 7)

Total revenue The total number of dollars a firm earns from the sale of a good or service, which is equal to its price multiplied by the quantity demanded. (Chapter 5)

Total utility The amount of satisfaction received from all the units of a good or service consumed. (Chapter 6)

Total variable cost (TVC) Costs that are zero when output is zero and vary as output varies. (Chapter 7)

Traditional economy A system that answers the What, How, and For Whom questions the way they always have been answered. (Chapter 29)

Transactions costs The costs of negotiating and enforcing a contract. (Chapter 14)

Transactions demand for money The stock of money people hold to pay everyday predictable expenses. (Chapter 26)

Transfer payment A government payment to individuals not in exchange for goods or services currently produced. (Chapter 15)

Trough The phase of the business cycle in which real GDP reaches its minimum after falling during a recession. (Chapter 16)

Trust A combination or cartel consisting of firms that place their assets in the custody of a board of trustees. (Chapter 13)

U

Unemployment compensation The government insurance program that pays income for a short time period to unemployed workers. (Chapter 12)

Unemployment rate The percentage of people in the labor force who are without jobs and are actively seeking jobs. (Chapter 16)

Unit of account The function of money to provide a common measurement of the relative value of goods and services. (Chapter 24)

Unitary elastic demand A condition in which the percentage change in quantity demanded is equal to the percentage change in price. (Chapter 5)

Utility The satisfaction, or pleasure, that people receive from consuming a good or service. (Chapter 6)

V

Variable input Any resource for which the quantity can change during the period of time under consideration. (Chapter 7)

Velocity of money The average number of times per year a dollar of the money supply is spent on final goods and services. (Chapter 26)

Vertical merger A merger of a firm with its suppliers. (Chapter 13)

Vicious circle of poverty The trap in which countries are poor because they cannot afford to save and invest, but they cannot save and invest because they are poor. (Chapter 30)

W

Wage and price controls Legal restrictions on wage and price increases. Violations can result in fines and imprisonment. (Chapter 27)

Wage and price guidelines Voluntary standards set by the government for "permissible" wage and price increases. (Chapter 27)

Wage-price spiral A situation that occurs when increases in nominal wage rates are passed on in higher prices, which, in turn, result in even higher nominal wage rates and prices. (Chapter 17)

Wealth The value of the stock of assets owned at some point in time. (Chapter 17)

World Bank The lending agency that makes long-term low-interest loans and provides technical assistance to less-developed countries. (Chapter 30)

Index

Photo Credits

ECONOMICS for Today
Internet Resource Sites

SITE	DESCRIPTION
The Adam Smith Institute http://www.adamsmith.org.uk	Promotes market-based economic reform ideas founded on the writings of Adam Smith.
Antitrust Policy http://www.antitrust.org/	An online resource linking antitrust research, policy, and cases.
BEA: International Accounts Data http://www.bea.doc.gov/bea/di1.htm	Comprehensive international accounts data from the Survey of Current Business.
BEA: National Accounts Data http://www.bea.doc.gov/bea/dn1.htm	Comprehensive national accounts data from the Survey of Current Business.
BLS: Economy at a Glance http://www.bls.gov/eag/eag.us.htm	Current data on key BLS economic indicators with icons for graphs of data over recent years.
BLS: Most Requested Series http://stats.bls.gov/data/top20.html	Bureau of Labor Statistics historical data on unemployment, prices, and productivity.
BLS: Other Statistical Sites on World Wide Web http://stats.bls.gov/bls/other.htm	Links to statistics and information from U.S. and international agencies.
Business Cycle Indicators http://www.conference-board.org/economics/index.cfm	The Conference Board provides charts and analysis of economic indicators.
Capitalism FAQ http://www.ocf.berkeley.edu/~shadab/	Answers accusations against capitalism in terms of theory and practice.
Congressional Budget Office http://www.cbo.gov/index.cfm	Free text search of Congressional Budget Office reports.
CCER National Budget Simulation http://garnet.berkeley.edu:3333/budget/budget.html	A federal budget game that allows you to balance the federal budget.
Concord Coalition Federal Budget Information http://www.concordcoalition.org/	A nonpartisan grassroots organization dedicated to eliminating federal budget deficits.
Consumer Research Center http://www.conference-board.org/search/ dpress.cfm?pressid=4683	The Conference Board's Consumer Confidence Index latest press release.
Economagic http://www.economagic.com	Historical monthly and quarterly graphs and tables for numerous economic datasets.
Economic Outlook http://www.oecd.org/eco/out/eo.htm	A summary of policy, and projections of output, employment, and prices of OECD countries.
Economic Report of the President http://w3.access.gpo.gov/eop/	Full online access to articles and data for current and past editions of the Economic Report of the President.
Economics Statistics Briefing Room http://www.whitehouse.gov/fsbr/esbr.html	Selected most recent federal economic indicators with icons for graphs of data over recent years.
Federal Reserve Board http://www.federalreserve.gov/	General information and historical data from the Federal Reserve.
FRED: Federal Reserve Economic Data http://www.stls.frb.org/fred/	Data for banking, monthly produces indexes, and other monthly monetary data. Also, provides federal reserve board statistical releases.
History of Money http://minneapolisfed.org/econed/curric/history.html	History of money from 700 B.C. to 1934.